THE
B&B
GUIDE
2015

AA Lifestyle Guides

Every effort has been made to trace copyright holders, and we apologise in advance for any unintentional omissions or errors. We would be pleased to apply any corrections in a following edition of this publication.

Typeset by Servis Filmsetting Ltd, Stockport
Printed in Italy by Printer Trento SRL, Trento

Directory compiled by the AA Lifestyle Guides Department and managed in the Librios Information Management System and generated from the AA establishment database system.

Maps prepared by the Mapping Services Department of AA Publishing.

Maps © AA Media Limited 2014.

Contains Ordnance Survey data © Crown copyright and database right 2014.

Licence number 100021153.

This is based upon Crown Copyright and is reproduced with the permission of Land & Property Services under delegated authority from the Controller of Her Majesty's Stationery Office.
© Crown copyright and database rights 2014 PMLPA No.100497

Republic of Ireland mapping based on © Ordnance Survey Ireland/Government of Ireland Copyright Permit number MP000314

Information on National Parks in England provided by the Countryside Agency (Natural England).

Information on National Parks in Scotland provided by Scottish Natural Heritage.

Information on National Parks in Wales provided by The Countryside Council for Wales.

A CIP catalogue record for this book is available from the British Library.

ISBN: 978-0-7495-7619-6
A05151

Contents

Welcome to the AA B&B Guide 2015

We know that people use the AA B&B Guide for finding many different types of accommodation for a variety of reasons. As the AA inspects such a wide range of establishments, we hope that this guide will prove an invaluable asset in helping you to find just the right place to stay.

Who's in the guide?

From the most stylish and sophisticated of the UK's urban boutique accommodation to family-run homes in the British countryside; from ultra-chic luxury to charmingly rustic home-from-home comfort and many points between, *The AA B&B Guide 2015* has it all. Throughout the year, our specially trained team of expert inspectors are visiting, grading and advising the Guest Accommodation that appears in this guide. Each one is judged on its presentation, quality of accommodation, leisure facilities, breakfasts and evening meals, service, hospitality, conference facilities and cleanliness and housekeeping. They are then rated according to our Classification System (see pages 8 and 9).

Our inspectors also choose their Guest Accommodation of the Year for England, Scotland, Wales, Northern Ireland and the Republic of Ireland, as well as the Friendliest B&B of the Year and the Funkiest B&B of the Year.

Gold Stars

All of the Guest Accommodation in this guide should be of a high standard, but some are a cut above, and those with Gold Stars are in the top ten percent of their star rating. At these establishments you can expect a little more of everything: more comfort, more extras, and more attention. From three Gold Stars to five Gold Stars, these are the best of British Guest Accommodation.

Premier Collection

All five star establishments, whether Gold or black Stars, are part of the Premier Collection, and these entries are highlighted in the guide. This allows the reader to see at a glance those Guest Accommodations that have met all the criteria required by the Guest Accommodation Scheme and have reached the highest rating possible.

Rosettes

Some of the B&Bs in this guide have their own restaurants, and many of them serve food that has attained the award of AA Rosettes; including a few that have reached the four and five Rosette level, making them among the finest restaurants in the world. These are regularly visited by the AA inspectorate and awarded Rosettes strictly on the basis of the inspector's experience alone.

Many establishments in the guides designated as Restaurants with Rooms have been awarded AA Rosettes for the quality of their food.

Anonymous inspection

Any Guest Accommodation applying for AA recognition receives a regular unannounced visit by one of the AA's team of professional inspectors to check standards. The inspector always pays his or her own bill (rather than it being paid by the establishment).

After staying overnight at the Guest House, the inspector will make themselves known to a member of staff and ask to speak to the manager. Once a rating is awarded, regular visits are made by our inspectors to check that standards are being maintained.

If the accommodation changes hands, the new owners must reapply for classification, as AA recognition is not transferable.

Tell us what you think

We welcome your feedback about the B&Bs included in this guide, and about the guide itself. You can write to us at: B&B Guide, 13th floor, Fanum House, Basing View, Basingstoke, Hampshire RG21 4EA or email us at **lifestyleguides@theaa.com**

How to use the AA B&B Guide

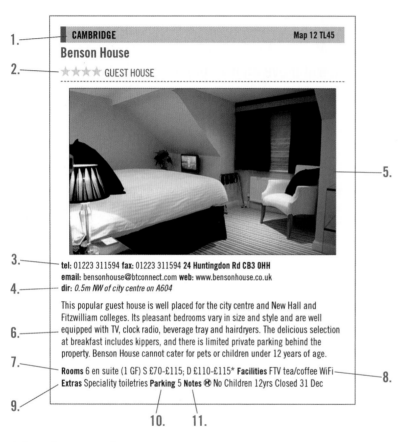

1. **CAMBRIDGE**   Map 12 TL45

   Benson House

2. ★★★★ GUEST HOUSE

3. **tel:** 01223 311594 **fax:** 01223 311594 **24 Huntingdon Rd CB3 0HH**
   email: bensonhouse@btconnect.com **web:** www.bensonhouse.co.uk

4. *dir: 0.5m NW of city centre on A604*

6. This popular guest house is well placed for the city centre and New Hall and Fitzwilliam colleges. Its pleasant bedrooms vary in size and style and are well equipped with TV, clock radio, beverage tray and hairdryers. The delicious selection at breakfast includes kippers, and there is limited private parking behind the property. Benson House cannot cater for pets or children under 12 years of age.

7. **Rooms** 6 en suite (1 GF) S £70-£115; D £110-£115* **Facilities** FTV tea/coffee WiFi
   Extras Speciality toiletries **Parking** 5 **Notes** ⊗ No Children 12yrs Closed 31 Dec

10. 11.

1. Location, map reference & name

Each country is listed in alphabetical order by county then town/village. The Channel Islands and Isle of Man follow the England section and the Scottish Islands follow the Scotland section. Establishments are listed alphabetically in descending order of Stars with Gold Stars appearing first in each rating.

The map page number refers to the atlas at the back of the guide and is followed by the National Grid Reference. To find the town/village, read the first figure across and the second figure vertically within the lettered square. Farmhouse entries also have a six-figure National Grid Reference, which can be used with Ordnance Survey maps or **www.ordnancesurvey.co.uk**.

You can find routes at **theAA.com** or **www.AAbookings.ie**. London has its own Plans (see end of atlas), and London establishments have a Plan number based on these.

If the establishment's name is shown in italics, then details have not been confirmed by the proprietor for this edition.

2. Classification & designator

See pages 8 and 9.

Five Star establishments are highlighted as Premier Collection, and they are listed on page 26.

⊛ **Rosettes** The AA's food award, see page 11.

🥚 **Egg cups and** 🥧 **pies** These symbols indicate that, in the experience of the inspector, either breakfast or dinner (or both) are really special, and have an emphasis on freshly prepared local ingredients.

3. Email address & website

Email and website addresses are included where they have been specified by the establishment. Such websites are not under the control of AA Media Limited, who cannot accept any responsibility or liability in respect of any and all matters whatsoever relating to such websites.

4. Directions & distances

Distances in **directions** are given in miles (m) and yards (yds), or kilometres (km) and metres (mtrs) in the Republic of Ireland.

5. Photographs

Establishments may choose to include a photograph

6. Description

Written by the inspector at the time of his or her visit.

7. Rooms

The number of letting bedrooms (rms), or rooms with a bath or shower en suite are shown. Bedrooms that have a private bathroom (pri facs) adjacent are indicated.

The number of bedrooms in an annexe of equivalent standard are also shown. Charges are per night:

S bed and breakfast per person

D bed and breakfast for two people sharing a room. If an asterisk (∗) follows the prices this indicates 2014 prices.

The euro is the currency of the Republic of Ireland.

Prices are indications only, so check before booking. Some places may offer free accommodation to children provided they share their parents' room.

8. Facilities

Most bedrooms will have TV. If this is important to you, please check when booking. If **TV4B** appears, this means that there are TVs in four bedrooms.

If **Dinner** is shown, you may have to order in advance. Please check when booking.

For other abbreviations and symbols, see legend opposite.

9. Extras

Anything the establishment offers in rooms that are more than expected e.g. specialist toiletries, trouser press, mineral water, home-made biscuits etc.

10. Parking

Parking is usually followed by the number of spaces. Motorists should be aware that some establishments may charge for parking. Please check when booking.

11. Notes

Although many establishments allow dogs, they may be excluded from some areas of the accommodation and some breeds, particularly those requiring an exceptional license, may not be accepted at all. Under the Equality Act 2010, access should be allowed to guide dogs and assistance dogs. Please check the establishment's policy when making your booking.

No children children cannot be accommodated, or a minimum age may be specified, e.g. No Children 4yrs means no children under four years old.

Establishments with special facilities for children (**ch fac**) may include a babysitting service or baby-intercom system, playroom or playground, laundry facilities, drying and ironing facilities, cots, high chairs and special meals. If you have very young children, check facilities before booking.

No coaches is published in good faith from details supplied by the establishment. Inns have well-defined legal obligations towards travellers; in the event of a query the customer should contact the proprietor or local licensing authority.

Additional facilities such as lifts or any leisure activities available are also listed.

LB indicates that Short or Leisure Breaks are available. Contact the establishment for details.

Establishments are open all year unless **Closed** days/dates/months are shown. Some places are open all year but offer a restricted service (**RS**) in low season. If the text does not say what the restricted services are you should check before booking.

Civ Wed 50 The establishment is licensed for civil weddings and can accommodate 50 guests for the ceremony.

⊜ shows that **credit/debit cards are not accepted**, but check when booking. Where credit cards are accepted there may be an extra charge.

Smoking Since July 1st 2007 smoking has been banned by law in all public places in the United Kingdom and Ireland. However, the proprietor can designate one or more bedrooms with ventilation systems where the occupants can smoke, but communal areas must be smoke-free. Communal areas include the interior bars and restaurants in pubs and inns. We indicate number of smoking rooms (if any).

Conference facilities Conf indicates that facilities are available. The total number of delegates that can be accommodated is shown, plus maximum numbers in various settings.

Key to Symbols and abbreviations

★☆	Classification (see page 8–9)
◉	AA Rosette award (see page 11)
A	Associate entry (see page 9)
U	Unclassified rating (see page 9)
⌕	A very special breakfast, with an emphasis on freshly prepared local ingredients
⊝	A very special dinner, with an emphasis on freshly prepared local ingredients
S	Single room
D	Double room (2 people sharing)
pri fac	Private facilities
fmly	Family bedroom
GF	Ground floor bedroom
LB	Short/Leisure breaks
∗	2014 prices
ch fac	Special facilities for children
TVL	Lounge with television
Lounge	Lounge without television
TV4B	Television in four bedrooms
STV	Satellite television
FTV	Freeview television
WiFi	Wireless internet
⊜	Credit/debit cards not accepted
tea/coffee	Tea and coffee-making facilities
Conf	Conference facilities
rms	Bedrooms in main building
Etr	Easter
fr	From
RS	Restricted service
⬗	Secure storage
⊗	No dogs
⊡	Indoor swimming pool
⊡	Heated indoor swimming pool
⌇	Outdoor swimming pool
⌇	Heated outdoor swimming pool
⚐	Croquet lawn
⚲	Tennis court
⚑	Golf (followed by number of holes)

AA Inspected Guest Accommodation

The AA inspects and classifies more than 2,500 guest houses, farmhouses, inns and restaurants with rooms for its Guest Accommodation Scheme, under common quality standards agreed between the AA, VisitBritain, VisitScotland and VisitWales. AA recognised establishments pay an annual fee according to the classification and the number of bedrooms. The classification is not transferable if an establishment changes hands.

The AA presents several awards within the Guest Accommodation Scheme, including the **AA Friendliest B&B of the Year**, which showcases the very finest hospitality in the country, **AA Guest Accommodation of the Year Awards**, presented to establishments in Scotland, Northern Ireland, Wales and England, **AA London B&B of the Year**, and **AA Funkiest B&B of the Year**. See pages 12-16 for this year's winners.

Stars

AA Stars classify guest accommodation at five levels of quality, from one at the simplest, to five offering the highest quality. In order to achieve a one Star rating an establishment must meet certain minimum entry requirements. For example:
- A cooked breakfast, or substantial continental option is provided
- The proprietor and/or staff are available for your arrival, departure and at all meal times
- Once registered, guests have access to the establishment at all times unless previously notified
- All areas of operation meet minimum quality requirements for cleanliness, maintenance and hospitality as well as facilities and the delivery of services
- A dining room or similar eating area is available unless meals are served in bedrooms

To obtain a higher Star rating, an establishment must provide increased quality standards across all areas, with particular emphasis in four key areas:
- Cleanliness and housekeeping
- Hospitality and service
- Quality and condition of bedrooms, bathrooms and public rooms
- Food quality

There are also particular requirements in order for an establishment to achieve three, four or five Stars, for example:

Three Stars and above
- access to both sides of all beds for double occupancy
- bathrooms/shower rooms cannot be used by the proprietor
- there is a washbasin in every guest bedroom (either in the bedrooms or the en suite/private facility)

Four Stars
- half of bedrooms must be en suite or have private facilities

Five Stars
- all bedrooms must be en suite or have private facilities

Establishments applying for AA recognition are visited by one of the AA's qualified accommodation inspectors as a mystery guest. Inspectors stay overnight to make a thorough test of the accommodation, food, and hospitality. After paying the bill the following morning they identify themselves and ask to be shown round the premises. The inspector completes a full report, resulting in a recommendation for the appropriate Star rating. After this first visit, the establishment will receive a regular visit to check that standards are maintained. If it changes hands, the new owners must re-apply for classification, as standards can change.

Guests can expect to find the following minimum standards at all levels:
- Pleasant and helpful welcome and service, and sound standards of housekeeping and maintenance
- Comfortable accommodation equipped to modern standards
- Bedding and towels changed for each new guest, and at least weekly if the room is taken for a long stay
- Adequate storage, heating, lighting and comfortable seating
- A sufficient hot water supply at reasonable times
- A full cooked breakfast. (If this is not provided, the fact must be advertised and a substantial continental breakfast must be offered)

When an AA inspector has visited a property, and evaluated all the aspects of the accommodation for comfort, facilities, attention to detail and presentation, you can be confident the Star rating will allow you to make the right choice for an enjoyable stay.

★ Highly Commended
AA Gold Stars are awarded to the very best Guest Accommodation within the 3, 4, or 5 star ratings.

Accommodation Designators
Along with the Star ratings, six designators have been introduced. The proprietors, in discussion with our inspectors, choose which designator best describes their establishment:

Bed & Breakfast
A private house run by the owner with accommodation for no more than six paying guests.

Guest House
Run on a more commercial basis than a B&B, the accommodation provides for more than six paying guests and there are usually more services; for example staff as well as the owner may provide dinner.

Farmhouse
The B&B or guest house accommodation is part of a working farm or smallholding.

Inn
The accommodation is provided in a fully licensed establishment. The bar will be open to non-residents and can provide food in the evenings.

Restaurant with Rooms
This is a destination restaurant offering overnight accommodation, with dining being the main business and open

to non-residents. The restaurant should offer a high standard of food and restaurant service at least five nights a week. A liquor licence is necessary and there is a maximum of 12 bedrooms.

Guest Accommodation
Any establishment that meets the minimum entry requirements is eligible for this general category.

[U] Unclassified entries
A small number of establishments in this guide have this symbol because their Star classification was not confirmed at the time of going to press. This may be due to a change of ownership or because the establishment has only recently joined the AA rating scheme. For up-to-date information on these and other new establishments check **theAA.com**.

[A] Associate entries
These establishments have been inspected and rated by VisitBritain, VisitScotland or VisitWales, and have joined the AA scheme on a marketing-only basis.

AA Advertised
These establishments are not rated or inspected by the AA, but are displayed for advertising purposes only.

Useful information

What follows is a selection of things we think it is worth bearing in mind when planning a stay. We hope you'll find them useful.

Arriving at the accommodation
There may be restricted access to some establishments, particularly in the late morning and the afternoon, so do check when booking.

Booking
Book as early as possible, particularly for the peak holiday period (early June to the end of September) and for Easter and other public holidays. In some parts of Scotland the skiing season is also a peak holiday period.

Some establishments only accept weekly bookings from Saturday, and some require a deposit on booking.

Prices
Minimum and maximum prices are shown for one (S) and two people (D) per night and include a full breakfast. If dinner is also included this is indicated in brackets (incl dinner). Where prices are for the room only, this is indicated.

Prices in the guide include VAT (and service where applicable), except the Channel Islands where VAT does not apply.

Where proprietors have been unable to provide us with their 2015 charges we publish the 2014 price as a rough guide (shown by an asterisk *). Where no prices are given, please make enquiries direct.

London prices
London prices tend to be higher than outside the capital, and normally only bed and breakfast is provided, although some establishments do provide a full meal service.

Cancellation
If you have to cancel a booking, let the proprietor know at once. If the room cannot be re-let you may be held legally responsible for partial payment; you could lose your deposit or be liable for compensation, so consider taking out cancellation insurance.

Food and drink
Some guest accommodation provides evening meals, ranging from a set meal to a full menu. Some even have their own restaurant. You may have to arrange dinner in advance, at breakfast or on the previous day, so do ask when booking.

If you book on bed, breakfast and evening meal terms, you may find that the tariff includes only the set menu. If there is a carte you may be able to order from this and pay a supplement.

On Sundays, many establishments serve the main meal at midday, and provide only a cold supper in the evening. In some parts of Britain, particularly in Scotland, high tea (i.e. a savoury dish followed by bread and butter, scones and cakes) is sometimes served instead of, or as an alternative to, dinner.

Farmhouses: Sometimes the land has been sold and only the house remains, but many are working farms and some farmers are happy to allow visitors to look around, or even to help feed the animals. However, you should always exercise care and never leave children unsupervised. Although the directory entry states the acreage and the type of farming, do check when booking to make sure that it matches your expectations. The farmhouses are listed under towns or villages, but do ask for directions when booking.

Inns: Traditional inns often have a cosy bar, convivial atmosphere, and good beer and pub food. Those listed in the guide will provide breakfast in a suitable room, and should also serve light meals during licensing hours. The character of the properties vary according to whether they are country inns or town establishments. Check before you book, including arrival times as these may be restricted to licensed opening hours.

Facilities for disabled guests

The Equality Act 2010 provides legal rights for disabled people including access to goods, services and facilities, and means that service providers may have to consider making adjustments to their premises. For more information about the Act see www.gov.uk/definition-of-disability-under-equality-act-2010 or www.gov.uk/government/policies/creating-a-fairer-and-more-equal-society.

We recommend that you always telephone in advance to ensure that the establishment you have chosen has appropriate facilities. The establishments in this guide should be aware of their obligations under the Act.

Please note: AA inspectors are not accredited to make inspections under the National Accessibility Scheme. We indicate in entries if an establishment has ground floor rooms; and if a B&B tells us they have disabled facilities this is included in the description.

AA Rosette Awards

The AA awards Rosettes to over 2,000 restaurants that we regard as the best in the UK & Ireland

@

Excellent local restaurants serving food prepared with care, understanding and skill, using good quality ingredients.

@@

The best local restaurants, which aim for and achieve higher standards and better consistency, and where a greater precision is apparent in the cooking. There will be obvious attention to the selection of quality ingredients.

@@@

Outstanding restaurants that demand recognition well beyond their local area.

@@@@

Among the very best restaurants in the British Isles, where the cooking demands national recognition.

@@@@@

The finest restaurants in the British Isles, where the cooking compares with the best in the world.

AA Bed &Breakfast Awards

Each year the AA celebrates the best that our Guest Accommodation scheme has to offer. Our inspectors nominate those places that they feel to be a cut above the rest, and award winners are chosen from these nominations. Held this year at St Ermins Hotel, London, the AA Bed and Breakfast Awards 2014-2015 recognised and rewarded more than 30 very deserving finalists, for demonstrating all-round excellence and unfailing standards and for providing outstanding service to their guests. All finalists were treated to a drinks reception, followed by a formal four-course celebratory luncheon. They also received a personalised certificate and an engraved Villeroy & Boch decanter, as well as a goody bag to take home with them.

FRIENDLIEST B&B OF THE YEAR

RIVER GARTH GUEST HOUSE ★★★★★
PENRITH page 100

After the last visit to River Garth, our inspector was most impressed. "It was a pleasure to return to River Garth ... the building, gardens and setting can not fail but to offer positive impressions on arrival." Set on the banks of the River Eamont, close to the bridge, the house is just a short walk from Penrith, but still maintains a village feel. Owned and run by Irene and Brian Nixon, River Garth is their latest project, after many successful years running guest houses in Penrith. Irene thought she'd retired when she and Brian moved to Eamont Bridge, but before long she found herself unable to do without the pleasure of looking after people. Unfortunately the riverside setting has not always been an advantage, as the B&B has been flooded twice, in 2005 and 2009, but on both occasions the Nixons have come back to full strength, and now oversee a delightful and popular guest house. There are three bedrooms; two doubles with balconies which overlook the river, and a family room. There is a comfortable lounge for relaxation, and Irene's Full English is not to be missed.

See page 16 for an interview with Irene Nixon

FUNKY B&B OF THE YEAR

THE BULL INN ★★★★★ ❀
MILDENHALL page 332

The Bull Inn a 17th-century coaching inn that has been given a modern, quirky make-over by the somewhat eccentric (by her own admission) owner, Cheryl Hickman. Passionate about quality, service and good food, Cheryl also has a penchant for unusual and sometimes startling design. Bedrooms themes include 'Zebra', 'Gold' and 'Aubergine'. One room – 'Lazy Cow' – has many pictures of cows including a rather surprising one of a heifer with its tongue out in the huge walk-in monsoon shower. Some rooms have hand-made furnishings, while all boast unique features, top quality beds and excellent en suite bathrooms. The dining room has been awarded an AA Rosette, and focuses on quality ingredients from small and often local suppliers. There are many innovative dishes on offer, as well as some old-school pub classics, which basically means something for everyone. Cheryl is always looking for new ideas, and all the decor and furniture is down to her imagination and determination to pursue a boutique style in a sympathetic traditional setting. Husband Wayne is the "Jack of all trades" who does his best to make it all physically happen.

GUEST ACCOMMODATION OF THE YEAR FOR LONDON

SYDNEY HOUSE CHELSEA ★★★★★ 🕯
LONDON SW3 page 245

Located in the heart of Chelsea, just minutes from the King's Road and South Kensington tube station, this smart Georgian townhouse has a lovely, contemporary feel and offers stylish accommodation. Launched in 2009, Sydney House was the first townhouse in the ABode Hotel Group, which has hotels in Canterbury, Exeter, Manchester and Glasgow. The emphasis here is on a good night's sleep, and a freshly cooked, quality breakfast. Beds have Vi-Spring mattresses, goose-down duvets and Egyptian cotton bed linen. There are 21 rooms, and if you're lucky you may be able to bag the top-floor double room known as 'The Room at the Top', which has its own private roof garden. The staff here are friendly and helpful, and although interiors are very stylish and well designed, the property maintains a home-from-home, intimate feel. Breakfast is French-style and includes home-baked pastries, sourdough bread, French jams and butter, as well as their famous Poilâne pain de mie. There are plenty of other choices as well, including the 'Full English', and American-style pancakes served with maple syrup.

AA Guest Accommodation of the Year 2014-2015

ENGLAND

PRAWLES COURT B&B ★★★★★ 🏠
EWHURST GREEN page 344

Elizabethan in origin, with extensions and rebuilding overseen by architect Nataniel Lloyd in the early 20th century, this delightful B&B run by Rob and Candida Machin is set in 27 acres of gardens and grounds. On offer are four unique rooms, each of which is individually furnished and full of character. The beds are dressed in the finest linen, and the en suite bathrooms boast Gilchrist & Soames toiletries. Furniture is an eclectic but perfectly balanced mix of antique and contemporary. Each room has lovely views over the extensive lawns, or the gardens and the distant hills. The hospitality trays are equally impressive, loaded with fresh fruit, home-made biscuits and confectionery, and a selection of teas and coffees. Guests can relax in a delightful drawing room with sumptuous sofas and a warming log fire. Home-made cakes are served on arrival as a treat, and the breakfasts have gained an AA Breakfast award, using the best of local or home-grown produce. Apart from making a great place for a relaxing stay, Prawles Court is also well equipped to cater for weddings and other special events.

SCOTLAND

AIKENSHILL HOUSE ★★★★★
ELLON page 422

Aikenshill House is set in two acres, and enjoys a prominent position on a hill overlooking the new Trump International Golf Links at Menie on the outskirts of Aberdeen. The traditional white painted exterior of this splendid farmhouse conceals a highly modern interior. Run by a family passionate about hospitality, a warm welcome and helpful, attentive service are a definite feature. The property is laid out over three floors, offering four stylish en suite bedrooms with modern amenities and technology. There is also a beautifully appointed lounge complete with a wood-burning stove, and a spacious dining room where breakfast is served. The landscaped gardens are a delight, and owners Jim and Shona generate rave reviews for their helpful, friendly and welcoming approach to guests, and it appears that nothing is too much trouble.

WALES

TYDDYNMAWR FARMHOUSE ★★★★★
DOLGELLAU page 476

Tyddynmawr (which means 'Large homestead' in Welsh) has an enviable location at the foot of Cader Iris mountain. Breathtaking views and peaceful surroundings, just a few miles away from the bustling market town of Dolgellau, make this a very special place which cannot fail to make a lasting impression. Established in 1986 and lovingly restored by Olwen Evans and her family, Tyddynmawr has original oak beams and open fireplaces, alongside two charming and spacious bedrooms. Bedrooms have either a private patio or a balcony with lovely views. The oversized half-tester beds come complete with the finest Egyptian cotton linen and the rooms have plenty of accessories. Olwen offers a warm welcome with tea and home-made cake on arrival. Breakfast is not to be missed, with five courses of the best local produce on offer; an ideal start to a day of walking and cycling in this beautiful area.

NORTHERN IRELAND

WHITEPARK HOUSE ★★★★★
BUSHMILLS page 496

Set in a stunning location on the North Antrim coast, Whitepark House overlooks the famous beaches of White Park Bay, long sweeping sands which are framed on either side by rugged coastline. Parts of the house date back to the 18th century, and first impressions when turning into the driveway are delightful. The gardens are a real feature, and during the summer months guests are able to fully enjoy great views of the grounds, as breakfast is served in the large conservatory at the far side of the building. Inside the house is a wealth of artefacts, paintings and art, many of which were collected by the owners during their extensive world travels. Each bedroom is individually designed and presented and the hospitality and service is of a consistently high standard. The proprietor, Bob Isles, won the AA Landlady of the Year Award back in 2003, and is still doing his best to make visitors welcome and create an ideal place for his guests to relax and get the most out of this beautiful coastal area.

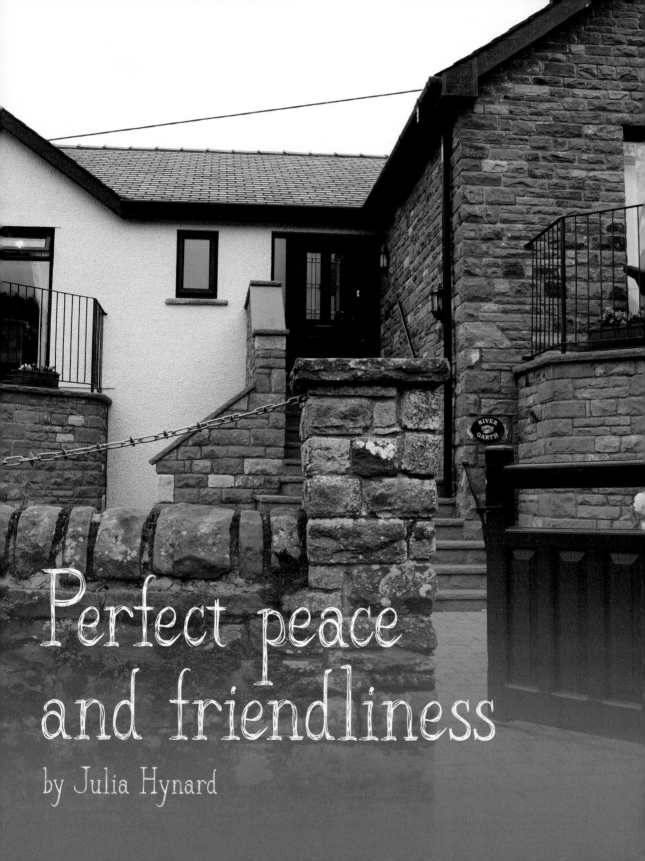

Perfect peace and friendliness

by Julia Hynard

Julia Hynard speaks to Irene Nixon, owner of River Garth, Penrith, winner of the AA Friendliest Bed and Breakfast Award 2014–2015, who says that welcoming people into her home has helped her overcome the trauma of the floods in 2005 and 2009.

Irene Nixon ran two B&Bs in Penrith for many years, deciding to retire when she moved with her husband Brian to a delightful bungalow on the south bank of the River Eamont in the village of Eamont Bridge. Six months later she realised she was bored and decided to open their new home, River Garth, to bed and breakfast guests. She simply missed the pleasure of looking after people and at 66 she still very much enjoys what she does.

Just a couple of years ago she registered with the AA and went straight to a five-Star rating and this year she received the AA's coveted accolade of Friendliest Bed and Breakfast 2014-2015. This was one of seven AA Bed and Breakfast Awards presented at the St Ermins Hotel in London on Tuesday 13 May 2014. Irene was chosen from a shortlist of 25 finalists, nominated by the AA's Hotel Inspectors. Other categories include the Funkiest Bed and Breakfast and AA Guest Accommodation of the Year.

The award presentations followed a Champagne reception and celebratory lunch. Irene, with no idea that she might actually win, felt 'very proud' and thoroughly enjoyed the occasion. Speaking of her nomination, she said: 'It is wonderful to have received so many thank you cards and positive reviews over the years that I already feel like a winner.'

Irene is very much at home with people. She is a friendly but modest person with a highly attuned sensitivity to the needs of others. She enjoys nothing more than meeting and greeting the 'wonderful people' who are her guests, and is entirely comfortable socialising and putting people at their ease. This comes naturally to her – however, the press, television and radio attention she's experienced since receiving the award is a completely different matter!

It is several years – post retirement – since Irene opened for business at River Garth, but it hasn't all been plain sailing. The riverside location which provides much of the property's charm has also made it vulnerable to some freak climatic conditions. In early 2005, the River Eamont flooded and the bungalow was badly affected. At this point they hadn't yet moved into the house, which they had earmarked for their retirement, and they were renting it out. However, it was full of their personal effects.

Heartbreaking as it was, a flood like this was deemed only to happen once in a hundred years, so Irene and Brian set about the laborious business of putting the bungalow back to how it had been before. Then they moved in, and after six months of retirement Irene asked Brian if he'd mind if she started doing bed and breakfast again. He happily agreed.

Three and half years later, unbelievably, they were flooded a second time and once more they lost everything. Irene says she had worked extremely hard to build up her business and had made many friends who had returned

"It is wonderful to have received so many thank you cards and positive reviews over the years that I already feel like a winner"

year on year to stay with them and she was determined to carry on. This time, when it came to restore the property, Irene and Brian decided to make some changes and build upwards, higher above the river. Sorting out the planning permissions and arrangements for raising electricity pylons and so on made this a rather protracted and frustrating process. However, after 18 months in rented accommodation in Penrith, they had created an attractive retreat in the same idyllic setting.

Irene and Brian altered the house so that their living quarters were raised to first floor level with a large garage area underneath. An extra bedroom was built above the garage and they now have three luxurious en suite guest bedrooms which can be used as either single, twin, double or family rooms. The dining area provides views of both the countryside and the river and the first floor has four exterior balconies making the most of the views.

Moments that become memories

A prospect of a riverside balcony proved a clincher for one of Irene's guests, a young professional footballer who, last year, was looking for an appropriately romantic spot to make a proposal of marriage to his girlfriend. Irene was happy to advise on a good local restaurant and assumed the proposal would happen there but, no, this was to happen later on the balcony of their room at River Garth. Brian drove the couple to the restaurant and collected them later, and Irene had a variety of drinks chilling in expectation of a happy outcome. Sure enough she heard the explosion of excitement and happy chatter and the newly engaged young woman rushed in to show Irene the ring and to phone her mum and dad to share the good news, and so Irene and Brian were included in the celebrations.

Irene very much enjoyed the part she played in this most special of occasions, helping to create the moments memories are made from.

Not being a football fan, Irene had not recognised the footballer, and of course she would never divulge his identity, but husband Brian clocked him straight away. While definitely a sporty chap, Brian is more of a cricket fan

and umpires at weekends. He is always happy to chat to fellow aficionados among their guests and to show off his cricketing mementoes.

The bed and breakfast business is very much Irene's. Brian works in haulage, but he is always happy to lend a hand, carrying in luggage and so on, and contributing to the warm and welcoming atmosphere.

Getting your teeth into it

Irene insists there are no negatives to running the business, but there is a funny side. She recalls the couple who were all packed up by breakfast time, but returned to their room to clean their teeth before leaving. Mid-brush, the husband received a call on his mobile phone, rushed to answer it, and then the pair made their goodbyes and headed off. When Irene went to service the room half an hour later, she found the toothbrush still on the sink enmeshed with the gentleman's dental bridge.

The wife was soon back at the door to retrieve the invaluable face gear – her husband was mortified with embarrassment and stayed in the car – while the grateful wife and Irene were able to appreciate the humour of the situation.

The right kind of experience

Asked why she'd gone into the B&B business in the first place, Irene explained that her mother had offered bed and breakfast at the family home in the Scottish Highlands in the early 1960s, while she'd been in her teens. She recalls with a chuckle that in those days it was a £1 a night for a bed and a hearty Scottish breakfast! She'd always had it in mind that when her three children had left home she'd do it herself, knowing that it would suit her.

Her employment choices prior to that have stood her in good stead for the business, giving her the right kind of experience for her ultimate career. From school, aged 15, she went to work in housekeeping at Floors Castle, near Kelso in south-east Scotland for the Duke and Duchess of Roxburgh. Another important job for her, which helped develop both her customer service and interior design skills, was working for many years at Horizon Tiles in Workington, for Mr and Mrs Hodgson, from whom she learned a lot. She loved the shop because it was so beautiful and had a great atmosphere, and had such good outcomes in terms of customer satisfaction.

Relax and unwind

Irene has been blessed with the nicest of people among her guests, including many regulars. She says she has no typical guest – they come from all around the world and all walks of life and might be travelling for business or pleasure. The one thing they have in common is that they all appreciate the peace and quiet of the location, by the river, a few hundred yards from the historic bridge that gives the village its name. They are at the edge of the Lake District, away from the hubbub, and with no traffic noise to disturb the tranquillity, but close enough to all the attractions the area has to offer. A real plus is that the house is just a short walk from the lovely old market town of Penrith, and that there are good pubs in the village that serve food.

Irene loves to see her guests visibly relax and unwind, whether from the day's business or travels, and to enjoy her home and the delights of the area, with the Lake District to the west and the Eden Valley and North Pennines to the east.

Over and above, not over the top

The best thing for Irene about running a bed and breakfast business is meeting people and providing a really good experience for them. She likes to make sure that her guests are comfortable by attending to the little details, like a turn down service, so that guests return each day to a tidy and inviting room.

When I asked Irene for the secret of her success, she answered without hesitation: 'Being natural and being helpful.' She thinks the little touches are important: hot water bottles on a cold night, even though the rooms are well heated, because they are comforting; providing a complimentary laundry service rather than directing guests to a launderette; and offering assistance, particularly to people from overseas, to make the most of their trip with advice on places to visit and things to do. As she puts it so well: 'Going over and above, but not over the top'.

▽ AA Restaurant Inspector Giovanna Grossi, award-winner Irene Nixon and Mark Croston, Chief Sales & Marketing Officer, eviivo

19

Staying in the Cotswolds

by Sean Callery

Ask anyone who lives there, and they'll tell you that The Cotswolds is a marvelous place to live: great walking, beautiful scenery and amazing architecture. Sean Callery takes a look at the past and present of this fascinating region.

Built to last

The Cotswolds region stands on a large bedrock of limestone that has been quarried to build its characteristic golden-hued cottages and walls. Chunks of that limestone form one of the earliest monuments in the area, the Rollright Stones, in the northeast Cotswolds. This is a circle of 77 (or is it? – count them again and you get a different number!) heavily weathered stones that welcome visitors intrigued by stories of witches, ancient ceremonies and kings turned to stone.

Roman development

Above the limestone the rolling grasslands are perfect pasture for sheep, something the Romans exploited during their rule. You're bound to come across a Roman road on your travels here, for example the famous Fosse Way forms the A429 running through it. The Romans built Cirencester to be the second largest city in Britain at the time. Known as Corinium, it was their military headquarters and became the centre for the new wool trade.

Chedworth Roman Villa offers a rare insight into Roman Britain, for it was home to some of the richest people in the country in the 4th century. Visitors can get up close to mosaics, two bath houses, latrines, and a temple. It's also worth taking time to wonder at and admire the marvelous underfloor heating system. There are regular special events bringing the Roman world to life.

Fleeces and churches

It is possible that the Cotswolds got their name after the Romans left, during the Saxon period when sheep continued to graze in enclosures known as 'cots' in the wolds – the Old English name for hills. Over the next few centuries, the area became a massive sheep pasture and gained riches from selling the harvested wool. The profits were used to build large manor houses and 'wool churches' funded by wealthy wool traders.

There are particularly good examples at Chipping Campden and Northleach. By the way, towns and villages with the prefix 'Chipping' were named after their origins as market places and many have narrow alleyways to allow farmers to herd their sheep into the town's central market square.

Clothed beauty

When the wool trade declined in the 15th century, cloth became the region's big earner, and about 150 water-powered mills spread along the Five Valleys around Stroud. But Yorkshire rivals eventually took over this trade because they had local supplies of coal to power their factories, and the Cotswolds did not see full-scale industrial development. This is probably why it is today an Area of Outstanding Natural Beauty, at 790 square miles the second largest protected landscape in England (after the Lake District).

"The town has a fabulous choice of restaurants, tea rooms and pubs"

Lauren O'Hara of East House, Broadway comments: "The town has a fabulous choice of restaurants, tea rooms and pubs. But it is also so beautiful here, with a very different landscape to the southern Cotswolds. The rolling valleys and escarpments create a wonderful landscape that takes your breath away – just as stunning as the scenery of the Yorkshire Dales, which we also love."

Chocolate boxes

The sheep are still there, but today you are more likely to see tourists flocking into the chocolate box towns and villages such as Bourton-on-the-Water. It's pretty, but pretty busy, too, with attractions such as Birdland (see below), a model village, a perfume factory, a motor museum, maze and a model railway exhibition. If you can, go on a weekday out of season when you will have more chance to explore without the queues.

Rob Kreisler of Woodlands Guest House, Upper Swell, suggests visitors have many alternatives to the famous village: "Obviously Bourton-on-the-Water is a big attraction, but we also recommend Chipping Campden for its history and architecture, and Broadway Tower for its view of five counties. This area also attracts a lot of walkers who enjoy the natural beauty – we tell them they will see something to smile about every ten minutes."

Indeed, Broadway is another of the top village attractions, named after its wide main street which is lined with many houses from the 16th to 18th centuries. It also has the Gordon Russell Museum, dedicated to the work of a furniture maker schooled in the Arts and Crafts tradition that has many connections in the Cotswolds. Overlooking the village is Broadway Tower, a Gothic folly offering views over a 62-mile radius on a good day.

Film stars

The combination of scenic landscape and time-warped villages appeals to film-makers, too. Castle Combe earns a living as a film set because it is so beautifully preserved, with 15th-century honey stone cottages, a medieval manor house and a fast-flowing stream in the main street.

Nick Westington, of Avalon Lodge in Devizes, says: "Castle Combe is a local favourite, but another is the quintessentially English village of Lacock. It is incredibly picturesque and has appeared in many TV programmes and films such as *Pride and Prejudice*, *Cranford* and *Moll Flanders*. We get people who want to visit it and see if it is really as pretty as it looks in the movies."

The sense of a time-warp is even more potent at Stanton, often listed as the prettiest Cotswold village, because when it was restored early last century by a Lancashire mill architect, Sir Philip Stott, he ensured that it looked the same as it had for the last 300 years.

Life after sheep

Sheep may have been the source of the wealth that built many Cotswold towns, but other animals are important to the area now. Just south of Burford is the Cotswold Wildlife Park where more than 260 species of exotic animals are housed in 160 acres of parkland. It's a good day out, with rare animals, an adventure playground, children's farmyard and train rides in the summer.

If you want to see more penguins and their pals, take off for Birdland, in Bourton-on-the-Water, where there are more than 50 aviaries and at least 500 birds, including flamingoes, pelicans, penguins and storks. More rare animals are on show at Adam Henson's Cotswold Farm Park, where there are more than 50 breeding flocks and herds of rare British farm animals. Children can get hands-on with rabbits, guinea pigs, lambs and goat kids, or if they want to get mechanical, they can work diggers, drive electric tractors or ride self-propelled roller racers.

Floral delight

If you like flora more than fauna, the Cotswolds is a treat. For those who like to see nature on a truly grand scale, try Westonbirt Arboretum, where more than 16,000 trees from around the world are planted across 600 acres and can be admired from 17 miles of footpaths. There's much to admire all year, but the Enchanted Christmas illuminated trails are a winter highlight.

Hidcote Manor Garden was the first property taken on by the National Trust solely because of its value as a garden. A maze of narrow pathways bordered by tall hedges leads the visitor through a set of garden rooms each with a distinctive personality. Created by Lawrence Johnston more than 100 years ago, it embodies the ideas of the Arts and Crafts movement in landscape. The movement's theorist William Morris lived at Kelmscott Manor in the region and there's a similar influence evident in the gardens there.

Arbors and armour

The Arts and Crafts movement also inspired the garden at Snowshill, where a series of interconnecting 'rooms' nestles in a set of terraces on a steep hill. However, there is more here than just a garden, for the house contains a truly eccentric museum. You'll chance across Samurai warriors in full armour, a vast collection of bicycles and prams, musical instruments and model ships. It's a bizarre collection from around the world, bought by sugar plantation owner Charles Wade – who dictated where each object should be displayed in his house and then ran out of living space and moved into the old Priest's House in the garden. As an aside, if you're a fan of quirky museums, make sure you wind up at Keith Harding's World of Mechanical Music in Northleach.

One site with fine gardens but an even more interesting building is Sudeley Castle. It is actually more of a medieval mansion than a castle, but has seen some right royal visitors. It was twice owned by Richard II, welcomed Henry VIII and two of his wives (Catherine Parr is buried in the church), plus it protected Charles I during the Civil War.

Eat on the hoof

You'd expect to find plenty of lamb in the Cotswolds, and it is also home to the Gloucester Old Spot pig so pork is all around. Other local meaty delights include deer, including sometimes the smaller species muntjac. There are lots of cheese makers, including, famously, Blur bassist Alex James who runs a farm near the foodie mecca of Kingham. Check out the farmer's markets for the region's fruits – there's a big one at Stroud, and others at Cirencester, Stow-on-the-Wold and Chipping Norton.

There's a long tradition of fine ales in the Cotswolds, including beers made in Hook Norton (where you can also tour the pretty much unchanged Victorian brewery), the Patriot range brewed in a pub in Whichford, and Witney's Wychwood brewery.

Unlikely sports

Oh, and if you want to nurse a pint near some strange sports, try the Olympick Games at Chipping Campden, the eccentric football at Bourton-on-the-Water Cotswoldian Football, or the cheese-rolling contest at Brockworth in south Gloucestershire. If that sounds like the Cotswolds are for summer only, think again:

"We get a lot of visitors through all twelve months of the year, because it doesn't matter what the weather is doing, the Cotswolds are always beautiful." says Ian Hawkins, of Burford House. "And being nicely placed between Oxford and Cheltenham, with Blenheim Palace not too far away, Burford is a great base from which to explore the whole Cotswolds area."

Another good base is Cheltenham, from where Alan Bishop of Beaumont House has a few suggestions: "I recommend the Wilson Art Gallery, which re-opened recently and has a lot of material about the Arts and Crafts movement. And the Slimbridge Wetland Trust is a brilliant attraction where you can ride on a trailer and see all sorts of unusual wildlife." That proves it: there really is something for everyone in the Cotswolds!

A bed for the night

by Jim Barker

What are the two aspects of a B&B stay that might make or break the experience? The clue's in the name. A decent breakfast might set you up for the day, but a good night's sleep is just as important. From four-poster extravaganzas to wide-ranging pillow menus, we take a look at what guests might encounter in their search for the perfect slumber.

You'd think a bed should be pretty easy to define. A single bed or a double? Sheets and blankets or a duvet? That's pretty much all you need to know for basic requirements, but if you want a more memorable night's sleep, what about a sleigh bed or a four-poster? Perhaps a queen-size bed, or a half-tester is more your thing? There's a lot more to it than you'd first expect.

Behind closed curtains

Many guest accommodation bedrooms offer four-poster beds. They're seen by many as the height of romantic luxury and are commonly associated with ideas of royalty and opulence. There's a post at each corner, usually wooden, which is topped with a canopy that has curtains attached, allowing the sleeper to inhabit a room within a room. It's an altogether warmer environment – remember, this was an invention from the days before central heating. It was also an effective means of ensuring a level of privacy and intimacy from the prying eyes of servants. Many four-posters these days are unadorned with curtains, which reduces function, but nevertheless makes for a dramatic statement.

Design over function?

A lesser four-poster, a kind of 'two-poster', if you will, is called a half-tester. It has a canopy extending over only around half the bed so that curtains could be drawn around the top half of the sleeper, thus keeping them warm, but not affording the same kind of privacy as a four-poster. This style, like the four-poster is these days more a matter of design than function and gives a Victorian feel to a room, but may not even have curtains.

A sleigh bed is pretty self-explanatory. It's a bed that looks like an old-fashioned sleigh, characterised by a high headboard and footboard, usually both made of heavy wood. This design is very much of the early 19th century, and again connect the sleeper with a luxurious and, often idealised, 'olde worlde' past. It's not just about what

"It's not just about what you're sleeping on..."

you're sleeping on, but where and when you feel you're sleeping.

Good memories

Modern beds, by contrast, are all about innovative materials and design with a particular focus on the mattress. The promise of a perfect and refreshing night's sleep, is important to any weary traveller who wants the familiar comforts and nested feel of their own home.

Memory foam has become one way to achieve this over the old spring-filled mattress. A kind of dense chemical foam slowly moulds to the shape of the sleeper, ostensibly offering a more comforting night's kip. Developed for NASA in the 1960s, and released to the public in the 1980s, it is now pretty much everywhere.

Head first

Pillow menus are a reasonably recent development, offering choice, for example, over hardness and the type of stuffing. As sleepers are in such close facial proximity to their pillow for hours at a time, allergies and respiratory issues are now taken into account by many B&B proprietors.

Among typical choices are pillows with hollow fibre filling, ideal for those with neck problems and allergies; adjustable pillows, with removable stuffing, so you can make it just the right thickness; traditional feather pillows, and pillows suitable for 'hot headed people' who need to keep cool.

Covering all bases

What you sleep under varies as well, but the majority choose between sheets and blankets, and what used to be known as the 'continental' option of the duvet,

although this is now pretty much standard for every household in the land, mainly due to the ease of making the bed. No longer is time spent with hospital corners, tucking in and turning down, just shake the duvet so it fills the cover and away you go. What is in the duvet can vary widely, from the wonderfully natural feel of goose or duck feathers to synthetic microfibre fillings, which not only offer many allergy sufferers the chance of an undisturbed night's sleep, but also make the duvet easier to wash. Duvets also come in a variety of tog ratings; 'tog' being a unit measuring the amount of body heat retained by the duvet, rather than a simple measure of thickness.

Size matters

The size of a bed is also an important consideration, particularly for couples. Some people are used to sleeping close together and others as far apart as the bed will possibly allow. A normal double bed is around 4' 6" wide and 6' 3" long, which is fine for normal use, but when you're on holiday, it's nice to spread out a bit. A king-size bed is another six inches wide and three inches long, and the queen (or Super King) is another foot wider, but if you really want to indulge in extravagant imperial sleeping spaces, you could look for a Caesar-sized bed, which is apparently wider than it is long; eight feet wide and 7' 3" long.

Hopefully whatever the type of bed you sleep in at one of our rated accommodations, you'll get what everyone hopes for when they turn out the light, put their head on the pillow and close their eyes – a refreshing night's sleep that sets you up for the day ahead.

★★★★★ The Premier Collection

ENGLAND

BERKSHIRE
HURLEY
The Olde Bell Inn

WINDSOR
Magna Carta

BRISTOL
BRISTOL
Berwick Lodge

BUCKINGHAMSHIRE
BEACONSFIELD
Crazy Bear Beaconsfield

CAMBRIDGESHIRE
ELTON
The Crown Inn

CHESHIRE
BURWARDSLEY
The Pheasant Inn

CHESTER
DODLESTON MANOR
Mitchell's of Chester
  Guest House
Stone Villa Chester

MALPAS
Tilston Lodge

WARMINGHAM
The Bear's Paw

CORNWALL
LAUNCESTON
Primrose Cottage
Wheatley Farm

LOOE
The Beach House

MEVAGISSEY
Pebble House

PADSTOW
The Seafood Restaurant

PENZANCE
Camilla House
The Summer House

PERRANUTHNOE
Ednovean Farm

POLPERRO
Trenderway Farm

ST AUSTELL
Anchorage House
Highland Court Lodge
Lower Barn

ST BLAZEY
Penarwyn House

CUMBRIA
AMBLESIDE
Nanny Brow

BORROWDALE
Hazel Bank Country House

BRAMPTON
Lanercost Bed and Breakfast

CARTMEL
L'enclume

CONISTON
Wheelgate Country Guest House

CROSTHWAITE
The Punchbowl Inn
  at Crosthwaite

GLENRIDDING
Glenridding House

GRASMERE
Moss Grove Organic

KESWICK
The Grange Country
  Guest House

KIRKBY LONSDALE
Hipping Hall
Plato's
The Sun Inn

LORTON
The Old Vicarage

LUPTON
The Plough Inn Lupton

NEAR SAWREY
Ees Wyke Country House

NEWBY BRIDGE
Hill Crest Country Guest House
The Knoll Country House

PENRITH
Brooklands Guest House
River Garth

TROUTBECK
(NEAR WINDERMERE)
Broadoaks Country House

WINDERMERE
Applegarth Villa & Restaurant
Dome House
The Howbeck
Oakbank House
Windermere Suites
The Woodlands

DERBYSHIRE
BELPER
Dannah Farm Country House

BRADWELL
The Samuel Fox Country Inn

BUXTON
Buxton's Victorian Guest House

HOPE
Underleigh House

MATLOCK
Holmefield Guest House

NEWHAVEN
The Smithy

DEVON
AXMINSTER
Kerrington House

CHAGFORD
Parford Well

CHILLATON
Tor Cottage

CULLOMPTON
Muddifords Court Country House

DARTMOUTH
Appletree Court House
Campbells
Mounthaven
Nonsuch House

ERMINGTON
Plantation House

LUSTLEIGH
Eastwrey Barton

LYDFORD
Moor View House

LYNMOUTH
The Heatherville

PAIGNTON
The P&M Paignton RESIDENCE

PLYMOUTH
Warleigh House

SIDMOUTH
The Salty Monk

STRETE
Strete Barton House

TEDBURN ST MARY
Frogmill Bed & Breakfast

TEIGNMOUTH
Thomas Luny House

TIVERTON
Fernside Bed and Breakfast

TORQUAY
The Briarfields
Carlton Court
The Cary Arms
Kingston House
Lanscombe House
Linden House
The Marstan

TOTNES
Stoke Gabriel Lodgings -
    Badgers Retreat

DORSET
BRIDPORT
The Roundham House
The Shave Cross Inn

BROADWINDSOR
Crosskeys House

CHRISTCHURCH
Druid House
The Lord Bute & Restauran

DORCHESTER
Little Court

FARNHAM
Farnham Farm House

SHAFTESBURY
The Old Chapel

SHERBORNE
The Kings Arms
Munden House
The Rose and Crown Inn, Trent

SWANAGE
Swanage Haven

WIMBORNE MINSTER
Les Bouviers Restaurant with
    Rooms

ESSEX
DEDHAM
The Sun Inn

GESTINGTHORPE
The Pheasant

STANSTED MOUNTFITCHET
Linden House

WIX
Dairy House Farm

GLOUCESTERSHIRE
BARNSLEY
The Village Pub

BLOCKLEY
Lower Brook House

BOURTON-ON-THE-WATER
Cranbourne House

CHELTENHAM
Beaumont House
The Bradley
Cleeve Hill House
Georgian House

CIRENCESTER
The Fleece at Cirencester

LOWER SLAUGHTER
The Slaughters Country Inn

NETHER WESTCOTE
The Feathered Nest Country Inn

STOW-ON-THE-WOLD
The Porch House

HAMPSHIRE
ALTON
The Anchor Inn

BARTON-ON-SEA
Pebble Beach

OVERTON
Mallards

SOUTHAMPTON
Ennio's Restaurant
    & Boutique Rooms
White Star Tavern,
    Dining and Rooms

WINCHESTER
Giffard House
Orchard House
29 Christchurch Road

HEREFORDSHIRE
BOLSTONE
Prickett's Place

HEREFORD
Somerville House

LEINTWARDINE
The Lion
Upper Buckton

LEOMINSTER
Hills Farm
The Old Rectory Pembridge

ROSS-ON-WYE
Wilton Court Restaurant
    with Rooms

HERTFORDSHIRE
HERTFORD
Rigsbys Guest House

WELWYN
The Wellington

ISLE OF WIGHT
GODSHILL
Koala Cottage

NITON
Enchanted Manor

TOTLAND BAY
Sentry Mead

VENTNOR
The Hambrough
The Leconfield

KENT
CANTERBURY
Magnolia House

DEAL
Sutherland House

DODDINGTON
The Old Vicarage

DOVER
The Marquis at Alkham

EGERTON
Frasers

MARDEN
Merzie Meadows

ROYAL TUNBRIDGE WELLS
Danehurst House

LANCASHIRE
BLACKBURN
The Millstone at Mellor

WHITEWELL
The Inn at Whitewell

LEICESTERSHIRE
BELVOIR
Vale House
EAST MIDLANDS AIRPORT
Kegworth House

LINCOLNSHIRE
HEMSWELL
Hemswell Court

HOUGH-ON-THE-HILL
The Brownlow Arms

LINCOLN
Corner Oak

MARKET RASEN
The Advocate Arms

STAMFORD
Meadow View

WINTERINGHAM
Winteringham Fields

LONDON
SW3
San Domenico House
Sydney House Chelsea

W1
The Marble Arch by Montcalm

NORFOLK
BLAKENEY
Blakeney House

GREAT YARMOUTH
3 Norfolk Square

NORWICH
Brasteds
38 St Giles

SHERINGHAM
Ashbourne House
Cleat House
The Eiders Bed & Breakfast

THORPE MARKET
The Green House B&B

THURSFORD
Holly Lodge

NORTHAMPTONSHIRE
BADBY
Bunkers Hill House

NORTHUMBERLAND
BELFORD
Market Cross Guest House

NOTTINGHAMSHIRE
ELTON
The Grange

HOLBECK
Browns

NOTTINGHAM
Restaurant Sat Bains
   with Rooms

OXFORDSHIRE
ABINGDON-ON-THAMES
B&B Rafters

BANBURY
Treetops Guest House

BURFORD
Burford House

FARINGDON
Buscot Manor B&B

OXFORD
The Bocardo
Burlington House

STADHAMPTON
The Crazy Bear

WITNEY
Old Swan & Minster Mill

WOODSTOCK
The Glove House

SHROPSHIRE
CHURCH STRETTON
Field House

LUDLOW
The Clive Bar & Restaurant
   with Rooms
Old Downton Lodge

MARKET DRAYTON
Ternhill Farm House &
   The Cottage Restaurant

OSWESTRY
Greystones

SHREWSBURY
Drapers Hall
Porter House SY1

SOMERSET
BATH
Apsley House
Chestnuts House
Dorian House
One Three Nine
Paradise House
River House and Friary
   Coach House
The Windsor Townhouse

DULVERTON
Tarr Farm Inn

FROME
Lullington House

HOLCOMBE
The Holcombe Inn

LYMPSHAM
Batch Country House

MINEHEAD
The Old Stables B&B
WELLS
Beaconsfield Farm

WESTON-SUPER-MARE
Church House

WITHYPOOL
Kings Farm

YEOVIL
Little Barwick House

STAFFORDSHIRE
LICHFIELD
Netherstowe House
Pipe Hill House

RUGELEY
Colton House

TAMWORTH
Oak Tree Farm

SUFFOLK
BURY ST EDMUNDS
Clarice House

ELVEDEN
The Elveden Inn

HOLTON
Valley Farm

IXWORTH
Ixworth House

LAVENHAM
Lavenham Great House
   'Restaurant With Rooms'

MILDENHALL
The Bull Inn

NEWMARKET
The Packhorse Inn

SOUTHWOLD
Sutherland House

THORNHAM MAGNA
Thornham Hall

YAXLEY
The Auberge

SURREY

CHIDDINGFOLD
The Crown Inn

SUSSEX, EAST

BOREHAM STREET
Boreham House

DITCHLING
Tovey Lodge

EASTBOURNE
Ocklynge Manor

EWHURST GREEN
Prawles Court B&B

HASTINGS & ST LEONARDS
The Cloudesley
Stream House

HERSTMONCEUX
Wartling Place

NORTHIAM
Knelle Dower B&B

RYE
Jeake's House
Manor Farm Oast
White Vine House
Willow Tree House

SUSSEX, WEST

CHICHESTER
Rooks Hill
The Royal Oak Inn

LITTLEHAMPTON
Berry House

LODSWORTH
The Halfway Bridge Inn

ROGATE
Mizzards Farm

SIDLESHAM
The Crab & Lobster

TYNE & WEAR

SUNNISIDE
Hedley Hall Bed & Breakfast
 & Country Cottages

WARWICKSHIRE

STRATFORD-UPON-AVON
Cherry Trees

WEST MIDLANDS

SOLIHULL
Hampton Manor

WILTSHIRE

BOX
The Northey Arms

BURTON
The Old House at Home

CORSHAM
The Methuen Arms

DEVIZES
Blounts Court Farm

EDINGTON
The Three Daggers

MARLBOROUGH
Poulton Grange

PEWSEY
Red Lion Freehouse

WORCESTERSHIRE

BEWDLEY
Kateshill House
Number Thirty

BROADWAY
Abbots Grange
East House
Mill Hay House
Russell's

WICHENFORD
Laughern Hill Estate

YORKSHIRE, EAST RIDING OF

BEVERLEY
Newbegin House

BRIDLINGTON
Marton Grange

YORKSHIRE, NORTH

AMPLEFORTH
Shallowdale House

ASENBY
Crab Manor

BAINBRIDGE
Yorebridge House

BOROUGHBRIDGE
The Crown Inn

FILEY
All Seasons Guesthouse

GOLDSBOROUGH
Goldsborough Hall

GRASSINGTON
Ashfield House
Grassington House

HARROGATE
The Grafton Boutique B&B

HETTON
The Angel Inn

KEXBY
Kexby House

KIRKBY FLEETHAM
The Black Horse

KNARESBOROUGH
General Tarleton Inn

LEVISHAM
Moorlands Country House

LEYBURN
Braithwaite Hall
Capple Bank Farm
Low Mill Guest House

OLDSTEAD
The Black Swan at Oldstead

OSMOTHERLEY
Cleveland Tontine

PICKERING
17 Burgate

RIPON
Mallard Grange

THIRSK
Spital Hill

WEST WITTON
The Wensleydale Heifer

★★★★★ The Premier Collection *continued*

YORKSHIRE, WEST
HAWORTH
Ashmount Country House

HUDDERSFIELD
315 Bar and Restaurant
CHANNEL ISLANDS

JERSEY
ST AUBIN
The Panorama

ISLE OF MAN

ISLE OF MAN
PORT ST MARY
Aaron House

SCOTLAND

ABERDEENSHIRE
ELLON
Aikenshill House

ARGYLL & BUTE
BARCALDINE
Ardtorna

CONNEL
Ards House

OBAN
Blarcreen House

AYRSHIRE, SOUTH
AYR
26 The Crescent

CITY OF EDINBURGH
EDINBURGH
Kew House
Six Brunton Place

23 Mayfield
21212
The Witchery by the Castle

FIFE
PEAT INN
The Peat Inn

ST ANDREWS
The Paddock

HIGHLAND
BRACHLA
Loch Ness Lodge

DORNOCH
2 Quail

GRANTOWN-ON-SPEY
The Dulaig

INVERNESS
Daviot Lodge
Trafford Bank

KINGUSSIE
The Cross

POOLEWE
Pool House

LOTHIAN, WEST
LINLITHGOW
Arden Country House

PERTH & KINROSS
ALYTH
Tigh Na Leigh Guesthouse

SCOTTISH BORDERS
MELROSE
Fauhope Country House

STIRLING
STRATHYRE
Creagan House
SCOTTISH ISLANDS

ISLE OF SKYE
STRUAN
Ullinish Country Lodge

WALES

ANGLESEY, ISLE OF
BEAUMARIS
Ye Olde Bulls Head Inn

CARMARTHENSHIRE
LLANARTHNE
Llwyn Helyg Country House

LLANWRDA
Tyllwyd Hir Bed & Breakfast

ST CLEARS
Coedllys Country House

CEREDIGION
ABERAERON
Feathers Royal
Ty Mawr Mansion

ABERYSTWYTH
Awel-Deg
Nanteos Mansion

CONWY
ABERGELE
The Kinmel Arms

BETWS-Y-COED
Penmachno Hall

CONWY
The Groes Inn

LLANDUDNO
Bryn Derwen

RHOS-ON-SEA
Plas Rhos

TREFRIW
Yr Hafod Country House
and Grill

DENBIGHSHIRE
LLANDYRNOG
Pentre Mawr Country House

RUTHIN
Firgrove Country House B&B

ST ASAPH
Tan-Yr-Onnen Guest House

GWYNEDD
CAERNARFON
Plas Dinas Country House

DOLGELLAU
Tyddynmawr Farmhouse

PWLLHELI
The Old Rectory

MONMOUTHSHIRE
SKENFRITH
The Bell at Skenfrith

WHITEBROOK
The Crown at Whitebrook

PEMBROKESHIRE
FISHGUARD
Erw-Lon Farm

HAVERFORDWEST
The Paddock

NARBERTH
The Grove

NEWPORT
Y Garth Boutique B&B

ST DAVIDS
Ramsey House

SOLVA
Crug-Glas Country House
Lochmeyler Farm Guest House

POWYS
BRECON
Peterstone Court

KNIGHTON
Pilleth Oaks

SWANSEA
MUMBLES
Little Langland

REYNOLDSTON
Fairyhill

VALE OF GLAMORGAN
HENSOL
Llanerch Vineyard

NORTHERN IRELAND

COUNTY ANTRIM
BUSHMILLS
Causeway Lodge
Whitepark House

COUNTY LONDONDERRY
COLERAINE
Greenhill House

REPUBLIC OF IRELAND

COUNTY CLARE
CRATLOE
Highbury House

LAHINCH
Moy House

COUNTY CORK
KINSALE
Friar's Lodge

KINSALE
The Old Bank House

SHANAGARRY
Ballymaloe House

DUBLIN
DUBLIN
Glenogra Town House
Harrington Hall

COUNTY KERRY
DINGLE
Gormans Clifftop House
 & Restaurant

KILLARNEY
Fairview Guest House
Foleys Town House
Old Weir Lodge

KILLORGLIN
Carrig House Country House
 & Restaurant

COUNTY KILDARE
ATHY
Coursetown Country House

COUNTY MEATH
SLANE
Tankardstown

COUNTY MONAGHAN
GLASLOUGH
The Castle at Castle
 Leslie Estate

COUNTY TIPPERARY
THURLES
The Castle
Inch House Country House
 & Restaurant

COUNTY WATERFORD
BALLYMACARBRY
Hanoras Cottage

COUNTY WEXFORD
CAMPILE
Kilmokea Country Manor
 & Gardens

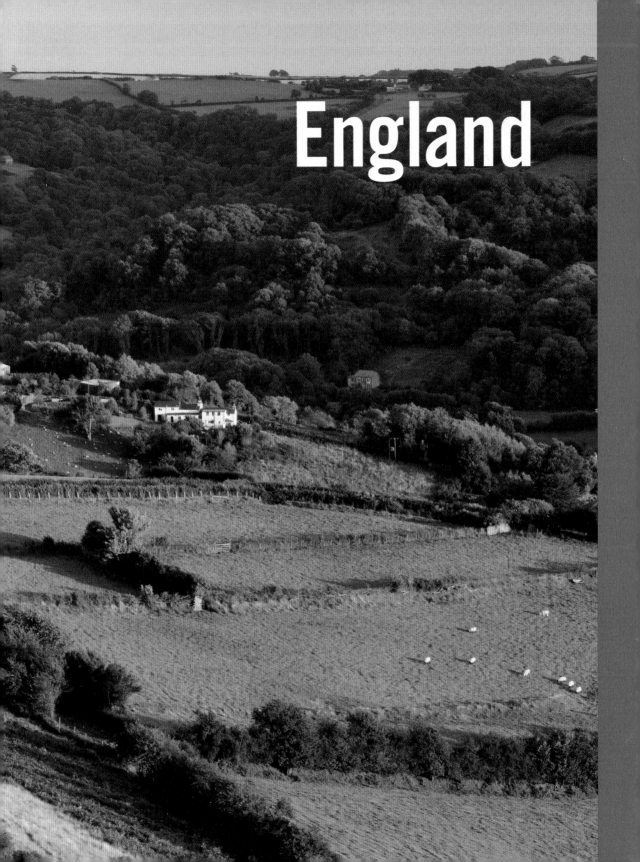

England

BEDFORDSHIRE

BEDFORD
Map 12 TL04

The Knife and Cleaver

★★★★ ⇔ INN

tel: 01234 930789 & 07554 790130   fax: 01234 930365
The Grove, Houghton Conquest MK45 3LA
email: info@theknifeandcleaver.com web: www.theknifeandcleaver.com
dir: *S of Bedford on A6, turn right to Houghton Conquest. Over rdbt, pass post office, right at next rdbt. Left to The Knife and Cleaver*

This charming inn has been totally refurbished to a high standard and offers guests a choice of spacious, well appointed bedrooms and sleek modern bathrooms. Set in the heart of the pretty village of Houghton Conquest it is very popular with locals and serves an extensive choice of seasonal dishes for lunch and dinner. Free WiFi is available throughout and pets are accepted by prior arrangement.

Rooms 9 en suite (9 GF) D £89-£99* **Facilities** FTV tea/coffee Dinner available WiFi **Conf** Max 20 Thtr 20 Class 20 Board 20 **Parking** 25 **Notes** LB No coaches

BLETSOE
Map 11 TL05

North End Barns

★★★★ GUEST ACCOMMODATION

tel: 01234 781320 **fax:** 01234 781320 **North End Farm MK44 1QT**
email: forstergriz@btconnect.com web: www.northendbarns.co.uk
dir: *A6 from Bedford, turn right signed Riseley & Thurleigh Business Park. After 0.75m turn left to Riseley, on left*

Situated in the quiet countryside of Bletsoe, bedrooms are in a delightful barn conversion and offer practical accommodation, with purpose built attractive rooms. A separate kitchen area is also available complete with fridge and microwave.

Rooms 8 annexe en suite (1 GF) S £45-£50; D £70-£80* **Facilities** FTV Lounge tea/coffee WiFi ⇔ 🔒 **Conf** Max 16 Board 14 **Parking** 12 **Notes** Closed Xmas

DUNSTABLE
Map 11 TL02

The Highwayman

★★★ INN

tel: 01582 601122 **fax:** 01582 603812 **London Rd LU6 3DX**
email: 6466@greeneking.co.uk web: www.oldenglish.co.uk
dir: *N'bound: M1 junct 9, A5, 6m on right. S'bound: M1 junct 11, A505, left on A5 towards London. Property on left*

The Highwayman continues to prove popular with business guests, partly due to its convenient location just south of the town, and also for the ample parking space available. The accommodation is comfortable, well equipped and cheerfully decorated. The public areas include a large public bar where meals are available.

Rooms 51 en suite (6 fmly) (23 GF) **Facilities** STV FTV TVL tea/coffee Dinner available WiFi **Parking** 76 **Notes** LB ⊗

LEIGHTON BUZZARD
Map 11 SP92

The Heath Inn

★★★ INN

tel: 01525 237816 & 237390   **fax:** 01525 237818
76 Woburn Rd, Heath and Reach LU7 0AR
email: enquiries@theheathinn.com web: www.theheathinn.com

Situated in the quiet village of Heath and Reach, close to Leighton Buzzard, this traditional inn offers comfortable accommodation. Good quality dishes and a range of cask ales are available, in both the bar and restaurant.

Rooms 16 en suite (5 fmly) (8 GF) S £50-£59.50; D £60-£69.50 **Facilities** FTV TVL tea/coffee Dinner available WiFi Pool table 🔒 **Parking** 50

MILTON ERNEST
Map 11 TL05

The Queens Head

★★★ INN

tel: 01234 822412 **fax:** 01234 822337 **2 Rushden Rd MK44 1RU**
email: 6495@greeneking.co.uk web: www.oldenglish.co.uk
dir: *From Bedford follow A6 towards Kettering, on left entering Milton Ernest*

The staff are friendly and polite at this character inn, which provides good accommodation and ample parking. The cosy bar is stocked with real ales and there is a wide range of dishes on the imaginative menu.

Rooms 13 en suite (4 GF) **Facilities** tea/coffee Direct Dial WiFi **Parking**

WOBURN
Map 11 SP93

The Bell

★★★★ INN

tel: 01525 290280 **fax:** 01525 290017 **21 Bedford St MK17 9QB**
email: bell.woburn@oldenglishinns.co.uk web: www.oldenglish.co.uk
dir: *M1 junct 13/A507 to Woburn Sands. Take 1st left, then next left. At T-junct turn right*

The bar, restaurant and some of the bedrooms are housed in this charming inn, where many of the original features have been retained. The rest of the bedrooms, together with a comfortable lounge, are located in a Georgian building directly opposite. Ample parking is provided behind both buildings.

Rooms 24 en suite (4 GF) **Facilities** FTV Lounge TVL tea/coffee Dinner available Direct Dial WiFi **Parking** 50

BERKSHIRE

BEENHAM
Map 5 SU56

The Six Bells

★★★★ ⇔ INN

tel: 0118 971 3368 **The Green RG7 5NX**
email: info@thesixbells.co.uk web: www.thesixbells.co.uk
dir: *Exit A4 between Reading & Newbury, follow signs for Beenham*

Not far from Thatcham and Newbury, The Six Bells is a friendly, traditional pub that has comfortable, well-appointed bedrooms and good service. Dinner is recommended here; the restaurant serves a range of excellent, well-prepared dishes.

Rooms 4 en suite **Facilities** FTV tea/coffee Dinner available **Conf** Max 40 Thtr 40 Class 40 Board 25 **Parking** 20 **Notes** ⊗ No Children 16yrs No coaches

BOXFORD
Map 5 SU47

High Street Farm Barn Bed & Breakfast (SU424714)
★★★★ FARMHOUSE

tel: 01488 608783 & 07768 324707 **RG20 8DD**
email: nboden@uk2.net **web:** www.highstreetfarmbarn.com
dir: 0.5m W of village centre. Off B4000 to Boxford, farm 1st on left opposite pub

Housed in a converted barn on a smallholding in the village of Boxford, this farmhouse offers comfortable accommodation in its smartly furnished bedrooms. Breakfast, which is served at one table, includes free-range eggs from the farm and home-made breads and marmalades.

Rooms 2 en suite (2 GF) S £55; D £80* **Facilities** FTV Lounge tea/coffee WiFi **Parking** 4 **Notes** ⊗ ⊜ 15 acres sheep

White Hart Cottage
★★★ BED AND BREAKFAST

tel: 01488 608410 **Westbrook RG20 8DN**
email: gillian@jones-parry.orangehome.co.uk
dir: 0.3m NW of Boxford. Off B4000 to Boxford, left for Westbrook, premises on right

Guests are ensured a friendly welcome at this pretty cottage, peacefully located in the delightful village of Boxford. Newbury and the M4 are both just a short drive away. Bedrooms are attractively appointed and guests have access to a small TV lounge. A hearty breakfast is served at the large kitchen table.

Rooms 3 rms (1 en suite) (2 pri facs) S £35-£45; D £65-£70* **Facilities** DVD TVL TV2B tea/coffee 🔒 **Parking** 6 **Notes** ⊗ No Children Closed 12 Dec-12 Jan ⊜

Bell@Boxford
★★★ 🅰 INN

tel: 01488 608721 **fax:** 01488 658502 **Lambourn Rd RG20 8DD**
email: paul@bellatboxford.com **web:** www.bellatboxford.com
dir: M4 junct 14, A338 towards Wantage. Right onto B4000 to x-rds signed Boxford

Paul and Helen Lavis have been the hosts at this traditional Berkshire inn for over twenty years. The restaurant offers a varied and comprehensive menu, seven days a week, along with relaxed service and good value prices. The bedrooms all come complete with power shower, HDTV, WiFi, trouser press and hairdryers, and the location is ideal for Newbury and Hungerford.

Rooms 9 en suite (4 GF) S £45-£80; D £60-£90* **Facilities** FTV DVD tea/coffee Dinner available Direct Dial WiFi Pool table **Conf** Max 12 Board 12 **Parking** 35

CHIEVELEY
Map 5 SU47

The Crab at Chieveley
★★★★★ ⊛⊛ RESTAURANT WITH ROOMS

tel: 01635 247550 **fax:** 01635 247440 **Wantage Rd RG20 8UE**
email: info@crabatchieveley.com **web:** www.crabatchieveley.com
dir: 1.5m W of Chieveley on B4494

The individually-themed bedrooms at this former pub have been appointed to a very high standard and include a full range of modern amenities. Ground-floor rooms have a small private patio area complete with a hot tub. The warm and cosy restaurant offers an extensive and award-winning range of fish and seafood dishes.

Rooms 9 en suite 5 annexe en suite (8 GF) **Facilities** FTV DVD tea/coffee Dinner available Direct Dial WiFi Hot tub Japanese spa suite **Extras** Home-made biscuits, slippers, robes **Conf** Max 14 Thtr 14 Class 14 Board 14 **Parking** 80 **Notes** No coaches

Ye Olde Red Lion
★★★★ ⊜ INN

tel: 01635 248379 & 07764 579808 **Green Ln RG20 8XB**
email: redlion@toucansurf.com **web:** www.yeolderedlion.com
dir: M4 junct 13 N towards Oxford for 300yds, onto slip road signed Chieveley. Left at junct, 300yds on left

Situated in the quiet village of Chieveley, just five miles north of Newbury, this traditional inn offers comfortable en suite accommodation in the adjoining 15th-century house. The cosy pub offers a good range of real ales, and dinner can be enjoyed in the restaurant where good use is made of local and seasonal produce.

Rooms 5 annexe en suite (3 GF) S £80; D £90* **Facilities** FTV tea/coffee Dinner available WiFi **Parking** 30

EAST GARSTON
Map 5 SU37

Queens Arms
★★★★ INN

tel: 01488 648757 **RG17 7ET**
email: info@queenshotel.co.uk **web:** www.queensarmshotel.co.uk
dir: From A338 into Shefford, then follow signs to East Garston. On right as you enter village

The perfect location for lovers of country pursuits, the Queens Arms is located in the beautiful Lambourn Valley. The individually themed bedrooms are well appointed and offer sumptuous beds, flat-screen TVs and WiFi. The bar is well stocked, and the restaurant serves good British food that is based on local produce.

Rooms 8 en suite (1 fmly) (1 GF) **Facilities** FTV DVD tea/coffee Dinner available Direct Dial WiFi ⅃ 18 Fishing Riding **Parking** 30 **Notes** Closed 25 Dec

HUNGERFORD
Map 5 SU36

The Swan Inn
★★★★ 🖥 ⊜ INN

tel: 01488 668326 **fax:** 01488 668306 **Craven Rd, Inkpen RG17 9DX**
email: enquiries@theswaninn-organics.co.uk **web:** www.theswaninn-organics.co.uk
dir: 3.5m SE of Hungerford. S on Hungerford High St past rail bridge, left to Hungerford Common, right signed Inkpen

This delightful village inn dates back to the 17th century, has open fires and beams in the bar, and the bonus of a smart restaurant. Bedrooms are generally spacious and well equipped. Organic produce is available from the on-site farm shop, so the bar, restaurant and breakfast menus all feature local organic produce too.

Rooms 10 en suite (2 fmly) S £70-£80; D £85-£105* **Facilities** FTV tea/coffee Dinner available Direct Dial WiFi 🔒 **Extras** Trouser press **Conf** Max 40 Thtr 40 Class 40 Board 12 **Parking** 50 **Notes** ⊗ Closed 25-26 Dec

HURLEY
Map 5 SU88

Premier Collection

The Olde Bell Inn
★★★★★ ◉◉ INN

tel: 01628 825881 **fax:** 01628 825939 **High St SL6 5LX**
email: oldebellreception@coachinginn.co.uk
dir: M4 junct 8/9 follow signs for Henley. At rdbt take A4130 to Hurley, turn right to Hurley Village, 800yds on right

Originally built in 1135, this charming coaching inn has lots of original features, with timber framed buildings and extensive landscaped gardens. Dinner can be enjoyed in the award-winning restaurant, and the kitchen uses some of the inn's own home-grown seasonal produce. There is a range of individually-styled bedrooms, each with a modern well-equipped bathroom. Both The Tithe Barn and Malthouse cater for functions and private parties, and there are a range of business facilities.

Rooms 48 en suite (21 GF) **Facilities** FTV tea/coffee Dinner available Direct Dial WiFi ⬇ **Conf** Max 130 Thtr 130 Class 80 Board 52 **Parking** 80 **Notes** LB Civ Wed 160

KNOWL HILL
Map 5 SU87

Bird in Hand Country Inn
★★★★ ⚠ INN

tel: 01628 826622 & 822781 **fax:** 01628 826748 **Bath Rd RG10 9UP**
email: info@birdinhand.co.uk **web:** www.birdinhand.co.uk
dir: M4 junct 8/9, A404 towards Henley. At junct 9b onto A4 towards Reading, 3m, Knowl Hill on right after BP garage

The Bird in Hand Country Inn is just four miles from Maidenhead, and dates back, in part, to the 14th century. Bedrooms are arranged around a brick courtyard and all are well equipped. Guests can relax in the Oak Lounge Bar, which has plenty of traditional charm and old English character, and dining is available either in the bar or the restaurant.

Rooms 10 en suite 12 annexe en suite (1 fmly) (6 GF) S £60-£120; D £80-£200* **Facilities** FTV iPod docking station tea/coffee Dinner available Direct Dial WiFi 🔒 **Extras** Robes & slippers in some rooms **Conf** Max 50 Thtr 50 Class 30 Board 40 **Parking** 80 **Notes** LB

MAIDENHEAD
Map 6 SU88

Pinkneys Court Mews
★★★★ 🛏 BED AND BREAKFAST

tel: 01628 633253 & 07989 572167 **Lee Ln SL6 6PE**
email: pinkneyscourtmews@outlook.com **web:** www.bedbreakfastmaidenhead.co.uk
dir: M4 junct 8/9 onto A404(M) to Maidenhead West. Exit after 2m & at rdbt onto A4 towards Maidenhead. Left at next rdbt, then right to Pinkneys Green. At Pinkneys Arms pub left into Lee Ln, on left

Situated within easy reach of Henley, Marlow, Maidenhead and Windsor, this attractive country house bed and breakfast offers convenient but quiet and tranquil surroundings. Attractively furnished bedrooms with designer fabrics provide a homely touch. Finish your stay with an enjoyable breakfast featuring locally sourced, fresh ingredients. A conservatory, terrace and garden are available.

Rooms 4 en suite S £65-£80; D £85-£95* **Facilities** FTV DVD Lounge tea/coffee WiFi ⬇ 18 **Extras** Speciality toiletries, snacks **Parking** 4 **Notes** ⊗

NEWBURY
Map 5 SU46

Pilgrims Guest House
★★★★ GUEST ACCOMMODATION

tel: 01635 40694 **fax:** 01635 44873 **Oxford Rd RG14 1XB**
email: office@pilgrimsgh.co.uk **web:** www.pilgrimsnewbury.co.uk
dir: In Newbury exit A4 at Waitrose rdbt onto B4494 towards Wantage, 0.5m on left

Located close to the town centre, this smartly presented house has comfortable bedrooms with modern bathrooms; some rooms are located in an annexe. WiFi is provided throughout the property and breakfast is served in the bright dining room. Parking is available.

Rooms 13 rms (9 en suite) 4 annexe en suite (1 fmly) (3 GF) S £45-£58; D £56-£65* **Facilities** FTV Lounge tea/coffee WiFi 🔒 **Parking** 17 **Notes** ⊗ Closed 24 Dec-2 Jan

Rookwood Farm House
★★★★ GUEST ACCOMMODATION

tel: 01488 608676 **fax:** 01488 657961 **Stockcross RG20 8JX**
email: charlotte@rookwoodfarmhouse.co.uk **web:** www.rookwoodfarmhouse.co.uk
dir: 2m W of Newbury, at junct A4 & A34 onto B4000, 0.75m to Stockcross, 1st right signed Woodspeen, bear left, 1st on right

Rookwood Farm House enjoys wonderful views and is very much a family home. Bedrooms are attractively presented and feature fine pieces of furniture. Breakfast is served at one large table in the kitchen. The coach house has a kitchen and sitting room and, during the summer, visitors can enjoy the beautiful gardens and outdoor pool.

Rooms 2 rms (1 en suite) (1 pri facs) 2 annexe en suite (1 fmly) S £65-£70; D £95-£100* **Facilities** TVL tea/coffee WiFi 🔦 ⬇ ⚡ 9 🔒 **Conf** Max 16 Board 16 **Parking** 4 **Notes** ⊗ Civ Wed 200

The Lord Lyon
Ⓤ

tel: 01488 657578 **Stockcross RG20 8LL**

Currently the rating for this establishment is not confirmed. This may be due to a change of ownership or because it has only recently joined the AA rating scheme. Owned by Arkell's family brewers, a great range of traditionally brewed beers is available.

Rooms 5 rms

PANGBOURNE
Map 5 SU67

Weir View House
★★★★ GUEST ACCOMMODATION

tel: 0118 984 2120 **fax:** 0118 984 3777 **9 Shooters Hill RG8 7DZ**
email: info@weirview.co.uk **web:** www.weirview.co.uk
dir: A329 N from Pangbourne, after mini rdbt under rail bridge, opposite The Swan pub

A warm welcome is guaranteed at this delightful house, overlooking the River Thames in the village of Pangbourne. The spacious modern bedrooms have been finished to a very high standard and the thoughtful extras include a well-stocked mini-bar. A continental breakfast is served in the bright and airy dining room, and freshly cooked meals can be delivered to your room from the pub across the road.

Rooms 9 en suite (6 fmly) (3 GF) **Facilities** FTV DVD TVL tea/coffee Direct Dial WiFi 🔒 **Extras** Mini-bar - chargeable; robes/slippers in some rooms **Conf** Max 10 Board 10 **Parking** 10 **Notes** ⊗

READING — Map 5 SU77

The French Horn

★★★★ ◎◎ RESTAURANT WITH ROOMS

tel: 0118 969 2204 **fax:** 0118 944 2210 **Sonning RG4 6TN**
email: info@thefrenchhorn.co.uk **web:** www.thefrenchhorn.co.uk
dir: *From A4 into Sonning, follow B478 through village over bridge, on right, car park on left*

This long established Thames-side establishment has a lovely village setting and retains the traditions of classic hospitality. The restaurant is a particular attraction and provides attentive service. Bedrooms, including four cottage suites, are spacious and comfortable; many offer stunning views over the river. A private boardroom is available for corporate guests.

Rooms 12 en suite 8 annexe en suite (4 GF) (4 smoking) S £125-£170; D £160-£215* **Facilities** FTV iPod docking station Lounge tea/coffee Dinner available Direct Dial WiFi ⅃ 18 Fishing ⚲ **Conf** Max 14 Board 14 **Parking** 43 **Notes** ✆ Closed 1-2 Jan RS 25 Dec eve closed for dinner No coaches

Chestnuts Bed & Breakfast

★★★ BED AND BREAKFAST

tel: 0118 988 6171 & 07903 956397 **Basingstoke Rd, Spencers Wood RG7 1AA**
email: chestnuts4bb@hotmail.com **web:** www.chestnutsbandb.co.uk
dir: *M4 junct 11, A33 for Basingstoke, next rdbt onto B3349 (Three Mile Cross), over white-spot rdbt. Chestnuts 1m on left between chemist & bakery*

This detached Georgian house is well placed for the business parks of Reading, just 1.5 miles from the M4 and with easy access to the M3. The house provides spacious bedrooms, warm hospitality, a good breakfast, and off-road parking.

Rooms 2 rms 2 annexe en suite **Facilities** FTV tea/coffee WiFi **Parking** 4 **Notes** ✆ No Children 16yrs ⊜

The Wee Waif

★★★ INN

tel: 0118 944 0066 **fax:** 0118 969 1525 **Old Bath Rd, Charvil RG10 9RJ**
web: www.oldenglish.co.uk

The Wee Waif can be found on the outskirts of Reading and has easy access to popular transport networks. The lodge-style accommodation is appointed with guest comfort in mind. All-day dining is available from the popular Hungry Horse restaurant and bar, where breakfast is also served. Ample parking is provided.

Rooms 42 en suite S £50-£75; D £50-£75* **Facilities** FTV tea/coffee Dinner available WiFi Pool table **Conf** Max 30 Thtr 30 Class 30 Board 30 **Parking** 50 **Notes** ✆

SLOUGH — Map 6 SU97

Furnival Lodge

★★★★ ⓐ GUEST HOUSE

tel: 01753 570333 **fax:** 01753 670038 **53-55 Furnival Av SL2 1DH**
email: info@furnival-lodge.co.uk **web:** www.furnival-lodge.co.uk
dir: *Just off A355 (Farnham Rd), adjacent to BP garage*

In operation for more than twenty years, Furnival Lodge offers modern and spacious rooms, complete with power showers in the en suite bathrooms. Bedrooms are pleasantly decorated and guests have the use of a comfortable lounge.

Rooms 10 en suite (1 fmly) (3 GF) **Facilities** TVL WiFi **Parking** 7 **Notes** ✆

WINDSOR — Map 6 SU97

Magna Carta

★★★★★ ⊜ GUEST ACCOMMODATION

tel: 07836 551912 **Thames Side SL4 1QN**
email: dominic@magna-carta.co.uk **web:** www.magna-carta.co.uk
dir: *M4 junct 5 follow signs to Datchet, then Windsor. At Windsor & Eton riverside station turn right & down to river*

An exciting way to experience life afloat, this superbly equipped barge offers bed and breakfast when not charter-cruising on the Thames. Accommodation is particularly comfortable and pleasantly spacious. The lounge and deck space is notable too, not only for the river views of course, but for the wealth of facilities provided; there is a hot tub on deck, and an impressive range of books, DVDs and music. The well-stocked bar has large picture windows which look out onto the tranquil river. Breakfasts, using local produce, are cooked in the barge's galley.

Rooms 4 en suite **Facilities** DVD Lounge tea/coffee Licensed WiFi Hot tub **Conf** Max 8 Board 8 **Notes** LB ✆ RS pre-booked cruises

Rainworth House

★★★★ GUEST ACCOMMODATION

tel: 01753 856749 **fax:** 01753 859192 **Oakley Green Rd SL4 5UL**
email: info@rainworthhouse.com **web:** www.rainworthhouse.com
dir: *Off A308 Windsor to Maidenhead road*

Near to Windsor and in well-kept grounds, this smart property has six individually styled bedrooms. The richly decorated rooms are well equipped and are ideal for both business and leisure guests. Public areas include a comfortable lounge, and the dining area is a sociable setting for breakfast. Parking is available.

Rooms 6 rms (5 en suite) (1 pri facs) (2 fmly) S £65-£90; D £95-£120* **Facilities** FTV Lounge tea/coffee Direct Dial WiFi ⚲ **Parking** 10

Innkeeper's Lodge Old Windsor

★★★★ INN

tel: 0845 112 6104 **Staright Rd, Old Winsdor SL4 2RR**
email: info@innkeeperslodge.com **web:** www.innkeeperslodge.com

At Innkeeper's Lodge you'll find accommodation with comfort and character in equal measure, and everything needed for a relaxing stay, from easy check-in and free parking to complimentary breakfast and a cosy pub serving great value food and drink on the doorstep. Each Lodge has quality rooms, and there are Lodges in a variety of locations from towns and cities to countryside settings across the UK.

Rooms 15 en suite (2 fmly) (7 GF) **Facilities** FTV tea/coffee Dinner available Direct Dial WiFi **Parking**

WINDSOR *continued*

Park Farm

★★★★ GUEST ACCOMMODATION

tel: 01753 866823 **St Leonards Rd SL4 3EA**
email: stay@parkfarm.com **web:** www.parkfarm.com
dir: *M4 junct 6, at end of dual-carriageway take 3rd exit. At T-junct, turn right, Park Farm on left*

Ideally situated between Windsor and Legoland, Park Farm offers a warm welcome and traditionally styled accommodation. Each bedroom has a range of useful facilities. Bunk beds can be added for children. The owners aim to offer guests a friendly and personal service including advice and information on where to eat or what to do in the area.

Rooms 4 rms (3 en suite) (1 pri facs) (2 fmly) (2 GF) **Facilities** FTV DVD iPod docking station tea/coffee WiFi **Parking** 8 **Notes** ⊗ ⊜

Clarence Guest House

★★★ GUEST HOUSE

tel: 01753 864436 **fax:** 01753 857060 **9 Clarence Rd SL4 5AE**
email: clarence.hotel@btconnect.com **web:** www.clarence-hotel.co.uk
dir: *M4 junct 6, dual carriageway to Windsor, left at 1st rdbt into Clarence Rd*

This Grade II listed Victorian house is in the heart of Windsor. Space in some rooms is limited, but all are well maintained and offer excellent value for money. Facilities include a lounge with a well-stocked bar, and a steam room. Breakfast is served in the dining room overlooking attractive gardens.

Rooms 20 en suite (6 fmly) (2 GF) (8 smoking) S £45-£84; D £49-£97* **Facilities** FTV DVD TVL tea/coffee Licensed WiFi Sauna 🛁 Steam room **Parking** 4 **Notes** LB

The Windsor Trooper

★★★ INN

tel: 01753 670123 **97 St Leonards Rd SL4 3BZ**
email: thewindsortrooper@live.co.uk **web:** www.thetrooperinnwindsor.com
dir: *M4 junct 6, at rdbt follow signs for Windsor, then straight over next 2 rdbts signed Staines-on-Thames, take 1st road on left*

Located close to many popular attractions and within walking distance of the town centre, this traditional inn provides comfortable annexed accommodation, including some rooms suitable for families. Dinner is available in the bright and airy conservatory, where a range of daily specials are often available. A freshly prepared breakfast is served and limited secure parking is available.

Rooms 4 en suite 5 annexe en suite (3 fmly) (5 GF) **Facilities** FTV tea/coffee Dinner available WiFi **Parking** 9 **Notes** ⊗

76 Duke Street B&B

[U]

tel: 01753 620636 & 07884 222225 **76 Duke St SL4 1SQ**
email: bedandbreakfast@76dukestreet.co.uk **web:** www.76dukestreet.co.uk
dir: *M4 junct 6 onto A332. Keep in left lane, take 1st slip road into Maidenhead Rd. At rdbt turn left, at 2nd set of lights turn left into Vansittart Rd. Duke St 1st turn on right, No 76 5th house on left*

Currently the rating for this establishment is not confirmed as it has only recently joined the AA rating scheme.

Rooms 1 rm (1 pri facs) D £85-£95 **Facilities** FTV Lounge tea/coffee WiFi **Notes** ⊗ No Children

WOKINGHAM	Map 5 SU86

Quarters

★★★★ GUEST ACCOMMODATION

tel: 0118 979 7071 **fax:** 0118 977 0057 **14 Milton Rd RG40 1DB**
email: elaineizod@hotmail.com **web:** www.quarterswokingham.com
dir: *From town centre on A321 towards Henley & Twyford. Left at 1st mini rdbt into Milton Rd*

Located just a short walk from the town centre, a warm welcome is assured at Quarters. Stylishly decorated bedrooms are well equipped and spacious. A hearty breakfast is served around the communal dining table.

Rooms 3 en suite S £45-£55; D £65-£75* **Facilities** FTV DVD iPod docking station tea/coffee WiFi **Notes** ⊗ No Children ⊜

The Emmbrook Inn

★★★ INN

tel: 0118 978 2552 **fax:** 0118 977 1728 **Emmbrook Rd RG41 1HG**
email: embrookinn@btconnect.com **web:** emmbrookinn.com
dir: *M4 junct 10 onto A329, 2m to inn*

Situated close to the M4 motorway with direct routes to London and the south west, this traditional English pub offers comfortable en suite accommodation, which is situated adjacent to the pub. Home-cooked meals can be enjoyed, along with a good range of real cask conditioned ales. An enclosed garden and front patio are available for summer drinks. Ample parking to the rear.

Rooms 12 en suite (6 GF) S £53-£69; D £63-£79 (room only)* **Facilities** STV FTV tea/coffee Dinner available WiFi **Parking** 24 **Notes** ⊗ No Children No coaches

BRISTOL

BRISTOL Map 4 ST57

Premier Collection

Berwick Lodge

★★★★★ ◉◉ GUEST ACCOMMODATION

tel: 0117 958 1590 **Berwick Dr, Henbury BS10 7TD**
email: info@berwicklodge.co.uk **web:** www.berwicklodge.co.uk
dir: *M5 junct 17, A4018 (Westbury-on-Trym). At 2nd rdbt 1st left (Westbury-on-Trym). At next rdbt double back on dual carriageway (signed M5 (M4)). Left after brown Clifton RFC sign. At x-rds straight on, follow Berwick Lodge signs*

This delightful building was built in the late 1890s as a private manor house and is surrounded by rose and woodland gardens. A five-year renovation project has been recently completed to provide very high standards of quality and comfort throughout the building, with luxurious bedrooms and bathrooms offering a range of shapes and sizes. Fine dining can be experienced in the opulent restaurant where both dinner and breakfast will be sure to delight the most discerning of guests.

Rooms 10 en suite 2 annexe en suite (2 fmly) S £85-£90; D £125-£145 **Facilities** STV FTV DVD Lounge tea/coffee Dinner available Direct Dial Lift Licensed WiFi ⏺ **Extras** Robes, fruit **Conf** Max 100 Thtr 100 Class 60 Board 30 **Parking** 100 **Notes** ⊗ Civ Wed 100

Westfield House

★★★★ ⌂ ⏺ BED AND BREAKFAST

tel: 0117 962 6119 **fax:** 0117 325 9965 **37 Stoke Hill, Stoke Bishop BS9 1LQ**
email: admin@westfieldhouse.net **web:** www.westfieldhouse.net
dir: *1.8m NW of city centre in Stoke Bishop*

A genuine welcome is assured at Westfield House, a friendly, family-run B&B in a quiet location on the edge of Durdham Downs. The very well-equipped bedrooms offer high levels of quality and comfort. Home-cooked dinners are available by arrangement, and in summer these can be enjoyed on the patio overlooking the large rear garden.

Rooms 3 en suite S £65-£110; D £89-£140* **Facilities** FTV DVD TVL tea/coffee Dinner available Direct Dial WiFi ⏺ **Conf** Max 10 Board 10 **Parking** 5 **Notes** LB ⊗ No Children 11yrs

Find out more about the AA's guest accommodation rating scheme on page 8

Downs Edge

★★★★ GUEST HOUSE

tel: 0117 968 3264 & 07885 866463 **fax:** 0117 968 7063
Saville Rd, Stoke Bishop BS9 1JA
email: welcome@downsedge.com **web:** www.downsedge.com
dir: *M5 junct 17, A4018, at 4th rdbt right onto B4054 (Parrys Ln), 1st left into Saville Rd, 3rd right into Hollybush Ln, left after 2nd speed ramp into Downs Edge Drive*

This attractive country house has a quiet parkland setting in the heart of the city, on the edge of Durdham Downs. It stands in glorious gardens and is furnished with period pieces and paintings. The pleasant, well-equipped bedrooms enjoy sweeping views across the Downs, and a basket of little extras will be found in each room, which provides a nice finishing touch. For breakfast there is an impressive variety of hot and cold dishes. The drawing room has an open fire, and a library containing many books about Bristol.

Rooms 4 en suite 3 annexe en suite **Facilities** FTV DVD Lounge tea/coffee WiFi **Extras** Home-made biscuits/cakes - complimentary **Conf** Board 12 **Parking** 8 **Notes** ⊗ No Children 6yrs Closed Xmas & New Year

See advert on page 40

BRISTOL *continued*

Valley Farm

★★★★ BED AND BREAKFAST

tel: 01275 332723 & 07799 768161 **Sandy Ln BS39 4EL**
email: valleyfarm2010@btinternet.com

(For full entry see Stanton Drew (Somerset))

Westbury Park Guest House

★★★★ GUEST HOUSE

tel: 0117 962 0465 **37 Westbury Rd, Westbury-on-Trym BS9 3AU**
email: westburypark@btconnect.com **web:** www.westburyparkguesthouse.co.uk
dir: *M5 junct 17, A4018, 3.5m opposite gates of Badminton School*

On the edge of Durdham Downs, this detached guest house is ideally located for many of Bristol's attractions. Breakfast is served in the spacious dining room overlooking the front garden. Bedrooms and bathrooms come in a range of shapes and sizes, including one room on the ground floor.

Rooms 8 en suite (1 fmly) (1 GF) **Facilities** tea/coffee WiFi **Parking** 3 **Notes** ⊗ No Children 5yrs

Mayfair Lodge

★★★ GUEST HOUSE

tel: 0117 962 2008 **fax:** 0117 962 2008 **5 Henleaze Rd, Westbury-on-Trym BS9 4EX**
email: enquiries@mayfairlodge.co.uk **web:** www.mayfairlodge.co.uk
dir: *M5 junct 17, A4018, after 3rd rdbt into Henleaze Rd. Lodge 50yds on left*

This charming Victorian house is in a residential area close to Durdham Downs and Bristol Zoo. Mayfair Lodge has well-equipped bedrooms of varying sizes and a relaxed, friendly atmosphere. Breakfast is served at separate tables in the bright dining room. Off-road parking is available behind the property.

Rooms 9 rms (6 en suite) S £40-£60; D £78-£85 **Facilities** FTV DVD tea/coffee WiFi **Parking** 6 **Notes** ⊗ No Children 10yrs Closed Xmas & New Year

The Washington

★★★ GUEST HOUSE

tel: 0117 973 3980 **fax:** 0117 973 4740 **11-15 St Pauls Rd, Clifton BS8 1LX**
email: washington@cliftonhotels.com **web:** www.cliftonhotels.com/bristolhotels/washington/
dir: *A4018 into city, right at lights opposite BBC, house 200yds on left*

This large terraced house is within walking distance of the city centre and Clifton Village. The bedrooms are well equipped for business guests. Public areas include a modern reception lounge and a bright basement breakfast room. The property has secure parking and a rear patio garden.

Rooms 46 rms (40 en suite) (4 fmly) (10 GF) S £41-£74; D £52-£103 **Facilities** FTV tea/coffee Direct Dial Licensed WiFi Reduced rate pass local health club & Bristol Zoo **Extras** Fresh fruit - complimentary **Parking** 16 **Notes** Closed 23-31 Dec

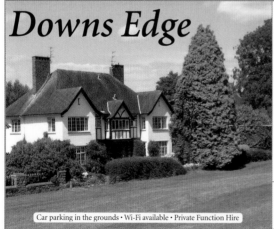

BUCKINGHAMSHIRE

AMERSHAM
Map 6 SU99

The Crown

★★★★★ ◉ 🏚 INN

tel: 01494 721541 **16 High St HP7 0DH**
email: reception@thecrownamersham.com **web:** www.thecrownamersham.com
dir: *M40 junct 2 onto A355, continue to Amersham. Onto Gore Hill, left into The Broadway*

Originally a 16th-century coaching inn, The Crown now offers a mix of quirky, modern minimalist style blended with the character of the original building. High quality food is served daily along with a notable breakfast that will set your day off to a good start.

Rooms 29 en suite 9 annexe en suite (1 fmly) (9 GF) S £99-£275; D £99-£275*
Facilities STV FTV Lounge TVL tea/coffee Dinner available Direct Dial WiFi 🐾 🔔
Extras Speciality toiletries, snacks **Conf** Max 120 Thtr 120 Class 100 Board 18
Parking 38 **Notes** No coaches Civ Wed 50

The Potters Arms

★★★ ⬤ INN

tel: 01494 726222 **Fagnall Ln, Winchmore Hill HP7 0PH**
email: info@pottersarms.co.uk **web:** www.pottersarms.co.uk
dir: *From Beaconsfield on A355, left into Magpie Ln. Follow road to Winchmore Hill*

Situated in a rural location in Buckinghamshire, close to Amersham, this traditional pub offers comfortable accommodation. A warm welcome will be received, and guests can enjoy a range of classic pub favourites in the bar and restaurant. The inn has become well known for its popular Comedy Nights, attracting some top comedians.

Rooms 4 en suite S £65-£85; D £75-£85* **Facilities** FTV TVL tea/coffee Dinner available WiFi **Parking** 20

ASTON CLINTON
Map 5 SP81

Innkeeper's Lodge Aylesbury (East)

★★★★ INN

tel: 0845 112 6094 **London Rd HP22 5HP**
email: info@innkeeperslodge.com **web:** www.innkeeperslodge.com

At Innkeeper's Lodge you'll find accommodation with comfort and character in equal measure, and everything needed for a relaxing stay, from easy check-in and free parking to complimentary breakfast and a cosy pub serving great value food and drink on the doorstep. Each Lodge has quality rooms, and there are Lodges in a variety of locations from towns and cities to countryside settings across the UK.

Rooms 11 en suite (4 fmly) (3 GF) **Facilities** FTV tea/coffee Dinner available Direct Dial WiFi **Parking**

AYLESBURY
Map 11 SP81

Innkeeper's Lodge Aylesbury (South)

★★★★ ⬤ INN

tel: 0845 112 6095 **40 Main St, Weston Turville HP22 5RW**
email: info@innkeeperslodge.com **web:** www.innkeeperslodge.com

At Innkeeper's Lodge you'll find accommodation with comfort and character in equal measure, and everything needed for a relaxing stay, from easy check-in and free parking to complimentary breakfast and a cosy pub serving great value food and drink on the doorstep. Each Lodge has quality rooms, and there are Lodges in a variety of locations from towns and cities to countryside settings across the UK.

Rooms 16 en suite (5 GF) **Facilities** FTV tea/coffee Dinner available Direct Dial WiFi **Parking**

BEACONSFIELD
Map 6 SU99

Premier Collection

Crazy Bear Beaconsfield

★★★★★ ◉ GUEST ACCOMMODATION

tel: 01494 673086 **fax:** 01494 730183 **75 Wycombe End, Old Town HP9 1LX**
email: enquiries@crazybear-beaconsfield.co.uk **web:** www.crazybeargroup.co.uk
dir: *M40 junct 2, 3rd exit from rdbt, next rdbt 1st exit. Over 2 mini rdbts, on right*

Located in the heart of the old town, this former inn dating from Tudor times has been completely restored to create an exciting and vibrant environment. Good food in both the Thai and the English restaurants, classic cocktails and an extensive wine list can all be enjoyed. The bedrooms are individually appointed with unusual fabrics and dazzling colours schemes.

Rooms 6 en suite 11 annexe en suite (2 GF) **Facilities** STV Dinner available Direct Dial Licensed WiFi 🎣 Jacuzzi **Extras** Fruit, mineral water - complimentary **Conf** Max 100 Thtr 100 Class 100 Board 60 **Parking** 12 **Notes** ⊗ Civ Wed 100

BRILL
Map 11 SP61

Poletrees Farm *(SP660160)*

★★★★ FARMHOUSE

tel: 01844 238276 **fax:** 01844 238276 **Ludgershall Rd HP18 9TZ**
email: poletrees.farm@btinternet.com
dir: *Exit S from A41 signed Ludgershall/Brill, after railway bridge 0.5m on left*

Located between the villages of Ludgershall and Brill, this 16th-century farmhouse retains many original features including a wealth of exposed beams. The bedrooms are in converted outbuildings, and the cosy dining room is the setting for a wholesome breakfast.

Rooms 4 annexe en suite (4 GF) **Facilities** FTV TVL tea/coffee **Parking** 6 **Notes** ⊗ No Children 10yrs 110 acres beef/sheep

CHALFONT ST GILES   Map 6 SU99

The White Hart

★★★ INN

tel: 01494 872441 & 0845 608 6040 **Three Households HP8 4LP**
email: 5630@greeneking.co.uk **web:** www.oldenglish.co.uk

A popular inn at the heart of a beautiful village, The White Hart offers modern, well-equipped bedrooms, while public areas feature a spacious lounge bar and a relaxed dining/conservatory area where a varied selection of dishes is available. Parking is available adjacent to the inn and there are also pleasant grounds.

Rooms 11 en suite (5 GF) **Facilities** FTV tea/coffee Dinner available WiFi ⅃ 18
Conf Max 50 Thtr 50 Class 20 Board 20 **Parking** 34 **Notes** LB

DENHAM   Map 6 TQ08

The Falcon Inn

★★★★ ⇔ INN

tel: 01895 832125 **Village Rd UB9 5BE**
email: mail@falcondenham.com **web:** www.falcondenham.com
dir: M40 junct 1, follow A40 & Gerrards Cross signs. Approx 200yds, right into Old Mill Rd, pub opposite village green

This 18th-century inn stands in the heart of the picturesque village of Denham, opposite the green. The en suite bedrooms, with smart shower rooms, are well equipped and display original features. Carefully prepared dishes, together with a good selection of wines, are served at both lunch and dinner in the cosy restaurant.

Rooms 4 en suite **Facilities** FTV DVD tea/coffee Dinner available WiFi ⅃ 18 ⬤
Extras Fresh fruit, bottled water - complimentary **Notes** LB No Children 10yrs

GREAT MISSENDEN   Map 6 SP80

Nags Head Inn & Restaurant

★★★★ ⊛ INN

tel: 01494 862200 **fax:** 01494 862685 **London Rd HP16 0DG**
email: goodfood@nagsheadbucks.com **web:** www.nagsheadbucks.com
dir: N of Amersham on A413, left at Chiltern hospital into London Rd signed Great Missenden

This delightful 15th-century inn, located in the picturesque Chiltern Hills, has a great reputation locally thanks to its extensive menu of local produce and carefully prepared dishes. Individually-designed bedrooms are comfortable with a modern twist ensuring a home-from-home feel. Ample parking is available.

Rooms 5 en suite (1 fmly) **Facilities** FTV tea/coffee Dinner available WiFi ⬤
Extras Speciality toiletries **Conf** Max 50 **Parking** 40 **Notes** Closed 25 Dec

See advert on opposite page

HAMBLEDEN   Map 5 SU78

The Stag & Huntsman

★★★★ INN

tel: 01491 571227 **RG9 6RP**
email: enquiries@thestagandhuntsman.co.uk

Set in the pretty estate village of Hambleden, between Henley and Marlow, this refurbished establishment provides all the character of a true local inn. The accommodation is pleasing with impressive levels of quality and comfort. Menus feature local estate produce when in season along with traditional pub favourites.

Rooms 9 en suite **Facilities** FTV DVD iPod docking station tea/coffee Dinner available Direct Dial WiFi **Parking** 40

HIGH WYCOMBE   Map 5 SU89

Clifton Lodge

★★★ GUEST HOUSE

tel: 01494 440095 **fax:** 01494 536322 **210 West Wycombe Rd HP12 3AR**
email: mail@cliftonlodgehotel.com **web:** www.cliftonlodgehotel.com
dir: A40 from town centre towards Aylesbury, on right after BP station & opposite phone box

Located west of the town centre, this long-established, owner-managed establishment provides a range of bedrooms, popular with a regular commercial clientele. Public areas include an attractive conservatory-dining room and a cosy lounge. Ample parking behind the property.

Rooms 32 rms (20 en suite) (1 fmly) (7 GF) **Facilities** FTV Lounge tea/coffee Dinner available Licensed WiFi **Conf** Max 25 Thtr 25 Class 20 Board 15 **Parking** 28 **Notes** LB ⊛

IVINGHOE
Map 11 SP91

The Brownlow B&B

★★★★ GUEST ACCOMMODATION

tel: 01296 668787 **LU7 9DY**
email: info@thebrownlow.com **web**: www.thebrownlow.com
dir: *A41 to Tring then B488 to Ivinghoe/Dunstable. Follow Leighton Buzzard signs*

The Brownlow at Ivinghoe was built in the early 1800s to serve the newly finished Grand Union Canal, and it has remained in the same family ever since. The old stables have been converted into well-appointed bedrooms which offer plenty of modern amenities. Breakfast is served at the communal table overlooking the canal.

Rooms 5 en suite (5 GF) S £50-£60; D £77.50-£87.50* **Facilities** FTV TVL tea/coffee WiFi 🔒 **Parking** 6 **Notes** ⊗ No Children 6yrs

MARLOW
Map 5 SU88

The Prince of Wales

★★★ INN

tel: 01628 482970 **1 Miller Rd SL7 1PX**
email: prince-of-wales@tiscali.co.uk **web**: www.the-prince-of-wales.co.uk

The Prince of Wales offers well-appointed bedrooms that meet the needs of both business and leisure travellers; some rooms are annexed and have private access. The traditional inn offers a range of ales and an appealing Thai and British menu. There is a large patio that proves ideal for relaxation in the warmer months. Ample, secure parking is available.

Rooms 3 en suite 3 annexe en suite (1 GF) S £65-£75; D £70-£90 (room only) **Facilities** FTV tea/coffee Dinner available WiFi **Parking** 22

MILTON KEYNES
Map 11 SP83

The Cock

★★★ INN

tel: 01908 567733 **fax**: 01908 562109 **72-74 High St, Stony Stratford MK11 1AH**
email: 6432@greeneking.co.uk **web**: www.oldenglish.co.uk
dir: *In village centre*

This historic, 15th-century coaching inn is situated in the picturesque market town of Stony Stratford with the Silverstone circuit nearby. All the bedrooms are en suite and equipped with modern amenities. Food is served all day and the function room is an ideal venue for many different occasions. Parking is available.

Rooms 31 en suite (4 fmly) (7 GF) **Facilities** tea/coffee Dinner available Direct Dial WiFi **Conf** Max 100 Thtr 100 Class 50 Board 45 **Parking Notes** ⊗ Civ Wed 100

NEWTON BLOSSOMVILLE
Map 11 SP95

The Old Mill

★★★ INN

tel: 01234 881273 **Clifton Rd MK43 8AN**
email: enquiries@oldmill.uk.com **web**: www.oldmill.uk.com
dir: *M1 junct 14 onto A509 towards Wellingborough. In Emberton right into Newton Rd*

In the quiet and attractive village of Newton Blossomville, in the Borough of Milton Keynes, this traditional inn offers comfortable accommodation. The inn remains a friendly locals' pub and guests can also enjoy a game of skittles. A traditional pub menu offers a good range of dishes, and a selection of real ales is on offer.

Rooms 5 en suite (2 fmly) **Facilities** FTV tea/coffee Dinner available WiFi 🔒 **Extras** Bottled water, fresh milk **Notes** LB No coaches

PRINCES RISBOROUGH   Map 5 SP80

The George and Dragon
★★★★ INN

tel: 01844 343087 & 346785 **High St HP27 0AX**
email: info@gndpubco.co.uk **web:** www.gndprincesrisborough.co.uk

The George and Dragon is a Grade II listed building, situated on Princes Risborough's historic high street. Recently taken over by Ian and Elle, a warm welcome awaits guests to this traditional pub. The rooms are recently refurbished and modern in design, offering good comfort. A range of pub classics is available for dinner, along with a good range of ales.

Rooms 3 en suite **Facilities** FTV tea/coffee Dinner available WiFi **Parking**

WADDESDON   Map 11 SP71

The Five Arrows
★★★★ ◉◉ ≜ RESTAURANT WITH ROOMS

tel: 01296 651727 **fax:** 01296 655716 **High St HP18 0JE**
email: five.arrows@nationaltrust.org.uk **web:** www.thefivearrows.com
dir: On A41 in Waddesdon. Into Baker St for car park

This Grade II listed building with its elaborate Elizabethan-style chimney stacks stands at the gates of Waddesdon Manor and was named after the Rothschild family emblem. Individually styled en suite bedrooms are comfortable and well appointed. Friendly staff are on hand to offer a warm welcome. Alfresco dining is possible in the warmer months.

Rooms 11 en suite (3 GF) **Facilities** FTV tea/coffee Dinner available Direct Dial WiFi **Conf** Max 20 Thtr 20 Class 20 Board 20 **Parking** 40 **Notes** Civ Wed 60

CAMBRIDGESHIRE

BALSHAM   Map 12 TL55

The Black Bull Inn
★★★★ ◉ INN

tel: 01223 893844 **27 High St CB21 4DJ**
email: info@blackbull-balsham.co.uk **web:** www.blackbull-balsham.co.uk
dir: M11 junct 9 signed Balsham, in centre of village

This privately owned 16th-century, Grade II listed free house is set in the pretty village of Balsham. There are five spacious en suite bedrooms located alongside the pub which provide very high levels of quality and comfort. Very good food is served at lunch and dinner every day.

Rooms 5 annexe en suite (1 fmly) (5 GF) S £85-£109; D £109-£129* **Facilities** FTV DVD Lounge tea/coffee Dinner available WiFi **Conf** Max 30 Thtr 30 Class 24 Board 20 **Parking** 30 **Notes** LB

BURWELL   Map 12 TL56

Deerview
★★★★ BED AND BREAKFAST

tel: 01638 741885 & 07554 300501 **133A North St CB25 0BB**
email: bookings@deerview.biz **web:** www.deerview.biz
dir: A14 junct 35 onto A1303 then B1102. Through Burwell, take last turn on right, at end turn left, 500yds to Deerview

Deerview enjoys a prominent position in the heart of the peaceful village of Burwell. Bedrooms are all spacious, attractively presented and very well equipped. A warm welcome is guaranteed from the friendly owners, and the freshly prepared breakfasts are not to be missed. The house is ten minutes from the famous Wicken

Fen and a short drive from Newmarket, Ely, and Cambridge. Secure parking is available, and there is free WiFi for guests.

Rooms 4 en suite (1 fmly) (2 GF) S fr £38; D £70-£80* **Facilities** FTV DVD tea/coffee WiFi ≜ **Extras** Bottled water, snacks - complimentary **Parking** 4 **Notes** ⊗

CAMBRIDGE   Map 12 TL45

Benson House
★★★★ GUEST HOUSE

tel: 01223 311594 **fax:** 01223 311594 **24 Huntingdon Rd CB3 0HH**
email: bensonhouse@btconnect.com **web:** www.bensonhouse.co.uk
dir: 0.5m NW of city centre on A604

This popular guest house is well placed for the city centre and New Hall and Fitzwilliam colleges. Its pleasant bedrooms vary in size and style and are well equipped with TV, clock radio, beverage tray and hairdryers. The delicious selection at breakfast includes kippers, and there is limited private parking behind the property. Benson House cannot cater for pets or children under 12 years of age.

Rooms 6 en suite (1 GF) S £70-£115; D £110-£115* **Facilities** FTV tea/coffee WiFi **Extras** Speciality toiletries **Parking** 5 **Notes** ⊗ No Children 12yrs Closed 31 Dec

Rose Corner
★★★★ BED AND BREAKFAST

tel: 01223 563136 & 07733 027581 **42 Woodcock Close, Impington CB24 9LD**
email: enquiries@rose-corner.co.uk **web:** www.rose-corner.co.uk
dir: 4m N of Cambridge. A14 junct 32, B1049 N into Impington, exit Milton Rd into Woodcock Close

Rose Corner is a detached property in a quiet cul-de-sac in the popular village of Impington, north of the city. Its spacious bedrooms are carefully furnished and thoughtfully equipped, and breakfast is served in the comfortable lounge/dining room overlooking the rear gardens.

Rooms 5 rms (3 en suite) S £35-£40; D £70-£75 **Facilities** FTV TVL tea/coffee WiFi ≜ **Parking** 5 **Notes** ⊗ No Children 11yrs

The Alpha Milton Guest House
★★★ GUEST ACCOMMODATION

tel: 01223 311625 **fax:** 01223 565100 **61-63 Milton Rd CB4 1XA**
email: info@alphamilton.com **web:** www.alphamilton.com
dir: 0.5m NE of city centre

The Alpha Milton Guest House is in a residential area just a short walk from the city centre. The attractive lounge-dining room overlooks the rear garden, and the pleasant bedrooms all have a good range of facilities.

Rooms 8 rms (7 en suite) (1 pri facs) (2 fmly) (2 GF) S fr £50; D fr £90 (room only)* **Facilities** FTV DVD tea/coffee WiFi **Parking** 8 **Notes** ⊗

The Carpenters Arms

★★★ ⊛ INN

tel: 01223 367050 **182-186 Victoria Rd CB4 3DZ**
email: carpentersarms2013@hotmail.com

The Carpenters Arms has recently re-opened as a family-friendly gastropub, and is located only ten minutes' walk from the centre of Cambridge. Accommodation is available, and guests can enjoy award-winning meals in the vibrant and friendly restaurant below, alongside a good selection of real ales and craft beers. Guests can also enjoy home-made stone-baked pizza from the wood-burning pizza oven.

Rooms 5 rms (2 en suite) (3 pri facs) (3 fmly) S £65-£85; D £85-£110* **Facilities** FTV tea/coffee Dinner available WiFi 🛁 **Extras** Mineral water - complimentary **Conf** Max 30 Thtr 30 Class 15 Board 15 **Parking** 6 **Notes** LB

Hamden Guest House

★★★ GUEST HOUSE

tel: 01223 413263 **89 High St, Cherry Hinton CB1 9LU**
email: info@hamdenguesthouse.co.uk **web:** www.hamdenguesthouse.co.uk
dir: *3m SE of city centre. From M11 exit A1134 to Cherry Hinton; from A14 exit N on A1303 signed Cambridge & Cherry Hinton*

Expect a warm welcome at this small, family-run guest house, which is just a short drive from the city centre. The pleasant bedrooms are generally quite spacious and equipped with many thoughtful extras. Public rooms include a large kitchen-dining room where breakfast is served at individual tables.

Rooms 3 en suite (2 fmly) (1 GF) S £40; D £60* **Facilities** FTV tea/coffee WiFi **Parking** 6 **Notes** LB ⊗ No Children 5yrs

See advert on page 46

Southampton Guest House

★★★ GUEST HOUSE

tel: 01223 357780 **fax:** 01223 314297 **7 Elizabeth Way CB4 1DE**
email: southamptonhouse@btinternet.com **web:** www.southamptonguesthouse.com
dir: *0.5m E of city centre*

The proprietors provide a friendly service at this terraced guest house which is situated on the city's inner ring road, and is just a short walk from the Grafton Centre. Guests can expect well-equipped bedrooms and a comprehensive choice at breakfast.

Rooms 5 en suite (3 fmly) (1 GF) S £40-£55; D £50-£60* **Facilities** tea/coffee Direct Dial WiFi **Parking** 8 **Notes** ⊗ ⊜

CHATTERIS Map 12 TL38

Kings Barn Farmhouse Bed & Breakfast (TL443862)

★★★★ FARMHOUSE

tel: 01354 694535 & 07739 647784 **Langwood Fen PE16 6XF**
email: enquiries@kingsbarn-bandb.co.uk **web:** www.kingsbarn-bandb.co.uk
dir: *From Chatteris on A142 then onto B1098 (New Rd). At end take right hand fork & straight over into Langwood Fen. Left at end of road, follow to end then left*

A very warm welcome is assured at this delightful farmhouse located at the heart of an arable working farm. Kings Barn really is a peaceful rural retreat. There are two en suite bedrooms which have their own side entrances. A hearty breakfast is served in the spacious dining room that overlooks the outdoor swimming pool; guests can use the pool in the summer months.

Rooms 2 en suite (1 fmly) S fr £55; D fr £80* **Facilities** FTV DVD iPod docking station tea/coffee WiFi 🛁 3-hole putting green **Extras** Fresh milk **Parking** 9 **Notes** Closed Xmas & New Year 700 acres arable/sheep

| ELTON | Map 12 TL09 |

Premier Collection

The Crown Inn

★★★★★ INN

tel: 01832 280232 **8 Duck St PE8 6RQ**
email: inncrown@googlemail.com **web:** www.thecrowninn.org
dir: A1 junct 17, A605 W. In 3.5m right signed Elton, 0.9m, left signed Nassington. On village green

Expect a warm welcome at this delightful village pub, situated opposite the village green. The property dates back to the 16th century. It retains many of its original features, such as a large inglenook fireplace and oak-beamed ceilings. The smartly decorated bedrooms are tastefully appointed and thoughtfully equipped. Public rooms include a large open-plan lounge bar, a small relaxed dining area to the front, and a tastefully appointed circular restaurant.

Rooms 3 en suite 2 annexe en suite (2 fmly) (2 GF) **Facilities** FTV DVD tea/coffee Dinner available Direct Dial WiFi ⚓ **Conf** Max 40 Thtr 25 Class 40 Board 25 **Parking** 15 **Notes** RS Sun eve & Mon (ex BH) Restaurant only closed No coaches

| ELY | Map 12 TL58 |

Lazy Otter Pub Restaurant

★★★★ INN

tel: 01353 649780 **Cambridge Rd, Stretham CB6 3LU**
email: thelazyotter@btconnect.com **web:** www.lazy-otter.com

The Lazy Otter enjoys an idyllic position, nestled on the banks of the River Ouse, ideally located between Cambridge and Ely. Bedrooms are all of a high standard and most comfortable. The restaurant overlooks the river with its boats and barges, and enjoys some lovely Fen scenery. The bar offers a range of real ales and guests can relax by roaring log fires in the cooler months. There is a very popular restaurant and the freshly cooked breakfasts are enjoyable. This is an ideal base from which to explore the countryside and delightful historic market towns.

Rooms 3 en suite S £65; D £110* **Facilities** FTV DVD iPod docking station tea/coffee Dinner available WiFi ⚓ **Parking** 60

The Anchor Inn

★★★★ ⊛ ⌂INN

tel: 01353 778537 **fax:** 01353 776180 **Sutton Gault CB6 2BD**
email: anchorinn@popmail.bta.com **web:** www.anchor-inn-restaurant.co.uk
dir: W of Ely. Sutton Gault signed from B1381 at S end of Sutton

Located beside the New Bedford River with stunning country views, this 17th-century inn has a wealth of original features complemented by period furniture, and the spacious bedrooms are tastefully appointed and equipped with many thoughtful touches. The friendly team of staff offer helpful and attentive service.

Rooms 4 en suite (2 fmly) **Facilities** FTV tea/coffee Dinner available Direct Dial WiFi **Parking** 16 **Notes** ⊗ No coaches

The Nyton

★★★★ ⌂ GUEST ACCOMMODATION

tel: 01353 662459 **fax:** 01353 666217 **7 Barton Rd CB7 4HZ**
email: thenyton@yahoo.co.uk **web:** www.thenyton.co.uk
dir: From S, A10 into Ely on Cambridge Rd, pass golf course, 1st right

Set in two acres of mature gardens, this family-run establishment offers comfortable bedrooms in a range of sizes and styles. The pleasant public rooms include a wood-panelled restaurant, a smart bar, and a conservatory-lounge overlooking the gardens. Meals are available in the dining room and informal light meals are served in the lounge bar.

Rooms 10 en suite (3 fmly) (2 GF) S £55-£65; D £90* **Facilities** FTV TVL tea/coffee Dinner available Direct Dial Licensed WiFi ⚓ 18 ⚓ **Conf** Max 40 Thtr 40 Class 20 Board 40 **Parking** 25 **Notes** LB ⊗ Civ Wed 100

The Three Pickerels

★★★★ INN

tel: 01353 777777 **fax:** 01353 777891 **19 Bridge Rd, Mepal CB6 2AR**
email: info@thethreepickerels.co.uk **web:** www.thethreepickerels.co.uk

Situated in the tranquil village of Mepal on the outskirts of Ely, this property sits on the banks of the New Bedford River and has views of the surrounding grassland. Public rooms include a smart bar, a dining room and a lovely lounge overlooking the river. The smartly appointed bedrooms are comfortable and well equipped.

Rooms 4 en suite (1 fmly) **Facilities** FTV TVL tea/coffee Dinner available WiFi Fishing Pool table **Parking** 40 **Notes** ⊗

Grove Barn Guest Rooms

★★★★ A GUEST ACCOMMODATION

tel: 01353 778311 & 07778 747132 **Bury Ln, Sutton Gault CB6 2BD**
email: info@grovebarncambridgeshire.com web: www.grovebarncambridgeshire.com
dir: *M11 junct 14 onto A14 to Bar Hill, then B1050. At 2nd rdbt straight over, then straight over at double mini rdbt, 4m to Sutton*

Located on the charming Isle of Ely, Grove Barn Guest Rooms is in an ideal location for bird watchers, walkers and anglers. There are also plenty of stately homes and other attractions in the area, and lots of places to just relax. On offer are luxuriously appointed bedrooms in a converted outbuilding, with king-size beds and a wealth of useful facilities. The three rooms include two doubles and a triple/family room. The newest double has a jacuzzi bathroom.

Rooms 3 annexe en suite (1 fmly) (2 GF) S £60-£75; D £85-£105* **Facilities** FTV DVD tea/coffee WiFi 🛜 **Extras** Speciality toiletries, chocolates - complimentary **Parking** 4 **Notes** LB

The Castle

★★★ GUEST ACCOMMODATION

tel: 01353 662276 **50 New Barns Rd CB7 4PW**
email: reservations@castlehotelely.com web: www.castlehotelely.co.uk

Conveniently located close to the centre of Ely, The Castle offers a range of bedrooms including several family rooms. There is a comfortable lounge bar, and breakfasts are served at individual tables in the spacious well-appointed breakfast room.

Rooms 15 rms (9 en suite) (6 pri facs) (4 fmly) (3 GF) S £45-£65; D £65-£85* **Facilities** FTV tea/coffee Dinner available Direct Dial Licensed WiFi 🛜 **Conf** Max 80 Thtr 80 Class 25 Board 25 **Parking** 3 **Notes** ⊗

The Village Inn

★★★ INN

tel: 01353 663763 **80 Main St, Witchford CB6 2HQ**
email: tarobinson@hotmail.co.uk

The Village Inn offers two comfortable, well-appointed bedrooms and is located in the peaceful village of Witchford. Dinner is available in the evenings and the bar has a good choice of ales and beers. The historic town of Ely and the city of Cambridge are a short drive away. Free WiFi is available along with secure parking.

Rooms 2 rms S £40-£45; D £50-£55*

HINXTON   Map 12 TL44

The Red Lion Inn

★★★★ INN

tel: 01799 530601 fax: 01799 252601 **32 High St CB10 1QY**
email: info@redlionhinxton.co.uk web: www.redlionhinxton.co.uk
dir: *Nbound only: M11 junct 9, towards A11, left onto A1301. Left to Hinxton. Or M11 junct 10, A505 towards A11/Newmarket. At rdbt 3rd exit onto A1301, right to Hinxton*

The Red Lion Inn is a 16th-century free house pub and restaurant, set in the pretty conservation village of Hinxton and offering high quality purpose-built accommodation. In the winter guests can relax by the well-stoked fire, while in summer they can relax in the attractive walled garden which overlooks the village church.

Rooms 8 annexe en suite (2 fmly) (8 GF) S £90-£115; D £115-£135* **Facilities** FTV DVD Lounge tea/coffee Dinner available Direct Dial WiFi 🛜 **Parking** 43 **Notes** LB

HOLYWELL   Map 12 TL37

The Old Ferryboat Inn

★★★ INN

tel: 01480 463227 fax: 01480 463245 **Back Ln PE27 4TG**
email: 8638@greeneking.co.uk web: www.oldenglish.co.uk
dir: *Phone for directions*

This delightful thatched inn sits in a tranquil setting beside the Great Ouse river, on the periphery of the village of Holywell. Said to be the oldest inn in England, with foundations dating back to 560AD, the inn retains much original character and charm. Bedrooms are soundly appointed, and the open-plan public rooms have a relaxed atmosphere. The extensive gardens, with views of the river, prove popular in the summer months.

Rooms 7 en suite **Facilities** tea/coffee Dinner available WiFi **Conf** Max 60 Thtr 60 Class 32 Board 24 **Parking** 70

HUNTINGDON   Map 12 TL27

Cheriton House

★★★★★ A BED AND BREAKFAST

tel: 01480 464004 fax: 01480 496960 **Mill St, Houghton PE28 2AZ**
email: sales@cheritonhousecambs.co.uk web: www.cheritonhousecambs.co.uk
dir: *In village of Houghton, through village square, signed to river & mill*

Cheriton House is a large Victorian country house close to the River Ouse in a picturesque village. You are assured of a warm welcome, along with friendly and efficient service from Liz and Chris during your stay. Locally sourced ingredients are included at breakfast; dinner is available at local pubs and restaurants.

Rooms 1 en suite 3 annexe en suite (3 GF) S £65-£75; D £70-£88* **Facilities** FTV DVD Lounge tea/coffee WiFi 🛜 🛴 12 🛜 **Extras** Speciality toiletries, chocolate - complimentary **Parking** 7 **Notes** LB ⊗ No Children 14yrs

The Abbot's Elm

★★★★ ◉◉ INN

tel: 01487 773773 **Abbots Ripton PE28 2PA**
email: info@theabbotselm.co.uk web: www.theabbotselm.co.uk
dir: *A1(M) junct 13 onto A14 towards Huntingdon. At 1st rdbt straight on (A141 Spittals Way). Left at 2nd rdbt signed Abbots Ripton. 3m in village centre*

This Grade II listed thatched country inn is situated in the quiet village of Abbots Ripton, near to the ancient market town of Huntingdon. Recently renovated after a fire, this property now boasts modern and comfortable rooms. Guests can enjoy a range of real ales and fine wines in the spacious and smartly appointed bar and restaurant, with a range of enjoyable meals cooked by chef-patron Julia.

Rooms 3 en suite (3 GF) S £60-£70; D £75-£85 **Facilities** STV Lounge tea/coffee Dinner available WiFi **Extras** Robes; filtered water - complimentary **Parking** 50 **Notes** No coaches

LINTON
Map 12 TL54

The Three Hills

★★★ 🛏 INN

tel: 01223 891259 & 07966 233330 **Ashdon Rd, Bartlow CB21 4PW**
email: 3hills@mail.com
dir: *Off A1307 between Cambridge & Haverhill*

This charming, authentic 17th-century coaching inn is just a short drive from Cambridge city centre. The purpose-built bedrooms are all attractively presented, comfortable and well appointed. There is a good selection of real ales, and the dinner menu has a good choice of home-cooked traditional food. A warm welcome is guaranteed and the oak beamed bar has log fires on cooler evenings. The inn is very popular with cyclists and walkers and is close to the main motorway network.

Rooms 4 en suite (2 GF) D £85-£100* **Facilities** FTV tea/coffee Dinner available ⚓ 18 **Parking** 12 **Notes** ⊗ No coaches

LITTLEPORT
Map 12 TL58

The Gate House

★★★★ BED AND BREAKFAST

tel: 01353 863840 & 07940 120023 **2B Lynn Rd CB6 1QG**
email: edna@thegatehousebandb.co.uk web: www.thegatehousebandb.co.uk
dir: *On A10 between Ely & King's Lynn. Cross railway line in Littleport, next right into Lynn Rd, last house on left*

This new-build house has a range of beautifully presented, stylish bedrooms and is a short walk from Littleport railway station. Rear-facing rooms have lovely views of a spur on the Great River Ouse. Conveniently located close to Cambridge, Newmarket and Ely, it is an ideal base to explore this lovely region. The freshly prepared breakfasts include award-winning local produce and should not be missed. Both ample secure parking and free WiFi are available.

Rooms 3 rms (2 en suite) (1 pri facs) **Facilities** FTV DVD Lounge tea/coffee WiFi **Extras** Robes, slippers, home-made biscuits **Parking** 4 **Notes** ⊗

MELBOURN
Map 12 TL34

The Sheene Mill

★★★★ 🛏 RESTAURANT WITH ROOMS

tel: 01763 261393 **39 Station Rd SG8 6DX**
email: enquiries@thesheenemill.com web: www.thesheenemill.com
dir: *M11 junct 10 onto A505 towards Royston. Right to Melbourn, pass church on right, on left before old bridge*

This 16th-century watermill is ideally situated just off the A10, a short drive from both Cambridge and Royston. The bedrooms are individually decorated and well equipped; some rooms overlook the mill pond and terrace. Public rooms include a comfortable lounge, a bar, conservatory and a delightful restaurant overlooking the pond.

Rooms 9 en suite (3 fmly) S £85-£95; D £105-£120 **Facilities** FTV Lounge tea/coffee Dinner available WiFi ⚓ 18 Sauna ⚓ **Extras** Speciality toiletries - complimentary **Conf** Max 180 Thtr 120 Class 120 Board 60 **Parking** 60 **Notes** Civ Wed 120

PIDLEY
Map 12 TL37

The Old Grain Store B&B

★★★★ BED AND BREAKFAST

tel: 01487 840627 & 07752 080369 **Fen Rd PE28 3DF**
email: louise@theoldgrainstore.co.uk web: www.theoldgrainstore.co.uk
dir: *From Warboys Rd into Fen Rd at duck pond. Follow signs to Lakeside Lodge Golf Club, 1.1m*

This newly-constructed bed and breakfast is in a rural location just 10 minutes from Huntingdon and St Ives, and proves convenient for both the business and leisure guests. There are five en suite double rooms, all individually designed and offering many thoughtful extras. Hearty breakfasts are served in the open-plan, airy dining room.

Rooms 5 en suite (1 GF) S £50-£60; D £80-£90* **Facilities** FTV Lounge tea/coffee WiFi ⚓ 18 ⚓ **Extras** Bottled water **Parking** 6 **Notes** ⊗

UFFORD
Map 12 TF00

The White Hart

★★★★ 🛏 INN

tel: 01780 740250 fax: 01780 740927 **Main St PE9 3BH**
email: info@whitehartufford.co.uk web: www.whitehartufford.co.uk

Just five miles from Stamford and ten miles from Peterborough, this charming 17th-century inn is home to Ufford Ales, which are served in the bar. The property is built from local stone and retains many of its original features. The delightful bedrooms are tastefully furnished and thoughtfully equipped. Public rooms include a lounge bar, conservatory and restaurant.

Rooms 6 en suite (2 GF) **Facilities** tea/coffee Dinner available WiFi ⚓ 18 ⚓ **Conf** Max 30 Thtr 30 Class 20 Board 20 **Parking** 30 **Notes** Civ Wed 30

WOODHURST
Map 12 TL37

Falcon's Nest

★★★ GUEST ACCOMMODATION

tel: 01487 741140 **The Raptor Foundation, The Heath, St Ives Rd PE28 3BT**
email: info@raptorfoundation.org.uk web: www.raptorfoundation.org.uk

Located just a few miles from St Ives, Falcon's Nest is in the grounds of The Raptor Foundation estate. There are eight en suite rooms all with kitchenette facilities. As a resident you also get free entry into the Raptor centre and can see many different birds of prey. Breakfasts are available at an additional cost and served in the Silent Wings Tea Room.

Rooms 8 en suite (1 fmly) (8 GF) D £45-£75 (room only)* **Facilities** FTV DVD tea/coffee WiFi ⚓ 18 Entry to The Raptor Foundation Bird of Prey Park **Conf** Class 50 **Parking** 56 **Notes** LB ⊗ Closed 25-26 Dec & 1 Jan

CHESHIRE

ALDERLEY EDGE
Map 16 SJ87

Innkeeper's Lodge Alderley Edge
★★★★ INN

tel: 0845 112 6020 & 01625 599959 **5-9 Wilmslow Rd SK9 7QN**
email: info@innkeeperslodge.com **web:** www.innkeeperslodge.com

Situated between Wilmslow and picturesque Alderley Edge, and only 12 miles from Manchester. Bedrooms are modern and offer good space and comfort. The cosy pub and restaurant offer of wide range of drinks and food. Complimentary WiFi is provided and there is on-site parking.

Rooms 10 en suite (2 fmly) **Facilities** FTV tea/coffee Dinner available WiFi **Extras** Speciality toiletries **Parking** 50 **Notes** ✿

BURWARDSLEY
Map 15 SJ55

Premier Collection

The Pheasant Inn
★★★★★ ✿ INN

tel: 01829 770434 **fax:** 01829 771097 **Higher Burwardsley CH3 9PF**
email: info@thepheasantinn.co.uk **web:** www.thepheasantinn.co.uk
dir: *From A41, left to Tattenhall, right at 1st junct & left at 2nd Higher Burwardsley. At post office left, signed*

This delightful 300-year-old inn sits high on the Peckforton Hills and enjoys spectacular views over the Cheshire Plain. Well-equipped, comfortable bedrooms are housed in an adjacent converted barn. Creative dishes are served either in the stylish restaurant or in the traditional, beamed bar where real fires are lit in the winter months.

Rooms 2 en suite 10 annexe en suite (2 fmly) (5 GF) S £65-£135; D £85-£135* **Facilities** FTV tea/coffee Dinner available Direct Dial WiFi ⅃ 18 **Parking** 80

CHESTER
Map 15 SJ46

See also Malpas

Premier Collection

Mitchell's of Chester Guest House
★★★★★ GUEST HOUSE

tel: 01244 679004 **28 Hough Green CH4 8JQ**
email: welcome@mitchellsofchester.com **web:** www.mitchellsofchester.com
dir: *1m SW of city centre. A483 onto A5104, 300yds on right in Hough Green*

A warm welcome is assured at this delightfully restored and elegant Victorian house, located on the south side of the Dee and the city. Bedrooms are very well equipped and delightfully furnished, and there is a comfortable guests' lounge where an open fire burns on colder days. Substantial breakfasts are served in the bright, south-facing dining room, and special diets can be catered for.

Rooms 3 en suite D £82-£98* **Facilities** FTV DVD TVL tea/coffee Licensed WiFi **Extras** Speciality toiletries, honesty bar **Parking** 5 **Notes** LB ✿ No Children 8yrs Closed 21 Dec-2 Jan

Premier Collection

Stone Villa Chester
★★★★★ GUEST ACCOMMODATION

tel: 01244 345014 & 07764 282015 **Stone Place, Hoole Rd CH2 3NR**
email: info@stonevillachester.co.uk **web:** www.stonevillachester.co.uk
dir: *0.5m NE of city on A56 Hoole Rd*

Stone Villa Chester is a welcoming retreat, away from the bustling city, yet within walking distance of city centre attractions. Bedrooms have comfortable beds and a wealth of accessories which creates a home-from-home experience. Hearty breakfasts feature local produce and home-made jams. Secure parking is a bonus.

Rooms 10 en suite (4 fmly) (3 GF) S £45-£70; D £80-£125* **Facilities** FTV DVD iPod docking station Lounge tea/coffee WiFi ⅃ **Extras** Fruit, chocolates in some rooms **Conf** Max 10 Board 10 **Parking** 10 **Notes** ✿

CHESTER *continued*

Dodleston Manor *(SJ373590)*

★★★★★ FARMHOUSE

tel: 01244 660206 & 07514 657687 **fax:** 01244 660206
Dodleston Ln, Dodleston CH4 9DS
email: rachel@dodlestonmanor.co.uk **web:** www.dodlestonmanor.co.uk
dir: *A55 junct 38 onto A483, then 1st exit onto B5445. Right into Dodleston Ln*

Dodleston Manor is a beautifully appointed, peaceful 19th-century farmhouse on a working dairy farm. Bedrooms are very well appointed with modern touches offering comfortable and modern accommodation in a traditional style. Expect a very warm welcome and a hearty farmer's breakfast.

Rooms 3 en suite (1 fmly) S £65-£85; D £80-£100* **Facilities** FTV DVD iPod docking station TVL tea/coffee WiFi 🔒 **Extras** Speciality toiletries **Parking** 3 **Notes** LB ⊗ 🖼 Civ Wed 20 220 acres dairy

Coach House Inn

★★★★ 🍴 INN

tel: 01244 351900 & 351143 **29 Northgate St CH1 2HQ**
email: info@coachhousechester.co.uk **web:** www.coachhousechester.co.uk
dir: *Phone for detailed directions*

Ideally located in the centre of the city, this inn has been appointed to provide high standards of comfort and good facilities. Its sumptuous bedrooms have a wealth of thoughtful extras; some have views over the Town Hall Square and the cathedral. Imaginative food is served in the bistro-style restaurant and in the cosy bar area. Staff offer informal service and a warm welcome.

Rooms 8 en suite (3 fmly) **Facilities** FTV tea/coffee Dinner available Direct Dial WiFi **Notes** ⊗ Closed 25 Dec

Cheltenham Lodge

★★★★ GUEST ACCOMMODATION

tel: 01244 346767 **58 Hoole Rd, Hoole CH2 3NL**
email: cheltenhamlodge@btinternet.com **web:** www.cheltenhamlodge.co.uk
dir: *1m NE of city centre on A56*

This personally-run guest accommodation lies midway between the city centre and the M53. The attractive bedrooms are well appointed and equipped with a wealth of extras. Family rooms and rooms on the ground floor are available. Substantial breakfasts are served in the smart dining room.

Rooms 5 en suite (2 fmly) (2 GF) **Facilities** FTV DVD tea/coffee WiFi 🔒 **Parking** 5 **Notes** ⊗ Closed 23 Dec-7 Jan 🖼

Green Gables

★★★★ GUEST HOUSE

tel: 01244 372243 **fax:** 01244 376352 **11 Eversley Park CH2 2AJ**
email: perruzza_d@hotmail.com **web:** www.greengableschester.co.uk
dir: *Off A5116 Liverpool Rd signed Countess of Chester Hospital, right at 3rd pedestrian lights to Eversley Park*

Green Gables is an attractive Victorian house with pretty gardens, set in a quiet residential area close to the city centre. The well-equipped bedrooms include a family room, and there is a large, comfortable sitting room. The bright breakfast room is strikingly decorated. Off-street parking is a bonus.

Rooms 2 en suite (1 fmly) S £50-£75; D £80-£100* **Facilities** FTV DVD TVL tea/coffee WiFi 🔒 **Parking** 8 **Notes** ⊗ 🖼

Hamilton Court

★★★★ GUEST HOUSE

tel: 01244 345387 **fax:** 01244 317404 **Hamilton St, Hoole CH2 3JG**
email: hamiltoncourth@aol.com

This friendly guest house offers a peaceful street location just a few minutes walk from Chester railway station and city centre. Bedrooms are spacious and comfortable, and equipped with a range of thoughtful extras. Hearty breakfasts are served in the traditionally decorated dining room. Off-road parking is available.

Rooms 11 en suite (4 fmly) (1 GF) **Facilities** FTV Lounge tea/coffee Licensed WiFi ⅃ 18 **Parking** 6

Lavender Lodge

★★★★ GUEST ACCOMMODATION

tel: 01244 323204 **fax:** 01244 329821 **46 Hoole Rd CH2 3NL**
email: bookings@lavenderlodgechester.co.uk **web:** www.lavenderlodgechester.co.uk
dir: *1m NE of city centre on A56, opposite All Saints Church*

A warm welcome is assured at this smart, late Victorian house located within easy walking distance of Chester's central attractions. The comfortable bedrooms are equipped with thoughtful little extras and have modern bathrooms. Hearty breakfasts are served in the attractive dining room.

Rooms 5 rms (4 en suite) (1 pri facs) (2 fmly) S £35-£50; D £70-£80* **Facilities** FTV tea/coffee WiFi 🔒 **Parking** 7 **Notes** LB ⊗ Closed 24 Dec-2 Jan

The Old Farmhouse B&B

★★★★ BED AND BREAKFAST

tel: 01244 332124 & 07949 820119 **9 Eggbridge Ln, Waverton CH3 7PE**
email: jmitchellgreenwalls@hotmail.com **web:** www.chestereggbridgefarm.co.uk
dir: *From A41 at Waverton left into Moor Ln, left into Eggbridge Ln, over canal bridge, house on right before shops*

The Old Farmhouse, dating from the 18th century, is located in a village community three miles south of the city centre. The cosy bedrooms are equipped with a wealth of thoughtful extras, and the hearty breakfasts feature local and home-made produce.

Rooms 2 rms (1 en suite) (1 pri facs) S £35-£45; D £70-£75* **Facilities** FTV TVL tea/coffee WiFi 🔒 **Parking** 6 **Notes** LB ⊗ No Children 10yrs Closed 13-28 Feb RS Xmas & New Year continental breakfast only

George & Dragon

★★★ INN

tel: 01244 380714 **fax:** 01244 378461 **1 Liverpool Rd CH2 1AA**
email: 7783@greeneking.co.uk **web:** www.oldenglish.co.uk

This former old coaching inn with its black and white Tudor façade, is situated just five minutes from the city centre. This is a traditional inn with sports viewing, cask ales, dining and weekly entertainment, and a late bar until midnight. Bedrooms vary in size. Parking is available on site.

Rooms 14 en suite (2 fmly) **Facilities** FTV tea/coffee Dinner available WiFi **Parking** 20 **Notes** ⊗ No coaches

Glen Garth

★★★ GUEST ACCOMMODATION

tel: 01244 310260 **fax:** 01244 559073 **59 Hoole Rd CH2 3NJ**
email: glengarthguesthouse@btconnect.com **web:** www.glengarthguesthouse.co.uk
dir: *Exit M53 onto A56, 0.5m E of city*

Situated within easy walking distance of the city, family-run Glen Garth provides well-equipped bedrooms, and hearty breakfasts served in the pleasant rear dining room. Friendly, attentive service is a strength here.

Rooms 5 rms (3 en suite) (2 pri facs) (3 fmly) S £35-£40; D £75-£85* **Facilities** FTV DVD tea/coffee WiFi ⅃ 18 **Parking** 5 **Notes** LB ⊗

Innkeeper's Lodge Chester Christleton

★★★ INN

tel: 0845 112 6022 **Whitchurch Rd CH3 6AE**
email: info@innkeeperslodge.com **web:** www.innkeeperslodge.com

Innkeeper's Lodge Chester Christleton (locally known as The Cheshire Cat) offers guests comfortable bedrooms with classic decor and thoughtful amenities; some in the main house, and some in converted cottages alongside the canal. A popular lunch venue with locals, the inn provides well cooked meals served in cosy rooms, each with its own style, and most with a real fire. Large attractive outside areas are available for dining in warmer weather, with access to the canalside to walk off your meal.

Rooms 14 en suite (3 fmly) (4 GF) **Facilities** FTV tea/coffee Dinner available Direct Dial WiFi **Parking**

The Oaklands

★★ INN

tel: 01244 345528 **93 Hoole Rd, Hoole CH2 3NB**
email: 7878@greeneking.co.uk **web:** www.oldenglish.co.uk

This busy and popular public house is conveniently located for access to both the city centre and the M56. A wide range of food is available in the stylish open-plan bar and dining area. Bedrooms vary in size, and service is friendly and attentive.

Rooms 14 rms (13 en suite) (1 pri facs) (2 fmly) (4 GF) **Facilities** FTV TVL tea/coffee Dinner available WiFi **Parking** 30 **Notes** ⊗

CONGLETON	Map 16 SJ86

Egerton Arms Country Inn

★★★★ INN

tel: 01260 273946 **fax:** 01260 277273 **Astbury Village CW12 4RQ**
email: egertonastbury@totalise.co.uk **web:** www.egertonarms.com
dir: *1.5m SW of Congleton off A34, by St Mary's Church Astbury*

This traditional country inn dates to the 15th century and stands opposite the church in the pretty village of Astbury. The creative, good-value menus in the bars and restaurant attract a strong local following, and the bedrooms provide high standards of comfort and facilities.

Rooms 6 en suite (1 fmly) S £60; D £70-£85 **Facilities** FTV tea/coffee Dinner available WiFi 🐾 **Conf** Max 40 Thtr 40 Class 30 Board 20 **Parking** 100 **Notes** LB ⊗ No coaches

The Plough At Eaton

★★★★ ⊜ INN

tel: 01260 280207 **fax:** 01260 298458 **Macclesfield Rd, Eaton CW12 2NH**
email: theploughinn@hotmail.co.uk **web:** www.theploughinnateaton.com
dir: *On A536 (Congleton to Macclesfield road), 1.5m from Congleton town centre*

The Plough At Eaton is a renovated traditional inn offering high quality meals and very comfortable bedrooms in an adjacent building. The bedrooms vary in style, some are contemporary and others more traditionally furnished yet all have very good en suite bathrooms. The spacious bar is appealing and there are also attractive outdoor seating areas.

Rooms 17 annexe en suite (2 fmly) (8 GF) S £60; D £75 **Facilities** Lounge tea/coffee Dinner available Direct Dial WiFi ⅃ 18 **Extras** Snacks **Conf** Max 110 Thtr 90 Class 110 Board 60 **Parking** 78 **Notes** LB RS 25-26 Dec & 1 Jan Close at 6pm Civ Wed 60

FARNDON   Map 15 SJ45

The Farndon

★★★★ ⏝ INN

tel: 01829 270570 **fax:** 01829 271842 **High St CH3 6PU**
email: enquiries@thefarndon.co.uk **web:** www.thefarndon.co.uk
dir: *Just off A534 in village on main street*

Located close to Chester and the north Wales coast, The Farndon is a family-run, traditional, 16th-century coaching inn with a modern twist. The attractive bedrooms are well equipped, and downstairs the bar offers a selection of real ales and fine wines, together with a wide range of imaginative dishes and welcoming log fires.

Rooms 5 en suite S £70-£75; D £85-£125 **Facilities** STV FTV Lounge TVL tea/coffee Dinner available Direct Dial WiFi **Parking** 15 **Notes** LB No coaches

KNUTSFORD   Map 15 SJ77

The Hinton Guest House

★★★★ GUEST HOUSE

tel: 01565 873484 **fax:** 01565 873484 **Town Ln, Mobberley WA16 7HH**
email: thehinton@chessmail.co.uk **web:** www.thehinton.com
dir: *1m NE on B5085 in Mobberley*

The Hinton Guest House is a spacious, family-run, detached house in the village of Mobberley, close to historic Knutsford. There is a range of comfortable, well furnished bedrooms that are thoughtfully equipped. Comprehensive breakfasts are served in the attractive dining room, and a lounge is also available to guests. Complimentary WiFi is provided.

Rooms 6 en suite (1 fmly) S £45-£48; D £68-£72* **Facilities** FTV DVD TVL tea/coffee Licensed WiFi 🦮 **Extras** Robes **Parking** 8 **Notes** ⊗

The Cottage Restaurant & Lodge

★★★ GUEST ACCOMMODATION

tel: 01565 722470 **fax:** 01565 722749 **London Rd, Allostock WA16 9LU**
email: reception@thecottageallostock.com **web:** www.thecottageallostock.com
dir: *M6 junct 18/19 onto A50, between Holmes Chapel & Knutsford*

This well presented family-run establishment enjoys a peaceful location on the A50 between Knutsford and Holmes Chapel. Smart, spacious lodge-style bedrooms complement an attractive open-plan restaurant and bar lounge. Bedrooms are thoughtfully equipped and offer good levels of comfort. Conference and meeting facilities, as well as ample parking, are available.

Rooms 11 annexe en suite (4 fmly) (5 GF) S £60-£79; D £75-£95* **Facilities** FTV tea/coffee Dinner available Direct Dial Licensed WiFi **Conf** Max 40 Thtr 40 Class 25 Board 25 **Parking** 40 **Notes** LB ⊗

LOWER WITHINGTON   Map 15 SJ86

Holly Tree Farm *(SJ802709)*

★★★★ FARMHOUSE

tel: 01477 571257 & 07979 910800   **fax:** 01477 571257 **Holmes Chapel Rd SK11 9DT**
email: davidathollies@aol.com **web:** www.hollytreefarm.org
dir: *On A535 Holmes Chapel Rd in front of Jodrell Bank*

Situated close to Jodrell Bank, Holly Tree Farm offers a good base for both business travellers or for those visiting the local attractions. Bedrooms are located in the adjacent house and are attractive and well equipped. Hearty breakfasts, served in the farmhouse, are based on local produce from the farm's own shop.

Rooms 4 en suite (1 fmly) (1 GF) S £35-£40; D £65-£70* **Facilities** FTV TVL tea/coffee WiFi ch fac 🦮 **Extras** Mini-fridge **Parking** 3 **Notes** LB ⊗ 100 acres beef/sheep/poultry

Who are the AA's award-winning B&Bs? For details see pages 12-16

MALPAS
Map 15 SJ44

Premier Collection

Tilston Lodge

★★★★★ GUEST ACCOMMODATION

tel: 01829 250223 **fax:** 01829 250223 **Tilston SY14 7DR**
email: kathie.ritchie@yahoo.co.uk
dir: A41 S from Chester for 10m, turn right for Tilston. Left at T-junct. Lodge 200yds on right

A former hunting lodge, Tilston Lodge is an impressive Victorian house standing in 16 acres of orchards and rolling pastures, which are home to rare breeds of sheep and poultry. The spacious bedrooms are furnished with fine period pieces and have many thoughtful extras. Ground-floor areas overlook immaculate gardens, and a choice of lounges is available in addition to the elegant dining room, the setting for memorable breakfasts.

Rooms 3 en suite (1 fmly) S £55-£60; D £90-£100* **Facilities** FTV DVD Lounge TVL tea/coffee WiFi 18 Hot tub **Extras** Chocolate, fruit - complimentary **Parking** 8 **Notes** LB

Hampton House Farm (SJ505496)

★★★★ FARMHOUSE

tel: 01948 820588 **Stevensons Ln, Hampton SY14 8JS**
email: enquiries@hamptonhousefarm.co.uk **web:** www.hamptonhousefarm.co.uk
dir: 2m NE of Malpas. Exit A41 into Cholmondeley Rd, next left

Hampton House is located on a quiet farm and offers thoughtfully appointed accommodation and a warm welcome. Parts of the house are reputed to date from 1600, and its stylish decor highlights the many retained period features, including a wealth of exposed beams.

Rooms 2 en suite S £45-£50; D £70* **Facilities** TVL tea/coffee WiFi **Parking** 12 **Notes** No Children 12yrs 180 acres mixed

The Paddock Bed and Breakfast

★★★★ BED AND BREAKFAST

tel: 01829 250569 & 07754 857057 **Malpas Rd, Tilston SY14 7DR**
email: info@thepaddocktilston.com **web:** www.thepaddocktilston.com
dir: Turn off A4, on entering Tilston, left at T-junct, 200mtrs on left, 1st drive after 40mph speed limit sign, with lampost at bottom of drive

The Paddock is set in the small village of Tilston, with easy access to Chester and Wrexham, and is just a short distance from ten golf courses. A warm welcome is assured at this family home, which offers three comfortable and well-equipped bedrooms, all with excellent bathroom facilities. There is a large summer house at the bottom of the garden where hosts Gail and Steve offer afternoon tea to arriving guests on warmer days. Well-cooked breakfasts feature locally sourced ingredients. WiFi is available, and the property has its own parking.

Rooms 3 rms (2 en suite) (1 pri facs) (1 fmly) S £40-£50; D £70-£90* **Facilities** FTV DVD iPod docking station Lounge tea/coffee WiFi **Extras** Bottled water, chocolates **Parking** 3 **Notes**

MIDDLEWICH
Map 15 SJ76

The Sandhurst

★★★★ GUEST ACCOMMODATION

tel: 01606 834125 **fax:** 0870 928 1111 **69 Chester Rd CW10 9EU**
email: sandhursthotel@aol.com **web:** www.sandhurst-hotel.co.uk
dir: M6 junct 18 towards Middlewich, over rdbt, straight ahead at lights. At junct take 2nd turn (Chester Rd), on left after mini rdbt

Guests will find a quintessentially English atmosphere at this Edwardian-themed, family-run house. The bedrooms are comfortable; the first-floor rooms more traditional while those on the top floor rooms are more modern. The elegant dining room is the setting for imaginative dinners, and a comfortable lounge bar is also available. Parking is available along with picturesque gardens at the rear of the property. Theme nights are a speciality.

Rooms 7 en suite 5 annexe rms 3 annexe en suite (4 fmly) (3 GF) **Facilities** FTV Lounge tea/coffee Dinner available Licensed WiFi **Parking** 20 **Notes** Civ Wed 55

NANTWICH
Map 15 SJ65

See also Wybunbury

Henhull Hall (SJ641536)

★★★★ FARMHOUSE

tel: 01270 624158 **fax:** 01270 624158 **Welshmans Ln CW5 6AD**
email: philippercival@hotmail.com **web:** www.cheshirefarmstay.co.uk
dir: M6 junct 16, A500 towards Nantwich, then A51 past Reaseheath, left into Welshmans Ln, 0.25m on left

Expect a friendly welcome at Henhull Hall, which has been in the Percival family since 1924. The Hall stands on the site of the Battle of Nantwich, fought in 1644. The farmhouse is surrounded by beautiful grounds and gardens amidst acres of farmland. Bedrooms are spacious and individually decorated. Breakfast is served in the attractive dining room and features fresh farm produce.

Rooms 2 rms (1 en suite) (1 pri facs) (1 fmly) S £40; D £80* **Facilities** DVD Lounge TVL TV1B tea/coffee WiFi **Conf** Max 10 Thtr 10 Class 10 Board 10 **Parking** 4 **Notes** 345 acres dairy/arable

The Cheshire Cat

★★★★ INN

tel: 01270 623020 **fax:** 01270 613350 **26 Welsh Row CW5 5ED**
email: hello@thecatatnantwich.com **web:** www.thecat.at
dir: M6 junct 15 follow signs to Nantwich. Left off B5341 onto Welsh Row, right into First Wood St

Originally built in the early 17th century as almshouses for six widows, this property has been restored with a modern 21st-century twist. The inn offers comfortable, attractive accommodation. Imaginative dinners are served in the restaurant with its oak beams and glass atrium. Weekends are lively with a bustling bar.

Rooms 11 en suite 1 annexe en suite (1 fmly) (5 GF) S £80-£110; D £90-£120* **Facilities** FTV TVL tea/coffee Dinner available Direct Dial WiFi **Extras** Speciality toiletries **Conf** Max 30 **Parking** 20 **Notes** LB

NANTWICH *continued*

Oakland House

★★★★ GUEST ACCOMMODATION

tel: 01270 567134 **252 Newcastle Rd, Blakelow, Shavington CW5 7ET**
email: enquiries@oaklandhouseonline.co.uk **web:** www.oaklandhouseonline.co.uk
dir: *2m E of Nantwich. Off A500 into Shavington, house 0.5m W of village*

Oakland House offers a friendly and relaxed atmosphere. Bedrooms, some of which are in a separate chalet, are attractively furnished and well equipped. There is a spacious sitting room, and a modern conservatory overlooks the pretty garden and the Cheshire countryside beyond. Substantial breakfasts are served either around one large table or at separate tables.

Rooms 2 en suite 6 annexe en suite (2 fmly) (6 GF) **Facilities** FTV TVL tea/coffee WiFi **Parking** 13 **Notes** LB Closed 31 Dec

NORTHWICH
Map 15 SJ67

The Red Lion

★★★ INN

tel: 01606 74597 **277 Chester Rd, Hartford CW8 1QL**
email: cathy.iglesias@tesco.net **web:** www.redlionhartford.com
dir: *From A556 take Hartford exit. Red Lion at 1st junct on left next to church*

At the heart of the village community opposite the parish church, this popular inn provides a range of real ales and traditional pub food, all served in the cosy public areas or well-tended beer garden. Smart bedrooms feature many thoughtful extras in addition to efficient en suite shower rooms.

Rooms 3 en suite (1 fmly) S £40-£44.95; D £50-£60* **Facilities** FTV tea/coffee Dinner available WiFi Pool table 🔒 **Parking** 6 **Notes** No coaches

SANDBACH
Map 15 SJ76

Innkeeper's Lodge Sandbach, Holmes Chapel

★★★ INN

tel: 0845 112 6026 **Brereton Green CW11 1RS**
email: info@innkeeperslodge.com **web:** www.innkeeperslodge.com

Peacefully located in rural Cheshire, close to historic Sandbach, the lodge provides comfortable, modern bedrooms. It is attached to the Bears Head Vintage Inn, an attractive black-and-white building that has real fires, spacious dining areas and a wide choice of cask ales and food. A continental buffet breakfast is complimentary for all guests.

Rooms 25 en suite (6 fmly) (10 GF) **Facilities** FTV tea/coffee Dinner available Direct Dial WiFi **Parking**

TARPORLEY
Map 15 SJ56

Alvanley Arms Inn

★★★★ INN

tel: 01829 760200 **Cotebrook CW6 9DS**
email: info@alvanleyarms.co.uk **web:** www.alvanleyarms.co.uk
dir: *M56 junct 10, follow signs for Whitchurch then A49*

This historic inn, bedecked with flowers in summer, dates back to the 17th century and the bar and dining areas still feature the original beams. Bedrooms are well equipped with complimentary WiFi access. The Alvanley Arms offers a wide choice of home-cooked meals that utilise local produce. The inn is perfectly placed for visiting the adjoining Shire Horse Centre and Countryside Park, which is popular with families, and also Delamere Forest Park and Oulton Park race circuit.

Rooms 7 en suite S £62-£78; D £100-£115* **Facilities** FTV DVD Lounge TVL tea/coffee Dinner available WiFi ♿ 18 🔒 **Parking** 30 **Notes** ⊗

WARMINGHAM
Map 15 SJ76

Premier Collection

The Bear's Paw

★★★★★ ⊛ INN

tel: 01270 526317 **School Ln CW11 3QN**
email: info@thebearspaw.co.uk **web:** www.thebearspaw.co.uk
dir: *M6 junct 17, A534, A533 signed Middlewich & Northwich. Continue on A533, left into Mill Ln, left into Warmingham Ln. Right into Plant Ln, left into Green Ln*

Located beside a small river in a rural Cheshire village, this 19th-century inn provides very comfortable and well-equipped boutique bedrooms that have a wealth of thoughtful and practical extras. The friendly team serves imaginative food, which utilises quality seasonal produce, in an attractive open-plan dining room; sumptuous lounge areas are also available.

Rooms 17 en suite (4 fmly) S £95-£120; D £105-£140* **Facilities** STV FTV iPod docking station Lounge tea/coffee Dinner available Direct Dial WiFi **Extras** Apple TV - deposit required **Parking** 75 **Notes** LB

WYBUNBURY
Map 15 SJ64

Lea Farm *(SJ717489)*

★★★ FARMHOUSE

tel: 01270 841429 **Wrinehill Rd CW5 7NS**
email: leafarm@hotmail.co.uk **web:** www.leafarm.co.uk
dir: *1m E of Wybunbury church on unclassified road*

This working dairy farm is surrounded by delightful gardens and beautiful Cheshire countryside. The spacious bedrooms have modern facilities and there is a cosy lounge. Hearty breakfasts are served in the attractive dining room, which looks out over the garden with its resident peacocks.

Rooms 3 rms (2 en suite) (1 pri facs) (1 fmly) S £30-£38; D £50-£64* (incl.dinner) **Facilities** FTV Lounge TVL tea/coffee WiFi Fishing Pool table 🔒 **Extras** Home-made biscuits **Parking** 24 **Notes** LB 🐾 150 acres dairy/beef

CORNWALL & ISLES OF SCILLY

BODINNICK
Map 2 SX15

The Old Ferry Inn

★★★ 🏠 INN

tel: 01726 870237 **fax:** 01726 870116 **PL23 1LX**
email: info@oldferryinn.co.uk **web:** www.oldferryinn.co.uk
dir: *From Liskeard on A38 to Dobwalls, left onto A390. After 3m left onto B3359 signed Looe. Right at sign for Lerryn/Bodinnick/Polruan*

The Old Ferry Inn has stood for over four hundred years on the edge of the Fowey River estuary, overlooking the Bodinnick to Fowey ferry service. 'Ferryside', the childhood home of Daphne du Maurier, is at the bottom of the hill. There are plenty of coastal walks, historical buildings, fishing and wildlife nearby, with the famous Eden Project just a few miles away. A range of local beers and Cornish ciders are available, and meals can be enjoyed while gazing out over the amazing river views.

Rooms 12 rms (10 en suite) (2 pri facs) (1 fmly) D £75-£140* **Facilities** FTV Lounge TVL tea/coffee Dinner available WiFi **Parking** 6 **Notes** LB No coaches

BODMIN
Map 2 SX06

Castle Canyke Farm

 BED AND BREAKFAST

tel: 01208 79109 **Priors Barn Rd PL31 1HG**
email: bookings@castlecanykefarm.co.uk **web:** www.castlecanykefarm.co.uk
dir: *On A389/A38 Priory Rd between church & Carminow Cross rdbt*

This is a traditional bed and breakfast operation run by very friendly hosts, and is in a handy location that benefits from off-street parking. The bedrooms are well appointed; guests have their own lounge, and hearty breakfasts are served in the conservatory. There is a pretty garden to the rear.

Rooms 3 en suite (1 fmly) **Facilities** FTV TVL tea/coffee WiFi **Parking** 3 **Notes** ⊗ No Children 8yrs 🐾

Mennabroom Farm *(SX161703)*

★★★★ 🏠 🏠 FARMHOUSE

tel: 01208 821272 **Warleggan PL30 4HE**
email: enquiries@mennabroom.com **web:** www.mennabroom.co.uk
dir: *A30 take exit signed Colliford Lake. After 2.8m turn right signed Mennabroom Farm and Cottages, turn right into Mennabroom*

In the heart of Bodmin Moor this extremely comfortable farmhouse offers a haven of peace and tranquillity for visitors to the beautiful West Country. Rooms are well appointed with quality furnishings and very comfortable beds. Guests are welcomed with afternoon tea, dinner is available upon request and breakfast uses the farm's home-produced eggs, bacon and sausages. Self-catering cottages are also available.

Rooms 2 en suite S £55; D £80* **Facilities** FTV DVD Lounge tea/coffee Dinner available WiFi 🔒 **Extras** Speciality toiletries - complimentary **Parking** 6 **Notes** LB 40 acres sheep/pigs/beef

Roscrea

★★★★ 🏠 BED AND BREAKFAST

tel: 01208 74400 **18 Saint Nicholas' St PL31 1AD**
email: roscrea@btconnect.com **web:** www.roscrea.co.uk
dir: *From Bodmin take B3268 to Lostwithiel. Roscrea 0.25m on left*

Dating back to 1805, this fascinating house was once the home of a celebrated local schoolmaster. Now sympathetically restored to its former glory, this is an excellent location for anyone wishing to explore all that Cornwall has to offer. Comfort and quality are evident throughout all areas, matched by the warmth of the welcome. Breakfast is a treat here, featuring local produce and eggs from the resident hens. Dinner is also available by prior arrangement.

Rooms 3 rms (2 en suite) (1 pri facs) S £47.50-£53; D £75-£85* **Facilities** FTV DVD TVL tea/coffee Dinner available WiFi 🔒 Facilities for drying **Parking** 2 **Notes** LB ⊗ 🐾

The Crown Inn

★★★ INN

tel: 01208 872707 **Lanlivery PL30 5BT**
email: thecrown@wagtailinns.com **web:** www.wagtailinns.com
dir: *Just off A390 between Lostwithiel & St Austell*

One of the oldest country pubs in Cornwall, The Crown Inn serves quality food and Cornish real ales in a traditional setting. The outbuildings have been converted into en suite bedrooms; all retaining some original features but appointed in a contemporary style to meet the needs of today's travellers. During the warmer months, guests can enjoy the tranquillity of the garden.

Rooms 9 en suite D £40-£80* **Facilities** tea/coffee Dinner available WiFi **Parking**

BODMIN *continued*

Mount Pleasant Farm

★★★ GUEST ACCOMMODATION

tel: 01208 821342 **Mount PL30 4EX**
email: info@mountpleasantcottages.co.uk **web:** www.mountpleasantcottages.co.uk
dir: *A30 from Bodmin towards Launceston for 4m, right signed Millpool, continue 3m*

Set in ten acres, this is a wonderfully peaceful base from which to explore the delights of Cornwall. Originally a farmhouse, dating back to the 17th century, there is something here for all the family, with extensive facilities including a games barn and heated swimming pool. Cosy bedrooms are well furnished, while public areas include a spacious sun lounge and extensive gardens. Breakfast, served in the well-appointed dining room, features local produce; home-cooked evening meals are available by prior arrangement.

Rooms 6 en suite (3 fmly) S £42; D £74* **Facilities** FTV Lounge tea/coffee Dinner available WiFi ⓣ Pool table 🐾 Games barn **Parking** 8 **Notes** LB

BUDE   Map 2 SS20

Bangors Organic

★★★★ 👄 GUEST HOUSE

tel: 01288 361297 **Poundstock EX23 0DP**
email: info@bangorsorganic.co.uk **web:** www.bangorsorganic.co.uk
dir: *4m S of Bude. On A39 in Poundstock*

Situated a few miles south of Bude, this renovated Victorian establishment offers elegant accommodation with a good level of comfort. Bedrooms are furnished to a high standard with bathrooms worthy of special mention, being impressively spacious and luxurious. Breakfast and dinner, featuring organic, local and home-made produce, are served in the pleasant dining room. The establishment is certified as organic by the Soil Association.

Rooms 2 en suite **Facilities** TVL tea/coffee Dinner available Licensed WiFi 🐾 Badminton **Parking** 10 **Notes** ⊗ No Children 10yrs

Dylan's Guest House

★★★★ GUEST HOUSE

tel: 01288 354705 **12 Downs View EX23 8RF**
email: dylansbude@tiscali.co.uk **web:** www.dylansbude.co.uk
dir: *From A39 onto A3073 at Stratton, at 2nd rdbt right to town centre, through town centre, signed Downs View*

Appointed to a high standard, this late Victorian house overlooks the golf course and is just a five-minute walk from the beach. There is a refreshing and appealing style here, derived from a combination of original features and a crisp, contemporary decor. The well-equipped bedrooms are light and airy with impressive levels of comfort. Plenty of choice is offered at breakfast, which is carefully prepared from quality produce and served in the attractive dining room.

Rooms 4 rms (3 en suite) (1 pri facs) (1 fmly) **Facilities** FTV TVL tea/coffee **Notes** LB ⊗ 🚭

Fairway House

★★★★ GUEST HOUSE

tel: 01288 355059 **8 Downs View EX23 8RF**
email: enquiries@fairwayguesthouse.co.uk **web:** www.fairwayguesthouse.co.uk
dir: *N through town to Flexbury, follow brown tourist signs to Downs View from golf course*

Genuine hospitality and attentive service await at this delightful Victorian terrace property, which overlooks the golf course and is close to the beach, the South West Coast Path and the town centre. The comfortable bedrooms are of a high standard and have many thoughtful extra facilities. Breakfast uses local produce, including free range local farm eggs and extra thick back bacon, and is served at separate tables. Full English, omelettes, kippers or continental options are available.

Rooms 7 rms (5 en suite) (2 pri facs) (1 fmly) S fr £35; D £60-£72* **Facilities** FTV Lounge tea/coffee WiFi 🐾 **Notes** LB ⊗ Closed Dec-Jan 🚭

Pencarrol Guest House

★★★★ GUEST HOUSE

tel: 01288 352478 **21 Downs View EX23 8RF**
email: pencarrolbude@aol.com
dir: *0.5m N of Bude. N from Bude into Flexbury village*

This cosy late-Victorian guest house is only a short walk from Bude centre and Crooklets Beach, and has glorious views over the golf course. Bedrooms are attractively furnished and there is a first-floor lounge. Breakfast is served at separate tables in the dining room.

Rooms 5 rms (3 en suite) (2 pri facs) (2 fmly) S £33-£35; D £70-£74* **Facilities** FTV tea/coffee 🔒 **Notes** LB ⊗ Closed Nov-Feb 📶

The Old Wainhouse Inn

★★★ INN

tel: 01840 230711 **Wainhouse Corner, St Gennys EX23 0BA**
email: wainhouse10@yahoo.co.uk **web:** www.oldwainhouseinn.co.uk
dir: *On A39 between Bude & Camelford*

This popular roadside pub provides an ideal base from which to explore the wonderful countryside and dramatic coastline; the South West Coast Path is close by. The convivial bar is the focus here, with plenty of friendly banter always on offer and helpful local advice readily available. Bedrooms and bathrooms provide good levels of comfort with simple styling. Food in the bar and restaurant includes a Sunday roast and vegetarian options.

Rooms 4 en suite S £50-£55; D £81-£90* **Facilities** FTV tea/coffee Dinner available WiFi Pool table 🔒 **Conf** Max 50 Class 50 **Parking** 25

Sea Jade Guest House

★★★ GUEST ACCOMMODATION

tel: 01288 353404 & 07737 541540 **15 Burn View EX23 8BZ**
email: seajadeguesthouse@yahoo.co.uk **web:** www.seajadeguesthouse.co.uk
dir: *A39 turn right follow signs for Bude & golf course*

A warm welcome awaits at this popular establishment which is well located within a few minutes' walk of both the town and beaches. Bedrooms are light and airy with a simple, contemporary styling; some have views across the golf course. Breakfast is a generous offering and guaranteed to get the day off to a satisfying start.

Rooms 8 rms (7 en suite) (1 pri facs) (4 fmly) (2 GF) S £32-£40; D £64-£71* **Facilities** FTV TVL tea/coffee WiFi ⚡ 18 **Notes** LB ⊗ 📶

CALLINGTON Map 3 SX36

Woodpeckers

★★★★ GUEST HOUSE

tel: 01579 363717 **Rilla Mill PL17 7NT**
email: alisonmerchant@virgin.net **web:** www.woodpeckersguesthouse.co.uk
dir: *5m NW of Callington. Exit B3254 at Upton Cross x-rds for Rilla Mill*

Set in a conservation village, in a wooded valley, by a tumbling stream, this modern, detached house offers cosy, well-equipped bedrooms with numerous thoughtful extras. Home-cooked dinners, using the best of local ingredients, are available by prior arrangement. The hot tub in the garden is an additional feature.

Rooms 3 en suite S £45-£60; D £60 **Facilities** STV FTV tea/coffee Dinner available Gym 🔒 Spa/Hot tub **Parking** 7 **Notes** LB ⊗ 📶

CRACKINGTON HAVEN Map 2 SX19

Lower Tresmorn Farm *(SX164975)*

★★★★ FARMHOUSE

tel: 01840 230667 & 07786 227437 **EX23 0NU**
email: rachel.crocker@talk21.com **web:** www.lowertresmorn.co.uk
dir: *Take Tresmorn turn off coast road, 2m N of Crackington Haven*

Set in north Cornwall's heritage coast area, parts of this charming farmhouse date back to medieval times. The welcome is warm and genuine with a reviving cup of tea and piece of cake always on offer. Bedrooms are located in the main house and an adjacent converted barn; all provide plenty of comfort. Breakfast makes use of local and farm produce.

Rooms 3 rms (2 en suite) (1 pri facs) 3 annexe en suite (2 fmly) (2 GF) S £45-£60; D £64-£84* **Facilities** FTV TVL TV4B tea/coffee WiFi 🔒 **Parking** 6 **Notes** ⊗ No Children 8yrs RS 20 Dec-5 Jan B&B only 222 acres beef/sheep

Trevigue *(SX137956)*

★★★★ FARMHOUSE

tel: 01840 230492 & 07903 110037 **Trevigue Farm EX23 0LQ**
email: trevigue@talk21.com

Peace and tranquillity are two of the many qualities of Trevigue, a beautiful 16th-century farmhouse set in 600 acres of stunning north Cornish cliff land. Your hosts will make you feel at home and cater for all your needs in order to make your stay as stress-free as possible. Rooms are beautifully appointed and equipped. Dinner and breakfast use the freshest of local produce. There is also a self-catering cottage.

Rooms 4 en suite (1 fmly) **Facilities** FTV iPod docking station Lounge TVL TV3B tea/coffee Dinner available Licensed WiFi 🔒 **Conf** Max 45 Class 45 Board 20 **Parking** 8 **Notes** ⊗ No Children 8yrs Civ Wed 45 500 acres beef

Bears & Boxes Country Guest House

★★★★  GUEST HOUSE

tel: 01840 230318 **Penrose, Dizzard EX23 0NX**
email: rwfrh@btinternet.com **web:** www.bearsandboxes.com
dir: *1.5m NE of St Gennys in Dizzard*

Dating in part from the mid 17th century, Bears & Boxes is a small, family-run guest house situated 500 yards from the coastal path. Guests are welcomed with a tray of tea and home-made cake, and the caring owners are always around to give advice on the local area. The cosy bedrooms have numerous thoughtful extras, and evening meals are served by prior arrangement.

Rooms 2 en suite **Facilities** FTV DVD Lounge tea/coffee Dinner available WiFi 🔒 **Parking** 6

CRAFTHOLE Map 3 SX35

The Liscawn

[U]

tel: 01503 230863 **PL11 3BD**
email: enquiries@liscawn.co.uk

Currently the rating for this establishment is not confirmed. This may be due to a change of ownership or because it has only recently joined the AA rating scheme.

Rooms 11 en suite

CRANTOCK
Map 2 SW76

Carrek Woth

★★★ GUEST ACCOMMODATION

tel: 01637 830530 **West Pentire Rd TR8 5SA**
web: www.carrekwoth.co.uk
dir: W from Crantock towards West Pentire

Many guests return to this friendly, family-run house where hospitality and service are noteworthy. Carrek Woth takes its name from the Cornish for Goose Rock, which can be seen in Crantock Bay. All the bedrooms are on the ground floor and neatly furnished; some have good views. The lounge looks towards Newquay and the sea. Breakfast is served in the attractive dining room; Sunday lunch is also available.

Rooms 6 en suite (1 fmly) (6 GF) S £50-£51; D £78-£80* **Facilities** FTV TVL tea/coffee **Parking** 6 **Notes** LB Closed mid Oct-mid Nov 🐾

FALMOUTH
Map 2 SW83

Bosanneth Guest House

★★★★ 🏅 🍴 GUEST HOUSE

tel: 01326 314649 **fax:** 01326 219337 **Gyllyngvase Hill TR11 4DW**
email: stay@bosanneth.co.uk **web:** www.bosanneth.co.uk
dir: From Truro on A39 follow signs for beaches/docks, 3rd right mini rdbt Melvil Rd, 3rd right into Gyllyngvase Hill

This is a well situated property just a two-minute walk from the beach, offers stylish and individually decorated bedrooms and a very warm welcome from the friendly hosts. Some bedrooms have a sea view and dinner is served each evening. A full Cornish breakfast is served in the dining room.

Rooms 8 en suite S £45-£65; D £80-£130* **Facilities** FTV Lounge tea/coffee Dinner available Licensed WiFi **Extras** Speciality toiletries, robes **Parking** 7 **Notes** LB 🚫 No Children Closed Nov

Prospect House

★★★★ GUEST ACCOMMODATION

tel: 01326 373198 **fax:** 01326 373198 **1 Church Rd, Penryn TR10 8DA**
email: stay@prospecthouse-penryn.co.uk **web:** www.prospecthouse-penryn.co.uk
dir: Exit A39 at Treluswell rdbt onto B3292, right at Penryn town centre sign. Left at junct to town hall, left into Saint Gluivas St, at bottom on left

Prospect House is an attractive building close to the waterside, and was built in 1820 for a ship's captain. The original charm of the house has been carefully maintained and the attractive bedrooms are well equipped. A comfortable lounge is available, and freshly cooked breakfasts are served in the elegant dining room.

Rooms 3 en suite S £45-£50; D £80-£85* **Facilities** FTV Lounge tea/coffee WiFi **Parking** 4 **Notes** 🚫

The Rosemary

★★★★ GUEST ACCOMMODATION

tel: 01326 314669 **22 Gyllyngvase Ter TR11 4DL**
email: stay@therosemary.co.uk **web:** www.therosemary.co.uk
dir: A39 Melvill Rd signed to beaches & seafront, right into Gyllyngvase Rd, 1st left

Just a short walk from the beach, this welcoming establishment is conveniently located for exploring the local area. The well-equipped bedrooms all provide impressive levels of comfort and quality, with many having the added bonus of wonderful views across Falmouth Bay. Breakfast is a generous and tasty start to the day, and is served in the light and airy dining room. Other facilities include a bar and guest lounge, while outside a decked area and rear garden are also available for guests.

Rooms 8 en suite (2 fmly) S £48-£53; D £77-£105* **Facilities** FTV DVD Lounge tea/coffee Licensed WiFi 🔒 **Extras** Speciality toiletries **Parking** 2 **Notes** LB Closed end Oct-9 Feb

See advert on opposite page

Anacapri

★★★★ GUEST ACCOMMODATION

tel: 01326 311454 **fax:** 01326 311474 **Gyllyngvase Rd TR11 4DJ**
email: anacapri@btconnect.com **web:** www.hotelanacapri.co.uk
dir: *A39 (Truro to Falmouth), straight on at lights. Over next 2 rdbts into Melvill Rd, down hill, 2nd right into Gyllyngvase Rd, Anacapri on right*

In an elevated position overlooking Gyllyngvase Beach with views of Falmouth Bay beyond, this family-run establishment extends a warm welcome to all. Bedrooms have high standards of comfort and quality, and the majority have sea views. Public areas include a convivial bar, a lounge and a smart breakfast room with ocean views.

Rooms 16 en suite **Facilities** FTV Lounge TVL tea/coffee Licensed WiFi **Parking** 16 **Notes** ⊗ No Children 10yrs Closed mid Dec-mid Jan

Melvill House

★★★★ GUEST ACCOMMODATION

tel: 01326 316645 **fax:** 01326 211608 **52 Melvill Rd TR11 4DQ**
email: melvillhouse@btconnect.com **web:** www.melvill-house-falmouth.co.uk
dir: *On A39 near town centre & docks*

Well situated for the beach, the town centre and the National Maritime Museum on the harbour, Melvill House is a family-run establishment with a relaxed atmosphere. Some bedrooms have four-poster beds, and breakfast is served in the smart dining room. Ample parking.

Rooms 7 en suite (2 fmly) (1 GF) S £35-£50; D £70-£85 **Facilities** FTV TVL tea/coffee WiFi 🔒 **Parking** 8 **Notes** LB ⊗

The Rathgowry

★★★★ GUEST HOUSE

tel: 01326 313482 **Gyllyngvase Hill TR11 4DN**
email: enquiries@rathgowry.co.uk **web:** www.rathgowry.co.uk
dir: *A39 into Falmouth, over 1st & 2nd rdbts. After 300mtrs turn right into Gyllyngvase Hill, half way down on left*

Located in a quieter residential area yet only a few minutes' stroll from the beach and 15 minutes from the town centre, this traditionally styled property offers a range of differently sized, well-equipped bedrooms and bathrooms. There are extra thoughtful touches in the rooms, and free WiFi is provided throughout the property. A varied menu is offered at breakfast including ample choice of cereals and preserves, with a bumper full English cooked option.

Rooms 9 rms (7 en suite) (2 pri facs) (1 fmly) S £38-£45; D £76-£90* **Facilities** FTV tea/coffee WiFi 🔒 **Extras** Bottled water **Parking** 7 **Notes** ⊗ Closed Dec-Feb

Rosemullion

★★★★ GUEST ACCOMMODATION

tel: 01326 314690 **fax:** 01326 210098 **Gyllyngvase Hill TR11 4DF**
email: gail@rosemullionhotel.co.uk **web:** www.rosemullionhotel.co.uk

Recognisable by its mock-Tudor exterior, this warm and friendly establishment is well situated for both the town centre and the beach. Some of the comfortable bedrooms are on the ground floor, while a few rooms on the top floor have views to Falmouth Bay. Breakfast, served in the panelled dining room, is freshly cooked and there is a well appointed lounge.

Rooms 13 rms (11 en suite) (2 pri facs) (3 GF) **Facilities** FTV Lounge tea/coffee WiFi **Parking** 18 **Notes** ⊗ No Children Closed 23-31 Dec

FALMOUTH *continued*

Trevoil Guest House

★★★ GUEST HOUSE

tel: 01326 314145 & 07966 409782 fax: 01326 314145 **25 Avenue Rd TR11 4AY**
email: alan.jewel@btconnect.com **web:** www.trevoil-falmouth.co.uk
dir: *Exit A39 (Melvill Rd) left into Avenue Rd, 150yds from Maritime Museum*

Located within walking distance of the town centre, the friendly Trevoil is a comfortable and relaxed place to stay. Breakfast is enjoyed in the light, pleasant dining room.

Rooms 8 rms (4 en suite) (3 fmly) (1 GF) S £25-£30; D £50-£60 **Facilities** FTV tea/coffee WiFi **Parking** 6 **Notes** LB

Eden Lodge

★★ GUEST HOUSE

tel: 01326 212989 & 07715 696218 **54 Melvill Rd TR11 4DQ**
email: edenlodge@hotmail.co.uk **web:** www.edenlodgefalmouth.co.uk
dir: *On A39, on left 200yds past Fox Rosehill Gardens*

Very well located on Melvill Road with off-road parking, Eden Lodge boasts comfortable rooms and a swimming pool. The friendly hosts serve dinner by arrangement and do all they can to ensure a comfortable stay for their guests.

Rooms 5 rms (4 en suite) (2 fmly) (1 GF) **Facilities** FTV TVL tea/coffee Dinner available Licensed WiFi ⓣ Gym 🔥 Massage & aromatherapy by appointment **Parking** 9 **Notes** LB ⊜

| **FOWEY** | **Map 2 SX15** |

Trevanion Guest House

★★★★ GUEST ACCOMMODATION

tel: 01726 832602 **70 Lostwithiel St PL23 1BQ**
email: alisteve@trevanionguesthouse.co.uk **web:** www.trevanionguesthouse.co.uk
dir: *A3082 into Fowey, down hill, left into Lostwithiel St. Trevanion on left*

This 16th-century merchant's house provides friendly, comfortable accommodation within easy walking distance of the historic town of Fowey and is also convenient for visiting the Eden Project. A hearty farmhouse-style cooked breakfast, using local produce, is served in the attractive dining room; other menu options are available.

Rooms 5 rms (4 en suite) (1 pri facs) (2 fmly) (1 GF) S £45-£50; D £65-£85* **Facilities** FTV DVD tea/coffee Dinner available WiFi 🔥 **Parking** 6 **Notes** LB ⊜

| **GWEEK** | **Map 2 SW72** |

Black Swan

★★★★ INN

tel: 01326 221502 **TR12 6TU**
dir: *In village centre*

The Black Swan inn is in the picturesque village of Gweek, a stone's throw from the popular Cornish Seal Sanctuary. This delightful inn has been restored to its former glory, and the stylish en suite bedrooms are comfortable and enhanced with homely touches. Food is sourced with care, ensuring local produce is used whenever possible; an extensive blackboard menu showcases pub classics and favourites. The selection of Cornish ales is not to be missed.

Rooms 4 en suite S £55-£60; D £70-£80* **Facilities** FTV tea/coffee Dinner available WiFi Pool table **Parking** 15

| **HAYLE** | **Map 2 SW53** |

Rosewarne Manor

★★★★★ ⓢ ⓢ RESTAURANT WITH ROOMS

tel: 01209 610414 & 07966 090341 **20 Gwinear Rd TR27 5JQ**
email: enquiries@rosewarnemanor.co.uk **web:** www.rosewarnemanor.co.uk
dir: *A30 Camborne West towards Connor Downs, left into Gwinear Rd. 0.75m to Rosewarne Manor*

Rosewarne Manor offers a flexible suite, which can be booked for bed and breakfast or self catering; it is well appointed and well equipped. The award-winning restaurant, overlooking the garden, offers menus that are created from fresh, local produce. The Manor can also be booked for a range of functions. Parking is available.

Rooms 1 annexe en suite S £70-£100; D £80-£110* **Facilities** FTV DVD iPod docking station Lounge tea/coffee Dinner available WiFi **Conf** Max 80 Thtr 80 Class 50 Board 12 **Parking** 50 **Notes** LB ⊗ No Children Civ Wed 70

The Penellen

★★★★ GUEST ACCOMMODATION

tel: 01736 753777 **64 Riviere Towans, Phillack TR27 5AF**
email: penellen@btconnect.com **web:** www.penellen.co.uk
dir: *From A30 onto B3301 through Hayle. Turn opposite petrol station, road bears to left, into private road*

Superbly situated at the water's edge, this personally run, friendly property has splendid views of the beach and coastline. Bedrooms are well equipped and comfortable, many with patio doors and stunning views to wake up to each morning. The dining room is spacious with a bright and airy feel. The cheerful hosts provide attentive service. Food is a strength, with good quality produce on offer. AA Friendliest B&B of the Year Finalist 2014-2015.

Rooms 5 en suite (2 fmly) S £59-£85; D £80-£100* **Facilities** FTV tea/coffee WiFi **Parking** 10 **Notes** ⊗ Closed Nov-Feb

Star Inn

★★★ INN

tel: 01736 752068 & 07984 319108 **1 Church St, St Erth TR27 6HP**
email: starinn.st.erth@gmail.com **web:** www.starinnst-erth.co.uk
dir: *From Hayle on A30 towards Penzance. After major rdbt 1st left signed St Erth. At T-junct left signed St Erth. Over river bridge into Chapel Hill. Inn on right on corner of Church St*

Situated in the very heart of St Erth, the Star Inn has been totally renovated to provide modern comforts within a traditional and convivial environment. The spacious, comfortable bedrooms are well appointed, as are the en suite shower rooms. A good choice of dishes is offered at lunch and dinner in the atmospheric restaurant-bar. This establishment is a popular venue for locals and tourists alike.

Rooms 2 annexe en suite (1 fmly) (1 GF) S £50-£70; D £70-£100* **Facilities** FTV Lounge tea/coffee Dinner available WiFi Pool table **Extras** Fresh milk **Parking** 30 **Notes** LB No coaches

HELFORD
Map 2 SW72

Prince of Wales
★★★★ INN

tel: 01326 231247 **Newtown, St Martin TR12 6DP**
email: mail@princeofwalesnewtown.co.uk

The Prince of Wales is a traditional pub in a quiet village setting, privately owned and run with care and much pride. The bedrooms are bright, comfortable and well furnished and include such extras as iPod docking stations. Dinner is served every evening and breakfast features locally sourced quality produce.

Rooms 3 en suite (2 fmly) S £85; D £95* **Facilities** FTV iPod docking station TVL tea/coffee Dinner available WiFi ⚲ 18 ⚓ **Parking** 70 **Notes** LB No coaches

HELSTON
Map 2 SW62

See also St Keverne

Tregaddra Farmhouse B&B *(SW697216)*
★★★★ FARMHOUSE

tel: 01326 240235 & 07773 518223 **Cury Cross Lanes TR12 7BB**
email: june@tregaddra.co.uk **web:** www.tregaddra.co.uk
dir: *From Helston on B3083, at Wheel Inn turn left at x-rds. 1st farm on left after 0.5m*

This 18th-century farmhouse, on a working farm, offers the perfect base for exploring the Lizard Peninsula and southwest Cornwall. All bedrooms are individually appointed and very comfortable; two have balconies overlooking the open countryside. A farmhouse Aga breakfast is served at individual tables in the attractive dining room. A swimming pool (seasonal) and tennis court are also available.

Rooms 4 en suite D £80-£90* **Facilities** FTV DVD Lounge TVL tea/coffee Dinner available WiFi ⚲ ⚓ 18 ⚓ **Extras** Speciality toiletries **Parking** 4 **Notes** LB ⊗ No Children 12yrs 300 acres beef/arable

LANEAST
Map 2 SX28

Stitch Park B&B
★★★★ ⛿ ⚑ BED AND BREAKFAST

tel: 01566 86687 **Stitch Park PL15 8PN**
email: katehandford@btinternet.com **web:** www.stitchpark.co.uk
dir: *A30 from Exeter. At Kennards House junct follow signs for North Cornwall & Wadebridge (A395). After 4m, pass through Pipers Pool then left for Laneast, village signed. Pass church on right, Church Way on left. Around corner, Stitch Park next bungalow on left*

Located just a few miles from Launceston, this modern bungalow is a perfect base from which to explore the beautiful coast and countryside. The views along the Inny Valley to Dartmoor beyond are breathtaking and always changing with the seasons. There is a comfortable lounge in which to relax, while bedrooms offer high quality and a host of extras; likewise bathrooms with a range of toiletries, fluffy towels and robes. Breakfast is a real treat, with eggs from the resident hens and other tasty local produce. Dinner is also available by prior arrangement.

Rooms 3 en suite (3 GF) D £66-£75* **Facilities** FTV DVD TVL tea/coffee Dinner available WiFi ⚓ **Extras** Speciality toiletries, chocolates - complimentary **Parking** 4 **Notes** ⊗ No Children 14yrs ⊜

LAUNCESTON
Map 3 SX38

Premier Collection

Primrose Cottage
★★★★★ ⛿ ⚑ BED AND BREAKFAST

tel: 01566 773645 **Lawhitton PL15 9PE**
email: enquiry@primrosecottagesuites.co.uk **web:** www.primrosecottagesuites.co.uk
dir: *Exit A30 Tavistock, follow A388 through Launceston for Plymouth then B3362, Tavistock 2.5m*

Originally a cottage, this impressive property has been imaginatively developed to provide stylish accommodation. From its elevated position, views across the lush countryside are wonderful. All bedrooms provide high levels of comfort with separate seating areas; two of the spacious suites have external entrances. Breakfast is a highlight of any stay here and makes use of excellent local produce. There is a garden to enjoy, or perhaps a stroll down to the River Tamar for a spot of fishing might appeal.

Rooms 2 en suite 1 annexe en suite (1 GF) S £70-£90; D £90-£130 **Facilities** FTV Lounge TVL tea/coffee Dinner available Licensed WiFi Fishing ⚓ **Extras** Wine, home-made cakes - complimentary **Parking** 5 **Notes** LB ⊗ No Children 12yrs Closed 23-28 Dec

Premier Collection

Wheatley Farm *(SX245926)*
★★★★★ ⛿ FARMHOUSE

tel: 01566 781232 **Maxworthy PL15 8LY**
email: valerie@wheatley-farm.co.uk **web:** www.wheatley-farm.co.uk
dir: *From A39 at Wainhouse Corner follow signs to Canworthy Water. At T-junct, left & after 1.5m turn left at sign to Wheatley Farm. 1st farm on left*

This working dairy farm dates back to 1871 and was originally part of the estate of Lord Bedford. Surrounded by wonderful rolling countryside, the family have been farming here for five generations. A pot of tea is always on offer for arriving guests with every effort made to ensure a relaxing and rewarding stay. Bedrooms all provide high levels of comfort, likewise the modern bathrooms. Breakfast is a treat, served in the lovely dining room complete with original slate floor and imposing granite fireplace. Additional facilities include a guest lounge, heated indoor swimming pool, spa and sauna.

Rooms 4 en suite D £76-£78 **Facilities** FTV DVD TVL tea/coffee Dinner available WiFi ⚲ Sauna Pool table ⚓ Spa bath **Parking** 4 **Notes** LB ⊗ Closed Nov-Mar 232 acres dairy

LAUNCESTON *continued*

Hurdon Farm *(SX333828)*

★★★★ 🏚 FARMHOUSE

tel: 01566 772955 **PL15 9LS**
email: hurdonfarm@hotmail.co.uk **web:** www.hurdonfarm.weebly.com
dir: *A30 onto A388 to Launceston, at rdbt exit for hospital, 2nd right signed Trebullett, premises 1st on right*

Genuine hospitality is assured at this delightful 18th-century granite farmhouse. The bedrooms are individually furnished and decorated, and equipped with numerous extras. The delicious dinners, by arrangement, use only the best local produce, and include home-made puddings and the farm's own clotted cream.

Rooms 6 en suite (1 fmly) (1 GF) S £35-£37; D £68-£70* **Facilities** FTV TVL tea/coffee Dinner available WiFi **Parking** 10 **Notes** LB ⊗ Closed Nov-Apr ⊜ 400 acres mixed

Bradridge Farm *(SX328938)*

★★★★ FARMHOUSE

tel: 01409 271264 & 07748 253346   **fax:** 01409 271331 **PL15 9RL**
email: angela@bradridgefarm.co.uk **web:** www.bradridgefarm.co.uk
dir: *5.5m N of Launceston. Exit B3254 at Ladycross sign for Boyton, Bradridge 2nd farm on right after Boyton school*

This late Victorian farmhouse stands in glorious countryside on the border of Devon and Cornwall. The well-presented bedrooms have many considerate extras, and the Aga-cooked breakfasts feature farm-fresh eggs.

Rooms 4 rms (3 en suite) (1 fmly) S £33-£40; D £66-£80* **Facilities** FTV Lounge TVL tea/coffee WiFi Fishing **Parking** 6 **Notes** LB Closed Nov-Mar ⊜ 250 acres arable/beef/sheep/hens

Middle Tremollett Farm B&B *(SX297757)*

★★★★ 🏚 FARMHOUSE

tel: 01566 782416 & 07973 435529 **Coad's Green PL15 7NA**
email: btrewin@btinternet.com **web:** www.tremollett.com
dir: *A30 onto B3257, through village of Coad's Green. Turn right signed Tremollett, 1st on left at bottom of hill*

Genuine hospitality is assured at this delightful granite farmhouse surrounded with breath-taking views of the countryside. The bedrooms are individually furnished and decorated, and equipped with numerous extras. The delicious breakfasts use only the best local produce, and include home-made produce and the farm's own eggs.

Rooms 2 en suite **Facilities** STV TVL tea/coffee WiFi ⏍ 🛁 **Extras** Speciality toiletries **Parking** 3 **Notes** LB ⊗ No Children Closed Dec-Feb arable/beef/sheep

Tyne Wells House

★★★★ BED AND BREAKFAST

tel: 01566 775810 **Pennygillam PL15 7EE**
email: btucker@talktalk.net **web:** www.tynewells.co.uk
dir: *0.6m SW of town centre. Exit A30 onto Pennygillam rdbt, house off rdbt*

Situated on the outskirts of town, Tyne Wells House has panoramic views over the countryside. There's a relaxed and friendly atmosphere and the bedrooms are neatly furnished. A hearty breakfast is served in the dining room, which overlooks the garden.

Rooms 3 rms (2 en suite) (1 pri facs) (1 fmly) S £35-£50; D £60-£80 **Facilities** FTV DVD tea/coffee WiFi 🛁 **Parking** 4 **Notes** LB ⊗ ⊜

Racehorse Inn

★★★ INN

tel: 01566 786916 **North Hill PL15 7PG**
email: theracehorseinn@hotmail.co.uk

A friendly welcome greets everyone at the Racehorse, a warm and inviting traditional inn set in a tranquil, pretty village, privately owned and run with care and much pride. The bedrooms are bright and well furnished and include many thoughtful extra touches. Dinner is served every evening and breakfast features locally sourced, quality produce. There's a good selection of beers and wines to choose from.

Rooms 3 rms D £80* **Facilities** Dinner available

| **LEEDSTOWN** | Map 2 SW63 |

Little Pengelly Farm *(SW614327)*

★★★★ FARMHOUSE

tel: 01736 850452 **Trenwheal TR27 6BP**
email: maxine@littlepengelly.co.uk **web:** www.littlepengelly.co.uk
dir: *From Hayle on B3302 towards Helston. Through Leedstown, after 2m at top of hill turn left. 1st house on right*

Little Pengelly Farm is situated in beautiful countryside about five miles from both the north and south coasts of the Cornwall peninsula. B&B and self-catering accommodation are on offer, as well as a tea-room serving freshly baked scones with home-made jam. The three guest rooms are bright and comfortable and enjoy views of the garden or courtyard. A farmhouse breakfast is served in the conservatory overlooking the gardens. Considerate pet owners are welcome, a laundry service and free WiFi are available, and there is ample parking on site.

Rooms 3 rms (2 en suite) (1 pri facs) (1 fmly) D £60-£100* **Facilities** FTV tea/coffee WiFi 🛁 **Extras** Speciality toiletries - complimentary **Parking** 10 **Notes** LB Closed 24-26 Dec 10 acres arable

LISKEARD
See also Callington

Map 2 SX26

Redgate Smithy

★★★★ 🛏 BED AND BREAKFAST

tel: 01579 321578 **Redgate, St Cleer PL14 6RU**
email: enquiries@redgatesmithy.co.uk web: www.redgatesmithy.co.uk
dir: *3m NW of Liskeard. Exit A30 at Bolventor/Jamaica Inn into St Cleer Rd for 7m, B&B just past x-rds*

This 200-year-old converted smithy is on the southern fringe of Bodmin Moor near Golitha Falls. The accommodation offers smartly furnished, cottage-style bedrooms with many extra facilities. A wide choice of freshly cooked breakfasts is served in the conservatory, and there are several eating options nearby.

Rooms 3 rms (2 en suite) (1 pri facs) S £55-£65; D £73-£83* **Facilities** FTV tea/coffee WiFi 🅿 **Parking** 3 **Notes** LB No Children 12yrs Closed Nov-Feb

Trecarne House

★★★★ GUEST ACCOMMODATION

tel: 01579 343543 & 07950 262682   fax: 01579 343543
Penhale Grange, St Cleer PL14 5EB
email: trish@trecarnehouse.co.uk web: www.trecarnehouse.co.uk
dir: *B3254 N from Liskeard to St Cleer. Right at Post Office, 3rd left after church, 2nd right, house on right*

A warm welcome awaits at Trecarne House, a large family home, peacefully located on the edge of the village. The stylish and spacious bedrooms enjoy magnificent country views and have many thoughtful extras. The buffet-style breakfast offers a wide choice, which can be enjoyed in the dining room or bright conservatory overlooking rolling countryside.

Rooms 3 en suite (2 fmly) S £65-£75; D £90-£100* **Facilities** DVD iPod docking station TVL tea/coffee WiFi Table tennis Trampoline **Conf** Max 25 **Parking** 6 **Notes** LB ⊗

Cheesewring

★★★ INN

tel: 01579 362321 **Minions PL14 5LE**
email: thecheesewring@gmail.com

This attractive, historic inn has an imposing position on the edge of Dartmoor, a great location for some beautiful walks and observation of the abundant wildlife. Each of the guest rooms is warm and inviting, and all have impressive modern facilities. A good choice of dishes is offered at lunch and dinner in the atmospheric restaurant-bar, and there are lovely open fires to relax in front of.

Rooms 3 rms S £30; D £60* **Facilities** Dinner available

Elnor Guest House

★★★ GUEST HOUSE

tel: 01579 342472 fax: 01579 345673 **1 Russell St PL14 4BP**
email: infoelnorguesthouse50@talktalk.net web: www.elnorguesthouse.co.uk
dir: *Exit A38 from Plymouth into town centre, house on right opposite florist on road to railway station, pass British Legion & The Railway pub*

Elnor is a well-established, friendly guest house, close to the town centre and railway station, and just a short drive from Bodmin Moor and other places of interest. Bedrooms are neatly presented and well equipped, and some are on the ground floor. A cosy lounge is available to guests.

Rooms 6 rms (4 en suite) 3 annexe en suite (3 fmly) (4 GF) S £35-£40; D £70-£80* **Facilities** FTV TVL tea/coffee Direct Dial WiFi 🅿 **Parking** 7 **Notes** ⊗ ⊠

LOOE
Map 2 SX25

Premier Collection

The Beach House
★★★★★ 🛏 GUEST ACCOMMODATION

tel: 01503 262598 **Marine Dr, Hannafore PL13 2DH**
email: enquiries@thebeachhouselooe.co.uk web: www.thebeachhouselooe.co.uk
dir: *From Looe W over bridge, left to Hannafore & Marine Drive, on right after Tom Sawyers B&B*

As its name would suggest this property has panoramic sea views and is just a short walk from the harbour, restaurants and town. Some rooms have stylish handmade furniture, and the bedrooms are well equipped and have many extras. Hearty breakfasts are served in the first-floor dining room providing a good start for walking the South West Coast Path which passes right by the house.

Rooms 5 en suite (4 GF) S £75; D £100-£130* **Facilities** FTV Lounge tea/coffee WiFi ♨ Beauty treatment room **Parking** 6 **Notes** LB ⊗ No Children 16yrs Closed Xmas

Barclay House
★★★★★ ◉◉ GUEST ACCOMMODATION

tel: 01503 262929 **fax:** 01503 262632 **St Martin's Rd PL13 1LP**
email: reception@barclayhouse.co.uk **web:** www.barclayhouse.co.uk
dir: *1st house on left on entering Looe from A38*

Barclay House stands in six acres of grounds overlooking Looe Harbour, and is within walking distance of the town. The thoughtfully furnished bedrooms have modern facilities, and there is a sitting room, a spacious bar, and a terrace where guests can enjoy an aperitif in the summer. The delicious, freshly prepared dinners are served in the light and airy restaurant and prove popular with locals and tourists alike. A heated swimming pool is also available.

Rooms 11 en suite 1 annexe en suite (1 fmly) (1 GF) S £45-£75; D £75-£170* **Facilities** FTV Lounge tea/coffee Dinner available Direct Dial Licensed WiFi ch fac ⊀ ⌣ 18 Sauna Gym 🛁 Hair salon Massage & beauty treatments **Extras** Speciality toiletries, chocolates - complimentary **Conf** Max 40 Thtr 20 Class 10 Board 18 **Parking** 25 **Notes** LB ⊗ Civ Wed 70

Bay View Farm *(SX282548)*
★★★★ 🚜 FARMHOUSE

tel: 01503 265922 & 07967 267312   **fax:** 01503 265922 **St Martins PL13 1NZ**
email: mike@looebaycaravans.co.uk **web:** www.looedirectory.co.uk/bay-view-farm.htm
dir: *2m NE of Looe. Off B3253 for Monkey Sanctuary, farm signed*

Bay View Farm is a renovated and extended bungalow, which has a truly spectacular location with ever-changing views across Looe Bay. The spacious bedrooms have many thoughtful extras. Add a genuine Cornish welcome, tranquillity and great food, and it's easy to see why guests are drawn back again and again to this special place.

Rooms 3 en suite (3 GF) S £40-£45; D £60-£65* **Facilities** TVL tea/coffee Dinner available WiFi **Extras** Fridges in bedrooms **Parking** 3 **Notes** LB ⊗ No Children ⊜ 56 acres mixed/shire horses

Bucklawren Farm (SX278540)

★★★★ FARMHOUSE

tel: 01503 240738 **St Martin-by-Looe PL13 1NZ**
email: bucklawren@btopenworld.com **web:** www.bucklawren.co.uk
dir: 2m NE of Looe. Off B3253 to Monkey Sanctuary, 0.5m right to Bucklawren, farmhouse 0.5m on left

This spacious 19th-century farmhouse stands in 400 acres of farmland just a mile from the beach. The attractive bedrooms, including one on the ground floor, are well equipped, and the front-facing rooms have spectacular views across fields to the sea. Breakfast is served in the elegant dining room and locally sourced produce is used whenever possible.

Rooms 6 en suite 1 annexe rm (1 pri facs) (3 fmly) (1 GF) S £40-£55; D £72-£84
Facilities FTV Lounge TVL tea/coffee WiFi 🐾 **Extras** Fridge **Parking** 7 **Notes** LB ⊗ No Children 5yrs Closed Nov-Feb 400 acres arable/beef

Meneglaze

★★★★ 🏠 BED AND BREAKFAST

tel: 01503 269227 & 07708 808323   **fax:** 0872 115 7468 **Shutta PL13 1LU**
email: stay@meneglaze.com **web:** www.looebedandbreakfast.com
dir: A387, opposite railway station turn into Shutta, 100yds on left

Built in 1860, this delightful B&B was formerly a sea captain's house. It has a private parking area for guests, and offers modern comfort and style just a five-minute, easy walk from the centre of Looe. Meneglaze maintains elements of its seafaring days with hints of the nautical throughout the decor. All rooms have tea and coffee making facilities, mini-bar fridges, sumptuous towelling gowns, Egyptian cotton bedding, flat-screen TV with Freeview and free WiFi. Breakfasts are hearty and proudly Cornish. Expect the best quality home-made marmalades and jams and the finest (award winning) Hog's Pudding available each morning.

Rooms 4 en suite S £65-£75; D £79-£84* **Facilities** FTV iPod docking station tea/coffee WiFi 🍴 **Extras** Speciality toiletries, home-made biscuits - free **Parking** 5 **Notes** ⊗ No Children 16yrs

Polgover Farm (SX277586)

★★★★ FARMHOUSE

tel: 01503 240248 **Widegates PL13 1PY**
email: enquiries@polgoverfarm.co.uk **web:** www.polgoverfarm.co.uk
dir: 4m NE of Looe. A38 S onto B3251 & B3252, 0.5m on right

The welcoming proprietors of Polgover Farm ensure that guests feel at home when they arrive at this attractive house which stands in acres of farmland and enjoys country views all around. The comfortable bedrooms are tastefully decorated with numerous thoughtful extras, and hearty breakfasts are served in the very pleasant lounge.

Rooms 3 rms (2 en suite) (1 pri facs) **Facilities** FTV Lounge tea/coffee WiFi **Extras** Bottled water **Parking** 9 **Notes** ⊗ No Children 12yrs Closed Nov-Feb 93 acres arable/sheep

Polraen Country House

★★★★ 🏠 🍴 GUEST ACCOMMODATION

tel: 01503 263956 **Sandplace PL13 1PJ**
email: enquiries@polraen.co.uk **web:** www.polraen.co.uk
dir: 2m N of Looe at junct A387 & B3254

This 18th-century stone house, formerly a coaching inn, sits in the peaceful Looe Valley. The charming hosts provide friendly service in a relaxed atmosphere, and the bedrooms and public areas are stylishly co-ordinated and well equipped. The licensed bar, lounge and dining room overlook the garden, and there are facilities for children. The excellent evening meals feature local produce and are served Wednesday to Saturday from March to October.

Rooms 5 en suite (2 fmly) D £80-£112* **Facilities** FTV Lounge TVL tea/coffee Dinner available Licensed WiFi 🎣 18 🏠 **Conf** Max 20 Thtr 16 Class 16 Board 16 **Parking** 20 **Notes** LB ⊗ Closed 23-28 Dec

LOOE *continued*

Trehaven Manor

★★★★ GUEST ACCOMMODATION

tel: 01503 262028 **fax:** 01503 265613 **Station Rd PL13 1HN**
email: enquiries@trehavenhotel.co.uk **web:** www.trehavenhotel.co.uk
dir: *In East Looe between railway station & bridge. Trehaven's drive adjacent to The Globe public house*

Run by a charming family, this former rectory is in a stunning location with magnificent views of the estuary. Many of the attractive bedrooms have views, and all are particularly well equipped. There is also a cosy lounge bar. Dinner, by arrangement, specialises in Oriental cuisine, and breakfast features traditional fare; the meals are memorable.

Rooms 7 en suite (1 fmly) (1 GF) **Facilities** TVL tea/coffee Dinner available Licensed **Parking** 8 **Notes** ®

Tremaine Farm *(SX194558)*

★★★★ FARMHOUSE

tel: 01503 220417 **Pelynt PL13 2LT**
email: rosemary@tremainefarm.co.uk **web:** www.tremainefarm.co.uk
dir: *5m NW of Looe. B3359 N from Pelynt, left at x-rds*

Convenient for Fowey, Looe and Polperro, this pleasant working farm offers a relaxing and rewarding stay. The proprietors provide friendly hospitality and attentive service, and the spacious and stylish bedrooms are well equipped with impressive bathrooms. A hearty breakfast is served in the dining room and there is also a spacious and comfortable guest lounge.

Rooms 3 en suite (1 fmly) S £38-£40; D £72-£76 **Facilities** FTV DVD iPod docking station TVL tea/coffee WiFi **Extras** Fridge **Parking** 6 **Notes** LB ® 250 acres arable/sheep/potatoes

Dovers House

★★★★ GUEST ACCOMMODATION

tel: 01503 265468 **St Martin's Rd PL13 1PB**
email: dovershouse@btconnect.com **web:** www.dovershouse.co.uk
dir: *From Saltash on A38, at Trerulefoot rdbt turn left onto A374. After 1m right onto A387, at Widegates stay on B3253, pass Tregoad Park, on left*

Within a rural setting on the outskirts of Looe, making it an ideal centre for exploring the stunning Cornish coastline. Dovers House is a comfortable house which provides a good base to relax. Bedrooms are light and airy and furnished to a consistently high standard. Breakfast is served in the dining room, which faces the beautiful gardens. Private parking is also provided.

Rooms 3 en suite (1 fmly) S £60; D £80-£95* **Facilities** FTV Lounge tea/coffee WiFi **Extras** Fridge, fresh milk **Parking** 4 **Notes** ® No Children 6yrs

Down Ende

★★★★ GUEST ACCOMMODATION

tel: 01503 240213 **fax:** 01503 240213 **Widegates PL13 1QN**
email: teresa@downende.com **web:** www.downende.com
dir: *A374 towards Looe, right A387 road becomes B3253 on left after Coombe Farm*

Set in its own grounds, guests are assured of a warm welcome at this young family's home. Bedrooms are comfortable and well equipped, the majority overlooking the gardens to the front of the property. Home-cooked evening meals are a highlight and use the best of local produce, prepared with care and skill.

Rooms 6 en suite 1 annexe en suite (1 fmly) (2 GF) S £40-£45; D £70-£80* **Facilities** Lounge tea/coffee Dinner available Licensed WiFi 18 **Conf** Max 20 **Parking** 9 **Notes** LB ® Closed 21-28 Dec

Shutta House

★★★★ GUEST ACCOMMODATION

tel: 01503 264233 **Shutta PL13 1LS**
email: enquiries@shuttahouse.co.uk **web:** www.shuttahouse.co.uk
dir: *From A58 Liskeard, follow A387 to Looe, opposite railway station*

This fine Victorian house was once the vicarage, and the current owners have created appealing and contemporary accommodation for their guests. All bedrooms offer high standards of comfort with elegant styling and original character. Breakfasts, served in the light and airy dining room, utilise locally sourced produce whenever possible. Guests are also welcome to use the garden which overlooks the East Looe River.

Rooms 3 en suite S £40-£68; D £50-£90* **Facilities** FTV tea/coffee WiFi **Extras** Bottled water, snacks - complimentary **Conf** Max 6 Thtr 6 Class 6 Board 6 **Parking** 1 **Notes** ® No Children 11yrs

Little Harbour

★★★ GUEST HOUSE

tel: 01503 262474 & 07846 575262 **fax:** 01503 262474 **Church St PL13 2EX**
email: littleharbour@btinternet.com **web:** www.littleharbour.co.uk
dir: *From harbour West Looe, right into Princess Sq, guest house on left*

Little Harbour is situated almost on Looe's harbour in the historic old town; it is in a pleasant and convenient spot and parking is available. The proprietors are friendly and attentive, and bedrooms are well appointed and attractively decorated. Breakfast is served, freshly cooked, in the dining room.

Rooms 5 en suite (1 fmly) S £30-£50; D £50-£80* **Facilities** STV FTV Lounge tea/coffee WiFi **Conf** Max 14 **Parking** 3 **Notes** LB No Children 5yrs

The Ship Inn

★★★ INN

tel: 01503 263124 fax: 01503 263624 Fore St PL13 1AD
email: reservations@smallandfriendly.co.uk web: www.smallandfriendly.co.uk

This lively family pub is located in the very heart of bustling East Looe and has a local following. The bedrooms are comfortable and equipped with all the expected facilities. A wide range of popular dishes is served at lunch times and during the evenings, with light refreshments available throughout the day.

Rooms 8 en suite (1 fmly) S £32.50-£40; D £65-£80* Facilities FTV tea/coffee Dinner available WiFi Pool table 🔒 Notes LB

Tom Sawyers B&B

★★★ GUEST ACCOMMODATION

tel: 01503 262782 Marine Dr, Hannafore PL13 2DQ
email: tom.sawyers@hotmail.co.uk web: www.tomsawyerslooe.co.uk

Both the bar and the rooms of Tom Sawyers B&B enjoy panoramic views of Looe Bay and St George's Island. The annexe rooms are well appointed and equipped.

Rooms 5 annexe rms 3 annexe en suite (1 fmly) (4 GF) Facilities FTV tea/coffee Licensed WiFi Parking 5 Notes LB

The Sea Breeze Guest House

[U]

tel: 01503 263131 & 07880 701584 3/4 Lower Chapel St PL13 1AT
email: seabreezelooe@live.co.uk web: www.seabreezelooe.com
dir: From A38 follow signs for Looe. Proceed through town to seafront. Turn right after chapel, on left

Currently the rating for this establishment is not confirmed. This may be due to a change of ownership or because it has only recently joined the AA rating scheme.

Rooms 5 en suite D £50-£80 Facilities FTV tea/coffee WiFi Notes LB ⊗
No Children 14yrs

| LOSTWITHIEL | Map 2 SX15 |

Hazelmere House

★★★★ 🏠 BED AND BREAKFAST

tel: 01208 873315 58 Grenville Rd PL22 0RA
email: hazelmerehouse@aol.com

Hazelmere House is a professionally run B&B where guests are welcomed with a smile and made to feel at home. The rooms are very well appointed and equipped. All three rooms offer great views over the beautiful Fowey Valley and beyond. The award-winning breakfast is served at the communal table in the formal dining room. The garden offers peace and tranquillity.

Rooms 3 en suite S £50; D £85 Facilities STV FTV iPod docking station TVL tea/coffee WiFi ch fac 🍳 🐾 🎣 18 Riding 🔒 Extras Speciality toiletries Parking 6 Notes 🖂

The King's Arms

★★★★ INN

tel: 01208 872383 & 07812 545036 Fore St PL22 0BL
email: info@thekingsarmslostwithiel.co.uk web: www.thekingsarmslostwithiel.co.uk
dir: On A390, at junct with Fore St

This welcoming and traditional pub is located in the heart of bustling Lostwithiel and is an ideal location for touring the beautiful Cornish countryside and coast. Popular with locals, the convivial bar offers a range of excellent local ales, and live music events are regularly staged. Bedrooms provide good levels of comfort and have all the expected necessities. The tasty breakfasts make use of Cornish produce as much as possible.

Rooms 4 en suite (1 fmly) S £45-£65; D £60-£75* Facilities FTV tea/coffee WiFi 🎣 18 Pool table 🔒 Extras Bottled water Notes LB Closed Xmas-New Year No coaches

Penrose B&B

★★★★ GUEST ACCOMMODATION

tel: 01208 871417 & 07766 900179 fax: 01208 871101 1 The Terrace PL22 0DT
email: enquiries@penrosebb.co.uk web: www.penrosebb.co.uk
dir: In Lostwithiel on A390 (Edgcumbe Rd) into Scrations Ln, turn 1st right for parking

Just a short walk from the town centre, this grand Victorian house offers comfortable accommodation and a genuine homely atmosphere. Many of the bedrooms have the original fireplaces and all are equipped with thoughtful extras. Breakfast is a generous offering and is served in the elegant dining room, with views over the garden. WiFi access is also available.

Rooms 7 en suite (3 fmly) (2 GF) Facilities FTV DVD TVL tea/coffee WiFi 🔒 Parking 8 Notes 🖂

Tremont House

★★★ BED AND BREAKFAST

tel: 01208 873055 2 The Terrace PL22 0DT
email: tremonthouse@aol.com web: www.tremonthouse.co.uk
dir: From A30 onto B3268 (Lostwithiel), at Sweetshouse, bear right onto B3269 & continue to T junct. Left onto A390, down steep hill, turn left into Scrations Ln. 2nd house on right

Situated on the outskirts of Lostwithiel, Tremont House has panoramic views over the countryside. There's a relaxed and friendly atmosphere and the bedrooms are neatly furnished. A hearty breakfast is served in the dining room, which overlooks the garden. Located perfectly to explore all the glorious attractions which are on the doorstep.

Rooms 3 rms (2 en suite) (1 pri facs) S £40-£45; D £55-£75* Facilities TVL tea/coffee WiFi Extras Bottled water - complimentary Parking 3 Notes ⊗ 🖂

LOSTWITHIEL *continued*

Hartswell Farm *(SX119597)*

★★★ FARMHOUSE

tel: 01208 873419 **St Winnow PL22 0RB**
email: hartswell@connexions.co.uk **web:** www.cornish-connexions.co.uk/hartswell
dir: *1m E of Lostwithiel. S off A390 at Downend Garage, farm 0.25m up hill on left*

This 17th-century farmhouse has a wonderfully peaceful setting, and offers generous hospitality and a homely atmosphere. The cosy bedrooms look across rolling countryside, and breakfast includes tasty eggs fresh from the farm. A self-catering barn conversion is available. Hartswell Farm boasts a small herd of Red Poll cattle.

Rooms 2 rms (1 en suite) (1 pri facs) D £60-£80 **Facilities** STV TVL TV1B tea/coffee WiFi ♨ Sailing days for 5 night stays **Parking** 3 **Notes** LB ⊗ No Children 6yrs ☻ 52 acres beef/rare breed cattle

---

LUXULYAN   Map 2 SX05

Ivy Cottage

★★★★ BED AND BREAKFAST

tel: 01726 850796 & 07707 038966   **PL30 5DW**
web: www.ivycottage-luxulyan.co.uk
dir: *A30 exit at Innis Downs onto A391. Follow signs to Eden Project. At rdbt take 1st exit signed Luxulyan. Pass Kings Arms pub, over rail bridge to top of hill. Turn right & at church sharp left, 1st cottage on right*

This welcoming cottage is surrounded by countryside and is an ideal base for touring Cornwall. Bedrooms have considerate finishing touches and there is a picturesque garden to relax in with abundant wildlife, and you can watch the friendly cows in the farmers' fields. Breakfast, using local produce, is enjoyed in the cosy dining room. Private parking is provided.

Rooms 2 en suite S £50-£60; D £75* **Facilities** FTV TVL tea/coffee Lift WiFi ⚓ 18 ♨ **Parking** 3 **Notes** ⊗ Closed 15 Oct-Mar ☻

MARAZION   Map 2 SW53

Blue Horizon

★★★★ BED AND BREAKFAST

tel: 01736 711199 **Fore St TR17 0AW**
email: stay@bluehorizon-marazion.co.uk **web:** www.bluehorizon-marazion.co.uk
dir: *E end of village centre*

Located in the heart of this market town, the rear of this establishment is almost at the water's edge and offers superb views of the sea from its garden, some of the bedrooms and the breakfast room. The atmosphere is laidback and relaxed. There are a number of additional facilities available (charged), including a laundry room, sauna cabin and barbeque facilities. Ample parking is also available.

Rooms 6 rms (5 en suite) (1 pri facs) S £40-£45; D £70-£90* **Facilities** FTV tea/coffee WiFi Sauna ♨ Hot tub in cabin **Parking** 6 **Notes** ⊗ Closed 16 Dec-13 Jan RS Oct-Feb continental bkst only

Marazion

★★★★ INN

tel: 01736 710334 **The Square TR17 0AP**
email: stephanie@marazionhotel.co.uk **web:** www.marazionhotel.co.uk
dir: *In village square opposite Out of Blue gallery*

Within 50 metres of one of Cornwall's safest beaches, this family-run establishment offers a relaxed atmosphere with friendly service. The individually furnished and decorated bedrooms are comfortable, and many have the benefit of stunning views across to St Michael's Mount. The Cutty Sark public bar is a great place to sit and enjoy a drink and listen to local banter, while the restaurant provides a wide range of meals to suit all tastes and budgets.

Rooms 10 en suite (3 fmly) **Facilities** FTV tea/coffee Dinner available WiFi **Conf** Max 20 **Parking** 20 **Notes** LB ⊗ No coaches

St Michaels Bed and Breakfast

★★★★ ▦ BED AND BREAKFAST

tel: 01736 711348 & 07518 945279 **The Corner House, Fore St TR17 0AD**
email: stmichaelsbandb@hotmail.com **web:** www.stmichaels-bedandbreakfast.co.uk
dir: *From A30 at Newtown rdbt, exit signed Marazion. At T-junct turn left, into Marazion, 800mtrs on left next to methodist chapel*

A relaxed yet professional approach, comfortable accommodation and award-winning breakfasts make St Michaels the ideal place to stay when visiting the ancient market town of Marazion, the sandy beaches of Mount's Bay or St Michael's Mount. Top floor rooms enjoy sea views, and parking is available. AA Friendliest B&B of the Year Finalist 2014-2015.

Rooms 6 en suite (1 GF) S £80-£95; D £90-£105* **Facilities** FTV DVD tea/coffee WiFi ♨ **Extras** Bottled water **Parking** 6 **Notes** ⊗ No Children 12yrs

Glenleigh House

★★★ GUEST HOUSE

tel: 01736 710308 **Higher Fore St TR17 0BQ**
email: glenleighbandb@hotmail.co.uk **web:** www.glenleigh-marazion.co.uk
dir: *A394 to Penzance, opposite Fire Engine Inn*

Glenleigh House, overlooking St Michael's Mount and the sweeping panorama of Mount's Bay, has been owned and run by the Hales family for more than 30 years. With nine comfortable and well-appointed bedrooms (many with views to the Mount and the sea), you can be assured of a comfortable stay. Built in 1898 as the home of a prosperous farmer, the house retains its original Victorian charm while providing modern amenities such as free WiFi. Expect a filling breakfast of your choice to set you up for the day.

Rooms 9 en suite (1 fmly) (1 GF) **Facilities** FTV TVL tea/coffee WiFi **Extras** Speciality toiletries **Parking** 9 **Notes** ⊗ No Children 8 yrs Closed Nov-Mar

| MEVAGISSEY | Map 2 SX04 |

Premier Collection

Pebble House

★★★★★ ≘ GUEST ACCOMMODATION

tel: 01726 844466 & 07973 714392 **Polkirt Hill PL26 6UX**
email: hello@pebblehousecornwall.co.uk **web:** www. pebblehousecornwall.co.uk
dir: *B3273 to Mevagissey, into village & follow one-way system. Pass Ship Inn on right, up hill keeping sea on left to T-junct. Pebble House on right*

This brand new property is affectionately known as 'THE house with THE view' which certainly provides an accurate description. All rooms are en suite and individual in design; modern, contemporary, quirky and providing excellent comfort. You can buy pretty much everything you see in the house if you wish. Light snacks, picnics, cream teas and a range of beverages are available, along with a hearty breakfast featuring daily specials.

Rooms 7 en suite (2 GF) S £100-£190; D £105-£195* **Facilities** STV FTV DVD iPod docking station tea/coffee Dinner available Licensed WiFi ♨ **Extras** Speciality toiletries, fridges in 2 rooms **Parking** 6 **Notes** ⊗ No Children 16yrs

Kerryanna Country House

★★★★ BED AND BREAKFAST

tel: 01726 843558 **fax:** 01726 843558 **Treleaven Farm, Valley Rd PL26 6SA**
email: enquiries@kerryanna.co.uk **web:** www.kerryanna.co.uk
dir: *B3273 St Austell to Mevagissey road, right at bottom of hill, next to playground*

Located on the peaceful outskirts of this little fishing village, Kerryanna stands in two acres of gardens and looks across the countryside to the sea. The attractive bedrooms are comfortably furnished, and guests can relax in the three cosy lounges and use the swimming pool.

Rooms 3 en suite D £77* **Facilities** FTV Lounge TVL tea/coffee WiFi ⸲ **Parking** 6 **Notes** LB ⊗ No Children 15yrs Closed Oct-Apr ⊛

Tanglewood House B&B

★★★★ ≘ BED AND BREAKFAST

tel: 01726 843657 **Valley Rd PL26 6SB**
email: stay@tanglewoodbandb.co.uk **web:** www.tanglewoodbandb.co.uk
dir: *From St Austell follow signs to Mevagissey on B3273, Tanglewood on right*

Just a short stroll from Mevagissey, this is a perfect base from which to explore popular attractions such as The Eden Project and The Lost Gardens of Heligan. Set within attractive and peaceful grounds, Tanglewood offers a warm welcome, and every effort is made to ensure an enjoyable and memorable stay. Bedrooms provide impressive levels of quality with all expected modern comforts, while bathrooms come complete with robes and cosseting towels. Breakfast uses locally sourced produce, including free-range eggs, and is served downstairs in the dining room, overlooking the garden.

Rooms 3 en suite **Facilities** FTV Lounge tea/coffee WiFi ⚓ 18 **Parking** 7 **Notes** ⊗ No Children 8yrs

---

The Plume of Feathers

A 16th Century coaching Inn set in the leafy village of Mitchell, just off the A30, The Plume is a destination venue with AA 4 star rooms. The menu takes inspiration from the great Cornish larder using fresh fish, locally reared meats and small organic suppliers.

With its roaring log fires, beamed ceilings and friendly, cosy ambience on one side and a cool, contemporary conservatory space on the other, the Plume of Feathers is the ideal venue for many occasions. Why not take breakfast in the conservatory from 8am? Or pop in for lunch in the beer garden (if the weather allows!). Or how about dinner next to the warm log burner on a cold winter's day? Serving fabulous food all-day every day of the year, we have a space to suit your every mood.

Our seasonal menu and twice daily changing specials use the very best local and organic ingredients. Head chef, Paul McKenna, has long established himself in Cornwall for cooking classic British dishes with a modern Mediterranean influence. Paul and his passionate team love using the freshest fish, traceable/properly reared meats and fine fruit and vegetables - some of which come from Mitchell's own fruit farm.

We are more than happy to cater for children, vegetarians, coeliacs and those with other dietary requirements. Dogs are also welcome!

Mitchell, Cornwall TR8 5AX • Tel: 01872 510387
Email: theplume@hospitalitycornwall.com • **Website:** www.hospitalitycornwall.com/theplumeoffeathers

MITCHELL
Map 2 SW85

The Plume of Feathers
★★★★ INN

tel: 01872 510387 & 511122   fax: 01872 511124 **TR8 5AX**
email: theplume@hospitalitycornwall.co.uk web: www.theplumemitchell.co.uk
dir: *Just off A30 & A3076, follow signs*

The Plume of Feathers is a very popular inn, with origins dating back to the 16th century, situated close to Newquay and the beaches. The restaurant offers a varied menu which relies heavily on local produce. The stylish bedrooms are decorated in neutral colours and have wrought-iron beds with quality linens. The garden makes an ideal place to enjoy a meal or a Cornish tea. Staff are very friendly.

Rooms 7 annexe en suite (1 fmly) (5 GF) **Facilities** FTV tea/coffee Dinner available WiFi **Conf** Max 65 **Parking** 40 **Notes** LB No coaches

See advert on page 69

MORWENSTOW
Map 2 SS21

West Point B&B
★★★★ BED AND BREAKFAST

tel: 01288 331594 **West Point, Crimp EX23 9PB**
email: bramhill@hotmail.co.uk web: www.budebedandbreakfast.co.uk
dir: *A361 to Barnstaple onto A39 towards Bude. 7m after Clovelly rdbt on right*

Ideally placed for exploring the beautiful countryside and coasts of north Cornwall and north Devon, this smartly appointed establishment is surrounded by colourful gardens with far-reaching views to the rear. Guests are assured of a genuine welcome plus the freedom of all-day access. Both bedrooms are comfortable, light and airy; one has a four-poster bed and patio doors leading to the garden. Additional facilities include a guest lounge and dining room where local farm produce is on offer whenever possible.

Rooms 2 en suite (1 fmly) (2 GF) S £42; D £70 **Facilities** FTV TVL tea/coffee WiFi 🛁 **Extras** Speciality toiletries - complimentary **Parking** 4 **Notes** LB ⊗ Closed 22 Dec-2 Jan ⊛

MULLION
Map 2 SW61

Colvennor Farmhouse
★★★★ BED AND BREAKFAST

tel: 01326 241208 fax: 01326 241208 **Cury TR12 7BJ**
email: colvennor@btinternet.com web: www.colvennorfarmhouse.com
dir: *A3083 (Helston-Lizard), over rdbt at end of airfield, next right to Cury/Poldhu Cove, farm 1.4m on right at top of hill*

This peacefully located Grade II listed former farmhouse is a wonderfully relaxing base from which to explore the picturesque delights of The Lizard. Parts of the house date back to the 17th century, but modern comforts are now in place, with bedrooms and bathrooms offering high levels of quality and character. Breakfast utilises excellent local produce and is served in the attractive dining room. Guests also have a lovely lounge at their disposal that has a log burner to keep the chill off in cooler months. There is also a large garden.

Rooms 3 en suite (1 GF) S £50-£55; D £66-£75* **Facilities** FTV DVD TVL tea/coffee ⚓ 18 🛁 **Parking** 3 **Notes** ⊗ No Children 10yrs ⊛

NEWQUAY
Map 2 SW86

Lewinnick Lodge
★★★★ RESTAURANT WITH ROOMS

tel: 01637 878117 **Pentire Headland TR7 1QD**
email: thelodge@hospitalitycornwall.com
web: www.hospitalitycornwall.com/lewinnicklodge
dir: *From A392, at rdbt exit into Pentire Rd then Pentire Ave. Turn right to Lewinnick Lodge*

Set above the cliffs of Pentire Headland, looking out across the mighty Atlantic, guests are guaranteed amazing coastal views here at Lewinnick Lodge. The bedrooms were designed by Guy Bostock and are these are modern, spacious, and offer many thoughtful extras; some have open-plan bathrooms. Modern British food (with an emphasis on fresh fish) is served all day.

Rooms 10 en suite **Facilities** FTV iPod docking station tea/coffee Dinner available Direct Dial Lift WiFi 🛁 Surf board store **Extras** Speciality toiletries, bottled water - free **Parking** 50 **Notes** No coaches

The Cove Guesthouse
★★★★ GUEST HOUSE

tel: 01637 875311 & 07922 621759   fax: 01637 800545
19 Alexandra Rd, Porth TR7 3ND
email: info@thecoveguesthouse.co.uk web: www.thecoveguesthouse.co.uk
dir: *From A392, at Quintrell Downs rdbt take 3rd exit (A3058). At double mini rdbt, turn right to Porth (B3276). 800mtrs on right*

The Cove Guesthouse sits overlooking the coast in Porth. The house has benefited from investment and while the size of rooms vary, all are smartly appointed. Bathrooms are well presented, though shower cubicles are on the compact side. The dining room enjoys a wonderful view out across the sea and is the ideal venue for home-cooked breakfasts. Guests are free to relax on the outside decking too and private parking is available on-site.

Rooms 5 rms (4 en suite) (1 pri facs) (3 fmly) S £45-£65; D £65-£105* **Facilities** FTV DVD tea/coffee WiFi 🛁 Body board hire **Extras** Speciality toiletries, bottled water - free **Parking** 7 **Notes** LB ⊗

The Windward

★★★★ GUEST ACCOMMODATION

tel: 01637 873185 **Alexandra Rd, Porth Bay TR7 3NB**
email: enquiries@windwardhotel.co.uk **web:** www.windwardhotel.co.uk
dir: 1.5m NE of town centre. A3508 towards Newquay, right onto B3276 (Padstow road), 1m on right

The Windward is pleasantly located almost on Porth Beach and is also convenient for the airport. It offers spectacular views, friendly hospitality, and a pleasant bar and terrace for relaxing. The spacious bedrooms are well equipped; some have balconies, and many have sea views. Breakfast is served in the restaurant overlooking the beach.

Rooms 13 en suite (3 fmly) (3 GF) S £78-£88; D £98-£140 **Facilities** FTV DVD TVL tea/coffee Licensed WiFi 🔒 **Parking** 15 **Notes** LB ⊗

Meadow View

★★★ GUEST ACCOMMODATION

tel: 01637 873132 **135 Mount Wise TR7 1QR**
email: meadowview135@hotmail.com **web:** www.meadowviewnewquay.co.uk
dir: A392 into Newquay to Mountwise, Meadow View on left before rdbt to Pentire

Expect a warm welcome at Meadow View, which is just a short walk from Newquay, and Fistral Beach which is famous for surfing. The bedrooms are comfortable and some have countryside views. A hearty breakfast is served in the pleasant dining room and there is a cosy sun lounge to relax in. Waterworld, The Eden Project, and the Pentire Peninsula with its rolling green coastline are all just a short drive away.

Rooms 7 en suite (2 fmly) S £30-£45; D £60-£75* **Facilities** FTV tea/coffee WiFi 🔒 **Parking** 7 **Notes** LB ⊗ No Children 5yrs Closed 7 Nov-mid Feb ⊜

The Three Tees

★★★ GUEST ACCOMMODATION

tel: 01637 872055 **fax:** 01637 820200 **21 Carminow Way TR7 3AY**
email: greg@3tees.co.uk **web:** www.3tees.co.uk
dir: A30 onto A392 signed Newquay. Right at Quintrell Downs rdbt signed Porth, over x-rds, 3rd right

Located in a quiet residential area just a short walk from the town and beach, this friendly family-run establishment is comfortable and well equipped. Guests have use of a lounge, a bar and a sun lounge, and breakfast is served in the dining room, where snacks are available throughout the day. The bar serves light snacks in the evenings. In addition to the bedrooms in the main house, a family annexe is also available, and offers flexible, level-access accommodation.

Rooms 8 rms (7 en suite) (1 pri facs) 1 annexe en suite (4 fmly) (2 GF) D £70-£80* **Facilities** FTV DVD TVL tea/coffee Licensed WiFi 🔒 **Parking** 9 **Notes** LB Closed Nov-Feb

Tregarthen Guest House

★★★ GUEST ACCOMMODATION

tel: 01637 873554 **1 Arundel Way TR7 3BB**
email: info@tregarthen.co.uk **web:** www.tregarthen.co.uk
dir: A30 onto A392, at Quintrell onto A3058 (Henver Rd), Arundel Way 4th right

Tregarthen Guest House is located in a peaceful location close to town and beaches. The owners of this delightful detached property provide warm hospitality along with comfortable accommodation which is smartly furnished and well equipped. Guests can look forward to a hearty breakfast served at individual tables in the spacious ground-floor dining room. Ample parking is available.

Rooms 6 en suite 1 annexe en suite (1 fmly) (6 GF) D £55-£75* **Facilities** FTV DVD iPod docking station tea/coffee WiFi 🔒 **Parking** 7 **Notes** LB ⊗ No Children 7yrs Closed Xmas

Wenden Guest House

★★★ GUEST HOUSE

tel: 01637 872604 **fax:** 01637 872604 **11 Berry Rd TR7 1AU**
email: wenden@newquay-holidays.co.uk **web:** www.newquay-holidays.co.uk
dir: In town centre off seafront Cliff Rd, near station

The family-run guest house offers bright, modern accommodation close to both the beach and the town centre. Bedrooms have been carefully designed to make best use of space, and each is individually styled. Breakfast, served in the stylish dining room, provides a filling start to the day.

Rooms 6 en suite D £55-£85* **Facilities** FTV DVD iPod docking station tea/coffee WiFi 🔒 **Extras** Mini-fridge **Parking** 6 **Notes** LB ⊗ No Children 16yrs Closed 1wk Xmas RS Nov-Feb 2 nights stay minimum

Avalon

★★★ GUEST ACCOMMODATION

tel: 01637 877522 & 07870 320346 **4 Edgcumbe Gardens TR7 2QD**
email: enquiries@avalonnewquay.co.uk **web:** www.avalonnewquay.co.uk
dir: From A30 at Quintrell Downs rdbt onto A3058 signed St Columb Minor. Left in 1m opposite Rocklands

Conveniently situated within walking distance of the town centre and the beaches, in a quiet residential area, Avalon provides comfortable accommodation, and enjoys the benefit of on-site parking. Guests may enjoy the front-facing sun terrace during summer months. Golfing holiday offers are available.

Rooms 6 rms (5 en suite) (1 pri facs) (1 fmly) **Facilities** FTV tea/coffee WiFi 🔒 **Parking** 6 **Notes** LB

The Croft

★★★ GUEST ACCOMMODATION

tel: 01637 871520 **fax:** 01637 871520 **37 Mount Wise TR7 2BL**
email: info@the-crofthotel.co.uk **web:** www.the-crofthotel.co.uk
dir: In town centre nr Towan Beach, junct Mount Wise & Mayfield Rd

Located just minutes away from the town centre and beach, The Croft is a comfortable place to stay, and the friendly hosts create a homely atmosphere. A full English breakfast is served in the informal bar-dining room.

Rooms 7 rms (5 en suite) (2 pri facs) (3 fmly) D £50-£75* **Facilities** FTV tea/coffee Licensed 🔒 **Parking** 7 **Notes** LB ⊗ No Children 3yrs

Dewolf Guest House

★★★ GUEST HOUSE

tel: 01637 874746 **100 Henver Rd TR7 3BL**
email: holidays@dewolfguesthouse.com **web:** www.dewolfguesthouse.com
dir: A392 onto A3058 at Quintrell Downs rdbt, guest house on left just past mini rdbts, before crossing

Making guests feel welcome and at home is the priority here. The bedrooms in the main house are bright and well equipped, and there are two more in a separate single storey building at the rear. The guest house is just a short walk from Porth Beach and all the local attractions.

Rooms 3 en suite 2 annexe en suite (1 GF) S £30-£45; D £60-£90* **Facilities** FTV tea/coffee Licensed WiFi **Extras** Mini-fridge - complimentary **Parking** 6 **Notes** LB

NEWQUAY *continued*

Milber Guest House

★★★ GUEST HOUSE

tel: 01637 872825 **11 Michell Av TR7 1BN**
email: suemilber@aol.com **web:** www.milberguesthouse.com
dir: *A392 to Newquay. From Quintrell rdbt onto A3058 (Quintrell Rd then Henver Rd) left into Narrowcliffe, becomes Cliff Rd. Left into Berry Rd, right into Mount Wise. 2nd right into Michell Av, house on left*

This small, friendly guest house is situated in the centre of Newquay, and has an on-site bar that is open most reasonable times. Bedrooms are comfortable and offer lots of useful facilities. Guests are given their own keys so they can come and go as they please.

Rooms 6 rms (4 en suite) (6 fmly) (1 GF) S £22.50-£30; D £40-£60* **Facilities** FTV iPod docking station tea/coffee Licensed WiFi 🔒 **Notes** LB ⊗ ➰

Pencrebar

★★★ GUEST ACCOMMODATION

tel: 01637 872037 **4 Berry Rd TR7 1AT**
email: enquiries@pencrebar.com **web:** www.pencrebar.com
dir: *A30 onto A392, right at boating lake on entering Newquay*

This friendly family-run house is a short walk from Newquay's popular beaches and the town centre. Bedrooms are all spacious and well planned. Delicious breakfasts are served in the attractive dining room. Nearby secure parking is available for guests.

Rooms 7 en suite (2 fmly) S £28-£35; D £48-£60 **Facilities** FTV DVD tea/coffee WiFi 🔒 Off site private parking - charged all year **Extras** Mini-fridge - complimentary **Notes** LB ⊗

Porth Lodge

★★★ INN

tel: 01637 874483 **Porth Bean Rd TR7 3LT**
email: info@porthlodgehotel.co.uk **web:** www.porthlodgehotel.co.uk

Porth Lodge is a popular venue with its own bowling alley. Staff here are friendly and helpful, and the bedrooms are very comfortable and well equipped. Meals are available every day.

Rooms 16 en suite (1 fmly) S £30-£50; D £60-£90* **Facilities** FTV tea/coffee Dinner available WiFi ⚗ 18 Pool table 🔒 Ten pin bowling alley **Conf** Thtr 40 Class 30 Board 20 **Parking** 20 **Notes** LB

Rolling Waves

★★★ GUEST HOUSE

tel: 01637 873236 **fax:** 01637 873236 **Alexandra Rd, Porth TR7 3NB**
email: enquiries@rollingwaves.co.uk **web:** www.rollingwaves.co.uk
dir: *A30 onto A392, A3058 towards Newquay. B3276 to Porth, pass Mermaid public house*

Rolling Waves is a family-owned and run guest house with great views across the bay. The bedrooms are comfortable, the hosts friendly and welcoming, and dinner is available on request.

Rooms 8 rms (7 en suite) (1 pri facs) (2 fmly) (4 GF) S £32-£40; D £64-£80* **Facilities** FTV TVL tea/coffee Dinner available Licensed WiFi **Parking** 7 **Notes** LB ⊗

St Breca

★★★ GUEST HOUSE

tel: 01637 872745 **22 Mount Wise TR7 2BG**
email: enquiries@stbreca.co.uk **web:** www.stbreca.co.uk
dir: *A30 onto A392. Follow signs to Newquay, then to Mount Wise*

This friendly guest house is conveniently located a few minutes' walk from the town centre, beaches and other amenities. It provides soundly maintained, modern bedrooms, and separate tables are provided in the attractive breakfast room.

Rooms 10 rms (8 en suite) (2 pri facs) (3 fmly) (2 GF) S £20-£35; D £40-£70* **Facilities** FTV DVD tea/coffee WiFi **Parking** 3 **Notes** LB ⊗

The Silver Jubilee

★★★ GUEST HOUSE

tel: 01637 874544 & 07779 518484 **13 Berry Rd TR7 1AU**
email: igali0andy@gmail.com **web:** www.silverjubileeguesthouse.co.uk
dir: *Follow A3058 into Newquay. After railway station, left at lights, 3rd house on left*

The Silver Jubilee is a small establishment situated on the level in the heart of Newquay. All amenities including shopping centre and beaches are about three minutes' walk away. Breakfast is served in the dining room. There is also a bar/lounge for a drink and relaxation.

Rooms 7 en suite (3 fmly) S £35-£50; D £50-£80* **Facilities** FTV Lounge tea/coffee Licensed WiFi 🔒 **Parking** 4 **Notes** LB ⊗

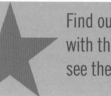

Find out more about this county with the AA Guide to Cornwall — see theAA.com/shop

Tir Chonaill

★★★ GUEST ACCOMMODATION

tel: 01637 876492 & 07918 663934 **106 Mount Wise TR7 1QP**
email: tirchonailhotel@talk21.com **web:** www.tirchonaill.co.uk
dir: *A392 into Newquay, at last rdbt right into Mount Wise, signed*

Expect a warm welcome at the long-established and family-owned Tir Chonaill, situated close to the beaches and the town centre. Some of the neat bedrooms have wonderful views across town to the sea, and the hearty breakfasts are sure to satisfy.

Rooms 9 en suite (9 fmly) (1 GF) S £35-£55; D £65-£80 **Facilities** FTV TVL tea/coffee WiFi ⚓ 18 **Parking** 10 **Notes** LB Closed Nov

Find out more about
the AA's awards for food
excellence on page 11

Premier Collection

The Seafood Restaurant

★★★★★ ◉◉◉ ☰ RESTAURANT WITH ROOMS

tel: 01841 532700 **fax:** 01841 532942 **Riverside PL28 8BY**
email: reservations@rickstein.com **web:** www.rickstein.com
dir: *Into town centre down hill, follow round sharp bend, restaurant on left*

Food lovers continue to beat a well-trodden path to this well-known restaurant. Situated on the edge of the harbour, just a stone's throw from the shops, The Seafood Restaurant offers chic and comfortable bedrooms that boast numerous thoughtful extras; some have views of the estuary and a couple have private balconies with stunning sea views. Service is relaxed and friendly; booking is essential for both accommodation and a table in the restaurant.

Rooms 14 en suite 6 annexe en suite (6 fmly) (3 GF) S £150-£282; D £150-£285* **Facilities** FTV DVD iPod docking station tea/coffee Dinner available Direct Dial Lift WiFi ⚓ Cookery School **Extras** Mini-bar - chargeable **Parking** 10 **Notes** LB Closed 24-26 Dec RS 24 Dec & 1 May restaurant limited service times No coaches

The Old Mill House

★★★★ ☰ GUEST HOUSE

tel: 01841 540388 **fax:** 01841 540406 **PL27 7QT**
email: enquiries@theoldmillhouse.com **web:** www.theoldmillhouse.com
dir: *2m S of Padstow. In centre of Little Petherick on A389*

Situated in an Area of Outstanding Natural Beauty, The Old Mill House is a Grade II listed 16th-century converted corn mill. Next to the attractive secluded gardens is a stream that runs into the Camel Estuary - if you're lucky you might see kingfishers. Bedrooms are well equipped and comfortable, and breakfast is served in the room where the mill wheel still turns.

Rooms 7 en suite S £70-£105; D £85-£120* **Facilities** FTV Lounge TVL tea/coffee Direct Dial Licensed WiFi ⚓ **Parking** 20 **Notes** LB ⊗ No Children 14yrs Closed Nov-Feb

Penjoly Guest House

★★★★ ☰ GUEST HOUSE

tel: 01841 533535 **Padstow Rd PL28 8LB**
email: penjoly.padstow@btopenworld.com **web:** www.penjolypadstow.co.uk
dir: *1m S of Padstow. Off A389 near Padstow Holiday Park*

Penjoy is a very professionally run establishment, where attention to detail and quality are noteworthy throughout. Bedrooms are delightfully decorated and complemented by an impressive range of extras. Breakfast is served in the attractive breakfast room or in the conservatory, and a guest lounge is also available. This is a perfect base for exploring the West Country's delights, and for seeking out the great restaurants of Cornwall. Guests have the convenience of off-road parking.

Rooms 3 en suite (3 GF) S £79.20-£85.50; D £88-£95* **Facilities** STV FTV DVD iPod docking station TVL tea/coffee WiFi **Extras** Robes **Parking** 10 **Notes** ⊗ No Children 16yrs ▨

PADSTOW *continued*

Rick Stein's Café

★★★★ BED AND BREAKFAST

tel: 01841 532700 **fax:** 01841 532942 **10 Middle St PL28 8AP**
email: reservations@rickstein.com **web:** www.rickstein.com
dir: *A389 into town, one way past church, 3rd right*

Another Rick Stein success story, this is a lively café by day, restaurant by night, and offers good food and quality accommodation just a short walk from the harbour. Three bedrooms are available - each is quite different but all have high standards of comfort. Friendly and personable staff are always on hand.

Rooms 3 en suite (1 fmly) S £110-£150; D £110-£150* **Facilities** FTV DVD iPod docking station tea/coffee Dinner available Direct Dial Licensed WiFi 🔒 Cookery school **Extras** Mini-bar - chargeable **Notes** LB Closed 25-26 Dec RS 24 Dec & 1 May limited service times

Wingfield House

★★ BED AND BREAKFAST

tel: 01841 532617 **Dennis Ln PL28 8DP**
email: besidetheseaside@btinternet.com
dir: *Into Padstow on A389, 1st right into Sarahs Ln. At bottom of hill, right into Dennis Ln, 3rd entrance on right*

Wingfield House is a very friendly, traditional bed and breakfast a few minutes' walk from Padstow town centre. The comfortable bedrooms are well appointed and have shared or private facilities. Hearty breakfasts are served at a large table in the dining room, and guests have the use of a TV lounge. There is off-road parking.

Rooms 3 rms (1 pri facs) (2 fmly) **Facilities** FTV TVL tea/coffee WiFi **Parking** 5 **Notes** ⊗

PAR
Map 2 SX05

The Britannia Inn & Restaurant

★★★★★ INN

tel: 01726 812889 & 815796 **fax:** 01726 812089 **St Austell Rd PL24 2SL**
email: info@britanniainn.com **web:** www.britanniainn.com
dir: *On A390 between Par & St Austell, next to Cornish Market World*

This long established inn is situated between Par and St Austell and is just a five-minute drive from The Eden Project. There is a very genuine welcome here and a collective effort to ensure guests are well looked after and enjoy their stay. A choice of bars is available, together with attractive gardens, function room and range of dining options. The extensive menu features plenty of Cornish produce with a range of daily specials also offered. Bedrooms offer contemporary style and comfort with impressive, high quality bathrooms.

Rooms 7 en suite (4 fmly) S £65-£85; D £75-£95* **Facilities** FTV tea/coffee Dinner available Direct Dial WiFi 🔒 **Conf** Max 75 Thtr 60 Class 45 Board 50 **Parking** 105

Elmswood House

★★★★ GUEST ACCOMMODATION

tel: 01726 814221 **73 Tehidy Rd, Tywardreath PL24 2QD**
email: info@elmswoodhouse.co.uk **web:** www.elmswoodhouse.co.uk
dir: *Right from Par station, then 1st left to top of hill, opposite village church*

Elmswood House is a fine Victorian building set in the middle of the village opposite the church. Many guests return to stay here time and again. Bedrooms have quality furnishings and many extra facilities, and the attractive dining room, lounge and bar overlook a beautiful garden.

Rooms 6 en suite (1 fmly) (1 GF) S £55-£65; D £75-£85* **Facilities** FTV Lounge TVL tea/coffee Licensed WiFi **Parking** 6 **Notes** ⊗ No Children 10yrs Closed Jan

Penarth Guest House

★★★★ 🏠 GUEST ACCOMMODATION

tel: 01726 810146 **St Austell Rd, St Blazey Gate PL24 2EF**
email: penarthgh@yahoo.com

Penarth Guest House is an ideal base for exploring Cornwall's spectacular coastline, gardens and countryside. The comfortable bedrooms are furnished in a contemporary style and are equipped with numerous facilities. There is a wide variety on offer at breakfast, from full English or continental, to scrambled eggs with smoked salmon. The award-winning breakfast, which includes local produce, is served in the spacious dining room. Off-road parking is available.

Rooms 3 rms **Parking Notes** Closed Dec-Mar

The Royal Inn

★★★★ INN

tel: 01726 815601 **fax:** 01726 816415 **66 Eastcliffe Rd, Tywardreath PL24 2AJ**
email: info@royal-inn.co.uk **web:** www.royal-inn.co.uk
dir: *Adjacent to Par railway station*

Situated next to the railway station on the edge of Tywardreath, this free house provides high standards of comfort and quality. Only five minutes from Par Sands and four miles from The Eden Project, it is an ideal base for exploring Cornwall. The open-plan bar area has slate floors and a large open fire; the atmosphere is relaxed and diners can choose from the bar menu or dine more formally in the restaurant or conservatory. All twin rooms have sofa beds (suitable for children under 14), and the family suite is suitable for families of four or five.

Rooms 15 en suite (8 fmly) (4 GF) **Facilities** STV FTV tea/coffee Dinner available Direct Dial WiFi 🎱 Pool table **Conf** Max 20 Thtr 8 Class 8 Board 20 **Parking** 17 **Notes** Closed 23-26 Dec & 30 Dec-1 Jan

PENZANCE   Map 2 SW43

Premier Collection

Ednovean Farm (SW538295)

★★★★★ ≜ FARMHOUSE

tel: 01736 711883 **TR20 9LZ**
email: info@ednoveanfarm.co.uk **web:** www.ednoveanfarm.co.uk

(For full entry see Perranuthnoe)

Premier Collection

The Summer House

★★★★★ ≜ ➔ GUEST ACCOMMODATION

tel: 01736 363744 **fax:** 01736 360959 **Cornwall Ter TR18 4HL**
email: reception@summerhouse-cornwall.com **web:** www.summerhouse-cornwall.com
dir: *A30 to Penzance, at rail station follow along harbour onto Promenade, pass Jubilee Pool, right after Queens Hotel. Summer House 30yds on left*

The Summer House, set in a delightful residential area close to the seafront and harbour, is decorated in a Mediterranean style. Expect warm hospitality and attentive service in tastefully furnished surroundings. The walled garden also reflects the theme, with sub-tropical plantings and attractive blue tables and chairs; dinner and drinks are served here on summer evenings.

Rooms 5 en suite S £95-£160; D £120-£160* **Facilities** FTV DVD Lounge TVL tea/coffee Dinner available Licensed WiFi 🔒 **Extras** Speciality toiletries, mineral water **Parking** 6 **Notes** LB ⊗ No Children 13yrs Closed Nov-Mar

Premier Collection

Camilla House

★★★★★ ≜ GUEST ACCOMMODATION

tel: 01736 363771 **fax:** 01736 363771 **12 Regent Ter TR18 4DW**
email: enquiries@camillahouse.co.uk **web:** www.camillahouse.co.uk
dir: *A30 to Penzance, at rail station follow road along harbourfront into Promenade Rd. Opposite Jubilee Bathing Pool, Regent Terrace 2nd right*

A warm welcome is assured at this charming Victorian property, located in a quiet, residential area facing the sea and only a short walk from Penzance's beach and town centre attractions. Bedrooms, some with views towards the coast, are spacious and attractively appointed. There's a stylish guest lounge with many homely features, and breakfast should not be missed. Secure car parking provided.

Rooms 8 rms (7 en suite) (1 pri facs) (1 GF) S £35-£40; D £77-£89*
Facilities FTV DVD TVL tea/coffee Licensed WiFi 🔒 **Parking** 7 **Notes** ⊗
RS Jan closed for refurbishment

The Dunedin

★★★★ GUEST ACCOMMODATION

tel: 01736 362652 **fax:** 01736 360497 **Alexandra Rd TR18 4LZ**
email: info@dunedinhotel.co.uk **web:** www.dunedinhotel.co.uk
dir: *A30 to Penzance, at rail station along harbour front into Promenade Rd, right into Alexandra Rd, Dunedin on right*

The Dunedin is in a tree-lined avenue just a stroll from the promenade and town centre. The friendly proprietors provide a relaxed atmosphere, and bedrooms that are well equipped and smartly decorated to a high standard. There is a cosy lounge, and hearty breakfasts are served in the dining room.

Rooms 8 en suite (2 fmly) (2 GF) S £50-£65; D £70-£90 **Facilities** FTV DVD TVL tea/coffee WiFi 🔒 **Notes** LB ⊗ No Children 5yrs Closed 31 Oct-3 Jan 📷

Mount Royal

★★★★ GUEST ACCOMMODATION

tel: 01736 362233 **fax:** 01736 362233 **Chyandour Cliff TR18 3LQ**
email: mountroyal@btconnect.com
dir: *From A30 onto coast road into town*

Part Georgian and part Victorian, the spacious Mount Royal has splendid views over Mount's Bay and is convenient for the town's attractions. There's a gracious elegance throughout with the impressive dining room retaining its original fireplace and ornate sideboard. Parking available to the rear of the property.

Rooms 6 en suite (1 fmly) (1 GF) S £80-£100; D £100-£130 **Facilities** Lounge tea/coffee WiFi 🔒 **Extras** Speciality toiletries **Parking** 8 **Notes** LB ⊗ Closed Oct-May 📷

The Old Vicarage

★★★★ BED AND BREAKFAST

tel: 01736 711508 & 07736 101230 **fax:** 01736 711508
Churchtown, St Hilary TR20 9DQ
email: johnbd524@aol.com **web:** www.oldvicaragepenzance.co.uk
dir: *5m E of Penzance. Off B3280 in St Hilary*

Guests will certainly feel very much at home after the friendly welcome they'll receive on arrival at The Old Vicarage. The spacious bedrooms are thoughtfully equipped, and there is a comfortable lounge and extensive gardens. Guests can also take advantage of the trekking and riding school, run by the proprietors who own a small stud farm.

Rooms 4 en suite (2 fmly) (1 GF) **Facilities** FTV TVL tea/coffee WiFi ⚵ 18 Riding **Parking** 8

The Coldstreamer Inn

★★★ 🏵 INN

tel: 01736 362072 **fax:** 01736 322072 **Gulval TR18 3BB**
email: info@coldstreamer-penzance.co.uk **web:** www.coldstreamer-penzance.co.uk
dir: *1m NE of Penzance on B3311, right into School Ln in Gulval, opposite church*

Standing opposite the picturesque church in the pretty village of Gulval, this local hostelry offers plenty of atmosphere and banter. Public areas have homely charm and the restaurant is the venue for impressive cuisine, prepared with skill, passion and excellent produce. After a relaxing evening, comfortable bedrooms offer a good night's sleep in preparation for a tasty, freshly cooked, breakfast.

Rooms 3 en suite S £60-£75; D £70-£85* **Facilities** FTV tea/coffee Dinner available WiFi 🔒 **Notes** LB

PENZANCE *continued*

The Dolphin Tavern

★★★ INN

tel: 01736 364106 **Quay St TR18 4BD**
email: dolphintavern@tiscali.co.uk web: www.dolphintavern.co.uk
dir: *Opposite Penzance harbour*

The Dolphin Tavern is a traditional inn just a few yards away from Penzance harbour, usefully located for the Scillonian ferry. Rooms are comfortable and well presented, and the staff are friendly and attentive. Food is available in the bar and restaurant daily from a wide menu which also offers daily-changing specials.

Rooms 2 en suite **Facilities** FTV tea/coffee Dinner available WiFi Pool table in winter only **Notes** ⊗ No coaches

Mount View

★★★ INN

tel: 01736 710416 **fax:** 01736 710416 **Longrock TR20 8JJ**
email: mountviewhotel@hotmail.co.uk web: www.mountviewhotelcornwall.co.uk
dir: *Exit A30 at Marazion/Penzance rdbt, 3rd exit signed Longrock. On right after pelican crossing*

This Victorian inn, just a short walk from the beach and half a mile from the Isles of Scilly heliport, is a good base for exploring west Cornwall. Bedrooms are well equipped, including a hospitality tray, and the bar is popular with locals. Breakfast is served in the dining room, and a dinner menu is available.

Rooms 5 rms (3 en suite) (2 fmly) (2 smoking) **Facilities** FTV tea/coffee Dinner available WiFi Pool table 🔒 **Conf** Max 20 **Parking** 8 **Notes** RS Sun closed 4.30pm-7pm

See advert on opposite page

Penmorvah

★★★ GUEST ACCOMMODATION

tel: 01736 363711 **61 Alexandra Rd TR18 4LZ**
email: penmorvah_penzance@talktalk.net web: www.penmorvah.net
dir: *A30 to Penzance, at railway station follow road along harbourfront, pass Jubilee pool. At mini rdbt, right into Alexandra Rd*

Penmorvah is just a few minutes' walk from the seafront with convenient on-street parking nearby. Rooms are comfortable and all are en suite. A warm welcome is assured with every effort made to ensure a relaxing and rewarding stay.

Rooms 7 en suite (1 fmly) (3 GF) **Facilities** FTV tea/coffee 🔒 **Notes** No Children 5yrs 🚗

The Swordfish Inn

★★★ INN

tel: 01736 362830 **The Strand, Newlyn TR18 5HN**
email: info@swordfishinn.co.uk web: www.swordfishinn.co.uk
dir: *1m SW of Penzance*

Situated in the very heart of the fishing village of Newlyn, The Swordfish has been totally renovated to provide modern comforts in a traditional and convivial environment. The spacious, comfortable bedrooms are well appointed, as are the en suite shower rooms. This establishment is a popular venue for locals and tourists alike.

Rooms 4 en suite **Facilities** FTV tea/coffee WiFi **Notes** ⊗ No coaches

The Carlton

★★ GUEST HOUSE

tel: 01736 362081 **fax:** 01736 362081 **Promenade TR18 4NW**
email: carltonhotelpenzance@talk21.com
dir: *From A30 signs for harbour & Newlyn, on right after rdbt*

Situated on the pleasant promenade and enjoying sea views from some of its rooms, The Carlton is an easy stroll from the town centre and amenities. Bedrooms are traditionally styled, and there is a guest lounge and spacious dining room, both sea facing.

Rooms 12 rms (9 en suite) (3 smoking) S £35-£40; D £70-£80* **Facilities** FTV TVL tea/coffee **Notes** ⊗

Ennys

U

tel: 01736 740262 **fax:** 01736 740099 **Trewhella Ln TR20 9BZ**
email: info@ennys.co.uk **web:** www.ennys.co.uk
dir: *1m N of B3280 (Leedstown to Goldsithney road) at end of Trewhella Ln*

Currently the rating for this establishment is not confirmed. This may be due to a change of ownership or because it has only recently joined the AA rating scheme.

Rooms 2 en suite (1 GF) D £150-£160* **Facilities** DVD iPod docking station tea/coffee WiFi ⊰ ♖ Riding **Extras** Speciality toiletries **Parking** 10 **Notes** LB ⊗ No Children 1-14yrs Closed Nov-1 Apr

Fountain Tavern

U

tel: 01736 369340 **Saint Clare St TR18 2PD**
email: contact@fountaintavernpenzance.co.uk

Currently the rating for this establishment is not confirmed. This may be due to a change of ownership or because it has only recently joined the AA rating scheme.

Rooms 5 rms (4 en suite)

PERRANPORTH   **Map 2 SW75**

St Georges Country House

★★★★ GUEST ACCOMMODATION

tel: 01872 572184 **St Georges Hill TR6 0ED**
email: info@stgeorgescountryhouse.co.uk **web:** www.stgeorgescountryhouse.co.uk

Situated in an elevated position above Perranporth, St Georges Country House is a very friendly and comfortable establishment. The owners and staff are attentive and very welcoming. Food is served most evenings and there is also a bar and large sitting room with comfy sofas and lots of books.

Rooms 7 en suite (2 fmly) **Facilities** FTV TVL tea/coffee Dinner available Licensed WiFi **Conf** Max 20 Board 20 **Parking** 10 **Notes** Closed 23-30 Dec

Seascape

★★★★ BED AND BREAKFAST

tel: 01872 858956 & 07833 975892 **Trevalga Close TR6 0HH**
email: nerleigh@gmail.com
dir: *From A3075, through 1st rdbt, at next rdbt take 2nd exit onto B3285. Continue onto Boscawen Rd (B3284)*

Just a short stroll from the centre of Perranporth and its magnificent beach, this is an ideal location for those wishing to relax, unwind and explore the magnificent north Cornish coast. A warm welcome is assured with helpful local information always readily available. The stylish bedrooms have private, external access with outside terraces providing lovely views across the town to the sea beyond. Breakfast is served either in the bedrooms or alfresco in the summer.

Rooms 2 en suite (2 GF) D £65-£95* **Facilities** FTV DVD iPod docking station tea/coffee WiFi ⌀ 18 ⚑ **Extras** Mineral water - complimentary **Parking** 2 **Notes** LB ⊗

The Mount View

Longrock, Penzance, Cornwall TR20 8JJ • Tel: 01736 710416
Email: mountviewhotel@hotmail.co.uk • Website: mountviewhotelcornwall.co.uk

The Mount View is an excellent base from which to explore West Cornwall. It has a private car park and bicycle storage can be arranged. Longrock is 3 miles from Penzance and only 1 mile from the picturesque town of Marazion and *St Michael's Mount*, there is a regular bus service through the village and the coastal footpath around Mount's Bay is 10 minutes' walk away. There are 5 well-appointed bedrooms and family rooms are available. The tariff includes a full Cornish breakfast and a full menu is also available, including a Sunday Roast Lunch and weekly specials in the dining room or picnics can be ordered. Dogs are welcome at no additional charge.

Rooms: 3 en-suite, 2 standard £30.00 and £24.00 per person per night. Free for Children under 2 and children under 16 sharing with parents are charged half price.
All prices are the same throughout the year except in July and August when a £5 single occupancy supplement applies.
Facilities: TV, Tea/Coffee, Wi-fi, Licensed Bar, Dinner available, Private Parking/Bike Storage

PERRANUTHNOE   Map 2 SW52

Premier Collection

Ednovean Farm (SW538295)

★★★★★ ≘ FARMHOUSE

tel: 01736 711883 **TR20 9LZ**
email: info@ednoveanfarm.co.uk **web:** www.ednoveanfarm.co.uk
dir: Off A394 towards Perranuthnoe at Dynasty Restaurant, farm drive on left on bend by post box

Tranquillity is guaranteed at this 17th-century farmhouse, which looks across the countryside towards Mount's Bay. The bedrooms are individually styled and are very comfortable. The impressive, Mediterranean-style gardens are ideal for relaxing and taking in the superb views. In addition to the sitting room, there is also a garden room and several patios. Breakfast is served at a magnificent oak table.

Rooms 3 en suite (3 GF) S £100-£130; D £100-£130* **Facilities** FTV DVD iPod docking station Lounge tea/coffee WiFi **Extras** Speciality toiletries, slippers **Parking** 4 **Notes** LB ⊗ No Children 16yrs Closed 24-28 Dec 22 acres grassland/stud

The Victoria Inn

★★★ ◉◉ ≘ INN

tel: 01736 710309 **TR20 9NP**
email: enquiries@victoriainn-penzance.co.uk **web:** www.victoriainn-penzance.co.uk
dir: Off A394 into village

This attractive and friendly inn, popular with locals and visitors alike, reputedly began trading in the Middle Ages. The food on offer should not be missed. The skilled kitchen team produces consistently impressive dishes which are served either in the cosy bar or the restaurant. The menus feature fresh produce, including locally-landed fish. The bedrooms are well presented and provide good levels of comfort.

Rooms 2 en suite S £50-£75; D £75* **Facilities** FTV DVD tea/coffee Dinner available WiFi **Extras** Fruit, magazines **Parking** 10 **Notes** No Children 18yrs Closed 1wk Jan No coaches

POLPERRO   Map 2 SX25

Premier Collection

Trenderway Farm (SX214533)

★★★★★ ≘ FARMHOUSE

tel: 01503 272214 **Pelynt PL13 2LY**
email: stay@trenderwayfarm.com **web:** www.trenderwayfarm.co.uk
dir: Take A387 from Looe to Polperro, right at signpost to Pelynt. 3rd left at signed junct to farm. Continue down lane to gravel car park

Warm hospitality awaits at this delightful 16th-century farmhouse set on a 200-acre working farm. Stylish bedrooms, both in the farmhouse and in the adjacent barns, offer high levels of comfort and include WiFi access. Hearty breakfasts are served in the conservatory overlooking the lake, and free-range eggs from the farm, as well as high quality local produce, are served.

Rooms 2 en suite 5 annexe en suite (2 GF) S £99-£175; D £99-£175* **Facilities** FTV DVD TVL tea/coffee Licensed WiFi ⬦ Lakes Falconry school **Extras** Speciality toiletries; mini-bar - chargeable **Conf** Max 100 Thtr 100 Class 50 Board 15 **Parking** 8 **Notes** LB No Children 16yrs Civ Wed 120 200 acres beef/sheep/orchards

Trenake Manor Farm (SX190555)

★★★★ FARMHOUSE

tel: 01503 220835 **fax:** 01503 220835 **Pelynt PL13 2LT**
email: lorraine@cornishfarmhouse.co.uk **web:** www.cornishfarmhouse.co.uk
dir: A38 onto A390 then B3359. Right at small x-rds, signed Trenake Farm

This welcoming 15th-century farmhouse is surrounded by countryside and is a good base for touring Cornwall. Bedrooms have considerate finishing touches and there is a comfortable lounge. Breakfast, using local produce, is enjoyed in the cosy dining room. You may just spot the milking cows quietly passing the end of the garden.

Rooms 3 en suite (1 fmly) D £80* **Facilities** FTV TVL tea/coffee Dinner available WiFi **Parking** 10 **Notes** LB ⊗ ⊜ 1000 acres dairy/beef/arable

Penryn House

★★★★ GUEST ACCOMMODATION

tel: 01503 272157 **fax:** 01503 273055 **The Coombes PL13 2RQ**
email: enquiries@penrynhouse.co.uk **web:** www.penrynhouse.co.uk
dir: *A387 to Polperro, at mini rdbt left down hill into village (ignore restricted access). 200yds on left*

Penryn House has a relaxed atmosphere and offers a warm welcome. Every effort is made to ensure a memorable stay. Bedrooms are neatly presented and reflect the character of the building. After a day exploring, enjoy a drink at the bar and relax in the comfortable lounge.

Rooms 12 en suite (3 fmly) S £45-£60; D £75-£105* **Facilities** FTV Lounge tea/coffee Licensed WiFi 🔒 **Parking** 13 **Notes** LB

PORTHLEVEN   Map 2 SW62

Kota Restaurant with Rooms

★★★ ◉◉ RESTAURANT WITH ROOMS

tel: 01326 562407 **fax:** 01326 562407 **Harbour Head TR13 9JA**
email: info@kotakai.co.uk **web:** www.kotarestaurant.co.uk
dir: *B3304 from Helston into Porthleven. Kota on harbour opposite slipway*

Overlooking the water, this 300-year-old building is the home of Kota Restaurant ('kota' being the Maori word for 'shellfish'). The bedrooms are approached from a granite stairway to the side of the building. The family room is spacious and has the benefit of harbour views, while the smaller, double room is at the rear of the property. The enthusiastic young owners ensure guests enjoy their stay here, and a meal in the restaurant should not be missed. Breakfast features the best local produce.

Rooms 2 annexe en suite (1 fmly) S £50-£85; D £60-£95 **Facilities** FTV DVD tea/coffee Dinner available WiFi ⚓ 18 🔒 **Parking** 1 **Notes** ⊗ Closed 10 Nov-10 Mar No coaches

---

PORTLOE   Map 2 SW93

The Lugger

★★★★★ ◉◉ INN

tel: 01872 501322 **TR2 5RD**
email: reservations.lugger@bespokehotels.com **web:** www.bespokehotels.com/thelugger
dir: *A390 to Truro, B3287 to Tregony, A3078 (St Mawes Rd), left for Veryan, left for Portloe*

This delightful inn enjoys a unique setting adjacent to the slipway of the harbour, where fishing boats still come and go. Bedrooms, some in adjacent buildings and cottages, are contemporary in style and are well equipped. There is a sitting room which reflects the original character of the property with beams and open fireplaces that create a cosy atmosphere. The modern restaurant enjoys superb views, and in warmer months, a sun terrace overlooking the harbour proves a popular place to enjoy a meal.

Rooms 5 en suite 17 annexe en suite (1 GF) **Facilities** FTV tea/coffee Dinner available Direct Dial WiFi **Parking** 26 **Notes** Civ Wed 50

Carradale

★★★★ BED AND BREAKFAST

tel: 01872 501508 **TR2 5RB**
email: barbara495@btinternet.com
dir: *Off A3078 into Portloe, B&B 200yds from Ship Inn*

Carradale lies on the outskirts of this picturesque fishing village, a short walk from the South West Coast Path. It provides warm hospitality, a good level of comfort and well equipped bedrooms. There is an upper-floor lounge with a TV, and breakfast is served around a communal table in the pleasant dining room.

Rooms 2 en suite (1 fmly) (1 GF) **Facilities** TVL tea/coffee WiFi 🔒 **Parking** 5 **Notes** ⊗ ⊛

REDRUTH   Map 2 SW64

Old Railway Yard

★★★★ BED AND BREAKFAST

tel: 01209 314514 & 07970 595598 **Lanner Hill TR16 5TZ**
email: g.s.collier@btinternet.com **web:** www.old-railway-yard.co.uk
dir: *A393 Redruth/Falmouth road, at brow of hill before Lanner village, turn right into Tram Cross Ln, 125mtrs on right*

The Old Railway Yard is a traditional bed and breakfast situated off Lanner Hill, with easy access to the A30. The hosts are friendly and attentive and really make their guests feel at home. The bedrooms are very well appointed; there is a small guest lounge and a conservatory, as well as a garden for guests to enjoy.

Rooms 3 rms (2 en suite) (1 pri facs) (1 GF) S £45-£65; D £55-£85* **Facilities** FTV DVD TVL tea/coffee Dinner available WiFi 🔒 **Parking** 8 **Notes** LB ⊗ No Children 6yrs

REDRUTH *continued*

Lanner Inn

★★ INN

tel: 01209 215611 **fax:** 01209 214065 **The Square, Lanner TR16 6EH**
email: info@lannerinn.co.uk **web:** www.lannerinn.co.uk
dir: *2m SE of Redruth. In Lanner on A393*

Conveniently situated for access to Redruth and the A30, this traditional inn is situated in the centre of Lanner and has a good local following. The property has a dining room and a bar in addition to the comfortable bedrooms. This inn is owner-run and managed, and the team of staff are very friendly.

Rooms 3 en suite 1 annexe en suite (2 fmly) (1 GF) **Facilities** FTV tea/coffee WiFi Pool table 🐾 **Parking** 16

| ST AGNES | Map 2 SW75 |

Driftwood Spars

★★★★ 🍴 GUEST ACCOMMODATION

tel: 01872 552428 **Trevaunance Cove TR5 0RT**
email: info@driftwoodspars.co.uk **web:** www.driftwoodspars.co.uk
dir: *A30 to Chiverton rdbt, right onto B3277, through village. Driftwood Spars 200yds before beach*

Partly built from shipwreck timbers, this 18th-century building attracts locals and visitors alike. The attractive bedrooms, some in an annexe, are decorated in a bright, seaside style with many interesting features. Local produce, including delicious seafood, is served in the informal dining room and in the restaurant, together with a range of hand-pulled beers.

Rooms 9 en suite 6 annexe en suite (4 fmly) (5 GF) S £50-£70; D £86-£102*
Facilities tea/coffee Dinner available Direct Dial Licensed WiFi Pool table Table football **Conf** Max 70 Thtr 70 Class 25 Board 20 **Parking** 40 **Notes** LB RS 25 Dec no lunch/dinner, no bar in evening Civ Wed 76

Penkerris

★★ GUEST HOUSE

tel: 01872 552262 **fax:** 01872 552262 **Penwinnick Rd TR5 0PA**
email: penkerris@gmail.com **web:** www.penkerris.co.uk
dir: *A30 onto B3277 to village, Penkerris on right after village sign*

Set in gardens on the edge of the village, this Edwardian house has a relaxed and welcoming atmosphere. Period features abound, and the best possible use is made of space in the bedrooms. Home-cooked evening meals are served by prior arrangement. Ample parking is available.

Rooms 7 rms (4 en suite) (3 fmly) **Facilities** FTV TVL tea/coffee Dinner available Licensed WiFi Badminton Volleyball **Parking** 9 **Notes** LB

| ST AUSTELL | Map 2 SX05 |

See also St Blazey

Premier Collection

Anchorage House

★★★★★ 🛏 ☕ GUEST ACCOMMODATION

tel: 01726 814071 **fax:** 01726 814071 **Nettles Corner, Tregrehan Mills PL25 3RH**
email: info@anchoragehouse.co.uk **web:** www.anchoragehouse.co.uk
dir: *2 m E of town centre off A390, opposite St Austell Garden Centre*

Georgian-style Anchorage House is set in an acre of carefully landscaped gardens at the end of a private lane. Guests are met upon arrival with afternoon tea, often served on the patio; dinner is served in the evening by arrangement. The luxurious and elegant bedrooms are equipped to the highest standard with sumptuous beds, and include satellite TV, fresh fruit, magazines, bottled water and chocolates. Guests also have use of the indoor heated pool, hot tub and gym. The house is a short distance from many of Cornwall's major tourist attractions.

Rooms 4 en suite 1 annexe en suite (1 GF) S £65-£75; D £85-£125*
Facilities STV FTV DVD Lounge tea/coffee Dinner available WiFi 🏊 Gym 🛁 Hot tub **Extras** Speciality toiletries **Parking** 6 **Notes** ⊗ No Children 16yrs Closed Dec-Feb

Premier Collection

Penarwyn House

★★★★★ 🛏 GUEST ACCOMMODATION

tel: 01726 814224 **fax:** 01726 814224 **PL24 2DS**
email: stay@penarwyn.co.uk **web:** www.penarwyn.co.uk

(For full entry see St Blazey)

Premier Collection

Highland Court Lodge

★★★★★ ≙ GUEST ACCOMMODATION

tel: 01726 813320 **fax:** 01726 813320 **Biscovey Rd, Biscovey, Par PL24 2HW**
email: enquiries@highlandcourt.co.uk **web:** www.highlandcourt.co.uk
dir: 2m E of St Austell. A390 E to St Blazey Gate, right into Biscovey Rd, 300yds on right

This is an extremely well presented and maintained contemporary building with stunning views over St Austell Bay, and is just over one mile from the Eden Project. Its impressive en suite bedrooms have luxurious fabrics and each room opens onto a private patio. There is a lounge with deep sofas, and the terrace shares the fine views. Breakfasts are served in the attractive dining area, and include porridge, the Full Cornish (with Cornish hog's pudding) and kippers.

Rooms 3 en suite (2 fmly) (3 GF) S £90-£125; D £120-£190* **Facilities** FTV DVD TVL tea/coffee Licensed WiFi 🔒 **Extras** Mini-bar, speciality toiletries, bath robes **Conf** Max 12 Class 12 Board 12 **Parking** 10 **Notes** LB ⊗

Premier Collection

Lower Barn

★★★★★ ≙ GUEST ACCOMMODATION

tel: 01726 844881 & 07825 270962 **Bosue, St Ewe PL26 6ET**
email: janie@bosue.co.uk **web:** www.bosue.co.uk
dir: 3.5m SW of St Austell. Off B3273 at x-rds signed Lost Gardens of Heligan, Lower Barn signed 1m on right

This converted barn, tucked away in the countryside, yet with easy access to local attractions, has huge appeal. Warm colours throughout create a Mediterranean feel, and staff offer informal and genuine hospitality. Bedrooms have a host of extras. Breakfast is served around a large table or on the patio deck overlooking the garden, which has a hot tub.

Rooms 3 en suite (1 fmly) (1 GF) S £50-£75; D £75-£140* **Facilities** FTV DVD tea/coffee Dinner available WiFi Sauna Hot tub Spa treatments Sauna in Nook suite **Parking** 7 **Notes** LB ⊗ Closed Jan

Ancient Shipbrokers

★★★★ BED AND BREAKFAST

tel: 01726 843370 **1 Higher West End, Pentewan PL26 6BY**
email: shipbrokers1@btinternet.com **web:** www.pentewanbedandbreakfast.com

The Ancient Shipbrokers overlooks Pentewan harbour and one of the best sandy beaches in Cornwall. The house has bags of history and character, and has been decorated tastefully and sympathetically. A large area of the garden is given over to wild flowers and trees, and there is also a kitchen garden. The dining room enjoys a wonderful view out across the harbour and the beach, and is the ideal venue for home-cooked breakfasts. Private parking is available on-site or in the village car park. Help with luggage and free WiFi is provided. There is also space for storing bicycles, surf boards and wetsuits. Self-catering is available.

Rooms 3 en suite (1 fmly) S £52-£60; D £80-£88* **Facilities** FTV DVD tea/coffee WiFi 🔒 **Parking** 3 **Notes** LB ⊗ Closed 20 Dec-5 Jan

The Grange

★★★★ ≙ BED AND BREAKFAST

tel: 01726 73351 & 07854 923262 **19 Southbourne Rd PL25 4RU**
email: enquiries@accommodationstaustell.co.uk
web: www.accommodationstaustell.co.uk
dir: A391 towards St Austell onto B3274. After 2m left onto A3058, then A390. At rdbt continue on A390 (Trevanion Rd), on left

The Grange is a period house, which has been lovingly restored and now offers comfortable and contemporary accommodation. It is ideally located for the Eden Project and Lost Gardens of Heligan, as well as the Cornish Riviera. An award-winning breakfast is served at the communal table in the attractive dining room.

Rooms 3 en suite (1 GF) S £49-£75; D £55-£130* **Facilities** FTV DVD iPod docking station Lounge tea/coffee Dinner available WiFi ⅃ 18 🔒 **Extras** Speciality toiletries, mineral water, chocolates **Parking** 3 **Notes** LB ⊗ No Children 14yrs Closed 23 Dec-2 Jan

Hunter's Moon

★★★★ GUEST HOUSE

tel: 01726 66445 **Chapel Hill, Polgooth PL26 7BU**
email: enquiries@huntersmooncornwall.co.uk **web:** www.huntersmooncornwall.co.uk
dir: 1.5m SW of town centre. Off B3273 into Polgooth, pass village shop on left, 1st right

Hunter's Moon lies in a quiet village just a few miles from Heligan and within easy reach of The Eden Project. Service is friendly and attentive and the bedrooms are well equipped for business or leisure. There is a conservatory-lounge and a pretty garden to enjoy during warmer weather. Breakfast is served in the cosy dining room and the nearby village inn serves freshly prepared meals.

Rooms 4 en suite (2 fmly) S fr £60; D fr £80 **Facilities** FTV Lounge tea/coffee WiFi 🔒 **Extras** Fridge for guest use **Parking** 5 **Notes** ⊗ No Children 14yrs ⊜

The Elms

★★★★ BED AND BREAKFAST

tel: 01726 74981 **fax:** 0872 115 7481 **14 Penwinnick Rd PL25 5DW**
email: pete@edenbb.co.uk **web:** www.edenbb.co.uk
dir: 0.5m SW of town centre. On A390 at junct with Pondhu Rd

Well located for The Eden Project or for touring Cornwall, this bed and breakfast offers a relaxed and friendly environment for leisure and business guests. Bedrooms, one with a four-poster bed, are well equipped and there is an inviting lounge. Breakfast is served in the conservatory dining room.

Rooms 3 en suite 1 annexe en suite (1 GF) S £37; D £60-£80* **Facilities** FTV Lounge TVL tea/coffee WiFi ⅃ 18 🔒 **Parking** 4 **Notes** LB ⊗

Elmswood House

★★★★ GUEST ACCOMMODATION

tel: 01726 814221 **73 Tehidy Rd, Tywardreath PL24 2QD**
email: info@elmswoodhouse.co.uk **web:** www.elmswoodhouse.co.uk

(For full entry see Par)

ST AUSTELL *continued*

The Gables

★★★★ GUEST ACCOMMODATION

tel: 01726 72638 & 07971 821854   **fax:** 0871 978 3459 **1 Edgcumbe Rd PL25 5DU**
email: barbara@gablesguesthousebnb.co.uk **web:** www.gablesguesthousebnb.co.uk

A warm welcome is assured at The Gables. The house offers a range of bedrooms with en suite or private facilities. A superb location for those wishing to visit The Eden Project, The Lost Gardens of Heligan and many other Cornish destinations. Memorable breakfasts are served in the conservatory or delightful gardens.

Rooms 4 rms (2 en suite) (2 pri facs) **Facilities** FTV Lounge tea/coffee WiFi
Extras Home-made biscuits - complimentary **Parking** 4 **Notes** ⊗ No Children 12yrs
RS Xmas wk

Langdale House

★★★★ BED AND BREAKFAST

tel: 01726 71404 & 07764 531050   **fax:** 01726 63798 **1A Southbourne Rd PL25 4RU**
email: stay@langdalehousecornwall.co.uk **web:** www.langdalehousecornwall.co.uk
dir: On A390 St Austell bypass, 0.5m S of town centre

Handy for the town centre, this is an ideal choice for both business and leisure guests and a great place to relax, unwind and re-charge the batteries. Quality and comfort levels are high throughout, both within the elegant bedrooms and the impressive bathrooms. The welcome is warm and friendly with every effort made to ensure an enjoyable and rewarding stay. Breakfast is served in the attractive dining room, with a good range of dishes offered. Super-fast WiFi is provided.

Rooms 3 en suite **Facilities** FTV tea/coffee WiFi ♿ **Extras** Speciality toiletries
Parking 3 **Notes** LB ⊗ No Children 5yrs

Nanscawen Manor House

★★★★ GUEST ACCOMMODATION

tel: 01726 814488 & 07811 022423 **Prideaux Rd, Luxulyan Valley PL24 2SR**
email: keith@nanscawen.com **web:** www.nanscawen.com

(For full entry see St Blazey)

Polgreen Farm *(SX008503)*

★★★★ FARMHOUSE

tel: 01726 75151 **London Apprentice PL26 7AP**
email: polgreen.farm@btinternet.com **web:** www.polgreenfarm.co.uk
dir: 1.5m S of St Austell. Exit B3273, left on entering London Apprentice & signed

Guests regularly return for the friendly welcome at this peaceful establishment located just south of St Austell. The spacious and well-equipped bedrooms are divided between the main house and an adjoining property, and each building has a comfortable lounge. Breakfast is served in a pleasant conservatory overlooking the garden.

Rooms 2 rms (1 en suite) (1 pri facs) 4 annexe en suite (1 fmly) (1 GF) S £35-£45;
D £66-£74* **Facilities** FTV Lounge TVL tea/coffee WiFi **Parking** 8 **Notes** LB ⊗ 🐾
64 acres livestock

T'Gallants

★★★★ GUEST HOUSE

tel: 01726 70203 **fax:** 01726 70203 **6 Charlestown Rd, Charlestown PL25 3NJ**
email: enquiries@tgallants.co.uk **web:** www.tgallants.co.uk
dir: 0.5m SE of town off A390 rdbt signed Charlestown

This fine Georgian house partly dates from 1630, and overlooks the historic port of Charlestown, where a fleet of square-rigged sailing ships is docked. The bedrooms are well presented and spacious, and one has a four-poster bed and views of the port. Breakfast is served in the attractive dining room with both traditional or continental options on offer. A guest lounge is available.

Rooms 7 en suite S fr £50; D £75-£100* **Facilities** FTV TVL tea/coffee WiFi 🐾
Notes ⊗

The Bugle Inn

★★★ INN

tel: 01726 850307 **57 Fore St, Bugle PL26 8PD**

The Bugle Inn is a warm and inviting establishment, with its origins dating back to the 17th century. It's situated in the heart of the Cornish countryside, between Bodmin and St Austell, handy for The Eden Project. Traditional pub food and drink are served in a characterful building with a lovely open fire. Bedrooms are attractive with a cosy feel.

Rooms 5 en suite S £45-£50; D £64-£75*

| ST BLAZEY | Map 2 SX05 |

Premier Collection

Penarwyn House

★★★★★ 🛏 GUEST ACCOMMODATION

tel: 01726 814224 **fax:** 01726 814224 **PL24 2DS**
email: stay@penarwyn.co.uk **web:** www.penarwyn.co.uk
dir: A390 W through St Blazey, left before 2nd speed camera into Doubletrees School, Penarwyn straight ahead

Impressive Penarwyn House stands in tranquil surroundings close to main routes, with The Eden Project, The Lost Gardens of Heligan, Fowey, the coastal footpath and National Trust properties all close by. Painstakingly restored, the spacious house offers a host of facilities, and the bedrooms are particularly comfortable and delightfully appointed. On arrival, guests are welcomed with afternoon tea and cake, and breakfast is always a highlight. Jan and Mike are great hosts and place a strong emphasis on service.

Rooms 3 en suite (1 fmly) S £75-£115; D £80-£160 **Facilities** FTV DVD Lounge tea/coffee WiFi 3/4 size snooker table **Extras** Speciality toiletries, fresh milk - free; fridge **Parking** 6 **Notes** LB ⊗ No Children 10yrs

Nanscawen Manor House

★★★★ GUEST ACCOMMODATION

tel: 01726 814488 & 07811 022423 **Prideaux Rd, Luxulyan Valley PL24 2SR**
email: keith@nanscawen.com **web:** www.nanscawen.com
dir: A390 W to St Blazey, right after railway, Nanscawen 0.75m on right

This gracious manor house has 14th-century origins and provides a high standard of accommodation, with elegant bedrooms and bathrooms complete with spa baths. There are extra luxurious touches throughout. Guests have a spacious lounge in which to relax, while outside there are five acres of pleasant gardens with splendid woodland views. Breakfast, served in the conservatory, features fresh local produce.

Rooms 4 en suite (4 fmly) S £40-£88; D £50-£98* **Facilities** STV FTV DVD Lounge tea/coffee Direct Dial WiFi ⚡ 🔥 Hot tub **Parking** 8 **Notes** ⊗ No Children 12yrs

| ST BURYAN | Map 2 SW42 |

Tregurnow Farm (SW444242)

★★★★ FARMHOUSE

tel: 01736 810255 **TR19 6BL**
email: tregurnow@lamorna.biz **web:** www.lamorna.biz
dir: From Newlyn take B3315, after 4m black & white sign on left just past turn for Lamorna Cove

Tucked away near St Buryan, Tregurnow Farm offers traditional, quality farmhouse bed and breakfast and self-catering facilities. Peace and quiet, stunning views and hearty breakfasts are hallmarks of a stay here. Close to Mousehole, Minack Theatre and Penzance, this is a good base for touring the far south-west of the county.

Rooms 3 en suite S £50-£70; D £72-£85* **Facilities** FTV TVL WiFi Pool table 🔥 **Parking** 10 **Notes** ⊗ No Children 5yrs Closed Xmas 100 acres mixed

| ST IVES | Map 2 SW54 |

Lamorna Lodge

★★★★ GUEST ACCOMMODATION

tel: 01736 795967 & 07837 638620 **Boskerris Rd, Carbis Bay TR26 2NG**
email: lamorna@tr26.wanadoo.co.uk **web:** www.lamorna.co.uk
dir: A30 onto A3074, right after playground in Carbis Bay, establishment 200yds on right

A warm welcome is assured at Lamorna Lodge, which is just a short walk from Carbis Bay beach. Wonderful views over St Ives Bay to Godrevy Lighthouse can be enjoyed from the spacious lounge, a view also shared by some of the stylish bedrooms. Breakfast utilises local Cornish produce and is served in the elegant surroundings of the dining room. The stylish terrace enjoys lovely sea views.

Rooms 9 en suite (2 fmly) (2 GF) S £57-£67; D £94-£104* **Facilities** FTV DVD Lounge tea/coffee WiFi 🔥 **Conf** Max 18 Thtr 18 Class 18 Board 18 **Parking** 9 **Notes** LB ⊗ Closed 5 Nov-10 Mar

The Nook

★★★★ GUEST ACCOMMODATION

tel: 01736 795913 **Ayr TR26 1EQ**
email: info@nookstives.co.uk **web:** www.nookstives.co.uk
dir: A30 to St Ives left at NatWest, right at rdbt & left at top of hill

The Nook is an ideal base for exploring Cornwall's spectacular coastline, gardens and countryside. The comfortable bedrooms are furnished in a contemporary style and are equipped with numerous facilities. There is a wide variety on offer at breakfast, from full English or continental, to scrambled eggs with smoked salmon.

Rooms 11 en suite (1 fmly) (1 GF) **Facilities** FTV DVD TVL tea/coffee WiFi **Parking** 10 **Notes** LB ⊗

Wheal-e-Mine Bed & Breakfast

★★★★ 🛏 BED AND BREAKFAST

tel: 01736 795051 & 07523 332018 **fax:** 01736 795051 **9 Belmont Ter TR26 1DZ**
email: whealemine@btinternet.com **web:** www.stivesbedandbreakfast.com
dir: A3074 into town, left at x-rds onto B3306, right at rdbt, left at top of hill

Guests are assured of a warm, friendly welcome at this Victorian terraced property, which over the last few years has been fully upgraded with style and flair. Bedrooms are well appointed and each boasts distant sea views. A hearty breakfast is served each morning in the attractive dining room. On-site parking at the rear of the property is an added bonus.

Rooms 3 en suite D £80-£110* **Facilities** FTV DVD tea/coffee WiFi 🔥 **Parking** 3 **Notes** LB ⊗ No Children 18yrs Closed Oct-Mar

ST IVES *continued*

Chy Conyn

★★★★ BED AND BREAKFAST

tel: 01736 798068 **8 Ayr Ter TR26 1ED**
email: chyconyn@hotmail.co.uk **web:** www.chyconyn.co.uk

Located in a pleasant residential area, just above the town, Chy Conyn offers accommodation in a range of sizes. All rooms come with plenty of useful extras. Breakfast is served in the relaxing and well-presented dining room. WiFi is available, and there is a car park to the rear of the property.

Rooms 4 rms (3 en suite) (1 pri facs) (1 fmly) **Facilities** FTV DVD tea/coffee WiFi **Parking** 3 **Notes** ⊗ No Children 3yrs Closed Nov-28 Dec

Coombe Farmhouse

★★★★ BED AND BREAKFAST

tel: 01736 740843 **TR27 6NW**
email: coombefarmhouse@aol.com **web:** www.coombefarmhouse.com
dir: *1.5m W of Lelant. Exit A3074 to Lelant Downs*

Built of sturdy granite, this early 19th-century farmhouse is in a delightful location tucked away at the southern foot of Trencrom Hill, yet convenient for St Ives. The comfortable bedrooms are attractively decorated. There is a conservatory lounge, and substantial breakfasts, featuring farm-fresh eggs, are served in the dining room overlooking the garden.

Rooms 3 rms (2 en suite) (1 pri facs) S £50; D £80-£85* **Facilities** FTV Lounge TV2B tea/coffee **Extras** Bottled water - complimentary **Parking** 3 **Notes** ⊗ No Children 12yrs Closed Dec ➂

The Mustard Tree

★★★★ GUEST HOUSE

tel: 01736 795677 & 07840 072323
Sea View Meadows, St Ives Rd, Carbis Bay TR26 2JX
email: enquiries@mustard-tree.co.uk **web:** www.stivesbnb.co.uk
dir: *A3074 to Carbis Bay, The Mustard Tree on right opposite Methodist church*

Set in delightful gardens and with sea views, this attractive house is just a short drive from the centre of St Ives, and the coastal path that leads from Carbis Bay to St Ives. The pleasant bedrooms are very comfortable and have many extras. A splendid choice is offered at breakfast, with vegetarian and continental options. A range of 'lite bites' is available in the early evening.

Rooms 9 rms (8 en suite) (1 pri facs) (2 fmly) (4 GF) S £35-£45; D fr £69* **Facilities** FTV DVD TVL tea/coffee Dinner available WiFi ⌚ **Extras** Guest PC available, fridge **Conf** Max 20 **Parking** 9 **Notes** ⊗

The Old Count House

★★★★ GUEST HOUSE

tel: 01736 795369 & 07853 844777 **1 Trenwith Square TR26 1DQ**
email: counthouse@btconnect.com **web:** www.theoldcounthouse-stives.co.uk
dir: *Follow signs to St Ives, house between leisure centre & school*

Situated in a quiet residential area with on-site parking, The Old Count House is a granite house, where Victorian mine workers collected their wages. Guests are assured of a warm welcome and an extensive choice at breakfast. Bedrooms vary in size, with all rooms being well equipped. The town centre, with all its restaurants, is only a five-minute walk away.

Rooms 10 rms (9 en suite) (1 pri facs) (2 GF) S £48-£55; D £85-£98 **Facilities** FTV DVD Lounge TVL tea/coffee WiFi Sauna ⌚ Excercise bike Massage chair **Parking** 9 **Notes** ⊗ No Children Closed Nov & 20-29 Dec

Old Vicarage

★★★★ ⌂ GUEST HOUSE

tel: 01736 796124 **Parc-an-Creet TR26 2ES**
email: stay@oldvicarage.com **web:** www.oldvicarage.com
dir: *From A3074 in town centre take B3306, 0.5m right into Parc-an-Creet*

This former Victorian rectory stands in secluded gardens in a quiet part of St Ives and is convenient for the seaside, town and Tate St Ives. The bedrooms are enhanced by modern facilities. A good choice of local produce is offered at breakfast, plus home-made yogurt and preserves.

Rooms 6 en suite (4 fmly) S £57-£75; D £76-£100 **Facilities** FTV TVL tea/coffee Licensed WiFi **Parking** 12 **Notes** LB Closed Dec-Jan Civ Wed 40

The Regent

★★★★ GUEST ACCOMMODATION

tel: 01736 796195 **fax:** 01736 794641 **Fernlea Ter TR26 2BH**
email: keith@regenthotel.com **web:** www.regenthotel.com
dir: *In town centre, near bus & railway station*

This popular and attractive property stands on an elevated position convenient for the town centre and seafront. The Regent has well-equipped bedrooms, some with spectacular sea vistas, and the comfortable lounge also has great views. The breakfast choices, including vegetarian, are excellent.

Rooms 10 rms (8 en suite) (1 fmly) **Facilities** TVL tea/coffee WiFi **Parking** 12 **Notes** ⊗ No Children 16yrs

The Rookery

★★★★ GUEST ACCOMMODATION

tel: 01736 799401 **8 The Terrace TR26 2BL**
email: therookerystives@hotmail.com **web:** www.rookerystives.com
dir: *A3074 through Carbis Bay, right fork at Porthminster Hotel, The Rookery 500yds on left*

Aptly named, The Rookery stands in an elevated position overlooking the town and sandy beach. The attractive bedrooms include one which is on the ground floor and a luxurious suite, all of which are well equipped and offer a good level of comfort. Breakfast is served in the first-floor dining room at separate tables.

Rooms 7 en suite (2 fmly) (1 GF) **Facilities** FTV tea/coffee WiFi 🔔 **Parking** 7 **Notes** ⊗ No Children 7yrs

Thurlestone Guest House

★★★★ GUEST ACCOMMODATION

tel: 01736 796369 **St Ives Rd, Carbis Bay TR26 2RT**
email: thurlestoneguesthouse@yahoo.co.uk **web:** www.thurlestoneguesthouse.co.uk
dir: *A3074 to Carbis Bay, pass convenience store on left, 0.25m on left next to Carbis Bay Holidays Office*

This granite former chapel, built in 1843, now offers stylish, comfortable accommodation. The welcoming proprietors provide a relaxed environment, and many guests return regularly. The property offers a cosy lounge bar and well-equipped bedrooms, some with sea views.

Rooms 7 en suite (1 fmly) (1 GF) S £40-£45; D £70-£89 **Facilities** STV FTV DVD TVL tea/coffee Licensed WiFi **Extras** Safe **Parking** 5 **Notes** LB ⊗ Closed Nov-Mar

Portarlington

★★★ GUEST ACCOMMODATION

tel: 01736 797278 **fax:** 01736 797278 **11 Parc Bean TR26 1EA**
email: info@portarlington.co.uk **web:** www.portarlington.co.uk

Portarlington is within easy reach of the town, beaches and Tate St Ives. The friendly proprietors have long welcomed guests to their home and many return regularly. Bedrooms are well furnished and some have sea views. There is a comfortable lounge, and enjoyable breakfasts are served in the attractive dining room.

Rooms 4 en suite (3 fmly) **Facilities** FTV TVL tea/coffee WiFi 🔔 **Extras** Fridge **Parking** 4 **Notes** ⊗ No Children 3yrs Closed Nov-Mar 🐾

The Sloop Inn

★★★ INN

tel: 01736 796584 **fax:** 01736 793322 **The Wharf TR26 1LP**
email: sloopinn@btinternet.com **web:** www.sloop-inn.co.uk
dir: *On St Ives harbour by middle slipway*

This attractive, historic inn has an imposing position on the harbour. Each of the guest rooms has a nautical name, many with pleasant views, and all have impressive modern facilities. A good choice of dishes is offered at lunch and dinner in the atmospheric restaurant-bar.

Rooms 18 en suite (6 fmly) (3 GF) (3 smoking) S £65-£80; D £100-£112*
Facilities FTV tea/coffee Dinner available WiFi 🔔 **Parking** 8 **Notes** LB No coaches

---

ST KEVERNE Map 2 SW72

Gallen-Treath Guest House

★★★ 🛏 GUEST HOUSE

tel: 01326 280400 & 07579 967836 **Porthallow TR12 6PL**
email: gallentreath@btclick.com **web:** www.gallen-treath.com
dir: *1.5m SE of St Keverne in Porthallow*

Gallen-Treath Guest House has super views over the countryside and sea from its elevated position above Porthallow. Bedrooms are individually decorated and feature many personal touches. Guests can relax in the large, comfortable lounge complete with balcony. Hearty breakfasts and dinners (by arrangement) are served in the bright dining room.

Rooms 5 rms (4 en suite) (1 pri facs) (1 fmly) (1 GF) **Facilities** FTV TVL tea/coffee Dinner available Licensed **Parking** 6

The Three Tuns

★★★ INN

tel: 01326 280949 **The Square TR12 6NA**
email: thethreetuns@mail.com **web:** www.thethreetunscornwall.co.uk

Located in the tranquil village square of St Keverne, the inn offers comfortable accommodation and complimentary WiFi. Local ales can be enjoyed in the bar whilst locally caught fish can be found on the menu. Ample parking is available.

Rooms 4 en suite (2 fmly) **Facilities** FTV DVD tea/coffee Dinner available WiFi Pool table 🔔 **Parking** 15

ST KEW Map 2 SX07

Tregellist Farm

★★★★ BED AND BREAKFAST

tel: 01208 880537 & 07970 559637 **Tregellist PL30 3HG**
email: mail@tregellistfarm.co.uk **web:** www.tregellistfarm.co.uk
dir: *On B3314 between Pendoggett & St Endellion, take turn brown signed to St Kew & Tregellist*

Tregellist Farm is located in beautiful countryside close to Port Isaac, and convenient for Lanhydrock, Pencarrow, The Lost Gardens of Heligan, Padstow and The Eden Project. All bedrooms are en suite, with flat-screen TVs, hospitality trays with fresh milk daily. Served at separate tables in the dining room, breakfast is sourced locally and includes fresh eggs from the farm.

Rooms 2 en suite 2 annexe en suite (1 fmly) (2 GF) S £42-£44; D £80-£84*
Facilities FTV DVD TVL tea/coffee WiFi 🔔 **Parking** 6 **Notes** ⊗ Closed Xmas & New Year

---

ST MARY'S (ISLES OF SCILLY) Map 2 SV91

Crebinick House

★★★★ GUEST HOUSE

tel: 01720 422968 **Church St TR21 0JT**
email: aa@crebinick.co.uk **web:** www.crebinick.co.uk
dir: *House 500yds from quay through Hugh Town; (airport bus to house)*

Many guests return time and again to this friendly, family-run house close to the town centre and the seafront. The granite-built property dates from 1760 and has smart, well-equipped bedrooms; two are on the ground floor. There is a quiet lounge for relaxing.

Rooms 4 en suite (2 GF) **Facilities** FTV Lounge tea/coffee WiFi **Notes** ⊗ No Children 10yrs Closed Nov-Mar

ST MAWGAN Map 2 SW86

The Falcon Inn

★★★★ INN

tel: 01637 860225 **TR8 4EP**
email: thefalconinnstmawgan@gmail.com **web:** www.thefalconinnstmawgan.co.uk
dir: *A30 towards Newquay airport, follow signs for St Mawgan. Turn right, signed, Falcon Inn at bottom of hill*

The Falcon is a traditional village pub offering good food and drink along with two well-presented and comfortable en suite bedrooms. The owners and friendly staff create a pleasant atmosphere. Its quiet location, along with plenty of off-street parking, make this a popular venue. Please note that the pub is closed 3-6pm; access for the accommodation will be arranged for these times.

Rooms 3 en suite S £50; D £90 **Facilities** FTV tea/coffee Dinner available Direct Dial WiFi ♪ 18 ♨ **Conf** Thtr 30 Class 20 Board 20 **Parking** 20 **Notes** LB

ST WENN Map 2 SW96

Tregolls Farm B&B *(SW983661)*

★★★★ FARMHOUSE

tel: 01208 812154 & 07807 687430 **Tregolls Farm PL30 5PE**
email: tregollsfarm@btclick.com **web:** www.tregollsfarm.co.uk
dir: *A30, pass Innis Downs exit. Take next slip road, signed Victoria Interchange. At rdbt, 3rd exit, follow signs to Withiel, through village, down steep hill for 1m. 1st left turn before T-junct, signed St Wenn, farm 1m on right*

The farmhouse is a Grade II listed building and offers all the character expected of such a property. It is located within a picturesque area and both en suite rooms offer attractive views over the surrounding area. Breakfast and evening meals are served in the dining room, and self-catering cottages are available.

Rooms 2 en suite (1 fmly) D £62-£74* **Facilities** FTV TVL tea/coffee Dinner available WiFi Pool table ♨ Games room **Parking** 4 **Notes** LB ⊗ Closed 20 Dec-5 Jan 107 acres beef/sheep

SALTASH Map 3 SX45

Smeaton Farm *(SX387634)*

★★★★ 🏠 🍴 FARMHOUSE

tel: 01579 351833 **fax:** 01579 351833 **PL12 6RZ**
email: info@smeatonfarm.co.uk **web:** www.smeatonfarm.co.uk
dir: *1m N of Hatt & 1m S of St Mellion just off A388*

This elegant Georgian farmhouse is surrounded by 450 acres of rolling Cornish farmland, providing a wonderfully peaceful place to stay. Home to the Jones family, the atmosphere is relaxed and hospitable, with every effort made to ensure that guests have a comfortable and rewarding break. Bedrooms are spacious, light and airy. Enjoyable dinners often feature home-reared meats, and the sausages at breakfast come highly recommended.

Rooms 3 en suite (1 fmly) S £50-£70; D £75-£90 **Facilities** FTV DVD Lounge TVL tea/coffee Dinner available Licensed WiFi ♪ 18 Riding ♨ Cornish maze Guided farm tours **Extras** Speciality toiletries, snacks, fruit **Conf** Max 10 Board 10 **Parking** 8 **Notes** LB ⊗ 450 acres arable/beef/sheep

Crooked Inn

★★★★ INN

tel: 01752 848177 **fax:** 01752 843203 **Stoketon Cross, Trematon PL12 4RZ**
email: info@crooked-inn.co.uk **web:** www.crooked-inn.co.uk
dir: *1.5m NW of Saltash. A38 W from Saltash, 2nd left to Trematon, sharp right*

The friendly animals that freely roam the courtyard add to the relaxed country style of this delightful inn. The spacious bedrooms are well equipped, and freshly cooked dinners are available in the bar and conservatory. Breakfast is served in the cottage-style dining room.

Rooms 18 annexe rms 15 annexe en suite (5 fmly) (7 GF) **Facilities** tea/coffee Dinner available ⚲ **Conf** Max 60 **Parking** 45 **Notes** Closed 25 Dec

Hay Lake Farm Bed & Breakfast

★★★★ BED AND BREAKFAST

tel: 01752 851209 & 07989 426306 **Landrake PL12 5AE**
email: ianbiffen@hotmail.co.uk **web:** www.haylakefarm.co.uk
dir: *A38 at Landrake turn into West Ln. 0.75m on left before x-rds*

This modern, comfortable bed and breakfast offers spacious and well-equipped en suite accommodation. Hay Lake Farm is ideal for those exploring both north and south coasts of Cornwall, and is within easy reach of many National Trust properties as well as The Eden Project. Stables are available.

Rooms 3 en suite (2 fmly) (1 GF) S £38-£45; D £68-£75* **Facilities** FTV DVD tea/coffee WiFi ♨ **Extras** Speciality toiletries - complimentary **Parking** 6 **Notes** ⊛

ISLES OF SCILLY

See St Mary's & Tresco

SENNEN
Map 2 SW32

Mayon Farmhouse
★★★★ BED AND BREAKFAST

tel: 01736 871757 **TR19 7AD**
email: mayonfarmhouse@hotmail.co.uk **web:** www.mayonfarmhouse.co.uk
dir: A30 to Sennen, pass school on left. Over mini rdbt, after 400mtrs turn left opposite Post Office

Guests receive a genuine welcome and a cream tea on arrival at this 19th-century, granite former farmhouse. About one mile from Land's End, and conveniently situated for visiting the Minack Theatre, it has country and distant coastal views. The attractive bedrooms are comfortable and well equipped, and an imaginative choice is offered at breakfast.

Rooms 4 rms (3 en suite) (1 pri facs) (1 fmly) S £65; D £90 **Facilities** FTV DVD TVL tea/coffee WiFi 🏌 **Extras** Fruit, chocolates, home-made biscuits **Parking** 30 **Notes** LB ⊗ No Children 14yrs

TINTAGEL
Map 2 SX08

Pendrin House
★★★★ GUEST HOUSE

tel: 01840 770560 **Atlantic Rd PL34 0DE**
email: info@pendrintagel.co.uk **web:** www.pendrintintagel.co.uk
dir: Through village, pass entrance to Tintagel Castle, last house on right before Headlands Caravan Park

Located close to coastal walks, the castle and the town centre, this Victorian house provides comfortable accommodation with most rooms having sea or country views. Additional facilities include a cosy lounge and ample off-road parking.

Rooms 9 rms (5 en suite) (4 pri facs) S £30-£35; D £60-£70* **Facilities** FTV TVL tea/coffee WiFi **Parking** 6 **Notes** ⊗ No Children 12yrs

TORPOINT
Map 3 SX45

The Devon and Cornwall
★★★ INN

tel: 01752 822320 **1 West St, Millbrook PL10 1AA**
email: thedevonandcornwall@hotmail.com **web:** www.thedevonandcornwall.co.uk
dir: From Torpoint Ferry onto A374, follow signs for Antony. Turn left into village & follow road to T-junct. Turn left to Millbrook, follow road

This cosy village inn, popular with the locals, offers a great location for those wishing to explore Devon and the south Cornwall coastline. All bedrooms are en suite, comfortable and modern following a recent refurbishment. Meals are served daily.

Rooms 5 en suite (2 fmly) S £50-£55; D £70-£80* **Facilities** FTV tea/coffee Dinner available WiFi 🏌 **Notes** LB

TRESCO (ISLES OF SCILLY)
Map 2 SV81

New Inn
★★★★★ ◉ INN

tel: 01720 422849 & 423006 **fax:** 01720 423200 **TR24 0QQ**
email: contactus@tresco.co.uk **web:** www.tresco.co.uk
dir: By New Grimsby Quay

This friendly, popular inn is located at the island's centre point and offers bright, attractive and well-equipped bedrooms, many with splendid sea views. Guests have an extensive choice from the menu at both lunch and dinner and can also choose where they take their meals - either in the airy bistro-style Pavilion, the popular bar which serves real ales, or the elegant restaurant. A heated outdoor pool is also available.

Rooms 16 en suite (2 fmly) (2 GF) S £60-£120; D £120-£240* **Facilities** FTV DVD Lounge tea/coffee Dinner available Direct Dial WiFi ⤳ 🏊 Fishing Pool table **Extras** Speciality toiletries **Notes** LB ⊗ No coaches

TRURO
Map 2 SW84

Bissick Old Mill
★★★★ GUEST HOUSE

tel: 01726 882557 **Ladock TR2 4PG**
email: enquiries@bissickoldmill.plus.com **web:** www.bissickoldmill.co.uk
dir: 6m NE of Truro. Exit B3275 in Ladock centre by Falmouth Arms pub

This charming family-run guest house in a former mill dates back some 300 years. Low ceilings, beams, stone walls and an impressive fireplace all contribute to its character. Equally inviting is the hospitality extended to guests, who are instantly made welcome. The high-spec bedrooms are all en suite and feature Egyptian cotton sheets along with many extras. The breakfast is a memorable aspect of any stay with the menu offering a range of freshly prepared hot dishes.

Rooms 3 en suite 1 annexe en suite (1 fmly) (1 GF) S fr £60; D fr £70* **Facilities** FTV DVD TVL tea/coffee Direct Dial WiFi **Parking** 6 **Notes** LB ⊗

Bodrean Manor Farm *(SW851480)*
★★★★ FARMHOUSE

tel: 07970 955857 **Trispen TR4 9AG**
email: bodrean@hotmail.co.uk **web:** www.bodreanmanorfarm.co.uk
dir: 3m NE of Truro. A30 onto A39 towards Truro, left after Trispen signed Frogmore & Trehane, farm drive 100yds

This friendly farmhouse is located in peaceful countryside, convenient for Truro or as a touring base. It has all the charm of an historic house but is styled and fitted with modern facilities. Bedrooms are thoughtfully and extensively equipped, and the bathrooms are well provisioned with soft towels and a host of toiletries. The home-cooked breakfast is served around a large, communal table in the smartly appointed dining room. Storage for motorbikes and cycles is available.

Rooms 3 rms (2 en suite) (1 pri facs) (1 fmly) **Facilities** FTV TVL tea/coffee WiFi **Parking** 6 **Notes** ⊗ ⊜ 220 acres mixed

The Haven
★★★★ BED AND BREAKFAST

tel: 01872 264197 & 07977 815177 **Truro Vean Ter TR1 1HA**
email: thehaven7@btinternet.com **web:** www.thehaven-truro.co.uk
dir: Entering Truro from A39 or A390, right at 1st rdbt, through 2 sets of lights, next right then immediately left. On left (no through road)

A warm and genuine welcome is assured at The Haven, an extended property within a few minutes' walk of the city centre. Bedrooms are bright and well furnished; beds are very comfortable and bathrooms well equipped. Freshly cooked, hearty breakfasts are served at a large table, in either the separate breakfast room or the conservatory, which leads on to a balcony. The Haven benefits from off-street parking and views of the cathedral.

Rooms 3 rms (2 en suite) (1 pri facs) (3 GF) **Facilities** FTV Lounge tea/coffee WiFi **Parking** 3 **Notes** ⊗ No Children 7yrs Closed Nov-Feb ⊜

TRURO *continued*

Oxturn House

★★★★ BED AND BREAKFAST

tel: 01726 884348 **Ladock TR2 4NQ**
email: oxturnhouse@hotmail.com **web:** www.oxturnhouse.co.uk
dir: *6m NE of Truro. B3275 into Ladock, take lane opposite Falmouth Arms, up hill 200yds, 1st right after end 30mph sign, Oxturn on right*

A friendly welcome is assured at Oxturn House, a large family house, set slightly above the village and close to a pub and several dining venues. Bedrooms are spacious and a pleasant lounge is available. In summer you can enjoy the country views from the patio. Hearty breakfasts are served in the dining room.

Rooms 2 rms (1 en suite) (1 pri facs) D £74-£82* **Facilities** FTV TVL tea/coffee WiFi **Parking** 4 **Notes** ✖ No Children 12yrs Closed Nov-Feb ⊜

Upper Lemon Villas

★★★★ BED AND BREAKFAST

tel: 01872 262293 & 07786 636827   **fax:** 01872 262293 **1 Upper Lemon Villas TR1 2PD**
email: susan.warrillow@btinternet.com
dir: *A390 to Truro. At 1st rdbt 3rd exit signed Redruth (A390). At next rdbt 3rd exit into St Aubyns Rd (up hill - becomes Strangways Terrace). At next T-junct, B&B on corner*

This charming Georgian villa is located in a quiet, residential area, only a short walk from Truro's cathedral and town centre attractions. Bedrooms, some with views towards Lemon Street, are spacious and attractively appointed. There is also an enclosed courtyard where guests can relax, as well as secure car parking. Breakfast, and the warm welcome, are delights not to be missed.

Rooms 3 en suite S £70-£80; D £80-£95* **Facilities** FTV Lounge WiFi **Parking** 2 **Notes** ✖ No Children ⊜

Donnington Guest House

★★★ GUEST ACCOMMODATION

tel: 01872 222552 & 07787 555475 **43 Treyew Rd TR1 2BY**
email: info@donnington-guesthouse.co.uk **web:** www.donnington-guesthouse.co.uk

A well located property within a 12-minute walk of the city centre. It is actually two houses operating as one, with breakfast being taken in the breakfast room of one of them. Well-appointed bedrooms, a friendly host and good off-road parking make this a very popular venue.

Rooms 14 rms (12 en suite) (2 pri facs) (2 fmly) (2 GF) S £25-£35; D £50-£65 **Facilities** FTV DVD tea/coffee WiFi ⅃ 18 🔒 **Extras** Fridge **Parking** 11 **Notes** ⊜

The Laurels

★★★ BED AND BREAKFAST

tel: 07794 472171 **Penwethers TR3 6EA**
email: annie.toms@hotmail.com **web:** www.thelaurelsbedandbreakfast.com
dir: *From A39 onto A390 (Tregolls Rd), through 3 rdbts. Take exit towards Redruth (Treyew Rd) next left to Penwethers*

The Laurels is a traditional bed and breakfast operation offering comfortable accommodation in a home-from-home environment. It is ideally located in a quiet location, yet is just minutes from the cathedral city of Truro. Off-road parking is available.

Rooms 3 rms (1 en suite) (1 pri facs) (2 fmly) S £45; D £65* **Facilities** FTV Lounge TV2B tea/coffee WiFi 🔒 **Extras** Chocolates **Parking** 3 **Notes** ✖ ⊜

Merchant House

★★★ GUEST ACCOMMODATION

tel: 01872 272450 **fax:** 01872 223938 **49 Falmouth Rd TR1 2HL**
email: reception@merchant-house.co.uk **web:** www.merchant-house.co.uk
dir: *A39 Truro, on approaching centre proceed across 1st & 2nd rdbts onto bypass. At top of hill turn right at twin mini rdbt into Falmouth Rd. 100mtrs on right*

Merchant House is just a short stroll from the city centre. A range of bedrooms are offered, some of which have benefited from the ongoing refurbishment programme, all offering good levels of comfort. Public areas are smartly appointed with period features retained where possible. The bar provides an engaging venue for a refreshing glass of something, perhaps accompanied by a tasty dish from the bar menu, and the friendly team are flexible and helpful.

Rooms 27 en suite (3 fmly) (4 GF) S £55; D £70-£90* **Facilities** FTV TVL tea/coffee Direct Dial Licensed WiFi 🔒 Drying room **Conf** Max 64 Thtr 64 Class 48 Board 36 **Parking** 31 **Notes** LB Closed 24-27 Dec

Resparveth Farm *(SW914499)*

★★★ FARMHOUSE

tel: 01726 882382 & 07929 234206 **Grampound Rd TR2 4EF**
email: resparveth.farm@gmail.com **web:** www.resparvethfarmbnb.co.uk
dir: *A30 exit signed Fraddon/Grampound Road (B3275). Continue on A3058, through Grampound Road village, turn right at B&B sign*

The young owners of this traditional farmhouse bed and breakfast do all they can to make a stay as comfortable as possible. This is a handy location for St Austell, The Eden Project and Truro, offering comfortable rooms and freshly cooked breakfasts at one large table in the breakfast room featuring an original Cornish range.

Rooms 3 en suite D £55-£75* **Facilities** FTV DVD TVL tea/coffee WiFi ⅋ 🔒 **Parking** 6 **Notes** LB ✖ 60 acres beef/sheep/bees

The Bay Tree

★★ GUEST ACCOMMODATION

tel: 01872 240274 **28 Ferris Town TR1 3JH**
web: www.baytree_guesthouse.co.uk

A well established, friendly property within a few minutes' walk of the railway station and the city centre. The bedrooms are comfortable and have shared facilities, and breakfast is served at large tables in the dining room. AA Friendliest B&B of the Year Finalist 2014-2015.

Rooms 3 rms (2 fmly) **Facilities** tea/coffee WiFi **Notes** RS proprietors' holidays ⊜

WADEBRIDGE   **Map 2 SW97**

Wadebridge B&B

★★★★ BED AND BREAKFAST

tel: 01208 816837 & 07740 255092 **Orchard House, Elmsleigh Rd PL27 7HA**
email: info@wadebridgebedandbreakfast.net **web:** www.wadebridgebedandbreakfast.net
dir: *From Bodmin A389 into Wadebridge. Pass Trelawney Garden Centre on right, continue to rdbt. Exit onto A39. At next rdbt left into West Hill. After phone box on left, take next left into Elmsleigh Rd*

This contemporary house is just a short walk from the town centre and provides an ideal base from which to explore the area. Bedrooms offer impressive levels of comfort and quality, and one has a balcony with lovely views over the town and countryside. Bathrooms offer all the expected mod cons with under floor heating, invigorating showers and fluffy towels. Generous and tasty breakfasts are served in the dining room with a garden patio available for alfresco dining. Secure storage is available for bikes and surf boards.

Rooms 3 en suite S £60-£80; D £60-£110 **Facilities** FTV DVD TVL tea/coffee WiFi   **Extras** Bottled water, fresh milk - complimentary **Parking** 3 **Notes** LB ⊗ No Children

CUMBRIA

ALSTON   Map 18 NY74

See also Cowshill (Co Durham)

Alston House

★★★★ RESTAURANT WITH ROOMS

tel: 01434 382200 **fax:** 01434 382493 **Townfoot CA9 3RN**
email: alstonhouse@fsmail.net **web:** www.alstonhouse.co.uk
dir: *On A686 opposite Spar garage*

Located at the foot of the town, this family-owned restaurant with rooms provides well-equipped, stylish and comfortable accommodation. The kitchen serves both modern and traditional dishes with flair and creativity. Alston House runs a café during the day serving light meals and afternoon teas.

Rooms 7 en suite (3 fmly) **Facilities** DVD tea/coffee Dinner available WiFi ⌁ 9 Fishing **Conf** Max 70 Thtr 70 Class 30 Board 30 **Parking** 20 **Notes** Civ Wed

Lowbyer Manor Country House

★★★★ GUEST HOUSE

tel: 01434 381230 **fax:** 01434 381425 **Hexham Rd CA9 3JX**
email: stay@lowbyer.com **web:** www.lowbyer.com
dir: *250yds N of village centre on A686. Pass South Tynedale Railway on left, turn right*

This Grade II listed Georgian building retains many original features, enhanced by the appropriate style of furnishings and decor. Cosy bedrooms are filled with a wealth of thoughtful extras and day rooms include an elegant dining room, a comfortable lounge and a bar containing lots of historical artefacts.

Rooms 9 en suite (1 fmly) S £38-£60; D £76-£90* **Facilities** FTV DVD Lounge tea/coffee Licensed WiFi   **Parking** 9 **Notes** LB

AMBLESIDE   Map 18 NY30

Premier Collection

Nanny Brow

★★★★★ GUEST ACCOMMODATION

tel: 015394 33232 & 07746 103008 **Clappersgate LA22 9NF**
email: unwind@nannybrow.co.uk **web:** www.nannybrow.co.uk
dir: *M6 junct 36 onto A590 & A591 through Windermere. At lights bear left onto A593, left again at rugby pitch & left over bridge. Through Clappersgate, 0.5m on right*

Nanny Brow provides high quality throughout. Each room is thoughtfully decorated with contemporary furnishings, antique furniture, and original arts and crafts. The property is situated in Clappersgate, close to Ambleside, standing high above the road overlooking the beautiful Langdale Valley. A drink from the bar menu can be enjoyed in the quiet guest lounge where you will find plenty of information regarding local walks.

Rooms 11 en suite 2 annexe en suite (2 GF) S £115-£265; D £130-£280 **Facilities** FTV DVD Lounge tea/coffee Licensed WiFi Fishing   Discounted use of nearby spa & gym **Extras** Robes - chargeable **Conf** Max 26 Thtr 26 Class 12 Board 12 **Parking** 15 **Notes** LB ⊗ No Children 12yrs Civ Wed 32

Riverside

★★★★ GUEST HOUSE

tel: 015394 32395 **fax:** 015394 32440 **Under Loughrigg LA22 9LJ**
email: info@riverside-at-ambleside.co.uk **web:** www.riverside-at-ambleside.co.uk
dir: *A593 from Ambleside to Coniston, over stone bridge, right into Under Loughrigg Ln, Riverside 150yds left*

A friendly atmosphere prevails at Riverside, a Victorian house situated on a quiet lane by the River Rothay, below Loughrigg Fell. Bedrooms, all with lovely views, are very comfortable, stylishly furnished and feature homely extras; some have spa baths. A log-burning stove warms the lounge in winter. Guests can use the garden, which has seating for morning and evening sun.

Rooms 6 en suite (1 fmly) **Facilities** TVL tea/coffee Licensed Fishing Jacuzzi **Parking** 15 **Notes** ⊗ No Children 10yrs Closed Xmas & New Year

Broadview Guest House

★★★★ GUEST HOUSE

tel: 015394 32431 **Lake Rd LA22 0DN**
email: enquiries@broadviewguesthouse.co.uk **web:** www.broadviewguesthouse.co.uk
dir: *On A591 S side of Ambleside, on Lake Rd opposite Garden Centre*

Just a short walk from the centre of Ambleside, a warm welcome is assured at this popular guest house, where regular improvements enhance the guest experience. Bedrooms are thoughtfully furnished and comprehensive breakfasts provide an excellent start to the day.

Rooms 6 rms (3 en suite) (1 pri facs) D £50-£80* **Facilities** FTV tea/coffee WiFi Access to nearby leisure club **Notes** LB ⊗

AMBLESIDE *continued*

Lake House

★★★★ GUEST ACCOMMODATION

tel: 015394 32360 **fax:** 015394 31474 **Waterhead Bay LA22 0HD**
email: info@lakehousehotel.co.uk **web:** www.lake-house.co.uk
dir: *From S: M6 junct 36, A590, then A591 towards Kendal & Windermere. House 3m N of Windermere. From N: M6 junct 40, A66 to Keswick, then A591 to Ambleside. House just S of town*

Set on a hillside with lake views, this delightful house has very stylish accommodation and a homely atmosphere. The bedrooms are all individual in style and include many homely extras. Dinner is available at the nearby sister property with complimentary transport, and leisure facilities are available there too. Breakfast is an interesting and substantial cold buffet.

Rooms 11 en suite 7 annexe en suite (4 GF) S £65-£119; D £75-£129 **Facilities** FTV DVD TVL tea/coffee Licensed WiFi 🔒 **Parking** 18 **Notes** LB No Children 14yrs

Lakes Lodge

★★★★ GUEST ACCOMMODATION

tel: 015394 33240 **fax:** 015394 31474 **Lake Rd LA22 0DB**
email: info@lakeslodge.co.uk **web:** www.lakeslodge.co.uk
dir: *Enter Ambleside on A591, right around one-way system, on exiting town turn right into Lake Rd*

Lakes Lodge is located in the centre of Ambleside. Friendly service and simply furnished, contemporary bedrooms in a range of sizes are available here. Wine, beer and champagne can be served to bedrooms during the day and evening, until 9pm. A continental breakfast buffet is served in the café-style breakfast room. Guests can arrange use of an indoor pool at a nearby hotel.

Rooms 16 en suite (4 fmly) (6 GF) S £60-£119; D £70-£129 **Facilities** FTV DVD Lounge tea/coffee Licensed WiFi 🔒 **Parking** 14 **Notes** LB Closed 23-27 Dec

Wanslea Guest House

★★★★ GUEST HOUSE

tel: 015394 33884 **fax:** 015394 33884 **Low Fold, Lake Rd LA22 0DN**
email: information@wanslea.co.uk **web:** www.wanslea.co.uk
dir: *On S side of town, opposite garden centre*

Located between town centre and lakeside pier, this Victorian house provides a range of thoughtfully furnished bedrooms, some of which are individually themed and equipped with spa baths. Comprehensive breakfasts are served in the spacious dining room and a cosy lounge is available.

Rooms 8 en suite (1 fmly) S £30-£50; D £60-£84 **Facilities** FTV Lounge tea/coffee WiFi 🔒 **Notes** LB ⊗ No Children 6yrs Closed 23-26 Dec

The Old Vicarage

★★★★ 🅰 GUEST ACCOMMODATION

tel: 015394 33364 **fax:** 015394 34734 **Vicarage Rd LA22 9DH**
email: info@oldvicarageambleside.co.uk **web:** www.oldvicarageambleside.co.uk
dir: *In town centre. Exit Compston Rd left into Vicarage Rd*

This charming early Victorian house stands in quiet landscaped grounds with private parking, close to the town centre. Bedrooms are mostly spacious, some having four posters and spa baths, and all have video players, fridges and CD players. There also is a splendid pool, sauna and a hot tub.

Rooms 15 en suite (4 fmly) (2 GF) D fr £76* **Facilities** FTV DVD Lounge tea/coffee WiFi 🔍 🏊 Riding Sauna Pool table 🔒 Hot tub **Extras** Mini-fridge **Parking** 17 **Notes** LB Closed 23-28 Dec

Innkeeper's Lodge Ambleside, Lake District

🅄

tel: 015394 39901 **The White Lion, Market Place LA22 9DB**
email: info@innkeeperslodge.com **web:** www.innkeeperslodge.com

Currently the rating for this establishment is not confirmed. This may be due to a change of ownership or because it has only recently joined the AA rating scheme.

Rooms 7

BOOT	Map 18 NY10

Brook House Inn

★★★★ 🍴 INN

tel: 01946 723288 **fax:** 01946 723160 **CA19 1TG**
email: stay@brookhouseinn.co.uk **web:** www.brookhouseinn.co.uk
dir: *In village centre. 0.5m NE of Dalegarth station*

Located in the heart of Eskdale, this impressive inn dates from the early 18th century and has been renovated to offer comfortable accommodation with smart, modern bathrooms for weary walkers and travellers. Wholesome meals using local produce are served in the traditionally furnished dining room or attractive bar - the latter features real ales and country memorabilia.

Rooms 8 en suite (2 fmly) **Facilities** FTV tea/coffee Dinner available WiFi **Conf** Max 35 **Parking** 24 **Notes** LB Closed 25 Dec

BORROWDALE	Map 18 NY21

Premier Collection

Hazel Bank Country House

★★★★★ 🛏 🍴 GUEST ACCOMMODATION

tel: 017687 77248 & 07775 701069 **fax:** 017687 77373 **Rosthwaite CA12 5XB**
email: info@hazelbankhotel.co.uk **web:** www.hazelbankhotel.co.uk
dir: *B5289 from Keswick towards Borrowdale, left after sign for Rosthwaite*

Set on an elevated position surrounded by four acres of gardens and woodland, Hazel Bank Country House enjoys wonderful views of Borrowdale. The approach to this grand Victorian house is impressive, reached via a picturesque hump back bridge and a winding drive. Bedrooms are sumptuous and all are en suite. Carefully cooked dishes are served in the elegant dining room; the daily changing four-course menu features fresh local ingredients. There is a friendly atmosphere here and the proprietors are very welcoming.

Rooms 7 en suite (2 GF) S £80-£95; D £120-£150* **Facilities** STV Lounge tea/coffee Dinner available Licensed WiFi 🔌 **Extras** Speciality toiletries, chocolates, bottled water **Parking** 9 **Notes** LB ⊗ No Children 12yrs Closed 30 Nov-30 Jan

BOWNESS-ON-WINDERMERE

See Windermere

BRAITHWAITE
Map 18 NY22

The Cottage in the Wood

★★★★ ◉◉ RESTAURANT WITH ROOMS

tel: 017687 78409 **Whinlatter Pass CA12 5TW**
email: relax@thecottageinthewood.co.uk **web:** www.thecottageinthewood.co.uk
dir: M6 junct 40, A66 W. After Keswick exit for Braithwaite via Whinlatter Pass (B5292), establishment at top of pass

This charming property sits on wooded hills with striking views of Skiddaw, and is conveniently placed for Keswick. The owners provide excellent hospitality in a relaxed manner. The award-winning food, freshly prepared and locally sourced, is served in the bright and welcoming conservatory restaurant that has stunning views. The comfortable bedrooms are well appointed and have many useful extras.

Rooms 9 en suite **Facilities** FTV Lounge tea/coffee Dinner available Direct Dial WiFi 🔒 **Parking** 15 **Notes** LB ⊗ No Children 10yrs Closed Jan RS Mon closed No coaches

The Royal Oak

★★★★ INN

tel: 017687 78533 **fax:** 017687 78533 **CA12 5SY**
email: info@royaloak-braithwaite.co.uk **web:** www.royaloak-braithwaite.co.uk
dir: In village centre

The Royal Oak, in the pretty village of Braithwaite, has delightful views of Skiddaw and Barrow, and is a good base for tourists and walkers. Some of the well-equipped bedrooms are furnished with four-poster beds. Hearty meals and traditional Cumbrian breakfasts are served in the restaurant, and there is an atmospheric, well-stocked bar.

Rooms 10 en suite (1 fmly) **Facilities** STV FTV tea/coffee Dinner available WiFi 🌣 **Parking** 20 **Notes** LB

BRAMPTON
Map 21 NY56

Premier Collection

Lanercost Bed and Breakfast

★★★★★ 🏠 🍴 GUEST ACCOMMODATION

tel: 016977 42589 & 07976 977204 **Lanercost CA8 2HQ**
email: info@lanercostbedandbreakfast.co.uk **web:** www.lanercostbedandbreakfast.co.uk
dir: Follow signs to Lanercost Priory, then signs to B&B

Built in 1840 in the grounds of Lanercost Priory, close to Hadrian's Wall, this property offers individually designed bedrooms of a good size with quality fixtures and fittings. Public areas are welcoming and enhanced with artwork and objets d'art. The hearty, award-winning breakfasts use local produce and make a wonderful start to the day, and dinners are equally good.

Rooms 4 en suite S £83-£88; D £93-£98 **Facilities** FTV iPod docking station Lounge tea/coffee Dinner available Licensed WiFi 🔒 18 Fishing Riding 🔒 **Extras** Speciality toiletries, home-made biscuits - free **Conf** Max 10 Thtr 10 Class 10 Board 10 **Parking** 10 **Notes** LB ⊛

The Blacksmiths Arms

★★★★ INN

tel: 016977 3452 & 42111 **fax:** 016977 3396 **Talkin Village CA8 1LE**
email: blacksmithsarmstalkin@yahoo.co.uk **web:** www.blacksmithstalkin.co.uk
dir: B6413 from Brampton to Castle Carrock, after level crossing 2nd left signed Talkin

Dating from the early 19th century and used as a smithy until the 1950s, this friendly village inn offers good home-cooked fare and real ales, with two Cumbrian cask beers always available. Bedrooms are well equipped, and three are particularly smart. An extensive menu and daily specials are offered in the cosy bar lounges or the smart, panelled Old Forge Restaurant.

Rooms 5 en suite 3 annexe en suite (2 fmly) (3 GF) S £55-£60; D £75-£85 **Facilities** FTV tea/coffee Dinner available Direct Dial WiFi 🔒 18 🔒 **Parking** 20 **Notes** ⊗ No coaches

CARLISLE
Map 18 NY35

See also Brampton

Cambro House

★★★★ GUEST ACCOMMODATION

tel: 01228 543094 **173 Warwick Rd CA1 1LP**
email: davidcambro@aol.com **web:** www.cambrohouse.co.uk
dir: M6 junct 43, into Warwick Rd, 1m on right before St Aidan's Church

This smart Victorian house is close to the town centre and is handy for the motorway. The spacious bedrooms are brightly decorated, smartly appointed and thoughtfully equipped. A hearty Cumbrian breakfast is served in the cosy morning room.

Rooms 3 en suite (1 GF) S £35-£40; D £60-£65* **Facilities** FTV tea/coffee WiFi **Parking** 2 **Notes** LB ⊗ No Children 5yrs

No1 Guest House

★★★★ BED AND BREAKFAST

tel: 01228 547285 & 07899 948711 **1 Etterby St CA3 9JB**
email: sheila@carlislebandb.co.uk **web:** www.carlislebandb.co.uk
dir: M6 junct 44 onto A7, right at 7th lights into Etterby St, house 1st on left

This small friendly house is on the north side of the city within walking distance of the centre. The attractive, well-equipped en suite bedrooms consist of a double, a twin and a single room. Hearty traditional breakfasts featuring the best of local produce, are served in the ground-floor dining room.

Rooms 3 en suite S £35-£42; D £62* **Facilities** FTV tea/coffee Dinner available WiFi **Parking** 1 **Notes** LB ⊗

The Angus

★★★ GUEST ACCOMMODATION

tel: 01228 523546 **fax:** 01228 531895 **14-16 Scotland Rd CA3 9DG**
email: hotel@angus-hotel.co.uk **web:** www.angus-hotel.co.uk
dir: 0.5m N of city centre on A7

Situated just north of the city, this family-run establishment is ideal for business and leisure. A warm welcome is assured and the accommodation is well equipped. The restaurant provides enjoyable food and home baking, and there is also a lounge and a large meeting room.

Rooms 10 en suite (2 fmly) **Facilities** FTV Lounge tea/coffee Dinner available Direct Dial Licensed WiFi 🔒 **Notes** LB

CARTMEL — Map 18 SD37

Premier Collection

L'enclume

★★★★★ ◉◉◉◉◉ RESTAURANT WITH ROOMS

tel: 015395 36362 **Cavendish St LA11 6PZ**
email: info@lenclume.co.uk **web:** www.lenclume.co.uk
dir: From A590 turn left for Cartmel before Newby Bridge

L'enclume is a delightful 13th-century property in the heart of a lovely village, and offers top notch 21st-century cooking that draws foodies from far and wide. Once the village forge (l'enclume is French for 'the anvil') it's now the location for some of Britain's best food, and Simon Rogan's imaginative and adventurous cooking may be sampled in the stylish restaurant. Individually designed, modern, en suite rooms vary in size and style, and are either in the main property or dotted about the village only a few moments' walk from the restaurant.

Rooms 6 en suite 11 annexe en suite (3 fmly) (3 GF) S £69-£169; D £99-£199* **Facilities** STV DVD iPod docking station tea/coffee Dinner available Direct Dial WiFi **Parking** 4 **Notes** ⊗ No coaches

CONISTON — Map 18 SD39

Premier Collection

Wheelgate Country Guest House

★★★★★ ≊ GUEST HOUSE

tel: 015394 41418 **Little Arrow LA21 8AU**
email: enquiry@wheelgate.co.uk **web:** www.wheelgate.co.uk
dir: 1.5m S of Coniston, on W side of road

Linda and Steve Abbott invite their guests to relax and unwind in the friendly atmosphere of their 17th-century country house. Guests can look forward to an award-winning breakfast, individually designed en suite bedrooms, and perhaps a drink in the cosy bar. Situated in a peaceful rural location amidst the breathtaking lake and mountain scenery of Coniston, Wheelgate is the ideal location for exploring the beautiful Lake District.

Rooms 4 en suite 1 annexe en suite (1 GF) S £33-£38; D £60-£76* **Facilities** FTV Lounge tea/coffee Licensed **Parking** 5 **Notes** LB ⊗ No Children 8yrs Closed Nov-Mar

CROSTHWAITE — Map 18 SD49

Premier Collection

The Punchbowl Inn at Crosthwaite

★★★★★ ◉◉ INN

tel: 015395 68237 **fax:** 015397 68875 **Lyth Valley LA8 8HR**
email: info@the-punchbowl.co.uk **web:** www.the-punchbowl.co.uk
dir: M6 junct 36 signed Barrow, on A5074 towards Windermere, turn right for Crosthwaite. At E end of village beside church

Located in the stunning Lyth Valley alongside the village church, this historic inn has been renovated to provide excellent standards of comfort and facilities. Its sumptuous bedrooms have a wealth of thoughtful extras, and imaginative food is available in the elegant restaurant or in the rustic-style bar with open fires. A warm welcome and professional service is assured.

Rooms 9 en suite S £95-£115; D £105-£305* **Facilities** FTV Dinner available Direct Dial WiFi **Extras** Speciality toiletries, jam & scones **Parking** 25 **Notes** No coaches Civ Wed 50

GLENRIDDING — Map 18 NY31

Premier Collection

Glenridding House

★★★★★ ≊ GUEST ACCOMMODATION

tel: 017684 82874 & 07966 486701 **CA11 0PH**
email: stay@glenriddinghouse.com **web:** www.glenriddinghouse.com
dir: M6 junct 40 onto A66, then A592 to Glenridding. Turn sharp second left

Glenridding House is a wonderful Georgian Lakeside villa which sits right on the shores of Ullswater. Used as a holiday home by Charles Darwin, this once derelict building has been lovingly restored. Bedrooms differ in size, and a number boast stunning views of the lake and surrounding fells. An excellent location for those touring this unspoilt area of the Lake District.

Rooms 7 rms (7 pri facs) (3 GF) S £130-£350; D £150-£350* **Facilities** FTV Lounge tea/coffee Dinner available Licensed WiFi Fishing **Packed lunches available **Conf** Max 30 Thtr 30 Class 30 Board 30 **Parking** 30 **Notes** LB ⊗ No Children 18yrs Civ Wed 50

GRANGE-OVER-SANDS — Map 18 SD47

Birchleigh Guest House

★★★★ GUEST HOUSE

tel: 015395 32592 & 07527 844403 **fax:** 015395 32592 **Kents Bank Rd LA11 7EY**
email: birchleigh@btinternet.com **web:** www.birchleighguesthouse.com
dir: M6 junct 36, A590 signed Windermere, then Barrow. At Meathop Rdbt left onto B5277 to Grange-Over-Sands. At 1st rdbt left, at 2nd rdbt right. At T-junct left into Kents Bank Rd. 4th house on left after car park

This homely and welcoming guest house is situated in the heart of town providing four comfortable and tastefully-decorated modern bedrooms. Expect a hearty breakfast served in the well appointed dining room with a separate lounge area available for guests.

Rooms 4 en suite (1 fmly) S £42-£55; D £65-£85* **Facilities** FTV Lounge tea/coffee WiFi **Extras** Fresh milk **Parking** 2 **Notes** ⊗

Greenacres Country Guest House

★★★★ 🅰 GUEST HOUSE

tel: 015395 34578 & 07776 211616   **fax:** 015395 34578 **Lindale LA11 6LP**
email: greenacres.lindale@gmail.com **web:** www.greenacres-lindale.co.uk
dir: *M6 junct 36, A590 signed Kendal/Barrow. After 3m 1st exit at rdbt, continue on A590, 1st exit at rdbt onto B5277, house on right before mini rdbt*

This lovely 18th-century cottage was once the village police station and is now a friendly guest house with a relaxed atmosphere. It is set in the pretty village of Lindale which is just two miles from the Edwardian resort of Grange-over-Sands. A warm welcome includes afternoon tea with freshly baked, home-made cakes, while breakfast is made from excellent Cumbrian produce.

Rooms 4 en suite 1 annexe en suite S £64; D £76-£84* **Facilities** FTV iPod docking station TVL TV4B tea/coffee WiFi 🛀 Packed lunches available, drying facilities **Parking** 5 **Notes** LB ⊗ No Children 12yrs

GRASMERE   Map 18 NY30

Premier Collection

Moss Grove Organic

★★★★★ 🍽 GUEST ACCOMMODATION

tel: 015394 35251 **fax:** 015394 35306 **LA22 9SW**
email: enquiries@mossgrove.com **web:** www.mossgrove.com
dir: *From S: M6 junct 36 onto A591 signed Keswick. From N: M6 junct 40 onto A591 signed Windermere*

Located in the centre of Grasmere, this impressive Victorian house has been appointed using as many natural products as possible, as part of an ongoing dedication to cause minimal environmental impact. The stylish bedrooms are decorated with beautiful wallpaper and natural clay paints, featuring hand-made beds and furnishings. Bose home entertainment systems, flat-screen TVs and luxury bathrooms add further comfort. Extensive continental breakfasts are served in the spacious kitchen, where guests can help themselves and dine at the large wooden dining table.

Rooms 11 en suite (2 GF) S £84-£154; D £99-£259 **Facilities** STV DVD iPod docking station Lounge tea/coffee Licensed WiFi 🛀 **Extras** Speciality toiletries **Parking** 11 **Notes** LB No Children 14yrs Closed 24-25 Dec

GRIZEDALE   Map 18 SD39

Grizedale Lodge

★★★★ GUEST HOUSE

tel: 015394 36532 **LA22 0QL**
email: enquiries@grizedale-lodge.com **web:** www.grizedale-lodge.com
dir: *From Hawkshead follow signs S to Grizedale. Lodge 2m on right*

Set in the heart of Grizedale Forest Park, close to the Go Ape centre and two miles away from the village of Hawkshead, this lovely property offers quiet and tranquil surroundings, ideal for a relaxing break away. Hospitality is key here, and Richard and Debs will be keen to welcome you into their home. The comfortable lounge with open log fire and views of the forest, makes this an ideal place to relax. All the rooms are well decorated and some offer four-poster beds. Expect good home-cooked dinners and appetising breakfasts. Mountain bike storage also available.

Rooms 8 en suite (1 fmly) (2 GF) D £95-£120* **Facilities** FTV DVD Lounge tea/coffee Dinner available Licensed WiFi 🛀 **Extras** Speciality toiletries **Parking** 12

HAWKSHEAD   Map 18 SD39
See also Near Sawrey

Premier Collection

Ees Wyke Country House

★★★★★ ◎ 🍽 GUEST HOUSE

tel: 015394 36393 **LA22 0JZ**
email: mail@eeswyke.co.uk **web:** www.eeswyke.co.uk

(For full entry see Near Sawrey)

The Queen's Head Inn & Restaurant

★★★★ 🍽 INN

tel: 015394 36271 **fax:** 015394 36722 **Main St LA22 0NS**
email: info@queensheadhawkshead.co.uk **web:** www.queensheadhawkshead.co.uk
dir: *M6 junct 36, then A590 to Newby Bridge. Over rdbt, 1st right into Hawkshead*

This 16th-century inn features a wood-panelled bar with low, oak-beamed ceilings and an open log fire. An excellent selection of quality dishes and local ales are served throughout the day. Accommodation has benefited from a complete refurbishment and bedrooms are comfortable and stylishly decorated with modern amenities.

Rooms 10 en suite 3 annexe en suite (1 fmly) (2 GF) D £95-£175* **Facilities** FTV DVD iPod docking station tea/coffee Dinner available WiFi 🛀
Extras Speciality toiletries, robes

Kings Arms

★★★ INN

tel: 015394 36372 **fax:** 015394 36006 **LA22 0NZ**
email: info@kingsarmshawkshead.co.uk **web:** www.kingsarmshawkshead.co.uk
dir: *M6 junct 36, A591, left onto A593 at Waterhead. 1m, onto B5286 to Hawkshead, Kings Arms in main square*

The Kings Arms is a traditional Lakeland inn in the heart of a conservation area. The cosy, thoughtfully equipped bedrooms retain much character and are traditionally furnished. A good choice of freshly prepared food is available in the lounge bar and the neatly presented dining room.

Rooms 8 en suite (3 fmly) S £55-£65; D £80-£96 **Facilities** FTV DVD tea/coffee Dinner available Direct Dial WiFi 🎣 Fishing Riding 🛀 Bowling green **Notes** LB Closed 25 Dec

HOLMROOK   Map 18 SD09

The Lutwidge Arms

★★★ INN

tel: 019467 24230 **fax:** 019467 24100 **CA19 1UH**
email: mail@lutwidgearms.co.uk **web:** www.lutwidgearms.co.uk
dir: *M6 junct 36, A590 towards Barrow. Follow A595 towards Whitehaven & Workington, property in village centre*

This Victorian roadside inn is family run and offers a welcoming atmosphere. Its name comes from the Lutwidge family of Holmrook Hall, whose lineage included Charles Lutwidge Dodgson, better known as Lewis Carroll. The bar and restaurant offer a wide range of meals during the evening. Bedrooms have been refurbished and present very well. A new Orangery has been built, and this has transformed the garden and dining areas.

Rooms 11 en suite 5 annexe en suite (5 fmly) (5 GF) **Facilities** FTV TVL tea/coffee Dinner available WiFi Pool table 🛀 **Parking** 30 **Notes** LB ⊗

IREBY   Map 18 NY23

Woodlands Country House

★★★★ ☖ ⌂ GUEST HOUSE

tel: 016973 71791 **fax:** 016973 71482 **CA7 1EX**
email: stay@woodlandsatireby.co.uk **web:** www.woodlandsatireby.co.uk
dir: *M6 junct 40, A66, pass Keswick, at rdbt right onto A591. At Castle Inn right signed Ireby, 2nd left signed Ireby. Pass church on left, last house in village*

Previously a vicarage, this lovely Victorian home is set in well tended gardens that attract lots of wildlife. Guests are given a warm welcome by the friendly owners and delicious home-cooked evening meals are available by prior arrangement. A peaceful lounge and cosy bar with snug are also available. Bedrooms are attractively furnished and thoughtfully equipped.

Rooms 4 en suite 3 annexe en suite (3 fmly) (3 GF) S £55-£75; D £75-£96
Facilities FTV Lounge TVL tea/coffee Dinner available Licensed WiFi ⚓
Extras Home-made shortbread, sweets, mineral water - free **Parking** 11 **Notes** LB

KENDAL   Map 18 SD59

The Punch Bowl

★★★★ ⌂ INN

tel: 015395 60267 **fax:** 015395 60267 **Barrows Green LA8 0AA**
email: punch_bowl@hotmail.co.uk **web:** www.thepunchbowla65.com
dir: *M6 junct 36 onto A65 signed Kendal. After 4m, on left*

Expect a warm welcome at a friendly pub within easy reach of local transport links and perfectly situated at the gateway to the Lake District. Two tasteful letting rooms are comfortable and well equipped for the modern traveller. Dinner is traditional and wholesome 'pub grub' whilst breakfasts are a hearty affair!

Rooms 2 en suite S fr £64.95; D fr £89.95* **Facilities** FTV Lounge TVL tea/coffee Dinner available WiFi Pool table ⚓ **Extras** Bottled water, Kendal mintcake **Parking** 40

KESWICK   Map 18 NY22

See also Lorton

Premier Collection

The Grange Country Guest House

★★★★★ ☖ GUEST HOUSE

tel: 017687 72500 **fax:** 07075 004885 **Manor Brow, Ambleside Rd CA12 4BA**
email: info@grangekeswick.com **web:** www.grangekeswick.com
dir: *M6 junct 40, A66, 15m. Left onto A591, 0.25m, right into Manor Brow*

This stylish Victorian residence stands in beautiful gardens just a stroll from the town centre and offers a relaxed atmosphere and professional service. The spacious bedrooms are well equipped and some have beams and mountain views. Spacious lounges and ample parking are available. The proprietors are keen to give advice on walks and local activities.

Rooms 10 en suite (1 GF) **Facilities** FTV Lounge tea/coffee Direct Dial Licensed WiFi **Extras** Speciality toiletries **Parking** 10 **Notes** LB ⊗ No Children 10yrs Closed Jan

Amble House

★★★★ ☖ GUEST HOUSE

tel: 017687 73288 **23 Eskin St CA12 4DQ**
email: info@amblehouse.co.uk **web:** www.amblehouse.co.uk
dir: *400yds SE of town centre. Exit A5271 (Penrith Rd) into Greta St & Eskin St*

An enthusiastic welcome awaits you at this Victorian mid-terrace house, close to the town centre. The thoughtfully equipped bedrooms have co-ordinated decor and are furnished in pine. Healthy breakfasts are served in the attractive dining room.

Rooms 5 en suite **Facilities** tea/coffee WiFi ⚓ **Extras** Speciality toiletries **Notes** ⊗ No Children 16yrs Closed 24-26 Dec

Badgers Wood

★★★★ GUEST HOUSE

tel: 017687 72621 **fax:** 017687 72621 **30 Stanger St CA12 5JU**
email: enquiries@badgers-wood.co.uk **web:** www.badgers-wood.co.uk
dir: *In town centre off A5271 (main street)*

The team at Badgers Wood welcomes guests to this delightful Victorian terrace house, located in a quiet area close to the town centre. The smart bedrooms are furnished to a high standard and are well equipped and have lovely views; the attractive breakfast room at the front of the house overlooks the fells. Off-road parking is an added benefit. Special diets gladly catered for.

Rooms 6 en suite S £41-£45; D £75-£80* **Facilities** FTV DVD tea/coffee WiFi ⚓ **Parking** 6 **Notes** ⊗ No Children 12yrs Closed Nov-Jan ⌨

Dalegarth House

★★★★ ⌂ GUEST ACCOMMODATION

tel: 017687 72817 **Portinscale CA12 5RQ**
email: allerdalechef@aol.com **web:** www.dalegarth-house.co.uk
dir: *Off A66 to Portinscale, pass Farmers Arms, 500yds on left*

This friendly, family-run establishment stands in an elevated position in the village of Portinscale, and has fine views from the well-tended garden. The attractive bedrooms are well equipped, and there is a peaceful lounge, a well-stocked bar, and a spacious dining room where the resident owner-chef produces hearty breakfasts and delicious evening meals.

Rooms 8 en suite 2 annexe en suite (1 fmly) (2 GF) S £45; D £88-£110*
Facilities FTV Lounge tea/coffee Dinner available Licensed WiFi ⚓ **Extras** Home-made cakes - complimentary **Parking** 10 **Notes** LB ⊗ No Children 12yrs Closed 24 Nov-1 Mar

The Edwardene

★★★★ ☖ GUEST ACCOMMODATION

tel: 017687 73586 **26 Southey St CA12 4EF**
email: info@edwardenehotel.com **web:** www.edwardenehotel.com
dir: *M6 junct 40, A66 follow 1st sign to Keswick, right into Penrith Rd. Sharp left by war memorial into Southey St, 150mtrs on right*

Located close to the heart of the town centre, this Victorian Lakeland stone building retains many of its original features. Bedrooms are well equipped with many thoughtful extras provided throughout. A comfortable lounge is available, and the generous Cumbrian breakfast is served in the stylish dining room.

Rooms 11 en suite (1 fmly) S £47-£48; D £86-£98* **Facilities** FTV TVL tea/coffee Licensed WiFi ⚓ **Extras** Speciality toiletries **Parking** 1 **Notes** LB ⊗ No Children 2yrs

Rooms 36

★★★★ GUEST ACCOMMODATION

tel: 017687 72764 & 74416 **36 Lake Rd CA12 5DQ**
email: andy@rooms36.co.uk **web:** www.rooms36.co.uk
dir: M6 junct 40, A66 to Keswick. From Main St in Keswick follow Borrowdale (B5289) signs. Right at next mini rdbt into Heads Rd (B5289), 4th right into The Heads, left at end into Lake Rd

Refurbished to a high standard, Rooms 36 overlooks Hope Park at the end of Lake Road. Modern bedrooms feature iPod docking stations, Tassimo coffee machines, comfortable beds and Herdwick wool carpets as standard. En suites are well appointed and public area decor is enhanced with wonderful artwork by local artist Tessa Kennedy.

Rooms 6 en suite (4 fmly) **Facilities** STV FTV iPod docking station Lounge TVL tea/coffee WiFi ⬤ **Parking** 2

Sunnyside Guest House

★★★★ GUEST HOUSE

tel: 017687 72446 **25 Southey St CA12 4EF**
email: enquiries@sunnysideguesthouse.com **web:** www.sunnysideguesthouse.com
dir: 200yds E of town centre. Exit A5271 (Penrith Rd) into Southey St. Sunnyside on left

This stylish guest house is in a quiet area close to the town centre. Bedrooms have been appointed to a high standard and are comfortably furnished and well equipped. There is a spacious and comfortable lounge with plenty of books and magazines. Breakfast is served at individual tables in the airy and attractive dining room. Private parking is available.

Rooms 7 en suite S fr £49; D fr £84* **Facilities** FTV DVD iPod docking station Lounge tea/coffee WiFi ⬤ **Parking** 7 **Notes** LB ⊗ No Children 12yrs Closed 3 Jan-10 Feb

Brundholme

★★★★ 🏠 GUEST ACCOMMODATION

tel: 017687 73305 **The Heads CA12 5ER**
email: bazaly@hotmail.co.uk **web:** www.brundholme.co.uk

Centrally located, overlooking Hope Park with some bedrooms boasting wonderful views of surrounding fells, this Victorian property is just minutes' walk from the town centre in one direction and the theatre in the other. Limited off-road parking is available. Bedrooms are comfortable and well appointed, and the well cooked traditional Lakeland breakfast will set you up for the day. Service is relaxed and friendly.

Rooms 4 en suite (1 GF) D £72* **Facilities** FTV tea/coffee WiFi **Parking** 6 **Notes** ⊗

Claremont House

★★★★ GUEST ACCOMMODATION

tel: 017687 72089 **Chestnut Hill CA12 4LT**
email: info@claremonthousekeswick.co.uk **web:** www.claremonthousekeswick.co.uk
dir: A591 N into Chestnut Hill. Pass Manor Brow on left, Claremont House 100yds on right

This impressive 19th-century house has commanding views over Keswick and beyond, and is set in mature grounds where red squirrels regularly visit. It is within walking distance of the town and is ideal for walkers. Guests can expect comfortable bedrooms, a hearty breakfast and friendly service. The resident owners also offer a hot drink and cake on your arrival. Free WiFi is also available.

Rooms 6 en suite (1 fmly) (1 GF) S £40-£50; D £60-£80* **Facilities** FTV tea/coffee WiFi ⬤ **Extras** Flowers, wine, chocolate - chargeable **Parking** 8 **Notes** LB ⊗ No Children 8yrs Closed 24-26 Dec

Craglands Guest House

★★★★ GUEST ACCOMMODATION

tel: 017687 74406 **Penrith Rd CA12 4LJ**
email: craglands@msn.com **web:** www.craglands-keswick.co.uk
dir: 0.5m E of Keswick centre on A5271 (Penrith Rd) at junct A591

This Victorian house occupies an elevated position within walking distance of the town centre. The good value accommodation provides attractive, well equipped bedrooms. Pauline and Mark offer a warm welcome and serve delicious breakfasts with local produce and home-made breads.

Rooms 7 rms (5 en suite) S £27-£50; D £54-£100* **Facilities** FTV tea/coffee Dinner available WiFi ⬤ **Parking** 6 **Notes** LB ⊗ No Children 8yrs

Cragside

★★★★ GUEST ACCOMMODATION

tel: 017687 73344 **fax:** 017687 20020 **39 Blencathra St CA12 4HX**
email: cragside-keswick@hotmail.com **web:** www.cragside-keswick.co.uk
dir: A591 Penrith Rd into Keswick, under rail bridge, 2nd left

Expect warm hospitality at Cragside, located within easy walking distance of the town centre. The attractive bedrooms are well equipped, and many have fine views of the fells. Hearty Cumbrian breakfasts are served in the breakfast room, which overlooks the small front garden. Visually or hearing impaired guests are catered for, with Braille information, televisions with teletext, and a loop system installed in the dining room.

Rooms 4 en suite (1 fmly) S £45-£60; D £60-£80 **Facilities** FTV DVD tea/coffee WiFi **Notes** No Children 5yrs

Dorchester House

★★★★ GUEST ACCOMMODATION

tel: 017687 73256 **17 Southey St CA12 4EG**
email: dennis@dorchesterhouse.co.uk **web:** www.dorchesterhouse-keswick.co.uk
dir: 200yds E of town centre. Exit A5271 (Penrith Rd) into Southey St, 150yds on left

A warm welcome awaits at Dorchester House, just a stroll from the town centre and its amenities. The comfortably proportioned, well-maintained bedrooms offer pleasing co-ordinated decor. Hearty breakfasts are served in the attractive ground-floor dining room.

Rooms 8 rms (7 en suite) (1 pri facs) (2 fmly) S £37-£48; D £78-£84* **Facilities** FTV tea/coffee WiFi **Notes** LB ⊗ No Children 6yrs

Eden Green Guest House

★★★★ GUEST HOUSE

tel: 017687 72077 **fax:** 017687 80870 **20 Blencathra St CA12 4HP**
email: enquiries@edengreenguesthouse.com **web:** www.edengreenguesthouse.com
dir: A591 Penrith Rd into Keswick, under railway bridge, 2nd left, house 500yds on left

This mid-terrace house, faced with local stone, offers well-decorated and furnished bedrooms, some with fine views of Skiddaw. Traditional English and vegetarian breakfasts are served in the neat breakfast room, and packed lunches can be provided on request.

Rooms 5 en suite (1 fmly) (1 GF) S £37.50-£40; D £70-£80* **Facilities** FTV DVD iPod docking station tea/coffee WiFi ⬤ **Notes** LB ⊗ No Children 8yrs

KESWICK *continued*

Elm Tree Lodge

★★★★ GUEST ACCOMMODATION

tel: 017687 71050 & 07980 521079 **16 Leonard St CA12 4EL**
email: info@elmtreelodge-keswick.co.uk **web:** www.elmtreelodge-keswick.co.uk
dir: *Exit A66, pass ambulance depot, left before pedestrian crossing, left into Southey St. 3rd left into Helvellyn St, 1st right into Leonard St, property 3rd on right*

Close to the town centre, Elm Tree Lodge is a tastefully decorated Victorian house that offers a variety of rooms. Bedrooms feature stripped pine, period furniture, crisp white linen and modern en suites or private shower room. Hearty breakfasts are served in the charming dining room and feature local produce. A friendly welcome is guaranteed.

Rooms 4 rms (3 en suite) (1 pri facs) D £60-£75* **Facilities** FTV tea/coffee WiFi
Parking 2 **Notes** LB ⊗ No Children 8yrs

The George

★★★★ 🛏 INN

tel: 017687 72076 **fax:** 017687 75968 **Saint Johns St CA12 5AZ**
email: rooms@thegeorgekeswick.co.uk **web:** www.thegeorgekeswick.co.uk
dir: *M6 junct 40, A66, take left filter road signed Keswick, pass pub on left. At x-rds left into Station St, 150yds on left*

Located in the centre of town, this property is Keswick's oldest coaching inn. There is an abundance of character with wooden beamed bar, cosy seating areas and an atmospheric, candle-lit dining room. Food is a highlight with a wide choice of freshly prepared dishes. Bedrooms are simply presented and comfortable. Parking permits and storage for cycles are available.

Rooms 12 en suite (2 fmly) S £60-£100; D £100* **Facilities** FTV tea/coffee Dinner available **Parking** 4 **Notes** No coaches

Hazelmere

★★★★ GUEST ACCOMMODATION

tel: 017687 72445 **Crosthwaite Rd CA12 5PG**
email: info@hazelmerekeswick.co.uk **web:** www.hazelmerekeswick.co.uk
dir: *Exit A66 left at Crosthwaite road (A591 junct) for Keswick, Hazelmere 400yds on right*

Hazelmere is peacefully located overlooking the River Greta and perfect for walking in the surrounding fells or to the shores of Derwentwater. The market place is only a short stroll away. The house has recently been completely refurbished by the friendly owners, who can offer advice on local walks and cycle routes. All bedrooms have stunning views and are well equipped. Guests can also enjoy watching the birds and other wildlife visiting the garden.

Rooms 6 en suite (1 fmly) S £35-£38; D £75-£85* **Facilities** FTV DVD tea/coffee WiFi **Parking** 7 **Notes** LB ⊗ No Children 8yrs

Hedgehog Hill Guest House

★★★★ GUEST HOUSE

tel: 017687 80654 **18 Blencathra St CA12 4HP**
email: keith@hedgehoghill.co.uk **web:** www.hedgehoghill.co.uk
dir: *M6 junct 40, A66 to Keswick. Left into Blencathra St*

Expect warm hospitality at this Victorian terrace house. Hedgehog Hill Guest House is convenient for the town centre, local attractions and many walks. Bedrooms are comfortably equipped and offer thoughtful extras. Hearty breakfasts are served in the light and airy dining room with vegetarians well catered for.

Rooms 6 rms (4 en suite) S £31-£33; D £68-£78* **Facilities** FTV tea/coffee WiFi
Extras Fair Trade snacks **Notes** ⊗ No Children 12yrs Closed 23-26 Dec

Keswick Park

★★★★ GUEST ACCOMMODATION

tel: 017687 72072 **fax:** 017687 74816 **33 Station Rd CA12 4NA**
email: reservations@keswickparkhotel.com **web:** www.keswickparkhotel.com
dir: *200yds NE of town centre. Exit A5271 Penrith Rd into Station Rd*

A friendly welcome awaits at Keswick Park, a comfortable Victorian house, situated a short walking distance from the town centre. Bedrooms are mostly of a good size and have homely extras. The breakfast room is divided into two sections and there is also a cosy bar. Guests might like to sit on the front garden patio while enjoying refreshments.

Rooms 16 en suite (2 fmly) **Facilities** FTV TVL tea/coffee Direct Dial Licensed WiFi
Parking 8 **Notes** ⊗

Rickerby Grange

★★★★ GUEST ACCOMMODATION

tel: 017687 72344 **Portinscale CA12 5RH**
email: stay@rickerbygrange.co.uk **web:** www.rickerbygrange.co.uk
dir: *W of Keswick on A66, turn left at Portinscale junct. Pass The Farmers public house, then 2nd right into Rickerby Ln. 50yds on right*

Rickerby Grange is ideally positioned in a private lane in the pretty village of Portinscale one mile from Keswick. This family-run property offers a genuine warm welcome to all, including walkers and cyclists (by prior arrangement). Even the family dog is welcome. Bedrooms are pleasantly furnished and most are en suite. A small but well-stocked bar is available, and drinks can be enjoyed in the lounge area or in the garden.

Rooms 9 rms (8 en suite) (1 pri facs) 1 annexe en suite (3 fmly) (1 GF) **Facilities** FTV tea/coffee Licensed WiFi **Parking** 14

The Royal Oak at Keswick

★★★★ INN

tel: 017687 74584 **Main St CA12 5HZ**
email: relax@keswicklodge.co.uk **web:** www.keswicklodge.co.uk
dir: *M6 junct 40, A66 to Keswick town centre to war memorial x-rds. Left into Station St. Inn 100yds*

Located on the corner of the vibrant market square this large, friendly 18th-century coaching inn offers a wide range of meals throughout the day and evening. There is a fully stocked bar complete with well-kept cask ales. Bedrooms vary in size but all are contemporary, smartly presented and feature quality accessories such as LCD TVs. There is also a drying room.

Rooms 19 en suite (2 fmly) **Facilities** FTV tea/coffee Dinner available

Salisbury Guest House

★★★★ GUEST HOUSE

tel: 017687 72230 & 07850 500723   **fax:** 017687 72230 **36 Blencathra St CA12 4HT**
email: enquiries@salisburyguesthouse.com **web:** www.salisburyguesthouse.com
dir: *M6 junct 40 onto A66. Take 1st exit into Keswick (Penrith Road), 3rd left after BP garage into Blencathra St*

Within easy walking distance of the town centre, Salisbury Guest House offers high standards of hospitality. It has comfortable surroundings with bedrooms that cater well for guest needs, and have many thoughtful extras provided as standard. Breakfast uses quality locally sourced produce and is served on individual tables in a bright and welcoming dining room.

Rooms 4 en suite (1 fmly) **Facilities** FTV DVD tea/coffee WiFi 🐾

Avondale Guest House

★★★★ 🅰 GUEST ACCOMMODATION

tel: 017687 72735 **20 Southey St CA12 4EF**
email: enquiries@avondaleguesthouse.com **web:** www.avondaleguesthouse.com
dir: *A66 to Keswick. A591 towards town centre, left at war memorial into Station St. Sharp left into Southey St, 100yds on right*

Just a two minute walk from Keswick town centre, Avondale Guest House is an ideal base for walkers and cyclists. Full English, Scottish and vegetarian cooked breakfasts are served in the attractive dining room. An extensive upgrade of all rooms and en suites has just been completed, so this would be the ideal time to sample the hospitality on offer.

Rooms 6 en suite S £40-£46; D £80-£92 **Facilities** FTV DVD Lounge tea/coffee WiFi 🐾 **Notes** ⊗ No Children 12yrs

Sandon Guesthouse

★★★★ 🅰 GUEST HOUSE

tel: 017687 73648 **13 Southey St CA12 4EG**
email: enquiries@sandonguesthouse.com **web:** www.sandonguesthouse.com
dir: *200yds E of town centre. Exit A5271 (Penrith Rd) into Southey St*

This spacious Victorian residence close to the market square offers en suite bedrooms (except the single room) thoughtfully equipped with many extras. Expect warm hospitality from the friendly resident owners.

Rooms 6 rms (5 en suite) (1 pri facs) S £38-£42; D £76-£84* **Facilities** FTV DVD tea/coffee WiFi 🐾 **Notes** ⊗ No Children 4yrs Closed 24 Dec (day), 25-26 Dec

Springs Farm B&B *(NY274227)*

★★★ FARMHOUSE

tel: 017687 72144 & 07816 824253 **Springs Farm, Springs Rd CA12 4AN**
email: springsfarmkeswick@gmail.com **web:** www.springsfarmcumbria.co.uk
dir: *A66 into Keswick, left at T-junct onto Chestnut Hill. After 200yds right on Manor Brow, then left into Springs Road. 0.5m at end of road*

Part of a working dairy farm, the farmhouse was built around 150 years ago. Guests can expect comfortable accommodation and a well-cooked breakfast with eggs from the farm's own hens. Springs Farm B&B is ideally located in the heart of the countryside but surprising close to the town centre, which is an easy 10-minute walk away.

Rooms 3 en suite S £42-£45; D £73-£75* **Facilities** STV FTV DVD iPod docking station TVL tea/coffee WiFi 🐾 Farm shop, tea room **Parking** 6 **Notes** LB Closed 19-29 Dec ⊛ 180 acres dairy/beef

KIRKBY IN FURNESS Map 18 SD28

Low Hall Farm *(SD232812)*

★★★★ FARMHOUSE

tel: 01229 889220 **LA17 7TR**
email: tracey.edmondson@btinternet.com **web:** www.low-hall.co.uk
dir: *M6 junct 36 onto A590. At rdbt signed Workington follow A595, through Askam in Furness. After 2.5m turn right, signed Low Hall Farm then 1st left*

Low Hall is a lovely Victorian farmhouse owned by Holker Hall Estates and run by Peter and Tracey Edmondson. The farm is a working beef and sheep farm set in peaceful countryside, offering spectacular views of the Duddon Estuary and Lakeland fells. Low Hall is a very spacious farmhouse, with all rooms offering high quality furnishings. A traditional farmhouse English breakfast is served in the bright and airy dining room, which is joined by a comfortable living room with wood burning stove. Ironing facilities are available.

Rooms 3 en suite S £40; D £65* **Facilities** FTV TVL tea/coffee WiFi **Extras** Speciality toiletries - complimentary **Parking** 4 **Notes** ⊗ No Children 14yrs 366 acres beef/sheep

KIRKBY LONSDALE Map 18 SD67

Premier Collection

Hipping Hall

★★★★★ ⑩⑩⑩ 🍽 RESTAURANT WITH ROOMS

tel: 015242 71187 **fax:** 015242 72452 **Cowan Bridge LA6 2JJ**
email: info@hippinghall.com **web:** www.hippinghall.com
dir: *M6 junct 36, A65 through Kirkby Lonsdale towards Skipton. On right after Cowan Bridge*

Close to the market town of Kirkby Lonsdale, Hipping Hall offers spacious bedrooms, designed using soft shades with sumptuous textures and fabrics; the bathrooms use natural stone, slate and limestone to great effect. There are also three spacious cottage suites that create a real hideaway experience. The sitting room, with large, comfortable sofas has a traditional feel. The 3 AA Rosette-worthy restaurant is a 15th-century hall with tapestries and a minstrels' gallery that is as impressive as it is intimate.

Rooms 6 en suite 3 annexe en suite (1 GF) **Facilities** FTV Lounge Dinner available Direct Dial WiFi 🦶 **Parking** 30 **Notes** No Children 12yrs No coaches Civ Wed 42

Premier Collection

Plato's

★★★★★ 🍽 RESTAURANT WITH ROOMS

tel: 015242 74180 **2 Mill Brow LA6 2AT**
email: hello@platoskirkby.co.uk **web:** www.platoskirkbylonsdale.co.uk
dir: *M6 junct 36, A65 Kirkby Lonsdale, after 5m at rdbt take 1st exit, onto one-way system*

Tucked away in the heart of the popular market town, Plato's is steeped in history. Sumptuous bedrooms have a wealth of thoughtful extras, and imaginative food is available in the elegant restaurant with its open-plan kitchen. The lounge bar is more rustic in style with fires to relax by. A warm welcome and professional service is assured. The Pop Shop offers Plato's cuisine to take away.

Rooms 8 en suite **Facilities** FTV TVL tea/coffee Dinner available WiFi 🦶 18 **Notes** LB No coaches

KIRKBY LONSDALE *continued*

The Sun Inn

★★★★★ ◉ RESTAURANT WITH ROOMS

tel: 015242 71965 **fax:** 015242 72485 **6 Market St LA6 2AU**
email: email@sun-inn.info **web:** www.sun-inn.info
dir: *From A65 follow signs to town centre. Inn on main street*

The Sun is a 17th-century inn situated in a historic market town, overlooking St Mary's Church. The atmospheric bar features stone walls, wooden beams and log fires with real ales available. Delicious meals are served in the bar or the more formal, modern restaurant. Traditional and modern styles are blended together in the beautifully appointed rooms with excellent en suites.

Rooms 11 en suite (1 fmly) S £78-£158; D £104-£178 **Facilities** FTV tea/coffee Dinner available WiFi ⌚ ♿ 18 ♨ **Extras** Bath robes, speciality toiletries **Notes** LB No coaches

Pheasant Inn

★★★★ ⌚ INN

tel: 015242 71230 **Casterton LA6 2RX**
email: info@pheasantinn.co.uk

This friendly family-run inn is perfectly situated in a quiet village near the picturesque market town of Kirkby Lonsdale. Real ales are a speciality, along with hearty but refined cooking served in the oak-panelled dining room. Spacious and comfortable accommodation is provided.

Rooms 10 rms S £40-£55; D £80-£100* **Facilities** Dinner available **Notes** Closed 5-28 Jan

The Copper Kettle

★★★ 🅰 GUEST ACCOMMODATION

tel: 015242 71714 **fax:** 015242 71714 **3-5 Market St LA6 2AU**
email: gamble_p@btconnect.com
dir: *In town centre, down lane by Post Office*

Built between 1610 and 1640 The Copper Kettle is situated in the heart of this small quaint market town, which nestles on the banks of the River Lune. The bedrooms, all of which retain their old world 17th-century charm, are comfortable and atmospheric. Home-cooked meals and hearty breakfasts are served in the cosy restaurant.

Rooms 5 en suite (2 fmly) S £35; D £49-£59* **Facilities** FTV tea/coffee Dinner available Licensed WiFi ♨ **Parking** 3 **Notes** LB

KIRKBY STEPHEN   Map 18 NY70

Tranna Hill

★★★★ 🏠 GUEST ACCOMMODATION

tel: 015396 23227 & 07989 892368 **Newbiggin-on-Lune CA17 4NY**
email: trannahill@hotmail.com **web:** www.trannahill.co.uk
dir: *M6 junct 38 onto A685 towards Brough. After 5m turn left towards Great Asby then immediately left to Kelleth. 100mtrs on right*

Tranna Hill is set in its own grounds on the edge of the village of Newbiggin-on-Lune, a short distance from the M6 and A66. This period building offers fantastic views of the surrounding fells. Bedrooms are comfortable, well appointed and

equipped with lots of books, maps and guides. The sitting/dining room has a log-burning stove and the gardens have seating on the patio.

Rooms 3 en suite (1 fmly) S £43-£45; D £66-£70* **Facilities** FTV DVD TVL tea/coffee WiFi ⌚ 9 ♨ **Extras** Speciality toiletries, chocolates **Parking** 8 **Notes** LB ⊗ Closed Nov-Feb ⊛

LITTLE LANGDALE   Map 18 NY30

Three Shires Inn

★★★★ ⌚ INN

tel: 015394 37215 **fax:** 015394 37127 **LA22 9NZ**
email: enquiry@threeshiresinn.co.uk **web:** www.threeshiresinn.co.uk
dir: *Exit A593, 3m from Ambleside at 2nd junct signed Langdales. 1st left after 0.5m, 1m along lane*

Enjoying an outstanding rural location, this family-run inn was built in 1872. The brightly decorated bedrooms are individual in style and many offer panoramic views. The attractive lounge features a roaring fire in the cooler months and there is a traditional style bar with a great selection of local ales. Meals can be taken in either the bar or cosy restaurant.

Rooms 10 en suite (1 fmly) D £92-£125* **Facilities** FTV Lounge TVL tea/coffee Dinner available WiFi ♨ Use of local country club **Parking** 15 **Notes** LB Closed 25 Dec RS Dec & Jan wknds & New Year only No coaches

LONGTOWN   Map 21 NY36

The Sycamore Tree

★★★★ BED AND BREAKFAST

tel: 01228 791919 **fax:** 01228 792202 **40/42 Bridge St CA6 5UD**
email: jfothergill2008@googlemail.com **web:** www.sycamoretreelongtown.co.uk
dir: *On A7*

The Sycamore Tree is located on the high street of Longtown just four miles from Gretna and the Scottish Border. Choose from a four-poster or a king-size family room. If you are staying on one of the 'steak nights' be sure to reserve a table for dinner.

Rooms 2 en suite (2 fmly) **Facilities** FTV tea/coffee Dinner available Licensed WiFi **Extras** Robes, slippers, bottled water **Notes** ⊗ Closed 1st 2wks Sep & 26 Dec

LORTON   Map 18 NY12

The Old Vicarage

★★★★★ 🍴 ⌚ GUEST HOUSE

tel: 01900 85656 **Church Ln CA13 9UN**
email: info@oldvicarage.co.uk **web:** www.oldvicarage.co.uk
dir: *B5292 onto B5289 N of Lorton. 1st left signed Church. House 1st on right*

This delightful Victorian house offers spacious accommodation in the peaceful Lorton Vale, at the heart of the Lake District National Park. A converted coach-house offers two rooms with exposed stone walls, and is ideal for families with older children. Bedrooms in the main house are well equipped and have excellent views of the distant mountains. Delicious home cooking is served in the bright dining room.

Rooms 6 en suite 2 annexe en suite (1 GF) **Facilities** FTV DVD Lounge tea/coffee Dinner available Licensed WiFi ♨ **Parking** 10 **Notes** ⊗ No Children 8yrs Closed mid Nov-Jan

LOWESWATER
Map 18 NY12

Kirkstile Inn

★★★★ INN

tel: 01900 85219 **CA13 0RU**
email: info@kirkstile.com **web:** www.kirkstile.com
dir: *A66 onto B5292 into Lorton, left signed Buttermere. Follow signs to Loweswater, left signed Kirkstile Inn*

This historic 16th-century inn lies in a valley surrounded by mountains. Serving great food and ale, its rustic bar and adjoining rooms are a mecca for walkers. There is also a cosy restaurant offering a quieter ambiance. Bedrooms retain their original character. There is a spacious family suite in an annexe, with two bedrooms, a lounge and a bathroom.

Rooms 7 en suite 3 annexe en suite (1 fmly) (2 GF) S £63.50-£90; D £103-£113* **Facilities** TVL TV3B tea/coffee Dinner available WiFi **Parking** 30 **Notes** LB Closed 25 Dec No coaches

Grange Country House

★★★★ GUEST ACCOMMODATION

tel: 01946 861211 & 861570 **CA13 0SU**
email: info@thegrange-loweswater.co.uk **web:** www.thegrange-loweswater.co.uk
dir: *Exit A5086 for Mockerkin, through village. After 2m left signed Loweswater Lake. Grange Country House at bottom of hill on left*

The delightful Grange Country House is set in extensive grounds in a quiet valley at the north western end of Loweswater and proves popular with guests seeking peace and quiet. It has a friendly relaxed atmosphere and cosy public areas which include a small bar serving a great range of local beers; a residents' lounge and an attractive dining room with dinner served by prior arrangement. The bedrooms are well equipped and comfortable, some with four-poster beds.

Rooms 8 en suite (2 fmly) (1 GF) S £48-£68; D £90-£110* **Facilities** FTV Lounge TVL tea/coffee Dinner available Licensed WiFi **Extras** Speciality toiletries **Conf** Max 25 Thtr 25 Class 25 Board 25 **Parking** 20 **Notes** LB

LUPTON
Map 18 SD58

Premier Collection

The Plough Inn Lupton

★★★★★ INN

tel: 015395 67700 **Cow Brow LA6 1PJ**
email: info@theploughatlupton.co.uk **web:** www.theploughatlupton.co.uk
dir: *M6 junct 36 onto A65 towards Kirkby Lonsdale. Through Nook, up hill, inn on right*

This delightful inn's interior is open plan and a real delight; modern but with a rustic farmhouse appearance. There are large beams, and a log-burning stove in the lounge surrounded by large comfortable sofas where you can relax and read the papers. The bedrooms are well proportioned and reflect the inn's high standards; all have feature bathrooms with roll-top baths and walk-in showers. The staff are excellent and guests are made to feel like part of the family. The inn is open all year and serves food every day.

Rooms 6 en suite (2 fmly) **Facilities** FTV Dinner available Direct Dial WiFi 18 **Extras** Speciality toiletries, bottled water **Conf** Max 8 Thtr 8 Board 8 **Parking** 50 **Notes** No coaches Civ Wed

MILNTHORPE
Map 18 SD48

The Cross Keys

★★★★ INN

tel: 015395 62115 **fax:** 015395 65732 **1 Park Rd LA7 7AB**
email: stay@thecrosskeyshotel.co.uk **web:** www.thecrosskeyshotel.co.uk

This early 19th century coaching inn has a wealth of history and is located in the heart of the town. In its' modern incarnation it offers well-equipped and comfortable accommodation and a pub serving good food and a range of cask ales. Ample parking is provided and there is a large function space and separate snooker and pool games rooms.

Rooms 8 en suite (2 fmly) S £47.50-£60; D £65-£70* **Facilities** STV FTV tea/coffee Dinner available Direct Dial WiFi 18 Fishing Snooker Pool table **Conf** Max 60 Thtr 60 Class 30 Board 40 **Parking** **Notes** LB

NEAR SAWREY
Map 18 SD39

Premier Collection

Ees Wyke Country House

★★★★★ GUEST HOUSE

tel: 015394 36393 **LA22 0JZ**
email: mail@eeswyke.co.uk **web:** www.eeswyke.co.uk
dir: *On B5285 on W side of village*

A warm welcome awaits at this elegant Georgian country house with views over Esthwaite Water and the surrounding countryside. The thoughtfully equipped bedrooms have been decorated and furnished with care. There is a charming lounge with an open fire, and a splendid dining room where a carefully prepared five-course dinner is served. Breakfasts have a fine reputation due to the skilful use of local produce.

Rooms 8 en suite (1 GF) S £79-£115; D £99-£160 **Facilities** FTV Lounge tea/coffee Dinner available Licensed WiFi **Extras** Sherry, peanuts **Parking** 12 **Notes** LB No Children 12yrs

NEWBY BRIDGE
Map 18 SD38

Premier Collection

The Knoll Country House

★★★★★ GUEST ACCOMMODATION

tel: 015395 31347 **fax:** 015395 30850 **Lakeside LA12 8AU**
email: info@theknoll-lakeside.co.uk **web:** www.theknoll-lakeside.co.uk
dir: *A590 W to Newby Bridge, over rdbt, signed right for Lake Steamers, house 0.5m on left*

This delightful Edwardian villa stands in a leafy dell on the western side of Windermere. Public areas have many original features, including open fires in the cosy lounge and dining room. The attractive bedrooms vary in style and outlook, but are all very stylish. Proprietor and chef Jenny Mead and her enthusiastic team extend a very caring and natural welcome. Jenny also prepares a very good range of excellent dishes at breakfast and dinner.

Rooms 8 en suite 1 annexe rm (1 pri facs) S £75-£110; D £95-£160 **Facilities** STV FTV DVD iPod docking station Lounge TVL tea/coffee Dinner available Direct Dial Licensed WiFi Use of nearby hotel leisure spa **Extras** Fruit & wine in 1 room **Conf** Max 30 Thtr 30 Class 18 Board 12 **Parking** 9 **Notes** LB No Children 16yrs Closed 24-26 Dec Civ Wed 40

NEWBY BRIDGE *continued*

modern bedrooms are light and airy, and there is a cosy lounge. Breakfast is served in a converted stable.

Rooms 3 rms (2 en suite) (1 pri facs) S £40–£45; D £60–£65 **Facilities** FTV DVD TVL tea/coffee WiFi ⚓ **Parking** 3 **Notes** LB ⊗ No Children 10yrs

---

Premier Collection

Hill Crest Country Guest House

★★★★★ 🏠 GUEST HOUSE

tel: 015395 31766 **fax:** 015395 31986 **Brow Edge LA12 8QP**
email: enquiries@hotelnewbybridge.co.uk **web:** www.hillcrestnewbybridge.co.uk
dir: *M6 junct 36 follow signs for Barrow (A590). 1m after Newby Bridge, turn left into Brow Edge Rd, continue on up incline. 4th house on right*

Hill Crest Country Guest House is set in picturesque surroundings with stunning views, and offers a high standard of en suite accommodation. All rooms are individual and well maintained. A cosy guest lounge leads into the conservatory breakfast room, where breakfast is served, making good use of fresh local produce. Warm and genuine hospitality is guaranteed.

Rooms 3 en suite (1 fmly) (1 GF) S £60–£85; D £80–£110* **Facilities** iPod docking station TVL tea/coffee WiFi Discounted rAtes at nearby health & fitness club **Extras** Speciality toiletries **Parking** 3 **Notes** LB ⊗ Closed 23-26 Dec

---

Lakes End Guest House

★★★★ GUEST HOUSE

tel: 015395 31260 **fax:** 015395 31260 **LA12 8ND**
email: info@lakes-end.co.uk **web:** www.lakes-end.co.uk
dir: *On A590 in Newby Bridge, 100yds from rdbt*

In a sheltered, wooded setting away from the road, Lakes End is convenient for the coast and the lakes. The bedrooms have been thoughtfully furnished and equipped. Traditional English breakfasts are served, and delicious home-cooked evening meals can be provided by arrangement.

Rooms 4 en suite (1 fmly) (1 GF) S £45–£60; D £65–£85* **Facilities** STV FTV tea/coffee Dinner available Licensed WiFi ⚓ Membership to local hotel spa **Parking** 6 **Notes** LB ⊗

Lyndhurst Country House

★★★★ 🏠 GUEST HOUSE

tel: 015395 31245 **LA12 8ND**
email: chris@lyndhurstcountryhouse.co.uk **web:** www.lyndhurstcountryhouse.co.uk
dir: *On junct of A590 & A592 at Newby Bridge rdbt*

This 1920s house is situated close to the southern tip of Lake Windermere. Accommodation consists of three comfortable, tastefully decorated bedrooms, each with en suite shower room. Hearty breakfasts feature local produce and are served in the pleasant dining room, which also has a lounge area opening onto the garden.

Rooms 3 en suite D £79–£88* **Facilities** FTV Lounge tea/coffee WiFi **Parking** 3 **Notes** LB ⊗ No Children 8yrs Closed 23-28 Dec

---

The Coach House

★★★★ BED AND BREAKFAST

tel: 015395 31622 **Hollow Oak LA12 8AD**
email: coachho@talk21.com **web:** www.coachho.com
dir: *2.5m SW of Newby Bridge. A590 onto B5278 signed Cark, 1st left into rear of white house*

This converted coach house stands in delightful gardens south of Lake Windermere. The hosts offer a warm welcome and are a good source of local knowledge. The

---

PENRITH	Map 18 NY53

Premier Collection

Brooklands Guest House

★★★★★ 🏠 GUEST HOUSE

tel: 01768 863395 **fax:** 01768 863395 **2 Portland Place CA11 7QN**
email: enquiries@brooklandsguesthouse.com **web:** www.brooklandsguesthouse.com
dir: *M6 junct 40, follow sign for TIC, left at town hall, 50yds on left*

In the bustling market town of Penrith, this beautifully appointed house offers individually furnished bedrooms with high quality accessories and some luxury touches. Nothing seems to be too much trouble for the friendly owners and, from romantic breaks to excellent storage for cyclists, all guests are very well looked after. Delicious breakfasts featuring Cumbrian produce are served in the attractive dining room.

Rooms 6 en suite (1 fmly) S £40–£70; D £80–£90 **Facilities** FTV DVD iPod docking station tea/coffee WiFi ⚓ **Extras** Speciality toiletries, fresh fruit **Parking** 2 **Notes** LB ⊗ Closed 24 Dec-4 Jan

---

AA FRIENDLIEST B&B OF THE YEAR 2014–2015

Premier Collection

River Garth

★★★★★ GUEST HOUSE

tel: 01768 863938 & 07718 763273 **Eamont Bridge CA10 2BH**
email: rivergarth@hotmail.co.uk **web:** www.rivergarth.co.uk
dir: *M6 junct 40, A66 E towards Scotch Corner. At rdbt 4th exit to Shap, 150yds over bridge & continue for 200yds, turn right at "Keep Clear" road marking. Last bungalow facing river*

The River Garth is in an elevated position overlooking the River Eamont. Spacious and well-presented bedrooms cater well for the needs of the guest, and two of them have balconies looking out on the river. The lounge dining room is comfortable and breakfast uses the finest local produce. Read an interview with Irene Nixon, landlady of River Garth, on page 17.

Rooms 3 en suite (1 fmly) S £55–£60; D £70–£85* **Facilities** STV FTV TVL tea/coffee WiFi ⚓ **Extras** Speciality toiletries, bottled water, sweets - free of charge **Parking** 6 **Notes** LB ⊗ 🐾

Albany House

★★★★ 🏠 GUEST HOUSE

tel: 01768 863072 **5 Portland Place CA11 7QN**
email: info@albany-house.org.uk **web:** www.albany-house.org.uk
dir: *Left at town hall into Portland Place. 30yds on left*

A well-maintained Victorian house which has been completely refurbished by the present owners, Albany House is close to Penrith town centre. Bedrooms are comfortable and thoughtfully equipped. Wholesome breakfasts using local ingredients are served in the attractive breakfast room. Good quality dinners are served at the weekend advance bookings are a necessity.

Rooms 5 rms (3 en suite) (2 pri facs) (1 fmly) D £70-£75 **Facilities** FTV tea/coffee Dinner available WiFi 🔒 **Extras** Speciality toiletries, bottled water, chocolates **Notes** LB ⊗

Brandelhow Guest House

★★★★ 🏠 GUEST HOUSE

tel: 01768 864470 **1 Portland Place CA11 7QN**
email: enquiries@brandelhowguesthouse.co.uk **web:** www.brandelhowguesthouse.co.uk
dir: In town centre on one-way system, left at town hall

Situated within easy walking distance of central amenities, this friendly guest house is also convenient for the Lakes and M6. The bedrooms are thoughtfully furnished and some are suitable for families. Breakfasts, utilising quality local produce, are served in a Cumbria-themed dining room overlooking the pretty courtyard garden. Afternoon and high teas are available by arrangement.

Rooms 5 rms (4 en suite) (1 pri facs) (2 fmly) **Facilities** FTV tea/coffee WiFi **Notes** ⊗ Closed 31 Dec & 1 Jan

Acorn Guest House

★★★★ GUEST HOUSE

tel: 01768 868696 **fax:** 08721 135465 **Scotland Rd CA11 9HL**
email: acornguesthouse@fsmail.net **web:** www.acorn-guesthouse.co.uk

Located within easy walking distance of the town centre, Acorn Guest House is ideal for walkers and cyclists as well as guests using Penrith as their base to tour the area. Bedrooms are en suite and are all well presented and spacious. Breakfast makes good use of quality local produce whilst dinners are available by prior arrangement. A small bar, along with drying facilities, is also available.

Rooms 7 en suite (2 fmly) S £38-£55; D £76-£100* **Facilities** FTV TVL tea/coffee Licensed WiFi 🔒 **Conf** Max 20 Thtr 12 Class 18 Board 20 **Parking** 8 **Notes** ⊗

Glendale Guest House

★★★★ GUEST HOUSE

tel: 01768 210061 **4 Portland Place CA11 7QN**
email: glendaleguesthouse@yahoo.co.uk **web:** www.glendaleguesthouse.com
dir: M6 junct 40, follow town centre signs. Pass castle, turn left before town hall

This friendly, family-run guest house is part of a Victorian terrace only a stroll from the town centre and convenient for the lakes and Eden Valley. Drying facilities are available. Bedrooms vary in size, but all are attractive, well equipped and well presented. Hearty breakfasts are served at individual tables in the charming ground-floor dining room.

Rooms 7 en suite (3 fmly) **Facilities** FTV tea/coffee WiFi

Sockbridge Mill Bed and Breakfast

★★★★ BED AND BREAKFAST

tel: 01768 895850 & 07734 886196 **Sockbridge CA10 2JT**
email: debbyakam@yahoo.co.uk **web:** www.sockbridgemill.com
dir: M6 junct 40, then A6 towards Shap. Onto B5320 signed Sockbridge/Tirril. In village, take lane towards River Eamont

A long narrow lane leads to Sockbridge Mill, a converted 18th-century watermill where peace and tranquillity are the order of the day. Many original features remain including wooden beams, and hardwood and slate floors. The guest experience is enhanced by a wonderful cooked breakfast. Guests should note that inside the property is a no-shoe zone but slippers can be provided if needed.

Rooms 2 rms (1 en suite) (1 pri facs) S £75; D £85* **Facilities** TVL tea/coffee WiFi 🔒 **Parking** 3 **Notes** Closed 23-27 Dec ⊛

RAVENSTONEDALE   Map 18 NY70

The Black Swan

★★★★ 🏠 🍴 INN

tel: 015396 23204 **fax:** 015396 23204 **CA17 4NG**
email: enquiries@blackswanhotel.com **web:** www.blackswanhotel.com
dir: M6 junct 38. Black Swan on A685, W of Kirkby Stephen

Set in the heart of this quiet village, the inn is popular with visitors and locals and offers a very friendly welcome. Bedrooms are individually styled and comfortably equipped. There is an informal atmosphere in the bar areas and home-made meals can be taken in the bar or the stylish dining room. Relax by the fire in the cooler months and enjoy the riverside garden in the summer.

Rooms 10 en suite 5 annexe en suite (3 fmly) (3 GF) S £65-£130; D £80-£130* **Facilities** FTV iPod docking station Lounge tea/coffee Dinner available WiFi ch fac 🏊 ⛳ 9 Fishing Riding Snooker 🔒 **Extras** Speciality toiletries, snacks, water, robes **Conf** Max 14 Thtr 14 Class 14 Board 14 **Parking** 20 **Notes** LB

The Fat Lamb

★★★★ INN

tel: 015396 23242 **fax:** 015396 23285 **Crossbank CA17 4LL**
email: enquiries@fatlamb.co.uk **web:** www.fatlamb.co.uk
dir: On A683, between Kirkby Stephen & Sedbergh

Solid stone walls and open fires feature at this 17th-century inn. The bedrooms are comfortable and all are en suite. An accessible ground-floor room with en suite wet room is available. Guests can enjoy a choice of dining options: well-cooked dishes using local produce are served in either the traditional bar or the more formal dining room. There is also a beer garden.

Rooms 12 en suite (4 fmly) (5 GF) S £56-£62; D £96-£104* **Facilities** Lounge TVL tea/coffee Dinner available WiFi ⛳ 18 🔒 Private 5-acre nature reserve **Conf** Thtr 60 Class 30 Board 30 **Parking** 60 **Notes** LB

RYDAL

See Ambleside

SEDBERGH   Map 18 SD69

The Garsdale Bed and Breakfast

★★★★ 🏠 BED AND BREAKFAST

tel: 01969 667096 & 07853 848116 **Garsdale House LA10 5PU**
email: stay@thegarsdale.com **web:** www.thegarsdale.com
dir: On A684, close to junct with B6259

On arrival at The Garsdale you'll be welcomed with complimentary tea or coffee and offered help with your luggage. The B&B is joined to the owners' home but has its own separate entrance, giving guests privacy and the freedom to come and go as they please. Bedrooms are air-conditioned, have HD-TVs, luxury Egyptian cotton bath robes, guest slippers, en suites with power showers, fridge, and free WiFi. There is a small licensed bar in the dining area, and evening meals are available if ordered in advance. The area is ideal for walkers, and a free taxi service is available to and from the local train station.

Rooms 3 en suite (1 fmly) (1 GF) **Facilities** STV DVD TVL tea/coffee Dinner available Licensed WiFi ch fac 🔒 **Extras** Robes, slippers **Parking** 6

SHAP
Map 18 NY51

Brookfield Guest House

★★★★ GUEST HOUSE

tel: 01931 716397 **fax:** 01931 716397 **CA10 3PZ**
email: info@brookfieldshap.co.uk **web:** www.brookfieldshap.co.uk
dir: *M6 junct 39, A6 towards Shap, 1st accommodation off motorway, on right*

In a quiet rural location within easy reach of the M6, inviting Brookfield Guest House stands in well-tended, attractive gardens. Bedrooms are thoughtfully appointed and well maintained. There is a comfortable lounge, and a small bar area next to the traditional dining room where substantial, home-cooked breakfasts are served at individual tables.

Rooms 4 rms (3 en suite) (1 pri facs) **Facilities** FTV TVL tea/coffee Licensed WiFi
Parking 20 **Notes** ⊗ No Children 12yrs Closed Nov-1 Mar ⊜

TEMPLE SOWERBY
Map 18 NY62

The Kings Arms

★★★★ ⊜ INN

tel: 017683 62944 **CA10 1SB**
email: enquiries@kingsarmstemplesowerby.co.uk
web: www.kingsarmstemplesowerby.co.uk
dir: *M6 junct 40, E on A66 to Temple Sowerby, Kings Arms in village*

The Kings Arms is located in the peaceful village of Temple Sowerby, just a couple of minutes from the A66 bypass and a short drive from Centre Parcs. The property dates back over 400 years and offers a good deal of charm and character. Quality food is served in the small restaurant or in the bar itself which has an open fire. Comfortable, well-appointed accommodation makes this an ideal base for touring this delightful area.

Rooms 8 en suite (5 fmly) S £60-£70; D £80-£120* **Facilities** FTV Lounge tea/coffee Dinner available WiFi Fishing **Parking** 20 **Notes** LB

Skygarth Farm *(NY612261)*

★★★ FARMHOUSE

tel: 017683 61300 **CA10 1SS**
email: skygarth@outlook.com **web:** www.skygarth.co.uk
dir: *Off A66 at Temple Sowerby for Morland, Skygarth 500yds on right, follow signs*

Skygarth is just south of the village, half a mile from the busy main road. The house stands in a cobbled courtyard surrounded by cowsheds, with gardens to the rear, where red squirrels feed. There are two well-proportioned bedrooms and an attractive lounge where tasty breakfasts are served.

Rooms 2 rms (2 fmly) S £35-£42; D £55-£62* **Facilities** FTV TVL tea/coffee WiFi
Extras Bottled water, biscuits - complimentary; robes **Parking** 4 **Notes** ⊗ Closed Dec-Jan ⊜ 200 acres mixed

TROUTBECK (NEAR WINDERMERE)
Map 18 NY40

Premier Collection

Broadoaks Country House

★★★★★ ⊜ GUEST ACCOMMODATION

tel: 015394 45566 **fax:** 015394 88766 **Bridge Ln LA23 1LA**
email: enquiries@broadoakscountryhouse.co.uk **web:** www.broadoakscountryhouse.co.uk
dir: *Exit A591 junct 36 pass Windermere. Filing station on left, 1st right 0.5m*

This impressive Lakeland stone house has been restored to its original Victorian grandeur and is set in seven acres of landscaped grounds with stunning views of the Troutbeck Valley. Individually furnished bedrooms are well appointed and en suite bathrooms feature either whirlpool or Victorian roll top baths. Spacious day rooms include the music room, featuring a Bechstein piano. Meals are served by friendly and attentive staff in the elegant dining room.

Rooms 11 en suite 8 annexe en suite (8 fmly) (7 GF) **Facilities** STV FTV DVD iPod docking station tea/coffee Dinner available Direct Dial Licensed WiFi Fishing Arrangement with local leisure facility **Extras** Speciality toiletries **Conf** Max 62 Thtr 40 Class 45 Board 45 **Parking** 40 **Notes** LB Civ Wed 100

The Queen's Head

★★★★ ⊜ INN

tel: 015394 32174 **fax:** 015394 31938 **Townhead LA23 1PW**
email: reservations@queensheadtroutbeck.co.uk **web:** www.queensheadtroutbeck.co.uk
dir: *M6 junct 36 onto A591, past Windermere towards Ambleside. At mini rdbt, right onto A592 for Ullswater, 3m on left*

This 17th-century coaching inn has stunning views of the Troutbeck Valley. The delightful bedrooms, several with four-poster beds, are traditionally furnished and equipped with modern facilities. Beams, flagstone floors, and a bar that was once an Elizabethan four-poster, provide a wonderful setting in which to enjoy imaginative food, real ales and fine wines.

Rooms 10 en suite 5 annexe en suite (1 fmly) (2 GF) S £100; D £150 (room only)* **Facilities** FTV tea/coffee Dinner available WiFi **Conf** Max 30 **Parking** 65 **Notes** LB RS 25 Dec pre-booked lunch only & 31 Dec pre-booked dinner only

WASDALE HEAD
Map 18 NY10

Wasdale Head Inn

★★★★ INN

tel: 019467 26229 & 26333 **CA20 1EX**
email: reception@wasdale.com **web:** www.wasdale.com
dir: *Leave A595 at Santon Bridge or Gosforth if travelling S. Follow signs for Wasdale*

Wasdale Head is known as the birthplace of British climbing for good reason. The setting of this popular inn is breathtaking, surrounded by the fells with the brooding West Water close by. Inside, the decor is enhanced with objets d'art and photos of climbers and mountains. Bedrooms and public areas are comfortable, and the service is relaxed and informal. Real ales and good food are served in the rustic bar while a separate restaurant is available for residents.

Rooms 11 en suite 9 annexe en suite (2 fmly) (3 GF) **Facilities** FTV Lounge tea/coffee Dinner available Direct Dial WiFi **Extras** Bath salts, robes - complimentary **Conf** Max 20 Thtr 20 Class 20 Board 20 **Parking** 30 **Notes** LB No coaches

WHITEHAVEN — Map 18 NX91

Glenfield Guest House
★★★★ GUEST HOUSE

tel: 01946 691911 & 07810 632890 **Back Corkickle CA28 7TS**
email: glenfieldgh@gmail.com web: www.glenfield-whitehaven.co.uk
dir: *0.5m SE of town centre on A5094*

The imposing, family-run Victorian house is in a conservation area close to the historic town centre and harbour. Margaret and Andrew provide a relaxed environment with friendly but unobtrusive service, and this is a good start point for the Sea to Sea (C2C) cycle ride.

Rooms 6 en suite (2 fmly) S £50; D £80* **Facilities** FTV DVD Lounge tea/coffee Dinner available Licensed WiFi 🔒 **Notes** ⊗

WINDERMERE — Map 18 SD49

Premier Collection

The Howbeck
★★★★★ GUEST HOUSE

tel: 015394 44739 **New Rd LA23 2LA**
email: relax@howbeck.co.uk web: www.howbeck.co.uk
dir: *A591 through Windermere town centre, left towards Bowness*

The Howbeck is a delightful Victorian villa, convenient for the village and the lake. Bedrooms are well appointed and feature lovely soft furnishings, along with luxurious spa baths in some cases. There is a bright lounge with internet access and an attractive dining room where home-prepared hearty Cumbrian breakfasts are served at individual tables.

Rooms 10 en suite 1 annexe en suite (3 GF) **Facilities** STV FTV TVL tea/coffee Dinner available Licensed WiFi Free membership to spa & leisure club 0.5m **Parking** 12 **Notes** ⊗ Closed 24-25 Dec

Premier Collection

Windermere Suites
★★★★★ BED AND BREAKFAST

tel: 015394 47672 & 43356 **New Rd LA23 2LA**
email: reservations@windermeresuites.co.uk web: www.windermeresuites.co.uk
dir: *Through village on one-way system towards Bowness-on-Windermere. 50mtrs past The Ellerthwaite*

Close to Windermere and Bowness, Windermere Suites is a very special boutique town house which offers eight individual suites, all combining contemporary designer furniture with cutting edge entertainment technology and sheer elegance. Each suite has its own lounge area, and the bathrooms have large spa baths complete with TV, mood lighting and power showers. Rooms also have mini-bars, and room service is available up to 10pm. An unusual feature is the "living showroom" element, if you like an item of furniture or decoration you can order it to buy at a discount.

Rooms 8 en suite (3 GF) **Facilities** STV FTV DVD iPod docking station TVL tea/coffee Licensed WiFi Free use of spa & leisure club 0.5m **Extras** Mini-bar, safe **Parking** 9 **Notes** ⊗

Premier Collection

Applegarth Villa & Restaurant
★★★★★ GUEST ACCOMMODATION

tel: 015394 43206 **fax:** 015394 46636 **College Rd LA23 1BU**
email: info@lakesapplegarth.co.uk web: www.lakesapplegarth.co.uk
dir: *M6 junct 36, A591 towards Windermere. On entering town left after NatWest Bank into Elleray Rd. 1st right into College Rd, Applegarth on right*

This period building set in the heart of Windermere, offers elegantly furnished accommodation with luxurious bathrooms. The attractive conservatory dining room offers stunning views of the mountains and serves locally sourced produce. The oak-panelled bar has an open fire and is a perfect retreat on a winter evening. Private off-road parking and spa facilities are a bonus.

Rooms 15 en suite S £70-£160; D £100-£310* **Facilities** FTV iPod docking station Lounge tea/coffee Dinner available Direct Dial Licensed WiFi 🔒 Complimentary leisure facilities at nearby hotel **Extras** Speciality toiletries, bottled water - free **Parking** 16 **Notes** LB ⊗ No Children 18yrs

Premier Collection

Dome House
★★★★★ BED AND BREAKFAST

tel: 015394 47244 **Brantfell Rd, Bowness LA23 3AE**
email: domehouse@rocketmail.com web: www.domehouselakedistrict.co.uk

Featured on Channel 4's *Grand Designs*, Dome House is ecologically sympathetic, showcases modern design ideas, and provides very comfortable accommodation. The boutique suites offer panoramic lake views, private outdoor seating, and a wealth of modern amenities. A welcome hamper filled with local and organic goodies provides all you need to enjoy a healthy breakfast in your room. The Dome is a Runner-up in the AA Funkiest B&B of the Year 2014-2015.

Rooms 5 en suite

Premier Collection

Oakbank House
★★★★★ GUEST HOUSE

tel: 015394 43386 **Helm Rd LA23 3BU**
email: info@oakbankhouse.co.uk web: www.oakbankhouse.co.uk
dir: *Exit A591 through town centre into Bowness. Helm Rd 100yds on left after cinema*

Oakbank House is just off the main street in Bowness village, overlooking Windermere and the fells beyond. Bedrooms are individually styled, attractive and very well equipped; most have stunning lake views. There is an elegant lounge with a perpetual coffee pot, and delicious breakfasts are served at individual tables in the dining room.

Rooms 12 rms (11 en suite) (1 pri facs) (3 GF) S £75-£115; D £80-£120 **Facilities** FTV Lounge tea/coffee WiFi Free membership of local country club **Extras** Speciality toiletries **Parking** 14 **Notes** LB ⊗ RS 20-26 Dec

WINDERMERE *continued*

The Woodlands

★★★★★ GUEST HOUSE

tel: 015394 43915 **fax:** 015394 43915 **New Rd LA23 2EE**
email: enquiries@woodlands-windermere.co.uk
web: www.woodlands-windermere.co.uk
dir: *One-way system through town down New Rd towards lake, premises by war memorial clock*

Guests can expect stylish accommodation and friendly, attentive service at The Woodlands, just a short walk from Lake Windermere. Bedrooms (including two contemporary four-poster rooms) have been individually decorated and feature quality furnishings and accessories, such as flat-screen TVs. Guests are welcome to relax in the comfortable lounge where there is also a well-stocked bar offering beers, wine, champagnes and rich Italian coffees. A wide choice is offered at breakfast, served in the spacious dining room.

Rooms 14 en suite (2 fmly) (3 GF) **Facilities** tea/coffee Dinner available Licensed Free facilities at local leisure/sports club **Parking** 17

The Cottage

★★★★ ▩ GUEST ACCOMMODATION

tel: 015394 44796 **Elleray Rd LA23 1AG**
email: enquiries@thecottageguesthouse.com **web:** www.thecottageguesthouse.com
dir: *A591, past Windermere Hotel, in 150yds left into Elleray Rd. The Cottage 150yds on left*

Built in 1847, this attractive house is one of the oldest in Windermere and offers a blend of modern and traditional styles. The tastefully furnished bedrooms are well equipped and comfortable. A wide choice of freshly cooked breakfasts is served in the spacious dining room at individual tables.

Rooms 8 en suite (2 GF) S £30-£48; D £60-£100* **Facilities** FTV DVD tea/coffee **Parking** 8 **Notes** ⊗ No Children 11yrs Closed Nov-Jan

Dene House

★★★★ GUEST ACCOMMODATION

tel: 015394 48236 **fax:** 08721 153685 **Kendal Rd LA23 3EW**
email: denehouse@ignetics.co.uk **web:** www.denehouse-guesthouse.co.uk
dir: *From Lake Rd, turn opposite St Martins Church into Kendal Rd. 400yds on right*

Detached property situated on the edge of the village a short walk from pubs, restaurants and Lake Windermere. Bedrooms are individually furnished and tastefully decorated, one room is situated on the ground floor offering ease of access; facilities include wine chillers, iPod docking stations and WiFi. Breakfast is served at individual tables in the smart dining room and the property has a beautiful terrace garden.

Rooms 7 rms (6 en suite) (1 pri facs) (1 GF) **Facilities** FTV iPod docking station tea/coffee WiFi Gym Use of pool at nearby hotel - charged **Parking** 7 **Notes** LB ⊗ No Children 12yrs

Fairfield House and Gardens

★★★★ ▩ GUEST HOUSE

tel: 015394 46565 **fax:** 015394 46564 **Brantfell Rd, Bowness-on-Windermere LA23 3AE**
email: tonyandliz@the-fairfield.co.uk **web:** www.the-fairfield.co.uk
dir: *Into Bowness town centre, turn opposite St Martin's Church & sharp left by Spinnery restaurant, house 200mtrs on right*

Situated just above Bowness and Lake Windermere, this Lakeland country house is tucked away in a half acre of secluded, peaceful gardens. The house has been beautifully appointed to combine Georgian and Victorian features with stylish, contemporary design. Guests are shown warm hospitality and can relax in the delightful lounge. Bedrooms are well furnished, varying in size and style with some featuring luxurious bathrooms. Delicious breakfasts are served in the attractive dining room or on the terrace in warmer weather.

Rooms 10 en suite (1 fmly) (1 GF) **Facilities** FTV DVD Lounge tea/coffee Licensed WiFi 🛝 ⚓ 18 ⚓ **Conf** Max 20 Thtr 20 Class 10 Board 12 **Parking** 10 **Notes** No Children 10yrs

The Hideaway at Windermere

★★★★ GUEST ACCOMMODATION

tel: 015394 43070 **Phoenix Way LA23 1DB**
email: eatandstay@thehideawayatwindermere.co.uk
web: www.thehideawayatwindermere.co.uk
dir: Exit A591 at Ravensworth B&B, into Phoenix Way, The Hideaway 100mtrs on right

Quietly tucked away, this beautiful Victorian Lakeland house is personally run by owners Richard and Lisa. Delicious food, individually designed bedrooms and warm hospitality ensure an enjoyable stay. There is a beautifully appointed lounge looking out to the garden, and the dining area is split between two light and airy rooms. Breakfast is freshly prepared using the best local ingredients and service is attentive and friendly. Bedrooms vary in size and style; the larger rooms feature luxury bathrooms. Tea and home-made cake is included and served each day.

Rooms 10 en suite 1 annexe en suite S £70-£110; D £70-£180* **Facilities** FTV Lounge tea/coffee Direct Dial Licensed WiFi 🛁 Off-site spa facilities available **Parking** 15 **Notes** LB ⊗ No Children 12yrs Closed Jan-mid Feb

Holly-Wood Guest House

★★★★ GUEST HOUSE

tel: 015394 42219 **Holly Rd LA23 2AF**
email: info@hollywoodguesthouse.co.uk **web:** www.hollywoodguesthouse.co.uk
dir: M6 junct 36 left onto A590 signed Kendal then A591 towards Windermere, left into town, left again into Ellerthwaite Rd, next left into Holly Rd

This attractive Victorian end terrace is located in a quiet residential area just a few minutes' walk from Windermere town centre. Guests are offered a friendly welcome, comfortable, well equipped bedrooms and a freshly prepared breakfast. Limited off-street parking is also available.

Rooms 6 en suite (1 fmly) S £37.50-£42.50; D £65-£85* **Facilities** FTV iPod docking station tea/coffee WiFi 🛁 **Extras** Speciality toiletries, home-made snacks **Parking** 3 **Notes** ⊗ No Children 10yrs Closed 23-27 Dec

Rockside Guest House

★★★★ 🛏 GUEST HOUSE

tel: 015394 45343 **25 Church St LA23 1AQ**
email: enquiries@rockside-guesthouse.co.uk

Rockside Guest House was built in 1847 from Lakeland stone, and is owner-managed by Martin and Caroline. They have modernised the building to provide all mod cons, yet retained many of the original features. Situated at the head of the village, Rockside is a two minute walk from local transport links, restaurants, pubs and shops, and only 20 minutes' walk from Lake Windermere. Breakfast offers a range of options for all tastes, from a substantial full breakfast to lighter bites and vegetarian alternatives, all prepared with quality local produce and served with home-made marmalade and jams.

Rooms 9 en suite **Facilities** FTV tea/coffee WiFi **Parking** 9 **Notes** ⊗ No Children 14yrs

The Wild Boar Inn, Grill & Smokehouse

★★★★ INN

tel: 015394 45225 **fax:** 015394 42498 **Crook LA23 3NF**
email: thewildboar@englishlakes.co.uk **web:** www.thewildboarinn.co.uk
dir: 2.5m S of Windermere on B5284. From Crook 3.5m, on right

Steeped in history, this former coaching inn enjoys a peaceful rural location close to Windermere. Public areas include a welcoming lounge and a cosy bar where an extensive choice of wines, ales and whiskies are served. The Grill & Smokehouse features quality local and seasonal ingredients. Bedrooms, some with four-poster beds, vary in style and size. Leisure facilities are available close by.

Rooms 33 en suite (2 fmly) (9 GF) S £78-£120; D £96-£160* **Facilities** FTV tea/coffee Dinner available Direct Dial WiFi Use of leisure facilities at sister hotel **Conf** Thtr 40 Class 10 Board 20 **Parking** 60 **Notes** LB

Blenheim Lodge

★★★★ GUEST ACCOMMODATION

tel: 015394 43440 **Brantfell Rd, Bowness-on-Windermere LA23 3AE**
email: enquiries@blenheim-lodge.com **web:** www.blenheim-lodge.com
dir: From Windermere to Bowness village, left at mini rdbt, next 2 lefts, then up to top of Brantfell Rd & turn right

From a peaceful position above the town of Bowness, Blenheim Lodge has stunning panoramic views of Lake Windermere. Bedrooms are well equipped featuring antique furnishings and pocket-sprung mattresses. Most beds are antiques themselves and include two William IV four-posters and three Louis XV examples. There is a comfortable lounge and a beautifully decorated dining room.

Rooms 11 rms (10 en suite) (1 pri facs) (2 fmly) (2 GF) S £60-£64; D £88-£152* **Facilities** FTV TVL tea/coffee Licensed WiFi 🛁 Free fishing permits & c-club membership **Parking** 11 **Notes** LB ⊗ Closed 25 Dec RS 24-27 Dec may open, phone for details

Cambridge House

★★★★ GUEST HOUSE

tel: 015394 43846 & 07553 345943 **9 Oak St LA23 1EN**
email: d.lupton@btconnect.com **web:** www.cambridgehousewindermere.co.uk

Located in the heart of Windermere this comfortable and friendly guest house offers a warm welcome and modern accommodation close to transport links and local amenities. A hearty breakfast uses local produce, and complimentary leisure facilities are available to guests staying two nights or more.

Rooms 6 en suite (1 fmly) (1 GF) S £45-£75; D £70-£95 **Facilities** STV DVD iPod docking station tea/coffee WiFi **Notes** LB ⊗ No Children 8yrs

WINDERMERE *continued*

The Coach House

★★★★ GUEST ACCOMMODATION

tel: 015394 44494 **Lake Rd LA23 2EQ**
email: enquiries@lakedistrictbandb.com **web:** www.lakedistrictbandb.com
dir: *A591 to Windermere, house 0.5m on right opposite St Herbert's Church*

Expect a relaxed and welcoming atmosphere at this stylish house, which has a minimalist interior with bright decor and cosmopolitan furnishings. Well equipped bedrooms are individually decorated in bright colours, keeping a cottage feel. There is a reception lounge, and a breakfast room where freshly prepared breakfasts feature the best of local produce.

Rooms 5 en suite D £60-£85* **Facilities** FTV iPod docking station tea/coffee WiFi 🛁 Use of local health & leisure club **Parking** 5 **Notes** LB ⊗ No Children 12yrs Closed 24-26 Dec

The Coppice

★★★★ 🛌 GUEST HOUSE

tel: 015394 88501 **fax:** 015394 42148 **Brook Rd LA23 2ED**
email: chris@thecoppice.co.uk **web:** www.thecoppice.co.uk
dir: *0.25m S of village centre on A5074*

This attractive detached old vicarage lies between Windermere and Bowness. There are brightly decorated public rooms and bedrooms, and breakfast is served in the delightful dining room. On offer is an excellent choice including a full Lakeland breakfast, a vegetarian choice, kippers, smoked salmon, and more. The bedrooms vary in size and style and have good facilities, some including in-room baths and mood lighting.

Rooms 9 en suite (1 GF) **Facilities** DVD Lounge tea/coffee Licensed WiFi Private leisure club membership **Extras** Sherry **Parking** 9 **Notes** LB No Children 12yrs

Fir Trees

★★★★ GUEST HOUSE

tel: 015394 42272 **fax:** 015394 42512 **Lake Rd LA23 2EQ**
email: enquiries@fir-trees.co.uk **web:** www.fir-trees.co.uk
dir: *Exit A591 through town, Lake Rd in 0.5m, Fir Trees on left after clock tower*

Located halfway between Windermere town and the lake, this spacious Victorian house offers attractive and well equipped accommodation. Bedrooms are generously proportioned and have many thoughtful extra touches. Breakfasts, featuring the best of local produce, are served at individual tables in the smart dining room.

Rooms 9 en suite (2 fmly) (3 GF) S £55-£60; D £68-£76* **Facilities** FTV tea/coffee WiFi Fishing 🛁 **Parking** 9 **Notes** LB ⊗ No Children 5yrs

Glencree

★★★★ GUEST HOUSE

tel: 015394 45822 & 07974 697114 **fax:** 05603 420040 **Lake Rd LA23 2EQ**
email: h.butterworth@btinternet.com **web:** www.glencreelakes.co.uk
dir: *From town centre signs for Bowness & The Lake, Glencree on right after large wooded area on right*

Colourful hanging baskets and floral displays adorn the car park and entrance to Glencree, which lies between Windermere and Bowness. Bedrooms are brightly decorated and individually furnished. The attractive lounge, with an honesty bar, is next to the dining room, where breakfasts are served at individual tables.

Rooms 6 en suite (1 fmly) (1 GF) S £60-£80; D £70-£90* **Facilities** FTV TVL tea/coffee Licensed WiFi 🛁 **Parking** 6 **Notes** LB ⊗ No Children 6yrs

Glenville House

★★★★ GUEST HOUSE

tel: 015394 43371 **fax:** 015394 48457 **Lake Rd LA23 2EQ**
email: mail@glenvillehouse.co.uk **web:** www.glenvillehouse.co.uk
dir: *At Windermere station/tourist info centre, turn left into village. Straight through, on right opposite vets*

Glenville House is very conveniently located in a pleasant area, and good parking is a bonus. The house is well appointed and the bedrooms have comfortable beds and many accessories to make your stay relaxing and enjoyable. The friendly proprietors make guests welcome, and breakfast is taken in a pleasant room at individual tables.

Rooms 7 en suite S £60-£110; D £65-£120* **Parking** 7 **Notes** LB No Children 18yrs Closed 6-30 Dec

The Haven

★★★★ BED AND BREAKFAST

tel: 015394 44017 **10 Birch St LA23 1EG**
email: stay@thehavenwindermere.co.uk **web:** www.thehavenwindermere.co.uk
dir: *On A5074 enter one-way system, 3rd left into Birch St*

Built from Lakeland slate and stone, The Haven is just a stroll from the town centre and shops. The bright, spacious bedrooms offer en suite facilities, and one has a Victorian brass bed. A hearty Cumbrian breakfast is served in the well-appointed dining room that doubles as a lounge.

Rooms 3 en suite (1 fmly) S £67-£76; D £70-£85* **Facilities** FTV DVD Lounge tea/coffee WiFi 🛁 **Parking** 3 **Notes** LB ⊗ No Children 7yrs

The Old Court House

★★★★ GUEST HOUSE

tel: 015394 45096 **Lake Rd LA23 3AP**
email: alison@theoch.co.uk **web:** www.theoch.co.uk
dir: *On Windermere-Bowness road at junct Longlands Rd*

Guests are given a warm welcome at this attractive former Victorian police station and courthouse, located in the centre of Bowness. Comfortable, pine-furnished bedrooms offer a good range of extra facilities. Freshly prepared breakfasts are served in the bright ground-floor dining room.

Rooms 6 en suite (2 GF) S £40-£70; D £65-£85* **Facilities** tea/coffee WiFi **Parking** 6 **Notes** LB ⊗ No Children 10yrs

Brook House

★★★ GUEST HOUSE

tel: 015394 44932 **30 Ellerthwaite Rd LA23 2AH**
email: stay@brookhouselakes.co.uk **web:** www.brookhouselakes.co.uk
dir: *M6 junct 36, A591, through one-way system. Ellerthwaite Rd 2nd left, 200yds on right*

Brook House is a Lakeland stone Victorian guest house set in a quiet part of Windermere and offers a very relaxed friendly atmosphere. Accessible with or without a car and close to all amenities, it is a perfect base for exploring the Lake District. Bedrooms include a family room and a single. Private parking and a guest lounge are also available. 'Whisky Warmer' weekends are run throughout the winter.

Rooms 5 en suite (1 fmly) S £35; D £60* **Facilities** FTV Lounge tea/coffee WiFi **Extras** Speciality toiletries - complimentary **Parking** 5 **Notes** ⊗ No Children 8yrs

Adam Place Guest House

★★★ GUEST HOUSE

tel: 015394 44600 & 07879 640757 **fax:** 015394 44600 **1 Park Av LA23 2AR**
email: adamplacewindermere@yahoo.co.uk **web:** www.adamplacelakedistrict.co.uk
dir: *Exit A591 into Windermere, through town centre, left into Ellerthwaite Rd & Park Av*

Located in a mainly residential area within easy walking distance of lake and town centre, this stone-built Victorian house has been renovated to provide comfortable and homely bedrooms. Comprehensive breakfasts are served in the cosy dining room and there is a pretty patio garden.

Rooms 5 en suite (2 fmly) S £30-£50; D £50-£75* **Facilities** FTV DVD tea/coffee WiFi 🔒 **Notes** LB ⊗ No Children 6yrs

Bonny Brae Guest House

★★★ GUEST HOUSE

tel: 015394 22699 & 07765 778046 **fax:** 015394 22699
West Beck, 11 Oak St LA23 1EN
email: stay@bonnybraewindermere.com **web:** www.bonnybraewindermere.com

A warm and genuine welcome awaits you at Bonny Brae, situated in the heart of Windermere village, just a short walk from cafés, shops and travel links. Accommodation is comfortable, and breakfast makes good use of local produce.

Rooms 5 en suite (1 fmly) S £40-£50; D £70-£85 **Facilities** FTV DVD iPod docking station tea/coffee WiFi 🔒 **Notes** ⊗ No Children 7yrs

Ellerdene Guesthouse

★★★ GUEST HOUSE

tel: 015394 43610 **12 Ellerthwaite Rd LA23 2AH**
web: www.ellerdene.co.uk
dir: *M6 junct 36 follow signs for Kendal then Windermere (A591). Follow one-way system, take 2nd left after pedestrian crossing into Ellerthwaite Rd. On right opposite Holly Rd*

Ellerdene is a welcoming guest house situated in the heart of Windermere, perfectly situated for all local amenities. Accommodation features modern, stylishly designed rooms which are comfortable and thoughtfully equipped. Expect a generous, freshly cooked breakfast served in the bright and spacious dining room.

Rooms 6 rms (5 en suite) (1 pri facs) (1 fmly) (1 GF) S £30-£45; D £60-£78* **Facilities** FTV DVD tea/coffee WiFi 🔒 **Extras** Fridge **Notes** LB No Children 6yrs Closed 27 Dec-14 Nov, 8-11 Dec, 22-27 Dec

Green Gables Guest House

★★★ GUEST HOUSE

tel: 015394 43886 **37 Broad St LA23 2AB**
email: info@greengablesguesthouse.co.uk **web:** www.greengablesguesthouse.co.uk
dir: *A591 into Windermere, 1st left after pelican crossing, opposite car park*

Aptly named, Green Gables is a friendly guest house looking onto Elleray Gardens. Just a short walk from the centre, the house is attractively furnished and offers bright, fresh and well appointed bedrooms. There is a comfortable bar-lounge, and substantial breakfasts are served in the spacious dining room.

Rooms 7 rms (4 en suite) (3 pri facs) (3 fmly) (1 GF) **Facilities** TVL tea/coffee Licensed **Notes** ⊗ Closed 23-27 Dec

WORKINGTON
Map 18 NY02

The Sleepwell Inn
★★★★ GUEST ACCOMMODATION

tel: 01900 65772 **fax:** 01900 68770 **Washington St CA14 3AX**
email: kawildwchotel@aol.com **web:** www.washingtoncentralhotelworkington.com
dir: M6 junct 40, W on A66. At bottom of Ramsay Brow left into Washington St, 300yds on left opposite church

The Sleepwell Inn offers comfortable and well-appointed accommodation and is situated just 100 metres from its sister property, the Washington Central Hotel. Guests have full use of the Washington's facilities and that is where breakfast is served. Limited off-road parking is available to the rear. Rooms differ in size and style at The Sleepwell, with some inter-connecting rooms available. A calming, natural colour scheme has been used in the bedrooms to create a chic, contemporary feel.

Rooms 24 en suite (4 fmly) (12 GF) S £50-£60; D £70 (room only) **Facilities** FTV Lounge TVL tea/coffee Dinner available Direct Dial Licensed WiFi ⅃ 18 ♨ Facilities available at Washington Central Hotel **Parking** 32 **Notes** LB ⊗ Civ Wed 300

DERBYSHIRE

ALFRETON
Map 16 SK45

Park Farm (SK370541)
★★★★ FARMHOUSE

tel: 01773 853072 & 07968 235371 **Park Ln, South Wingfield DE55 7LR**
email: parkfarm@w3z.co.uk **web:** www.parkfarmbandb.com
dir: At Ripley on A38 take A610 towards Matlock. Right onto B6013 (Higham). Left into Park Lane (signed Fritchley). Park Lane also acccessed from B5035

Located in an elevated position offering stunning views of the surrounding countryside, this working farm provides very good standards within easy reach of many local attractions. Guest accommodation, situated in a sympathetic renovation of a former milking barn, is equipped with spacious comfortable bedrooms, complemented by smart modern en suite bathrooms. The attractive ground floor dining area includes a lounge area and an adjacent kitchen for guest use, when not being used for the freshly prepared breakfasts, featuring quality locally sourced produce.

Rooms 3 en suite (1 GF) S £50-£55; D £70-£75* **Facilities** FTV DVD TVL tea/coffee WiFi **Parking** 6 **Notes** ⊗ No Children 8yrs 200 acres beef/arable

ASHBOURNE
Map 10 SK14

Compton House
★★★★ GUEST ACCOMMODATION

tel: 01335 343100 **27-31 Compton DE6 1BX**
email: jane@comptonhouse.co.uk **web:** www.comptonhouse.co.uk
dir: A52 from Derby into Ashbourne, over lights at bottom of hill, house 100yds on left opposite garage

Within easy walking distance of the central attractions, this conversion of three cottages has resulted in a house with good standards of comfort and facilities. Bedrooms are filled with homely extras and comprehensive breakfasts are served in the cottage-style dining room.

Rooms 5 en suite (2 fmly) (1 GF) **Facilities** FTV TVL tea/coffee WiFi **Parking** 6

Mercaston Hall (SK279419)
★★★★ FARMHOUSE

tel: 01335 360263 & 07836 648102 **Mercaston DE6 3BL**
email: mercastonhall@btinternet.com **web:** www.mercastonhall.com
dir: Exit A52 in Brailsford into Luke Ln, 1m, right at 1st x-rds, house 1m on right

Located in a pretty hamlet, this medieval building retains many original features. Bedrooms are homely, and additional facilities include an all-weather tennis court and a livery service. WiFi access is also available. This is a good base for visiting local stately homes, the Derwent Valley mills and Dovedale.

Rooms 3 en suite S £55; D £75* **Facilities** FTV DVD Lounge tea/coffee WiFi ⅃ Fishing ♨ **Extras** Fridge **Parking** 3 **Notes** Closed Xmas ⊛ 60 acres mixed

The Wheel House
★★★★ BED AND BREAKFAST

tel: 01335 372837 **fax:** 01335 372837 **Belper Rd, Hulland Ward DE6 3EE**
email: thewheelhouse@btinternet.com **web:** www.thewheelhouse.co.uk
dir: Between Ashbourne & Belper on A517

This comfortably furnished house is set in open countryside on the main road between Ashbourne and Belper. The bedrooms are furnished in a country style and are named after authors. A cosy lounge is available. Breakfasts are hearty, and guests can expect friendly and attentive service.

Rooms 3 en suite S £50; D £65-£75* **Facilities** FTV TVL tea/coffee WiFi ♨ **Extras** Bottled water, jar of sweets - complimentary **Parking** 5 **Notes** LB ⊗

Homesclose House
★★★ BED AND BREAKFAST

tel: 01335 324475 **DE6 2DA**
email: gilltomlinson@tiscali.co.uk **web:** www.ashbourne-town.com
dir: Off A52 into village centre

Stunning views of the surrounding countryside and manicured gardens are a feature of this beautifully maintained dormer bungalow. Bedrooms are filled with homely extras, and an attractive dining room with one family table is the setting for breakfast.

Rooms 3 rms (2 en suite) (1 fmly) (1 GF) **Facilities** FTV tea/coffee WiFi ♨ **Parking** 4 **Notes** LB Closed Dec-Jan ⊛

BAKEWELL
Map 16 SK26

Wyedale Bed & Breakfast
★★★★ BED AND BREAKFAST

tel: 01629 812845 **Wyedale House, 25 Holywell DE45 1BA**
web: www.wyedale.co.uk
dir: 500yds SE of town centre, off A6 (Haddon Rd)

Wyedale is close to the town centre and is ideally based for a relaxing stay or touring. Bedrooms, one of which is on the ground floor, are spacious and pleasantly decorated. Breakfast is served in the attractive dining room, which overlooks the rear patio.

Rooms 4 en suite (1 fmly) (1 GF) **Facilities** tea/coffee WiFi ⅃ Fishing ♨ **Parking** 4 **Notes** ⊗ Closed 31 Dec RS 24 Dec ⊛

Wyeclose

★★★ BED AND BREAKFAST

tel: 01629 813702 **5 Granby Croft DE45 1ET**
email: h.wilson@talk21.com **web:** www.wyeclosebnb.co.uk
dir: *Exit A6 (Matlock St) into Granby Rd & Granby Croft*

Located in a quiet cul-de-sac in the town centre, this Edwardian house provides thoughtfully furnished bedroom accommodation with smart modern bathrooms, and an attractive dining room, which is the setting for comprehensive breakfasts. Original family art is a feature in the ground-floor areas.

Rooms 2 rms (1 en suite) (1 pri facs) S £40; D £60* **Facilities** FTV DVD tea/coffee WiFi 🔒 **Parking** 3 **Notes** ⊗ No Children 8yrs Closed Xmas & New Year

BEELEY   Map 16 SK26

The Devonshire Arms at Beeley

★★★★★ ⑳⑳ INN

tel: 01629 733259 & 01756 718111   **fax:** 01629 734542 **Devonshire Square DE4 2NR**
email: enquiries@devonshirebeeley.co.uk **web:** www.devonshirebeeley.co.uk
dir: *B6012 towards Matlock, pass Chatsworth House. After 1.5m turn left, 2nd entrance to Beeley*

The Devonshire Arms is a picturesque country inn at the heart of village life. It offers all the charm and character of a historic hostelry with a warm and comfortable interior, full of oak beams and stone crannies, but venture inside a little further and the decor is the startlingly different; the brasserie has a contemporary bar, glass-fronted wine store and colourful furnishings. For the ultimate escape, there are four stylish cottage bedrooms.

Rooms 4 en suite 4 annexe en suite (1 fmly) (2 GF) **Facilities** STV tea/coffee Dinner available Direct Dial WiFi **Conf** Max 80 Thtr 80 Board 25 **Parking** 40 **Notes** No coaches Civ Wed 80

BELPER   Map 11 SK34

Premier Collection

Dannah Farm Country House

★★★★★ 🏠 GUEST ACCOMMODATION

tel: 01773 550273 & 550630   **fax:** 01773 550590 **Bowmans Ln, Shottle DE56 2DR**
email: slack@dannah.co.uk **web:** www.dannah.co.uk
dir: *A517 from Belper towards Ashbourne, 1.5m right into Shottle after Hanging Gate pub on right, over x-rds & right*

Part of the Chatsworth Estates at Shottle, in an elevated position with stunning views, this impressive Georgian house and its outbuildings have been renovated to provide luxurious, individually styled bedrooms. Two have private hot tubs, one has a sauna, and there is a Spa Cabin that can be booked separately. The elegant dining room is the setting for memorable breakfasts, which make use of the finest local produce.

Rooms 8 en suite (1 fmly) (2 GF) S £89-£105; D £185-£285* **Facilities** FTV DVD iPod docking station Lounge tea/coffee Licensed WiFi Sauna 🔒 Leisure cabin Hot tub **Extras** Bath robes, speciality toiletries **Parking** 20 **Notes** LB ⊗ Closed 24-26 Dec

BRADWELL   Map 16 SK18

Premier Collection

The Samuel Fox Country Inn

★★★★★ ⑳⑳ INN

tel: 01433 621562 **fax:** 01433 623770 **Stretfield Rd S33 9JT**
email: thesamuelfox@hotmail.co.uk **web:** www.samuelfox.co.uk
dir: *M1 junct 29, A617 towards Chesterfield, A619 signed Baslow & Buxton, 2nd rdbt A623 for 7m, take B6049 to Bradwell, through village on left*

Named after Bradwell's most famous son, industrial magnate Samuel Fox, who built the steelworks at Stocksbridge, The Samuel Fox Country Inn is modern and stylish yet retains its rustic charm. Bedrooms are both immaculately presented and extensively equipped, and service is highly attentive. Modern British cuisine is served in the restaurant which has breathtaking views over Bradwell.

Rooms 4 en suite S £95-£120; D £130-£180* (incl.dinner) **Facilities** FTV tea/coffee Dinner available Direct Dial WiFi 🔒 **Conf** Max 20 Thtr 12 Class 12 Board 10 **Parking** 15 **Notes** LB ⊗ Closed 2-17 Jan

BUXTON   Map 16 SK07

Premier Collection

Buxton's Victorian Guest House

★★★★★ 🏠 GUEST HOUSE

tel: 01298 78759 **3A Broad Walk SK17 6JE**
email: buxtonvictorian@btconnect.com **web:** www.buxtonvictorian.co.uk
dir: *Follow signs to Opera House, proceed to Old Hall Hotel, right into Hartington Rd, car park 100yds on right*

Standing in a prime position overlooking the Pavilion Gardens, this delightfully furnished house has an interesting Victorian style. Bedrooms are individually themed and have many thoughtful extras. A comfortable lounge is available. Excellent breakfasts are served in the Oriental breakfast room and hospitality is first class. Complimentary WiFi access is provided.

Rooms 4 en suite (1 fmly) S £60; D £86-£104* **Facilities** FTV Lounge tea/coffee WiFi ⚲ 18 Riding 🔒 **Extras** Speciality toiletries, sweets, sherry decanter **Parking** 6 **Notes** LB ⊗ No Children 4yrs Closed 22 Dec-12 Jan

Alpine Lodge Guest House

★★★★ GUEST HOUSE

tel: 01298 26155 & 07808 283408 **1 Thornsett, Hardwick Mount SK17 6PS**
email: sales@alpinelodgebuxton.co.uk **web:** http://alpinelodgebuxton.co.uk
dir: *A515 onto Hardwick St. Take right hand fork into Hardwick Mount, just past church on left*

Alpine Lodge is particularly welcoming to walkers and cyclists. It offers elegant, stylishly furnished accommodation on a tree-lined residential road close to the town centre. All rooms have en suite shower facilities or private bathrooms with large baths, separate showers and luxurious toiletries. A hospitality tray with fresh milk is provided in each room. Non-allergenic duvets and pillows are available on request, and all beds have fresh crisp cotton sheets and duvet covers. Buxton Opera House and the tranquil Pavilion Gardens are 10 minutes stroll away. The Peak District National Park and Derbyshire Dales are on the doorstep.

Rooms 5 rms (4 en suite) (1 pri facs) (1 fmly) S £38-£70; D £76-£95* **Facilities** FTV TV4B tea/coffee WiFi 🔒 **Extras** Speciality toiletries, bottled water - free **Parking** 4 **Notes** ⊗ No Children 1yr ⑳

BUXTON *continued*

Oldfield Guest House

★★★★ 🏠 GUEST HOUSE

tel: 01298 78264 **8 Macclesfield Rd SK17 9AH**
email: avril@oldfieldhousebuxton.co.uk **web:** www.oldfieldhousebuxton.co.uk
dir: *On B5059 0.5m SW of town centre*

Located within easy walking distance of the centre, Oldfield Guest House is an impressive Victorian house with some original stained-glass windows, providing spacious bedrooms with modern en suites. Comprehensive breakfasts are served in the bright dining room, and a cosy lounge is available, making this a home-from-home experience.

Rooms 5 en suite (1 GF) D £80-£90* **Facilities** FTV DVD TVL tea/coffee WiFi ♨ 18 🅿
Extras Speciality toiletries, bottled water **Parking** 7 **Notes** LB ⊗ No Children 8yrs Closed Xmas

The Church Inn

★★★★ INN

tel: 01298 85319 **Main St, Chelmorton SK17 9SL**
email: justinsatur@gmail.com **web:** www.thechurchinn.co.uk
dir: *From A6 or A515 onto A5270 signed Chelmorton. In village opposite church*

The Church Inn is set in an historic Peak District village, and opened in 1742 as an alehouse called The Blacksmith's Arms. It was renamed in 1884 and the name has stayed the same since then. It is ideally located for visiting nearby Buxton and the Peak District. Lunch and dinner are offered from a tasty menu, and are complemented by a good range of beers, wines and spirits in the bar. Breakfast is served in a dedicated breakfast room; English and continental options are on offer. There are three double bedrooms, and one twin bedroom, which is equipped with

two single beds. These are in an annexe, not above the pub. All have pine furnishings and en suite shower rooms.

Rooms 4 annexe en suite S £55-£80; D £80* **Facilities** FTV DVD tea/coffee Dinner available WiFi 🅿 **Extras** Speciality toiletries **Parking** 4 **Notes** LB

Roseleigh

★★★★ GUEST HOUSE

tel: 01298 24904 **fax:** 01298 24904 **19 Broad Walk SK17 6JR**
email: enquiries@roseleighhotel.co.uk **web:** www.roseleighhotel.co.uk
dir: *A6 to Morrisons rdbt, into Dale Rd, right at lights, 100yds left by Swan pub, down hill, right into Hartington Rd*

This elegant property has a prime location overlooking Pavilion Gardens, and the quality furnishings and decor highlight the many original features. The thoughtfully furnished bedrooms have smart modern shower rooms, and a comfortable lounge is also available.

Rooms 14 rms (12 en suite) (2 pri facs) (1 GF) S £41-£94; D £70-£94* **Facilities** FTV Lounge tea/coffee WiFi **Parking** 9 **Notes** ⊗ No Children 6yrs Closed 16 Dec-16 Jan

CASTLETON	Map 16 SK18

Innkeeper's Lodge Castleton, Peak District

★★★ INN

tel: 0845 112 6046 **Castle St S33 8WG**
email: info@innkeeperslodge.com **web:** www.innkeeperslodge.com

This property enjoys an excellent location, nestled amongst the hills of Hope Valley and surrounded by the wild moors and sheer rock edges. Dating back to the 1800s this coaching inn provides modern spacious accommodation. The welcoming lounge bar is a popular place to eat with food served all day. Free WiFi available along with on-site car parking.

Rooms 15 en suite (4 fmly) (3 GF) **Facilities** FTV tea/coffee Dinner available Direct Dial WiFi **Parking**

CHESTERFIELD   Map 16 SK37

Church Villa B&B

★★★ BED AND BREAKFAST

tel: 01246 850254 **29 Church Ln, Temple Normanton S42 5DB**
email: churchvilla@btinternet.com **web:** www.churchvilla29.co.uk
dir: *M1 junct 29 onto A617. After 2m turn to Temple Normanton. Take 3rd right signed Holmewood, right again into Birkin Ln. Next right into Church Ln, opposite church notice board*

Church Villa B&B is a charming cottage situated on the outskirts of Chesterfield, ideally placed for visiting the Peak District. It has comfortable, well-equipped bedrooms which come complete with many thoughtful extras. Breakfast and home-cooked dinners are served in the dining room, which has a 100-year old vine, and overlooks the country garden. A guest lounge is also available.

Rooms 3 en suite S £42-£60; D £62-£72* **Facilities** FTV DVD TVL tea/coffee Dinner available WiFi 🔒 **Parking** 3 **Notes** LB ⊗

Dusty Miller Inn

★★★ INN

tel: 01246 810507 **Sheffield Rd, Barlborough S43 4TW**
email: adrian.fazakerley@virgin.net **web:** www.dustymiller.co.uk
dir: *M1 junct 30, on Sheffield road*

Dusty Miller is set in the village of Barlborough, in the countryside, yet only two minutes' drive from the M1, convenient for Sheffield and Chesterfield. This family-run inn offers live music nights, a games area with a pool table and free WiFi throughout. Bedrooms are situated above the inn with en suite facilities. Carvery dining proves very popular along side classic pub food. On-site parking available.

Rooms 5 en suite (1 fmly) S fr £34.95; D fr £49.95 (room only) **Facilities** FTV tea/coffee Dinner available WiFi Pool table 🔒 **Parking** 30

CHINLEY   Map 16 SK08

The Old Hall Inn

★★★★ 🅰 INN

tel: 01663 750529 **Whitehough SK23 6EJ**
email: info@old-hall-inn.co.uk **web:** www.old-hall-inn.co.uk

This 16th-century, family-run inn is located in some prime walking country. The rooms are all en suite and one has a balcony overlooking the garden. All rooms have flat-screen TVs and WiFi. Breakfast comes as full English or continental style, while other meals can be eaten in the Old Hall's Minstrel Gallery restaurant. The bar features many ales from local breweries as well as an extensive wine list.

Rooms 4 en suite 4 annexe en suite S £69-£75; D £79-£105* **Facilities** FTV DVD tea/coffee Dinner available WiFi 🔒 **Parking** 20 **Notes** LB

CROMFORD   Map 16 SK25

Alison House

★★★★ GUEST ACCOMMODATION

tel: 01629 822211 **fax:** 01629 822316 **Intake Ln DE4 3RH**
email: info@alison-house-hotel.co.uk **web:** www.alison-house-hotel.co.uk
dir: *From A6, SE of Cromford, right into Intake Ln*

This well furnished and spacious 18th-century house stands in seven acres of well-tended grounds just a short walk from the village. Public rooms are comfortable and charming, and bedrooms come in a variety of sizes. All are furnished to a high standard, and The Arkwright Suite is a favourite with honeymooners.

Rooms 15 en suite (2 fmly) (4 GF) **Facilities** TVL tea/coffee Dinner available Direct Dial Licensed WiFi ⤵ 🔒 **Conf** Max 40 Thtr 40 Class 40 Board 40 **Parking** 30 **Notes** LB Civ Wed 80

DALBURY   Map 10 SK23

The Black Cow

★★★★ ◉ INN

tel: 01332 824297 **The Green, Dalbury Lees DE6 5BE**
email: enquiries@theblackcow.co.uk **web:** www.theblackcow.co.uk
dir: *From Derby A52 signed Ashbourne, Kirk Langley; turn into Church Lane, then Long Lane, follow signs to Dalbury Lees*

The Black Cow is set in the centre of the village overlooking the green. It is a traditional pub with friendly staff and hand-pulled ales. There is a beer garden and children's play area. Comfortable bedrooms come with flat-screen TVs and complimentary WiFi. The en suite bathrooms are well equipped with high standards of decor. Bar and dining room areas are very comfortable.

Rooms 6 en suite (1 fmly) S £49; D £65* **Facilities** FTV Lounge tea/coffee Dinner available WiFi ⟟ 18 Pool table 🔒 **Extras** Speciality toiletries, bottled water **Parking** 22

DERBY
Map 11 SK33

See also Belper & Melbourne

The Derby Conference Centre

★★★★ GUEST ACCOMMODATION

tel: 01332 861842 **fax:** 0870 890 0030 **London Rd DE24 8UX**
email: enquiries@thederbyconferencecentre.com
web: www.thederbyconferencecentre.com
dir: *M1 junct 25, A52 towards Derby. Filter left onto A5111 signed Ring Road. At Raynesway Park rdbt 3rd exit signed Ring Road/Alvaston. At next rdbt A6 towards Derby centre. Pass Wickes, left into entrance*

Formerly a railway training centre, this Grade II listed art deco building has modern public areas, meeting rooms and accommodation, yet original features such as the wall paintings by Norman Wilkinson still remain. Extensive conference facilities include a lecture theatre, and the grounds are perfect for events or weddings. Complimentary WiFi access is provided.

Rooms 50 en suite (10 GF) S £40-£65; D £45-£75* **Facilities** FTV Lounge TVL tea/coffee Dinner available Licensed WiFi 🔒 **Conf** Max 1000 Thtr 350 Class 60 Board 40 **Parking** 250 **Notes** ⊗ Closed 24 Dec-4 Jan Civ Wed 250

EYAM
Map 16 SK27

Crown Cottage

★★★★ BED AND BREAKFAST

tel: 01433 630858 **Main Rd S32 5QW**
email: janet@eatonfold.demon.co.uk **web:** www.crown-cottage.co.uk
dir: *From A623 in village at top of hill, 1st left & left again. Follow brown tourist signs to Eyam Hall. Pass church on right then Eyam Hall on right. Round right hand bend, 50yds on left*

Crown Cottage enjoys a prominent position in the pretty village of Eyam, in the heart of the Peak District National Park. Formerly a coaching inn, built in 1780, the cottage has undergone major refurbishment under its current owners. Bedrooms are all very comfortable and well equipped, while delicious breakfasts are served in the light-filled breakfast room. Secure parking is available at the rear of the cottage and free WiFi is available for guests.

Rooms 4 en suite S £50-£55; D £70-£75 **Facilities** FTV DVD Lounge tea/coffee WiFi 🔒 **Parking** 4 **Notes** ⊗

Barrel Inn

★★★ 🍴 INN

tel: 01433 630856 **Bretton S32 5QD**
email: barrelinn@btconnect.com
dir: *From Baslow on A623, turn right signed Foolow. At next T junct, turn left & immediately right opposite pond. 1m on left*

Laying claim to be the highest pub in Derbyshire, the Barrel Inn dates back to 1597 and provides the visitor was a warm and homely base from which to explore the area. Oak-beamed ceiling and flagstones are a feature in the bar area, while the restaurant offers a wide selection of meals. On a clear day it is possible to see five counties.

Rooms 4 annexe en suite (1 fmly) (1 GF) **Facilities** DVD tea/coffee Dinner available WiFi **Parking** 20 **Notes** ⊗

FENNY BENTLEY
Map 16 SK14

Bentley Brook Inn

★★★ INN

tel: 01335 350278 **fax:** 01335 350422 **DE6 1LF**
email: all@bentleybrookinn.co.uk **web:** www.bentleybrookinn.co.uk
dir: *2m N of Ashbourne at junct of A515 & B5056*

The Bentley Brook Inn is set in delightful grounds, and offers comfortable bedrooms including a two bedroom family suite. The restaurant is open daily for lunch and dinner, and all day at weekends and during the school holidays. There's a carvery on Sunday afternoon, and the Toe Wrestling World Championship has been held here every year since 2003. Dogs and children are more than welcome.

Rooms 9 en suite 2 annexe en suite (1 fmly) (2 GF) S £50-£90; D £75-£130* **Facilities** FTV tea/coffee Dinner available WiFi 🔒 **Conf** Max 200 Thtr 200 Class 120 Board 30 **Parking** 80 **Notes** LB Civ Wed 60

FOOLOW
Map 16 SK17

The Bulls Head Inn

★★★★ INN

tel: 01433 630873 **fax:** 01433 631738 **S32 5QR**
email: wilbnd@aol.com **web:** www.thebullatfoolow.co.uk
dir: *Off A623 into Foolow*

Located in the village centre, this popular inn retains many original features and offers comfortable, well-equipped bedrooms. Extensive and imaginative bar meals are served in the traditionally furnished dining room or in the cosy bar areas. The inn welcomes well-behaved dogs in the bar (and even muddy boots on the flagstone areas).

Rooms 3 en suite (1 fmly) **Facilities** tea/coffee Dinner available ♿ 18 **Parking** 20

FROGGATT
Map 16 SK27

The Chequers Inn

★★★★ ◉ INN

tel: 01433 630231 **fax:** 01433 631072 **S32 3ZJ**
email: info@chequers-froggatt.com **web:** www.chequers-froggatt.com
dir: *On A625 between Sheffield & Bakewell, 0.75m from Calver*

The Chequers Inn is a very popular 16th-century inn offering an extensive range of well-cooked food. The bedrooms are comprehensively equipped with all modern comforts and the hospitality is professional and sincere. This is a good location for touring Derbyshire, the Peak Park, and visiting Chatsworth.

Rooms 6 en suite S £85-£115; D £85-£115* **Facilities** FTV tea/coffee Dinner available WiFi **Parking** 45 **Notes** LB ⊗ Closed 25 Dec No coaches

GREAT HUCKLOW
Map 16 SK17

The Queen Anne
★★★ ⌷ INN

tel: 01298 871246 **fax:** 01298 873504 **SK17 8RF**
email: angelaryan100@aol.com **web:** www.queenanneinn.co.uk
dir: Exit A623 onto B6049 to Great Hucklow

Set in the heart of this pretty village, The Queen Anne has been a licensed inn for over 300 years and the public areas retain many original features. Well cooked meals are served in the cosy inn or in the pretty garden in fine weather. The bedrooms are in a separate building with direct access, and have modern shower rooms en suite.

Rooms 2 annexe en suite (2 GF) S £53; D £69* **Facilities** FTV DVD TVL tea/coffee Dinner available WiFi **Parking** 20 **Notes** LB ⊗ No Children 10yrs Closed Xmas & New Year

HARDSTOFT
Map 16 SK46

The Shoulder at Hardstoft
★★★★★ ⊚⊚ ⌷ INN

tel: 01246 850276 **Deep Ln S45 8AF**
email: info@thefamousshoulder.co.uk **web:** www.thefamousshoulder.co.uk
dir: B6039 follow signs for Hardwick Hall, 1st right after turning off B6039

This 300-year-old country pub offers a friendly atmosphere along with real ales and log fires. Delicious, home-cooked meals are skilfully prepared and served throughout the informal bar and the stylish restaurant; breakfasts include home-made sausages and black pudding. Bedrooms vary in size but all are well furnished and complimentary WiFi is provided. There is also a function room available.

Rooms 4 en suite (1 fmly) **Facilities** FTV tea/coffee Dinner available WiFi **Extras** Bottled water, home-made biscuits **Conf** Max 80 Thtr 80 Class 40 Board 40 **Parking** 50

HARTINGTON
Map 16 SK16

Bank House Guest House
★★★★ GUEST ACCOMMODATION

tel: 01298 84465 **Market Place SK17 0AL**
web: www.visitbankhouse.co.uk
dir: B5054 into village centre

Bank House is a very well-maintained Grade II listed Georgian building that stands in the main square of this delightful village. Bedrooms are neat and fresh in appearance, and there is a comfortable television lounge. A hearty breakfast is served in the ground-floor cottage-style dining room.

Rooms 5 rms (3 en suite) (3 fmly) S £36-£40; D £58-£66* **Facilities** FTV TVL tea/coffee WiFi ⌷ **Parking** 2 **Notes** LB ⊗ Closed Xmas RS 22-28 Dec

Find out more about this county with the AA Guide to The Peak District – see theAA.com/shop

HARTSHORNE
Map 10 SK32

The Mill Wheel
★★★★ ⊚ INN

tel: 01283 550335 **fax:** 01283 552833 **Ticknall Rd DE11 7AS**
email: info@themillwheel.co.uk **web:** www.themillwheel.co.uk
dir: M42 junct 2, A511 to Woodville, left onto A514 towards Derby to Hartshorne

The Mill Wheel offers a wide range of well-prepared food in the Rosette award-winning restaurant and the large mill wheel has been retained in the comfortable bar. Decor in the bar and dining room includes deep red walls, leather and wood seating and welcoming log fires. Bedrooms are modern and well-equipped while friendly and attentive service is provided.

Rooms 4 en suite (2 GF) **Facilities** FTV tea/coffee Dinner available WiFi **Conf** Max 24 Thtr 24 Board 12 **Parking** 55 **Notes** ⊗

HATHERSAGE
Map 16 SK28

The Plough Inn
★★★★ ⊚ INN

tel: 01433 650319 **fax:** 01433 651049 **Leadmill Bridge S32 1BA**
email: sales@theploughinn-hathersage.co.uk **web:** www.theploughinn-hathersage.co.uk
dir: 1m SE of Hathersage on B6001. Over bridge, 150yds beyond at Leadmill

This delightful 16th-century inn with beer garden has an idyllic location by the River Derwent. A selection of real ales and imaginative food is served in the spacious public areas, and original fireplaces and exposed beams have been preserved. The attractive, well-equipped bedrooms include several luxury rooms, and WiFi access is available throughout.

Rooms 3 en suite 2 annexe en suite (1 GF) S £75-£100; D £105-£140* **Facilities** FTV DVD iPod docking station tea/coffee Dinner available Direct Dial WiFi ⌷ 18 ⌷ **Extras** Fruit, water - complimentary **Parking** 50 **Notes** LB Closed 25 Dec No coaches

HOPE
Map 16 SK18

Premier Collection

Underleigh House

★★★★★ 🏠 GUEST ACCOMMODATION

tel: 01433 621372 **fax:** 01433 621324 **Lose Hill Ln S33 6AF**
email: info@underleighhouse.co.uk **web:** www.underleighhouse.co.uk
dir: *From village church on A6187 into Edale Rd, 1m left into Lose Hill Ln*

Situated at the end of a private lane, surrounded by glorious scenery, Underleigh House was converted from a barn and cottage that dates from 1873, and now offers carefully furnished and attractively decorated bedrooms with modern facilities. One room has a private lounge and others have access to the gardens. There is a very spacious lounge with comfortable chairs and a welcoming log fire. Memorable breakfasts are served at one large table in the dining room.

Rooms 5 en suite (2 GF) S £70-£90; D £90-£110* **Facilities** DVD TVL tea/coffee Direct Dial Licensed WiFi 🔒 **Extras** Speciality toiletries, fruit, sweets - free **Parking** 6 **Notes** LB No Children 12yrs Closed Xmas, New Year & Jan

Stoney Ridge

★★★★ 🏠 GUEST ACCOMMODATION

tel: 01433 620538 **Granby Rd, Bradwell S33 9HU**
email: info@stoneyridge.org.uk **web:** www.stoneyridge.org.uk
dir: *From N end of Bradwell on B6049 into Gore Ln, uphill, pass Ye Olde Bowling Green Inn, left into Granby Rd*

This large, split-level bungalow stands in attractive mature gardens at the highest part of the village and has extensive views. Hens roam freely in the landscaped garden, and their fresh eggs add to the hearty breakfasts. Bedrooms are attractively furnished and thoughtfully equipped, and there is a spacious comfortable lounge and a superb indoor swimming pool (may be closed November to March).

Rooms 4 rms (3 en suite) (1 pri facs) S £50-£58; D £50-£78* **Facilities** STV FTV TVL tea/coffee WiFi 🐾 🔒 **Extras** Sweets **Parking** 6 **Notes** LB No Children 14yrs RS Nov-Mar Pool may be closed for maintenance

Round Meadow Barn

★★★ BED AND BREAKFAST

tel: 01433 621347 & 07836 689422 **fax:** 01433 621347 **Parsons Ln S33 6RB**
email: geof@harrisrmb.freeserve.co.uk **web:** www.mysite.freeserve.com/rmbarn
dir: *Exit A625 (Hope Rd) N onto Parsons Ln, over rail bridge, in 200yds right into hay barnyard, through gates, across 3 fields, house on left*

This converted barn, with original stone walls and exposed timbers, stands in open fields in the picturesque Hope Valley. The bedrooms are large enough for families and there are two modern bathrooms. Breakfast is served at one large table adjoining the family kitchen.

Rooms 3 rms (1 en suite) (2 pri facs) (1 fmly) **Facilities** FTV tea/coffee Direct Dial 🔒 **Parking** 8 **Notes** 🐾

MATLOCK
Map 16 SK35

Premier Collection

Holmefield Guest House

★★★★★ 🍽 GUEST HOUSE

tel: 01629 735347 **Dale Road North, Darley Dale DE4 2HY**
email: holmefieldguesthouse@btinternet.com **web:** www.holmefieldguesthouse.co.uk
dir: *Between Bakewell & Matlock on A6. 1m from Rowsley & Chatsworth Estate, 0.5m from Peak Rail*

Standing in mature grounds between Matlock and Bakewell, this elegant Victorian house has been furnished with flair to offer good levels of comfort and facilities. Imaginative dinners feature seasonal local produce, including some from the Chatsworth Estate. Warm hospitality and attentive service are assured.

Rooms 4 en suite 3 annexe en suite (1 fmly) (2 GF) **Facilities** tea/coffee Dinner available Direct Dial WiFi Pool table **Parking** 10 **Notes** ⊗

Castle Green B&B

★★★★ BED AND BREAKFAST

tel: 01629 581349 & 07584 162988 **fax:** 01629 501050 **Butts Dr DE4 3DJ**
email: info@castlegreenbandb.co.uk **web:** www.castlegreenbandb.co.uk
dir: *A615 into Matlock, pass British Red Cross on left, opposite Castle Green & Butts Drive*

Located in the peaceful grounds of the former Ernest Bailey mansion, the property is nestled in a wooded valley with views of Riber Castle; the house is within walking distance of Matlock. A warm welcome awaits and the accommodation is well equipped and very comfortable. Breakfast is served in the dining room on the ground floor. A lounge is available complete with television and daily newspapers. Other facilities include WiFi and on site parking.

Rooms 6 en suite (1 fmly) (1 GF) S £45-£50; D £80* **Facilities** FTV tea/coffee WiFi 🔒 **Parking** 8 **Notes** LB ⊗

Hearthstone Farm *(SK308583)*

★★★★ 🏠 FARMHOUSE

tel: 01629 534304 **Hearthstone Ln, Riber DE4 5JW**
email: enquiries@hearthstonefarm.co.uk **web:** www.hearthstonefarm.co.uk
dir: *A615 at Tansley (2m E of Matlock), turn opposite Royal Oak towards Riber, at gates to Riber Hall left into Riber Rd, 1st left into Hearthstone Ln, farmhouse on left*

Situated in a stunning elevated location, this traditional stone farmhouse retains many original features and is stylishly decorated throughout. Bedrooms are equipped with a wealth of homely extras and comprehensive breakfasts feature the farm's organic produce. There is a very comfortable lounge, and the farm animals in the grounds are an attraction.

Rooms 3 en suite S £55-£60; D £75-£80* **Facilities** FTV TVL tea/coffee WiFi **Parking** 6 **Notes** LB Closed Xmas & New Year ⊛ 150 acres beef/lamb

The Pines

★★★★ BED AND BREAKFAST

tel: 01629 732646 **12 Eversleigh Rd, Darley Bridge DE4 2JW**
email: info@thepinesbandb.co.uk **web:** www.thepinesbandb.co.uk
dir: *From Bakewell or Matlock take A6 to Darley Dale. Turn at Whitworth Hotel onto B5057, pass Square & Compass pub & The 3 Stags Heads, The Pines on right*

Dating from the 1820s, this home as been authentically restored and stands in a secluded and pretty garden. Three spacious en suite bedrooms are stylishly furnished using rich fabrics. Comprehensive breakfasts, making use of quality local produce, offer a hearty start to the day. The Pines makes an ideal location for visiting the Peak District. The Pines is a Runner Up in the AA Friendliest B&B of the Year 2014-2015.

Rooms 3 en suite S £50-£60; D £70-£80* **Facilities** FTV tea/coffee Dinner available WiFi 🔒 **Parking** 5 **Notes** LB

The Red Lion

★★★ INN

tel: 01629 584888 **Matlock Green DE4 3BT**
dir: *500yds SE of town centre on A632*

This comfortable free house is a good base for exploring Matlock and the surrounding Derbyshire countryside. Each bedroom is comfortably furnished, and one comes complete with a four-poster. Public areas include a games area with open fires, and a restaurant where a wide selection of meals is on offer. Private parking is a bonus.

Rooms 6 en suite **Facilities** tea/coffee Dinner available WiFi Pool table **Parking** 20 **Notes** ⊗

Farley Farm *(SK294622)*

★★★ FARMHOUSE

tel: 01629 582533 & 07801 756409   **fax:** 01629 584856 **Farley DE4 5LR**
email: eric.brailsford@btconnect.com **web:** www.farleyfarm.co.uk
dir: *1m N of Matlock. From A6 rdbt towards Bakewell, 1st right, right at top of hill, left up Farley Hill, 2nd farm on left*

Guests can expect a warm welcome at this traditional stone farmhouse. In addition to farming, the proprietors also breed dogs and horses. The bedrooms are pleasantly decorated and equipped with many useful extras. A hearty farmhouse breakfast offers a good start to any day.

Rooms 2 en suite (3 fmly) D £60-£65 **Facilities** FTV TVL tea/coffee Riding 🔒 **Parking** 8 **Notes** LB ⊛ 165 acres arable/beef/dairy

Red House Carriage Museum

★★★ GUEST ACCOMMODATION

tel: 01629 733583 **fax:** 01629 733583 **Old Rd, Darley Dale DE4 2ER**
email: redhousestables@hotmail.co.uk **web:** www.workingcarriages.com
dir: *2m N of Matlock, left from A6, 200yds on left*

Located in a famous carriage-driving school and museum, this detached house provides homely and thoughtfully equipped bedrooms, including one on the ground floor and two in a former stable. Comprehensive breakfasts are served at a family table in an attractive dining room, and the comfortable lounge area overlooks the spacious gardens.

Rooms 2 rms (1 en suite) 2 annexe en suite (1 fmly) (1 GF) **Facilities** tea/coffee 🔒 Horse & carriage trips **Parking** 5 **Notes** ⊗ RS Nov-Mar Mon-Sat 10-4 & Sun 10-2 ⊛

MELBOURNE	Map 11 SK32

The Coach House

★★★★ GUEST HOUSE

tel: 01332 862338 **fax:** 01332 695281 **69 Derby Rd DE73 8FE**
email: enquiries@coachhouse-hotel.co.uk **web:** www.coachhouse-hotel.co.uk
dir: *Off B587 in village centre*

The Coach House sits in the heart of a conservation area, close to Donington Park and East Midlands Airport. This traditional cottage has been restored to provide good standards of comfort and facilities. Bedrooms are thoughtfully furnished, and a lounge and secure parking are available.

Rooms 6 en suite (1 fmly) (3 GF) S £41-£46; D £56-£66* **Facilities** FTV TVL tea/coffee WiFi 🔒 **Parking** 5 **Notes** LB ⊗

MICKLEOVER   Map 10 SK33

The Great Northern

★★★★ INN

tel: 01332 514288 **Station Rd DE3 9FB**
email: greatnorthernderby@yahoo.co.uk **web:** www.thegreatnorthern.co.uk
dir: *From N - A38 to Markeaton Island, take 3rd exit. Then 2nd left into Radbourne Ln, 3rd left into Station Rd*

Bedrooms at The Great Northern in a converted barn; the three boutique-style rooms are well appointed and thoughtfully equipped. This modern inn with friendly staff provides imaginative food, and a selection of local cask ales. Free WiFi and ample parking are provided. A meeting room is available for small parties or private dining.

Rooms 3 en suite (1 fmly) (1 GF) S £80; D £80* **Facilities** FTV DVD tea/coffee Dinner available WiFi **Conf** Max 25 Thtr 15 Class 15 Board 25 **Parking** 80 **Notes** ⊗

NEWHAVEN   Map 16 SK16

Premier Collection

The Smithy

★★★★★ ⌂ GUEST ACCOMMODATION

tel: 01298 84548 **SK17 0DT**
email: lynnandgary@thesmithybedandbreakfast.co.uk
web: www.thesmithybedandbreakfast.co.uk
dir: *0.5m S of Newhaven on A515. Adjacent to Biggin Ln, private driveway opposite Ivy House*

Set in a peaceful location close to the Tissington and High Peak trails, this 17th-century drovers' inn and blacksmith's workshop has been carefully renovated. Bedrooms, which are in a former barn, are well equipped. Enjoyable breakfasts, which include free-range eggs and home-made preserves, are served in the forge, which features the original bellows on the vast open hearth.

Rooms 4 en suite (2 GF) S £45-£50; D £75-£90* **Facilities** FTV DVD TVL tea/coffee WiFi 🛁 **Conf** Max 20 Thtr 15 Board 10 **Parking** 8 **Notes** LB ⊗ No Children ⊠

NEW MILLS   Map 16 SK08

Pack Horse Inn

★★★★ Ⓐ INN

tel: 01663 742365 **fax:** 01663 741674 **Mellor Rd SK22 4QQ**
email: info@packhorseinn.co.uk

The Pack Horse Inn sits on the edge of the Peak District, ideally located within easy reach of Stockport, Manchester and Sheffield. Some bedrooms are in a converted barn and still have some original oak beams. The other rooms are in the main building. The friendly bar has at least three hand-pulled, regularly changing guest ales together with Tetley bitter. Traditional bar meals and snacks are available, or a more formal meal is served in the dining room which overlooks the patio area, where guests can eat and drink in the warmer weather.

Rooms 12 en suite

PILSLEY   Map 16 SK27

Holly Cottage

★★★★ ⌂ BED AND BREAKFAST

tel: 01246 582245 **DE45 1UH**
email: hollycottagebandb@btinternet.com **web:** www.hollycottagebandb.co.uk
dir: *Follow brown tourist signs for Chatsworth & Pilsley. Holly Cottage next to post office in Pilsley*

A warm welcome is assured at this mellow stone cottage, part of a combined Post Office and shop in the conservation area of Pilsley, which is owned by the adjacent Chatsworth Estate. The cosy bedrooms feature a wealth of thoughtful extras, and comprehensive breakfasts, utilising quality local produce, are taken in an attractive pine-furnished dining room.

Rooms 3 en suite **Facilities** FTV iPod docking station tea/coffee WiFi **Notes** LB ⊗ No Children 10yrs

The Devonshire Arms at Pilsley

★★★ INN

tel: 01246 583258 **The High St DE45 1UL**
email: marketing@devonshirehotels.co.uk **web:** www.devonshirepilsley.co.uk
dir: *From A619, in Baslow, at rdbt take 1st exit onto B6012. Follow signs to Chatsworth, 2nd right to Pilsley*

The newest addition to the Devonshire Hotels and Restaurants group, The Devonshire Arms at Pilsley is just two miles from Chatsworth House, and also a minute's walk from the Chatsworth farm shop which provides much of the food served. All rooms are en suite, quite individual in design and offer very impressive quality and comfort.

Rooms 7 en suite (1 fmly) S £85-£125; D £85-£165* **Facilities** DVD tea/coffee Dinner available WiFi **Parking** 10 **Notes** ⊗ No coaches

TIDESWELL   Map 16 SK17

The George

★★★ ⊜ INN

tel: 01298 871382 **Commercial Rd SK17 8NU**
email: andrewrowe@rowe-erices.cl **web:** www.georgeinntideswell.co.uk

A warm welcome and a well cooked meal await you at The George, where traditional values mix well with modern convenience. The comfortable spacious bedrooms are decorated in warm tones and are well equipped with thoughtful extras. A log fire burns in the dining room on cooler days and there is a popular bar. A function room is also available.

Rooms 4 en suite (2 fmly) **Facilities** FTV DVD tea/coffee Dinner available WiFi Pool table 🔒 **Conf** Max 50 Thtr 50 Class 40 **Parking** 10

WINSTER   Map 16 SK26

Brae Cottage

★★★★ Ⓐ GUEST ACCOMMODATION

tel: 01629 650375 **East Bank DE4 2DT**
web: www.braecottagewinster.co.uk
dir: *A6 onto B5057, driveway on right past pub*

Brae Cottage lies in the heart of this Peak District village, a stone's throw from the Old Bowling Green Inn. The bedrooms are in converted outbuildings and have a wealth of thoughtful extras. Comprehensive breakfasts, featuring home-made or local produce, are served at an antique table in the carefully furnished cottage.

Rooms 2 annexe en suite (1 fmly) (2 GF) S £55-£65; D £65-£75* **Facilities** tea/coffee 🔒 **Extras** Mineral water - complimentary **Parking** 2 **Notes** ⊗ No Children 11yrs ⊛

YOULGREAVE   Map 16 SK26

The George

★★★ INN

tel: 01629 636292 **fax:** 01632 636292 **Church St DE45 1UW**
dir: *3m S of Bakewell in Youlgreave, opposite church*

The public bars of the 17th-century George are popular with locals and tourists. Bedroom styles vary, and all have shower rooms en suite. Breakfast is served in the lounge bar, and a range of bar meals and snacks is available.

Rooms 3 en suite (1 fmly) S £40-£44; D £72-£80* **Facilities** tea/coffee Dinner available WiFi Fishing **Parking** 12 **Notes** ⊛

DEVON

APPLEDORE   Map 3 SS43

Appledore House

★★★★ GUEST ACCOMMODATION

tel: 01237 421471 & 07825 141459 **Meeting St EX39 1RJ**
email: info@appledore-house.co.uk **web:** www.appledore-house.co.uk
dir: *A361 N Devon Link Road, follow signs to Bideford, then Appledore. Turn left into Staddon Rd, Appledore House at junct with Meeting St*

This imposing house is set on the hill overlooking the town and across the water towards Instow; a number of rooms enjoy these impressive views. Furnishings and comfort are of a high standard, and the proprietors have a genuine concern for their guests' comfort and wellbeing.

Rooms 5 en suite (1 fmly) S £60-£65; D £80-£115* **Facilities** FTV tea/coffee WiFi 🔒 Drying area **Extras** Cream teas **Conf** Max 20 Thtr 20 Class 20 Board 12 **Parking** 3 **Notes** LB ⊗

ASHBURTON   Map 3 SX77

Greencott

★★★★ GUEST HOUSE

tel: 01803 762649 **Landscove TQ13 7LZ**
dir: *3m SE of Ashburton. Exit A38 at Peartree junct, Landscove signed on slip road, village green 2m on right, opposite village hall*

Greencott has a peaceful village location and superb country views. Your hosts extend a very warm welcome and there is a relaxed home-from-home atmosphere. Service is attentive and caring and many guests return time and again. Bedrooms are attractive, comfortable and very well equipped. Delicious breakfasts are served around an oak dining table.

Rooms 2 en suite S £25; D £50* **Facilities** TVL tea/coffee **Parking** 3 **Notes** LB ⊗ Closed 25-26 Dec ⊛

ASHBURTON *continued*

Gages Mill Country Guest House

★★★★ GUEST ACCOMMODATION

tel: 01364 652391 **Buckfastleigh Rd TQ13 7JW**
email: katestone@gagesmill.co.uk **web:** www.gagesmill.co.uk
dir: *Off A38 at Peartree junct, turn right then left at fuel station, Gages Mill 500yds on left*

Conveniently situated within easy access of the A38, this Grade II listed building was formerly a woollen mill. Very much a family home, there is a relaxed and welcoming feel here with every effort made to ensure a rewarding and memorable stay. The bedrooms provide good standards of comfort and many have lovely views across the surrounding fields. Breakfast provides a substantial and enjoyable start to the day with plenty of choice for all appetites.

Rooms 7 en suite (1 fmly) (1 GF) S £60; D £80-£85* **Facilities** iPod docking station TVL tea/coffee Licensed WiFi 🔒 **Parking** 7 **Notes** ⊗ Closed Nov-Feb 🐾

The Rising Sun

★★★ INN

tel: 01364 652544 **Woodland TQ13 7JT**
email: enquiries@therisingsunwoodland.co.uk **web:** www.therisingsunwoodland.co.uk
dir: *From A38 take exit signed Woodland & Denbury, 1.5m on left*

Conveniently situated for access to Dartmoor and the stunning countryside, The Rising Sun is situated in woodland, perfect for the keen walker. The property has a dining room and a bar in addition to its comfortable bedrooms. The inn is owner-run and managed, with friendly staff. There's an ample range offered on the menu, along with a good selection of wines and beers. Lovely open fires on the winter evenings create a cosy relaxed atmosphere.

Rooms 4 en suite (1 fmly) (2 GF) S fr £55; D fr £75* **Facilities** FTV tea/coffee Dinner available WiFi 🔒 **Parking** 20

West Down *(SS582228)*

★★★★ 🏠 FARMHOUSE

tel: 01769 560551 **fax:** 01769 560551 **Little Eastacombe EX37 9HP**
email: info@westdown.co.uk **web:** www.westdown.co.uk
dir: *0.5m from Atherington on B3227 to Torrington, turn right, 100yds on left*

Set within 25 acres of lush Devon countryside, this establishment makes a good base for exploring the area. A peaceful atmosphere and caring hospitality are assured. Bedrooms are equipped with a host of thoughtful extras, and every effort is made to ensure an enjoyable stay. One bedroom has wheelchair access and a

large wet room. A choice of homely lounges is available; breakfast and scrumptious dinners are served in the sun lounge.

Rooms 2 en suite 2 annexe en suite (2 GF) S £50-£55; D £80-£84* **Facilities** Lounge TVL tea/coffee Dinner available WiFi 🔒 **Parking** 8 **Notes** LB ⊗ 🐾 25 acres sheep/chickens

Premier Collection

Kerrington House

★★★★★ 🏠 🏠 GUEST ACCOMMODATION

tel: 01297 35333 **fax:** 01297 35345 **Musbury Rd EX13 5JR**
email: info@kerringtonhouse.com **web:** www.kerringtonhouse.com
dir: *0.5m from Axminster on A358 towards Seaton, house on left*

This former Victorian gentleman's residence has been decorated and furnished to very high standards to make guests as comfortable as possible. Bedrooms and bathrooms include a range of welcome extras. Afternoon tea may be enjoyed in the comfortably furnished lounge or, in the warmer months, outside overlooking the landscaped gardens. Locally sourced produce is used both at breakfast and at dinner which is available by prior arrangement.

Rooms 5 en suite (2 fmly) (2 GF) S £85; D £125* **Facilities** FTV DVD iPod docking station Lounge tea/coffee Dinner available Licensed WiFi 🔒 **Extras** Speciality toiletries, sherry, chocolates - free **Conf** Max 12 Board 12 **Parking** 6 **Notes** LB ⊗

The Bark House

★★★★ 🏠 GUEST ACCOMMODATION

tel: 01398 351236 **Oakfordbridge EX16 9HZ**
web: www.thebarkhouse.co.uk
dir: *A361 to rdbt at Tiverton onto A396 for Dulverton, then onto Oakfordbridge. House on right*

Located in the stunning Exe Valley and surrounded by wonderful unspoilt countryside, this is a perfect place to relax and unwind. Hospitality is the hallmark here and a cup of tea by the fireside is always on offer. Both breakfast and dinner make use of the excellent local produce, and are served in the attractive dining room, overlooking fields and the river. Bedrooms have a homely, cottage-style feel with comfortable beds to ensure a peaceful night's sleep.

Rooms 5 rms (4 en suite) (1 pri facs) S £40-£65; D £70-£98* **Facilities** Lounge tea/coffee Dinner available Licensed WiFi **Parking** 10 **Notes** LB

Newhouse Farm *(SS892228)*

★★★★ 🏠 🏠 FARMHOUSE

tel: 01398 351347 **EX16 9JE**
email: anne.boldry@btconnect.com **web:** www.newhouse-farm-holidays.co.uk
dir: *5m W of Bampton on B3227*

Set in 42 acres of rolling farmland, this delightful farmhouse provides a friendly and informal atmosphere. The smart, rustic-style bedrooms are well equipped with modern facilities, and imaginative and delicious home-cooked dinners, using the best local produce, are available by arrangement. Home-made bread and preserves feature at breakfast which can be enjoyed outside on the patio in the summer months.

Rooms 3 en suite (1 GF) S £42.50-£50; D £65-£80* **Facilities** FTV tea/coffee Dinner available WiFi Fishing **Parking** 3 **Notes** LB ⊗ No Children 10yrs Closed Xmas & New Year 🐾 42 acres beef/sheep

Blackberries

★★★★ 🍽 GUEST ACCOMMODATION

tel: 01398 331842 & 07712 615480 **19 Fore St EX16 9ND**
email: blackberries@btconnect.com **web:** www.blackberries-bampton.co.uk
dir: M5 junct 27 onto A361, then A396 to Bampton

Situated in the charming town of Bampton, this is an ideal base from which to explore the beautiful countryside and coast, with Exmoor just a short drive away. A warm and genuine welcome is assured, with every effort made to help ensure a relaxed and enjoyable stay. Bedrooms all provide good standards of comfort and quality, as do the bathrooms. Downstairs, the inviting bar and restaurant are the main focus. A range of skilfully prepared dishes is offered, and the satisfying breakfasts provide a great start to the day.

Rooms 6 en suite (2 fmly) (1 GF) **Facilities** FTV tea/coffee Dinner available Licensed WiFi **Parking** 6 **Notes** LB

The Swan

★★★★ 🍽 INN

tel: 01398 332248 **Station Rd EX16 9NG**
email: info@theswan.co **web:** www.theswan.co

The Swan is a traditional hostelry offering good food, good beer and a wide selection of wines coupled with comfortable, well-equipped bedrooms and en suite bathrooms. Each bedroom has a flat-screen TV, and other modern media staples. Staff are very friendly and do all they can to make a stay comfortable. Breakfast is a hearty affair using good local ingredients, and the menu in the evening offers a great choice for all.

Rooms 3 en suite S £65-£75; D £80-£95* **Facilities** FTV iPod docking station tea/coffee Dinner available WiFi Fishing Riding Gym 🔒 **Extras** Speciality toiletries, espresso machine, snacks **Notes** LB Closed 25-26 Dec

Weston House

★★★★ BED AND BREAKFAST

tel: 01398 332094 & 07958 176799 **6 Luke St EX16 9NF**
email: peter@westonhousedevon.co.uk **web:** www.westonhousedevon.co.uk
dir: On B3227, in village, opposite church

Located in the heart of Bampton within easy reach of many local attractions and gardens, Weston House offers comfortable, well-equipped bedrooms and hearty breakfasts using quality local ingredients. Owner Catherine Stott is an artist who teaches, and many of her pieces are tastefully displayed throughout the house. Public parking is available within a few minutes' walk.

Rooms 3 rms (2 en suite) (1 pri facs) S £50-£55; D £60-£75* **Facilities** FTV DVD tea/coffee WiFi ⌚ 18 🔒 Drying facilities **Extras** Speciality toiletries, home-made biscuits - free **Notes** LB ⊗ Closed 20-28 Dec

BARNSTAPLE	Map 3 SS53

The Spinney

★★★★ GUEST ACCOMMODATION

tel: 01271 850282 & 07775 335654 **Shirwell EX31 4JR**
email: stay@thespinneyshirwell.co.uk **web:** www.thespinneyshirwell.co.uk
dir: From Barnstaple on A39, past hospital towards Lynton

This elegant, 18th-century former rectory is located in the heart of north Devon, three miles from the historic market town of Barnstaple. The Spinney offers stylishly decorated, en suite accommodation in muted colours with thoughtful extras. Local

farm sausages feature at breakfast which is served in the conservatory. Ample private parking is available.

Rooms 5 rms (4 en suite) (1 pri facs) (1 fmly) S £70-£80; D £80-£93 **Facilities** FTV DVD Lounge tea/coffee WiFi 🔒 **Extras** Chocolates, water - complimentary **Parking** 7 **Notes** LB ⊗ No Children 10yrs

Cedars Lodge

★★★★ INN

tel: 01271 371784 **fax:** 01271 325733 **Bickington Rd EX31 2HP**
email: cedars.barnstaple@oldenglishinns.co.uk **web:** www.oldenglish.co.uk

Once a private country house, Cedars Lodge stands in three acres of gardens, situated just outside Barnstaple and within easy reach of the M5 and major roads. Bedrooms are located in the adjacent lodge which is set around a courtyard facing the main house; all rooms offer generous levels of comfort and modern facilities. The popular conservatory restaurant serves a wide choice of dishes.

Rooms 2 en suite 32 annexe en suite (7 fmly) **Facilities** FTV TVL tea/coffee Dinner available Direct Dial WiFi ⌚ 18 🔒 **Conf** Max 250 Thtr 250 Class 100 Board 100 **Parking** 200 **Notes** LB Civ Wed

Lower Yelland Farm Guest House

★★★★ GUEST HOUSE

tel: 01271 860101 & 07803 933642 **Fremington EX31 3EN**
email: peterday@loweryellandfarm.co.uk **web:** www.loweryellandfarm.co.uk
dir: Approaching Barnstaple on A361, at 1st rdbt take 1st exit A39 (Bideford). Straight over next 2 rdbts, at 3rd rdbt take 3rd exit. Over 2 mini rdbts, at 3rd take 1st exit onto B3233. Through Fremington, 1st turn on right

Lower Yelland Farm is a well established property close to Instow and within easy reach of Barnstaple and North Devon. Peter Day does all he can to make his guests welcome and serves a high quality, traditional farmhouse breakfast which features home-made jams, marmalades and bread in the attractive breakfast room. En suite bedrooms are well presented and appointed, and there is ample off-road parking for guests.

Rooms 7 en suite (1 fmly) (1 GF) S £27.50-£37.50; D £50-£70 (room only)* **Facilities** FTV Lounge tea/coffee WiFi ⌚ 18 🔒 **Parking** 7 **Notes** LB

BARNSTAPLE *continued*

Cresta Guest House

★★★ GUEST HOUSE

tel: 01271 374022 **26 Sticklepath Hill EX31 2BU**
email: contact@crestaguesthouse.co.uk **web:** www.crestaguesthouse.co.uk
dir: *On A3215, 0.6m W of town centre, top of hill on right*

A warm welcome is assured at this family-run establishment, situated on the western outskirts of Barnstaple. The well-equipped, individually styled bedrooms are smartly appointed and include ground-floor rooms. A hearty breakfast is served in the modern and comfortable dining room.

Rooms 6 en suite 2 annexe en suite (2 fmly) (2 GF) **Facilities** FTV tea/coffee WiFi 🛁
Parking 6 **Notes** ❸ Closed 2wks Xmas

BEER	Map 4 SY28

Anchor Inn

★★★★ INN

tel: 01297 20386 **fax:** 01297 24474 **Fore St EX12 3ET**
email: 6403@greeneking.co.uk **web:** www.oldenglish.co.uk
dir: *A3052 at Hangmans Stone onto B3174 into Beer, located on slipway*

Overlooking the sea in the idyllic village of Beer, this perennially popular inn has a well deserved reputation for the warmth of its welcome and convivial atmosphere. A number of the well appointed bedrooms have the added bonus of sea views. The menu makes plentiful use of the excellent local fish, much of which is landed just yards away. The cliff-top beer garden is a wonderful spot in summer months to soak up some sun whilst enjoying freshly barbecued food.

Rooms 6 rms (5 en suite) (1 pri facs) **Facilities** STV FTV tea/coffee Dinner available WiFi **Notes** LB

BEESANDS	Map 3 SX84

The Cricket Inn

★★★★ ⊛ INN

tel: 01548 580215 **TQ7 2EN**
email: enquiries@thecricketinn.com **web:** www.thecricketinn.com
dir: *From Kingsbridge follow A379 towards Dartmouth, at Stokenham mini rdbt turn right for Beesands*

Dating back to 1867 this charming seaside inn is situated almost on the beach at Start Bay. The well-appointed bedrooms have fantastic views, comfortable beds and flat-screen TVs. The daily-changing fish menu includes locally-caught crabs, lobster and perhaps hand-dived scallops.

Rooms 8 en suite (1 fmly) **Facilities** FTV tea/coffee Dinner available WiFi **Parking** 30 **Notes** No coaches

BIDEFORD	Map 3 SS42

The West Country Inn

★★★ INN

tel: 01237 441724 **Bursdon Moor EX39 6HB**
email: thewestcinn@aol.com **web:** www.westcountryinn.co.uk
dir: *On A39 S of Clovelly*

Originally a coaching inn, dating back to the 16th century, this traditional and welcoming establishment is ideally placed for exploring this picturesque area. Bedrooms provide good levels of comfort with all the necessities to ensure a relaxing stay. The well-stocked bar has a range of local ales and provides a convivial focal point with plenty of good-natured banter always on offer. A range of good, honest dishes are served either in the bar or adjacent dining room. Additional facilities include a newly opened spa and gym.

Rooms 9 en suite (1 fmly) S £50-£59; D £85-£99* **Facilities** FTV Lounge tea/coffee Dinner available WiFi Gym Pool table 🛁 Hot tub **Conf** Max 100 Thtr 100 Class 70 Board 70 **Parking** 100

The Pines at Eastleigh

Ⓤ

tel: 01271 860561 **The Pines, Eastleigh EX39 4PA**
web: www.thepinesateastleigh.co.uk
dir: *A39 onto A386 signed East-the-Water. 1st left signed Eastleigh, 500yds next left, 1.5m to village, house on right*

Currently the rating for this establishment is not confirmed. This may be due to a change of ownership or because it has only recently joined the AA rating scheme.

Rooms 10 en suite (1 fmly) (4 GF) S £70; D £95* **Conf** Max 25 Thtr 20 Board 20

BITTADON	Map 3 SS54

Centery Farm

★★★★ BED AND BREAKFAST

tel: 01271 879603 **EX31 4HN**
email: stay@centeryfarm.co.uk **web:** www.centeryfarm.co.uk
dir: *From Barnstaple on A39, left onto B3230 signed Ilfracombe. Pass through Muddiford & Bittadon, at 1st staggered x-rds on right*

Centery Farm can be found just outside Ilfracombe, set back from the main road and with easy access to the town and Barnstaple. The very friendly hosts offer a genuinely warm welcome with home-made scones and local jam and clotted cream. Bedrooms are well equipped, beds are very comfortable and en suites are well appointed. Breakfast offers quality, locally sourced ingredients and makes a great start to the day.

Rooms 4 rms (3 en suite) (1 pri facs) S £46.55-£49; D £80.75-£85* **Facilities** STV TVL tea/coffee WiFi 🦶 **Parking** 20 **Notes** LB ⊗ No Children 16yrs Closed Dec-1 Mar

---

▮ BLACKAWTON — Map 3 SX85

The Normandy Arms

★★★★ INN

tel: 01803 712884 **Chapel St TQ9 7BN**
email: info@thenormandyarms.co.uk **web:** www.thenormandyarms.co.uk
dir: On A3122 Kingsbridge to Dartmouth road, turn right at Forces Tavern

Situated midway between Totnes and Dartmouth, this charming inn is in the heart of the village and provides a perfect setting from which to explore the beautiful coast and countryside of the South Hams. There is a stylish simplicity throughout both public areas and bedrooms, the latter offering high standards of comfort with contemporary bathrooms. The menu is a showcase for produce from the local area, presenting elegant dishes packed with flavour, and skilfully executed. Similar qualities are also evident at breakfast, a satisfying start to the day. In addition to the bar, there is also a south-facing garden in which to enjoy a relaxing drink.

Rooms 4 en suite D £85-£95 **Facilities** FTV tea/coffee Dinner available WiFi **Extras** Speciality toiletries **Conf** Max 24 Class 24 Board 20 **Parking** 3 **Notes** LB ⊗ Closed Jan-1 Feb No coaches

---

The George Inn

★★★ INN

tel: 01803 712342 **Main St TQ9 7BG**
email: tgiblackawton@yahoo.co.uk **web:** www.blackawton.com
dir: From Totnes on A381 through Halwell. Left onto A3122 towards Dartmouth, turn right to Blackawton

Situated in the heart of Blackawton, this village local offers a warm welcome to all. A proper, unspoilt pub, it enjoys an engaging traditional atmosphere and a real sense of community. Bedrooms offer good levels of comfort and quality, likewise the modern bathrooms; while public areas have an inviting, rustic charm. A wide range of food options are offered, with local produce used as much as possible. Lovely views across the rolling countryside can be enjoyed from the terrace and garden.

Rooms 4 en suite (1 fmly) **Facilities** FTV DVD tea/coffee Dinner available WiFi 🦶 **Parking** 12 **Notes** No coaches

---

▮ BOVEY TRACEY — Map 3 SX87

Courtenay House

★★★ BED AND BREAKFAST

tel: 01626 835363 **fax:** 01626 835363 **76 Fore St TQ13 9AE**
email: info@courtenayhouse.co.uk **web:** www.courtenayhouse.co.uk
dir: A38 from Exeter towards Plymouth. Follow B3344 Chudleigh Knighton signs. At T-junct in Bovey Tracey, right, follow Town Centre signs into Fore St. House on left after Orchard Terrace

Courtenay House is located in the heart of the historic town of Bovey Tracey and is the perfect base to explore the area. The bedrooms are well furnished and equipped with a range of useful amenities. A freshly cooked breakfast is served in the Tea Room just off the Antique Shop.

Rooms 3 rms (2 en suite) (1 pri facs) (1 GF) S £42-£45; D £75-£80* **Facilities** FTV tea/coffee WiFi **Notes** LB No Children 16yrs Closed 24 Dec-6 Jan

---

▮ BRIXHAM — Map 3 SX95

Anchorage Guest House

★★★★ GUEST HOUSE

tel: 01803 852960 & 07950 536362 **170 New Rd TQ5 8DA**
email: enquiries@brixham-anchorage.co.uk **web:** www.brixham-anchorage.co.uk
dir: A3022, enter Brixham, left at lights at junct with Monksbridge Rd. Pass Toll House immediately on right

Conveniently located within walking distance of the town centre and harbour, this is an excellent choice for anyone looking to explore the many attractions of this popular holiday area. The dining room and the bedrooms have a light, bright contemporary style with many extra facilities provided to ensure a comfortable stay. Guests are welcome to use the delightful garden, and on-site parking is also a bonus. AA Friendliest B&B of the Year Finalist 2014-2015.

Rooms 7 rms (6 en suite) (1 pri facs) (4 GF) S £34-£38; D £60-£75* **Facilities** FTV tea/coffee WiFi 🦶 **Parking** 6 **Notes** ⊗ No Children

---

▮ BUCKFAST — Map 3 SX76

Furzeleigh Mill

★★★ GUEST ACCOMMODATION

tel: 01364 643476 **fax:** 01364 643476 **Old Ashburton Rd TQ11 0JP**
email: enquiries@furzeleigh.co.uk **web:** www.furzeleigh.co.uk
dir: Exit A38 at Dartbridge junct, right at end slip road, right signed Ashburton/Prince Town (NB do not cross River Dart bridge), 200yds right

This Grade II listed, 16th-century converted corn mill stands in its own grounds and is a good base for touring Dartmoor. Spacious family rooms are available as well as a lounge and a bar. All meals are served in the dining room and use local produce.

Rooms 14 en suite (2 fmly) S £35-£59; D £65-£89 **Facilities** FTV TVL tea/coffee Dinner available Licensed WiFi 🦶 **Conf** Max 20 Thtr 20 **Parking** 32 **Notes** LB Closed 23 Dec-2 Jan

---

▮ BUCKFASTLEIGH — Map 3 SX76

Kilbury Manor

★★★★  GUEST ACCOMMODATION

tel: 01364 644079 **Colston Rd TQ11 0LN**
email: info@kilburymanor.co.uk **web:** www.kilburymanor.co.uk
dir: Off A38 onto B3380 to Buckfastleigh, left into Old Totnes Rd, at bottom turn right, Kilbury Manor on left

Dating back to the 17th century, this charming Devon longhouse is situated in the tranquil surroundings of the Dart Valley with access to the river across the meadow. Bedrooms have an abundance of character and are located in the main house and in adjacent converted barns; all provide high levels of comfort. The stylish bathrooms are also appointed to impressive standards. Breakfast is served in the elegant dining room with local produce very much in evidence.

Rooms 4 rms (3 en suite) (1 pri facs) (1 GF) S £65-£70; D £79-£95* **Facilities** FTV DVD tea/coffee WiFi **Parking** 5 **Notes** No Children 7yrs ⊛

BUCKFASTLEIGH *continued*

Dartbridge Inn
★★★ 🅰 INN

tel: 01364 642214 **fax:** 01364 643839 **Totnes Rd TQ11 0JR**
email: dartbridgeinn@oldenglishinns.co.uk **web:** www.oldenglish.co.uk
dir: *0.5m NE of town centre. A38 onto A384, 250yds on left*

Situated close to the beautiful River Dart, this popular inn has a friendly and relaxed atmosphere, with open fires and oak beams adding to the charm. Bedrooms are soundly appointed and an extensive menu is offered along with daily specials.

Rooms 10 en suite (1 fmly) **Facilities** FTV Lounge tea/coffee Dinner available Direct Dial WiFi 🔒 **Conf** Max 150 Thtr 150 Class 75 Board 40 **Parking** 100

CHAGFORD   Map 3 SX78

Premier Collection

Parford Well
★★★★★ BED AND BREAKFAST

tel: 01647 433353 **Sandy Park TQ13 8JW**
email: tim@parfordwell.co.uk **web:** www.parfordwell.co.uk
dir: *A30 onto A382, after 3m left at Sandy Park towards Drewsteignton, house 50yds on left*

Set in delightful grounds on the edge of Dartmoor, this attractive house is a restful and friendly home. Quality and style combine in the comfortable bedrooms. The lounge overlooks the well-tended gardens and breakfast is served at tables laid with crisp linen and silverware in one of two dining rooms. Carefully cooked local ingredients are hallmarks of a breakfast that makes the perfect start to a day exploring the moors.

Rooms 3 rms (2 en suite) (1 pri facs) D £85-£105 **Facilities** TVL tea/coffee WiFi **Extras** Speciality toiletries **Parking** 4 **Notes** ⊗ No Children 8yrs Closed Jan-Feb ⊛

CHILLATON   Map 3 SX48

Premier Collection

Tor Cottage
★★★★★ 🏠 GUEST ACCOMMODATION

tel: 01822 860248 **fax:** 01822 860126 **PL16 0JE**
email: info@torcottage.co.uk **web:** www.torcottage.co.uk
dir: *A30 Lewdown exit through Chillaton towards Tavistock, 300yds after Post Office right signed 'Bridlepath No Public Vehicular Access' to end*

Tor Cottage, located in its own valley with 18 acres of grounds, is a welcome antidote to the fast pace of everyday life. Rooms are spacious and elegant; the cottage-wing bedroom has a separate sitting room, and the garden rooms have their own wood burners. The gardens are delightful, with a stream and heated outdoor pool. An exceptional range of dishes is offered at breakfast, which can be enjoyed either in the conservatory dining room or on the terrace.

Rooms 1 en suite 3 annexe en suite (3 GF) S £98; D £150-£155 **Facilities** FTV DVD TVL tea/coffee WiFi 🎣 🔒 **Parking** 8 **Notes** LB ⊗ No Children 14yrs Closed mid Dec-beg Feb

CHRISTOW   Map 3 SX88

Hyner Farm *(SX835820)*
★★★★ FARMHOUSE

tel: 01647 252923 **EX6 7NT**
email: preston916@btinternet.com **web:** www.hynerfarm-bandb-devon.co.uk

This beautiful rural farmhouse, located in the middle of the Teign Valley has 3 highly individual bedrooms. The richly decorated rooms are well equipped and are ideal for business or leisure use. Public areas include a comfortable lounge and the dining area with its inglenook fire place is a sociable setting for breakfast. There is also parking, all in characterful grounds.

Rooms 3 en suite S fr £50; D £70-£80* **Facilities** FTV DVD TVL tea/coffee WiFi 🐾 18 🔒 **Parking** 3 **Notes** LB 120 acres beef/grass

CHULMLEIGH   Map 3 SS61

The Old Bakehouse
★★★★ 🏠 GUEST HOUSE

tel: 01769 580074 & 580137 **South Molton St EX18 7BW**
email: holly@oldbakehousedevon.co.uk **web:** www.oldbakehousedevon.co.uk
dir: *A377 onto B3096 into village centre, left into South Molton St, 100yds on left*

This 16th-century, thatched house is situated in the centre of Chulmleigh, a hilltop town which stands above a beautiful river valley. The charming bedrooms are equipped with many extras such as DVD players (library available) and are located across a pretty, secluded courtyard garden in the former village bakery. A wealth of beams, thick cob walls and wood-burning stove all contribute to the character and comfort. A generous choice is offered at breakfast with an emphasis on excellent local produce.

Rooms 3 en suite (1 GF) S £55; D £80* **Facilities** FTV DVD Lounge tea/coffee 🐾 18 🔒 **Extras** Home-made biscuits - complimentary **Notes** LB ⊗ No Children 11yrs

CLOVELLY	Map 3 SS32

East Dyke Farmhouse *(SS312235)*

★★★★ 🏠 FARMHOUSE

tel: 01237 431216 **East Dyke Farm, Higher Clovelly EX39 5RU**
email: helen.goaman@btinternet.com **web:** www.bedbreakfastclovelly.co.uk
dir: *A39 onto B3237 at Clovelly Cross rdbt, farm 500yds on left*

Adjoining an Iron Age hill fort, this working farm has glorious views of Bideford Bay in the distance. The farmhouse has a friendly atmosphere and the open fires, beams and stone floors add to its charm and character. The three bedrooms are spacious and furnished in co-ordinated fabrics with thoughtful little extras. A key feature here is the breakfast - local produce and delicious home-made preserves are served around one large table.

Rooms 3 rms (2 en suite) (1 pri facs) (1 fmly) S £40-£45; D £60-£70* **Facilities** FTV TVL tea/coffee WiFi 🔒 **Extras** Fridge **Parking** 6 **Notes** ⊗ Closed 24-26 Dec ☻ 350 acres beef/arable

COLEFORD	Map 3 SS70

The New Inn

★★★★ INN

tel: 01363 84242 **fax:** 01363 85044 **EX17 5BZ**
email: enquiries@thenewinncoleford.co.uk **web:** www.thenewinncoleford.co.uk
dir: *Exit A377 into Coleford, 1.5m to inn (signed)*

Originally dating back to the 13th century, The New Inn is a charming thatched village inn with much to offer, and is a relaxing base from which to explore this beautiful corner of Devon. Bedrooms are spacious, comfortable and well appointed with lovely beds and lots of period features. Roaring fires, flagged floors and Captain, the resident parrot, all combine to create an engaging atmosphere. A choice of carefully prepared dishes is on offer in the restaurant and bar lounges, with local produce strongly featured.

Rooms 6 en suite (4 fmly) (1 GF) S £65-£70; D £85-£95* **Facilities** DVD tea/coffee Dinner available Direct Dial WiFi ⚓ 18 🔒 **Extras** Bottled water - complimentary **Parking** 50 **Notes** LB Closed 25-26 Dec No coaches

CROYDE	Map 3 SS43

The Whiteleaf

★★★★ 🏠 GUEST HOUSE

tel: 01271 890266 **Croyde Rd EX33 1PN**
web: www.thewhiteleaf.co.uk
dir: *On B3231 entering Croyde, on left at 'Road Narrows' sign*

A warm family welcome awaits guests at this attractive house within easy walking distance of the pretty village and the sandy beach. Each of the well-equipped bedrooms has its own charm, and three rooms have decked balconies. Ambitious and imaginative dinners, using fresh seasonal produce, are served in the elegant restaurant.

Rooms 5 en suite (2 fmly) S £65-£72; D £82-£140* **Facilities** FTV Lounge tea/coffee Dinner available Direct Dial Licensed 🔒 **Extras** Mini-bar **Parking** 10 **Notes** LB ⊗ Closed 24-27 Dec

CULLOMPTON	Map 3 ST00

Premier Collection

Muddifords Court Country House

★★★★★ 🏠 GUEST ACCOMMODATION

tel: 01884 820023 & 07969 668849 **Willand EX15 2QG**
email: info@muddifords.co.uk **web:** www.muddifordscourt.co.uk
dir: *M5 junct 27 onto A38 (Wellington). After 1m at rdbt right onto B3181, at rdbt (4m) right signed Halberton/Willand. Over mini rdbt, 500mtrs turn right (Sampford Peverell). 200mtrs on right*

Muddifords Court has been developed into a high quality establishment, with the added benefit of a range of flexible meeting space to accommodate weddings, conferences and special events. The rooms have been finished to a high standard and are sumptuously appointed; some offer attractive views over the Culm Valley and beyond. A choice of freshly prepared breakfasts is served in the main dining room. Self-catering huts are available in the private copse.

Rooms 5 en suite 2 annexe en suite (1 GF) D £65-£125 (room only)* **Facilities** FTV DVD TVL tea/coffee Licensed WiFi 🔒 **Extras** Sherry **Conf** Max 100 Thtr 100 Class 80 Board 60 **Parking** 70 **Notes** ⊗ Closed 24-26 Dec Civ Wed 120

Lower Ford Farm *(SS978095)*

★★★★ 🏠 FARMHOUSE

tel: 01884 252354 **EX15 1LX**
email: lowerfordfarm@hotmail.com **web:** www.lowerfordfarm-accommodation.co.uk
dir: *M5 junct 28 Cullompton, take road by HSBC bank. At Whitedown x-rds turn left then 1st left*

A peacefully located 15th-century farmhouse, Lower Ford Farm offers naturally welcoming hospitality with a real home-from-home atmosphere. Surrounded by delightful countryside, this working farm provides a peaceful retreat. Bedrooms are comfortably furnished and equipped with some welcome extras to add to guest comfort. A spacious lounge is also available. In addition to the large, farmhouse breakfast, the home-cooked dinners (available by prior arrangement) should not be missed.

Rooms 3 en suite (1 fmly) **Facilities** FTV TVL tea/coffee Dinner available WiFi 🔒 **Parking** 6 **Notes** ⊗ Closed Nov-Jan ☻ 350 acres beef/sheep/arable

Weir Mill Farm *(ST040108)*

★★★★ FARMHOUSE

tel: 01884 820803 **Jaycroft, Willand EX15 2RE**
email: rita@weirmill-devon.co.uk **web:** www.weirmill-devon.co.uk
dir: *2m N of Cullompton. M5 junct 27, B3181 to Willand, left at rdbt onto B3340 signed Uffculme, 50yds right into Willand Moor Rd, after Lupin Way left into lane*

Set in extensive farmland, this charming 19th-century farmhouse offers comfortable accommodation with a relaxed and homely atmosphere. The spacious bedrooms are attractively decorated and equipped with an impressive range of thoughtful extras. A good choice is offered at breakfast in the well-appointed dining room.

Rooms 3 en suite (1 fmly) S £40; D £70 **Facilities** FTV tea/coffee WiFi 🔒 **Parking** 5 **Notes** ⊗ ☻ 100 acres arable/beef

DARTMEET
Map 3 SX67

Brimpts Farm
★★★ GUEST ACCOMMODATION

tel: 01364 631450 **PL20 6SG**
email: info@brimptsfarm.co.uk web: www.brimptsfarm.co.uk
dir: *Dartmeet at E end of B3357, establishment signed on right at top of hill*

A popular venue for walkers and lovers of the great outdoors, Brimpts Farm is peacefully situated in the heart of Dartmoor and has been a Duchy of Cornwall farm since 1307. Bedrooms are simply furnished and many have wonderful views across the moor. Dinner is served by arrangement. Additional facilities include a sauna and spa, and a children's play area. Brimpts Farm is also home to the Dartmoor Pony Heritage Trust.

Rooms 10 en suite 3 annexe rms (3 pri facs) (2 fmly) (7 GF) S £35; D £60-£80*
Facilities Lounge TVL TV1B tea/coffee Dinner available Licensed WiFi Sauna Pool table 🌡 Farm walks & trails Hot tub **Conf** Max 60 Thtr 60 Class 40 Board 25 **Parking** 50 **Notes** LB

DARTMOUTH
Map 3 SX85

Nonsuch House
★★★★★ 🔔 🍴 GUEST ACCOMMODATION

tel: 01803 752829 fax: 01803 752357 **Church Hill, Kingswear TQ6 0BX**
email: enquiries@nonsuch-house.co.uk web: www.nonsuch-house.co.uk
dir: *A3022 onto A379 2m before Brixham. Fork left onto B3205. Left up Higher Contour Rd, down Ridley Hill, house on bend on left at top of Church Hill*

Nonsuch House is a delightful Edwardian property with fabulous views across the Dart estuary. The marvellous hosts combine friendliness with unobtrusive service. Bedrooms are spacious and superbly appointed, each with a spectacular panorama of the harbour. Fresh, local ingredients are served at dinner, including top-quality meat, fish, and farmhouse cheeses. Breakfast, served on the patio in good weather, features freshly squeezed juice, local sausages and home-baked bread.

Rooms 4 en suite (2 fmly) (2 GF) S £100-£165; D £125-£190* **Facilities** FTV DVD iPod docking station tea/coffee Dinner available WiFi 🌡 **Extras** Speciality toiletries, home-made biscuits - free **Parking** 4 **Notes** LB ⊗ No Children 12yrs RS Sat & Tue-Wed no dinner available

Strete Barton House
★★★★★ 🔔 GUEST HOUSE

tel: 01803 770364 fax: 01803 771182 **Totnes Rd TQ6 0RU**
email: info@stretebarton.co.uk web: www.stretebarton.co.uk

(For full entry see Strete)

Appletree Court House
★★★★★ 🔔 BED AND BREAKFAST

tel: 01803 414621 & 07768 534335 **4c Church Rd TQ6 9HQ**
email: enquiries@appletreecourthouse.co.uk web: www.appletreecourthouse.co.uk
dir: *Follow signs for town centre, down hill, turn right into Townstal Rd. 1st right into Church Rd, signed*

Appletree Court House is a very high quality bed and breakfast tucked away in a quiet location, yet just a few minutes' walk from the centre of Dartmouth. Hosts John and Christine are very experienced and do all they can to make their guests feel relaxed and at home. Service is very attentive and breakfast is a real treat - a great start to the day.

Rooms 1 en suite (1 fmly) S £70; D £99-£115* **Facilities** FTV DVD Lounge tea/coffee WiFi ⛳ 27 🌡 Leisure facilities at golf & country club **Extras** Robes - complimentary **Parking** 2 **Notes** ⊗ No Children 18yrs

Campbells
★★★★★ BED AND BREAKFAST

tel: 01803 833438 **5 Mount Boone TQ6 9PB**
email: campbelldartmouth@yahoo.com
dir: *A38 exit signed Buckfastleigh/Dartmouth. In Totnes follow signs to Dartmouth, cross 2 rdbts. Top of the hill turn right into Townstal Rd. At x-rds turn left, Mount Boone. B&B on right*

This property is located just minutes from Dartmouth seafront with impressive views. Accommodation is traditional in style with modern fixtures and furnishings including free WiFi. Guests can enjoy the use of the lounge or the terrace during the warmer months. A cooked or continental breakfast is available which consists of homemade and local ingredients.

Rooms 1 en suite (1 fmly) S £75-£100; D £75-£100 **Facilities** TVL tea/coffee Dinner available WiFi **Parking** 2 **Notes** Closed Oct-1 Apr ⊕

Premier Collection

Mounthaven

★★★★★ BED AND BREAKFAST

tel: 01803 839061 & 07919 274751 **fax:** 01803 839061 **Mount Boone TQ6 9PB**
email: enquiries@mounthavendartmouth.co.uk **web:** www.mounthavendartmouth.co.uk
dir: A379, right into Townstal Rd, opposite Royal Naval College gates. 1st left into Mount Boone, halfway down on right

Set on the hillside of Mount Boone, Mounthaven has a superb view of the town and the estuary yet is only a few minutes' walk from the town centre. The hosts are experienced and professional, offering a very friendly welcome and doing all they can to make a stay memorable. Bedrooms are individually decorated and each enjoys a view of historic Dartmouth or the sea.

Rooms 3 en suite S £60-£115; D £96-£120* **Facilities** STV FTV DVD TVL tea/coffee WiFi ♨ 18 🔒 **Parking** 5 **Notes** LB ⊗ No Children 16yrs ⊜

Hill View House

★★★★ GUEST ACCOMMODATION

tel: 01803 839372 **76 Victoria Rd TQ6 9DZ**
email: enquiries@hillviewdartmouth.co.uk **web:** www.hillviewdartmouth.co.uk
dir: Phone for detailed directions

Centrally located, Hill View House is a fully refurbished five-storey late Victorian town house. A warm welcome is guaranteed and is located only minutes from the heart of Dartmouth. Bedrooms are comfortably furnished, serviced to a high standard, and come equipped with a range of accessories. Breakfast is served in the light and airy dining room. Free WiFi is accessible throughout.

Rooms 4 en suite 1 annexe en suite S £42-£47; D £70* **Facilities** TVL tea/coffee WiFi ♨ 18 **Extras** Speciality toiletries **Parking** 3 **Notes** ⊗ No Children 14yrs

Bayards Cove Inn

★★★★ 🏠 GUEST ACCOMMODATION

tel: 01803 839278 **27 Lower St TQ6 9AN**
email: bayardscove@gmail.com **web:** www.bayardscoveinn.co.uk

There is a real sense of history at this charming waterside establishment, once a Tudor merchant's house, located a few steps from where the Pilgrims set sail on the Mayflower in 1621. Every effort is made to ensure guests have a relaxed and rewarding stay. A café and wine bar by day, there is a contended buzz here; evening opening times vary, with a tapas menu available on selected nights. Bedrooms are comfortable, and individually styled. Bathrooms provide all the expected modern necessities with cosseting towels and quality toiletries. Breakfast is a generous affair, with a range of continental and cooked options, all showcasing the best of local produce.

Rooms 7 en suite (2 fmly) S £85-£150; D £90-£170* **Facilities** FTV DVD Lounge tea/coffee Dinner available Licensed WiFi ♨ 18 🔒 **Extras** Magazines - complimentary

Cherub's Nest

★★★★ GUEST ACCOMMODATION

tel: 01803 832482 **15 Higher St TQ6 9RB**
email: cherubsnest4bb@aol.com **web:** www.cherubsnest.co.uk
dir: From Lower Dartmouth ferry along Lower St, left into Smith St, left into Higher St, Cherub's Nest 50yds on left

Dating from 1710, this former merchant's house, bedecked with flowers during the summer, is located in the very heart of historic Dartmouth. Full of character, the individually decorated bedrooms vary in size, but all are attractive and well equipped. A choice of breakfasts is served in the cosy dining room.

Rooms 3 en suite **Facilities** FTV tea/coffee WiFi **Notes** ⊗ No Children 10yrs

| DAWLISH | Map 3 SX97 |

Manor Farm (SX952749)

★★★★ 🅰 FARMHOUSE

tel: 01626 863020 & 07581 499825 **Holcombe EX7 0JT**
email: humphreyclem@aol.com **web:** www.farmaccom.com
dir: A379 through Dawlish, after 1.5m turn right into Fordens Ln. Entrance opposite Castle Inn

Manor Farm is a Victorian farmhouse on a working beef farm, which is also home to horses, ponies and chickens. There are three bedrooms, all of which have sea or field views, and breakfast offers free-range eggs, local produce and home-made preserves and honey. The garden is ideal for relaxing and casual bird-watching. Guests are free to walk around the farm, and there is also a beach and an inn nearby.

Rooms 3 rms (2 en suite) (1 pri facs) (1 fmly) S £40-£45; D £66* **Facilities** FTV DVD tea/coffee WiFi ⌖ Riding Pool table 🔒 **Parking** 6 **Notes** ⊗ ⊜ 135 acres beef/livery

| DODDISCOMBSLEIGH | Map 3 SX88 |

The Nobody Inn

★★★★ ⊚ INN

tel: 01647 252394 **fax:** 01647 252978 **EX6 7PS**
email: info@nobodyinn.co.uk **web:** www.nobodyinn.co.uk
dir: From A38 turn off at top of Haldon Hill, follow signs to Doddiscombsleigh

Dating back to the 16th century, this fascinating inn is something of a mecca for lovers of wine, whisky and local ale - the choices are extensive. Let's not forget the impressive food, much of which is sourced locally including an extensive cheese selection. Bedrooms and bathrooms have been appointed to provide high levels of quality, comfort and individuality. Reassuringly, the bars and lounges remain unchanged with charmingly mis-matched furniture, age-darkened beams and an inglenook fireplace.

Rooms 5 rms (4 en suite) (1 pri facs) S £50-£75; D £70-£105 **Facilities** FTV DVD tea/coffee Dinner available Direct Dial WiFi 🔒 **Conf** Max 24 **Parking** 50 **Notes** No Children 5yrs Closed 1 Jan No coaches

| DUNKESWELL | Map 3 ST10 |

The Old Kennels

★★★★ BED AND BREAKFAST

tel: 01823 681138 **Stentwood EX14 4RW**
email: info@theoldkennels.co.uk **web:** www.theoldkennels.co.uk

Located in the heart of the beautiful Blackdown Hills, on the Devon-Somerset border, The Old Kennels is in a quiet rural location and makes an ideal base for exploring this vibrant area. Accommodation includes a cosy two bedroom loft apartment, furnished with antique and vintage details. It has a compact lounge area with TV, microwave, fridge, kettle and sink. The roof terrace and garden area have far-reaching views across the fields and valley. A continental breakfast is served in the main house, from which the resident alpacas can be seen grazing in the fields.

Rooms 2 annexe rms 1 annexe en suite (1 pri facs) (1 fmly) S £40-£45; D £80-£90* **Facilities** TVL tea/coffee WiFi ♨ 18 🔒 25 acres of woodland Arts & crafts courses **Conf** Max 12 Board 12 **Parking** 10 **Notes** LB ⊗

ERMINGTON   Map 3 SX65

Premier Collection

Plantation House
★★★★★ ⊛ 🍴 RESTAURANT WITH ROOMS

tel: 01548 831100 & 830741 **Totnes Rd PL21 9NS**
email: info@plantationhousehotel.co.uk **web:** www.plantationhousehotel.co.uk

Peacefully situated within the picturesque South Hams, this former parish rectory now provides an intimate and relaxing base from which to explore the area. Quality, comfort and individuality are hallmarks throughout, with bedrooms offering impressive standards and a host of thoughtful extras. The stylish bathrooms come equipped with fluffy towels, robes and under-floor heating. A drink beside the crackling log fire is the ideal prelude to dinner, where skill and passion underpin menus focusing upon wonderful local produce. Breakfast is equally enjoyable, with superb eggs provided by the resident hens.

Rooms 8 en suite S £55-£75; D £105-£230* **Facilities** DVD iPod docking station Lounge tea/coffee Dinner available Direct Dial WiFi ⌂ ⅃ 18 Fishing Riding Massage & Therapies **Extras** Fruit, robes, snacks, mineral water **Conf** Max 12 **Parking** 25 **Notes** LB No coaches

EXETER   Map 3 SX99

Chi Restaurant & Bar with Accommodation
★★★★ 🍴 RESTAURANT WITH ROOMS

tel: 01626 890213 **fax:** 01626 891678 **Fore St, Kenton EX6 8LD**
email: enquiries@chi-restaurant.co.uk **web:** www.chi-restaurant.co.uk
dir: 5m S of Exeter. M5 junct 30, A379 towards Dawlish, in village centre

This former pub has been spectacularly transformed into a chic and contemporary bar, allied with a stylish Chinese restaurant. Dishes are beautifully presented with an emphasis on quality produce and authenticity, resulting in a memorable dining experience. Bedrooms are well equipped and all provide good levels of space and comfort, along with modern bathrooms.

Rooms 5 en suite (1 fmly) S £45; D £58-£64 (room only) **Facilities** FTV DVD TVL tea/coffee Dinner available Direct Dial WiFi 🌣 **Parking** 26 **Notes** ⊗ No coaches

Mill Farm (SX959839)
★★★★ FARMHOUSE

tel: 01392 832471 **Kenton EX6 8JR**
email: info@millfarmstay.co.uk **web:** www.millfarmstay.co.uk
dir: A379 from Exeter towards Dawlish, over mini rdbt by Swans Nest, farm 1.75m on right

Located just a short drive from the Powderham Estate, this imposing farmhouse is surrounded by pasture. Each of the spacious bedrooms (single, twin, double or family) is stylishly co-ordinated and comfortably furnished; all rooms have countryside views. Breakfast (including vegetarian options) is served in the sunny dining room and a lounge is also provided. A packed breakfast can be prepared if a very early start is required.

Rooms 5 en suite (3 fmly) **Facilities** FTV TVL tea/coffee WiFi **Parking** 12 **Notes** ⊗ No Children 6yrs Closed Xmas 30 acres horses

Raffles
★★★★ 🅐 GUEST ACCOMMODATION

tel: 01392 270200 **fax:** 01392 270200 **11 Blackall Rd EX4 4HD**
email: raffleshtl@btinternet.com
dir: M5, exit at Exeter services, follow signs for Middlemore & City Centre

Raffles is a centrally located Victorian townhouse, and is the ideal base for visits to Exeter as well as the coast, estuaries and countryside of this beautiful part of East Devon. The house is furnished with antiques and has been restored in keeping with the age and character of the building. Meals use organic ingredients where possible, and off-street parking is available.

Rooms 6 en suite (2 fmly) S fr £48; D fr £78* **Facilities** FTV TVL tea/coffee WiFi 🌣 **Parking** 12

Innkeeper's Lodge Exeter, Clyst St George
★★★ INN

tel: 0845 112 6086 **Clyst St George EX3 0QJ**
email: info@innkeeperslodge.com **web:** www.innkeeperslodge.com

This welcoming inn is just a short drive from the centre of Exeter and very convenient for access to the M5. Surrounded by rolling fields, this is an excellent base for exploring the East Devon coast, with Exmouth close by and Topsham also worth a visit. Bedrooms all provide impressive levels of comfort and quality with all the requirements for the business and leisure guest. The pub has a warm and inviting atmosphere with crackling log fires and cosy hideaways, so sit back and enjoy a drink and a satisfying meal.

Rooms 21 en suite (6 fmly) (8 GF) **Facilities** FTV tea/coffee Dinner available Direct Dial WiFi **Parking**

EXMOUTH   Map 3 SY08

Barn
★★★★ GUEST ACCOMMODATION

tel: 01395 224411 **fax:** 01395 225445 **Foxholes Hill, Marine Dr EX8 2DF**
email: exmouthbarn@gmail.com **web:** www.barnhotel.co.uk
dir: From M5 junct 30 take A376 to Exmouth, then follow signs to seafront. At rdbt last exit into Foxholes Hill. Located on right

This is a Grade II listed establishment that enjoys a prime location, close to miles of sandy beaches. There is an immaculate rear garden, which is sea-facing and features a terrace and swimming pool for use during the summer. Service is attentive and friendly, and spectacular sea views are enjoyed from most of the well-equipped bedrooms and public rooms. Breakfast is served in the elegant dining room.

Rooms 11 en suite (4 fmly) **Facilities** FTV DVD Lounge tea/coffee Direct Dial Licensed WiFi ⌁ **Extras** Speciality toiletries - complimentary **Parking** 30 **Notes** LB Closed 23 Dec-10 Jan

The Devoncourt

★★★★ GUEST ACCOMMODATION

tel: 01395 272277 **fax:** 01395 269315 **16 Douglas Av EX8 2EX**
email: enquiries@devoncourt.com **web:** www.devoncourthotel.com
dir: *M5/A376 to Exmouth, follow seafront to Maer Rd, right at T-junct*

The Devoncourt stands in four acres of mature, subtropical gardens, sloping gently towards the sea and overlooking two miles of sandy beaches. It offers extensive leisure facilities, and the smartly furnished bedrooms are exceptionally well equipped. The spacious public areas are available to timeshare owners as well as guests. For meals there is a choice between the informal bar and the restaurant.

Rooms 52 en suite 2 annexe en suite (35 fmly) (8 GF) S £59-£77; D £69-£109 (room only)* **Facilities** FTV DVD TVL tea/coffee Dinner available Direct Dial Lift Licensed WiFi ⓣ ⚲ ⦾⦾⚑ 18 Snooker Sauna Gym Sun shower Jacuzzi **Parking** 50 **Notes** LB ⊗ Civ Wed 100

The Swallows

★★★★ BED AND BREAKFAST

tel: 01395 263937 **11 Carlton Hill EX8 2AJ**
email: coulsonlowes@googlemail.com

The Swallows is located in a quiet residential area, yet within walking distance of the seafront, beach and town centre. It is a family home, that offers comfortable accommodation within a relaxed setting. A freshly cooked breakfast, using local produce, is served in the spacious dining room overlooking the front garden.

Rooms 3 en suite (1 fmly) D £72-£80* **Facilities** FTV tea/coffee WiFi 🔒 **Parking** 3 **Notes** ⊗

GREAT TORRINGTON Map 3 SS41

Locksbeam Farm (SS483205)

★★★★ FARMHOUSE

tel: 01805 623213 & 07891 246839 **EX38 7EZ**
email: tracey@locksbeamfarm.co.uk **web:** www.locksbeamfarm.co.uk
dir: *In Great Torrington turn opposite church & follow signs for golf course. Pass course, 1st turn on right*

Locksbeam is a traditional working dairy farm offering warm hospitality and good quality accommodation. The en suite rooms are thoughtfully appointed with comfortable beds. Breakfast uses quality local produce such as sausages, eggs and bacon, and local jams and marmalades are also on offer.

Rooms 5 en suite (1 fmly) **Facilities** FTV DVD iPod docking station TVL tea/coffee WiFi ⚲⚑ 9 🔒 **Parking** 5 **Notes** ⊗ Closed Xmas 300 acres organic dairy

---

HALWELL Map 3 SX75

Stanborough Farm (SX767527)

★★★★ FARMHOUSE

tel: 01548 821306 & 07807 787327 **Halwell TQ9 7JQ**
email: stanboroughfarm@hotmail.com **web:** www.stanboroughfarm.co.uk
dir: *From Halwell turn right signed Moreleigh, farm on left*

A warm welcome is received on arrival at this working dairy farm. After a comfortable night's sleep, a freshly cooked farmhouse breakfast, using produce from the farm whenever possible, is served in the attractive breakfast room overlooking the garden. Both en suite bedrooms have been appointed to a high standard and offer all the comforts required by the modern traveller. An ideal location for exploring the South Hams. There are two country pubs within walking distance.

Rooms 3 en suite S fr £45; D fr £65 **Facilities** FTV Lounge TV2B tea/coffee WiFi **Parking** 4 **Notes** ⊗ ⊜ 130 acres dairy/poultry

HAYTOR VALE Map 3 SX77

Rock Inn

★★★★ ◉ INN

tel: 01364 661305 & 661465 **fax:** 01364 661242 **TQ13 9XP**
email: inn@rock-inn.co.uk **web:** www.rock-inn.co.uk
dir: A38 onto 382 to Bovey Tracey, in 0.5m left onto B3387 to Haytor

Dating back to the 1750s, this former coaching inn is in a pretty hamlet on the edge of Dartmoor. Each named after a Grand National winner, the individually decorated bedrooms have some nice extra touches. Bars are full of character, with flagstone floors and old beams, and offer a wide range of dishes, cooked with imagination.

Rooms 9 en suite **Facilities** STV Lounge Dinner available 🔒 **Parking** 10 **Notes** LB Closed 25-26 Dec No coaches

HELE Map 3 SS90

The Arlington

★★★ GUEST ACCOMMODATION

tel: 01392 882005 **Hillside House EX5 4PW**
email: thearlington@talktalk.net **web:** www.thearlingtonhotel.co.uk
dir: M5 junct 28 onto B3181 to Hele

The Arlington is a well maintained and comfortable establishment with good access to the M5, Cullompton and Exeter. The National Trust Woodland walk is just across the road and other attractions are only a few miles away. The en suite rooms are spacious and well equipped, and a self-service breakfast is served in the attractive dining room.

Rooms 5 en suite S £50-£70; D £55-£80* **Facilities** tea/coffee WiFi 🔒 **Conf** Max 10 **Parking Notes** ⊗ No Children 16yrs

HOLSWORTHY Map 3 SS30

The Hollies Farm Guest House (SS371001)

★★★★ FARMHOUSE

tel: 01409 253770 & 07972 510014 **Clawton EX22 6PN**
email: theholliesfarm@hotmail.com **web:** www.theholliesfarm.co.uk
dir: Exit A388 at Clawton signed vineyard, left in 2m. The Hollies in lane on left, by farm buildings, after T-junct, signed. At end of farm lane, fork right

This sheep and beef farm offers comfortable, modern accommodation with a family atmosphere. There are pleasant views across the countryside from some bedrooms, and all are well appointed. Breakfast is served in the conservatory, and dinner is available by arrangement. There is also a barbecue area with a gazebo.

Rooms 3 en suite (2 fmly) **Facilities** FTV DVD TVL tea/coffee Dinner available WiFi ⌖ 18 🔒 **Parking** 6 **Notes** LB ⊗ Closed 24-25 Dec ⊜ 25 acres beef/sheep

Thorne Park Farmhouse Accommodation (SS342061)

★★★★ FARMHOUSE

tel: 01409 253339 & 07969 381239 **Thorne Park EX22 7BL**
email: thornepark@farming.co.uk **web:** www.thornepark-devon.co.uk

Thorne Park Farmhouse is in a great position and enjoys both countryside and coast, being just over a mile from the village of Holsworthy and ten miles from the Devon coastline. Guests have a choice of two comfortable en suite bedrooms and breakfast is served in the conservatory with lovely views over the surrounding area. Ample parking is available.

Rooms 2 en suite (1 fmly) (1 GF) S £40-£47; D £70-£76* **Facilities** FTV DVD Lounge TVL tea/coffee Dinner available WiFi ⌖ 18 🔒 **Extras** Cream tea on arrival **Parking** 7 **Notes** LB ⊗ Closed Xmas 110 acres mixed

HONITON Map 4 ST10

Threshays

★★★ BED AND BREAKFAST

tel: 01404 43551 & 07811 675800 **fax:** 01404 43551 **Awliscombe EX14 3QB**
email: threshays@btinternet.com **web:** www.stayat.co.uk/threshays
dir: 2.5m NW of Honiton on A373

A converted threshing barn, situated on a non-working farm, Threshays has wonderful views over open countryside. With tea and cake offered on arrival, this family-run establishment provides comfortable accommodation in a friendly atmosphere. The lounge-dining room is a light and airy setting for enjoying breakfasts. Ample parking is a bonus.

Rooms 2 rms (1 fmly) S £35; D £60 **Facilities** TVL tea/coffee WiFi **Parking** 4 **Notes** ⊗ ⊜

HOPE COVE Map 3 SX64

Cottage

★★★★ GUEST ACCOMMODATION

tel: 01548 561555 **fax:** 01548 561455 **TQ7 3HJ**
email: info@hopecove.com **web:** www.hopecove.com
dir: From Kingsbridge on A381 to Salcombe. 2nd right at Marlborough, left for Inner Hope

Glorious sunsets can be seen over the attractive bay from this popular accommodation. Friendly and attentive service from the staff and management mean many guests return here. Bedrooms, many with sea views and some with balconies, are well equipped. The restaurant offers an enjoyable dining experience.

Rooms 32 rms (31 en suite) (1 pri facs) (5 fmly) (5 GF) S £53.50-£79; D £118.80-£180* (incl.dinner) **Facilities** FTV DVD Lounge TVL tea/coffee Dinner available Direct Dial Licensed WiFi ch fac ⌖ 18 🔒 Table tennis **Conf** Max 70 Thtr 60 Class 60 Board 30 **Parking** 50 **Notes** LB Closed early Jan-early Feb

ILFRACOMBE Map 3 SS54

Strathmore

★★★★ GUEST ACCOMMODATION

tel: 01271 862248 **fax:** 08444 849387 **57 St Brannock's Rd EX34 8EQ**
email: info@the-strathmore.co.uk **web:** www.the-strathmore.co.uk
dir: A361 from Barnstaple to Ilfracombe, Strathmore 1.5m from Mullacot Cross entering Ilfracombe

Situated within walking distance of the town centre and beach, this charming Victorian property offers a very warm welcome. The attractive bedrooms are comfortably furnished, while public areas include a well-stocked bar, an attractive terraced garden, and an elegant breakfast room.

Rooms 8 en suite (3 fmly) S £40; D £75* **Facilities** FTV DVD Lounge tea/coffee Licensed WiFi 🔒 **Extras** Mini-fridges in family rooms **Parking** 5 **Notes** LB

Collingdale Guest House

★★★★ 🏠 GUEST HOUSE

tel: 01271 863770 **13 Larkstone Ter EX34 9NU**
email: thecollingdale@gmail.com web: www.thecollingdale.co.uk
dir: *Take A399 E through Ilfracombe, on left past B3230 turning*

Overlooking the harbour, this Victorian guest house is within easy walking distance of the town centre and seafront. The well-presented bedrooms, many with sweeping sea views, are furnished to a high standard with many thoughtful extras. The comfortable lounge and elegant dining room share the magnificent views. A cosy bar is also available for a tipple before bedtime.

Rooms 9 rms (8 en suite) (1 pri facs) (3 fmly) S £50-£62; D £75-£88* **Facilities** FTV TVL tea/coffee Licensed WiFi ⚓ 18 **Extras** Mineral water - complimentary **Notes** LB ⊗ No Children 8yrs Closed Nov-Feb

Marine Court

★★★★ GUEST HOUSE

tel: 01271 862920 & 07791 051778 **Hillsborough Rd EX34 9QQ**
email: info@marinecourthoteldevon.co.uk web: www.marinecourthoteldevon.co.uk
dir: *M5 junct 27, A361 to Barnstaple, continue to Ilfracombe*

Marine Court is a well-established guest house offering comfortable, well appointed rooms in a handy location. Guests are assured a very warm welcome from the hosts who do all they can to ensure a comfortable stay. Guests have use of a small bar lounge where drinks can be served, and off-road parking is a bonus.

Rooms 8 en suite (1 fmly) S £50; D £70-£95* **Facilities** FTV DVD iPod docking station Lounge tea/coffee Licensed WiFi **Parking** 8 **Notes** ⊗ No Children 8yrs Closed Nov-Mar

Norbury House

★★★★ GUEST HOUSE

tel: 01271 863888 **Torrs Park EX34 8AZ**
email: info@norburyhouse.co.uk web: www.norburyhouse.co.uk
dir: *From A399 to end of High St/Church St. At mini rdbt after lights take 1st exit into Church Rd. Bear left into Osbourne Rd. At T-junct left into Torrs Park. House at top of hill on right*

This detached Victorian residence has a refreshingly different, contemporary style, and the genuinely warm welcome is allied with a helpful and attentive approach. A variety of bedroom styles is offered but all provide impressive levels of comfort and quality. An elegant lounge leads through to a conservatory which has an honesty bar. Outside, the peaceful terraced gardens have lovely views. Cuisine is taken seriously here, with breakfast featuring quality, local produce.

Rooms 6 en suite (2 fmly) **Facilities** FTV tea/coffee Licensed WiFi **Conf** Max 18 Thtr 14 Class 14 Board 12 **Parking** 6 **Notes** ⊗

KENTISBEARE Map 3 ST00

Orway Crescent Farm Bed & Breakfast

★★★★ BED AND BREAKFAST

tel: 01884 266876 & 0845 658 8472 **fax:** 01884 266876
Orway Crescent Farm, Orway EX15 2EX
email: orway.crescentfarm@btinternet.com web: www.orway-crescent-farm.co.uk
dir: *M5 junct 28, A373 towards Honiton. 5m, Keepers Cottage pub on right, next left for Sheldon & Broad Rd. 3rd left to Orway, farm at bottom of hill*

Located in a sleepy rural hamlet, this welcoming home is appointed to an impressive standard and is just five miles from the M5. Bedrooms combine comfort and quality in equal measure, and have numerous useful extras which typify the caring and helpful approach here. The stylish modern bathrooms are simply superb, either for an invigorating shower or relaxing soak in the bath. The dining room is the venue for substantial breakfasts with lovely views across the fields to woodland beyond.

Rooms 3 en suite (1 fmly) (1 GF) **Facilities** STV FTV tea/coffee WiFi **Parking** 3 **Notes** ⊗

KENTISBURY Map 3 SS64

Nightingails

★★★★ 🏠 GUEST ACCOMMODATION

tel: 01271 883545 **Kentisbury Mill EX31 4NF**
email: info@nightingails.co.uk web: www.nightingails.co.uk
dir: *M5 junct 27, A361 towards Barnstaple, then A399 to Blackmoor Gate. Left at Blackmoor Gate onto A39, right onto B3229 at Kentisbury Ford, 1m on right*

Originally consisting of an 18th-century cottage and mill, this relaxing hideaway has been sympathetically renovated to provide impressive levels of comfort, allied with caring hospitality. Bedrooms offer an appealing blend of old and new, with views over the extensive gardens. A guest lounge is also provided with plenty of local information for those wanting to explore the dramatic coast and countryside. Breakfast is Aga-cooked and includes eggs laid by the resident hens, together with other wonderful local produce.

Rooms 5 en suite S £37.50; D £68-£75* **Facilities** FTV DVD Lounge tea/coffee Dinner available WiFi 🔒 **Parking** 6 **Notes** LB ⊗ Closed Xmas

---

LEWDOWN Map 3 SX48

Lobhill Farmhouse

★★★★ BED AND BREAKFAST

tel: 01566 783542 & 07817 244687 **EX20 4DT**
email: jane.colwill@btopenworld.com web: www.lobhillbedandbreakfast.co.uk
dir: *Exit A30 at Sourton Cross, follow signs for Lewdown onto old A30. Lobhill 1m before Lewdown*

Ideally situated for easy access to moorland and the Devon and Cornwall coasts, this stone farmhouse dates back some 130 years. Peacefully located, its renovation has resulted in impressive levels of quality, yet it still retains a reassuringly traditional and homely feel. Bedrooms (including one on the ground floor with separate access) have free WiFi and views of the countryside. Tasty and satisfying breakfasts are cooked on the Aga and served either in the dining room or at the kitchen table. Guests are welcome to make use of the lovely gardens and summerhouse, or explore the woodland walks.

Rooms 4 en suite (1 fmly) (1 GF) S £50; D £70-£90* **Facilities** FTV DVD tea/coffee WiFi Fishing 🔒 **Extras** Home-made biscuits **Parking** 8 **Notes** LB

LIFTON
Map 3 SX38

Tinhay Mill Guest House

★★★★ BED AND BREAKFAST

tel: 01566 784201 **fax:** 01566 784201 **Tinhay PL16 0AJ**
email: tinhay.mill@talk21.com **web:** www.tinhaymillrestaurant.co.uk
dir: *A30/A388 approach Lifton, establishment at bottom of village on right*

These former mill cottages have been transformed into a delightful and relaxing place that makes the most of the peace and tranquillity of the area. Charming rooms offers impressive levels of comfort, with a good nights sleep guaranteed. Beams and open fireplaces set the scene with a guest lounge also provided. Breakfast is a tasty treat with excellent local produce utilised.

Rooms 5 en suite (1 GF) **Facilities** FTV DVD Lounge tea/coffee Licensed WiFi 🔒
Parking 10 **Notes** LB ⊗ No Children 14yrs Closed Nov-Feb

LUSTLEIGH
Map 3 SX78

Premier Collection

Eastwrey Barton

★★★★★ 🖙 GUEST ACCOMMODATION

tel: 01647 277338 **Moretonhampstead Rd TQ13 9SN**
email: info@eastwreybarton.co.uk **web:** www.eastwreybarton.co.uk
dir: *On A382 between Bovey Tracey & Moretonhampstead, 6m from A38 (Drumbridges junct)*

Warm hospitality and a genuine welcome are hallmarks at this family-run establishment, situated inside the Dartmoor National Park. Built in the 18th century, the house retains many original features and has views across the Wray Valley. Bedrooms are spacious and well equipped, while public areas include a cosy lounge warmed by a crackling log fire. Breakfast and dinner showcase local produce with an impressive wine list to accompany the latter.

Rooms 5 en suite (1 fmly) S £95-£115; D £120-£140* **Facilities** FTV Lounge tea/coffee Dinner available Licensed WiFi 🔒 **Parking** 18 **Notes** ⊗ No Children 10yrs

LYDFORD
Map 3 SX58

Premier Collection

Moor View House

★★★★★ 🖙 GUEST ACCOMMODATION

tel: 01822 820220 **fax:** 01822 820220 **Vale Down EX20 4BB**
email: moorviewhouse@yahoo.co.uk
dir: *4m from Sourton A30/A386, signed Tavistock, NE of Lydford*

Built around 1870, this charming house once changed hands over a game of cards. The elegant bedrooms are furnished with interesting pieces and retain many original features. Breakfast, and dinner by arrangement, are served house-party style at a large oak table. The two acres of moorland gardens give access to Dartmoor.

Rooms 3 en suite 1 annexe en suite (1 pri facs) (1 GF) S £45-£50; D £70-£85*
Facilities FTV DVD Lounge TVL tea/coffee Dinner available Licensed WiFi 🐾 🔒
Extras Fruit - complimentary **Parking** 15 **Notes** LB ⊗ No Children 12yrs Closed 23 Dec-2 Jan 🅿

LYNMOUTH
Map 3 SS74

Premier Collection

The Heatherville

★★★★★ 🖵 🖙 GUEST ACCOMMODATION

tel: 01598 752327 & 753893 **Tors Park EX35 6NB**
email: theheatherville@aol.com **web:** www.heatherville.co.uk
dir: *Exit A39 into Tors Rd, 1st left fork into Tors Park*

This wonderful Victorian establishment stands high above Lynmouth, and the views across the wooded valley are quite superb. There is an abundance of charm and quality here at The Heatherville, and bedrooms are individually styled with comfort and character. Public rooms are also inviting with an elegant lounge and snug bar, whilst the dining room is the attractive venue for skilfully prepared dinners and substantial breakfasts.

Rooms 6 en suite D £90-£125* **Facilities** FTV DVD Lounge tea/coffee Dinner available Licensed WiFi 🔒 **Parking** 6 **Notes** LB ⊗ No Children 16yrs Closed Nov-Mar

Rock House

★★★★ GUEST ACCOMMODATION

tel: 01598 753508 **fax:** 0800 756 6964 **Manor Green EX35 6EN**
email: enquiries@rock-house.co.uk **web:** www.rock-house.co.uk
dir: *From A39, at foot of Countisbury Hill right into drive, pass Manor Green (play area) to Rock House*

Located next to the river with wonderful views of the harbour and out to sea, this enchanting establishment dates back to the 18th century and has much to offer. Bedrooms are well appointed, and many have the benefit of wonderful views of the rolling waves. A choice of menus is offered, either in the spacious lounge/bar or in the smart dining room. The garden is a popular venue for cream teas in the summer.

Rooms 8 en suite (1 GF) **Facilities** FTV DVD iPod docking station TVL tea/coffee Dinner available Licensed WiFi 🔒 **Parking** 8 **Notes** Closed 24-25 Dec

East Lyn House

★★★ GUEST HOUSE

tel: 01598 752540 **17 Watersmeet Rd EX35 6EP**
email: eastlynhousehotel@gmail.com **web:** www.eastlynhouse.co.uk

Just a short stroll from the centre of the village and the harbour, this is a perfect place to stay, relax and enjoy this picturesque location. Bedrooms provide all the expected comforts with comfy beds ensuring a good rest before the day's activities. Public areas include a bar and lounge, while outside a wonderful terrace looks out over the River Lyn, with stunning views up the densely wooded valley. Breakfast is a tasty start to the day, and can be served on the terrace in summer months. Parking is also available.

Rooms 8 en suite (1 fmly) S £70-£80; D £80-£100* **Facilities** FTV DVD Lounge TVL tea/coffee Licensed WiFi 🔒 **Parking** 8 **Notes** No Children 8yrs

| LYNTON | Map 3 SS74 |

The Denes

★★★★ GUEST HOUSE

tel: 01598 753573 **15 Longmead EX35 6DQ**
email: j.e.mcgowan@btinternet.com **web:** www.thedenes.com

With the dramatic Valley of the Rocks just down the road, this is an ideal base from which to explore the superb landscape of Exmoor. The welcome is always warm and genuine with every effort made to ensure a stay is relaxing, rewarding and memorable. Within a short stroll of the village centre, there is a real homeliness about this establishment with bedrooms and bathrooms all offering extra comforts. Breakfast is a generous offering, served in the well-appointed dining room.

Rooms 5 rms (4 en suite) (1 pri facs) (2 fmly) S £40-£55; D £65-£75* **Facilities** DVD TVL tea/coffee Licensed WiFi Pool table 🔒 **Parking** 5 **Notes** LB ⊗

Gable Lodge Guest House

★★★★ GUEST ACCOMMODATION

tel: 01598 752367 **35 Lee Rd EX35 6BS**
email: gablelodge@btconnect.com **web:** www.gablelodgelynton.co.uk
dir: M5 junct 23 onto A39 to Lynmouth. Right up hill to Lynton, right at top of hill signed Lynton. Continue through town, Gable Lodge on right

Gable Lodge is a Grade II listed, family-run, Victorian establishment just a short stroll from the centre of this small town. The welcome is warm and genuine with plenty of local information, help and advice always available to help ensure a memorable stay. Bedrooms all provide good levels of comfort and quality with lovely views an added bonus. Generous breakfasts are served in the dining room, and evening meals also available on request. Additional facilities include a guest lounge and parking.

Rooms 6 en suite (2 fmly) S £37.50-£45; D £59-£70* **Facilities** FTV DVD iPod docking station TVL tea/coffee Dinner available Licensed WiFi 🔒 **Extras** Mini-fridge, fresh milk **Parking** 5 **Notes** LB ⊗ Closed Xmas

Pine Lodge Guest House

★★★★ GUEST ACCOMMODATION

tel: 01598 753230 **Lynway EX35 6AX**
email: info@pinelodgelynton.co.uk

Peacefully located within a few minutes' walk of the town centre, Pine Lodge offers very comfortable, well-equipped bedrooms and bathrooms plus off-road parking. Hearty breakfasts, using local quality ingredients, are served in the breakfast room

and include seasonal fresh fruit. The hosts do all they can to make a stay here as enjoyable and as relaxing as possible.

Rooms 5 en suite **Facilities** FTV Lounge tea/coffee Licensed WiFi 🔒 **Parking** 5 **Notes** ⊗ No Children 12yrs

Sinai House

★★★★ GUEST HOUSE

tel: 01598 753227 **Lynway EX35 6AY**
email: enquiries@sinaihouse.co.uk **web:** www.sinaihouse.co.uk
dir: A39 onto B3234 through town, pass church, house on right overlooking main car park

Originally built in 1850, this grand house stands in half an acre of terraced gardens, just a short stroll from the centre of town. Spectacular views can be enjoyed from many of the comfy, well-appointed bedrooms, likewise from the elegant guest lounge. The welcome is warm and genuine with every effort made to ensure a relaxed and rewarding stay. In addition to the satisfying breakfasts, dinner and bar snacks are also available, served either in the spacious dining room or snug bar.

Rooms 8 rms (6 en suite) (2 pri facs) S £40; D £74-£76* **Facilities** FTV DVD Lounge tea/coffee Licensed WiFi 🔒 **Parking** 8 **Notes** ⊗ No Children 12yrs Closed Xmas

Southcliffe Guest House

★★★★ BED AND BREAKFAST

tel: 01598 753328 **fax:** 08721 139542 **34 Lee Rd EX35 6BS**
email: info@southcliffe.co.uk **web:** www.southcliffe.co.uk
dir: A39 into town, just past post office

Perfectly located for exploring the delights of this spectacular area, Southcliffe is an ideal base for rest, relaxation and a genuine welcome. Helpful advice is always available with every effort made to ensure a rewarding and enjoyable stay. Bedrooms provide all the comforts required with two rooms having the added bonus of balconies with wonderful views. Breakfast and dinner (by arrangement) are served in the elegant dining room with tasty produce on offer. Additional facilities include a guest lounge and ample parking.

Rooms 6 en suite S £45-£52; D £70-£84* **Facilities** FTV Lounge tea/coffee Dinner available Licensed WiFi 🔒 **Extras** Speciality toiletries, chocolates **Parking** 6 **Notes** LB No Children 10yrs Closed Dec-Feb

The Fernery

★★★ BED AND BREAKFAST

tel: 01598 753265 & 07970 857459 **Lydiate Ln EX35 6AJ**
email: info@thefernerylynton.com **web:** www.thefernerylynton.com
dir: B3234 to Lynton into Castle Hill. Then Lee Rd, turn left into Cross St. Left into Lydiate Ln, 300mtrs on right

Nestled in a quiet street within a few minutes' walk of the town centre, The Fernery provides a comfortable, convenient base for exploring the North Devon coast and Exmoor. Rooms are bright and have very comfortable beds, and breakfast features local quality produce. There is on-street parking nearby and two main public car parks close by.

Rooms 3 en suite S £40.50-£51; D £54-£68* **Facilities** FTV DVD Lounge tea/coffee WiFi 🔒 **Notes** ⊗

LYNTON *continued*

Waterloo House

★★★ ◎ GUEST ACCOMMODATION

tel: 01598 752575 **Lydiate Ln EX35 6AJ**
email: info@waterloohousehotel.com **web:** www.waterloohousehotel.com
dir: *A39 into Lynton, road bends to Lydiate Ln*

Waterloo House is a traditional establishment in a quiet setting within easy reach of the town. Rooms are comfortably furnished and guests have use of a pleasant lounge. Dinner is a treat and best use is made of local, fresh ingredients.

Rooms 5 en suite S £32.50-£37.50; D £65-£99* **Facilities** FTV Lounge tea/coffee Dinner available Licensed WiFi 🔒 **Extras** Mini-fridge, fresh milk **Parking** 1 **Notes** LB No Children 18yrs

▮ MORETONHAMPSTEAD   Map 3 SX78

Great Sloncombe Farm *(SX737864)*

★★★★ ▲ FARMHOUSE

tel: 01647 440595 **fax:** 01647 440595 **TQ13 8QF**
email: hmerchant@sloncombe.freeserve.co.uk **web:** www.greatsloncombefarm.co.uk
dir: *A382 from Moretonhampstead towards Chagford, 1.5m left at sharp double bend & farm 0.5m up lane*

This attractive farmhouse is set in a peaceful valley and is surrounded by beautiful meadows and woodland. Ideal as a base for visiting the area or for a relaxing break this is a most pleasant home where guests are made to feel comfortable and welcome. The bedrooms enjoy splendid views and are comfortable and spacious.

Rooms 3 en suite S £40-£45; D £76-£84* **Facilities** FTV DVD tea/coffee WiFi 🔒 **Parking** 3 **Notes** 170 acres beef/horses

▮ NEWTON ABBOT   Map 3 SX87

Bulleigh Barton Manor

★★★★ BED AND BREAKFAST

tel: 01803 873411 & 07973 422678 **Ipplepen TQ12 5UA**
email: liz.lamport@escapetosouthdevon.co.uk **web:** www.escapetosouthdevon.co.uk
dir: *From A381 follow signs to Bulleigh and Compton Castle. Bear left along narrow lane, after 1.5m Bickley Mill signed on left, drive directly opposite turning*

Warm hospitality and a genuine welcome are hallmarks at this family-run establishment. This wonderful house dates back to the 1400s and is steeped in history. Today it offers en suite bedrooms providing comfortable accommodation in a peaceful countryside location. Breakfast is a hearty affair featuring locally sourced produce.

Rooms 3 en suite S £70-£90; D £80-£110* **Facilities** FTV DVD Lounge tea/coffee Dinner available WiFi ⚑ ✿ 🔒 **Extras** Home-made fudge & cakes, fresh milk - free **Parking** 3 **Notes** LB No Children 16yrs ✉

Bulleigh Park Farm *(SX860660)*

★★★★ ◎ FARMHOUSE

tel: 01803 872254 **fax:** 01803 872254 **Ipplepen TQ12 5UA**
email: bulleigh@lineone.net **web:** www.southdevonaccommodation.co.uk
dir: *3.5m S of Newton Abbot. Exit A381 at Parkhill Cross, by petrol station, for Compton, 1m, signed*

Bulleigh Park is a working farm; stock includes a rare breed of sheep, the Devon Closewool. Expect a warm friendly welcome at this family home set in glorious tranquil countryside, but centrally located for the coast and Dartmoor. The breakfasts are notable for their wealth of fresh, local and home-made produce, and

the porridge is cooked using a secret recipe. Home-made tea and cakes greet guests on arrival. The local inn is just a short stroll away.

Rooms 2 en suite (1 fmly) S £48-£50; D £78-£84* **Facilities** FTV iPod docking station Lounge TVL tea/coffee WiFi 🔒 **Extras** Mini-fridge **Parking** 6 **Notes** LB Closed Dec-1 Feb 60 acres beef/sheep/hens

Dunkeld House

★★★★ BED AND BREAKFAST

tel: 01626 821306 & 07773 719221 **Exeter Cross TQ12 6EY**
email: susan.small12@btinternet.com **web:** www.dunkeldhouse-bedandbreakfast.co.uk
dir: *A38 onto A382, at rdbt 3rd exit signed Liverton. Pass post office on left, Dunkeld House on left*

Dunkeld House is newly built, with ample parking and manicured borders, ideally located to explore the Dartmoor National Park. The two rooms are well appointed and offer comfortable accommodation and a range of amenities. Breakfast is served in the conservatory at individual tables.

Rooms 2 rms (1 en suite) (1 pri facs) S £60-£68; D £65-£85* **Facilities** FTV DVD Lounge TVL tea/coffee WiFi 🔒 **Parking** 5 **Notes** ⊗ No Children 12yrs

▮ NOSS MAYO   Map 3 SX54

Worswell Barton Farmhouse B&B *(SX549464)*

★★★★ FARMHOUSE

tel: 01752 872977 **Worswell Barton PL8 1HB**
email: info@worswellbarton.co.uk **web:** www.worswellbarton.co.uk
dir: *M5 onto A38, exit at Smithaleigh & follow signs to Yealmpton (B3186). Continue to Newton Ferrers then Noss Mayo. At Bridgend, up hill to church then Stoke Rd/Cross Rd continue to end*

Worswell Barton is very much a working farm, owned by the National Trust and home to the family for over 65 years. The farmhouse can trace its roots back to the Domesday Book with period features adding to the charm and character. Bedrooms and bathrooms are up-to-date and provide all the necessary contemporary comforts. Breakfast is served around the dining table with wonderful eggs from the farm and locally produced bacon and sausages. The setting is quite spectacular, a haven for those wishing to relax and unwind, surrounded by stunning coastal scenery. There are many local walks, with the South West Coast Path just a short walk from the farm.

Rooms 4 rms (2 en suite) (2 pri facs) S £40-£55; D £85-£110 **Facilities** FTV TVL tea/coffee WiFi ⌇ **Extras** Robes, slippers **Parking** 4 **Notes** LB ⊗ ⊛ 1000 acres mixed

▮ OAKFORD   Map 3 SS92

Harton Farm *(SS905222)*

★★★ FARMHOUSE

tel: 01398 351209 **EX16 9HH**
email: lindy@hartonfarm.co.uk **web:** www.hartonfarm.co.uk
dir: *M5 junct 27 onto A361 towards Barnstaple. At 1st rdbt onto A396 towards Minehead. Bear left at Exeter Inn & again at Black Cat garage. 2m on right, after crossing River Exe*

Good food and warm hospitality characterise this comfortable old stone farmhouse on the fringes of Exmoor. Harton Farm lies hidden amongst fields and trees at the end of a quiet lane. Home-reared, additive-free meat, with fruit and vegetables from the secluded walled garden, is used in the evening meals. Guests are welcome to walk the farm trail of this working - mainly sheep - farm in the company of canine guides. Gold awards from both Green Tourism and Devon Wildlife Trust demonstrate a strong commitment to a sustainable Exmoor. Maps and local information are freely available.

Rooms 2 rms (1 pri facs) (1 fmly) S £40; D £60* **Facilities** TVL tea/coffee Dinner available 🔌 Farm walk with nature notes Lamb feeding in spring **Parking** 3 **Notes** LB No Children 4yrs Closed Nov-Mar 🐾 63 acres sheep

OKEHAMPTON   Map 3 SX59

See also Holsworthy

Meadowlea Guest House

★★★★ GUEST HOUSE

tel: 01837 53200 **65 Station Rd EX20 1EA**
email: meadowleaguesthouse@tiscali.co.uk **web:** www.meadowleaguesthouse.co.uk
dir: *From A30 onto B3260, after 2m left at lights, then 3rd right into Station Rd. 200yds on left*

A well-presented period house, Meadowlea has been modernised over the years but still retains its Victorian essence. A range of comfortably appointed rooms for all budgets, some with shared facilities, is offered. There is a well appointed sitting room in which to relax and local produce is used on the breakfast menu. Should you wish to eat in, after a long day exploring the local area, guests are welcome to use the breakfast room, which is suitably equipped. Secure storage for bicycles is available.

Rooms 7 rms (4 en suite) (1 fmly) S £29-£45; D £53-£70* **Facilities** FTV Lounge tea/coffee WiFi 🔌 Drying room for boots & coats **Extras** Bottled water - complimentary **Parking** 2 **Notes** ⊗

OTTERY ST MARY   Map 3 SY19

Fluxton Farm

★★ BED AND BREAKFAST

tel: 01404 812818 **fax:** 01404 814843 **Fluxton EX11 1RJ**
email: ann@fluxtonfarm.co.uk **web:** www.fluxtonfarm.co.uk
dir: *2m SW of Ottery St Mary. B3174, W from Ottery over river, left, next left to Fluxton*

A haven for cat lovers, Fluxton Farm offers comfortable accommodation with a choice of lounges and a large garden, complete with pond and ducks. Set in peaceful farmland four miles from the coast, this 16th-century longhouse has a wealth of beams and open fireplaces.

Rooms 7 en suite S fr £32.50; D fr £65* **Facilities** FTV Lounge TVL tea/coffee WiFi 🔌 **Parking** 15 **Notes** LB No Children 8yrs RS Nov-Apr pre-booked & wknds only 🐾

PAIGNTON   Map 3 SX86

Premier Collection

The P&M Paignton RESIDENCE

★★★★★ BED AND BREAKFAST

tel: 01803 523118 & 07803 290568 **fax:** 01803 523118 **2 Kernou Rd TQ4 6BA**
email: mail@paignton-residence.com **web:** www.paignton-residence.com
dir: *Follow signs to seafront, into Kernou Rd, close to cinema*

A warm welcome is guaranteed in this smart B&B, very conveniently located within walking distance of Paignton seafront. All eight bedrooms are comfortably furnished, serviced to a high standard, and come equipped with a range of accessories. Breakfast is served in the light and airy dining room. Free WiFi is available throughout.

Rooms 8 en suite (1 GF) S £67.50-£91; D £67.50-£91* **Facilities** FTV DVD iPod docking station tea/coffee WiFi 🔌 Sauna in 1 room **Conf** Max 10 Thtr 10 Class 10 Board 10 **Parking** 2 **Notes** ⊗ No Children 16yrs

Beaches B&B

★★★★ BED AND BREAKFAST

tel: 01803 459656 **9 Manor Rd TQ3 2HT**
email: mikemitchell21@hotmail.com

Situated just a few hundred metres from Paignton seafront, this bed and breakfast offers bright, spacious, well-equipped rooms with comfortable beds. Breakfast is served in the light, airy breakfast rooms and guests have use of complimentary WiFi, a well-appointed guest lounge, and free off-road parking.

Rooms 4 rms S £50-£65; D £60-£99*

The Clydesdale

★★★★ GUEST HOUSE

tel: 01803 558402 **fax:** 01803 558402 **5 Polsham Park TQ3 2AD**
email: theclydesdale@hotmail.co.uk **web:** www.theclydesdale.co.uk
dir: *Exit A3022 (Torquay Rd) into Lower Polsham Rd, 2nd right into Polsham Park*

Tucked away in a quiet residential area, this is an ideal location from which to explore the varied attractions of Paignton and the wider Torbay area. The welcome is warm and genuine, with every effort made to ensure a relaxed and rewarding stay. The bedrooms are well appointed and provide all the expected modern comforts. Breakfast is served in the dining room; a separate guest lounge is also available.

Rooms 7 en suite (1 fmly) (2 GF) S £25-£30; D £50-£60 **Facilities** FTV TVL tea/coffee WiFi 🔌 **Parking** 6 **Notes** LB ⊗ Closed Xmas & New Year 🐾

Collerton Lodge Bed and Breakfast

★★★★ BED AND BREAKFAST

tel: 01803 554018 & 669045 **332 Totnes Rd TQ4 7HD**
email: sandra.singleton@sky.com **web:** www.collertonlodge.co.uk
dir: *A3022 to Paignton then left onto A385 towards Totnes. 100yds on right*

Ideally situated for access to the Torbay area, this warm and welcoming establishment offers high standards of accommodation, with every effort made to ensure an enjoyable stay. Bedrooms all provide impressive levels of comfort and quality with all the expected necessities, likewise the modern bathrooms with robes also provided. Breakfast is a generous and tasty offering, served in the conservatory with lovely views over the surrounding houses and fields. Ample parking is also provided, along with a guest lounge.

Rooms 5 en suite (1 fmly) **Facilities** FTV DVD Lounge TVL tea/coffee WiFi ⚡ 18 🔌 **Parking** 5 **Notes** ⊗ No Children 5yrs

PAIGNTON *continued*

Devon House Guest House

★★★★ GUEST HOUSE

tel: 01803 445570 **20 Garfield Rd TQ4 6AX**
email: naomi@devonhouseguesthouse.co.uk **web:** www.devonhouseguesthouse.co.uk

Devon House has been lovingly restored by the present owners and is conveniently located to explore Paignton and its surrounding area. All rooms offer comfortable beds and a range of facilities to meet the needs of a varied clientele, including families. A freshly cooked breakfast is served in the attractive dining rooms on the ground floor.

Rooms 8 en suite (3 fmly) S £40; D £80* **Facilities** FTV tea/coffee WiFi **Notes** LB ⊗ Closed Dec-Jan ⓐ

Merritt House B&B

★★★★ ≙ GUEST ACCOMMODATION

tel: 01803 528959 **7 Queens Rd TQ4 6AT**
email: bookings@merritthouse.co.uk **web:** http://merritthouse.co.uk
dir: *From Paignton seafront, right into Torbay Rd, 1st left into Queens Rd, house on right*

Just a five-minute stroll from the seafront and town centre, this elegant Victorian property is ideally situated to make the most of this traditional resort. The owners take great pride in their establishment and will assist in any way possible to make sure your stay is relaxed and rewarding. Bedrooms and bathrooms are thoughtfully furnished and generously equipped, and breakfast is a real treat, with plenty of choice and an emphasis on local and home-made produce.

Rooms 7 en suite (3 GF) S £34-£42; D £53-£73* **Facilities** FTV DVD tea/coffee WiFi ⓐ Drying room **Conf** Max 7 Board 7 **Parking** 4 **Notes** No Children 14yrs Closed Dec-Jan

The Wentworth Guest House

★★★★ GUEST HOUSE

tel: 01803 557843 **18 Youngs Park Rd, Goodrington TQ4 6BU**
email: enquiries@wentworthguesthouse.co.uk **web:** www.wentworthguesthouse.co.uk
dir: *Through Paignton on A378, 1m left at rdbt, sharp right into Roundham Rd, right & right again into Youngs Park Rd*

Quietly located opposite a pretty park, this is an ideal location for exploring the many and varied attractions of the English Riviera. Goodrington's lovely beaches are just a short stroll, and the town centre is a 10-15 minute walk away. The caring owners are always on hand to assist with local information. Bedrooms offer good levels of comfort and include both a dog-friendly room and family rooms. Breakfast is served in the informal dining room with a cosy guest lounge also provided.

Rooms 10 en suite (2 fmly) S £30-£47; D £55-£72* **Facilities** FTV TVL tea/coffee Licensed WiFi **Parking** 5 **Notes** LB Closed 16 Dec-2 Jan

St Edmunds Guest House

★★★ GUEST ACCOMMODATION

tel: 01803 558756 **fax:** 01803 390364 **25 Sands Rd TQ4 6EG**
email: info@stedmunds-guesthouse.co.uk **web:** www.stedmunds-guesthouse.co.uk
dir: *Follow signs for Paignton via A380, turn left over level crossing then 2nd right into Queens Rd, last house on right*

Located just a short stroll from the beach, town centre and harbour, this is a perfect choice for anyone looking to explore the many attractions in the area. The welcome is always genuine, with every effort made to help guests enjoy their stay. Bedrooms all provide good levels of comfort with ground floor rooms available. Good, honest,

home-cooked dinners are offered, while breakfast provides a tasty and satisfying start to the day.

Rooms 7 en suite (2 fmly) (3 GF) S £26-£32; D £52-£64* **Facilities** FTV tea/coffee Dinner available WiFi ⓐ **Extras** Sweets **Parking** 7 **Notes** LB

Bay Cottage

★★★ GUEST HOUSE

tel: 01803 525729 **4 Beach Rd TQ4 6AY**
web: www.baycottagepaignton.co.uk
dir: *Along B3201 Esplanade Rd past Paignton Pier, Beach Rd 2nd right*

Quietly located in a level terrace, the seafront, park, harbour and shops are all just a short stroll away. Run in a friendly and relaxed manner, Bay Cottage offers a range of bedrooms of various shapes and sizes, with a guest lounge also made available. Dinner is offered by prior arrangement and includes enjoyable home cooking in hearty portions.

Rooms 8 en suite (3 fmly) S £22-£25; D £44-£50* **Facilities** FTV TVL tea/coffee Dinner available WiFi **Notes** LB ⊗

Merriedale Guest House

★★★ GUEST HOUSE

tel: 01803 553013 & 07950 819716 **fax:** 01803 553013 **21 Garfield Rd TQ4 6AX**
email: merriedale@gmx.co.uk **web:** www.merriedale.com
dir: *A380 to Torquay, 2nd exit at rdbt (Kerswell Gdns). 1st exit at next rdbt Churscombe Cross into Marldon Rd (B3060). Right into Torquay Rd (A3022), bear left into Hyde Rd, left into Torbay Rd & left into Garfield Rd*

Overlooking Victoria Park, this friendly and welcoming establishment is perfectly situated to explore the local area, as it's just a short walk from the town centre and the wonderful sandy beach. Every effort is made to help guests enjoy a relaxing stay, with local information and advice readily offered. Bedrooms and bathrooms all offer good levels of quality and all the expected comforts. Breakfast is a satisfying start to the day and is served in the well-appointed dining room.

Rooms 6 rms (5 en suite) (1 pri facs) **Facilities** FTV tea/coffee WiFi **Extras** Bottled water - complimentary **Parking** 6 **Notes** LB ⊗

The Park

★★★ GUEST ACCOMMODATION

tel: 01803 557856 **fax:** 01803 555626 **Esplanade Rd TQ4 6BQ**
email: stay@theparkhotel.net **web:** www.theparkhotel.net
dir: *On Paignton seafront, nearly opposite pier*

This large establishment has a prominent position on the seafront with excellent views of Torbay. The pleasant bedrooms are spacious and available in a number of options, and several have sea views. Entertainment is provided in the lounge on some evenings. Dinner and breakfast are served in the spacious dining room, which overlooks the attractive front garden.

Rooms 47 en suite (5 fmly) (3 GF) **Facilities** tea/coffee Dinner available Lift Licensed WiFi Pool table 🛁 Games room with 3/4 snooker table & table tennis **Conf** Max 120 Thtr 80 Class 120 Board 40 **Parking** 38 **Notes** LB

PLYMOUTH	Map 3 SX45

Premier Collection

Warleigh House

★★★★★ BED AND BREAKFAST

tel: 01752 767218 & 07971 220152 **Horsham Ln, Tamerton Foliot PL5 4LG**
email: parkhallmanor@hotmail.co.uk **web:** www.warleighhouse.co.uk

This stunning country house enjoys a unique location in 140 acres of its own grounds, in the beautiful surroundings of the Tavy estuary. Carefully restored and full of character, it is the perfect base for visiting Plymouth and South Devon. Accommodation and public areas are well appointed and comfortable, retaining an air of elegance along with every modern convenience.

Rooms 3 en suite S £79-£140; D £79-£140* **Facilities** FTV DVD iPod docking station Lounge TVL tea/coffee WiFi Fishing **Parking** 10 **Notes** LB

Brittany Guest House

★★★★ GUEST ACCOMMODATION

tel: 01752 262247 **28 Athenaeum St, The Hoe PL1 2RQ**
email: thebrittanyguesthouse@btconnect.com **web:** www.brittanyguesthouse.co.uk
dir: A38/City Centre follow signs for Pavillions, left at mini rdbt, left at lights into Athenaeum St

Situated in a pleasant street, within walking distance of Plymouth's many attractions, this well presented house offers comfortable and well-equipped accommodation. The proprietors provide friendly hospitality, and many guests return frequently. Freshly cooked breakfast is served in the attractive dining room. Parking available.

Rooms 10 en suite (3 fmly) (1 GF) **Facilities** FTV tea/coffee WiFi **Parking** 6 **Notes** ⊗ No Children 5yrs Closed 20 Dec-2 Jan

Jewell's

★★★★ GUEST ACCOMMODATION

tel: 01752 254760 **fax:** 01752 254760 **220 Citadel Rd, The Hoe PL1 3BB**
email: jewellsguest@btconnect.com **web:** www.jewellsguesthouse.com
dir: A38 towards city centre, follow sign for The Barbican, then The Hoe. Left at lights, right at top of road into Citadel Rd. Jewell's 0.25m

This smart, comfortable, family-run establishment is only a short walk from The Hoe and is convenient for the city centre, the Citadel and the Barbican. Bedrooms come with a wide range of extra facilities, and breakfast is served in the pleasant dining room. Some secure parking is available.

Rooms 10 rms (7 en suite) (5 fmly) **Facilities** FTV tea/coffee WiFi **Parking** 3 **Notes** LB ⊗

Rainbow Lodge Guest House

★★★★ GUEST HOUSE

tel: 01752 229699 **29 Athenaeum St, The Hoe PL1 2RQ**
email: info@rainbowlodgeplymouth.co.uk **web:** www.rainbowlodgeplymouth.co.uk
dir: A38 onto A374. Follow City Centre signs for 3m, into Exeter St. Bear left into Breton Side at lights, follow road, left into Athenaeum St at Walrus pub

Just a short stroll from The Hoe, this small and friendly establishment is well placed for exploring the city. Bedrooms vary in size and style, and two are suitable for family use. Substantial breakfasts are served in the homely dining room. Please note that children under five years of age are not accepted.

Rooms 11 rms (7 en suite) (1 pri facs) (2 fmly) (1 GF) S £32-£59; D £49-£72* **Facilities** FTV tea/coffee WiFi 🛁 **Extras** Speciality toiletries **Parking** 3 **Notes** LB ⊗ No Children 5yrs Closed 22 Dec-5 Jan

Devonshire Guest House

★★★ GUEST ACCOMMODATION

tel: 01752 220726 **fax:** 01752 220766 **22 Lockyer Rd, Mannamead PL3 4RL**
email: devonshiregh@blueyonder.co.uk **web:** www.devonshiregh.pwp.blueyonder.co.uk
dir: At Hyde Park pub on traffic island turn left into Wilderness Rd. After 60yds left into Lockyer Rd

This comfortable Victorian house is located in a residential area close to Mutley Plain high street, from where there is a regular bus service to the city centre. The well-proportioned bedrooms are bright and attractive, and guests can use the comfy lounge. Parking is available.

Rooms 10 rms (5 en suite) (4 fmly) (3 GF) **Facilities** FTV TVL tea/coffee Licensed WiFi **Parking** 6 **Notes** ⊗

The Firs Guest Accommodation

★★★ GUEST ACCOMMODATION

tel: 01752 262870 & 300010 **13 Pier St, West Hoe PL1 3BS**
email: thefirsguesthouseinplymouthdevon@hotmail.com
web: www.thefirsinplymouth.co.uk
dir: A374 into city centre, follow signs to The Hoe. Continue on Hoe Rd, with sea on left, 1st right at mini rdbt into Pier St

A well located and well established house on the West Hoe with convenient on-street parking. Friendly owners and comfortable rooms make it a popular destination.

Rooms 7 rms (3 en suite) (2 fmly) S £25-£45; D £55-£85* **Facilities** FTV tea/coffee Dinner available WiFi 🛁 Fishing trips can be arranged **Notes** LB

PLYMOUTH *continued*

The Lamplighter

★★★ GUEST ACCOMMODATION

tel: 01752 663855 **103 Citadel Rd, The Hoe PL1 2RN**
email: stay@lamplighterplymouth.co.uk **web:** www.lamplighterplymouth.co.uk
dir: *Near war memorial*

With easy access to The Hoe, The Barbican and the city centre, this comfortable house provides a good base for leisure or business. Bedrooms, including family rooms, are light and airy and furnished to a consistent standard. Breakfast is served in the dining room, which has an adjoining lounge area.

Rooms 9 rms (7 en suite) (2 pri facs) (2 fmly) S £40-£60; D £60 **Facilities** FTV TVL tea/coffee WiFi 🔒 **Parking** 4

SEATON

Map 4 SY29

Mariners

★★★★ 🏅 🍽 GUEST ACCOMMODATION

tel: 01297 20560 **East Walk Esplanade EX12 2NP**
web: www.marinershotelseaton.co.uk
dir: *Off A3052 signed Seaton, Mariners on seafront*

Located just yards from the beach and cliff paths, this comfortable establishment has a friendly and relaxed atmosphere. Bedrooms, some with sea views, are well equipped, and public rooms are light and airy. The dining room is the venue for enjoyable breakfasts that utilise quality local produce; afternoon teas are also available on the seafront terrace.

Rooms 10 en suite (1 fmly) (2 GF) **Facilities** FTV Lounge tea/coffee Dinner available Licensed WiFi 🔒 **Parking** 9 **Notes** ⊗ No Children 5yrs RS Nov-Jan Closed at certain times

Beaumont Guest House

★★★★ GUEST HOUSE

tel: 01297 20832 & 07775 713667 **Castle Hill EX12 2QW**
email: beaumont.seaton@talktalk.net **web:** www.beaumont-seaton.co.uk
dir: *In Seaton, from Harbour Rd head W to Marine Place on seafront. Beaumont Guest House at beginning of Castle Hill*

Dating back to the days of Victorian splendour, this elegant establishment is just a few steps away from the wonderful beach at Seaton. A warm and genuine welcome awaits with plenty of helpful local advice always on offer. Bedrooms have great sea views and provide all the expected modern comforts with a ground floor room also being available. Breakfast provides a tasty start to the day, served in the attractive dining room.

Rooms 5 en suite (2 fmly) (1 GF) **Facilities** FTV tea/coffee WiFi ch fac **Parking** 6 **Notes** ⊗ Closed Xmas & New Year

SHALDON

See Teignmouth

SIDMOUTH

Map 3 SY18

See also Ottery St Mary

Premier Collection

The Salty Monk

★★★★★ ◉◉ 🍽 RESTAURANT WITH ROOMS

tel: 01395 513174 **Church St, Sidford EX10 9QP**
email: saltymonk@btconnect.com **web:** www.saltymonk.co.uk
dir: *On A3052 opposite church in Sidford*

Set in the village of Sidford, this attractive property dates from the 16th century. There's oodles of style and appeal here and each bedroom has a unique identity. Bathrooms are equally special with multi-jet showers, spa baths and cosseting robes and towels. The output from the kitchen is impressive with excellent local produce very much in evidence, served in the elegant surroundings of the restaurant. A mini spa facility is available.

Rooms 5 en suite 1 annexe en suite (3 GF) S £85-£120; D £130-£180* **Facilities** FTV Lounge tea/coffee Dinner available WiFi 🛝 18 Sauna Gym 🔒 Outdoor Hot tub **Extras** Speciality toiletries - complimentary **Parking** 20 **Notes** LB Closed 1wk Nov & Jan RS Nov-15 Mar closed Sun night & Mon night No coaches

The Groveside

★★★★ GUEST HOUSE

tel: 01395 513406 **Vicarage Rd EX10 8UQ**
email: info@thegroveside.co.uk **web:** www.thegroveside.co.uk
dir: *0.5m N of seafront on A375*

Conveniently situated a short, level walking distance from the town centre, The Groveside offers boutique-style accommodation. A number of influences, such as art deco, have been used to impressive effect in the bedrooms, while bathrooms also show individuality and flair. Guests are assured of attentive service and a relaxed and friendly atmosphere. Home-cooked evening meals are served by prior arrangement. On-site parking is a bonus.

Rooms 9 en suite **Facilities** FTV TVL tea/coffee Dinner available WiFi Pamper wknds in Nov **Conf** Max 14 Class 14 Board 14 **Parking** 9 **Notes** ⊗ No Children 12yrs

The Old Farmhouse

★★★★ GUEST ACCOMMODATION

tel: 01395 512284 **Hillside Rd EX10 8JG**
web: www.theoldfarmhousesidmouth.co.uk
dir: *A3052 from Exeter to Sidmouth, right at Bowd x-rds, 2m left at rdbt, left at mini rdbt, next right, over hump-back bridge, bear right on the corner*

This beautiful 16th-century thatched farmhouse, in a quiet residential area just a stroll from the Esplanade and shops, has been lovingly restored. Bedrooms are attractively decorated, and the charming public rooms feature beams and an inglenook fireplace. The welcoming proprietors provide memorable dinners, (by prior arrangement) using traditional recipes and fresh local ingredients.

Rooms 3 en suite 3 annexe en suite (1 fmly) (1 GF) S £49-£58; D £66-£78* **Facilities** FTV Lounge TVL tea/coffee Dinner available WiFi ♨ 18 **Parking** 4 **Notes** LB ⊗ No Children 12yrs Closed Nov-Feb ⊛

Cheriton Guest House

★★★★ GUEST ACCOMMODATION

tel: 01395 513810 & 07899 793314 **Vicarage Rd EX10 8UQ**
email: info@cheriton-guesthouse.co.uk **web:** www.cheriton-guesthouse.co.uk

Located just a 10-minute stroll from the seafront, Cheriton Guest House is a convenient base for exploring Sidmouth. A flexible approach to guest requirements is adopted here, and every effort is made to ensure guests have a comfortable stay. Bedrooms provide good levels of comfort with all the expected extras; public rooms include a stylish lounge and airy breakfast room.

Rooms 8 en suite **Facilities** FTV Lounge tea/coffee WiFi **Parking** 7 **Notes** LB ⊗

Dukes

★★★★ ⚲ INN

tel: 01395 513320 **fax:** 01395 519318 **The Esplanade EX10 8AR**
email: dukes@sidmouthinn.co.uk **web:** www.dukessidmouth.co.uk
dir: *Exit A3052 to Sidmouth, left onto Esplanade*

Situated in the heart of Sidmouth, this stylish inn offers a relaxed and convivial atmosphere created by a great team of attentive staff. Bedrooms provide good levels of comfort and a number have the benefit of sea views. The menu utilises the seasonal produce that this area has to offer. A choice of dining areas is available including the patio garden - perfect for soaking up the sun.

Rooms 13 en suite (5 fmly) S £46-£56; D £92-£145* **Facilities** FTV DVD iPod docking station tea/coffee Dinner available Direct Dial WiFi **Parking** 9 **Notes** LB RS 25 Dec

Glendevon

★★★★ GUEST HOUSE

tel: 01395 514028 **Cotmaton Rd EX10 8QX**
email: geraldcorr@gmail.co.uk **web:** www.glendevonsidmouth.co.uk
dir: *A3052 onto B3176 to mini rdbt. Right, house 100yds on right*

Located in a quiet residential area just a short walk from the town centre and beaches, this stylish Victorian house offers neat, comfortable bedrooms. Guests are assured of a warm welcome from the resident owners, who provide attentive service and wholesome home-cooked evening meals by arrangement.

Rooms 8 en suite S £38-£44; D £76-£88* **Facilities** FTV Lounge tea/coffee Dinner available Licensed WiFi **Notes** LB ⊗ No Children ⊛

Rose Cottage Guest House

★★★★ GUEST HOUSE

tel: 01395 597357 **fax:** 01395 597898 **Greenhead, Sidbury EX10 0RH**
web: www.rosecottagesidbury.co.uk
dir: *At junct of A375 & Greenhead*

Rose Cottage is a very well appointed, comfortable property in the quiet village of Sidbury, with the resort of Sidmouth close by. Roz, and son Luke, do all they can to make you feel very welcome and at home. Rooms are well appointed, there is a guest lounge to enjoy, and there is off-road parking. Very good quality, locally sourced produce is used for breakfast, which is served in the well appointed dining room.

Rooms 6 en suite S £38-£48; D £76-£90* **Facilities** FTV Lounge tea/coffee WiFi **Parking** 6 **Notes** LB

SOURTON	Map 3 SX59

Bearslake Inn

★★★★ ⚲ INN

tel: 01837 861334 **fax:** 01837 861108 **Lake EX20 4HQ**
email: enquiries@bearslakeinn.com **web:** www.bearslakeinn.com
dir: *A30 from Exeter onto A386 signed Sourton & Tavistock, 2m on left from junct*

Situated on the edge of the Dartmoor National Park, this thatched inn is believed to date back to the 13th century and was originally part of a working farm. There is character in abundance here with beams, flagstone floors and low ceilings, all of which contribute to an engaging atmosphere. Bedrooms have great individuality and provide period features combined with contemporary comforts. Local produce is very much in evidence on the menu, with dinner served in the attractive Stable Restaurant. The beer garden is bordered by a moorland stream with wonderful views across open countryside.

Rooms 6 en suite (3 fmly) (1 GF) S £80-£95; D £115-£130* **Facilities** FTV DVD tea/coffee Dinner available WiFi ⚓ **Parking** 35 **Notes** LB No coaches

SOUTH MOLTON

Map 3 SS72

Kerscott Farm *(SS789256)*

★★★★ FARMHOUSE

tel: 01769 550262 & 07793 526260 **Bishop's Nympton EX36 4QG**
web: www.devon-bandb-kerscott.co.uk
dir: *From A361 onto B3227, 1.5m E of junct*

Kerscott Farm is mentioned in the Domesday Book, and has been farmed continuously for more than a thousand years. The present house dates from the early 15th century, with some parts being even older. Full of character, with beams, sloping floors, a branch staircase and many other original features, the house retains a walled cottage garden and cobblestone paths. The sitting room has a large inglenook fireplace and breakfast is produced on the trusty Aga. Evening meals are available by prior arrangement. Obviously all meals are prepared using local produce, mainly from the farm itself. Unusually the farm's water comes from its own springs and wells. Kerscott is a traditional livestock farm, and does not accept under 14s or dogs.

Rooms 3 en suite S £50; D £70-£76* **Facilities** FTV Lounge tea/coffee Dinner available WiFi **Parking Notes** ⊗ No Children 14yrs 200 acres beef/sheep

Sampson Barton Guest House

★★★★ 🍴 GUEST HOUSE

tel: 01769 572466 **Kings Nympton EX37 9TG**
email: mail@sampsonbarton.co.uk **web:** www.sampsonbarton.co.uk
dir: *From South Molton follow signs for George Nympton & Kings Nympton. Through George Nympton, down hill, over bridge, 1st right into lane signed Sampson & Sletchcott. Up hill, 0.75m on left*

Dating back some 400 years, this charming former farmhouse is the perfect place to relax. A reviving cup of tea on arrival in front of the warming woodburner sets the scene, with helpful local information always on hand. Bedrooms offer good levels of comfort, likewise the contemporary bathrooms. Dinner is a treat, with wonderful local produce on offer. Breakfast is also impressive with eggs supplied by the resident hens. A stroll around the wonderful gardens is a must; find a peaceful vantage point and gaze over the rolling Devon countryside.

Rooms 6 rms (5 en suite) (1 pri facs) S £50-£60; D £76-£90* **Facilities** FTV TVL TV4B tea/coffee Dinner available Licensed WiFi ♨ **Extras** Speciality toiletries - complimentary **Parking** 6 **Notes** LB ⊗

The Coaching Inn

★★★ INN

tel: 01769 572526 **Queen St EX36 3BJ**
web: www.thecoaching-inn.co.uk
dir: *In town centre*

This long-established former coaching inn has been providing a warm welcome to weary travellers for many years. Situated in the heart of this bustling town, guests are assured of a relaxing stay in a genuine, family-friendly atmosphere. Bedrooms provide good levels of comfort. An extensive menu is provided with an emphasis on quality and value for money.

Rooms 10 en suite (2 fmly) S fr £35; D fr £70* **Facilities** FTV tea/coffee Dinner available WiFi Pool table ♨ **Conf** Max 100 Thtr 80 Class 50 Board 60 **Parking** 40

West Down Guest House & Farm *(SS749259)*

★★★ FARMHOUSE

tel: 01769 550839 & 07919 054746 **Whitechapel, Bishops Nympton EX36 3EQ**
email: enquiries@westdown-devon.co.uk **web:** www.westdown-devon.co.uk
dir: *M5 junct 27 onto A361 towards Barnstaple. At 2nd rdbt, 3rd exit & 150yds over bridge, immediate right*

A friendly welcome awaits at this spacious "Arts and Crafts" country house, built in the 1920s and set in 30 acres of rolling Devon countryside. Bedrooms all provide the expected necessities with comfortable beds ensuring a contented nights sleep. Breakfast provides a tasty start to the day, and is served either in the dining room or conservatory, which overlooks the lush gardens. West Down Guest House is excellent base from which to explore the picturesque delights of North Devon.

Rooms 5 en suite (3 fmly) **Facilities** FTV DVD Lounge TVL tea/coffee Dinner available WiFi ♨ **Extras** Fridge, robes **Parking** 5 **Notes** 30 acres beef/sheep

STRETE

Map 3 SX84

Premier Collection

Strete Barton House

★★★★★ 🏠 GUEST HOUSE

tel: 01803 770364 **fax:** 01803 771182 **Totnes Rd TQ6 0RU**
email: info@stretebarton.co.uk **web:** www.stretebarton.co.uk
dir: *Off A379 coastal road into village, just below church*

This delightful 16th-century former farmhouse blends stylish accommodation with original character. The bedrooms are very comfortably furnished and well equipped with useful extras. Breakfast utilises quality local produce and is served in the spacious dining room. Guests are also welcome to use the comfortable lounge, complete with log-burning stove. The village lies between Dartmouth and Kingsbridge and has easy access to the beautiful South Hams as well as many local pubs and restaurants.

Rooms 5 rms (4 en suite) (1 pri facs) 1 annexe en suite D £105-£160* **Facilities** FTV DVD iPod docking station Lounge tea/coffee WiFi ⌟ 18 ♨ **Extras** Speciality toiletries, guest fridge **Parking** 4 **Notes** LB No Children 8yrs

TAVISTOCK   Map 3 SX47

Premier Collection

Tor Cottage

★★★★★ 🛏 GUEST ACCOMMODATION

tel: 01822 860248 **fax:** 01822 860126 **PL16 0JE**
email: info@torcottage.co.uk **web:** www.torcottage.co.uk

(For full entry see Chillaton)

Beera Farmhouse *(SX399764)*

★★★★ 🛏 FARMHOUSE

tel: 01822 870216 & 07974 957966 **Milton Abbot PL19 8PL**
email: hilary@beera-farm.co.uk **web:** www.beera-farm.co.uk
dir: *From Tavistock on B3362 towards Lamerton, through Milton Abbot. 1st left, after 2.2m, farm on left*

Tucked away in the midst of the rolling Devon countryside, this traditional family farm is a wonderful place to get away from the pressures of a hurly burly existence and savour some rest and relaxation. Beera is very much a working farm, with lush fields occupied by contentedly grazing sheep and cows. Bedrooms all provide the necessary comforts with more besides, likewise the bathrooms have cosy robes and

cosseting towels. Breakfast is a treat, with eggs fresh from the farm, whilst dinner (by prior arrangement) is also highly recommended, with local produce used as much as possible.

Rooms 3 en suite S £55-£65; D £80-£95 **Facilities** FTV DVD iPod docking station TVL tea/coffee Dinner available WiFi 🐾 **Extras** Robes, fresh fruit, bottled water **Parking** 4 **Notes** LB Closed 18 Feb-5 Mar 300 acres beef/sheep

Tavistock Inn

★★★★ INN

tel: 01822 615736 **19 Brook St PL19 0HD**
email: tavistockinn@live.com **web:** www.thetavistockinn.co.uk

Tavistock is an ancient stannary and market town in west Devon, situated on the River Tavy, from which its name derives. It traces its recorded history back to at least 961AD when Tavistock Abbey, whose ruins lie in the centre of the town, was founded, and its most famous son is Sir Francis Drake. The Tavistock Inn is situated in the centre of this busy little town, surrounded by shops and restaurants. A very warm welcome awaits the guest upon arrival, and the accommodation offered is stylish, comfortable and very clean. Great value pub food and drink is available all day.

Rooms 4 en suite (1 fmly) **Facilities** FTV tea/coffee Dinner available WiFi 🏌 18 Pool table 🐾 **Notes** LB

Symbols and abbreviations are explained on page 7

Find out more about the AA Friendliest B&B of the Year on page 17

TEDBURN ST MARY
Map 3 SX89

Premier Collection

Frogmill Bed & Breakfast

★★★★★ BED AND BREAKFAST

tel: 01647 272727 & 24088 fax: 08721 152577 **EX6 6ES**
email: frogmillbandb@btinternet.com web: www.frogmillbandb.co.uk
dir: *From A30 take exit signed Cheriton Bishop. Take Tedburn road, then left towards Crediton. After 1m left to Froggy Mill, 1m on left*

Situated in the heart of Devon, this former mill house is as picturesque as could be, complete with thatch and babbling brook. The grounds are spectacular, with around 10 acres of woodland and pasture, and the welcome is as impressive as the location, with a cream tea in the garden being offered on arrival. Bedrooms offer comfort, quality and individuality and include a separate, self-contained suite, away from the main building; the bathrooms have soft towels and invigorating showers. Food is a treat here with eggs for breakfast contributed by the resident hens. In addition to the elegant dining room, a guest lounge is provided with deep leather sofas and a woodburner.

Rooms 2 en suite 1 annexe en suite (1 fmly) (1 GF) S £60-£70; D £75-£95*
Facilities FTV iPod docking station Lounge tea/coffee WiFi ⚓ Extras Fruit, chocolates - free; robes Parking 6 Notes LB

TEIGNMOUTH
Map 3 SX97

Premier Collection

Thomas Luny House

★★★★★ GUEST ACCOMMODATION

tel: 01626 772976 Teign St **TQ14 8EG**
email: alisonandjohn@thomas-luny-house.co.uk web: www.thomas-luny-house.co.uk
dir: *A381 to Teignmouth, at 3rd lights right to quay, 50yds left into Teign St, after 60yds right through white archway*

Built in the late 18th century by marine artist Thomas Luny, this charming house offers unique and comfortable accommodation in the old quarter of Teignmouth. Bedrooms are individually decorated and furnished, and all are well equipped with a good range of extras. The elegant drawing room has French windows which open to a walled garden with a terraced sitting area. A superb breakfast, featuring local produce, is served in the attractive dining room.

Rooms 4 en suite S £60-£75; D £80-£105* Facilities FTV Lounge tea/coffee Direct Dial Licensed WiFi Parking 8 Notes LB ⊗ No Children 12yrs

Potters Mooring

★★★★ GUEST ACCOMMODATION

tel: 01626 873225 fax: 01626 872982 **30 The Green, Shaldon TQ14 0DN**
email: info@pottersmooring.co.uk
dir: *A38 onto A380 signed Torquay, B3192 to Teignmouth & Shaldon, over river, follow signs to Potters Mooring*

A former sea captain's residence dating from 1625, Potters Mooring has been appointed to provide charming accommodation of a very high standard, including a four-poster room. The friendly proprietors make every effort to ensure an enjoyable stay, and the Captain Potter's breakfast features tasty local produce.

Rooms 9 en suite

TIVERTON
Map 3 SS91

Premier Collection

Fernside Bed and Breakfast

★★★★★ BED AND BREAKFAST

tel: 01884 860025 & 07885 192331 Fernside Cottage, Templeton **EX16 8BP**
email: enquiries@fernsidecottage-bed-and-breakfast.co.uk
web: www.fernsidecottage-bed-and-breakfast.co.uk
dir: *M25 junct 27, A361 signed Barnstaple. In approx 4m at Stonelands Cross left signed Rackenford & Templeton. Left at T-junct signed Templeton. 2nd right signed Templeton. In Templeton Bridge at T-junct right signed Witheridge. B&B up hill on right*

This charming thatched cottage is within easy reach of Tiverton and the M5, and sits in rolling countryside which is a haven of peace and tranquillity. Expect high quality bedrooms with wonderful beds, smart bathrooms, Aga-cooked breakfasts and a really warm welcome from two very caring hosts.

Rooms 2 en suite Facilities FTV iPod docking station Lounge tea/coffee WiFi Riding ⚓ Extras Speciality toiletries, robes, home-made biscuits Parking 3 Notes ⊗ No Children 18yrs Closed 12 Dec-6 Jan ⊜

Hornhill Farmhouse *(SS965117)*

★★★★ FARMHOUSE

tel: 01884 253352 Exeter Hill **EX16 4PL**
email: hornhill@tinyworld.co.uk web: www.hornhill-farmhouse.co.uk
dir: *Signs to Grand Western Canal, right fork up Exeter Hill. Farmhouse on left at top of hill*

Hornhill has a peaceful hilltop setting with panoramic views of the town and the Exe Valley. Elegant decor and furnishings enhance the character of the farmhouse, which in part dates from the 18th century. Bedrooms are beautifully equipped with modern facilities and there is a lovely sitting room with a log fire. Breakfast is served at one large table in the spacious dining room.

Rooms 3 rms (1 en suite) (2 pri facs) (1 GF) S £40-£45; D £70-£80 **Facilities** FTV Lounge tea/coffee WiFi ⚘ **Parking** 5 **Notes** ⊗ No Children 12yrs Closed Nov-Feb ⊛ 75 acres beef/sheep

Stoodleigh B&B

★★★★ BED AND BREAKFAST

tel: 01398 351163 & 07789 982305 **Barton House, Stoodleigh EX16 9PP**
email: bookings@stoodleighbandb.co.uk **web:** www.stoodleighbandb.co.uk
dir: A361 from Tiverton towards Barnstaple. At Stoodleigh Cross turn right, follow signs to Stoodleigh, left bend into Long Ln, then West End Ln. Behind hall in village

Within easy reach of Exmoor National Park, this is a perfect choice for anyone looking for a peaceful base from which to explore some beautiful countryside. Rest and relaxation are assured, with a warm welcome always on offer. Bedrooms provide all the expected contemporary comforts, likewise the well-appointed bathrooms. Breakfast makes use of wonderful local produce, served in the attractive dining room.

Rooms 3 en suite (1 fmly) D £75-£85* **Facilities** FTV TVL tea/coffee WiFi ⚘ **Parking** 4 **Notes** LB ⊛

Quoit-At-Cross (ST923188)

★★★ FARMHOUSE

tel: 01398 351280 **Stoodleigh EX16 9PJ**
email: quoit-at-cross@hotmail.co.uk **web:** www.quoit-at-cross.co.uk
dir: M5 junct 27 for Tiverton. A396 N for Bampton, after 3.5m turn left over bridge for Stoodleigh, farmhouse on 1st junct in village centre

This delightful stone-built farmhouse commands lovely views over rolling Devonshire countryside and is a great place from which to explore this picturesque area. A warm and genuine welcome is assured, along with a homely and relaxed atmosphere. The comfortable, attractive bedrooms are well furnished and have many extra facilities. A crackling fire keeps the lounge snug and warm during colder nights, while in the summer the pretty garden is available to guests.

Rooms 4 en suite (2 fmly) S £40; D £66-£76* **Facilities** FTV DVD TVL tea/coffee Dinner available WiFi Fishing Riding Pool table ⚘ Wildlife garden & farm wildlife trail **Extras** Speciality toiletries, snacks, fridge available **Conf** Max 15 **Parking** 4 **Notes** LB Closed Xmas ⊛ 160 acres mixed

TORBAY

See Brixham, Paignton and Torquay

TORQUAY
Map 3 SX96

Premier Collection

Carlton Court

★★★★★ BED AND BREAKFAST

tel: 01803 297318 & 07794 613051 **fax:** 08717 142207 **18 Cleveland Rd TQ2 5BE**
email: stay@carlton-court.co.uk **web:** www.carlton-court.co.uk
dir: A380 onto A3022, straight ahead at 3 sets of lights. Stay in left lane, straight ahead at 2 sets of lights. Into right lane at Torre station, down hill. After 100yds left into Cleveland Rd, straight over at x-rds, 700yds on right

This elegant detached Victorian villa has been sensitively refurbished to provide impressive levels of quality and comfort, while retaining many original period features. Service and hospitality are very much hallmarks here and every effort is made to ensure guests feel both welcomed and relaxed, with helpful local information always on offer. Bedrooms provide high standards with a range of types available, including suites and ground-floor rooms. Quality is equally high in bathrooms, with lovely warm towels and robes waiting after a long soak in the bath or an invigorating shower. All rooms also feature chiller fridges. Breakfast is served in the well-appointed dining room, overlooking the garden, and provides a wonderful start to the day.

Rooms 6 en suite (2 GF) S £70-£75; D £90-£99* **Facilities** FTV DVD tea/coffee WiFi **Extras** Fresh milk, bottled water - complimentary **Parking** 7 **Notes** ⊗ No Children 14yrs

Premier Collection

The Marstan

★★★★★ GUEST HOUSE

tel: 01803 292837 **fax:** 01803 299202 **Meadfoot Sea Rd TQ1 2LQ**
email: enquiries@marstanhotel.co.uk **web:** www.marstanhotel.co.uk
dir: A3022 to seafront, left onto A379 Torbay Rd & Babbacombe Rd, right into Meadfoot Rd, Marstan on right

This elegant, mid-19th-century villa provides high levels of comfort and quality throughout. The hospitality and service are excellent, and every effort is made to create a relaxed atmosphere. Public areas include an impressive dining room, a bar and a comfortable lounge. Outdoors, guests can enjoy a heated swimming pool and hot tub in the secluded garden.

Rooms 9 en suite (1 fmly) (2 GF) **Facilities** FTV iPod docking station Lounge tea/coffee Direct Dial Licensed WiFi ⚡ Hot tub **Parking** 8 **Notes** LB ⊗

TORQUAY *continued*

Premier Collection

The Briarfields

★★★★★ GUEST ACCOMMODATION

tel: 01803 297844 **84-86 Avenue Rd TQ2 5LF**
email: info@briarfields.co.uk
dir: *Into Torquay on A3022, follow signs for seafront and Riviera Centre. Filter right at Torre railway station, straight on at lights into Avenue Rd*

The Briarfields offers a choice of well appointed bedrooms, some with air conditioning, and well designed bathrooms for a relaxing and enjoyable stay. Both bedrooms and bathrooms are well equipped to ensure a flawless experience, and six bedrooms have air-conditioning. The award-winning breakfast, which includes local produce, is served in the spacious dining room. Off-road parking is available.

Rooms 8 en suite S £70; D £83-£115 **Facilities** FTV DVD tea/coffee WiFi ⅃ 18 **Parking** 8 **Notes** LB ⊗ No Children 16yrs Closed 15 Dec-15 Jan

Premier Collection

The Cary Arms

★★★★★ INN

tel: 01803 327110 **fax:** 01803 323221 **Babbacombe Beach TQ1 3LX**
email: enquiries@caryarms.co.uk **web:** www.caryarms.co.uk
dir: *A380 at Ashcombe Cross onto B3192 to Teignmouth. Right at lights to Torquay on A379, left at lights to Babbacombe. Left into Babbacombe Downs Rd, left into Beach Rd*

Located on the water's edge at Babbacombe, this seaside retreat is very well appointed; the rooms have sea views and nearly all have terraces or balconies. Bedrooms and bathrooms are fitted to a high standard with many thoughtful extras and unique touches to make a stay memorable. This is a popular dining venue whether eating inside, or on the terraces that lead down to the water's edge; in summer there's a BBQ and wood-fired oven. The dedicated staff will assist in planning your day, or simply share local knowledge.

Rooms 8 en suite (1 fmly) (3 GF) S £155-£195; D £195-£275* **Facilities** FTV Lounge tea/coffee Dinner available WiFi ⅃ 18 Pool table Spa treatment room Sea fishing **Extras** Speciality toiletries, sloe gin, confectionery **Conf** Max 24 Thtr 24 Class 24 Board 24 **Parking** 15 **Notes** LB No coaches Civ Wed 40

Premier Collection

Kingston House

★★★★★ GUEST ACCOMMODATION

tel: 01803 212760 **75 Avenue Rd TQ2 5LL**
email: stay@kingstonhousetorquay.co.uk **web:** www.kingstonhousetorquay.co.uk
dir: *From A3022 to Torquay, turn right at Torre Station down Avenue Rd, Kingston House approx 0.4m on left*

Dating from around 1870, this elegant Victorian house, just a short stroll from the seafront, is well positioned for those visiting the area for business or pleasure. There is always plenty of helpful advice and information readily available. Tea and cakes on arrival are served in the inviting guest lounge, an ideal way to start a relaxing break. Bedrooms offer impressive quality with wonderfully comfortable beds, likewise bathrooms come equipped with cosseting towels and robes. Breakfast offers a number of tasty options, served in the well-appointed dining room. Kingston House is a Runner-Up in the AA Friendliest B&B of the Year 2014-2015.

Rooms 5 en suite (1 GF) S £65-£70; D £80-£90 **Facilities** FTV DVD TVL tea/coffee WiFi **Extras** Speciality toiletries, chocolates, bottled water **Parking** 5 **Notes** ⊗ No Children 16yrs Closed 20 Dec-10 Feb

Premier Collection

Lanscombe House

★★★★★ GUEST ACCOMMODATION

tel: 01803 606938 & 07928 928570 **Cockington Village TQ2 6XA**
email: stay@lanscombehouse.co.uk **web:** www.lanscombehouse.co.uk
dir: *From Torquay seafront, turn right towards Paignton. At Livermead turn right signed Cockington Village & Country Park. 0.5m along valley, at entrance to village*

Located in the peaceful village of Cockington, in the heart of Cockington Country Park, and close to the attractions of Torquay, Lanscombe House offers sumptuous en suite accommodation. The building is surrounded by lovely secluded gardens that are perfect on a summer's day, or guests may choose to relax in the elegant lounge. Ample private parking is available. Lanscombe House does not accept dogs, or children under 16 years of age.

Rooms 7 en suite (1 GF) S £60-£100; D £75-£125* **Facilities** FTV Lounge tea/coffee Licensed WiFi 🍴 🔒 **Extras** Speciality toiletries, local confectionery - free **Parking** 10 **Notes** LB ⊗ No Children 16yrs Closed mid Oct-Etr

Premier Collection

Linden House

★★★★★ GUEST ACCOMMODATION

tel: 01803 212281 & 07786 075359 **31 Bampfylde Rd TQ2 5AY**
email: susanelliott488@btinternet.com **web:** www.lindenhousetorquay.co.uk
dir: *Phone for directions*

This grand Victorian house has timeless elegance and charm, and has been refurbished throughout to provide impressive levels of contemporary comfort combined with stylish period features. Tea and cake is always on offer to arriving guests, along with a friendly welcome and the offer of help with local information and advice. Bedrooms and bathrooms offer high levels of quality with individual styling and all the expected necessities to ensure a relaxing and rewarding stay. Spacious public areas include a lovely lounge with views over the garden; and a light and airy dining room is the venue for the wonderful breakfasts that guarantee to get the day off to a tasty and satisfying start. AA Friendliest B&B of the Year Finalist 2014-2015.

Rooms 6 en suite 1 annexe en suite (1 GF) **Facilities** FTV TVL tea/coffee WiFi **Extras** Home-made chocolates, toiletries **Parking** 6 **Notes** LB No Children 16yrs Closed 21 Dec-6 Jan

Headland View

★★★★ 🏠 GUEST HOUSE

tel: 01803 312612 & 07762 960230 **37 Babbacombe Downs Rd, Babbacombe TQ1 3LN**
email: reception@headlandview.com **web:** www.headlandview.com
dir: Follow signs for Babbacombe Theatre & Model Village

Positioned on Babbacombe Downs, this elegant Victorian house boasts superb views of the coast of Lyme Bay, a World Heritage Site. Bedrooms are individually styled with most having French doors leading onto balconies overlooking the spectacular bay. The many period features enhance the character and appeal of the building. A spacious guest lounge is available, whilst the excellent breakfasts are served in the pretty dining room.

Rooms 6 rms (4 en suite) (2 pri facs) S £47-£57; D £62-£72* **Facilities** FTV DVD iPod docking station Lounge TVL tea/coffee WiFi 🔋 **Extras** Speciality toiletries, bottled water **Parking** 4 **Notes** LB ⊗ No Children 12yrs Closed Dec

Meadfoot Bay Guest House

★★★★ 🏠 GUEST ACCOMMODATION

tel: 01803 294722 **Meadfoot Sea Rd TQ1 2LQ**
email: stay@meadfoot.com **web:** www.meadfoot.com
dir: A3022 to seafront, onto A379, right into Meadfoot Rd, 0.5m on right

The Meadfoot Bay Guest House is a family-run guest house situated in the Meadfoot conservation area, just north of Torquay harbour, and only 200 metres from a delightful Blue Flag beach. Rooms vary in size and facilities, and include standard, superior, superior deluxe and The St Andrews Suite. Free parking is available in the private car park, and free WiFi is a bonus. Meadfoot Bay is completely non-smoking.

Rooms 15 en suite (2 GF) S £49.50-£55; D £80-£89 **Facilities** FTV Lounge TVL tea/coffee Licensed WiFi ⚡ 18 Access to nearby health club **Parking** 15 **Notes** LB ⊗ No Children 14yrs

Orestone Manor

★★★★★ ◉◉ RESTAURANT WITH ROOMS

tel: 01803 328098 **Rockhouse Ln, Maidencombe TQ1 4SX**
email: info@orestonemanor.com **web:** www.orestonemanor.com
dir: N of Torquay on A379, on sharp bend in village of Maidencombe

Set in an fabulous location overlooking the bay, Orestone Manor has a long history of providing fine food and very comfortable accommodation, coupled with friendly, attentive service. Log fires burn in cooler months, and there is a conservatory, a bar and a sitting room for guests to enjoy. AA Rosettes have been awarded for the uncomplicated modern cuisine which is based on quality local produce.

Rooms 9 en suite 1 annexe en suite (6 fmly) (1 GF) S £80-£140; D £100-£200* **Facilities** FTV DVD Lounge tea/coffee Dinner available Direct Dial WiFi 🔋 **Extras** Speciality toiletries **Conf** Max 90 Thtr 90 Class 60 Board 30 **Parking** 38 **Notes** LB Closed Jan Civ Wed 90

Aveland House

★★★★ 🏠 GUEST ACCOMMODATION

tel: 01803 326622 **Aveland Rd, Babbacombe TQ1 3PT**
email: avelandhouse@aol.com **web:** www.avelandhouse.co.uk
dir: A3022 to Torquay, left onto B3199 (Hele Rd) into Westhill Rd. Then Warbro Rd, 2nd left into Aveland Rd

Set in well-tended gardens in a peaceful area of Babbacombe, close to the South West Coast Path, beaches, shops and attractions, Aveland House is within easy

walking distance of Torquay harbour and town. This family-run house offers warm and attentive service. The attractive bedrooms are well equipped, with free WiFi throughout. A pleasant bar and two comfortable TV lounges are available. Hearing-impaired visitors are especially welcome, as both the proprietors are OCSL signers. Evening meals and bar snacks are available by arrangement. Coeliacs and special diets can be catered for.

Rooms 10 en suite S £45; D £76-£86 **Facilities** Lounge TVL tea/coffee Dinner available Licensed WiFi 🔋 **Parking** 10 **Notes** LB ⊗ No Children 12yrs RS Sun no evening meals

Babbacombe Palms Guest House

★★★★ GUEST HOUSE

tel: 01803 327087 **2 York Rd, Babbacombe TQ1 3SG**
email: reception@babbacombepalms.com **web:** www.babbacombepalms.com
dir: A379 to Torquay, pass golf club on left. Follow signs to St Marychurch, straight over at lights. 3rd turning on left into York Rd

Babbacombe Palms has a convenient location, in a pleasant residential area within strolling distance of the town's many attractions. There is a very friendly atmosphere here and guests made to feel welcome. Bedrooms are comfortably appointed. There is a cosy bar where guests can relax and a spacious dining room where freshly cooked breakfasts are served.

Rooms 8 rms (7 en suite) (1 pri facs) (2 fmly) (1 GF) S fr £36; D fr £55* **Facilities** FTV TVL tea/coffee Licensed WiFi **Notes** LB

Barclay Court

★★★★ GUEST ACCOMMODATION

tel: 01803 292791 **29 Castle Rd TQ1 3BB**
email: enquiries@barclaycourt.co.uk **web:** www.barclaycourt.co.uk
dir: M5 onto A38 then A380 to Torquay. A3022 Newton Rd left onto Upton Rd, right towards Lymington Rd. Right to Castle Circus, Castle Rd on left

The delightful, personally-run Barclay Court is within easy walking distance of Torquay's attractions and offers a friendly, relaxed atmosphere. Individually decorated rooms vary in size, but all are en suite and well equipped. There is a games room on the lower-ground floor and the garden is a quiet retreat, especially in the summer months.

Rooms 4 en suite 6 annexe en suite (1 fmly) (1 GF) S £25-£35; D £50-£90 **Facilities** FTV TVL tea/coffee WiFi 🔋 Games room **Parking** 7 **Notes** ⊗ Closed 25 Dec & New Year RS Nov-Mar Limited rooms available

Braddon Hall

★★★★ 🏠 GUEST ACCOMMODATION

tel: 01803 293908 **fax:** 01803 200722 **70 Braddons Hill Road East TQ1 1HF**
email: stay@braddonhallhotel.co.uk **web:** www.braddonhallhotel.co.uk
dir: A380 to Torquay. At 1st rdbt, take 1st exit onto A3022. Left onto A379 (Torbay Rd), then left into Braddons Hill Road East

Braddon Hall offers a choice of well appointed and very spacious bedrooms, some with lovely views. Located in close to the town, within walking distance to the sea. Both bedrooms and bathrooms are well equipped to ensure a flawless experience. The award-winning breakfast, which includes local produce, is served in the spacious dining room. Off-road parking is available.

Rooms 9 en suite (1 fmly) S £38-£50; D £55-£78* **Facilities** FTV Lounge tea/coffee Licensed WiFi **Parking** 6 **Notes** Closed Xmas wk

TORQUAY *continued*

Brooklands

★★★★ GUEST HOUSE

tel: 01803 296696 & 07900 417855   **fax:** 01803 296696 **5 Scarborough Rd TQ2 5UJ**
email: enquiries@brooklandsguesthousetorquay.com **web:** www.
brooklandsguesthousetorquay.com
dir: *From seafront into Belgrave Rd. Scarborough Rd 300mtrs on right*

This personally-run Victorian terraced property is convenient for the seafront, town centre and Princess Theatre, making it an ideal base for exploring the English Riviera. The en suite bedrooms have good facilities with a thoughtful range of extras including a fridge in each room and a selection of toiletries. Generous breakfasts are served at individual tables in the attractive breakfast room, and there is also a separate lounge. On-street parking is available at the rear on request. Guests are welcome to drink in the neighbouring RAF Association Social Club (by prior arrangement).

Rooms 5 en suite (1 fmly) S £30-£45; D £50-£60* **Facilities** FTV tea/coffee Dinner available WiFi Use of nearby health and fitness centre **Extras** Snacks, beverages - complimentary **Parking** 1 **Notes** LB ⊗ No Children 5yrs

Burleigh House

★★★★ GUEST HOUSE

tel: 01803 291557 **25 Newton Rd TQ2 5DB**
email: nigelharris10@sky.com

Burleigh House is a friendly, family-run guest house just a short distance from the town centre, harbour and beaches; offering good quality accommodation, great food and hospitality. Bedrooms are well equipped, offering comfortable, attractively dressed beds. Families are very welcome, and nothing is too much trouble for the friendly hosts, making this a great location to explore the region. Ample, secure parking is a bonus.

Rooms 8 rms (6 en suite) (2 pri facs) (4 GF) S £28-£35; D £56-£60* **Facilities** FTV Lounge tea/coffee WiFi 🛝 **Extras** Sweets **Parking** 8 **Notes** ⊗

The Coppice

★★★★ GUEST ACCOMMODATION

tel: 01803 297786 & 211085   **fax:** 01803 211085 **Barrington Rd TQ1 2QJ**
email: reservations@coppicehotel.co.uk **web:** www.coppicehotel.co.uk
dir: *1m from harbour on Babbacombe Rd, opposite St Matthias Church*

Friendly and comfortable, The Coppice is a popular choice and occupies a convenient location within walking distance of the beaches and shops. In addition to the indoor and outdoor swimming pools, evening entertainment is often provided in the spacious bar. Bedrooms are bright and airy with modern amenities.

Rooms 39 en suite (10 fmly) (28 GF) S £30-£60; D £60-£120 (incl.dinner)
Facilities FTV Lounge tea/coffee Dinner available Licensed WiFi ⊗ ⤴ ⚓ 9 Sauna Gym Pool table **Conf** Max 60 Thtr 60 Class 60 Board 60 **Parking** 20 **Notes** LB ⊗

The Downs, Babbacombe

★★★★ 🏠 🍴 GUEST ACCOMMODATION

tel: 01803 328543 **41-43 Babbacombe Downs Rd, Babbacombe TQ1 3LN**
email: manager@downshotel.co.uk **web:** www.downshotel.co.uk
dir: *From Torquay, A329 to Babbacombe. Off Babbacombe road turn left into Princes St. Left into Babbacombe Downs Rd, 20mtrs on left*

Originally built in the 1850s, this elegant building forms part of a seafront terrace with direct access to the promenade and Babbacombe Downs. The warmth of welcome is matched by attentive service, with every effort made to ensure a rewarding and relaxing stay. Bedrooms offer impressive levels of comfort and most have spectacular views across Lyme Bay with balconies being an added bonus. For guests with limited mobility, assisted access is available to the first floor. Additional facilities include the convivial lounge/bar and spacious restaurant where enjoyable dinners and breakfasts are offered.

Rooms 12 en suite (4 fmly) **Facilities** FTV TVL tea/coffee Dinner available Direct Dial Licensed WiFi **Parking** 8

See advert on opposite page

TORQUAY *continued*

The Elmington

★★★★ GUEST ACCOMMODATION

tel: 01803 605192 **fax:** 01803 690488 **St Agnes Ln, Chelston TQ2 6QE**
email: mail@elmington.co.uk **web:** www.elmington.co.uk
dir: *At rear of rail station*

Set in sub-tropical gardens with views over the bay, this splendid Victorian villa has been lovingly restored. The comfortable bedrooms are brightly decorated and vary in size and style. There is a spacious lounge, bar and dining room. Additional facilities include an outdoor pool and terrace.

Rooms 19 en suite S £50; D £70-£90* **Facilities** FTV Lounge tea/coffee Dinner available Licensed WiFi ↘ ☕ ♨ Pool table 🔒 **Parking** 24 **Notes** LB ⊗ Closed Nov-Mar

Garway Lodge Guest House

★★★★ 🛏 GUEST HOUSE

tel: 01803 293126 & 07711 552878 **79 Avenue Rd TQ2 5LL**
email: info@garwaylodge.co.uk **web:** www.garwaylodge.co.uk
dir: *On A3022, 100mtrs past Torre Station on left*

Garway Lodge is in the heart of Torquay and offers accommodation exclusively for adults. The bedrooms are spacious and stylish and include a ground floor room. Business guests are particularly welcomed and there is free on-site parking and free WiFi. Residents have use of a small honesty bar and an extensive breakfast menu is offered. The seafront and harbourside restaurants are only a level walk away.

Rooms 6 en suite (1 GF) S £30-£45; D £60-£85 **Facilities** FTV DVD iPod docking station tea/coffee Licensed WiFi 🔒 **Extras** Speciality toiletries, honesty bar **Parking** 6 **Notes** LB No Children

Glenorleigh

★★★★ GUEST ACCOMMODATION

tel: 01803 292135 **fax:** 01803 213717 **26 Cleveland Rd TQ2 5BE**
email: glenorleighhotel@btinternet.com **web:** www.glenorleigh.co.uk
dir: *A380 from Newton Abbot onto A3022, at Torre station lights right into Avenue Rd, 1st left, across 1st junct, 200yds on right*

Situated in a residential area, the Glenorleigh provides a range of smart bedrooms including some on ground-floor level. Offering guests a solarium, a heated outdoor pool with terrace and a convivial bar, this family-run establishment is ideal for both leisure or business guests. Breakfast provides a hearty start to the day, and dinner is available with prior notice.

Rooms 15 rms (14 en suite) (6 fmly) (7 GF) S £35-£45; D £70-£90 **Facilities** FTV TVL tea/coffee Dinner available Licensed WiFi ↘ Pool table 🔒 Solarium **Parking** 10 **Notes** LB ⊗

The Iona

★★★★ 🛏 GUEST ACCOMMODATION

tel: 01803 294918 **fax:** 01803 294918 **5 Cleveland Rd TQ2 5BD**
email: stay@hoteliona.co.uk **web:** www.hoteliona.co.uk
dir: *A380 to Riviera rdbt, 1st exit onto A3022 towards seafront. Take left into Vine Rd, right into Cleveland Rd*

Dating back to the 1860s, this grand Victorian villa is situated in a quiet location just a short stroll from the town centre, harbour and many attractions. A variety of

bedroom sizes is offered; all provide good levels of comfort and the expected necessities. Public areas are elegant with a number of period features retained. Dinner and breakfast are served in the light and airy conservatory, and a bar is also provided.

Rooms 8 en suite S £37.50-£50; D £62-£85* **Facilities** FTV DVD iPod docking station Lounge TVL tea/coffee Dinner available Licensed WiFi **Parking** 8 **Notes** LB No Children

Kelvin House

★★★★ GUEST ACCOMMODATION

tel: 01803 209093 **fax:** 01803 209093 **46 Bampfylde Rd TQ2 5AY**
email: kelvinhousehotel@hotmail.com **web:** www.kelvinhousehotel.co.uk
dir: *M5 junct 31, A380, A3032 (Newton Rd) into Torquay. At lights at Torre Station right into Avenue Rd. Bampfylde Rd on left*

This attractive Victorian house was built in the 1880s and sits on a lovely tree-lined road. It is a family-run property with a relaxed, friendly home-from-home atmosphere. All bedrooms are en suite and have been appointed to a high standard with many extras. A large elegant sitting room is available for guests, and hearty breakfasts are served in the dining room, or on the patio in good weather. Close to good transport links, it makes an ideal base for touring the Torquay Riviera.

Rooms 8 en suite (1 fmly) (2 GF) **Facilities** FTV TVL tea/coffee Licensed WiFi **Parking** 6 **Notes** ⊗

Kingsholm

★★★★ GUEST ACCOMMODATION

tel: 01803 297794 **fax:** 01803 897121 **539 Babbacombe Rd TQ1 1HQ**
email: thekingsholm@virginmedia.com **web:** www.kingsholmhotel.co.uk
dir: *From A3022 left onto Torquay seafront, left at clock tower rdbt, Kingsholm 400mtrs on left*

An elegant, personally-run establishment situated in a conservation area, only 350 metres from the bustling harbour, this fine Edwardian house offers excellent accommodation that is appointed to a high standard; many rooms overlook Torwood Gardens. All bedrooms have Freeview TV, free WiFi, hairdryers and hospitality trays. There is also a guest lounge, a spacious dining room with separate tables and a licensed bar. Parking is free. Owners June and Carl offer a friendly welcome.

Rooms 9 en suite S £35-£40; D £50-£70 **Facilities** FTV TVL tea/coffee Licensed WiFi **Parking** 9 **Notes** ⊗ No Children 10yrs Closed 17 Dec-17 Feb

Newton House

★★★★ GUEST ACCOMMODATION

tel: 01803 297520 **fax:** 01803 297520 **31 Newton Rd TQ2 5DB**
email: newtonhouse_torquay@yahoo.com **web:** www.newtonhouse-tq.co.uk
dir: *From Torre station bear left at lights, Newton House 40yds on left*

You are assured of a warm welcome at Newton House, which is close to the town centre and attractions. The comfortable bedrooms, some on the ground floor, have thoughtful extras, and a lounge is available. Breakfast is enjoyed in the pleasant dining room.

Rooms 9 en suite (3 fmly) (5 GF) **Facilities** FTV Lounge tea/coffee WiFi 🔒 Drying room for hikers **Extras** Snacks - complimentary **Parking** 15 **Notes** ⊗

Peppers

★★★★ GUEST ACCOMMODATION

tel: 01803 293856 **fax:** 07006 037547 **551 Babbacombe Rd TQ1 1HQ**
email: enquiries@hotel-peppers.co.uk **web:** www.hotel-peppers.co.uk
dir: *A3022 to seafront, left on to B3199 towards harbour. At clock tower rdbt, turn left, 250mtrs on left*

Peppers is a very well-placed property near the harbour and town centre, with free off-road parking. The bedrooms are bright and comfortable, and there is a well-appointed guest lounge. Hearty breakfasts are served in the light and airy breakfast room.

Rooms 10 rms (9 en suite) (1 pri facs) S £30-£42; D £52-£85 **Facilities** FTV TVL tea/coffee Licensed WiFi **Extras** Bottled water - complimentary **Parking** 9 **Notes** LB ⊗ No Children 10yrs Closed 18 Dec-9 Jan

Robin Hill

★★★★ GUEST ACCOMMODATION

tel: 01803 214518 **fax:** 01803 291410 **74 Braddons Hill Road East TQ1 1HF**
email: reservations@therobinhill.co.uk **web:** www.robinhillhotel.co.uk
dir: *From A38 to seafront then left to Babbacombe. Pass theatre to Clock Tower rdbt, take 1st exit & through 2 sets of lights, Braddons Hill Road East on left*

Dating back to 1896, this fascinating building has character in abundance and is located a short stroll from the harbour and shops. Every effort is made to ensure a stay is enjoyable; assistance is readily available at all times. Bedrooms, in varying styles, provide all the expected necessities. Public areas include the inviting lounge, plus a light and airy dining room where breakfast is served.

Rooms 10 en suite (2 fmly) (1 GF) **Facilities** FTV Lounge TVL tea/coffee Licensed WiFi ♨ ♿ 18 **Parking** 10 **Notes** Closed Nov-Mar

Summerlands

★★★★ GUEST ACCOMMODATION

tel: 01803 299844 **19 Belgrave Rd TQ2 5HU**
email: summerlands@fsmail.net **web:** www.summerlandsguesthousetorquay.com
dir: *A3022 into Newton Rd, towards seafront & town centre, into Belgrave Rd. Summerlands on left just past lights*

Located just five minutes walk from the seafront, Summerlands offers a friendly and relaxed environment. There are six well equipped, modern and comfortable bedrooms, all of which are en suite. Breakfasts are served on the lower-ground floor and provide a satisfying start to the day.

Rooms 6 en suite (2 fmly) (1 GF) S £35-£45; D £55-£70* **Facilities** FTV tea/coffee WiFi **Parking** 4 **Notes** ⊗ No Children 5yrs

Tyndale Guest House

★★★★ GUEST ACCOMMODATION

tel: 01803 380888 **68 Avenue Rd TQ2 5LF**
email: info@tyndaletorquay.co.uk **web:** www.tyndaletorquay.co.uk
dir: *A380 onto A3022, follow sea front signs into Avenue Rd, on right hand side of 1st lights*

Tyndale is a traditional operation within walking distance of the town and beach, with good off-road parking. Bedrooms are comfortable and well presented, breakfast is cooked to order, and the hosts are friendly and helpful.

Rooms 5 en suite (1 GF) S £30-£35; D £50-£70* **Facilities** FTV DVD tea/coffee WiFi **Parking** 7 **Notes** LB ⊗

The Norwood

★★★★ Ⓐ GUEST ACCOMMODATION

tel: 01803 294236 & 07741 662861 **60 Belgrave Rd TQ2 5HY**
email: enquiries@norwoodhoteltorquay.co.uk **web:** www.norwoodhoteltorquay.co.uk
dir: *From Princess Theatre towards Paignton, at 1st lights right into Belgrave Rd, over x-rds, 3rd building on left*

The Norwood is just a short walk from the seafront, town centre and Conference Centre. All the individually decorated bedrooms are en suite and four-poster rooms are available. There are excellent choices at breakfast, from traditional full English to lighter options; dinner is available by prior arrangement, and the hosts are happy to cater for special dietary requests. Packed lunches and takeaway breakfasts are also available.

Rooms 10 en suite (5 fmly) (1 GF) S £32-£42; D £50-£62* **Facilities** FTV tea/coffee Dinner available Licensed WiFi **Extras** Speciality toiletries - complimentary **Parking** 3 **Notes** LB

The Sandpiper Guest House

★★★★ Ⓐ GUEST HOUSE

tel: 01803 292779 **fax:** 01803 292806 **Rowdens Rd TQ2 5AZ**
email: enquiries@sandpiperguesthouse.co.uk **web:** www.sandpiperguesthouse.co.uk
dir: *From A380 onto A3022 (Riviera Way) follow signs for seafront along Avenue Rd. Left into Bampfylde Rd, right into Rowdens Rd*

The Sandpiper Guest House is in a peaceful tree-lined cul-de-sac, just a short walk away from the Riviera International Centre, Torre Abbey Gardens and the seafront. Guests may relax in the lounge, in the cellar bar or decked patio area. Breakfast is served in the dining room, and evening meals are available for an extra charge. Ample parking is a bonus, or a pick up from the rail or bus stations can be arranged.

Rooms 11 rms (9 en suite) (2 pri facs) (1 fmly) (2 GF) **Facilities** FTV TVL tea/coffee Dinner available Licensed WiFi **Parking** 8

Lindum Lodge

Ⓤ

tel: 01803 292795 **105 Abbey Rd TQ2 5NP**
email: enquiries@lindumlodge.co.uk

Currently the rating for this establishment is not confirmed. This may be due to a change of ownership or because it has only recently joined the AA rating scheme.

Rooms 15 en suite S £30-£50; D £60-£75* **Notes** Closed Oct-Feb

TOTNES
Map 3 SX86

Premier Collection

Stoke Gabriel Lodgings - Badgers Retreat

★★★★★ BED AND BREAKFAST

tel: 01803 782003 & 07785 710225 **2 Orchard Close, Stoke Gabriel TQ9 6SX**
email: info@stokegabriellodgings.com **web:** www.stokegabriellodgings.com
dir: *In Stoke Gabriel, pass Baptist church, take left fork into Paignton Rd. 100mtrs to entrance on left by public bench*

Stoke Gabriel Lodgings is an attractive example of contemporary architecture, positioned high above the River Dart just outside Stoke Gabriel, near Totnes. It was only completed in 2010 and has been designed to take full advantage of its location. David and Helen offer a warm welcome as well as a delicious Devon cream tea on arrival. Bedrooms are spacious and lavishly furnished with comfortable seating, and en suites that come complete with wet shower areas and heated towel rails. Patio doors open to a private balcony overlooking the garden and countryside. Outside, the newly planted garden landscape can be enjoyed from the large terrace or conservatory. Breakfast is a delight, while dinner can be taken at one of many local pubs and restaurants.

Rooms 3 en suite (1 fmly) S £70-£75; D £90-£100 **Facilities** STV FTV DVD iPod docking station Lounge TVL tea/coffee WiFi ☕ **Extras** Speciality toiletries, fruit/snacks, mineral water **Parking** 6 **Notes** ⊗ ☺

Steam Packet Inn

★★★★ ☕ INN

tel: 01803 863880 **fax:** 01803 862754 **St Peter's Quay TQ9 5EW**
email: steampacket@buccaneer.co.uk **web:** www.steampacketinn.co.uk
dir: *Off A38 at Totnes to Dartington & Totnes. Over 1st lights, pass railway station, signs for town centre at next rdbt. Over mini rdbt, River Dart on left, inn 100yds on left*

This friendly and popular riverside inn offers a warm welcome to visitors and locals alike. Bedrooms are well equipped and comfortable, and some have river views. Public areas have open fires and a choice of dining options including the heated waterside patio area, ideal for relaxing on warmer days. Interesting and well-cooked dishes are offered at lunch and dinner, while breakfast provides a satisfying start to the day. Complete with its own quay, the property has a long and interesting history.

Rooms 4 en suite (1 fmly) S £65-£75; D £75-£95* **Facilities** FTV tea/coffee Dinner available WiFi ☕ 4 private moorings **Extras** Speciality toiletries, water - complimentary **Parking** 15 **Notes** LB

YELVERTON
Map 3 SX56

Burrator Inn

★★★★ ☕ ☕ INN

tel: 01822 853121 **Dousland PL20 6NP**
email: reservations@theburratorinn.co.uk **web:** www.theburratorinn.com
dir: *From Yelverton on B3212 to Dousland*

This lively family pub is located in the very heart of Dousland, near Yelverton, and has a local following. The bedrooms are comfortable and equipped with all the expected facilities. A wide range of popular dishes served all day. Very cheerful and upbeat staff are ready and willing to meet the needs of their guests. Good selection of wines and local beers. Great for all ages and families.

Rooms 7 en suite S £55; D £75-£85* **Facilities** FTV DVD tea/coffee Dinner available WiFi Pool table **Parking** 40 **Notes** Closed 25 Dec

Overcombe House

★★★★ ⚠ GUEST HOUSE

tel: 01822 853501 **Old Station Rd, Horrabridge PL20 7RA**
email: enquiries@overcombehotel.co.uk **web:** www.overcombehotel.co.uk
dir: *Signed 100yds off A386 at Horrabridge*

Many guests return on a regular basis to enjoy this delightful, family-run establishment. Genuine hospitality is a great strength, and every effort is taken to ensure an enjoyable and memorable stay. Given its location, this is a perfect base for exploring the rugged beauty of the Dartmoor National Park, just on the doorstep. Bedrooms are all neatly presented; many have lovely views across the countryside.

Rooms 8 en suite (2 GF) S £67.50-£85; D £77.50-£95 **Facilities** FTV tea/coffee Licensed WiFi ☕ **Parking** 7 **Notes** ⊗ No Children 12yrs Closed 25 Dec

Tor Royal

Ⓤ

tel: 01822 890189 & 07892 910666 **Princetown PL20 6SL**
email: stay@torroyal.co.uk **web:** www.torroyal.co.uk
dir: *A38 exit at Ashburton, follow signs to Princetown/Two Bridges. Turn right to Princetown & left opposite Country Charm shop, Tor Royal on right*

Currently the rating for this establishment is not confirmed. This may be due to a change of ownership or because it has only recently joined the AA rating scheme.

Rooms 5 en suite (1 GF) S £55; D £80-£100 **Facilities** FTV DVD Lounge TV4B Dinner available WiFi ☕ **Conf** Max 30 Class 25 Board 20 **Parking** 10 **Notes** LB RS Xmas & New Year Civ Wed 50

DORSET

ASKERSWELL   Map 4 SY59

The Spyway Inn
★★★★ INN

tel: 01308 485250 fax: 01308 485250 **DT2 9EP**
email: spywaytim@hotmail.com web: www.spyway-inn.co.uk
dir: *From A35 follow Askerswell sign, then follow Spyway Inn sign*

Peacefully located in the rolling Dorset countryside, this family-run inn offers a warm and genuine welcome. Bedrooms are spacious and well appointed with a number of extras provided, including bath robes. Real ales are on tap in the bar, where locals congregate to put the world to rights. Menus feature home-cooked food, with many dishes utilising local produce both at dinner and breakfast. The extensive beer garden, with wonderful views, is popular in summer.

Rooms 3 en suite (1 fmly) S £50; D £80* **Facilities** FTV tea/coffee Dinner available WiFi **Parking** 40 **Notes** LB ⊗

BLANDFORD FORUM   Map 4 ST80

Portman Lodge
★★★★ BED AND BREAKFAST

tel: 01258 453727 **Whitecliff Mill St DT11 7BP**
email: enquiries@portmanlodge.co.uk web: www.portmanlodge.co.uk
dir: *One-way system, follow signs from town centre to Shaftesbury & hospital. On right past Our Lady of Lourdes church (on left)*

Built in the Victorian period and once used as a music school, this substantial detached house now provides elegant accommodation and a warm welcome. All bedrooms and bathrooms are well decorated and comfortably furnished. Breakfast utilises good quality ingredients and is served at a communal table.

Rooms 3 en suite 2 annexe en suite (1 fmly) S £65; D £80-£90 **Facilities** STV tea/coffee WiFi ♨ **Parking** 8 **Notes** No Children 10yrs ⊛

See advert on page 150

The Anvil Inn
★★★★ INN

tel: 01258 453431 fax: 01258 480182 **Salisbury Rd, Pimperne DT11 8UQ**
email: theanvil.inn@btconnect.com web: www.anvilinn.co.uk
dir: *2m NE of Blandford on A354 in Pimperne*

Dating back to the 16th century, this picturesque thatched inn is in the village of Pimperne, just a couple of miles from Blandford. There's a warm and welcoming atmosphere here, and a convivial bar and choice of dining areas in which to enjoy a meal from the extensive menu. Bedrooms and bathrooms offer impressive standards of comfort for both business and leisure guests. This is a great location for exploring the many historic towns, countryside and coastline which the region has to offer.

Rooms 12 en suite S £60-£110; D £95-£130* **Facilities** FTV tea/coffee Dinner available Direct Dial WiFi **Parking** 18 **Notes** LB No coaches

St Martin's House
★★★★ BED AND BREAKFAST

tel: 01258 451245 & 07818 814381 **White Cliff Mill St DT11 7BP**
email: info@stmartinshouse.co.uk web: www.stmartinshouse.co.uk
dir: *Market Place into Salisbury St, left into White Cliff Mill St, on right before traffic island*

This restored 19th-century property was once part of the choristers' house for a local church. The bedrooms are comfortable, homely and well equipped. The hosts offer warm hospitality and attentive service. Breakfast, which features local and home-made items, is served at a communal table.

Rooms 2 rms (2 pri facs) (1 fmly) S £45-£80; D £65-£80* **Facilities** FTV DVD tea/coffee WiFi ♨ **Parking** 3 **Notes** LB ⊗ ⊛

BLANDFORD FORUM *continued*

The Old Bakery Bed & Breakfast

★★★ BED AND BREAKFAST

tel: 01258 455173 & 07799 853784 **Church Rd, Pimperne DT11 8UB**
email: jjtanners@hotmail.com **web:** www.theoldbakerydorset.co.uk
dir: *2m NE of Blandford. Off A354 into Pimperne*

This family home, in what was once the village bakery, offers comfortable accommodation in a convenient location. Popular with business travellers, families can also be accommodated, with cots available. Substantial breakfasts featuring home-made bread and marmalade are served in the dining room.

Rooms 3 en suite (1 GF) **Facilities** TVL tea/coffee Dinner available WiFi **Parking** 2 **Notes** ⊗ ⊜

| BOURNEMOUTH | Map 5 SZ09 |

The Maples

★★★★ BED AND BREAKFAST

tel: 01202 529820 **1 Library Rd, Winton BH9 2QH**
email: jeffreyhurrell@yahoo.co.uk **web:** www.themaplesbnb.com
dir: *1.5m N of town centre. Exit A3060 (Castle Ln West) into Wimborne Rd. The Maples 1m on right after police station*

A friendly greeting awaits you at The Maples, which is just off Winton High Street. The atmosphere is informal and bedrooms are quiet, comfortable and equipped with considerate extras. Breakfast is enjoyed in the pleasant dining room around a communal table.

Rooms 2 en suite (1 fmly) S £25-£30; D £50-£60 **Facilities** FTV Lounge tea/coffee WiFi 🍴 **Parking** 2 **Notes** ⊗ No Children 7yrs ⊜

Newlands

★★★★ GUEST ACCOMMODATION

tel: 01202 761922 **fax:** 01202 769872 **14 Rosemount Rd, Alum Chine BH4 8HB**
email: newlandshotel@totalise.co.uk **web:** www.newlandsguesthouse.com
dir: *A338, A35 to Liverpool Victoria rdbt, exit for Alum Chine, left at lights, right at small rdbt into Alumhurst Rd, 3rd left*

A warm welcome is guaranteed at this attractive Edwardian house which is in a quiet area near Alum Chine beach and within easy driving distance of Bournemouth and Poole centres. Newlands offers comfortable accommodation with WiFi and a guest lounge.

Rooms 8 en suite (3 fmly) **Facilities** TVL tea/coffee WiFi **Parking** 8 **Notes** ⊗ Closed Dec, Jan & Feb

Blue Palms

★★★★ 🅐 BED AND BREAKFAST

tel: 01202 554968 **fax:** 01202 294197 **26 Tregonwell Rd, West Cliff BH2 5NS**
email: bluepalmshotel@btopenworld.com **web:** www.bluepalmshotel.com
dir: *Exit A338 at Bournemouth West rdbt signed town centre, Triangle, at next rdbt into Durley Chine Rd, at rdbt into West Hill Rd. Tregonwell Rd 3rd left*

The proprietor's collection of Hollywood memorabilia makes this an interesting place to stay. All the rooms are en suite and come in different sizes. Public areas are well presented and airy, and you can enjoy breakfast alfresco in the summer.

Rooms 7 en suite D £70-£98* **Facilities** FTV DVD TVL tea/coffee Licensed WiFi **Parking** 8 **Notes** LB ⊗ No Children 5yrs Closed Dec-14 Jan

---

Portman Lodge

Built in 1873, *Portman Lodge* is the main wing and entrance into a large Victorian property, originally part of Lord Portman's estate. It is thought to have been a residence for choristers for St Martin's Church. Many of the original fixtures and fittings remain, in particular the attractive Victorian tiled floor in the entrance hall and corridor.

The individually decorated bedrooms, with twin, double or kingsize beds, are supremely comfortable, with ensuite rooms, plentiful hot water, powerful showers and white fluffy towels.

Substantial cooked tasty breakfasts, including a varied range of locally sourced produce, are served around a large table in our lovely dining room.

There is a good choice of pubs and restaurants for lunch and dinner in the beautiful Georgian market town of Blandford, just five minutes walk away, so no need to get into your car.

Recommended in the area: Kingston Lacy, Lulworth Cove, Jurassic Coast, Corfe Castle, Abbotsbury Swannery and Gardens

Whitecliff Mill Street, Blandford Forum, Dorset DT11 7BP
Tel: 01258 453727
Mobile: 07860 424235 (Gerry) • 07785 971743 (Pat)
Website: www.portmanlodge.co.uk
Email: enquiries@portmanlodge.co.uk

Burley Court

★★★ GUEST ACCOMMODATION

tel: 01202 552824 & 556704 **fax:** 01202 298514 **Bath Rd BH1 2NP**
email: info@burleycourthotel.co.uk **web:** www.burleycourthotel.co.uk
dir: *Off A338 at St Pauls rdbt, 3rd exit at next rdbt into Holdenhurst Rd, 3rd exit at next rdbt into Bath Rd, over crossing, 1st left*

Burley Court is a large family-owned business that has been well established for many years. It's close to the East Cliff with good parking facilities, an outdoor swimming pool and serves dinner in the main season.

Rooms 40 rms (38 en suite) (10 fmly) (4 GF) S £25-£75; D £25-£150* **Facilities** FTV Lounge TVL tea/coffee Dinner available Direct Dial Lift Licensed WiFi ⚲ ᴸ 18 Pool table ⚑ **Conf** Thtr 30 Class 15 Board 15 **Parking** 40 **Notes** LB

Commodore

★★★ INN

tel: 01202 423150 **fax:** 01202 423519 **Overcliff Dr, Southbourne BH6 3TD**
email: 7688@greeneking.co.uk **web:** www.oldenglish.co.uk
dir: *1m E of town centre on seafront*

Situated on the cliff top at Southbourne, the Commodore is adjacent to Fisherman's Walk. Popular with locals, the bar boasts spectacular views across Poole Bay and serves an extensive range of dishes.

Rooms 12 en suite (1 fmly) **Facilities** tea/coffee Dinner available Lift ᴸ 18 **Conf** Max 30 Thtr 30 Class 18 Board 20 **Parking** 12 **Notes** ⊗

Pinedale

★★★ GUEST ACCOMMODATION

tel: 01202 553733 & 292702 **40 Tregonwell Rd, West Cliff BH2 5NT**
email: thepinedalehotel@btconnect.com **web:** www.thepinedalehotel.co.uk
dir: *A338 at Bournemouth West rdbt, signs to West Cliff, Tregonwell Rd 3rd left after passing Wessex Hotel*

This friendly place is enthusiastically run by two generations of the same family, and offers comfortable accommodation within a short walk of the seafront and local attractions. The fresh-looking bedrooms are equipped with useful extras. There is also an attractive licensed bar and an airy dining room where you can enjoy wholesome home-cooked breakfasts.

Rooms 15 rms (10 en suite) (1 fmly) S £20-£40; D £40-£80* **Facilities** FTV TVL tea/coffee Direct Dial Licensed WiFi ⚑ **Parking** 15 **Notes** ⊗ Closed 24 Dec-2 Jan

Trouville Lodge

★★★ GUEST ACCOMMODATION

tel: 01202 552262 **fax:** 01202 293324 **9 Priory Rd BH2 5DF**
email: reception@trouvillehotel.com **web:** www.trouvillehotel.com

Professionally run, this well-managed establishment offers an impressive standard of accommodation and facilities. Bedrooms are situated in an annexe to the Trouville Hotel next door. All rooms are stylishly appointed and comfortably furnished. Facilities are in the hotel. The Deauville restaurant offers a very good menu choice, and the well-stocked Le Café Bar provides an informal and pleasant environment. There is also a large pool and sauna as well as a resident beautician.

Rooms 19 en suite (4 fmly) (4 GF) **Facilities** FTV tea/coffee WiFi Leisure facilities available at Trouville Hotel **Parking** 14

The Westbrook

★★★ BED AND BREAKFAST

tel: 01202 761081 & 07871 174892 **fax:** 01202 761081
64 Alum Chine Rd, Westbourne BH4 8DZ
email: info@thewestbrookhotel.co.uk **web:** www.thewestbrookhotel.co.uk
dir: *At County Gates rdbt exit signed Compton Acres. At lights turn left. At mini rdbt take 2nd exit, on left*

The Westbrook sits in one of the quieter suburbs of Bournemouth a little less than a mile away from the town centre. The house has been decorated tastefully in sympathy with its age and bedrooms are smartly presented and all are en suite. Home-cooked breakfasts are served in the light dining room and private parking, whilst limited is available on-site. Free WiFi is also available.

Rooms 6 en suite (3 fmly) (1 GF) S £29-£65; D £45-£75* **Facilities** FTV DVD tea/coffee WiFi ⚑ **Parking** 6 **Notes** ⊗ No Children 6yrs

Ingledene Guest House

★★ GUEST HOUSE

tel: 01202 291914 & 07005 810914 **18-20 Gardens View BH1 3QA**
email: ingledenehouse@yahoo.com **web:** www.ingledenehouse.co.uk

Ingledene Guest House offers practical, comfortable accommodation at reasonable prices. Breakfast and dinner is served in the dining room with the pre-order dinner menu offering ample choice. The house is well placed for Bournemouth town centre, with the train station a few minutes' walk away. Off-road parking is available.

Rooms 12 en suite (8 fmly) (1 GF) **Facilities** FTV TVL tea/coffee Dinner available Licensed WiFi ⚲ **Conf** Max 20 Class 20 Board 20 **Parking** 5 **Notes** ⊗

| BRIDPORT | Map 4 SY49 |

See also Chideock

Premier Collection

The Roundham House

★★★★★ GUEST ACCOMMODATION

tel: 01308 422753 **fax:** 01308 421500
Roundham Gardens, West Bay Rd DT6 4BD
email: cyprencom@compuserve.com **web:** www.roundhamhouse.co.uk
dir: *A35 into Bridport, at Crown Inn rdbt take exit signed West Bay. House 400yds on left*

The hosts here are always on hand to welcome guests to their lovely home, which has well-tended gardens and views to the coast. Bedrooms come in a variety of sizes and are filled with useful extras. Public areas include a comfortable lounge and well-appointed dining room.

Rooms 8 rms (7 en suite) (1 fmly) **Facilities** FTV Lounge tea/coffee Licensed WiFi **Parking** 10 **Notes** No Children 5yrs Closed Nov-Apr

BRIDPORT *continued*

Premier Collection

The Shave Cross Inn

★★★★★ ⬤ INN

tel: 01308 868358 **fax:** 01308 867064 **Marshwood Vale DT6 6HW**
email: roy.warburton@virgin.net **web:** www.theshavecrossinn.co.uk
dir: *From B3165 turn at Birdsmoorgate & follow brown signs*

This historic inn has been providing refreshment to weary travellers for centuries and continues to offer a warm and genuine welcome. The snug bar is dominated by a wonderful fireplace with crackling logs creating just the right atmosphere. Bedrooms are located in a separate Dorset flint and stone building. Quality is impressive throughout with wonderful stone floors and oak beams, combined with feature beds and luxurious bathrooms. Food, using excellent local produce, has a distinct Caribbean and international slant, including a number of authentic dishes.

Rooms 7 en suite (1 fmly) (3 GF) **Facilities** STV FTV tea/coffee Dinner available Direct Dial WiFi Pool table **Parking** 29 **Notes** No Children RS Mon (ex BH) closed for lunch & dinner No coaches

Britmead House

★★★★ GUEST ACCOMMODATION

tel: 01308 422941 & 07973 725243 **West Bay Rd DT6 4EG**
email: britmead@talk21.com **web:** www.britmeadhouse.co.uk
dir: *1m S of town centre, exit A35 into West Bay Rd*

Britmead House is located south of Bridport, within easy reach of the town centre and West Bay harbour. Family-run, the atmosphere is friendly and the accommodation well appointed and comfortable. As it is suitable for business and leisure, many guests return regularly. A choice of breakfast is served in the light and airy dining room.

Rooms 8 en suite (2 fmly) (2 GF) S £48-£64; D £68-£86 **Facilities** FTV iPod docking station Lounge tea/coffee WiFi ⬤ **Parking** 12 **Notes** LB Closed 24-27 Dec

Oxbridge Farm (SY475977)

★★★★ ⬤ FARMHOUSE

tel: 01308 488368 & 07766 086543 **DT6 3UA**
email: jojokillin@hotmail.com **web:** www.oxbridgefarm.co.uk
dir: *From A3066 Bridport to Beaminster. Take 1st right signed Oxbridge 1m*

Oxbridge Farm sits in the rolling hills of west Dorset in an Area of Outstanding Natural Beauty. The bedrooms are well equipped and offer a very good level of comfort. A hearty breakfast is served in the attractive dining room which benefits from wonderful countryside views.

Rooms 4 rms (3 en suite) (1 pri facs) (2 fmly) (1 GF) **Facilities** FTV Lounge TVL TV3B tea/coffee Dinner available WiFi ⬤ 18 **Parking** 6 **Notes** LB ⊗ ⬤ 40 acres sheep

Premier Collection

Crosskeys House

★★★★★ BED AND BREAKFAST

tel: 01308 868063 **High St DT8 3QP**
email: robin.adeney@care4free.net **web:** www.crosskeyshouse.com
dir: *From Beaminster to Broadwindsor. Enter one-way system, last house on right before x-rds*

Crosskeys House is a Grade II listed building set in the heart of this peaceful village, and is an ideal base from which to explore the Dorset countryside and coast. Over the years the site has been home to a pub, blacksmith and a cobbler's shop. These days a warm welcome is extended to guests, and bedrooms provide high levels of quality with a host of thoughtful extras, while bathrooms come complete with fluffy towels and cosseting robes. Breakfast is a generous and tasty offering served in the elegant dining room. A lounge is also provided, and breakfast can be taken in the wonderful garden during the summer.

Rooms 3 rms (2 en suite) (1 pri facs) S £60-£75; D £90-£105* **Facilities** FTV DVD Lounge tea/coffee WiFi ⬤ **Extras** Speciality toiletries, bottled water - free **Parking** 3 **Notes** LB ⊗ No Children 12yrs

Abbots

★★★ BED AND BREAKFAST

tel: 01300 341349 **7 Long St DT2 7JF**
email: info@abbotsbedand breakfast.co.uk **web:** www.abbotsbedandbreakfast.co.uk
dir: *From A352 follow signs to village centre, next to village stores opposite New Inn public house*

Located in the pleasant village of Cerne Abbas, guests here can enjoy a cream tea in the downstairs tea room before retiring upstairs to the relaxing bedrooms. A choice of pubs offering a selection of evening meals is just a few minutes' stroll away. Home-cooked breakfasts are also served in the comfortable tea room.

Rooms 5 rms (4 en suite) (1 pri facs) (1 fmly) S £55-£60; D £75-£85* **Facilities** FTV tea/coffee Licensed WiFi ⬤

The White House

★★★★ ⬤ ⬤ GUEST HOUSE

tel: 01297 560411 **The Street DT6 6PJ**
email: ian@whitehousehotel.com **web:** www.whitehousehotel.com
dir: *From Lyme Regis rdbt on A35 take exit signed Charmouth. On Main St opposite St Andrew's Church*

Located only five minutes' walk from the beach and a short drive to Lyme Regis, this old Regency building offers four luxury en suite rooms. They serve quality dishes, at breakfast and dinner, that make the best use of locally sourced meat and fish, as well as herbs from their own garden and eggs laid by the resident chickens. Off-street parking is available.

Rooms 4 en suite (1 fmly) (1 GF) S £90-£120; D £120-£140* **Facilities** FTV DVD iPod docking station Lounge tea/coffee Dinner available Licensed WiFi ⬤ **Extras** Mineral water **Parking** 8 **Notes** LB RS Nov-Feb B&B only mid wk

CHIDEOCK
Map 4 SY49

Rose Cottage
★★★★ BED AND BREAKFAST

tel: 01297 489994 & 07980 400904 **Main St DT6 6JQ**
email: enquire@rosecottage-chideock.co.uk **web:** www.rosecottage-chideock.co.uk
dir: *On A35 in village centre, on left in W direction*

Located in the centre of a charming village, this 300-year-old cottage provides very well-appointed, attractive accommodation and a friendly welcome is assured. Breakfast can be enjoyed in the renovated dining room which has many interesting features, and in finer weather guests can relax in the pretty garden.

Rooms 2 en suite S £55; D £75* **Facilities** FTV tea/coffee WiFi ⚓ **Parking** 2 **Notes** LB ⊗ No Children 12yrs Closed 23-24 & 31 Dec

CHRISTCHURCH
Map 5 SZ19

Druid House
★★★★★ ⌂ GUEST ACCOMMODATION

tel: 01202 485615 **fax:** 01202 473484 **26 Sopers Ln BH23 1JE**
email: reservations@druid-house.co.uk **web:** www.druid-house.co.uk
dir: *From A35 exit at Christchurch main rdbt into Sopers Ln, establishment on left*

Overlooking the park, this delightful family-run establishment is just a stroll from the high street, the priory and the quay. Bedrooms, some with balconies, are very comfortably furnished, and have many welcome extras including CD players. There is a pleasant rear garden, patio and relaxing lounge and bar areas.

Rooms 8 en suite (3 fmly) (4 GF) **Facilities** FTV DVD iPod docking station tea/coffee Direct Dial Licensed WiFi **Parking** 8 **Notes** ⊗

The Lord Bute & Restaurant
★★★★★ ◉ GUEST ACCOMMODATION

tel: 01425 278884 **fax:** 01425 279258 **179-181**
Lymington Rd, Highcliffe on Sea BH23 4JS
email: mail@lordbute.co.uk **web:** www.lordbute.co.uk
dir: *A337 towards Highcliffe*

The elegant Lord Bute stands directly behind the original entrance lodges of Highcliffe Castle, close to the beach and historic town of Christchurch. Bedrooms have been finished to a very high standard with many thoughtful extras including spa baths. Excellent, award-winning food is available in the smart restaurant. Conferences and weddings are catered for.

Rooms 9 en suite 4 annexe en suite (1 fmly) (6 GF) **Facilities** FTV tea/coffee Dinner available Direct Dial Licensed **Conf** Max 25 Thtr 25 Class 15 Board 18 **Parking** 40 **Notes** LB RS Mon Restaurant closed (open bkfst) Civ Wed 120

Grosvenor Lodge
★★★★ GUEST HOUSE

tel: 01202 499008 **fax:** 01202 486041 **53 Stour Rd BH23 1LN**
email: bookings@grosvenorlodge.co.uk **web:** www.grosvenorlodge.co.uk
dir: *A35 from Christchurch to Bournemouth, at 1st lights left into Stour Rd. Lodge on right*

Grosvenor House is a friendly and popular guest house near the centre of this historic town. The bedrooms are brightly and individually decorated and have lots of useful extras. Hearty breakfasts are served in the cheerful dining room and there are many local restaurants for lunch and dinner to head for. AA Friendliest B&B of the Year Finalist 2014-2015.

Rooms 7 en suite (4 fmly) (1 GF) S £35-£50; D £50-£100* **Facilities** FTV iPod docking station tea/coffee WiFi ⚓ **Parking** 10 **Notes** LB ⊗

CHRISTCHURCH *continued*

Avon Breeze

★★★★ ☱ BED AND BREAKFAST

tel: 01425 279102 & 07896 128026 **21 Fulmar Rd BH23 4BJ**
email: info@avonbreeze.co.uk **web:** http://avonbreeze.co.uk
dir: *A35 follow signs for Christchurch. At Sainsburys, signs for Mudeford. At Mudeford quay, turn into Falcon Dr, left & left again*

Avon Breeze is situated on the edge of the New Forest, a few minutes' level walk to the harbour, beach and local pubs. This contemporary home offers two comfortable en suite rooms as well as the use of a conservatory. Breakfast consists of locally sourced organic ingredients. Ample off street parking is available.

Rooms 2 en suite (2 GF) D £80–£95 **Facilities** FTV DVD iPod docking station tea/coffee WiFi 🔒 **Extras** Bottled water, chocolate - complimentary **Parking** 3 **Notes** LB ⊗ No Children Closed Oct-Mar RS Apr 1 room only open ⊜

Bure Farmhouse

★★★★ BED AND BREAKFAST

tel: 01425 275498 **107 Bure Ln, Friars Cliff BH23 4DN**
web: www.burefarmhouse.co.uk
dir: *A35 & A337 E from Christchurch towards Highcliffe, 1st rdbt right into The Runway. Bure Ln 3rd turn sharp right into service road, farmhouse on left*

A friendly welcome is assured at Bure Farmhouse, an Edwardian family home offering individually decorated, comfortable bedrooms with plenty of useful extras. Hearty breakfasts are served farmhouse-style in the dining room overlooking the attractive gardens. Ideally located for exploring Christchurch and the New Forest, and just a short walk from Highcliffe Castle.

Rooms 3 rms (2 en suite) (1 pri facs) (1 fmly) S £45; D £65–£70 **Facilities** DVD tea/coffee WiFi 🔒 **Parking** 3 **Notes** LB ⊗ No Children 4yrs ⊜

Riversmead

★★★★ GUEST ACCOMMODATION

tel: 01202 487195 **61 Stour Rd BH23 1LN**
email: riversmead.dorset@googlemail.com
dir: *A338 to Christchurch. Left turn to town centre, turn right over railway bridge*

Ideally located close to the town centre, beaches and the New Forest with excellent access to all local transport, Riversmead is the perfect base for a short break or longer stay. This comfortable house offers a range of facilities including enclosed off-road parking, fridges in rooms and an excellent breakfast.

Rooms 3 en suite (1 fmly) S £45–£50; D £60–£70* **Facilities** FTV tea/coffee WiFi **Parking** 9 **Notes** LB

The Rothesay

★★★★ GUEST ACCOMMODATION

tel: 01425 274172 **175, Lymington Rd, Highcliffe BH23 4JS**
email: reservations@therothesayhotel.com **web:** www.therothesayhotel.com
dir: *A337 to Highcliffe towards The Castle, 1m on left*

Set on the edge of Highcliffe, The Rothesay is a great base for exploring the Dorset and Hampshire coast. Highcliffe Castle is just a five-minute walk away, and there are cliff-top walks and views to the Isle of Wight. The indoor pool is a real bonus, as are the pretty gardens and large car park.

Rooms 12 en suite 3 annexe en suite (1 fmly) (7 GF) **Facilities** FTV TVL tea/coffee Licensed WiFi 🕲 Sauna Pool table **Conf** Max 30 Thtr 30 Class 30 Board 30 **Parking** 21 **Notes** ⊗ No Children 8yrs

The White House

★★★★ GUEST ACCOMMODATION

tel: 01425 271279 **fax:** 01425 276900 **428 Lymington Rd, Highcliffe on Sea BH23 5HF**
email: enquiries@thewhitehouse-christchurch.co.uk **web:** www.thewhitehouse-christchurch.co.uk
dir: *Off A35, signs to Highcliffe. After rdbt The White House 200yds on right*

This charming Victorian house is just a short drive from Highcliffe beach, the New Forest and the historic town of Christchurch. Comfortable, well-appointed accommodation is provided, and a generous, freshly-cooked breakfast is served in the cosy dining room.

Rooms 6 en suite **Facilities** tea/coffee WiFi **Parking** 6 **Notes** LB ⊗

Brantwood Guest House

★★★ GUEST ACCOMMODATION

tel: 01202 473446 **fax:** 01202 473446 **55 Stour Rd BH23 1LN**
email: brantwoodbookings@gmail.com **web:** www.brantwoodguesthouse.com
dir: *A338 Bournemouth, 1st exit to Christchurch, right after railway bridge, cross lights, 200yds on right*

Brantwood Guest House offers relaxed and friendly guest accommodation where the proprietors create a home-from-home atmosphere. Bedrooms and bathrooms are all well decorated and comfortably furnished. The town centre is just a stroll away and off-road parking is available.

Rooms 5 rms (4 en suite) (1 pri facs) (2 fmly) (1 GF) **Facilities** tea/coffee WiFi **Parking** 5 **Notes** ⊗ ⊜

Southern Comfort Guest House

★★★ GUEST ACCOMMODATION

tel: 01202 471373 **51 Stour Rd BH23 1LN**
email: scomfortgh@aol.com **web:** www.christchurchguesthouse.co.uk
dir: *A338 onto B3073 towards Christchurch, 2m onto B3059 (Stour Rd)*

Convenient for Bournemouth, Christchurch and Southbourne, this practical and friendly guest accommodation offers spacious bedrooms. Breakfast, served in the bright lounge-dining room, is a relaxed affair with a good choice of hot items.

Rooms 3 en suite (3 fmly) **Facilities** FTV TVL tea/coffee WiFi **Parking** 4 **Notes** LB ⊗

CORFE MULLEN   Map 4 SY99

Kenways

★★★ BED AND BREAKFAST

tel: 01202 280620 **90a Wareham Rd BH21 3LQ**
email: eileen@kenways.com **web:** www.kenways.com
dir: *2m SW of Wimborne. Off A31 to Corfe Mullen. Over B3074 rdbt, B&B 0.3m on right*

Expect to be welcomed as one of the family at this homely bed and breakfast situated between Wimborne Minster and Poole. The spacious bedrooms are well provisioned with thoughtful extras, and breakfast is served in the pleasant conservatory overlooking attractive gardens.

Rooms 3 rms (3 pri facs) (2 GF) **Facilities** FTV DVD TVL tea/coffee WiFi Table tennis Snooker table **Parking** 4

CRANBORNE
Map 5 SU01

The Inn at Cranborne

★★★★ ≘ INN

tel: 01725 551249 **fax:** 01725 350001 **5 Wimborne St BH21 5PP**
email: info@theinnatcranborne.co.uk **web:** www.theinnatcranborne.co.uk
dir: *On B3078 in centre of village*

A delightful 17th-century inn, lovingly restored and full of special touches, The Inn at Cranborne is located in a peaceful village just a short drive from the New Forest and the Jurassic Coast. Nine comfortable and beautifully appointed en suite rooms are available. Breakfast (a real treat here), lunch and dinner are served in the bar and dining room areas. Off-street parking is available.

Rooms 9 en suite (2 fmly) S £75-£95; D £85-£140* **Facilities** FTV DVD iPod docking station tea/coffee Dinner available WiFi ⚘ 18 ⚑ **Extras** Speciality toiletries
Conf Max 10 Thtr 15 Board 10 **Parking** 25 **Notes** LB Closed 2-7 Jan

DORCHESTER
Map 4 SY69

Premier Collection

Little Court

★★★★★ ≘ GUEST ACCOMMODATION

tel: 01305 261576 **fax:** 01305 261359 **5 Westleaze, Charminster DT2 9PZ**
email: info@littlecourt.net **web:** www.littlecourt.net
dir: *A37 from Dorchester, 0.25m right at Loders Garage, Little Court 0.5m on right*

Built in 1909 in the style of Lutyens, Little Court sits in over four acres of attractive grounds and gardens, complete with tennis courts and swimming pool. The property has been appointed to a very high standard and the friendly proprietors are on hand to ensure a pleasant stay. A delicious breakfast, including home-grown produce, can be enjoyed in the stylish dining room.

Rooms 8 en suite (1 fmly) **Facilities** FTV Lounge tea/coffee Licensed WiFi ⚘ ⚘ ⚘ 18 Gym **Parking** 10 **Notes** LB ⊗ Closed Xmas & New Year

Baytree House Dorchester

★★★★ BED AND BREAKFAST

tel: 01305 263696 **4 Athelstan Rd DT1 1NR**
email: info@baytreedorchester.com **web:** www.bandbdorchester.co.uk
dir: *0.5m SE of town centre*

Baytree House Dorchester is friendly, family-run bed and breakfast situated in the heart of the town, not far from the village of Higher Bockham, birthplace of Thomas Hardy. The bedrooms are furnished in an appealing contemporary style and provide high levels of comfort. Breakfast is served farmhouse style in the open-plan kitchen/dining area. Parking is available.

Rooms 6 en suite S fr £40; D £65-£75 **Facilities** FTV iPod docking station tea/coffee **Parking** 3 **Notes** LB ⊗

Westwood House

★★★★ GUEST ACCOMMODATION

tel: 01305 268018 **29 High West St DT1 1UP**
email: reservations@westwoodhouse.co.uk **web:** www.westwoodhouse.co.uk
dir: *On B2150 in town centre*

Originally built in 1815, Westwood House is centrally located in this historic town and is ideal for leisure visitors as well as business travellers. Run by a husband and wife team, this attractive property offers well-appointed rooms with modern facilities presented in an informal, stylish environment.

Rooms 7 rms (5 en suite) (2 pri facs) (2 fmly) **Facilities** FTV DVD tea/coffee WiFi ⚑ **Extras** Speciality toiletries, fresh milk **Notes** ⊗

The Brewers Arms

★★★ INN

tel: 01305 889361 **Martinstown DT2 9LB**
email: contact@thebrewersarms.com **web:** www.thebrewersarms.com
dir: *W of Dorchester on A35, after 2m turn left signed Martinstown. Right into village, 0.5m on right*

The Brewers Arms is very much a traditional country local, situated in the heart of a picturesque village. A warm welcome is assured and the atmosphere at the bar is good-natured and friendly. Bedrooms are located in an adjacent building and are entirely self-contained. Each one is spacious and well appointed with all the necessities to ensure a comfortable and relaxing stay. The menu offers a range of popular favourites, served either in the restaurant or the bar area. An extensive garden is also available.

Rooms 2 annexe en suite (2 GF) S £80-£90; D £90* **Facilities** FTV tea/coffee Dinner available WiFi **Extras** Speciality toiletries, bottled water **Parking** 20 **Notes** LB

EVERSHOT
Map 4 ST50

The Acorn Inn

★★★★ ⊛ INN

tel: 01935 83228 **fax:** 01935 83707 **DT2 0JW**
email: stay@acorn-inn.co.uk **web:** www.acorn-inn.co.uk
dir: *From A37 between Yeovil & Dorchester, follow Evershot & Holywell signs, 0.5m to inn*

This delightful 16th-century coaching inn is located in the heart of the village. Many of the bedrooms feature interesting four-poster beds, and all the rooms have been individually decorated and furnished. The public areas retain many original features including oak panelling, open fires and stone-flagged floors. Fresh local produce is included on the varied menu.

Rooms 10 en suite (2 fmly) **Facilities** STV FTV TVL tea/coffee Dinner available Direct Dial WiFi ch fac ⚑ Use of spa opposite - charged **Conf** Max 30 Thtr 30 Board 30 **Parking** 40

FARNHAM
Map 4 ST91

Premier Collection

Farnham Farm House

★★★★★ GUEST ACCOMMODATION

tel: 01725 516254 **fax:** 01725 516306 **DT11 8DG**
email: info@farnhamfarmhouse.co.uk **web:** www.farnhamfarmhouse.co.uk
dir: *Exit A354 Thickthorn x-rds into Farnham, continue NW from village centre T-junct, 1m bear right at sign*

Farnham Farm House sits in 350 acres of arable farmland, offering a high level of quality, comfort and service. The atmosphere is friendly and the accommodation charming and spacious. In winter, a log fire burns in the attractive dining room, where a delicious breakfast, featuring local produce, is served; views across the rolling countryside can be enjoyed while you eat your meal. Added features include an outdoor pool and the Sarpenela Natural Therapies Centre in the converted stable.

Rooms 3 en suite (1 fmly) S £80; D £90 **Facilities** FTV Lounge TVL tea/coffee WiFi ⚘ ⚘ ⚑ Holistic Therapies Centre **Parking** 7 **Notes** ⊗ Closed 25-26 Dec

FARNHAM *continued*

Museum Inn

★★★★ ◎◎ INN

tel: 01725 812702 **DT11 8DE**
email: enquiries@museuminn.co.uk **web:** www.museuminn.co.uk
dir: *Off A354 between Salisbury & Blandford Forum*

Located in a peaceful Dorset village, this traditional inn offers cosy log fires, flagstone floors and a welcoming bar combined with efficient service and a friendly welcome. Bedrooms include larger, stylish rooms in the main building or a selection of cosy rooms in an adjacent building. Food here, whether dinner or breakfast, uses the finest quality produce and really should not be missed.

Rooms 4 en suite 4 annexe en suite (2 fmly) (4 GF) S £90-£110; D £90-£130*
Facilities FTV Lounge tea/coffee Dinner available Direct Dial WiFi ↕ 18 Fishing Riding **Extras** Speciality toiletries **Conf** Max 30 Thtr 30 Class 24 Board 20 **Parking** 24 **Notes** LB

FERNDOWN	Map 5 SU00

City Lodge

★★★★ GUEST ACCOMMODATION

tel: 01202 578828 **fax:** 01202 572620 **Ringwood Rd BH22 9AN**
email: bournemouth@citylodge.co.uk **web:** www.citylodge.co.uk

Close to Bournemouth and the airport, City Lodge provides an ideal base for exploring the Dorset coastline. Situated on the edge of the River Stour, many of the rooms have the benefit of beautiful riverside views. The bedrooms offer modern facilities and en suite bathrooms. The large bar and restaurant serve meals and snacks. Parking is gated and secure.

Rooms 45 en suite (4 fmly) (11 GF) S £49.95-£89.95; D £49.95-£89.95 (room only)*
Facilities FTV Lounge tea/coffee Dinner available Licensed WiFi Fishing 🔒 **Conf** Max 120 Thtr 80 Class 60 Board 40 **Parking** 300 **Notes** LB ⊗

HIGHCLIFFE	

For accommodation details see Christchurch

LYME REGIS	Map 4 SY39

See also Axminster (Devon)

Old Lyme Guest House

★★★★ GUEST ACCOMMODATION

tel: 01297 442929 **29 Coombe St DT7 3PP**
email: oldlymeguesthouse@gmail.com **web:** www.oldlymeguesthouse.co.uk
dir: *In town centre into Coombe St at lights*

Comfort is a high priority at this delightful 18th-century former post office, which is just a short walk from the seafront. Bedrooms, which vary in size, are all well equipped and include many thoughtful extras. A wide choice is offered at breakfast, served in the cheerful dining room.

Rooms 5 rms (4 en suite) (1 pri facs) (1 fmly) D £85-£90* **Facilities** FTV TVL tea/coffee WiFi **Notes** LB ⊗ No Children 5yrs Closed Xmas & New Year

St Cuthberts

★★★★ BED AND BREAKFAST

tel: 01297 445901 **Charmouth Rd DT7 3HG**
email: info@stcuthbertsoflyme.co.uk **web:** www.stcuthbertsoflyme.co.uk
dir: *A35 from Dorchester, at Charmouth rdbt onto B3052 for 2m. Establishment on opposite side of road to "Welcome to Lyme Regis" sign*

Located just a ten minute walk above the main town and harbour, this detached home is set within mature gardens and has its own parking. Bedrooms and bathrooms offer plenty of quality and comfort, as well as many thoughtful extras. A lounge with a log-burning stove and a decked terrace are available for guests. Breakfast, served around one large table, offers a varied choice including delicious pancakes, with bacon and maple syrup.

Rooms 3 en suite (1 GF) S fr £65; D fr £85* **Facilities** FTV DVD TVL tea/coffee ↕ 18 **Parking** 3 **Notes** ⊗ No Children 7yrs ◉

The White House

★★★★ 🏠 ☕ GUEST HOUSE

tel: 01297 560411 **The Street DT6 6PJ**
email: ian@whitehousehotel.com **web:** www.whitehousehotel.com

(For full entry see Charmouth)

The Mariners

★★★★ ◎ INN

tel: 01297 442753 **fax:** 01297 442431 **Silver St DT7 3HS**
email: enquiry@hotellymeregis.co.uk **web:** www.hotellymeregis.co.uk
dir: *A35 onto B3165 (Lyme Rd). Mariners is pink building opposite road to The Cobb (Pound Rd)*

This delightful building combines traditional character and ambience with a modern and stylish upgrade. Bedrooms and bathrooms vary in size, but include a range of welcome extras; many have views over the bay. Public areas include a relaxing lounge, comfortable bar and modern restaurant. Guests can choose a full dinner, utilising local fish and seafood, or a varied range of lighter options from the bar menu. Outdoor seating is available.

Rooms 14 en suite (2 fmly) **Facilities** FTV Lounge tea/coffee Dinner available Direct Dial WiFi ↕ 18 Fishing **Conf** Max 30 Thtr 24 Class 16 Board 30 **Parking** 20

MATCHAMS	Map 5 SU10

Little Paddock B&B

★★★★ 🏠 BED AND BREAKFAST

tel: 01425 470889 **218 Hurn Rd BH24 2BT**
email: enquiries@little-paddock.com **web:** www.little-paddock.com

Little Paddock B&B is an adults-only getaway on the edge of the New Forest. It is in a secluded setting, yet still conveniently close to the busy town of Ringwood, and only a short distance from the popular seaside towns of Bournemouth, Poole and Christchurch. The three double rooms offer impressive levels of comfort with a host of thoughtful extras; all have French doors leading out onto the terrace. There is a unique glass dome for guests to relax in, as well as a swimming pool, sauna and hot tub. Breakfast is served either in the guest lounge or in the Retreat and includes home-baked bread, eggs from the owners' chickens and home-made jams, marmalade and local honey.

Rooms 3 en suite (3 GF) S £65-£80; D £77.50-£95* **Facilities** FTV DVD Lounge TVL tea/coffee Licensed WiFi ⚲ ☀ Sauna 🔒 Hot tub Table tennis **Parking** 12 **Notes** LB ⊗ No Children 18yrs

MILTON ABBAS — Map 4 ST80

Fishmore Hill Farm *(ST799013)*

 FARMHOUSE

tel: 01258 881122 & 07708 003561 **fax:** 01258 881122 **DT11 0DL**
email: sarah@fishmorehillfarm.com **web:** www.fishmorehillfarm.com
dir: *Off A354 signed Milton Abbas, 3m left on sharp bend, up steep hill, 1st left*

This working sheep farm and family home is surrounded by beautiful Dorset countryside, close to historic Milton Abbas and only a short drive from the coast. Bedrooms, which vary in size, are comfortable and have useful extras. The atmosphere is friendly and relaxed. Breakfast is served in the smart dining room around a communal table.

Rooms 3 en suite S fr £35; D fr £70 **Facilities** FTV TVL tea/coffee WiFi **Parking** 4 **Notes** Closed Xmas & New Year 🐑 50 acres sheep/horses

MOTCOMBE — Map 4 ST82

The Coppleridge Inn

★★★ INN

tel: 01747 851980 **fax:** 01747 851858 **SP7 9HW**
email: thecoppleridgeinn@btinternet.com **web:** www.coppleridge.com
dir: *Exit A350 to Motcombe, under railway bridge, 400yds, right to Mere, inn 300yds on left*

This village inn set within its own 15 acres of land offers ten en suite bedrooms located in a pretty courtyard. All bedrooms have been appointed to a very high standard to provide a very comfortable stay. Staff offer a warm welcome, and the inn serves good food with many daily specials. There are tennis courts and boules, plus a children's play area. Clay pigeon shooting can also be arranged.

Rooms 10 en suite (2 fmly) (10 GF) **Facilities** FTV DVD TVL tea/coffee Dinner available Direct Dial WiFi ch fac 🎱 🔒 Boules pitch **Extras** Mini-bar **Conf** Max 60 Thtr 60 Class 60 Board 30 **Parking** 100 **Notes** Civ Wed 80

PIDDLEHINTON — Map 4 SY79

Longpuddle

★★★★ BED AND BREAKFAST

tel: 01300 348532 **4 High St DT2 7TD**
email: ann@longpuddle.co.uk **web:** www.longpuddle.co.uk
dir: *From Dorchester (A35) take B3143, after entering village 1st thatched house on left after village cross*

This purpose-built annexed accommodation is perfectly located for exploring the delightful Dorset countryside and coast. Bedrooms are spacious, very well furnished and equipped with thoughtful extras such as mini-fridges. Breakfast is served in the dining room of the main house, where a guest lounge is also located overlooking the lovely gardens.

Rooms 2 annexe en suite (2 fmly) S £40-£50; D £80-£100* **Facilities** FTV TVL tea/coffee WiFi **Parking** 3 **Notes** RS Dec-Jan Prior bookings only

PLUSH — Map 4 ST70

The Brace of Pheasants

★★★★ 🍴 INN

tel: 01300 348357 **DT2 7RQ**
email: info@braceofpheasants.co.uk **web:** www.braceofpheasants.co.uk
dir: *A35 onto B3142, right to Plush 1.5m*

Situated in the heart of Dorset, this picturesque thatched pub offers a warm and genuine welcome to both visitors and locals alike. Very much a traditional pub, the atmosphere is convivial, with plenty of good-natured conversation. Bedrooms are split between the main building and the former skittle alley - all offer exceptional standards of comfort and individual style, with wonderful bathrooms. The food here should not be missed, with excellent local produce used to create an appealing menu.

Rooms 4 en suite 4 annexe en suite (4 GF) **Facilities** FTV tea/coffee Dinner available Direct Dial WiFi **Parking** 15 **Notes** Closed 25 Dec

POOLE — Map 4 SZ09

Acorns Guest House

★★★★ GUEST ACCOMMODATION

tel: 01202 672901 **fax:** 01202 672901 **264 Wimborne Rd, Oakdale BH15 3EF**
email: enquiries@acornsguesthouse.co.uk **web:** www.acornsguesthouse.co.uk
dir: *On A35, approx 1m from town centre, opposite Esso station*

A warm welcome is assured at Acorns Guest House, located with easy access to the town, ferry terminal, business parks and attractions. The bedrooms are furnished to a high standard, and an English breakfast is served in the charming dining room. There is also a quiet cosy lounge.

Rooms 4 en suite (1 GF) D £65-£72 **Facilities** FTV DVD TVL tea/coffee WiFi 🔒 **Parking** 6 **Notes** LB ⊗ No Children 14yrs Closed 23 Dec-1 Jan 🌐

Milsoms Poole

★★★★ 🍴 RESTAURANT WITH ROOMS

tel: 01202 609000 **47 Haven Rd, Canford Cliffs BH13 7LH**
email: poole@milsomshotel.co.uk **web:** www.milsomshotel.co.uk

Milsoms Poole is located in the Canford Cliffs area, moments from some of the country's best beaches and the picturesque Purbeck Hills. Comfortable and stylish en suite accommodation is situated above the popular seafood Loch Fyne Restaurant. The friendly and helpful team provide a warm welcome. Limited on-site parking is available.

Rooms 8 en suite (1 GF) **Facilities** FTV tea/coffee Dinner available WiFi **Parking** 12 **Notes** ⊗ No coaches

Towngate Guest House

★★★ GUEST HOUSE

tel: 01202 668552 **58 Wimborne Rd BH15 2BY**
email: ayoun19@ntlworld.com **web:** www.towngateguesthouse.net
dir: *B3093 from town centre, guest house on right*

Guests are assured of a warm welcome at this centrally located house, within walking distance of the town centre and harbour, and just a short drive from the ferry terminal. The well-equipped bedrooms are comfortable and nicely furnished.

Rooms 3 en suite S £45-£48; D £60-£65* **Facilities** FTV tea/coffee WiFi 🔒 **Parking** 4 **Notes** ⊗ No Children 10yrs Closed mid Dec-mid Jan 🌐

Antelope Inn

★★★ INN

tel: 01202 672029 **fax:** 01202 678286 **8 High St BH15 1BP**
email: 6603@greeneking.co.uk **web:** www.oldenglish.co.uk

Close to Poole Quay, which is one of the town's main attractions, this famous old coaching inn is the oldest licensed premises in Poole, and has long been a popular meeting point. All rooms are furnished to a good standard with modern facilities, and include some feature rooms. Public areas include a busy bar and a restaurant.

Rooms 23 en suite

POOLE *continued*

Seacourt

★★★ GUEST ACCOMMODATION

tel: 01202 674995 **249 Blandford Rd, Hamworthy BH15 4AZ**
email: seacourtguesthouse@hotmail.co.uk
dir: *Off A3049/A35 signed to Hamworthy*

Within a short distance of the ferry port and town centre, this friendly establishment is well maintained and efficiently run. The comfortable bedrooms, some located on the ground floor, are all nicely decorated and equipped with useful extra facilities. Breakfast is served in the pleasant dining room at separate tables.

Rooms 5 en suite (1 fmly) (3 GF) (5 smoking) **Facilities** FTV tea/coffee WiFi **Parking** 5 **Notes** ⊗ No Children 5yrs ⊛

PORTESHAM   Map 4 SY68

Kings Arms

★★★ INN

tel: 01305 871342 **2 Front St DT3 4ET**
web: www.kingsarmsportesham.co.uk
dir: *On B3157 coastal road*

Situated on the coast road, approximately half way between Weymouth and Dorchester, this long established, and popular village local is a great base from which to explore the local area. The atmosphere is warm and welcoming with good-natured banter at the bar. Local produce features on the menu with a range of dishes for all tastes. Bedrooms are located to the side of the pub, all with level access and private entrance.

Rooms 3 en suite (1 fmly) (3 GF) S £50-£70; D £70-£95* **Facilities** tea/coffee Dinner available WiFi **Extras** Speciality toiletries **Parking** 20

PORTLAND   Map 4 SY67

Queen Anne House

★★★★ GUEST ACCOMMODATION

tel: 01305 820028 **2/4 Fortuneswell DT5 1LP**
email: margaretdunlop@tiscali.co.uk **web:** www.queenannehouse.com
dir: *A354 to Portland then Fortuneswell. House on left 200mtrs past Royal Portland Arms*

This delightful Grade II listed building is a charming and comfortable place to stay; particularly delightful are the Italianate gardens to the rear. Ideal for business and leisure travellers, Queen Anne House is close to Portland Bill, Weymouth and Chesil Beach. The bedrooms are particularly attractive and pleasantly furnished. Breakfast, taken at one large table, offers a wide choice of options.

Rooms 3 en suite S £50-£60; D £80-£95* **Facilities** FTV TVL tea/coffee WiFi **Parking** 4 **Notes** ⊗ ⊛

Portland Lodge

★★★ GUEST ACCOMMODATION

tel: 01305 820265 **fax:** 01305 860359 **Easton Ln DT5 1BW**
email: info@portlandlodge.com **web:** www.portlandlodge.com
dir: *Signs to Easton/Portland Bill, rdbt at Portland Heights Hotel 1st right. Portland Lodge 200yds*

Situated on the fascinating island of Portland, this modern, lodge-style establishment provides comfortable accommodation including a number of ground-floor bedrooms. Breakfast is served in the spacious dining room with a friendly team of staff on hand. This is an ideal location for those wishing to explore the World Heritage coastline.

Rooms 30 annexe en suite (15 fmly) (7 GF) S £32-£52; D £45-£64 (room only)* **Facilities** FTV tea/coffee WiFi **Parking** 50 **Notes** LB ⊗

POWERSTOCK   Map 4 SY59

Three Horseshoes Inn

★★★★ ⊛ INN

tel: 01308 485328 **fax:** 01308 485760 **DT6 3TF**
email: threehorseshoespowerstock@live.co.uk **web:** www.threeshoesdorset.co.uk
dir: *3m from Bridport. Powerstock signed off A3066 Bridport to Beaminster*

The Three Horseshoes overlooks rolling hills from its elevated position in the village. The unpretentious bar and cosy dining room appeal to locals and visitors alike. Dinner offers a selection of traditional pub classics with a stylish twist, to suit a wide variety of tastes. Two of the spacious bedrooms have been recently refurbished to provide high levels of quality and comfort.

Rooms 1 en suite 2 annexe en suite (3 fmly) (2 GF) **Facilities** FTV DVD tea/coffee Dinner available WiFi **Parking** 20 **Notes** No coaches

PUNCKNOWLE   Map 4 SY58

Offley Bed & Breakfast

★★★★ GUEST ACCOMMODATION

tel: 01308 897044 & 07792 624977 **Looke Ln DT2 9BD**
dir: *Off B3157 into village centre, left after Crown Inn into Looke Ln, 2nd house on right*

With magnificent views over the Bride Valley, this village house provides comfortable, quality accommodation. Guests are assured of a warm, friendly welcome, and this is an ideal base from which to enjoy the numerous local attractions. There are several local inns, one in the village which is just a gentle stroll away.

Rooms 3 rms (2 en suite) (1 pri facs) **Facilities** FTV TVL tea/coffee ♿ 🔒 **Extras** Fruit, flowers - complimentary **Parking** 4 **Notes** LB ⊛

ST LEONARDS   Map 5 SU10

St Leonards

★★★ INN

tel: 01425 471220 **fax:** 01425 480274 **Ringwood Rd BH24 2NP**
email: 9230@greeneking.co.uk **web:** www.oldenglish.co.uk
dir: *At end of M27 continue to 1st rdbt. Take slip road on left*

Close to Ringwood and Bournemouth, this inn has an attractive bar and restaurant offering an extensive menu of popular dishes as well as a children's menu. The spacious bedrooms are furnished to a high standard with modern facilities; two are particularly well appointed. The lounge bar features pillars inscribed with the names of World War II pilots who flew from the wartime airfields in the New Forest area.

Rooms 35 en suite (5 fmly) (15 GF) **Facilities** tea/coffee Dinner available Direct Dial Lift **Parking** 500 **Notes** Civ Wed 60

Map 4 ST82

SHAFTESBURY

Premier Collection

The Old Chapel

★★★★★ ☰ BED AND BREAKFAST

tel: 01747 852404 **9 Breach Ln SP7 8LE**
email: info@theoldchapelbb.co.uk **web:** www.theoldchapelbb.co.uk

The Old Chapel is exactly that; a lovingly and dramatically converted chapel with spacious and well-appointed accommodation. Bedrooms are particularly comfortable, excellent beds are attractively dressed and the rooms have a host of thoughtful extras. Bathrooms too are very well fitted, with power showers and delightful towels and toiletries. There is a pleasant garden and a lounge area. Breakfasts are a highlight, featuring fresh and local produce. The welcome is also outstanding.

Rooms 2 en suite S £60; D £90* **Facilities** FTV tea/coffee WiFi **Parking** 2 **Notes** ⊗ No Children 15yrs

La Fleur de Lys Restaurant with Rooms

★★★★ ⑧⑧ RESTAURANT WITH ROOMS

tel: 01747 853717 **fax:** 01747 853130 **Bleke St SP7 8AW**
email: info@lafleurdelys.co.uk **web:** www.lafleurdelys.co.uk
dir: From junct of A30 & A350, 0.25m towards town centre

Located just a few minutes' walk from the famous Gold Hill, this light and airy restaurant with rooms combines efficient service in a relaxed and friendly

atmosphere. Bedrooms, which are suitable for both business and leisure guests, vary in size but all are well equipped, comfortable and tastefully furnished. A relaxing guest lounge and courtyard are available for afternoon tea or pre-dinner drinks.

Rooms 8 en suite (2 fmly) (1 GF) S £85-£105; D £100-£160* **Facilities** FTV Lounge tea/coffee Dinner available Direct Dial WiFi 🔒 **Extras** Home-made biscuits, fresh milk - complimentary **Conf** Max 12 Board 10 **Parking** 10 **Notes** LB ⊗ Closed 1-21 Jan No coaches

The Fontmell

★★★★ ☕ INN

tel: 01747 811441 **Crown Hill, Fontmell Magna SP7 0PA**
email: info@thefontmell.com **web:** www.thefontmell.com

This warm and welcoming pub was formerly known as The Crown, but was re-named following extensive refurbishment in 2010. The result is a stylish and comfortable environment, complete with a stream flowing between the bar and the dining room. Relaxation is guaranteed; a great place to linger over a pint at the bar, or curl up on the sofa and peruse the newspapers. Bedrooms offer impressive quality and comfort, and each has its own unique identity. The kitchen presents a range of flavour-packed dishes, based on the best of local, seasonal produce.

Rooms 6 rms (6 pri facs) S £65-£145; D £75-£155* **Facilities** FTV DVD TVL tea/coffee Dinner available Direct Dial WiFi 🔒 **Parking** 30 **Notes** Closed 25 Dec eve-26 Dec No coaches

SHERBORNE

Map 4 ST61

See also Corton Denham (Somerset)

The Queens Arms

Corton Denham, Sherborne, Somerset DT9 4LR • Tel: 01963 220317
Website: www.thequeensarms.com • Email: relax@thequeensarms.com
Facebook: www.facebook.com/thequeensarms • Twitter: @queensarmspub

Taste of Somerset Best Pub 2013, Best National Freehouse 2012 and former AA Pub of the Year 2008–9, this proper inn is located in peaceful countryside and complete with roaring log fire, a friendly greeting from the staff and a welcoming sign stating muddy boots and dogs welcome in the bar. Eight luxury ensuite bedrooms with state of the art bathrooms, 100% Egyptian linen and all are well decorated and comfortably furnished. In addition to a very good selection of real ales, this is a paradise for bottled beer lovers with a great choice from around the world. A choice of two menus for customers to choose from, a restaurant menu with wine and beer matches and a classic bar menu offering local, fresh seasonal produce.

SHERBORNE *continued*

Premier Collection

The Kings Arms

★★★★★ ⊛ INN

tel: 01963 220281 **fax:** 01963 220496 **Charlton Horethorne DT9 4NL**
email: admin@thekingsarms.co.uk **web:** www.thekingsarms.co.uk
dir: *From A303 follow signs for Templecombe & Sherborne onto B3145 to Charlton Horethorne*

Situated in the heart of this engaging village, The Kings Arms offers impressive standards throughout. The experienced owners have created something for everyone with a convivial bar, snug and choice of dining environments, including the garden terrace with lovely countryside views. Bedrooms have individuality, quality and style with marble bathrooms, robes and wonderful showers. Food is taken seriously here, with an assured team producing a menu showcasing the best of local produce.

Rooms 10 en suite (1 fmly) D £135* **Facilities** FTV DVD tea/coffee Dinner available Direct Dial Lift WiFi 📶 ⚽ 18 Discounted rates at sports centre **Conf** Thtr 70 Class 45 Board 50 **Parking** 30 **Notes** Closed 25 Dec RS 26 Dec no dinner served No coaches

Premier Collection

Munden House

★★★★★ ☜ GUEST ACCOMMODATION

tel: 01963 23150 **Munden Ln, Alweston DT9 5HU**
email: stay@mundenhouse.co.uk **web:** www.mundenhouse.co.uk
dir: *A352 from Sherborne, left onto A3030 to Alweston, at Oxfords Bakery sign, turn left into Mundens Ln. Munden House 100yds on right*

Delightful property set in a quiet lane away from the main road, with pleasant views over the surrounding countryside. Bedrooms and bathrooms come in a variety of shapes and styles but all are very well decorated and furnished; the beds are especially comfortable. Guests are welcome to use the lounge and garden, and delicious home-cooked dinners (accompanied by an Italian wine list) are available by prior arrangement. Breakfast includes a selection of high quality hot and cold dishes, all carefully prepared to order.

Rooms 5 en suite 3 annexe en suite (2 fmly) (4 GF) S £75-£120; D £85-£135* **Facilities** FTV Lounge tea/coffee Dinner available Licensed WiFi 📶 🔒 **Extras** Speciality toiletries, mineral water - free **Parking** 15 **Notes** LB

Premier Collection

The Rose and Crown Inn, Trent

★★★★★ ☜ INN

tel: 01935 850776 **Trent DT9 4SL**
email: info@theroseandcrowntrent.co.uk **web:** www.theroseandcrowntrent.co.uk
dir: *Just off A30 between Sherborne & Yeovil*

The Rose and Crown is a quintessential country inn with a long and interesting history, starting with its construction in the 14th century. Packed full of character this is a place where relaxation comes easily, with crackling fires adding to the atmosphere and charm. Bedrooms are accessed externally, each having high levels of comfort and quality with stylish bathrooms and cosseting extras such as bathrobes; each also has a patio area with lovely views across the rolling countryside. Food is taken seriously here with an experienced kitchen producing creative and flavoursome dishes in tune with the locale and seasons.

Rooms 3 annexe en suite (3 GF) S £75-£95; D £85-£110* **Facilities** FTV DVD iPod docking station Lounge tea/coffee Dinner available WiFi **Parking** 30 **Notes** No coaches

The Alders

★★★★ BED AND BREAKFAST

tel: 01963 220666 **Sandford Orcas DT9 4SB**
email: info@thealdersbb.com **web:** www.thealdersbb.com
dir: *3m N of Sherborne. Off B3148 signed Sandford Orcas, near Manor House in village*

Located in the charming conservation area of Sandford Orcas and set in a lovely walled garden, this delightful property offers attractive, well-equipped bedrooms. Guests have their own entrance leading from the garden. A large inglenook fireplace with a wood-burning stove can be found in the comfortable sitting room, which also features the owner's watercolours. Massage therapies are available.

Rooms 3 en suite (1 fmly) D £65-£80* **Facilities** FTV TVL tea/coffee WiFi 🔒 **Parking** 4 **Notes** ⊗ ⊜

Venn Farm (ST684183)

★★★ FARMHOUSE

tel: 01963 250598 **fax:** 01963 250598 **Milborne Port DT9 5RA**
email: info@colintizzard.co.uk
dir: 3m E of Sherborne on A30 on edge of Milborne Port

Set in a good location for exploring west Dorset, the owners of this farmhouse specialise in training National Hunt racehorses, and extend a friendly welcome. The individually furnished bedrooms are comfortable, and bathrooms are fitted with power showers. Downstairs, a farmhouse breakfast is served in the lounge-dining room.

Rooms 2 en suite D fr £60* **Facilities** FTV TVL tea/coffee Fishing **Parking** 6 **Notes** ⊗ No Children 5yrs Closed Xmas ⊛ 375 acres dairy/mixed/racehorses

| STURMINSTER NEWTON | Map 4 ST71 |

The Old Post Office

★★★ BED AND BREAKFAST

tel: 01258 475590 **fax:** 01258 475590 **Marnhull Rd, Hinton St Mary DT10 1NG**
email: info@northdorsetbandb.co.uk **web:** www.northdorsetbandb.co.uk
dir: A30 onto B3092 signed Sturminster Newton, on right after 5m

Built in the 1830s, The Old Post Office provides pleasant and relaxing accommodation with charming features such as low doorways and unusual angles in the floors and walls. Comfortable beds are provided in the two rooms; one is en suite and the other has private facilities. Guests are welcome to use the pleasant rear garden and relaxing guest lounge where a TV is provided (rather than in the bedrooms). Off-street parking is available.

Rooms 2 rms (1 en suite) (1 pri facs) S £50-£55; D £65-£70* **Facilities** TVL tea/coffee WiFi 🛁 **Parking** 2 **Notes** ⊗ No Children 16yrs ⊛

| SWANAGE | Map 5 SZ07 |

Premier Collection

Swanage Haven

★★★★★ 🏠 GUEST HOUSE

tel: 01929 423088 **fax:** 01929 421912 **3 Victoria Rd BH19 1LY**
email: info@swanagehaven.com **web:** www.swanagehaven.com

Swanage Haven is a boutique-style guest house close to Swanage Beach and the coastal path. Exclusively for adults, the accommodation is modern and contemporary with many extras such as fluffy robes, slippers, WiFi and a hot tub. Hands-on owners provide excellent hospitality with relaxed and friendly service. Breakfasts are superb; top quality organic and local produce from an extensive menu.

Rooms 7 en suite **Facilities** FTV TVL tea/coffee Dinner available Licensed WiFi ⚲ 🛁 18 Hot tub Holistic treatment room **Parking** 7 **Notes** ⊗ No Children 16yrs

Clare House

★★★★★ 🅰 GUEST HOUSE

tel: 01929 422855 **fax:** 01929 422855 **1 Park Rd BH19 2AA**
web: www.clare-house.com
dir: From Swanage town centre, fork left at the White Swan pub, 2nd right at Red Brick Pizza restaurant

Clare House is a Victorian building, set just off the High Street, and is ideally placed for those visiting the beach, the pier, restaurants and bars. Bedrooms have plenty of useful facilities and extras, while the bathrooms include quality toiletries.

The breakfast, served in the elegant dining room, features local produce where possible.

Rooms 6 en suite D £80-£105* **Facilities** FTV DVD iPod docking station tea/coffee WiFi **Notes** LB ⊗

The Castleton

★★★★ GUEST ACCOMMODATION

tel: 01929 423972 **1 Highcliffe Rd BH19 1LW**
email: stay@thecastleton.co.uk **web:** www.thecastleton.co.uk
dir: From town centre follow seafront towards Studland Rd, 110yds after leaving Promenade on right

A charming and luxurious Victorian house, full of character and located just 100 metres from Swanage's glorious beach. The Castleton provides elegant, well-equipped bedrooms and bathrooms, and is just a short stroll along the seafront from the town centre and its many attractions. Breakfast is served at separate tables in the light-filled dining area.

Rooms 10 en suite (2 fmly) S fr £55; D fr £100* **Facilities** FTV DVD TVL tea/coffee WiFi 🛁 18 🛁 **Parking** 4 **Notes** ⊗ Closed Dec-2 Jan

Rivendell

★★★★ 🏠 GUEST HOUSE

tel: 01929 421383 **58 Kings Rd BH19 1HR**
email: kevin@rivendell-guesthouse.co.uk **web:** www.rivendell-guesthouse.co.uk

This beautiful period house, located within easy reach of the beach and town centre, has been lovingly restored to retain many of the original features. The bedrooms have been upgraded to a very good standard and can accommodate a diverse clientele. An award-winning breakfast is served in the cosy dining room.

Rooms 9 en suite (1 fmly) **Facilities** FTV DVD TVL tea/coffee WiFi **Notes** ⊗

Corner Meadow

★★★★ BED AND BREAKFAST

tel: 01929 423493 & 07930 486347 **fax:** 0871 266 8496 **24 Victoria Av BH19 1AP**
email: geogios@hotmail.co.uk **web:** www.cornermeadow.co.uk
dir: In Victoria Av, opposite main beach car park

Diane and Roy make guests feel very welcome at their comfortable and well appointed bed and breakfast, just five minutes' level walk from the beach, steam railway and town centre. All bedrooms are en suite, and private parking is available at the rear of the premises.

Rooms 3 en suite (1 fmly) (1 GF) D £70-£88 **Facilities** FTV DVD Lounge WiFi 🛁 **Extras** Fridge **Parking** 4 **Notes** ⊗ Closed Nov-Feb ⊛

The Limes

★★★★ GUEST HOUSE

tel: 01929 422664 **48 Park Rd BH19 2AE**
email: info@limeshotel.net **web:** www.limeshotel.net
dir: Follow one-way system, signed to Durlston Country Park. Pass Trattoria restaurant on left, right into Park Rd, 200mtrs on right

Ideally located for both the town centre and the seafront, this comfortable establishment offers a variety of different bedroom shapes and sizes. In addition to the pleasant dining room, guests are free to use a small bar area and a popular games room.

Rooms 12 rms (10 en suite) (7 fmly) S £44-£55; D £94-£95* **Facilities** FTV DVD Lounge tea/coffee Licensed WiFi ch fac Pool table 🛁 **Conf** Max 25 Thtr 25 Class 20 Board 16 **Parking** 8 **Notes** LB

SWANAGE *continued*

Amber Lodge

★★★ GUEST HOUSE

tel: 01929 426446 **34 Victoria Av BH19 1AP**
email: stay@amberlodge-swanage.co.uk **web:** www.amberlodge-swanage.co.uk
dir: *On A351 into town, pass pitch & putt, on left before main beach car park*

Situated just five minutes' walk from the seafront, the atmosphere at Amber Lodge is friendly, and the bedrooms are quiet, comfortable and equipped with considerate extras. There is a small guest lounge, and breakfast is enjoyed in the spacious rear dining room at individual tables. On-site parking is an added bonus, and half board rates are available.

Rooms 7 en suite 1 annexe en suite (3 fmly) (3 GF) S £40-£80; D £60-£80*
Facilities FTV TVL tea/coffee Dinner available WiFi **Parking** 9 **Notes** ⊗

Oxford House

★★★ GUEST ACCOMMODATION

tel: 01929 422247 **5 Park Rd BH19 2AA**
email: enquiries@theoxfordswanage.com **web:** www.theoxfordswanage.com
dir: *Follow signs for town centre, pass Mowlem Theatre on left. Turn left opposite White Swan, 2nd right into Park Rd*

Located just a three-minute walk from Swanage pier, Oxford House offers relaxed and informal accommodation. The property benefits from being close to the town centre and beach. Cooked breakfasts are served in the front dining room.

Rooms 6 rms (5 en suite) (1 pri facs) (2 fmly) S £40-£42; D £65-£80 **Facilities** FTV DVD tea/coffee WiFi **Notes** ⊗ No Children 5yrs Closed Nov-Mar

Southover Bed and Breakfast

★★★ BED AND BREAKFAST

tel: 01929 426773 & 07798 622462 **Southover, Southcliffe Rd BH19 2JF**
email: southover@hotmail.co.uk **web:** www.southoverswanage.co.uk
dir: *A351 into Swanage, follow signs for Durlston Country Park. Into unmade Sunnydale Rd*

Situated in a quiet, semi-rural location on the edge of town, this welcoming home has a country park and coastal walks just a short stroll from the doorstep. A warm welcome is assured and helpful local information is always on offer. Bedrooms are both on the ground floor, one room has a spa bath. Breakfast is a tasty treat with eggs from the resident hens, served either around the dining room table or on the terrace in the summer.

Rooms 2 en suite (1 fmly) (2 GF) S £40-£70; D £75-£80* **Facilities** FTV DVD tea/coffee WiFi ☖ **Notes** LB ⊗

SYDLING ST NICHOLAS	Map 4 SY69

The Greyhound Inn

★★★★ ☖ INN

tel: 01300 341303 **26 High St DT2 9PD**
email: info@dorsetgreyhound.co.uk **web:** www.dorsetgreyhound.co.uk
dir: *Off A37 into village centre*

Located in the peaceful and quintessentially English village of Sydling St Nicholas, this comfortable inn is certainly the place to escape to. Bedrooms and bathrooms, in an adjacent building, are decorated and furnished to high standards. A choice of tempting dishes is available at both lunch and dinner, including dishes based on the daily fish deliveries. Pleasant outdoor seating is available.

Rooms 6 en suite (1 fmly) (2 GF) **Facilities** FTV tea/coffee Dinner available WiFi **Parking** 15

TARRANT MONKTON	Map 4 ST90

The Langton Arms

★★★★ INN

tel: 01258 830225 **fax:** 01258 830053 **DT11 8RX**
email: info@thelangtonarms.co.uk **web:** www.thelangtonarms.co.uk
dir: *Exit A354 in Tarrant Hinton to Tarrant Monkton, through ford, Langton Arms opposite*

Tucked away in this sleepy Dorset village, The Langton Arms offers stylish, light and airy accommodation and is a good base for touring this attractive area. Bedrooms, all at ground-floor level in the modern annexe, are very well equipped and comfortable. Diners can choose between the relaxed bar-restaurant and the more formal Stables Restaurant, offering innovative and appetising dishes. Breakfast is served in the conservatory dining room just a few steps through the pretty courtyard.

Rooms 6 annexe en suite (6 fmly) (6 GF) S £70; D £90* **Facilities** FTV tea/coffee Dinner available Direct Dial WiFi **Conf** Max 70 Thtr 70 Class 70 Board 70 **Parking** 100 **Notes** Civ Wed 60

WAREHAM	Map 4 SY98

Frome Corner

★★★★ BED AND BREAKFAST

tel: 01929 551550 & 07773 205053 **10 Frome Rd BH20 4QA**
web: www.fromecornerbandb.co.uk
dir: *From town centre into West Street. After 0.25m turn left, after fire station, into Stowell Crescent. Next right, then 1st left into Frome Rd*

Located in a peaceful residential area within walking distance of the town, Frome Corner offers two large and comfortable en suite bedrooms and an extensive breakfast menu that includes a full English option. The B&B will appeal especially to cyclists and walkers as there are facilities for storage and cleaning. There is ample off-road parking.

Rooms 3 rms (2 en suite) (1 pri facs) (1 fmly) S £60-£70; D £85-£95* **Facilities** FTV DVD tea/coffee WiFi ☖ **Extras** Fresh milk **Parking** 6 **Notes** ⊗

Hyde Cottage Bed & Breakfast

★★★★ BED AND BREAKFAST

tel: 01929 553344 **Furzebrook Rd, Stoborough BH20 5AX**
email: hydecottagebb@gmail.com **web:** www.hydecottage.com
dir: *2m S of Wareham. Exit at A351 rdbt for Furzebrook/Blue Pool, premises on right*

Easy to find, on the Corfe Castle side of Wareham, this friendly bed and breakfast is in a great location. All the bedrooms are large with lounge seating and some are suitable for families; all are well equipped with extras such as fridges. Meals are served en famille in the dining area downstairs.

Rooms 3 en suite (2 fmly) (1 GF) S £35-£50; D £64-£80* **Facilities** FTV tea/coffee Dinner available WiFi ☖ **Parking** 4 **Notes** LB ⊗ Closed 24-27 Dec ☺

Kingston Country Courtyard

★★★★ GUEST ACCOMMODATION

tel: 01929 481066 **fax:** 01929 481256
Greystone Court, Kingston, Corfe Castle BH20 5LR
email: relax@kingstoncountrycourtyard.com **web:** www.kingstoncountrycourtyard.com
dir: *Through Corfe Castle towards Swanage (A351), turn right onto B3069. Through village, Kingston Country Courtyard on right*

Situated amid the beautiful Purbeck Hills, the views from this house include historic Corfe Castle and the distant shores of the Isle of Wight. A variety of comfortable guest bedrooms is on offer and breakfast served in the spacious dining hall.

Rooms 25 en suite (3 fmly) (21 GF) **Facilities** tea/coffee Licensed WiFi 🔔 **Conf** Max 100 Thtr 100 Class 100 Board 50 **Parking** 100 **Notes** LB Closed 24 Dec-3 Jan RS wknds may be closed due to weddings Civ Wed 120

Norden House (SY950828)

★★★★ FARMHOUSE

tel: 01929 480177 **fax:** 01929 480177 **Norden Farm, Norden, Corfe Castle BH20 5DS**
email: info@nordenhouse.com
dir: Phone for directions

Set in its own grounds, this Georgian farmhouse offers eight en suite bedrooms. Located in the heart of Purbeck and surrounded by farmland and beautiful countryside, the historic village of Corfe Castle is only half a mile from the old port town of Wareham. There is an on-site farm shop selling local produce and everyday necessities.

Rooms 8 en suite **Notes** Closed Jan-1 Mar

The Red Lion

★★★★ 🏚 INN

tel: 01929 550099 **1 North St BH20 4AB**
email: redlionbookings@btconnect.com **web:** www.redlionwareham.co.uk
dir: Phone for directions

Standing in the heart of the town centre, this former coaching inn has been tastefully restored to its former glory with modern amenities and guests' comfort in mind. Bedrooms are well appointed and benefit from deeply comfortable beds and well appointed en suite bathrooms. The popular brasserie-style restaurant and bar uses local ingredients where possible on the menus and makes an ideal place to meet for a drink. Limited parking is available but can be discussed at time of booking.

Rooms 10 en suite (4 fmly) (2 GF) S £75-£85; D £90-£115* **Facilities** FTV tea/coffee Dinner available WiFi 🔔 **Extras** Filtered water **Parking** 8

Bishops

★★★★ 🍴 GUEST ACCOMMODATION

tel: 01929 400552 **Lulworth Cove BH20 5RQ**
email: bishopscottagelulworth@gmail.com **web:** www.bishopscottage.co.uk

Bishops is located 100 metres from beautiful Lulworth Cove and offers high quality en suite bedrooms, a bar that opens daily and a restaurant offering fish and vegetarian dishes. During spring and summer guests can enjoy afternoon tea outside. Breakfast served in the contemporary dining room with dishes based on locally sourced ingredients.

Rooms 3 en suite 2 annexe en suite (2 fmly) S fr £110; D fr £160* **Facilities** STV FTV TVL tea/coffee Dinner available Licensed WiFi ⚓ Riding 🔔 **Extras** Robes, snacks **Notes** Civ Wed

See also Portland

Swallows Rest

★★★★ BED AND BREAKFAST

tel: 01305 785244 & 07747 753656 **Martleaves Farm, South Rd, Wyke Regis DT4 9NR**
email: jane.furlong@btinternet.com **web:** www.swallowsrestselfcatering.co.uk
dir: From Weymouth on Portland road, follow brown tourism signs

This beautiful rural B&B with coastal views has 4 highly individual bedrooms. The richly decorated rooms are well equipped and are ideal for any break. Public areas include a comfortable lounge and the dining area, which is a sociable setting for breakfast. There is also parking, all in characterful grounds. There is also a campsite, some self catering apartments and the owners have their own pigs, chickens, ducks and alpacas.

Rooms 4 rms (3 en suite) (1 pri facs) S £50-£60; D £75-£98* **Facilities** FTV TVL tea/coffee Licensed WiFi 🔔 **Extras** Speciality toiletries, home-made cakes, chocolates **Parking** 16 **Notes** LB ⊗ No Children Closed 24-26 Dec Civ Wed 30

The Esplanade

★★★★ 🏚 GUEST ACCOMMODATION

tel: 01305 783129 & 07515 657116 **fax:** 01305 783129 **141 The Esplanade DT4 7NJ**
email: stay@theesplanadehotel.co.uk **web:** www.theesplanadehotel.co.uk
dir: On seafront, between Jubilee Clock & pier bandstand

Dating from 1835, this attractive property is located on the seafront and offers wonderful views from the elegant dining room and stylish first-floor lounge. There's a genuine enthusiasm here, with a warm welcome assured. The comfortable bedrooms are thoughtfully equipped, including Egyptian cotton sheets and towels, and many rooms have sea views. Breakfast is a showcase of local produce with an extensive menu.

Rooms 11 en suite (3 fmly) (2 GF) **Facilities** FTV TVL tea/coffee Licensed WiFi **Parking** 9 **Notes** ⊗ Closed Nov-Feb

Florian Guest House

★★★★ GUEST HOUSE

tel: 01305 773836 & 07900 158300 **fax:** 01305 898545 **59 Abbotsbury Rd DT4 0AQ**
email: enquiryflorian@aol.com **web:** www.florianguesthouse.co.uk
dir: At junct of A354 & A353 into Abbotsbury Rd. 500yds on left after St Pauls Church

Situated just 10-15 minutes' walk from the town centre, beach and local attractions, this welcoming property offers bedrooms in a range of shapes and sizes, and is ideally situated for a family seaside holiday or a short break. Breakfast is taken in the comfortably furnished downstairs dining area.

Rooms 5 en suite (1 fmly) (1 GF) **Facilities** FTV DVD tea/coffee WiFi 🔔 **Extras** Fridge **Parking** 5 **Notes** ⊗ No Children 3yrs

WEYMOUTH *continued*

Kingswood

★★★★ GUEST ACCOMMODATION

tel: 01305 784926 **55 Rodwell Rd DT4 8QY**
email: kingwood55@sky.com **web:** www.kingswoodhotel.com
dir: *On A354 up hill towards Portland from inner harbour, on left after lights*

Handily located for both Weymouth and Portland, this welcoming establishment provides spacious guest accommodation, including larger suites with jacuzzi baths. The building has a long and interesting history and was even commandeered during World War II for American officers. The bedrooms are well appointed and comfortable, as are the public areas. Breakfast is served in the attractive dining room. Just a stroll away is Brewers Quay, a lovely area in which to while away an hour or two.

Rooms 10 rms (9 en suite) (1 pri facs) (2 GF) S £50-£60; D £69-£99* **Facilities** FTV Lounge tea/coffee WiFi **Extras** Fridges in some rooms **Parking** 20 **Notes** LB ⊗

Old Manor House

★★★★ GUEST ACCOMMODATION

tel: 01305 816652 & 07789 938555 **Mill St DT3 5DN**
email: manorhouseweymouth@gmail.com **web:** www.the-old-manor-house.com

Situated a couple of miles from Weymouth, this wonderful Grade II listed property was originally built around 1840. In recent years, the owners have lovingly restored the house while retaining many original features, thus adding to the charm and elegance. Bedrooms all provide impressive levels of comfort with a number of combinations are available, including ground floor and family rooms. Breakfast provides a satisfying start to the day and is served in the attractive dining room where a crackling fire burns during the winter months.

Rooms 6 en suite (1 fmly) (2 GF) S £38-£45* **Facilities** FTV Lounge tea/coffee WiFi ⚓ **Extras** Bottled water - complimentary **Parking** 6 **Notes** Closed Feb

St John's Guest House

★★★★ GUEST ACCOMMODATION

tel: 01305 775523 **7 Dorchester Rd DT4 7JR**
email: stjohnsguesthouse@googlemail.com **web:** www.stjohnsguesthouse.co.uk
dir: *Opposite St John's Church*

Located just 70 yards from the beach, St John's is an elegant building from around 1880. Hospitality here is warm and genuine, and the property has an appealing, uncluttered style. Standards are high throughout. Bedrooms are all well equipped with such extras as DVD players, WiFi access and comfy beds. Breakfast is served in the light and airy dining room with a lounge area also available for guests.

Rooms 7 en suite (2 fmly) (2 GF) **Facilities** FTV DVD tea/coffee WiFi **Parking** 10 **Notes** ⊗ No Children 4yrs

Find out more about the AA's guest accommodation rating scheme on page 8

Barnes's Rest Weymouth

★★★ BED AND BREAKFAST

tel: 01305 779354 & 07582 707749 **165 Dorchester Rd DT4 7LE**
email: barnessrest@hotmail.co.uk **web:** www.bandbbarnessrestweymouth.co.uk
dir: *A354 into Weymouth. At Manor rdbt 1st exit onto B3159 (Dorchester Rd), on right just past doctors surgery*

This Victorian family home is ideally located for those visiting Weymouth for either business or pleasure. The welcome is warm and inviting with every effort made to ensure a relaxing and rewarding stay. The handy location is just a 10 minute stroll from the seafront. Bedrooms and bathrooms are light and airy with modern facilities and all the required necessities. Breakfast is served around the dining table with ample choice for all appetites. Safe storage facilities are available for bikes and outdoor gear.

Rooms 3 en suite S £35-£95; D £35-£95 **Facilities** FTV tea/coffee WiFi ⚓ **Parking** 2 **Notes** LB ⊗

Kimberley Guest House

★★★ GUEST HOUSE

tel: 01305 783333 **fax:** 01305 839603 **16 Kirtleton Av DT4 7PT**
email: kenneth.jones918@btconnect.com
dir: *Exit A384 (Weymouth road) into Carlton Rd North, opposite Rembrandt Hotel, Kirtleton Av on left*

This friendly guest house is in a quiet residential area near the seafront and has an informal atmosphere. The bedrooms are well presented, and the hearty breakfasts make use of fresh, locally sourced produce. There is on-site parking to the front and rear of the property.

Rooms 11 rms (10 en suite) (1 pri facs) (1 fmly) (1 GF) S £34-£35; D £68-£70* **Facilities** FTV tea/coffee Dinner available WiFi **Parking** 8 **Notes** LB ⊗ Closed 1-29 Dec ☺

Beaufort Guesthouse

★★★ GUEST HOUSE

tel: 01305 782088 **24 The Esplanade DT4 8DN**
web: www.beaufortguesthouse.co.uk

Just a few steps from the sandy beach, this friendly, family-run establishment is ideally located for a seaside break. Bedrooms are soundly appointed with all the necessary essentials, likewise the modern showers. Some of the rooms have the added bonus of sea views. Breakfast is served in the lounge diner, which also has a bar to refresh and revive after a hard day enjoying the many and varied local attractions.

Rooms 6 rms (5 en suite) (1 fmly) S £30-£35; D £60-£70 **Facilities** FTV TVL tea/coffee Licensed WiFi **Notes** LB ⊗ No Children 6months Closed 23 Dec-1 Jan

The Bedford Guest House

★★★ BED AND BREAKFAST

tel: 01305 786995 **17 The Esplanade DT4 8DT**
email: info@thebedfordweymouth.co.uk **web:** www.thebedfordweymouth.co.uk
dir: *Along The Esplanade W towards harbour, turn right around amusement gardens (one-way), Bedford Guest House on left*

Ideally located right on the seafront and with the added bonus of voucher parking for guests, this welcoming accommodation offers bedrooms in a range of shapes and sizes, with most enjoying sea or harbour views. Breakfast is taken in the comfortably furnished downstairs dining area.

Rooms 8 en suite (2 fmly) **Facilities** FTV TVL tea/coffee WiFi **Notes** ⊗ No Children 5yrs Closed Dec-Jan

The Cavendale

★★★ BED AND BREAKFAST

tel: 01305 786960 **10 The Esplanade DT4 8EB**
email: thecavendale@gmail.com **web:** http://weymouth.co.uk
dir: *Phone for directions*

Conveniently located right on the seafront with splendid views from some of the bedrooms, this cosy bed and breakfast offers a range of bedroom sizes, some with private bathrooms. Guests are welcome to use the lounge, where in addition to a large range of videos, they can join in with the current on-the-go jigsaw. Helpfully, parking permits for nearby car parks are available.

Rooms 9 rms (6 en suite) (3 pri facs) (5 fmly) S £30-£35; D £64-£72* **Facilities** FTV DVD TVL tea/coffee WiFi **Notes** LB ⊗ Closed 24 Dec-2 Jan

The Edenhurst

★★★ GUEST HOUSE

tel: 01305 771255 **122 The Esplanade DT4 7ER**
email: enquiries@edenhurstweymouth.com **web:** www.edenhurstweymouth.com
dir: *Phone for directions*

Just a step across the road from the beach and within walking distance of the railway and bus stations, this smartly presented establishment is a perfect base from which to explore the local area. A number of bedroom styles are offered, some having balconies and wonderful sea views; all have modern bathrooms. Breakfast is served in the elegant, sea-facing dining room, a guest lounge is also provided.

Rooms 12 rms (11 en suite) (1 pri facs) (4 fmly) S £38-£46; D £76-£100* **Facilities** FTV TVL tea/coffee WiFi **Extras** Bottled water - complimentary **Notes** LB ⊗

The Lugger Inn

★★★ INN

tel: 01305 766611 & 07787 872737 **fax:** 01305 766014 **30 West St, Chickerell DT3 4DY**
email: info@theluggerinn.co.uk **web:** www.theluggerinn.co.uk
dir: *Follow B3157 coastal road to Bridport. 3m from centre of Weymouth turn right at Chickerell Hill into West St*

The Lugger is a charming inn, within easy reach of Weymouth that offers comfortable accommodation in a peaceful setting. Carefully prepared dinners are enjoyed in the warm atmosphere of the bar-restaurant. The inn benefits from outside seating and ample parking space.

Rooms 14 en suite (6 fmly) (3 GF) S £60-£75; D £70-£85* **Facilities** STV FTV TVL tea/coffee Dinner available WiFi ♿ 18 🍴 **Conf** Max 50 Class 50 Board 30 **Parking** 30

Preecelands Guest House

★★★ 🏠 BED AND BREAKFAST

tel: 01305 783951 **13 Holland Rd DT4 0AL**
email: preecelands@gmail.com

Located close to the town and seafront with the beautiful beaches of Weymouth, this guest house offers a genuine warm welcome. The comfortable bedrooms are brightly decorated. Breakfast is enjoyed in the smart dining room. Off-road parking to the front of the property is a bonus.

Rooms 4 en suite (2 fmly) S £45; D £50-£70* **Facilities** FTV DVD tea/coffee WiFi **Parking** 4 **Notes** LB ⊗

Tara Guest House

★★★ GUEST HOUSE

tel: 01305 766235 **10 Market St DT4 8DD**
web: www.taraweymouth.co.uk
dir: *From Alexandra Gardens on The Esplanade right into Belle Vue, right & left into Market St*

Neatly presented, this welcoming establishment is set just back from the seafront at the harbour end of town. Strictly non-smoking, the guest house provides a relaxed and friendly atmosphere. Bedrooms offer good levels of comfort.

Rooms 6 en suite (1 fmly) S £30-£32; D £60-£64 **Facilities** FTV tea/coffee **Notes** LB ⊗ No Children 4yrs 🐾

Wadham Guesthouse

★★★ GUEST HOUSE

tel: 01305 779640 & 07717 899213 **22 East St DT4 8BN**
email: shirleyoma@talktalk.net **web:** www.wadhamhouse.co.uk
dir: *Off S end of A353 The Esplanade*

This pleasant, town centre property offers a range of rooms, and is a good base for touring or for a short stay. The comfortable bedrooms are attractively decorated, and home-cooked breakfasts are served in the ground-floor dining room. Parking permits are available.

Rooms 9 en suite (2 fmly) (1 GF) S £30-£42; D £65-£80* **Facilities** FTV tea/coffee WiFi **Notes** LB ⊗ No Children 5yrs Closed Xmas

WIMBORNE MINSTER
Map 5 SZ09

Premier Collection

Les Bouviers Restaurant with Rooms

★★★★★ ◉◉ 🍽 RESTAURANT WITH ROOMS

tel: 01202 889555 **fax:** 01202 639428
Arrowsmith Rd, Canford Magna BH21 3BD
email: info@lesbouviers.co.uk **web:** www.lesbouviers.co.uk
dir: A31 onto A349. Left in 0.6m. In approx 1m right into Arrowsmith Rd.
Establishment approx 100yds on right

Les Bouviers is an excellent restaurant with rooms in a great location, set in five
and a half acres of grounds. Food is a highlight of any stay here as is the
friendly, attentive service. Chef patron James Coward's team turn out impressive
cooking, which has been recognised with two AA Rosettes. The bedrooms are
extremely well equipped and the beds are supremely comfortable. Cream teas
can be taken on the terrace.

Rooms 6 en suite (4 fmly) S £77-£183; D £88-£215* **Facilities** FTV DVD Lounge
tea/coffee Dinner available Direct Dial WiFi All bathrooms have steam showers
or air baths **Extras** Robes, slippers **Conf** Max 120 Thtr 100 Class 100 Board 100
Parking 50 **Notes** LB RS Sun eve restricted opening & restaurant closed Civ Wed
120

The Kings Head

★★★ INN

tel: 01202 880101 **fax:** 01202 881667 **The Square BH21 1JG**
email: 6474@greeneking.co.uk **web:** www.oldenglish.co.uk
dir: From A31 Dorchester take B3073 into Wimborne. Follow signs to town centre, in
square on left

Situated in the town square, this establishment offers accommodation that
includes one room with a four-poster and also a family room. The restaurant
specialises in seafood and there is also Laing's Bar that serves bar food and real
ales. There are facilities for small meetings and wedding receptions.

Rooms 27 en suite (1 fmly) **Facilities** tea/coffee Dinner available Direct Dial Lift

Who are the AA's award-
winning B&Bs? For details
see pages 12-16

COUNTY DURHAM

AYCLIFFE
Map 19 NZ22

The County

★★★★ 🍽 RESTAURANT WITH ROOMS

tel: 01325 312273 **fax:** 01325 317131 **12 The Green DL5 6LX**
email: info@thecountyaycliffevillage.com **web:** www.thecountyaycliffevillage.com
dir: A1(M) junct 59, A167 towards Newton Aycliffe. In Aycliffe turn onto village green

Located overlooking the pretty village green yet convenient for the A1, the focus
here is on fresh, home-cooked meals, real ales and friendly service. There is a
relaxed atmosphere in the bar area, and the restaurant where attractive artwork is
displayed. The bedrooms in the smart town house next door are all furnished to a
high standard.

Rooms 7 en suite (3 GF) S £49; D £70-£110* **Facilities** FTV Lounge tea/coffee Dinner
available WiFi **Parking** 25 **Notes** LB ⊗ Closed 25-26 Dec & 1 Jan No coaches

BARNARD CASTLE
Map 19 NZ01

Homelands Guest House

★★★★ 🏠 GUEST HOUSE

tel: 01833 638757 & 07725 363330 **85 Galgate DL12 8ES**
email: enquiries@homelandsguesthouse.co.uk **web:** www.homelandsguesthouse.co.uk
dir: From A1(M) onto A67 to Barnard Castle. Guest house on left on A67(Galgate)

This beautiful Victorian town house is conveniently located for the Yorkshire Dales
and is only 20 minutes from the A1(M). Guests are welcome to use the attractive
lounge, where there is an honesty bar and complimentary WiFi is also provided. The
attractively presented bedrooms are thoughtfully equipped and include a garden
room. Breakfast features a wide choice of hot and cold items and high quality,
locally sourced ingredients. The friendly proprietors also welcome families.

Rooms 4 rms (3 en suite) (1 pri facs) 1 annexe en suite (1 fmly) (1 GF) **Facilities** FTV
Lounge tea/coffee Dinner available Licensed WiFi

Three Horseshoes

★★★★ INN

tel: 01833 631777 **fax:** 01833 638806 **5-7 Galgate DL12 8EQ**
email: info@three-horse-shoes.co.uk **web:** www.three-horse-shoes.co.uk

The Three Horseshoes is a family owned and run inn. It is modern with very good
design throughout the refurbished and modernised bedrooms, en suite bathrooms,
and public areas. Real ales and home-cooked food are a feature, with an ever-
changing menu and competitively priced wine list. Private parking and sun terrace
add to the features of this beautifully restored inn.

Rooms 7 en suite 4 annexe en suite (1 fmly) (2 GF) S £70-£90; D £80-£100*
Facilities FTV DVD tea/coffee Dinner available Direct Dial WiFi 🐾 **Parking** 12
Notes ⊗

Strathmore Lawn East

[U]

tel: 01833 637061 & 07790 006920 **81 Galgate DL12 8ES**
email: strathmorelawn@gmail.com **web:** www.strathmorelawneast.co.uk
dir: From A66 to Barnard Castle, through town centre into Galgate. On right opposite
chemist

Currently the rating for this establishment is not confirmed. This may be due to a
change of ownership or because it has only recently joined the AA rating scheme.

Rooms 3 rms (2 en suite) (1 pri facs) S £51; D £76* **Facilities** Lounge 🐾 **Notes** LB
No Children 2yrs Closed 22 Dec-4 Jan

COWSHILL   Map 18 NY84

Low Cornriggs Farm (NY845413)

★★★★ 🏠 FARMHOUSE

tel: 01388 537600 & 07760 766794 Cowshill-in-Weardale DL13 1AQ
email: cornriggsfarm@btconnect.com web: www.cornriggsfarm.co.uk
dir: 0.6m NW of Cowshill on A689

Situated in the heart of Weardale yet also close to Cumbria, this delightful farmhouse has stunning views. Original stone and stripped pine are combined to provide a house with real character. Excellent home-cooked dinners are offered along with charming hospitality. Bedrooms are attractive and thoughtfully equipped with many homely extras.

Rooms 3 en suite 4 annexe en suite (3 GF) S £44-£45; D £66-£68* Facilities STV FTV TVL tea/coffee Dinner available WiFi ♿ 9 🅿 Parking 6 Notes LB ⊗ 42 acres beef/sheep

DURHAM   Map 19 NZ24

The Old Mill

★★★★ ☕ INN

tel: 01740 652928 fax: 01740 657230 Thinford Rd, Metal Bridge DH6 5NX
email: office@oldmilldurham.co.uk web: www.oldmilldurham.co.uk
dir: 5m S of Durham. A1(M) junct 61, A688 S for 1.5m, left at rdbt, sharp right

This traditional, family-owned inn is in a countryside setting yet is only a mile from the A1. There is a friendly atmosphere and the bar and dining areas are full of character. Food is served throughout the day and evening, with the vast menu displayed on chalkboards. Bedrooms are spacious and well equipped. Complimentary WiFi is provided.

Rooms 8 en suite S £60; D £70* Facilities STV FTV DVD tea/coffee Dinner available Direct Dial WiFi 🅿 Conf Max 40 Thtr 40 Class 40 Board 25 Parking 40 Notes ⊗ Closed 2 Jan RS 25 Dec

FROSTERLEY   Map 19 NZ03

Newlands Hall (NZ043372)

★★★★ 🏠 FARMHOUSE

tel: 01388 529233 & 07970 032517 DL13 2SH
email: carol@newlandshall.co.uk web: www.newlandshall.co.uk
dir: 1.5m W of Wolsingham on A689 on right. Follow drive over cattle grid, fork right onto concrete drive, over cattle grid

Newlands Hall is a spacious, traditional farmhouse in a peaceful location with panoramic views over Weardale in the North Pennines. The two family rooms can sleep three people comfortably, and a fourth person can potentially be accommodated in each. Breakfast is a highlight with freshly baked bread and

locally sourced ingredients; afternoon tea is also available. Complimentary WiFi is provided. Walkers, cyclists and classic car owners are very welcome, with secure storage provided.

Rooms 2 en suite (2 fmly) S £55-£65; D £75-£85 Facilities FTV TVL tea/coffee WiFi 🅿 Extras Bottled water, fruit juice Parking 8 Notes LB Closed Dec-Jan 380 acres mixed

PETERLEE   Map 19 NZ44

The Ship Inn

★★★★ ☕ INN

tel: 01429 836453 & 07760 767448 High Hesleden TS27 4QD
email: sheila@theshipinn.net web: www.theshipinn.net
dir: A19 onto B1281 signed Blackhall. Follow Hesleden signs to High Hesleden

Totally refurbished by the current owners, The Ship Inn has some wonderful sea views from its well-appointed and comfortable bedrooms. The bar is cosy and welcoming and has an impressive selection of well-kept real ales. Dinner is served in the spacious, comfortable restaurant and log fires burn brightly on cooler evenings. Sympathetically restored over a number of years, many of the original features of this fine old property are still in place. Free WiFi and secure parking is provided for guests.

Rooms 6 en suite 3 annexe en suite (3 fmly) (6 GF) S £65; D £75* Facilities STV FTV DVD TV7B tea/coffee Dinner available WiFi 🅿 Extras Fruit - complimentary Conf Max 45 Thtr 45 Class 25 Board 25 Parking 25 Notes ⊗ RS Mon

SEAHAM   Map 19 NZ44

The Seaton Lane Inn

★★★★ INN

tel: 0191 581 2038 Seaton Ln, Seaton Village SR7 0LP
email: info@seatonlaneinn.com web: www.seatonlaneinn.com
dir: A19 S of Sunderland on B1404 between Seaham & Houghton

Set on the edge of the quiet village of Seaton, yet close to Seaham and the A19, the inn is popular with visitors and locals alike and is a blend of modern and traditional. The emphasis is on food here with interesting home-made dishes offered in the restaurant and bar. The bedrooms, located in the adjoining building, are modern, spacious and smartly furnished.

Rooms 18 en suite (1 GF) S £69.95-£100; D £89.95-£120 Facilities FTV TVL tea/coffee Dinner available Direct Dial WiFi ♿ 18 Fishing Extras Speciality toiletries Parking 36 Notes ⊗

STOCKTON-ON-TEES   Map 19 NZ41

Vane Arms

★★★★ ☕ INN

tel: 01642 580401 & 07760 618121 Darlington Rd, Long Newton TS21 1DB
email: thevanearms@hotmail.com web: www.vanearms.com
dir: W end of village off A66

This gem of a pub is located in the village of Long Newton. The friendly owners have fully refurbished the property and there is a welcoming atmosphere. The traditional bar features real ales and an open fire. The pub restaurant is smartly presented with a wide choice of delicious, skilfully prepared home-cooked meals served at lunchtimes and evenings. Bedrooms are stylish and contemporary with complimentary WiFi provided. There is also a large beer garden with stunning views across open fields to the Yorkshire Moors.

Rooms 4 en suite S £50-£55; D £65-£70* Facilities FTV DVD iPod docking station tea/coffee Dinner available WiFi 🅿 Parking 14 Notes ⊗ No Children 16yrs No coaches

STOCKTON-ON-TEES *continued*

The Parkwood Inn

★★★ INN

tel: 01642 587933 **64-66 Darlington Rd, Hartburn TS18 5ER**
email: theparkwoodhotel@aol.com **web:** www.theparkwoodhotel.com
dir: *1.5m SW of town centre. A66 onto A137 signed Yarm & Stockton West, left at lights onto A1027, left into Darlington Rd*

Expect a very friendly welcome at this family-run establishment. The well-equipped, en suite bedrooms come with many homely extras, and a range of professionally prepared meals are served in the cosy bar lounge, conservatory, or the attractive dining room.

Rooms 6 en suite **Facilities** tea/coffee Dinner available **Parking** 36 **Notes** No coaches

ESSEX

CHELMSFORD   Map 6 TL70

The Lion Inn

★★★★ 🍴 INN

tel: 01245 394900 **fax:** 01245 394999 **Main Rd, Boreham CM3 3JA**
email: info@lioninnhotel.co.uk
dir: *A12 junct 19 onto B1137 to Maldon. 0.75m on right*

The Lion Inn offers stylish and comfortably appointed accommodation; well-equipped with flat-screen TVs, free WiFi, and full air-conditioning it appeals to leisure and business guests alike. Many rooms benefit from balconies or direct access to the private garden. The spacious bar and restaurant is open-plan style with additional seating in the Victorian conservatory. Guests can enjoy a wide selection of good classic pub dishes with a continental twist; a cooked and continental breakfast is served daily.

Rooms 15 en suite (1 fmly) (4 GF) D £105-£200* **Facilities** tea/coffee Dinner available Direct Dial WiFi **Conf** Thtr 40 Board 20 **Parking** 150 **Notes** ⊗ Closed 24-26 Dec No coaches

CLACTON-ON-SEA   Map 7 TM11

The Chudleigh

★★★★ GUEST ACCOMMODATION

tel: 01255 425407 **fax:** 01255 470280 **13 Agate Rd, Marine Parade West CO15 1RA**
email: chudleighhotel@btconnect.com **web:** www.thechudleighhotel.com
dir: *With sea on left, cross lights at pier, turn into Agate Rd at mini rdbt*

Conveniently situated for the seafront and shops, this immaculate property has been run by the friendly owners Peter and Carol Oleggini for more than 50 years. Bedrooms are most attractive with co-ordinating decor and well chosen fabrics. Breakfast is served in the smart dining room and there is a cosy lounge with plush sofas.

Rooms 10 en suite (2 fmly) (2 GF) S £50-£55; D £80-£85 **Facilities** FTV TVL tea/coffee Direct Dial Licensed WiFi 🛁 **Extras** Speciality toiletries, chocolates **Parking** 7 **Notes** No Children 1.5yrs Closed Oct RS 1wk Mar/Apr

Pond House *(TM143164)*

★★★★ 🏡 FARMHOUSE

tel: 01255 820458 & 07855 914064 **Earls Hall Farm, Earls Hall Dr CO16 8BP**
email: brenda_lord@farming.co.uk **web:** www.earlshallfarm.info
dir: *A133 onto B1027 signed St Osyth, after 2m turn right into Earls Hall Drive. Follow to end & signs for Pond House*

This charming Victorian farmhouse is surrounded by mature gardens and enjoys lovely countryside views. Bedrooms are all attractively presented, very comfortable and equipped with a host of thoughtful little extras. Guests can enjoy woodland walks on this working farm, or watch the birds while enjoying a hearty breakfast from the extensive menu (sourced locally wherever possible). Home-made cake and refreshments are offered in the sitting room on arrival, and on return from days out.

Rooms 2 en suite S £50-£55; D £70-£75* **Facilities** FTV DVD Lounge tea/coffee WiFi 🎣 18 Fishing 🛁 **Extras** Juice, snacks **Parking** 3 **Notes** LB ⊗ No Children 12yrs 300 acres arable/beef

COLCHESTER   Map 13 TL92

Black Bond Hall Bed and Breakfast

★★★★ BED AND BREAKFAST

tel: 01206 735776 & 07909 516013 **Lodge Ln, Langenhoe CO5 7LX**
email: gill@blackbondhall.co.uk **web:** www.blackbondhall.co.uk
dir: *A12 junct 26 signed to Mersea (B1025). Through Abberton & Langenhoe pass x-rds & garage, 1st left into School Rd & Fingringhoe Range. 1st right into Lodge Ln, on right*

Black Bond Hall is ideally situated for Colchester and attractions such as The Beth Chatto Gardens, Dedham, Rowhedge, Abberton Reservoir, Mersea Island and Fingringhoe Nature Reserves. The two comfortable double rooms provide tea- and coffee-making facilities, colour TV, WiFi and hairdryer. Guests can expect a warm welcome with home-made cake on arrival, as well as tea and coffee. Breakfast is sourced from local produce and is served in either the modern breakfast room overlooking the garden, or the traditional dining room. There are several local pubs for evening meals.

Rooms 2 en suite D fr £80* **Facilities** FTV tea/coffee WiFi 🛁 **Extras** Snacks **Parking** 8 **Notes** LB ⊗ No Children 12yrs 🅿

Fridaywood Farm (TL985213)

★★★★ FARMHOUSE

tel: 01206 573595 & 07970 836285   **fax:** 01206 547011 **Bounstead Rd CO2 0DF**
email: lochorem8@aol.com **web:** www.fridaywoodfarm.co.uk
dir: *From A12 follow signs to zoo, pass on right. Onto B1026 signed Mersea Cross, after 1m turn right into Bounstead Rd. 0.75m on right*

Fridaywood Farm is a traditional farmhouse surrounded by wooded countryside. Bedrooms are generally quite spacious, and each one is carefully decorated, furnished with well-chosen pieces and equipped with many thoughtful touches. Public rooms include an elegant dining room where breakfast is served at a large communal table, and a cosy sitting room.

Rooms 2 en suite S £65-£75; D £75-£90 **Facilities** FTV DVD Lounge tea/coffee WiFi
⚓ 🔒 **Extras** Bottled water, sweets **Parking** 6 **Notes** ⊗ No Children 12yrs 🐾
500 acres sheep/arable/roots

The George

★★★★ INN

tel: 01206 578494 & 08431 787153   **116 High St CO1 1TD**
email: reservations.thegeorgehotel@bespokehotels.com
web: www.bespokehotels.com/thegeorgehotel
dir: *Exit A12 at Colchester junct, follow town centre signs. Located in High St*

This former coaching inn enjoys a prominent position in the heart of Colchester, England's oldest Roman town. Individually styled bedrooms are all spacious and well equipped. The cosy bar has real fires and is very comfortable. Secure parking is available for guests and free WiFi is also provided. Evening meals are served in the well-appointed restaurant and delicious breakfasts are not to be missed.

Rooms 47 en suite (7 fmly) **Facilities** FTV Lounge tea/coffee Dinner available Direct Dial WiFi **Conf** Max 50 Thtr 50 Class 25 Board 30 **Parking** 50 **Notes** LB ⊗ No coaches

DEDHAM   Map 13 TM03

Premier Collection

The Sun Inn

★★★★★ 🏵🏵 🛏 INN

tel: 01206 323351 **High St CO7 6DF**
email: office@thesuninndedham.com **web:** www.thesuninndedham.com
dir: *In village centre opposite church*

The Sun Inn is a charming 15th-century coaching inn situated in the centre of Dedham, opposite the church. The carefully decorated bedrooms include four-poster and half tester beds, along with many thoughtful touches. The open-plan public rooms have a wealth of character with inglenook fires, oak beams and fine oak panelling.

Rooms 7 en suite **Facilities** DVD iPod docking station tea/coffee Dinner available
⚓ **Parking** 15 **Notes** Closed 25-28 Dec

Marlborough Head Inn

★★★ INN

tel: 01206 323250 **Mill Ln CO7 6DH**
email: jen.pearmain@tiscali.co.uk **web:** www.marlborough-head.co.uk
dir: *0.5m off A12 in village centre*

A period building with many original features, the Marlborough Head Inn is ideally located to explore "Constable Country". The three en suite bedrooms are traditionally appointed and offer modern amenities. There are two bars, two restaurants and a comfortable lounge. In addition parking is provided as well as a well maintained garden.

Rooms 3 en suite S £45-£90; D £45-£100 (room only)* **Facilities** FTV Lounge TVL tea/coffee Dinner available WiFi ⚓ **Parking** 20 **Notes** ⊗ No Children 16yrs Closed 24-28 Dec

FRINTON-ON-SEA   Map 7 TM22

Uplands Guest House

★★★ GUEST ACCOMMODATION

tel: 01255 674889 & 07921 640772   **fax:** 01255 674889 **41 Hadleigh Rd CO13 9HQ**
email: info@uplandsguesthouse.co.uk **web:** www.uplandsguesthouse.co.uk
dir: *B1033 into Frinton, over level crossing, Hadleigh Rd 3rd left, Uplands 250yds on left*

This large Edwardian house stands in a peaceful side road just a short walk from the shops and seafront. Bedrooms are pleasantly decorated and thoughtfully equipped with a good range of useful extras. Public rooms include a large lounge-dining room where breakfast is served at individual tables.

Rooms 6 rms (4 en suite) (1 fmly) S £35-£45; D £62-£66* **Facilities** FTV TVL tea/coffee WiFi ⚓ **Parking** 4 **Notes** LB ⊗

GESTINGTHORPE   Map 13 TL83

Premier Collection

The Pheasant

★★★★★ 🏵 🛏 INN

tel: 01787 465010 & 461196   **Audley End CO9 3AU**
email: thepheasantpb@aol.com **web:** www.thepheasant.net
dir: *Phone for directions*

Close to the Suffolk/Essex border, The Pheasant enjoys stunning countryside views and a lovely location in the heart of the charming village of Gestingthorpe. The bar is charming and features wood-burning stoves, low ceilings and a good choice of local real ales. Dinner is not to be missed and much of the produce is grown on the pub's own plot of land. The five spacious bedrooms in the coach house are beautifully presented and are all individually designed. An ideal base from which to explore the surrounding countryside and pretty Suffolk villages. The Pheasant is the AA Pub of the Year for England 2014-2015.

Rooms 5 en suite (2 fmly) (2 GF) S £85-£105; D £95-£165* **Facilities** FTV tea/coffee Dinner available Direct Dial WiFi ⚓ 18 🔒 **Extras** Speciality toiletries **Parking** 25 **Notes** LB Closed 1st 2wks Jan No coaches

GREAT DUNMOW   Map 6 TL62

Dunmow Guest House

★★★★ BED AND BREAKFAST

tel: 01371 859138 & 07740 724626   **46 Stortford Rd CM6 1DL**
email: enquiries@dunmowguesthouse.com **web:** www.dunmowguesthouse.co.uk
dir: *On Stortford Rd, 100yds from Queen Victoria pub, on opposite side of road*

Dunmow Guest House is conveniently located, close to Stansted Airport and a short walk into the pretty market town of Great Dunmow. The historic villages of Thaxted and Saffron Walden are nearby, as are many historic houses and the Freeport designer village. Spacious modern bedrooms are beautifully presented and feature super king-size beds. The indoor pool is very popular with guests as are the games room and fantastic home cinema.

Rooms 3 rms (2 en suite) (1 pri facs) S £89-£119; D £89-£119* **Facilities** FTV DVD TVL tea/coffee WiFi 📺 Private cinema Games room **Extras** Speciality toiletries, soft drinks - complimentary **Parking** 3 **Notes** ⊗ No Children 18yrs

GREAT DUNMOW *continued*

Harwood House

★★★★ GUEST ACCOMMODATION

tel: 01371 874627 **52 Stortford Rd CM6 1DN**
email: info@harwoodhousestansted.com **web:** www.harwoodhousestansted.com
dir: *M11 junct 8 onto A120 signed Stansted/Colchester. Exit onto B1256 signed Great Dunmow, over 3 rdbts & take 1st exit at 4th. Harwood House on left*

A charming period house located in the quaint market town of Great Dunmow. Harwood House offers guests large comfortable bedrooms and a warm welcome is guaranteed from the friendly proprietors. Ample secure parking is available and the house is conveniently located close to the main road network and a short drive from Stansted Airport. Free WiFi is available throughout the house and freshly cooked breakfasts are served in conservatory breakfast room.

Rooms 8 en suite (1 fmly) (3 GF) S £55-£70; D £65-£80* **Facilities** FTV iPod docking station Lounge TVL tea/coffee Licensed WiFi 🔒 **Parking** 20 **Notes** ⊗

GREAT TOTHAM
Map 7 TL81

The Bull at Great Totham

★★★★★ ⑳⑳ RESTAURANT WITH ROOMS

tel: 01621 893385 & 894020 **fax:** 01621 894029 **2 Maldon Rd CM9 8NH**
email: reservations@thebullatgreattotham.co.uk **web:** www.thebullatgreattotham.co.uk
dir: *Exit A12 at Witham junct to Great Totham*

A 16th-century coaching inn located in the village of Great Totham, The Bull is now a very stylish restaurant with rooms that offers en suite bedrooms with satellite TVs with Freeview; WiFi is available throughout. Guests can enjoy dinner in the gastro-pub or in the award-winning, fine dining restaurant, The Willow Room.

Rooms 4 en suite (2 GF) S £75; D £85* **Facilities** STV FTV Lounge tea/coffee Dinner available WiFi ⚡ 18 **Conf** Max 60 Thtr 40 Class 40 Board 16 **Parking** 80 **Notes** LB

GREAT YELDHAM
Map 13 TL73

The White Hart

★★★★★ ⑳⑳ RESTAURANT WITH ROOMS

tel: 01787 237250 **fax:** 01787 238044 **Poole St CO9 4HJ**
email: mjwmason@yahoo.co.uk **web:** www.whitehartyeldham.com
dir: *On A1017 in village*

The White Hart is a large timber-framed character building that includes the main restaurant and bar areas while the bedrooms are located in the converted coach house; all are smartly appointed and well equipped with many thoughtful extras. The comfortable lounge and bar and the beautifully landscaped gardens provide areas for relaxation. Locally sourced produce is used on menus in the main house restaurant which is popular with local residents and guests alike.

Rooms 11 en suite (2 fmly) (6 GF) **Facilities** FTV TVL tea/coffee Dinner available Direct Dial WiFi **Conf** Max 200 Thtr 200 Class 200 Board 50 **Parking** 80 **Notes** Civ Wed 130

HALSTEAD
Map 13 TL83

The Bull

★★★ INN

tel: 01787 472144 **fax:** 01787 472496 **Bridge St CO9 1HU**
email: bull.halstead@oldenglishinns.co.uk **web:** www.oldenglish.co.uk
dir: *Off A131 at bottom of hill on High St*

This charming inn is situated at the heart of this bustling town between Sudbury and Braintree. Public areas include a large lounge bar, cosy restaurant and meeting rooms. Bedrooms are full of original character; each one is pleasantly decorated and equipped with modern facilities.

Rooms 10 en suite 6 annexe en suite **Facilities** tea/coffee Direct Dial **Parking** 25 **Notes** Civ Wed 50

HATFIELD HEATH
Map 6 TL51

Lancasters Farm (TL544149)

★★★★ FARMHOUSE

tel: 01279 730220 **fax:** 01279 730220 **Chelmsford Rd CM22 7BB**
dir: *A1060 from Hatfield Heath for Chelmsford, 1m left on sharp right bend, through white gates*

Guests are made to feel at home at this delightfully spacious house, which is at the heart of this large working arable farm close to Stansted Airport. Bedrooms vary in size and style, but all are smartly decorated and thoughtfully equipped. Garaging can be arranged, as can transport to and from the airport.

Rooms 4 rms (2 en suite) (2 pri facs) S fr £48; D fr £84* **Facilities** FTV Lounge tea/coffee WiFi **Parking** 6 **Notes** ⊗ No Children 12yrs Closed 14 Dec-4 Jan ⊜ 260 acres arable

MALDON
Map 7 TL80

The Bell

★★★ GUEST HOUSE

tel: 01621 843208 **2 Silver St CM9 4QE**
email: info@thebellmaldon.co.uk **web:** www.thebellmaldon.co.uk
dir: *Phone for directions*

Centrally located to explore the historic town of Maldon and surrounding areas, this attractive guest house used to be a pub in a previous life and many original features can still be found around the property. The bedrooms offer good accommodation, while breakfast is served in the former cellar. Limited parking is available.

Rooms 4 rms (2 en suite) (2 pri facs) **Facilities** FTV DVD TVL tea/coffee Direct Dial WiFi ⚡ 18 🔒 **Parking** 2 **Notes** ⊗ No Children 6yrs ⊜

MANNINGTREE
Map 13 TM13

Premier Collection

Dairy House Farm (TM148293)

★★★★★ FARMHOUSE

tel: 01255 870322 & 07749 073974 **Bradfield Rd CO11 2SR**
email: bridgetwhitworth353@gmail.com **web:** www.dairyhousefarm.info

(For full entry see Wix)

SAFFRON WALDEN   Map 12 TL53

Bush Farm Bed & Breakfast

★★★★ BED AND BREAKFAST

tel: 01799 586636 **Bush Rd, Little Sampford CB10 2RY**
email: angelabushfarm@yhaoo.co.uk

Set in a peaceful rural location Bush Farm offers a range of comfortable well-appointed bedrooms. Lots of original features in this period house and a charming lounge is available for guests. Freshly cooked breakfasts are not to be missed and free WiFi is available along with secure parking.

Rooms 3 en suite **Notes** Closed Nov-May

The Cricketers Arms

★★★ ⇔ INN

tel: 01799 543210 **Rickling Green CB11 3YG**
email: info@thecricketersarmsricklinggreen.co.uk
web: www.thecricketersarmsricklinggreen.co.uk
dir: M11 junct 8 onto A120 then B1383. Follow signs for Newport then Rickling Green

The Cricketers Arms is a popular inn located in the heart of a peaceful Essex village and overlooks the green and historic cricket ground. The property is within easy driving distance of Stansted Airport and the major road networks. The modern bedrooms are smartly appointed and comfortable with a range of useful extras. Public rooms include a large open plan bar and a restaurant.

Rooms 10 en suite (3 fmly) (3 GF) D £49-£135* **Facilities** FTV iPod docking station tea/coffee Dinner available WiFi **Conf** Max 30 Thtr 20 Class 20 Board 20 **Parking** 50

The Crown Inn

★★★ ⇔ INN

tel: 01799 522475 **Little Walden CB10 1XA**
email: pippathecrown@aol.com **web:** www.thecrownlittlewalden.co.uk
dir: M11 junct 9 follow signs for Saffron Walden. In Saffron Walden, left at lights signed Thaxted. At mini rdbt left towards Little Walden (B1052)

This charming country inn enjoys a prominent position in the pretty village of Little Walden and has a choice of three cosy, comfortable bedrooms. All are individually styled and well equipped. Free WiFi is available throughout the property and there is secure parking for guests. There's a great atmosphere in the authentic bar, and an extensive choice of home-cooked meals on the evening menu.

Rooms 3 en suite **Facilities** FTV tea/coffee Dinner available WiFi **Conf** Max 40 Thtr 40 Class 30 Board 30 **Parking** 30

SOUTHEND-ON-SEA   Map 7 TQ88

Hamiltons Boutique

★★★★ GUEST ACCOMMODATION

tel: 01702 332350 **6 Royal Ter SS1 1DY**
email: enquiries@hamiltonsboutiquehotel.co.uk **web:** www.hamiltonsboutiquehotel.co.uk

This Grade II Georgian building is located on the historic Royal Terrace and enjoys excellent views over the Thames estuary and the seafront. The individually styled bedrooms are all beautifully presented, and very well equipped. Free WiFi is available for guests. The house has been sympathetically refurbished and the original features make an immediate impact. Afternoon tea can be arranged (minimum of four people) and delicious breakfasts are served in the light-filled breakfast room.

Rooms 7 en suite D £65-£130* **Facilities** FTV DVD TVL tea/coffee WiFi **Extras** Bottled water - complimentary **Notes** ⊗ Closed 21-30 Dec

The Ilfracombe House

★★★★ GUEST ACCOMMODATION

tel: 01702 351000 **fax:** 01702 393989 **9-13 Wilson Rd SS1 1HG**
email: info@ilfracombe-hotel.co.uk **web:** www.ilfracombe-hotel.co.uk
dir: 500yds W of town centre. Exit A13 at Cricketers pub into Milton Rd, 3rd left into Cambridge Rd, 4th right, car park in Alexandra Rd

The Ilfracombe House lies in Southend's conservation area, just a short walk from the cliffs, gardens and the beach. The public rooms include a dining room, lounge and a cosy bar, and the well-equipped bedrooms include deluxe options and two four-poster rooms.

Rooms 20 en suite (4 fmly) (2 GF) **Facilities** STV FTV DVD TVL tea/coffee Dinner available Direct Dial Licensed WiFi **Extras** Mini-fridge **Conf** Max 15 **Parking** 9 **Notes** ⊗

STANSTED AIRPORT   Map 6 TL52

See also Bishop's Stortford (Hertfordshire)

The White House

★★★★ GUEST ACCOMMODATION

tel: 01279 870257 **fax:** 01279 870423 **Smiths Green CM22 6NR**
email: enquiries@whitehousestansted.co.uk **web:** www.whitehousestansted.co.uk
dir: M11 junct 8, B1256 towards Takeley. Through lights at Four Ashes x-rds. 400yds, corner of B1256 & Smiths Green

The White House is a delightful 16th-century property situated close to Stansted Airport (but not on the flight path). The stylish bedrooms feature superb beds, luxurious bathrooms and many thoughtful touches. Traditional breakfasts, served in the farmhouse-style kitchen, are made from local ingredients; evening meals are available at the Lion and Lamb, a nearby pub/restaurant owned by the proprietors, who can usually provide transport to and from The White House.

Rooms 3 rms (2 en suite) (1 pri facs) (3 fmly) **Facilities** FTV DVD tea/coffee Dinner available WiFi **Conf** Max 25 **Parking** 6 **Notes** ⊗ Closed 24-25, 31 Dec & 1 Jan

STANSTED MOUNTFITCHET   Map 12 TL52

Premier Collection

Linden House

★★★★★ ⊛ ≜ RESTAURANT WITH ROOMS

tel: 01279 813003 **1-3 Silver St CM24 8HA**
email: stay@lindenhousestansted.co.uk **web:** www.lindenhousestansted.co.uk
dir: M11 junct 8 towards Newport on A120, on right after windmill

Linden House enjoys a prominent position in the heart of Stansted Mountfitchet and is a short drive from the airport. This fine property has individually designed bedrooms, all beautifully presented and very luxurious. The cosy bar is ideal for pre-dinner drinks with a good choice of local ales and an extensive wine list. The award-winning restaurant serves great food, service is attentive and there is a lovely atmosphere in the evenings. Visitors arriving late should note that on Sundays last orders in the restaurant is at 6pm. Freshly cooked breakfasts are not to be missed. Free WiFi is available throughout the property and there is parking nearby.

Rooms 9 en suite (2 GF) S £94-£149; D £94-£149 (room only)* **Facilities** DVD iPod docking station tea/coffee Dinner available Direct Dial WiFi **Extras** Speciality toiletries, home-made cookies **Notes** LB ⊗

THORPE BAY

See Southend-on-Sea

THAXTED Map 12 TL63

Steepleview Bed & Breakfast

★★★ BED AND BREAKFAST

---

tel: 01371 831263 & 07949 589325 **Steepleview, 61 Newbiggen St CM6 2QS**
email: info@steepleviewthaxted.co.uk **web:** www.steepleviewthaxted.co.uk

Steepleview is a charming family run B&B in the pretty village of Thaxted and offers guests a choice of beautifully presented, well equipped and comfortable bedrooms. Breakfast is served in the well-appointed breakfast room and the conservatory lounge is available for guests. Free WiFi is available along with secure parking and Steepleview is ideally located for trips to Stansted Airport.

Rooms 2 en suite D £45-£70* **Facilities** FTV iPod docking station Lounge tea/coffee WiFi ᕕ **Parking** 2 **Notes** ⊗ No Children 6yrs ⊜

The Farmhouse Inn

★★★ INN

---

tel: 01371 830864 **fax:** 01371 831196 **Monk St CM6 2NR**
email: info@farmhouseinn.org **web:** www.farmhouseinn.org
dir: *M11 to A120 to B184, 1m from Thaxted, between Thaxted & Great Dunmow*

This 16th-century inn overlooks the Chelmer Valley, and is surrounded by open countryside. The property is ideally situated in the quiet hamlet of Monk Street about two miles from the historic town of Thaxted. Bedrooms are pleasantly decorated and equipped with modern facilities. Public rooms include a cosy lounge bar and a large, smartly appointed restaurant.

Rooms 11 annexe en suite **Facilities** FTV tea/coffee Dinner available WiFi **Conf** Max 80 Thtr 80 Class 60 Board 50 **Parking** 35

The Swan

★★★ INN

---

tel: 01371 830321 **fax:** 01371 831186 **Bullring, Watling St CM6 2PL**
email: swan.thaxted@greeneking.co.uk **web:** www.oldenglish.co.uk
dir: *M11 junct 8, A120 to Great Dunmow, then B164 to Thaxted. At N end of high street, opposite church*

The Swan is a popular inn situated in the village centre opposite the parish church. Public areas feature a large open-plan beamed bar/restaurant serving real ales and appealing dishes. Bedrooms are located in the main building or the more peaceful rear annexe; each one is pleasantly decorated and well equipped.

Rooms 13 en suite 6 annexe en suite (2 fmly) (3 GF) **Facilities** FTV tea/coffee Dinner available WiFi **Conf** Max 20 Thtr 20 Class 20 Board 20 **Parking** 15

THORPE BAY

See Southend-on-Sea

TOPPESFIELD Map 12 TL73

Ollivers Farm

★★★ BED AND BREAKFAST

---

tel: 01787 237642 **fax:** 01787 237602 **C09 4LS**
web: www.essex-bed-breakfast.co.uk
dir: *500yds SE of village centre. Off A1017 in Great Yeldham to Toppesfield, farm 1m on left before T-junct to village*

Full of charm and character, this impressive 16th-century farmhouse is set amid pretty landscaped gardens in a peaceful rural location. Bedrooms are pleasantly decorated and thoughtfully equipped. Public rooms have a wealth of original

features including exposed beams and there is a huge open fireplace in the reception hall.

Rooms 3 rms (1 en suite) (1 pri facs) S £50; D £70-£80* **Facilities** FTV Lounge tea/coffee WiFi ᕕ Shed for bikes **Parking** 4 **Notes** ⊗ No Children 10yrs Closed 23 Dec-1 Jan ⊜

WALTON ON THE NAZE Map 7 TM22

The Royal Albion Public House

★★ INN

---

tel: 01255 677122 **The Parade C014 8AS**
email: theroyalalbion@btconnect.com **web:** www.theroyalalbion.co.uk
dir: *Phone for directions*

Popular with families, The Royal Albion Public House offers good value accommodation with lovely sea views. Bedrooms are comfortable, spacious and an in-room continental breakfast is provided for guests.

Rooms 3 rms (1 en suite) (2 pri facs) (3 fmly) S £50-£60; D £50-£60* **Facilities** FTV DVD tea/coffee Pool table **Parking** 3 **Notes** ⊗ No coaches

---

WIX Map 13 TM12

Premier Collection

Dairy House Farm *(TM148293)*

★★★★★ FARMHOUSE

---

tel: 01255 870322 & 07749 073974 **Bradfield Rd CO11 2SR**
email: bridgetwhitworth353@gmail.com **web:** www.dairyhousefarm.info
dir: *Exit A120 into Wix, turn at x-rds to Bradfield, farm 1m on left*

This Georgian house stands amid 550 acres of arable land, and is blessed with stunning views of the surrounding countryside. Extensively renovated in the Victorian style, it has original decorative tiled floors, moulded cornices and marble fireplaces. The spacious bedrooms are carefully furnished and equipped with many thoughtful touches. Breakfast is served in the elegant antique-furnished dining room and there is a cosy lounge.

Rooms 3 en suite S £50-£55; D £72-£85 **Facilities** FTV DVD TVL tea/coffee WiFi ⤵ ᕕ Farm reservoir fishing **Extras** Home-made cake - complimentary **Parking** 8 **Notes** ⊗ No Children 12yrs ⊜ 550 acres arable

---

GLOUCESTERSHIRE

ALDERTON Map 10 SP03

Corner Cottage Bed and Breakfast

★★★★ BED AND BREAKFAST

---

tel: 01242 620630 **Stow Rd GL20 8NH**
email: info@stayatcornercottage.co.uk **web:** www.stayatcornercottage.co.uk
dir: *M5 junct 9 E onto A46 to rdbt then B4077 (Stow). Turn left opposite Alderton garage into Willowbank Rd, left again into drive & follow signs to car park*

There is a warm and genuine welcome for all guests arriving at Corner Cottage, with helpful local advice always on offer if required. The location is an ideal base from which to explore this picturesque area, with Tewkesbury only a short drive away. Bedrooms offer good levels of comfort, with modern, well-appointed bathrooms. Breakfast is a generous and tasty offering, served around the dining table in the lounge-diner.

Rooms 3 en suite S £50-£80; D £70-£80* **Facilities** FTV TVL tea/coffee WiFi **Parking** 8 **Notes** ⊗ No Children Closed Xmas/New Year

Tally Ho Bed & Breakfast

★★★★ BED AND BREAKFAST

tel: 01242 621482 & 07966 593169 **20 Beckford Rd GL20 8NL**
email: tallyhobb@aol.com **web:** www.cotswolds-bedandbreakfast.co.uk
dir: *M5 junct 9, A46 signed Evesham, through Ashchurch. Take B4077 signed Stow-on-the-Wold & Alderton. Left in 1.5m opposite garage signed Alderton*

Convenient for the M5, this friendly establishment stands in a delightful quiet village. Bedrooms, including two on the ground floor, offer modern comforts and attractive co-ordinated furnishings. Breakfast is served in the stylish dining room, and for dinner, the village pub is just a stroll away.

Rooms 3 en suite (1 fmly) (2 GF) S £45-£50; D £65-£70 **Facilities** FTV DVD tea/coffee WiFi **Parking** 3 **Notes** LB

See advert below

| ARLINGHAM | Map 4 SO71 |

The Old Passage Inn

★★★★ ◉◉ 🍽 RESTAURANT WITH ROOMS

tel: 01452 740547 **Passage Rd GL2 7JR**
email: oldpassage@btconnect.com **web:** www.theoldpassage.com
dir: *A38 onto B4071 through Frampton on Severn. 4m to Arlingham, through village to river*

Delightfully located on the very edge of the River Severn, this relaxing restaurant with rooms combines high quality food with an air of tranquillity. Bedrooms and bathrooms are decorated in a modern style and include a collection of welcome extras such as air conditioning and a well-stocked mini-bar. The menu offers a wide range of seafood and shellfish dishes including crab, oysters and lobsters from Cornwall (kept alive in seawater tanks) and has been recognised for its excellence with two AA Rosettes. An outdoor terrace is available in warmer months.

Rooms 3 en suite S £60-£130; D £80-£130* **Facilities** FTV DVD Lounge tea/coffee Dinner available WiFi 🛝 **Extras** Mini-bar - chargeable **Parking** 30 **Notes** Closed 25 & 26 Dec RS Jan-Feb closed for dinner Tue & Wed No coaches

BARNSLEY
Map 5 SP00

Premier Collection

The Village Pub
★★★★★ ◉ INN

tel: 01285 740000 & 740241   **fax:** 01285 740925 **GL7 5EF**
email: reservations@barnsleyhouse.com **web:** www.thevillagepub.co.uk
dir: *On B4425 in centre of village*

With a village location as its name suggests, this delightful establishment provides high quality accommodation and an efficient but relaxed style of hospitality and service. Owned by the same company as Barnsley House Hotel (across the road), guests here can enjoy an informal stay with high standards. The bar-dining room serves an excellent choice of top quality, seasonal produce and a varied choice of wines and ales. The bedrooms and bathrooms come in a range of sizes and all are comfortably furnished and equipped.

Rooms 6 rms (6 pri facs) (1 fmly) **Facilities** STV FTV DVD iPod docking station tea/coffee Dinner available Direct Dial WiFi ⚘ ⚘ ⚘ 18 Riding **Parking** 20 **Notes** LB

BERKELEY
Map 4 ST69

The Malt House
★★★ INN

tel: 01453 511177 **fax:** 01453 810257 **22 Marybrook St GL13 9BA**
email: the-malthouse@btconnect.com **web:** www.themalthouse.uk.com
dir: *A38 into Berkeley, at town hall follow road to right, premises on right past hospital & opposite school*

Conveniently located for business and leisure travellers, this family-run inn has a convivial atmosphere. Bedrooms are soundly appointed while public areas include a

choice of bars, a skittle alley and an attractive restaurant area. Local attractions include Berkeley Castle, and the Wildfowl & Wetlands Trust at Slimbridge.

Rooms 9 en suite (2 fmly) **Facilities** FTV tea/coffee Dinner available WiFi Pool table Skittle Alley **Parking** 30 **Notes** ⊗

BIBURY
Map 5 SP10

The Catherine Wheel
★★★★ ⌂ INN

tel: 01285 740250 **Arlington GL7 5ND**
email: rooms@catherinewheel-bibury.co.uk **web:** www.catherinewheel-bibury.co.uk
dir: *On B4425 between Burford & Cirencester*

This family-run inn provides a pleasant welcome and traditional country pub ambience. A range of seating is available in the cosy bar, or in the more formal dining room where a selection of carefully prepared dishes is offered throughout the day and evening. Bedrooms are in an adjacent building and include smaller standard rooms or larger superior rooms - all comfortably furnished and with some welcome extras.

Rooms 4 annexe en suite (4 GF) S £59-£93; D £65-£99* **Facilities** FTV DVD TVL tea/coffee Dinner available WiFi ⚘ **Parking** 23

BLOCKLEY
Map 10 SP13

Premier Collection

Lower Brook House
★★★★★ ⌂ ⌂ GUEST ACCOMMODATION

tel: 01386 700286 **fax:** 01386 701400 **Lower St GL56 9DS**
email: info@lowerbrookhouse.com **web:** www.lowerbrookhouse.com
dir: *In village centre*

Dating from the 17th century, this enchanting house is the perfect place to relax. Genuine hospitality and attentive service are hallmarks here, and bedrooms come in all shapes and sizes. The public areas have a lot of character, with beams, flagstone floors, a huge fireplace and deep stone walls. Enjoy a delicious breakfast and an aperitif in the garden, but leave room for the skilfully prepared dinner.

Rooms 6 en suite **Facilities** FTV Lounge tea/coffee Dinner available Licensed WiFi ⚘ 18 ⚘ **Extras** Mineral water, fruit **Parking** 6 **Notes** ⊗ No Children 10yrs Closed Xmas

BOURTON-ON-THE-WATER | Map 10 SP12

Premier Collection

Cranbourne House

★★★★★ 🛏 BED AND BREAKFAST

tel: 01451 821883 **Moore Rd GL54 2AZ**
email: info@cranbournehousebandb.co.uk **web:** www.cranbournehousebandb.co.uk
dir: *From A429 into Station Rd towards Bourton-on-the-Water. 0.5m on right turn into Moore Rd, 1st house on right*

Known as the 'Venice of the Cotswolds', there is something very special about Bourton-on-the-Water, and this wonderful Cotswold Arts and Crafts house is a perfect base from which to explore the locale. Bedrooms offer impressive levels of quality and comfort, likewise the modern bathrooms. Breakfast provides a substantial and rewarding start to the day with plentiful use of local produce. Guests have both an elegant lounge and conservatory in which to relax and enjoy this peaceful and relaxing environment.

Rooms 4 en suite 2 annexe en suite (1 GF) S £115-£135; D £130-£150 **Facilities** FTV iPod docking station TVL tea/coffee WiFi 🛁 **Parking** 6 **Notes** ⊗ No Children 12yrs

Larks Rise

★★★★ BED AND BREAKFAST

tel: 01451 822613 & 07884 438498 **Old Gloucester Rd GL54 3BH**
email: larks.rise@virgin.net **web:** www.larksrisehouse.co.uk
dir: *0.5m W of village. A249 onto A436, 1st driveway on left*

Larks Rise is a relaxed and welcoming establishment that sits in an acre of gardens on the edge of the village. Comfort and style are of paramount importance at this delightful property where the proprietors offer a very warm welcome. The bedrooms are really comfortable with cotton sheets on pocket-sprung mattresses and high quality, en suite facilities. Breakfasts feature locally sourced produce, and there is ample parking.

Rooms 3 rms (2 en suite) (1 pri facs) (1 GF) **Facilities** FTV tea/coffee WiFi **Parking** 6 **Notes** ⊗ No Children 12yrs

The Mousetrap Inn

★★★ INN

tel: 01451 820579 **Lansdowne GL54 2AR**
email: thebatesies@gmail.com **web:** www.mousetrap-inn.co.uk

The Mousetrap Inn is a traditional and informal Cotswold hostelry located on the edge of this idyllic village just a few minutes' stroll from the centre. A selection of real ales and also home-cooked dinners (except Sundays and Mondays) are offered in the relaxed bar. Bedrooms and bathrooms vary in size and include three at ground floor level. Breakfast includes home-made sausages and free-range eggs.

Rooms 10 en suite (3 GF) **Facilities** tea/coffee Dinner available WiFi **Parking** 10 **Notes** ⊗ No Children 10yrs

Old Manse

★★★ INN

tel: 01451 820082 **fax:** 01451 810381 **Victoria St GL54 2BX**
email: 6488@greeneking.co.uk **web:** www.oldenglish.co.uk
dir: *A429 Bourton turn off, property at far end of village high street next to Cotswold Motor Museum*

During the 18th century the Old Manse was a residence for Baptist ministers. It has lots of traditional Cotswold charm, and is located close to the River Windrush. There is an extensive bar menu and a good restaurant menu. Bedrooms are modern and well equipped with comfortable beds. In the winter guests can relax by a roaring log fire, and in the summer enjoy the beer garden overlooking the river.

Rooms 12 en suite 3 annexe en suite **Facilities** FTV tea/coffee Dinner available Direct Dial WiFi **Conf** Max 40 Thtr 40 Class 20 Board 16 **Parking** 12

The Red House East

★★★ BED AND BREAKFAST

tel: 01451 821406 **Station Rd GL54 2EN**
email: ktcunningham21@yahoo.co.uk

Conveniently located just off the main high street, this former doctor's house now provides comfortable well equipped bedrooms complimented by good quality bathrooms. The friendly hosts offer a warm welcome, with the property providing an ideal base to explore the surrounding area.

Rooms 3 rms S £60-£100; D £100-£140*

CHELTENHAM | Map 10 SO92

Premier Collection

Beaumont House

★★★★★ GUEST ACCOMMODATION

tel: 01242 223311 **fax:** 01242 520044 **56 Shurdington Rd GL53 0JE**
email: reservations@bhhotel.co.uk **web:** www.bhhotel.co.uk
dir: *S side of town on A46 to Stroud*

Built as a private residence, popular Beaumont House exudes genteel charm. Public areas include a large lounge and an elegant dining room which overlooks the garden. The accommodation includes studio bedrooms on the top floor. These complement the 'Out of Asia' and 'Out of Africa' bedrooms, which are luxuriously furnished and very well equipped. Bedrooms situated to the rear of the building have views over Leckhampton Hill and there are also bedrooms on the lower ground floor.

Rooms 16 en suite (3 fmly) S £72-£82; D £105-£199* **Facilities** STV FTV Lounge tea/coffee Dinner available Direct Dial Licensed WiFi 🛁 **Extras** Fruit, mineral water - free; mini-bar - chargeable **Parking** 16 **Notes** ⊗ RS 25-26 Dec No housekeeping services

CHELTENHAM *continued*

The Bradley

★★★★★ GUEST ACCOMMODATION

tel: 01242 519077 **fax:** 01242 650800 **19 Bayshill Rd GL50 3AY**
email: thebradleyguesthouse@gmail.com **web:** www.thebradleyhotel.co.uk

The Bradley is a boutique town house in the centre of Regency Cheltenham, just a few minutes' stroll from the local shops and the town centre. Bedrooms and bathrooms offer plenty of quality and comfort and come in a range of shapes and sizes. Breakfast utilises the best quality produce and is served in the elegant dining room. Parking permits can generally be arranged if booked in advance.

Rooms 7 en suite (1 GF) **Facilities** FTV iPod docking station WiFi **Extras** Still & sparkling water, chocolate **Parking** 2 **Notes** ⊗ No Children 11yrs

Cleeve Hill House

★★★★★ GUEST ACCOMMODATION

tel: 01242 672052 **fax:** 01242 679969 **Cleeve Hill GL52 3PR**
email: info@cleevehill-hotel.co.uk **web:** www.cleevehill-hotel.co.uk
dir: 3m N of Cheltenham on B4632

Many of the bedrooms and the lounge at this Edwardian property have spectacular views across to the Malvern Hills. Room shapes and sizes vary but all are comfortably furnished with many welcome extras; some have four-poster beds. There is a relaxing guest lounge, and an honesty bar is in place. Breakfast, served in the pleasant conservatory, offers a good selection of carefully presented hot and cold items.

Rooms 10 en suite (1 GF) S £55-£65; D £90-£98* **Facilities** STV FTV DVD Lounge tea/coffee Direct Dial Licensed WiFi **Parking** 11 **Notes** ⊗ No Children 8yrs

Georgian House

★★★★★ BED AND BREAKFAST

tel: 01242 515577 **fax:** 01242 545929 **77 Montpellier Ter GL50 1XA**
email: penny@georgianhouse.net **web:** www.georgianhouse.net
dir: M5 junct 11, A40 into town centre, into Montpellier Terrace. Georgian House on right after park

Dating from 1807, this elegant Georgian House is located in the fashionable area of Montpellier. The accommodation is delightful with the accent on quality and comfort throughout. Bedrooms are individually styled, blending contemporary style with period furnishings to great effect. Warm hospitality and attentive service ensure a memorable stay.

Rooms 3 en suite S £75-£85* **Facilities** FTV Lounge tea/coffee WiFi
Extras Fridge, milk & complimentary drinks **Parking** 2 **Notes** ⊗ No Children 16yrs Closed Xmas & New Year

The Battledown Bed and Breakfast

★★★★ BED AND BREAKFAST

tel: 01242 233881 & 07807 142069 **125 Hales Rd GL52 6ST**
email: info@thebattledown.co.uk **web:** www.thebattledown.co.uk
dir: 0.5m E of town centre. A40 onto B4075, 0.5m on right

Simon, Sarah and their daughter Isabella welcome you to their home, The Battledown, a French colonial-style villa that was built in 1855. It is conveniently located for the town centre, all of the events in Cheltenham and the surrounding Cotswold countryside.

Rooms 7 en suite (2 fmly) **Facilities** FTV DVD Lounge tea/coffee WiFi **Parking** 7 **Notes** ⊗

Clarence Court

★★★★ GUEST ACCOMMODATION

tel: 01242 580411 **fax:** 01242 224609 **Clarence Square GL50 4JR**
email: enquiries@clarencecourthotel.com **web:** www.clarencecourthotel.com

Situated in an attractive, tree-lined Georgian square, this property was once owned by the Duke of Wellington. The building is charming and its elegant public rooms reflect the grace of a bygone age. Spacious bedrooms offer ample comfort and quality, and have many original features. The convenience of the peaceful location is a great asset, only a five-minute stroll from the town centre. A varied range of carefully prepared dishes is offered in the relaxing café-restaurant from noon to 9pm.

Rooms 20 en suite (3 fmly) (7 GF) **Facilities** FTV DVD TVL tea/coffee Dinner available Direct Dial Licensed WiFi **Parking** 21

Cotswold Grange

★★★★ GUEST ACCOMMODATION

tel: 01242 515119 **fax:** 01242 241537 **Pittville Circus Rd GL52 2QH**
email: info@cotswoldgrange.co.uk **web:** www.cotswoldgrange.co.uk
dir: From town centre, follow Prestbury signs. Right at 1st rdbt, next rdbt straight over, 100yds on left

A delightful building located in a quiet, mainly residential area of Cheltenham, Cotswold Grange is near Pittville Park and just a short walk from the town centre. There's a relaxed and welcoming atmosphere here, and the bedrooms come with many useful extras. A range of carefully cooked and presented dishes is served in the comfortable restaurant.

Rooms 24 en suite (3 fmly) D £85-£115* **Facilities** FTV TVL tea/coffee Dinner available Direct Dial Licensed WiFi 18 Complimentary access to nearby gym **Conf** Max 60 Board 30 **Parking** 21 **Notes** LB Closed 25-31 Dec

Hilden House B&B

★★★★ GUEST ACCOMMODATION

tel: 01242 515181 & 07795 245943   **fax:** 01242 650670 **20 Evesham Rd GL52 2AB**
email: info@hildenhouse.co.uk **web:** www.hildenhouse.co.uk
dir: *From Cheltenham on Evesham Road towards racecourse, on left*

Conveniently located just a short stroll from the town centre and racecourse, this elegant Regency town house offers impressive levels of comfort and quality. Bedrooms are well appointed and equipped meet the needs of both business and leisure guests, likewise the modern bathrooms. Charming public areas include a bar and the specious dining room where breakfast is a real treat.

Rooms 8 en suite 4 annexe en suite (1 fmly) (2 GF) S £55-£65; D £82-£130*
Facilities FTV tea/coffee Licensed WiFi **Notes** ❸ No Children 5yrs RS 11-15 Mar Festival wk

Hilden Lodge

★★★★ GUEST ACCOMMODATION

tel: 01242 583242 **fax:** 01242 650271 **271 London Rd GL52 6YG**
email: hildenlodgecheltenham@gmail.com **web:** www.hildenlodgecheltenham.co.uk

Located a few minutes' drive outside Cheltenham, smartly presented Hilden Lodge makes a perfect base from which to explore the beautiful Cotswold villages and countryside. There is an intimate and friendly atmosphere here with guests well looked after by the committed team. Bedrooms and bathrooms are well equipped and provide all the expected comforts to ensure a relaxing and enjoyable stay. A bar and restaurant are also available here, with dinner well worth a try. A plentiful choice is offered at breakfast.

Rooms 12 en suite (1 fmly) (2 GF) S £45-£65; D £55-£95 **Facilities** FTV DVD TVL tea/coffee Dinner available Licensed WiFi 👙 **Extras** Bottled water - chargeable **Conf** Max 25 Thtr 25 Class 15 Board 20 **Parking** 8 **Notes** ❸

Hope Orchard

★★★★ GUEST ACCOMMODATION

tel: 01452 855556 **Gloucester Rd, Staverton GL51 0TF**
email: info@hopeorchard.com **web:** www.hopeorchard.com
dir: *A40 onto B4063 at Arlecourt rdbt. Hope Orchard 1.25m on right*

Situated midway between Gloucester and Cheltenham, Hope Orchard is a good base for exploring the area. The comfortable bedrooms are next to the main house, all are on the ground floor and each has its own separate entrance. There is a large garden, and ample off-road parking is available.

Rooms 8 en suite (8 GF) **Facilities** FTV DVD tea/coffee Direct Dial WiFi 👙
Extras Fridge, microwave **Parking** 10 **Notes** Closed 23 Dec-2 Jan

Malvern View

★★★★ GUEST ACCOMMODATION

tel: 01242 672017 **Cleeve Hill GL52 3PR**
web: www.malvernview.com
dir: *B4632 from Cheltenham towards Winchcombe & Stratford-upon-Avon. Through Southam & Cleeve Hill, Malvern View on right*

This family-run guest accommodation is located just four miles north of Cheltenham. The property backs onto the Cotswold Way and Cleeve Common, which has amazing views that reach as far as the Black Mountains in Wales. The six bedrooms, mostly en suite, are all individually styled and offer an impressive level of quality and comfort.

Rooms 7 rms (6 en suite) (1 pri facs) S £55-£105; D £90-£135* **Facilities** FTV Lounge TV6B tea/coffee Dinner available Licensed WiFi ⌔ 18 🔓 **Extras** Speciality toiletries **Conf** Max 30 Thtr 18 Class 30 Board 18 **Parking** 15 **Notes** LB ❸ Closed 2-15 Jan

The Beaufort Arms

★★★ INN

tel: 01242 526038 & 07758 400110   **fax:** 01242 526038 **184 London Rd GL52 6HJ**
email: lisa@the-beaufort-arms.co.uk **web:** www.the-beaufort-arms.co.uk

This traditional inn is located on the main road, a level walk of around ten minutes from town. Meals are available during the day and evenings, although only up to lunch time on Sundays. Bedrooms and bathrooms are traditionally furnished and offer a range of shapes and sizes. A good welcome is offered from the helpful staff both in the bar and at breakfast.

Rooms 6 rms (2 en suite) (4 pri facs) (1 fmly) **Facilities** FTV tea/coffee Dinner available WiFi Pool table Skittle alley **Parking** 6

Kingsmuir

Ⓤ

tel: 01242 245397 & 020 8643 6854 **Pittville Circus GL52 2PU**
web: www.kingsmuirhotel.co.uk
dir: *0.5m N of town centre, E of Evesham Rd*

Currently the rating for this establishment is not confirmed. This may be due to a change of ownership or because it has only recently joined the AA rating scheme.

Rooms 6 en suite (1 fmly) S £35-£50; D £52-£70* **Facilities** FTV tea/coffee WiFi **Parking** 3 **Notes** ❸ Closed mid Dec-mid Jan

---

CHIPPING CAMPDEN   **Map 10 SP13**

See also Blockley

The Kings

★★★★ ⓦⓦ ⌂ RESTAURANT WITH ROOMS

tel: 01386 840256 & 841056   **fax:** 01386 841598 **The Square GL55 6AW**
email: info@kingscampden.co.uk **web:** www.kingscampden.co.uk
dir: *In centre of town square*

Located in the centre of this delightful Cotswold town, The Kings effortlessly blends a relaxed and friendly welcome with efficient service. Bedrooms and bathrooms come in a range of shapes and sizes and all are appointed to a high level of quality and comfort. Dining options, whether in the main restaurant or the comfortable bar area, serve a tempting menu to suit all tastes, from light salads and pasta, to meat and fish dishes.

Rooms 14 en suite 5 annexe en suite (3 fmly) (3 GF) S £95-£200; D £120-£325 **Facilities** FTV tea/coffee Dinner available Direct Dial WiFi **Conf** Thtr 30 Class 20 Board 20 **Parking** 8 **Notes** LB ❸ Civ Wed 60

CHIPPING CAMPDEN *continued*

Catbrook House

★★★★ BED AND BREAKFAST

tel: 01386 841499 **Catbrook GL55 6DE**
email: m.klein@virgin.net **web:** www.chippingcampden.co.uk/catbrook.htm
dir: *B4081 into Chipping Campden, signs for Broad Campden until Catbrook House on right*

Along with stunning rural views and close proximity to the town centre, this mellow-toned stone house provides comfortable, homely bedrooms. The attentive hosts extend a friendly welcome, and serve traditional English breakfasts in the comfortably furnished dining room.

Rooms 2 rms (1 en suite) (1 pri facs) S fr £45; D fr £63* **Facilities** FTV DVD tea/coffee 🔒 **Parking** 3 **Notes** ⊗ No Children 9yrs Closed Xmas ✉

Holly House

★★★★ BED AND BREAKFAST

tel: 01386 593213 **Ebrington GL55 6NL**
email: jeffreyhutsby@yahoo.co.uk **web:** www.hollyhousebandb.co.uk
dir: *B4035 from Chipping Campden towards Shipston on Stour, 0.5m left to Ebrington & signed*

Set in the heart of the pretty Cotswold village of Ebrington, this late Victorian house offers thoughtfully equipped accommodation. Bedrooms are housed in buildings that were formerly used by the local wheelwright, and offer level access, seclusion and privacy. Quality English breakfasts are served in the light and airy dining room. For other meals, the village pub is just a short walk away.

Rooms 2 en suite 1 annexe en suite (2 fmly) (3 GF) S £55-£85; D £75-£85* **Facilities** FTV Lounge tea/coffee WiFi **Parking** 5 **Notes** ⊗ ✉

Lygon Arms

★★★★ 🛎 ⇌ INN

tel: 01386 840318 & 840089 **fax:** 01386 841088 **High St GL55 6HB**
email: sandra@lygonarms.co.uk **web:** www.lygonarms.co.uk
dir: *In town centre near church*

This charming and welcoming inn sits on Chipping Campden's high street - a tranquil location with lots of tempting antique shops. Well managed by a friendly team, the inn has a cosy bar with open log fires and oak beams. Spacious and very well-appointed accommodation is provided in the main building and in mews houses. Both breakfast and dinner are hearty and should not be missed.

Rooms 10 en suite (3 fmly) (1 GF) **Facilities** FTV tea/coffee Dinner available Direct Dial WiFi **Parking** 12 **Notes** No coaches

Manor Farm *(SP124412)*

★★★★ FARMHOUSE

tel: 01386 840390 & 07889 108812 **Weston-sub-Edge GL55 6QH**
email: lucy@manorfarmbnb.demon.co.uk **web:** www.manorfarmbnb.demon.co.uk
dir: *2m NW of Chipping Campden. On B4632 in Weston-sub-Edge*

A genuine welcome is extended at Manor Farm, a 17th-century honey-coloured stone farmhouse. Bedrooms are comfortable and homely with thoughtful extras. Facilities include a lounge with a wood-burning stove, and an elegant dining room where mouth-watering breakfasts are served.

Rooms 3 en suite S £65-£75; D £75-£80* **Facilities** STV FTV iPod docking station TVL tea/coffee WiFi 🌡 18 **Parking** 8 **Notes** LB ⊗ 800 acres arable/cattle/horses/sheep

▌ CHIPPING SODBURY   Map 4 ST78

The Moda House

★★★★ GUEST ACCOMMODATION

tel: 01454 312135 **fax:** 01454 850090 **1 High St BS37 6BA**
email: enquiries@modahouse.co.uk **web:** www.modahouse.co.uk
dir: *In town centre*

This popular Grade II listed Georgian house has an imposing position at the top of the High Street. It has been appointed to provide modern bedrooms of varying shapes and sizes and comfortable public areas, while retaining many original features. Room facilities include satellite TV and phones.

Rooms 8 en suite 3 annexe en suite (3 GF) S £62-£67; D £75-£95* **Facilities** STV Lounge TVL tea/coffee Direct Dial Licensed WiFi **Conf** Max 20 Thtr 10 Board 10

▌ CIRENCESTER   Map 5 SP00

The Fleece at Cirencester

★★★★★ ⇌ INN

tel: 01285 658507 **Market Place GL7 2NZ**
email: relax@thefleececirencester.co.uk **web:** www.thefleececirencester.co.uk

Located in the heart of the market town of Cirencester, this country inn has been finished to a high standard with guests and comfort in mind. Bedrooms are sumptuous, and many thoughtful touches add to the stay. Public areas include a traditional bar featuring Thwaites cask ales, a cosy lounge and a popular restaurant.

Rooms 28 en suite (1 fmly) **Facilities** FTV Lounge tea/coffee Dinner available WiFi **Parking** 8

Greensleeves

★★★★ BED AND BREAKFAST

tel: 01285 642516 & 07971 929259 **Baunton Ln, Stratton GL7 2LN**
email: johnps1@tesco.net **web:** www.greensleeves4u.co.uk
dir: *From Cirencester, follow signs for Stratton. Right into Baunton Ln*

Guests are ensured of a warm and friendly welcome from proprietor John, at this delightful property, just a short drive from Cirencester. Smart en suite accommodation, with off street parking, is well equipped with a host of facilities to ensure both leisure and corporate guests feel at home. Delicious breakfasts feature home baked bread. AA Friendliest B&B of the Year Finalist 2014-2015.

Rooms 3 en suite S £50-£55; D £65-£75* **Facilities** FTV DVD tea/coffee WiFi ⚓ 🐾
Parking 5

CLEEVE HILL   Map 10 SO92

Rising Sun

★★★ INN

tel: 01242 676281 **fax:** 01242 673069 **GL52 3PX**
email: 9210@greeneking.co.uk **web:** www.oldenglish.co.uk
dir: *On B4632, 4m N of Cheltenham*

This popular establishment is situated on Cleeve Hill and offers commanding views across the Severn Vale to the Malvern Hills and beyond. There is a pleasant range of public rooms which include a large bar-bistro and a reception lounge. Bedrooms are well equipped and smartly presented, and many have glorious views. A large garden is also available for summer drinking and dining.

Rooms 24 en suite (3 fmly) (6 GF) **Facilities** STV Lounge tea/coffee Dinner available Direct Dial WiFi ⚓ 18 **Parking** 70 **Notes** LB

COLEFORD   Map 4 SO51

Dryslade Farm *(SO581147)*

★★★★ FARMHOUSE

tel: 01594 860259 & 07766 631988 **English Bicknor GL16 7PA**
email: daphne@drysladefarm.co.uk **web:** www.drysladefarm.co.uk
dir: *3m N of Coleford. A4136 onto B4432, right towards English Bicknor, farm 1m*

Visitors are warmly welcomed at this 184-acre working farm, which dates from 1780 and has been in the same family for almost 100 years. The en suite bedrooms are attractively furnished in natural pine and are well equipped. The lounge leads onto a conservatory where hearty breakfasts are served.

Rooms 3 en suite (1 GF) S £45-£50; D £68-£74* **Facilities** FTV DVD Lounge TVL tea/coffee WiFi 🐾 **Extras** Use of fridge **Parking** 6 **Notes** LB 🐾 184 acres beef

The Rock B&B

★★★★ GUEST ACCOMMODATION

tel: 01594 837893 **GL16 7NY**
email: chris@stayattherock.com **web:** www.stayattherock.com
dir: *A40 at Monmouth onto A4136. 5m, left at Five Acres into Park Rd. At Christchurch right, immediately left towards Symonds Yat Rock, 0.75m S of Symonds Yat Rock*

The Rock B&B offers stylish modern accommodation and is located on the outskirts of Coleford, near the famous Symonds Yat Rock. Bedrooms are attractively presented and very comfortable, with new garden rooms making the most of the spectacular views over the Wye Valley. Very popular with walkers, The Rock also caters well for business guests. Breakfasts are served in the spacious dining room overlooking the garden.

Rooms 7 annexe en suite (5 GF) **Facilities** FTV Lounge tea/coffee WiFi 🐾 Hot tub **Parking** 20 **Notes** LB No Children 12yrs

---

The Miners Country Inn

★★★ 🛏 INN

tel: 01594 836632 **Chepstow Rd, Sling GL16 8LH**

The Miners is a real family affair, set in the Heart of the Forest of Dean. First impressions are of a quintessential pub with beamed ceilings, stone flooring and a bar stocking an array of local ales. A strong local trade makes for a bustling atmosphere, but really it's the food that's important. With an impressive pedigree the chef-patron focuses on locally sourced ingredients. Suppliers are championed on blackboards and menus, with most supplying the inn exclusively. Dishes offer classic hearty fare with a modern twist. Bedrooms are light and airy, with modern en suite bathrooms.

Rooms 4 en suite **Facilities** Dinner available

COWLEY   Map 10 SO91

The Green Dragon Inn

★★★★ 🛏 INN

tel: 01242 870271 **fax:** 01242 870171 **Cockleford GL53 9NW**
email: green-dragon@buccaneer.co.uk **web:** www.green-dragon-inn.co.uk

The Green Dragon offers all the charm and character of an English country pub combined with a relaxed atmosphere and carefully prepared food made from local produce; dinner is particularly recommended. Bedrooms, some at ground floor level, are individually furnished and vary in size. There is a terrace to the front where guests may enjoy a drink on warm sunny days.

Rooms 9 en suite (4 GF) S £70-£105; D £95-£175* **Facilities** iPod docking station tea/coffee Dinner available Direct Dial WiFi **Conf** Max 100 Thtr 100 Class 65 Board 65 **Parking** 11 **Notes** LB Closed 25 Dec eve-26 Dec eve & 1 Jan eve

---

DIDMARTON   Map 4 ST88

The Kings Arms

★★★★ 🛏 INN

tel: 01454 238245 **The Street GL9 1DT**
email: enquiries@kingsarmsdidmarton.co.uk

The Kings Arms is a real gem of a find. Situated in a rural village it boasts many features which include rooms named after hounds of the local hunt from former days. Bedrooms are sumptuous in quality, and retain all the character of the stables that they once were. Locally sourced produce is cooked with passion and presented with flair. The inn has been fully restored but retains its stone flagged floors and heavy wooden tables, rustic walls and simple decoration. Real ales are also a feature. Outside the garden provides a great space in the summer.

Rooms 4 en suite 4 annexe en suite (2 fmly) (2 GF) **Facilities** FTV DVD tea/coffee Dinner available WiFi Fishing **Parking** 25

Find out more about Staying in the Cotswolds see page 21

EBRINGTON — Map 10 SP14

The Ebrington Arms

★★★★★ ◉◉ ≘ INN

tel: 01386 593223 **GL55 6NH**
email: info@theebringtonarms.co.uk **web:** www.theebringtonarms.co.uk
dir: *From Chipping Campden take B4035 towards Shipston on Stour, left to Ebrington*

Nestled in the quiet, unspoilt village of Ebrington, just a couple of miles from Chipping Campden, this 17th-century inn offers an excellent selection of real ales, fine wines and really enjoyable award-winning cuisine utilising the finest of produce. Food is served in the friendly bar or in the cosy dining room where the open fire roars on chilly days. Bedrooms are full of character and include some welcome extras. A large beer garden and car park are also available.

Rooms 3 en suite **Facilities** FTV tea/coffee Dinner available **Conf** Max 32 Thtr 32 Class 32 Board 25 **Parking** 10

EWEN — Map 4 SU09

The Wild Duck

★★★★ INN

tel: 01285 770310 **fax:** 01285 770492 **Drakes Island GL7 6BY**
email: duckreservations@aol.com **web:** www.thewildduckinn.co.uk
dir: *From Cirencester take A429 towards Malmesbury, at Kemble left to village centre*

This lovely 16th-century family-run inn sits in a delightful Cotswold village and offers a wealth of character and interest. Log fires crackle, and there are heaps of nooks and crannies in the bar and restaurant where guests can enjoy hearty cuisine and an extensive choice of beers and wines. There is a lovely courtyard for alfresco dining in the warmer weather. The individually designed bedrooms have a contemporary look, and each has a black, lacquered four-poster; the Chinese Suite is in the oldest part of the building.

Rooms 4 en suite 8 annexe en suite (8 GF) **Facilities** FTV Lounge tea/coffee Dinner available Direct Dial WiFi ⅃ 18 **Parking** 50 **Notes** Closed 25 Dec evening

FRAMPTON MANSELL — Map 4 SO90

The Crown Inn

★★★★ INN

tel: 01285 760601 **GL6 8JG**
email: enquiries@thecrowninn-cotswolds.co.uk **web:** www.thecrowninn-cotswolds.co.uk
dir: *Off A419 signed Frampton Mansell, 0.75m at village centre*

This establishment was a cider house in the 17th century, and guests today will find that roaring log fires, locally brewed ales and traditional, home-cooked food are all on offer. The comfortable, well-equipped bedrooms are in an annexe, and ample parking is available.

Rooms 12 annexe en suite (1 fmly) (4 GF) S £67.50-£87.50; D £87.50* **Facilities** tea/coffee Dinner available WiFi **Conf** Max 40 **Parking** 35 **Notes** LB

GLOUCESTER — Map 10 SO81

The Wharf House Restaurant with Rooms

★★★★ ◉ RESTAURANT WITH ROOMS

tel: 01452 332900 **fax:** 01452 332901 **Over GL2 8DB**
email: thewharfhouse@yahoo.co.uk **web:** www.thewharfhouse.co.uk
dir: *From A40 between Gloucester & Highnam exit at lights for Over. Establishment signed*

The Wharf House was built to replace the old lock cottage and, as the name suggests, it is located at the very edge of the river; it has pleasant views and an outdoor terrace. The bedrooms and bathrooms have been finished to a high standard, and there are plenty of guest extras. Seasonal, local produce can be enjoyed both at breakfast and dinner in the delightful AA Rosetted restaurant.

Rooms 7 en suite (1 fmly) (1 GF) S £79-£149; D £85-£149* **Facilities** STV FTV DVD Lounge tea/coffee Dinner available WiFi Fishing ⓑ **Extras** Mini-bar - chargeable **Parking** 37 **Notes** Closed 24 Dec-4 Jan No coaches

See advert on opposite page

HYDE
Map 4 SO80

The Ragged Cot
★★★★ ⬚ INN

tel: 01453 884643 & 07976 011198 **Cirencester Rd GL6 8PE**
email: info@theraggedcot.co.uk **web:** www.theraggedcot.co.uk
dir: M5 junct 13 onto A419 signed Stroud/Cirencester. At Ashton Down Airfield rdbt, right signed Minchinhampton. 2m on left

Originally a 17th century coaching inn, the property has over time been extended to offer a modern large airy bar and restaurant with a selection of good quality bedrooms well equipped for the modern day traveller. An extensive collection of ever changing artwork provides an interesting feature. This friendly inn serves a wide selection of real ales with the menu focusing on locally sourced ingredients.

Rooms 9 en suite (4 GF) D £80-£125* **Facilities** FTV DVD tea/coffee Dinner available WiFi ⬚ 36 **Extras** Speciality toiletries **Parking** 30 **Notes** No coaches

LECHLADE ON THAMES
Map 5 SU29

The Riverside
★★★ INN

tel: 01367 252534 **Park End Wharf GL7 3AQ**

Located on the banks of the Thames, with an unrivalled position in Lechlade, this traditional inn is within easy reach of Swindon, Cirencester and the Cotswolds. Comfortable accommodation is located adjacent to the inn with its own entrance, all rooms are en suite some suitable for families. Great British fare is served either in the main bar and dining rooms or weather permitting outside. Owned by the Arkell's family brewers, a great range of traditionally brewed beers are available.

Rooms 6 en suite

LOWER SLAUGHTER
Map 10 SP12

Premier Collection

The Slaughters Country Inn
★★★★★ ◉◉ INN

tel: 01451 822143 **GL54 2HS**
email: info@theslaughtersinn.co.uk **web:** www.theslaughtersinn.co.uk
dir: Exit A429 at 'The Slaughters' sign, between Stow-on-the-Wold & Bourton-on-the-Water. In village centre

This attractive 17th-century inn is set in beautiful grounds beside the River Eye. Inside, contemporary high quality bedrooms, all with modern bathrooms, blend well with the more traditional bar area with its beamed ceilings, open fires, and flagstone floors. The recently refurbished Eton Restaurant is an attractive setting where modern British cooking sits next to more classical dishes and there's a comfortable lounge in which to relax. Parking is a bonus.

Rooms 19 en suite 11 annexe en suite (2 fmly) (5 GF) S £85-£325; D £95-£345 **Facilities** FTV DVD tea/coffee Dinner available Direct Dial WiFi ⬚ **Conf** Thtr 80 Class 50 Board 36 **Parking** 45 **Notes** Civ Wed 80

NAILSWORTH
Map 4 ST89

Wild Garlic Restaurant and Rooms
★★★★ ◉◉ RESTAURANT WITH ROOMS

tel: 01453 832615 **3 Cossack Square GL6 0DB**
email: info@wild-garlic.co.uk **web:** www.wild-garlic.co.uk
dir: M4 junct 18, A46 towards Stroud. Enter Nailsworth, left at rdbt, immediately left. Establishment opposite Britannia pub

Situated in a quiet corner of charming Nailsworth, this restaurant with rooms offers a delightful combination of welcoming, relaxed hospitality and serious cuisine. The spacious and well-equipped bedrooms are situated above the award-winning restaurant. The small and friendly team of staff ensure guests are very well looked after throughout their stay.

Rooms 3 en suite (2 fmly) **Facilities** STV FTV DVD tea/coffee Dinner available WiFi ⬚ 18 Fishing Riding Shooting **Extras** Spring water - complimentary **Notes** ⊗ No coaches

NAUNTON — Map 10 SP12

Mill View Guest House

★★★★ GUEST HOUSE

tel: 01451 850586 & 07887 553571 **2 Mill View GL54 3AF**
email: patricia@millview.myzen.co.uk **web:** www.millviewguesthousecotswolds.com
dir: Exit B4068 to E end of village

Standing opposite a historic watermill, this former family home is geared towards guests and aims to provide every comfort. A warm welcome and attentive care is assured in this non-smoking house, which has one ground floor bedroom, equipped for easier access. The accommodation provides a good base for walkers or for touring Gloucestershire.

Rooms 3 en suite (1 GF) S fr £50* **Facilities** FTV DVD iPod docking station TVL tea/coffee Dinner available WiFi ♨ **Extras** Snacks, sherry - complimentary **Parking** 4 **Notes** LB ⊗ ⊜

NETHER WESTCOTE — Map 10 SP22

Premier Collection

The Feathered Nest Country Inn

★★★★★ ⦿⦿⦿ INN

tel: 01993 833030 **fax:** 01993 833031 **OX7 6SD**
email: info@thefeatherednestinn.co.uk **web:** www.thefeatherednestinn.co.uk
dir: A424 between Burford & Stow-on-the-Wold, follow signs

Located in the picturesque Cotswold village of Nether Westcote, with rolling views over the Evenlode Valley, this charming village inn offers a cosy base from which to explore the pretty countryside. There are four luxurious en suite bedrooms, all individually designed combining quality antiques and modern extras. Service is attentive and helpful while the food is a delight, offering a selection of carefully crafted dishes using the best of quality, seasonal produce. Fish is delivered fresh from the coast, and meals can be enjoyed on the charming outdoor terrace in warmer weather.

Rooms 4 en suite **Facilities** STV FTV DVD TVL tea/coffee Dinner available Direct Dial WiFi **Extras** Home-made biscuits, fruit - complimentary; robes **Parking** 45 **Notes** ⊗ Closed 25 Dec RS Mon (ex BHs) No coaches Civ Wed 200

NEWENT — Map 10 SO72

Kilcot Inn

★★★★ INN

tel: 01989 720707 **Ross Rd GL18 1NA**
web: www.kilcotinn.com

The inviting Kilcot Inn deals in the best traditions of hospitality, food and drink. From the selection of real ales and local ciders on tap, to the high quality produce used in the delicious dishes in the bar/restaurant there is something for everyone. The bedrooms and bathrooms above the inn provide high levels of quality and comfort. Outdoor seating is also available, including a pleasant garden area to the rear of the property.

Rooms 4 en suite **Facilities** FTV Lounge tea/coffee Dinner available WiFi ♨ **Parking** 40

Three Choirs Vineyards

★★★★ ⦿ RESTAURANT WITH ROOMS

tel: 01531 890223 **fax:** 01531 890877 **GL18 1LS**
email: info@threechoirs.com **web:** www.threechoirs.com
dir: On B4215 N of Newent, follow brown tourist signs

This thriving vineyard continues to go from strength to strength and provides a wonderfully different place to stay. The restaurant, which overlooks the 100-acre estate, enjoys a popular following thanks to well-executed dishes that make good use of local produce. Spacious, high quality bedrooms are equipped with many extras, and each opens onto a private patio area which has wonderful views.

Rooms 11 annexe en suite (1 fmly) (11 GF) S £130-£155; D £135-£160* **Facilities** FTV DVD Lounge tea/coffee Dinner available Direct Dial WiFi Wine tasting Vineyard Tours **Conf** Max 20 Thtr 20 Class 15 Board 20 **Parking** 11 **Notes** LB Closed 24 Dec-5 Jan No coaches

OLD SODBURY — Map 4 ST78

The Sodbury House

★★★★ GUEST HOUSE

tel: 01454 312847 **fax:** 01454 273105 **Badminton Rd BS37 6LU**
email: info@sodburyhouse.co.uk **web:** www.sodburyhouse.co.uk
dir: M4 junct 18, A46 N, 2m left onto A432 to Chipping Sodbury, house 1m on left

This comfortably furnished 19th-century farmhouse stands in six acres of grounds. The bedrooms, some located on the ground floor and in buildings adjacent to the main house, have many extra facilities. Breakfast offers a varied choice and is served in the spacious breakfast room.

Rooms 6 en suite 3 annexe en suite (1 fmly) (2 GF) **Facilities** FTV Lounge TVL tea/coffee WiFi ♨ ♨ **Conf** Thtr 40 Class 25 Board 20 **Parking** 30 **Notes** ⊗ Closed 24 Dec-3 Jan

The Cross Hands

★★★ INN

tel: 01454 313000 **fax:** 01454 324409 **BS37 6RJ**
email: 6435@greeneking.co.uk **web:** www.oldenglish.co.uk
dir: M4 junct 18 signed to Cirencester/Stroud on A46. After 1.5m, on right at 1st lights

The Cross Hands is a former posting house dating back to the 14th century and can be found just off the main road, within easy reach of both Bath and Bristol. The bedrooms are well equipped and some are at ground-floor level. The public areas include a bar, comfortable seating area and a spacious split-level restaurant which offers a selection of home-cooked dishes. Alternatively, guests may choose to eat from the extensive menu in the bar area.

Rooms 21 en suite (1 fmly) (9 GF) S £30-£80; D £50-£105* **Facilities** FTV tea/coffee Dinner available Direct Dial WiFi **Extras** Chocolates, flowers, champagne - chargeable **Conf** Max 80 Thtr 80 Class 24 Board 16 **Parking** 120 **Notes** Civ Wed 80

| PAINSWICK | Map 4 SO80 |

The Falcon

★★★★ 🏠 🍽 INN

tel: 01452 814222 New St GL6 6UN
email: info@falconpainswick.co.uk web: www.falconpainswick.co.uk
dir: On A46 in centre of Painswick

This imposing Cotswold stone building dates back to 1554, and sits on the main street of this attractive Cotswold village. The Falcon overlooks St Mary's church with its famous clipped yews, and is also within easy driving distance of Cheltenham Racecourse. Bedrooms are all individually designed and well equipped with comfortable beds, crisp white linen and very good quality toiletries. There is a spacious bar and dining area. With an eclectic mix of furnishings, and chalky white and muted duck egg blue walls, this popular place has a really good atmosphere with a good mix of locals and tourists. The kitchen serves an accomplished bistro style menu awash with locally sourced seasonal ingredients.

Rooms 8 en suite 3 annexe en suite (2 fmly) (1 GF) S £69-£95; D £79-£125*
Facilities FTV tea/coffee Dinner available WiFi ⅃ 18 ♣ Extras Speciality toiletries
Conf Max 30 Thtr 30 Class 20 Board 20 Parking 20

| PUCKLECHURCH | Map 4 ST77 |

Orchard Cottage Bed & Breakfast

AA Advertised

tel: 0117 937 3284 18 Homefield Rd BS16 9QD
email: davidmstacey@gmail.com web: www.orchardcottagebandb.co.uk

Orchard Cottage is set adjacent to Pucklechurch conservation area, and is a completely private duplex apartment with its own entrance and free parking, available for B&B or self-catering rental. The apartment includes a private lounge with designer furniture, LCD TV, WiFi, iPod dock, fridge and tea/coffee making facilities. The bedroom has a fully tiled en suite shower-room, and a round window with a lovely view of the conservation area barn. The apartment is suitable for adults only.

Rooms 1 en suite S £53.10-£59; D £62.10-£69* Facilities STV FTV DVD iPod docking station TVL tea/coffee WiFi ♣ Parking 4 Notes ⊗ No Children 18yrs

| ST BRIAVELS | Map 4 SO50 |

The Florence

★★★★ GUEST ACCOMMODATION

tel: 01594 530830 fax: 01594 530830 Bigsweir GL15 6QQ
email: enquiries@florencehotel.co.uk web: www.florencehotel.co.uk
dir: On A466 between Monmouth & Chepstow

Located on the Wye Valley road, The Florence has delightful views across the river and stands in more than five acres of gardens with woodland walks. Bedrooms, some in the main house and the others in an adjacent cottage, come in a range of sizes and styles. Guests can enjoy cream teas in the garden, a drink in the snug, and choose from a wide selection of carefully prepared dishes at both lunch and dinner.

Rooms 4 en suite 4 annexe en suite (1 fmly) (2 GF) Facilities Lounge tea/coffee Dinner available Licensed WiFi Fishing ♣ Parking 30 Notes LB ⊗ No Children 10yrs Closed Nov-Feb

| STOW-ON-THE-WOLD | Map 10 SP12 |

Premier Collection

The Porch House

★★★★★ ◉◉ 🏠 INN

tel: 01451 870048 Digbeth St GL54 1BN

Originally built in 975AD the Porch House is reputed to be England's oldest inn and many of the original features can be seen today in the beautifully presented public areas. The inn was sympathetically refurbished in 2013 and has thirteen individually styled bedrooms. All are equipped to a high standard and WiFi is available throughout. Guests have a choice of cosy authentic bars, with exposed stonewalls and log fires, for casual dining. The award-winning restaurant is very well appointed and the unmissable breakfast features lots of local produce.

Rooms 13 en suite Facilities Dinner available

Woodlands Guest House

★★★★ GUEST ACCOMMODATION

tel: 01451 832346 Upper Swell GL54 1EW
email: amandak247@talktalk.net web: www.woodlands-guest-house.co.uk
dir: Upper Swell 1m from Stow-on-the-Wold, take B4077 (Tewkesbury Road)

Situated in the small hamlet of Upper Swell, Woodlands provides an ideal base for exploring the many charming nearby villages. This establishment enjoys delightful rural views and has comfortably appointed bedrooms with a good range of extra accessories. Breakfast is served in the welcoming dining room around the communal dining table. Off-road parking is available.

Rooms 5 en suite (2 GF) S £50-£65; D £75-£90* Facilities FTV tea/coffee WiFi
Parking 8 Notes LB ⊗

Aston House

★★★★ BED AND BREAKFAST

tel: 01451 830475 Broadwell GL56 0TJ
email: fja@astonhouse.net web: www.astonhouse.net
dir: A429 from Stow-on-the-Wold towards Moreton-in-Marsh, 1m right at x-rds to Broadwell, Aston House 0.5m on left

Peacefully located on the edge of the village of Broadwell, this is an ideal base from which to explore the Cotswolds. A warm and genuine welcome is guaranteed and every effort is made to ensure a relaxed and enjoyable stay. Great care and attention are hallmarks here, and bedrooms come equipped with many thoughtful extras such as electric blankets.

Rooms 2 en suite D £80-£90 Facilities FTV tea/coffee WiFi ♣ Stairlift
Extras Chocolates Parking 3 Notes ⊗ No Children 10yrs Closed Nov-Feb 🍽

Corsham Field Farmhouse (SP217249)

★★★★ FARMHOUSE

tel: 01451 831750 Bledington Rd GL54 1JH
email: farmhouse@corshamfield.co.uk web: www.corshamfield.co.uk
dir: A436 from Stow towards Chipping Norton. After 1m bear right onto B4450 (Bledington Rd), 1st farm on right in 0.5m

Corsham Field Farmhouse, which has views of the surrounding countryside from its elevated position, is a popular choice with walking groups and families. The modern bedrooms are practically equipped and located in two separate houses. Enjoyable breakfasts are taken in the spacious dining room, which also provides a lounge. The local pub is just a short walk away and has a reputation for good food.

Rooms 7 rms (5 en suite) (2 pri facs) (3 fmly) (2 GF) S £45-£60; D £55-£75*
Facilities FTV Lounge tea/coffee WiFi **Extras** Speciality toiletries, sweets **Parking** 10
Notes LB ⊗ ⊜ 100 acres arable

The Kings Head Inn

★★★★ ⊚ INN

tel: 01608 658365 **fax:** 01608 658902 **The Green, Bledington OX7 6XQ**
email: info@kingsheadinn.net **web:** www.kingsheadinn.net
dir: 4m SE off B4450

In prime village position on the delightful village green near the river, this 16th-century inn has spacious public areas with open fires, wobbly floors, beams and wood furnishings. The comfortable restaurant offers an excellent dining experience and the bedrooms have been creatively decorated and well furnished; some rooms are in a converted annexe.

Rooms 6 en suite 6 annexe en suite (3 GF) **Facilities** FTV TVL tea/coffee Dinner available Direct Dial WiFi **Parking** 24 **Notes** ⊗ Closed 25-26 Dec RS wkdays Closed every afternoon 3-6 low season No coaches

1 Woodchester Lodge

★★★★ ⊜ BED AND BREAKFAST

tel: 01453 872586 **Southfield Rd, North Woodchester GL5 5PA**
email: anne@woodchesterlodge.co.uk **web:** www.woodchesterlodge.co.uk
dir: A46 into Selsley Rd, 2nd left, house 200yds on left

Close to the newly re-routed Cotswold Way, this late Victorian former timber merchant's house is set in the peaceful village of North Woodchester and is just a short drive from Stroud. In its own landscaped gardens, this large house has spacious, sympathetically restored bedrooms and a comfortable lounge. Evening meals and freshly prepared breakfasts are not to be missed.

Rooms 3 rms (1 en suite) (2 pri facs) (1 fmly) S £55-£60; D £80-£85* **Facilities** FTV DVD Lounge TVL tea/coffee Dinner available WiFi ⊕ **Extras** Speciality toiletries **Parking** 4 **Notes** ⊗ Closed Xmas & Etr

Hunters Hall

★★★★ INN

tel: 01453 860393 **fax:** 01453 860707 **Kingscote GL8 8XZ**
email: huntershall.kingscote@greeneking.co.uk **web:** www.oldenglish.co.uk
dir: M4 junct 18, take A46 towards Stroud. Turn left signed Kingscote, to T-junct left, 0.5m on left

Situated close to Tetbury, this 16th-century inn has a wealth of charm and character, enhanced by beamed ceilings and open fires. There are three bars and a restaurant offering freshly prepared, home-cooked traditional food from an extensive menu. The bedrooms, situated in the converted stable block, are comfortable with a good range of extras. One of the ground-floor rooms has facilities for disabled guests. There is a large garden and play area.

Rooms 12 annexe en suite (1 fmly) (8 GF) **Facilities** tea/coffee Direct Dial Pool table **Parking** 100

The Great Tythe Barn Accommodation

★★★ GUEST ACCOMMODATION

tel: 01666 502475 **fax:** 01666 502358 **Folly Farm, Long Newton GL8 8XA**
email: info@gtb.co.uk **web:** www.gtb.co.uk
dir: M4 junct 17, B4014 signed Tetbury, on right after Welcome to Tetbury sign

Folly Farm is located amidst rolling countryside just a 10-minute walk from Tetbury. The well-equipped bedrooms are adjacent to the huge tithe barn, that together with the pleasant grounds surrounding it, makes this a popular wedding venue. Breakfast taken in the comfortable and relaxing Orangery, offers a well-presented continental selection.

Rooms 12 en suite (2 fmly) (6 GF) **Facilities** FTV tea/coffee Licensed WiFi ⊕ **Extras** Wine, flowers - chargeable **Conf** Max 180 Thtr 100 Class 64 Board 65 **Parking** 100 **Notes** ⊗ Civ Wed 180

The Bell

★★★★ INN

tel: 01684 293293 **fax:** 01684 295938 **52 Church St GL20 5SA**
email: 6408@greeneking.co.uk **web:** www.oldenglish.co.uk
dir: M5 junct 9, follow brown tourist signs for Tewkesbury Abbey, directly opposite Abbey

This 14th-century former coaching house is situated on the edge of the town, opposite the Norman abbey. The bar and lounge are the focal point of this atmospheric and friendly place where the large open fire provides warmth. Bedrooms offer good levels of comfort and quality with some welcome extra facilities provided.

Rooms 24 en suite (1 fmly) (4 GF) **Facilities** tea/coffee Direct Dial WiFi **Parking** 20

TEWKESBURY *continued*

Willow Cottages

★★★ GUEST ACCOMMODATION

tel: 01684 298599 **fax:** 01684 298599 **Shuthonger Common GL20 6ED**
email: RobBrd1@aol.com **web:** www.tewkesburybedandbreakfast.co.uk
dir: *1m N of Tewkesbury, on A38, house on right; or 1m S of M50 junct 1, on A38 house on left*

Located to the north of Tewkesbury in pretty rural surroundings, this welcoming house offers comfortable, homely bedrooms with efficient modern bathrooms and a cosy, pine-furnished breakfast room. Willow Cottages makes an excellent base for those visiting this picturesque area whether for work or pleasure.

Rooms 3 en suite (1 fmly) S fr £35; D fr £65* **Facilities** DVD tea/coffee Dinner available 🔒 **Parking** 6 **Notes** LB ⊗ ⊕

THORNBURY	Map 4 ST69

Thornbury Lodge

★★★★ GUEST ACCOMMODATION

tel: 01454 281144 **fax:** 01454 281177 **Bristol Rd BS35 3XL**
email: info@thornburygc.co.uk **web:** www.thornburygc.co.uk
dir: *M5 junct 16, A38 towards Thornbury. At lights (Berkeley Vale Motors) turn left, 1m on left*

With good access to both the M4 and M5, this lodge offers a popular retreat for both business and leisure guests, and is surrounded by pleasant scenery including a golf course. Dinner and breakfast can be enjoyed in the clubhouse-style dining area where an abundant choice is offered. Spacious and comfortable bedrooms are located in a lodge adjacent to the main clubhouse. An excellent golf driving range is also available.

Rooms 11 en suite (11 fmly) (7 GF) S £65-£80; D £80-£110 (room only)*
Facilities FTV TVL tea/coffee Dinner available Direct Dial Licensed WiFi ♿ 36 Driving

range Practice putting green **Conf** Max 165 Thtr 165 Class 60 Board 40 **Parking** 200 **Notes** LB ⊗ Civ Wed 120

WICK	Map 4 ST77

Southwood House B&B

★★★ BED AND BREAKFAST

tel: 0117 937 2649 & 07792 980087 **fax:** 0117 937 3361 **2 Bath Rd BS30 5RL**
email: mail@southwoodhouse.com **web:** www.southwoodhouse.com

Conveniently located with easy access to both Bristol and Bath, this welcoming, family-run B&B offers a peaceful ambience and comfortable rooms. Two rooms are located in the main house, and one larger room in an adjacent building. Breakfasts utilise fresh, local produce including eggs from the hens in the back garden, and also home-made jams. There's a good choice of pubs nearby including a couple within easy walking distance.

Rooms 2 en suite 1 annexe en suite S £50-£55; D £70-£75* **Facilities** FTV Lounge tea/coffee WiFi ♿ 18 🔒 **Parking** 3 **Notes** LB ⊗

WINCHCOMBE	Map 10 SP02

Sudeley Hill Farm (SP038276)

★★★★ 🏠 FARMHOUSE

tel: 01242 602344 **fax:** 01242 602344 **GL54 5JB**
email: scudamore4@aol.com
dir: *Exit B4632 in Winchcombe into Castle St. White Hart Inn on corner, farm 0.75m on left*

Located on an 800-acre mixed arable and sheep farm, this 15th-century stone farmhouse is full of original features including fires and exposed beams. Genuine hospitality is always on offer here together with a relaxed and welcoming atmosphere. The comfortable bedrooms are filled with thoughtful extras, and memorable breakfasts are served in the elegant dining room that overlooks the immaculate gardens.

Rooms 3 en suite (1 fmly) **Facilities** FTV DVD TVL tea/coffee 🔒 **Parking** 10 **Notes** ⊗ Closed Xmas ⊕ 800 acres sheep/arable

Wesley House

★★★★ ⊛⊛ 🏠 RESTAURANT WITH ROOMS

tel: 01242 602366 **fax:** 01242 609046 **High St GL54 5LJ**
email: enquiries@wesleyhouse.co.uk **web:** www.wesleyhouse.co.uk
dir: *In town centre*

This 15th-century, half-timbered property is named after John Wesley, founder of the Methodist Church, who stayed here while preaching in the town. Bedrooms are small but full of character. In the rear dining room, a unique lighting system changes colour to suit the mood required, and also highlights the various floral displays created by a world-renowned flower arranger. A glass atrium covers the outside terrace.

Rooms 5 en suite S £65-£75; D £75-£100* **Facilities** FTV Lounge tea/coffee Dinner available WiFi 🌐 **Conf** Thtr 30 Class 40 **Notes** ⊗ RS Sun eve & Mon Restaurant closed Civ Wed 60

See advert below

WITHINGTON   Map 10 SP01

Willowside House and Farm

[U]

tel: 01242 890557 **GL54 4DA**
email: info@willowside-estate.co.uk

Currently the rating for this establishment is not confirmed. This may be due to a change of ownership or because it has only recently joined the AA rating scheme.

Rooms 4 rms S £85-£95; D £120* **Notes** ⊛

GREATER MANCHESTER

ALTRINCHAM   Map 15 SJ78

Ash Farm Country House

★★★★ GUEST ACCOMMODATION

tel: 0161 929 9290 **Park Ln, Little Bollington WA14 4TJ**
email: ashfarm@googlemail.com **web:** www.ashfarm.co.uk
dir: *M56 junct 7 onto A56 at Lymm Rd into Park Ln, house at bottom of lane on right, just before The Swan with Two Nicks pub*

A warm welcome is guaranteed at this charming 18th-century National Trust farmhouse, which enjoys a peaceful location along a quiet country lane. The bedrooms are attractively presented and public areas include a book-filled lounge with its crackling log fire and cosy sofas. Free WiFi is available and the house is equally popular with business and leisure guests. The Dunham Massey Hall and Deerpark is a short stroll from the house while Manchester Airport is just a 15-minute drive away.

Rooms 3 en suite 1 annexe en suite (1 GF) S £49-£69; D £81-£96* **Facilities** FTV Lounge tea/coffee Licensed WiFi 🌐 **Extras** Robes **Conf** Max 10 Class 10 **Parking** 12 **Notes** LB ⊗ No Children 12yrs Closed 22 Dec-2 Jan

ASHTON-UNDER-LYNE   Map 16 SJ99

Broadoak

★★★★ INN

tel: 0161 330 2764 **fax:** 0161 339 6463 **69 Broadoak Rd OL6 8QD**
email: broadoakhotel@googlemail.com **web:** www.broadoakhotel.co.uk
dir: *M60 junct 23 follow signs to Oldham (A627). Right at lights into Wilshaw Ln. Right at rdbt, Broadoak on right*

This inn is popular with locals, and ideally situated for Manchester, with excellent transport links to the ring road and the city. Hearty meals are served in the pub restaurant by friendly staff, often accompanied by live jazz. Accommodation is comfortable with a traditional feel, equipped with modern travellers in mind. Family suite available. Functions are also catered for.

Rooms 7 en suite (1 fmly) S £55-£85; D £70-£100* **Facilities** FTV Lounge TVL tea/coffee Dinner available Direct Dial WiFi 🌐 **Conf** Max 100 Thtr 100 Class 50 Board 50 **Parking** 25 **Notes** LB ⊗ No coaches

The Governors House

★★★ INN

tel: 0161 488 4222 **43 Ravenoak Rd, Cheadle Hulme SK8 7EQ**
email: 4718@greeneking.co.uk web: www.oldenglish.co.uk

Located close to Manchester and Stockport, this establishment is an ideal base for exploring the Cheshire countryside. Bedrooms are tastefully decorated and furnished, with a good range of accessories. The bar and restaurant are popular with residents and locals, and alfresco dining can be enjoyed in the summer months. Children are welcome. Park and Fly Manchester service is available.

Rooms 9 en suite (1 fmly) **Facilities** FTV tea/coffee Dinner available Direct Dial WiFi **Conf** Thtr 20 Class 14 Board 14 **Parking** 87 **Notes** ⊗ No coaches

Wellcroft House

★★★★ 🏠 GUEST ACCOMMODATION

tel: 01457 875017 **Bleak Hey Nook OL3 5LY**
email: wellcrofthouse@hotmail.co.uk web: www.wellcrofthouse.co.uk
dir: *Off A62 on Standedge Foot Rd near A670 junct*

Commanding superb views down the valley below, this former weaver's cottage offers warm traditional hospitality to walkers on the Pennine Way and those touring the Pennine towns and villages. Modern comforts are provided in all bedrooms. Transport from local railway or walks is routinely provided by the friendly proprietors.

Rooms 3 rms (2 en suite) (1 pri facs) (1 GF) S £40-£50; D £60-£70* **Facilities** FTV TVL tea/coffee Dinner available WiFi Pool table 🔒 **Parking** 1 **Notes** LB ⊛

The Ascott

★★★★ GUEST ACCOMMODATION

tel: 0161 950 2453 fax: 0161 661 7063 **6 Half Edge Ln, Ellesmere Park, Eccles M30 9GJ**
email: ascotthotelmanchester@yahoo.co.uk web: www.ascotthotelmanchester.co.uk
dir: *M602 junct 2, left into Wellington Rd, 0.25m, right into Abbey Grove & left into Half Edge Ln*

Set in a mainly residential area close to major routes, this early Victorian house, once the home of the Mayor of Eccles, provides thoughtfully furnished bedrooms with smart modern bathrooms. A choice of breakfast rooms is available and there is an elegant lounge.

Rooms 14 en suite (1 fmly) (4 GF) S £45-£75; D £65-£95 (room only)* **Facilities** FTV Lounge TVL tea/coffee Direct Dial WiFi **Parking** 12 **Notes** ⊗ Closed 22 Dec-2 Jan RS Sun & Fri Closed 1-5pm

Thistlewood

★★★ GUEST HOUSE

tel: 0161 865 3611 fax: 0161 866 8133 **203 Urmston Ln, Stretford M32 9EF**
email: iain.campbell30@ntlworld.com web: www.thethistlewood.co.uk
dir: *M60 junct 7, A56 towards Stretford, left onto A5181 & Sandy Ln, left onto A5213*

Thistlewood is a grand Victorian house, set in attractive grounds in a residential area close to the M60, and within easy reach are Old Trafford football and cricket

grounds, as well as the airport. The bedrooms are well equipped, and the public rooms, including a lounge, are spacious and comfortable. Complimentary WiFi is also provided.

Rooms 9 en suite **Facilities** FTV DVD TVL tea/coffee Licensed WiFi 🔒 **Parking** 12 **Notes** ⊗

The Moorfield Arms

★★★★ INN

tel: 0161 427 1580 fax: 0161 427 1582 **Shiloh Rd SK6 5NE**
email: moorfieldarms@gmail.com web: www.moorfieldarms.co.uk
dir: *1m NE of Mellor. Exit A6015 towards Mellor, right into Shiloh Rd, 0.3m on left*

Located in an elevated position this 400-year old property enjoys stunning views of the surrounding countryside including Kinder Scout. Well-cooked meals and hearty breakfasts are served in spacious, comfortable public areas. The tastefully furnished, modern bedrooms are situated in a sympathetic barn conversion.

Rooms 4 annexe en suite (1 fmly) (3 GF) S £60; D £80-£100* **Facilities** FTV tea/coffee Dinner available **Conf** Max 90 Class 40 Board 25 **Parking** 100 **Notes** LB ⊗ Closed Mon (ex BHs)

The Old Bell Inn

★★★★★ 🅖 INN

tel: 01457 870130 fax: 01457 876597 **5 Huddersfield Rd, Delph OL3 5EG**
email: info@theoldbellinn.co.uk web: www.theoldbellinn.co.uk
dir: *M62 junct 22 onto A672. In Denshaw onto A6052, through Delph to x-rds with A62. Turn left, 100yds on left*

Situated in a rural village yet close to motorway links, the Old Bell has a village ambiance allied with refined service. Hospitality is a real strength of the young and enthusiastic team. Formerly a coaching inn dating back to 1835, it has been fully refurbished to a high standard. Bedrooms offer space, quality and comfort. The conservatory lounge is the perfect way to finish the evening after dinner in the modern restaurant.

Rooms 18 en suite (1 fmly) S £57.50; D £95-£120* **Facilities** FTV TVL tea/coffee Dinner available Direct Dial WiFi **Parking** 20 **Notes** ⊗

Innkeeper's Lodge Stockport

★★★ INN

tel: 0845 112 6027 **271 Wellington Rd, North Heaton Chapel SK4 5BP**
email: info@innkeeperslodge.com web: www.innkeeperslodge.com

At Innkeeper's Lodge you'll find accommodation with comfort and character in equal measure, and everything needed for a relaxing stay, from easy check-in and free parking to complimentary breakfast and a cosy pub serving great value food and drink on the doorstep. Each Lodge has quality rooms, and there are Lodges in a variety of locations from towns and cities to countryside settings across the UK.

Rooms 22 en suite (1 fmly) (1 GF) **Facilities** FTV tea/coffee Dinner available Direct Dial WiFi **Parking**

WIGAN
Map 15 SD50

The Beeches
★★★ RESTAURANT WITH ROOMS

tel: 01257 426432 & 421316   fax: 01257 427503 **School Ln, Standish WN6 0TD**
email: mail@beecheshotel.co.uk web: www.beecheshotel.co.uk
dir: *M6 junct 27, A5209 into Standish & into School Ln*

Just a mile away from junction 27 of the M6, this privately owned, spacious Victorian property is set in pleasant gardens. Bedrooms are well equipped and offer modern facilities. A wide choice of food is offered in the brasserie. The beautifully presented Piano Lounge also offers live entertainment on Friday and Saturday evenings.

Rooms 10 en suite (4 fmly) **Facilities** FTV Lounge tea/coffee Dinner available WiFi **Conf** Max 120 Thtr 100 Board 40 **Parking** 120 **Notes** ✖ Civ Wed 60

HAMPSHIRE

ALRESFORD
See New Alresford

ALTON
Map 5 SU73

Premier Collection

The Anchor Inn
★★★★★ ◉◉ RESTAURANT WITH ROOMS

tel: 01420 23261 **Lower Froyle GU34 4NA**
email: info@anchorinnatlowerfroyle.co.uk web: www.anchorinnatlowerfroyle.co.uk
dir: *From A3 follow Bentley signs & inn signs*

The Anchor Inn is located in the tranquil village of Lower Froyle. Luxury rooms are designed to reflect the traditional English inn style with charming decor, pictures and a selection of books. The restaurant welcomes both residents and non-residents with classic pub cooking, in impressive surroundings that feature wooden floors and period furnishings.

Rooms 5 en suite D £120-£150* **Facilities** STV FTV DVD tea/coffee Dinner available Direct Dial WiFi **Parking** 30 **Notes** Closed 25 Dec Civ Wed 60

The Angel
★★★★ GUEST ACCOMMODATION

tel: 01730 828111 fax: 01730 828057 **City Lodge, Gosport Rd GU34 3NN**
email: alton@citylodge.co.uk web: www.citylodge.co.uk
dir: *On A32 between Alton & West Meon*

The Angel is conveniently located on the A32 and has easy access to Alton, Winchester and Petersfield. The en suite bedrooms are very comfortable and have Hypnos beds, flat-screen TVs and free WiFi. Breakfast, lunch and dinner are served in the pub-style restaurant, and a popular carvery is offered each day.

Rooms 21 en suite 19 annexe en suite (2 fmly) (27 GF) S £49.95-£89.95; D £49.95-£89.95 (room only)* **Facilities** FTV Lounge tea/coffee Dinner available Licensed WiFi **Conf** Thtr 120 Class 60 Board 40 **Parking** 100 **Notes** LB ✖

The Swan
★★★ INN

tel: 01420 83777 fax: 01420 87975 **High St GU34 1AT**
email: 6518@greeneking.co.uk web: www.oldenglish.co.uk
dir: *B3004 into Alton, follow signs for town centre*

Located in the centre of the town, The Swan is a traditional coaching inn where guests have been welcomed for centuries. Bedrooms and bathrooms vary in size but are generally comfortably furnished and include some welcome extras. A varied choice of enjoyable meals is available from the all-day menu, and a good selection of well-prepared dishes is offered at breakfast.

Rooms 37 en suite (1 fmly) **Facilities** STV FTV TVL tea/coffee Dinner available Direct Dial WiFi ♿ 9 **Conf** Max 120 Thtr 120 Class 80 Board 80 **Parking** 50 **Notes** Civ Wed 120

ANDOVER
Map 5 SU34

May Cottage
★★★★ ⚑ BED AND BREAKFAST

tel: 01264 771241 & 07768 242166   fax: 01264 771770 **SP11 8LZ**
email: info@maycottage-thruxton.co.uk web: www.maycottage-thruxton.co.uk
dir: *3.5m W of Andover. Off A303 signed Thruxton (Village Only), opposite George Inn*

Excellent customer care is assured at this 18th-century, part-thatched house, which stands in pretty gardens in the heart of the village. Fine art and furnishings enhance the original features, and bedrooms are filled with a wealth of thoughtful extras. Comprehensive breakfasts are served in the attractive dining room.

Rooms 3 en suite (1 GF) **Facilities** STV FTV TVL tea/coffee WiFi ♿ 18 🔒 **Parking** 5 **Notes** ✖ 📧

The White Horse
★★★ 🍽 INN

tel: 01264 772401 & 07823 320043 **Thruxton SP11 8EE**
email: enquiries@whitehorsethruxton.co.uk web: www.whitehorsethruxton.co.uk
dir: *Off A303, 4m from Andover town centre*

Situated in the heart of the Test Valley, this 15th-century Grade II listed inn is ideally situated for both business and leisure guests. Beneath the thatch, a warm welcome is assured, with every effort made to ensure a relaxing and rewarding stay. Bedrooms are well appointed with good levels of comfort while public areas include a spacious bar, a choice of dining areas and some lovely gardens. Food is a delight with quality local produce utilised in flavoursome and creative dishes.

Rooms 4 en suite (2 fmly) S £55-£65; D £60-£75* **Facilities** FTV DVD TVL tea/coffee Dinner available WiFi 🔒 **Extras** Mineral water **Parking** 50 **Notes** No coaches

ANDOVER *continued*

The Hatchet Inn

★★★ INN

tel: 01264 730229 fax: 01264 730212 **Lower Chute SP11 9DX**
email: info@thehatchetinn.co.uk
dir: *A303 exit signed Weyhill/Monxton onto A343. Follow signs for The Chutes*

Dating back to the 13th century, this picturesque thatched inn is very much the traditional village local, providing a warm welcome to all. Bedrooms offer good levels of comfort with all the necessities required to ensure a relaxing and rewarding stay. A good choice is offered at dinner, whilst breakfast provides a tasty start to the day. Many original features remain within the bar and public areas, all adding to the unique charms of this popular hostelry.

Rooms 7 annexe en suite (2 fmly) (3 GF) S £70; D £80 **Facilities** FTV TVL tea/coffee Dinner available WiFi 🔒 **Conf** Max 20 Board 20 **Parking** 50 **Notes** LB

ASHURST | Map 5 SU31

Kingswood Cottage

★★★★ 🏠 BED AND BREAKFAST

tel: 023 8029 2582 & 07866 455322 **10 Woodlands Rd SO40 7AD**
email: kingswoodcottage@yahoo.co.uk web: www.kingswoodcottage.co.uk
dir: *Off A35 Lyndhurst to Ashurst, in village turn right over bridge signed Woodlands. Gates on right after 1st turning*

Kingswood Cottage is located in Ashurst village, a quiet area just three miles from Lyndhurst yet with easy access to Southampton, just six miles away. Bedrooms are comfortably appointed with traditional-style decor and furnishings. Bedrooms also benefit from views of the spacious well tended gardens which guests can enjoy year round. A hearty cooked or continental breakfast is served in the dining room and conservatory area. Guests can enjoy home-made refreshments on arrival.

Rooms 3 en suite S £35-£55; D £65-£80* **Facilities** FTV TVL tea/coffee WiFi 🔒
Extras Bottled water - complimentary; robes **Parking** 3 **Notes** LB ⊗ No Children 5yrs Closed 12 Dec-2 Jan ⊕

Forest Gate Lodge

★★★★ BED AND BREAKFAST

tel: 023 8029 3026 fax: 023 8029 3026 **161 Lyndhurst Rd SO40 7AW**
email: forestgatelodge161@hotmail.co.uk web: www.forestgatelodge.co.uk

Forest Gate Lodge is located in Ashurst, just a short drive from all that the New Forest has to offer. Bedrooms have modern decor and furnishings, and come equipped with digital TV, DVD and free WiFi access. There is a guest lounge on the ground floor and guests can enjoy a cooked or continental breakfast daily in the dining room. Off-road parking is available, and both restaurants and pubs are within a short walking distance from the property.

Rooms 5 en suite (1 fmly) **Facilities** FTV DVD iPod docking station TVL tea/coffee WiFi ⛷ Riding 🔒 **Parking** 6 **Notes** LB ⊗ No Children 5-12yrs ⊕

The Willows

★★★ BED AND BREAKFAST

tel: 023 8029 2745 & 07980 937862 **72 Lyndhurst Rd SO40 7BE**
email: thewillowsashurst@hotmail.com web: www.thewillowsbandb.co.uk
dir: *M27 junct 3 onto M271. 1.5m, at rdbt take A35 signed Lyndhurst. In Ashurst, The Willows on right before bus stop*

This property is on the edge of the New Forest, and is convenient for Ashurst railway station and the M27. The bedrooms are traditional in style but with modern fixtures

and furnishings including free WiFi; the bathrooms have high-quality fixtures. Guests can enjoy a cooked or continental breakfast in the dining room.

Rooms 3 en suite (1 fmly) S £42-£47; D £67-£72* **Facilities** FTV tea/coffee WiFi **Parking** 4 **Notes** No Children 5yrs Closed 2wks Xmas & New Year

---

BARTON-ON-SEA | Map 5 SZ29

Premier Collection

Pebble Beach

★★★★★ ◎ 🍴 RESTAURANT WITH ROOMS

tel: 01425 627777 fax: 01425 610689 **Marine Dr BH25 7DZ**
email: mail@pebblebeach-uk.com web: www.pebblebeach-uk.com
dir: *A35 from Southampton onto A337 to New Milton, left into Barton Court Av to clifftop*

Situated on the clifftop, the restaurant at Pebble Beach boasts stunning views towards The Needles. Bedrooms and bathrooms (situated above the restaurant) are well equipped and provide a range of accessories to enhance guest comfort. A freshly cooked breakfast is served in the main restaurant.

Rooms 4 rms (3 en suite) (1 pri facs) S £69.95; D £89.95-£99.95* **Facilities** FTV tea/coffee Dinner available WiFi **Extras** Speciality toiletries **Conf** Max 8 Thtr 8 Class 8 Board 8 **Parking** 20 **Notes** ⊗ RS 25 Dec & 1 Jan dinner not available No coaches

---

BASINGSTOKE | Map 5 SU65

Innkeeper's Lodge Basingstoke

★★★ INN

tel: 0845 112 6113 **Andover Rd, Clerken Green, Oakley RG23 7EP**
email: info@innkeeperslodge.com web: www.innkeeperslodge.com

Located on the quiet outskirts of the town, Innkeeper's Lodge Basingstoke provides a good level of comfort and quality through the recently refurbished accommodation and public areas. Bedrooms are well appointed and fitted with extras tailored to the modern traveller. Meals and drinks are served in The Beach Arms, adjacent to the Lodge; a wide choice on the menu is sure to suit any appetite and all tastes.

Rooms 22 en suite (4 fmly) (22 GF) **Facilities** FTV tea/coffee Dinner available Direct Dial WiFi **Parking** 45

BRANSGORE | Map 5 SZ19

Tothill House

★★★★ BED AND BREAKFAST

tel: 01425 674414 **Black Ln, off Forest Rd BH23 8EA**
email: enquiries@tothillhouse.com web: www.tothillhouse.com
dir: *M27 onto A31 or A35, house is 0.75m NE of Bransgore centre*

Built for an admiral in 1908, Tothill House is located in the southern part of the New Forest. The garden backs on to the forest, and is frequently visited by deer, ponies and other wildlife. The spacious bedrooms are furnished to a high standard, reflecting the character of the house. There is an elegant library, and a generous breakfast is served in the dining room.

Rooms 3 rms (2 en suite) (1 pri facs) D £80* **Facilities** STV FTV Lounge tea/coffee WiFi 🔒 **Parking** 6 **Notes** ⊗ No Children 16yrs Closed Nov-Feb ⊕

BROCKENHURST
Map 5 SU30

The Filly Inn

★★★★ INN

tel: 01590 623449 **Lymington Rd SO42 7UF**
web: www.fillyinn.co.uk

The Filly Inn has been thoughtfully refurbished to offer comfortable accommodation especially after walking one of the many local routes across the heathland and woodland of the New Forest. Local produce features heavily on the menu with local ales and ciders on offer at the bar.

Rooms 5 en suite **Facilities** FTV tea/coffee Dinner available WiFi **Parking** 40

CLANFIELD
Map 5 SU71

The Rising Sun Inn

★★★ INN

tel: 023 9259 6975 & 07702 262339 **North Ln PO8 0RN**
email: enquiries@therisingsunclanfield.co.uk **web:** www.therisingsunclanfield.co.uk
dir: A3 between Petersfield & Horndean, exit signed Clanfield/Chalton. Follow brown signs

The family-run Rising Sun Inn is in the quiet village of Clanfield yet just off the A3 and so within a short drive of both Portsmouth and Chichester. The three bedrooms are fresh and modern with comfortable accommodation, well equipped with both digital TVs and WiFi. Food is served daily and guests can enjoy a selection of traditional pub classics. A cooked and continental breakfast is served each morning in the restaurant.

Rooms 3 en suite **Facilities** FTV iPod docking station tea/coffee Dinner available WiFi 🏐 **Parking** 24 **Notes** No coaches

COSHAM
Map 5 SU60

Red Lion

[U]

tel: 023 9238 2041 **London Rd PO6 3EE**
email: redlionhotel@orchidpubs.co.uk

Currently the rating for this establishment is not confirmed. This may be due to a change of ownership or because it has only recently joined the AA rating scheme.

Rooms 16 en suite S £60; D £60 (room only)* **Facilities** FTV DVD TVL tea/coffee Licensed WiFi **Parking** 20 **Notes** ⊗

DUMMER
Map 5 SU54

Tower Hill House

★★★ BED AND BREAKFAST

tel: 01256 398340 **fax:** 01256 398340 **Tower Hill, Winchester Rd RG25 2AL**
email: martin.hyndman@virgin.net **web:** www.accommodationinbasingstoke.co.uk
dir: In village. M3 junct 7, A30 towards Winchester, 2nd left, opposite sign for North Waltham

Ideally situated for access to the M3 and A30, while overlooking fields and countryside, this family-run bed and breakfast is in the pretty village of Dummer, just 10 minutes away from the centre of Basingstoke. Bedrooms are simply, but comfortably furnished and a well-prepared breakfast is served in the cheerful dining room.

Rooms 4 rms (2 en suite) (1 pri facs) S £25-£35; D £50-£60* **Facilities** tea/coffee WiFi **Parking** 6

EMSWORTH
Map 5 SU70

36 on the Quay

★★★★★ ⊛⊛⊛ RESTAURANT WITH ROOMS

tel: 01243 375592 & 372257 **47 South St PO10 7EG**
web: www.36onthequay.co.uk
dir: Last building on right in South St, which runs from square in centre of Emsworth

Occupying a prime position with far-reaching views over the estuary, this 16th-century house is the scene for some accomplished and exciting cuisine. The elegant restaurant occupies centre stage with peaceful pastel shades, local art and crisp napery together with glimpses of the bustling harbour outside. The contemporary bedrooms offer style, comfort and thoughtful extras.

Rooms 5 en suite 2 annexe en suite **Facilities** FTV iPod docking station tea/coffee Dinner available WiFi **Parking** 6 **Notes** LB Closed 3wks Jan, 1wk late May & 1wk late Oct

Hollybank House

★★★★ BED AND BREAKFAST

tel: 01243 375502 **Hollybank Ln PO10 7UN**
email: anna@hollybankhouse.com **web:** www.hollybankhouse.com
dir: 1m N of town centre. A259 onto B2148, 1m right into Southleigh Rd, 3rd left into Hollybank Ln, house at top

This Georgian country house stands in a 10-acre woodland garden complete with tennis court on the outskirts of Emsworth, and looks out to Chichester Harbour. The attractive entrance hall leads into spacious lounge and dining rooms where light streams through the deep Georgian windows. Bedrooms are comfortable and home-made goods feature on the breakfast menu. Emsworth has a variety of restaurants, pubs and harbour walks.

Rooms 4 rms (3 en suite) (1 pri facs) (1 fmly) S £50-£65; D £75-£95* **Facilities** FTV DVD Lounge tea/coffee WiFi 🌣 🐾 🏐 **Parking** 85

The Jingles

★★★★ GUEST ACCOMMODATION

tel: 01243 373755 **fax:** 01243 431377 **77 Horndean Rd PO10 7PU**
email: info@thejingles.co.uk **web:** www.thejingles.co.uk
dir: A3 (M) junct 2, follow signs for Emsworth, 4m, 1st building in Emsworth on right

The Jingles is a family-run business, located in the charming maritime village of Emsworth. Situated adjacent to open farmland, it's a great location for discovering both Portsmouth and Chichester. All bedrooms are en suite and decorated to a high standard. The dining room is the setting for a cooked English breakfast, and a drawing room is available for relaxing in. WiFi is available if required.

Rooms 28 en suite (2 fmly) (7 GF) S £49-£79; D £69-£89 **Facilities** FTV Lounge tea/coffee Licensed WiFi 🏐 **Parking** 35 **Notes** LB ⊗ Closed 24 Dec-2 Jan

The Crown

★★★ INN

tel: 01243 372806 **fax:** 01243 370082 **High St PO10 7AW**
email: thecrownemsworth@aol.com

An historic property conveniently located in the centre of town with ample parking at the back. Long winding stairs and uneven corridors lead to well-appointed bedrooms which offer a range of amenities such as flat-screen TVs and WiFi. Freshly prepared food is served in the well-stocked bar and the restaurant.

Rooms 9 rms (7 en suite) (2 pri facs) (2 fmly) **Facilities** FTV tea/coffee Dinner available WiFi ♿ 18 **Conf** Max 48 Thtr 48 Class 36 Board 24 **Parking** 16

FAREHAM   Map 5 SU50

Wisteria House

★★★★ BED AND BREAKFAST

tel: 01329 511940 & 07742 400242 **14 Mays Ln, Stubbington PO14 2EP**
email: info@wisteria-house.co.uk web: www.wisteria-house.co.uk
dir: *M27 junct 9, A27 to Fareham. Right onto B3334, at rdbt left into Mays Ln*

Wisteria House is located on the edge of the village of Stubbington, just a short walk from local amenities, and only one mile from the beach at Lee-on-the-Solent. Attention to detail is key at this B&B, guaranteeing a return visit by those who stay here. The charming and comfortable bedrooms have en suite bathrooms, are located on the ground floor, and also have WiFi. Off-road parking is available.

Rooms 2 en suite (2 GF) S £50-£55; D £65-£70* **Facilities** FTV tea/coffee WiFi **Parking** 2 **Notes** ⊗ No Children 8yrs

The Bugle

★★ INN

tel: 01329 841888 **The Square, High St, Titchfield PO14 4AF**
email: reception@thebuglehotel.co.uk web: www.thebuglehotel.co.uk
dir: *M27 junct 9 onto A27 towards Fareham. Right into Titchfield village*

The Bugle is located in a beautiful village popular with visitors and locals alike. The accommodation consists of well equipped en suite rooms and two single rooms with shared facilities, all located in the main house. The restaurant has a friendly atmosphere and offers a wide range of freshly prepared dishes, and a large drinks selection including beers and wines which are available all day.

Rooms 8 rms (6 en suite) (1 fmly) S £45-£55; D £70-£95 (room only)* **Facilities** FTV DVD tea/coffee Dinner available WiFi 🎱 **Conf** Max 40 Thtr 40 Class 40 Board 30 **Parking** 15 **Notes** ⊗

HAVANT   Map 5 SU70

The Bear

★★★ INN

tel: 023 9248 6501 fax: 023 9247 0551 **15-17 East St PO9 1AA**
email: 9110@greeneking.co.uk web: www.oldenglish.co.uk

This Grade II listed former coaching inn is located in the heart of the town and has informal public rooms which include a small cocktail bar and the Elizabethan public bar. The fully equipped bedrooms are well laid out and are suited to both business and leisure guests.

Rooms 42 en suite (3 fmly) **Facilities** TVL tea/coffee Dinner available Direct Dial WiFi Pool table **Conf** Max 100 Thtr 100 Class 40 Board 40 **Parking** 80

HAWKLEY   Map 5 SU72

The Hawkley Inn

★★★★ ⬤ INN

tel: 01730 827205 **Pococks Ln GU33 6NE**
email: info@hawkleyinn.co.uk web: www.hawkleyinn.co.uk
dir: *A3 Liss rdbt towards Liss B3006. Right at Spread Eagle, follow brown tourist signs. After 3m, left to village centre*

The Hawkley Inn captures all that is required of a traditional inn and more. There are four beautifully appointed double rooms, which offer all the comforts required

by discerning travellers. The bar is well stocked including a range of real ales and the chef-proprietor is passionate about local produce and prepares award-winning dishes. The rear garden is a haven of tranquillity.

Rooms 4 en suite 1 annexe en suite (1 fmly) (1 GF) D £69-£119* **Facilities** FTV tea/coffee Dinner available WiFi ⬆ 18 **Parking** 4

HAYLING ISLAND   Map 5 SU70

Ravensdale

★★★★ BED AND BREAKFAST

tel: 023 9246 3203 & 07802 188259 **19 St Catherines Rd PO11 0HF**
email: phil.taylor@tayloredprint.co.uk web: www.ravensdale-hayling.co.uk
dir: *A27 onto A3023 at Langstone, cross Hayling Bridge, 3m to mini rdbt, right into Manor Rd, 1m. Right by Barley Mow into Station Rd, 3rd left into St Catherines Rd*

A warm welcome awaits you at this comfortable home, quietly situated near the beach and golf course. Bedrooms are attractive, very comfortable and enhanced with numerous thoughtful extras. One room is a triple and has its own separate facilities. Home cooking can be enjoyed at breakfast in the dining room, and there is also a lounge area.

Rooms 3 rms (2 en suite) (1 pri facs) S £45; D £70 **Facilities** FTV DVD TVL tea/coffee WiFi **Extras** Flowers, chocolates **Parking** 4 **Notes** ⊗ No Children 8yrs Closed last 2wks Dec 🚭

HIGHCLERE   Map 5 SU45

The Yew Tree

★★★★ ⬤ INN

tel: 01635 253360 **Hollington Cross RG20 9SE**
email: info@theyewtree.co.uk

Situated in Highclere, this attractive 17th-century country inn has recently undergone some refurbishment. Each room is decorated with William Morris print wallpaper, retaining traditional features, and giving an overall cosy feel. Great British cooking can be enjoyed in the attractively decorated restaurant, where good use is made of high quality produce and fresh ingredients.

Rooms 8 rms D £95-£120* **Facilities** Dinner available

HOOK   Map 5 SU75

Oaklea Guest House

★★★★ GUEST HOUSE

tel: 01256 762673 **London Rd RG27 9LA**
email: reception@oakleaguesthouse.co.uk web: www.oakleaguesthouse.co.uk
dir: *From village centre, 500yds on right on A30 towards Basingstoke*

You can be sure of a warm welcome at this Victorian house located just a short drive from the M3. Bedrooms are well appointed with modern facilities many with pine furniture. There is a comfortable lounge with soft, leather sofas, and the large dining room has a bar.

Rooms 15 en suite (2 fmly) (1 GF) **Facilities** FTV DVD TVL tea/coffee Licensed WiFi **Extras** Bottled water - complimentary **Parking** 15

The Poachers Inn

★★★★ ⬤ INN

tel: 01256 862218 **Alton Rd, South Warnborough RG29 1RP**
email: mail@thepoacherinn.com web: www.thepoacherinn.com

Located in the peaceful village of South Warnborough, this traditional village inn has been refurbished to a very high standard. Bedrooms are tastefully appointed, with quality fabrics and comfortable beds. The popular inn offers an enjoyable dining experience; menus feature a wide range of home-made dishes supplemented by a regular changing specials menu. Ample parking is available.

Rooms 5 en suite S £65; D £70-£85* **Facilities** FTV iPod docking station tea/coffee Dinner available WiFi **Parking** 20 **Notes** No coaches

Cherry Lodge Guest Accommodation

★★★ GUEST ACCOMMODATION

tel: 01256 762532 **Reading Rd RG27 9DB**
email: cherrylodge@btinternet.com
dir: *On B3349 (Reading Rd), next to Hook garden centre*

This pleasant bungalow is peacefully set back from the Reading Road, and is convenient for the M3. Cherry Lodge provides extremely friendly hospitality and is popular with business guests. Breakfast is served from 6.30am. A spacious lounge is provided and bedrooms are well equipped.

Rooms 7 en suite (7 GF) S £39-£49; D £60-£70* **Facilities** FTV DVD Lounge tea/coffee Direct Dial WiFi **Extras** Fridge **Parking** 15 **Notes** ⊗ Closed Xmas-New Year

HURSLEY   Map 5 SU42

The Kings Head

★★★★ ⬤ INN

tel: 01962 775208 **Main Rd SO21 2JW**
email: enquiries@kingsheadhursley.co.uk web: www.kingsheadhursley.co.uk

The Kings Head is a traditional inn a short drive from Winchester in an idyllic quiet village. Bar and restaurant areas are smart yet cosy, and quality food is available. Rooms are exceptionally well presented with comfortable beds and a host of extras to make your stay even more enjoyable. Full English breakfast can be enjoyed each morning in the Snug.

Rooms 8 rms **Facilities** Dinner available

HYTHE   Map 5 SU40

Four Seasons B&B

★★★★ GUEST ACCOMMODATION

tel: 023 8084 5151 & 07973 194660   fax: 023 8084 6285 **Hamilton Rd SO45 3PD**
email: the-four-seasons@btconnect.com web: www.the-four-seasons.co.uk
dir: *M27 junct 2 onto A326. Continue towards Fawley/Hythe, at 4th rdbt take exit signed Hythe & Marine Park, on left after 500mtrs*

The Four Seasons B&B is located in Hythe with easy access to both Southampton and the New Forest. Bedrooms are tastefully decorated with modern decor and furnishings, and rooms are equipped with Freeview TV and free WiFi throughout. The dining room and guest lounge is open plan. A cooked and continental breakfast is available and, for the early riser, is served from 6:30am on weekdays.

Rooms 11 rms (6 en suite) (1 fmly) (1 GF) S £30-£42; D £60-£72* **Facilities** FTV DVD TVL tea/coffee WiFi 🔒 **Parking** 11 **Notes** LB ⊗

ISLE OF WIGHT

See Isle of Wight (following Hertfordshire)

LEE-ON-THE-SOLENT   Map 5 SU50

West Wind Guest House

★★★★ GUEST ACCOMMODATION

tel: 023 9255 2550 **197 Portsmouth Rd PO13 9AA**
email: info@west-wind.co.uk web: www.west-wind.co.uk
dir: *M27 junct 11 follow Gosport & Fareham signs, B3385 for Lee-on-the-Solent. At seafront left along Marine Pde, 600mtrs left into Portsmouth Rd. West Wind on right*

This family-run guest accommodation is found in a quiet, residential area within walking distance of the beach and town centre. The bedrooms are comfortable and nicely appointed, some with flat-screen TV and all with free WiFi. There is an attractive breakfast room and off-street parking.

Rooms 6 en suite (1 GF) S fr £50; D fr £65* **Facilities** FTV DVD iPod docking station tea/coffee WiFi **Parking** 6 **Notes** ⊗ No Children 8yrs

LISS   Map 5 SU72

The Jolly Drover

★★★★ INN

tel: 01730 893137 fax: 0161 490 8048 **London Rd, Hillbrow GU33 7QL**
email: thejollydrover@googlemail.com web: www.thejollydrover.co.uk
dir: *From Liss on B3006, at junct with B2070*

Situated on the West Sussex/Hampshire border this traditional inn prides itself on local ales, good home-cooked food and a warm welcome. It is popular with both business and leisure guests due to its close proximity to Petersfield and transport links. Rooms are situated in the traditional outbuildings, and have been fitted in a comfortable modern style with all expected guest amenities. Free WiFi is available. A large beer garden to the rear of the inn is the perfect place to enjoy a summer's day, and ample parking is available.

Rooms 6 annexe rms (6 pri facs) (1 fmly) (6 GF) S £60-£70; D £80-£90* **Facilities** FTV tea/coffee Dinner available WiFi **Extras** Bottled water **Parking** 48 **Notes** LB ⊗ Closed 25-26 Dec & 1 Jan

LYMINGTON   Map 5 SZ39

Britannia House

★★★★ BED AND BREAKFAST

tel: 01590 672091 & 07808 792639 **Station St SO41 3BA**
email: enquiries@britannia-house.com web: www.britannia-house.com
dir: *Follow signs to railway station, at corner of Station St & Mill Ln*

Built in 1865 as the Britannia Commercial Hotel, today's Britannia House occupies a quiet location only two minutes' walk from the quay, waterfront and the High Street with its many shops, pubs and restaurants. Rooms are elegant with a refined air, there is a charming lounge and breakfast is taken in the homely kitchen.

Rooms 3 en suite 2 annexe en suite (2 GF) S £55-£95; D £85-£99 **Facilities** FTV Lounge tea/coffee WiFi 🔒 **Parking** 4 **Notes** LB ⊗ No Children 10yrs

LYNDHURST   Map 5 SU30

Little Hayes

★★★★ GUEST ACCOMMODATION

tel: 023 8028 3816 **43 Romsey Rd SO43 7AR**
email: wendy@littlehayes.co.uk **web:** www.littlehayes.co.uk
dir: *M27 junct 1, A337. On entering Lyndhurst, 200yds on right*

Little Hayes is a friendly, well-run establishment located a few moments' walk from the town centre, pubs and restaurants. Breakfast makes best use of local produce and is served in the cosy dining room. This is an ideal base for touring the New Forest National Park, and benefits from off-road parking.

Rooms 5 rms (4 en suite) (1 pri facs) S £60; D £70-£100* **Facilities** FTV DVD tea/coffee WiFi 🔒 **Parking** 6 **Notes** ⊗ No Children 14yrs Closed Dec-Jan

Temple Lodge

★★★★ 🏠 GUEST ACCOMMODATION

tel: 023 8028 2392 **fax:** 023 8000 0091 **2 Queens Rd SO43 7BR**
email: templelodge@btinternet.com **web:** www.templelodge-guesthouse.com
dir: *M27 junct 2/3 onto A35 to Ashurst & Lyndhurst. Temple Lodge on 2nd corner on right, opposite forest*

Temple Lodge is a well appointed Victorian house with very friendly hosts, who welcome back returning guests year after year. Guests will enjoy easy access to the New Forest and Lyndhurst town centre, with good off-road parking. The bedrooms are furnished with comfort in mind and feature lots of thoughtful extras including mini-bars, some bedrooms have sofas too. The breakfasts should not be missed.

Rooms 6 en suite (1 fmly) D £70-£120* **Facilities** FTV DVD TVL tea/coffee WiFi 🔒 **Extras** Mini-fridge with snacks/soft drinks - chargeable **Parking** 6 **Notes** LB ⊗ No Children 12yrs

Whitemoor House

★★★★ 🏠 GUEST ACCOMMODATION

tel: 023 8028 3043 **Southampton Rd SO43 7BU**
email: whitemoorhouse@talktalk.net **web:** www.whitemoorhouse.co.uk
dir: *0.5m NE of town centre on A35*

Situated just on the edge of Lyndhurst, this very well run establishment offers comfortable, smartly-decorated bedrooms, well equipped and all en suite. Breakfast is impressive, with home-made preserves and an extensive selection of cold items. There are plenty of hot options too, most sourced from local suppliers. Guests can relax in the cosy lounge, which opens onto the patio, overlooking the well-kept grounds. There is also an honesty bar, free WiFi and parking on site.

Rooms 6 en suite (1 fmly) S £56-£61; D £72-£92* **Facilities** FTV TVL tea/coffee Licensed WiFi 👣 18 🔒 **Extras** Home-made cake - complimentary **Parking** 7 **Notes** ⊗ No Children 12yrs Closed Nov-7 Jan 🐾

Clayhill House

★★★★ BED AND BREAKFAST

tel: 023 8028 2304 **SO43 7DE**
email: clayhillhouse@tinyworld.co.uk **web:** www.clayhillhouse.co.uk
dir: *Exit M27 junct 2. A35 to Lyndhurst then A337 signed Brockenhurst, 0.75m*

Set at the edge of this attractive town, and convenient for visiting the New Forest and coastal attractions nearby, Clayhill House is a well-appointed property, which offers friendly service and comfortable accommodation. The bedrooms are particularly well equipped with thoughtful extras. Freshly cooked breakfasts are served in the dining room.

Rooms 3 en suite (1 fmly) S £50-£80; D £70-£160* **Facilities** FTV tea/coffee WiFi **Parking** 6 **Notes** LB ⊗ No Children 14yrs Closed 22 Dec-4 Jan

The Rufus House

★★★★ 🏠 GUEST ACCOMMODATION

tel: 023 8028 2930 **Southampton Rd SO43 7BQ**
email: stay@rufushouse.co.uk **web:** www.rufushouse.co.uk
dir: *From Lyndhurst centre onto A35 (Southampton Rd), 300yds on left*

Located on the edge of town, this delightful family-run Victorian property is well situated for exploring the New Forest. The brightly decorated bedrooms are appointed to a high standard, while the turret lounge and the garden terrace are great spots for relaxing.

Rooms 10 en suite (1 fmly) (2 GF) **Facilities** tea/coffee WiFi 👣 18 **Parking** 12 **Notes** ⊗ No Children 5yrs

Heather House

★★★ GUEST ACCOMMODATION

tel: 023 8028 4409 **fax:** 023 8028 4431 **Southampton Rd SO43 7BQ**
email: enquiries@heatherhouse.co.uk **web:** www.heatherhouse.co.uk
dir: M27 junct 1, A337 to Lyndhurst. At lights in centre turn left, establishment 800yds on left

This impressive double-fronted Edwardian house stands in attractive gardens on the edge of town and enjoys views of the New Forest. Bedrooms are comfortably appointed with one especially good for families. Breakfast is served in the pleasant dining room.

Rooms 10 en suite (1 fmly) **Facilities** FTV TVL tea/coffee Licensed WiFi 🔒
Parking 12 **Notes** ⊗ No Children 7yrs Closed 23 Dec–2 Jan

■ NEW ALRESFORD — Map 5 SU53

Haygarth

★★★ ⚑ BED AND BREAKFAST

tel: 01962 732715 & 07986 372895 **82 Jack Lyns Ln SO24 9LJ**
dir: B3046 from New Alresford centre for Cheriton, Haygarth 0.5m on right

A family house, Haygarth is peacefully located, yet within easy reach of the M3 and is convenient for visiting Winchester. Cosy bedrooms are traditionally furnished and well equipped. Breakfast is served in the dining room or conservatory, overlooking the pretty garden complete with a fish pond. There is also a guest lounge.

Rooms 3 rms (2 en suite) (1 pri facs) (3 GF) **Facilities** TVL tea/coffee **Parking** 7
Notes ⊗ 🖃

■ OVERTON — Map 5 SU54

Premier Collection

Mallards

★★★★★ BED AND BREAKFAST

tel: 01256 770039 **Trims Court, High St RG25 3JZ**
email: info@mallardsoverton.co.uk **web:** www.mallardsoverton.co.uk
dir: M3 junct 8 onto A303 towards Andover. W of Popham Services onto Overton Road, N for 4m. Left at lights onto B3400 (High St), Trims Court on right

A warm reception is assured here. Mallards is ideally located for those wishing to explore Winchester and Highclere, with excellent rail and bus links just a few minutes away. There are three en suite bedrooms offering luxurious comfort and quality. The garden backs onto the River Test, well known as a "home of fly-fishing", and is a haven for birds and wildlife. A good breakfast is served around the family-style table.

Rooms 3 en suite (1 GF) S £50–£65; D £70–£80* **Facilities** FTV DVD iPod docking station tea/coffee WiFi Fishing 🔒 **Extras** Fridge **Parking** 3 **Notes** LB ⊗ No Children 16yrs

■ PETERSFIELD — Map 5 SU72

The Old Drum

★★★★★ 🏵 INN

tel: 01730 300544 **fax:** 0872 115 4202 **16 Chapel St GU32 3DP**
email: info@theolddrum.co.uk **web:** www.theolddrum.co.uk

The Old Drum is situated in the delightful market town of Petersfield, part of the South Downs National Park. A refurbished inn, contemporary in style yet keeping the warmth and tradition of a country pub; the three open fires are a welcome addition in the winter, while the eclectic style is refreshing. A range of real ales is available from the bar, many of which are supplied by local microbreweries. Bedrooms have been tastefully appointed and offer amenities for both the leisure and business traveller. Award-winning cuisine is served, with a true local and seasonal slant making this a memorable experience. Nothing is too much trouble for the hands-on proprietor and friendly staff, not forgetting Digby, the resident dog.

Rooms 2 en suite S £70–£90; D £80–£90* **Facilities** FTV tea/coffee Dinner available WiFi 🔒 **Notes** Closed 5–14 Jan No coaches

■ PORTSMOUTH & SOUTHSEA — Map 5 SU60

St Margaret's Lodge

★★★★ GUEST HOUSE

tel: 023 9282 0097 **fax:** 023 9282 0097 **3 Craneswater Gate PO4 0NZ**
email: enquiries@stmargarets-southsea.co.uk **web:** www.stmargarets-southsea.co.uk
dir: From South Parade Pier E along A288 St Helens Parade, 2nd left

This establishment is in a quiet residential area close to the seafront and town centre. The attractive bedrooms have co-ordinated soft furnishings and many thoughtful extras. Breakfast is served in the smart dining room and there are two lounges.

Rooms 14 en suite (1 fmly) S £40–£48; D £65–£95* **Facilities** FTV Lounge TVL tea/coffee WiFi **Parking** 5 **Notes** ⊗ No Children 3yrs Closed 21 Dec–2 Jan

■ RAKE — Map 5 SU82

The Flying Bull Inn

★★★★ INN

tel: 01730 892285 **fax:** 01730 893149 **London Rd GU33 7JB**
email: info@theflyingbull.com **web:** www.theflyingbull.com
dir: From A3 Sbound, take exit for Liphook & follow signs for B2070. In Rake on right hand side

This traditional inn is set in the village of Rake, near Liss in Hampshire and close to both Petersfield and Haslemere. Bedrooms and bathrooms are well appointed offering guests comfortable accommodation. There is plenty of parking available, and a well tended outside seating area in addition to the bar and restaurant. A cooked or continental breakfast is served in the restaurant; lunch and dinner are available daily.

Rooms 7 en suite (1 fmly) (5 GF) **Facilities** FTV Lounge tea/coffee Dinner available WiFi ⊕ ♨ 18 🔒 **Parking** 35

Little Forest Lodge

☆☆☆☆ GUEST HOUSE

tel: 01425 478848 **fax:** 01425 473564 **Poulner Hill BH24 3HS**
web: www.littleforestlodge.co.uk
dir: 1.5m E of Ringwood on A31

A warm welcome is given to guests, and their pets, at this charming Edwardian house where the manicured lawns run in two acres of woodland. Bedrooms are pleasantly decorated and equipped with thoughtful extras. Both the attractive wood-panelled dining room and the delightful lounge, with bar and wood-burning fire, overlook the gardens.

Rooms 6 en suite (3 fmly) (1 GF) S £45-£50; D £80 **Facilities** FTV Lounge tea/coffee Licensed ⅃ ⚿ **Parking** 10

Moortown Lodge

☆☆☆☆ GUEST ACCOMMODATION

tel: 01425 471404 **fax:** 01425 476527 **244 Christchurch Rd BH24 3AS**
email: enquiries@moortownlodge.co.uk **web:** www.moortownlodge.co.uk
dir: 1m S of Ringwood. Exit A31 at Ringwood onto B3347, follow signs to Sopley. Lodge adjacent to David Lloyds Leisure Club

Moortown Lodge was originally a Georgian hunting lodge and is conveniently located ten miles from the Dorset coast, not far from Christchurch, and just five minutes south of Ringwood. It offers free WiFi, well-equipped rooms with DVD players, and full English breakfasts. Rooms are individually decorated and have comfortable bedding, telephone, tea- and coffee-making facilities, and digital TV. Breakfasts are cooked to order.

Rooms 7 en suite (3 fmly) (2 GF) S £75; D £82-£88* **Facilities** FTV DVD Lounge tea/coffee Direct Dial WiFi ⚿ Access to facilities of adjoining leisure club **Extras** Speciality toiletries, robes **Parking** 9 **Notes** LB

Amberwood

★★★★ GUEST ACCOMMODATION

tel: 01425 476615 **fax:** 01425 476615 **3/5 Top Ln BH24 1LF**
email: maynsing1@sky.com **web:** www.amberwoodbandb.co.uk
dir: A31 onto B3347, over rdbt, left into School Ln, left into Top Ln

This delightful Victorian home is situated in a quiet residential area within easy walking distance of the town centre. Bedrooms are attractively furnished and decorated, with many thoughtful extras. A substantial breakfast is served around one large table in the conservatory, which overlooks the well-tended garden. A lounge is also available.

Rooms 2 en suite (1 fmly) **Facilities** FTV TVL tea/coffee Direct Dial WiFi **Parking** 2 **Notes** ⊗ No Children 12yrs Closed Xmas & New Year ✉

The Cromwell Arms Country Pub With Rooms

☆☆☆☆ RESTAURANT WITH ROOMS

tel: 01794 519515 **fax:** 01794 519516 **Mainstone SO51 8HG**
email: info@thecromwellarms.com **web:** www.thecromwellarms.com
dir: M27 junct 2 onto A3090 to Mainstone, on left

This charming country pub has a popular restaurant serving food all day and every day. In addition, there are luxury bedrooms, which are spacious, beautifully styled and come with a host of extras. Bathrooms are modern and equipped with high quality towels and toiletries. The grounds are well kept, there is ample parking and also great access to major roads.

Rooms 10 en suite (10 fmly) (10 GF) D £95-£125 **Facilities** FTV iPod docking station tea/coffee Dinner available Direct Dial WiFi **Extras** Speciality toiletries, mini-bar **Parking** 50

The Mill Arms

★★★★ ➡ INN

tel: 01794 340401 **fax:** 01794 342281 **Barley Hill, Dunbridge SO51 0LF**
email: millarms@btconnect.com **web:** www.themillarms.co.uk
dir: M27 junct 2 onto A3090 then left onto A27 (Salisbury road). Turn right into Danes Rd, straight over into Saunders Ln. At T-junct left into Barley Hill

The Mill Arms is a traditional inn set in a quiet village with easy access to the New Forest and surrounding towns, cities and the South Coast. Guests are assured of a warm welcome, friendly service and great food here. Bedrooms are comfortable, well equipped and furnished and there is free WiFi. Good on-site parking is a bonus.

Rooms 6 en suite (1 fmly) (6 GF) **Facilities** FTV tea/coffee Dinner available WiFi ⚿ **Extras** Home-made biscuits, mineral water - complimentary **Conf** Max 100 Thtr 70 Class 30 Board 30 **Parking** 60 **Notes** RS Sun closed after 4pm lunch & dinner not served Mon

Premier Collection

Ennio's Restaurant & Boutique Rooms

★★★★★ ➡ RESTAURANT WITH ROOMS

tel: 023 8022 1159 & 07748 966111　**fax:** 023 8039 9849
Town Quay Rd SO14 3AS
email: info@ennios.co.uk **web:** www.ennios.co.uk
dir: Opposite Red Funnel Ferry terminal

This fine property, lovingly converted from a Victorian former warehouse, offers luxurious accommodation on Southampton's waterfront. All rooms are en suite and are furnished to a very high standard, including mini-bars and over-sized showers. Downstairs, the popular Ennio's Restaurant and bar is the ideal setting in which to dine, offering an authentic Italian atmosphere and a wonderful selection of dishes. There is limited parking available to the rear of the building.

Rooms 10 en suite **Facilities** FTV iPod docking station tea/coffee Dinner available WiFi **Extras** Speciality toiletries, mini-bar **Parking** 6 **Notes** LB ⊗ No coaches

White Star Tavern, Dining and Rooms

★★★★★ ◉◉ INN

tel: 023 8082 1990 **fax:** 023 8090 4982 **28 Oxford St SO14 3DJ**
email: reservations@whitestartavern.co.uk **web:** www.whitestartavern.co.uk
dir: M3 junct 14, A33 towards Ocean Village

This stylish tavern is conveniently located in the popular Oxford Street area, a moment's walk to the city centre. Bedrooms take their name from the ships of the White Star Line and are smartly appointed and well equipped with many thoughtful extras. The main bar and restaurant areas provide comfortable seating in stylish surroundings. Award-winning cuisine is served in the White Star restaurant whilst in the morning an à la carte breakfast is served in the bar area. Private meeting space is also available.

Rooms 13 en suite **Facilities** FTV DVD iPod docking station TVL tea/coffee Dinner available Direct Dial WiFi **Extras** Mini-bar, fresh milk & bottled water **Conf** Max 12 Thtr 12 Board 12 **Notes** LB ⊗ Closed 25-26 Dec

Alcantara Guest House

★★★★ ▤ GUEST ACCOMMODATION

tel: 023 8033 2966 **fax:** 023 8049 6163 **20 Howard Rd, Shirley SO15 5BN**
email: alcantaraguesthouse@sky.com **web:** www.alcantaraguesthouse.co.uk
dir: 0.5m NW of city centre. Exit A3057 into Howard Rd

A warm welcome is assured at this Victorian property, named after an ocean liner to reflect the establishment's shipping connections. Bedrooms are comfortable and well decorated and have many thoughtful extras. An appetising breakfast can be served in the bright and airy dining room. Secure off-road parking is available.

Rooms 9 rms (6 en suite) (1 fmly) (2 GF) S fr £34; D fr £70* **Facilities** FTV tea/coffee WiFi ⬤ **Parking** 7 **Notes** ⊗ No Children 12yrs RS 2wks Xmas

Hunters Lodge

★★★★ GUEST ACCOMMODATION

tel: 023 8022 7919 **25 Landguard Rd, Shirley SO15 5DL**
email: hunterslodge.hotel@virgin.net **web:** www.hunterslodgehotel.net
dir: 500yds NW of Southampton Central station. Exit A3057 (Shirley Rd) into Languard Rd

Located in a leafy residential area close to the city centre and convenient for the docks, ferry terminal, university and hospital, this double-fronted Victorian house provides business and leisure guests with comfortable, well-equipped bedrooms. Full English breakfast is served at shared tables in the elegant dining room. There is also a television lounge and a well-stocked bar.

Rooms 14 en suite (1 fmly) (1 GF) **Facilities** FTV DVD TVL tea/coffee Direct Dial Licensed WiFi **Parking** 16 **Notes** ⊗

Landguard Lodge

★★★★ GUEST HOUSE

tel: 023 8063 6904 **fax:** 023 8063 2258 **21 Landguard Rd SO15 5DL**
email: info@landguardlodge.co.uk **web:** www.landguardlodge.co.uk
dir: 500yds NW of Southampton Central station. Off A3057 Shirley Rd into Landguard Rd, between Hill Ln & Shirley Rd

This smart and well cared for Victorian house is in a quiet residential area, just a 10-15 minute walk from the railway station, or there is off-street parking available. The bedrooms are bright, comfortable and well equipped with many thoughtful extras. Breakfast is served in the sunny breakfast room.

Rooms 11 en suite (1 fmly) (2 GF) S £44-£48; D £70* **Facilities** FTV tea/coffee WiFi ⬤ **Parking** 3 **Notes** ⊗ No Children 5yrs

Prince Consort

★★★ INN

tel: 023 8045 2676 **Victoria Rd, Netley SO31 5DQ**
email: info@theprinceconsortpub.co.uk **web:** www.theprinceconsortpub.co.uk

Situated just five minutes' walk from the seafront, the atmosphere here is friendly, bedrooms are quiet, comfortable and well equipped, with food available every evening. Outdoor seating is a real bonus, as is the on-site parking.

Rooms 7 annexe en suite (1 fmly) (5 GF) S £50; D £65* **Facilities** STV FTV tea/coffee Dinner available WiFi **Conf** Max 40 Class 40 Board 20 **Parking** 25

Mayview Guest House

★★★ ◭ GUEST ACCOMMODATION

tel: 023 8022 0907 & 07973 874194 **fax:** 0845 127 4055 **30 The Polygon SO15 2BN**
email: info@mayview.co.uk **web:** www.mayview.co.uk

Mayview Guest House is only a 10-minute walk from the city centre. The bedrooms are spread over three floors and include a family room. Public areas comprise a light and airy dining room where breakfast is served.

Rooms 9 rms (1 en suite) (1 fmly) (1 GF) **Facilities** FTV tea/coffee WiFi **Notes** ⊗ Closed 25 Dec

The Brimar Guest House

★★ GUEST ACCOMMODATION

tel: 023 8086 2950 **fax:** 023 8086 1301 **10-14 High St, Totton SO40 9HN**
email: info@brimar-guesthouse.co.uk **web:** www.brimar-guesthouse.co.uk
dir: 3m W of city centre, exit A35 (Totton bypass) into Totton High St

This property offers practical, comfortable accommodation at reasonable prices. Not all rooms are en suite but bathrooms are well situated. Breakfast is served in the dining room or as a take-away option. The Brimar is well placed for the M27 and Southampton docks, and off-road parking is available.

Rooms 21 rms (8 en suite) (13 pri facs) (2 fmly) (8 GF) **Facilities** FTV WiFi **Parking** 20 **Notes** ⊗

SOUTHAMPTON *continued*

City Park Guest House

Ⓤ

tel: 023 8022 5391 fax: 023 8057 8744 **4-6 The Polygon SO15 2BN**
email: info@cityparkguesthouse.com web: www.cityparkguesthouse.com

Currently the rating for this establishment is not confirmed. This may be due to a change of ownership or because it has only recently joined the AA rating scheme.

Rooms 12 rms (9 en suite) (1 fmly) (2 GF) S £30-£47; D £45-£75* **Facilities** FTV DVD tea/coffee WiFi ☗ **Parking** 2 **Notes** ⊗

SOUTHSEA

See Portsmouth & Southsea

STOCKBRIDGE — Map 5 SU33

The Greyhound on the Test

★★★★ ◉◉ 🍴 RESTAURANT WITH ROOMS

tel: 01264 810833 **31 High St SO20 6EY**
email: info@thegreyhoundonthetest.co.uk web: www.thegreyhoundonthetest.co.uk
dir: *9m NW of Winchester, 8m S of Andover. Off A303*

This charming restaurant with rooms has the River Test at its rear and serves great food. In addition, the luxury bedrooms are generally spacious, beautifully styled and come with a host of extras. Bathrooms are modern and come with high quality towels and toiletries. There is also ample parking and well kept grounds.

Rooms 7 en suite S £75-£80; D £110-£155* **Facilities** FTV DVD Lounge tea/coffee Dinner available WiFi ⚓ Fishing Riding **Conf** Max 12 Board 12 **Parking** 28 **Notes** Closed 24-25 Dec No coaches

The Peat Spade Inn

★★★★ ◉ INN

tel: 01264 810612 **Village St, Longstock SO20 6DR**
email: info@peatspadeinn.co.uk web: www.peatspadeinn.co.uk
dir: *M3 junct 8, A303 W approx 15m, then take A3057 Stockbridge/Andover*

Located in a delightfully tranquil setting between the historic cities of Winchester and Salisbury, Longstock is a well placed village just north of Stockbridge in the heart of the Test Valley, known for its fly fishing and picture-postcard villages. The inn has lots of character, with bedrooms located in the main building and the adjacent former peat house; all are comfortable and furnished in a modern style in keeping with the date of the original building. The inn is popular for both dining and drinking; the modern British menus are well balanced and utilise seasonal ingredients sourced from the local area.

Rooms 8 en suite **Facilities** FTV DVD tea/coffee Dinner available Direct Dial WiFi Fishing Riding ⚓ **Extras** Bottled water, mini-fridge **Conf** Board 22 **Parking** 16 **Notes** Closed 25 Dec Civ Wed 32

The Three Cups Inn

★★★★ ◉ INN

tel: 01264 810527 **High St SO20 6HB**
email: manager@the3cups.co.uk web: www.the3cups.co.uk

Standing on Stockbridge high street, The Three Cups Inn is a 15th-century former coaching inn that has bags of charm and character. A free house, there are many cask ales to try in the cosy bar. The bedrooms are individually furnished, comfortable and equipped to a high standard. Excellent food is available every evening, served in both the cosy, snug-like dining room and the Orangery overlooking the garden.

Rooms 8 en suite (3 fmly) **Facilities** tea/coffee Dinner available WiFi Fishing **Parking** 15

The Grosvenor

★★★ INN

tel: 01264 810606 fax: 01264 810747 **23 High St SO20 6EU**
email: 9180@greeneking.co.uk web: www.oldenglish.co.uk

The Grosvenor provides en suite accommodation within the traditional setting of this Georgian building. Bedrooms have been designed with comfort in mind. The Tom Cannon Restaurant is popular with both residents and locals alike, and provides a good range of locally sourced produce including game (when in season).

Rooms 14 en suite 12 annexe en suite (6 GF) **Facilities** FTV tea/coffee Dinner available Direct Dial WiFi Fishing ⚓ **Conf** Max 105 Thtr 105 Class 85 Board 40 **Parking** 16 **Notes** Civ Wed 85

WARNFORD — Map 5 SU62

George & Falcon

★★★★ INN

tel: 01730 829623 fax: 01730 352222 **Warnford Rd SO32 3LB**
email: reservations@georgeandfalcon.com web: www.georgeandfalcon.com
dir: *Adjacent to A32 in village*

Set within the picturesque village of Warnford, located close to major transport links to Winchester, Portsmouth and Southampton. The bedrooms are tastefully appointed to retain the charm and character of a coaching inn yet provide modern facilities. Traditional fare is served in the popular restaurant and bar, and there is a large decking area which proves a useful addition in summer months.

Rooms 6 en suite (1 fmly) **Facilities** FTV Lounge tea/coffee Dinner available WiFi ⚓ 18 Fishing Riding ⚓ **Extras** Speciality toiletries **Conf** Max 30 Thtr 30 Class 15 Board 15 **Parking** 47 **Notes** LB Closed Xmas & 1 Jan Civ Wed 135

WHERWELL — Map 5 SU34

The White Lion

★★★ ⊜ INN

tel: 01264 860317 **Winchester Rd SP11 7JF**
web: www.thewhitelionwherwell.co.uk

Located in the tranquil village of Wherwell, yet close to transport links, The White Lion was built in 1611 and is full of charm and character. Rooms are tastefully appointed, and equipped with modern amenities and wash hand basins. Shower rooms and toilets are located on each floor. There is also a popular bar and dining room.

Rooms 6 rms **Facilities** tea/coffee Dinner available WiFi **Parking** 22

WHITCHURCH Map 5 SU44

White Hart Whitchurch

★★★ INN

tel: 01256 892900 **The Square RG28 7DN**

Located in the centre of Whitchurch the White Hart is steeped in history having served the local community for over 500 years. En suite rooms are well equipped some of which are located in an adjacent building. The inn is very popular with locals and diners alike. A very warm welcome from the friendly team is assured. Owned by Arkell's family brewers, a great range of traditionally brewed beers are available.

Rooms 10 en suite

WINCHESTER Map 5 SU42

Premier Collection

Giffard House

★★★★★ GUEST HOUSE

tel: 01962 852628 **50 Christchurch Rd SO23 9SU**
email: giffardhotel@aol.com **web:** www.giffardhotel.co.uk
dir: M3 junct 11, at rdbt 3rd exit onto A333 (St Cross road) for 1m. Pass BP garage on right, next left, 2nd right. 150mtrs on left

Expect a warm welcome at Giffard House, a stunning 19th-century Victorian property, close to the university. The accommodation is luxurious, comfortable and well equipped for both the business and leisure traveller. Beds are made up with crisp linen, and breakfast is served in the dining room. There is also a fully licensed bar set in the elegant conservatory. Plentiful parking is a real bonus.

Rooms 13 en suite (1 fmly) (4 GF) S £74-£126; D £99-£136* **Facilities** STV FTV Lounge tea/coffee Direct Dial Licensed WiFi **Extras** Speciality toiletries **Conf** Max 15 Thtr 15 Class 15 Board 13 **Parking** 13 **Notes** ⊗ Closed 24 Dec-2 Jan

Premier Collection

Orchard House

★★★★★ ≙ BED AND BREAKFAST

tel: 01962 861544 & 07763 759494 **fax:** 01962 861988
3 Christchurch Gardens, St Cross SO23 9TH
email: h.hope@hotmail.co.uk **web:** www.winchesterbedbreakfast.co.uk
dir: B3335 to Winchester & St Cross, after 2nd lights left into Barnes Close, right into Christchurch Rd, right again into Christchurch Gdns, last house on right

This friendly, family-run B&B is in a peaceful cul-de-sac, close to Winchester and its famous college, yet within easy reach of the M3. Orchard House offers a relaxed atmosphere, professional service and warm hospitality. The bedrooms are spacious, comfortable and very well equipped. Gardens are well tended, and breakfast can be taken on the balcony overlooking the rear garden on warmer summer mornings. There is parking for two cars.

Rooms 2 en suite (1 fmly) S £60-£70; D £90-£100* **Facilities** STV FTV DVD TVL tea/coffee WiFi **Extras** Speciality toiletries, fruit, snacks - free **Parking** 2 **Notes** ⊗ No Children 6yrs ⊛

Premier Collection

29 Christchurch Road

★★★★★ BED AND BREAKFAST

tel: 01962 868661 **fax:** 01962 868661 **29 Christchurch Rd SO23 9SU**
email: dilke@waitrose.com **web:** www.fetherstondilke.com
dir: M3 junct 11 follow signs for Winchester & St Cross (B3335), through 2 sets of lights, pass BP garage, left into Ranelagh Rd. 2nd right into Christchurch Rd, house at junct with Grafton Rd

Located a short distance from the historic centre of Winchester, this quality accommodation is tastefully appointed and offers comfortable bedrooms and bathrooms. The guest terrace is the ideal place to relax on a summer's afternoon within the well kept garden. A wide selection of breakfast items are served in the dining room around the communal table. Ample on-street parking is available.

Rooms 3 rms (2 en suite) (1 pri facs) S £65-£80; D £90-£100* **Facilities** FTV Lounge tea/coffee WiFi **Notes** ⊗ No Children 5yrs ⊛

The Old Vine

★★★★ INN

tel: 01962 854616 **8 Great Minster St SO23 9HA**
email: reservations@oldvinewinchester.com **web:** www.oldvinewinchester.com
dir: M3 junct 11 towards St Cross, right at Green Man Pub, left into Symonds St, left into Little Minster St

Overlooking the cathedral, this Grade II listed 18th-century inn mixes the elegance of days gone by with chic, modern comfort. The beautifully appointed bedrooms are named after designers and blend antique with contemporary, and the attractive dining room serves quality fare using local produce. There is permit parking.

Rooms 5 en suite 1 annexe en suite (2 fmly) S £110-£160; D £120-£195* **Facilities** FTV tea/coffee Dinner available WiFi **Extras** Speciality toiletries, water, fruit juices - free **Notes** No coaches

The Wykeham Arms

★★★★ ◎◎ ≙ INN

tel: 01962 853834 **fax:** 01962 854411 **75 Kingsgate St SO23 9PE**
web: www.wykehamarmswinchester.co.uk
dir: Immediately S of Cathedral, by Kingsgate and opposite Winchester College

This is one of the oldest and best-loved public houses in Hampshire and is situated just south of the ancient cathedral. Bedrooms are sited in both the main house and annexe. All areas are furnished to a high standard with excellent facilities. Dining in the restaurant or bar is recommended - walls are adorned from top to bottom with every kind of bijouterie imaginable and the regularly changing menu uses fresh ingredients.

Rooms 14 en suite S £87-£102; D £104-£190* **Facilities** FTV Lounge tea/coffee Dinner available Direct Dial WiFi ♨ 18 **Extras** Mineral water - complimentary; robes in some rooms **Conf** Max 20 Thtr 20 Class 20 Board 20 **Parking** 10 **Notes** No Children 14yrs

WINCHESTER *continued*

Running Horse Inn

★★★★ ◉◉ INN

tel: 01962 880218 **fax:** 01962 886596 **88 Main Rd, Littleton SO22 6QS**
email: runninghorseinn@btconnect.com **web:** www.runninghorseinn.co.uk
dir: *B3049 from Winchester 1.5m, turn right into Littleton after 1m, Running Horse on right*

Situated in a pretty rural location, yet with easy access to the M3, this is a great location for business and leisure travellers visiting Hampshire. Offering quality accommodation, the Running Horse Inn is minimalist in its design, and provides comfortable beds and a small workstation area. Highlights of a stay here are a meal in the smart restaurant or a drink in the bar.

Rooms 9 annexe en suite (1 fmly) (9 GF) **Facilities** FTV tea/coffee Dinner available WiFi **Parking** 40 **Notes** No coaches

24 Clifton Road

★★★ BED AND BREAKFAST

tel: 01962 851620 **SO22 5BU**
email: a.williams1997@btinternet.com
dir: *500yds NW of city centre. B3090 Romsey Rd W from city centre, Clifton Rd 2nd right*

This delightful house is in a quiet residential area close to the railway station and High Street. It combines town-house elegance with a homely cottage charm, and is handy for local walks. The bedroom is comfortably furnished and the bathroom has a deep claw-foot bath. There is a lounge and a dining room.

Rooms 1 rm (1 pri facs) S £40; D £65 **Facilities** TVL tea/coffee WiFi 🔒 **Parking** 2 **Notes** ⊗ No Children 6yrs ⊛

The Westgate Inn

★★★ INN

tel: 01962 820222 **fax:** 01962 820222 **2 Romsey Rd SO23 8TP**
email: wghguy@yahoo.co.uk **web:** www.westgateinn.co.uk
dir: *M3 junct 9 follow signs to city centre, on corner of Romsey Rd & Upper High St*

The Westgate Inn is well placed at the west end of the city near the castle. A popular restaurant serves good, home-prepared Indian meals and snacks. The traditional bar is always busy. The attractive and good-sized bedrooms on two floors are well equipped.

Rooms 8 rms (6 en suite) D £75-£90* **Facilities** FTV DVD iPod docking station tea/coffee Dinner available WiFi **Conf** Max 12 Board 12 **Notes** No Children 10yrs No coaches

▌ADFORTON
Map 9 SO47

Brick House Farm

★★★★ 🏠 BED AND BREAKFAST

tel: 01568 770870 **SY7 0NF**
email: info@adforton.com **web:** www.adforton.com
dir: *On A4110 in Adforton opposite St Andrew's Church*

Very much at the heart of the village community, this 16th-century longhouse provides high standards of comfort and good facilities. Superb beds and smart, modern private bathrooms can be found in the thoughtfully furnished accommodation. Comprehensive breakfasts featuring locally-sourced produce are served in the cosy, combined sitting and dining room. A warm welcome is assured.

Rooms 2 rms (2 pri facs) D £79* **Facilities** STV FTV Lounge tea/coffee WiFi **Parking** 2 **Notes** LB No Children 12yrs

▌ASTON INGHAM
Map 10 SO62

New House Farm B&B *(SO685229)*

★★★★ FARMHOUSE

tel: 01452 830484 & 07811 707487   **fax:** 01452 830484 **Barrel Ln GL17 0LS**
email: scaldbrain@btinternet.com **web:** www.newhousefarm-accommodation.co.uk
dir: *A40 onto B4222, Barrel Ln on right before Aston Ingham; or M50 junct 3 towards Newent, right at Kilcot to Aston Ingham (B4222)*

Located in tranquil wooded countryside, this working farm is a good spot for a touring base on the Gloucestershire-Herefordshire border. Set in 80 acres, the welcoming farmhouse will certainly appeal to nature lovers, and there is a comfortable lounge. Breakfast consists of a good selection of carefully prepared local produce.

Rooms 3 en suite (1 fmly) **Facilities** FTV DVD Lounge TVL tea/coffee Dinner available WiFi ⅋ 🔒 Clay pigeon shooting **Conf** Max 15 **Parking** 10 **Notes** LB ⊗ Closed Xmas & New Year 80 acres sheep/cattle/woodland

▌AYMESTREY
Map 9 SO46

Mount Pleasant Lodge

★★★★ BED AND BREAKFAST

tel: 01568 708031 **HR6 9SU**
email: mountpleasantlodge@gmail.com **web:** www.mplaymestrey.co.uk

Mount Pleasant Lodge is a detached family home offering plenty of quality and comfort throughout, ideally located for guests visiting the many nearby attractions which include a number of National Trust properties. Bedrooms and bathrooms provide good space and comfort along with some welcome extras. The freshly cooked breakfast offers a range of good quality local produce. Off-street parking, a comfortable guest conservatory and a pleasant garden are all available for guests.

Rooms 3 en suite **Facilities** FTV DVD Lounge tea/coffee WiFi 🔒 **Extras** Snacks, filtered water - complimentary **Parking** 5 **Notes** ⊗ Closed Xmas & New Year ⊛

BODENHAM
Map 10 S055

The Coach House at England Gate's Inn
★★★★ ⌂ INN

tel: 01568 797286 **HR1 3HU**
email: englandsgate@btconnect.com **web:** www.englandsgate.co.uk
dir: *Just off A417*

This fine black and white 16th-century inn is run by the McNeil family, who pride themselves on quality service. The inn is set in attractive gardens which are perfect for alfresco dining on warmer days. The detached coach house has comfortable bedrooms with modern en suite facilities; the views are spectacular from the upstairs rooms. Continental breakfast is served in the coach house dining area on weekdays, and a full cooked breakfast is available at weekends.

Rooms 7 en suite (2 fmly) (4 GF) S £82-£90; D £82-£123* **Facilities** FTV DVD tea/coffee Dinner available Direct Dial WiFi 🔒 **Extras** Bottled water **Conf** Max 12 Board 12 **Parking** 30

BOLSTONE
Map 10 S053

Premier Collection

Prickett's Place
★★★★★ ⌂ BED AND BREAKFAST

tel: 01432 870221 **HR2 6LZ**
email: prickettsplace@btinternet.com **web:** www.prickettsplace.com
dir: *M50 junct 4 onto A49, right towards Hoarwithy. Follow signs for Cottage of Content public house, turn left then turn right, Prickett's Place on left*

Surrounded by magnificent countryside in the beautiful Wye Valley, Prickett's Place is peacefully located just seven miles from Hereford and nine miles from Ross-on-Wye. Bedrooms are very well furnished and equipped with welcome extras. Guests can enjoy tea in the garden upon arrival and also have use of a comfortable lounge. An excellent selection of high-quality ingredients is offered at breakfast.

Rooms 1 en suite 1 annexe en suite (1 fmly) **Facilities** FTV TVL tea/coffee WiFi 🔒 Canoeing **Extras** Speciality toiletries, fruit **Parking** 6 **Notes** ⊗ No Children 10yrs Closed Xmas & New Year

BREDWARDINE
Map 9 S034

Red Lion
★★★ INN

tel: 01981 500303 **HR3 6BU**
email: info@redlion-hotel.com **web:** www.redlion-hotel.com
dir: *Off A438, Hereford to Brecon road*

This traditionally styled inn is set in a pleasant village and provides an ideal base for exploring the local countryside and river walks. Popular with anglers, the inn has a fishing theme running throughout the public areas. Bedrooms offer a range of shapes and sizes, and are located either above the inn or in an adjacent annexe. Home cooked meals are served at both lunch and dinner.

Rooms 7 en suite 3 annexe en suite (1 fmly) (2 GF) S £45-£60; D £60-£88* **Facilities** FTV TVL tea/coffee Dinner available Direct Dial WiFi Fishing **Parking** 20 **Notes** LB Closed Dec-1 Mar RS Mar-May closed Sun eve to Wed am

BROCKHAMPTON
Map 10 S053

Ladyridge Farm
★★★★ ⌂ GUEST HOUSE

tel: 01989 740220 **fax:** 01989 740220 **HR1 4SE**
email: carolgrant@ladyridgefarm.fsworld.co.uk **web:** www.ladyridge.co.uk
dir: *Exit B4224 signed Brockhampton Church between How Caple & Fownhope. 400yds on right after thatched church*

This working farm, set in delightful countryside, provides a peaceful haven for visitors, and is also home to rare breed ducks, poultry and sheep. The traditional-styled bedrooms are spacious and thoughtfully equipped. Meals are served family-style in the attractive dining room, and use local, fresh ingredients, as well as home-produced free-range eggs.

Rooms 3 rms (2 pri facs) (1 fmly) **Facilities** DVD tea/coffee Dinner available WiFi 🔒 **Extras** Robes **Parking** 6 **Notes** ⊗

GARWAY
Map 9 S042

Garway Moon Inn
★★★★ ⌂ INN

tel: 01600 750270 **HR2 8RQ**
email: info@garwaymooninn.co.uk **web:** www.garwaymooninn.co.uk
dir: *From Hereford, S on A49. Right onto A466, right again onto B4521. At Broad Oak turn right to Garway*

This traditional old hostelry is situated in peaceful and picturesque surroundings. Bedrooms are located above the inn and have been recently refurbished to provide good quality and comfort. This "proper" pub offers a selection of real ales and ciders, with a relaxed and welcoming ambience in the bar. Dinner should not be missed with high quality produce from local suppliers - many of whom might be found sitting in the bar. The home-made burgers are especially recommended.

Rooms 3 en suite (2 fmly) D £70-£90* **Facilities** STV FTV DVD Lounge tea/coffee Dinner available WiFi **Extras** Bottled water - complimentary **Conf** Max 12 Board 12 **Parking** 20

HEREFORD
Map 10 S053

See also Little Dewchurch

Premier Collection

Somerville House
★★★★★ GUEST ACCOMMODATION

tel: 01432 273991 **fax:** 01432 268719 **12 Bodenham Rd HR1 2TS**
email: enquiries@somervillehouse.net **web:** www.somervillehouse.net
dir: *A465, at Aylestone Hill rdbt towards city centre, left at Southbank Rd, leading to Bodenham Rd*

Situated in a quiet, tree-lined residential road, Somerville House is a detached late-Victorian villa that provides a boutique-style experience. Expect a warm and friendly welcome from Rosie and Bill who offer quality accommodation with high standards of luxury and comfort. All bedrooms are spacious, with a good range of quality extras. Breakfast is served in the light and contemporary dining room at individual tables. There is a terraced garden to the rear where guests can sit and relax, or indoors, they can make use of the comfortable lounge. There is ample parking.

Rooms 12 en suite (2 fmly) (1 GF) S £55-£87; D £70-£112* **Facilities** FTV DVD Lounge tea/coffee Licensed WiFi 🔒 Arrangement with health spa **Extras** Speciality toiletries, chocolate, bottled water **Conf** Max 10 Thtr 10 Class 10 Board 10 **Parking** 10 **Notes** LB ⊗

HEREFORD *continued*

The Bay Horse Inn

★★★★ INN

tel: 01432 273351 **236 Kings Acre Rd HR4 0SD**
email: info@bayhorseinnhereford.co.uk **web:** www.bayhorseinnhereford.co.uk
dir: *On A438, pass Wyevale garden centre, 100yds on left*

Located just outside the city centre, The Bay Horse Inn combines comfortable bedrooms and bathrooms with an excellent range of food available during the day and evening. There is a relaxed ambience and welcoming service throughout. Guests also benefit from the use of a car park and a range of outdoor seating in warmer weather. A good selection of real ales, wine and bottled ciders are available.

Rooms 8 annexe en suite (3 fmly) (4 GF) S fr £59; D fr £69* **Facilities** FTV TVL tea/coffee Dinner available WiFi **Conf** Max 60 Thtr 35 Class 60 Board 20 **Parking** 56 **Notes** ⊗

No 21

★★★★ GUEST ACCOMMODATION

tel: 01432 279897 & 07967 525403 **21 Aylestone Hill HR1 1HR**
email: jane@21aylestonehill.co.uk
dir: *On A4103 from Worcester to rdbt at approach to Hereford. Take 1st exit to town centre (A465)*

A warm welcome from Ken and Jane awaits at this peaceful detached property, not far from the train station. The property has been totally renovated, and all bedrooms and smart modern bathrooms are appointed to a high standard. The bedrooms are spacious with many extras; one ground-floor room, with a wet room, is ideal for guests that have difficulty with stairs. Breakfast is served in the spacious dining room at the front of the property. There is ample secure parking.

Rooms 4 en suite (1 fmly) (1 GF) S £40-£50; D £60-£75* **Facilities** FTV TVL tea/coffee WiFi 🔒 **Extras** Orange juice, bottled water, fresh milk - free **Parking** 8 **Notes** ⊛

Sink Green Farm *(SO542377)*

★★★★ FARMHOUSE

tel: 01432 870223 **fax:** 01432 870223 **Rotherwas HR2 6LE**
email: enquiries@sinkgreenfarm.co.uk **web:** www.sinkgreenfarm.co.uk
dir: *3m SE of city centre. Exit A49 onto B4399 for 2m*

This charming 16th-century farmhouse stands in attractive countryside and has many original features, including flagstone floors, exposed beams and open fireplaces. Bedrooms are traditionally furnished and one has a four-poster bed. The pleasant garden has a comfortable summer house, hot tub and barbecue.

Rooms 3 en suite S £40-£80; D £80-£90* **Facilities** FTV iPod docking station Lounge TVL tea/coffee WiFi Hot tub **Extras** Home-made biscuits **Parking** 10 **Notes** LB ⊛ 180 acres beef

Heron House

★★★ 🅰 BED AND BREAKFAST

tel: 01432 761111 **fax:** 01432 760603 **Canon Pyon Rd, Portway HR4 8NG**
email: info@theheronhouse.com **web:** www.theheronhouse.com
dir: *A4103 onto A4110 to Portway x-rds, Heron House 200yds on left*

Originally an 18th-century cottage, Heron House was considerably extended about 30 years ago. It is quietly located at Burghill, some four miles north of Hereford. The accommodation consists of one twin and one double bedded room, both with modern furnishings and equipment. Separate tables are provided in the cosy breakfast room.

Rooms 2 rms (1 en suite) S £30; D £64* **Facilities** DVD tea/coffee **Parking** 5 **Notes** ⊗ No Children 10yrs ⊛

The Steppes

U

tel: 01432 851536 **Hemhill, Lumber Ln HR1 4AL**
email: lin@thesteppeshereford.co.uk

Currently the rating for this establishment is not confirmed. This may be due to a change of ownership or because it has only recently joined the AA rating scheme.

Rooms 4 rms S £55-£75; D £65-£110*

LEDBURY   Map 10 SO73

The Lodge at Orchard Cottage

★★★★ BED AND BREAKFAST

tel: 01531 660646 & 07748 832344 **Orchard Cottage, Much Marcle HR8 2NU**
email: orchardcottagemuchmarcle@gmail.com
web: www.orchardcottagemuchmarcle.co.uk
dir: *From Ledbury on A449, right at Much Marcle post office, up hill. Left at 1st x-rds towards Yatton & Ross-on-Wye. 3rd cottage on left (0.5m)*

Delightful views over the surrounding countryside can be enjoyed from the recently completed lodge-style rooms located in the garden next to the main house. These two rooms are comfortably furnished and equipped and include some welcome extras. A further bedroom is available in the main house where guests are offered a good selection of carefully prepared dishes at breakfast - all served in the comfortable dining room. Off-street car parking is also provided.

Rooms 1 en suite 2 annexe en suite (2 GF) S £65-£85; D £85-£170* **Facilities** FTV TVL TV2B tea/coffee WiFi 🔒 **Extras** Speciality toiletries **Parking** 4 **Notes** ⊗ Closed 23-26 Dec & 31 Dec-1 Jan ⊛

Moor Court Farm (SO639447)

★★★★ FARMHOUSE

tel: 01531 670408 **fax:** 01531 670408 **Stretton, Grandison HR8 2TP**
web: www.moorcourtfarm.co.uk
dir: *1.5m E of A417 at Upper Eggleton*

Moor Court Farm has a 15th-century farmhouse and is a mixed farm with working oast houses where hops are dried. Bedrooms are thoughtfully equipped and furnished, and one has a four-poster. Public areas include a comfortable lounge with an impressive stone fireplace and a dining room, where breakfast includes local produce and eggs from the farm.

Rooms 3 en suite **Facilities** tea/coffee Dinner available Licensed Fishing **Parking** 5
Notes ⊗ No Children 8yrs ⊜ 200 acres mixed/livestock/hops

The Seven Stars

★★★★ ⊜ INN

tel: 01531 635800 **11 The Homend HR8 1BN**
email: paulford@sevenstars.co.uk **web:** www.sevenstarsledbury.co.uk
dir: *4m from M50*

The Seven Stars inn is reputedly the oldest in this picturesque market town - the inn dates back to the 16th century. Owners Paul and Sharon are welcoming and friendly. The interior of the inn is modern and contemporary with a stylish dining area to the rear. The bedrooms have very comfortable beds and good space with some thoughtful extras. Breakfast is freshly prepared and hearty. Parking is available at the nearby public car park.

Rooms 3 en suite (2 fmly) **Facilities** STV tea/coffee Dinner available WiFi **Notes** ⊗
No coaches

Verzon House

tel: 01531 670381 **Trumpet HR8 2PZ**

Currently the rating for this establishment is not confirmed. This may be due to a change of ownership or because it has only recently joined the AA rating scheme.

Rooms 8 en suite

LEINTWARDINE   **Map 9 SO47**

Premier Collection

The Lion

 **RESTAURANT WITH ROOMS**

tel: 01547 540203 & 540747   **fax:** 01547 540747 **High St SY7 0JZ**
email: enquiries@thelionleintwardine.co.uk **web:** www.thelionleintwardine.co.uk
dir: *Beside bridge on A4113 (Ludlow to Knighton road) in Leintwardine*

This quiet country restaurant with rooms in the picturesque village of Leintwardine, set beside the River Teme, is just a short distance from Ludlow and Craven Arms. The interior is stylish and all the contemporary bedrooms are en suite. Dining is taken seriously here and the modern, imaginative food uses the freshest local ingredients. The well-stocked bar offers a selection of real ales and lagers and there is a separate drinkers' bar too. The Lion is particularly popular with families as the garden has a secure children's play area, and in warmer months guests can eat alfresco. The friendly staff help to make any visit memorable.

Rooms 8 en suite (1 fmly) **Facilities** FTV Lounge tea/coffee Dinner available
Direct Dial WiFi Fishing 🔒 **Extras** Home-made shortbread - complimentary
Conf Max 25 Class 25 Board 25 **Parking** 25 **Notes** ⊗ Closed 25 Dec

Premier Collection

Upper Buckton (SO384733)

★★★★★ ⊜ FARMHOUSE

tel: 01547 540634 **Buckton SY7 0JU**
email: ghlloydco@btconnect.com **web:** www.upperbuckton.co.uk
dir: *From Leintwardine on A4113 to Walford. Right into narrow road signed Buckton. 2nd farm on left*

Upper Buckton is a Georgian house surrounded by beautiful grounds that slope gently down to the mill stream and out to the motte. Beyond this lies the ha-ha, old fashioned meadowland, the River Teme and the forested Wigmore Rolls. The house is comfortably furnished with interesting paintings and antique furniture. Of the three bedrooms, two have an en suite bathroom and one has private facilities and beds are fitted with electric blankets. An enjoyable home-cooked dinner is available by prior arrangement. In the cooler months the sitting room is a pleasant place to take afternoon tea and enjoy an after-dinner coffee around the log fire.

Rooms 3 rms (2 en suite) (1 pri facs) S £63-£70; D £96-£110* **Facilities** FTV
Lounge tea/coffee Dinner available Licensed WiFi Table tennis **Extras** Speciality
toiletries **Parking** 3 **Notes** LB ⊗ ⊜ 360 acres arable/potatoes/sheep

LEOMINSTER   **Map 10 SO45**

Premier Collection

The Old Rectory Pembridge

★★★★★ BED AND BREAKFAST

tel: 01544 387968 **Bridge St, Pembridge HR6 9EU**
email: lynnpickard@hotmail.co.uk **web:** www.theoldrectorypembridge.co.uk
dir: *A44 to Pembridge into Bridge St towards river, house on right before bridge*

Set in a peaceful location close to the River Arrow on the Black and White Village Trail, this 1852 Gothic building provides luxurious accommodation, and a warm welcome. The bedrooms have antique furniture and quality soft furnishings, along with a range of thoughtful extras. The spacious en suite bathrooms add to the experience. Public areas include a large lounge with a log fire, and an elegant dining room where excellent breakfasts are served around a communal table.

Rooms 3 en suite **Facilities** FTV DVD TVL tea/coffee WiFi 🔒 **Parking** 6 **Notes** ⊗
No Children

Premier Collection

Hills Farm (SO564638)

★★★★★ FARMHOUSE

tel: 01568 750205 **Leysters HR6 0HP**
email: info@thehillsfarm.co.uk **web:** www.thehillsfarm.co.uk
dir: *Off A4112 (Leominster to Tenbury Wells), on outskirts of Leysters*

Set in a peaceful location with views over the countryside, this property dates in part from the 16th century. The friendly, attentive proprietors provide a relaxing and homely atmosphere. The attractive bedrooms, in the converted barns, are spacious and comfortable. Breakfasts, served in the dining room and conservatory, feature fresh local produce.

Rooms 3 annexe en suite (1 GF) D £86* **Facilities** FTV iPod docking station
Lounge tea/coffee WiFi 🔒 **Parking** 8 **Notes** ⊗ No Children 12yrs Closed Nov-Mar
120 acres arable

LITTLE DEWCHURCH
Map 10 SO53

Cwm Craig Farm *(SO535322)*

★★★★ FARMHOUSE

tel: 01432 840250 **HR2 6PS**
email: cwmcraigfarm@gmail.com **web:** www.cwmcraigfarm.co.uk
dir: *Exit A49 into Little Dewchurch, right in village, Cwm Craig 1st farm on left*

Cwm Craig Farm is a spacious Georgian farmhouse situated on the outskirts of the village amid unspoilt countryside. Bedrooms and bathrooms are comfortable, homely and well equipped, while a hearty breakfast includes eggs from the farm's hens and is served in the large dining room. A games and sitting room are also available for guests use.

Rooms 3 en suite S £40-£45; D £65-£75 **Facilities** FTV TVL tea/coffee WiFi Pool table Games room **Parking** 6 **Notes** ⊗ Closed Nov-Feb ⊜ 190 acres organic/arable

ROSS-ON-WYE
Map 10 SO52

Premier Collection

Wilton Court Restaurant with Rooms

★★★★★ ⚙⚙ 🏠 RESTAURANT WITH ROOMS

tel: 01989 562569 **fax:** 01989 768460 **Wilton Ln HR9 6AQ**
email: info@wiltoncourthotel.com **web:** www.wiltoncourthotel.com
dir: *M50 junct 4, A40 towards Monmouth at 3rd rdbt left signed Ross-on-Wye, 1st right, on right*

Dating back to the 16th century, Wilton Court has great charm and a wealth of character. Standing on the banks of the River Wye, just a short walk from the town centre, there is a genuinely relaxed, friendly and unhurried atmosphere created by hosts Roger and Helen Wynn and their reliable team. Bedrooms are tastefully furnished and well equipped, while public areas include a comfortable lounge, traditional bar and pleasant restaurant with a conservatory extension overlooking the garden. High standards of food, using fresh, locally sourced ingredients, are offered.

Rooms 10 en suite (1 fmly) S £100-£155; D £135-£185* **Facilities** FTV DVD TVL tea/coffee Dinner available Direct Dial WiFi ⇌ ⏃ 18 Fishing 🔒 **Extras** Kimonos, bottled water **Conf** Thtr 50 Class 20 Board 20 **Parking** 20 **Notes** LB Closed 3-15 Jan Civ Wed 50

Benhall Farm

★★★★ 🏠 BED AND BREAKFAST

tel: 01989 563900 & 07900 264612 **fax:** 01989 563900 **Wilton HR9 6AG**
email: info@benhallfarm.co.uk **web:** www.benhallfarm.co.uk
dir: *From Wilton rdbt (A40 & A49 junct), take exit towards M50. On dual-carriageway immediately left at No Through Road sign. Benhall Farm at end of lane*

A warm welcome can be expected at Benhall Farm, a modern working dairy and arable farm of 335 acres which forms part of the Duchy of Cornwall Estate. The farm is on the outskirts of Ross-on-Wye on the banks of the River Wye and has easy access to the M50, Hereford, Abergavenny, Monmouth, and the Forest of Dean. The bedrooms are comfortable, spacious and many guest extras are provided, including WiFi. A lounge is available for guests' use and the dining room is the venue for hearty breakfasts served at the communal table. Parking is available to the front of the property.

Rooms 3 en suite S £50-£84; D £76-£80* **Facilities** FTV TVL tea/coffee WiFi Fishing 🔒 **Extras** Fridge, home-made biscuits, fresh milk **Parking** 6 **Notes** LB ⊗ Closed 20 Dec-10 Jan

The Coach House

★★★★ BED AND BREAKFAST

tel: 01989 780339 **Old Gore HR9 7QT**
email: iolafass@btinternet.com **web:** www.thecoachhousebandb.com
dir: *M50/A40 junct 4 onto A449 to Ledbury. After 3m fork left to Hereford, over x-rds in 500yds, Coach House 200yds on right*

Peacefully located in its own gardens, this attractive accommodation includes well furnished bedrooms with very comfortable beds. Breakfast is served in the smart dining room and includes home-made breads and jams, along with freshly squeezed orange juice. Guests have use of the large garden with seating, and plenty of off-road parking is available.

Rooms 3 rms (2 en suite) (1 pri facs) **Facilities** FTV DVD Lounge tea/coffee WiFi ⚒ **Parking** 3 **Notes** ⊜

Forest View Guest House

★★★★ GUEST HOUSE

tel: 01600 890210 & 07881 247068 **fax:** 01600 890210 **Symonds Yat East HR9 6JL**
email: forestviewguesthouse@gmail.com **web:** www.forestviewguesthouse.co.uk
dir: *A40 onto B4229 signed Goodrich, then B4432 for Symonds Yat East*

Delightfully located on the banks of the river, guests here have a range of activities such as walking and canoeing literally on the doorstep. Bedrooms and bathrooms are comfortably furnished and most have views over the river and the forest beyond. In addition to carefully prepared breakfast, guests also have the option of a range of home-cooked dinners served in the pleasant dining room. A small bar and lounge is provided.

Rooms 10 en suite (2 GF) S £40-£55; D £50-£95 **Facilities** FTV DVD Lounge TVL tea/coffee Dinner available Licensed WiFi ⏃ 18 Fishing 🔒 **Extras** Speciality toiletries, snacks **Conf** Max 20 Thtr 20 Class 20 Board 26 **Parking** 15 **Notes** ⊗ No Children 12yrs

Lea House

★★★★ 🏠 🍴 GUEST ACCOMMODATION

tel: 01989 750652 **fax:** 01989 750652 **Lea HR9 7JZ**
email: enquiries@leahouse.co.uk **web:** www.leahouse.co.uk
dir: *4m SE of Ross on A40 towards Gloucester, in Lea*

This former coaching inn, near Ross-on-Wye, has a relaxed atmosphere and makes a good base for exploring the Forest of Dean and the Wye Valley. The individually furnished bedrooms are thoughtfully equipped and very homely. Breakfast in the oak-beamed dining room offers home-made breads, freshly squeezed juice, fresh fruit platters, local sausages and fish choices. Home-cooked dinners are available by prior arrangement.

Rooms 3 rms (2 en suite) (1 pri facs) (1 fmly) S £50-£65; D £70-£90* **Facilities** FTV TVL tea/coffee Dinner available WiFi 🏊 **Parking** 4 **Notes** LB

Thatch Close

★★★★ GUEST ACCOMMODATION

tel: 01989 770300 **Llangrove HR9 6EL**
email: info@thatchclose.co.uk **web:** www.thatchclose.co.uk
dir: *Off A40 at Symonds Yat West/Whitchurch junct to Llangrove, right at x-rds after Post Office & before school. Thatch Close 0.6m on left*

Standing in 13 acres, this sturdy 18th-century farmhouse is full of character. Expect a wonderfully warm atmosphere with a genuine welcome from your hosts. The homely bedrooms are equipped for comfort with many thoughtful extras. Breakfast is served in the elegant dining room, and a lounge is available. The extensive patios and gardens are popular in summer, providing plenty of space to find a quiet corner and relax with a good book.

Rooms 3 en suite S £50-£55; D £70-£75* **Facilities** TVL tea/coffee WiFi 🏊 **Parking** 8 **Notes** LB

The Old Court House

★★★ BED AND BREAKFAST

tel: 01989 762275 & 07946 413901 **53 High St HR9 5HH**
email: theoldcourthouse@hotmail.com **web:** www.theoldcourthousebandb.co.uk
dir: *From heritage centre take road to Hereford. 100mtrs on left (Lloyds bank on corner)*

As the name suggests, there is plenty of character within this charming building located right on the High Street of the town. Narrow and quite steep stairs lead to bedrooms and bathrooms offering a range of shapes and sizes and all with comfortable beds and bedding. Breakfast is served in the main dining room on the ground floor and parking is usually available on one of the nearby streets.

Rooms 4 en suite (2 fmly) S £30-£50; D £80-£90* **Facilities** FTV DVD tea/coffee WiFi ♨ 🏊 **Extras** Fridge, microwave **Notes** LB ⊗ Closed 19 Dec-5 Jan

The White House Guest House

★★★ GUEST HOUSE

tel: 01989 763572 & 07824 531906 **Wye St HR9 7BX**
email: whitehouseross@aol.com **web:** www.whitehouseross.com
dir: *Exit A40 dual-carriageway at Wilton, pass over bridge, take 1st left White House on right*

A warm welcome awaits at The White House Guest House, an 18th-century guest house which is located adjacent to the River Wye and just a short walk from the town centre. The bedrooms are tastefully appointed and provide a thoughtful range of extras including WiFi access. There are four-poster rooms and single rooms available. A hearty breakfast is provided at individual tables in the dining room, and evening meals are available with prior notice. Parking is on the road to the front.

Rooms 7 en suite (2 fmly) (2 smoking) S fr £50; D fr £70* **Facilities** FTV tea/coffee Dinner available Licensed WiFi 🏊 **Extras** Sweets - complimentary **Notes** LB Closed 24-25 Dec

Brampton Cottage Bed & Breakfast

U

tel: 01989 564295 & 07521 136500 **Brampton Abbotts HR9 7JD**
email: rachelt3uk@yahoo.co.uk **web:** www.bramptonabbottsbedandbreakfast.co.uk
dir: *M50 junct 4, at rdbt 2nd exit towards Ledbury (A449). After 500mtrs take 1st left to Brampton Abbotts. At T-junct turn left, 1st right, then 1st right again. On left*

Currently the rating for this establishment is not confirmed. This may be due to a change of ownership or because it has only recently joined the AA rating scheme.

Rooms 3 rms (1 en suite) (1 pri facs) (2 fmly) S £50-£55; D £60-£65* **Facilities** FTV tea/coffee WiFi **Parking** 2 **Notes** ⊗ 🚭

ST OWENS CROSS   **Map 10 SO52**

Little Treaddow Farm House B&B *(SO540242)*

★★★★ FARMHOUSE

tel: 01989 730372 & 07739 976513 **fax:** 01989 730557 **HR2 8LQ**
email: sleep@treaddow.co.uk **web:** www.treaddow.co.uk
dir: *A49 from Ross-on-Wye towards Hereford for 2.5m. Turn left signed Abergavenny. End of road turn right 500mtrs on right*

This historic and welcoming farmhouse accommodation includes parking and a garden. Bedrooms and bathrooms are well equipped and a guest lounge is also available. Breakfast utilises plenty of local and good quality produce and is served in the comfortable dining room/lounge area.

Rooms 2 en suite (1 fmly) S £60-£70; D £70-£80* **Facilities** FTV DVD TVL tea/coffee WiFi 🐾 18 🏊 **Extras** Fridge **Parking** 10 **Notes** LB 10 acres

---

SYMONDS YAT (EAST)   **Map 10 SO51**

See also Coleford (Gloucestershire)

The Royal Lodge

★★★★ 🏠 🍴 GUEST ACCOMMODATION

tel: 01600 890238 **fax:** 01600 891425 **HR9 6JL**
email: info@royalhotel-symondsyat.com **web:** www.royallodgesymondsyat.co.uk
dir: *Midway between Ross and Monmouth exit A40 at signs for Goodrich & B4229 to Symonds Yat East*

The Royal Lodge stands at the top end of the village overlooking the River Wye. Bedrooms are spacious and comfortable, and come complete with flat-screen TVs and many guest extras; the bathrooms offer modern facilities. There is a cosy lounge with an open fireplace and two bars are available. Meals are offered in the welcoming restaurant, which provides carefully prepared meals using fresh and local ingredients. Staff are pleasant and friendly.

Rooms 21 en suite (5 fmly) S £45-£59; D £55-£135 **Facilities** FTV DVD TVL tea/coffee Dinner available Direct Dial Licensed WiFi Fishing 🏊 **Extras** Mineral water **Conf** Max 70 Thtr 70 Class 20 Board 30 **Parking** 150 **Notes** LB Civ Wed 80

SYMONDS YAT (EAST) *continued*

Saracens Head Inn
★★★★ ⊜ INN

tel: 01600 890435 **HR9 6JL**
email: contact@saracensheadinn.co.uk web: www.saracensheadinn.co.uk
dir: *Exit A40 at South Herefordshire Motorcaravan Centre, signed Symonds Yat East, 2m*

Dating from the 16th century, the friendly, family-run Saracens Head faces the River Wye and has wonderful views. The well-equipped bedrooms are decorated in a cottage style, and there is a cosy lounge, an attractive dining room, and a popular public bar onto a riverside patio. All meals are offered from a regularly changing and comprehensive menu, that includes locally-sourced produce.

Rooms 8 en suite 2 annexe en suite (1 GF) S £59-£75; D £89-£138* **Facilities** FTV TVL tea/coffee Dinner available Direct Dial WiFi Fishing ⓐ **Conf** Max 25 Thtr 25 Class 25 Board 25 **Parking** 35 **Notes** LB No Children 7yrs No coaches

See advert below

| WHITCHURCH | Map 10 SO51 |

Norton House Bed & Breakfast & Cottages
★★★★ ⌂ BED AND BREAKFAST

tel: 01600 890046 & 07805 260890   fax: 08723 526284 **Old Monmouth Rd HR9 6DJ**
email: enquiries@norton-house.com web: www.norton-house.com

Built as a farmhouse, Norton House dates back some 300 years and has retained a lot of character, with flagstone floors and beamed ceilings. A warm and friendly welcome awaits all guests from hosts Jayne and Bill. The bedrooms, including a four-poster room, are individually styled and furnished for maximum comfort. Charming public areas include a snug lounge with a wood-burning stove, and a breakfast room with a communal table. Excellent local produce is used to create an imaginative range of breakfast dishes. Parking is off-road, and self-catering cottages are also available.

Rooms 3 en suite **Facilities** FTV iPod docking station Lounge TVL tea/coffee WiFi ⓐ **Extras** Fruit - complimentary **Parking** 5 **Notes** LB

WHITNEY-ON-WYE
Map 9 SO24

The Rhydspence Inn
★★★★ INN

tel: 01497 831262 & 831751 fax: 01497 831751 HR3 6EU
email: info@rhydspence-inn.co.uk web: www.rhydspence-inn.co.uk
dir: N side of A438 1m W of Whitney

This traditional inn is full of character and history. Parts of the building date from 1380, and extensions were added from the 17th to 20th centuries. A friendly welcome and relaxing ambience is provided in both the bar and the dining room where locals and guests mingle well. Bedrooms offer a variety of shapes and sizes and are all located above the inn. Both dinner and breakfast offer a good selection of homemade, carefully prepared dishes. The inn is generally open throughout the day for a variety of food and drink.

Rooms 6 en suite Facilities tea/coffee Dinner available WiFi 🔒 Extras Snacks, bottled water Parking 30

YARKHILL
Map 10 SO64

Garford Farm (SO600435)
★★★★ FARMHOUSE

tel: 01432 890226 fax: 01432 890707 HR1 3ST
email: garfordfarm@btconnect.com
dir: Exit A417 at Newtown x-rds onto A4103 for Hereford, farm 1.5m on left

This black and white, timber-framed farmhouse, set on a large arable holding, dates from the 17th century. Its character is enhanced by period furnishings, and fires burn in the comfortable lounge during colder weather. The traditionally furnished bedrooms, including a family room, have modern facilities.

Rooms 2 en suite (1 fmly) D fr £60* Facilities Lounge tea/coffee WiFi 🐾 🔒 Parking 6 Notes No Children 2yrs Closed 25-26 Dec ⊛ 700 acres arable

HERTFORDSHIRE

BALDOCK
Map 12 TL23

The White House
★★★★ BED AND BREAKFAST

tel: 01462 742745 & 07836 260865 Newnham SG7 5JU
email: info@thenewnhamwhitehouse.com web: www.thenewnhamwhitehouse.com
dir: A1(M) junct 10 onto A507 towards Baldock. After 500yds turn left signed Newnham & Ashwell. At T-junct turn right, last house on left before narrow bridge

A warm welcome is assured at this delightful home. On arrival, refreshments can be served either in the drawing room or, weather permitting, on the terrace. All bedrooms are well appointed and offer guests a good range of amenities with comfort in mind. A quality breakfast, featuring local sourced ingredients, is served around a communal table in the dining room.

Rooms 2 rms (1 en suite) (1 pri facs) (2 fmly) S £60; D £60-£70* Facilities FTV Lounge tea/coffee WiFi Extras Fruit & snacks - complimentary Parking 3 Notes ⊛ Closed 20 Dec-5 Jan ⊛

BISHOP'S STORTFORD
Map 6 TL42

The PitStop
★★★★ GUEST ACCOMMODATION

tel: 01279 725725 & 07803 290000 fax: 01279 726901
The Morgan Garage, Little Hallingbury CM22 7RA
email: mr@melvyn-rutter.net web: www.the-pitstop.net
dir: 3m S of Bishop's Stortford, signed Melvyn Rutter Ltd - Morgan Garage

The PitStop offers four individually styled en suite rooms. Located above The Morgan Garage, guests can enjoy a good night's sleep, as well as hire a modern classic Morgan car for the day. All rooms are very well equipped and meet the needs of a varied clientele. Self-service continental breakfast can be taken in the American-style diner.

Rooms 4 en suite (1 fmly) D £85-£99* Facilities FTV iPod docking station TVL Lift WiFi Hire of Morgan sports car Parking 30 Notes ⊛ Closed 24-29 Dec

See advert on page 208

BISHOP'S STORTFORD *continued*

Bonningtons Guest House

★★★ GUEST HOUSE

tel: 01279 507472 & 07815 704830   **fax:** 01279 507472
George Green, Little Hallingbury CM22 7SP
email: info@bonningtons.net **web:** www.bonningtons.net
dir: *M11 junct 8 onto A120 towards Bishop's Stortford. Left at next rdbt, at lights left onto A1060 towards Hatfield Heath. In centre of Little Hallingbury, turn right opposite The George pub*

Set in its own grounds, Bonningtons is a stylish guest house with a range of individually designed modern bedrooms. All bedrooms are well equipped, free WiFi is available along with secure parking. Stansted Airport is a short drive away and daily rates for parking are available. Continental style breakfasts are provided and there is a very good choice on offer. An ideal base from which to explore the Cambridgeshire and Essex countryside.

Rooms 6 annexe en suite (1 fmly) (4 GF) **Facilities** FTV Lounge tea/coffee WiFi 🔌
Extras Chocolates **Parking** 20

BUNTINGFORD   Map 12 TL32

Sword Inn Hand

★★★★ 🍺 INN

tel: 01763 271356 **Westmill SG9 9LQ**
email: theswordinnhandrestaurant@gmail.com **web:** www.theswordinnhand.co.uk
dir: *In Westmill, off A10 S of Buntingford*

Set within the peaceful village of Westmill amid rolling countryside, this charming 14th-century inn offers excellent accommodation in a friendly and relaxed atmosphere. The purpose-built, ground-floor bedrooms are located just off the rear gardens; all are very well-equipped and carefully appointed and have their own access. Character public rooms offer a choice of restaurant and bar dining options, along with a choice of draught ales.

Rooms 4 en suite (4 GF) S £65-£70; D £75-£95* **Facilities** STV FTV TVL tea/coffee Dinner available **Parking** 25 **Notes** ⊗

HARPENDEN
Map 6 TL11

The Silver Cup
★★★★ INN

tel: 01582 713095 & 07545 977442 **5 St Albans Rd AL5 2JF**
email: info@silvercupinharpenden.co.uk web: www.silvercupinharpenden.co.uk

Serving customers since 1838 The Silver Cup enjoys a prominent position overlooking Harpenden Common. Harpenden is a very busy little town with a great range of shops and businesses along the main street. Bedrooms are all attractively presented, well equipped and comfortable. There is a very popular bar, which serves full selection of real ales along with evening meals. There is ample parking and free WiFi is available.

Rooms 6 en suite (1 fmly) S £75-£85; D £95-£105* **Facilities** FTV TVL tea/coffee Dinner available WiFi ⅃ 18 🍺 **Parking** 6

HERTFORD
Map 6 TL31

Premier Collection

Rigsbys Guest House
★★★★★ GUEST HOUSE

tel: 01992 535999 **25 Saint Andrew St SG14 1HZ**
email: morris@rigsbysguesthouse.com web: www.rigsbysguesthouse.com
dir: *In town centre*

This charming town house enjoys a prominent position in the busy market town of Hertford. Built in the 18th century it is very well appointed with luxurious spacious bedrooms and stylish modern bathrooms. There is a small courtyard at the rear and Rigsbys Restaurant is a popular venue for lunch or afternoon tea. Free WiFi is available in all bedrooms.

Rooms 5 en suite 2 annexe en suite (1 fmly) S £85-£95; D £95-£115*
Facilities FTV iPod docking station tea/coffee Licensed WiFi **Extras** Robes, slippers, bottled water **Conf** Max 15 Thtr 15 Class 10 Board 15 **Notes** LB ⊗

HITCHIN
Map 12 TL12

The Sun
★★★ INN

tel: 01462 432092 & 438411 fax: 01462 431488 **Sun St SG5 1AF**
email: sun.hitchin@greeneking.co.uk web: www.oldenglish.co.uk
dir: *A1(M) junct 8, A602 to Hitchin. At 1st rdbt 4th exit. Straight over at mini rdbt. 2nd left into Biggin Ln, to car park*

This attractive 16th-century coaching inn is situated in the centre of town. Bedrooms are equipped with modern facilities and some retain their original character including exposed beams. Public areas offer an informal restaurant and a comfortably appointed bar.

Rooms 26 en suite 6 annexe en suite (6 GF) (6 smoking) **Facilities** tea/coffee Dinner available Direct Dial **Conf** Max 100 Thtr 100 Class 60 Board 30 **Parking** 20 **Notes** Civ Wed 100

MUCH HADHAM
Map 6 TL41

High Hedges Bed & Breakfast
★★★★ BED AND BREAKFAST

tel: 01279 842505 **High Hedges, Green Tye SG10 6JP**
email: info@high-hedges.co.uk web: www.high-hedges.co.uk
dir: *From B1004 turn off to Green Tye at Prince of Wales pub, turn into private road, 1st on right*

Expect a warm welcome at High Hedges. Bedrooms are well presented and comfortable, and come with many thoughtful extra touches. A substantial breakfast is served in the pleasant dining room.

Rooms 3 rms (2 en suite) (1 pri facs) (1 fmly) (1 GF) S £55; D £70* **Facilities** FTV tea/coffee WiFi **Parking** 3 **Notes** ⊗ Closed 25-26 Dec & 31 Dec-1 Jan ⊜

NUTHAMPSTEAD
Map 12 TL43

The Woodman Inn
★★★ INN

tel: 01763 848328 fax: 01763 848328 **SG8 8NB**
email: woodman.inn@virgin.net web: www.thewoodman-inn.co.uk
dir: *M11 junct 20, A505 towards Royston, left onto B1368 to Barkway, 1st left past Tally Ho, right in 2m. Inn on left. Or from Royston take A505 signed motorway (M11) & Newmarket. Right onto B1368 & then as above*

This 17th-century inn has many fine features, and is close to the Duxford Imperial War Museum. The practical bedrooms are decorated in a traditional style. The kitchen offers a good range of British meals, plus a generous breakfast.

Rooms 2 annexe en suite (2 GF) **Facilities** tea/coffee Dinner available WiFi ⅃ 18 Pool table Shooting range by arrangement **Parking** 30 **Notes** ⊗ RS Sun eve & Mon bar & restaurant closed

ST ALBANS
Map 6 TL10

Innkeeper's Lodge St Albans, London Colney
★★★★ INN

tel: 0845 112 6058 **Barnet Rd, London Colney AL2 1BL**
email: info@innkeeperslodge.com web: www.innkeeperslodge.com

Conveniently located close to the historic town of St Albans, the Colney Fox is a favourite with leisure and business guests. The charming original bar is warm and welcoming, and the log fires burn brightly on cooler evenings. The Fox is a very popular dining venue, and the extensive dinner menu caters for most tastes. The stylish bedrooms are all attractively presented while still retaining many of the inn's original features. Free WiFi is provided, ample secure parking is available and the M25 is close by.

Rooms 13 en suite **Facilities** FTV tea/coffee Dinner available Direct Dial WiFi **Parking**

STAPLEFORD Map 6 TL31

Papillon Woodhall Arms

★★★ INN

tel: 01992 535123 **fax:** 01992 587030 **17 High Rd SG14 3NW**
email: papillonwoodhall@aol.com **web:** www.papillonrestaurant.co.uk
dir: *2.5m from Hertford town on A119 (Hertford to Stevenage road)*

Located in the village centre, this Victorian house has been sympathetically
renovated and extended to provide good standards of comfort and facilities.
Bedrooms are equipped with both practical and thoughtful extras, and public areas
include a spacious restaurant which offers a wide range of international dishes.

Rooms 10 en suite (1 fmly) **Facilities** Lounge TVL tea/coffee Dinner available WiFi
Conf Max 50 Thtr 50 Class 30 Board 20 **Parking** 33 **Notes** ⊗

WARE Map 6 TL31

Feathers Inn

★★★ INN

tel: 01920 462606 **fax:** 01920 469994 **Wadesmill SG12 0TN**
email: feathers.wadesmill@newbridgeinns.co.uk **web:** www.oldenglish.co.uk

This coaching inn is situated beside the A10 on the Cambridge side of Ware. An
adjacent modern annexe provides cottage-style rooms and a good array of modern
facilities. Meals are taken in the inn where there is a choice of a carvery and
informal restaurant operations; the bar remains open all day.

Rooms 31 en suite

WELWYN Map 6 TL21

Premier Collection

The Wellington

★★★★★ ⊛ INN

tel: 01438 714036 **High St AL6 9LZ**
email: info@wellingtonwelwyn.co.uk **web:** www.wellingtonatwelwyn.co.uk
dir: *A1(M) junct 6 follow signs to Welwyn. In the High St opposite St Mary Church*

Enjoying a prominent position in the heart of the pretty village of Welwyn, The
Wellington has undergone a major refurbishment and offers a range of
beautifully presented, individually styled bedrooms. The most is made of the
eye-catching original features in the charming restaurant, and log fires on
colder evenings add to the ambiance. There is a cosy bar area along with a
sheltered terrace at the rear of the property. Ample secure parking is available
along with free WiFi for guests.

Rooms 6 en suite S £85–£105; D £95–£120* **Facilities** FTV DVD iPod docking
station tea/coffee Dinner available WiFi **Extras** Bottled water **Parking** 34 **Notes** ⊗
No coaches

The White Hart

★★★★ ⌂ ⌂ INN

tel: 01438 715353 **2 Prospect Place AL6 9EN**
email: bookings@thewhitehartel.net **web:** www.thewhitehartel.net

This 17th-century coaching inn is located in the heart of the pretty village of
Welwyn and offers a very good choice of well-appointed bedrooms. The very popular
bar serves a good choice of Cask Marque traditional real ales. The bar is used for
casual dining and the restaurant has a warm, welcoming atmosphere.

Rooms 13 rms (3 en suite) (10 pri facs) **Facilities** Dinner available

WELWYN GARDEN CITY Map 6 TL21

The Fairway Tavern

★★★ INN

tel: 01707 336007 & 339349 **fax:** 01707 376154 **Old Herns Ln AL7 2ED**
email: info@fairwaytavern.co.uk **web:** www.fairwaytavern.co.uk
dir: *Exit A1 junct 6 to B1000 through Digswell for 2m, follow signs for golf complex*

Enjoying a picturesque location, this property is located on Panshanger Golf
Complex, with lodge-style bedrooms opening out onto views of the golf course and
rolling countryside. Bedrooms are smartly presented and are well equipped for
business and leisure guests. Breakfast and evening meals are served by the
friendly staff in the adjacent pub. Evening meals are available Monday to Thursday,
between 6.30pm and 9.30pm. A large peaceful garden and a function room for
private hire are available.

Rooms 7 en suite (2 fmly) (7 GF) S £45–£55; D £55–£65 (room only)* **Facilities** FTV
tea/coffee Dinner available Direct Dial Lift WiFi ⅃ 18 **Extras** Bottled water -
complimentary **Conf** Thtr 120 Class 80 Board 25 **Parking** 200 **Notes** ⊗ Civ Wed 100

ISLE OF WIGHT

ARRETON Map 5 SZ58

Blandings

★★★★ BED AND BREAKFAST

tel: 01983 865720 & 865331 **fax:** 01983 862099 **Horringford PO30 3AP**
email: robin.oulton@horringford.com **web:** www.horringford.com/bedandbreakfast.htm
dir: *S through Arreton (B3056), pass Stickworth Hall on right, 300yds on left farm
entrance signed Horringford Gdns. U-turn to left, at end of poplar trees turn right.
Blandings on left*

Blandings is a detached home in the grounds of Horringford Gardens. Set in a small
group of farm buildings, it was formerly the piggery and wainhouse, where the farm
carts were kept. The guest bedroom has private access and a decking area for
warm summer evenings. Breakfast is a highlight with local island produce gracing
the table.

Rooms 1 en suite (1 GF) D £69–£79* **Facilities** FTV tea/coffee WiFi **Parking** 3
Notes LB ⊛

■ BEMBRIDGE   Map 5 SZ68

The Crab & Lobster Inn

★★★★ INN

tel: 01983 872244 **fax:** 01983 873495 **32 Forelands Field Rd PO35 5TR**
email: info@crabandlobsterinn.co.uk **web:** www.crabandlobsterinn.co.uk
dir: *From High St in Bembridge, 1st left after Boots into Forelands Rd. At right bend, left into Lane End Rd, 2nd right into Egerton Rd. At T-junct left into Howgate Rd. Road bears right & becomes Forelands Field Rd, follow brown inn signs*

The Crab & Lobster is a traditional beamed inn enjoying a coastal location overlooking Bembridge Ledge and has panoramic sea views. Bedrooms and bathrooms are traditionally fitted, comfortable and spacious, offering a good range of accessories. Locally-caught crab and lobster is the specialty during lunch and dinner at this popular dining destination.

Rooms 5 en suite (1 fmly) S £35-£75; D £70-£110* **Facilities** FTV DVD tea/coffee
Dinner available WiFi **Parking** 20 **Notes** RS 24-26 Dec B&B only No coaches

■ BONCHURCH   Map 5 SZ57

The Lake

★★★★ GUEST ACCOMMODATION

tel: 01983 852613 **Shore Rd PO38 1RF**
email: enquiries@lakehotel.co.uk **web:** www.lakehotel.co.uk
dir: *0.5m E of Ventnor. Exit A3055 to Bonchurch, opposite village pond*

A warm welcome is assured at this friendly, family-run property set in two acres of well-tended gardens close to the sea. Bedrooms are equipped with modern facilities and the elegant public rooms offer a high standard of comfort. The breakfast menu lists a good choice of hot and cold options.

Rooms 11 en suite 9 annexe en suite (7 fmly) (4 GF) S £55; D £80-£98*
Facilities FTV Lounge TVL tea/coffee Licensed WiFi ⅃ 9 ⚬ **Parking** 20 **Notes** LB
No Children 3yrs Closed 20 Dec-15 Jan

■ CHALE   Map 5 SZ47

The Old House

★★★★ 🛏 BED AND BREAKFAST

tel: 01983 551368 & 07746 453398 **Gotten Manor, Gotten Ln PO38 2HQ**
email: aa@gottenmanor.co.uk **web:** www.gottenmanor.co.uk
dir: *1m N of Chale. Turn right from B3399 into Gotten Ln (opposite chapel), house at end*

Located in countryside close to the coast, this 17th-century house has 18th- and 19th-century additions. The charming rustic bedrooms have antique bathtubs. Comprehensive breakfasts using the finest ingredients are served in the cosy dining room, and there is a spacious lounge with an open fire.

Rooms 2 en suite S £70-£80; D £85-£95 **Facilities** STV FTV iPod docking station
Lounge tea/coffee WiFi ⅃ ⚬ **Parking** 3 **Notes** LB ⊗ No Children 12yrs ▣

■ COWES   Map 5 SZ49

Mimosa Lodge

★★★★ BED AND BREAKFAST

tel: 01983 241490 & 07775 742361 **59 Baring Rd PO31 8DW**
email: info@mimosa-lodge.co.uk **web:** www.mimosa-lodge.co.uk
dir: *From East Cowes on chain ferry to West Cowes, into Mill Hill Rd. Right into Victoria Rd, at end right into Park Rd then immediately left into Ward Ave. At bottom of road, left into Baring Rd*

Located just a short distance from Cowes, this Regency-style house offers spacious and comfortable en suite bedrooms boasting many original features, alongside modern decor and fixtures that include WiFi and digital TVs. Just a short distance from the Isle of Wight Coast Path, this B&B is also ideal for walkers. Guests can expect a friendly arrival where refreshments can be enjoyed in the conservatory. A cooked and continental breakfast is served daily in the dining room.

Rooms 3 en suite (1 GF) **Facilities** FTV DVD tea/coffee WiFi **Parking** 3 **Notes** ⊗ No Children 12yrs Closed 22 Dec-2 Jan

COWES *continued*

Duke of York Inn

★★★ INN

tel: 01983 295171 **fax:** 01983 295047 **Mill Hill Rd PO31 7BT**
email: bookings@dukeofyorkcowes.co.uk **web:** www.dukeofyorkcowes.co.uk

This family-run inn is situated very close to the town centre of Cowes. Comfortable bedrooms are divided between the main building and a separate building only seconds away. Home-cooked meals, with a number of fish and seafood dishes, feature on the menu every evening and are served in the bar and dining area; outdoor covered dining is also an option. Parking is a bonus.

Rooms 8 en suite 5 annexe en suite (1 fmly) (1 GF) **Facilities** FTV tea/coffee Dinner available WiFi **Parking** 10

The Fountain Inn

★★★ INN

tel: 01983 292397 **fax:** 01983 299554 **High St PO31 7AW**
email: fountain.cowes@oldenglishinns.co.uk **web:** www.oldenglish.co.uk
dir: *Adjacent to Red Jet passenger ferry in town centre*

The Fountain Inn, located in the heart of this harbourside town, offers a number of bedrooms that have beautiful views across the water. Bedrooms and bathrooms are modern in design and provide comfortable accommodation. Substantial bar meals are served in the public areas, and breakfast offers a wide range of options. There is a regular transport service with a convenient drop-off point at the rear of the inn; a pay-and-display car park is a short walk away.

Rooms 20 en suite **Facilities** FTV tea/coffee Dinner available Direct Dial WiFi **Notes** No coaches

FISHBOURNE   Map 5 SZ59

The Fishbourne

★★★★ INN

tel: 01983 811784 **fax:** 01983 884779 **111 Fishbourne Ln PO33 4EU**
email: info@thefishbourne.co.uk **web:** www.thefishbourne.co.uk
dir: *Off A3054 Newport to Ryde road, next to Wightlink Ferry Terminal*

The Fishbourne is conveniently located just along from the Wightlink Fishbourne terminal. The inn offers five stylishly decorated bedrooms with light and airy decor and modern fixtures, including LCD TV and free WiFi. Guests can enjoy breakfast, lunch or dinner served in the open-plan bar and restaurant area. On offer are a wide range of traditional pub dishes, with all produce locally sourced.

Rooms 5 en suite (2 fmly) S £55-£75; D £100-£120 **Facilities** FTV DVD iPod docking station tea/coffee Dinner available WiFi ⌁ 9 **Parking** 40 **Notes** LB No coaches

GODSHILL   Map 5 SZ58

Premier Collection

Koala Cottage

★★★★★ 🏠 BED AND BREAKFAST

tel: 01983 842031 **Church Hollow PO38 3DR**
email: info@koalacottage.co.uk **web:** www.koalacottage.co.uk
dir: *From Ryde on A3055, after 7m onto A3056 then A3020, left into Church Hollow*

Located in the heart of the picturesque village of Godshill, Koala Cottage offers three spacious and comfortably appointed bedrooms, all with external access and on-site parking. Bedrooms and bathrooms are of a high quality and guests can expect a number of thoughtful extras on arrival, including locally-made chocolates plus wine and flowers. There is a patio area and indoor hot tub for guests to enjoy. Both cooked and continental breakfasts are served in the conservatory. There are a number of good pubs within a couple of minutes walking distance for evening meals.

Rooms 3 en suite (3 GF) **Facilities** FTV DVD tea/coffee Direct Dial Licensed WiFi Sauna 🛁 Jacuzzi **Extras** Chocolates, wine - complimentary **Parking** 3 **Notes** No Children 18yrs

Arndale

★★★★ BED AND BREAKFAST

tel: 01983 842003 **High St PO38 3HH**
email: arndalebandb@aol.com
dir: *On A3020 High St*

Arndale is situated in the pretty village of Godshill. Expect a warm welcome from the proprietors as well as the resident dogs, Bayley and Arrow. Breakfast is served in the private lounge-dining room. Guests have access to the patio and garden during the warmer months of the year.

Rooms 2 rms (2 pri facs) (1 GF) **Facilities** FTV TVL WiFi Riding **Extras** Fruit - complimentary **Parking** 4 **Notes** ⊗ No Children 14yrs ⊛

NEWPORT   Map 5 SZ58

The Stag

★★★★ INN

tel: 01983 522709 & 811784   **fax:** 01983 521307 **Stag Ln PO30 5TW**
email: info@thestagiow.co.uk **web:** www.thestagiow.co.uk
dir: *From Newport N on A3020 signed Cowes. Pass St Mary's Hospital, up Horsebridge Hill. On corner of Stag Ln*

Located a few minutes from the town of Newport, this inn has recently been refurbished to offer guests stylish and modern bedrooms and bathrooms. Guests can enjoy breakfast, lunch or dinner in the bar and restaurant area, and there is a large outside seating area for alfresco dining during the warmer months. There is ample free parking on site.

Rooms 4 en suite (1 fmly) S £55-£75; D £90-£110 **Facilities** FTV DVD iPod docking station tea/coffee Dinner available WiFi **Extras** Speciality toiletries - complimentary **Parking Notes** LB No coaches

Castle Lodge

★★★ GUEST ACCOMMODATION

tel: 01983 527862 & 07789 228203 **54 Castle Rd PO30 1DP**
email: castlelodge@hotmail.co.uk **web:** www.castlelodgeiow.co.uk
dir: *0.5m SW of town centre. On B3323 towards Carisbrooke Castle*

Well-presented Castle Lodge is located in a quiet residential area within close walking distance of the famous Carisbrooke Castle. A comfortable stay is assured in attractive and restful bedrooms, together with a bright and airy dining room where a substantial breakfast can be enjoyed.

Rooms 2 en suite 5 annexe en suite (1 fmly) (5 GF) S £35-£45; D £55-£75*
Facilities FTV DVD tea/coffee WiFi 🔒 **Parking** 5 **Notes** ⊗

NITON   Map 5 SZ57

Premier Collection

Enchanted Manor

★★★★★ GUEST ACCOMMODATION

tel: 01983 730215 **Sandrock Rd PO38 2NG**
email: info@enchantedmanor.co.uk **web:** www.enchantedmanor.co.uk

Enchanted Manor is a delightful property, set in charming grounds, and enjoys an enviable location within walking distance of the sea. The unusual theme of magic and enchantment prevails throughout the beautifully appointed suites and spacious public areas, all of which are furnished and decorated to a very high standard. A host of extra touches are provided such as DVD players, well-stocked mini-fridges and welcome baskets. Guests are ensured of friendly, attentive service and an excellent breakfast.

Rooms 7 en suite (2 GF) **Facilities** STV FTV tea/coffee Licensed WiFi Snooker Pool table Spa/hot tub Massage beauty treatment room **Conf** Max 30 Board 30 **Parking** 15 **Notes** LB No Children Civ Wed 50

RYDE   Map 5 SZ59

Lisle Court

★★★★ BED AND BREAKFAST

tel: 01983 882860 & 07773 870376 **Woodside, Wootton PO33 4JR**
email: welcome@lislecourt.org.uk **web:** www.lislecourt.org.uk
dir: *A3054 to Wootton Bridge. In High St into New Rd, 1m to Lisle Court*

In a prime location with views of Wooton Creek, this Victorian property offers comfortably appointed bedrooms and bathrooms. The house stands in approximately two acres of garden, mainly mature trees, shrubs and lawns with a small pond and swimming pool. For anyone with a boat the property has its own jetty and pontoons which dry out at low tide. A small boat/summer house on the foreshore provides a tranquil spot to sit and watch boats and wildlife on the creek.

Rooms 3 en suite S £55-£65; D £90-£100 **Facilities** FTV Lounge TVL tea/coffee WiFi ⚲ Fishing 🔒 Private jetty & pontoons **Parking** 12 **Notes** LB No Children 16yrs Closed 24 Dec-4 Jan ⊛

SANDOWN   Map 5 SZ58

Carisbrooke House

★★★★ GUEST HOUSE

tel: 01983 402257 **fax:** 01983 402257 **11 Beachfield Rd PO36 8NA**
email: wmch583@aol.com **web:** www.carisbrookehousehotel.co.uk
dir: *Opposite Ferncliff Gardens*

Expect a friendly welcome at this family-run guest house situated opposite Ferncliff Gardens, and within walking distance of the town centre and seafront. A full English breakfast is served in the dining room overlooking the sun terrace. Enjoy a drink in the bar-lounge. Dinner by arrangement.

Rooms 11 rms (9 en suite) (2 pri facs) (3 fmly) (3 GF) **Facilities** TVL tea/coffee Dinner available Licensed WiFi **Parking** 3

The Sandhill

★★★ Ⓐ GUEST ACCOMMODATION

tel: 01983 403635 **fax:** 01983 403695 **6 Hill St PO36 9DB**
email: sandhillsandown@aol.com **web:** www.sandhill-hotel.co.uk
dir: *In Sandown on main broadway, into Leed St. The Sandhill at top of road*

Set in a pleasant residential area of Sandown, with all main amenities within walking distance, Sandhill is a great base for exploring the island. Guests have use of a TV lounge and a sun lounge, and can enjoy a drink in the bar.

Rooms 16 en suite (5 fmly) (4 GF) S £30-£40; D £60-£80* **Facilities** FTV Lounge TVL tea/coffee Direct Dial Licensed WiFi 🔒 **Parking** 10 **Notes** LB

SEAVIEW   Map 5 SZ69

The Boathouse

★★★★ 🍽 INN

tel: 01983 811784 **fax:** 01983 811784 **Springvale Rd PO34 5AW**
email: info@theboathouseiow.co.uk **web:** www.theboathouseiow.co.uk
dir: *From Seaview follow sea road, The Boathouse on corner of Springvale Rd & Puckpool Hill*

This very pleasant inn has a shore-side location and is a relaxing, friendly and comfortable place to stay. Food is a focus here with fresh, local produce and speciality lobster and crab dishes. The inn provides a contemporary style throughout; bedrooms are pleasantly spacious and most have beach views. There is ample parking and a garden, where in warmer times food and drink are served.

Rooms 4 en suite (1 fmly) S £55-£75; D £105-£125 **Facilities** FTV DVD iPod docking station tea/coffee Dinner available WiFi **Parking** 20 **Notes** LB No coaches

SHANKLIN   Map 5 SZ58

The Fawley

★★★★ GUEST ACCOMMODATION

tel: 01983 868898 **fax:** 01983 719313 **12 Hope Rd PO37 6EA**
email: info@thefawley.co.uk **web:** www.thefawley.co.uk
dir: *300mtrs from beach on main approach road*

Relax and unwind in this stylish accommodation just a stone's throw from cliff-top walks and sandy beaches. The Fawley is committed to ensuring your stay is relaxed and enjoyable. All rooms and communal areas have been refurbished to a high standard, to provide guests with a boutique experience without the price tag. The Fawley is ideally situated just ten minutes from the town centre, train station and the old village with its thatched cottages and tea rooms.

Rooms 9 en suite (1 fmly) S £40-£55; D £70-£85 **Facilities** STV FTV iPod docking station TVL tea/coffee WiFi 🔒 **Extras** Speciality toiletries, bottled water - free **Parking** 8 **Notes** LB ⊗ No Children 5yrs

SHANKLIN *continued*

Fernbank

★★★★ ≋ GUEST ACCOMMODATION

tel: 01983 862790 **6 Highfield Rd PO37 6PP**
email: fernbank2010@btconnect.com **web:** www.fernbank-iow.co.uk
dir: *Approaching Shanklin on A3020, right into Highfield Rd. 300yds on left*

Located in the Shanklin Old Village, Fernbank offers modern, comfortable and spacious accommodation. Home-made refreshments are available throughout the afternoon and guests can enjoy a wide range of both cooked and continental breakfasts in the airy dining room. There is an indoor swimming pool and plenty of outside space within the landscaped gardens in which to relax. Free WiFi is available throughout.

Rooms 17 en suite (1 fmly) (2 GF) S £46-£51; D £80-£108 **Facilities** FTV DVD tea/coffee Licensed WiFi ☯ Petanque **Parking** 13 **Notes** LB ⊗ No Children 12yrs Closed Nov-Feb

The Avenue

★★★★ GUEST ACCOMMODATION

tel: 01983 862746 **6 Avenue Rd PO37 7BG**
email: info@avenuehotelshanklin.co.uk **web:** www.avenuehotelshanklin.co.uk
dir: *A3055 from Sandown, through Lake, right into Avenue Rd before x-rds lights*

This friendly, family-run guest accommodation is in a quiet location just a five-minute walk from the town centre and beaches. The well-equipped bedrooms are generally spacious, and there is a bar-lounge, a conservatory and a comfortable breakfast room. The attractive terraced courtyard lies to the rear.

Rooms 10 en suite (2 GF) S £39-£49; D £69-£79* **Facilities** FTV Lounge tea/coffee Licensed WiFi 🔒 **Parking** 6 **Notes** LB ⊗ Closed Nov-Feb

The Belmont

★★★★ ≋ GUEST ACCOMMODATION

tel: 01983 862864 & 867875 **8 Queens Rd PO37 6AN**
email: enquiries@belmont-iow.co.uk **web:** www.belmont-iow.co.uk
dir: *From Sandown (on A3055), half turn left at Fiveways lights signed Ventnor. Belmont 400mtrs on right, opposite St Saviour's Church*

Situated less than ten minutes' walk from Shanklin beach and only five minutes from Shanklin Old Village, The Belmont offers comfortable accommodation and several rooms with stunning sea views. The Belmont is licensed, and drinks and sandwiches are available during the day and evening. Off-road parking is a benefit, and during summer months guests can enjoy the outdoor swimming pool.

Rooms 13 en suite (2 GF) **Facilities** FTV TVL tea/coffee Dinner available Licensed WiFi ☯ Sauna 🔒 **Parking** 9 **Notes** LB ⊗ No Children 16yrs

The Birkdale

★★★★ GUEST ACCOMMODATION

tel: 01983 862949 & 07508 591889 **fax:** 01983 862949 **5 Grange Rd PO37 6NN**
email: birkdale-iow@hotmail.co.uk **web:** www.birkdalehotel.com
dir: *Follow signs for Shanklin Old Village, Grange Rd opposite car park. The Birkdale on right opposite dance school*

Located right in the heart of Shanklin Old Village, The Birkdale offers spacious and stylishly decorated accommodation, well equipped and with well-stocked beverage trays, digital TV and free WiFi access. There is a traditional guest lounge and extensive range of both cooked and continental dishes for breakfast. Ample off-road parking is available, and a number of shops, cafés, pubs and restaurants are right on the doorstep of this establishment.

Rooms 7 en suite (3 GF) S £39-£46; D £60-£78* **Facilities** STV DVD TVL tea/coffee WiFi 🔒 **Parking** 7 **Notes** LB ⊗ No Children 16yrs

The Grange

★★★★ GUEST ACCOMMODATION

tel: 01983 867644 **fax:** 01983 865537 **9 Eastcliff Rd PO37 6AA**
email: jenni@thegrangebythesea.com **web:** www.thegrangebythesea.com
dir: *Off A3055, High St*

This delightful house specialises in holistic breaks and enjoys a tranquil yet convenient setting among manicured grounds, close to the seafront and village centre. Care has been taken over the beautifully presented bedrooms and spacious public areas. Breakfast is taken en famille (outside in fine weather).

Rooms 16 en suite (2 fmly) (6 GF) S £69-£83; D £88-£116* **Facilities** Lounge TVL tea/coffee Licensed WiFi Sauna Beauty treatments & massage **Extras** Speciality toiletries **Parking** 8 **Notes** LB ⊗ Civ Wed 100

Hayes Barton

★★★★ ≋ GUEST ACCOMMODATION

tel: 01983 867747 **7 Highfield Rd PO37 6PP**
email: williams.2000@virgin.net **web:** www.hayesbarton.co.uk
dir: *A3055 onto A3020 Victoria Ave, 3rd left*

Hayes Barton has the relaxed atmosphere of a family home and provides well-equipped bedrooms and a range of comfortable public areas. Dinner is available from a short selection of home-cooked dishes, and there is a cosy bar-lounge. Shanklin Old Village, beach and promenade are all within walking distance.

Rooms 9 en suite (4 fmly) (2 GF) S £45-£55; D £80-£90* **Facilities** FTV DVD TVL tea/coffee Dinner available Licensed WiFi **Parking** 9 **Notes** LB No Children 7yrs Closed Oct-Apr

The Rowborough

★★★★ GUEST ACCOMMODATION

tel: 01983 866072 **32 Arthurs Hill PO37 6EX**
email: info@rowboroughhotel.com web: www.rowboroughhotel.com
dir: *Off A3055 Sandown Rd, on corner of Arthurs Hill & Wilton Park Rd*

A warm welcome is guaranteed at this family-run Victorian house, set in beautifully tended gardens within walking distance of Shanklin Village, Chine and beaches. All nine bedrooms are comfortably furnished, serviced to a high standard, and come equipped with Freeview TV and DVD. Breakfast and dinner are served in the light and airy dining room, which has doors leading out to the patio and gardens. Guests can enjoy a drink at the well-stocked bar or simply relax in either the guest lounge or modern conservatory. Free WiFi is accessible throughout. Children of all ages and small dogs are all welcome.

Rooms 9 en suite (2 fmly) (1 GF) S £34-£42; D £68-£84 **Facilities** FTV DVD Lounge TVL tea/coffee Dinner available Licensed WiFi 🛜 **Parking** 5 **Notes** LB Closed 5 Jan-9 Feb

St Georges House

★★★★ GUEST ACCOMMODATION

tel: 01983 863691 fax: 01983 861597 **2 St Georges Rd PO37 6BA**
email: info@stgeorgesiow.com web: www.stgeorgesiow.com
dir: *S from Fiveways turn 2nd right off A3055, next right*

This very friendly family-run property is located in a quiet area between the town centre and cliff top. Dating back to 1870, St Georges House retains much of its period charm and style. Bedrooms vary in size but all are comfortable and well appointed. Guests have use of the lounge and bar, and hosts Jan and Mick make every effort to ensure your stay is relaxing.

Rooms 9 en suite (1 fmly) (1 GF) S £32-£47; D £64-£94* **Facilities** FTV TVL tea/coffee Licensed WiFi 🛜 **Parking** 7 **Notes** LB Closed mid Dec-mid Jan

The St Leonards

★★★★ GUEST ACCOMMODATION

tel: 01983 862121 fax: 0872 115 0272 **22 Queens Rd PO37 6AW**
email: info@thestleonards.co.uk web: www.thestleonards.co.uk
dir: *Off A3055 into Queens Rd*

The St Leonards is located in the heart of Shanklin just a short walk away from Shanklin Old Village and nearby beach. This traditional style guest accommodation offers spacious and comfortably appointed rooms, all well equipped with well-stocked beverage trays, free WiFi access and digital TV. There is a comfortable guest lounge and bar on the ground floor where guests can enjoy refreshments on arrival. Breakfast is served daily and offers a good selection of both cooked and continental dishes. Evening meals are available over the winter months. Off-road parking is also available.

Rooms 7 en suite (2 fmly) **Facilities** FTV Lounge TVL tea/coffee Licensed WiFi 🛜 **Parking** 6 **Notes** LB ⊗

TOTLAND BAY	Map 5 SZ38

Sentry Mead

★★★★★ 🛏 GUEST ACCOMMODATION

tel: 01983 753212 fax: 01983 754710 **Madeira Rd PO39 0BJ**
email: info@sentrymead.co.uk web: www.sentrymead.co.uk
dir: *From Yarmouth onto A3054 to Freshwater, 2m, straight over at rdbt, right at next rdbt into Madeira Rd, 300yds on right*

This country house is located in Totland Bay, the West Wight part of the Isle of Wight. Bedrooms have been tastefully decorated to offer guests traditional yet stylish accommodation, all well equipped with WiFi and digital TV. Public areas are spacious; guests can relax in the main lounge or conservatory area, both with views of the large, well-tended garden. A selection of cooked breakfasts and continental dishes is available each morning in the dining room.

Rooms 11 en suite S £55-£60; D £80-£120* **Facilities** FTV iPod docking station Lounge tea/coffee Dinner available Licensed WiFi ⌗ 18 🛜 Day membership to West Bay Country Club **Extras** Speciality toiletries **Parking** 9 **Notes** LB Closed 21 Dec-6 Feb

The Hoo

★★★★ BED AND BREAKFAST

tel: 01983 753592 fax: 01983 753592 **Colwell Rd PO39 0AB**
email: the.hoo@btinternet.com web: www.thehoo.co.uk
dir: *From Yarmouth ferry right onto A3054, 2.25m enter Colwell Common. The Hoo on corner of Colwell Rd & Warden Rd*

Located close to the port and beaches, this friendly, family home provides a peaceful setting. The house has many Japanese features and guests are asked to wear slippers. The spacious bedrooms are well equipped and comfortably furnished. English breakfast is most enjoyable and is served overlooking the attractive gardens.

Rooms 3 rms (1 en suite) (2 fmly) **Facilities** FTV tea/coffee WiFi **Parking** 1 **Notes** No Children 5yrs

The Hermitage

★★★ GUEST ACCOMMODATION

tel: 01983 752518 **Cliff Rd PO39 0EW**
email: blake_david@btconnect.com web: www.thehermitagebnb.co.uk
dir: *From Church Hill (B3322), right into Eden Rd, left into Cliff Rd, 0.5m on right*

The Hermitage is an extremely pet- and people-friendly establishment which occupies a stunning and unspoilt location near to the cliff top in Totland Bay. Extensive gardens are well maintained and off-road parking is a bonus. Accommodation is comfortable and guests are assured of a genuinely warm welcome here. A range of delicious items at breakfast provide a substantial start to the day.

Rooms 6 rms (5 en suite) (1 pri facs) (1 fmly) **Facilities** FTV Lounge TVL tea/coffee Dinner available 🛜 **Parking** 6 **Notes** LB

VENTNOR
Map 5 SZ57

Premier Collection

The Hambrough

★★★★★ ◉◉◉ RESTAURANT WITH ROOMS

tel: 01983 856333 **fax:** 01983 857260 **Hambrough Rd PO38 1SQ**
email: info@thehambrough.com **web:** www.thehambrough.com
dir: *Phone for directions*

A former Victorian villa set on the hillside above Ventnor and with memorable views out to sea, The Hambrough has a modern, stylish interior with well-equipped and boutique-style accommodation. The kitchen team's passion for food is clearly evident in the superb cuisine served in the minimalist restaurant. Head Chef Darren Beevers' cooking has recently been awarded 3 AA Rosettes.

Rooms 7 en suite (3 fmly) **Facilities** STV DVD Lounge tea/coffee Dinner available Direct Dial WiFi 🛝 **Extras** Speciality toiletries - free; mini-bar - charged **Notes** LB ⊗ No coaches Civ Wed 40

Premier Collection

The Leconfield

★★★★★ ◉ 🛏 GUEST ACCOMMODATION

tel: 01983 852196 **85 Leeson Rd, Upper Bonchurch PO38 1PU**
email: enquiries@leconfieldhotel.com **web:** www.leconfieldhotel.com
dir: *On A3055, 3m from Shanklin Old Village*

This country house is situated on an elevated position with panoramic sea views above the historic village of Bonchurch. Luxury bedrooms and suites are spacious and individually styled. Public rooms include two lounges and a conservatory, in addition to the Sea Scape restaurant, (named after the views) where freshly prepared breakfast and imaginative dinner menus are served. Additional facilities include the outdoor pool, terrace area and ample off-road parking.

Rooms 6 en suite 5 annexe en suite (3 GF) S £40-£195; D £70-£200 **Facilities** FTV DVD iPod docking station Lounge tea/coffee Dinner available Licensed WiFi 🛝 **Extras** Bath robes - complimentary **Parking** 14 **Notes** LB ⊗ No Children 16yrs Closed 24-26 Dec & 3-27 Jan

Little Rannoch

★★★★ 🛏 BED AND BREAKFAST

tel: 01983 852263 **1 Steephill Court Rd PO38 1UH**
email: littlerannoch@btinternet.com **web:** www.littlerannoch.co.uk
dir: *From Ventnor town centre onto A3055 to St Lawrence. After 1.3m turn right after botanic gardens into Steephill Court Rd, on left*

Little Rannoch is a south-facing bungalow less than a mile from Ventnor, close to Ventnor Botanic Gardens, Cricket Ground and Steephill Cove. The accommodation comprises one self-contained suite comprising of double bedroom, dining/kitchenette, shower room and patio with garden and sea views. The resorts of Shanklin and Sandown are within eight miles of Little Rannoch. Breakfast features local and home-made items. Off street parking available.

Rooms 1 en suite (1 GF) S £45; D £90 **Facilities** STV FTV iPod docking station tea/coffee 🛝 **Extras** Snacks, home-made biscuits **Parking** 1 **Notes** ⊗ No Children Closed Nov-1 Mar

St Maur

★★★★ GUEST ACCOMMODATION

tel: 01983 852570 & 853645 **fax:** 01983 852306 **Castle Rd PO38 1LG**
email: sales@stmaur.co.uk **web:** www.stmaur.co.uk
dir: *Exit A3055 at end of Park Av into Castle Rd, premises 150yds on left*

A warm welcome awaits at this Victorian villa, which is pleasantly and quietly located in an elevated position overlooking the bay. The well-equipped bedrooms are traditionally decorated, while public areas include a spacious lounge and cosy residents' bar. The gardens here are a delight.

Rooms 9 en suite (2 fmly) **Facilities** STV FTV Lounge tea/coffee Dinner available Licensed WiFi 🛝 **Parking** 9 **Notes** ⊗ No Children 5yrs Closed Dec

KENT

ASHFORD
Map 7 TR04

Downsview Guest House

★★★★ GUEST ACCOMMODATION

tel: 01233 621391 & 07968 978581 **fax:** 01233 620364 **Willesborough Rd TN24 9QP**
email: downsviewguesthouse@msn.com **web:** www.ashforddownsview.co.uk
dir: *M20 junct 10, at rdbt take 1st exit onto A2070 signed Canterbury. Downsview on right hand side*

This spacious and well appointed guest house is located within minutes of Ashford town centre and easy access to both the M20 and Ashford International Station. Bedrooms are traditional throughout yet comfortably appointed with digital TVs and free WiFi access. There is plenty of parking available and many rooms benefit from fantastic views of the Stour Valley. Guests can enjoy a cooked or continental breakfast served in the dining room.

Rooms 12 en suite 2 annexe rms (2 pri facs) (4 fmly) (6 GF) **Facilities** FTV Lounge TVL tea/coffee Licensed WiFi 🛝 **Extras** Speciality toiletries - complimentary **Parking** 41 **Notes** ⊗

BENENDEN
Map 7 TQ83

Apple Trees B&B

★★★★ BED AND BREAKFAST

tel: 01580 240622 **Goddards Green TN17 4AR**
email: garryblanch@aol.com **web:** www.appletreesbandb.co.uk
dir: *3m E of Cranbrook. Exit A262 at Sissinghurst S into Chaple Ln, over x-rds, 2m left to Goddards Green, 1m on right*

This spacious cottage is situated in the heart of the Kentish countryside, and is convenient for those visiting Sissinghurst Castle and Great Dixter. Bedrooms are attractively presented and include plenty of thoughtful extras such as flat-screen TVs and internet connection. Breakfast is served in the rustic dining room overlooking the garden.

Rooms 3 rms (1 en suite) (2 pri facs) (3 GF) S £50-£70; D £65-£80* **Facilities** TVL TV1B tea/coffee WiFi 🛝 18 **Parking** 6 **Notes** ⊗ ⊜

BIDDENDEN　　　　　　　　　　Map 7 TQ83

Heron Cottage

★★★★ GUEST ACCOMMODATION

tel: 01580 291358 **fax:** 01580 291358 **TN27 8HH**
email: susantwort@hotmail.com **web:** www.heroncottage.info
dir: *1m NW of Biddenden. A262 W from Biddenden, 1st right, 0.25m across sharp left bend through stone pillars, left into unmade road*

Expect a warm welcome at this picturesque cottage, set in immaculate, mature gardens in the peaceful Kent countryside. The bedrooms are thoughtfully equipped and have co-ordinated soft furnishings. Breakfast is served in the smart dining room, and the cosy sitting room has an open fireplace.

Rooms 7 rms (6 en suite) (2 fmly) (1 GF) S £65-£75; D £75-£85* **Facilities** FTV Lounge TVL tea/coffee Dinner available WiFi 🎣 Fishing **Parking** 8 **Notes** Closed Dec-Feb ⊛

BROADSTAIRS　　　　　　　　Map 7 TR36

Bay Tree Broadstairs

★★★★ GUEST ACCOMMODATION

tel: 01843 862502 **fax:** 01843 860589 **12 Eastern Esplanade CT10 1DR**
email: enquiries@baytreebroadstairs.co.uk **web:** www.baytreebroadstairs.co.uk
dir: *A255 into Rectory Rd & Eastern Esplanade*

Bay Tree Broadstairs is a family-run concern, situated on an elevated position overlooking East Cliff. The attractive bedrooms are well equipped and some have a balcony with a sea view. There is a comfortable lounge bar, and a good breakfast menu is offered in the dining room.

Rooms 10 en suite (1 GF) **Facilities** FTV TVL tea/coffee Licensed **Parking** 11 **Notes** ⊗ No Children 10yrs Closed Xmas & New Year

The Victoria Bed and Breakfast

★★★★ BED AND BREAKFAST

tel: 01843 871010 **23 Victoria Pde CT10 1QL**
email: helen.kemp2@virgin.net **web:** www.thevictoriabroadstairs.co.uk
dir: *A299 into Broadstairs, pass train station & continue on High St. Turn right into Charlotte St, 1st left then right into Victoria Parade*

The Victoria Bed and Breakfast offers very comfortable seaside accommodation in an excellent location. The breakfast room/lounge and top floor bedroom have stunning sea views and the house is just thirty metres from the beach. All bedrooms are well furnished with en suite bathrooms, Freeview TV and tea/coffee making facilities. Breakfast is cooked to order, and a range of breakfast options is available with most items locally sourced. Private parking or nearby permit parking available at no charge.

Rooms 3 en suite (1 fmly) S £70; D £85-£135* **Facilities** FTV DVD Lounge tea/coffee WiFi 🔒 **Extras** Fridge, fresh milk, mineral water **Parking** 1 **Notes** LB ⊗ RS Xmas

BROOKLAND　　　　　　　　　Map 7 TQ92

Dean Court

★★★★ BED AND BREAKFAST

tel: 01797 344244 **fax:** 01797 344102 **TN29 9TD**
email: anne_furnival@hotmail.com **web:** www.deancourtromneymarsh.co.uk
dir: *M20 junct 10, A2070 towards Hastings (follow Brenzett signs). At Brenzett take A259 signed Hastings & Rye. Through Brookland, sharp left bend, on right 0.5m to house*

Expect a warm welcome at Dean Court, a Victorian farmhouse on a busy working farm. The Furnival family have lived and farmed here since the 1950s. A hearty breakfast will set you up for a day of exploring the nearby countryside and sandy beaches; Romney Marsh is a lovely area for walking and cycling. Dogs are welcome if crated in the house.

Rooms 3 en suite S fr £55; D fr £170* **Facilities** FTV iPod docking station Lounge tea/coffee WiFi 🔒 **Parking** 5 **Notes** No Children 12yrs Closed 20 Dec-1 Feb ⊛

CANTERBURY   Map 7 TR15

Premier Collection

Magnolia House

★★★★★ GUEST ACCOMMODATION

tel: 01227 765121 & 07776 236459   fax: 0872 111 7681
36 St Dunstans Ter CT2 8AX
email: info@magnoliahousecanterbury.co.uk
web: www.magnoliahousecanterbury.co.uk
dir: *A2 E onto A2050 for city centre, left at 1st rdbt signed University of Kent. St Dunstans Terrace 3rd right*

This charming Georgian property dates from around 1830 and combines a warm welcome with quality accommodation. Bedrooms are superbly appointed and luxurious, equipped with lots of extra amenities including WiFi. A wide range of items is offered at breakfast. Magnolia House is just a ten-minute stroll from the city centre.

Rooms 6 en suite (1 GF) S £50-£55; D £95-£135 **Facilities** FTV DVD Lounge tea/coffee WiFi **Extras** Hand-made toiletries, fridge, complimentary drinks **Parking** 5 **Notes** ⊗ No Children 12yrs Closed 23-28 Dec

House of Agnes

★★★★ GUEST ACCOMMODATION

tel: 01227 472185 fax: 01227 470478 **71 Saint Dunstans St CT2 8BN**
email: info@houseofagnes.co.uk web: www.houseofagnes.co.uk
dir: *On A290 between London Rd & Orchard St, 300mtrs from West Gate*

This historic 14th-century property has been appointed to provide luxury guest accommodation and offers individually themed rooms, ranging from the traditional to the more exotic. All bedrooms have a good range of amenities such as flat-screen TVs and WiFi. This establishment is also licensed for weddings.

Rooms 8 en suite 8 annexe en suite (2 fmly) (8 GF) S £69-£92; D £75-£135* **Facilities** FTV DVD Lounge TVL tea/coffee Licensed WiFi ⇩ ⅃ 18 ⚫ Boules Badminton **Conf** Thtr 30 Class 12 Board 20 **Parking** 13 **Notes** LB ⊗ No Children 6yrs Closed 24-26 Dec Civ Wed 46

The White House

★★★★ GUEST ACCOMMODATION

tel: 01227 761836 **6 St Peters Ln CT1 2BP**
email: info@whitehousecanterbury.co.uk web: www.whitehousecanterbury.co.uk
dir: *A2 into Canterbury. At London Rd rdbt take 2nd exit (A2050), at next rdbt 1st exit into St Peters Pl. Right at Westgate Tower rdbt, right before next rdbt. Left at end, St Peters Ln on right*

The White House is an ideally located Regency property in the heart of Canterbury, within a two-minute walk of the famous cathedral. All bedrooms are modern with bright, airy decor and have LCD TVs and WiFi. Breakfast can be enjoyed in the ground-floor dining room and there's additional space for guests to relax during their stay.

Rooms 7 en suite S £60-£75; D £80-£140* **Facilities** FTV DVD tea/coffee WiFi **Notes** ⊗ No Children 16yrs Closed Jan

Yorke Lodge

★★★★ GUEST ACCOMMODATION

tel: 01227 451243 **fax:** 01227 462006 **50 London Rd CT2 8LF**
email: info@yorkelodge.com web: www.yorkelodge.com
dir: *M2 junct 7, A2, exit left signed Canterbury. At 1st rdbt turn left into London Rd*

Yorke Lodge stands in a tree-lined road just a ten-minute walk from the town centre and railway station. The spacious bedrooms are thoughtfully equipped and carefully decorated using a calming palette of neutral and pastel shades. Some rooms have four-poster beds. The stylish dining room leads to a conservatory-lounge, which opens onto a superb terrace.

Rooms 8 en suite (1 fmly) S £60-£75; D £90-£130 **Facilities** FTV tea/coffee WiFi **Parking** 5 **Notes** LB No Children 5yrs

The City of Canterbury Guest House

★★★★ GUEST ACCOMMODATION

tel: 01227 457455 **27 St Thomas Hill CT2 8HW**
email: t.mills@thecityofcanterbury.co.uk web: www.thecityofcanterbury.co.uk

This guest house is located less than one mile from the city centre of historic Canterbury. There is a large open plan lounge and dining room where guests can relax in front of the log burner and also where both cooked or continental breakfasts are served daily. Bedrooms are spacious, many with views of Canterbury and all offer comfortably equipped accommodation including digital TV and free WiFi. There is plenty of parking available for guests.

Rooms 9 en suite (2 fmly) (2 GF) S £45-£55; D £65-£80* **Facilities** FTV TVL tea/coffee WiFi **Parking** 7 **Notes** ⊗ Closed 31 Dec-1 Jan ⊛

Peregrine House

★★★★ GUEST ACCOMMODATION

tel: 01227 761897 **18 Hawks Ln CT1 2NU**
email: enquiries@castlehousehotel.co.uk

Peregrine House is centrally located right in the heart of Canterbury. This is a sister property to Castle House. Guests register at Castle House and then take a short walk to Peregrine House, alternatively a courtesy car is available to help transport guests and their luggage. Bedrooms and bathrooms offer clean, modern comfortable accommodation. Close to the main high street, Canterbury Cathedral, shops and restaurants.

Rooms 13 rms (11 en suite) (2 pri facs) (5 fmly) (3 GF) **Facilities** TVL tea/coffee Dinner available Licensed WiFi **Parking** 14 **Notes** ⊗

Cathedral Gate

★★★ GUEST ACCOMMODATION

tel: 01227 464381 fax: 01227 462800 **36 Burgate CT1 2HA**
email: cgate@cgate.demon.co.uk web: www.cathgate.co.uk
dir: *In city centre. Next to main gateway into cathedral precincts*

Dating from 1438, this house has an enviable central location next to the cathedral. Old beams and winding corridors are part of the character of the property. Bedrooms are traditionally furnished, equipped to modern standards and many have cathedral views. Luggage can be unloaded at reception before parking in a nearby car park.

Rooms 13 rms (2 en suite) 12 annexe rms 10 annexe en suite (5 fmly) **Facilities** FTV tea/coffee Dinner available Direct Dial Licensed WiFi

Duke Of Cumberland

★★★ INN

tel: 01227 831396 & 01303 844663 **The Street, Barham CT4 6NY**
email: info@dukeofcumberland.co.uk **web:** www.dukeofcumberland.co.uk
dir: S of Canterbury on A2. Exit signed Barham, 100yds on The Street, off Valley Rd

This traditional English pub is located in the village of Barham just a few miles outside historic Canterbury. There are three comfortably appointed en suite bedrooms, traditional in style with all modern amenities including WiFi and digital TVs. A hearty cooked breakfast is served daily and guests can enjoy lunch or dinner in the main bar and restaurant area.

Rooms 3 en suite (1 fmly) S £50; D £70* **Facilities** FTV DVD iPod docking station tea/coffee Dinner available WiFi 🐾 **Parking** 30

Ersham Lodge

 ★★★ GUEST ACCOMMODATION

tel: 01227 463174 **12 New Dover Rd CT1 3AP**
email: info@ersham-lodge.co.uk **web:** www.ersham-lodge.co.uk
dir: From Canterbury ring road take A2050 (signs for Dover, A2) premises on right 40mtrs after lights opposite road entrance to Canterbury College

This attractive twin-gabled Victorian house is just a short walk from the college, cathedral and the city's attractions. Bedrooms are smartly decorated and comfortable, and there is a cosy lounge and a spacious breakfast room which looks out onto the well-kept patio and garden. Free guest parking is available.

Rooms 10 en suite (1 fmly) (5 GF) **Facilities** Lounge tea/coffee WiFi 🐾 **Conf** Max 30 Class 30 Board 20 **Parking** 10 **Notes** ⊗

Innkeeper's Lodge Canterbury

★★★ INN

tel: 0845 112 6099 **162 New Dover Rd CT1 3EL**
email: info@innkeeperslodge.com **web:** www.innkeeperslodge.com

At Innkeeper's Lodge you'll find accommodation with comfort and character in equal measure, and everything needed for a relaxing stay, from easy check-in and free parking to complimentary breakfast and a cosy pub serving great value food and drink on the doorstep. Each Lodge has quality rooms, and there are Lodges in a variety of locations from towns and cities to countryside settings across the UK.

Rooms 9 en suite (1 fmly) **Facilities** FTV tea/coffee Dinner available Direct Dial WiFi **Parking**

St Stephens Guest House

★★★ GUEST ACCOMMODATION

tel: 01227 767644 **100 St Stephens Rd CT2 7JL**
email: info@ststephensguesthouse.co.uk **web:** www.ststephensguesthouse.co.uk
dir: A290 from city, Westgate & sharp right into North Ln, 2nd rdbt left into St Stephens Rd, right into Market Way, car park on right

St Stephens Guest House offers well-appointed accommodation. Rooms are well equipped. It is located just ten minutes' walk from Canterbury town centre and conveniently located near the University of Kent and Christchurch College. The dining room is traditionally decorated and has views of the garden; guests can enjoy a cooked or continental breakfast.

Rooms 1 en suite 8 annexe en suite (1 fmly) (3 GF) S fr £52; D fr £73* **Facilities** FTV tea/coffee WiFi **Parking** 8 **Notes** ⊗ Closed mid Dec-mid Jan

The Black Horse

Ⓤ

tel: 01227 455411 **11-12 Orchard St CT2 8AP**
email: caroline@hillpropertyltd.com

Currently the rating for this establishment is not confirmed. This may be due to a change of ownership or because it has only recently joined the AA rating scheme.

Rooms 9 en suite

DARTFORD	Map 6 TQ57

The Rising Sun Inn

★★★ INN

tel: 01474 872291 **fax:** 01474 872779 **Fawkham Green DA3 8NL**
email: enquiries@risingsun-fawkham.co.uk **web:** www.risingsun-fawkham.co.uk
dir: M25 junct 3, A20 Brands Hatch. Turn into Scratchers Ln until sign for Fawkham. Left into Brandshatch Rd, inn on left

This popular inn overlooks the village green and is just a short drive from Brands Hatch. All the en suite bedrooms are spacious, pleasantly decorated and comfortable. There is a busy character bar, restaurant, and a patio for alfresco dining in warmer weather.

Rooms 5 en suite (1 fmly) (2 GF) S fr £55; D fr £85 **Facilities** FTV tea/coffee Dinner available WiFi **Parking** 20 **Notes** ⊗ No coaches

DEAL
Map 7 TR35

Premier Collection

Sutherland House

★★★★★ GUEST ACCOMMODATION

tel: 01304 362853 fax: 01304 381146 **186 London Rd CT14 9PT**
email: info@sutherlandhouse.fsnet.co.uk web: www.sutherlandhousehotel.co.uk
dir: *0.5m W of town centre/seafront on A258*

This stylish accommodation demonstrates impeccable taste with its charming, well-equipped bedrooms and a comfortable lounge. A fully stocked bar, books, free WiFi, Freeview TV and radio are some of the many amenities offered. The elegant dining room is the venue for a hearty breakfast and dinner is available by prior arrangement.

Rooms 4 en suite (1 GF) S £65-£75; D £80-£90* **Facilities** FTV DVD iPod docking station Lounge tea/coffee Dinner available Direct Dial Licensed WiFi 🔒 **Extras** Speciality toiletries, honesty bar **Conf** Max 12 Thtr 12 Class 12 Board 12 **Parking** 7 **Notes** LB No Children 5yrs

Sondes Lodge

★★★ GUEST ACCOMMODATION

tel: 01304 368741 & 07817 178186 **14 Sondes Rd CT14 7BW**
email: info@sondeslodge.co.uk web: www.sondeslodge.co.uk
dir: *From Dover take A258 to Deal, pass Deal Castle, towards town centre. 4th right into Sondes Rd. Lodge on right*

Expect a warm welcome at this smart guest accommodation situated in a side road just off the seafront and a short walk from the town centre. The pleasant bedrooms have co-ordinated fabrics and many thoughtful touches. Breakfast is served at individual tables in the lower ground-floor dining room.

Rooms 3 en suite (1 fmly) (1 GF) S £40-£50; D £60-£70* **Facilities** FTV DVD TVL tea/coffee WiFi **Extras** Bath robes, bottled water, fruit/snacks - free **Notes** ⊗

DODDINGTON
Map 7 TQ95

Premier Collection

The Old Vicarage

★★★★★ GUEST ACCOMMODATION

tel: 01795 886136 fax: 01795 886136 **Church Hill ME9 0BD**
email: claire@oldvicaragedoddington.co.uk web: www.oldvicaragedoddington.co.uk
dir: *From A2 take Faversham Rd signed Doddington for 4.4m. Turn right towards church*

The Old Vicarage is a stunning Grade II listed property, situated at the edge of Doddington, beside the old church. Spacious rooms come with flat-screen TVs, and special touches such as binoculars and bird reference books. Guests can relax in the elegant lounge, and a bountiful breakfast is served in the stylish dining room overlooking a vista of endless trees and green fields.

Rooms 3 en suite (2 fmly) S £57-£72; D £82-£93* **Facilities** FTV Lounge tea/coffee WiFi 🔒 **Parking** 6 **Notes** ⊗ No Children 3yrs Closed 25 Dec-2 Jan

DOVER
Map 7 TR34

Premier Collection

The Marquis at Alkham

★★★★★ ◉◉◉ 🍴 RESTAURANT WITH ROOMS

tel: 01304 873410 & 822945 fax: 01304 873418 **Alkham Valley Rd, Alkham CT15 7DF**
email: info@themarquisatalkham.co.uk web: www.themarquisatalkham.co.uk
dir: *A256 from Dover, at rdbt 1st exit into London Rd, left into Alkham Rd, Alkham Valley Rd. Establishment 1.5m after sharp bend*

Located between Dover and Folkestone, this contemporary restaurant with rooms offers luxury accommodation with modern features, including flat-screen TVs, WiFi, power showers and bathrobes to name but a few. All the stylish bedrooms are individually designed and have fantastic views of the Kent Downs. The award-winning restaurant, open for lunch and dinner, specialises in modern British cuisine guided by Head Chef Charlie Lakin. Both continental and a choice of cooked breakfasts are offered.

Rooms 10 en suite (3 fmly) (1 GF) **Facilities** FTV DVD Lounge TVL Dinner available Direct Dial WiFi **Conf** Max 20 Thtr 20 Class 20 Board 16 **Parking** 22 **Notes** ⊗ Civ Wed 55

Beulah House

★★★★ GUEST ACCOMMODATION

tel: 01304 824615 fax: 01304 828850 **94 Crabble Hill, London Rd CT17 0SA**
email: owen@beulahhouse94.freeserve.co.uk web: www.beulahguesthouse.co.uk
dir: *On A256*

An impressive Victorian house located just a stroll from the town centre and close to the ferry port. The spacious bedrooms are pleasantly decorated and thoughtfully equipped. Public rooms include two conservatories and a comfortable lounge. The impressive garden has an interesting display of topiary and a small menagerie.

Rooms 8 en suite **Facilities** TVL tea/coffee WiFi **Parking** 8 **Notes** LB ⊗ No Children 12yrs

Hubert House Guesthouse

★★★★ GUEST HOUSE

tel: 01304 202253 fax: 01304 210142 **9 Castle Hill Rd CT16 1QW**
email: stay@huberthouse.co.uk web: www.huberthouse.co.uk
dir: *On A258 by Dover Castle, down hill, 1st left. Next to White Horse pub*

This charming Georgian house is within walking distance of the ferry port and the town centre. Bedrooms are sumptuously decorated and furnished with an abundance of practical extras. Breakfast, including full English and healthy options, is served in the smart bistro. Families are especially welcome.

Rooms 6 en suite (4 fmly) S £40-£50; D £65-£100 **Facilities** FTV tea/coffee Licensed WiFi 🔒 **Extras** Robes, fridges **Parking** 6 **Notes** LB Closed 24-27 Dec & 31 Dec-2 Jan

Castle Guest House

★★★★ GUEST HOUSE

tel: 01304 201656 **10 Castle Hill CT16 1QW**
email: info@castle-guesthouse.com **web:** www.castle-guesthouse.co.uk
dir: *A20 Dover, follow signs for Dover Castle. At foot of hill, on right*

Castle Guest House is located in the centre of Dover just minutes from the town centre, Dover ferry port and Channel Tunnel terminal. Bedrooms are modern and comfortably appointed and include digital TV and free WiFi access. A cooked and continental breakfast is served daily in the dining room. Free off-road parking available and secure parking is available for motorbikes or bicycles (on request).

Rooms 6 en suite (2 fmly) S £40-£50; D £65-£75 **Facilities** FTV DVD tea/coffee WiFi
🅿 **Parking** 5 **Notes** LB

Maison Dieu Guest House

★★★★ GUEST ACCOMMODATION

tel: 01304 204033 **fax:** 01304 242816 **89 Maison Dieu Rd CT16 1RU**
email: info@brguest.co.uk **web:** www.brguest.co.uk
dir: *M20/A20 to Dover. Left into York St, at rdbt 2nd exit. Right at lights into Ladywell, right at next lights, 100yds on left*

Maison Dieu is ideally located to offer the perfect stop over en route to and from Dover and mainland Europe. Dover ferry and cruise terminals and The White Cliffs of Dover are just 5 minutes away and the Channel Tunnel is 10 minutes by car. Bedrooms are comfortably decorated and come well equipped with WiFi and digital TV. Guests can enjoy a cooked or continental breakfast daily in the dining room.

Rooms 7 rms (4 en suite) (1 pri facs) (4 fmly) S £32-£38; D £48-£68 (room only)*
Facilities FTV tea/coffee WiFi 🅿 **Parking** 6 **Notes** LB ⊗ No Children 4yrs

Bleriot's

★★★ GUEST ACCOMMODATION

tel: 01304 211394 **Belper House, 47 Park Av CT16 1HE**
email: info@bleriotsguesthouse.co.uk **web:** www.bleriotsguesthouse.co.uk
dir: *A20 to Dover, left into York St, right at lights into Ladywell. Left at next lights into Park Av*

This large, family-run Victorian property is convenient for the ferry port and town centre. Guests receive a warm welcome and can enjoy a range of comfortable, spacious en suite bedrooms. The attractive dining room is the venue for a wholesome breakfast to set you up for the day.

Rooms 8 en suite (2 fmly) S £35; D £60 (room only)* **Facilities** FTV Lounge tea/coffee WiFi 🅿 **Parking** 8 **Notes** LB ⊗

Ardmore Guest House

★★★ GUEST ACCOMMODATION

tel: 01304 205895 **fax:** 01304 208229 **18 Castle Hill Rd CT16 1QW**
email: res@ardmoreph.co.uk **web:** www.ardmoreph.co.uk
dir: *On A258 by Dover Castle*

Dating from 1796, this delightful house is adjacent to Dover Castle. Convenient for the town centre and ferry port, the Ardmore offers comfortable accommodation and friendly hospitality. The non-smoking bedrooms are spacious and airy. Public rooms include a comfortable lounge and a well-appointed breakfast room.

Rooms 4 en suite (1 fmly) D £60-£70* **Facilities** FTV Lounge tea/coffee WiFi **Notes** ⊗ Closed Xmas

St Martins Guest House

★★★ GUEST ACCOMMODATION

tel: 01304 205938 **fax:** 01304 208229 **17 Castle Hill Rd CT16 1QW**
email: res@stmartinsgh.co.uk **web:** www.stmartinsgh.co.uk
dir: *On A258 by Dover Castle*

Located close to the castle, ferry port and town centre, this smart guest accommodation offers a friendly welcome. The thoughtfully equipped en suite bedrooms are attractively decorated, and most rooms enjoy a sunny aspect. Breakfast is served in the pine-furnished dining room, and there is also a comfortable lounge.

Rooms 6 en suite (3 fmly) D £60-£70* **Facilities** FTV Lounge tea/coffee WiFi **Notes** ⊗ Closed Xmas

EGERTON	Map 7 TQ94

Premier Collection

Frasers

★★★★★ ◉ 🏠 GUEST ACCOMMODATION

tel: 01233 756122 **fax:** 01233 756770 **Coldharbour Farm TN27 9DD**
email: lisa@frasers-events.co.uk
dir: *Please contact Frasers for detailed directions*

Frasers is nestled at the end of a private drive on a working farm set deep in beautiful Kent countryside, halfway between Maidstone and Ashford. Bedrooms are spacious and individual in style with excellent quality furnishings ensuring a comfortable stay. Guests can enjoy an extensive cooked or continental breakfast in the main restaurant; this is also where the AA Rosette-worthy dinner is served.

Rooms 8 en suite S £85-£100; D £160-£295 **Facilities** tea/coffee Dinner available Licensed WiFi ♿ 18 Fishing 🅿 **Extras** Speciality toiletries, robes, slippers **Conf** Max 150 Thtr 150 Class 50 Board 50 **Parking** 50 **Notes** LB ⊗ Civ Wed 100

FAVERSHAM
Map 7 TR06

Garden Cottage

★★★★ GUEST ACCOMMODATION

tel: 01795 531167 **Stonebridge Lodge, West St ME13 7RU**
email: lizandtonysharp@mac.com **web:** www.stonebridgelodgefaversham.com
dir: *M2 junct 6 onto A251, left onto A2. Right into Ospringe Rd, left into Napleton Rd, right into Tanners St, left into West St. 1st house on right*

Located in the centre of Faversham within easy walking distance of the town and restaurants, Garden Cottage is in the garden of Stonebridge Lodge. Accommodation is spacious and comfortably appointed with modern decor and furnishings. A substantial continental breakfast can be provided in the room and there is a dining area in the room where guests can eat. The spacious gardens surrounding the cottage are dotted with ponds and waterways.

Rooms 1 annexe en suite (1 fmly) (1 GF) S £90; D £90* **Facilities** STV FTV tea/coffee WiFi 🛁 Outdoor hot tub (in season) **Extras** Fruit, snacks, fridge **Parking** 3 **Notes** Closed 15 Dec-15 Jan ⊜

The White Horse Inn

★★★★ ⌂ INN

tel: 01227 751343 **fax:** 01227 751090 **246 The Street, Boughton-under-Blean ME13 9AL**
email: whitehorseinn@live.co.uk **web:** www.whitehorsecanterbury.co.uk
dir: *M2 junct 7, slip road left towards Channel Tunnel/Canterbury/Dover. At rdbt 4th exit onto A2 then slip road left to Boughton. On left on entering village*

This traditional inn is located in the picturesque village of Boughton-under-Blean, yet just a short drive from Canterbury city centre. The White Horse Inn has a spacious pub and restaurant area where lunch, dinner and breakfast are served daily. Bedrooms are all modern in style and comfortably appointed, and come well equipped with digital TV and free WiFi.

Rooms 13 en suite (3 fmly) (2 GF) S £55-£70; D £70-£105 (room only)*
Facilities FTV DVD TVL tea/coffee Dinner available Direct Dial WiFi ⚲ 18 🛁
Extras Speciality toiletries, water - free; slippers **Parking** 31 **Notes** LB

Judd's Folly

★★★ GUEST ACCOMMODATION

tel: 01795 591818 & 532595 **fax:** 01795 532595 **Syndalie Park, London Rd ME13 0RH**
email: jason@juddsfollyhotel.co.uk **web:** www.juddsfollyhotel.co.uk
dir: *M2 junct 6 follow signs for Faversham. Onto A2 towards Sittingbourne, through Ospringe, over mini rdbt, 50yds on left*

High on an elevated position with far-reaching views, Judd's Folly is just a five minute drive from the market town of Faversham and just a couple of minutes' drive from the M2. Bedrooms are all tastefully decorated with modern decor and soft furnishings, and are split between courtyard buildings and the main building which hosts the bar and restaurant area. Dinner is served here daily and is also the venue for cooked and continental breakfasts. Functions and weddings can also be accommodated.

Rooms 16 en suite 13 annexe en suite (4 fmly) (16 GF) **Facilities** FTV Lounge TVL tea/coffee Dinner available Direct Dial Licensed WiFi Arrangement with gym, charges payable **Conf** Max 100 Thtr 80 Class 30 Board 30 **Parking** 100 **Notes** LB Civ Wed 100

FOLKESTONE
Map 7 TR23

Rocksalt Rooms

★★★★ ◉◉ RESTAURANT WITH ROOMS

tel: 01303 212070 **2 Back St CT19 6NN**
email: info@rocksaltfolkestone.co.uk **web:** www.rocksaltfolkestone.co.uk
dir: *M20 junct 13 follow signs to harbour (A259). At harbour left onto Fish Market*

Overlooking the busy harbour, often crowded with small leisure boats, and having wonderful sea views, Rocksalt enjoys a great location in Folkestone. Bedrooms are stylish, well appointed with original antique beds and equipped with a host of thoughtful little extras. Continental breakfasts are delivered promptly to the guests' rooms each morning, and dinner is served in the award-winning restaurant that is also blessed with panoramic views.

Rooms 4 en suite (1 fmly) S £85-£115; D £85-£115* **Facilities** FTV iPod docking station tea/coffee Dinner available WiFi **Notes** ⊗ No coaches

The Wycliffe

★★★ GUEST HOUSE

tel: 01303 252186 **fax:** 01303 252186 **63 Bouverie Rd West CT20 2RN**
email: wycliffehotel@gmail.com **web:** www.wycliffehotel.com
dir: *M20 junct 13 onto A20. 2nd set of lights take middle lane & proceed straight over. After 1km turn right signed A259 Sandgate/Hastings into Earls Av. Then 2nd left into Bouverie Road West, 200mtrs on right*

The Wycliffe is located in the heart of Folkestone, just a short walk into the town centre and main promenade. Bedrooms are spacious and traditional in style with modern amenities including digital TV and free WiFi access. There is a bar on the ground floor and a large dining room where guests can enjoy breakfast and evening meals.

Rooms 13 rms (9 en suite) (3 fmly) S £25-£45; D £45-£100 (room only)*
Facilities FTV TVL tea/coffee Dinner available Licensed WiFi 🛁 **Parking** 10 **Notes** LB

GOUDHURST

Map 6 TQ73

The Star & Eagle

★★★★ ◠ INN

tel: 01580 211512 **fax:** 01580 212444 **High St TN17 1AL**
email: starandeagle@btconnect.com **web:** www.starandeagle.co.uk
dir: *Off A21 to Hastings rd, take A262, inn at top of village next to church*

A warm welcome is assured at the 15th-century Star & Eagle, located in the heart of this delightful village. Within easy reach of Royal Tunbridge Wells and the Weald, this is a great base for walkers. Both bedrooms and public areas boast original features and much character. A wide range of delicious home-made dishes is available in the restaurant and bar.

Rooms 10 rms (8 en suite) (2 pri facs) S £85-£160; D £90-£160 **Facilities** FTV tea/coffee Dinner available Direct Dial WiFi 🔒 **Extras** Speciality toiletries, home-made shortbread **Conf** Max 30 Thtr 30 Class 15 Board 12 **Parking** 20 **Notes** ⊗ RS 25-26 Dec eve closed Civ Wed 50

GRAFTY GREEN
Map 7 TQ84

Who'd A Thought It

★★★★ ◉ GUEST ACCOMMODATION

tel: 01622 858951 **Headcorn Rd ME17 2AR**
email: joe@whodathoughtit.com **web:** www.whodathoughtit.com
dir: *M20 junct 8 onto A20 towards Lenham. After 1m take turn signed Grafty Green, follow brown tourism signs for 4-5m*

The unusually named Who'd A Thought It is located in the quiet village of Grafty Green, yet convenient for both Maidstone and Ashford. Bedrooms and bathrooms are spacious and individually designed, using eclectic furnishings and stylish decor. Bathrooms feature hot tubs or jacuzzi baths, along with speciality toiletries. The restaurant offers an intimate and comfortable ambiance along with some bold fabrics that reflect the style of bedrooms into public spaces. Restaurant meals are served daily and there is a bar menu also available. Who'd A Thought It was the AA Funkiest B&B of the Year for 2013-14.

Rooms 11 annexe en suite (11 GF) S £45-£60; D £70-£375* **Facilities** STV FTV DVD iPod docking station Lounge tea/coffee Dinner available Licensed WiFi ⚓ 18 Fishing **Extras** Chocolates, champagne, bottled water **Conf** Max 30 Thtr 30 Class 30 Board 20 **Parking** 40 **Notes** ⊗

HALSTEAD
Map 6 TQ46

7 Motel Diner

★★★★ GUEST ACCOMMODATION

tel: 01959 535890 **London Rd, Polhill TN14 7AA**
email: reservations@7hoteldiner.co.uk **web:** www.7hoteldiner.co.uk
dir: *M25 junct 4, 2m towards Sevenoaks*

This guest accommodation is conveniently located off the M25 and is just a short drive from Sevenoaks. The well-equipped bedrooms have been stylishly decorated to offer modern, comfortable accommodation; all have custom-made furniture, flat-screen TVs and free WiFi. There is an American-themed diner complete with authentic jukebox and leather booths, and all-day dining is available from 7am in the 7 Lounge.

Rooms 26 en suite (2 fmly) (6 GF) S £29.95-£60; D £39.95-£89* **Facilities** FTV TVL tea/coffee Dinner available Direct Dial Licensed WiFi ⚓ **Parking** 50 **Notes** ⊗

HAWKHURST
Map 7 TQ73

Tudor Rose Bed and Breakfast

★★★★ BED AND BREAKFAST

tel: 01580 754830 & 07831 620172 **1 Tudor Hall TN18 5DB**
email: rosemarie_imago@hotmail.com **web:** www.tudor-rose-bnb.com

Tudor Rose is a family-run B&B, located on the outskirts of Hawkhurst. It has three double rooms, two en suite and one with a private bathroom; the family room is en suite, and has a double bed and single bed. All rooms have tea and coffee making facilities, Freeview TV, CD/DVD and WiFi. Thoughtful touches include dressing gowns, slippers, and toiletries. Full English or continental breakfast is served in the dining room.

Rooms 3 rms (2 en suite) (1 pri facs) (1 fmly) S £55-£65; D £65-£85* **Facilities** FTV DVD Lounge tea/coffee WiFi 🔒 **Extras** Robes, slippers **Parking** 4 **Notes** LB ⊗

Applebloom Bed and Breakfast

★★★★ BED AND BREAKFAST

tel: 01580 753347 **White Rose Cottage TN18 5DZ**
email: enquiries@applebloom.co.uk **web:** www.applebloom.co.uk
dir: *A21 onto A268 at Flimwell. Through Hawkhurst, after 1.1m turn right at x-rds into Conghurst Ln. 400mtrs on right*

Applebloom Bed and Breakfast is set in its own attractive garden and surrounded by the beautiful Kent countryside. The two bedrooms are individually appointed and offer style, quality and comfort. Guests can relax either in the lounge, or in the garden during the warm months of the year. Breakfast is served at a communal table overlooking the garden; expect home-made and locally sourced items of the highest quality.

Rooms 2 rms (1 en suite) (1 pri facs) S £50-£75; D £60-£85 **Facilities** FTV Lounge tea/coffee WiFi **Parking** 2 **Notes** ⊗ No Children 12yrs ◉

Summerhill

★★★★ BED AND BREAKFAST

tel: 01580 754378 & 07887 764538 **Cranbrook Rd TN18 4AT**
email: info@summerhillkent.co.uk **web:** www.summerhillkent.co.uk
dir: *A21 onto A268 at Flimwell lights. In Hawkhurst, left at lights, then left into Western Rd. At end of road on left*

Located in the centre of Hawkhurst, this B&B offers comfortably appointed bedrooms with a traditional style. Guest can enjoy home-made refreshments on arrival in the conservatory lounge looking over the garden. Breakfast is served daily and offers a good selection of both cooked and continental dishes. Off-road parking is available and guests are just a short stroll from the heart of Hawkhurst.

Rooms 2 rms (1 en suite) (1 pri facs) D £60-£85* **Facilities** FTV Lounge TVL tea/coffee WiFi ⚓ 9 **Extras** Home-made cookies/biscuits, bottled water - free **Parking** 2 **Notes** LB ⊗ ◉

LEYSDOWN-ON-SEA   Map 7 TR07

The Ferry House Inn

★★★★ INN

tel: 01795 510214 **Harty Ferry Rd ME12 4BQ**
email: info@theferryhouseinn.co.uk **web:** www.theferryhouseinn.co.uk

The Ferry House Inn is on the Isle of Sheppey, and offers spacious and comfortable accommodation as well as some fantastic views. All rooms have modern fixtures, fittings and decor. Guests can enjoy dinner in the main restaurant or in the bar area with lots of local produce sourced from surrounding farms. A cooked or continental breakfast is served daily.

Rooms 4 en suite **Facilities** FTV DVD iPod docking station Lounge tea/coffee Dinner available WiFi **Conf** Max 80 Thtr 80 Class 40 Board 40 **Parking** 50 **Notes** ⊗ No Children 12yrs Civ Wed 150

MAIDSTONE   Map 7 TQ75

See also Marden

The Black Horse Inn

★★★★ ⇨ INN

tel: 01622 737185 & 630830   **fax:** 01622 739170 **Pilgrims Way, Thurnham ME14 3LD**
email: info@wellieboot.net **web:** www.wellieboot.net
dir: M20 junct 7, N A249. Right into Detling, opposite pub into Pilgrims Way for 1m

This charming inn dates from the 17th century, and the public areas showcase a wealth of oak beams, exposed brickwork and open fireplaces. The stylish bedrooms are in a series of cosy cabins behind the premises; each one is attractively furnished and thoughtfully equipped, and the bathrooms are of an equally high standard.

Rooms 27 annexe en suite (8 fmly) (27 GF) D £65-£95* **Facilities** FTV tea/coffee Dinner available WiFi 🔥 **Conf** Max 80 Thtr 80 Class 40 Board 28 **Parking** 40 **Notes** LB No coaches Civ Wed 80

Innkeeper's Lodge Maidstone

★★★ INN

tel: 0845 112 6103 **Sandling Rd ME14 2RF**
email: info@innkeeperslodge.com **web:** www.innkeeperslodge.com

Known as The White Rabbit Sandling, this Innkeeper's Lodge is situated close to the centre of town, and dates back to 1797 when it was built to house the officers' quarters of the Invicta Barracks. Lodge bedrooms are modern, spacious and well appointed with a good range of facilities. Public rooms feature plush seating and dining areas where a good choice of food is available.

Rooms 12 en suite (1 fmly) **Facilities** FTV tea/coffee Dinner available Direct Dial WiFi **Parking**

Follow us on Facebook
www.facebook.com/TheAAUK

MARDEN   Map 6 TQ74

Premier Collection

Merzie Meadows

★★★★★ BED AND BREAKFAST

tel: 01622 820500 & 07762 713077 **Hunton Rd TN12 9SL**
email: pamela@merziemeadows.co.uk **web:** www.merziemeadows.co.uk
dir: A229 onto B2079 for Marden, 1st right into Underlyn Ln, 2.5m at large Chainhurst sign, right onto drive

Merzie Meadows is a detached property set in 20 acres of mature gardens in the Kent countryside. The generously proportioned bedrooms are housed in two wings, which overlook a terrace; each room is carefully decorated, thoughtfully equipped and furnished with well-chosen pieces. The attractive breakfast room has an Italian tiled floor and superb views of the garden.

Rooms 2 en suite (1 fmly) (2 GF) S £98-£100; D £100-£110* **Facilities** STV FTV TVL tea/coffee WiFi **Extras** Speciality toiletries, chocolates - complimentary **Parking** 4 **Notes** ⊗ No Children 15yrs Closed mid Dec-mid Feb ⊛

NEW ROMNEY   Map 7 TR02

The Ship

★★★ INN

tel: 01797 362776 **83 High St TN28 8AZ**
email: theshiphotelandrestaurant@gmail.com **web:** www.the-ship-hotel.co.uk
dir: M20 junct 10 onto A2070 to Brenzett. At rdbt 1st exit onto A259 to New Romney. Next to petrol station on right

This traditional inn is located in the very centre of Romney Marsh, bedrooms are traditional in style and are all located above the main pub area. The restaurant is spacious, seating up to 70 people and is ideal for events and functions. Main bar area, conservatory and fully heated patio offer a good array of seating areas for guests to enjoy. Breakfast, lunch and dinner are served here daily.

Rooms 10 en suite (1 fmly) S fr £40; D fr £50* **Facilities** FTV DVD tea/coffee Dinner available WiFi ⛳ 18 Pool table 🔥 **Conf** Max 130 Thtr 130 Class 80 Board 40 **Parking** 20 **Notes** LB

PEMBURY   Map 6 TQ64

Camden Arms

★★★★ INN

tel: 01892 822012 **1 High St TN2 4PH**
email: food@camdenarms.co.uk **web:** www.camdenarms.co.uk
dir: Off A21, opposite village green

Located in a central position and just a couple of minutes' drive from Tunbridge Wells, this inn offers comfortable, well-equipped accommodation with LCD TVs, free WiFi throughout, and spacious en suite bathrooms. The large garden has outdoor seating, and the restaurant and bar area serve a large variety of local beers which change on a regular basis and pub meals are available seven days a week. Guests can enjoy a continental breakfast in the morning, or, for an extra charge, a hearty traditional English breakfast.

Rooms 15 annexe en suite (1 fmly) (8 GF) **Facilities** FTV tea/coffee Dinner available WiFi 🔥 **Extras** Trouser press **Conf** Max 50 Thtr 50 Class 24 Board 16 **Parking** 68

PLUCKLEY   Map 7 TQ94

Elvey Farm

★★★★ GUEST ACCOMMODATION

tel: 01233 840442 fax: 01233 841037 **Elvey Ln TN27 0SU**
email: bookings@elveyfarm.co.uk web: www.elveyfarm.co.uk
dir: *M20 junct 8 onto A20 to Charing. Right into Station Rd signed Pluckley. At bottom of Forge Hill turn right. 1st right into Mundy Bois Rd, then 1st right into Elvey Ln*

Located in a very quiet and picturesque part of the Kentish countryside, a number of period outbuildings have been converted to offer stylish and comfortable accommodation. There is a restaurant on site with outside seating area open for afternoon tea and dinner every night. Some meeting rooms also make this ideal for small functions, weddings or business meetings. A hearty cooked or continental breakfast is served daily in the main restaurant.

Rooms 11 en suite (6 GF) S £40-£140; D £70-£275* **Facilities** FTV DVD Lounge tea/coffee Dinner available Licensed WiFi ☕ **Conf** Max 20 Thtr 20 Class 15 Board 12 **Parking** 30 **Notes** No Children 8yrs Closed 1st 2wks Jan Civ Wed 60

SANDWICH   Map 7 TR35

The New Inn

★★★ INN

tel: 01304 612335 fax: 01304 619133 **2 Harnet St CT13 9ES**
email: new.inn@thorleytaverns.com web: www.thenewinnsandwich.com
dir: *Off A256, one-way system into town centre, inn on right*

The New Inn is situated in the heart of busy Sandwich. The large open-plan lounge bar offers an extensive range of beers and an interesting choice of home-made dishes. Bedrooms are furnished in pine and have many useful extras.

Rooms 5 en suite (3 fmly) (2 smoking) **Facilities** STV tea/coffee Dinner available Direct Dial WiFi ☕ **Parking** 17 **Notes** No coaches

SITTINGBOURNE   Map 7 TQ96

Dadmans

★★★★ ☕ BED AND BREAKFAST

tel: 01795 521293 & 07931 153253 **Lynsted ME9 0JJ**
email: info@dadmans.co.uk web: www.dadmans.co.uk
dir: *M20 junct 8 E on A20 to Lenham. Turn left to Doddington, at The Chequers pub turn left. 1.7m on left*

This country house bed and breakfast is located in a quiet area just south of Lynsted village. Bedrooms are comfortable and traditional in style, and all benefit from views of the gardens and local countryside. There is a guest's lounge where refreshments are served on arrival, while dinner is available by prior arrangement and can be enjoyed in the Aga-heated kitchen or in the dining room. Guests are more than welcome to explore the acres of well tended gardens. Rare breed hens wander the gardens and provide eggs for the hearty cooked breakfast.

Rooms 3 rms (2 en suite) (1 pri facs) **Facilities** Lounge TVL TV1B tea/coffee Dinner available WiFi ☕ ☕ **Parking** 6 **Notes** ⊗ No Children 3yrs ☕

Sandhurst Farm Forge

★★★★ BED AND BREAKFAST

tel: 01795 886854 **Seed Rd, Newnham ME9 0NE**
email: rooms.forge@btinternet.com web: www.sandhurstfarmforge.co.uk
dir: *Exit A2 into Newnham, into Seed Rd by church, establishment 1m on right*

A warm welcome is assured at this peaceful location, which also features a working forge. The spacious bedrooms are in a converted stable block and provide smartly

furnished accommodation. Breakfast is served in the dining room adjoining the bedrooms. The owner has won an award for green tourism by reducing the impact of the business on the environment.

Rooms 2 annexe en suite (2 GF) S £45; D £75* **Facilities** STV DVD tea/coffee WiFi Riding ☕ **Extras** Fruit, snacks, bottled water **Parking** 6 **Notes** LB No Children 12yrs Closed 23 Dec-2 Jan

TENTERDEN   Map 7 TQ83

Little Dane Court

★★★★ BED AND BREAKFAST

tel: 01580 763389 & 07776 193399 **1 Ashford Rd TN30 6AB**
email: littledanecourt@gmail.com web: www.littledanecourt.co.uk
dir: *A28 to Tenterden, after 1m pass 2 red telephone boxes. Little Dane 4th house on right*

Little Dane Court has a long and fascinating history, and offers a range of well-appointed bedrooms that meet the needs of discerning travellers. All rooms are well equipped. For something a bit more individual, the Japanese-style cottage offers extra privacy and space. Breakfast is served at the communal table in the dining room or in the courtyard during the warm months of the year. The Japanese-style garden is a pocket of tranquillity.

Rooms 3 rms (2 en suite) (1 pri facs) 1 annexe en suite S £65-£95; D £95-£125* **Facilities** FTV DVD TVL tea/coffee Dinner available WiFi ☕ **Conf** Max 10 Thtr 10 Board 10 **Parking** 6 **Notes** LB

TUNBRIDGE WELLS (ROYAL)   Map 6 TQ53

Premier Collection

Danehurst House

★★★★★ ☕ BED AND BREAKFAST

tel: 01892 527739 fax: 01892 514804 **41 Lower Green Rd, Rusthall TN4 8TW**
email: info@danehurst.net web: www.danehurst.net
dir: *1.5m W of Tunbridge Wells in Rusthall. Exit A264 into Coach Rd & Lower Green Rd*

Situated in pretty gardens in a quiet residential area, this Victorian gabled house is located to the west of the historic spa town. The house retains many original features and is attractively decorated throughout. Public areas include a comfortable lounge with a small bar. The homely bedrooms come with a wealth of thoughtful extras, and excellent breakfasts are served in the conservatory.

Rooms 4 en suite (1 fmly) **Facilities** TVL tea/coffee Licensed **Parking** 6 **Notes** ⊗ No Children 8yrs Closed Xmas

Salomons

★★★★ GUEST ACCOMMODATION

tel: 01892 515152 **Salomons Estate, Broomhill Rd, Southborough TN3 0TG**
email: reception@salomons-estate.com web: www.salomons-estate.com
dir: *M25 junct 5, A21 signed Hastings. Then A26 (Southborough & Tunbridge Wells). In Southborough right at 2nd lights into Speldhurst Rd. 2nd left into Broomhill Rd, entrance on right*

Salomons is located on a private, 36-acre estate just a short distance from Royal Tunbridge Wells. The bedrooms are all contemporary in style with modern decor and are well equipped ideal for both business and leisure guests. Guests can enjoy breakfast, lunch and dinner in the main Manor House daily. This is also a very popular wedding venue and a great range of conference rooms are available.

Rooms 47 en suite S £50-£60; D £75-£90* **Facilities** STV FTV tea/coffee Dinner available Direct Dial Licensed WiFi Gym **Conf** Max 230 Thtr 230 Class 100 Board 56 **Parking** 200 **Notes** Civ Wed 200

TUNBRIDGE WELLS (ROYAL) *continued*

The Victorian Bed & Breakfast

★★★★ BED AND BREAKFAST

tel: 01892 533633 & 07714 264489 **22 Lansdowne Rd TN1 2NJ**
email: haroldmbrown@hotmail.com

Be prepared to step back in time when arriving at The Victorian Bed & Breakfast; you host has taken great care in ensuring every detail is as accurate as possible. The rooms have been simply appointed but comfort and quality are not compromised. Tea and scones are served on arrival in the drawing room whilst breakfast and dinner are served in the formal dining room with its imposing portrait of Queen Victoria.

Rooms 3 en suite S fr £80; D fr £100* **Facilities** Lounge Dinner available WiFi 🛁 **Parking** 4 **Notes** ⊗ No Children 10yrs 🖼

Innkeeper's Lodge Tunbridge Wells

★★★ INN

tel: 0845 112 6109 **London Rd, Southborough TN4 0QB**
email: info@innkeeperslodge.com **web:** www.innkeeperslodge.com

At Innkeeper's Lodge you'll find accommodation with comfort and character in equal measure, and everything needed for a relaxing stay, from easy check-in and free parking to complimentary breakfast and a cosy pub serving great value food and drink on the doorstep. Each Lodge has quality rooms, and there are Lodges in a variety of locations from towns and cities to countryside settings across the UK.

Rooms 14 en suite (2 fmly) **Facilities** FTV tea/coffee Dinner available Direct Dial WiFi **Parking**

WESTERHAM   Map 6 TQ45

Kings Arms

★★★ INN

tel: 01959 562990 **fax:** 01959 561240 **Market Square TN16 1AN**
email: 6471@greeneking.co.uk **web:** www.oldenglish.co.uk
dir: *Exit M25 junct 6 & follow A25 to Westerham*

The Kings Arms is located in the centre of Westerham and is in close proximity to Sevenoaks, Tunbridge Wells and Maidstone. The bedrooms are spacious and feature original oak beams; some have four-poster beds. The bar and restaurant are modern, and breakfast can be enjoyed in the conservatory. Free WiFi is available throughout.

Rooms 18 en suite (4 fmly) **Facilities** STV tea/coffee Dinner available Direct Dial WiFi **Extras** Pamper packs - charged **Conf** Max 50 Thtr 50 Class 40 Board 24 **Parking** 33 **Notes** LB Civ Wed 50

WORTH   Map 7 TR35

Chilton Villa B&B

★★★★ BED AND BREAKFAST

tel: 01304 614415 **The Street CT14 0DD**
email: info@chiltonvilla.co.uk **web:** www.chiltonvilla.co.uk
dir: *A2 or A20 onto A256 towards Sandwich, then A258 towards Deal. Turn left to Worth*

Located in the heart of the village, just a mile from Sandwich and close to Canterbury, this former post office has two spacious en suite bedrooms offering very good quality and comfortable accommodation; each is equipped with modern fixtures including digital TV and free WiFi. There is a cosy dining room, with separate access, where a cooked and a continental breakfast is served daily.

Rooms 2 annexe en suite (2 fmly) (2 GF) S £60; D £75* **Facilities** FTV tea/coffee WiFi ⅃ 18 🅿 **Parking** 2

WROTHAM   Map 6 TQ65

The Bull

★★★★ 🏵 INN

tel: 01732 789800 **fax:** 01732 886288 **Bull Ln TN15 7RF**
email: info@thebullhotel.com **web:** www.thebullhotel.com
dir: *In centre of village*

Dating back to 1385 and first licensed in 1495, The Bull offers modern facilities yet retains many traditional features including original exposed beams. High quality meals can be enjoyed at breakfast, lunch and dinner; the inn sources local produce from nearby farms, south coast landed fish and real ales from Dark Star micro-brewery. The bedrooms, including one four-poster room, are decorated with modern furnishings. The Buttery function room was originally the village bakery.

Rooms 11 en suite (1 fmly) S £69-£139; D £79-£159* **Facilities** FTV tea/coffee Dinner available WiFi ⅃ 18 **Conf** Max 100 Thtr 60 Class 60 Board 40 **Parking** 30 **Notes** Civ Wed 60

LANCASHIRE

ACCRINGTON
Map 18 SD72

The Maple Lodge
★★★★ GUEST ACCOMMODATION

tel: 01254 301284 **fax:** 0560 112 5380 **70 Blackburn Rd, Clayton-le-Moors BB5 5JH**
email: info@stayatmaplelodge.co.uk **web:** www.stayatmaplelodge.co.uk
dir: M65 junct 7, follow signs for Clitheroe, right at T-junct into Blackburn Rd

This welcoming house is convenient for the M65, and provides comfortable, well-equipped bedrooms, as well as an inviting lounge with well-stocked bar. Freshly cooked dinners (by arrangement) and hearty breakfasts are served in the attractive dining room.

Rooms 4 en suite 4 annexe en suite (1 fmly) (4 GF) **Facilities** FTV TVL tea/coffee Dinner available Direct Dial Licensed WiFi 🏌 **Parking** 6 **Notes** LB

Pilkington's Guest House
★★★ GUEST HOUSE

tel: 01254 237032 **fax:** 01254 237032 **135 Blackburn Rd BB5 0AA**
email: pilkybuses@hotmail.com **web:** www.pilkingtonsbedandbreakfast.webs.com
dir: M65 junct 7 follow signs to Accrington town centre, establishment opposite railway station. M66 onto A56 to Accrington town centre

Positioned close to the railway station, this family-run property has two comfortable bedrooms in the main house and four further bedrooms in the terrace which is just a short way along the street. Home-cooked breakfasts are served in the main house.

Rooms 6 rms (6 pri facs) (2 fmly) (2 GF) S £25-£30; D £50-£60 **Facilities** FTV TVL tea/coffee Licensed WiFi Snooker Pool table 🏌 **Conf** Max 60 Thtr 60 Class 60 Board 60 **Parking** 6 **Notes** ⊗

BLACKBURN
Map 18 SD62

Premier Collection

The Millstone at Mellor
★★★★★ ⊛⊛ INN

tel: 01254 813333 **fax:** 01254 812628 **Church Ln, Mellor BB2 7JR**
email: relax@millstonehotel.co.uk **web:** www.millstonehotel.co.uk
dir: A677 from Blackburn (or from A59) follow signs to Mellor

Once a coaching inn, The Millstone is situated in a village just outside the town. It provides a very high standard of accommodation and professional and friendly service. Bedrooms, some in an adjacent house, are comfortable and generally spacious, and all are very well equipped. A room for less mobile guests is also available. Meals in the AA Rosetted restaurant make excellent use of the highest quality Ribble Valley produce.

Rooms 17 en suite 6 annexe en suite (5 fmly) (8 GF) **Facilities** STV tea/coffee Dinner available Direct Dial WiFi **Parking** 40 **Notes** ⊗ Civ Wed 60

BLACKPOOL
Map 18 SD33

Bona Vista
★★★★ GUEST ACCOMMODATION

tel: 01253 351396 **fax:** 01253 594985 **104-106 Queens Promenade FY2 9NX**
email: enquires@bonavistahotel.com **web:** www.bonavistahotel.com
dir: 0.25m N of Uncle Toms Cabin & Casino

The Bona Vista has a peaceful seafront location on North Shore within reach of Blackpool's amenities. Its attractive bedrooms are well equipped and some have sea views. There is a spacious dining room and a comfortable bar and lounges. Some 16 parking spaces are available, an absolute bonus in this busy town.

Rooms 19 rms (17 en suite) (4 fmly) **Facilities** FTV Lounge TVL tea/coffee Dinner available Licensed WiFi Pool table 🏌 **Conf** Max 50 Thtr 50 Class 50 Board 50 **Parking** 16

The Bromley
★★★★ BED AND BREAKFAST

tel: 01253 624171 & 07702 239890 **306 Promenade FY1 2EY**
email: bromleyhotel@virginmedia.com **web:** www.bromleyhotelblackpool.co.uk
dir: 0.1m N past Blackpool Tower, on right

Located on the North Shore promenade, just a short walk from many of the main attractions, The Bromley offers comfortable en suite accommodation. There is a licensed bar and lounge on the ground floor. Free WiFi is available in public areas, and off-road parking, provided at the front of the property, is a real bonus.

Rooms 13 en suite (6 fmly) (1 GF) S £30-£35; D £55-£65* **Facilities** FTV DVD iPod docking station TVL tea/coffee Licensed WiFi Pool table 🏌 **Parking** 9 **Notes** ⊗ Closed 21-27 Dec

BLACKPOOL *continued*

The Craigmore

★★★★ GUEST HOUSE

tel: 01253 355098 **8 Willshaw Rd, Gynn Square FY2 9SH**
email: enquiries@thecraigmore.com **web:** www.thecraigmore.com
dir: *1m N of Tower. A584 N over Gynn rdbt, 1st right into Willshaw Rd. The Craigmore 3rd on left*

This well-maintained property is in an attractive location overlooking Gynn Square gardens, with the Promenade and tram stops just metres away. Three of the smart modern bedrooms are suitable for families. There is a comfortable lounge, a sun lounge and patio, and the pretty dining room has a small bar.

Rooms 7 en suite (3 fmly) S £35-£50; D £55-£65* **Facilities** FTV Lounge TVL tea/coffee Licensed WiFi **Notes** LB ⊗ No Children 5yrs Closed Nov-Mar

The Fylde International

★★★★ GUEST HOUSE

tel: 01253 623735 **93 Palatine Rd FY1 4BX**
email: fyldeinternationalblackpool@gmail.com **web:** www.fyldehotel.com
dir: *A5099 (Central Dr) into town centre, right into Palatine Rd. Property on right before lights*

This family-run guest house has a prime central location close to all of Blackpool's attractions. Accommodation is comfortable and all rooms are equipped with modern facilities. Families are well catered for with a choice of family rooms and suites available. A spacious lounge and a separate dedicated children's area ensure all guests can enjoy the relaxed and welcoming environment. A substantial buffet breakfast is served. Parking is available.

Rooms 9 en suite (3 fmly) (2 GF) S £25-£39; D £50-£60 **Facilities** FTV TVL tea/coffee Licensed WiFi 🔒 **Parking** 6 **Notes** LB ⊗ RS Dec-1 Feb Groups only

Lynbar Guesthouse

★★★★ GUEST HOUSE

tel: 01253 294504 **32 Vance Rd FY1 4QD**
email: enquiries@lynbarhotel.co.uk **web:** www.lynbarhotel.co.uk
dir: *M55 until end, follow Yeadon Way/Seasiders Way to central car park. Exit car park into Central Dr, turn left then 2nd on right*

Lynbar is a welcoming guest house with a prime location just 300 metres from the promenade; an ideal position for the Tower, Winter Gardens and Grand Theatre.

There are comfortable beds and good in-room amenities. Dinner is served with advance notice and the hearty breakfast is of very good quality.

Rooms 8 rms (6 en suite) (2 pri facs) (3 fmly) S £30-£40; D £50-£80 **Facilities** FTV Lounge tea/coffee Dinner available Licensed WiFi **Notes** LB ⊗ No Children 2yrs Closed 22 Dec-4 Jan

Pelham Lodge

★★★★ GUEST ACCOMMODATION

tel: 01253 625127 **fax:** 0872 115 7127 **7-9 General St FY1 1RW**
email: info@pelhamlodge.co.uk **web:** www.pelhamlodge.co.uk

Situated towards the North End of Blackpool, and close to attractions such as Funny Girls, the Winter Gardens and Blackpool Tower, Pelham Lodge is only a 5 minute walk from the train station. Good quality and comfortable accommodation is promised and a friendly welcome on arrival guaranteed. Limited parking available to the rear.

Rooms 15 en suite (2 fmly) (2 GF) **Facilities** FTV TVL tea/coffee WiFi **Extras** Bottled water - complimentary **Parking** 5 **Notes** ⊗ Closed 24-25 Dec

The Ramsay

★★★★ GUEST ACCOMMODATION

tel: 01253 352777 **fax:** 01253 351207 **90-92 Queen Promenade FY2 9NS**
email: enquiries@theramsayhotel.co.uk **web:** www.theramsayhotel.co.uk
dir: *M55 exit towards Blackpool, left into Central Drive, 1st left towards promenade. Right at lights. At Gynn rdbt straight over, establishment just past Uncle Toms Cabin*

This family-run guest accommodation occupies a prime location on the North Shore promenade. The bedrooms are restful and those at the front enjoy panoramic sea views. The public rooms are spacious, and include a cosy lounge with comfortable seating providing an ideal area to relax and have a drink from the bar. Dinner is available on request.

Rooms 22 en suite (2 fmly) **Facilities** FTV TVL tea/coffee Dinner available Lift Licensed WiFi ♿ **Parking** 8 **Notes** ⊗

The Baron

★★★★ 🅰 GUEST ACCOMMODATION

tel: 01253 622729 **fax:** 0161 297 0464 **296 North Promenade FY1 2EY**
email: baronhotel@f2s.com

The Baron offers comfortable surroundings only a short walk from the North Pier, Tower and centre. All rooms come complete with thoughtful extras, including free WiFi. Guests can dine at individual tables, and vegetarians and other special diets can be catered for. A passenger lift is on hand for the dining room and first and second floor bedrooms. Free parking is a plus.

Rooms 21 en suite (1 fmly) (3 GF) (2 smoking) **Facilities** FTV tea/coffee Dinner available Lift Licensed WiFi **Conf** Max 20 Thtr 20 Class 20 Board 20 **Parking** 16 **Notes** ⊗ No Children 12yrs

Eden House

★★★ BED AND BREAKFAST

tel: 01253 297669 **91 Palatine Rd FY1 4BX**
email: info@edenhouseblackpool.com **web:** www.edenhouseblackpool.com
dir: *M55 junct 4 onto A583 pass windmill on left. Through 10 sets of lights, turn left into Palatine Rd*

A warm welcome is assured at Eden House, just off the beaten track in the centre of Blackpool, and within easy walking distance of attractions. Bedrooms are very comfortable, and are equipped with a wealth of extras for the modern traveller. Well-cooked, hearty breakfasts are served in the bright dining room.

Rooms 6 en suite (2 fmly) (1 GF) S £30-£35; D £45-£55* **Facilities** FTV tea/coffee 🛁 **Parking** 5 **Notes** LB ⊗

Hartshead

★★★ GUEST ACCOMMODATION

tel: 01253 353133 & 357111 **fax:** 01253 357111
17 King Edward Av, North Shore FY2 9TA
email: info@hartshead-hotel.co.uk **web:** www.hartshead-hotel.co.uk
dir: *M55 junct 4, A583, A584 to North Shore, exit Queens Promenade into King Edward Av*

Popular for its location near the seafront, the enthusiastically run Hartshead has modern bedrooms of various sizes, all equipped with a good range of practical extras. A veranda-sitting room is available, in addition to a comfortable lounge bar. Breakfast and pre-theatre dinner is served in the attractive dining room.

Rooms 9 en suite (3 fmly) S £24-£38; D £48-£60* **Facilities** FTV DVD Lounge TVL tea/coffee Dinner available Licensed WiFi **Parking** 6 **Notes** LB ⊗

All Seasons

★★★ GUEST HOUSE

tel: 01253 404906 **fax:** 01253 531031 **42 St Chad's Rd, South Shore FY1 6BP**
email: enquiries@allseasonshotelblackpool.co.uk
web: www.allseasonshotelblackpool.co.uk

Families and couples are welcome in this friendly guest house which has been recently refurbished and has a prime, central location close to the promenade and equal distance between the Tower and Pleasure Beach. Generous breakfasts are served in the modern dining room whilst at night a small bar is available to guests.

Rooms 8 en suite (2 fmly) D £36-£50 (room only)* **Facilities** STV FTV TVL tea/coffee Licensed WiFi 🛁 **Notes** LB ⊗ Closed 20-30 Dec

Bianca Guesthouse

★★★ GUEST ACCOMMODATION

tel: 01253 752824 **25 Palatine Rd FY1 4BX**
email: jnny5john@btinternet.com **web:** www.hotelbianca.co.uk

A warm welcome awaits at Bianca Guesthouse, situated centrally, and within easy walking distance of Blackpool's attractions and amenities. Accommodation is well equipped and comfortable, with family rooms available. There is a licensed bar.

Rooms 10 en suite (2 fmly) **Facilities** FTV tea/coffee Licensed WiFi **Notes** ⊗ Closed 20-27 Dec

Casablanca

★★★ GUEST ACCOMMODATION

tel: 01253 622574 **84 Hornby Rd FY1 4QS**
email: jdixon8969@aol.com **web:** www.casablancablackpool.com

A personally run and homely guest house, perfectly situated within easy reach of all of Blackpool's central attractions. Accommodation is fully en suite and features modern accessories and a choice of room types. There is a comfortable lounge, breakfasts are generous and limited parking is available.

Rooms 9 en suite (2 fmly) S £30; D £50-£55* **Facilities** FTV TVL tea/coffee WiFi 🛁 **Parking** 2 **Notes** LB ⊗ Closed 20 Dec-4 Jan

The Derby

★★★ GUEST ACCOMMODATION

tel: 01253 623708 & 07809 143248 **2 Derby Rd FY1 2JF**
email: tj52way@yahoo.com **web:** www.thederbyhotel.co.uk
dir: *From promenade, pass North Pier, heading N. Turn right next to Hilton Hotel into Derby Road, The Derby on right*

The Derby is a family-friendly establishment offering good value, modern accommodation in a variety of sizes. Dinner is available and guests have the use of a comfortable lounge and a separate bar. Breakfast is the highlight of any stay with high quality cooking and hearty portions to be expected.

Rooms 9 rms (5 en suite) (4 pri facs) (3 fmly) S £20-£35; D £40-£60 **Facilities** FTV TVL tea/coffee Dinner available Licensed WiFi 🛁 **Parking** 3 **Notes** LB

Funky Towers

★★★ GUEST ACCOMMODATION

tel: 01253 400123 **297 The Promenade FY1 6AL**
email: stay@funkytowers.com **web:** www.funkytowers.com
dir: *On seafront promenade halfway between The Tower & Pleasure Beach*

This friendly, family-run property has a distinctive style and a prime location facing the sea, between the Pleasure Beach and Central Pier. There is a spacious bar and lounge with direct access to the seafront. The bedrooms are equipped with lots of extras; some feature four-posters and others have great sea views.

Rooms 14 en suite (5 fmly) **Facilities** FTV DVD Lounge TVL tea/coffee Licensed WiFi Pool table 🛁 **Parking** 3 **Notes** ⊗

The Sandalwood

★★★ BED AND BREAKFAST

tel: 01253 351795 **3 Glynn Av FY1 2LD**
email: info@thesandalwood.co.uk **web:** www.thesandalwood.co.uk
dir: *From North Pier towards Fleetwood, after 1.5m turn right after Hilton hotel*

A warm, friendly welcome is assured at The Sandalwood, a small, family-run B&B situated in the quieter North Shore of Blackpool, yet within easy reach of all the local amenities and attractions. Comfortable accommodation is available, and a hearty cooked breakfast, using fresh farm produce, is provided.

Rooms 8 rms (7 en suite) (1 pri facs) (2 fmly) S £20-£30; D £40-£60* **Facilities** FTV TVL tea/coffee Dinner available WiFi **Notes** ⊗ Closed 19-29 Dec 🛒

BLACKPOOL *continued*

The Wilton

★★★ BED AND BREAKFAST

tel: 01253 346673 **22 Alexandra Rd, South Shore FY1 6BU**
email: enquiries@thewiltonhotel.co.uk **web:** www.thewiltonhotel.co.uk

Families and couples alike are very welcome at this comfortable accommodation, situated close to the promenade and within easy walking distance of Blackpool's central attractions, the south shore and the stadium. Hospitality is warm and personal. Dinner is served and a notable breakfast provided. A well stocked bar and private parking are among the facilities available.

Rooms 16 en suite (6 fmly) S £20-£35; D £40-£60* **Facilities** FTV tea/coffee Dinner available Licensed WiFi Pool table ☎ **Parking Notes** LB ⊗

The Fairway

★★★ 🅰 GUEST ACCOMMODATION

tel: 01253 623777 **fax:** 01253 297970 **34-36 Hull Rd FY1 4QB**
email: impulsedh@aol.com **web:** www.fairwayhotelblackpool.co.uk

Close to Blackpool's seafront and tower, The Fairway is run by friendly owners and is a traditional seaside property. It is ideal for families, or those attending dance festivals, conferences or other Blackpool entertainments. There is a licensed bar, and a games area with a pool table. A full English breakfast is served and free WiFi is a bonus.

Rooms 19 en suite **Facilities** FTV DVD TVL TV18B Licensed WiFi Pool table **Notes** LB ⊗

Beachwood Guest House

🅄

tel: 01253 401951 **30 Moore St FY4 1DA**
email: beachwoodguesthouse30@gmail.com **web:** www.beachwoodguesthouse.net

Currently the rating for this establishment is not confirmed. This may be due to a change of ownership or because it has only recently joined the AA rating scheme.

Rooms 6 en suite (2 fmly) (1 GF) S £15; D £30 **Facilities** STV FTV DVD tea/coffee WiFi **Extras** Mini fridge in all rooms **Parking** 4 **Notes** LB ⊗

Come Ye In

🅄

tel: 01253 625065 **85 Hornby FY1 4QP**
email: margery.tracey@virgin.net **web:** www.comeyein.co.uk
dir: *Follow Central Dr (A5099) into town centre, right into Hornby Rd. Through lights, on right*

Currently the rating for this establishment is not confirmed. This may be due to a change of ownership or because it has only recently joined the AA rating scheme.

Rooms 8 en suite (2 fmly) S £25-£30; D £50-£60* **Facilities** FTV TVL tea/coffee WiFi **Parking** 3 **Notes** LB ⊗

BOLTON-BY-BOWLAND — Map 18 SD74

Middle Flass Lodge

★★★★ 🍴 GUEST HOUSE

tel: 01200 447259 **fax:** 01200 447300 **Settle Rd BB7 4NY**
email: middleflasslodge@btconnect.com **web:** www.middleflasslodge.co.uk
dir: *2m N of Bolton by Bowland. Off A59 for Sawley, N to Forest Becks, over bridge, 1m on right*

Set in peaceful countryside in the Forest of Bowland, this smart house provides a warm welcome. Stylishly converted from farm outbuildings, exposed timbers feature throughout, as well as in the attractive restaurant and cosy lounge. The modern bedrooms include a family room, with stairlift access to the first floor. Thanks to the accomplished chef, the restaurant is very popular.

Rooms 5 en suite 2 annexe en suite (1 fmly) S £50-£55; D £70-£76* **Facilities** FTV TVL tea/coffee Dinner available Licensed WiFi ☎ **Parking** 14 **Notes** LB ⊗

CHORLEY

See Eccleston

ECCLESTON — Map 15 SD51

Parr Hall Farm

★★★★ GUEST ACCOMMODATION

tel: 01257 451917 **8 Parr Ln PR7 5SL**
email: enquiries@parrhallfarm.com **web:** www.parrhallfarm.com
dir: *M6 junct 27, B5250 N for 5m to Parr Ln on right. 1st property on left*

This attractive, well-maintained farmhouse, located in a quiet corner of the village yet close to the M6, dates back to the 18th century. The majority of bedrooms are located in a sympathetic barn conversion and include luxury en suite bathrooms and lots of thoughtful extras. A comprehensive continental breakfast is included in the room price.

Rooms 10 annexe en suite (1 fmly) (5 GF) S £45; D £70 **Facilities** FTV tea/coffee WiFi ♿ 9 ☎ Guided Walks **Parking** 20 **Notes** ⊗

LANCASTER — Map 18 SD46

Penny Street Bridge

★★★★ INN

tel: 01524 599900 **fax:** 01524 599901 **Penny St LA1 1XT**
email: relax@pennystreetbridge.co.uk **web:** www.pennystreetbridge.co.uk

Ideally situated in the heart of the city, Penny Street Bridge has been transformed from a typical Victorian property to one that is fresh and contemporary, yet retains all the elegance of its original era. Bedrooms are modern and very well equipped. The stylish bar and brasserie are popular with both guests and local residents, serving meals and light bites throughout the day.

Rooms 28 en suite (2 fmly) S £67-£98; D £67-£98* **Facilities** FTV tea/coffee Dinner available Lift WiFi ☎ **Conf** Max 20 Thtr 20 Board 20 **Parking** 3 **Notes** LB ⊗ No coaches

LANESHAW BRIDGE

Map 18 SD94

The Alma Inn

★★★★ ➡ INN

tel: 01282 857830 **fax:** 01282 857831 **Emmott Ln BB8 7EG**
email: reception@thealmainn.com **web:** www.thealmainn.com
dir: At end of M65 onto A6068 (Vivary Way) towards Skipton. At 3rd rdbt, 1st exit into Skipton Old Rd, after 0.5m right into Hill Ln. 0.5m on right

The Alma Inn nestles in the magnificent Pendle countryside, and dates back to 1725. This rural coaching inn features open fires, stone floor and original beams, and guests can dine well in the lounge-style bars or the restaurant. The stylish rooms come in a variety of sizes, and all are thoughtfully equipped. Function facilities are available along with ample parking and a helicopter landing pad.

Rooms 9 en suite (8 fmly) S £69.95-£109.95; D £79.95-£109.95 **Facilities** FTV DVD iPod docking station Lounge tea/coffee Dinner available Direct Dial WiFi ⌁ 9 ⌂
Extras Speciality toiletries - complimentary **Conf** Max 150 Thtr 100 Class 50 Board 40 **Parking** 45 **Notes** LB Civ Wed 170

Rye Flatt Bed & Breakfast

★★★★ BED AND BREAKFAST

tel: 01282 871565 **20 School Ln BB8 7JB**
email: info@rye-flatt.co.uk **web:** www.rye-flatt.co.uk
dir: M65 onto A6068 towards Keighley. Turn right at Emmott Arms, park on left, immediately after bridge

Situated on the Lancashire and Yorkshire border with great transport links, this B&B operates from a 17th-century farmhouse which has some fantastic original features. Ideally located for business or leisure, the house features cosy bedrooms and well-equipped bathrooms. Warm hospitality and a memorable breakfast are features of any stay here. There is also a garden for sunnier days.

Rooms 2 en suite S £40; D £70* **Facilities** FTV Lounge tea/coffee WiFi ⌂ **Parking** 2 **Notes** ⊗

LYTHAM ST ANNES

Map 18 SD32

Strathmore

★★★ GUEST ACCOMMODATION

tel: 01253 725478 **305 Clifton Drive South FY8 1HN**
dir: In centre of St Annes opposite Post Office

The long-established, family-run Strathmore has a central location close to the promenade, and offers smartly furnished and well-equipped bedrooms. There is an elegant lounge and a smart dining room.

Rooms 8 rms (5 en suite) S £24-£32; D £48-£64* **Facilities** Lounge tea/coffee WiFi ⌂ **Parking** 8 **Notes** LB ⊗ No Children 9yrs ⌸

MORECAMBE

Map 18 SD46

Yacht Bay View

★★★★ GUEST HOUSE

tel: 01524 414481 **359 Marine Road East LA4 5AQ**
email: yachtbayview@hotmail.com **web:** www.yachtbay.co.uk
dir: 0.5m NE of town centre on seafront promenade

Overlooking Morecambe Bay, this family-run property offers comfortable bedrooms, some with impressive views, and all with en suite shower rooms. Guests are given a warm welcome and breakfast is served in the dining room, which also has a lounge area.

Rooms 7 en suite S £34-£40; D £68-£75 **Facilities** FTV DVD TVL tea/coffee WiFi ⌂ **Extras** Speciality toiletries - complimentary **Parking** 1 **Notes** LB ⊗ Closed 15 Dec-7 Jan

Broadwater Guest House

★★★ GUEST HOUSE

tel: 01524 41333 **356 Marine Road East LA4 5AQ**
email: enquiries@thebroadwaterhotel.co.uk **web:** www.thebroadwaterhotel.co.uk
dir: M6 junct 34 follow signs for Morecambe, then signs for E Promenade

Located on Morecambe's seafront, Broadwater Guest House offers a refreshingly friendly welcome. Bedrooms vary in size, but all are en suite, and well equipped with thoughtful extras including free WiFi. Substantial breakfasts are served in the pleasant dining room which has sea views.

Rooms 8 en suite S £30-£33; D £62-£70* **Facilities** FTV DVD Lounge tea/coffee WiFi **Notes** ⊗

The Wimslow

★★★ GUEST ACCOMMODATION

tel: 01524 417804 & 07942 861948 **fax:** 01524 417804 **374 Marine Road East LA4 5AH**
email: thewimslow@yahoo.co.uk **web:** www.thewimslow.co.uk
dir: From S: M6 junct 34 follow signs for Lancaster/Morecambe. In Morecambe take A589, turn left at Broadway Hotel, 0.25m on left. From N: M6 junct 35 via Carnforth/Bolton-le-Sands, after 0.25m right at lights. After 3m, 200mtrs past Emmanuel Church

A very warm welcome is assured at The Wimslow, where the owner's first concern is your comfort and enjoyment. Bedrooms are comfortable, with modern decor and furnishings, and offer a range of guest amenities. Hearty breakfasts are served overlooking Morecambe Bay towards the Lake District on a fine day. Binoculars and guides are provided for breakfast birdwatching.

Rooms 7 en suite (2 GF) **Facilities** FTV Lounge tea/coffee WiFi ⌂ **Parking** 3 **Notes** LB No Children 18yrs Closed 24 Dec-2 Jan

Beach Mount

★★★ GUEST ACCOMMODATION

tel: 01524 420753 **395 Marine Road East LA4 5AN**
email: beachmounthotel@aol.com **web:** www.beachmounthotelmorecambe.co.uk
dir: M6 junct 34/35, follow signs to Morecambe. Beach Mount 0.5m from town centre on E Promenade

This spacious property overlooks the bay and features a range of room styles that includes a junior suite. Guests have use of a comfortable lounge with fully licensed bar, and breakfasts are served in a pleasant separate dining room.

Rooms 10 en suite (1 GF) (5 smoking) S £26.25-£29.50; D £54-£61* **Facilities** FTV DVD Lounge tea/coffee Licensed WiFi **Notes** LB Closed Nov-Mar

MORECAMBE *continued*

Belle Vue

★★★ GUEST ACCOMMODATION

tel: 01524 411375 & 411214   **fax:** 01524 411375 **330 Marine Rd LA4 5AA**
dir: *On seafront between lifeboat house & bingo hall*

With fine views over the promenade and Morecambe Bay, the Belle Vue provides a range of bedroom styles on three floors; most are accessible by lift. There are comfortable lounges, and a spacious lounge bar where entertainment is provided at peak times of the year. A choice of dishes is available in the large dining room.

Rooms 41 rms (34 en suite) (3 fmly) S £30; D £50–£60* **Facilities** FTV Lounge TVL tea/coffee Dinner available Lift Licensed **Parking** 3 **Notes** LB ⊗ Closed Jan-Mar

Silverwell

★★★ GUEST HOUSE

tel: 01524 410532 **20 West End Rd LA4 4DL**
email: silverwell.hotel@btconnect.com **web:** www.silverwellhotel.co.uk
dir: *Follow signs to West End, turn right at promenade, take 3rd on left, Silverwell on left*

Silverwell offers comfortable accommodation in a quiet residential street, with rooms in a range of sizes with singles and families catered for. There is a licensed bar and lounge for guests use. Evening meals are available by prior arrangement.

Rooms 14 rms (8 en suite) (6 pri facs) (3 fmly) (4 GF) (5 smoking) S £25–£30; D £50–£60* **Facilities** FTV Lounge tea/coffee Dinner available Licensed WiFi 🔒
Conf Max 20 Class 20 Board 12 **Notes** ⊗

See advert on opposite page

See advert on opposite page

Innkeeper's Lodge Ormskirk

★★★★ INN

tel: 0845 112 6177 **Springfield Rd, Aughton L39 6ST**
email: aughton@millerandcarter.co.uk

On the edge of the pretty village of Aughton, this luxurious lodge provides smart yet affordable accommodation ideally located for a country escape or as a quiet base away from the hustle and bustle of Liverpool or Southport, and in easy reach of attractions such as Knowsley Safari Park, Chester Zoo, Formby Golf Club and Aintree racecourse. The elegant en suite rooms offer many extras and there's a Miller & Carter steakhouse.

Rooms 12 en suite

Birch Croft Bed & Breakfast

★★★ BED AND BREAKFAST

tel: 01772 613174 & 07761 817187 **Gill Ln, Longton PR4 4SS**
email: johnsuts@btinternet.com **web:** www.birchcroftbandb.co.uk
dir: *From A59 right at rdbt to Midge Hall. Premises 4th on left*

Situated only ten minutes away from major motorway links (M6, M65, M61) Birch Croft is on the doorstep of many attractions and close to Southport, Preston and Blackpool. This is a friendly, family-run business which offers comfortable accommodation in a very peaceful location.

Rooms 3 en suite (1 fmly) S fr £30; D fr £50* **Facilities** FTV TVL tea/coffee WiFi **Parking** 11 **Notes** LB ⊗ ⌨

Ashton Lodge Guest House

★★ GUEST ACCOMMODATION

tel: 01772 728414 **fax:** 01772 720580 **37 Victoria Pde, Ashton PR2 1DT**
email: greathospitality@btconnect.com **web:** www.prestonaccommodation.org.uk
dir: *M6 junct 31, A59 onto A5085, 3.3m onto A5072 (Tulketh Rd), 0.3m, into Victoria Pde*

Ashton Lodge is a detached Victorian residence offering good value accommodation, with bedrooms in a variety of sizes; some are located on the ground floor. The dining room is the setting for hearty traditional breakfasts served at individual tables.

Rooms 8 rms (3 en suite) (5 fmly) (3 GF) **Facilities** FTV TVL tea/coffee WiFi 🔒 **Parking** 7 **Notes** ⊗

Samlesbury Hall Lodge

★★★★ GUEST ACCOMMODATION

tel: 01254 812010 **fax:** 01254 812174 **Preston New Rd PR5 0UP**
email: info@samlesburyhall.co.uk **web:** www.samlesburyhall.co.uk
dir: *M6 junct 31 onto A59 then A677 signed Blackburn*

The gate lodge of Samlesbury Hall provides a cosy getaway for small groups, or couples looking for a romantic retreat. Accommodation comprises a large suite with two sitting rooms on one level, making it accessible for guests with mobility issues. The sitting rooms can be converted, allowing up to six guests. Breakfasts are served in the Hall or in the suite by prior arrangement. The Hall serves hearty lunches and has an antiques saleroom and an art gallery, as well as the Hall and gardens themselves to explore.

Rooms 3 en suite (3 fmly) (3 GF) S £60; D £100 (room only)* **Facilities** FTV DVD Lounge TVL TV1B tea/coffee Licensed WiFi ♿ 9 🔒 Golf driving range Play trail

Historic house **Conf** Max 150 Thtr 150 Class 150 Board 150 **Parking** 4 **Notes** ⊗ Civ Wed 120

WARTON
Map 18 SD42

The Birley Arms

[U]

tel: 01772 679988 **fax:** 01772 679435 **Bryning Ln PR4 1TN**
email: birley@thebirleyarmshotel.co.uk **web:** www.thebirleyarmshotel.co.uk
dir: *M55 junct 3 (Kirkham), 1st left, then over 3 rdbts. Straight on at mini rdbt, at next rdbt left signed Warton. 2m on left*

Currently the rating for this establishment is not confirmed. This may be due to a change of ownership or because it has only recently joined the AA rating scheme.

Rooms 16 en suite (1 fmly) (8 GF) S £70; D £75* **Facilities** FTV DVD tea/coffee Dinner available Licensed WiFi 📶 **Extras** Speciality toiletries - complimentary **Parking** 60 **Notes** ⊗

WHITEWELL
Map 18 SD64

Premier Collection

The Inn at Whitewell
★★★★★ ⊛ INN

tel: 01200 448222 **fax:** 01200 448298 **Forest of Bowland, Clitheroe BB7 3AT**
email: reception@innatwhitewell.com **web:** www.innatwhitewell.com
dir: *M6 junct 31a, B6243 to Longridge. Left at mini rdbt. After 3 rdbts (approx 3m) sharp left (with white railings), then right. Approx 1m, left, right at T-junct. Next left, 3m to Whitewell*

This long-established culinary destination is hidden away in quintessential Lancashire countryside, just 20 minutes from the M6. The fine dining restaurant is complemented by two historic and cosy bars with roaring fires, real ales and polished service. Bedrooms are richly furnished with antiques and eye-catching bijouterie, while many of the bathrooms have Victorian brass showers.

Rooms 19 en suite 4 annexe en suite (1 fmly) (2 GF) S £90-£200; D £125-£248* **Facilities** STV FTV DVD iPod docking station tea/coffee Dinner available Direct Dial WiFi ⚓ 18 Fishing Riding 📶 Horse stabling can be arranged **Extras** Speciality toiletries - complimentary **Conf** Max 45 Thtr 45 Board 35 **Parking** 60 **Notes** Civ Wed 80

LEICESTERSHIRE

BELVOIR
Map 11 SK83

Premier Collection

Vale House
★★★★★ 🏠 GUEST HOUSE

tel: 01476 879365 & 07795 320095 **NG32 1PA**
email: stay@valehousebelvoir.com **web:** www.valehousebelvoir.com
dir: *Follow brown tourist signs for Belvoir Castle, opposite ticket office on corner of Belvoir & Woolsthorpe Rd*

Vale House is a grand house that has commanding views over the Leicestershire countryside and was originally built for the engineer at nearby Belvoir Castle. Each of the individually styled bedrooms are very spacious and beautifully presented. The award-winning breakfasts are not to be missed and the comfortable lounge with its log fire is very popular with guests. WiFi is available, along with secure parking.

Rooms 5 rms (4 en suite) (1 pri facs) (1 fmly) (1 GF) **Facilities** FTV DVD TVL TV4B tea/coffee WiFi 📶 **Extras** Bottled water **Conf** Max 10 Thtr 10 Class 10 Board 10 **Parking** 5 **Notes** LB ⊗

CROFT
Map 11 SP59

Fossebrook B&B
★★★★ GUEST ACCOMMODATION

tel: 01455 283517 **Coventry Rd LE9 3GP**
web: www.fossebrook.co.uk
dir: *0.6m SE of village centre on B4114*

Offering friendly guest accommodation, Fossebrook B&B stands in a quiet rural location with good access to major roads. Bedrooms are spacious, very comfortable and offer an excellent range of facilities including a range of videos in all rooms. Breakfast is served in the bright dining room, that overlooks pleasant gardens and grounds.

Rooms 4 en suite (4 GF) **Facilities** tea/coffee WiFi 📶 **Extras** Fruit, snacks - complimentary **Parking** 16 **Notes** ⊗ Closed 24 Dec-2 Jan

EAST MIDLANDS AIRPORT   Map 11 SK42

Premier Collection

Kegworth House

★★★★★ 🛏 GUEST HOUSE

tel: 01509 672575 **fax:** 01509 670645 **42 High St DE74 2DA**
email: info@kegworthhouse.co.uk **web:** www.kegworthhouse.co.uk
dir: *M1 junct 24, A6 to Loughborough. 0.5m 1st right onto Packington Hill. Left at junct, Kegworth House 50yds on left*

Convenient for major roads and East Midlands Airport, this impressive Georgian house with an immaculate walled garden is lovingly maintained. The individually styled bedrooms are luxuriously appointed and equipped with a wealth of thoughtful extras. The elegant dining room is the setting for memorable dinners (by arrangement for six or more), and wholesome breakfasts featuring local produce are served in the kitchen.

Rooms 11 en suite (1 fmly) (2 GF) S £87-£150; D £107-£210* **Facilities** FTV DVD Lounge tea/coffee Direct Dial Licensed WiFi Free access to health club & swimming pool **Conf** Max 12 Board 12 **Parking** 25 **Notes** LB ⊛ No Children 8yrs

HUSBANDS BOSWORTH   Map 11 SP68

Croft Farm B&B *(SP634860)*

★★★★ FARMHOUSE

tel: 01858 880679 **Leicester Rd LE17 6NW**
email: janesmith06@aol.com **web:** www.croftfarm.org.uk
dir: *A5199 from Husbands Bosworth towards Leicester. Croft Farm 0.25m on left*

This very spacious and delightfully furnished house stands on the edge of the village in well-tended grounds. Bedrooms are thoughtfully equipped and there is a comfortable guests' lounge. Expect a substantial breakfast together with friendly and attentive service.

Rooms 4 en suite S £35-£50; D £65-£70* **Facilities** DVD TVL tea/coffee WiFi **Parking** 15 **Notes** ⊛ No Children 10yrs 🐾 350 acres sheep/arable/beef/mixed

KEGWORTH

See East Midlands Airport

KNIPTON   Map 11 SK83

The Manners Arms

★★★★ 🍽 RESTAURANT WITH ROOMS

tel: 01476 879222 **fax:** 01476 879228 **Croxton Rd NG32 1RH**
email: info@mannersarms.com **web:** www.mannersarms.com
dir: *From A607 follow signs to Knipton; from A52 follow signs to Belvoir Castle*

Part of the Rutland Estate and built as a hunting lodge for the 6th Duke, The Manners Arms offers thoughtfully furnished bedrooms designed by the present Duchess. Public areas include the intimate Beater's Bar and attractive Red Coats Restaurant, popular for its imaginative menus.

Rooms 10 en suite (1 fmly) **Facilities** FTV TVL tea/coffee Dinner available Direct Dial WiFi ♨ 18 🎣 **Conf** Max 50 Thtr 50 Class 25 Board 20 **Parking** 60 **Notes** Civ Wed 50

LEICESTER   Map 11 SK50

Stoney Croft

★★★ GUEST ACCOMMODATION

tel: 0116 270 7605 **fax:** 0116 270 6067 **5-7 Elmfield Av, Off London Rd LE2 1RB**
email: reception@stoneycrofthotel.co.uk **web:** www.stoneycrofthotel.co.uk
dir: *Near city centre on A6 to Market Harborough*

Stoney Croft provides comfortable accommodation and staff offer helpful service. Public rooms include a foyer-lounge area, breakfast room and conference facilities. The modern bedrooms come with desks. There is also a large restaurant-bar where a good selection of freshly cooked dishes is available.

Rooms 41 en suite (4 fmly) (6 GF) **Facilities** FTV TVL tea/coffee Dinner available Direct Dial Licensed WiFi Pool table **Conf** Max 150 Thtr 40 Class 20 Board 30 **Parking** 30 **Notes** Civ Wed 120

LONG WHATTON   Map 11 SK42

The Royal Oak

★★★★ ⊛ 🛏 INN

tel: 01509 843694 **26 The Green LE12 5DB**
email: enquiries@theroyaloaklongwhatton.co.uk **web:** www.theroyaloaklongwhatton.co.uk

The Royal Oak is a popular gastro pub with rooms, located in a small village just four miles from East Midlands Airport. Members of the young team offer a warm welcome and service is attentive. The seven spacious en suite bedrooms are set to the rear of the property and have been designed with comfort and style in mind. There is plenty of parking available and a small garden for the warmer months.

Rooms 7 en suite (1 fmly) (7 GF) **Facilities** FTV tea/coffee Dinner available WiFi **Extras** Speciality toiletries, mineral water **Parking** 28 **Notes** ⊛

The Falcon Inn

★★★ INN

tel: 01509 842416 **fax:** 01509 646802 **64 Main St LE12 5DG**
email: enquiries@thefalconinnlongwhatton.com **web:** www.thefalconinnlongwhatton.com
dir: *M1 junct 23 N or junct 24 S, follow signs to Airport. After lights 1st left to Diseworth, left at T-junct, left towards Long Whatton, on right*

This late 18th-century traditional country pub sits in the quiet village of Long Whatton. Inside, the relaxed and friendly atmosphere is complemented by a good choice of freshly made meals, real ales and efficient service. Smartly appointed bedrooms are housed in a converted former school house and stable block at the rear of the main inn. Ample private parking is provided. Helicopter landing pad available.

Rooms 11 annexe en suite (5 GF) **Facilities** FTV tea/coffee Dinner available WiFi petanque pitch **Conf** Max 30 Thtr 20 Class 20 Board 20 **Parking** 46 **Notes** ⊛

MARKET BOSWORTH   Map 11 SK40

Softleys

★★★ 🍽 GUEST ACCOMMODATION

tel: 01455 290464 **2 Market Place CV13 0LE**
email: softleysrestaurant@gmail.com **web:** www.softleys.com
dir: *On B585 in Market Place*

Softleys is a Grade II listed building dating back to 1794. The bedrooms are en suite and set on the third floor offering picturesque views over Market Bosworth. Quality food is served using locally sourced ingredients.

Rooms 3 en suite (1 fmly) Facilities FTV tea/coffee Dinner available Direct Dial Licensed WiFi Conf Max 26 Thtr 26 Class 26 Board 26 Notes RS Sun eve & Mon no food available

■ SIBSON   Map 11 SK30

The Millers

★★★★ INN

tel: 01827 880223 fax: 01827 880990 Twycross Rd CV13 6LB
email: millerssibsonreservations@greeneking.co.uk web: www.oldenglish.co.uk
dir: A5 onto A444 towards Burton. Property 3m on right

This former bakery and water mill has been totally refurbished and most of the original features have been retained - the water wheel is a feature of the public bar along with the log-burning fireplace. The well-equipped bedrooms have modern facilities. The bar and restaurant are popular with the locals, and there is a conference suite in a separate building which is ideal for small groups.

Rooms 39 en suite (2 fmly) (15 GF) Facilities tea/coffee Dinner available Direct Dial WiFi Conf Max 60 Thtr 60 Class 30 Board 40 Parking 60 Notes ⊗ Civ Wed 60

■ SUTTON IN THE ELMS   Map 11 SP59

The Mill on the Soar

★★★ INN

tel: 01455 282419 fax: 01455 285937 Coventry Rd LE9 6QA
email: 1968@greeneking.co.uk web: www.oldenglish.co.uk
dir: M1 junct 21, follow signs for Narborough, 3m, inn on left

This is a popular inn that caters especially well for family dining, and is set in grounds with two rivers and a lake. The open-plan bar offers meals and snacks throughout the day, and is divided into family and adults-only areas; for the summer months, there is also an attractive patio. Practical bedrooms are housed in a lodge-style annexe in the grounds.

Rooms 20 en suite 5 annexe en suite (19 fmly) (13 GF) Facilities FTV tea/coffee Direct Dial Children's outdoor play area Pool room Parking 80 Notes ⊗

■ WOODHOUSE EAVES   Map 11 SK51

The Wheatsheaf Inn

★★★★ ⊜ INN

tel: 01509 890320 90 Brand Hill LE12 8SS
email: richard@wheatsheafinn.net web: www.wheatsheafinn.net

Originally built around 1800 by the local miners of Swithland slate mines, this charming inn offers a friendly service, good food and modern accommodation in the adjacent self-contained cottage. The first-floor restaurant proves very popular with locals, offering specials and bistro menus that include traditional English dishes, and fresh fish appears on the blackboard specials.

Rooms 2 annexe en suite Facilities FTV TVL tea/coffee Dinner available WiFi ⬤ Conf Thtr 18 Class 12 Board 14 Parking 70 Notes ⊗ No coaches

LINCOLNSHIRE

■ CLEETHORPES   Map 17 TA30

Adelaide

★★★★ GUEST ACCOMMODATION

tel: 01472 693594 fax: 01472 329717 41 Isaac's Hill DN35 8JT
email: adelaide.hotel@ntlworld.com
dir: 500yds W of seafront. At A180 & A46 junct onto A1098 (Isaac's Hill), house on right at bottom of hill

This beautifully presented house offers well-equipped bedrooms and comfortable public rooms. Hospitality is a major strength. Good home cooking is provided and there is a small lounge with a bar.

Rooms 5 rms (3 en suite) (1 fmly) Facilities STV TVL tea/coffee Dinner available Licensed Notes ⊗ No Children 4yrs

Aristocrat Guest House

★★★★ GUEST HOUSE

tel: 01472 234027 & 07957 388475 fax: 01472 318086 15 Clee Rd DN35 8AD
email: aristocrat@ntlworld.com web: www.aristocrat-guesthouse.co.uk
dir: From A180 follow signs for Cleethorpes, over flyover, through 3 sets of lights. At rdbt right into Clee Rd, 30yds on left

Family-run Aristocrat Guest House is located just a few minutes' walk from the seafront, restaurants, bars and main attractions. The attractively decorated bedrooms in this lovely house are well equipped with thoughtful accessories such as fridges and DVD players, and WiFi is available.

Rooms 4 rms (3 en suite) (1 pri facs) S £30-£35; D £60-£65 Facilities FTV tea/coffee WiFi ♨ 18 Parking 2 Notes LB ⊗

CLEETHORPES *continued*

The Comat

★★★★ GUEST ACCOMMODATION

tel: 01472 694791 **fax:** 01472 238113 **26 Yarra Rd DN35 8LS**
email: comat-hotel@ntlworld.com **web:** www.comat-hotel.co.uk
dir: *Exit A1098 (Alexandra Rd), left of library*

A short walk from the shops and seafront, the welcoming Comat offers cosy, well-equipped bedrooms. There are a range of rooms, including ground floor bedrooms and a family suite with all bedrooms featuring smart, modern en suite bath or shower rooms. Tasty English breakfasts are served in the bright dining room, and an attractive lounge is also available.

Rooms 5 en suite (2 fmly) (1 GF) S £60-£75; D £70-£80* **Facilities** FTV DVD TVL tea/coffee WiFi **Notes** LB ⊛

Brier Park Guest House

★★★ GUEST ACCOMMODATION

tel: 01472 605591 & 07849 639923 **27 Clee Rd DN35 8AD**
email: graham.sherwood2@ntlworld.com **web:** www.brierparks-guesthouse.co.uk
dir: *Left at bottom of Isaac's Hill, 150yds on left*

Brier Park is a private house personally managed by the owner, offering a friendly atmosphere and comfortable accommodation. Bedrooms are modern, some are en suite and all well equipped. Breakfast is freshly cooked to order, and convenient parking in front is a bonus. The house is just a short stroll to the seafront and town centre.

Rooms 6 rms (3 en suite) (3 pri facs) (1 fmly) (2 GF) S £25-£30; D £60-£70* **Facilities** FTV TVL tea/coffee WiFi **Parking** 2 **Notes** LB ⊛ No Children 5yrs

Ginnie's Guest House

★★★ 🅰 GUEST HOUSE

tel: 01472 694997 **27 Queens Pde DN35 0DF**
email: enquiries@ginnies.co.uk **web:** www.ginnies.co.uk
dir: *From Kingsway (seafront) into Queens Parade (A1098)*

Ginnie's Guest House is a Victorian terrace house situated in a quiet location close to the Winter Gardens, Playtower, and many other amenities. Well maintained by the resident proprietor who takes pride in the many guests who return for further visits.

Rooms 7 rms (5 en suite) (2 pri facs) (3 fmly) (1 GF) D £50-£65 **Facilities** FTV DVD iPod docking station TVL tea/coffee WiFi 🔒 **Extras** Speciality toiletries - complimentary **Parking** 4 **Notes** LB ⊛ RS 24 Dec-2 Jan 24-25 & 31 Dec room only

Holmhirst

★★ GUEST ACCOMMODATION

tel: 01472 692656 **fax:** 01472 692656 **3 Alexandra Rd DN35 8LQ**
email: holmhirst@aol.com

Overlooking the sea and the pier, this Victorian terraced house has simply furnished bedrooms, many with en suite shower rooms. The public areas are known as Apples Wine & Cider Bar Bistro and have a stylish New York theme. The bar is well stocked and a wide range of meals is available.

Rooms 8 rms (5 en suite) S £35-£40; D £50-£78* **Facilities** TVL TV7B tea/coffee Dinner available Licensed **Notes** ⊛

The Nottingham House

U

tel: 01472 505150 & 505152 **5-7 Sea View St DN35 8EU**
email: nottinghamhousehotel@gmail.com **web:** www.nottinghamhousehotel.com

Currently the rating for this establishment is not confirmed. This may be due to a change of ownership or because it has only recently joined the AA rating scheme.

Rooms 3 en suite (1 fmly) S £45; D £65 **Facilities** FTV tea/coffee Dinner available Licensed WiFi ⚡ 18 Sauna Gym Pool table **Notes** No Children 5yrs Closed 25-26 Dec

GRANTHAM	Map 11 SK93

The Cedars

★★★★ BED AND BREAKFAST

tel: 01476 563400 & 07947 022119 **Low Rd, Barrowby NG32 1DL**
email: pbcbennett@mac.com
dir: *From A1 onto A52, W of Grantham. Follow signs to Barrowby, at x-rds, turn into Main St to village green. Then Low Rd*

A very warm welcome awaits at The Cedars, not just from the proprietors but also from the family dog. This beautiful 300-year-old Grade II listed family home offers comfortable accommodation. Guests can enjoy the family lounge and also the garden in the warmer months. Breakfast is served family-style in the dining room.

Rooms 3 rms (2 en suite) (1 pri facs) (1 fmly) **Facilities** FTV Lounge TVL tea/coffee Dinner available WiFi 🔒 **Parking** 4 **Notes** ⊜

Beaver House

★★★ BED AND BREAKFAST

tel: 01476 565011 & 07779 002206 **School Ln, Old Somerby NG33 4AH**
email: cuttlers@btinternet.com **web:** www.beaverhouse.co.uk
dir: *From Grantham A52 E for 2m. At rdbt take exit signed Old Somerby, then 1st left, 1st house on right*

Beaver House is located on a mainly residential avenue in the quiet village of Old Somerby, just five minutes' drive from Grantham. The accommodation has been thoughtfully designed, and is well equipped and very comfortable. Breakfasts are served in the dining room overlooking the manicured garden, and there is a restaurant within walking distance. A highchair and travel cot can be provided.

Rooms 3 rms (1 en suite) (1 pri facs) **Facilities** FTV TVL tea/coffee WiFi **Parking** 3 **Notes** ⊛ ⊜

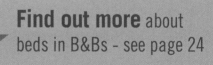

Find out more about beds in B&Bs - see page 24

HEMSWELL
Map 17 SK99

Premier Collection

Hemswell Court

★★★★★ 🍴 🏠 GUEST ACCOMMODATION

tel: 01427 668508 fax: 01427 667335 **Lancaster Green, Hemswell Cliff DN21 5TQ**
email: function@hemswellcourt.com web: www.hemswellcourt.com
dir: *1.5m SE of Hemswell on A631 in Hemswell Cliff*

Originally an officers' mess, Hemswell Court is a popular venue for conferences, weddings or private gatherings. The modern bedrooms and many suites are ideal for families or groups of friends, and all rooms are well equipped. The lounges and dining rooms are enhanced by many antique pieces.

Rooms 24 en suite (2 fmly) (5 GF) S £65-£95; D £85-£145* **Facilities** Lounge TVL tea/coffee Dinner available Licensed WiFi 🕭 🏊 **Conf** Max 200 Thtr 200 Class 150 Board 150 **Parking** 150 **Notes** ✖ Closed Xmas & New Year Civ Wed 200

HORNCASTLE
Map 17 TF26

Greenfield Farm (TF175745)

★★★★ FARMHOUSE

tel: 01507 578457 & 07768 368829   fax: 01507 578457 **Mill Ln/Cow Ln, Minting LN9 5PJ**
email: info@greenfieldfarm.net web: www.greenfieldfarm.net
dir: *A158 NW from Horncastle. 5m left at The New Midge pub, farm 1m on right*

Greenfield Farm's beautifully appointed, spacious farmhouse is located just one mile from the A158 and within easy reach of many attractions. The stunning grounds, wildlife pond and surrounding countryside ensure a peaceful stay. A warm welcome is certain along with comfortable, fully equipped bedrooms (two doubles and a twin room available) and a hearty Lincolnshire breakfast. There is also a lovely sitting room and complimentary WiFi access.

Rooms 3 en suite D £68-£74* **Facilities** FTV TVL tea/coffee WiFi 🔒 Farm trail **Parking** 12 **Notes** LB ✖ No Children 10yrs Closed Xmas & New Year 🐾 410 acres arable

HOUGH-ON-THE-HILL
Map 11 SK94

Premier Collection

The Brownlow Arms

★★★★★ 🏠 INN

tel: 01400 250234 fax: 01400 271193 **High Rd NG32 2AZ**
email: armsinn@yahoo.co.uk web: www.thebrownlowarms.com
dir: *Take A607 (Grantham to Sleaford road). Hough-on-the-Hill signed from Barkston*

The Brownlow Arms is a beautiful 16th-century property that enjoys a peaceful location in this picturesque village, located between Newark and Grantham. Tastefully appointed and spacious public areas have many original features, and include a choice of luxurious lounges and an elegant restaurant offering imaginative cuisine. The bedrooms are stylish, comfortable and particularly well equipped.

Rooms 4 en suite 2 annexe en suite (2 GF) S £65-£75; D £98-£110*
Facilities FTV DVD tea/coffee Dinner available Direct Dial WiFi 🔒 **Parking** 20
Notes ✖ No Children 8yrs Closed 25-27 Dec & 31 Dec-1 Jan No coaches

LINCOLN
Map 17 SK97

See also Horncastle & Marton (Village)

Premier Collection

Corner Oak

★★★★★ BED AND BREAKFAST

tel: 01522 684197 & 07729 577034   fax: 01522 684197
Old Wood, Skellingthorpe LN6 5UA
email: info@corner-oak.co.uk web: www.corner-oak.co.uk
dir: *From A46 to Skellingthorpe rdbt, follow road to village. Turn right at Co-op, left into Woodbank. Right at fork, 0.25m on left*

Corner Oak is just five miles from the centre of Lincoln, on the edge of 200 acres of woodland, hidden away in one and a half acres of garden. Accommodation comprises a luxurious ground-floor two-bedroom suite with a lounge, and a bathroom with a free-standing bath and separate shower. The suite has robes, slippers, toiletries and unlimited tea and coffee, and a large selection of DVDs, games and books as well as free WiFi and a mini fridge. Home-made cake and drinks are offered on arrival. A substantial continental breakfast can be served in the guest lounge, or you are welcome to join your hosts. Guests may enjoy the woodland walks or borrow the Corner Oak bicycles. There is a resident cat that frequents the guest lounge, and horses roam the grounds in winter. An abundance of wildlife can be found in the gardens and woodlands.

Rooms 2 annexe rms 1 annexe en suite (1 pri facs) (1 fmly) (2 GF) S fr £65; D fr £80* **Facilities** DVD TVL WiFi 🔒 Woodland play area **Extras** Mini-fridge **Parking** 10 **Notes** ✖ 🐾

St Clements Lodge

★★★★ GUEST ACCOMMODATION

tel: 01522 521532 & 07906 184266   fax: 01522 521532 **21 Langworth Gate LN2 4AD**
email: enquiries@stclementslodge.co.uk web: www.stclementslodge.co.uk
dir: *350yds E of cathedral, down Eastgate into Langworth Gate*

A warm welcome awaits at St Clements Lodge, which is just a short walk from Lincoln Cathedral and castle. This constantly improving accommodation offers three very comfortable bedrooms, two of which are en suite. There is also a family room, ideal for up to four people. A full English breakfast is served, along with home-made preserves, in the elegant breakfast room. Off-road parking is available.

Rooms 3 rms (2 en suite) (1 pri facs) (1 fmly) S £60; D £75-£80 **Facilities** FTV tea/coffee WiFi 🔒 **Parking** 3 **Notes** ✖ 🐾

Eagles Guest House

★★★★ GUEST ACCOMMODATION

tel: 01522 686346 **552A Newark Rd, North Hykeham LN6 9NG**
email: eaglesguesthouse@yahoo.co.uk web: www.eaglesguesthouse.co.uk
dir: *A46 onto A1434, signed Lincoln South, North Hykeham & South Hykeham. 0.5m on right opposite Cornflower Way*

This large, modern detached house is situated within easy access of the A46 and the historic city of Lincoln. The smartly appointed, thoughtfully equipped bedrooms are bright and fresh in appearance. A substantial breakfast is served in the pleasant dining room and free WiFi is available throughout the property.

Rooms 5 en suite (1 fmly) (1 GF) S £37-£42; D £50-£70* **Facilities** FTV tea/coffee WiFi **Parking** 6 **Notes** ✖ No Children 9yrs

LINCOLN *continued*

The Loudor

★★★★ GUEST ACCOMMODATION

tel: 01522 680333 fax: 01522 802770 **37 Newark Rd, North Hykeham LN6 8RB**
email: info@loudorhotel.co.uk web: www.loudorhotel.co.uk
dir: *3m from city centre. A46 onto A1434 for 2m, on left opposite shopping centre*

The Loudor can be found opposite the Forum shopping centre and a short walk from the sports centre. This friendly place offers well-equipped bedrooms, and breakfast is served at individual tables in the spacious dining room. There is some parking.

Rooms 9 en suite 2 annexe rms (1 fmly) (2 GF) S £40; D £60* **Facilities** FTV Lounge tea/coffee WiFi 🔒 **Extras** Home-made biscuits **Conf** Max 30 **Parking** 8 **Notes** ⊗

The Old Bakery

★★★★ ⍟⍟ RESTAURANT WITH ROOMS

tel: 01522 576057 & 07949 035554 **26/28 Burton Rd LN1 3LB**
email: enquiries@theold-bakery.co.uk web: www.theold-bakery.co.uk
dir: *Exit A46 at Lincoln North follow signs for cathedral. 3rd exit at 1st rdbt, 1st exit at next rdbt*

Situated close to the castle at the top of the town, this converted bakery offers recently refurbished, well-equipped bedrooms and a delightful dining operation. The cooking has gained two AA Rosettes, and uses much local produce. Expect good friendly service from the dedicated staff.

Rooms 4 rms (2 en suite) (2 pri facs) (1 fmly) S £55; D £75 **Facilities** FTV tea/coffee Dinner available WiFi 🔒 **Notes** ⊗ Closed 25-26 Dec, 1-16 Jan RS Mon closed No coaches

South Park Guest House

★★★★ GUEST HOUSE

tel: 01522 887136 fax: 01522 887136 **11 South Park LN5 8EN**
email: enquiry@southparkguesthouse.co.uk web: www.southparkguesthouse.co.uk
dir: *1m S of city centre on A15*

A Victorian house situated on the inner ring road facing South Park. The staff are friendly and attentive, and bedrooms, though compact, are well equipped. Breakfast is served in a modern dining room overlooking the park.

Rooms 6 en suite 1 annexe en suite (2 fmly) (1 GF) **Facilities** FTV tea/coffee Dinner available WiFi **Parking** 7 **Notes** ⊗

The Tennyson Guest House

★★★★ GUEST ACCOMMODATION

tel: 01522 521624 **7-8 South Park LN5 8EN**
email: enquiries@tennysonhotel.co.uk web: www.thetennyson.com
dir: *On A15 at S end of High St, adjacent to St Catherine's rdbt*

Adjacent to Lincoln's South Common, this well proportioned Victorian property is convenient for both business and leisure guests. Bedrooms are practical, with some situated on the ground floor. A guest lounge and complimentary WiFi are provided, as is off-road parking.

Rooms 8 en suite (2 GF) **Facilities** FTV Lounge tea/coffee WiFi 🔒 **Extras** Trouser press **Parking** 6 **Notes** ⊗

LOUTH
Map 17 TF38

The Manse B&B

★★★ BED AND BREAKFAST

tel: 01507 327495 **Middlesykes Ln, Grimoldby LN11 8TE**
email: knowles578@btinternet.com web: www.themansebb.co.uk
dir: *Grimoldby 4m from Louth on B1200. Into Tinkle St, right into Middlesykes Ln*

Located on a quiet country lane, this pleasantly appointed house offers comfortable accommodation and a warm welcome. Proprietors are enthusiastic and helpful, ensuring guests enjoy their stay. Bedrooms offer a range of homely extras, and freshly cooked evening meals are available by prior arrangement. The Manse is an ideal location for exploring the delights of the Wolds.

Rooms 4 rms (3 en suite) (1 pri facs) (1 fmly) (1 GF) S £45-£50; D £60-£75* **Facilities** FTV TVL tea/coffee Dinner available WiFi **Parking** 5 **Notes** LB ⊗ No Children 5yrs Closed 25 Dec ⊜

MABLETHORPE
Map 17 TF58

Park View Guest House

★★★ GUEST HOUSE

tel: 01507 477267 & 07906 847841 **48 Gibraltar Rd LN12 2AT**
email: malcolm@pvgh.freeserve.co.uk web: www.theparkview.co.uk
dir: *Take A1104 to Mablethorpe. At beach turn right into Gibraltar Rd*

This well-established guest house is set just beside Mablethorpe's golden beach and the Queens Park, and within easy walking distance of the town centre. Service is helpful and friendly, provided by the resident proprietors, Debbie and Malcolm. Bedrooms are soundly presented and of varying sizes, those on the ground-floor proving particularly popular. Enjoyable home-cooked dinners are available.

Rooms 5 rms (2 en suite) (3 GF) S £25-£27.50; D £50-£55* **Facilities** FTV TVL tea/coffee Dinner available Licensed WiFi ⍰ **Parking** 6 **Notes** LB ⊜

MARKET RASEN
Map 17 TF18

Premier Collection

The Advocate Arms

★★★★★ ⍟ RESTAURANT WITH ROOMS

tel: 01673 842364 **2 Queen St LN8 3EH**
email: info@advocatearms.co.uk web: www.advocatearms.co.uk
dir: *In town centre*

Appointed to a high standard, this 18th-century property is located in the heart of Market Rasen and combines historic character with contemporary design. The operation centres around the stylish restaurant where service is friendly yet professional and the food is a highlight. The attractive bedrooms are very well equipped and feature luxury bathrooms.

Rooms 10 en suite (2 fmly) S £42-£110; D £42-£110 (room only)* **Facilities** FTV tea/coffee Dinner available WiFi ⍰ 18 🔒 **Conf** Max 22 Thtr 18 Class 22 Board 18 **Parking** 6 **Notes** ⊗

East Farmhouse *(TF090847)*

★★★ FARMHOUSE

tel: 01673 842283 & 07836 331424 **Mill Ln, Middle Rasen LN3 5AQ**
email: emmalouise.grant@btconnect.com
web: www.eastfarmhousebedandbreakfast.co.uk
dir: *From A631 in Middle Rasen, turn opposite village shop into Mill Ln, signed Lissington. 2m on right*

This attractive Grade II listed building is just four miles from Market Rasen and is set in tranquil gardens and surrounding farmland. The comfortable accommodation offers lots of thoughtful extras and a warm welcome will be received from Gill and Jim, with an offer of tea and cake on arrival. Breakfast includes local produce, and home produced eggs and bread. A great base for walkers, with good walks in the area.

Rooms 2 rms (1 en suite) (1 pri facs) (1 fmly) S £40-£45; D £70-£80*
Facilities DVD TVL tea/coffee WiFi ⚘ 🐾 **Parking** 10 **Notes** LB ⊗ 410 acres arable/free range chickens

Wold View House B&B

★★★ 🏠 BED AND BREAKFAST

tel: 01673 838226 & 07976 563473 **Bully Hill Top, Tealby LN8 6JA**
email: enquiries@woldviewhouse.co.uk **web:** www.woldviewhouse.co.uk
dir: *A46 onto B1225 towards Horncastle, after 7m Wold View House at x-rds*

Situated at the top of Bully Hill with expansive views across The Wold, this smart bed and breakfast offers modern bedrooms and warm hospitality. Ideal for walking, riding, or touring the charming nearby villages and coastline, Wold View House is just a short drive from Lincoln.

Rooms 3 rms (2 en suite) (1 pri facs) (1 fmly) S £40-£45; D £70* **Facilities** FTV TVL tea/coffee Dinner available Licensed WiFi 🐾 **Parking** 15 **Notes** LB

MARTON (VILLAGE) — Map 17 SK88

Black Swan Guest House

★★★★ GUEST ACCOMMODATION

tel: 01427 718878 **21 High St DN21 5AH**
email: info@blackswanguesthouse.co.uk **web:** www.blackswanguesthouse.co.uk
dir: *On A156 in village centre at junct A1500*

Centrally located in the village, this 18th-century former coaching inn retains many original features, and offers good hospitality and homely bedrooms with modern facilities. Tasty breakfasts are served in the cosy dining room and a comfortable lounge with WiFi access is available. Transport to nearby pubs and restaurants can be provided.

Rooms 6 en suite 4 annexe en suite (3 fmly) (4 GF) **Facilities** FTV TVL tea/coffee Licensed WiFi 🐾 **Parking** 10

REVESBY — Map 17 TF36

The Red Lion

★★★ INN

tel: 01507 568665 **Main Rd PE22 7NU**
email: enquiries@redlion-revesby.co.uk **web:** www.redlion-revesby.co.uk
dir: *6m from Horncastle towards Boston*

Situated in the village of Revesby this traditional inn offers comfortable accommodation and all rooms are en suite. A good selection of freshly cooked meals can be enjoyed in the bar or dining room, and certainly won't disappoint those with a healthy appetite. A good range of Bateman's real ales is available.

Rooms 4 en suite S £55; D £80 **Facilities** FTV tea/coffee Dinner available WiFi Pool table 🐾 **Parking** 20 **Notes** ⊗ No coaches

SCOTTER — Map 17 SE80

The White Swan

★★★★ 🍴 RESTAURANT WITH ROOMS

tel: 01724 763061 **fax:** 01652 651493 **9 The Green DN21 3UD**
email: info@whiteswanscotter.com **web:** www.whiteswanscotter.com

This smartly presented property has been fully refurbished to provide stylish, contemporary accommodation in a peaceful village location. The restaurant is modern with vaulted ceilings and is split over three levels, whilst there is also a traditional pub called The Mucky Duck. A lounge bar and impressive garden add to the range of areas for guests to relax. Weddings and other special events are also well catered for. Accommodation rates include a continental breakfast but a choice of breakfast options are also available.

Rooms 11 en suite (1 fmly) D £55-£85* **Facilities** FTV tea/coffee Dinner available WiFi **Conf** Max 50 Thtr 50 Class 35 Board 35 **Parking** 35 **Notes** Civ Wed 110

SKILLINGTON — Map 11 SK82

The Cross Swords Inn

★★★ 🍴 INN

tel: 01476 861132 **The Square NG33 5HB**
email: harold@thecross-swordsinn.co.uk **web:** www.thecross-swordsinn.co.uk
dir: *Exit A1 at Colsterworth junct between Grantham & Stamford*

Very popular with the local community, this traditional inn offers three modern, well-equipped bedrooms, housed in an attractive cottage at the top of the courtyard, and named in keeping with the history of the village. All are very comfortable and coupled with smart modern bathrooms. The inn provides imaginative food and a range of real ales in a rustic period atmosphere.

Rooms 3 annexe en suite (3 GF) **Facilities** FTV tea/coffee Dinner available Gliding club **Parking** 12 **Notes** ⊗ No Children 10yrs RS Sun eve & Mon lunch bar & restaurant closed No coaches

| STAMFORD | Map 11 TF00 |

Premier Collection

Meadow View

★★★★★ BED AND BREAKFAST

tel: 01780 762133 & 07833 972577 **Wothorpe Rd PE9 2JR**
dir: *Off A1 signed Stamford, follow road past entrance to Burley House, bottom of hill, left at lights. Follow road round, 1st house on left*

Meadow View is a stylish property situated just a short walk from the town centre and Burghley House. The tastefully appointed bedrooms are contemporary in style with lovely co-ordinated soft furnishings and many thoughtful touches. Breakfast is served at a large communal table in the open-plan kitchen/dining room, and guests have the use of a smartly appointed lounge with plush sofas.

Rooms 3 en suite S £65; D £85* **Facilities** FTV iPod docking station TVL tea/coffee WiFi 🛁 **Extras** Chocolates, sherry, still/sparkling water **Notes** LB ⊗ ⊜

The Bull & Swan at Burghley

★★★★★ ⊚ 🍴 INN

tel: 01780 766412 **fax:** 01780 767061 **High St, St Martins PE9 2LJ**
email: enquiries@thebullandswan.co.uk **web:** www.thebullandswan.co.uk
dir: *A1 onto Old Great North Rd, left onto B1081, follow Stamford signs*

This delightful inn dates back to the 16th century when it is said to have been a gentlemen's drinking club. The public rooms include a large bar with a range of ales. There is also a separate restaurant serving great food. The stylish bedrooms are extremely well appointed with lovely soft furnishings and a range of thoughtful touches.

Rooms 7 en suite (2 fmly) **Facilities** FTV tea/coffee Dinner available Direct Dial WiFi **Parking** 7 **Notes** LB No coaches

Candlesticks

★★★ RESTAURANT WITH ROOMS

tel: 01780 764033 **fax:** 01780 756071 **1 Church Ln PE9 2JU**
email: info@candlestickshotel.co.uk **web:** www.candlestickshotel.co.uk
dir: *B1081 into Stamford. Left onto A43. Right into Worthorpe Rd, right into Church Ln*

Candlesticks is a 17th-century property situated in a quiet lane in the oldest part of Stamford, just a short walk from the centre of town. The bedrooms are pleasantly decorated and equipped with a good range of useful extras. Public rooms feature Candlesticks restaurant and a cosy bar.

Rooms 8 en suite S £50-£75; D £70-£90* **Facilities** STV FTV Lounge tea/coffee Dinner available Direct Dial WiFi 🛁 **Parking** 8 **Notes** LB ⊗ RS Mon No restaurant or bar service

| SWINESHEAD BRIDGE | Map 12 TF24 |

Boston Lodge

★★★ GUEST ACCOMMODATION

tel: 01205 820983 & 07436 269596 **fax:** 0872 111 5905 **Browns Drove PE20 3PX**
email: info@bostonlodge.co.uk **web:** www.bostonlodge.co.uk
dir: *From A17 onto A1121 to Boston, take 1st left into Browns Drove then immediate right*

A personal welcome is guaranteed at Boston Lodge. Located in a quiet village on the outskirts of Boston within easy reach of Sleaford and Lincoln, it is an ideal base for both the tourist and business traveller. Rooms are all en suite and individual in design. Ample off-road parking is a plus.

Rooms 8 en suite 1 annexe en suite (2 fmly) (3 GF) S £36; D £52* **Facilities** FTV TVL tea/coffee WiFi 🛁 **Parking** 30

| WHAPLODE | Map 12 TF32 |

Westgate House & Barn

★★★★ BED AND BREAKFAST

tel: 01406 370546 **Little Ln PE12 6RU**
email: enquiries@westgatehouseandb.co.uk **web:** www.westgatehouseandb.co.uk
dir: *Follow brown signs in Whaplode (on A151)*

Set in a peaceful rural location, in well-established cottage gardens and grounds, Westgate House offers comfortably appointed accommodation in a delightful barn conversion. Breakfast is taken in the main house, in a charming room with wood-burning stove and garden views. The freshly cooked breakfast includes good locally sourced ingredients and home-made preserves.

Rooms 2 annexe en suite S £40-£44; D £60-£65* **Facilities** FTV tea/coffee WiFi 🛁 **Extras** Fresh milk - complimentary **Parking** 2 **Notes** LB ⊗ No Children 6yrs ⊜

| WINTERINGHAM | Map 17 SE92 |

Premier Collection

Winteringham Fields

★★★★★ ⊚⊚⊚ RESTAURANT WITH ROOMS

tel: 01724 733096 **fax:** 01724 733898 **DN15 9ND**
email: reception@winteringhamfields.co.uk **web:** www.winteringhamfields.co.uk
dir: *In village centre at x-rds*

This highly regarded restaurant with rooms, located deep in the countryside at Winteringham village, is six miles west of the Humber Bridge. Public rooms and bedrooms, some of which are housed in renovated barns and cottages, are delightfully luxurious. There is an abundance of charm, and period features are combined with rich furnishings and fabrics. The award-winning food is a highlight of any stay and guests can expect highly skilled dishes, excellent quality and stunning presentation.

Rooms 4 en suite 7 annexe en suite (2 fmly) (3 GF) S £145-£180; D £180-£220* **Facilities** iPod docking station tea/coffee Dinner available Direct Dial WiFi 🛁 **Conf** Max 50 Thtr 50 Class 50 Board 50 **Parking** 14 **Notes** LB Closed 25 Dec for 2wks, last wk Oct, 2wks Aug No coaches Civ Wed 60

WOODHALL SPA
Map 17 TF16

Oglee Guest House

★★★★ GUEST HOUSE

tel: 01526 353512 **16 Stanhope Av LN10 6SP**
email: ogleeguesthouse@gmail.com **web:** www.oglee-guesthouse.co.uk
dir: *Close to junct of B1191 & B1192*

This Edwardian family home is ideally situated for exploring Lincolnshire. It is also within easy reach of several RAF bases and the well-regarded Hotchkin Golf Course. Spacious bedrooms offer a high level of comfort with modern amenities. Hearty breakfasts use local produce, feature hand-made jams and additional special dishes. Evening meals by prior arrangement.

Rooms 3 en suite (1 fmly) S £50; D £70* **Facilities** FTV DVD TVL tea/coffee Dinner available WiFi **Extras** Fruit **Parking** 4 **Notes** LB

WOOLSTHORPE
Map 11 SK83

Chequers Inn

★★★★ INN

tel: 01476 870701 **Main St NG32 1LU**
email: justinnabar@yahoo.co.uk **web:** www.chequersinn.net
dir: *From Melton Mowbray on A607 towards Grantham, follow brown heritage signs to Belvoir Castle. Turn left at x-rds & follow signs*

Situated in the picturesque village of Woolsthorpe in the unspoilt Vale of Belvoir, the Chequers Inn is a quintessentially English inn dating from the 17th century. It has roaring fires in the winter and a well-maintained garden for alfresco dining in the summer. The snug and bar was once the original village bakery. Bedrooms are situated in the adjacent stables and are tastefully decorated. Good food is served in the bar and in the restaurant.

Rooms 4 annexe en suite (1 fmly) (3 GF) **Facilities** FTV DVD tea/coffee Dinner available 18 **Conf** Max 80 Thtr 80 Class 80 Board 30 **Parking** 40 **Notes** Closed 25 Dec eve, 26 Dec eve & 1 Jan eve Civ Wed 80

Symbols and abbreviations are explained on page 7

LONDON

N4

BEST WESTERN London Highbury
PLAN 2 F5

★★★ GUEST ACCOMMODATION

tel: 020 8802 6551 **fax:** 020 8802 9461 **372-374 Seven Sisters Rd N4 2PG**
email: reservations@highbury.com **web:** www.bestwesternlondonhighbury.com
dir: *0.5m from Finsbury Park Station*

Opposite Finsbury Park and only a short tube ride from the centre of London, this establishment offers well-appointed and well-equipped accommodation. There is ample and secure parking; a well stocked bar and a buffet style continental breakfast is available daily.

Rooms 45 en suite (6 fmly) (7 GF) **Facilities** STV FTV TVL tea/coffee Direct Dial Lift Licensed WiFi **Parking** 20 **Notes** ⊗

N12
Map 6 TQ29

Glenlyn Guest House

★★★ GUEST ACCOMMODATION

tel: 020 8445 0440 **fax:** 020 8446 2902 **6 Woodside Park Rd N12 8RP**
email: contactus@glenlynhotel.com **web:** www.glenlynhotel.com
dir: *M25 junct 23 towards High Barnet, A1000 into North Finchley on right after Sainsbury's*

Located in the heart of Finchley and set in four large Victorian terraced houses, the Glenlyn Guest House offers a choice of rooms spanning from cosy loft rooms to interconnecting family rooms. Guests can relax in the private bar or unwind in the garden. Breakfast is served in the airy conservatory.

Rooms 27 en suite (4 fmly) (3 GF) **Facilities** FTV Lounge TVL tea/coffee Direct Dial Licensed WiFi **Parking** 14 **Notes** ⊗

NW1

TheWesley
PLAN 1 C5

★★★★ 🍽 GUEST ACCOMMODATION

tel: 020 7380 0001 **fax:** 020 7387 5300 **81-103 Euston St NW1 2EZ**
email: reservations@thewesley.co.uk **web:** www.thewesley.co.uk
dir: *Euston Rd left at lights into Melton St, 1st left into Euston St, 100yds on left*

Located within walking distance of Euston station, this smart property is convenient for central London. Stylish air-conditioned bedrooms are thoughtfully equipped for business and leisure. The airy Atrium Bar and Restaurant offers drinks, light snacks and an evening menu. Extensive conference and meeting facilities are available.

Rooms 100 en suite (2 fmly) **Facilities** STV FTV iPod docking station TVL tea/coffee Dinner available Direct Dial Lift Licensed WiFi **Extras** Speciality toiletries, safe **Conf** Max 150 Thtr 150 Class 50 Board 45 **Notes** ⊗ Civ Wed

NW3

The Langorf
PLAN 2 E4

★★★★ GUEST ACCOMMODATION

tel: 020 7794 4483 **fax:** 020 7435 9055 **20 Frognal, Hampstead NW3 6AG**
email: info@langorfhotel.com **web:** www.langorfhotel.com
dir: *Off A41 (Finchley Rd), near Finchley Road tube station*

Located on a leafy and mainly residential avenue within easy walking distance of shops and restaurants, this elegant Edwardian property has been appointed to provide high standards of comfort and facilities. Bedrooms are furnished with flair and a warm welcome is assured.

Rooms 31 en suite (4 fmly) (3 GF) D £75-£155* **Facilities** STV TVL tea/coffee Direct Dial Lift Licensed WiFi **Conf** Max 30 Thtr 30 Class 20 Board 15 **Parking Notes** LB ⊗

La Gaffe
PLAN 2 E5

★★★ 🍽 GUEST ACCOMMODATION

tel: 020 7435 8965 & 7435 4941 **fax:** 020 7794 7592 **107-111 Heath St NW3 6SS**
email: info@lagaffe.co.uk **web:** www.lagaffe.co.uk
dir: *On A502, 250yds N of Hampstead tube station*

This family-owned and run guest accommodation, just north of Hampstead High Street, offers charm and warm hospitality. The Italian restaurant, which is open most lunchtimes and for dinner, is popular with locals. Bedrooms are compact, but all are en suite.

Rooms 11 en suite 7 annexe en suite (2 fmly) (2 GF) S £75-£110; D £99-£129* **Facilities** FTV tea/coffee Dinner available Direct Dial Licensed WiFi **Conf** Max 10 Board 10 **Notes** ⊗ RS 25-26 Dec Restaurant closed 25 Dec eve & 26 Dec

NW9

Kingsland
PLAN 2 C5

★★★ GUEST ACCOMMODATION

tel: 020 8206 0666 **fax:** 020 8206 0555 **Kingsbury Circle, Kingsbury NW9 9RR**
email: stay@kingslandhotel.co.uk **web:** www.kingslandhotel.co.uk
dir: *Kingsbury Circle junct A4006 & A4140*

Easily located at the roundabout near Kingsbury Station, and handy for shops, restaurants and the Wembley complex, the Kingsland provides modern bedrooms with smart en suite bathrooms. A continental breakfast is supplied, and a passenger lift and car park are available.

Rooms 27 en suite (5 fmly) (5 GF) **Facilities** FTV tea/coffee Lift WiFi **Parking** 30 **Notes** ⊗

NW11

Martel Guest House
PLAN 2 D5

★★★ GUEST HOUSE

tel: 020 8455 1802 & 07587 655181 fax: 020 3137 6927 **27 The Ridgeway NW11 8QP**
email: reservations@martelguesthouse.co.uk web: www.bedbreakfastlondon.co.uk

Martel Guest House is in a quiet residential area of north London, just a 15 minute underground journey from central London, and only five minutes from the M1. Accommodation is nicely appointed and offers all modern comforts including air-conditioning and free WiFi. Secure parking offered.

Rooms 9 en suite (2 fmly) (3 GF) S £60; D £80* **Facilities** FTV tea/coffee Direct Dial WiFi **Extras** Fridge **Parking** 7 **Notes** ⊛

SE10

Innkeeper's Lodge London, Greenwich
PLAN 2 G3

★★★★ INN

tel: 020 8293 0037 **291 Greenwich High Rd, Greenwich SE10 8NA**
web: www.innkeeperslodge.com

At Innkeeper's Lodge you'll find accommodation with comfort and character in equal measure, and everything needed for a relaxing stay, from easy check-in and free parking to complimentary breakfast and a cosy pub serving great value food and drink on the doorstep. Each Lodge has quality rooms, and there are Lodges in a variety of locations from towns and cities to countryside settings across the UK.

Rooms 24 rms

SW1

The Windermere
PLAN 1 C1

★★★★ GUEST ACCOMMODATION

tel: 020 7834 5163 fax: 020 7630 8831 **142/144 Warwick Way, Victoria SW1V 4JE**
email: reservations@windermere-hotel.co.uk web: www.windermere-hotel.co.uk
dir: *B324 off Buckingham Palace Rd, on Warwick Way, at junct with Alderney St*

The Windermere is a relaxed, informal and family-run establishment within easy reach of Victoria station and many of the capital's attractions. Bedrooms, although varying in size, are stylish, comfortable and well equipped. The Pimlico restaurant serves delicious evening meals and hearty cooked breakfasts. The Windermere was the AA Guest Accommodation of the Year for London 2013-14.

Rooms 19 en suite (3 fmly) (3 GF) S fr £135; D fr £225* **Facilities** FTV iPod docking station TVL tea/coffee Dinner available Direct Dial Lift Licensed WiFi **Extras** Speciality toiletries **Notes** ⊛ No Children 3yrs

Sidney London-Victoria
PLAN 1 C1

★★★★ GUEST ACCOMMODATION

tel: 020 7834 2738 fax: 020 7630 0973 **68-76 Belgrave Rd SW1V 2BP**
email: reservations@sidneyhotel.com web: www.sidneyhotel.com
dir: *A202 (Vauxhall Bridge Rd) into Charlwood St & junct with Belgrave Rd*

This smart Grade II listed property near Pimlico is formed from five six-storey town houses, and offers brightly decorated bedrooms that are well equipped for business use. Several rooms are suitable for families. Public areas include a bar lounge and an airy breakfast room.

Rooms 80 en suite (13 fmly) (9 GF) **Facilities** STV Lounge TVL tea/coffee Direct Dial Lift Licensed WiFi **Conf** Max 30 Thtr 30 Class 15 Board 14 **Notes** ⊛

BEST WESTERN Victoria Palace
PLAN 1 C1

★★★ GUEST ACCOMMODATION

tel: 020 7821 7113 fax: 020 7630 0806 **60-64 Warwick Way SW1V 1SA**
email: info@bestwesternvictoriapalace.co.uk web: www.bestwesternvictoriapalace.co.uk

An elegant, 19th-century building located in the heart of London, near to Belgravia and a five minute walk from Victoria rail, underground and coach stations. The bedrooms have en suite shower rooms. A buffet-style breakfast is served in the basement dining room.

Rooms 50 en suite (4 fmly) (4 GF) **Facilities** STV TVL tea/coffee Direct Dial Lift **Notes** ⊛

The Lidos
PLAN 1 C1

★★★ GUEST ACCOMMODATION

tel: 020 7828 1164 fax: 020 7828 1165 **43-45 Belgrave Rd, Victoria SW1V 2BB**
email: reservations@lidoshotel.com web: www.lidoshotel.com
dir: *From Victoria railway station exit to Wilton Rd. After 2nd set of lights into Denbigh St. Left at next lights into Belgrave Rd. On left*

The Lidos offers affordable accommodation within walking distance of Victoria Station and the Tube. In addition, there's a bus stop right in front of the main entrance making access easy to all major sites. All rooms have en suite facilities and have been equipped with modern amenities. An inclusive continental breakfast is offered to all guests whilst a range of restaurants and pubs can be found nearby.

Rooms 39 en suite (2 fmly) (4 GF) S £45-£155; D £55-£195* **Facilities** FTV tea/coffee Lift WiFi **Notes** ⊛

BEST WESTERN Corona
PLAN 1 C1

★★★ GUEST ACCOMMODATION

tel: 020 7828 9279 & 7487 0673 fax: 020 7931 8576 **87-89 Belgrave Rd SW1V 2BQ**
email: info@coronahotel.co.uk web: www.coronahotel.co.uk
dir: *From Pimlico Station into Tachbrook St. 1st left into Moreton St, 1st right into Belgrave Rd*

Centrally located, this elegant Victorian property is appointed to a high standard. The smart, well-equipped bedrooms offer comfortable, modern accommodation. A continental breakfast is served in the basement dining room, and room service is also available.

Rooms 51 en suite (13 fmly) (7 GF) **Facilities** STV FTV Lounge Direct Dial Lift Licensed WiFi **Notes** ⊛

Central House
PLAN 1 C1

★★★ GUEST ACCOMMODATION

tel: 020 7834 8036 fax: 020 7900 2212 **39 Belgrave Rd SW1V 2BB**
email: info@centralhousehotel.co.uk web: www.centralhousehotel.co.uk
dir: *Near Victoria station*

Located a short walk from Victoria station, the Central House offers sound accommodation. Bedroom sizes vary, and each room is suitably appointed, with en suite compact modular shower rooms. A self-service continental breakfast is offered in the lower ground-floor dining room.

Rooms 54 en suite (4 fmly) **Facilities** TVL tea/coffee Direct Dial Lift WiFi **Notes** ⊛

SW1 *continued*

Comfort Inn

PLAN 1 C1

★★★ GUEST ACCOMMODATION

tel: 020 7834 2988 **fax:** 020 7821 5814 **8-12 St George's Dr SW1V 4BJ**
email: info@comfortinnbuckinghampalacerd.co.uk
web: www.comfortinnbuckinghampalacerd.co.uk
dir: *From Buckingham Palace Rd into St George's Dr. Comfort Inn on left*

Located just a short walk south from Victoria station, this establishment is a good base for visiting the capital's attractions. All bedrooms and public areas are smartly appointed and offer very good levels of comfort. An extensive continental breakfast is served.

Rooms 81 en suite (13 fmly) (15 GF) **Facilities** STV TVL tea/coffee Direct Dial Lift **Conf** Max 20 Thtr 20 Class 20 Board 20 **Notes** ⊗

Comfort Inn Victoria

PLAN 1 C1

★★★ GUEST ACCOMMODATION

tel: 020 7233 6636 **fax:** 020 7932 0538 **18-24 Belgrave Rd, Victoria SW1V 1QF**
email: stay@comfortinnvictoria.co.uk **web:** www.comfortinnvictoria.co.uk

With a prime location close to Victoria station, this property offers brightly appointed en suite accommodation that is thoughtfully equipped for business and leisure guests. A continental breakfast is offered in the basement dining room.

Rooms 50 rms (48 en suite) (16 fmly) (9 GF) **Facilities** STV FTV TVL tea/coffee Direct Dial Lift WiFi **Notes** ⊗

The Victoria Inn

PLAN 1 C1

★★★ GUEST HOUSE

tel: 020 7834 6721 & 7834 0182 **fax:** 020 7931 0201
65-67 Belgrave Rd, Victoria SW1V 2BG
email: welcome@victoriainn.co.uk **web:** www.victoriainn.co.uk
dir: *On A3213, 0.4m SE of Victoria station, near Pimlico tube station*

A short walk from Victoria station, this Victorian property offers modern, well-equipped accommodation for business and leisure guests. There is a comfortable reception lounge, and a limited self-service buffet breakfast is available in the basement breakfast room.

Rooms 43 en suite (7 fmly) **Facilities** STV tea/coffee Direct Dial Lift WiFi **Notes** ⊗

Stanley House

PLAN 1 C1

★★ ⚠ BED AND BREAKFAST

tel: 020 7834 5042 & 7834 7292 **fax:** 020 7834 8439
19-21 Belgrave Rd, Victoria SW1V 1RB
email: cmahotel@aol.com **web:** www.londonbudgethotels.co.uk
dir: *Near Victoria station*

Stanley House is conveniently situated close to Victoria station and within easy access of the West End. Plain, soundly appointed bedrooms of varying sizes are offered, with breakfasts served in the lower ground-floor dining room; guests also have use of a ground-floor television lounge area.

Rooms 44 rms (41 en suite) (7 fmly) (8 GF) S £45-£55; D £60-£70* **Facilities** FTV TVL Direct Dial WiFi **Notes** LB ⊗ No Children 5yrs

SW3

Premier Collection

San Domenico House

PLAN 1 B1

★★★★★ GUEST ACCOMMODATION

tel: 020 7581 5757 **fax:** 020 7584 1348 **29-31 Draycott Place SW3 2SH**
email: info@sandomenicohouse.com **web:** www.sandomenicohouse.com

This stunning property in the heart of Chelsea offers beautiful, individually styled bedrooms, all with antique and period pieces, and well appointed en suites complete with Italian Spa toiletries. A sumptuous drawing room with wonderful works of art is available for guests to relax in or maybe to enjoy afternoon tea. Breakfast is served either in guests' bedrooms or in the elegant lower ground-floor dining room. Staff are friendly and attentive.

Rooms 13 en suite (9 smoking) **Facilities** STV Direct Dial Lift Licensed **Notes** ⊗

Find out more about the AA Friendliest B&B of the Year on page 17

Premier Collection

Sydney House Chelsea
PLAN 1 A1

★★★★★ 🏠 GUEST ACCOMMODATION

tel: 020 7376 7711 & 7376 6900   **fax:** 020 7376 4233
Sydney St, Chelsea SW3 6PU
email: info@sydneyhousechelsea.co.uk **web:** www.sydneyhousechelsea.co.uk
dir: *A4 Cromwell Rd, pass Natural History Museum on left, turn next right. Sydney St on left*

Located in the heart of Chelsea, this smart Grade II listed Georgian town house offers stylish and very comfortable accommodation, well equipped for both corporate and leisure guests. There is a small bar and drawing room and room service is also available. Staff are attentive and are always on hand to ensure guests feel at home. Breakfast is a particular highlight.

Rooms 21 en suite S £125-£255; D £125-£355 (room only)* **Facilities** STV FTV DVD Lounge tea/coffee Dinner available Direct Dial Lift Licensed WiFi **Extras** Still mineral water **Notes** ⊗ Closed 24-30 Dec

---

SW5

BEST WESTERN The Boltons
PLAN 2 E3

★★★★ GUEST ACCOMMODATION

tel: 020 7373 8900 **fax:** 020 7244 6835 **19-21 Penywern Rd, Earls Court SW5 9TT**
email: reservations@theboltonshotel.co.uk **web:** www.theboltonshotel.co.uk
dir: *A3220 from Cromwell Rd, follow road past Earls Court station, 1st right into Penywern Rd. Located on left*

This smart property boasts an excellent location, just seconds' walk from Earls Court tube station and exhibition centre, and within easy reach of museums and major shopping areas. Both public areas and bedrooms have an airy, contemporary feel with stylish furnishings and fittings. En suite bedrooms have comfortable beds, flat-screen satellite TV and WiFi. 24-hour room service is available and a buffet breakfast is served.

Rooms 57 en suite (4 fmly) (4 GF) **Facilities** STV FTV iPod docking station TVL tea/coffee Direct Dial Lift WiFi **Notes** ⊗

The Mayflower
PLAN 2 E3

★★★★ GUEST ACCOMMODATION

tel: 020 7370 0991 **fax:** 020 7370 0994 **26-28 Trebovir Rd SW5 9NJ**
email: info@mayflower-group.co.uk **web:** www.mayflowerhotel.co.uk
dir: *Left from Earls Court tube station & 1st left into Trebovir Rd, premises on left in 50yds*

This smart guest accommodation is a short walk from Earls Court, and close to Olympia and West London's museums and attractions. Stylish, individually designed bedrooms vary in size but all are extremely well equipped and have smart, modern en suites. There is an airy dining room where breakfast is served.

Rooms 47 en suite (4 fmly) (5 GF) S £109-£159; D £139-£299* **Facilities** FTV iPod docking station tea/coffee Direct Dial Lift WiFi **Extras** Speciality toiletries **Conf** Max 25 Thtr 25 Class 25 Board 25 **Parking** 4 **Notes** LB ⊗

See advert on page 246

SW5 *continued*

The Park Grand London Kensington

PLAN 2 E3

★★★★ GUEST ACCOMMODATION

tel: 020 7370 6831 fax: 020 7373 6179 **33-37 Hogarth Rd, Kensington SW5 0QQ**
email: info@parkgrandlondon.com web: www.parkgrandkensington.co.uk

Well appointed to a high standard, this property has a smart modern feel and is conveniently located for the exhibition centre, the West End and local transport links. Bedrooms are furnished and decorated to a very high standard, offering guests a comprehensive range of modern facilities and amenities.

Rooms 132 en suite (7 GF) **Facilities** STV FTV iPod docking station tea/coffee Dinner available Direct Dial Lift Licensed WiFi Gym Fitness centre **Conf** Max 15 Board 15 **Notes** ⊗

SW7

BEST WESTERN The Cromwell

PLAN 1 A2

★★★★ GUEST ACCOMMODATION

tel: 020 7244 1720 fax: 020 7373 3706 **110-112 Cromwell Rd, Kensington SW7 4ES**
email: reception@thecromwell.co.uk web: www.thelordsgroup.co.uk
dir: *M4/A4 towards London, pass Cromwell Hospital, 0.5m*

Just minutes away from the tube station and within easy access of all main tourist attractions, this property offers comfortable, modern accommodation. Fully air-conditioned and with free WiFi, this is an ideal location for both leisure and business guests. Amenities include an on-site meeting room, and secure parking is available nearby.

Rooms 85 en suite (11 GF) **Facilities** STV TVL tea/coffee Direct Dial Lift Licensed WiFi Fitness room **Conf** Max 8 Board 8 **Notes** ⊗

The Gainsborough

PLAN 1 A2

★★★★ GUEST ACCOMMODATION

tel: 020 7957 0000 fax: 020 7970 1805
7-11 Queensberry Place, South Kensington SW7 2DL
email: reservations@eeh.co.uk web: www.eeh.co.uk
dir: *Off A4 (Cromwell Rd) opposite Natural History Museum, near South Kensington tube station*

This smart Georgian house is in a quiet street near South Kensington's museums. Bedrooms are individually designed with fine fabrics and quality furnishings in co-ordinated colours. A choice of breakfasts is offered in the attractive dining room. There is also a delightful lobby lounge, and 24-hour room service is available.

Rooms 48 en suite (5 fmly) (4 GF) **Facilities** STV Lounge tea/coffee Dinner available Direct Dial Lift Licensed WiFi **Conf** Max 40 Class 40 Board 30 **Notes** ⊗

The Gallery
PLAN 1 A2

★★★★ GUEST ACCOMMODATION

tel: 020 7915 0000 fax: 020 7970 1805
8-10 Queensberry Place, South Kensington SW7 2EA
email: reservations@eeh.co.uk web: www.eeh.co.uk
dir: *Exit A4 (Cromwell Rd) opposite Natural History Museum, near South Kensington tube station*

The Gallery can be found close to Kensington and Knightsbridge and offers friendly hospitality, attentive service and sumptuously furnished bedrooms; some have a private terrace. Public areas include a choice of lounges (one with internet access) and an elegant bar. There is an option of English or continental breakfast, and 24-hour room service is available.

Rooms 36 en suite **Facilities** STV Lounge tea/coffee Dinner available Direct Dial Lift Licensed WiFi **Conf** Max 40 Thtr 40 Board 30 **Notes** ⊗

SW14

The Victoria
PLAN 2 C2

★★★★ ⚛⚛ RESTAURANT WITH ROOMS

tel: 020 8876 4238 fax: 020 8878 3464 **10 West Temple Sheen SW14 7RT**
email: bookings@thevictoria.net web: www.thevictoria.net
dir: *Off Upper Richmond Rd West into Derby Rd, then into West Temple Sheen*

The Victoria is in a quiet residential area close to Richmond Park. The bedrooms are refreshingly stylish and thoughtfully equipped. The public areas consist of a small contemporary seating area, a modern bar, and an award-winning restaurant that serves imaginative and well sourced dishes. Alfresco dining is also an option.

Rooms 7 en suite (2 fmly) (3 GF) S fr £120; D fr £130* **Facilities** FTV iPod docking station tea/coffee Dinner available Direct Dial WiFi ⚓ **Parking** 10 **Notes** No coaches

W1

Premier Collection

The Marble Arch by Montcalm
PLAN 1 B4

★★★★★ GUEST ACCOMMODATION

tel: 020 7258 0777 fax: 020 7258 0999 **31 Great Cumberland Place W1H 7TA**

Located just a short walk from Marble Arch, this luxury boutique townhouse property offers elegant, stylish and comfortable accommodation. Bedrooms are well equipped for the modern traveller with all rooms offering media hub, WiFi and mini bar.

Rooms 43 en suite (1 fmly) **Facilities** STV FTV TVL tea/coffee Lift Licensed WiFi **Notes** ⊗

The Sumner
PLAN 1 B4

★★★★ GUEST ACCOMMODATION

tel: 020 7723 2244 fax: 0870 705 8767 **54 Upper Berkeley St, Marble Arch W1H 7QR**
email: hotel@thesumner.com web: www.thesumner.com

Centrally located and just five minutes' walk from Marble Arch, The Sumner is part of a Georgian terrace. Appointed throughout to a very high standard, this delightful property combines much of the original character of the building with modern comfort. The air-conditioned bedrooms have all been designer decorated and feature widescreen LCD TVs as well as a range of traditional amenities. The breakfast buffet is included in the rate and there is an elegant.

Rooms 20 en suite S £160-£275; D £160-£375* **Facilities** FTV Lounge Direct Dial Lift Licensed WiFi **Notes** ⊗ No Children 5yrs

BEST WESTERN PREMIER Shaftesbury
PLAN 1 D3

★★★★ GUEST ACCOMMODATION

tel: 020 7871 6000 fax: 020 7871 6001 **65-73 Shaftesbury Av W1D 6EX**
email: reservations@shaftesburyhotel.co.uk web: www.shaftesburyhotel.co.uk
dir: *From Piccadilly Circus 300yds up Shaftesbury Av, at junct with Dean St*

In the centre of the West End, this boutique property offers plenty of warm, traditional hospitality. The Shaftesbury is next to two major underground stations, with comfortably sized public areas, a refreshment lounge, the Premier Bar, restaurants, conference facilities, and a fitness room.

Rooms 67 en suite (2 fmly) **Facilities** STV FTV iPod docking station TVL tea/coffee Direct Dial Lift Licensed WiFi Gym **Extras** Fruit - complimentary; Mini-bar - chargeable **Conf** Max 12 Board 12 **Notes** LB ⊗

W2

Park Grand Paddington
PLAN 1 A4

★★★★ GUEST ACCOMMODATION

tel: 020 7298 9800 fax: 020 7262 5414 **1-2 Queens Gardens, Paddington W2 3BA**
email: info@parkgrandlondon.co.uk web: www.parkgrandlondon.co.uk
dir: *Exit Paddington station via Praed St, turn right. After 3 sets of lights right into Devonshire Terrace. 100mtrs to Park Grand Paddington*

Park Grand Paddington enjoys a central location moments walk from Paddington station and Hyde Park, not to mention the city's main shopping districts and attractions. Rooms vary in size and are appointed to a very high standard. A number of stylish suites are also available. The Atlantic bar serves a range of light snacks throughout the day and evening. Additional facilities include state-of-the-art technology with free internet access, TV and fridges.

Rooms 157 en suite (11 fmly) (23 GF) **Facilities** FTV TVL tea/coffee Dinner available Direct Dial Lift Licensed WiFi Fitness room **Notes** ⊗

BEST WESTERN Mornington
PLAN 1 A3

★★★★ GUEST ACCOMMODATION

tel: 020 7262 7361 fax: 020 7706 1028 **12 Lancaster Gate W2 3LG**
email: london@mornington.co.uk web: www.morningtonhotel.co.uk
dir: *N of Hyde Park, off A402 Bayswater Rd*

This fine Victorian building is located in a quiet road and close to Lancaster Gate station for easy access to the West End. The bedrooms have been appointed to provide comfortable, stylish accommodation. There is a lounge bar and an attractive dining room where an extensive Scandinavian-style breakfast is served.

Rooms 70 en suite (10 fmly) (4 GF) **Facilities** STV FTV tea/coffee Direct Dial Lift Licensed WiFi **Extras** Mini-bar **Conf** Max 14 Thtr 14 Class 14 Board 14 **Notes** ⊗

BEST WESTERN Shaftesbury Paddington Court London
PLAN 1 A4

★★★★ GUEST ACCOMMODATION

tel: 020 7745 1200 fax: 020 7745 1221 **27 Devonshire Ter W2 3DP**
email: info@paddingtoncourt.com web: www.paddingtoncourt.com
dir: *From A40 take exit before Paddington flyover, follow Paddington Station signs. Devonshire Ter is off Craven Rd*

This establishment benefits from its convenient location close to Paddington station which has links to the underground and the Heathrow Express terminal. Situated next to Hyde Park and Kensington Palace Gardens, the guest accommodation comprises smart and comfortable rooms and a substantial breakfast. Club Rooms are also available with additional extras including the

continued

W2 *continued*

exclusive use of the Club Lounge. A room is available for small meetings by prior arrangement.

Rooms 165 en suite 35 annexe en suite (43 fmly) **Facilities** STV TVL tea/coffee Direct Dial Lift Licensed

Grand Royale London Hyde Park
PLAN 2 E3

★★★★ GUEST ACCOMMODATION

tel: 020 7313 7900 **fax:** 020 7221 1169 **1 Inverness Ter W2 3JP**
email: info@shaftesburyhotels.com **web:** www.shaftesburyhotels.com
dir: *On A40 Bayswater Rd*

Located adjacent to Hyde Park, fashionable Notting Hill and within easy reach of the West End, the Grand Royale combines its rich heritage with the needs of the modern traveller. The accommodation is contemporary in style and very well equipped. Breakfast is served in the staterooms.

Rooms 188 en suite (2 GF) **Facilities** tea/coffee Direct Dial Lift Licensed WiFi **Conf** Max 20 Thtr 20 Class 20 Board 20 **Notes** ⊗

Hyde Park Radnor
PLAN 1 A4

★★★★ GUEST ACCOMMODATION

tel: 020 7723 5969 **fax:** 020 7262 8955 **7-9 Sussex Place, Hyde Park W2 2SX**
email: hydeparkradnor@btconnect.com **web:** www.hydeparkradnor.com
dir: *A402 (Bayswater Rd) into Lancaster Ter & Sussex Gardens, right into Sussex Place*

This smart property is within walking distance of Paddington station and close to all London's central attractions. The smart bedrooms are brightly appointed, well equipped and have modern en suites. English breakfast is served in the lower ground-floor dining room.

Rooms 36 en suite (10 fmly) (5 GF) S £55-£90; D £95-£120* **Facilities** STV TVL tea/coffee Direct Dial Lift WiFi **Notes** LB ⊗

Mercure London Paddington
PLAN 1 A4

★★★★ GUEST ACCOMMODATION

tel: 020 7835 2000 **fax:** 020 7706 8800 **144 Praed St, Paddington W2 1HU**
email: stay@mercurepaddington.com **web:** www.mercurepaddington.com

Contemporary and stylish, Mercure London Paddington enjoys a central location, adjacent to Paddington Station. Bedrooms and en suites vary in size but all are smartly appointed and boast a host of extra facilities including CD players, flat-screen TVs, room safes and internet access. A small gym, stylish lounge and meeting rooms are also available.

Rooms 83 en suite **Facilities** STV TVL tea/coffee Dinner available Direct Dial Lift Licensed **Conf** Max 22 Board 22 **Notes** ⊗

The New Linden
PLAN 2 E3

★★★★ GUEST ACCOMMODATION

tel: 020 7221 4321 **fax:** 020 7727 3156 **59 Leinster Square, Notting Hill W2 4PS**
email: newlindenhotel@mayflower-group.co.uk **web:** www.newlinden.co.uk
dir: *Off A402, Bayswater Rd into Palace Court, left into Moscow Rd. Right into Hereford Rd, 100mtrs on left*

The New Linden is a friendly place that has a good location north of Kensington Gardens. Its stylish en suite bedrooms are richly furnished and thoughtfully equipped with CD players and safes. A good continental breakfast is served in the basement dining room.

Rooms 50 en suite S £109-£159; D £139-£299* **Facilities** STV FTV iPod docking station TVL tea/coffee Direct Dial Lift WiFi **Conf** Max 25 **Parking** 4 **Notes** ⊗

See advert on opposite page

Park Grand London Hyde Park
PLAN 1 A4

★★★★ GUEST ACCOMMODATION

tel: 020 7262 4521 **fax:** 020 7262 7610 **78-82 Westbourne Ter, Paddington W2 6QA**
email: reservations@londonpremierhotels.co.uk **web:** www.parkgrandhydepark.co.uk
dir: *A40 into Lancaster Terrace, at crossing left onto slip road*

This attractive property enjoys a central location within easy reach of central London shops and attractions. The en suite bedrooms and public areas have a smart contemporary feel. Although rooms vary in size, all boast many useful facilities such as free internet access, mini-fridges and irons.

Rooms 119 en suite (10 fmly) (19 GF) **Facilities** FTV Lounge tea/coffee Direct Dial Lift Licensed WiFi **Parking** 11 **Notes** ⊗

Princes Square   PLAN 2 E3

★★★★ GUEST ACCOMMODATION

tel: 020 7229 9876 **fax:** 020 7229 4664
23-25 Princes Square, off Ilchester Gardens, Bayswater W2 4NJ
email: info@princesssquarehotel.co.uk **web:** www.princesssquarehotel.co.uk
dir: *From Bayswater 1st left into Moscow Rd, 3rd right into Ilchester Gardens*

This fine building is in a quiet road close to tube stations for easy access to the
West End. The comfortable bedrooms provide stylish accommodation, and there is a
small bar and an attractive dining room where a continental breakfast is served.

Rooms 50 en suite (3 fmly) (6 GF) **Facilities** STV FTV tea/coffee Direct Dial Lift WiFi
Notes LB ⊗

Quality Crown Hyde Park   PLAN 1 A4

★★★★ GUEST ACCOMMODATION

tel: 020 7262 6699 **fax:** 020 7723 3233 **8-14 Talbot Square W2 1TS**
email: res.hydepark@lth-hotels.com **web:** www.lth-hotels.com
dir: *SE of Paddington station off Sussex Gardens*

This well-presented property is convenient for Hyde Park, Paddington and Marble
Arch. The modern bedrooms are furnished to a good standard and the executive
rooms are particularly impressive. Public areas include a compact but stylish bar
and lounge, and a basement restaurant where hearty breakfasts are served.

Rooms 75 en suite (8 fmly) (8 GF) **Facilities** FTV TVL tea/coffee Direct Dial Lift
Licensed WiFi **Notes** ⊗

Shaftesbury Hyde Park International   PLAN 2 E3

★★★★ GUEST ACCOMMODATION

tel: 020 7985 8300 **fax:** 020 7792 0157 **52-55 Inverness Ter W2 3LB**
email: info@shaftesburyhotels.com **web:** www.shaftesburyhotels.com
dir: *Off A402 (Bayswater Rd)*

A smart, modern establishment near to Bayswater, Queensway and Paddington
underground stations, the Shaftesbury Hyde Park International is also within
walking distance of a myriad of dining options. Bedrooms and bathrooms are
decorated to a very high standard with a good range of in-room facilities including
flat-screen TV, iron and ironing board and complimentary internet or WiFi access.
Continental and cooked buffet breakfasts are served daily. There is a limited
number of off-road parking spaces.

Rooms 70 en suite (2 GF) **Facilities** STV TVL tea/coffee Direct Dial Lift Licensed WiFi
Gym **Parking** 3 **Notes** ⊗

Shaftesbury Metropolis London Hyde Park   PLAN 1 A4

★★★★ GUEST ACCOMMODATION

tel: 020 7723 7723 **fax:** 020 7402 6318 **78-84 Sussex Gardens, Hyde Park W2 1UH**
email: gurpreet@shaftesburymetropolitan.com **web:** www.shaftesburyhotels.com

This establishment is in an ideal location close to Paddington station with express
links to Heathrow Airport. Smartly decorated bedrooms with highly comfortable beds
are available in a range of sizes, all with stylish en suite provision. On-site
facilities include complimentary internet or WiFi, and continental and full English
breakfasts are served every day. Reception is staffed 24 hours a day.

Rooms 90 en suite (14 GF) **Facilities** STV FTV TVL tea/coffee Direct Dial Lift Licensed
WiFi Small fitness centre **Notes** ⊗

W2 *continued*

Shaftesbury Premier London Notting Hill   PLAN 2 E3

★★★★ GUEST ACCOMMODATION

tel: 020 7792 1414 **fax:** 020 7792 0099 **5-7 Princes Square, Bayswater W2 4NP**
web: www.shaftesburyhotels.com

Situated conveniently for many attractions yet peacefully located in a quiet, leafy square, this smart establishment offers friendly, professional service and comfortable rooms. The property has stylish public rooms and offers free WiFi as well as hard-wire connectivity in the extremely well-equipped bedrooms. Breakfast is served in the dining room and offers a good choice of freshly cooked traditional breakfast and continental items.

Rooms 68 en suite (2 GF) **Facilities** STV TVL tea/coffee Direct Dial Lift WiFi Gym

Shaftesbury Premier London Paddington   PLAN 1 A4

★★★★ GUEST ACCOMMODATION

tel: 020 7723 3434 **fax:** 020 7402 0433 **55-61 Westbourne Ter W2 6QA**
web: www.theshaftesbury.co.uk
dir: *Exit A40 into Lancaster Terrace*

This smart property enjoys a convenient location within walking distance of Hyde Park and of many of London's major shops and attractions. Bedrooms are smartly appointed and boast modern technology. A hearty breakfast is served in the airy dining room. Limited off-street parking (chargeable) is a bonus. The staff are friendly and attentive.

Rooms 118 en suite (7 fmly) (20 GF) S £330; D £390 (room only)* **Facilities** STV TVL tea/coffee Dinner available Direct Dial Lift Licensed WiFi **Parking** 12 **Notes** ⊗

Number 63 Soroptimist   PLAN 1 A3

★★★ GUEST ACCOMMODATION

tel: 020 7723 8575 **fax:** 020 7723 1061 **63 Bayswater Rd W2 3PH**
email: info@number63.co.uk **web:** www.number63.co.uk

Number 63 Soroptimist offers a surprisingly tranquil environment just a minute's walk from Lancaster Gate tube and directly opposite Hyde Park. All bedrooms are comfortable with en suite facilities and consist of a range of singles and twins; there is also a triple room. Hot snacks are available throughout the afternoon and evening (by prior arrangement) and a good continental or cooked breakfast is served in the mornings. A meeting/function room is available. Parking can be arranged.

Rooms 16 en suite (1 fmly) S fr £75.50; D fr £126* **Facilities** FTV Lounge TVL tea/coffee Dinner available Direct Dial Lift Licensed WiFi **Conf** Max 25 Thtr 25 Class 25 Board 25 **Notes** ⊗ Closed 23-26 Dec

Admiral   PLAN 1 A4

★★★ GUEST ACCOMMODATION

tel: 020 7723 7309 **fax:** 020 7723 8731 **143 Sussex Gardens, Hyde Park W2 2RY**
email: enquiries@admiral-hotel.com **web:** www.admiral-hotel.com

The Admiral is a short walk from Paddington station and is convenient for Hyde Park and the West End. The smart bedrooms are enhanced with attractive artworks, and a full English breakfast is provided.

Rooms 21 en suite (12 fmly) (1 GF) **Facilities** STV FTV TVL tea/coffee Dinner available Direct Dial Licensed WiFi **Conf** Max 30 Class 25 Board 25 **Parking** 3 **Notes** LB ⊗

Comfort Inn Hyde Park   PLAN 1 A3

★★★ GUEST ACCOMMODATION

tel: 020 7229 6424 **fax:** 020 7221 4772 **73 Queensborough Ter, Bayswater W2 3SU**
email: info@comforthydepark.com **web:** www.choicehotels.co.uk
dir: *Off Bayswater Rd near Queensway tube station*

A short walk from Kensington Gardens and fashionable Queensway, this property has been converted to provide practically equipped bedrooms, with bright and well appointed bathrooms. Breakfast is served in the basement dining room.

Rooms 29 en suite (1 fmly) (3 GF) **Facilities** STV FTV tea/coffee Direct Dial Lift WiFi **Notes** ⊗

Kingsway Park Guest Accommodation   PLAN 1 A4

★★★ GUEST ACCOMMODATION

tel: 020 7723 5677 & 7724 9346   **fax:** 020 7402 4352 **139 Sussex Gardens W2 2RX**
email: info@kingswaypark-hotel.com **web:** www.kingswaypark-hotel.com
dir: *A40 Ebound junct for Paddington, through to Sussex Gdns*

This Victorian property has a central location within walking distance of Marble Arch, Hyde Park and Paddington. Bedrooms offer well-equipped, good value accommodation. Public areas include a reception lounge and a basement breakfast room adorned with interesting artwork. A limited number of parking spaces is available.

Rooms 22 en suite (5 fmly) (2 GF) **Facilities** STV FTV TVL tea/coffee Direct Dial Licensed **Conf** Max 30 **Parking** 3 **Notes** LB ⊗

Barry House
PLAN 1 A4

★★★ A BED AND BREAKFAST

tel: 020 7723 7340 **fax:** 020 7723 9775 **12 Sussex Place, Hyde Park W2 2TP**
email: hotel@barryhouse.co.uk **web:** www.barryhouse.co.uk
dir: *300yds SE of Paddington station*

The family-run Barry House offers friendly accommodation, close to rail and tube stations and just a stroll from Hyde Park. Bedrooms are comfortably equipped and most are en suite.

Rooms 18 rms (16 en suite) (5 fmly) (2 GF) S £50-£90; D £85-£130 **Facilities** FTV tea/coffee Direct Dial WiFi **Notes** ⊗

W6

BEST WESTERN PLUS Seraphine
PLAN 2 D3

★★★★ GUEST ACCOMMODATION

tel: 020 8600 0555 & 020 8741 6464 **fax:** 020 8600 0556 **84 King St W6 0QW**
email: hammersmith@seraphinehotel.co.uk **web:** www.seraphinehotel.co.uk
dir: *A4 exit into Hammersmith Bridge Rd before Hammersmith flyover. Right into King St, on right*

Located just a short walk from Hammersmith Station, this establishment is a good base for visiting the capital's attractions. All bedrooms and public areas are smartly appointed and offer very good levels of comfort. An extensive continental breakfast is served.

Rooms 62 en suite (14 fmly) **Facilities** STV FTV iPod docking station Lounge TVL tea/coffee Direct Dial Lift Licensed WiFi **Extras** Bottled water **Conf** Thtr 24 Class 16 Board 16 **Notes** LB ⊗

W8

BEST WESTERN Seraphine, Kensington Gardens
PLAN 2 E3

★★★★ GUEST ACCOMMODATION

tel: 020 7368 2222 & 7938 5911 **fax:** 020 7368 2221 **7-11 Kensington High St W8 5NP**
email: info@seraphinehotel.co.uk **web:** www.seraphinehotel.co.uk
dir: *B325 Gloucester Road, continue for 0.5m, left at A315 Kensington Road*

This smart property enjoys a prime location opposite Kensington Palace and is ideally positioned for Hyde Park, The Royal Albert Hall, shops and museums. Bedrooms vary in size but all are well equipped with interactive flat-screen TV, iPod docking, laptop safes and free WiFi; the en suites are modern with power showers. An extensive continental breakfast is included.

Rooms 22 en suite **Facilities** STV FTV TVL tea/coffee Direct Dial Lift Licensed WiFi 🔔 **Notes** ⊗

BEST WESTERN Seraphine Kensington Olympia
PLAN 2 E3

★★★★ GUEST ACCOMMODATION

tel: 020 7938 5911 **fax:** 020 7938 5912 **225 Kensington High St W8 6SA**
email: olympia@seraphinehotel.co.uk **web:** www.seraphinehotel.co.uk
dir: *A4 left onto A330, then right onto A315. On corner of Kensington High St & Abingdon Rd*

This chic and intimate property enjoys a prime location in the heart of High Street Kensington, and is ideally positioned for Holland Park, local attractions, shops and museums. Bedrooms vary in size but all are well equipped with interactive flat-screen TV, iPod docking, laptop safes and free WiFi. En suites are modern with powerful showers. An extensive continental breakfast is included and full cooked breakfasts upon request.

Rooms 35 en suite (35 fmly) **Facilities** FTV iPod docking station TVL tea/coffee Direct Dial Lift Licensed WiFi **Extras** Bottled water **Notes** ⊗

Mercure London Kensington
PLAN 2 E3

★★★★ GUEST ACCOMMODATION

tel: 020 7244 2400 **fax:** 020 7244 2500 **1a Lexham Gardens, Kensington W8 5JJ**
email: stay@mercurekensington.com

Mercure London Kensington enjoys a prime location adjacent to the famous Cromwell Road Hospital, and is within easy reach of the V&A and the chic shops of Knightsbridge and South Kensington. Bedrooms are extremely well equipped and, along with the comfortable public areas, have a stylish, contemporary feel. The smart and popular bar is a feature.

Rooms 82 en suite **Facilities** STV TVL tea/coffee Dinner available Direct Dial Lift Licensed **Parking** 8 **Notes** ⊗

W13

BEST WESTERN Maitrise Suites
PLAN 2 C3

★★★★ GUEST ACCOMMODATION

tel: 020 8799 3850 **fax:** 020 8840 7661 **50-54 The Broadway, West Ealing W13 0SU**
email: info@maitrisesuites.com **web:** www.maitrisesuites.com

This establishment offers fully serviced accommodation. The rooms are made up of studio, one and two bedroom apartments, all with kitchens and lounge areas. Bedrooms are stylish and come fully equipped with all modern amenities including digital TV and free WiFi throughout. A continental room service breakfast can be enjoyed daily. This property has parking available and is just 10 minutes from Ealing Broadway Underground.

Rooms 17 en suite (17 fmly) **Facilities** FTV iPod docking station tea/coffee Direct Dial Lift WiFi **Parking** 8 **Notes** ⊗

WC1

The George
PLAN 1 D5

★★★ GUEST ACCOMMODATION

tel: 020 7387 8777 **fax:** 020 7387 8666 **58-60 Cartwright Gardens WC1H 9EL**
email: ghotel@aol.com **web:** www.georgehotel.com
dir: *From St Pancras 2nd left into Marchmont St & 1st left into Cartwright Gardens*

The George is within walking distance of Russell Square and the tube, and convenient for London's central attractions. The brightly appointed bedrooms vary in size, some have en suites, and some rooms are suitable for families. A substantial breakfast is served in the attractive ground-floor dining room.

Rooms 41 rms (15 en suite) (2 fmly) (5 GF) **Facilities** FTV Lounge TVL tea/coffee Direct Dial WiFi 🔔 **Notes** ⊗

GREATER LONDON

BARNET
Map 6 TQ29

Savoro Restaurant with Rooms
★★★★ ⊛ RESTAURANT WITH ROOMS

tel: 020 8449 9888 **fax:** 020 8449 7444 **206 High St EN5 5SZ**
email: savoro@savoro.co.uk **web:** www.savoro.co.uk
dir: *M25 junct 23, A1000. Establishment in crescent behind Hadley Green Jaguar Garage*

Set back from the main high street, the traditional frontage of this establishment belies the stylishly contemporary bedrooms within. Several have modern four-poster bed and all have well designed bathrooms. The award-winning restaurant is an additional bonus, serving food which is all freshly prepared in-house, from bread to ice cream.

Rooms 11 rms (9 en suite) (2 pri facs) (2 fmly) (3 GF) **Facilities** FTV tea/coffee Dinner available WiFi **Extras** Bottled water - complimentary **Parking** 9 **Notes** ⊛ No coaches

BECKENHAM
See London Plan 2 G1

Innkeeper's Lodge Beckenham
★★★ INN

tel: 0845 112 6126 **422 Upper Elmers End Rd BR3 3HQ**
email: info@innkeeperslodge.com **web:** www.innkeeperslodge.com

At Innkeeper's Lodge you'll find accommodation with comfort and character in equal measure, and everything needed for a relaxing stay, from easy check-in and free parking to complimentary breakfast and a cosy pub serving great value food and drink on the doorstep. Each Lodge has quality rooms, and there are Lodges in a variety of locations from towns and cities to countryside settings across the UK.

Rooms 24 en suite (1 fmly) (8 GF) **Facilities** FTV tea/coffee Dinner available Direct Dial WiFi **Parking** 40

CRANFORD
See London Plan 2 A3 For accommodation details see Heathrow Airport

CROYDON
Map 6 TQ36

Kirkdale
★★★ GUEST ACCOMMODATION

tel: 020 8688 5898 **fax:** 020 8680 6001 **22 St Peters Rd CR0 1HD**
email: reservations@kirkdalehotel.co.uk **web:** www.kirkdalehotel.co.uk
dir: *A23 onto A232 W & A212 (Lower Coombe St), 500yds right*

Close to the town centre, this Victorian property retains many original features. Public areas include a small lounge bar and an attractive breakfast room, and the bedrooms have good facilities. There is a sheltered patio for use in the summer.

Rooms 16 en suite (5 GF) **Facilities** FTV TVL tea/coffee Direct Dial Licensed WiFi **Parking** 12 **Notes** ⊛

Croham Park Bed and Breakfast

[U]

tel: 020 8680 1189 & 07901 926898 **18 Croham Park Av CR2 7HH**
email: enquiries@crohampark.com **web:** www.crohampark.com

Currently the rating for this establishment is not confirmed. This may be due to a change of ownership or because it has only recently joined the AA rating scheme.

Rooms 4 en suite S £75–£110; D £75–£120* **Facilities** FTV tea/coffee WiFi **Parking** 2 **Notes** ⊗ No Children 10yrs

ERITH
Map 6 TQ57

Julius Lodge - Thamesmead

★★ GUEST ACCOMMODATION

tel: 020 8312 9304 & 07582 141055 **27 Holstein Way DA18 4DQ**
web: www.juliuslodge.co.uk

Julius Lodge offers good-value rooms with shared facilities, as well as a self-contained studio. All rooms are equipped with flat-screen TVs with Freeview and free WiFi is available throughout the house. Guests can relax in the comfortable seating room and enjoy free parking after 5pm.

Rooms 9 rms (1 pri facs) (1 fmly) (2 GF) S £35–£40; D £50–£70* **Facilities** STV FTV DVD TVL WiFi **Notes** ⊗

HARROW ON THE HILL

See London Plan 2 B5

Old Etonian

★★★ 🍽 GUEST ACCOMMODATION

tel: 020 8423 3854 & 8422 8482   **fax:** 020 8423 1225 **36-38 High St HA1 3LL**
email: info@oldetonian.com **web:** www.oldetonian.com
dir: In town centre. On B458 opposite Harrow School

In the heart of this historic part of London and opposite the prestigious school, this friendly guest accommodation is a delight. Bedrooms are attractive, well appointed and comfortable. A continental breakfast is served in the dining room, which in the evening is home to a lively restaurant. On-road parking is available.

Rooms 9 en suite (1 GF) **Facilities** FTV tea/coffee Dinner available Direct Dial Licensed WiFi 🐾 **Extras** Snacks - complimentary **Conf** Max 30 Thtr 20 Class 20 Board 20 **Parking** 3 **Notes** ⊗

HEATHROW AIRPORT

Crompton Guest House
PLAN 2 B2

★★★★ GUEST HOUSE

tel: 020 8570 7090 **fax:** 020 8577 1975 **49 Lampton Rd TW3 1JG**
email: cromptonguesthouse@btconnect.com **web:** www.cromptonguesthouse.co.uk
dir: M4 junct 3, follow signs for Hounslow. Into Bath Rd (A3005), left at Yates pub. 200yds on right just before bridge

Located just a moment's walk away from Hounslow underground station this accommodation is popular with both business and leisure travellers. Bedrooms and bathrooms are comfortable and well equipped with good facilities including air conditioning. Breakfast is served in the intimate dining room where a freshly prepared breakfast is served. Parking is a bonus and is free for up to 15 days.

Rooms 11 en suite (7 fmly) (2 GF) S £90–£200; D £100–£250* **Facilities** STV FTV DVD iPod docking station tea/coffee Dinner available Direct Dial WiFi 🐾 **Extras** Speciality toiletries - complimentary; safe **Parking** 12 **Notes** LB ⊗

HEATHROW AIRPORT *continued*

The Cottage

PLAN 2 B3

★★★★ GUEST ACCOMMODATION

tel: 020 8897 1815 **150-152 High St TW5 9WB**
email: info@the-cottage.eu **web:** www.the-cottage.eu
dir: *M4 junct 3, A312 towards Feltham, left at lights, left after 1st pub on left*

This beautiful property is a peacefully situated, family-run oasis, within five minutes of Heathrow Airport. It offers comfortable and spacious accommodation, in the tastefully decorated main house and six bedrooms located at the rear of the garden, connected to the main building by a covered walkway overlooking the stunning courtyard.

Rooms 14 en suite 6 annexe en suite (4 fmly) (12 GF) S £60-£75; D £70-£85*
Facilities FTV tea/coffee WiFi **Parking** 16 **Notes** ⊗ Closed 24-26 Dec & 31 Dec-1 Jan

---

HORNCHURCH

Map 6 TQ58

Innkeeper's Lodge Hornchurch

★★★ INN

tel: 0845 112 6010 **Station Ln RM12 6SB**
email: info@innkeeperslodge.com **web:** www.innkeeperslodge.com

At Innkeeper's Lodge you'll find accommodation with comfort and character in equal measure, and everything needed for a relaxing stay, from easy check-in and free parking to complimentary breakfast and a cosy pub serving great value food and drink on the doorstep. Each Lodge has quality rooms, and there are Lodges in a variety of locations from towns and cities to countryside settings across the UK.

Rooms 12 en suite (1 fmly) **Facilities** FTV tea/coffee Dinner available Direct Dial WiFi **Conf** Max 60 **Parking** 40 **Notes** ⊗

HOUNSLOW

See London Plan 2 B2 For accommodation details see under Heathrow Airport

ILFORD

See London Plan 2 H5

BEST WESTERN Ilford

★★★★ GUEST ACCOMMODATION

tel: 020 8911 6083 **fax:** 020 8554 4726 **3-5 Argyle Rd IG1 3BH**
email: manager@expresslodging.co.uk **web:** www.expresslodging.co.uk
dir: *From A406 E towards Ilford, then A118 & 1st left after Ilford Station*

This establishment is conveniently located for easy access to the Queen Elizabeth II Olympic Park and central London. The accommodation is very comfortable and offers a range of amenities such as free internet and a new, state-of-the-art media hub. 24-hour room service and parking is also provided.

Rooms 34 en suite 26 annexe en suite (9 fmly) (15 GF) **Facilities** FTV Lounge TVL tea/coffee Dinner available Direct Dial WiFi & **Conf** Max 30 Thtr 30 Class 30 Board 30 **Parking** 12 **Notes** ⊗

KEW

See London Plan 2 C3

Kew Garden Studios

U

tel: 020 8940 8150 **269 Sandycombe Rd TW9 3LU**
email: geoffdobbie@hotmail.com

Currently the rating for this establishment is not confirmed. This may be due to a change of ownership or because it has only recently joined the AA rating scheme.

Rooms 4 rms S £75-£125; D £80-£130*

MERSEYSIDE

BIRKENHEAD
Map 15 SJ38

Shrewsbury Lodge

★★★ GUEST HOUSE

tel: 0151 652 4029 fax: 0151 653 3593 31 Shrewsbury Rd, Oxton CH43 2JB
email: info@shrewsbury-hotel.com web: www.shrewsbury-hotel.com

Modern accommodation situated in a quiet residential area but within easy walking distance of local amenities and close to travel links. Family-run, it provides well-equipped bedrooms and good breakfasts are served in the pleasant dining room. Friendly, attentive service is a strength here.

Rooms 15 rms (12 en suite) (3 pri facs) (3 fmly) (4 GF) S £38-£39; D £65-£72 (room only) Facilities FTV Lounge TVL tea/coffee Licensed WiFi ♨ 18 Parking 12 Notes LB ⊗

BOOTLE
Map 15 SJ39

Breeze Guest House

★★★ GUEST HOUSE

tel: 0151 933 2576 237 Hawthorne Rd L20 3AW
email: breezegh@googlemail.com web: www.breezeguesthouse.co.uk

This pleasant family-run guest house provides a friendly place to stay. With secure parking and great transport links, it is ideally located for Anfield and Goodison Park as well as being convenient for Aintree. Dinner is available and there is a pleasant bar too. Bedrooms are spacious and comfortable.

Rooms 10 en suite (1 fmly) (1 GF) S £35-£50; D £70-£150* Facilities FTV DVD TVL tea/coffee Dinner available Licensed WiFi Snooker Extras Bottled water Parking 8 Notes Closed 20 Dec-2 Jan

BROMBOROUGH
Map 15 SJ38

Pesto at the Dibbinsdale Inn

★★★★ ⬤ INN

tel: 0151 334 9818 Dibbinsdale Rd CH63 0HJ
email: pestodibbinsdale@hotmail.com web: www.pestorestaurants.co.uk
dir: M53 junct 5 onto A41 towards Birkenhead. After 2m left towards railway station, through 2 sets of lights, 2nd right into Dibbinsdale Rd. 600yds on right

Pesto at the Dibbinsdale Inn offers plenty of those little luxuries you'd expect from a larger establishment, combined with the relaxed comfort of an independently-run inn, all in a peaceful setting. With high standards of comfort and facilities, the stylish en suite bedrooms are equipped for both leisure and business guests. With real ales on tap and open fires, the restaurant also offers Pesto's unique informal Italian dining experience with its piattini menu of small plates, perfect for sharing. A special party menu is available for group bookings.

Rooms 12 en suite (1 fmly) S fr £59; D fr £75* Facilities FTV Lounge tea/coffee Dinner available WiFi ♨ 18 Parking 25 Notes LB ⊗ RS 25 Dec restaurant closed

IRBY
Map 15 SJ28

Manor Garden Lodge

★★★★ BED AND BREAKFAST

tel: 0151 648 7212 & 07855 512008 5 Manor Rd CH61 4UA
email: mark@broadscopefp.co.uk web: www.manorgardenlodge.co.uk
dir: M53 junct 3 onto A552 towards Heswall. Left into Arrowe Park Rd, then right into Thingwall Rd E. After 1m at T-junct turn right, then 1st right

Located in the heart of the Wirral and handy for transport into both Liverpool and Chester, this is a B&B with a difference. The two newly-built wooden lodges at the secluded end of a neat garden are spacious and well equipped, with modern facilities and thoughtful extras. Breakfast is taken in the main house. A warm and personal welcome and service is guaranteed.

Rooms 2 annexe en suite (2 GF) S £55-£75; D £65-£80* Facilities FTV tea/coffee WiFi ♨ 18 Parking 2 Notes LB ⊗ ⊛ ⊜

LIVERPOOL
Map 15 SJ39

Liverpool Gateway

★★★ GUEST ACCOMMODATION

tel: 0151 298 2288 & 07714 090842 95 St Oswald's St L13 5SB
email: andy@dmsnw.co.uk web: www.liverpoolgateway.co.uk
dir: End of M62 through 2 pedestrian lights, through next lights, on right opposite subway

Ideally situated for the M62 and with easy access to the city centre and its attractions, Liverpool Gateway provides comfortable accommodation, facilities and thoughtful extras for the modern traveller. Continental breakfasts are taken in a communal kitchen; secure off-road parking is provided.

Rooms 6 rms (1 pri facs) Facilities FTV WiFi ⬧ Conf Board 10 Parking 20 Notes ⊗ No Children 10yrs

Manor House

AA Advertised

tel: 0151 260 6177 91 Edge Ln L7 2PD
email: themanor.172pd@hotmail.com

The Manor House is a budget establishment offering a warm welcome and modern amenities close to Liverpool city centre. Guests can relax in the comfortable seating area in reception, and staff are happy to help with planning trips in the city. Rooms come in single, double, triple, twin and family sizes. On-site parking is available.

Rooms 15 rms S £32-£40; D £55-£60 (room only)* Notes ⊜

SOUTHPORT
Map 15 SD31

Bay Tree House B&B

★★★★ ⬤ GUEST ACCOMMODATION

tel: 01704 510555 fax: 0870 753 6318 No1 Irving St, Marine Gate PR9 0HD
email: info@baytreehousesouthport.co.uk web: www.baytreehousesouthport.co.uk
dir: 3rd road right off Leicester St, approaching from rdbt off Lord St

A warm welcome is assured at this immaculately maintained house, located a short walk from the promenade and central attractions. Bedrooms are equipped with a wealth of thoughtful extras, and delicious imaginative breakfasts are served in an attractive dining room overlooking the pretty front patio garden.

Rooms 6 en suite S £55-£65; D £80-£110* Facilities FTV DVD iPod docking station Lounge tea/coffee Direct Dial Licensed WiFi Discounts available for local swimming baths & gym Extras Speciality toiletries, mini-bar, snacks, robes Parking 2 Notes Closed 24 Dec-Jan

SOUTHPORT *continued*

The Baytrees

★★★★ GUEST ACCOMMODATION

tel: 01704 536513 **fax:** 01704 536513 **4 Queens Rd PR9 9HN**
email: baytreeshotel@hotmail.co.uk **web:** www.baytreeshotel.co.uk
dir: *From B565 (Lord St) towards fire station, right at rdbt into Manchester Rd, left at lights, 200yds on right*

Located a short walk from Lord Street, this elegant late Victorian house has been well appointed to provide thoughtfully furnished bedrooms with smart modern en suite bathrooms. Breakfast is served in the attractive dining room overlooking the pretty rear garden, and a lounge is also available.

Rooms 12 en suite (5 fmly) (2 GF) S £32.50-£49.50; D £59-£72.50* **Facilities** FTV DVD TVL tea/coffee WiFi 🅿 **Parking** 11 **Notes** ⊗ Closed Xmas

Bowden Lodge

★★★★ 🛏 GUEST ACCOMMODATION

tel: 01704 543531 **fax:** 01704 539112 **18 Albert Rd PR9 0LE**
email: stay@bowdenlodge.co.uk **web:** www.bowdenlodge.co.uk
dir: *A565 N from town centre, over rdbt, 150yds on right*

This stylish house is in a quiet residential area a short stroll from Lord Street and the town's attractions. Bedrooms, some suitable for families, are smartly furnished and well equipped. Day rooms include a lounge with deep sofas, and a bright dining room where hearty cooked breakfasts are served. Value for money and a friendly welcome are assured. Ideal venue for walkers and cyclists.

Rooms 10 en suite (3 fmly) S £35-£60; D £65-£100* **Facilities** FTV TVL tea/coffee Dinner available Licensed WiFi 🅿 **Parking** 10 **Notes** LB ⊗

NORFOLK

ALBURGH
Map 13 TM28

The Dove Restaurant with Rooms

★★★★ ⊛⊛ 🛏 RESTAURANT WITH ROOMS

tel: 01986 788315 **fax:** 01986 788315 **Holbrook Hill IP20 0EP**
email: info@thedoverestaurant.co.uk **web:** www.thedoverestaurant.co.uk
dir: *Between Harleston & Bungay at junct A143 & B1062*

A warm welcome awaits at The Dove Restaurant with Rooms. Bedrooms are pleasantly decorated, furnished with pine pieces and have modern facilities. Public rooms include a lounge area with a small bar, and a smart restaurant with well-spaced tables and excellent food.

Rooms 2 rms (1 en suite) (1 pri facs) (1 fmly) S £45; D £70* **Facilities** tea/coffee Dinner available WiFi ⚡ 18 🅿 **Parking** 20 **Notes** ⊗ No coaches

BLAKENEY
Map 13 TG04

Premier Collection

Blakeney House

★★★★★ GUEST HOUSE

tel: 01263 740561 **fax:** 01263 741750 **High St NR25 7NX**
email: admin@blakeneyhouse.com **web:** www.blakeneyhouse.com
dir: *In village centre*

Blakeney House is a stunning Victorian manor house set amid two acres of attractive landscaped grounds, just a short walk from the quay and town centre. The stylish, individually decorated bedrooms have co-ordinated fabrics and many thoughtful touches. Breakfast is served at individual tables in the smart dining room, which overlooks the well-stocked front garden.

Rooms 8 rms (7 en suite) (1 pri facs) (1 fmly) **Facilities** DVD tea/coffee WiFi ⚡ 18 🅿 **Parking** 8 **Notes** ⊗ No Children 12yrs

BROOKE
Map 13 TM29

The Old Vicarage

★★★★ BED AND BREAKFAST

tel: 01508 558329 **48 The Street NR15 1JU**
dir: *From Norwich on B1332, turn left after Kings Head pub. 1st left at fork in road to village. Immediately before church on right*

Set in mature gardens in a peaceful village, this charming house is within easy driving distance of Norwich. The individually decorated bedrooms are thoughtfully furnished and equipped, and one room has a lovely four-poster bed. There is an elegant dining room and a cosy lounge, and dinner is available by arrangement. Service is genuinely helpful, provided in a relaxed and friendly manner.

Rooms 2 en suite S £40; D £70* **Facilities** TVL tea/coffee Dinner available **Parking** 4 **Notes** LB ⊗ No Children 15yrs 🐾

BURNHAM MARKET
Map 13 TF84

The Nelson Country Inn

★★★★ INN

tel: 01328 738321 **4 Creake Rd PE31 8EN**
email: stay@the-nelson.com **web:** www.the-nelson.com
dir: *From Market Pl onto Front St (at lower end). 200yds, on Creake Rd*

This country inn is set in the pretty north Norfolk village of Burnham Market, within easy reach of King's Lynn, Norwich, Hunstanton and Cromer. There are four en suite double rooms available, all with an individual finish. Hearty meals are served daily, making good use of local and seasonal produce where possible.

Rooms 2 en suite 2 annexe en suite (2 GF) **Facilities** FTV tea/coffee Dinner available WiFi 🅿 **Extras** Sweets **Conf** Max 18 Thtr 12 Class 18 Board 14 **Parking** 20

CASTLE ACRE
Map 13 TF81

Ostrich Inn

★★★★ INN

tel: 01760 755398 **Stocks Green PE32 2AE**
email: info@ostrichcastleacre.com **web:** www.ostrichcastleacre.com
dir: *0.3m on right of Castle Acre Priory*

The 15th-century Ostrich Inn is situated adjacent to the village green in the centre of Castle Acre. The warm and inviting public areas have a wealth of original features such as exposed brickwork, oak beams and open fires. The spacious bedrooms are in an adjacent building; each room is equipped with modern facilities.

Rooms 6 en suite (1 fmly) (1 GF) **Facilities** FTV tea/coffee Dinner available Direct Dial WiFi **Conf** Max 25 Thtr 25 Class 25 Board 25 **Parking** 30 **Notes** LB

COLTON
Map 13 TG10

The Ugly Bug Inn

★★★★ INN

tel: 01603 880794 **High House Farm Ln NR9 5DG**
email: info@uglybuginn.co.uk **web:** www.uglybuginn.co.uk

Popular and friendly, The Ugly Bug Inn is located in a peaceful rural location on the edge of the village, close to the A47 with links to Norwich and the Norfolk coast. Public rooms include a large lounge bar and a smart restaurant. The bedrooms are smartly appointed with modern facilities, and most rooms have views of the countryside.

Rooms 4 en suite (1 GF) **Facilities** FTV tea/coffee Dinner available WiFi ⚲ 18 🔒 **Parking** 40 **Notes** No Children 16yrs

CROMER
Map 13 TG24

See also Sheringham

The Grove Cromer

★★★★★ ⚜⚜ GUEST ACCOMMODATION

tel: 01263 512412 **95 Overstrand Rd NR27 0DJ**
email: enquiries@thegrovecromer.co.uk **web:** www.thegrovecromer.co.uk
dir: *Into Cromer on A149, right at 1st mini rdbt into Cromwell Rd. At double mini rdbt straight over into Overstrand Rd, 200mtrs on left*

A charming Georgian house, The Grove Cromer sits in several acres of landscaped gardens and is a short walk from Cromer town centre, cliff walks and the beach. There are several bedroom styles to choose from; the well-appointed comfortable bedrooms are in the main house and stylish garden rooms. There is an indoor heated swimming pool available for guests along with a children's play area in the woodland walk. Delicious dinners are served in the restaurant and guests are guaranteed a warm welcome at this fine property.

Rooms 10 en suite 5 annexe en suite (4 fmly) (5 GF) S £40-£54; D £85-£130* **Facilities** FTV DVD TVL tea/coffee Dinner available Direct Dial Licensed WiFi 🏊 ⚲ 18 🔒 **Conf** Max 24 Thtr 24 Class 24 Board 18 **Parking** 25 **Notes** LB ⊗

The Red Lion Food and Rooms

★★★★ INN

tel: 01263 514964 **fax:** 01263 512834 **Brook St NR27 9HD**
email: info@redlion-cromer.co.uk **web:** www.redlion-cromer.co.uk
dir: *Follow one-way system, pass church on left & take next left into Brook St*

The Red Lion is a charming Victorian inn in an elevated position at the heart of the town centre, overlooking the beach and the sea. The open-plan public areas include a lounge bar, a popular restaurant and sunny conservatory. The spacious bedrooms are tastefully decorated with co-ordinated soft furnishings and include many thoughtful touches.

Rooms 15 en suite (1 fmly) S fr £65; D fr £110* **Facilities** FTV DVD iPod docking station tea/coffee Dinner available WiFi 🔒 **Extras** Honesty box incl chocolate, wine, snacks **Parking** 20 **Notes** LB

Shrublands Farm *(TG246393)*

★★★★ 🏠 FARMHOUSE

tel: 01263 579297 **fax:** 01263 579297 **Church St, Northrepps NR27 0AA**
email: youngman@farming.co.uk **web:** www.shrublandsfarm.com
dir: *Exit A149 to Northrepps, through village, past Foundry Arms, cream house 50yds on left*

Expect a warm welcome from the caring host at this delightful 18th-century farmhouse, set in landscaped grounds and surrounded by 300 acres of arable farmland. Public areas include a cosy lounge with a wood-burning stove, and breakfast is served at a communal table in the elegant dining room.

Rooms 2 rms (1 en suite) (1 pri facs) S £48-£50; D £76-£80* **Facilities** FTV DVD TVL tea/coffee WiFi 🔒 **Extras** Speciality toiletries, snacks, confectionery - free of charge **Parking** 5 **Notes** LB ⊗ No Children 12yrs Closed 25-26 Dec 300 acres arable

The White Horse Overstrand

★★★★★ ⚜⚜ INN

tel: 01263 579237 **34 High St, Overstrand NR27 0AB**
email: reservations@whitehorseoverstrand.co.uk **web:** www.whitehorseoverstrand.co.uk
dir: *From A140, before Cromer, turn right into Mill Rd. At bottom right into Station Rd. After 2m, bear left into High St, White Horse on left*

The White Horse Overstrand is a smartly appointed inn ideally situated in the heart of this popular village on the north Norfolk coast. The modern bedrooms are tastefully appointed and equipped with a good range of useful extras. Public rooms include a large open-plan lounge bar with comfortable seating and a relaxed dining area. Cooking is taken seriously here as is reflected in its award of two AA Rosettes.

Rooms 8 en suite (2 fmly) **Facilities** TVL tea/coffee Dinner available WiFi Pool table **Parking** 6 **Notes** LB

Bon Vista

★★★★ GUEST ACCOMMODATION

tel: 01263 511818 **12 Alfred Rd NR27 9AN**
email: jim@bonvista-cromer.co.uk **web:** www.bonvista-cromer.co.uk
dir: *From pier onto A148 (coast road), in 400yds left into Alfred Rd*

The owners extend a warm welcome to guests arriving at this delightful Victorian terraced house, situated in a peaceful side road adjacent to the seafront, just a short walk from the town centre. The individually decorated bedrooms have co-ordinated soft fabrics, and the public rooms include an attractive dining room and a spacious first-floor lounge.

Rooms 5 en suite (2 fmly) S £35-£60; D £68-£84 **Facilities** FTV TVL tea/coffee WiFi 🔒 **Extras** Mini fridge **Notes** LB ⊗

CROMER *continued*

Homefield Guest House

★★★★ GUEST HOUSE

tel: 01263 837337 **48 Cromer Rd, West Runton NR27 9AD**
email: homefield@hotmail.co.uk **web:** www.homefieldguesthouse.co.uk
dir: *On A149 (coast road) between Sheringham & Cromer*

This large Victorian house was previously owned by the Canon of Cromer and is situated in the peaceful village of West Runton between Cromer and Sheringham. The pleasantly co-ordinated bedrooms have many useful extras. Breakfast, which includes locally sourced produce, is served at individual tables in the smart dining room.

Rooms 6 en suite S £40-£60; D £60-£80 **Facilities** STV tea/coffee WiFi ⚓ **Parking** 8 **Notes** LB ⊗ No Children 14yrs

The Sandcliff

★★★ GUEST HOUSE

tel: 01263 512888 **fax:** 01263 512785 **Runton Rd NR27 9AS**
email: bookings@sandcliffcromer.co.uk **web:** www.sandcliffcromer.co.uk
dir: *500yds W of town centre on A149*

Ideally situated on the seafront just a short walk from the town centre, this guest house offers a large lounge bar with comfortable seating and a spacious dining room where breakfast and dinner are served. The bedrooms are pleasantly decorated, thoughtfully equipped and some have superb sea views.

Rooms 23 rms (17 en suite) (10 fmly) (3 GF) S £29-£49; D £48-£89 (room only)* **Facilities** FTV TVL tea/coffee Dinner available Licensed WiFi ⅃ 18 ⚓ **Parking** 10 **Notes** LB

Glendale Guest House

★★★ GUEST HOUSE

tel: 01263 513278 **33 Macdonald Rd NR27 9AP**
email: glendalecromer@btconnect.com
dir: *A149 (coast road) from Cromer centre, 4th left*

Glendale Guest House is a Victorian property situated in a peaceful side road adjacent to the seafront, just a short walk from the town centre. Bedrooms are pleasantly decorated, well maintained and equipped with a good range of useful extras. Breakfast is served at individual tables in the smart dining room.

Rooms 5 rms (1 en suite) S £30-£42; D £60-£84 **Facilities** FTV tea/coffee **Parking** 2 **Notes** LB Closed 14 Oct-2 Apr

---

DEREHAM   Map 13 TF91

Orchard Cottage

★★★★ BED AND BREAKFAST

tel: 01362 860265 **The Drift, Gressenhall NR20 4EH**
email: ann@walkers-norfolk.co.uk **web:** www.walkers-norfolk.co.uk
dir: *2m NE of Dereham. Exit B1146 in Beetley to Gressenhall, right at x-rds into Bittering St, right at x-rds, 2nd right*

Orchard Cottage is an attractive Norfolk flint building situated in the historic village of Gressenhall near Dereham. The comfortable, country style bedrooms are smartly decorated and situated on the ground floor; one of the rooms has a superb wet room. Public rooms include a lounge, a dining room and a study. Dinner is available by arrangement.

Rooms 2 en suite (2 GF) **Facilities** FTV Lounge TVL tea/coffee Dinner available WiFi ⚓ **Parking** 2 **Notes** ⊗ ✉

DOWNHAM MARKET   Map 12 TF60

Crosskeys Riverside House

★★★★ BED AND BREAKFAST

tel: 01366 387777 **fax:** 01366 387777 **Bridge St, Hilgay PE38 0LD**
email: crosskeyshouse@aol.com **web:** www.crosskeys.info
dir: *2m S of Downham Market. Off A10 into Hilgay, Crosskeys on bridge*

Situated in the small village of Hilgay, in its own grounds on the banks of the River Wissey, this former coaching inn offers comfortable accommodation that includes a number of four-poster bedrooms; all rooms have river views, as well as CD players and free WiFi. Public rooms include a dining room with oak beams and an inglenook fireplace.

Rooms 4 en suite (1 fmly) (2 GF) S £45-£65; D £65-£75* **Facilities** FTV DVD Lounge tea/coffee WiFi Fishing ⚓ Rowing boat for guests use **Extras** Flowers, champagne - chargeable **Parking** 10

EAST HARLING   Map 13 TL98

The George and Dragon

★★★★ ⊜ INN

tel: 01953 717918 **Market St NR16 2AD**
email: georgeharling@hotmail.co.uk **web:** www.georgeanddragonharling.co.uk
dir: *From A11 exit signed Watton, East Harling onto B1111. Continue into village located opposite market place*

This charming village pub has undergone major refurbishment in recent years and now offers four charming, well-appointed and cosy bedrooms. The George and Dragon has a prominent position within the village, and is very popular with locals. The authentic bar is full of character, there is a good choice of beers and the real fire is a welcome addition. The stylish bistro restaurant serves a range of home cooked meals and there is a very good choice on the breakfast menu. Secure parking is available along with WiFi and a patio beer garden for guests.

Rooms 4 en suite S £65; D £75 **Facilities** FTV Lounge TVL tea/coffee Dinner available WiFi Fishing Riding Gym **Parking** 15 **Notes** LB

GORLESTON ON SEA
Map 13 TG50

Avalon
★★★★ GUEST ACCOMMODATION

tel: 01493 662114 **fax:** 01493 668528 **54 Clarence Rd NR31 6DR**
email: avalon.hotel@btinternet.com **web:** www.avalon-gorleston.co.uk
dir: A12 past James Paget Hospital. Take 2nd exit at rdbt towards Gorleston. Next rdbt 2nd exit, 1st right

This Edwardian terraced house is just a short walk from the promenade and beach. Breakfast and evening meals are served in the smart dining room and there is a cosy lounge bar. Service is both helpful and friendly. Bedrooms are pleasantly appointed, thoughtfully equipped and well furnished.

Rooms 10 en suite (6 fmly) (1 GF) **Facilities** TVL tea/coffee Dinner available Licensed WiFi **Notes** ⊗

GREAT ELLINGHAM
Map 13 TM09

Aldercarr Hall
★★★★ GUEST ACCOMMODATION

tel: 01953 455766 & 07710 752213 **fax:** 01953 457993 **Attleborough Rd NR17 1LQ**
email: bedandbreakfast@aldercarr-limited.com **web:** www.aldercarrhall.co.uk
dir: On B1077 500yds SE of village

Aldercarr Hall is set in extensive grounds and surrounded by open countryside on the edge of Great Ellingham. Public rooms include a comfortably appointed conservatory and a delightful dining room where breakfast is served around a large table. The excellent facilities include a health, beauty and hairdressing studio, an indoor swimming pool, a jacuzzi and a large function suite.

Rooms 3 annexe en suite (1 fmly) (3 GF) **Facilities** FTV TVL tea/coffee Licensed WiFi ⓧ ♨ Fishing Riding Snooker Sauna Pool table 🅿 **Parking** 200

GREAT MASSINGHAM
Map 13 TF72

The Dabbling Duck
★★★ 🍴 INN

tel: 01485 520827 **11 Abbey Rd PE32 2HN**
email: info@thedabblingduck.co.uk **web:** www.thedabblingduck.co.uk

Situated in the quiet village of Great Massingham, the inn sits between two large duck ponds, inhabited by numerous 'dabbling ducks' hence the name. A traditional village inn, where guests can enjoy dinner in the relaxing surroundings of the bar and restaurant, with a good range of real ales available. Accommodation is provided upstairs; rooms are all tastefully decorated and offer a host of thoughtful accessories.

Rooms 6 en suite (1 fmly) S £65-£90; D £90-£100* **Facilities** FTV tea/coffee Dinner available WiFi **Extras** Home-made vodka **Conf** Max 50 Thtr 50 Class 40 Board 30 **Parking** 30 **Notes** LB

GREAT MOULTON
Map 13 TM19

South Norfolk Guest House
★★★★ GUEST HOUSE

tel: 01379 677359 & 07885 351212 **fax:** 01379 677359 **Frith Way NR15 2HE**
email: info@sngh.co.uk **web:** www.southnorfolkguesthouse.co.uk
dir: From A140 (N), in Long Stratton turn left at 1st set of lights. Through Wacton, pass sign to Coronation Hall on right. 1st property on right in Great Moulton, past house, turn right & right again

This former village school enjoys a peaceful rural location yet is only a short drive from Norwich. A warm welcome is guaranteed from the friendly proprietors and

bedrooms are all most comfortable. Ample secure parking is available for guests along with free WiFi. Delicious hot breakfasts are served in the conservatory breakfast room.

Rooms 9 en suite S £39-£69; D £59-£75* **Facilities** FTV DVD Lounge tea/coffee Dinner available WiFi 🅿 **Parking** 120 **Notes** LB

GREAT RYBURGH
Map 13 TF92

The Blue Boar Inn
★★★ 🍴 INN

tel: 01328 829212 **5 Station Rd NR21 0DX**
email: blueboarinnryburgh@gmail.com

Built in 1635, The Blue Boar has been in the heart of village life in Great Ryburgh for over three centuries. The cosy wood-beamed bar has an original inglenook fireplace and guests are guaranteed a warm welcome. Bedrooms are all comfortable, attractively presented and well equipped. The Blue Boar has been sympathetically restored in recent years and the restaurant serves an extensive choice of imaginative dishes using the best in local produce. Hearty breakfasts are cooked to order and not to be missed. Secure parking and free WiFi are available for guests.

Rooms 6 rms **Facilities** Dinner available

GREAT YARMOUTH
Map 13 TG50

Premier Collection

3 Norfolk Square
★★★★★ GUEST HOUSE

tel: 01493 843042 & 07734 735001 **fax:** 01493 857276
3 Norfolk Square NR30 1EE
email: info@3norfolksquare.co.uk **web:** www.3norfolksquare.co.uk
dir: From Britannia Pier, 200yds N along seafront, left into Albemarle Rd

A delightful property situated in a peaceful side road just a short walk from the seafront and town centre, 3 Norfolk Square offers smartly decorated bedrooms, with co-ordinated soft furnishings and many thoughtful touches. Breakfast is served in the lower ground floor dining room/bar, and guests also have the use of a large lounge.

Rooms 8 en suite (2 GF) S £55-£65; D £80-£110* **Facilities** FTV DVD TVL tea/coffee Licensed WiFi **Parking** 3 **Notes** LB ⊗ No Children 18yrs

The Classic Lodge
★★★★ BED AND BREAKFAST

tel: 01493 852851 **fax:** 01493 852851 **13 Euston Rd NR30 1DY**
email: classiclodge@uwclub.net **web:** www.classiclodge.com
dir: A12 to A47, follow signs for seafront. Turn left at Sainsbury's, ahead at lights 200mtrs on right, 100mtrs from seafront

The Classic Lodge is an impressive Victorian villa situated just a short stroll from the seafront and town centre. Breakfast is served at individual tables in the large lounge-dining room, and the spacious bedrooms are carefully furnished and equipped with a good range of facilities. Secure parking is provided at the rear of the property.

Rooms 3 en suite D £50-£60* **Facilities** FTV TVL tea/coffee WiFi **Parking** 5 **Notes** LB ⊗ No Children 18yrs Closed Nov-Mar 🍴

GREAT YARMOUTH *continued*

Marine Lodge

★★★★ 🐾 GUEST ACCOMMODATION

tel: 01493 331120 **19-20 Euston Rd NR30 1DY**
email: res@marinelodge.co.uk web: www.marinelodge.co.uk
dir: *Follow signs for seafront, 300mtrs N of Britannia Pier*

This establishment's enviable seafront position has panoramic views of the bowling greens and beach, and is within easy walking distance of Britannia Pier. Bright, modern bedrooms are complemented by smart public areas that include a bar area where light snacks are available during the evening. Guests also have complimentary use of the indoor swimming pool at the sister Palm Court Hotel.

Rooms 40 en suite (5 fmly) (5 GF) S £55-£59; D £60-£64 (room only)* **Facilities** FTV TVL tea/coffee Dinner available Lift Licensed WiFi **Conf** Thtr 50 Class 35 Board 25 **Parking** 38 **Notes** LB ⊗

All Seasons Guest House

★★★★ GUEST HOUSE

tel: 01493 852713 & 07543 036475 **10 Nelson Road South NR30 3JL**
email: mpilgrimmcd@hotmail.co.uk web: www.allseasons-guesthouse.co.uk
dir: *Enter Great Yarmouth on A47, at rdbt 2nd exit onto A149 for 0.3m. Next rdbt 3rd exit onto B1141 for 0.4m. Left into Queens Rd, after 0.2m left into Nelson Rd*

All Seasons Guest House is a smartly presented, family-run guest house that enjoys an ideal location close to the seafront and the historic South Quay area. A warm welcome is guaranteed and the freshly cooked breakfasts are not to be missed. There is a good range of comfortable well-appointed bedrooms available. Free WiFi is available and there is ample on-street parking.

Rooms 8 en suite (1 GF) S £30-£35; D £60-£70* **Facilities** FTV DVD TVL tea/coffee WiFi 🔒 **Extras** Snacks - complimentary **Notes** LB ⊗

The Chequers

★★★★ GUEST HOUSE

tel: 01493 853091 **27 Nelson Road South NR30 3JA**
email: mitchellsatchequers@hotmail.co.uk web: www.thechequersguesthouse.co.uk
dir: *Exit A47 signed seafront, right into Marine Parade & Kings Rd, 1st right*

Guests will receive a warm welcome from the caring hosts at this privately-run establishment, situated just a short walk from Wellington pier and the beach. Public rooms include a cosy bar, residents' lounge and a smart dining room. Bedrooms are cheerfully decorated and have many thoughtful touches.

Rooms 8 rms (7 en suite) (1 pri facs) (2 fmly) **Facilities** FTV TVL tea/coffee Dinner available Licensed WiFi **Notes** ⊗

The Hamilton

★★★★ GUEST HOUSE

tel: 01493 844662 **fax:** 01493 745772 **23-24 North Dr NR30 4EW**
email: enquiries@hamilton-hotel.co.uk web: www.hamilton-hotel.co.uk

Overlooking the beach with fantastic views of the sea, this property is ideally situated for the theatre, tourist attractions, town centre and Yarmouth Racecourse. Public rooms include a smart lounge bar with plush leather seating, a breakfast room and a residents' lounge with comfy sofas. Bedrooms are bright and airy with many thoughtful touches; most rooms have lovely sea views.

Rooms 21 en suite (4 fmly) (2 GF) **Facilities** FTV TVL tea/coffee Dinner available Licensed WiFi ⚡ 18 **Conf** Max 40 Thtr 40 Class 26 Board 26 **Parking** 20 **Notes** LB ⊗

Swiss Cottage Bed and Breakfast

★★★★ GUEST ACCOMMODATION

tel: 01493 855742 & 07986 399857 **fax:** 01493 843547 **31 North Dr NR30 4EW**
email: info@swiss-cottage.info web: www.swisscottagebedandbreakfast.co.uk
dir: *0.5m N of town centre. Exit A47 or A12 to seafront, 750yds N of pier. Left at Britannia Pier. Swiss Cottage on left opposite Water Gardens*

Swiss Cottage Bed and Breakfast is a charming detached property situated in the peaceful part of town overlooking the Venetian waterways and the sea beyond. The comfortable bedrooms are pleasantly decorated with co-ordinated fabrics and have many useful extras. Breakfast is served in the smart dining room and guests have use of an open-plan lounge area.

Rooms 8 en suite 1 annexe en suite (2 GF) S £38-£44; D £59-£75* **Facilities** FTV Lounge tea/coffee WiFi 🔒 **Parking** 9 **Notes** LB No Children 11yrs Closed Nov-Feb

The Winchester

★★★★ GUEST ACCOMMODATION

tel: 01493 843950 & 07807 733161 **12 Euston Rd NR30 1DY**
email: enquiries@winchesterprivatehotel.com web: www.winchesterprivatehotel.com
dir: *A12 onto A47, signs for seafront, left at Sainsbury's over lights, premises 400yds on right*

A warm welcome is assured from the friendly hosts at The Winchester, just off the seafront. The pleasant bedrooms vary in size and style and are thoughtfully equipped. Public rooms include a large lower ground-floor dining room, a small conservatory and a foyer with comfortable sofas.

Rooms 14 en suite (2 fmly) (5 GF) S £30-£36; D £60-£72* **Facilities** TVL tea/coffee Dinner available WiFi 🔒 **Parking** 10 **Notes** LB ⊗ No Children 12yrs Closed Dec-Jan RS Oct-Etr No evening meals ⊛

Dene House

★★★ 🛏 GUEST HOUSE

tel: 01493 844181 **89 North Denes Rd NR30 4LW**
email: denehouse@btinternet.com **web:** www.denehouse-greatyarmouth.co.uk

You are guaranteed a warm welcome at this family run guest house that enjoys a peaceful location on a quiet street in Great Yarmouth. Dene House is conveniently located and is a few minutes' walk from the seafront and the main tourist attractions of the town. Bedrooms are all comfortable, very well appointed and free WiFi is available throughout the house. Evening meals can be provided by prior arrangement.

Rooms 7 en suite (1 GF) S £24-£27; D £48-£54* **Facilities** FTV TVL tea/coffee Dinner available Licensed WiFi **Parking** 3 **Notes** LB ⊗

The Elmfield

★★★ GUEST HOUSE

tel: 01493 859827 & 07879 632529 **38 Wellesley Rd NR30 1EU**
email: stay@theelmfield.co.uk **web:** www.theelmfield.co.uk
dir: A47 into Great Yarmouth, left into St Nicholas Rd. Turn left into Wellesley Rd

The Elmfield is located in a quiet area within walking distance of the town centre and the many attractions that Great Yarmouth has to offer. It is also the perfect base for exploring the Norfolk countryside and the Broads. All rooms are comfortably appointed and some have sea views. Breakfast is cooked to order and served in the airy breakfast room.

Rooms 9 en suite (3 fmly) **Facilities** FTV tea/coffee WiFi 🔒 **Parking** 5 **Notes** ⊗

Haydee

★★★ GUEST HOUSE

tel: 01493 844580 **fax:** 01493 844580 **27 Princes Rd NR30 2DG**
email: info@haydee.co.uk **web:** www.haydee.co.uk
dir: Exit A47 to seafront, Princes Rd opposite Britannia Pier

The Haydee is in a side road just a stroll from the seafront, pier and town centre. The pleasant bedrooms vary in size and style, and all are well equipped. Breakfast is served in the smart dining room and there is a cosy lounge bar.

Rooms 8 en suite (2 fmly) (2 smoking) S £25-£28; D £50-£56* **Facilities** FTV DVD TVL tea/coffee Licensed WiFi 🔒 **Notes** LB ⊗

Senglea Lodge

★★★ GUEST ACCOMMODATION

tel: 01493 859632 & 07775 698819 **7 Euston Rd NR30 1DX**
email: senglealodge@fsmail.net **web:** www.senglealodge.com
dir: From A4 straight over 1st 2 rdbts. At lights left towards seafront. Through next lights, Lodge on right

Senglea Lodge is a delightful terrace property situated just off the seafront and very close to the town centre. Bedrooms are pleasantly decorated, have co-ordinated soft furnishings and a good range of useful extras. Breakfast is served at individual tables in the smart open-plan lounge/dining room.

Rooms 6 rms (4 en suite) (2 fmly) (2 smoking) S £22.50-£25; D £45-£50* **Facilities** FTV DVD TVL tea/coffee WiFi 🔒 **Notes** LB ⊗ Closed 23 Dec-2 Jan

Shemara Guest House

★★★ GUEST HOUSE

tel: 01493 844054 & 07771 882054 **11 Wellesley Rd NR30 2AR**
email: info@shemaraguesthouse.co.uk **web:** www.shemaraguesthouse.co.uk
dir: A47 to Great Yarmouth, follow signs for seafront, take 4th right, Shemara on right

Shemara Guest House is ideally situated in the heart of this busy resort, as it is just a short walk from the town centre and seafront. Bedrooms come in a variety of sizes and styles, each one is pleasantly decorated and well equipped. Breakfast is served at individual tables in the open-plan lounge/dining room.

Rooms 7 en suite (2 fmly) **Facilities** FTV tea/coffee Dinner available WiFi **Parking** 4 **Notes** ⊗

Silverstone House

★★★ GUEST ACCOMMODATION

tel: 01493 844862 **29 Wellesley Rd NR30 1EY**
email: silverstonehouse@yahoo.co.uk **web:** www.silverstone-house.co.uk
dir: A47 into Great Yarmouth. Over 2 rdbts, left at lights signed seafront. Over next lights, turn left

A warm welcome is guaranteed at this family-run property. Silverstone House is conveniently located close to the seafront and a short walk to the main shopping district. This four-storey Victorian terraced house has nine well-appointed, comfortable bedrooms. Freshly prepared hot breakfasts are served to individual tables in the charming breakfast room.

Rooms 9 en suite (4 fmly) (1 GF) (4 smoking) S £23-£25; D £45-£50* **Facilities** FTV tea/coffee WiFi **Extras** Mini-fridge - complimentary **Notes** LB ⊗

Victoria

★★★ GUEST ACCOMMODATION

tel: 01493 843872 & 842132 **fax:** 01493 718921 **2 Kings Rd NR30 3JW**
email: booking@hotelvictoria.org.uk **web:** www.hotelvictoria.org.uk
dir: Off seafront, opposite model village

The Victoria is a large detached property situated just off the seafront close to Wellington Pier and the town centre. Bedrooms come in a variety of sizes and styles; each one is pleasantly decorated and thoughtfully equipped. Dinner and breakfast are served in the open-plan lounge/dining room. There is also a smart outdoor swimming pool.

Rooms 35 en suite 10 annexe en suite (13 fmly) (2 GF) S £25-£42; D £49-£72* **Facilities** FTV DVD TVL tea/coffee Dinner available Lift Licensed WiFi 🏊 Pool table 🔒 **Conf** Max 50 Thtr 50 Class 50 Board 30 **Parking** 20 **Notes** LB ⊗

Rhonadean

★★ GUEST HOUSE

tel: 01493 842004 **110-111 Wellesley Rd NR30 2AR**
email: barbara473@msn.com
dir: 500yds N of town centre. A47 onto B1141 (Fuller's Hill) towards seafront, into St Nicholas Rd, 3rd right

Rhonadean is situated in a side road adjacent to the seafront and just a short walk from the town centre. Public rooms include a small lounge bar and a dining room where breakfast and dinner are served at individual tables. Bedrooms vary in size and style; each one is pleasantly decorated and well equipped.

Rooms 18 rms (17 en suite) (1 pri facs) (7 fmly) (8 GF) **Facilities** TVL tea/coffee Dinner available Licensed Pool table **Notes** ⊗ Closed 24-26 Dec

HARLESTON — Map 13 TM28

Heath Farmhouse

★★★★ BED AND BREAKFAST

tel: 01986 788417 **Homersfield IP20 0EX**
email: julia.john.hunt@googlemail.com
dir: A143 onto B1062 towards Flixton, over bridge past Suffolk sign, 2nd farm entrance on left at AA sign

This charming 16th-century farmhouse is set amid attractive landscaped grounds that include a croquet lawn. The property retains much of its original character with exposed beams, open fireplaces and wood-burning stoves. The pleasant bedrooms are carefully furnished and have many thoughtful touches. Breakfast and dinner are served in the smart dining room overlooking the garden.

Rooms 2 rms (1 fmly) S £35; D £65* **Facilities** Lounge TVL tea/coffee Dinner available WiFi ⏚ 🔒 Table tennis **Extras** Mineral water **Parking** 8 **Notes** ⊗ 🐾

HINDOLVESTON — Map 13 TG02

The Old Bakery B&B

★★★★ ⬚ BED AND BREAKFAST

tel: 01263 862802 & 07771 391967 **34 The Street NR20 5DF**
email: mike@theoldbakerynorfolk.co.uk **web:** www.theoldbakerynorfolk.co.uk
dir: From A148 exit at Little Snoring signed Fulmodeston, follow signs to Hindolveston. At next junct continue for 1.3m, house on corner of turn to Foulsham

The Old Bakery B&B is a delightful detached property which was originally the village bakery and dates back to the 17th century. The spacious, well-equipped bedroom has pine furniture and many thoughtful touches. Breakfast, which includes fresh local ingredients, is served at a large communal table in the smart dining room. Guests have the use of a comfortable lounge with leather sofas and a log fire.

Rooms 2 en suite S £55-£60; D £70-£85* **Facilities** FTV DVD iPod docking station TVL tea/coffee Dinner available WiFi ⏚ 🔒 **Extras** Cakes on arrival - complimentary; fridge **Parking** 4 **Notes** LB ⊗ No Children 🐾

HOLT — Map 13 TG03

The Lawns Wine Bar

★★★★ 🏵 RESTAURANT WITH ROOMS

tel: 01263 713390 **26 Station Rd NR25 6BS**
email: info@lawnshotelholt.co.uk **web:** www.lawnshotelholt.co.uk
dir: A148 (Cromer road). 0.25m from Holt rdbt, turn left, 400yds along Station Rd

The Lawns is a superb Georgian house situated in the centre of this delightful north Norfolk market town. The open-plan public areas include a large wine bar, a conservatory and a smart restaurant. The spacious bedrooms are tastefully appointed with co-ordinated soft furnishings and have many thoughtful touches.

Rooms 8 en suite 2 annexe en suite (2 GF) S £95; D £115-£140 **Facilities** FTV DVD TVL tea/coffee Dinner available WiFi **Extras** Speciality toiletries **Conf** Max 20 Thtr 20 Class 12 **Parking** 18

Holm Oaks

★★★★ GUEST HOUSE

tel: 01263 711061 & 07778 600600 **83a Cromer Rd NR25 6DY**
email: holmoaks@btinternet.com

Holm Oaks enjoys a very convenient location on the outskirts of the Georgian village of Holt. The four bedrooms are all attractively presented and free WiFi is available throughout the house. Breakfast is served at individual tables in the conservatory, which overlooks the landscaped gardens. Secure parking is available. This makes an ideal base from which to explore beautiful north Norfolk.

Rooms 4 en suite (4 GF) **Facilities** FTV DVD Lounge tea/coffee WiFi **Parking** 5 **Notes** LB No Children

The Feathers

★★★ INN

tel: 01263 712318 **6 Market Place NR25 6BW**
email: enquiries@thefeathershotel.com **web:** www.thefeathershotel.com

This former coaching inn enjoys a prominent position in the heart of this pretty village. Bedrooms have been refurbished along with much of the public areas. Bedrooms vary in size but all are well equipped and comfortable. The bar, with its real fire, is extremely popular with locals and the dinner menu offers an extensive choice.

Rooms 13 en suite (2 fmly) S £75; D £100* **Facilities** FTV Lounge Dinner available Direct Dial WiFi ⏚ 18 🔒 **Conf** Max 100 Thtr 100 Class 80 Board 80 **Parking** 15

HORNING — Map 13 TG31

Innkeeper's Lodge Norfolk Broads, Horning

★★★ INN

tel: 0845 112 6060 **10 Lower St NR12 8AA**
email: info@innkeeperslodge.com **web:** www.innkeeperslodge.com

At Innkeeper's Lodge you'll find accommodation with comfort and character in equal measure, and everything needed for a relaxing stay, from easy check-in and free parking to complimentary breakfast and a cosy pub serving great value food and drink on the doorstep. Each Lodge has quality rooms, and there are Lodges in a variety of locations from towns and cities to countryside settings across the UK.

Rooms 8 en suite (3 fmly) **Facilities** FTV tea/coffee Dinner available Direct Dial WiFi **Parking**

HUNSTANTON — Map 12 TF64

The Neptune Restaurant with Rooms

★★★★★ 🏵🏵🏵 RESTAURANT WITH ROOMS

tel: 01485 532122 **85 Old Hunstanton Rd, Old Hunstanton PE36 6HZ**
email: reservations@theneptune.co.uk **web:** www.theneptune.co.uk
dir: On A149, past Hunstanton, 200mtrs on left after post office

This charming 18th-century coaching inn, now a restaurant with rooms, is ideally situated for touring the Norfolk coastline. The smartly appointed bedrooms are brightly finished with co-ordinated fabrics and hand-made New England furniture. Public rooms feature white clapboard walls, polished dark wood floors, fresh flowers and Lloyd Loom furniture. Obviously, the food is very much a draw here with the carefully prepared, award-winning cuisine using excellent local produce; from oysters and mussels from Thornham to quinces grown on a neighbouring farm.

Rooms 6 en suite S £130-£155; D £210-£240* (incl.dinner) **Facilities** FTV tea/coffee Dinner available Direct Dial WiFi 🔒 **Parking** 6 **Notes** ⊗ No Children 10yrs Closed 2wks Nov & 3wks Jan RS Oct-Apr Closed Mon No coaches

Claremont Guest House

★★★★ GUEST HOUSE

tel: 01485 533171 **35 Greevegate PE36 6AF**
email: claremontgh@tiscali.co.uk
dir: *Exit A149 into Greevegate, house before St Edmund's Church*

This Victorian guest house, close to the shops, beach and gardens, has individually decorated bedrooms with a good range of useful extras. Accommodation includes a ground-floor room, two feature rooms, one with a four-poster, and another with a canopied bed.

Rooms 7 en suite (1 fmly) (1 GF) S £30-£39; D £60-£78 **Facilities** TVL tea/coffee **Parking** 4 **Notes** LB No Children 5yrs Closed 15 Nov-15 Mar ⊜

Gemini Lodge Guest House

★★★★ GUEST HOUSE

tel: 01485 533902 **5 Alexandra Rd PE36 5BT**

Gemini Lodge Guest House is in an elevated position close to the centre of town and seafront. The bedrooms are smartly decorated in neutral colours with lovely co-ordinated soft furnishings and fabrics; some rooms have lovely views of the sea. Public rooms include a smart lounge with plush sofas, and breakfast is served at a large communal table in the contemporary dining room.

Rooms 3 en suite **Facilities** FTV TVL tea/coffee **Parking** 3 **Notes** No Children ⊜

The King William IV Country Inn & Restaurant

★★★★ Ⓐ INN

tel: 01485 571765 **fax:** 01485 571743 **Heacham Rd, Sedgeford PE36 5LU**
email: info@thekingwilliamsedgeford.co.uk **web:** www.thekingwilliamsedgeford.co.uk
dir: *A149 to Hunstanton, right at Norfolk Lavender in Heacham onto B1454, signed Docking. 2m to Sedgeford*

Tucked away in the village of Sedgeford, amid rolling countryside yet close to Norfolk's beautiful coast line, this family-run inn has been welcoming travellers and locals since 1836. There are log fires throughout the winter, and a garden for the summer. The menu offers classic dishes, complemented by daily specials and seasonal offerings. Bedrooms are full of character and have plenty of useful facilities.

Rooms 9 en suite (4 fmly) S £70-£80; D £100-£125* **Facilities** Lounge tea/coffee Dinner available WiFi ⅃ 18 ⚓ **Extras** Speciality toiletries **Parking** 60 **Notes** LB No coaches

Rosamaly Guest House

★★★★ Ⓐ GUEST ACCOMMODATION

tel: 01485 534187 & 07775 724484 **14 Glebe Av PE36 6BS**
email: vacancies@rosamaly.co.uk **web:** www.rosamaly.co.uk
dir: *A149 to Hunstanton. At rdbt take 3rd exit staying on A149 towards Cromer. In 1m church on left, Glebe Av 2nd left, Rosamaly 50yds on left*

Rosamaly is a family-run guest house situated in a peaceful side road within easy walking distance of the seafront and town centre. The well equipped bedrooms are pleasantly decorated with co-ordinated soft furnishings and many thoughtful touches. Breakfast is served at individual tables in the smart breakfast room and guests have the use of a cosy TV lounge.

Rooms 6 en suite (1 fmly) (1 GF) S fr £44; D fr £72* **Facilities** FTV TVL tea/coffee **Notes** LB Closed 24 Dec-1 Jan ⊜

The White Cottage

★★★ GUEST ACCOMMODATION

tel: 01485 532380 **19 Wodehouse Rd PE36 6JW**

A charming cottage situated in a quiet side road in Old Hunstanton, The White Cottage has been owned and run by Mrs Burton for 30 years. The spacious bedrooms are attractively decorated, and some have lovely sea views. Dinner is served in the smart dining room and there is a cosy sitting room with a television.

Rooms 3 rms (1 en suite) **Facilities** TVL tea/coffee Dinner available ⚓ **Parking** 4 **Notes** LB No Children 10yrs ⊜

Richmond House Bed & Breakfast

★★★ GUEST HOUSE

tel: 01485 532601 **6-8 Westgate PE36 5AL**
dir: *Exit A149 into Westgate*

Conveniently situated for the seafront and town centre, Richmond House B&B has pleasant bedrooms in a variety of sizes and styles, but all are well equipped and some rooms have superb sea views. Public rooms feature a smart restaurant and a cosy lounge bar.

Rooms 14 rms (10 en suite) (5 GF) S £40-£45; D £65-£70* **Facilities** tea/coffee Dinner available Lift Licensed ⚓ **Notes** ⊗ No Children 18yrs Closed Nov-Etr ⊜

| **KING'S LYNN** | Map 12 TF62 |

Linden Bed & Breakfast

★★★★ 🖺 BED AND BREAKFAST

tel: 01485 609198 & 07867 686216 **fax:** 01485 205001 **Station Rd PE31 6DE**
email: info@lindenbedandbreakfast.co.uk **web:** www.lindenbedandbreakfast.co.uk
dir: *From A148 onto B1153 signed Congham, 200mtrs on left before St Mary's church*

In a modern house, Linden Bed & Breakfast offers three individual, highly appointed en suite bedrooms along with a spacious guest lounge, a pretty garden overlooking the Norfolk countryside and a family-style breakfast/dining room. In the warmer months, cream teas are available and light suppers can also be arranged with prior notice.

Rooms 3 en suite S £55-£60; D £70-£75* **Facilities** FTV iPod docking station TVL tea/coffee WiFi ⚓ **Extras** Speciality toiletries - complimentary **Parking** 5 **Notes** ⊗ No Children 12yrs

| **LITCHAM** | Map 13 TF81 |

Bramley

★★★★ BED AND BREAKFAST

tel: 01328 701592 **fax:** 01328 701592 **Weasenham Rd PE32 2QT**
email: bramleybandb@hotmail.co.uk **web:** www.bramley-litcham.co.uk
dir: *A1065 onto B1145. Left at x-rds, left at school, 4th house on left*

A warm welcome awaits at Bramley, a delightful detached house, set in a peaceful location on the fringe of the village, with ample safe parking in generous grounds. The mostly spacious bedrooms are thoughtfully furnished to ensure guest comfort and have smartly appointed en suite shower rooms. A hearty, freshly-cooked breakfast is served at individual tables in the separate, elegant dining room.

Rooms 4 en suite (1 fmly) S £30-£40; D £60-£75* **Facilities** FTV tea/coffee WiFi ⚓ **Parking** 4 **Notes** LB ⊗ ⊜

LITTLE PLUMSTEAD
Map 13 TG31

Wayside B&B

★★★★ BED AND BREAKFAST

tel: 01603 619188 fax: 08721 153306 Honeycombe Rd NR13 5HY
email: moira@littleplumsteadbedandbreakfast.com

Wayside B&B is a charming house conveniently located close to Norwich and the Norfolk Broads and is set in the pretty village of Little Plumstead. Bedrooms are comfortable and very well equipped. Guests can relax on the terrace, and the continental breakfast offer a very good choice. Free WiFi is available along with secure parking.

Rooms 2 en suite

MUNDESLEY
Map 13 TG33

Overcliff Lodge

★★★★ 🛏 GUEST HOUSE

tel: 01263 720016 & 07902 386865 46 Cromer Rd NR11 8DB
email: enquiries@overclifflodge.co.uk web: www.overclifflodge.co.uk
dir: On B1159 Mundesley to Cromer coast road, opposite garage

Overcliff Lodge is on the outskirts of Mundesley and is a short walk to the beach. The house has been totally refurbished by its current owners and bedrooms are all beautifully presented and very well equipped. The lounge is very comfortable and award-winning breakfasts are served at individual tables in the light-filled breakfast room. WiFi is available throughout the house and the garden patio area is a popular breakfast venue on warmer days.

Rooms 7 en suite S £50-£55; D £70-£80 Facilities FTV DVD Lounge TVL tea/coffee WiFi 🛜 Extras Chocolates, bottled water - complimentary Parking 7 Notes ⊗ No Children 15yrs Closed Jan

NORTH WALSHAM
Map 13 TG23

Scarborough Hill Country Inn

★★★★ 🍽 INN

tel: 01692 402151 fax: 01692 486686 Old Yarmouth Rd NR28 9NA
email: reservations@scarboroughhillcountryinn.co.uk web: www.scarboroughhillcountryinn.co.uk

Set in five acres of landscaped gardens, Scarborough Hill Country Inn enjoys a quiet rural setting and is a short drive from the historic village of North Walsham. Refurbished in 2013, the inn offers a range of individually styled well-appointed bedrooms. The charming bar has several local ales, a good wine list and guests can relax by the log fire on colder evenings. Dinner is served in the conservatory restaurant and there is an extensive menu with a strong emphasis on local produce. WiFi is available throughout the inn along with ample secure parking.

Rooms 8 en suite 1 annexe en suite (1 fmly) (1 GF) Facilities FTV DVD TVL tea/coffee Dinner available Direct Dial WiFi 🛜 Extras Speciality toiletries, hand-made fudge Conf Max 80 Thtr 60 Class 50 Board 22 Parking 50 Notes No coaches Civ Wed 70

NORWICH
Map 13 TG20

Brasteds

★★★★★ 🏵🏵 🛏 RESTAURANT WITH ROOMS

tel: 01508 491112 fax: 01508 491113
Manor Farm Barns, Framingham Pigot NR14 7PZ
email: enquiries@brasteds.co.uk web: www.brasteds.co.uk
dir: A11 onto A47 towards Great Yarmouth, then A146. 0.5m, right into Fox Rd, 0.5m on left

Brasteds is a lovely detached property set in 20 acres of mature, landscaped parkland on the outskirts of Norwich. The tastefully appointed bedrooms have beautiful soft furnishings and fabrics along with comfortable seating and many thoughtful touches. Public rooms include a cosy snug with plush sofas, and a smart dining room where breakfast is served. Dinner is available in Brasteds Restaurant, which can be found in an adjacent building.

Rooms 6 en suite (1 fmly) (3 GF) S £99-£130; D £115-£200* Facilities FTV DVD iPod docking station TVL tea/coffee Dinner available Direct Dial WiFi 🛜 Extras Mini-bar Conf Max 120 Thtr 120 Class 100 Board 40 Parking 50 Notes LB No coaches Civ Wed 160

38 St Giles

★★★★★ 🛏 BED AND BREAKFAST

tel: 01603 662944 38 Saint Giles St NR2 1LL
email: booking@38stgiles.co.uk web: www.38stgiles.co.uk

Enjoying a prominent position in the heart of Norwich this beautifully restored building is a little oasis of calm. 38 St Giles has a choice of individually styled and tastefully appointed bedrooms and secure parking for guests. The award-winning breakfasts are not to be missed and this grand old building oozes charm and character. All the main tourist attractions, business and shopping districts, are a short walk away.

Rooms 6 en suite

Gothic House Bed & Breakfast

★★★★ GUEST ACCOMMODATION

tel: 01603 631879 King's Head Yard, Magdalen St NR3 1JE
email: charvey649@aol.com web: www.gothic-house-norwich.com
dir: Follow signs for A147, exit at rdbt past flyover into Whitefriars. Right into Fishergate, at end, right into Magdalen St

Gothic House Bed & Breakfast is an elegant Grade II listed Regency town house set in a quiet courtyard in the heart of Norwich. The property retains much of its original character and the spacious bedrooms are individually decorated and have many thoughtful touches. Breakfast, which includes locally sourced produce, is served in the elegant dining room.

Rooms 2 rms (2 pri facs) S £65; D £95* Facilities STV FTV tea/coffee WiFi 🛜 Extras Speciality toiletries Parking 2 Notes ⊗ No Children 18yrs Closed Feb ⌨

Old Thorn Barn

★★★★ GUEST ACCOMMODATION

tel: 01953 607785 & 07894 203208
Corporation Farm, Wymondham Rd, Hethel NR14 8EU
email: enquiries@oldthornbarn.co.uk **web:** www.oldthornbarn.co.uk
dir: *6m SW of Norwich. Follow signs for Lotus Cars from A11 or B1113, on Wymondham Rd*

Old Thorn Barn is a delightful Grade II listed barn situated in a peaceful rural location just a short drive from the city centre. The property has stylish, thoughtfully equipped bedrooms with polished wood floors and antique pine furniture. Breakfast is served in the open-plan barn, which also has a wood-burning stove and a cosy lounge area.

Rooms 5 en suite 2 annexe en suite (7 GF) S £38-£42; D £68-£72 **Facilities** FTV TVL tea/coffee WiFi 🐾 **Parking** 14 **Notes** ⊗

Church Farm

★★★★ GUEST ACCOMMODATION

tel: 01603 898020 & 898582 **fax:** 01603 755010 **Church St, Horsford NR10 3DB**
email: churchfarmgh@aol.com **web:** www.churchfarmgh.co.uk
dir: *5m NW of city centre. A140 onto B1149, right at x-rds*

Church Farm is set in a peaceful rural location just a short drive from Norwich airport and the city centre. The spacious bedrooms are smartly decorated, pleasantly furnished and have many considerate extras. Breakfast is served at individual tables in the conservatory-style lounge-dining room, which overlooks the garden and sun terrace.

Rooms 10 en suite (1 fmly) (3 GF) S £40-£50; D £60-£70* **Facilities** FTV TVL tea/coffee WiFi **Parking** 20 **Notes** ⊗

Cringleford Guest House

★★★★ GUEST HOUSE

tel: 01603 451349 & 07775 725933 **1 Gurney Ln, Cringleford NR4 7SB**
email: robandkate@cringlefordguesthouse.co.uk **web:** www.cringlefordguesthouse.co.uk
dir: *From A11 & A47 Thickthorn rdbt follow signs to Norwich, 0.25m slip road to Cringleford, left at junct into Colney Ln. Gurney Ln 5th on right*

Cringleford Guest House is a delightful property, situated just a short drive from the hospital, University of East Anglia and major roads. The pleasant, well-equipped bedrooms have co-ordinated fabrics and pine furniture. Breakfast is served at individual tables in the smart dining room.

Rooms 6 en suite 1 annexe en suite (4 fmly) (2 GF) S £45-£60; D £60-£90* **Facilities** FTV DVD TVL tea/coffee WiFi 🐾 **Conf** Max 10 Thtr 10 Class 10 Board 10 **Parking** 7 **Notes** LB ⊗

Salhouse Lodge Inn

★★★★ INN

tel: 01603 782828 **Vicarage Rd, Salhouse NR13 6HD**
web: www.salhouselodge.co.uk
dir: *From A1042 (ring road), NE of Norwich centre, exit at lights into Salhouse Rd signed New Rackheath. Through New Rackheath to Salhouse. Left onto B1140 signed Wroxham. Right in Vicarage Rd at sign for inn*

Situated on the outskirts of Norwich, this former rectory has extensive gardens and enjoys a peaceful rural location close to the Norfolk Broads. All the bedrooms are of a high standard and are very well equipped. Evening meals are served in the cosy lounge and the log fire really comes into its own on cooler evenings.

Rooms 7 en suite (2 fmly) S £55; D £95-£125* **Facilities** FTV tea/coffee Dinner available WiFi ⚓ 18 Pool table 🐾 **Parking** 50 **Notes** LB

Innkeeper's Lodge Norwich

★★★ INN

tel: 0845 112 6063 & 01603 700600 **18-22 Yarmouth Rd NR7 0EF**
email: info@innkeeperslodge.com **web:** www.innkeeperslodge.com
dir: *A47 onto A1042 signed Thorpe St Andrew. Continue for 1.5m*

Ideally located close to the beautiful city of Norwich, with its medieval architecture, and the Norfolk Broads, this Innkeeper's Lodge has 14 well appointed bedrooms. All are attractively presented and well-equipped, and free WiFi is available. Set beside the banks of the River Yare the large garden really comes into its own in the warmer months. There is a very popular restaurant and the lounge is spacious and comfortable.

Rooms 14 en suite (5 fmly) **Facilities** FTV tea/coffee Dinner available Direct Dial WiFi **Parking** 16 **Notes** ⊗

Number 3 B&B

★★★ GUEST ACCOMMODATION

tel: 01603 619188 & 08721 153306 **3 Chalk Hill Rd NR1 1SL**

Number 3 B&B is ideally located close to Norwich city centre and the main shopping and business districts. This charming period house has a range of individually styled, comfortable and well-appointed bedrooms. Free WiFi is available throughout the house and a parking permit is provided for guests' use. The continental breakfast offers a very good choice and includes fresh fruits, yogurts and a range of baked goods. An ideal base to explore the historic city of Norwich.

Rooms 5 rms (2 en suite) (1 pri facs)

Find out more about this county with the AA Guide to Suffolk & Norfolk – see theAA.com/shop

See also Cromer

Premier Collection

Ashbourne House

★★★★★ 🏛 BED AND BREAKFAST

tel: 01263 821555 & 07807 629868   **1 Nelson Rd NR26 8BT**
email: nailligill@yahoo.co.uk **web:** www.ashbournehousesheringham.co.uk
dir: *Take A149 Cromer road towards Cromer, turn left over Beeston Common. Under bridge, at top of Curtis Ln turn left, situated on right*

This superb detached property has been tastefully appointed to a very high standard. The smart bedrooms have lovely soft furnishings and are full of thoughtful touches. Public rooms include a large entrance hall and a guest lounge. Breakfast is served in the stylish panelled dining room, which overlooks the landscaped gardens that slope upwards to the cliff top.

Rooms 3 en suite S £50-£60; D £70-£80* **Facilities** STV FTV DVD TVL tea/coffee WiFi 🔌 **Parking** 3 **Notes** ⊗ No Children 12yrs ⊛

Premier Collection

Cleat House

★★★★★ 🏛 BED AND BREAKFAST

tel: 01263 822765   **7 Montague Rd NR26 8LN**
email: roblinda@cleathouse.co.uk **web:** www.cleathouse.co.uk
dir: *A149 into Sheringham, left at rdbt & 2nd right over railway bridge. 1st left into The Boulevard, then 2nd left to North St. Cleat House at end of road*

Cleat House is a large period property that is situated on a quiet side street but is only a short walk from the town centre and a five-minute walk to the beach. Guests are guaranteed a warm welcome and the delicious breakfasts are not to be missed. Original artwork is used throughout the house and bedrooms are individually styled and very comfortable. Complimentary cream tea is served to guests on arrival and WiFi is available throughout.

Rooms 3 rms (2 en suite) (1 pri facs) S £80-£125; D £90-£125 **Facilities** FTV DVD TVL tea/coffee WiFi 🔌 **Extras** Bathrobes, bottled water, mini-bar **Conf** Max 15 Board 15 **Parking** 4 **Notes** LB ⊗ No Children 14yrs Closed Dec-18 Mar

Premier Collection

The Eiders Bed & Breakfast

★★★★★ BED AND BREAKFAST

tel: 01263 837280   **Holt Rd, Aylmerton NR11 8QA**
email: enquiries@eiders.co.uk **web:** www.eiders.co.uk
dir: *From Cromer on A148, enter Aylmerton, pass garage on left. After x-rds, 2nd entrance on right*

The Eiders Bed & Breakfast is just a short drive from the centre of Sheringham and is ideally placed for touring the north Norfolk coast. The tastefully appointed bedrooms have lovely co-ordinated fabrics and many extras. Breakfast is served at individual tables in the conservatory which overlooks the gardens and a duck pond. Guests have the use of a heated swimming pool which is open from May to September.

Rooms 6 en suite (2 fmly) (6 GF) S £75-£95; D £95-£140* **Facilities** FTV DVD iPod docking station TVL tea/coffee WiFi 🔌 🔌 **Extras** Bottled water - complimentary **Parking** 7 **Notes** LB ⊗

At-Knollside

★★★★ BED AND BREAKFAST

tel: 01263 823320 & 07771 631980   **43 Cliff Rd NR26 8BJ**
email: avril@at-knollside.co.uk **web:** www.at-knollside.co.uk
dir: *250yds E of town centre. A1082 to High St, into Wyndham St & Cliff Rd*

Expect a warm welcome from the caring hosts at this delightful Victorian house overlooking the beach and sea. Bedrooms are tastefully furnished, using co-ordinated fabrics and other thoughtful touches. Breakfast is served in the elegant dining room and features local produce. Guests also have the use of a comfortable lounge.

Rooms 3 en suite D £75-£85 **Facilities** STV FTV DVD Lounge tea/coffee WiFi 🔌 36 **Extras** Chocolates, sweets **Parking** 3 **Notes** LB ⊗ No Children 3yrs ⊛

Roman Camp Inn

★★★★ ⊜ INN

tel: 01263 838291 **fax:** 01263 837071 **Holt Rd, Aylmerton NR11 8QD**
email: enquiries@romancampinn.co.uk **web:** www.romancampinn.co.uk
dir: *On A148 between Sheringham & Cromer, approx 1.5m from Cromer*

Roman Camp Inn provides spacious, tastefully appointed bedrooms with a good range of useful facilities including hairdryers. Five rooms are presented as deluxe, and two are suitable for disabled guests. Public rooms include a smart conservatory-style restaurant, a comfortable open-plan lounge/bar and a dining area. Room service is available, guests have complimentary use of local leisure facilities, and there is ample free parking.

Rooms 15 en suite (1 fmly) (10 GF) **Facilities** FTV tea/coffee Dinner available Direct Dial WiFi Free use of nearby leisure complex & pool **Conf** Max 20 Thtr 20 Class 20 Board 20 **Parking** 50 **Notes** ⊗ Closed 25-26 Dec

Bay Leaf Guest House

★★★★ BED AND BREAKFAST

tel: 01263 823779 **10 St Peters Rd NR26 8QY**
email: bayleafgh@aol.com **web:** www.bayleafbandb.co.uk
dir: *A149 Cromer road into Station Rd. 1st left into Station Approach, 2nd right into St Peters Rd*

This lovely Victorian property is ideally situated just a short walk from the golf course, steam railway and town centre. There is a smart lounge bar, and breakfast is served in the conservatory-dining room which overlooks the patio. Bedrooms vary in size and style, all are comfortable.

Rooms 7 en suite (2 fmly) (2 GF) S £40-£50; D £62-£74 **Facilities** FTV tea/coffee Licensed **Parking** 5 **Notes** LB ⊗ No Children 8yrs ⊛

The Old Barn

★★★★ ⓐ BED AND BREAKFAST

tel: 01263 838285 **Cromer Rd, West Runton NR27 9QT**
email: mkelliott2@aol.com **web:** www.theoldbarnnorfolk.co.uk
dir: *A149 from Cromer to West Runton, 2m opposite church*

The Old Barn is a charming property situated in the picturesque village of West Runton, just a short drive from Sheringham. There is a smart dining room and a superb beamed drawing room. The attractive bedrooms are carefully furnished and thoughtfully equipped.

Rooms 3 rms (2 en suite) (1 pri facs) (1 GF) S £60-£75; D £75-£85* **Facilities** STV FTV DVD iPod docking station TVL tea/coffee WiFi **Parking** 6 **Notes** ⊗ No Children 18yrs

| **SNETTISHAM** | **Map 12 TF63** |

The Rose & Crown

★★★★ INN

tel: 01485 541382 **Old Church Rd PE31 7LX**
email: info@roseandcrownsnettisham.co.uk **web:** www.roseandcrownsnettisham.co.uk
dir: A149 towards Hunstanton. In village centre into Old Church Rd, 100yds on left

This lovely village inn provides comfortable, well-equipped bedrooms. A range of quality meals is served in the many dining areas, complemented by a good variety of real ales and wines. Service is friendly and a delightful atmosphere prevails. A walled garden is available on sunny days, as is a children's play area.

Rooms 16 en suite (4 fmly) (2 GF) S £80-£110; D £100-£125* **Facilities** FTV Lounge TVL tea/coffee Dinner available WiFi ch fac ⚓ **Extras** Speciality toiletries **Conf** Max 80 **Parking** 60 **Notes** No coaches

| **STALHAM** | **Map 13 TG32** |

The Ingham Swan

★★★★ ◉◉ RESTAURANT WITH ROOMS

tel: 01692 581099 **Sea Palling Rd, Ingham NR12 9AB**
email: info@theinghamswan.co.uk **web:** www.theinghamswan.co.uk
dir: From A149 Stalham, into Old Market Rd towards Upper Staithe Rd/Lower Staithe Rd. At rdbt 1st exit, 2nd exit at next rdbt into Ingham Rd. Continue to Town Rd

The Swan is a charming 14th century former coaching inn that has been sympathetically restored and enjoys a peaceful rural location in the heart of Norfolk. Stylish, very well equipped bedrooms are most comfortable and the eye-catching original features really add to the presentation. The award-winning restaurant serves the best of Norfolk produce and there is a small bar area for pre-dinner drinks. Secure parking is available along with free WiFi for guests.

Rooms 4 annexe en suite (2 fmly) (2 GF) S £75-£115; D £85-£125* **Facilities** FTV tea/coffee Dinner available WiFi **Parking** 12 **Notes** ⊗ Closed 25-26 Dec

| **SWAFFHAM** |

See Castle Acre

| **THETFORD** | **Map 13 TL88** |

The Bell

★★★ INN

tel: 01842 754455 **fax:** 01842 755552 **King St IP24 2AZ**
email: bell.thetford@oldenglishinns.co.uk **web:** www.oldenglish.co.uk
dir: From S exit A11, 2m to 1st lights, right onto A134. 100yds, left into Bridge St, 150yds over bridge

Situated in the heart of the old part of town, this 15th-century coaching inn oozes charm and character. The accommodation is split between the main building and the more modern bedroom wings. Public areas include a bar, a lounge, and a restaurant, as well as conference facilities.

Rooms 46 en suite (1 fmly) **Facilities** tea/coffee Direct Dial **Parking** 55

| **THORPE MARKET** | **Map 13 TG23** |

Premier Collection

The Green House B&B

★★★★★ ≅ ☕ GUEST ACCOMMODATION

tel: 01263 834701 & 07721 462905 **Cromer Rd NR11 8TH**
email: greenhouse.norfolk@btinternet.com **web:** www.greenhousenorfolk.co.uk
dir: A140 in village of Roughton, right at mini rdbt into Thorpe Market Rd. After 1.5m turn right at give way sign, 200yds on left

The Green House B&B, a 17th-century, flint-faced farmhouse, offers friendly hospitality and a relaxed atmosphere. Near to Cromer, it's ideal for exploring the north Norfolk coast, the Broads, or Norwich. Bedrooms are all doubles, with one being either a king or twin room. All have walk-in showers, and one room has a double-ended bath. In-room facilities include flat-screen TV with DVD player, bottled water, hairdryer, bath robes, slippers and duck-down feather quilts and pillows. The Green House is licensed and the bar is open to non-residents for drinks and light lunches, but resident guests are offered an evening meal, which can be served in the dining room. Children under 14 are not accommodated.

Rooms 5 en suite S £60-£80; D £70-£120* **Facilities** FTV DVD iPod docking station Lounge tea/coffee Dinner available Licensed WiFi ⚓ 18 ⚓ **Extras** Slippers, dressing gown **Parking** 6 **Notes** LB No Children 14yrs

The Barns at Thorpe Market

★★★★ ≅ GUEST ACCOMMODATION

tel: 01263 833033 **Common Ln NR11 8TP**
email: info@bedbreakfastnorfolk.com **web:** www.bedbreakfastnorfolk.com
dir: A140 at Roughton onto B1436. At end turn right onto A149, onto slip road just past bus stop

This charming 18th-century converted barn offers a range of beautifully presented bedrooms overlooking a central courtyard. The bedrooms are spacious and very comfortable, and original flint walls are a real feature of the property. Thorpe Market is a short drive from Norwich and is close to the Norfolk Broads as well as a number of National Trust properties. Breakfast is served in the vaulted breakfast room, and features the best in local produce. WiFi is available for guests along with secure bike storage.

Rooms 3 en suite **Facilities** FTV tea/coffee WiFi ⚓ **Parking** 3 **Notes** ⊗ No Children 14yrs

| **THURSFORD** | **Map 13 TF93** |

Premier Collection

Holly Lodge

★★★★★ ≅ ☕ BED AND BREAKFAST

tel: 01328 878465 **fax:** 01328 878465 **The Street NR21 0AS**
email: info@hollylodgeguesthouse.co.uk **web:** www.hollylodgeguesthouse.co.uk
dir: Exit A148 into Thursford (village green on left) 2nd driveway on left past green

Holly Lodge is an award-winning 18th-century property situated in a picturesque location surrounded by open farmland. The stylish cottage bedrooms are in a converted stable block, each room individually decorated, beautifully furnished and equipped with many useful extras. The attractive public rooms have a wealth of character, with flagstone floors, oak beams and open fireplaces. There are superb landscaped grounds to enjoy.

Rooms 3 en suite (3 GF) S £70-£100; D £90-£120* **Facilities** FTV DVD Lounge TVL tea/coffee Dinner available WiFi ⚓ **Extras** Speciality toiletries, wine, home-made cakes - free of charge **Parking** 5 **Notes** LB ⊗ No Children 14yrs

THURSFORD *continued*

The Old Forge Seafood Restaurant

★★★★ ⊛ RESTAURANT WITH ROOMS

tel: 01328 878345 **Fakenham Rd NR21 0BD**
email: sarah.goldspink@btconnect.com **web:** www.seafoodnorthnorfolk.co.uk
dir: *On A148 (Fakenham to Holt road)*

Expect a warm welcome at this delightfully relaxed restaurant with rooms. The open-plan public areas include a lounge bar with comfy sofas, and an intimate restaurant with pine tables. Bedrooms are pleasantly decorated and equipped with a good range of useful facilities.

Rooms 3 en suite S £30-£65; D £55-£80 **Facilities** STV FTV Lounge tea/coffee Dinner available WiFi Riding 🐾 **Parking** 14 **Notes** No Children 10yrs No coaches

---

TIVETSHALL ST MARGARET	**Map 13 TM18**

Red House Farm Bed & Breakfast

★★★★ BED AND BREAKFAST

tel: 01379 676566 & 07719 437007 **Station Rd NR15 2DJ**
email: office@redhousefarm.info **web:** www.redhousefarm.info
dir: *500mtrs from Pulham rdbt A140*

A warm welcome is assured at this delightful 17th-century barn conversion, situated on a small working farm in a peaceful rural location. The tastefully appointed bedrooms have modern furniture and lovely countryside views. Breakfast, which includes home-grown produce, is served at a large communal table in the smart kitchen.

Rooms 2 en suite 2 annexe en suite (4 GF) S £45-£50; D £70-£75* **Facilities** FTV TVL tea/coffee WiFi **Parking** 4 **Notes** ⊛

WELLS-NEXT-THE-SEA	**Map 13 TF94**

Kilcoroon

★★★★ BED AND BREAKFAST

tel: 01328 710270 & 07733 112108 **Chancery Ln NR23 1ER**
email: terry@kilcoroon.co.uk **web:** www.kilcoroon.co.uk
dir: *Exit B1105 into Mill Rd. 3rd right into Buttlands. Property on left of Crown Hotel*

Kilcoroon is a delightful, detached period property situated by the green, just off the Buttlands and a short walk from the town centre. The spacious bedrooms are pleasantly decorated with co-ordinated fabrics and equipped with modern facilities. Breakfast is served at a large communal table in the elegant dining room.

Rooms 2 en suite **Facilities** FTV DVD tea/coffee WiFi 🐾 **Notes** ⊗ No Children 10yrs Closed 23-31 Dec ⊛

NORTHAMPTONSHIRE

ASHBY ST LEDGERS	**Map 11 SP56**

Olde Coach House

★★★★ ⊜ INN

tel: 01788 890349 **Main St CV23 8UN**
email: info@oldecoachhouse.co.uk **web:** www.oldecoachhouse.co.uk
dir: *M1 junct 18 onto A428. Follow signs for Daventry (A361), Ashby St Ledgers signed on left*

The Olde Coach House has been totally renovated. The public areas are in keeping with the building's vintage, but with all the modern amenities expected by today's guests. There is a large bar area and a spacious raised dining area, with open fires and exposed beams. The accommodation is smartly presented; rooms vary in size but all are equipped to the same high standard with flat-screen TVs, iPod docking station and wonderfully comfortable beds. The property benefits from excellent parking and outside areas for dining and drinking.

Rooms 4 en suite 11 annexe en suite (6 GF) S £65-£85; D £65-£95* **Facilities** FTV iPod docking station Lounge tea/coffee Dinner available Direct Dial WiFi ♨ 18 **Extras** Robes, speciality toiletries, snacks **Parking** 30

BADBY
Map 11 SP55

Premier Collection

Bunkers Hill House

★★★★★ 🏠 🍴 BED AND BREAKFAST

tel: 01327 707927 & 07818 406240 **NN11 3AW**
email: info@bunkershillhouse.co.uk **web:** www.bunkershillhouse.co.uk
dir: From Daventry on A361 into Badby. Windmill Inn on right, Bunkers Hill House on right off farm track before Bunkers Hill

Located in the quiet village of Badby in the Northamptonshire countryside, a warm welcome awaits at this beautiful Georgian-style family home. Spacious bedrooms and large comfortable beds will offer a good night's sleep. Many thoughtful extras are provided and a kitchenette and small lounge are also available for use. A heated indoor pool and spa are available, and aromatherapy treatments can be pre-arranged. AA Friendliest B&B of the Year Finalist 2014-2015.

Rooms 2 en suite (1 GF) **Facilities** FTV iPod docking station TVL tea/coffee Dinner available WiFi 🕙 🔒 **Extras** Fruit, snacks **Parking** 4 **Notes** No Children 16yrs

EASTON-ON-THE-HILL
Map 11 TF00

The Exeter Arms

★★★★★ 🍴 INN

tel: 01780 756321 **fax:** 01780 753171 **21 Stamford Rd PE9 3NS**
email: reservations@theexeterarms.net **web:** www.theexeterarms.net
dir: A1 Nbound take exit signed Easton-on-the-Hill; A1 Sbound take exit signed A47/A43 Corby/Kettering, on left entering village

This lovely village inn is situated in north-eastern Northamptonshire just a short drive from Stamford. The public rooms have many original features such as stone walls and open fireplaces; they include a lounge bar and the Orangery Restaurant which opens out onto the terrace for alfresco dining. The modern, well-equipped bedrooms are very stylish.

Rooms 5 en suite 1 annexe en suite (2 fmly) S £70-£100; D £80-£120 **Facilities** FTV tea/coffee Dinner available Direct Dial WiFi ♿ 18 **Parking** 40

LONG BUCKBY
Map 11 SP66

Murcott Mill Farmhouse B&B

AA Advertised

tel: 01327 842236 & 07756 981085 **Murcott Mill, Murcott NN6 7QR**
email: carrie.murcottmill@virgin.net **web:** www.murcottmill.com

This Northamptonshire farmhouse has been run by Brian and Carrie Hart for more than twelve years. They offer full English breakfast, along with luxurious en suite bedrooms and a guest lounge with log fire. Murcott Mill is pet and family friendly, and evening meals are available by arrangement.

Rooms 3 en suite (1 fmly) **Facilities** FTV DVD iPod docking station Lounge tea/coffee Dinner available WiFi ch fac 🔒

NASSINGTON
Map 12 TL09

The Queens Head Inn

★★★★ 🍴🍴 INN

tel: 01780 784006 **fax:** 01780 781539 **54 Station Rd PE8 6QB**
email: info@queensheadnassington.co.uk **web:** www.queensheadnassington.co.uk
dir: A1 Nbound exit junct 17, follow signs for Yarwell, then Nassington. Queens Head on left on entering the village

The Queens Head Inn offers a friendly atmosphere and a warm welcome, situated on the banks of the River Nene in the picturesque village of Nassington. The adjacent bedrooms are constructed from local stone; each one is smartly appointed and well equipped. Public rooms include a smart lounge bar, a restaurant and a light-filled conservatory dining room.

Rooms 9 en suite (2 fmly) (9 GF) **Facilities** FTV tea/coffee Dinner available Direct Dial WiFi Fishing 🔒 **Extras** Bottled water **Conf** Max 50 Thtr 50 Class 20 Board 20 **Parking** 45 **Notes** LB ⊗ Civ Wed 70

TOWCESTER
Map 11 SP64

The Saracens Head

★★★ INN

tel: 01327 350414 & 0800 917 3085 **fax:** 01327 359879 **219 Watling St NN12 6BX**
email: saracenshead.towcester@greeneking.co.uk **web:** www.oldenglish.co.uk
dir: M1 junct 15a, A43, at rdbt 1st exit onto A5 signed Towcester, premises on right

This historic coaching inn is rumoured to be an inspiration for Dickens' *Pickwick Papers*, and provides smart bedrooms and a convivial bar and restaurant. Staff are young and friendly. The Saracens Head provides an excellent base for horse-racing enthusiasts visiting the Towcester course, and for motor-racing fans heading for Silverstone.

Rooms 21 en suite (5 fmly) **Facilities** FTV tea/coffee Direct Dial WiFi **Conf** Max 100 Thtr 100 Class 60 Board 50 **Parking** 32 **Notes** LB ⊗ No coaches Civ Wed 90

WEEDON
Map 11 SP65

Narrow Boat at Weedon

★★★★ 🍴 INN

tel: 01327 340333 **Stowe Hill, A5 Watling St NN7 4RZ**
email: info@narrowboatatweedon.co.uk **web:** www.narrowboatatweedon.co.uk
dir: M1 junct 16 follow signs to Flore & Weedon. In Weedon at x-rds turn left up hill, on left

The Narrow Boat at Weedon has a superb location beside the Grand Union Canal, just off the A5. Close to both Milton Keynes and Northampton, it makes an ideal location for those wishing to visit attractions such as Silverstone and the Althorp Estate. There are seven very comfortable en suite bedrooms at the rear of the property, each with external access. Modern British cuisine and traditional pub classics can be enjoyed in both the bar and the restaurant, or out on the heated decking area in the garden by the canal, weather permitting of course.

Rooms 7 annexe en suite (7 GF) S £55-£95; D £55-£95* **Facilities** FTV DVD tea/coffee Dinner available WiFi **Conf** Max 30 Class 30 Board 30 **Parking** 40

NORTHUMBERLAND

ALNWICK   Map 21 NU11

Bondgate House

★★★★ 🏠 GUEST HOUSE

tel: 01665 602025 **20 Bondgate Without NE66 1PN**
email: enquiries@bondgatehouse.co.uk **web:** www.bondgatehouse.co.uk
dir: A1 onto B6346 into town centre, 200yds past war memorial on right

Originally a doctor's house, this Georgian building stands close to the historic gateway into the town centre. An attractive breakfast room, memorable breakfasts and the cosy lounge are complemented by friendly, helpful service. Bedrooms are all well equipped and thoughtfully furnished and include some rooms in converted stables set in a secluded garden behind the house.

Rooms 3 en suite 2 annexe en suite **Facilities** FTV DVD iPod docking station TVL tea/coffee WiFi 🛇 **Parking** 8 **Notes** ⊗ No Children 12yrs Closed Xmas 🖾

The Hogs Head Inn

★★★ INN

tel: 01665 606576 **Hawfinch Dr, Cawledge NE66 2BF**
email: info@hogsheadinnalnwick.co.uk **web:** www.hogsheadinnalnwick.co.uk
dir: A1 to Alnwick, follow signs for Cawledge Park

Named after the inn featured in the Harry Potter books, the Hogs Head opened in July 2012. It is ideally located just off the A1, on the edge of Alnwick close to the castle and gardens. It offers comfortable, spacious and well-equipped bedrooms, and WiFi throughout the whole property. The bar and restaurant serve tasty dishes in comfortable, informal surroundings. This purpose-built inn also offers external seating and dining.

Rooms 53 en suite (9 fmly) (25 GF) S £60–£65; D £85–£95* **Facilities** FTV Lounge TVL tea/coffee Dinner available Lift WiFi 🛇 18 **Parking** 125

BARDON MILL   Map 21 NY76

Coach House Bed & Breakfast

★★★★ GUEST ACCOMMODATION

tel: 01434 344779 **NE47 7HZ**
email: mail@bardonmillcoachhouse.co.uk **web:** www.bardonmillcoachhouse.co.uk
dir: Turn off A69 for Bardon Mill. In village next to the pottery

Versatile and well-presented accommodation with private entrances, the Coach House is family run, within easy distance of Hadrian's Wall, and caters well for everyone, from walkers to wedding guests. Gardens are a feature with a bubbling stream running close by. A well-cooked breakfast is served family style in the main house.

Rooms 1 en suite 2 annexe en suite (2 fmly) (1 GF) S fr £47; D fr £74* **Facilities** FTV DVD tea/coffee WiFi 🛇 **Parking** 6 **Notes** LB

BEADNELL   Map 21 NU23

The Craster Arms

★★★★ INN

tel: 01665 720272 & 07958 678280 **fax:** 08712 668881 **The Wynding NE67 5AX**
email: michael@crasterarms.co.uk **web:** www.crasterarms.co.uk
dir: From A1 junct at Brownieside Head East, through Preston and Chathill to Beadnell

Parts of The Craster Arms date back to the 15th century. The property has it all - open fire, beer garden and spacious well-appointed, comfortable bedrooms. The bar serves real ales along with good quality food using local produce and offers generous portion sizes. Well located in the peaceful village of Beadnell and just a short drive to the beach, Seahouses and Bamburgh with world famous Craster kippers available for breakfast.

Rooms 3 en suite (2 fmly) (1 GF) **Facilities** FTV TVL tea/coffee Dinner available WiFi 🛇 18 Riding Pool table **Parking** 20

BELFORD   Map 21 NU13

Premier Collection

Market Cross Guest House

★★★★★ 🏠 ⊜ GUEST HOUSE

tel: 01668 213013 & 07595 453208 **1 Church St NE70 7LS**
email: info@marketcrossbelford.co.uk **web:** www.marketcrossbelford.co.uk
dir: Exit A1 into village, opposite church

Market Cross Guest House keeps going from strength to strength; the owners have refurbished to a high standard and added their own personal slant to the property. Comfortable bedrooms have a whole array of personal touches including Nespresso machines, home baking and mini-fridges. Dinner by prior arrangement is wonderful and comes highly recommended, but ensure space is left for the great breakfast in the morning.

Rooms 4 en suite S £60–£100; D £80–£110 **Facilities** FTV DVD iPod docking station tea/coffee Dinner available WiFi 🛇 **Extras** Home-made snacks, mini-fridge, robes **Parking** 4 **Notes** ⊗ No Children 10yrs Closed 23-28 Dec

Purdy Lodge

★★★★ GUEST ACCOMMODATION

tel: 01668 213000 **Adderstone Services NE70 7JU**
email: reception@purdylodge.co.uk **web:** www.purdylodge.co.uk
dir: A1 onto B1341 then immediately left

Purdy Lodge is located just off the A1 with Alnwick, Seahouses and Bamburgh all within easy striking distance. This comfortable accommodation has a bar and restaurant along with a 24 hour café for those late arrivals. This family-run business offers warm Northumbrian hospitality and good customer care.

Rooms 20 en suite (7 fmly) (10 GF) S £55.95–£65.95; D £55.95–£65.95 (room only)* **Facilities** FTV tea/coffee Dinner available Direct Dial Licensed WiFi 🛇 **Parking** 60 **Notes** Closed 25 Dec

BERWICK-UPON-TWEED   Map 21 NT95

The Old School House

★★★★ GUEST ACCOMMODATION

tel: 01289 382000 & 07795 022705 **Thornton TD15 2LP**
email: johnburton2@waitrose.com **web:** www.oshthornton.co.uk
dir: Turn off A1 at Berwick-upon-Tweed onto A698 (Coldstream Road). After 3m turn left to Thornton, 1st house on left

Set in the peaceful Northumbrian countryside but just four miles from Berwick-upon-Tweed. Hospitality is a great strength with tea and home-baking offered on arrival, which can be taken in either the conservatory area, or in the drawing room in front of the fire. The well-appointed bedrooms are comfortable and offer plenty of extras. Breakfasts use local produce and make for a good start to the day. The pleasant walled gardens are an enjoyable place to relax.

Rooms 3 rms (2 en suite) (1 pri facs) S £60–£65; D £80–£90* **Facilities** FTV Lounge tea/coffee WiFi 🛇 **Extras** Chocolate, snacks - complimentary **Parking** 5 **Notes** LB ⊗ No Children 12yrs Closed 23 Dec-2 Jan

The Rob Roy Inn

★★★★ INN

tel: 01289 306428 **Dock Rd, Tweedmouth TD15 2BE**
email: therobroy@hotmail.co.uk

Enjoying views over the Tweed estuary and across to the historical border town of Berwick-upon-Tweed, this family-run inn offers high standards of accommodation. The small bar is warm and welcoming and well used by guests and locals alike. Harbour Lights Restaurant offers good quality food served in comfortable surroundings. The town centre is only a five minute walk whilst Spittle beach and promenade is just ten minutes in the opposite direction.

Rooms 5 rms

Lindisfarne Inn

★★★ INN

tel: 01289 381223 **fax:** 01289 381223 **Beal TD15 2PD**
email: enquiries@lindisfarneinn.co.uk **web:** www.lindisfarneinn.co.uk
dir: Exit A1 for Holy Island

The Lindisfarne Inn stands on the site of the old Plough Hotel at Beal, on the road leading to Holy Island. The inn has a traditional bar, rustic-style restaurant and comfortably equipped, courtyard bedrooms in the adjacent wing. Food is available all day.

Rooms 21 annexe en suite (20 fmly) (10 GF) S £60; D £85* **Facilities** FTV TVL tea/coffee Dinner available WiFi **Parking** 25

| CRAMLINGTON | Map 21 NZ27 |

Innkeeper's Lodge Cramlington

★★★ INN

tel: 0845 112 6013 **Blagdon Ln NE23 8AU**
email: info@innkeeperslodge.com **web:** www.innkeeperslodge.com

At Innkeeper's Lodge you'll find accommodation with comfort and character in equal measure, and everything needed for a relaxing stay, from easy check-in and free parking to complimentary breakfast and a cosy pub serving great value food and drink on the doorstep. Each Lodge has quality rooms, and there are Lodges in a variety of locations from towns and cities to countryside settings across the UK.

Rooms 18 en suite (4 fmly) (10 GF) **Facilities** FTV tea/coffee Dinner available Direct Dial WiFi **Parking** 50

| FALSTONE | Map 21 NY78 |

The Blackcock Country Inn and Restaurant

★★★★ INN

tel: 01434 240200 **NE48 1AA**
email: thebcinn@yahoo.co.uk **web:** www.blackcockinn.co.uk
dir: From Hexham take A6079 to Bellingham, then left at church. In village centre, towards Kielder Water

This traditional, family-run village inn lies close to Kielder Water. A cosy pub, it has a homely atmosphere, with welcoming fires burning in the colder weather. The bedrooms are very comfortable and well equipped; evening meals are served here or in the restaurant. The inn is closed during the day on Wednesdays in winter.

Rooms 6 rms (4 en suite) (2 pri facs) (1 fmly) S £45-£65; D £85-£95* **Facilities** STV TVL tea/coffee Dinner available WiFi Fishing Riding Pool table 🐾 Children's play area Clay pigeon shooting **Extras** Robes, chocolates; pet menus - charged **Parking** 15 **Notes** LB RS Wed closed during low season

Pheasant Inn

★★★★ 🍴 INN

tel: 01434 240382 **fax:** 01434 240382 **Stannersburn NE48 1DD**
email: stay@thepheasantinn.com **web:** www.thepheasantinn.com
dir: From A69 (N of Hexham) take A6079 signed Otterburn & Bellingham. Left onto B6320 signed Bellingham. Before Bellingham follow Hesleyside sign, then signs for Kielder & Stannersburn

The Pheasant Inn epitomises the traditional, charming country inn; it has character, good food and warm hospitality. Bright modern bedrooms, some with their own entrances, can all be found in stone buildings adjoining the inn. Delicious home-cooked meals are served in the bar with its low-beamed ceilings and exposed stone walls, or in the attractive dining room.

Rooms 8 annexe en suite (1 fmly) (5 GF) S £65-£70; D £90-£100* **Facilities** tea/coffee Dinner available WiFi ch fac 🛝 18 🐾 **Parking** 40 **Notes** LB Closed 4 days Xmas RS Nov-Mar closed Mon & Tue No coaches

| FELTON | Map 21 NU10 |

Birchwood House

★★★★ 🏠 GUEST ACCOMMODATION

tel: 01670 787828 **fax:** 01670 787828 **Kitswell Dene NE65 9NZ**
email: gbblewitt@btinternet.com **web:** www.birchwood-house.co.uk
dir: Just off A1. Take 2nd Swarland exit, bear left, left again

Ideally located for the A1, this spacious house combines very high standards of accommodation with warmth and great hospitality. Modern bedrooms and en suites cater well for the needs of the guest, and a fantastic large lounge is also made available. A well-cooked breakfast will set you up for your day regardless of your planned activities.

Rooms 3 en suite (3 GF) **Facilities** FTV iPod docking station TVL tea/coffee WiFi **Parking** 20 **Notes** ⊗ No Children 14yrs Closed Nov-1 Mar

| FORD | Map 21 NT93 |

The Estate House

★★★★ GUEST HOUSE

tel: 01890 820668 & 07436 266951 **fax:** 0872 111 5428 **TD15 2PX**
email: admin@theestatehouse.info **web:** www.theestatehouse.info
dir: 1m from A697, follow signs to Ford on B6354

Located in the heart of peaceful Ford village, this Edwardian house is set in its own mature gardens. A pet-friendly house that offers spacious, well-appointed accommodation with well-dressed and comfortable beds. A guests' lounge is available and during the day, the property runs a popular tea room. A wonderful base from which to tour this area of Northumberland.

Rooms 4 rms (3 en suite) (1 pri facs) (1 fmly) S £45-£60; D £60-£75 **Facilities** FTV DVD iPod docking station TVL tea/coffee Dinner available Licensed WiFi ch fac 🐾 Fishing 🐾 **Extras** Bottled water - complimentary

HALTWHISTLE
Map 21 NY76

See also Brampton (Cumbria)

Glendale Mews

★★★ BED AND BREAKFAST

tel: 01434 320711 & 07971 691631 **Glendale, North Rd NE49 9ND**
email: jap352@aol.com **web:** www.glendaleleisure.co.uk
dir: *On B6318*

Ideally located close to Haltwhistle and even closer to Hadrian's Wall. A wonderful property if you are walking or cycling in and around this area or to use as a base to tour the many sights. The self-contained cottage-style properties have their own mini-kitchens where a continental breakfast is provided. Many extras available including a swimming pool (charges apply).

Rooms 1 en suite (1 GF) S £50-£60; D £70-£80 **Facilities** STV FTV DVD iPod docking station TVL tea/coffee WiFi ch fac 🌀 🏊 Fishing Snooker Gym Pool table ♨ Cinema Ten pin bowling Children's indoor soft play **Extras** Fresh fruit, flowers, snacks **Parking** 4 **Notes** LB

LONGFRAMLINGTON
Map 21 NU10

The Granby Inn

★★★ 🍽 INN

tel: 01665 570228 & 570362 **fax:** 01665 570736 **NE65 8DP**
email: info@thegranbyinn.co.uk **web:** www.thegranbyinn.co.uk
dir: *Off A1 onto A697 signed Coldstream. On right in Longframlington*

The Granby Inn is a traditional, family-run coaching inn dating back over 250 years, situated in the heart of the village. Bedrooms are comfortable and some have wonderful views right to the coast. Food is a real strength here and the team take great pride in their locally sourced produce. The bar is welcoming and reservations to eat are always recommended.

Rooms 5 en suite **Facilities** FTV DVD tea/coffee Dinner available Direct Dial WiFi 🌀 ♨ Complimentary use of nearby leisure facilities **Parking** 24 **Notes** LB ⊗ Closed 25-26 Dec, 1 Jan

LOWICK
Map 21 NU04

The White Swan Inn

★★★★ INN

tel: 01289 388249 **fax:** 01289 388241 **51 Main St TD15 2UD**
email: thewhiteswan73@yahoo.co.uk **web:** www.whiteswanlowick.co.uk

The White Swan is a traditional local pub in the heart of the village. The property has enjoyed a good deal of refurbishment, and offers comfortable, well-appointed, modern bedrooms. The bar is friendly and welcoming with good quality local produce that is also served in the restaurant. A great base for touring the Borders and Northumberland.

Rooms 4 en suite (1 GF) **Facilities** FTV DVD tea/coffee Dinner available WiFi Pool table ♨ **Extras** Speciality toiletries, bottled water - free **Conf** Max 30 Thtr 30 Class 20 Board 25 **Parking** 6

NEWTON-ON-THE-MOOR
Map 21 NU10

The Cook and Barker Inn

★★★★ 🍽 INN

tel: 01665 575234 **fax:** 01665 575234 **NE65 9JY**
email: info@cookandbarkerinn.co.uk **web:** www.cookandbarkerinn.co.uk
dir: *North on A1, pass Morpeth. A1 becomes single carriageway for 8m, then dual carriageway. Up slight incline 3m, follow signs on left to Newton-on-the-Moor*

Set in the heart of a quiet village, this inn is popular with visitors and locals. The emphasis is on food here with interesting home-made dishes offered in the restaurant and bar areas. Bedrooms are smartly furnished and well equipped, and are split between the main house and the adjacent annexe.

Rooms 4 en suite 14 annexe en suite (2 fmly) (7 GF) **Facilities** tea/coffee Dinner available Direct Dial WiFi **Conf** Max 50 Thtr 50 Class 50 Board 25 **Parking** 64 **Notes** ⊗

OTTERBURN
Map 21 NY89

Dunns Houses Farmhouse (NY868930)

★★★★ FARMHOUSE

tel: 01830 520677 & 07808 592701 **fax:** 01830 520677 **NE19 1LB**
email: dunnshouses@hotmail.com **web:** www.northumberlandfarmholidays.co.uk
dir: *Situated on the A68, 7m E of Bellingham & 3m W of Otterburn*

Dunns Houses Farmhouse stands on a working farm in 960 hectares of Northumberland National Park. Bedrooms are well appointed and there is a comfortable lounge and dining room. Breakfasts use locally sourced produce, as do the home-cooked dinners (by prior arrangement only). Warm hospitality and great on-site amenities are on offer here.

Rooms 3 en suite (1 fmly) S £45; D £75-£80* **Facilities** FTV TVL tea/coffee Dinner available WiFi 🦆 🎣 18 Fishing Pool table ♨ **Extras** Speciality toiletries **Parking** 6 **Notes** LB 2372 acres beef/sheep/horses

RIDING MILL
Map 21 NZ06

Low Fotherley Farm (NZ030581)

★★★★ FARMHOUSE

tel: 01434 682277 & 07707 821202 **fax:** 01434 682277 **NE44 6BB**
email: hugh@lowfotherley.fsnet.co.uk **web:** www.lowfotherleyfarmhouse.co.uk
dir: *1.5m N of Kilnpit Hill, on left*

Low Fotherley Farm is a traditional Victorian farmhouse on a working farm, just off the A68 in the heart of the Northumbrian countryside. Bedrooms are spacious and comfortable, while customer care and hospitality are very warm. A hearty breakfast is served family-style in the dining room.

Rooms 3 rms (2 en suite) (1 pri facs) S £45-£50; D £70-£75 **Facilities** FTV tea/coffee WiFi ♨ **Parking** 6 **Notes** ⊗ No Children 12yrs Closed Xmas & New Year 225 acres sheep

Map 21 NU23

The Olde Ship Inn

 ★★★★ INN

tel: 01665 720200 **fax:** 01665 721383 **NE68 7RD**
email: theoldeship@seahouses.co.uk **web:** www.seahouses.co.uk
dir: Lower end of main street above harbour

Under the same ownership since 1910, this friendly inn overlooks the harbour and is full of character. Lovingly maintained, its sense of history is evident by the amount of nautical memorabilia on display. Public areas include a character bar, cosy snug, restaurant and guests' lounge. The individual bedrooms are smartly presented. Two separate buildings contain executive apartments, all with sea views.

Rooms 12 en suite 6 annexe en suite (4 GF) S £47; D £94-£130* **Facilities** FTV Lounge TVL tea/coffee Dinner available Direct Dial WiFi Pool table ⚓ **Parking** 18 **Notes** LB ⊗ No Children 10yrs Closed Dec-Jan No coaches

Bamburgh Castle Inn

★★★ INN

tel: 01665 720283 **fax:** 01665 720284 **NE68 7SQ**
email: enquiries@bamburghcastleinn.co.uk **web:** www.bamburghcastleinn.co.uk
dir: A1 onto B1341 to Bamburgh, B1340 to Seahouses, follow signs to harbour

Situated in a prime location on the quayside, this establishment has arguably the best view along the coast. Dating back to the 18th century, the inn has superb dining and bar areas, with outside seating available in warmer weather. There are smart, comfortable bedrooms, many with views of the Farne Islands and the inn's famous namesake, Bamburgh Castle.

Rooms 27 en suite 2 annexe en suite (6 fmly) (8 GF) S £60-£65; D £85-£95* **Facilities** FTV TVL tea/coffee Dinner available **Conf** Max 50 **Parking** 35 **Notes** LB

Map 21 NZ37

The Waterford Arms

★★★★ INN

tel: 0191 237 0450 **Collywell Bay Rd NE26 4QZ**
email: waterfordarms@gmail.com

Overlooking the picturesque estuary The Waterford Arms is a wonderful family run small property with a great restaurant operation. Bedrooms are well presented with good quality decor and on-going work is showing very good results. The restaurant and bar are of a good size and offer great value for money. The inn is famous for its fish & chips - the 'whale' sized portion is not for the faint hearted.

Rooms 7 en suite (1 fmly) S £39.99-£49.99; D £59.99-£79.99* **Facilities** FTV Lounge TVL tea/coffee Dinner available WiFi Pool table ⚓ **Parking** 16 **Notes** LB

Map 21 NT90

The Holystone Estate

[U]

tel: 01669 640140 **Farnham Park NE65 7AQ**
email: info@holystonelodge.co.uk **web:** www.holystonelodge.co.uk

Currently the rating for this establishment is not confirmed. This may be due to a change of ownership or because it has only recently joined the AA rating scheme.

Rooms 4 en suite 1 annexe en suite S fr £65; D £100-£150* **Facilities** FTV TVL tea/coffee Dinner available Direct Dial Licensed WiFi ⚓ 18 Fishing ⚓ **Parking** 21 **Notes** LB ⊗ Closed Xmas-New Year RS Sun eve & Mon

Map 21 NU00

The Three Wheat Heads

★★★★ INN

tel: 01669 620262 **NE65 7LR**
email: info@threewheatheads.co.uk **web:** www.threewheatheads.co.uk

The Three Wheat Heads is located on the edge of the Northumberland National Park just a few miles from Rothbury. All bedrooms have been refurbished to a high standard, and most offer picture-postcard views of the local countryside. Good food is served in a choice of areas with a beer garden to the rear also available.

Rooms 5 en suite (1 fmly) **Facilities** FTV tea/coffee Dinner available WiFi ⚓ 18 Fishing ⚓ **Parking** 14 **Notes** LB

NOTTINGHAMSHIRE

COTGRAVE
Map 11 SK63

Jerico Farm (SK654307)
★★★★ ≝ FARMHOUSE

tel: 01949 81733 **Fosse Way NG12 3HG**
email: info@jericofarm.co.uk **web:** www.jericofarm.co.uk
dir: Off A46, signed Kinoulton. N of junct with A606

A friendly relaxed atmosphere is offered at Jerico Farm, an attractive building, which stands in the beautiful Nottinghamshire countryside just off the A46, close to Nottingham, Trent Bridge Cricket and the National Water Sports Centre. Day rooms include a comfortable lounge, and a separate dining room in which substantial, tasty breakfasts are served overlooking the gardens. Spacious bedrooms are individually appointed and thoughtfully equipped.

Rooms 3 en suite (1 fmly) **Facilities** FTV TVL tea/coffee WiFi Fishing **Extras** Speciality toiletries **Parking** 4 **Notes** ⊗ No Children 10yrs Closed 24 Dec-2 Jan 150 acres mixed

EASTWOOD
Map 11 SK44

The Sun Inn
★★★ INN

tel: 01773 712940 **fax:** 01773 531563 **6 Derby Rd NG16 3NT**
web: www.oldenglish.co.uk

Built in 1705, this Grade II listed building is located right in the centre of Eastwood, with easy access to the Derbyshire Dales for walkers, and Nottingham for shoppers. The well-equipped bedrooms are all en suite and offer modern facilities.

Rooms 15 en suite (1 fmly) **Facilities** FTV tea/coffee Dinner available WiFi Pool table **Conf** Max 15 Thtr 15 Class 8 Board 15 **Parking** 8 **Notes** ⊗

EDWINSTOWE
Map 16 SK66

The Forest Lodge
★★★★ INN

tel: 01623 824443 **fax:** 01623 824686 **Church St NG21 9QA**
email: reception@forestlodgehotel.co.uk **web:** www.forestlodgehotel.co.uk
dir: A614 into Edwinstowe. On B6034, opposite St Mary's church

Situated in the heart of Sherwood Forest, The Forest Lodge is a 17th-century coaching inn that provides the visitor with a warm and homely base from which to explore this fascinating and historic area. The bedrooms have been tastefully finished and the bar provides home comforts and good company. Food is served in the bar and in the restaurant.

Rooms 8 en suite 5 annexe en suite (2 fmly) (5 GF) S £75; D £80-£90* **Facilities** FTV tea/coffee Dinner available WiFi ⚲ 36 ⚑ **Extras** Speciality toiletries - complimentary **Conf** Max 75 Thtr 75 Class 45 Board 50 **Parking** 35

ELTON
Map 11 SK73

The Grange
★★★★★ ⚑ BED AND BREAKFAST

tel: 07887 952181 **Sutton Ln NG13 9LA**
web: www.thegrangebedandbreakfastnotts.co.uk
dir: From Grantham A1 onto A52 to Elton x-rds, left 200yds, B&B on right

Parts of this lovely house date back to the early 17th century and the rooms command fine views across the gardens and rolling open countryside. Bedrooms contain many thoughtful extras and fine hospitality is assured from the proprietors. There is also a lounge as well as a reading room for residents' use, both furnished in warm tones with welcoming soft sofas and wood-burning stoves.

Rooms 3 en suite S £45-£55; D £70-£79 **Facilities** FTV DVD Lounge TVL tea/coffee WiFi ⚑ **Extras** Chocolate, snacks, orange juice, water - free **Parking** 8 **Notes** ⊗ ⊜

HOLBECK
Map 16 SK57

Browns
★★★★★ ⚑ BED AND BREAKFAST

tel: 01909 720659 **fax:** 01909 720659
The Old Orchard Cottage, Holbeck Ln S80 3NF
email: browns.holbeck@btconnect.com **web:** www.brownsholbeck.co.uk
dir: 0.5m off A616 Sheffield-Newark road, turn for Holbeck at x-rds

Set amid beautifully tended gardens with lily-ponds and extensive lawns, this mid 18th-century cottage is a tranquil rural hideaway. Breakfasts are served in the Regency-style dining room, and the elegant bedrooms have four-poster beds and many extras. The friendly owners provide attentive service, including courtesy transport to nearby restaurants if required.

Rooms 3 annexe en suite (3 GF) S £59-£69; D £83-£93* **Facilities** FTV DVD tea/coffee WiFi Riding ⚑ **Extras** Robes, slippers, speciality toiletries, chocolates **Parking** 3 **Notes** ⊗ No Children 17yrs Closed Xmas wk ⊜

HOLME PIERREPONT
Map 11 SK63

Holme Grange Cottage
★★★ GUEST ACCOMMODATION

tel: 0115 981 0413 **Adbolton Ln NG12 2LU**
email: jean.colinwightman@talk21.com **web:** www.holmegrangecottage.co.uk
dir: Exit A52 SE of Nottingham onto A6011. After 500yds turn right into Regatta Way, 1.25m on right

A stone's throw from the National Water Sports Centre, Holme Grange Cottage has its own all-weather tennis court - ideal for the active guest. Indeed, when not providing warm hospitality and freshly cooked breakfasts, the proprietor is usually on the golf course.

Rooms 3 rms (1 en suite) (1 fmly) S £33-£39; D £56-£62* **Facilities** FTV TVL tea/coffee WiFi ⚲ ⚑ **Parking** 6 **Notes** Closed Xmas ⊜

MANSFIELD  Map 16 SK56

Bridleways Holiday Homes & Guest House

★★★★ GUEST HOUSE

tel: 01623 635725 fax: 01623 635725 **Newlands Rd, Forest Town NG19 0HU**
email: bridleways@outlook.com web: www.stayatbridleways.co.uk
dir: *From Mansfield take B6030 towards New Clipstone. Right at rdbt, follow Crown Farm Industrial Park sign. 1st left into Newlands Rd. Guest house on left*

Beside a quiet bridleway that leads to Vicar Water Country Park and Sherwood Pines Forest Park, this friendly guest house is a good touring base for walking, cycling or sightseeing. The double, twin and family bedrooms are particularly spacious and all are en suite. Lovely breakfasts are served in a cottage-style dining room.

Rooms 9 en suite (1 fmly) (2 GF) S £38; D £72* **Facilities** FTV tea/coffee WiFi
Parking 14 **Notes** ⊗

NEWARK-ON-TRENT Map 17 SK75

Compton House

★★★★ ☕ 🍴 GUEST HOUSE

tel: 01636 708670 **117 Baldertongate NG24 1RY**
email: info@comptonhousenewark.com web: www.comptonhousenewark.com
dir: *500yds SE of town centre. B6326 into Sherwood Av, 1st right into Baldertongate*

Located a short walk from Newark's central attractions, this elegant period house provides high standards of comfort. Individually themed bedrooms come with a wealth of thoughtful extras and smart modern bathrooms. Comprehensive breakfasts, and wholesome dinners (by arrangement), are served in the attractive dining room and a lounge is available.

Rooms 7 rms (6 en suite) (1 pri facs) (1 fmly) (1 GF) S £50-£80; D £95-£130* **Facilities** FTV Lounge tea/coffee Dinner available WiFi 🏋 **Extras** Magazines, mineral water - complimentary **Conf** Max 10 Thtr 10 Class 10 Board 10 **Parking** 2 **Notes** ⊗ Closed Xmas

NOTTINGHAM Map 11 SK53

See also Cotgrave

Premier Collection

Restaurant Sat Bains with Rooms

★★★★★ 🍴🍴🍴🍴🍴 ☕ RESTAURANT WITH ROOMS

tel: 0115 986 6566 fax: 0115 986 0343 **Trentside, Lenton Ln NG7 2SA**
email: info@restaurantsatbains.net web: www.restaurantsatbains.com
dir: *M1 junct 24, A453 Nottingham S. Over River Trent into central lane to rdbt. Left, left again towards river. Establishment on left after bend*

This charming restaurant with rooms, a stylish conversion of Victorian farm buildings, is situated on the river and close to the industrial area of Nottingham. The bedrooms create a warm atmosphere by using quality soft furnishings together with antique and period furniture; suites and four-poster rooms are available. Public areas are chic and cosy, and the delightful restaurant complements the truly outstanding, much acclaimed cuisine.

Rooms 4 en suite 4 annexe en suite (6 GF) **Facilities** STV Dinner available Direct Dial **Parking** 22 **Notes** ⊗ Closed 1st wk Jan & 2wks mid Aug RS Sun & Mon rooms & restaurant closed

Cockliffe Country House

★★★★ 🍴🍴 RESTAURANT WITH ROOMS

tel: 0115 968 0179 fax: 0115 968 0623
Burntstump Country Park, Burntstump Hill, Arnold NG5 8PQ
email: enquiries@cockliffehouse.co.uk web: www.cockliffehouse.co.uk
dir: *M1 junct 27, follow signs to Hucknall (A611), then B6011, right at T-junct, follow signs for Cockliffe House*

Expect a warm welcome at this delightful property situated in a peaceful rural location amid neat landscaped grounds, close to Sherwood Forest. Public areas include a smart breakfast room, a tastefully appointed restaurant serving great food, and a cosy lounge bar. The individually decorated bedrooms have co-ordinated soft furnishings and many thoughtful touches.

Rooms 7 en suite 4 annexe en suite (5 GF) **Facilities** FTV tea/coffee Dinner available Direct Dial WiFi ⏎ **Conf** Max 30 Thtr 30 Class 25 Board 30 **Parking** 60 **Notes** No coaches Civ Wed 60

Beech Lodge

★★★★ GUEST ACCOMMODATION

tel: 0115 952 3314 & 07961 075939 **222 Porchester Rd NG3 6HG**
email: paulinegoodwin222@hotmail.co.uk web: www.beechlodgeguesthouse.com
dir: *From A684 into Porchester Rd, 8th left, (Punchbowl pub on right corner), Beech Lodge on left corner*

A friendly welcome is assured at Beech Lodge and the modern accommodation is well presented and suitably equipped. The ground-floor lounge is particularly comfortable, and there is a small conservatory. Breakfast is a good choice of freshly cooked and carefully presented fare served in the dining area next to the lounge.

Rooms 4 en suite (1 fmly) S fr £35; D fr £65* **Facilities** FTV TVL tea/coffee WiFi
Parking 4 **Notes** ⊗

The Yellow House

★★★★ BED AND BREAKFAST

tel: 0115 926 2280 **7 Littlegreen Rd, Woodthorpe NG5 4LE**
email: suzanne.prewsmith1@btinternet.com web: www.bandb-nottingham.co.uk
dir: *Exit A60 (Mansfield Rd) N from city centre into Thackeray's Ln, over rdbt, right into Whernside Rd to x-rds, left into Littlegreen Rd, house on left*

This semi-detached private house is in an easily-accessible and quiet residential suburb to the north-east of the city. The one purpose-built bedroom contains many thoughtful extras. A warm welcome is assured here and the proprietors' pet dog is also very friendly.

Rooms 1 en suite S £45-£50; D £65-£69* **Facilities** FTV tea/coffee WiFi 🏋 **Parking** 1 **Notes** ⊗ No Children Closed Xmas & New Year 🐾

WORKSOP Map 16 SK57

Acorn Lodge

★★★★ GUEST ACCOMMODATION

tel: 01909 478383 fax: 01909 478383 **85 Potter St S80 2HL**
email: info@acornlodgeworksop.co.uk
dir: *A1 onto A57. Take B6040 (town centre) through Manton. Lodge on right, 100mtrs past Priory*

Originally part of the community house of the Priory Church, this property has been modernised to offer comfortable, well-appointed accommodation. Good breakfasts are served in the pleasant breakfast room and ample private parking is available at the rear.

Rooms 7 en suite (2 fmly) S fr £40; D fr £55 (room only)* **Facilities** FTV tea/coffee WiFi 🏋 **Parking** 15 **Notes** ⊗

OXFORDSHIRE

ABINGDON-ON-THAMES
Map 5 SU49

Premier Collection

B&B Rafters

★★★★★ 🏠 BED AND BREAKFAST

tel: 01865 391298 & 07824 378720   **fax:** 01865 391173
Abingdon Rd, Marcham OX13 6NU
email: enquiries@bnb-rafters.co.uk **web:** www.bnb-rafters.co.uk
dir: *A34 onto A415 towards Witney. Rafters on A415 in Marcham adjacent to pedestrian crossing, on right*

Set amid immaculate gardens, this modern house is built in a half-timbered style and offers spacious accommodation together with a warm welcome. Bedrooms are stylishly furnished and equipped in a boutique-style, and come with a range of homely extras. Comprehensive breakfasts feature local and organic produce when possible.

Rooms 4 en suite S £57-£119; D £119-£145 **Facilities** FTV DVD iPod docking station Lounge tea/coffee WiFi **Extras** Speciality toiletries, fruit, bottled water - free **Parking** 4 **Notes** ⊗

Abbey Guest House

★★★★ BED AND BREAKFAST

tel: 01235 537020 & 07976 627252   **fax:** 01235 537020 **136 Oxford Rd OX14 2AG**
email: info@abbeyguest.com **web:** www.abbeyguest.com
dir: *1m from A34 Sbound, exit at North Abingdon*

A warm welcome is assured at Abbey Guest House. This well maintained property offers very comfortable, modern bedrooms with many useful extras and a relaxed atmosphere. There are a couple of local pubs nearby as well as very good bus links to Oxford from just outside the property. Freshly prepared breakfasts are served in the airy dining room overlooking the garden. Free WiFi is available throughout the house and off road parking is provided for guests.

Rooms 7 en suite (1 fmly) (1 GF) S £50-£66; D £90-£99 **Facilities** FTV DVD Lounge tea/coffee WiFi 🐾 **Extras** Use of fridge & microwave **Parking** 7 **Notes** ⊗

The Dog House

★★★ INN

tel: 01865 390830 **fax:** 01865 390860 **Faringdon Rd, Frilford Heath OX13 6QJ**
email: doghouse.frilfordheath@oldenglishinns.co.uk **web:** www.oldenglish.co.uk

As its name suggests, The Dog House was once the kennels (and the stables) for a local manor house. Situated in the heart of the Oxfordshire countryside, this is a popular inn with a spacious bar and restaurant that offer a wide variety of meals and lighter options, with a carvery available on Sundays. Conference facilities are available and weddings are also catered for.

Rooms 20 en suite (2 fmly) (4 GF) **Facilities** tea/coffee Dinner available Direct Dial WiFi **Conf** Thtr 30 Class 10 Board 18 **Parking** 40

ADDERBURY
Map 11 SP43

Red Lion

★★★ INN

tel: 01295 810269 **fax:** 01295 811906 **The Green, Oxford Rd OX17 3LU**
email: 6496@greenking.co.uk **web:** www.oldenglish.co.uk
dir: *M40 junct 11 into Banbury, take A4260 towards Bodicote into Adderbury, on left*

This charming former coaching inn was once an important stop-over on the old Banbury to Oxford road. The atmosphere typifies an English inn, and dedicated staff provide a warm welcome. The comfortable and spacious bedrooms are attractively decorated; some rooms are split-level and one has a four-poster. Honest, fresh food is served in the restaurant and the bar.

Rooms 12 en suite (1 GF) **Facilities** FTV tea/coffee Direct Dial WiFi **Notes** ⊗

ASTON ROWANT
Map 5 SU79

Lambert Arms

★★★★ ⊚ 🏠 INN

tel: 01844 351496 **fax:** 01844 351893 **London Rd OX49 5SB**
email: info.lambertarms@bespokehotels.com **web:** www.bespokehotels.com
dir: *M40 junct 6, follow signs to Chinnor (B4009) then left to Thame (A40)*

Retaining original and historical features, this lovely coaching inn combines the feel of an old pub with a modern twist. You'll find a comfortable and friendly bar with log fires, real ales and a mouth-watering array of food, including favourite pub classics using fresh, seasonal locally sourced produce.

Rooms 9 rms (8 en suite) (1 pri facs) 35 annexe en suite (13 fmly) (16 GF) **Facilities** STV FTV tea/coffee Dinner available Direct Dial Lift WiFi ⅃ 18 Gym **Conf** Max 140 Thtr 120 Class 62 Board 38 **Parking** 75 **Notes** Civ Wed 120

BAMPTON
Map 5 SP30

Biztro at Wheelgate House

★★★★ RESTAURANT WITH ROOMS

tel: 01993 851151 & 07747 466151 **Wheelgate House, Market Square OX18 2JH**
email: enquiries@wheelgatehouse.co.uk **web:** www.wheelgatehouse.co.uk
dir: *In village centre opposite war memorial*

This restaurant with rooms is set in the pretty village of Bampton at the edge of the Cotswolds, and extends a warm and friendly welcome to all its guests. Bedrooms are individual in design offering a cosy experience. The ground floor is 'Biztro', where breakfast is served daily along with lunches and dinners available from Tuesday to Saturday.

Rooms 3 rms (2 en suite) (1 pri facs) S £59; D £89* **Facilities** FTV DVD tea/coffee Dinner available WiFi **Extras** Speciality toiletries, bottled water **Notes** No coaches

BANBURY

Map 11 SP44

Premier Collection

Treetops Guest House

★★★★★ GUEST ACCOMMODATION

tel: 01295 254444 & 07951 095479 **28 Dashwood Rd OX16 5HD**
email: enquiries@treetopsbanbury.co.uk **web:** www.treetopsbanbury.co.uk
dir: *M40 junct 11 onto A422. At Concord rdbt 1st exit onto A4260, next rdbt 1st exit. Over 1st set of lights, right at next lights into George St, 2nd left into Broad St. At junct of Newlands Rd & Dashwood Rd*

Located just a short walk from the town centre, a warm welcome is assured at Treetops. Stylishly decorated bedrooms are well equipped, spacious and are the perfect respite for the business traveller or the holidaymaker. Hearty breakfasts and daily specials are served at individual tables in the modern dining room. The guest house now has two electric vehicle charging stations, which can be used by EV drivers to charge their vehicles overnight.

Rooms 4 en suite S £49-£58; D £70-£88* **Facilities** FTV DVD tea/coffee WiFi 🛁 **Extras** Bottled water **Parking** 3 **Notes** ⊗ No Children 12yrs Closed 24 Dec-2 Jan

Ashlea Guest House

★★★★ GUEST HOUSE

tel: 01295 250539 & 07818 431429   **fax:** 0872 115 4458 **58 Oxford Rd OX16 9AN**
email: info@ashleaguesthouse.co.uk **web:** www.ashleaguesthouse.co.uk
dir: *M40 junct 11, follow signs to Banbury. At 2nd rdbt take 1st exit (Concord Avenue), next rdbt 1st exit. Through 3 sets of lights, then into right hand lane at 4th set of lights, opposite junction*

Ashlea Guest House is a family run establishment where husband and wife team ensure their guests are warmly welcomed and made to feel at home. There is a choice of well presented rooms to suit all budgets. The guest house is the perfect base to explore the historic town of Banbury or the beautiful Cotswold countryside.

Rooms 6 rms (3 en suite) 6 annexe en suite (1 fmly) (5 GF) S £45-£55; D £65-£76 **Facilities** FTV DVD tea/coffee WiFi 🛁 **Parking** 13 **Notes** ⊗

Find out more this area with the AA Guide to The Cotswolds — see theAA.com/shop

---

The Cromwell Lodge

★★★★ INN

tel: 01295 259781 **fax:** 01295 276619 **9-11 North Bar OX16 0TB**
email: 6434@greeneking.co.uk **web:** www.oldenglish.co.uk
dir: *M40 junct 11 towards Banbury, through 3 sets of lights, property on left just before Banbury Cross*

Enjoying a central location, this 17th-century property is full of character. Diners can choose to eat in the lounge, the smart restaurant or the delightful walled garden and patio in summer. The comfortable bedrooms are furnished and equipped to a good standard. Parking is available at the rear of the building.

Rooms 23 en suite (1 fmly) (3 GF) **Facilities** Direct Dial **Parking** 20

Horse & Groom Inn

★★★★ ⌣ INN

tel: 01295 722142 & 07774 210943 **Milcombe OX15 4RS**
email: horseandgroominn@gmail.com **web:** www.thehorseandgroominn.co.uk
dir: *M40 junct 11, A422 towards Banbury. Onto A361 signed Chipping Norton, past Bloxham turn right signed Milcombe. At end of village*

This 17th-century coaching house is a traditional village pub with a good atmosphere, friendly service and comfortable, well-appointed bedrooms. The restaurant offers a good choice of well-prepared and tasty dishes. The establishment is convenient for Banbury, Stratford-upon-Avon and the Cotswolds.

Rooms 4 en suite (1 fmly) S £60-£75; D £70-£85* **Facilities** FTV DVD iPod docking station tea/coffee Dinner available WiFi 🎣 18 Fishing 🛁 **Conf** Max 40 Thtr 40 Class 30 Board 20 **Parking** 20

The Blinking Owl

★★★ INN

tel: 01295 730650 **Main St, North Newington OX15 6AE**
email: theblinkingowl@btinternet.com **web:** www.theblinkingowl.co.uk
dir: *B4035 from Banbury, 2m, sharp bend, right to North Newington, inn opposite green*

An important part of the community in the pretty village of North Newington, this former 17th-century inn retains many original features including impressive open fires. Straightforward food and a range of real ales are served in the beamed bar-lounges. The converted barn houses the three bedrooms and the restaurant, which is open at weekends.

Rooms 3 en suite S £70; D £70 **Facilities** tea/coffee Dinner available WiFi **Parking** 14 **Notes** ⊗ ⊜

BURFORD
Map 5 SP21

Premier Collection

Burford House
★★★★★ 🏠 GUEST ACCOMMODATION

tel: 01993 823151 **fax:** 01993 823240 **99 High St OX18 4QA**
email: stay@burfordhouse.co.uk **web:** www.burford-house.co.uk
dir: *A40 onto A361, on right half way down hill*

This charming house provides superb quality with a professional and friendly welcome. The bedrooms offer very good quality, space and comfort and combine elegance and practicality well. Rich colours adorn the walls and add to the feeling of warmth here. Wonderful lunches and afternoon teas are served daily, while dinners are available by prior arrangement.

Rooms 8 en suite (1 fmly) (1 GF) **Facilities** STV tea/coffee Dinner available Direct Dial Licensed WiFi **Notes** ⊗

The Maytime Inn
★★★★ INN

tel: 01993 822068 & 822635   **fax:** 0871 522 6560 **Asthall OX18 4HW**
email: info@themaytime.com **web:** www.themaytime.com

This country inn, located just a few miles outside of Burford, known as 'The gateway to the Cotswolds', has recently undergone a full refurbishment. It has retained its country charm albeit with some modern enhancement. The six en suite bedrooms are all individual in design, and offer a very comfortable stay. Food is available every day.

Rooms 2 en suite 4 annexe en suite (6 GF) S £85-£150; D £95-£150* **Facilities** FTV iPod docking station tea/coffee Dinner available Direct Dial WiFi 🛁 **Extras** Speciality toiletries **Parking** 30 **Notes** LB

The Angel at Burford
★★★★ 🍽 INN

tel: 01993 822714 **14 Witney St OX18 4SN**
email: enquiries@theangelatburford.co.uk **web:** www.theangelatburford.co.uk

Just off the high street in the picturesque market town of Burford, this 16th-century coaching inn features beamed ceilings and open fires. Guests can dine well in the restaurant, and the character bedrooms are thoughtfully equipped. Service is friendly here and families, children and dogs are all welcome.

Rooms 3 en suite S £90-£160; D £90-£160* (incl.dinner) **Facilities** FTV DVD Lounge Dinner available WiFi 🛁 **Extras** Refreshments - complimentary **Notes** LB

The Bull at Burford
★★★★ 🍽🍽 🏠 INN

tel: 01993 822220 **fax:** 01993 824055 **105 High St OX18 4RG**
email: info@bullatburford.co.uk **web:** www.bullatburford.co.uk
dir: *In town centre*

Situated in the heart of a pretty Cotswold town, The Bull was originally built in 1475 as a rest house for the local priory. It now has stylish, attractively presented bedrooms that reflect plenty of charm and character. Dinner is a must and the award-winning restaurant has an imaginative menu along with an excellent choice of wines. Lunch is served daily and afternoon tea is popular. There is a residents' lounge, and free WiFi is available.

Rooms 13 en suite 2 annexe en suite (1 fmly) S £65-£80; D £80-£170* **Facilities** FTV Lounge tea/coffee Dinner available WiFi **Conf** Thtr 24 Class 12 Board 12 **Parking** 6 **Notes** LB

Potters Hill Farm *(SP300148)*
★★★★ FARMHOUSE

tel: 01993 878018 & 07711 045207   **fax:** 01993 878018 **Leafield OX29 9QB**
web: www.pottershillfarm.co.uk
dir: *4.5m NE of Burford. A361 onto B4437, 1st right, 1st left, 1.5m past entrance to farm buildings, on left*

Located on a working farm in peaceful parkland that's teaming with diverse wildlife, this converted coach house stands next to the farmhouse. It has been appointed to offer comfortable bedrooms with many original features. Breakfast is served in the main farmhouse and features fresh, local produce.

Rooms 3 annexe en suite (1 fmly) (2 GF) S £45-£55; D £75-£85* **Facilities** FTV Lounge tea/coffee Dinner available WiFi 🛁 **Extras** Snacks, speciality toiletries **Parking** 5 **Notes** ⊗ 770 acres mixed/sheep/arable

The Golden Pheasant Inn

★★★ INN

tel: 01993 823223 fax: 01993 822621 **91 High St OX18 4QA**
email: bournehospitality@hotmail.co.uk web: www.goldenpheasantburford.com

This attractive inn is set on Burford's main street and dates, in part, back to the 16th century. Bedrooms vary in size but are well furnished with attractive fabrics and some period furniture. The bar and open-plan restaurant is full of character, and lunch and dinner is served here daily.

Rooms 12 rms (11 en suite) (1 pri facs) (2 GF) S £50-£100; D £50-£150 **Facilities** FTV tea/coffee Dinner available **Parking** 8 **Notes** ⊗

The Inn for All Seasons

★★★ ⇌ INN

tel: 01451 844324 fax: 01451 844375 **The Barringtons OX18 4TN**
email: sharp@innforallseasons.com web: www.innforallseasons.com
dir: *3m W of Burford on A40 towards Cheltenham*

This charming 16th-century coaching inn is close to the pretty village of Burford. The individually styled bedrooms are comfortable, and include a four-poster room, as well as a family room that sleeps four. The public areas include a cosy bar with oak beams and real fires. There is a good choice on the bar menu, and evening meals feature the best of local Cotswold produce. The inn is a dog-friendly establishment and there are ground-floor bedrooms with direct access to the garden and an exercise area.

Rooms 9 en suite 1 annexe en suite (2 fmly) (1 GF) S £75-£105; D £105-£120 **Facilities** FTV DVD Lounge TVL tea/coffee Dinner available WiFi ⅃ 18 Fishing 🎱 **Conf** Max 40 Thtr 40 Class 20 Board 25 **Parking** 60 **Notes** LB

CHIPPING NORTON   Map 10 SP32

Premier Collection

The Feathered Nest Country Inn

☆☆☆☆☆ ●●● ⌂ INN

tel: 01993 833030 fax: 01993 833031 **OX7 6SD**
email: info@thefeatherednestinn.co.uk web: www.thefeatherednestinn.co.uk

(For full entry see Nether Westcote (Gloucestershire))

Wild Thyme Restaurant with Rooms

★★★★ ●● RESTAURANT WITH ROOMS

tel: 01608 645060 **10 New St OX7 5LJ**
email: enquiries@wildthymerestaurant.co.uk web: www.wildthymerestaurant.co.uk
dir: *On A44 in town centre off market square*

Set in the bustling Cotswold market town of Chipping Norton, this restaurant with rooms offers three en suite bedrooms that are individually designed, well equipped, and have many thoughtful extras. The restaurant serves exciting Modern British food that is presented with relaxed and friendly service.

Rooms 3 en suite S £65-£85; D £75-£100* **Facilities** FTV DVD tea/coffee Dinner available WiFi **Extras** Mineral water, home-made biscuits **Notes** ⊗ Closed 1wk Jan & 1wk spring No coaches

CULHAM   Map 5 SU59

The Railway Inn

★★★ INN

tel: 01235 528046 fax: 01235 525183 **Station Rd OX14 3BT**
email: info@railwayinnculham.co.uk web: www.railwayinnculham.co.uk
dir: *2.5m SE of Abingdon-on-Thames on A415. Turn left signed Culham railway station*

The Railway Inn is located beside Culham railway station and is the perfect base to explore Abingdon, Didcot and Oxford. The inn offers a choice of comfortable and affordable rooms, a selection of real ales and home cooked food. In addition, there is a permanent marquee in the garden, which is suitable for all occasions.

Rooms 5 en suite 4 annexe en suite (2 fmly) S £50; D £72* **Facilities** FTV Lounge TVL tea/coffee Dinner available WiFi Pool table 🎱 **Parking** 30

FARINGDON   Map 5 SU29

Premier Collection

Buscot Manor B&B

★★★★★ BED AND BREAKFAST

tel: 01367 252225 & 07973 831690 **SN7 8DA**
email: romneypargeter@hotmail.co.uk web: www.buscotmanor.co.uk

Delightfully located in a peaceful village, Buscot Manor, a Queen Anne manor house built in 1692, is full of character and quality. Guests are welcome to use the two comfortable lounges in addition to the pleasant gardens, where tea may be enjoyed in the summer months. The two upper-floor bedrooms have private bathrooms and traditional four-poster beds. A more contemporary room is located on the ground floor. Breakfast is taken around one large table in the elegant dining room.

Rooms 2 en suite 1 annexe en suite (3 fmly) (1 GF) **Facilities** FTV DVD Lounge TVL tea/coffee WiFi ch fac ⅃ Fishing Riding Sauna Gym 🎱 Watersports weekends available **Extras** Speciality toiletries, fruit, snacks **Conf** Max 12 Board 12 **Parking** 30

FARINGDON *continued*

Chowle Farmhouse Bed & Breakfast

★★★★ BED AND BREAKFAST

tel: 01367 241688 **SN7 7SR**
email: info@chowlefarmhouse.co.uk **web:** www.chowlefarmhouse.co.uk
dir: *From Faringdon rdbt on A420, 2m W on right. From Watchfield rdbt 1.5m E on left*

Chowle is a delightful modern farmhouse in a quiet setting, just off the A420 and ideally placed for visiting Oxford and Swindon. Bedrooms are very well equipped, and there is a charming and airy downstairs breakfast room. An outdoor pool and hot tub are available to guests. There is ample parking.

Rooms 4 en suite (1 GF) S fr £65; D fr £85* **Facilities** FTV tea/coffee WiFi ⚡ ⚓ 9 Fishing Riding Sauna Gym ⚓ Clay pigeon shooting Indoor hot tub **Parking** 10 **Notes** LB

The Eagle

★★★★ ⍟⍟ INN

tel: 01367 241879 **Little Coxwell SN7 7LW**
email: eaglelittlecoxwell@gmail.com **web:** www.eagletavern.co.uk
dir: *M4 junct 15, A419, A420 signed Oxford, right into village*

Located in the peaceful village of Little Coxwell, in the beautiful Vale of the White Horse, The Eagle is a traditional inn with a welcoming atmosphere and a selection of real ales. The upstairs bedrooms, in a range of shapes and sizes, are very stylish and offer good comfort and ease of use. At both breakfast and dinner there's a variety of carefully prepared, quality dishes to choose from.

Rooms 6 en suite S £60-£70; D £70-£90* **Facilities** FTV Lounge tea/coffee Dinner available WiFi ⚓ **Notes** LB No coaches

The Trout at Tadpole Bridge

★★★★ ⍟ INN

tel: 01367 870382 **fax:** 01367 870912 **Buckland Marsh SN7 8RF**
email: info@troutinn.co.uk **web:** www.troutinn.co.uk
dir: *A420 Swindon to Oxford road, turn signed Bampton. Inn 2m on right*

The Trout is located 'where the River Thames meets the Cotswolds'. The peaceful location offers riverside walks from the door and berthing for up to six boats. Bedrooms and bathrooms are located adjacent to the inn and all rooms are very comfortable and well equipped with welcome extras. The main bar and restaurant offer an excellent selection of carefully prepared local produce at both lunch and dinner, together with cask ales and a varied choice of wines by the glass.

Rooms 3 en suite 3 annexe en suite (1 fmly) (4 GF) **Facilities** FTV tea/coffee Dinner available WiFi Fishing **Conf** Max 20 Thtr 20 Class 20 Board 20 **Parking** 40 **Notes** Closed 25-26 Dec No coaches

---

HENLEY-ON-THAMES   Map 5 SU78

Badgemore Park Golf Club

★★★★ GUEST ACCOMMODATION

tel: 01491 637300 **Badgemore Park, Badgemore RG9 4NR**
email: info@badgemorepark.com

Located close to Henley-on-Thames, this property offers comfortable guest accommodation in quiet surroundings within the secluded and private walled gardens, situated just 100 metres away from the main clubhouse. In summer months, dinner and a bar are available until 6pm. The venue also caters well for business meetings complete with own lounge and kitchen. Free WiFi available.

Rooms 7 rms S £70-£90; D £70-£105*

The Baskerville

★★★★ ⍾ INN

tel: 0118 940 3332 **Station Rd, Lower Shiplake RG9 3NY**
email: enquiries@thebaskerville.com **web:** www.thebaskerville.com
dir: *2m S of Henley in Lower Shiplake. Exit A4155 into Station Rd, inn signed*

Located close to Shiplake station and just a short drive from Henley, this smart accommodation is perfect for a business or leisure break. It is a good base for exploring the Oxfordshire countryside, and the enjoyable hearty meals, served in the cosy restaurant, use good local produce.

Rooms 4 en suite (1 fmly) S £89-£175; D £99-£175* **Facilities** STV DVD tea/coffee Dinner available WiFi 🛁 **Extras** Bottled water, sweets - complimentary **Conf** Max 15 Thtr 15 Class 15 Board 15 **Parking** 15 **Notes** Closed 25 Dec & 1 Jan No coaches

The Cherry Tree Inn
★★★★ ⊛ INN

tel: 01491 680430 **Main St, Stoke Row RG9 5QA**
email: enquiries@thecherrytreeinn.co.uk **web:** www.thecherrytreeinn.co.uk
dir: On A4155 from Henley-on-Thames exit B481 to Sonning Common. Follow Stoke Row signs, turn right for inn

This 400 year-old building is located in a pretty village on the outskirts of Henley-on-Thames. There are four en suite bedrooms which offer modern comforts and are set adjacent to the public house. A range of high quality wines complement the menus which often feature local produce.

Rooms 4 annexe en suite (4 GF) S £65-£100; D £70-£200* **Facilities** FTV Lounge TVL tea/coffee Dinner available WiFi ⛳ 18 **Parking** 30 **Notes** LB

Leander Club
★★★★ 🛏 GUEST ACCOMMODATION

tel: 01491 575782 **fax:** 01491 410291 **Leander Way RG9 2LP**
email: events@leander.co.uk **web:** www.leander.co.uk
dir: M4 junct 8/9 follow signs for Henley (A404M & A4130). Turn right immediately before Henley Bridge to Club & car park

This historic rowing club has opened its doors and made its delightful facilities available to guests. The location is breathtaking, particularly in the morning, when the rowers can be seen setting out on the river. The rooms are each named after various colleges and universities, and each is packed with interesting photos and memorabilia linking them with the Leander Club. Public areas also feature lots of trophies, pictures and artefacts, and it all makes for a most interesting place to stay.

Rooms 11 en suite (1 fmly) **Facilities** STV FTV TVL tea/coffee Dinner available Direct Dial Lift Licensed WiFi **Conf** Max 120 Thtr 120 Class 40 Board 20 **Parking** 60 **Notes** ⊗ No Children 10yrs Closed Xmas-New Year RS 1st wk Jul Henley Royal Regatta Civ Wed 120

Milsoms Henley-on-Thames
★★★★ RESTAURANT WITH ROOMS

tel: 01491 845780 & 845789 **20 Market Place RG9 2AH**
email: henley@milsomshotel.co.uk **web:** www.milsomshotel.co.uk
dir: In centre of town, close to town hall

The seven en suite bedrooms are located in a listed building above the Loch Fyne Restaurant in Henley's Market Place. Each bedroom is individually appointed and equipped to meet the needs of the modern traveller; particular care has been taken to incorporate original features into the contemporary design. The restaurant has a commitment to offer ethically sourced seafood.

Rooms 7 en suite (2 fmly) (1 GF) D £60-£95* **Facilities** FTV tea/coffee Dinner available WiFi **Extras** Still & sparkling water - complimentary **Parking** 7 **Notes** ⊗ No coaches

Phyllis Court Club
★★★★ GUEST ACCOMMODATION

tel: 01491 570500 **fax:** 01491 570528 **Marlow Rd RG9 2HT**
email: enquiries@phylliscourt.co.uk **web:** www.phylliscourt.co.uk
dir: A404 onto A4130 into town centre. Follow A4155, 150mtrs on right

Phyllis Court was founded in 1906 as a private members' club and has welcomed many distinguished visitors over the years. Set in 18 acres, with lawns sweeping down to the Thames, it offers a unique blend of traditional elegance and modern comforts. The club takes centre stage during Henley Royal Regatta week, being positioned opposite the finishing line. The individually styled bedrooms are well appointed and very comfortable. There is restricted meal service two days before and after the regattas in June and July. An excellent range of function venues is available, and the Grade II listed Grandstand Pavilion is perfect for weddings.

Rooms 17 en suite D £145-£175* **Facilities** FTV Lounge TVL tea/coffee Dinner available Direct Dial Lift Licensed WiFi **Extras** Speciality toiletries, trouser press, magazines **Conf** Max 250 Thtr 250 Class 100 Board 30 **Parking** 200 **Notes** RS 26-28 Dec, 2-3 Jan, regattas Jun-Jul Civ Wed 250

Slater's Farm
★★★ 🅰 BED AND BREAKFAST

tel: 01491 628675 **Peppard Common RG9 5JL**
email: stay@slatersfarm.co.uk **web:** www.slatersfarm.co.uk
dir: 3m W of Henley. A4130 left onto B481 to Rotherfield Peppard, pass Ruchetta Restaurant, left to primary school, house 200yds on right

This Georgian farmhouse is set on the edge of the Chilterns. Bedrooms are delightfully decorated and well-equipped. Breakfasts cater for all dietary needs.

Rooms 3 rms (1 pri facs) **Facilities** FTV tea/coffee Dinner available WiFi ⛳ 18 **Parking** 7 **Notes** ⊗ Closed Xmas

HORNTON · Map 11 SP34

Hornton Grounds Country House (SP384443)

★★★★ FARMHOUSE

tel: 01295 678318 **OX15 6HH**
email: Catherine@horntongrounds.com **web:** www.horntongrounds.co.uk
dir: *From Banbury onto A422 signed Stratford. Through Wroxton, pass New Inn pub, next right & follow long drive*

A very warm welcome waits at Hornton Grounds Country House, an impressive retreat set on a busy working farm. It's an ideal setting for those wishing to explore the north Cotswold countryside. Guests are encouraged to enjoy the extensive grounds on foot, or you can even bring your own horse (stabling available). Evening meals are available by prior arrangement.

Rooms 4 rms (2 en suite) (2 pri facs) S £36-£60; D £72-£100* **Facilities** TVL tea/coffee Dinner available WiFi ☕ 🏇 ⛳ Riding 🐾 **Parking** 8 **Notes** 200 acres pigs/beef/sheep

IDBURY · Map 10 SP21

Bould Farm (SP244209)

★★★★ FARMHOUSE

tel: 01608 658850 **fax:** 01608 658850 **OX7 6RT**
email: meyrick@bouldfarm.co.uk **web:** www.bouldfarm.co.uk
dir: *Off A424 signed Idbury, through village, down hill, round two bends, on right*

Accommodation is in a delightful 17th-century farmhouse that stands amid pretty gardens between Stow-on-the-Wold and Burford. The spacious bedrooms are carefully furnished and thoughtfully equipped, and some have stunning views of the surrounding countryside. Breakfast is served in the cosy dining room which features a cast-iron stove and stone-flagged floors.

Rooms 3 rms (2 en suite) (1 pri facs) (1 fmly) S £55-£60; D £75-£80 **Facilities** FTV TVL tea/coffee WiFi **Parking** 6 **Notes** ⊗ Closed Nov-Feb 400 acres arable/sheep/beef cows

KINGHAM · Map 10 SP22

The Kingham Plough

★★★★★ ⊛⊛ 🍴 INN

tel: 01608 658327 **The Green OX7 6YD**
email: book@thekinghamplough.co.uk **web:** www.thekinghamplough.co.uk
dir: *From Chipping Norton, take B4450 to Churchill. Take 2nd right to Kingham, left at T-junct in Kingham. Pub on right.*

The Kingham Plough is a quintessential Cotswold inn set in the pretty village of Kingham, just minutes away from the well-known Daylesford Organic Estate. The en suite bedrooms have Cotswold character and offer impressive quality and comfort. Eating here is memorable both at breakfast or in the evening and has been recognised by achieving two AA Rosettes; the team deliver excellent results using locally sourced produce.

Rooms 4 en suite 3 annexe en suite (2 fmly) S £75-£125; D £95-£145* **Facilities** FTV DVD iPod docking station Lounge tea/coffee Dinner available WiFi 🐾
Extras Speciality toiletries, home-made biscuits **Parking** 25 **Notes** Closed 25 Dec No coaches

Moat End

★★★★ 🏠 BED AND BREAKFAST

tel: 01608 658090 & 07765 278399 **The Moat OX7 6XZ**
email: moatend@gmail.com **web:** www.moatend.co.uk
dir: *Exit B4450 or A436 into village centre*

This converted barn lies in a peaceful Cotswold village and has splendid country views. Its well-appointed bedrooms either have a jacuzzi or large shower cubicles, one with hydro-massage jets. The attractive dining room leads to a comfortable beamed sitting room with a stone fireplace. Quality local ingredients are used in the wholesome breakfasts. The owner has won an award for green tourism by reducing the impact of the business on the environment.

Rooms 3 en suite (1 fmly) S £60-£70; D £78-£85* **Facilities** FTV Lounge tea/coffee WiFi 🐾 **Parking** 4 **Notes** LB ⊗ Closed Xmas & New Year

The Wild Rabbit

★★★★ INN

tel: 01608 658389 **Church St OX7 6YA**
email: theteam@thewildrabbit.co.uk **web:** www.thewildrabbit.co.uk

Situated in the idyllic Cotswold village of Kingham, this Grade II listed Georgian building has been lovingly restored to provide a complete home-from-home among some of the most beautiful countryside in Britain. The Wild Rabbit provides comfortable, well-equipped accommodation in pleasant surroundings. A good choice of menu for lunch and dinner is available, with fine use made of fresh and local produce. You can also be sure of a hearty breakfast.

Rooms 10 en suite **Facilities** Dinner available

OXFORD · Map 5 SP50

Premier Collection

Burlington House

★★★★★ 🏠 GUEST ACCOMMODATION

tel: 01865 513513 **fax:** 01865 311785 **374 Banbury Rd, Summertown OX2 7PP**
email: stay@burlington-house.co.uk **web:** www.burlington-house.co.uk
dir: *Opposite Oxford Conference Centre on A4165 on corner of Hernes Rd & Banbury Rd*

Guests are assured of a warm welcome and attentive service at this smart, beautifully maintained Victorian house, within walking distance of Summertown's fashionable restaurants. Elegant, contemporary bedrooms are filled with a wealth of thoughtful extras, and some open onto a pretty patio garden. Memorable breakfasts, served in the delightful dining room, include home-made preserves, fruit breads, granola and excellent coffee.

Rooms 10 en suite 2 annexe en suite **Facilities** FTV tea/coffee Direct Dial WiFi **Parking** 5 **Notes** ⊗ No Children 12yrs Closed 24 Dec-2 Jan

Premier Collection

The Bocardo

★★★★★ GUEST ACCOMMODATION

tel: 01865 591234 **24-26 George St OX1 2AE**
email: reservations@thebocardo.co.uk **web:** www.thebocardo.co.uk

The Bocardo is right in the heart of the city centre on George Street and located directly above Jamie's Italian Restaurant. The bedrooms here have stylish decor; all have flat-screen TVs, free WiFi and high quality bathrooms with power showers. This is a room-only establishment so breakfast is not available, however there are numerous bars, restaurants and cafés right on the doorstep.

Rooms 10 en suite **Facilities** STV WiFi **Extras** Speciality toiletries **Notes** ⊗

Parklands

★★★★ GUEST ACCOMMODATION

tel: 01865 554374 **fax:** 01865 559860 **100 Banbury Rd OX2 6JU**
email: stay@parklandsoxford.co.uk **web:** www.parklandsoxford.co.uk

Parklands enjoys a prominent position along the tree-lined Banbury road and is only a short walk from the city centre. This beautiful Victorian building was once the home of an Oxford Don and has a range of individually designed, spacious bedrooms. Secure parking is available and free WiFi is provided. The walled garden is a peaceful retreat and the residents' lounge is very well appointed.

Rooms 14 rms (13 en suite) (1 pri facs) S £55-£85; D £80-£140* **Facilities** FTV Lounge tea/coffee Direct Dial Licensed WiFi **Extras** Bottled water - complimentary **Parking** 14 **Notes** ⊗ No Children 18yrs

Red Mullions Guest House

★★★★ GUEST HOUSE

tel: 01865 742741 **fax:** 01865 769944 **23 London Rd, Headington OX3 7RE**
email: stay@redmullions.co.uk **web:** www.redmullions.co.uk
dir: M40 junct 8, A40. At Headington rdbt, 2nd exit signed Headington into London Rd

Red Mullions Guest House takes its name from the brick columns between the windows of the building. Modern bedrooms provide comfortable accommodation set within easy reach of motorway networks and Oxford city centre. Hearty breakfasts provide a good start to any day.

Rooms 16 rms (15 en suite) (1 pri facs) (3 fmly) (7 GF) S £85-£95; D £95-£120* **Facilities** STV FTV DVD tea/coffee WiFi **Extras** Bottled water - complimentary **Parking** 9 **Notes** ⊗

Remont Oxford

★★★★ GUEST ACCOMMODATION

tel: 01865 311020 **fax:** 01865 552080 **367 Banbury Rd OX2 7PL**
email: info@remont-oxford.co.uk **web:** www.remont-oxford.co.uk

Remont Oxford is in the popular Summertown area, some two miles from the city centre. The well-equipped bedrooms and bathrooms are modern and stylish and come with flat-screen TVs, complimentary WiFi and well stocked beverage trays; rooms all offer high quality and comfort. Parking is available and there is a delightful garden for guests to enjoy. Cooked and continental buffet breakfasts are served in the light and airy dining room.

Rooms 25 en suite (2 fmly) (8 GF) D £89-£152 **Facilities** FTV Lounge tea/coffee Lift WiFi **Parking** 18 **Notes** ⊗

Conifers Guest House

★★★★ GUEST ACCOMMODATION

tel: 01865 763055 **fax:** 01865 742232 **116 The Slade, Headington OX3 7DX**
email: stay@conifersguesthouse.co.uk **web:** www.conifersguesthouse.co.uk
dir: Exit ring road onto A420 towards city centre. Left onto B4495 (Windmill Rd), straight over at lights, house on left past Nuffield Orthopaedic Centre

Situated in the Headington area, Conifers is within walking distance of the Headington Hospitals, the BMW plant, Cowley Business Park, and Oxford Brookes, as well as Shotover Country Park. It is an impressive Edwardian house that provides comfortable accommodation in pine-furnished bedrooms. Breakfast is served in a smart, front-facing dining room. A private car park and a large rear garden are bonuses.

Rooms 11 en suite (4 fmly) **Facilities** FTV tea/coffee WiFi **Parking** 8 **Notes** ⊗

Cotswold House

★★★★ GUEST ACCOMMODATION

tel: 01865 310558 **fax:** 08721 107068 **363 Banbury Rd OX2 7PL**
email: d.r.walker@talk21.com **web:** www.cotswoldhouse.co.uk
dir: A40 onto A423 into city centre, follow signs to Summertown, house 0.5m on right

Situated in a leafy avenue close to the northern ring road and Summertown, this well-maintained house offers comfortable, well-equipped bedrooms and a relaxed atmosphere. Enjoy a traditional, hearty breakfast with vegetarian choices, including home-made muesli and fresh fruit, served in the bright attractive dining room.

Rooms 8 en suite (2 fmly) (2 GF) S £78-£85; D £120-£130 **Facilities** FTV Lounge tea/coffee WiFi 🅿 **Parking** 6 **Notes** ⊗

OXFORD *continued*

Galaxie

★★★★ GUEST ACCOMMODATION

tel: 01865 515688 **fax:** 01865 556824 **180 Banbury Rd OX2 7BT**
email: info@galaxie.co.uk **web:** www.galaxie.co.uk
dir: *1m N of Oxford centre, on right before shops in Summertown*

In the popular Summertown area of the city, the Galaxie has a welcoming
atmosphere and good-quality accommodation. The well-equipped bedrooms are all
very comfortable and come with a range of extra facilities. The attractive
conservatory dining room looks over the Oriental garden.

Rooms 32 rms (28 en suite) (3 fmly) S £65-£85; D £102-£130* **Facilities** TVL TV31B
tea/coffee Direct Dial Lift WiFi **Parking** 30 **Notes** ⊗

Marlborough House

★★★★ GUEST ACCOMMODATION

tel: 01865 311321 **fax:** 01865 515329 **321 Woodstock Rd OX2 7NY**
email: enquiries@marlbhouse.co.uk **web:** www.marlbhouse.co.uk
dir: *1.5m N of city centre. Exit at A34 & A44 junct for city centre, onto A4144 (Woodstock
Rd), premises on right by lights*

Marlborough House is just 1.5 miles north of Oxford's historic city centre, and is
within easy reach of the M40 and the A34 ring road. Custom built in 1990 to a
traditional design, the house sits comfortably alongside its Victorian neighbours in
a predominantly residential area. All 17 bedrooms have en suite facilities,
kitchenettes and mini-bars. WiFi covers the lounge and many of the rooms.

Rooms 13 en suite 4 annexe en suite (3 fmly) (4 GF) S £65-£85; D £85-£110*
Facilities FTV Lounge tea/coffee Direct Dial Licensed WiFi **Extras** Mini-bar -
chargeable **Parking** 6 **Notes** ⊗

The Falcon B&B

★★★ GUEST ACCOMMODATION

tel: 01865 511122 **fax:** 01865 246642 **88-90 Abingdon Rd OX1 4PX**
email: stay@falconoxford.co.uk **web:** www.falconoxford.co.uk

Enjoying a central location in the heart of Oxford, and overlooking The Queen's
College playing fields, this is an ideal base to explore the city. Spread over two
Victorian town houses, The Falcon has a range of individually styled, spacious
bedrooms. Freshly prepared breakfasts are served at individual tables and service
is friendly and attentive. WiFi is available throughout the house and secure parking
is available for guests.

Rooms 16 en suite (3 fmly) S £50-£60; D £75-£105* **Facilities** FTV TVL tea/coffee
WiFi **Parking** 9 **Notes** ⊗

Green Gables

★★★ GUEST ACCOMMODATION

tel: 01865 725870 **fax:** 01865 723115 **326 Abingdon Rd OX1 4TE**
email: green.gables@virgin.net **web:** www.greengables.uk.com
dir: *Exit ring road onto B4144 towards city centre, Green Gables 0.5m on left*

A warm welcome is assured at Green Gables, located within easy walking distance
of the city centre. Bedrooms are equipped with a range of practical and homely
extras, and a comprehensive breakfast is served in the cosy dining room. Guests
have free access to the internet in the smart conservatory-lounge, and private
parking is available.

Rooms 11 en suite (2 fmly) (4 GF) S £50-£57; D £80-£92 **Facilities** FTV Lounge tea/
coffee Direct Dial WiFi **Parking** 9 **Notes** ⊗ Closed 23-31 Dec

The Osney Arms Guest House

★★★ BED AND BREAKFAST

tel: 01865 243498 **45 Botley Rd OX2 0BP**
email: info@theosneyarms.co.uk **web:** www.theosneyarms.co.uk
dir: *A34, take exit signed A420 (Oxford). On Botley Rd (A420)*

The Osney Arms is a delightful house set on the outskirts of Oxford, within a few
minutes' walk of the centre. A very warm welcome is always assured by the owners,
and the house is large and recently refurbished retaining many original features.
Bedrooms and bathrooms offer very good quality and comfort with high standards
of cleanliness. The continental breakfast is a relaxing experience, hosted by the
owners. Some private parking is available.

Rooms 10 rms (8 en suite) (2 pri facs) (2 GF) **Facilities** DVD Lounge tea/coffee WiFi
🔒 **Conf** Max 15 Board 15 **Parking** 2 **Notes** ⊗

Oxford Guest House

★★★ GUEST HOUSE

tel: 01865 308833 & 07855 737373 **228 London Rd, Headington OX3 9EG**
email: oxfordguesthouse@gmail.com **web:** www.theoxfordguesthouse.co.uk
dir: M40 junct 8 onto A40 towards Oxford. At Headington rdbt take 2nd exit signed
Headington into London Rd (A420). On left after 2nd set of lights

The newly-built Oxford Guest House is located in a quiet residential area, and offers
well configured rooms finished to a very good standard. All rooms have been
equipped with flat-screen TVs and free WiFi. A choice of breakfasts is served daily
in the well-appointed breakfast room. Off-street parking is available.

Rooms 6 en suite (1 fmly) (2 GF) **Facilities** STV FTV tea/coffee WiFi 🔒 **Parking** 6
Notes LB ⊗

All Seasons Guest House

★★★ GUEST ACCOMMODATION

tel: 01865 742215 **fax:** 01865 429667 **63 Windmill Rd, Headington OX3 7BP**
email: info@allseasonshouse.com **web:** www.allseasonshouse.com
dir: Exit ring road onto A420 towards city centre. 1m, left at lights into Windmill Rd,
house 300yds on left

Within easy walking distance of the suburb of Headington, this double-fronted
Victorian house provides comfortable, homely bedrooms equipped with practical
and thoughtful extras. The elegant dining room features an original fireplace, and
secure parking is available behind the property.

Rooms 7 rms (5 en suite) (2 pri facs) (1 fmly) (1 GF) **Facilities** FTV TVL tea/coffee
WiFi **Parking** 6 **Notes** ⊗

Athena Guest House

★★★ GUEST ACCOMMODATION

tel: 01865 425700 & 07748 837144   **fax:** 01865 389597 **255 Cowley Rd, Cowley
OX4 1XQ**
email: info@athenaguesthouse.com **web:** www.athenaguesthouse.com
dir: 1.5m SE of city centre on B480

Located close to the shops and amenities in Cowley, this Victorian brick house
offers smart modern bedrooms on three floors, with many useful extras. Breakfast is
served in the bright and relaxing dining room, and limited parking is available.

Rooms 6 en suite (2 fmly) (2 GF) S £40-£75; D £50-£83 **Facilities** STV FTV DVD TVL
tea/coffee WiFi 🔒 **Conf** Max 15 **Parking** 7 **Notes** LB ⊗

Sports View Guest House

★★★ GUEST ACCOMMODATION

tel: 01865 244268 **fax:** 01865 249270 **106-110 Abingdon Rd OX1 4PX**
email: stay@sportsviewguesthouse.co.uk **web:** www.sportsviewguesthouse.co.uk
dir: Exit Oxford S at Kennington rdbt towards city centre, 1.25m on left

This family-run Victorian property overlooks The Queen's College sports ground.
Situated south of the city, it is within walking distance of the centre. Rooms are
comfortable, and the property benefits from off-road parking.

Rooms 20 rms (19 en suite) (1 pri facs) (4 fmly) (5 GF) S £52-£60; D £75-£89*
Facilities FTV Lounge tea/coffee WiFi 🔒 **Parking** 10 **Notes** ⊗ No Children 3yrs
Closed 25-26 Dec & 1 Jan

Newton House

★★★ Ⓐ BED AND BREAKFAST

tel: 01865 240561 **fax:** 01865 244647 **82-84 Abingdon Rd OX1 4PL**
email: stay@newtonhouseoxford.co.uk **web:** www.newtonhouseoxford.co.uk
dir: On A4144 (Abingdon Rd)

Located a few minutes walk from central attractions, this sympathetic conversion
of two Victorian houses retains many original features; furniture styles and decor
enhance the character. Comprehensive breakfasts are taken in an attractive
cottage-style dining room.

Rooms 14 en suite (2 fmly) (4 GF) S £65-£92; D £75-£105* **Facilities** FTV tea/coffee
Direct Dial WiFi **Parking** 8 **Notes** LB ⊗

| SHRIVENHAM | Map 5 SU28 |

The White Horse View

★★★★ BED AND BREAKFAST

tel: 01793 780301 & 07967 497926 **Cherry Bungalow, Station Rd SN6 8JL**
email: colin@thewhitehorseview.com **web:** www.thewhitehorseview.com

Located in the pretty village of Shrivenham, this bed and breakfast offers three
modern en suite bedrooms set away from the main house, each with their own
external seating and spectacular countryside views. Breakfasts are served in the
conservatory and feature local produce. A good location for those wanting to walk
the Ridgeway or take in the sights of historic Marlborough. The delightful 'Seasons
Day Spa' is also located on site offering an opportunity to relax and be well and
truly pampered.

Rooms 3 en suite (1 fmly) (3 GF) S £59-£75; D £59-£75* **Facilities** FTV DVD TVL tea/
coffee WiFi Pool table **Parking** 3 **Notes** RS 25-26 Dec room only

The Rose and Crown

Ⓤ

tel: 01793 710222 & 07908 666196 **3 High St, Ashbury SN6 8NA**
email: bookings@roseandcrowninn.co.uk **web:** www.roseandcrowninn.co.uk
dir: 3m from Shrivenham on B4000 in Ashbury

Currently the rating for this establishment is not confirmed. This may be due to a
change of ownership or because it has only recently joined the AA rating scheme.

Rooms 8 rms (7 en suite) (1 pri facs) (2 fmly) S £45-£55; D £55-£70 (room only)
Facilities FTV Lounge TVL tea/coffee Dinner available Licensed WiFi ↥ 18 Pool table
🔒 Games room **Conf** Max 20 Thtr 20 Class 20 Board 18 **Parking** 30 **Notes** LB

| STADHAMPTON | Map 5 SU69 |

Premier Collection

The Crazy Bear

★★★★★★ ⊛⊛ ▣ GUEST ACCOMMODATION

tel: 01865 890714 **fax:** 01865 400481 **Bear Ln OX44 7UR**
email: enquiries@crazybear-stadhampton.co.uk **web:** www.crazybeargroup.co.uk
dir: M40 junct 7, A329. In 4m left after petrol station, left into Bear Ln

This popular and attractive guest accommodation successfully combines modern chic with old world character. Cuisine is extensive and varied, with award-winning Thai and English restaurants under the same roof (both with AA Rosettes). Those choosing to make a night of it can enjoy staying in one of the concept bedrooms, all presented to a very high standard and styled with exciting themes; the 'infinity suites' have state-of-the-art facilities.

Rooms 5 en suite 12 annexe en suite (3 fmly) (4 GF) S £199-£399;
D £199-£399* **Facilities** STV FTV Dinner available Direct Dial Licensed WiFi ✆
Conf Max 40 Thtr 30 Class 30 Board 30 **Parking** 100 **Notes** ⊛ Civ Wed 200

| SWINBROOK | Map 5 SP21 |

The Swan Inn

★★★★★ ⊛⊛ INN

tel: 01993 823339 **OX18 4DY**
email: swaninnswinbrook@btconnect.com **web:** www.theswanswinbrook.co.uk
dir: 1m from A40, 2m E of Burford

The idyllic location and award-winning food are only two of the reasons why this is the perfect place for a comfortable business visit or a relaxed weekend. The bar offers real ales, local lagers and an appealing wine list. The accommodation is sumptuous and combines modern facilities with traditional comfort.

Rooms 6 en suite (1 fmly) (4 GF) **Facilities** FTV tea/coffee Dinner available WiFi ⚲ 18 Riding **Parking** 20 **Notes** Closed 25 Dec No coaches

| UFFINGTON | Map 5 SU38 |

The Fox and Hounds

★★★★ INN

tel: 01367 820680 **High St SN7 7RP**
email: enquiries@uffingtonpub.co.uk **web:** www.uffingtonpub.co.uk
dir: From A420 (S of Faringdon) follow Fernham or Uffington signs

The Fox and Hounds is a traditional pub located in the charming village of Uffington, and an ideal base to explore the surrounding area. The two cottage-style bedrooms are well appointed and offer a range of amenities. The beamed bar is well stocked and includes a selection of real ales, while the restaurant offers a daily menu with an oriental twist.

Rooms 2 annexe en suite (2 fmly) (2 GF) S £75-£85; D £75-£85* **Facilities** FTV DVD tea/coffee Dinner available WiFi ⚿ **Parking** 14

| WANTAGE | Map 5 SU38 |

La Fontana Restaurant with Accommodation

★★★★ ▭ RESTAURANT WITH ROOMS

tel: 01235 868287 **fax:** 01235 868019 **Oxford Rd, East Hanney OX12 0HP**
email: anna@la-fontana.co.uk **web:** www.la-fontana.co.uk
dir: A338 from Wantage towards Oxford. Restaurant on right in East Hanney

Guests are guaranteed a warm welcome at this family-run Italian restaurant located on the outskirts of the busy town of Wantage. The stylish bedrooms are individually designed, well equipped and very comfortable. Dinner should not be missed - the menu features a wide range of regional Italian specialities.

Rooms 8 en suite 7 annexe en suite (2 fmly) (4 GF) **Facilities** FTV TVL tea/coffee Dinner available Direct Dial WiFi **Parking** 30 **Notes** ⊛

The Star Inn

★★★★ ⊛⊛ INN

tel: 01235 751873 **fax:** 01235 751539 **Watery Ln, Sparholt OX12 9PL**
email: info@thestarsparsholt.co.uk
dir: from B4507, 4m W of Wantage turn right to Sparsholt. The Star Inn is signposted

Located in the picturesque village of Sparsholt, at the foot of the famous Ridgeway. At the heart of the community for over 300 years, The Star Inn has been completely and sympathetically refurbished. Bedrooms are now peacefully situated in a converted barn at the rear of the property, each providing a very good level of comfort. Food is a highlight of any stay, excellent quality ingredients are skilfully prepared and carefully presented.

Rooms 8 en suite S £75-£85; D £85-£135*

Hill Barn (SU337852)

★★★ FARMHOUSE

tel: 01235 751236 & 07885 368918 **Sparholt Firs OX12 9XB**
email: jmw@hillbarn.plus.com **web:** www.hillbarnbedandbreakfast.co.uk
dir: W of B4001 on The Ridgeway, 4m N of Wantage

This working farm offers en suite bedrooms with beautiful far-reaching views over the countryside. The atmosphere is friendly, and guests are able to relax either in the sitting room or in the garden. Breakfast is a highlight with home-made jams and other produce from the farm (when available).

Rooms 3 rms (2 en suite) (1 pri facs) D £70-£80* **Facilities** Lounge TVL TV2B tea/coffee Dinner available WiFi **Parking** 3 **Notes** LB ⊛ 100 acres horses

Greensands Guest House

★★★ GUEST ACCOMMODATION

tel: 01235 833338 **fax:** 01235 821632 **Reading Rd, East Hendred OX12 8JE**
email: greensands@outlook.com. **web:** www.greensandsguesthouse.co.uk
dir: A4185 to Rowstock rdbt, take A417, 1m on right

Greensands Guest House is in a peaceful, rural setting with good access to local towns, attractions and transport networks. Bedrooms vary in size and are comfortably appointed. Hearty breakfasts are served overlooking the attractive gardens. Ample parking available.

Rooms 7 rms (6 en suite) (1 pri facs) (2 fmly) (3 GF) **Facilities** FTV tea/coffee WiFi **Parking** 9

WHEATLEY — Map 5 SP50

Gidleigh House

★★★★ BED AND BREAKFAST

tel: 01865 875150 & 07733 026882 **27 Old London Rd OX33 1YW**
web: www.gidleighhousebb.co.uk
dir: *M40 junct 8 follow signs to Wheatley. Pass Asda on left & right turn to Hotton/Waterperry. Next right, marked private road*

You are assured of a warm, personal welcome at this modern home which is located on a private road in a quiet village just ten minutes from Oxford city centre and has easy access to the M40. The two en suite rooms are spacious, very comfortable and equipped with thoughtful extras. Relax over a newspaper in the conservatory at the family-style table while your breakfast is freshly prepared.

Rooms 2 en suite (2 fmly) **Facilities** TVL tea/coffee **Extras** Fruit, chocolates **Parking** 4 **Notes** ⊗ No Children 10yrs Closed 18 Dec-5 Jan ☺

WITNEY — Map 5 SP31

Premier Collection

Old Swan & Minster Mill

★★★★★ ◉ ⌂ INN

tel: 01993 774441 **fax:** 01993 702002 **Old Minster OX29 0RN**
email: enquiries@oldswanandminstermill.com **web:** www.oldswanandminstermill.com
dir: *Exit A40 signed Minster Lovell, through village right T-junct, 2nd left*

Located within its own stunning grounds and gardens including a private stretch of the River Windrush, the Old Swan & Minster Mill are two distinct accommodation areas, both with quality and individuality. Check-in is at the Minster Mill, where guests are welcomed and escorted to their room or suite. Old Swan rooms are traditional, with old oak beams and fireplaces in some rooms, while Mill rooms are more contemporary in style, many of which feature great views of the river and grounds. Award-winning cuisine is served in the dining room.

Rooms 60 en suite (4 fmly) (19 GF) S £145-£355; D £165-£375* **Facilities** FTV Lounge tea/coffee Dinner available Direct Dial WiFi ⚓ 🚤 🎣 18 Fishing Riding Gym Pool table Petanque **Extras** Speciality toiletries, decanter of sloe gin **Conf** Thtr 55 Class 22 Board 24 **Parking** 70 **Notes** LB No coaches Civ Wed 50

Corncroft Guest House

★★★★ GUEST ACCOMMODATION

tel: 01993 773298 **fax:** 01993 773298 **69-71 Corn St OX28 6AS**
web: www.corncroftguesthouse.com
dir: *A40 to town centre, from Market Square into Corn Street, 400mtrs on left*

Located in the quieter end of town, yet close to the centre, Corncroft Guest House offers comfortable well-equipped accommodation in a friendly atmosphere. Substantial breakfasts featuring local produce are served in the attractive dining room.

Rooms 11 en suite (1 fmly) (2 GF) S £65-£79.99; D £79.99-£95* **Facilities** FTV DVD TVL tea/coffee WiFi **Extras** Sweets - complimentary **Notes** Closed 24-26 Dec

Crofters Guest House

★★★★ GUEST ACCOMMODATION

tel: 01993 778165 & 07930 539021 **29 Oxford Hill OX28 3JU**
email: countycolours@hotmail.co.uk **web:** www.bedandbreakfastwitney.co.uk
dir: *Off A40 onto B4022 (Witney East). On right just after 1st set of lights*

Crofters Guest House is located on the west side of Witney, just a ten minute walk from the centre of town. There are two ground floor double en suite rooms and two twin rooms with shared facilities upstairs. A family style breakfast table arrangement is provided in the conservatory. WiFi is available throughout and off-road parking is a bonus.

Rooms 4 rms (2 en suite) (1 fmly) (2 GF) S £50-£65; D £75-£90* **Facilities** FTV TVL tea/coffee WiFi 🔒 **Parking** 5 **Notes** ⊗

Find out more about the AA's guest accommodation rating scheme on page 8

WOODSTOCK   Map 11 SP41

Premier Collection

The Glove House

★★★★★ BED AND BREAKFAST

tel: 01993 813475 & 07447 012832   **fax:** 01993 813475 **24 Oxford St OX20 1TS**
email: info@theglovehouse.co.uk **web:** www.theglovehouse.co.uk
dir: *M40 junct 8 onto A40, then A44 signed to Evesham/Woodstock. Glove House on right*

The Glove House is a 17th-century Grade II listed property, which has been sympathetically renovated and enjoys a prime location; Blenheim Palace is within walking distance. The three en suite bedrooms are very well appointed and ooze style, quality and comfort. Breakfast can be served in walled garden during the summer.

Rooms 3 en suite (2 fmly) S £140-£205; D £155-£220* **Facilities** FTV DVD iPod docking station Lounge tea/coffee WiFi **Extras** Speciality toiletries, mini-bar **Notes** ⊗ No Children 10yrs

Duke of Marlborough Country Inn

★★★★ INN

tel: 01993 811460 **fax:** 01993 810165 **Woodleys OX20 1HT**
email: sales@dukeofmarlborough.co.uk **web:** www.dukeofmarlborough.co.uk
dir: *1m N of Woodstock on A44 x-rds*

The Duke of Marlborough is just outside the popular town of Woodstock, convenient for local attractions including Blenheim Palace. Bedrooms and bathrooms are in an adjacent lodge-style building and offer high standards of quality and comfort. Dinner includes many tempting home-cooked dishes, complemented by a good selection of ales and wines.

Rooms 13 annexe en suite (2 fmly) (7 GF) **Facilities** FTV tea/coffee Dinner available Direct Dial WiFi ⌂ **Conf** Max 20 Thtr 20 Class 16 Board 12 **Parking** 42 **Notes** ⊗

The Blenheim Guest House & Tea Rooms

★★★★ A GUEST ACCOMMODATION

tel: 01993 813814 **fax:** 01993 813810 **17 Park St OX20 1SJ**
email: theblenheim@aol.com **web:** www.theblenheim.com
dir: *Off A44 in Woodstock to County Museum, after museum on left*

Taking its name from the famous palace just a stroll away, this delightful venue is also well suited for touring the Cotswolds. The 200-year-old house, which featured in a Miss Marple film, has an appealing tea room serving traditional tea and tasty home-made cakes.

Rooms 6 rms (5 en suite) (1 pri facs) (1 fmly) S £55-£65; D £75-£90* **Facilities** tea/coffee Licensed WiFi ⌂

The Townhouse

★★★ GUEST ACCOMMODATION

tel: 01993 810843 **15 High St OX20 1TE**
email: townhousewoodstock@hotmail.co.uk **web:** www.woodstock-townhouse.com
dir: *Off A44 into High St*

This early 18th-century stone town house is full of character and offers five individually styled, cosy en suite bedrooms. Situated in the heart of the town just a short walk from Blenheim Palace, it is an ideal base for exploring many famous Cotswold locations. Breakfasts are cooked to order and served in the small conservatory room overlooking the walled garden.

Rooms 5 en suite (1 fmly) S £65; D £83* **Facilities** FTV TVL tea/coffee WiFi **Notes** ⊗

RUTLAND

CLIPSHAM   Map 11 SK91

Beech House

★★★★ ◉◉ ⌂ INN

tel: 01780 410355 **fax:** 01780 410000 **Main St LE15 7SH**
email: rooms@theolivebranchpub.com **web:** www.theolivebranchpub.com
dir: *From A1 take B668 signed Stretton & Clipsham*

Beech House stands over the road from the Olive Branch restaurant. Its bedrooms are furnished with style and finesse, combining crisp linens, natural wood and retro-style accessories with traditional and modern furniture. Breakfasts are served in the Olive Branch and should not be missed. Excellent lunches and dinners are also available.

Rooms 5 en suite 1 annexe en suite (2 fmly) (3 GF) S £97.50-£175; D £115-£195 **Facilities** FTV DVD tea/coffee Dinner available Direct Dial WiFi ⌂ 18 ⌂ **Extras** Speciality toiletries - free; fruit - charged **Conf** Max 20 Thtr 20 Class 12 Board 16 **Parking** 10 **Notes** LB No coaches

LYDDINGTON   Map 11 SP89

The Marquess of Exeter

★★★★ ◉ INN

tel: 01572 822477 **fax:** 08082 801159 **52 Main St LE15 9LT**
email: info@marquessexeter.co.uk **web:** www.marquessexeter.co.uk
dir: *M1 junct 19, A14 to Kettering, then A6003 to Caldecott. Right into Lyddington Rd, 2m to village*

Situated in the picturesque Rutland countryside, the inn is appointed with contemporary touches whilst retaining many original features such as timber beam ceilings, log fires and flagstone floors. The stylish bedrooms, situated across a courtyard, are individually decorated and comfortable. The food is imaginative with the chef's 'sharing dishes' being particularly noteworthy.

Rooms 17 rms (16 en suite) (1 pri facs) (3 fmly) (10 GF) S £79.50-£104.50; D £99.50-£134.50* **Facilities** FTV tea/coffee Dinner available Direct Dial WiFi **Conf** Max 50 Thtr 50 Class 40 Board 40 **Parking** 60

Old White Hart

★★★★ INN

tel: 01572 821703 fax: 01572 821978 **51 Main St LE15 9LR**
email: mail@oldwhitehart.co.uk web: www.oldwhitehart.co.uk
dir: *1m S of Uppingham on main street, opposite village green*

Set opposite the village green in the heart of Lyddington, the Old White Hart offers a personal, attentive welcome. The accommodation can be found in converted cottages alongside the public house. All bedrooms have been thoughtfully renovated, and each is individually designed to offer quality and comfort. Enjoy home-prepared food in one of the cosy restaurants or bar, or experience alfresco dining in the garden during the summer months.

Rooms 2 en suite 8 annexe en suite (1 fmly) (2 GF) S £65-£75; D £90-£100*
Facilities FTV Lounge tea/coffee Dinner available Direct Dial WiFi 🏊 Petanque
Conf Max 20 Thtr 15 Class 15 Board 18 **Parking** 50 **Notes** LB ⊗ Closed 25 Dec

■ OAKHAM
Map 11 SK80

The Finch's Arms

★★★★ ◡ INN

tel: 01572 756575 **Oakham Rd, Hambleton LE15 8TL**
email: info@finchsarms.co.uk

Set in a fantastic location overlooking Rutland Water, The Finch's Arms is a 17th-century inn that has been refurbished to a high standard, offering modern and luxury rooms. Guests can enjoy afternoon tea in the bar or outdoor terrace, and fine dining available in the elegant Garden Room restaurant with fabulous views across the water. A more casual dining menu is also available with a good range of cask ales.

Rooms 10 rms S £80-£110; D £100-£130* **Facilities** Dinner available

Kirkee House

★★★★ BED AND BREAKFAST

tel: 01572 757401 **35 Welland Way LE15 6SL**
email: carolbeech@kirkeehouse.demon.co.uk web: www.kirkeehouse.co.uk
dir: *S of town centre. Exit A606 (High St) into Mill St, over level crossing, 400yds on left*

Located on a leafy avenue a short walk from the town centre, this immaculately maintained modern house provides comfortable bedrooms filled with homely extras. Comprehensive breakfasts, including local sausages and home-made jams, are served in the elegant conservatory-dining room which overlooks the pretty garden.

Rooms 2 en suite D £70-£72* **Facilities** FTV tea/coffee WiFi 🏊 **Parking** 2 **Notes** ⊗
No Children 7yrs 🖥

■ UPPINGHAM
Map 11 SP89

The Lake Isle

★★★★ ◉◉ 🍽 RESTAURANT WITH ROOMS

tel: 01572 822951 fax: 01572 824400 **16 High Street East LE15 9PZ**
email: info@lakeisle.co.uk web: www.lakeisle.co.uk
dir: *From A47, turn left at 2nd lights, 100yds on right*

This attractive town house centres around a delightful restaurant and small elegant bar. There is also an inviting first-floor guest lounge, and the bedrooms are extremely well appointed and thoughtfully equipped; spacious split-level cottage suites situated in a quiet courtyard are also available. The imaginative cooking and an extremely impressive wine list are highlights here.

Rooms 9 en suite 3 annexe rms (3 pri facs) (1 fmly) (1 GF) **Facilities** FTV tea/coffee Dinner available Direct Dial WiFi **Conf** Max 16 Board 16 **Parking** 7 **Notes** ⊗ RS Sun eve & Mon lunch closed No coaches

■ WHITWELL
Map 11 SK90

The Noel@Whitwell

★★★ ◡ INN

tel: 01780 460347 fax: 01780 460956 **Main Rd LE15 8BW**
email: info@thenoel.co.uk web: www.thenoel.co.uk

The Noel is a busy inn set close to Rutland Water. Accommodation is simply furnished and quite spacious; all rooms have en suite bathrooms, WiFi and modern flat-screen TVs. The public areas are in keeping with the style and character of the inn and the food and hospitality is what brings guest back again and again. Ample free car parking is available to all customers.

Rooms 8 en suite S £57; D £80 **Facilities** FTV Lounge TVL tea/coffee Dinner available Direct Dial ♿ 9 🏊 **Conf** Max 12 **Parking** 30 **Notes** Civ Wed 60

■ WING
Map 11 SK80

Kings Arms Inn & Restaurant

★★★★ ◉◉ 🍽 INN

tel: 01572 737634 fax: 01572 737255 **13 Top St LE15 8SE**
email: info@thekingsarms-wing.co.uk web: www.thekingsarms-wing.co.uk
dir: *1.5m off A6003 in village centre*

This traditional village inn, with its open fires, flagstone floors and low beams, dates from the 17th century. The restaurant is more contemporary and offers a wide range of interesting, freshly produced dishes. Service is attentive and friendly. The spacious, well-equipped bedrooms are in The Old Bake House and Granny's Cottage, in the nearby courtyard.

Rooms 8 en suite (2 fmly) (4 GF) S £65-£75; D £80-£90 (room only)* **Facilities** FTV tea/coffee Dinner available WiFi **Parking** 30 **Notes** LB RS Nov-Apr closed Mon, Tue lunch & Sun eve (ex BHs)

SHROPSHIRE

BISHOP'S CASTLE   Map 15 SO38

Boars Head

★★★★ INN

tel: 01588 638521 **Church St SY9 5AE**
email: info@boarsheadhotel.co.uk **web:** www.boarsheadhotel.co.uk

The Boars Head is situated in the centre of Bishop's Castle, and is a traditional inn with comfortable and spacious bedrooms in a separate annexe. The inn incorporates a post office with a cash machine and phone top-up facilities, and a hair salon. Food is on offer all day and good quality ingredients are used to create a well-balanced menu. Parking is to the rear of the inn.

Rooms 3 annexe en suite (1 fmly) (3 GF) **Facilities** FTV DVD iPod docking station Lounge tea/coffee Dinner available WiFi **Extras** Fridge, digital safe, mineral water **Parking** 60 **Notes** ⊗

BRIDGNORTH   Map 10 SO79

The Halfway House Inn

★★★ INN

tel: 01746 762670 **fax:** 01746 802020 **Cleobury Mortimer Rd WV16 5LS**
email: info@halfwayhouseinn.co.uk **web:** www.halfwayhouseinn.co.uk
dir: *1.5m from town centre on B4363 to Cleobury Mortimer*

Located in a rural area, this 16th-century inn has been renovated to provide good standards of comfort, while retaining its original character. The bedrooms, some in converted stables and cottages, are especially suitable for families and groups.

Rooms 10 en suite (10 fmly) (6 GF) S £50-£65; D £65-£95* **Facilities** FTV TVL tea/coffee Dinner available WiFi ⚓ 18 Fishing Pool table ⚓ **Conf** Max 30 Thtr 30 Class 24 Board 20 **Parking** 30 **Notes** LB Closed 25-26 Dec RS Winter Sun eve (ex BHs) from 5pm

CHURCH STRETTON   Map 15 SO49

Premier Collection

Field House

★★★★★ GUEST HOUSE

tel: 01694 771485 **Cardington Moor, Cardington SY6 7LL**
email: pjsecrett@talktalk.net **web:** www.fieldhousebandb.co.uk
dir: *A49 onto B4371 at lights in Church Stretton. Left after 3.5m signed Cardington, left in 1m, house 0.5m on right*

This delightful old cottage stands in nine acres of grounds and gardens, and is quietly located in a picturesque valley. Field House provides tastefully appointed, modern accommodation which includes a bedroom on the ground floor. Separate tables are laid out for guests in the pleasant dining room where a hearty breakfast is served. There is also a conservatory lounge with views out to the well maintained gardens.

Rooms 3 en suite (1 GF) S £45; D £70-£80* **Facilities** FTV Lounge tea/coffee Direct Dial WiFi Pool table ⚓ Table tennis **Extras** Speciality toiletries, kitchen for guests' use **Parking** 3 **Notes** LB ⊗ Closed Nov-Feb

Court Farm *(SO514951)*

★★★★ 🏠 FARMHOUSE

tel: 01694 771219 **fax:** 01694 771219 **Gretton SY6 7HU**
email: alison@courtfarm.eu **web:** www.courtfarm.eu
dir: *Turn off B4371 at Longville, left at x-rds, 1st on left*

Located in the pretty village of Gretton, this Grade II listed stone-built Georgian house is on a 330-acre working farm, and its bedrooms overlook the pretty gardens. It has been home to the Norris family since 1898, and over the years they have sympathetically restored and modernised the building. Comprehensive breakfasts are served in an elegant dining room, and a comfortable guest lounge is also available. Court Farm is an ideal base for exploring Shropshire and surrounding areas.

Rooms 2 en suite S £50-£55; D £70-£80* **Facilities** FTV TVL tea/coffee WiFi ⚓ **Parking** 4 **Notes** ⊗ No Children 12yrs 🐾 330 acres mixed

Belvedere Guest House

★★★★ GUEST HOUSE

tel: 01694 722232 **Burway Rd SY6 6DP**
email: info@belvedereguesthouse.co.uk **web:** www.belvedereguesthouse.co.uk
dir: *Exit A49 into town centre, over x-rds into Burway Rd*

Popular with walkers and cyclists and located on the lower slopes of the Long Mynd, this impressive, well-proportioned Edwardian house has a range of homely bedrooms, equipped with practical extras and complemented by modern bathrooms. Ground-floor areas include a cottage-style dining room overlooking the pretty garden and a choice of lounges.

Rooms 7 rms (6 en suite) (2 fmly) S £35-£40; D £60-£68 **Facilities** TVL tea/coffee WiFi ⚓ **Extras** Mini-fridge, snacks, bottled water - chargeable **Parking** 9 **Notes** LB

The Bucks Head

★★★★ INN

tel: 01694 722898 & 07811 364416 **42 High St SY6 6BX**
email: lloyd.nutting@btconnect.com **web:** www.the-bucks-head.co.uk
dir: *A49 N or S, turn into Church Stretton. At top of town turn left, Bucks Head on right*

The Bucks Head enjoys a central location in the heart of historic Church Stretton, and is a vibrant modern inn. There are high levels of comfort and up-to-date facilities together with original charm and character. The comfortable bedrooms are complemented by smart en suite bathrooms, and the attractive open-plan public areas are the perfect setting for enjoying food and drinks. The hospitality is warm and genuine.

Rooms 4 en suite **Facilities** FTV tea/coffee Dinner available WiFi **Notes** ⊗ No Children 5yrs No coaches

North Hill Farm

★★★★ BED AND BREAKFAST

tel: 01694 771532 **Cardington SY6 7LL**
email: cbrandon@btinternet.com **web:** www.northhillfarmbandb.co.uk
dir: *From Cardington S onto Church Stretton road, right signed Cardington Moor, farm at top of hill on left*

Deep among the Shropshire hills, on a small farm, this delightful house offers comfortable accommodation with fabulous countryside views. There is a small, cosy sitting room for guests in the main house, and breakfast is served at one large table in the dining room. There are two bedrooms in the main house with another in an annexe, and a cottage room which provides high quality, spacious family accommodation.

Rooms 2 rms (2 pri facs) 2 annexe en suite (2 GF) S £40-£42; D £56-£90*
Facilities FTV Lounge tea/coffee WiFi ☕ Stabling & grazing for guests horses
Parking 6 **Notes** LB Closed Xmas ✆

| CRAVEN ARMS | Map 9 SO48 |

Strefford Hall Farm *(SO444856)*

★★★★ FARMHOUSE

tel: 01588 672383 **fax:** 0870 132 3818 **Strefford SY7 8DE**
email: strefford@btconnect.com **web:** www.streffordhall.co.uk
dir: *A49 from Church Stretton, S for 5.5m to Strefford, 0.25m past Travellers Rest Inn signed left. Strefford Hall 0.25m on right*

This well-proportioned Victorian house stands at the foot of Wenlock Edge. The spacious bedrooms, filled with homely extras, have stunning views of the surrounding countryside. Breakfast is served in the elegant dining room and a comfortable lounge is also available.

Rooms 3 en suite (1 fmly) S £40-£50; D £76-£80* **Facilities** DVD Lounge TVL tea/coffee WiFi **Parking** 3 **Notes** LB ✆ Closed end Oct-beg Apr ✆ 350 acres arable/beef/sheep

| DORRINGTON | Map 15 SJ40 |

Upper Shadymoor Farm *(SJ454021)*

★★★★ FARMHOUSE

tel: 01743 718670 **Stapleton SY5 7AL**
email: kevan@shadymoor.co.uk **web:** www.shadymoor.co.uk

Upper Shadymoor Farm has it all, the shabby-chic rooms, the formal dining room, the family atmosphere, the tranquil location, the farm animals, the deer park and much more. Expect a warm welcome from the Fox family and a truly enjoyable experience. Produce from the farm is used at dinner and breakfast.

Rooms 3 en suite (1 fmly) S £50-£65; D £80-£90* **Facilities** Lounge tea/coffee Dinner available WiFi Fishing ☕ **Parking** 20 **Notes** ✆ 200 acres beef/mixed/sheep

Caro's Bed & Breakfast

★★★ BED AND BREAKFAST

tel: 01743 718790 & 07739 285263 **1 Higher Netley SY5 7JY**
email: info@carosbandb.co.uk **web:** www.carosbandb.co.uk
dir: *1m SW of Dorrington. Exit A49 in Dorrington signed Picklescott, 1m left onto driveway by stone bridge, signed Higher Netley*

Self-contained accommodation is provided in this converted barn, south-west of Dorrington. Bedrooms, with smart modern bathrooms, are equipped with thoughtful

extras and the open-plan ground floor contains a dining area and a comfortable lounge with a wood-burning stove.

Rooms 2 en suite (1 fmly) D £65* **Facilities** FTV DVD Lounge tea/coffee WiFi ☕ **Parking** 4 **Notes** LB Closed 21-28 Dec ✆

| GRINSHILL | Map 15 SJ52 |

The Inn at Grinshill

★★★★★ ◉◉ ⊕ INN

tel: 01939 220410 **The High St SY4 3BL**
email: info@theinnatgrinshill.co.uk **web:** www.theinnatgrinshill.co.uk
dir: *N of Shrewsbury on A49, after 7m turn left, inn 500yds on left*

This inn is part Grade II listed and many areas have been uncovered to highlight the original features. It is located under the lee of Grinshill in a delightful village with beautiful countryside close by; the Welsh border is within easy driving distance as are Shrewsbury, Telford and Welshpool. The accommodation is comfortable, and real ales and award-winning food are available in the spacious restaurant. Guests are very welcome to make use of the grounds.

Rooms 6 en suite **Facilities** FTV TVL tea/coffee Dinner available WiFi ⬇ 36 **Parking** 30 **Notes** Closed 1st wk Jan RS Sun eve, Mon & Tue

| HADNALL | Map 15 SJ52 |

Saracens at Hadnall

★★★★ ◉◉ RESTAURANT WITH ROOMS

tel: 01939 210877 **fax:** 01939 210877 **Shrewsbury Rd SY4 4AG**
email: reception@saracensathadnall.co.uk **web:** www.saracensathadnall.co.uk
dir: *M54 onto A5 towards Shrewsbury, take A49 towards Whitchurch. In Hadnall, property diagonally opposite church*

This Georgian Grade II listed former farmhouse and village pub has been tastefully converted into a very smart restaurant with rooms, without any loss of original charm and character. The bedrooms are thoughtfully equipped. Skilfully prepared meals are served in either the elegant dining room or the adjacent conservatory, where there is a glass-topped well.

Rooms 5 en suite S £50; D £70-£85* **Facilities** FTV tea/coffee Dinner available **Parking** 20 **Notes** LB ✆ Closed 24-26 & 29-30 Dec No coaches

| IRONBRIDGE | Map 10 SJ60 |

Broseley House

★★★★ GUEST HOUSE

tel: 01952 882043 & 07790 732723 **1 The Square, Broseley TF12 5EW**
email: info@broseleyhouse.co.uk **web:** www.broseleyhouse.co.uk
dir: *1m S of Ironbridge in Broseley town centre*

A warm welcome is assured at this impressive Georgian house in the centre of Broseley. Quality, individual decor and soft furnishings highlight the many original features, and the thoughtfully furnished bedrooms are equipped with a wealth of homely extras. Comprehensive breakfasts are taken in an elegant dining room; a stylish apartment is also available.

Rooms 6 en suite (2 fmly) (1 GF) **Facilities** FTV DVD iPod docking station tea/coffee WiFi ☕ **Extras** Fridge **Notes** No Children 5yrs

LUDLOW   Map 10 SO57

Premier Collection

The Clive Bar & Restaurant with Rooms

★★★★★ ◉◉ RESTAURANT WITH ROOMS

tel: 01584 856565 & 856665   **fax:** 01584 856661 **Bromfield SY8 2JR**
email: info@theclive.co.uk **web:** www.theclive.co.uk
dir: *2m N of Ludlow on A49 in Bromfield*

The Clive is just two miles from the busy town of Ludlow and is a convenient base for visiting the local attractions or for business. The bedrooms, located in an annexe, are spacious and very well equipped; some are suitable for families and many are on the ground-floor level. Meals are available in the well-known Clive Restaurant or in the bar areas. The property also has a small meeting room.

Rooms 15 annexe en suite (9 fmly) (11 GF) S £70-£95; D £100-£125*
Facilities FTV tea/coffee Dinner available Direct Dial WiFi **Extras** Mini-bar with local produce **Conf** Max 40 Thtr 40 Class 40 Board 24 **Parking** 100 **Notes** LB ⊗ Closed 25-26 Dec

Premier Collection

Old Downton Lodge

★★★★★ ⌂ ☕ GUEST ACCOMMODATION

tel: 01568 771826 & 07797 475881   **fax:** 01568 630825
Downton on the Rock SY8 2HU
email: bookings@olddowntonlodge.com **web:** www.olddowntonlodge.com
dir: *From Ludlow onto A49 towards Shrewsbury, 1st left onto A4113. After 1.9m turn left signed Downton, 3m on single track road. Turn right, signed*

Originally a farm, this high-end establishment has kept bags of character, and is a stylish, comfortable and tranquil place to stay. Bedrooms are spacious and very well appointed, with comfortable beds and luxurious bathrooms. Old Downton Lodge is within easy reach of Ludlow's many attractions, yet has a peaceful country location with good parking, pleasant grounds, and is an ideal area for walks and country pursuits. There is an honesty bar and excellent wine list. Breakfast should not be missed, and excellent evening meals are available with 24 hours notice.

Rooms 9 en suite (5 GF) S £105-£160; D £105-£160* **Facilities** FTV DVD Lounge tea/coffee Dinner available Direct Dial Licensed WiFi **Extras** Speciality toiletries, home-made biscuits **Conf** Max 30 Thtr 30 Class 30 Board 30 **Parking** 20 **Notes** LB No Children Closed 24-26 Dec

37 Gravel Hill

★★★★ BED AND BREAKFAST

tel: 01584 877524 **SY8 1QR**
email: angelastraker@btinternet.com
dir: *Close to town centre*

This charming old house is within walking distance of the town centre. It provides good quality, thoughtfully equipped accommodation, and there is also a comfortable sitting room. Guests share one large table in the elegant breakfast room.

Rooms 2 rms (1 en suite) (1 pri facs) **Facilities** TVL tea/coffee WiFi ⌂ **Notes** ⊗

Angel House Bed and Breakfast

★★★★ BED AND BREAKFAST

tel: 01584 891377 & 07568 142626   **Angel Bank, Bitterley SY8 3HT**
email: angelhouse48@gmail.com **web:** www.angelhousecleehill.co.uk
dir: *On A4117 towards Kidderminster*

Angel House has a super location, set just outside the busy hustle and bustle of Ludlow; the house has plentiful parking and super views. The friendly proprietors are very attentive and provide a comfortable place to stay. Bedrooms are very well appointed with lots of thoughtful extras. The gardens are spacious and home to the chickens that provide breakfast eggs.

Rooms 2 en suite (1 fmly) **Facilities** FTV DVD Lounge tea/coffee Dinner available WiFi ⌂ **Extras** Speciality toiletries **Parking** 3 **Notes** No Children 7yrs

Haynall Villa *(SO543674)*

★★★★ FARMHOUSE

tel: 01584 711589 & 711061   **fax:** 01584 711589 **Little Hereford SY8 4BG**
email: bookings@haynallvilla.co.uk **web:** www.bedandbreakfastludlow.com
dir: *A49 onto A456, at Little Hereford right signed Leysters & Middleton on the Hill. Villa 1m on right*

Surrounded by immaculate gardens in the pretty hamlet of Little Hereford, this Victorian house retains many original features, which are enhanced by the furnishings and decor. Bedrooms are filled with lots of homely extras and the lounge has an open fire.

Rooms 3 rms (2 en suite) (1 pri facs) (1 fmly) S £33-£50; D £65-£75* **Facilities** FTV TVL tea/coffee Dinner available WiFi Fishing ⌂ **Parking** 3 **Notes** LB No Children 6yrs Closed mid Dec-mid Jan 72 acres arable

130 Corve Street

★★★★ BED AND BREAKFAST

tel: 01584 875548 **fax:** 08723 523397 **130 Corve St SY8 2PG**
email: info@130corvestreet.co.uk **web:** www.130corvestreet.co.uk
dir: *N side of town on B4361, adjacent to Tesco supermarket*

Expect a warm welcome at this Grade II listed building, situated within easy access of the town's many amenities and restaurants. The attractive bedrooms, situated on the ground floor at the rear, are comfortable and have independent entrances. Hearty breakfasts are served in the first-floor dining room. There is off-road parking close by.

Rooms 3 en suite (3 GF) D £75* **Facilities** FTV DVD tea/coffee WiFi **Parking** 3 **Notes** LB ⊗ No Children 12yrs

The Church Inn

★★★ INN

tel: 01584 872174 fax: 01584 877146 **The Buttercross SY8 1AW**
web: www.thechurchinn.com
dir: *In town centre at top of Broad St, behind Buttercross*

Set right in the heart of Ludlow, this Grade II listed inn has quality accommodation with smart modern bathrooms, some with spa baths. Other areas include a small lounge, a well-equipped meeting room, and cosy bar areas where imaginative food and real ales are served.

Rooms 10 en suite (3 fmly) **Facilities** TVL tea/coffee Dinner available Direct Dial
Conf Max 38 **Notes** No coaches

MARKET DRAYTON   Map 15 SJ63

Premier Collection

Ternhill Farm House & The Cottage Restaurant

★★★★★ ◉◉ 🍴 RESTAURANT WITH ROOMS

tel: 01630 638984 fax: 01630 638752 **Ternhill TF9 3PX**
email: info@ternhillfarm.co.uk web: www.ternhillfarm.co.uk
dir: *On junct A53 & A41, archway off A53 to back of property*

This elegant Grade II listed Georgian farmhouse stands in a large pleasant garden and offers quality accommodation. There is a choice of comfortable lounges, and The Cottage Restaurant features imaginative dishes using local produce. Dinner is served Tuesday to Saturday. Secure parking is an additional benefit.

Rooms 7 en suite **Facilities** FTV DVD Lounge tea/coffee Dinner available WiFi
Extras Speciality toiletries **Parking** 21 **Notes** LB ⊗ No Children 14yrs RS Sun & Mon restaurant closed

The Four Alls Inn

★★★ ➧ INN

tel: 01630 652995 fax: 01630 653930 **Woodseaves TF9 2AG**
email: inn@thefouralls.com web: www.thefouralls.com
dir: *On A529 1m S of Market Drayton*

This country inn provides spacious open-plan public areas and has a strong local following for its food and real ales. Bedrooms, which are in a purpose-built chalet block, offer a good balance between practicality and homeliness. The superb beer gardens are adorned with attractive floral displays in summer.

Rooms 9 annexe en suite (4 fmly) (9 GF) S £45-£47; D £65-£67* **Facilities** FTV tea/coffee Dinner available Direct Dial WiFi 🔒 **Conf** Max 100 Thtr 100 Class 100 Board 30 **Parking** 60 **Notes** LB ⊗ Closed 24-26 Dec

Who are the AA's award-winning B&Bs? For details see pages 12-16

The Tudor House

★★★ INN

tel: 01630 657523 & 01257 248012   fax: 01630 657806 **1 Cheshire St TF9 1PD**
email: tudor@alfatravel.co.uk web: www.thetudorhousehotel.com
dir: *A53 onto A529 (Adderley Rd), at next rdbt 2nd exit into Cheshire St*

This beautiful property and former coaching inn is located in the heart of the town and has a public bar full of character. The fully equipped bedrooms are well laid out and are equally suited to both business and leisure guests. Parking is shared with a hotel just a short distance away.

Rooms 10 en suite (3 fmly) **Facilities** FTV TVL tea/coffee Dinner available WiFi ⚐ 18
🔒 **Extras** Speciality toiletries - complimentary **Conf** Thtr 40 Class 6 Board 12
Notes ⊗ No coaches

MELVERLEY   Map 15 SJ31

Big Bear Lodge

★★★★ BED AND BREAKFAST

tel: 01691 682640 **Hendre Villa SY10 8PH**
web: www.bigbearlodge.co.uk

Big Bear Lodge offers comfortable accommodation in a purpose-built lodge, which has a very spacious lounge and dining area. Bedrooms are comfortably appointed, and bathrooms are stylishly finished. The proprietors are a friendly couple, who are keen to provide a relaxing environment, but also offer an impressive range of activities for the more adventurous. Breakfasts are very pleasant.

Rooms 3 en suite (1 fmly) (3 GF) S £50; D £75-£85* **Facilities** FTV DVD Lounge tea/coffee WiFi Fishing Riding 🔒 **Conf** Max 6 Class 6 **Parking** 3 **Notes** LB ⊗

MUCH WENLOCK   Map 10 SO69

Yew Tree Farm (SO543958)

★★★★ 🍴 FARMHOUSE

tel: 01694 771866 **Longville in the Dale TF13 6EB**
email: enquiries@yewtreefarmshropshire.co.uk web: www.yewtreefarmshropshire.co.uk
dir: *5m SW of Much Wenlock. N off B4371 at Longville, left at pub, right at x-rds, farm 1.2m on right*

Yew Tree Farm is peacefully located between Much Wenlock and Church Stretton, in ten acres of unspoiled countryside, where pigs, sheep and chickens are reared. Own produce is a feature on the comprehensive breakfast menu, bedrooms are equipped with thoughtful extras, and a warm welcome is assured.

Rooms 2 rms (1 en suite) (1 pri facs) S £35-£45; D £55-£75* **Facilities** FTV TVL tea/coffee WiFi ch fac 🔒 **Extras** Snacks, bottled water - complimentary **Parking** 4
Notes LB Closed 24-30 Dec ⊛ 10 acres small holding/sheep/pigs

Talbot Inn

★★★ Ⓐ INN

tel: 01952 727077 fax: 01952 728436 **High St TF13 6AA**
email: the_talbot_inn@hotmail.com web: www.thetalbotinnwenlock.co.uk
dir: *In village centre on A458*

Located on the historic High Street, this 17th-century timber-framed inn retains many original features. Public areas include cosy bars, a pretty enclosed courtyard, and the comfortable bedrooms are in a converted malt house.

Rooms 6 annexe en suite (1 GF) **Facilities** TVL tea/coffee Dinner available **Parking** 6
Notes ⊗ Closed 25 Dec

MUNSLOW   Map 10 SO58

Crown Country Inn

★★★★ ◉◉ ⌂ INN

tel: 01584 841205 **SY7 9ET**
email: info@crowncountryinn.co.uk **web:** www.crowncountryinn.co.uk
dir: *Off B4368 into village*

Located between Much Wenlock and Craven Arms, this impressive pastel-coloured and half-timbered Tudor inn is full of character and charm with stone floors, exposed beams and blazing log fires during winter. The smart pine-furnished bedrooms are in a converted stable block, and the spacious public areas include two dining rooms.

Rooms 3 en suite (1 GF) **Facilities** FTV DVD tea/coffee Dinner available WiFi 🐾 **Conf** Max 30 Thtr 30 Class 30 Board 20 **Parking** 20 **Notes** LB ⊗ No Children 12yrs Closed 25 Dec RS Closed Sun eve & Mon for food & drink No coaches

NORTON   Map 10 SJ70

The Hundred House

★★★★★ ◉◉ INN

tel: 01952 580240 & 0845 644 6100   **fax:** 01952 580260 **Bridgnorth Rd TF11 9EE**
email: reservations@hundredhouse.co.uk **web:** www.hundredhouse.co.uk
dir: *M54 junct 5, follow signs for Bridgnorth (A442), midway between Bridgnorth & Telford*

This interesting property has a genuine atmosphere of rural charm, setting it apart from the modern style of country 'food destination' pubs. A rabbit warren of public bars and restaurants, it provides respite for weary travellers and locals alike, many of whom come for the excellent meals. Bedrooms are individually designed, with quirky furnishings and decor, and are well equipped. A large beer garden provides for good weather, with well-stocked herb and flower gardens to encourage a wander.

Rooms 9 en suite (4 fmly) S £60-£79; D £69-£120* **Facilities** FTV tea/coffee Dinner available Direct Dial WiFi ⅃ 18 🐾 **Extras** Bottled water, sweets **Conf** Max 100 Thtr 80 Class 30 Board 35 **Parking** 50 **Notes** LB Civ Wed 120

OSWESTRY   Map 15 SJ22

Premier Collection

Greystones

★★★★★ ⌂ ⌂ GUEST HOUSE

tel: 07976 740141 **Crickheath SY10 8BW**
email: enquiry@stayatgreystones.co.uk **web:** www.stayatgreystones.co.uk
dir: *From A483 follow B4396, turn right through village take No Through Road, Greystones on right*

A warm welcome is assured at this impressive detached house, located on pretty, mature gardens in the hamlet of Crickheath. The bedrooms are equipped with a wealth of thoughtful extras and smart modern bathrooms. Comprehensive breakfasts and imaginative dinners, featuring the best seasonal produce, are available in the elegant dining room. A comfortable guest lounge is also available.

Rooms 4 en suite (1 fmly) S £75; D £85-£110* **Facilities** FTV DVD TVL tea/coffee Dinner available Licensed WiFi ⅃ 18 Fishing 🐾 **Extras** Espresso machine, robes, fridge, fruit **Conf** Board 10 **Parking** 20 **Notes** LB ⊗ No Children 14yrs

The Pentre

★★★★ ⌂ GUEST HOUSE

tel: 01691 653952 **Trefonen SY10 9EE**
email: helen@thepentre.com **web:** www.thepentre.com
dir: *4m SW of Oswestry. Exit Oswestry-Treflach road into New Well Ln, The Pentre signed*

A 500-year-old stone farmhouse, The Pentre retains many original features, including a wealth of exposed beams and a superb inglenook fireplace where the woodburner blazes during colder months. Bedrooms are equipped with a range of thoughtful extras, and breakfast and dinner are memorable, with quality produce cooked with flair on an Aga.

Rooms 3 en suite (1 fmly) (1 GF) S £40-£50; D £70-£76* **Facilities** FTV TVL tea/coffee Dinner available WiFi 🐾 **Parking** 10 **Notes** LB ⊗ ⊗ ⊗

Sebastians

★★★★ ◉◉ ⌂ RESTAURANT WITH ROOMS

tel: 01691 655444 **fax:** 01691 653452 **45 Willow St SY11 1AQ**
email: sebastians.rest@virgin.net **web:** www.sebastians-hotel.co.uk
dir: *From town centre, take turn signed Selattyn into Willow St. 400yds from junct on left opposite Willow Street Gallery*

Sebastians is an intrinsic part of the leisure scene in Oswestry and has built up a loyal local following. Meals feature French influences, with a multi-choice set menu as well as a simpler Market menu. Rooms are set around the pretty terrace courtyard, and provide very comfortable accommodation with all the comforts of home.

Rooms 1 en suite 4 annexe en suite (4 fmly) (2 GF) S £75; D £85 (room only) **Facilities** iPod docking station Lounge tea/coffee Dinner available Direct Dial WiFi **Extras** Speciality toiletries, fruit - complimentary **Parking** 6 **Notes** ⊗ Closed Xmas/ New Year & Etr Mon No coaches

Carreg-Y-big Farm

★★ BED AND BREAKFAST

tel: 01691 654754 **Carreg-y-big, Selattyn SY10 7HX**
email: info@carreg-y-bigfarm.co.uk **web:** www.carreg-y-bigfarm.co.uk
dir: *Off B4580 at Old Racecourse, signed Selattyn. 1m on right on Offa's Dyke*

Part of The Oswestry Equestrian Centre on the edge of Selattyn, this former farmhouse provides a range of simply appointed bedrooms. The farm is ideally located for anyone walking on nearby Offas's Dyke. Comprehensive breakfasts, and dinners by arrangement, are served at one table in an attractive, beamed dining room; a small guest lounge is also available.

Rooms 4 rms (1 pri facs) (1 GF) **Facilities** TVL Dinner available Riding **Parking** 10 **Notes** ⊗

SHIFNAL   Map 10 SJ70

The Anvil Lodge

★★★★ GUEST ACCOMMODATION

tel: 01952 460125 & 07918 163289   **22 Aston Rd TF11 8DU**
email: michaeldavies234@btinternet.com **web:** www.anvillodge.co.uk

A friendly welcome is assured at The Anvil Lodge, just a short stroll from the market town of Shifnal. Delicious, freshly cooked breakfasts are served around the dining room table. Bedrooms are spacious, fresh in appearance and very comfortable with modern bathrooms complete with bath and separate shower. Off-road secure parking is available.

Rooms 4 annexe en suite (2 fmly) (2 GF) **Facilities** FTV **Parking** 8 **Notes** ⊗

SHREWSBURY
Map 15 SJ41

See also Criggion (Powys), Wem & Westbury

Premier Collection

Drapers Hall
★★★★★ ◎◎ 🍴 RESTAURANT WITH ROOMS

tel: 01743 344679 **10 Saint Mary's Place SY1 1DZ**
email: goodfood@drapershallrestaurant.co.uk **web:** www.drapershallrestaurant.co.uk
dir: *From A5191 (Saint Mary's St) on one-way system into St Mary's Place*

This 16th-century, timber-framed property is situated in the heart of the market town of Shrewsbury. It provides high quality accommodation, including two suites, with modern facilities. Careful preservation of the original beams and wood panels, together with beautiful wooden furniture, has created real harmony between the past and present. Accomplished cooking from Nigel Huxley can be enjoyed in the main restaurant.

Rooms 6 en suite (2 fmly) **Facilities** FTV TVL tea/coffee Dinner available WiFi **Conf** Max 20 Thtr 20 Class 20 Board 20 **Notes** ⊛

Premier Collection

Porter House SY1
★★★★★ ◎ RESTAURANT WITH ROOMS

tel: 01743 358870 & 761220 **fax:** 01743 344422 **15 Saint Mary's St SY1 1EQ**
email: hello@porterhousesy1.co.uk **web:** www.porterhousesy1.co.uk
dir: *Follow one-way system around town, opposite St Mary's church*

This fine property is located in the heart of the town. The four individually designed bedrooms, including a suite, are very comfortable and have spacious and contemporary bathrooms. Downstairs the award-winning, vibrant bar and restaurant specialises in British food with a classic twist. Breakfast offers a range of quality dishes. Secure parking is available in a nearby public car park.

Rooms 4 en suite (1 fmly) **Facilities** tea/coffee Dinner available WiFi **Notes** LB ⊛ No coaches

The Old Station
★★★★ BED AND BREAKFAST

tel: 01939 290905 **Leaton, Bomere Heath SY4 3AP**
web: www.theoldstationshropshire.co.uk
dir: *M54 junct 7 onto A5 then A49 N. At Battlefield (A5124) over rdbt into Huffley Ln, left by cricket field, 100mtrs on right*

This former railway station, built in 1847, is set in the heart of the Shropshire countryside yet just four miles from Shrewsbury. The railway theme continues throughout the rooms, which offer a range of shapes and sizes. Stained-glass windows are a feature throughout the house. Breakfast is served in the well furnished dining room, with some tables located on what was previously the station platform. A garden and a small lounge are provided and there is ample parking.

Rooms 6 en suite (4 fmly) (1 GF) S £40-£45; D £65-£80* **Facilities** FTV TVL TV5B tea/coffee Dinner available WiFi 🔒 **Parking** 11 **Notes** LB Closed Dec-Feb ⊛

TELFORD
Map 10 SJ60

Church Farm Guest House
★★★★ 🏠 GUEST ACCOMMODATION

tel: 01952 251927 & 07976 897528 **fax:** 01952 427511
Wrockwardine Village, Wellington TF6 5DG
email: info@churchfarm-shropshire.co.uk **web:** www.churchfarm-shropshire.co.uk
dir: *M54 junct 7 towards Wellington, 1st left, 1st right, right at end of road. 0.5m on left opposite St Peters Church*

Located in the pretty rural village of Wrockwardine, this impressive period former farmhouse provides high standards of comfort and good facilities. Attractive bedrooms, attractively furnished, offer a wealth of thoughtful extras including complimentary WiFi. The spacious day rooms include a comfortable lounge and an elegant dining room. There is a sister restaurant in a nearby village, with transport arranged for guests wanting to dine there.

Rooms 4 rms (3 en suite) (1 pri facs) (2 fmly) S £60-£65; D £80-£90* **Facilities** FTV DVD Lounge tea/coffee Dinner available WiFi 🛝 18 🎣 **Conf** Max 20 Class 20 Board 14 **Parking** 12 **Notes** LB

The Lord Nelson
★★ GUEST ACCOMMODATION

tel: 01952 240055 **fax:** 01952 223452 **11-13 Park St, Wellington TF1 3AE**

This Grade II listed property is pleasantly located close to town and has lots of charm and character. Pleasant meals are served in the bar dining area, and service is friendly and relaxed. Bedrooms are available in a range of room sizes and are comfortably appointed.

Rooms 12 en suite **Notes** Closed 21 Dec-3 Jan

WELLINGTON
Map 10 SJ61

The Old Orleton Inn
★★★★★ 🅰 INN

tel: 01952 255011 & 07515 352538 **Holyhead Rd TF1 2HA**
email: info@theoldorleton.com **web:** www.theoldorleton.com
dir: *M54 junct 7, towards Wellington then 400yds on left on corner of Haygate Rd & Holyhead Rd*

Facing Wrekin Hill, this impressive 17th-century coaching inn has been appointed in a charming contemporary style. Each of the boutique-style bedrooms is unique in design and character, yet all retain original antique features. The kitchen has a good local reputation for its selection of carefully-prepared dishes. Fresh, quality produce, sourced locally whenever possible, is used in everything from snacks to three-course dinners, which are served in the three dining rooms.

Rooms 10 en suite S £69-£89; D £79-£119* **Facilities** FTV iPod docking station tea/coffee Dinner available Direct Dial WiFi 🛝 18 Discounted access to local gym/spa **Conf** Max 15 Thtr 15 Class 15 Board 15 **Parking** 25 **Notes** LB ⊛ No Children 5yrs Closed 1st 2wks Jan

WELLINGTON *continued*

Clairmont Guest House

★★★★ Ⓐ GUEST HOUSE

tel: 01952 414214 & 07590 335000   **fax:** 01952 897997 **54 Haygate Rd TF1 1QN**
email: info@clairmontguesthouse.co.uk **web:** www.clairmontguesthouse.co.uk

Clairmont Guest House offers bed and breakfast in a Victorian semi-detached property, and is suitable for both business and leisure visitors, and is only a short drive from the World Heritage Site of Ironbridge. All bedrooms are en suite, and two are on the ground floor. Breakfast is served in the pleasant breakfast room, and is made using local produce where possible. Free WiFi is a feature, and for those without their own laptop there is a PC in the study which can be used for free.

Rooms 5 en suite (1 fmly) (2 GF) S £45-£50; D £65-£70* **Facilities** FTV DVD iPod docking station tea/coffee WiFi 🛁 **Extras** Speciality toiletries, mini-bar, bottled water **Parking** 5 **Notes** ⊗

WEM | Map 15 SJ52

Soulton Hall

★★★★ 🏠 GUEST ACCOMMODATION

tel: 01939 232786 **fax:** 01939 234097 **Soulton SY4 5RS**
email: enquiries@soultonhall.co.uk **web:** www.soultonhall.co.uk
dir: *From A49 between Shrewsbury & Whitchurch take B5065 towards Wem. Soulton Hall 2m E of Wem*

Located two miles from historic Wem, this 16th-century manor house incorporates part of an even older building. The house stands in 560 acres and provides high levels of comfort. Bedrooms are equipped with homely extras and the ground-floor areas include a spacious hall-sitting room, lounge-bar and an attractive dining room, the setting for imaginative dinners.

Rooms 4 en suite 3 annexe en suite (2 fmly) (3 GF) **Facilities** FTV tea/coffee Dinner available Direct Dial Licensed WiFi ch fac 🛥️ ⚓ 18 Fishing Birdwatching in 50 acre private woodland **Conf** Max 100 Thtr 100 Class 60 Board 50 **Parking** 52 **Notes** Civ Wed 450

Aston Lodge Guest House

★★★★ BED AND BREAKFAST

tel: 01939 232577 **fax:** 01939 232577 **Soulton Rd SY4 5BG**
email: astonlodge@btconnect.com **web:** www.aston-lodge.co.uk
dir: *On B5065, close to Wem railway station*

Aston Lodge is an elegant Georgian house situated in a quiet, convenient position close to the train station in the heart of Wem. Some bedrooms are in the main house while the others are found in the adjoining coach house, where two are on the ground floor and the other has its own lounge. All rooms are of a high standard and

have free WiFi. Breakfast is served in the dining room using fine quality and, where possible, locally-sourced produce. Guests may use the lounge adjacent at certain times. There is ample off-road parking and a pleasant good-sized garden.

Rooms 3 rms (2 en suite) (1 pri facs) 3 annexe en suite (1 fmly) (2 GF) S £44-£49; D £69-£94* **Facilities** FTV DVD TVL tea/coffee WiFi **Parking** 6 **Notes** LB ⊗ No Children 10yrs Closed Oct-5 Nov, 22 Dec-7 Jan & 5-19 Jul

WESTBURY | Map 15 SJ30

Barley Mow House

★★★★ BED AND BREAKFAST

tel: 01743 891234 **Aston Rogers SY5 9HQ**
email: colinrigby@astonrogers.fsnet.co.uk **web:** www.barleymowhouse.co.uk
dir: *2m S of Westbury. Exit B4386 into Aston Rogers, house 400yds opposite Aston Hall*

Dating in part from the 17th century and extended in the 18th, this charming property has been restored to provide comfortable accommodation with modern facilities. The house stands in a peaceful village and is surrounded by beautifully maintained gardens.

Rooms 3 en suite (1 fmly) (1 GF) S £38-£40; D £66-£68* **Facilities** FTV TVL tea/coffee WiFi 🛁 **Parking** 4 **Notes** LB Closed Dec-1 Mar 🚭

WHITCHURCH | Map 15 SJ54

Sedgeford House

★★★★ GUEST ACCOMMODATION

tel: 01948 665598 & 07962 111679 **Sedgeford SY13 1EX**
email: enquiries@sedgefordhouse.com **web:** www.sedgefordhouse.com
dir: *From N - follow A41 to Tilstock Rd (B5476) turn left & left again. From S - into Whitchurch on B5395, straight ahead*

Conveniently located just a five minute walk from the centre of the market town of Whitchurch, this modern property offers spacious, well-equipped bedrooms with the addition of very good quality bathrooms. There is a genuine warm welcome from the friendly owners and they are always on hand to advise on local attractions and restaurants.

Rooms 3 en suite S £40; D £70* **Facilities** FTV TVL tea/coffee WiFi 🛁 **Parking** 3 **Notes** ⊗ Closed 23 Dec-4 Jan

SOMERSET

AXBRIDGE | Map 4 ST45

The Oak House

★★★★ ⓦ ⓦ RESTAURANT WITH ROOMS

tel: 01934 732444 **fax:** 01934 733112 **The Square BS26 2AP**
email: info@theoakhousesomerset.com **web:** www.theoakhousesomerset.com
dir: *M5 junct 22, A38 N, turn right towards Axbridge & Cheddar*

This impressive restaurant with rooms is located in the middle of the village and has undergone a considerable transformation in recent years. It now provides a relaxed, high quality experience, whether guests are coming to enjoy the restaurant or to stay in one of the nine bedrooms above. Hospitality and service are delivered in an efficient and helpful manner by a young and enthusiastic team. The kitchen has a serious approach and delivers delightful dishes full of flavour, utilising the best quality produce.

Rooms 9 en suite (2 fmly) S £40-£90; D £40-£90 (room only) **Facilities** FTV DVD Lounge tea/coffee Dinner available WiFi **Notes** ⊗ Closed 2-5 Jan RS Sun eve & Mon eve Restaurant closed

BABCARY Map 4 ST52

The Red Lion Inn

★★★★ ◯ INN

tel: 01458 223230 **fax:** 01458 224510 **Main St TA11 7ED**
email: redlionbabcary@btinternet.com **web:** www.redlionbabcary.co.uk
dir: Off A303 & A37

Tucked away in a sleepy village, this engaging country pub has so much to offer and provides an appealing blend of traditional and contemporary styles. Thatched roof, flagstone floors and crackling log fires all set the tone with a committed team dedicated to ensuring guests are properly looked after. Bedrooms are located in the adjacent barn and provide impressive levels of comfort and quality with all the necessities for a thoroughly relaxing stay. Food is not to be missed with a skilled kitchen team making excellent use of the best the area has to offer. An alternative option in spring and summer is The Den, a stylish function room within the gardens which houses a wood-fired pizza oven.

Rooms 6 annexe en suite (2 fmly) (4 GF) S fr £90; D £110-£120* **Facilities** DVD tea/coffee Dinner available Direct Dial WiFi **Extras** Speciality toiletries **Parking** 35

BALTONSBOROUGH Map 4 ST53

Lower Farm (ST572346)

★★★★ FARMHOUSE

tel: 01458 850206 & 07773 497188 **Lottisham BA6 8PF**
email: dboard51@btinternet.com
dir: From Shepton Mallet take A37 over Wraxall Hill past Queens Arms. Follow road 3rd turning on right to Lottisham, 1st on right

Peacefully located and surrounded by pleasant countryside, this working farm offers a genuine welcome and traditional farmhouse hospitality. The one en suite bedroom is spacious and well equipped, and is located on the ground floor at one end of the main building. Breakfast is taken in the comfortable dining room where a wood-burning fire adds to the ambience during the winter.

Rooms 1 en suite (1 GF) **Facilities** FTV TVL tea/coffee ⚓ **Notes** ⊗ beef/sheep

---

BATH Map 4 ST76

For other locations surrounding Bath see also Box (Wiltshire), Bradford on Avon (Wiltshire), Farmborough & Frome

---

Premier Collection

One Three Nine

★★★★★ GUEST ACCOMMODATION

tel: 01225 314769 **fax:** 01225 443079 **139 Wells Rd BA2 3AL**
email: info@139bath.co.uk **web:** www.139bath.co.uk
dir: M4 junct 19, A46. A4 towards Bath, A367 towards Wells & Shepton Mallet. Establishment on left 500mtrs up hill

Overlooking the historic city of Bath, this quality establishment pairs spacious accommodation with thoughtful design. The bedrooms are comfortably equipped with a very good range of accessories, and a number of feature bathrooms add a dash of luxury. Breakfast is served in the bright and airy dining room, where an excellent choice of continental and hot items is available. Off-street parking is an advantage.

Rooms 10 en suite (1 fmly) (2 GF) **Facilities** FTV DVD tea/coffee Direct Dial WiFi **Parking** 10 **Notes** ⊗ Closed 24-25 Dec

---

Premier Collection

Paradise House

★★★★★ GUEST ACCOMMODATION

tel: 01225 317723 **fax:** 01225 482005 **Holloway BA2 4PX**
email: info@paradise-house.co.uk **web:** www.paradise-house.co.uk
dir: A36 onto A367 (Wells Rd), 3rd left, down hill into cul-de-sac, house 200yds on left

Set in half an acre of lovely walled gardens, this Georgian house built of mellow Bath stone, is within walking distance of the city centre. Many bedrooms have fine views over the city, and all are decorated in opulent style. Furnishings are elegant and facilities modern. The lounge is comfortable and relaxing, and breakfast is served in the smart dining room. Hospitality and service are friendly and professional.

Rooms 12 en suite (2 fmly) (5 GF) S £65-£200; D £69-£210 **Facilities** FTV DVD Lounge tea/coffee Direct Dial Licensed WiFi **Parking** 10 **Notes** LB ⊗ Closed 24-25 Dec

---

Premier Collection

Apsley House

★★★★★ BED AND BREAKFAST

tel: 01225 336966 **fax:** 01225 425462 **Newbridge Hill BA1 3PT**
email: info@apsley-house.co.uk **web:** www.apsley-house.co.uk
dir: 1.3m W of city centre on A431

Built in 1830 for the Duke of Wellington, Apsley House is within walking distance (allow around half an hour) of the city centre. The house is extremely elegant, and the spacious bedrooms have pleasant views. Some rooms have four-poster beds, and there are two family rooms. A smart breakfast room and a delightful lounge are available.

Rooms 11 en suite (2 fmly) (1 GF) S £75-£165; D £80-£215* **Facilities** STV FTV DVD Lounge tea/coffee Direct Dial Licensed WiFi **Extras** Speciality toiletries, bottled water **Parking** 12 **Notes** LB ⊗ Closed 3 days Xmas

---

Premier Collection

Chestnuts House

★★★★★ GUEST ACCOMMODATION

tel: 01225 334279 **fax:** 01225 312236 **16 Henrietta Rd BA2 6LY**
email: reservations@chestnutshouse.co.uk **web:** www.chestnutshouse.co.uk
dir: Enter Bath on A46, under flyover, right at rdbt. Follow signs for A36 Warminster, over Cleveland Bridge & turn right. 50mtrs on left

Located just a few minutes' walk from the city centre and appointed using light shades and oak, Chestnuts' accommodation is fresh and airy. Bedrooms are attractively co-ordinated, well equipped and comfortable. Added enhancements, such as WiFi make the rooms suitable for both business and leisure guests. Breakfast, which features quite an extensive buffet and daily specials, is served in the dining room that opens onto the pretty rear garden. There is a cosy lounge, and the small car park is a bonus.

Rooms 5 en suite (1 fmly) (2 GF) **Facilities** STV FTV DVD TVL tea/coffee WiFi Riding **Extras** Speciality toiletries **Parking** 5 **Notes** ⊗

BATH *continued*

Premier Collection

Dorian House
★★★★★ GUEST ACCOMMODATION

tel: 01225 426336 **fax:** 01225 444699 **1 Upper Oldfield Park BA2 3JX**
email: info@dorianhouse.co.uk **web:** www.dorianhouse.co.uk
dir: *A36 onto A367 (Wells Rd), right into Upper Oldfield Park, 3rd building on left*

This elegant Victorian property has stunning views over the city. The atmosphere is welcoming, and the accommodation of high quality. Several of the rooms have fine period four-poster beds and all offer a range of extra facilities. The attractive lounge has an honesty bar and views of the terraced gardens.

Rooms 13 en suite (4 fmly) (2 GF) **Facilities** FTV iPod docking station Lounge tea/coffee Direct Dial Licensed WiFi 🔒 **Parking** 9 **Notes** LB ⊗ Closed 24-26 Dec

See advert on opposite page

Follow us on twitter
@TheAA_Lifestyle

Premier Collection

River House and Friary Coach House
★★★★★ GUEST ACCOMMODATION

tel: 01225 722252 & 07712 437478 **fax:** 01225 722252
Friary, Freshford BA2 7UE
email: info@riverhousebath.com **web:** www.riverhousebath.com
dir: *A36 S of Bath, pass signs for Freshford on left, take left turn at x-rds sign down narrow lane, "No through road"*

Set in eleven acres of delightfully peaceful former monastery grounds, River House offers views over the delightful gardens, and is just five miles from Bath. Accommodation consists of comfortable bedrooms in the main house with lounges and relaxing areas for guests to enjoy, and the separate Friary Coach House: a luxurious, self-contained building adjacent to the main house. Guests in the Coach House have the option of breakfast being delivered to their own dining room. Attentive service and a genuine welcome are assured.

Rooms 5 rms (4 en suite) (1 pri facs) (1 fmly) (1 GF) S fr £60; D fr £120*
Facilities STV FTV DVD iPod docking station Lounge TVL TV4B tea/coffee Dinner available Direct Dial Licensed WiFi 🏊🚣 Fishing Riding Pool table 🔒 Hot tub Badminton Art Nature Trail **Extras** Chocolates, fridge, speciality toiletries - free **Parking** 10 **Notes** LB ⊛

Premier Collection

The Windsor Townhouse
★★★★★ GUEST HOUSE

tel: 01225 422100 **fax:** 01225 422550 **69 Great Pulteney St BA2 4DL**
email: sales@bathwindsorguesthouse.com **web:** www.bathwindsorguesthouse.com

An easy two-minute walk from the city centre, shops, restaurants and attractions, The Windsor is a Grade I listed Georgian townhouse on Great Pulteney Street, one of the finest boulevards in Europe. Inside are fifteen individually styled, en suite bedrooms. Period features, free WiFi, air conditioning, flat-screen TVs, tea and coffee making facilities, hairdryer, mini-safe and ironing board come as standard. Breakfast offers a good selection of well prepared hot and cold dishes, and staff are well-known for their warmth and willingness to help. Parking permits are available to purchase for the street outside.

Rooms 15 en suite (1 fmly) S £69-£120; D £89-£189 **Facilities** STV FTV DVD iPod docking station tea/coffee Direct Dial Licensed WiFi **Extras** Speciality toiletries, mini-bar **Parking** 2 **Notes** ⊗ Closed 25 Dec & 1 Jan RS 24 & 31 Dec last check out 11am

Astor House
★★★★ BED AND BREAKFAST

tel: 01225 429134 & 07921 139558 **14 Oldfield Rd BA2 3ND**
email: astorhouse.visitus@virgin.net **web:** www.astorhouse-bath.co.uk
dir: *A4 into Bath to lights, then follow A36 (avoiding city centre). Onto A367, then 2nd right*

Astor House offers very comfortable accommodation and personal, friendly service. Rooms are understatedly elegant, and equipped with a wealth of extras for the modern traveller. Hearty breakfasts are served in the light dining room. The location, in a quiet street, is within easy distance of all central attractions, making it an ideal base from which to explore the city.

Rooms 7 en suite (3 fmly) S £60-£75; D £90-£110* **Facilities** FTV Lounge TVL tea/coffee Direct Dial WiFi 🔒 **Parking** 5 **Notes** ⊗

The Bailbrook Lodge

★★★★ ≜ GUEST HOUSE

tel: 01225 859090 **fax:** 01225 852299 **35-37 London Road West BA1 7HZ**
email: hotel@bailbrooklodge.co.uk **web:** www.bailbrooklodge.co.uk
dir: *M4 junct 18, A46 S to A4 junct, left signed Batheaston. Lodge 1st on left*

Set in extensive gardens on the east edge of the city, this imposing Georgian building provides smart accommodation. The well-equipped bedrooms include some with four-poster beds and period furniture, and service is professional and efficient. The inviting lounge has a small bar, and light snacks are available from noon until evening. Breakfast is served in the elegant dining room.

Rooms 15 rms (14 en suite) (1 pri facs) (5 fmly) (1 GF) **Facilities** FTV DVD iPod docking station Lounge tea/coffee Licensed WiFi 🛁 **Extras** Mineral water, bath robes in some rooms **Conf** Max 20 Thtr 20 Class 10 Board 12 **Parking** 15 **Notes** ⊗

Beckford House B&B

★★★★ BED AND BREAKFAST

tel: 01225 310005 **59 Upper Oldfield Park BA2 3LB**
email: info@beckford-house.com **web:** www.beckford-house.com
dir: *Turn off A36 (Warminster-Bristol road) opposite Skoda showroom, Upper Oldfield Park 3rd on left*

Close to the city's attractions, this charming Victorian house provides a relaxed and friendly welcome in a quiet location. The spacious bedrooms are elegantly furnished and beautifully decorated. The house is wonderfully proportioned and there are touches of grandeur throughout. A varied choice is offered at breakfast including local and organic produce.

Rooms 2 en suite (1 fmly) **Facilities** FTV DVD iPod docking station tea/coffee WiFi 🛁 **Parking** 2 **Notes** ⊗ No Children 11yrs Closed 25-31 Dec ☻

Corston Fields Farm *(ST674648)*

★★★★ FARMHOUSE

tel: 01225 873305 & 07900 056568 **Corston BA2 9EZ**
email: corston.fields@btinternet.com **web:** www.corstonfields.com
dir: *300mtrs off A39 between Corston & Marksbury on lane running adjacent to Wheatsheaf pub*

Located in peaceful countryside and surrounded by a variety of crops, this traditional farmhouse offers a relaxing stay. Spacious and well-furnished bedrooms are located in the main property, and there's an additional room in a separate building with its own entrance and patio. Guests are welcome to use the comfortable lounge, and walk the family dog in the fields if they feel like it. The breakfasts use high-quality ingredients including free-range eggs from the farm.

Rooms 1 en suite 2 annexe en suite (2 GF) S £62-£67; D £94-£105* **Facilities** STV FTV Lounge tea/coffee WiFi Walk around farm **Extras** Speciality toiletries, fridge **Parking** 4 **Notes** ⊗ No Children 13yrs Closed 23 Dec-2 Jan 312 acres arable

Cranleigh

★★★★ ≜ BED AND BREAKFAST

tel: 01225 310197 **fax:** 01225 423143 **159 Newbridge Hill BA1 3PX**
email: stay@cranleighbath.com **web:** www.cranleighbath.com
dir: *1.2m W of city centre on A431*

This pleasant Victorian house is in a quiet location near the city centre. The well-equipped bedrooms, some of which are on the ground floor, are decorated in the style of the period, and two rooms have four-poster beds. Breakfast is served in the elegant dining room, and there is also an attractive garden which includes a popular hot tub.

Rooms 9 en suite (3 fmly) (2 GF) **Facilities** FTV DVD iPod docking station tea/coffee Licensed WiFi Garden hot tub **Parking** 5 **Notes** ⊗ No Children 5yrs Closed 25-26 Dec

Dorian House

1 Upper Oldfield Park, Bath BA2 3JX • Tel: 01225 426336
Website: www.dorianhouse.co.uk • Email: info@dorianhouse.co.uk

Enter an atmosphere of period charm in Dorian House, built of Bath stone circa 1880. Extensively refurbished in 2009 with marble bathrooms and high pressure showers, a new Breakfast-Orangery and additional room "SLAVA" in memory of the great cellist Rostropovich. Characterful bedrooms have a restful ambience and views over the Royal Crescent or well-tended gardens. Some have traditional oak four-poster or super king size beds and are luxuriously decorated with opulent fabrics and stunning decor. Crisp cotton sheets, fluffy towels, tea/coffee making facilities, television, hairdryer and telephone ensure a comfortable stay.

BATH *continued*

The Kennard

★★★★ 🛏 GUEST ACCOMMODATION

tel: 01225 310472 **fax:** 01225 460054 **11 Henrietta St BA2 6LL**
email: reception@kennard.co.uk **web:** www.kennard.co.uk
dir: *A4 onto A36 (Bathwick St), 2nd right into Henrietta Rd & Henrietta St*

The Kennard, an attractive Georgian house, dates from 1794 and is situated just off famous Great Pulteney Street, making it convenient for the city centre. The house is decorated and furnished in keeping with the elegant architecture. Bedrooms, two located at ground-floor level, vary in style and size. Breakfast is served in the lower garden dining room and includes an excellent cold buffet, as well as a selection of hot items.

Rooms 12 rms (10 en suite) (2 GF) S £65-£70; D £110-£130* **Facilities** FTV tea/coffee Direct Dial Licensed WiFi 🔒 **Notes** ⊗ No Children 8yrs Closed 1wk Xmas

Marlborough House

★★★★ GUEST ACCOMMODATION

tel: 01225 318175 **fax:** 01225 466127 **1 Marlborough Ln BA1 2NQ**
email: mars@manque.dircon.co.uk **web:** www.marlborough-house.net
dir: *450yds W of city centre, at A4 junct with Marlborough Ln*

Marlborough House is situated opposite Royal Victoria Park and close to the Royal Crescent. Some original features remain and the rooms are decorated with period furniture and pictures. The atmosphere is relaxed, and service is attentive and friendly. The breakfast, served from an open-plan kitchen, is vegetarian and organic.

Rooms 6 en suite (3 fmly) (1 GF) S £95-£160; D £95-£170* **Facilities** FTV Lounge tea/coffee Direct Dial Licensed WiFi 🔒 **Extras** Organic toiletries; mini-bar - chargeable **Parking** 3 **Notes** LB Closed 24-26 Dec

Follow us on Facebook
www.facebook.com/TheAAUK

Oldfields

★★★★ GUEST ACCOMMODATION

tel: 01225 317984 **fax:** 01225 444471 **102 Wells Rd BA2 3AL**
email: info@oldfields.co.uk **web:** www.oldfields.co.uk
dir: *A4 to city centre, left at lights (A36/A367). At large rdbt, under railway viaduct, 1st exit A367 signed Radstock. After 0.5m 1st right, then left*

Located in an elevated position with excellent views over Bath from many of the bedrooms, Oldfields provides a range of rooms decorated and furnished to provide very good levels of quality and comfort. Guests are welcome to use the relaxing lounge, and a DVD library is available. At breakfast, taken in the relaxing dining room, there is a choice of high-quality cooked dishes. The property has a small car park.

Rooms 16 en suite (2 GF) **Facilities** FTV DVD Lounge tea/coffee Direct Dial WiFi **Parking** 14 **Notes** ⊗ No Children 14yrs Closed 25-26 Dec

School Cottages Bed & Breakfast

★★★★ 🛏 BED AND BREAKFAST

tel: 01761 471167 & 07989 349428 **The Street, Near Bath BA2 0AR**
email: tim@schoolcottages.co.uk **web:** www.schoolcottages.co.uk

(For full entry see Farmborough)

17 Lansdown Crescent

★★★★ BED AND BREAKFAST

tel: 01225 471741 **BA1 5EX**
email: derries@globalnet.co.uk **web:** www.bedandbreakfastbathuk.co.uk
dir: *From A4 into Lansdown Rd, 5th left into Lansdown Place East, into Lansdown Crescent*

17 Lansdown Crescent is an impressive Georgian building full of charm and elegance in a location that overlooks Bath. Grade I listed, it has very spacious bedrooms and a huge, tastefully decorated breakfast room. Guests are welcome to use the full-size snooker table, and parking permits are available. While not en suite due to the nature of the building, each bedroom has its own well-decorated bathroom.

Rooms 2 rms (2 pri facs) (2 fmly) **Facilities** FTV tea/coffee WiFi Snooker **Notes** LB ⊗ Closed 20-28 Dec 🖂

Villa Claudia

★★★★ BED AND BREAKFAST

tel: 01225 329670 **fax:** 01225 282601 **19 Forester Rd, Bathwick BA2 6QE**
email: claudiaamato77@aol.com **web:** www.villaclaudia.co.uk
dir: *From A4 into Cleveland Place East (A36), at next rdbt 1st exit into Beckford Rd, left into Forester Rd*

Villa Claudia is a beautiful Victorian property located on a quiet, tree-lined residential street within easy walking distance of the city centre's attractions and restaurants. The Italian owners of this family-run bed and breakfast provide attentive and personal service. The bedrooms and bathrooms are beautifully decorated and very comfortable; a four-poster room is available. Delicious breakfasts are served in the charming dining room at a communal table. AA Friendliest B&B of the Year Finalist 2014-2015.

Rooms 3 rms (1 en suite) (2 pri facs) (1 fmly) **Facilities** FTV DVD tea/coffee WiFi **Extras** Mineral water - complimentary **Parking** 4 **Notes** ⊗ Closed 21 Dec-1 Jan

Waterhouse

★★★★ GUEST ACCOMMODATION

tel: 01225 721999 **fax:** 01225 721998 **Waterhouse Ln, Monkton Combe BA2 7JB**
email: waterhouse@wilsher-group.com **web:** www.waterhousebath.co.uk
dir: *From Bath on A36 to Monkton Combe*

This 18th-century manor house is in a peaceful location just a couple of miles outside of Bath. It offers modern bedrooms and bathrooms with plenty of welcome guest extras, and a range of relaxing lounges. Guests can enjoy the garden, and country walks start straight from the front door. Breakfast is served in the contemporary dining room, and meeting rooms are also available.

Rooms 13 en suite (4 fmly) **Facilities** STV FTV Lounge TVL tea/coffee Lift Licensed WiFi ♨ 18 Fishing ♦ Arrangement with leisure centre **Conf** Max 40 Thtr 40 Class 20 Board 16 **Parking** 45 **Notes** LB ⊗

The Bath House

★★★★ GUEST ACCOMMODATION

tel: 07711 119847 & 0117 937 4495   **fax:** 0117 337 6791 **40 Crescent Gardens BA1 2NB**
email: info@thebathhouse.org **web:** www.thebathhouse.org
dir: *100yds from Queen Sq on A431*

Appointed to high specifications, this accommodation is stylish and just a few minutes' level walk from the city. Bedrooms are attractive, spacious, light and airy, and equipped with modern accessories, including flat-screen TVs. WiFi is also available. Breakfast is room service only and a full height dining table provided in the bedroom ensures guests enjoy their meal experience. Limited parking space is available.

Rooms 4 en suite (1 GF) S £69-£119; D £79-£129* **Facilities** FTV iPod docking station tea/coffee WiFi ♨ **Extras** Mini-fridge, air conditioning **Parking** 5 **Notes** LB ⊗ No Children 8yrs

Brocks Guest House

★★★★ GUEST ACCOMMODATION

tel: 01225 338374 **fax:** 01225 338425 **32 Brock St BA1 2LN**
email: brocks@brocksguesthouse.co.uk **web:** www.brocksguesthouse.co.uk
dir: *Just off A4 between Circus & Royal Crescent*

A warm welcome is extended at this delightful Georgian property, located in the heart of the city just a few hundred yards from Royal Crescent. All rooms reflect the comfortable elegance of the Georgian era. A traditional breakfast is served in the charming dining room, which also offers a lounge area with comfortable seating.

Rooms 6 en suite (2 fmly) **Facilities** FTV Lounge tea/coffee WiFi ♨ **Notes** ⊗ Closed 24 Dec-1 Jan

Devonshire House

★★★★ GUEST ACCOMMODATION

tel: 01225 312495 **143 Wellsway BA2 4RZ**
email: enquiries@devonshire-house.uk.com **web:** www.devonshire-house.uk.com
dir: *1m S of city centre. A36 onto A367 (Wells Rd becomes Wellsway)*

Located within walking distance of the city centre, this charming house has maintained its Victorian style, and the friendly proprietors make every effort to ensure a stay here is pleasant and memorable. The attractive bedrooms, some appointed to a very high standard, have many thoughtful extras. There is a small lounge area, and freshly cooked breakfasts are served in the pleasant dining room. Secure parking is available.

Rooms 4 en suite (1 fmly) (2 GF) S £68-£98; D £78-£98* **Facilities** FTV DVD iPod docking station tea/coffee WiFi ♨ **Parking** 6 **Notes** LB ⊗

Grove Lodge

★★★★ GUEST ACCOMMODATION

tel: 01225 310860 **fax:** 01225 429630 **11 Lambridge BA1 6BJ**
email: stay@grovelodgebath.co.uk **web:** www.grovelodgebath.co.uk
dir: *0.6m NE of city centre. Exit A4, 400yds W from junct A46*

This fine Georgian house lies within easy reach of the city centre and is accessed via a stone path through a neat garden surrounded by trees. The spacious bedrooms have period character and all are well equipped. There is an attractive breakfast room, and parking is available in nearby side streets. Guests can venture into the city for evening meals or alternatively, a short stroll along the canal will take you to an inn that serves food.

Rooms 4 rms (3 en suite) (1 pri facs) **Facilities** FTV tea/coffee WiFi ♨ **Notes** ⊗ No Children 7yrs Closed Xmas & New Year

Highways House

★★★★ GUEST ACCOMMODATION

tel: 01225 421238 **fax:** 01225 481169 **143 Wells Rd BA2 3AL**
email: stay@highwayshouse.co.uk **web:** www.highwayshouse.co.uk
dir: *A36 onto A367 (Wells Rd), 300yds on left*

Victorian Highways House is just a ten-minute walk from the city centre; alternatively, there is a frequent bus service. The bedrooms are individually styled, well equipped and homely. A spacious, attractive lounge is available, and breakfast is served in the dining room at separate tables. Parking is a bonus.

Rooms 5 en suite 2 annexe en suite (2 fmly) (3 GF) **Facilities** FTV Lounge tea/coffee WiFi **Parking** 7 **Notes** ⊗ No Children 8yrs

The Hollies

★★★★ GUEST ACCOMMODATION

tel: 01225 313366 **Hatfield Rd BA2 2BD**
email: davcartwright@lineone.net **web:** www.theholliesbath.co.uk
dir: *A36 onto A367 Wells Rd & Wellsway, 0.7m right opposite Devonshire Arms*

This delightful house stands in impressive gardens overlooking a magnificent church, and is within easy reach of the city centre. The individually decorated, themed bedrooms are appointed to provide excellent levels of comfort and have good facilities. Breakfast in the elegant dining room is an enjoyable start to the day.

Rooms 3 rms (2 en suite) (1 pri facs) S fr £85; D fr £105* **Facilities** FTV Lounge tea/coffee WiFi ♨ **Extras** Sweets **Parking** 3 **Notes** ⊗ No Children 16yrs Closed 15 Dec-15 Jan

BATH *continued*

Milsoms Bath

★★★★ 🍴 RESTAURANT WITH ROOMS

tel: 01225 750128 **fax:** 01225 750121 **24 Milsom St BA1 1DG**
email: bath@milsomshotel.co.uk **web:** www.milsomshotel.co.uk
dir: *M4 junct 18, A46 (Bath), 3m, through Pennsylvania. 3rd exit at rdbt onto A420 (Bristol). 1st left signed Hamswell/Park & Ride, left at junct towards Lansdown. Right at next T-junct. 5th right into George St. 1st left into Milsom St*

Located at the end of the main street in busy, central Bath, this stylish restaurant with rooms offers a range of comfortable, well-equipped accommodation. The ground-floor Loch Fyne Restaurant serves an excellent selection of dishes at both lunch and dinner, with an emphasis on freshest quality fish and shellfish. A good selection of hot and cold items is also available in the same restaurant at breakfast.

Rooms 9 en suite **Facilities** FTV tea/coffee Dinner available Direct Dial **Notes** LB ⊗ Closed 24-25 Dec No coaches

Milton House Bed & Breakfast

★★★★ BED AND BREAKFAST

tel: 01225 335632 & 07875 319567 **75 Wellsway BA2 4RU**
email: info@milton-house.co.uk **web:** www.milton-house.co.uk
dir: *A36 inner ring road onto A367 (Wells Road). After 0.5m, sharp right turn, Milton House 150yds on left*

Located in a residential area just 15 minutes' walk from the centre of Bath, this comfortable establishment is run by Gibson and Blessing Mutandwa, who offer a very warm welcome to all guests. Bedrooms come in a range of shapes and sizes and are all well furnished and equipped. A carefully prepared breakfast is provided in the comfortable dining room. Parking is available on the side streets nearby, or on main road outside. Milton House was the AA Friendliest B&B of the Year for 2013-14.

Rooms 4 en suite (1 fmly) S £50-£70; D £70-£120* **Facilities** FTV tea/coffee WiFi 🐾 **Notes** ⊗ No Children 8yrs

Poplar House

★★★★ BED AND BREAKFAST

tel: 01225 852629 **9 The Batch BA1 7DR**
email: poplarhousebath@gmail.com
dir: *M4 junct 18 onto A46 (London Rd). Left at rdbt, located on left*

Located a short drive from the centre of Bath, Poplar House is a very well-maintained property that offers comfortable accommodation in a peaceful setting. Bedrooms offer a range of shapes and sizes, and guests are also welcome to use the comfortable lounge and outdoor seating terrace. Breakfast utilises good quality produce and is served around one large table in the very pleasant dining room.

Rooms 3 en suite S £75-£125; D £80-£135* **Facilities** FTV TVL tea/coffee WiFi ♿ 🐾 **Extras** Robes, sweets - complimentary **Parking** 6 **Notes** ⊗

Find out more about beds in B&Bs - see page 24

Pulteney House

★★★★ GUEST ACCOMMODATION

tel: 01225 460991 **fax:** 01225 460991 **14 Pulteney Rd BA2 4HA**
email: pulteney@tinyworld.co.uk **web:** www.pulteneyhotel.co.uk
dir: *On A36*

This large detached property situated in a well-tended garden, is within walking distance of the city centre. Bedrooms vary in size including some annexe rooms, and are well equipped with useful facilities. Full English breakfasts are served in the dining room at individual tables. A guest lounge and car park are both welcome features.

Rooms 12 rms (11 en suite) (1 pri facs) 5 annexe en suite (3 fmly) (2 GF) S £55-£65; D £80-£140* **Facilities** STV FTV TVL tea/coffee WiFi 🐾 **Parking** 18 **Notes** LB ⊗ Closed 24-26 Dec

Rivers Street Rooms

★★★★ BED AND BREAKFAST

tel: 07787 500345 **39 Rivers St BA1 2QA**
email: sharonabrahams3@yahoo.co.uk **web:** www.riversstrooms.com
dir: *M4 junct 18, A46, through Pennsylvania to mini rdbt, right onto A420 signed Bristol. 0.5m, left at staggered x-rds into lane. Left at end, pass racecourse, 2m. At church right into Lansdown Rd towards city. Right into Julian Rd. 1st left into Rivers St. 50mtrs on left*

This centrally located, five-storey, 18th-century town house offers modern contemporary styling that blends seamlessly with a wealth of original features. The family suite has two rooms, and there is also a double room with king-size bed and the exclusive use of a small courtyard garden; both rooms have flat-screen Freeview TVs and refreshment trays. Breakfast is continental but very generous, offering a wide variety of delicious home-baked goodies such as mini-quiches, pastries, scones and fresh fruits.

Rooms 2 rms (1 en suite) (1 pri facs) (1 fmly) **Facilities** FTV tea/coffee WiFi **Notes** ☺

Sir Walter Elliot's House

★★★★ BED AND BREAKFAST

tel: 01225 469435 & 07737 793772 **95 Sydney Place BA2 6NE**
email: visitus@sirwalterelliotshouse.co.uk **web:** www.sirwalterelliotshouse.co.uk
dir: *A46 onto A4 for 2m. At lights left, over bridge, at next lights right, pass Holburne Museum, then immediately left*

Situated close to the city centre, this substantial Regency town house featured in the 1995 film version of Jane Austen's *Persuasion*. Architecturally restored with many original features, the house provides an insight into the 18th century. The en suite bedrooms are very spacious and decorated with period wallpapers. Breakfast is a choice of traditional English or the house special, an Austrian continental breakfast. Parking is by arrangement.

Rooms 3 rms (2 en suite) **Facilities** TVL TV1B tea/coffee WiFi 🔒 **Parking** 2 **Notes** ⊗

Walton Villa

★★★★ BED AND BREAKFAST

tel: 01225 482792 **fax:** 01225 313093 **3 Newbridge Hill BA1 3PW**
email: walton.villa@virgin.net **web:** www.waltonvilla.co.uk
dir: *M4 junct 18, A46 to Bath then A4. At lights take right fork onto A431, 50mtrs on left*

Located around half a mile from the centre of Bath this welcoming accommodation has the benefit of on-site parking and a number of inns and restaurants all within a short stroll. Bedrooms are comfortably furnished and a good choice is offered at breakfast which is served in the relaxing dining room.

Rooms 4 rms (3 en suite) (1 pri facs) S £55-£60; D £95-£98 **Facilities** FTV Lounge tea/coffee WiFi **Parking** 4 **Notes** ⊗ No Children 12yrs Closed 22 Dec-2 Jan

Wentworth House

★★★★ GUEST ACCOMMODATION

tel: 01225 339193 **fax:** 01225 310460 **106 Bloomfield Rd BA2 2AP**
email: stay@wentworthhouse.co.uk **web:** www.wentworthhouse.co.uk
dir: *From city centre on A367 (signed Shepton Mallet), right into Bloomfield Rd*

Set in an elevated position above Bath with views over the city, Wentworth House is a comfortable establishment that includes a relaxing guest lounge, bar and garden with pool and hot tub in the summer. Bedrooms offer a range of shapes and sizes - some with four posters. Breakfast is served in the spacious dining room overlooking the garden.

Rooms 19 rms (18 en suite) (1 pri facs) 1 annexe en suite (3 fmly) (9 GF) S £70-£100; D £75-£145 **Facilities** STV FTV TVL tea/coffee Dinner available Direct Dial Licensed WiFi ⤳ ♨ 🔒 Hot tub **Conf** Max 15 Class 15 Board 20 **Parking** 15 **Notes** LB ⊗

Elgin Villa

★★★ BED AND BREAKFAST

tel: 01225 424557 **6 Marlborough Ln BA1 2NQ**
email: elginvilla@hotmail.co.uk **web:** www.elginvilla.co.uk
dir: *From one way system at Queen Sq, exit NW & follow signs for A4, Bristol. By pedestrian crossing, right into car park, parking in far left corner behind wooden gate*

Located near the park and just a ten-minute walk from the centre of Bath, Elgin Villa offers a range of variously sized bedrooms. Most rooms have en suite facilities, although two have shower and washbasin in the room, and share a toilet. Continental breakfast, including scrambled eggs and croissants, is served in the comfortable dining room. Private parking is available to the rear of the property.

Rooms 6 rms (4 en suite) (2 fmly) D £85-£110* **Facilities** FTV tea/coffee WiFi **Parking** 6 **Notes** ⊗

Roman City Guest House

★★★ GUEST HOUSE

tel: 01225 463668 & 07899 777953 **18 Raby Place, Bathwick Hill BA2 4EH**
email: romancityguesthouse.fsnet.co.uk **web:** romancityguesthouse.co.uk
dir: *A4 onto A36 Bathwick St, turn right at lights, straight on at rdbt. Turn left at St Mary's church into Bathwick Hill, on left*

A warm welcome is assured at this 18th-century end-of-terrace house, located just a stroll from the heart of the historic city. The spacious bedrooms, some with four-poster beds, are comfortable and well equipped with many extra facilities. A pleasant lounge is also available.

Rooms 4 rms (3 en suite) (1 pri facs) (2 fmly) **Facilities** FTV DVD tea/coffee WiFi **Conf** Board 12 **Notes** ⊗

Waltons Guest House

★★★ GUEST HOUSE

tel: 01225 426528 **17-19 Crescent Gardens, Upper Bristol Rd BA1 2NA**
email: rose@waltonsguesthouse.co.uk **web:** www.bathguesthouse.com
dir: *On A4 350yds W of city centre*

There is a warm welcome at Waltons Guest House, situated within strolling distance of the centre of Bath. The cosy bedrooms come with useful extra facilities, and a traditional English breakfast is served at individual tables in the dining room.

Rooms 7 en suite **Facilities** FTV tea/coffee Direct Dial **Notes** ⊗

Apple Tree Guest House

Ⓤ

tel: 01225 337642 **fax:** 01225 337642 **7 Pulteney Gardens BA2 4HG**
email: enquiries@appletreeguesthouse.co.uk **web:** www.appletreeguesthouse.com
dir: *A4 onto A36 into Pulteney Rd. Under railway bridge, take 2nd left into Pulteney Gdns*

Currently the rating for this establishment is not confirmed. This may be due to a change of ownership or because it has only recently joined the AA rating scheme.

Rooms 4 en suite S £80-£150; D £90-£160* **Facilities** FTV tea/coffee WiFi Massage & beauty treatments **Extras** Speciality toiletries - complimentary **Parking** 2 **Notes** ⊗ No Children 11yrs Closed 14 Dec-9 Jan

BECKINGTON   Map 4 ST85

Woolpack Inn

★★★★ INN

tel: 01373 831244 **fax:** 01373 831223 **BA11 6SP**
email: 6534@greeneking.co.uk **web:** www.oldenglish.co.uk

This charming coaching inn dates back to the 16th century and retains many original features including flagstone floors, open fireplaces and exposed beams. The bar is popular with visitors and locals alike. There is a garden room lounge and a choice of places to eat: the bar for light snacks, the Oak Room for more substantial meals, or the Garden Room which leads onto a pleasant courtyard.

Rooms 12 en suite (3 fmly) S £44-£99; D £44-£99* **Facilities** FTV TV11B tea/coffee Dinner available Direct Dial WiFi ⌖ 18 **Conf** Max 40 Thtr 40 Class 20 Board 20 **Parking** 16 **Notes** LB

BRIDGWATER   Map 4 ST23

Ash-Wembdon Farm *(ST281382)*

★★★★ FARMHOUSE

tel: 01278 453097 **Hollow Ln, Wembdon TA5 2BD**
email: mary.rowe@btinternet.com **web:** www.farmaccommodation.co.uk
dir: M5, A38, A39 to Minehead, at rdbt 3rd exit into Homeburg Way, at lights take B3339, right into Hollow Ln

Near the Quantock Hills, this is a 17th-century farmhouse on a working beef and arable farm offering homely and comfortable accommodation. All rooms have en suite showers or private bathrooms, and English or continental breakfasts are served in the guest dining room. Guests also have use of a lounge and landscaped garden.

Rooms 3 rms (2 en suite) (1 pri facs) S £40-£45; D £60-£65 **Facilities** FTV Lounge tea/coffee WiFi ⌖ **Parking** 3 **Notes** LB ⊗ No Children 12yrs Closed 22 Dec-3 Jan 340 acres arable/beef

Blackmore Farm *(ST247385)*

★★★★ FARMHOUSE

tel: 01278 653442 **Blackmore Ln, Cannington TA5 2NE**
email: dyerfarm@aol.com **web:** www.blackmorefarm.co.uk
dir: 3m W of Bridgwater. Follow brown tourist signs on A39, before Cannington

Dating back to the 15th century, this Grade I listed manor house is truly unique; there is a wealth of original features such as oak beams, huge open fireplaces, stone archways and even a chapel. Bedrooms located in the main house are individual in style and one has a wonderful four-poster and a lofty oak-beamed ceiling. Additional, more conventional bedrooms are located in a separate courtyard area. Breakfast is taken in the grandeur of the dining room around one incredibly long table - a truly memorable experience.

Rooms 3 en suite 2 annexe en suite (1 fmly) (2 GF) D £100-£120* **Facilities** FTV TVL tea/coffee Licensed WiFi ⌖ 18 Fishing ⌖ Farm shop café **Extras** Fruit, bath robes in some rooms - complimentary **Conf** Max 30 Board 30 **Parking** 10 **Notes** LB ⊗ 900 acres dairy/arable

The Malt Shovel

★★★ INN

tel: 01278 653432 **Blackmore Ln, Cannington TA5 2NE**
email: maltshovel@butcombe.com **web:** www.maltshovel.butcombe.com
dir: A39 from Bridgwater, left into Blackmore Ln, just before Bridgwater Mowers

Located in a quiet rural area and just a couple of miles from Bridgwater, this popular hostelry has a broad appeal. There's plenty of character here with log fires, low beams and a warm, genuine welcome. The well-stocked bar offers a range of Butcombe Ales as well as guest beers, while the menu offers plenty of choice in addition to the impressive carvery. The bedrooms are located in an adjacent building, and provide good levels of space and comfort. Spacious gardens and patios make the perfect venues for a refreshing drink in the summer.

Rooms 8 annexe en suite (1 fmly) (8 GF) S £50; D £80* **Facilities** FTV tea/coffee Dinner available WiFi ⌖ 18 **Parking** 50 **Notes** LB

BROMPTON REGIS   Map 3 SS93

Holworthy Farm *(SS978308)*

★★★★ ⌑ FARMHOUSE

tel: 01398 371244 **fax:** 01398 371244 **TA22 9NY**
email: holworthyfarm@aol.com **web:** www.holworthyfarm.co.uk
dir: 2m E of Brompton Regis. Exit A396 on E side of Wimbleball Lake

Set in the south-east corner of Exmoor, this working livestock farm has spectacular views over Wimbleball Lake. Bedrooms are traditionally furnished and well equipped. The dining room overlooking the garden is an attractive setting for breakfast. Dinner is available by arrangement.

Rooms 5 rms (3 en suite) (2 pri facs) (2 fmly) (1 GF) **Facilities** DVD Lounge TVL tea/coffee Dinner available WiFi **Extras** Bottled water - complimentary **Conf** Max 20 Class 20 **Parking** 8 **Notes** LB ⊗ 200 acres beef/sheep

BRUTON

Map 4 ST63

Turks Hall

★★★ BED AND BREAKFAST

tel: 01749 813725 & 07807 193450 **Lusty BA10 0BX**
email: carolinenolder@gmail.com **web:** www.turkshall.co.uk
dir: *Exit A303 signed Bruton, in town follow signs for Yeovil. At T-junct turn left, 3rd house on left*

Located in the historic market town of Bruton, Turks Hall is a Victorian townhouse within easy walking distance of the local shops, pubs and restaurants. The double bedroom is located on the second floor and is comfortably furnished and equipped. A range of leaf teas and a glass of sherry are among the pleasant extras provided by the very welcoming hosts.

Rooms 1 en suite (1 fmly) S £70; D £80* **Facilities** STV iPod docking station WiFi **Extras** Sherry - complimentary **Notes** ⊗ ⌂

BURNHAM-ON-SEA

Map 4 ST34

Magnolia House

★★★★ GUEST HOUSE

tel: 01278 792460 **26 Manor Rd TA8 2AS**
email: enquiries@magnoliahouse.gb.com **web:** www.magnoliahouse.gb.com
dir: *M5 junct 22, follow signs to Burnham-on-Sea, at 2nd rdbt, Magnolia House on right*

Within walking distance of the town centre and beach, this elegant Edwardian house has been appointed to an impressive standard. Contemporary bedrooms offer comfort and quality with many extras such as WiFi and a large DVD film library. Bathrooms are also modern and stylish with invigorating showers. A family suite is offered with separate, interconnecting bedrooms. Traditional full English breakfasts are served in the attractive, air-conditioned breakfast room, with vegetarian and continental options also available.

Rooms 4 en suite (2 fmly) **Facilities** FTV tea/coffee WiFi ⚓ 18 **Parking** 7 **Notes** ⊗ No Children 5yrs

The Victoria

★★★ INN

tel: 01278 783085 **25 Victoria St TA8 1EQ**
web: www.the-victoria-hotel.co.uk

Just a short walk from the seafront at Burnham-on-Sea, the Victoria is a well established hostelry providing comfortable rooms and serving pub fare in the bar and restaurant. Some off-road parking is available on a first-come, first-served basis.

Rooms 6 rms (4 en suite) **Facilities** FTV tea/coffee Dinner available WiFi Pool table ⚓ **Parking** 6 **Notes** No Children 15yrs

CASTLE CARY

Map 4 ST63

The Pilgrims

★★★★★ ◉◉ 🍴 RESTAURANT WITH ROOMS

tel: 01963 240600 **Lovington BA7 7PT**
email: jools@thepilgrimsatlovington.co.uk **web:** www.thepilgrimsatlovington.co.uk
dir: *On B3153, 1.5m E of lights on A37 at Lydford*

The Pilgrims describes itself as 'the pub that thinks it's a restaurant', which is pretty accurate. With a real emphasis on fresh, local and carefully prepared produce, both dinner and breakfast are the focus of any stay here. In addition, the

resident family proprietors provide a friendly and relaxed atmosphere. Comfortable and well-equipped bedrooms are available in the adjacent converted cider barn.

Rooms 5 annexe en suite (5 GF) S £80-£110; D £95-£120* **Facilities** FTV DVD Lounge tea/coffee Dinner available WiFi **Extras** Speciality toiletries **Parking** 5 **Notes** LB No Children 14yrs RS Sun lunch-Tue lunch Restaurant & bar closed to non-residents No coaches

CHARD

Map 4 ST30

Hornsbury Mill

★★★★ Ⓐ GUEST ACCOMMODATION

tel: 01460 63317 **fax:** 01460 67758 **Eleighwater TA20 3AQ**
email: info@hornsburymill.co.uk **web:** www.hornsburymill.co.uk

Hornsbury Mill is a charming example of an early 19th-century corn mill, built of local flint with hamstone mullion windows. The waterwheel has been lovingly restored and turns during daylight hours; and there are four acres of beautiful gardens, making this a popular wedding venue. Bedrooms include a ground-floor room with good disabled access and facilities, and the delightful Crown Wheel Suite with four-poster bed and separate sitting room.

Rooms 10 en suite (2 fmly) (1 GF) S £70-£75; D £99-£165* **Facilities** STV FTV Lounge tea/coffee Dinner available Direct Dial Licensed WiFi ⚓ 18 **Conf** Max 150 Thtr 150 Class 50 Board 50 **Parking** 80 **Notes** ⊗ Closed 24 Dec-10 Jan RS Sun eve closed Civ Wed 120

CHEDDAR

See Draycott

CLUTTON

Map 4 ST65

The Hunters Rest

★★★★ 🍺 INN

tel: 01761 452303 **fax:** 01761 453308 **King Ln, Clutton Hill BS39 5QL**
email: paul@huntersrest.co.uk **web:** www.huntersrest.co.uk
dir: *Off A37 onto A368 towards Bath, 100yds right into lane, left at T-junct, inn 0.25m on left*

This establishment was originally built around 1750 as a hunting lodge for the Earl of Warwick. Set in delightful countryside, it is ideally located for Bath, Bristol and Wells. Bedrooms and bathrooms are furnished and equipped to excellent standards, and the ground floor combines the character of a real country inn with an excellent range of home-cooked meals.

Rooms 5 en suite (2 fmly) S £67.50-£77.50; D £95-£130* **Facilities** FTV iPod docking station tea/coffee Dinner available Direct Dial WiFi ⚓ 18 Fishing Riding 🔔 **Conf** Max 40 Thtr 40 Class 25 Board 25 **Parking** 90 **Notes** LB

Mezzé at the Warwick Arms

★★★★ 🍺 INN

tel: 01761 451200 **Upper Bristol Rd BS39 5TA**
email: clutton@mezzerestaurants.com **web:** www.mezzerestaurants.com/clutton
dir: *S of Bristol on A37*

Part of the Mezzé chain of inns, this delightful property has been fully refurbished throughout to provide high levels of quality and comfort. Conveniently located for Bristol Airport, the inn offers an excellent selection of dishes at dinner including a mezze selection to tempt all tastes. Both dinner and breakfast are taken in the very comfortable dining room. Outdoor seating in the garden is also provided.

Rooms 8 en suite (1 fmly) **Facilities** FTV tea/coffee Dinner available WiFi **Conf** Max 20 **Parking** 30 **Notes** ⊗

COMBE HAY
Map 4 ST75

The Wheatsheaf Combe Hay
★★★★ ® INN

tel: 01225 833504 **BA2 7EG**
email: info@wheatsheafcombehay.com **web:** www.wheatsheafcombehay.com
dir: *From Bath take A369 (Exeter road) to Odd Down, left at park & ride & immediately right towards Combe Hay. 2m to thatched cottage, turn left*

Peacefully located in the Somerset countryside yet just a short drive from the centre of Bath, this delightful country inn has much to offer. Accommodation is in the luxuriously converted cowshed adjacent to the main inn. King-sized beds and quality showers are included, along with a range of welcome extras. Award-winning cuisine is prepared by the talented young chef and complemented by a range of beers, lagers and ciders as well as an extensive wine list with a heavy French bias.

Rooms 3 annexe en suite D £120-£150* **Facilities** FTV tea/coffee Dinner available WiFi **Conf** Max 26 Class 26 **Parking** 80 **Notes** LB Closed 1st wk Jan RS Sun eve & Mon (ex BHs) closed No coaches

COMPTON MARTIN
Map 4 ST55

Ring O Bells
★★★★ ➝ INN

tel: 01761 221284 **BS40 6JE**
email: ring_o_bells@btconnect.com **web:** www.ringobellscomptonmartin.co.uk
dir: *On A368 between Blagdon & Chew Valley*

The Ring O Bells is a delightful village inn that offers a rare combination of traditional character and hospitality with some more modern, quirky additions. The bar and dining areas are full of interest, and along with a good selection of real ales, a range of excellent dishes is offered. Bedrooms include very comfortable king-sized beds and quality showers in the bathrooms. Outdoor seating in the rear garden, and car parking are both welcome features.

Rooms 1 en suite 1 annexe en suite (2 GF) S £60; D £90* **Facilities** FTV iPod docking station Lounge tea/coffee Dinner available WiFi ⚡ 18 ♠ **Parking** 60 **Notes** LB RS Mon-Wed closed 3-6pm

CONGRESBURY
Map 4 ST46

Mezzé at the Ship and Castle
★★★★ ➝ INN

tel: 01934 833535 **High St BS49 5BN**
email: congresbury@mezzerestaurants.com **web:** www.mezzerestaurants.com

Part of the Mezzé group, this pleasant inn offers good quality bedrooms and bathrooms in a range of shapes and sizes. The restaurant is very well decorated and furnished in a contemporary style and provides guests with good comfort for all day dining. The extensive menu offers the popular range of tapas dishes in addition to a more traditional menu. The pleasant rear garden is especially popular for outdoor dining.

Rooms 6 en suite (2 fmly) **Facilities** FTV DVD iPod docking station tea/coffee Dinner available WiFi **Parking** 60 **Notes** ⊗ No coaches

CORTON DENHAM
Map 4 ST62

The Queens Arms
★★★★★ ® ⌂ INN

tel: 01963 220317 **fax:** 01963 220797 **DT9 4LR**
email: relax@thequeensarms.com **web:** www.thequeensarms.com
dir: *A303 exit Chapel Cross signed South Cadbury & Corton Denham. Follow signs to South Cadbury. Through village, after 0.25m turn left up hill signed Sherborne & Corton Denham. Left at top of hill, pub at end of village on right*

This is a proper inn located in peaceful countryside. Staff are friendly and welcoming, and the pub dog can usually be found in front of the roaring log fire in the bar. Bedrooms and bathrooms have benefited from recent refurbishment and offer impressive levels of comfort, style and quality. In addition to a very good selection of real ales, this is a paradise for bottled beer lovers with a great choice from around the world. Excellent, quality local produce is utilised to provide a choice of delicious dinners which may be enjoyed in the traditional bar or character restaurant.

Rooms 5 en suite 3 annexe en suite (1 GF) S £85-£130; D £110-£130* **Facilities** FTV DVD iPod docking station Lounge tea/coffee Dinner available Direct Dial WiFi ⚡ 18 Riding ♠ **Extras** Speciality toiletries, robes/slippers, sweets **Conf** Max 35 Thtr 35 Class 25 Board 30 **Parking** 20 **Notes** LB

See advert on page 159

CREWKERNE
Map 4 ST40

Manor Farm
★★★★ GUEST ACCOMMODATION

tel: 01460 78865 & 07767 620031　**fax:** 01460 78865 **Wayford TA18 8QL**
email: theresaemery@hotmail.com **web:** www.manorfarm.biz
dir: B3165 from Crewkerne to Lyme Regis. 3m, in Clapton right into Dunsham Ln, Manor Farm 0.5m up hill on right

Just off the beaten track and well worth seeking out, this fine Victorian country house has extensive views over Clapton towards the Axe Valley. The comfortably furnished bedrooms are well equipped, and front-facing rooms enjoy splendid views. Breakfast is served at separate tables in the dining room, and a spacious lounge is also provided.

Rooms 4 en suite 1 annexe en suite (2 fmly) S £40-£45; D £80 **Facilities** STV FTV TVL TV4B tea/coffee WiFi Fishing Riding 🐾 **Parking** 14 **Notes** ⊗ ⊜

The George
★★★ INN

tel: 01460 73650 **fax:** 01460 72974 **Market Square TA18 7LP**
email: georgecrewkerne@btconnect.com **web:** www.thegeorgehotelcrewkerne.co.uk
dir: In town centre on A30

Situated in the heart of town, this welcoming inn has been providing rest and sustenance for over 400 years. The atmosphere is warm and inviting, and the bar is the ideal place for a natter and a refreshing pint. Comfortable bedrooms are traditionally styled and include four-poster rooms. A choice of menus is available, served either in the bar or the attractive restaurant.

Rooms 13 rms (8 en suite) (2 pri facs) (2 fmly) S £40-£100; D £70-£150
Facilities FTV DVD TVL tea/coffee Dinner available Direct Dial WiFi 🐾 George Suite has a hydro-therapy spa bath **Conf** Max 100 Thtr 100 Class 100 Board 50 **Notes** LB ⊗

DRAYCOTT
Map 4 ST45

Oakland House
★★★★ ⊜ GUEST ACCOMMODATION

tel: 01934 744195 **fax:** 01934 744195 **Wells Rd BS27 3SU**
email: enquiries@oakland-house.co.uk **web:** www.oakland-house.co.uk
dir: Off A371 at S end of village

Situated a short distance from Cheddar, this friendly home provides comfortable and spacious accommodation. There are splendid views of the Somerset Moors and Glastonbury Tor from the sun lounge and the well-appointed and attractive bedrooms. Dinner features fresh fruit and vegetables from the garden.

Rooms 3 en suite (1 fmly) S £45-£50; D £75-£85 (incl.dinner) **Facilities** FTV DVD TVL tea/coffee Dinner available Pool table 🐾 **Parking** 6 **Notes** LB ⊗

DULVERTON
Map 3 SS92

Tarr Farm Inn
★★★★★ ⊛ INN

tel: 01643 851507 **fax:** 01643 851111
Tarr Steps, Exmoor National Park TA22 9PY
email: enquiries@tarrfarm.co.uk **web:** www.tarrfarm.co.uk
dir: 4m NW of Dulverton. Off B3223 signed Tarr Steps, signs to Tarr Farm Inn

Tarr Farm, dating from the 16th century, nestles on the lower slopes of Exmoor overlooking the famous old clapper bridge, Tarr Steps. The majority of rooms are in the bedroom block that provides very stylish and comfortable accommodation with an impressive selection of thoughtful touches. Tarr Farm Inn, with much character and traditional charm, draws the crowds for cream teas and delicious dinners which are prepared from good local produce.

Rooms 9 en suite (4 GF) S £75-£90; D £100-£150* **Facilities** STV DVD iPod docking station TVL tea/coffee Dinner available Direct Dial WiFi Fishing Riding 🐾 **Extras** Bottled water, fruit **Conf** Max 30 Thtr 30 Class 18 Board 18 **Parking** 10 **Notes** LB No Children 10yrs No coaches

EXEBRIDGE
Map 3 SS92

Anchor Inn
★★★ INN

tel: 01398 323433 **TA22 9AZ**
email: info@theanchorinnexebridge.co.uk **web:** www.theanchorinnexebridge.co.uk
dir: M5 junct 27, take 3rd exit onto A361, signed Tiverton. Left at Exeter Inn & follow signs for Dulverton. Straight across at junct. In Exebridge left at the round house. Follow Anchor Inn signs

This popular riverside inn is perfect for exploring Exmoor's stunning countryside and coast. The welcome is always warm and inviting, with the convivial bar a great place for a pint. Bedrooms provide good levels of comfort with lovely views of the countryside or the River Exe. An extensive menu is offered, with an emphasis on local seafood and seasonal game. Riverside gardens are an added bonus, a wonderful spot to enjoy an alfresco meal.

Rooms 6 en suite (1 fmly) S £50-£70; D £70-£90 **Facilities** FTV tea/coffee Dinner available WiFi Fishing 🐾 **Conf** Max 50 Thtr 50 Class 40 Board 30 **Parking** 50

EXFORD
Map 3 SS83

Stockleigh Lodge
★★★★ BED AND BREAKFAST

tel: 01643 831500 **TA24 7PZ**
email: stay@stockleighexford.co.uk **web:** www.stockleighexford.co.uk
dir: On B3224 through Wheddon Cross to Exford. Over river bridge into Simonsbath Rd, up hill on right

Situated at the very heart of Exmoor, this grand lodge dates from around 1900 and provides a perfect base from which to explore this spectacular area. Whether exploration is by car, foot, cycle or horseback, your hosts will be only too pleased to help with local information. Bedrooms offer good comfort with lovely views being an added bonus, while public areas include a spacious guest lounge warmed by a crackling fire in cooler months. Aga-cooked breakfasts will get the day off to a satisfying start. Stabling is also available for those wishing to bring their horses on holiday.

Rooms 9 en suite (2 fmly) S £35-£40; D £70-£80* **Facilities** TVL tea/coffee WiFi Riding 🐾 Stabling available **Parking** 10

FARMBOROUGH
Map 4 ST66

School Cottages Bed & Breakfast

★★★★ ≜ BED AND BREAKFAST

tel: 01761 471167 & 07989 349428 **The Street, Near Bath BA2 0AR**
email: tim@schoolcottages.co.uk **web:** www.schoolcottages.co.uk
dir: *Exit A39 in Farmborough into The Street, 1st left opposite village school*

This lovingly-restored country house is conveniently located to the south-west of Bath, in the pretty Somerset village of Farmborough. The contemporary, stylish bedrooms are equipped with WiFi, while the excellent bathrooms may include a power shower or a spa bath. Home-made jams and freshly-laid eggs contribute to the delicious breakfasts served in a charming conservatory overlooking the garden.

Rooms 3 en suite **Facilities** FTV TVL tea/coffee WiFi ⌕ 18 ♨ **Extras** Bottled water - complimentary **Parking** 3 **Notes** ⊗ No Children 10yrs

FROME
Map 4 ST74

Premier Collection

Lullington House

★★★★★ BED AND BREAKFAST

tel: 01373 831406 & 07979 290146 **fax:** 01373 831406 **Lullington BA11 2PG**
email: info@lullingtonhouse.co.uk **web:** www.lullingtonhouse.co.uk
dir: *2.5m N of Frome. Off A36 into Lullington*

Built in 1866 as a rectory, this quintessentially English stone country house stands in extensive grounds and gardens which convey an air of peace, quiet and tranquillity. The luxurious large bedrooms, some with four-poster beds, are decorated to high standards using beautiful fabrics, fine antique furniture and many extras such as WiFi, decanters of sherry, fresh flowers and well-stocked beverage trays. Breakfast is served in the impressive dining room with an excellent selection of dishes available.

Rooms 3 en suite S fr £70; D £100-£120* **Facilities** FTV tea/coffee WiFi ⌕ 18 ♨ **Parking** 4 **Notes** ⊗ Closed Xmas & New Year ⊜

GLASTONBURY
Map 4 ST53

See also Somerton

The Glastonbury Town House

★★★★ BED AND BREAKFAST

tel: 01458 831040 **Hillclose, Street Rd BA6 9EG**
email: stay@glastonburytownhouse.co.uk **web:** www.glastonburytownhouse.co.uk
dir: *M5 junct 23 towards Glastonbury. Continue on A39, at B&Q rdbt 3rd exit, 200yds on right*

A very warm welcome is guaranteed at The Glastonbury Town House, where guests can expect to have a comfortable night's rest followed by a hearty breakfast. Thanks to Greg's love of the area and its history, visitors are not left wanting for information to help plan their day. Centrally located with off-street parking, the house is well placed for exploring Glastonbury Tor and the Chalice Well.

Rooms 3 en suite S £55-£75; D £60-£85* **Facilities** FTV tea/coffee Dinner available WiFi **Parking** 3 **Notes** LB ⊗ No Children 12yrs

HIGHBRIDGE
Map 4 ST34

Woodlands Country House

★★★★ ⌖ GUEST ACCOMMODATION

tel: 01278 760232 & 769071 **fax:** 01278 769090 **Hill Ln, Brent Knoll TA9 4DF**
email: info@woodlands-hotel.co.uk **web:** www.woodlands-hotel.co.uk
dir: *M5 junct 22 onto A38 towards Bristol. Turn left opposite Fox & Goose pub, through Brent Knoll. Right into Church Ln, then left into Hill Ln*

This charming, elegant and traditional country house is an ideal place to relax and enjoy the lovely setting and genuine hospitality. Bedrooms offer plenty of comfort and quality with all the necessities to ensure a satisfying and rewarding stay. Public areas include a drawing room and snug bar with crackling fires on cooler nights. The elegant dining room is the venue for accomplished cuisine with a range of skilfully prepared dishes on offer. In the summer, the terrace is a popular option to sit, enjoy a drink and appreciate the views.

Rooms 10 en suite (1 fmly) (2 GF) S £79.95-£109.95; D £89.95-£145.95* **Facilities** FTV DVD Lounge tea/coffee Dinner available Direct Dial Licensed WiFi ⌕ 18 ♨ **Conf** Max 50 Thtr 50 Class 30 Board 36 **Parking** 40 **Notes** Closed 24-30 Dec Civ Wed 50

HOLCOMBE
Map 4 ST64

Premier Collection

The Holcombe Inn

★★★★★ ◉ INN

tel: 01761 232478 **Stratton Rd BA3 5EB**
email: bookings@holcombeinn.co.uk **web:** www.holcombeinn.co.uk
dir: *From Bath or Shepton Mallet take A367 (Fosse Way) to Stratton. Follow inn signs*

Dating back to the 16th century, this inn has views towards Downside Abbey in the distance. The attentive owners and pleasant staff create a friendly and relaxed atmosphere. Bedrooms are individually furnished and very comfortable. Real ales are served in the open-plan bar which has an attractive split-level restaurant.

Rooms 8 en suite (5 fmly) S £75-£120; D £100-£120* **Facilities** FTV DVD Lounge tea/coffee Dinner available Direct Dial WiFi **Extras** Speciality toiletries - complimentary **Conf** Thtr 40 Class 40 **Parking** 40 **Notes** LB

ILCHESTER
Map 4 ST52

Liongate House

★★★★ ≜ BED AND BREAKFAST

tel: 01935 841741 & 07951 538692 **Northover BA22 8NG**
email: info@liongatehouse.co.uk **web:** www.liongatehouse.com

Located in the centre of this pleasant village and a short stroll to a selection of inns and restaurants for dinner, this very comfortable accommodation demonstrates high quality throughout the bedrooms and bathrooms. The proprietors offer a genuine welcome and are very focused on customer care. Breakfast offers a range of top local produce and includes home-made bread, and jams made with fruit from the garden. AA Friendliest B&B of the Year Finalist 2014-2015.

Rooms 3 en suite (1 fmly) (1 GF) **Facilities** FTV DVD tea/coffee WiFi ⌕ ♨ **Parking** 5 **Notes** LB ⊗ Closed Xmas

ILMINSTER
Map 4 ST31

The New Inn
★★★★ ⊜ INN

tel: 01460 52413 **Dowlish Wake TA19 0NZ**
email: newinn-ilminster@btconnect.com **web:** www.newinn-ilminster.co.uk
dir: A358 or A303, follow signs for Perry's Cider, well-signed in village

Situated in the tranquil and unspoilt village of Dowlish Wake, The New Inn is a proper local pub with a warm welcome to be had at the bar. All the bedrooms are on the ground floor; they are contemporary in style and located to the rear overlooking the garden. The menu offers a range of enduring favourites and daily specials, with good local produce used whenever possible. Breakfast is a substantial offering, just right for healthy appetites.

Rooms 4 annexe en suite (4 GF) **Facilities** FTV tea/coffee Dinner available **Parking** 20

Square & Compass
★★★★ INN

tel: 01823 480467 **fax:** 01823 480467 **Windmill Hill, Ashill TA19 9NX**
email: squareandcompass@tiscali.co.uk **web:** www.squareandcompasspub.com
dir: M5 junct 25 onto A358. After 5m, turn right into Wood Rd, signed Windmill Hill; From Ilminster, 2m N on A358

This peacefully located inn provides a genuinely warm welcome and traditional hospitality. The bedrooms and modern bathrooms provide high standards of quality and comfort, and are situated in converted stables adjacent to the main building. In addition to a range of excellent home-cooked meals, a selection of real ales is also available. Outdoor seating is provided in the warmer months.

Rooms 8 en suite (8 fmly) (8 GF) S £49-£65; D £69-£85* **Facilities** FTV Lounge tea/coffee Dinner available WiFi **Conf** Max 100 Class 100 Board 50 **Parking** 50 **Notes** Closed 24-26 Dec No coaches Civ Wed 120

KEYNSHAM
Map 4 ST66

Grasmere Court
★★★★ GUEST ACCOMMODATION

tel: 0117 986 2662 **fax:** 0117 986 2762 **22-24 Bath Rd BS31 1SN**
email: reception@grasmerecourt.co.uk **web:** www.grasmerecourthotel.com
dir: On B3116 just off A4 between Bath & Bristol

This very friendly establishment is located between Bath and Bristol. Bedrooms vary in size, with one room boasting a four-poster bed. A comfortable lounge and a well stocked bar are available, and good value, freshly prepared food is served in the attractive dining room overlooking the garden. Functions also catered for.

Rooms 16 en suite (1 fmly) (4 GF) S £64.50-£70; D £79.95-£90* **Facilities** FTV DVD TVL tea/coffee Dinner available Direct Dial Licensed WiFi **Conf** Max 30 **Parking** 13 **Notes** ⊗

LOWER LANGFORD
Map 4 ST46

The Langford Inn
★★★★ ⊜ INN

tel: 01934 863059 **fax:** 01934 863539 **BS40 5BL**
email: langfordinn@aol.com **web:** www.langfordinn.com
dir: M5 junct 21, A370 towards Bristol. At lights right onto B3133 to Langford, at mini rdbt left signed Lower Langford

Located in a peaceful village on the edge of the Mendips, this traditional country pub offers a varied selection of real ales, well-chosen wines and carefully prepared, home-made dishes. Bedrooms and bathrooms, appointed to a high standard, are housed in two converted 17th-century barns that are adjacent to the inn. They feature exposed beams, original brickwork and oak floors combined with modern luxuries.

Rooms 7 annexe en suite (3 fmly) (6 GF) S £79-£110; D £79-£110 (room only)* **Facilities** FTV DVD TVL Dinner available WiFi **Conf** Max 30 Thtr 30 Class 20 Board 20 **Parking** 20

LOWER VOBSTER
Map 4 ST74

The Vobster Inn
★★★★ ⊛⊛ INN

tel: 01373 812920 **fax:** 01373 812247 **BA3 5RJ**
email: info@vobsterinn.co.uk **web:** www.vobsterinn.co.uk
dir: From A361 follow signs for Whatley & Mells, then Vobster

Peacefully located in four acres, this is a village inn where the resident proprietors offer a genuine welcome and personal attention. Bedrooms and bathrooms provide high levels of quality and comfort. Dinner menus place an emphasis on high quality, simply prepared dishes with regular seasonal changes; several dishes demonstrate the Spanish heritage of the chef proprietor.

Rooms 4 annexe en suite (2 fmly) (4 GF) S £55-£70; D £90-£100 **Facilities** FTV tea/coffee Dinner available WiFi **Petanque Extras** Home-made cookies - complimentary **Conf** Max 40 Thtr 25 Class 32 Board 32 **Parking** 60 **Notes** LB RS Sun eve & Mon (ex BH lunch) No food or drinks available

LYMPSHAM
Map 4 ST35

Batch Country House
★★★★★ ⊜ GUEST ACCOMMODATION

tel: 01934 750371 **fax:** 01934 750501 **Batch Ln BS24 0EX**
web: www.batchcountryhouse.co.uk
dir: M5 junct 22, take last exit on rdbt signed A370 to Weston-Super-Mare. After 3.5m, left into Lympsham, 1m, sign at end of road

In a rural location between Weston-Super-Mare and Burnham-on-Sea, Batch Country House is a former farmhouse that offers a relaxed, friendly and peaceful environment. Bedrooms have been refurbished to provide high levels of quality and comfort, while spacious lounges overlook the extensive, well-tended gardens. The function room makes this a popular venue for wedding ceremonies. Guests can relax with a drink in the bar where orders are taken for delicious home-cooked dinners.

Rooms 19 en suite (3 fmly) (9 GF) **Facilities** Lounge TVL tea/coffee Dinner available Direct Dial Licensed WiFi **Conf** Max 250 Thtr 250 Class 200 Board 200 **Parking** 140 **Notes** ⊗ RS 25-26 Dec bookings only Civ Wed 260

MILVERTON
Map 3 ST12

The Globe
★★★ @ INN

tel: 01823 400534 **Fore St TA4 1JX**
email: adele@theglobemilverton.co.uk **web:** www.theglobemilverton.co.uk
dir: M5 junct 27 follow B3277 to Milverton. In village centre

This popular village local was once a coaching inn, and even though it has been given contemporary styling it still retains much traditional charm. The welcome is warm and genuine with a convivial atmosphere always guaranteed. Bedrooms are appointed in a similar modern style and have comfy beds. The hard-working kitchen is committed to quality, with excellent locally-sourced produce used in impressive dishes. Continental breakfast is served.

Rooms 3 en suite (1 fmly) **Facilities** tea/coffee Dinner available WiFi **Parking** 4 **Notes** ⊗ Closed 20 Dec-2 Jan No coaches

MINEHEAD
Map 3 SS94

Premier Collection

The Old Stables B&B
★★★★★ BED AND BREAKFAST

tel: 07435 964882 **Northfield Rd TA24 5QH**
email: info@theoldstablesminehead.co.uk **web:** www.theoldstablesminehead.co.uk

Originally dating back to 1901, this B&B, as the name suggests, was formerly used as stables. The welcome is warm and genuine with every effort made to ensure a relaxed and rewarding stay. Hosts Nina and Andrew have introduced a Finnish-British style with a simple, elegant and uncluttered approach. Bedrooms provide impressive levels of comfort with cosseting beds, while the sparkling bathrooms include fluffy towels and robes. Breakfast is served in the light and airy dining room with carefully sourced, local produce on offer and a range of temptations to start off the day. The location is a short stroll from the town centre and minutes from the seafront.

Rooms 3 rms (2 en suite) (1 pri facs) (2 fmly) (1 GF) S £60; D £85-£90 **Facilities** FTV DVD tea/coffee WiFi ♿ 18 🔒 **Extras** Hand-made chocolate, fruit juice/soft drinks - free of charge **Parking** 3 **Notes** LB ⊗ No Children 6yrs

Alcombe House
★★★★ GUEST ACCOMMODATION

tel: 01643 705130 & 07549 887456 **Bircham Rd, Alcombe TA24 6BG**
email: info@alcombehouse.co.uk **web:** www.alcombehouse.co.uk
dir: A39, pass junct for Dunster, straight over at floral rdbt. Alcombe House on left

This elegant, period house is a perfect base from which to explore the many and varied delights of the area. The welcome is warm and genuine with plenty of attentive service. Bedrooms provide impressive levels of quality and comfort with ample space to relax and unwind. Public areas combine contemporary and traditional styling, and include a wonderful lounge where indulgent afternoon teas can be sampled. The attractive dining room is the venue for breakfast and dinner (by prior arrangement) with quality produce very much to the fore.

Rooms 7 en suite S £39-£65; D £78-£130* **Facilities** FTV DVD Lounge TVL tea/coffee Dinner available Licensed WiFi ♿ 🔒 **Parking** 8 **Notes** LB No Children

Kenella House
★★★★ GUEST ACCOMMODATION

tel: 01643 703128 & 07710 889079 **fax:** 01643 703128 **7 Tregonwell Rd TA24 5DT**
email: kenellahouse@fsmail.net **web:** www.kenellahouse.co.uk
dir: Off A39 into Townsend Rd & right into Ponsford Rd & Tregonwell Rd

A warm welcome and a relaxed atmosphere is found at Kenella House. Located close to the town centre, this property is also convenient for visitors to the steam railway, and walkers (a heated boot cupboard is available). The well-maintained bedrooms are very comfortable and have many extras. Hearty breakfasts are served in the smart dining room.

Rooms 6 en suite (1 GF) D £58.50-£70* **Facilities** FTV tea/coffee WiFi 🔒 **Parking** 8 **Notes** LB ⊗ No Children 14yrs Closed 23-26 Dec 🐾

Exmoor Owl & Hawk Centre
★★★ BED AND BREAKFAST

tel: 01643 862816 **West Lynch Farm, Allerford TA24 8HJ**
email: exmoor.falcon@virgin.net
dir: W of Minehead, turn right at Allerford Corner. 0.75m on left

This wonderful National Trust farmhouse dates back to the 15th century and offers a fascinating base from which to explore the stunning scenery of Exmoor. Bedrooms are full of charm and character and offer good levels of comfort, likewise the bathrooms, with all the required necessities to ensure a relaxing stay. Breakfast is served in the spacious dining room, or outside in the charming garden during summer months. This is home to an impressive collection of birds of prey and owls, with horse riding also available.

Rooms 2 rms (1 en suite) (1 pri facs) (2 fmly) **Facilities** FTV Lounge tea/coffee WiFi Riding 🔒 Bird of prey activities Alpaca walking **Conf** Max 15 Class 15 Board 15 **Parking** 4 **Notes** LB

Stones
★★★ INN

tel: 01643 709717 **48 The Avenue TA24 5AN**
email: stonesminehead@yahoo.co.uk

Located in the heart of town and just a short stroll from the seafront, this lively bar and restaurant has much to recommend it. A wide ranging menu is offered, supplemented with daily specials, which can be sampled either within the main bar area, or the stylish restaurant. Bedrooms are light, bright and modern, likewise bathrooms with good levels of comfort throughout.

Rooms 19 rms S £39-£65; D £49-£88*

■ **MONKSILVER** Map 3 ST03

The Notley Arms Inn

★★★★★ @ INN

tel: 01984 656095 **Front St TA4 4JB**
email: uksi@hotmail.com
dir: *From A358 at Bishop's Lydeard, onto B3224. After 5m right onto B3188 to Monksilver*

The Notley Arms was re-built around 1870 and more recently has benefited from extensive refurbishment, resulting in a warm, friendly and inviting village inn. Crackling log fires, comfy sofas and attentive service all contribute to a relaxing atmosphere. Bedrooms are located in the adjacent coach house and all provide impressive levels of quality, comfort and sophistication. The bar comes well stocked with local ales; likewise the menu focuses upon sourcing the best the region has to offer with a range of flavoursome and thoroughly enjoyable dishes. A garden is also available.

Rooms 6 en suite (2 fmly) (3 GF) S £60-£110; D £70-£120* **Facilities** FTV Lounge tea/coffee Dinner available ♨ Petanque court **Extras** Speciality toiletries, home-made biscuits - free **Parking** 18 **Notes** LB

■ **NORTH WOOTTON** Map 4 ST54

Crossways

★★★★ @ INN

tel: 01749 899000 **fax:** 01749 890476 **Stocks Ln BA4 4EU**
email: enquiries@thecrossways.co.uk **web:** www.thecrossways.co.uk
dir: *Exit M5 junct 22 towards Shepton Mallet, 0.2m from Pilton*

This family-run establishment is tucked away down a quiet lane, yet within easy reach of Wells and Glastonbury. The bedrooms and bathrooms are spacious and provide high levels of quality and comfort. There is a large bar-restaurant and a smaller dining room where breakfast is served. The extensive menu (served Wednesday to Sunday) features high quality produce with a choice of traditional pub classics or à la carte.

Rooms 13 en suite (3 fmly) **Facilities** tea/coffee Dinner available WiFi Pool table ♨ **Conf** Max 40 Thtr 40 Class 40 Board 25 **Parking** 100 **Notes** ⊗ Closed 25 Dec RS 26 Dec-2 Jan Civ Wed 100

■ **OAKHILL** Map 4 ST64

The Oakhill Inn

★★★★ @ INN

tel: 01749 840442 **fax:** 01749 840289 **Fosse Rd BA3 5HU**
email: info@theoakhillinn.com **web:** www.theoakhillinn.com
dir: *On A367 between Stratton-on-the-Fosse & Shepton Mallet*

A welcoming country inn, offering warm hospitality, locally sourced food and a wide selection of fine ales from local micro breweries. The comfortable bedrooms include luxuries such as Egyptian cotton sheets and DVD players. Dinner here should not be missed. In addition to lighter bar snacks, a full range of high-quality dishes utilising fresh local produce is also available.

Rooms 5 en suite (1 fmly) S £65-£95; D £90-£120 **Facilities** FTV DVD Lounge tea/coffee Dinner available WiFi ⌖ 18 ♨ **Extras** Mineral water - complimentary **Parking** 12 **Notes** LB

■ **PORLOCK** Map 3 SS84

Glen Lodge Country House

★★★★ 🏠 ➾ BED AND BREAKFAST

tel: 01643 863371 & 07786 118933 **Hawkcombe TA24 8LN**
email: glenlodge@gmail.com **web:** www.glenlodge.net
dir: *A39 in Porlock, turn into Parsons St at church. After 0.5m turn left over small bridge, property drive opposite*

The approach to this grand country house whets the appetite for the stunning views back down the densely wooded valley to the sea beyond. This is a perfect place to relax and unwind, a cup of tea and home-made cake on the deck sets the scene with helpful advice always readily offered. Bedrooms offer impressive levels of comfort and quality, with a number of thoughtful extras, typifying the commitment to guest welfare. Bathrooms come complete with robes and cosseting fluffy towels. Wonderful local and home-made produce features at breakfast, likewise at dinner, which is available by prior arrangement.

Rooms 5 rms (3 en suite) (2 pri facs) **Facilities** FTV DVD Lounge TVL tea/coffee Dinner available WiFi ➾ ⌖ 18 Fishing Riding ♨ **Extras** Speciality toiletries, robes **Parking** 6 **Notes** Closed 23 Dec-5 Jan

---

Tudor Cottage

★★★★ GUEST ACCOMMODATION

tel: 01643 862255 & 07855 531593 **TA24 8HQ**
email: tudorcottagebossington@btconnect.com **web:** www.tudorcottage.net
dir: *M5 junct 25, A358, A39 through Minehead. 5m, follow signs for Allerford & Bossington. 1m, 1st house on left*

Parts of this engaging cottage date back to the 15th century, and many period features have been retained. The welcome couldn't be warmer with tea and cakes in the lovely garden to get a stay off to a relaxing start. The setting is a haven of peace and tranquillity with a wonderful wooded hillside as a backdrop. Bedrooms are reassuringly cosy with all the expected modern comforts. Breakfast features a host of locally-sourced produce, and light snacks are offered in the evenings.

Rooms 3 rms (1 en suite) (2 pri facs) S £50; D £70-£80* **Facilities** FTV DVD TVL tea/coffee Dinner available Licensed WiFi ♨ **Extras** Books; mini-bar - chargeable **Parking** 3 **Notes** LB ⊗ No Children 10yrs

---

■ **RUDGE** Map 4 ST85

The Full Moon Inn

★★★ ➾ INN

tel: 01373 830936 **BA11 2QF**
email: info@thefullmoon.co.uk **web:** www.thefullmoon.co.uk
dir: *From A36 S from Bath, 10m, left at Standerwick by The Bell pub. 4m from Warminster*

Peacefully located in the quiet village of Rudge, this traditional inn offers a warm welcome and a proper country pub atmosphere. In the bar area, guests mix happily with the locals to enjoy a selection of real ales, and a log fire in the colder months. In addition to bar meals, a comfortable restaurant serving excellent home-cooked dishes is also available. Bedrooms include some at the main inn and more in an adjacent annexe - all are comfortable and well equipped.

Rooms 5 en suite 12 annexe en suite (2 fmly) (3 GF) **Facilities** tea/coffee Dinner available ⌖ **Conf** Max 65 Thtr 30 Class 12 Board 18 **Parking** 25

Roses Farm

★★★★ BED AND BREAKFAST

tel: 01749 860261 **Wraxall BA4 6RQ**
email: info@rosesfarm.com **web:** www.rosesfarm.com

Roses Farm is both peaceful and homely, and enjoys fine views of the Somerset countryside. It is convenient for Wells, Glastonbury, Bath, the Royal Bath & West Showground, and many National Trust properties. Rooms are nicely decorated, having comfortable five-foot double beds, free WiFi, tea and coffee making facilities, and TV. A guests' sitting room is available for quiet relaxation. There are excellent pubs and restaurants nearby.

Rooms 3 rms (2 en suite) (1 pri facs) S £50-£65; D £80-£85* **Facilities** FTV DVD Lounge tea/coffee WiFi ⚓ 🔒 **Parking** 6 **Notes** ⊗ No Children 14yrs

Cannards Grave Farmhouse

★★★★ GUEST ACCOMMODATION

tel: 01749 347091 **fax:** 01749 347091 **Cannards Grave BA4 4LY**
email: sue@cannardsgravefarmhouse.co.uk **web:** www.cannardsgravefarmhouse.co.uk
dir: On A37 between Shepton Mallet & The Bath and West Showground, 100yds from Highwayman pub towards showground on left

Conveniently located for the Royal Bath & West Showground, Longleat, Glastonbury and Wells, this 17th-century house provides thoughtfully equipped en suite bedrooms. There is also a well-furnished lounge, and breakfast is served in the conservatory dining room. The proprietors provide warm hospitality.

Rooms 4 en suite 1 annexe en suite (2 fmly) (1 GF) **Facilities** FTV DVD iPod docking station TVL tea/coffee WiFi **Extras** Mineral water **Parking** 6 **Notes** ⊗

Longbridge House Bed & Breakfast

★★★★ BED AND BREAKFAST

tel: 01749 572311 & 07809 437325 **78 Cowl St BA4 5EP**
email: longbridgehouse@gmail.com **web:** www.longbridgehouse.co.uk

There is plenty of history attached to this building. The Duke of Monmouth is reputed to have stayed here after the Battle of Sedgemoor in 1685; during the 19th century, the house was the childhood home of one John Lewis, founder of the eponymous department store; and more recently the house has belonged to the Bishop of London, who gave the sermon at the wedding of Prince William and the Duchess of Cambridge. Breakfast is freshly cooked on the Aga, and is served either at one large table in the comfortable kitchen or in the adjacent conservatory.

Rooms 2 en suite S £70-£90; D £80-£100 **Facilities** FTV iPod docking station tea/coffee WiFi **Extras** Bottled water **Notes** ⊗ No Children 🐾

The Natterjack Inn

★★★★ 🍴 INN

tel: 01749 860253 **fax:** 01749 860757 **Evercreech Junction BA4 6NA**
email: natterjack@btconnect.com **web:** www.thenatterjackinn.co.uk
dir: On A371 between Bath & Castle Cary, 2m past Bath & West Showground heading towards Castle Cary

The Natterjack Inn offers plenty of traditional character and hospitality with log fire, cosy seating and an excellent range of real ales and ciders. Dinner is another highlight with a varied menu to suit all tastes. Bedrooms are located in the adjacent converted cider barn, in a range of shapes and sizes that all come with very good quality bathrooms and showers. Breakfast is served in the pleasant dining room overlooking the large garden.

Rooms 5 en suite (3 GF) S £60; D £85* **Facilities** FTV tea/coffee Dinner available WiFi ⚓ 18 **Extras** Speciality toiletries, home-made biscuits - free **Parking** 20 **Notes** ⊗ No coaches

The Thatched Cottage Inn

★★★★ ⍟ INN

tel: 01749 342058 **fax:** 01749 901100 **63-67 Charlton Rd BA4 5QF**
email: enquiries@thatchedcottageinn.com **web:** www.thatchedcottageinn.com
dir: 0.6m E of town centre on A361

This popular inn offers a warm welcome and traditional hospitality. Bedrooms and bathrooms come in a range of shapes and sizes but all are comfortably furnished. There is a choice of seating areas for either drinking or dining, in addition to outdoor seating in the pleasant garden. Guests have a choice of carefully prepared quality food at dinner from menus of pub classics to a more fine-dining option - all meals are served in a welcoming atmosphere.

Rooms 8 en suite (1 fmly) **Facilities** FTV Lounge Dinner available Direct Dial WiFi 🔒 **Conf** Max 45 Thtr 45 Class 25 Board 35 **Parking** 48 **Notes** ⊗

The Devonshire Arms

★★★★ ⍟ INN

tel: 01458 241271 **fax:** 01458 241037 **Long Sutton TA10 9LP**
email: mail@thedevonshirearms.com **web:** www.thedevonshirearms.com
dir: A303 onto A372 at Podimore rdbt. After 4m left onto B3165, signed Martock & Long Sutton

This popular village inn offers an appealing blend of traditional and contemporary styling throughout the spacious public areas and accommodation. Bedrooms are individually designed and provide impressive levels of comfort and quality. Public areas include a convivial bar and an elegant restaurant where excellent local produce is utilised in skilfully executed dishes.

Rooms 7 en suite 2 annexe en suite (1 fmly) (2 GF) S £85-£145; D £100-£145 **Facilities** FTV tea/coffee Dinner available WiFi ⚓ 18 🔒 **Conf** Max 14 Board 14 **Parking** 6 **Notes** LB Closed 25-26 Dec & 1 Jan

Somerton Court Country House

★★★★ GUEST ACCOMMODATION

tel: 01458 274694 **fax:** 01458 274694 **TA11 7AH**
email: enquiries@somertoncourt.com **web:** www.somertoncourt.com
dir: From A303 onto A372 at Podimore rdbt. In 3m right onto B3151 to Somerton & follow signs

Dating back to the 17th century and set in extensive gardens and grounds, this house provides a tranquil haven away from the pressures of modern life. The comfortable bedrooms have lovely views, and breakfast is served in a delightful dining room that overlooks the gardens.

Rooms 4 en suite 2 annexe en suite (1 fmly) (2 GF) S fr £60; D fr £90*
Facilities Lounge tea/coffee WiFi Riding **Parking** 30 **Notes** LB Closed Xmas & New Year

Redlake Farm

★★★ BED AND BREAKFAST

tel: 01458 270086 & 07740 196645 **Littleton TA11 6NS**
email: redlakefarm@btinternet.com **web:** www.redlakebedandbreakfast.co.uk
dir: M5 junct 23 onto A39 (Glastonbury). Onto B3153 signed Somerton. At Marshalls Elm x-rds turn right, farmhouse on right

Located just outside Somerton, Redlake Farm is a perfect place to relax and unwind. The house is surrounded by five and half acres of attractive grounds, with camping facilities also offered and a lake for fly-fishing enthusiasts. Bedrooms offer all the required comforts, and breakfast is a generous offering, served in the delightful conservatory with eggs supplied by the resident hens.

Rooms 3 rms (2 en suite) (1 pri facs) (1 fmly) (1 GF) S £40-£45; D £55-£65*
Facilities FTV tea/coffee Licensed WiFi ⅃ 18 Fishing 🔒 **Conf** Max 8 Thtr 8 Class 8 Board 8 **Parking** 6 **Notes** LB ☜

SOUTH PETHERTON
Map 4 ST41

New Farm Restaurant

★★★★ ☜ GUEST ACCOMMODATION

tel: 01460 240584 & 07808 563885 **Over Stratton TA13 5LQ**
email: dine@newfarmrestaurant.co.uk **web:** www.newfarmrestaurant.co.uk
dir: From A303, at South Petherton rdbt 4th exit (travelling E) or 2nd exit (travelling W), pass Esso garage on left. Turn next left, 500mtrs on right

Situated in the picturesque village of Over Stratton, New Farm provides an ideal base from which to explore the many surrounding attractions of Somerset and Dorset, including several nearby National Trust properties. Bedrooms vary in size and all are comfortably furnished and decorated. Dinner (restaurant menu available Tuesday - Saturday nights and other times by prior arrangement) is a highlight, as is the range of well-cooked and presented dishes served at breakfast.

Rooms 3 en suite **Facilities** FTV Lounge tea/coffee Dinner available Licensed WiFi **Extras** Mineral water - complimentary **Parking** 11

STANTON DREW
Map 4 ST56

Valley Farm

★★★★ BED AND BREAKFAST

tel: 01275 332723 & 07799 768161 **Sandy Ln BS39 4EL**
email: valleyfarm2010@btinternet.com
dir: Exit B3130 into Stanton Drew, right into Sandy Ln

Located on a quiet country lane, Valley Farm offers relaxing and friendly accommodation. All bedrooms are comfortable and well equipped, and each has pleasant views over the countryside. Breakfast is served around a communal table in the dining room and, although dinner is not available here, a number of village pubs are just a stroll away. Also conveniently located for Bath and Bristol.

Rooms 3 en suite (1 fmly) (1 GF) **Facilities** FTV TVL tea/coffee WiFi **Parking** 6 **Notes** ⊗ No Children 12yrs ☜

STAPLE FITZPAINE
Map 4 ST21

Greyhound Inn

★★★★ ☜ INN

tel: 01823 480227 **fax:** 01823 481117 **TA3 5SP**
email: thegreyhound-inn@btconnect.com **web:** www.thegreyhoundinn.biz
dir: M5 junct 25, A358 signed Yeovil. In 3m turn right, signed Staple Fitzpaine

Set in the Blackdown Hills in the heart of Somerset, this picturesque village inn has great atmosphere and character, complete with flagstone floors and open fires. An imaginative choice of freshly-prepared seasonal dishes using locally sourced ingredients is featured on the ever-changing blackboard menu. The delightful bedrooms are spacious, comfortable, and well equipped, with many extra facilities.

Rooms 4 en suite S £65; D £90* **Facilities** FTV tea/coffee Dinner available Direct Dial WiFi Pool table **Conf** Max 60 Thtr 60 Class 30 Board 20 **Parking** 40 **Notes** No Children 10yrs

Wick House

★★★★ GUEST ACCOMMODATION

tel: 01984 656422 **Brook St TA4 3SZ**
email: sheila@wickhouse.co.uk **web:** www.wickhouse.co.uk
dir: Off A358 into village, left at x-rds, Wick House 3rd on left

Wick House offers homely accommodation, in a pretty village on the edge of Exmoor National Park. The cosy lounge has a wood-burning stove, there is a television room, and breakfast is enjoyed in the pleasant dining room overlooking the garden. One bedroom is designed for easier access.

Rooms 9 en suite (1 GF) S £45-£55; D £75-£85 **Facilities** FTV Lounge TVL tea/coffee Licensed WiFi ⚓ **Extras** Sweets - complimentary **Parking** 6 **Notes** LB ⊗

The Two Brewers

★★★★ INN

tel: 01458 442421 **38 Leigh Rd BA16 0HB**
email: thetwobrewers@yahoo.com **web:** www.thetwobrewers.co.uk

The Two Brewers is a traditional inn that is very popular with locals and tourists alike and offers a genuine welcome, excellent home-cooked food and a selection of fine, real ales. The bedrooms are located in an annexe to the rear of the inn and are well equipped and comfortable. The absence of music and machines in the bar adds to the relaxing atmosphere, and the menu choices include regularly-changing blackboard specials and guest real ales.

Rooms 3 annexe en suite (1 GF) **Facilities** FTV tea/coffee Dinner available WiFi ⚓ Skittle alley **Parking** 20 **Notes** LB ⊗ Closed 25-26 Dec No coaches

Kasuli Bed & Breakfast

★★★ BED AND BREAKFAST

tel: 01458 442063 **71 Somerton Rd BA16 0DN**
dir: B3151 from Street rdbt for Somerton, house 400yds past Street Inn on left, on corner of Downside

Kasuli Bed & Breakfast is family-run and located close to Clarks Village Outlet Centre and with easy access to local places of historical interest. Friendliness and a homely atmosphere are offered, and bedrooms are neatly presented. An enjoyable traditional breakfast is served in the dining room around the family dining table.

Rooms 2 rms S £30-£35; D £58-£65 **Facilities** FTV tea/coffee WiFi ⚓ **Parking** 2 **Notes** ⊗ No Children 10yrs ⊜

See also Staple Fitzpaine

Meryan House

★★★★ ⬭ GUEST ACCOMMODATION

tel: 01823 337445 **fax:** 01823 322355 **Bishop's Hull TA1 5EG**
email: meryanhousehotel@yahoo.co.uk **web:** www.meryanhouse.co.uk
dir: 1.5m W of town centre. Off Silk Mills Rd (A358)

Set in its own grounds, just over a mile from the town centre, this 17th-century property has delightful, individually furnished rooms featuring antiques and modern facilities. Interesting dishes are available at dinner, and there is also a cosy bar and a spacious lounge.

Rooms 12 en suite (2 fmly) (2 GF) **Facilities** STV FTV DVD iPod docking station TVL tea/coffee Dinner available Licensed WiFi ⚓ **Conf** Max 25 Thtr 25 Class 25 Board 18 **Parking** 17 **Notes** LB RS Sun No evening meal

Wick House B&B

★★★★★ BED AND BREAKFAST

tel: 01823 289614 & 07535 259473 **Norton Fitzwarren TA4 1BT**
email: info@wick-house.co.uk **web:** www.wick-house.co.uk
dir: From Taunton take B3227 through Norton Fitzwarren, after old railway bridge, 1st house on right

This family-run establishment is handily placed just a few minutes from Taunton and within 15 minutes of the M5. Bedrooms are located away from the main house, allowing guests the flexibility to come and go as they please. All bedrooms provide impressive levels of comfort and quality, including spacious wet rooms and a kitchenette area for making drinks. Breakfast is taken in the well-appointed dining room which has lovely views across the orchard.

Rooms 3 annexe en suite (3 GF) S £45-£55; D £65-£85* **Facilities** FTV DVD tea/coffee WiFi ⚓ **Extras** Bottled water, orange juice **Parking** 3 **Notes** ⊗ No Children

Blorenge House

★★★★ GUEST ACCOMMODATION

tel: 01823 283005 **fax:** 01823 283005 **57 Staple Grove Rd TA1 1DG**
email: enquiries@blorengehouse.co.uk **web:** www.blorengehouse.co.uk
dir: M5 junct 25, towards cricket ground & Morrisons on left, left at lights, right at 2nd lights, house 150yds on left

A fine Victorian property, Blorenge House offers spacious accommodation and is within walking distance of the town centre. The bedrooms, two at ground-floor level and some with four-poster beds, are individually furnished and vary in size. A lounge is available, and the garden, with an outdoor swimming pool, is open to guests during daytime hours, most days of the week. There is also ample parking.

Rooms 20 rms (17 en suite) (3 pri facs) (2 fmly) (2 GF) S £56-£85; D £80-£100* **Facilities** FTV TVL tea/coffee WiFi ⚓ **Conf** Max 20 **Parking** 20 **Notes** LB

Brookfield House

★★★★ GUEST HOUSE

tel: 01823 272786 **fax:** 01823 240003 **16 Wellington Rd TA1 4EQ**
email: info@brookfieldguesthouse.uk.com **web:** www.brookfieldguesthouse.uk.com
dir: From town centre follow signs to Musgrove Hospital, onto A38 (Wellington Rd), on right opposite turn to hospital

This charming Grade II listed Georgian house is just a five-minute level walk from the town centre. The family take great pride in caring for guests, and the brightly decorated bedrooms are well equipped. Breakfast, featuring local produce, is served in the attractive dining room. The property is entirely non-smoking.

Rooms 7 en suite (1 fmly) S £65-£72; D £78-£105* **Facilities** FTV Lounge tea/coffee Dinner available WiFi **Parking** 8 **Notes** ⊗ No Children 7yrs

Creechbarn Bed & Breakfast

★★★★ BED AND BREAKFAST

tel: 01823 443955 **Vicarage Ln, Creech St Michael TA3 5PP**
email: mick@somersite.co.uk **web:** www.somersite.co.uk
dir: M5 junct 25, A358 to Creech St Michael, follow canal boat signs to end Vicarage Ln. Through brick gateposts, turn right

Located next to the canal and on a Sustrans cycle route, this traditional Somerset barn is lovingly cared for by its owners. Bedrooms are comfortable and there is a spacious sitting room with books and TV. Breakfast is well prepared using free-range eggs and home-made bread.

Rooms 2 rms (1 en suite) (1 pri facs) **Facilities** TVL TV1B tea/coffee Direct Dial WiFi ⚓ **Parking** 6 **Notes** Closed 20 Dec-6 Jan ⊜

Lower Farm (ST281241)

★★★★ FARMHOUSE

tel: 01823 443549 & 07811 565309 **Thornfalcon TA3 5NR**
email: doreen@titman.eclipse.co.uk web: www.thornfalcon.co.uk
dir: M5 junct 25, 2m SE on A358, left opposite Nags Head pub, farm signed 1m on left

This charming, thatched 15th-century farmhouse is set in lovely gardens and surrounded by open countryside. Hearty breakfasts, served in the farmhouse kitchen, feature home-produced eggs. Some bedrooms are located in the converted granary, some on the ground floor. There is a comfortable sitting room with a log fire.

Rooms 2 rms (1 en suite) (1 pri facs) 9 annexe rms 7 annexe en suite (2 pri facs) (2 fmly) (7 GF) S £45-£50; D £75-£80* **Facilities** FTV TVL TV9B tea/coffee WiFi 🛁 **Parking** 14 **Notes** LB ⊗ No Children 5yrs 10 acres beef/cows/poultry

Lower Marsh Farm (ST224279)

★★★★ FARMHOUSE

tel: 01823 451331 **fax**: 01823 451331 **Kingston St Mary TA2 8AB**
email: info@lowermarshfarm.co.uk web: www.lowermarshfarm.co.uk
dir: M5 junct 25. B&B between Taunton & Kingston St Mary just past King's Hall School on right

Located at the foot of the Quantock Hills, this delightful family-run farm provides a warm welcome with a pot of tea and a slice of cake ready and waiting. Bedrooms are individually styled and reflect the traditional charm of the house; an impressive level of quality is complemented by numerous thoughtful extras. The Aga-cooked breakfast is a real treat, served in the dining room around one grand table, and evening meals are available by prior arrangement. There is a spacious lounge warmed by a crackling log fire in winter.

Rooms 3 en suite (2 fmly) S fr £40; D fr £80 **Facilities** TVL tea/coffee Dinner available WiFi 🛁 **Parking** 6 **Notes** ⊗ 300 acres arable

---

TINTINHULL | Map 4 ST41

Crown & Victoria

★★★★ ⊛ INN

tel: 01935 823341 **fax**: 01935 825786 **Farm St BA22 8PZ**
email: info@thecrownandvictoria.co.uk web: www.thecrownandvictoria.co.uk
dir: Off A303, signs for Tintinhull Gardens

Appointed to a high standard, the light and airy property has very well-equipped bedrooms. The staff ensure guests are well cared for, and the contemporary bar and restaurant provide a good selection of carefully prepared dishes. The food here has been awarded an AA Rosette.

Rooms 5 en suite **Facilities** FTV DVD tea/coffee Dinner available WiFi 🛁 **Extras** Bottled water **Parking** 60 **Notes** No coaches

---

WALTON | Map 4 ST43

The Walton Gateway

★★★★ ⊜ INN

tel: 01458 447733 **160 Main St BA16 9QU**
email: info@waltongateway.co.uk web: www.waltongateway.co.uk
dir: M5 junct 23 towards Glastonbury on A39. In village of Walton on right

The Walton Gateway provides very good quality accommodation in a modern inn. Bedrooms are comfortable, with some very spacious rooms, and cater to the modern traveller whilst providing home comfort. Hearty, well-cooked meals are served in the bar; there is a brasserie for a more formal dining experience or large party, and a large beer garden for sunnier days.

Rooms 6 en suite (3 fmly) S £59-£149; D £79-£149* **Facilities** FTV TVL tea/coffee Dinner available WiFi **Extras** Speciality toiletries **Conf** Max 40 Thtr 40 Class 40 Board 20 **Parking** 50 **Notes** LB ⊗

WATCHET
Map 3 ST04

The Georgian House
★★★★ GUEST HOUSE

tel: 01984 639279 **28 Swain St TA23 0AD**
email: georgianhouse_watchet@virgin.net
dir: *From A39 over railway bridge into main street*

This elegant Georgian property is situated in the heart of the increasingly popular coastal resort and is within a short walk of the impressive marina. The comfortable bedrooms combine quality and individuality. Breakfast (and dinner by arrangement) is served in the well-appointed dining room. Additional facilities for guests include a lounge and the use of the garden.

Rooms 3 en suite S £35-£40; D £60-£100* **Facilities** Dinner available **Parking** 2 **Notes** LB ⊗

Langtry Country House
★★★★ 🏡 🍴 BED AND BREAKFAST

tel: 01984 641200 & 07500 366184 **Washford TA23 0NT**
email: langtrycountryhouse@icloud.com **web:** www.langtrycountryhouse.co.uk
dir: *From A39 in Williton onto Minehead road. 2m on right just before Washford*

Dating from the early 1900s and originally a farmhouse, this grand house is a convenient base from which to explore this picturesque area. A pot of tea and home-made cake on arrival is on offer, and typifies the whole-hearted commitment to ensure guests are comfortable, relaxed and genuinely welcome. Bedrooms provide very good levels of comfort, likewise bathrooms, complete with fluffy towels and robes. The elegant dining room is the venue for the superb dinners and wonderful breakfasts, with high quality produce cooked with care and skill. A guest lounge is also provided, while outside, extensive gardens can be enjoyed.

Rooms 3 en suite S £50-£72.50; D £85-£95* **Facilities** FTV DVD Lounge tea/coffee Dinner available WiFi 🏌 **Extras** Speciality toiletries; snacks - chargeable **Parking** 8 **Notes** LB ⊗ No Children 12yrs

WEDMORE
Map 4 ST44

The George
★★★★ 🍴 INN

tel: 01934 712124 **Church St BS28 4AB**
email: info@thegeorgewedmore.co.uk **web:** www.thegeorgewedmore.co.uk
dir: *M5 junct 22, follow Bristol/Cheddar signs (A38). From dual carriageway right, follow signs for Mark, then Wedmore. In village centre*

The George is a traditional inn offering plenty of character, log fires and a fine selection of ales. Bedrooms offer a range of shapes and sizes and are located on the first floor above the inn. A range of dishes are offered at lunch and dinner to suit all tastes and may be taken in the cosy bar or more formal dining areas. Outdoor seating and car parking are also available.

Rooms 4 en suite S £80-£90; D £80-£100* **Facilities** FTV DVD iPod docking station Lounge tea/coffee Dinner available WiFi 🏌 18 🏌 **Extras** Speciality toiletries **Conf** Max 60 Thtr 30 Class 30 Board 30 **Parking** 30 **Notes** Civ Wed 100

WELLINGTON
Map 3 ST12

The Cleve Spa
★★★★ GUEST ACCOMMODATION

tel: 01823 662033 **fax:** 01823 660874 **Mantle St TA21 8SN**
email: reception@clevehotel.com **web:** www.clevehotel.com
dir: *M5 junct 26 follow signs to Wellington town centre. Continue for 600mtrs, entrance on left*

This elegant Victorian country house is situated in an elevated position with commanding views. Bedrooms provide high levels of comfort and quality, with well appointed and stylish bathrooms. Dinner and breakfast are served in the attractive restaurant, after which a stroll around the extensive grounds may be appropriate. An impressive array of leisure facilities is also offered, including indoor pool, spa bath, steam room and fully-equipped fitness studio.

Rooms 21 en suite (5 fmly) (3 GF) S £70-£120; D £80-£135* **Facilities** FTV Lounge tea/coffee Dinner available Direct Dial Licensed WiFi 🕯 Sauna Gym Spa beauty treatments **Conf** Max 250 Thtr 250 Class 100 Board 60 **Parking** 100 **Notes** LB Civ Wed 200

WELLS
Map 4 ST54

Premier Collection

Beaconsfield Farm
★★★★★ 🏡 BED AND BREAKFAST

tel: 01749 870308 **Easton BA5 1DU**
email: carol@beaconsfieldfarm.co.uk **web:** www.beaconsfieldfarm.co.uk
dir: *2.5m from Wells on A371, on right just before Easton*

Set in pleasant, well-tended gardens on the west side of the Mendip Hills, Beaconsfield Farm is a convenient base for exploring this attractive area. The welcoming hosts are really friendly and attentive, and many guests return on a regular basis. The comfortable bedrooms are delightfully decorated with co-ordinated fabrics and have many guest extras. A choice of well-cooked dishes featuring fresh local produce is offered at breakfast.

Rooms 3 en suite **Facilities** FTV TVL tea/coffee WiFi **Parking** 10 **Notes** ⊗ No Children 8yrs Closed 22 Dec-3 Jan ●

Beryl
★★★★★ 🅰 BED AND BREAKFAST

tel: 01749 678738 **fax:** 01749 670508 **Hawkers Ln BA5 3JP**
email: stay@beryl-wells.co.uk **web:** www.beryl-wells.co.uk
dir: *Exit B3139 (Radstock Rd), signed The Horringtons, into Hawkers Ln opposite BP garage, to end*

Beryl is a small country mansion built in the Gothic Revival style, quietly located just one mile from the cathedral city of Wells. Bedrooms include welcome extras and enjoy splendid views of the surrounding countryside. The fine lounge (including honesty bar) and separate dining room are both suitably in keeping with the country mansion feel.

Rooms 13 rms (12 en suite) (1 pri facs) (4 fmly) S £80-£100; D £100-£160* **Facilities** FTV DVD Lounge TVL tea/coffee Direct Dial Lift Licensed WiFi ⚲ ❧ 🏌 childrens play area **Parking** 20 **Notes** LB Closed 24-27 Dec

Coxley House

★★★★ ≜ BED AND BREAKFAST

tel: 01749 675527 & 07836 751294 **Upper Coxley BA5 1QS**
email: info@coxleyhouse.co.uk **web:** www.coxleyhouse.co.uk
dir: *A39 from Wells, after 2m turn left into Stoppers Ln. Coxley House after 2nd bend through gates*

Peacefully located in a quiet area with pleasant views and a large garden, this detached accommodation provides guests with plenty of quality and comfort throughout. While Coxley House is ideal for exploring the surrounding areas of Wells, Glastonbury and Street, guests also have use of a large lounge and delightful outdoor seating area in warmer weather. Breakfast offers an excellent range of high quality produce and is served around one large table in the well furnished dining room.

Rooms 2 en suite D £100-£115* **Facilities** FTV TVL tea/coffee WiFi ⮕
Extras Speciality toiletries **Parking** 2 **Notes** No Children 10yrs

Double-Gate Farm (ST484424)

★★★★ FARMHOUSE

tel: 01458 832217 & 07843 924079 **fax:** 01458 835612 **Godney BA5 1RZ**
email: doublegatefarm@aol.com **web:** www.doublegatefarm.com
dir: *A39 from Wells towards Glastonbury, at Polsham right signed Godney/Polsham. 2m to x-rds, continue to farmhouse on left after inn*

Expect a warm welcome not only from the owners, but also their friendly Labradors. Set on the banks of the River Sheppey on the Somerset Levels, this comfortable farmhouse is well known for its attractive summer flower garden, as well as delicious breakfasts. Guests have use of a games room and free internet access in the lounge.

Rooms 1 en suite 7 annexe en suite (4 fmly) (5 GF) S £60-£85; D £70-£110*
Facilities FTV DVD TVL tea/coffee Direct Dial WiFi Fishing Snooker ⬤ Table tennis
Extras Mini-fridges in some rooms **Parking** 9 **Notes** ⊗ Closed 22 Dec-5 Jan
100 acres mixed

See advert below

The Crown at Wells

★★★★ ⇌ INN

tel: 01749 673457 **fax:** 01749 679792 **Market Place BA5 2RP**
email: stay@crownatwells.co.uk **web:** www.crownatwells.co.uk
dir: *On entering Wells follow signs for Hotels & Deliveries, in Market Place, car park at rear*

Retaining its original features and period charm, this historic inn is situated in the heart of the city, just a short stroll from the cathedral. The building's frontage has been used in many film productions. Bedrooms, all with modern facilities, vary in size and style. Public areas focus around Anton's, the popular bistro, which has a light, airy environment and relaxed atmosphere. The Penn Bar offers an alternative eating option and real ales.

Rooms 15 en suite (2 fmly) S fr £65; D £90-£115* **Facilities** FTV Lounge tea/coffee Dinner available WiFi ⬩ 18 ⬤ **Extras** Speciality toiletries, filtered water - free **Parking** 10 **Notes** LB

WELLS *continued*

Highfield

★★★★ BED AND BREAKFAST

tel: 01749 675330 **93 Portway BA5 2BR**
web: www.highfieldbandb.net
dir: *Enter Wells & signs for A371 Cheddar, Highfield on Portway after last lights at top of hill*

Within walking distance of the city and cathedral, this delightful home maintains Edwardian style and provides comfortable accommodation. Pleasant views of the countryside can be enjoyed and some bedrooms have balconies. A carefully prepared breakfast is served around one large table in the well furnished breakfast room. Welcome extra features include the well-tended garden and off-street parking.

Rooms 3 en suite (1 fmly) S £45-£50; D £70-£75* **Facilities** FTV tea/coffee WiFi ⌕ 18 **Parking** 7 **Notes** LB ⊗ No Children 2yrs Closed 23 Dec-1 Jan ⊛

Amber House

★★★ BED AND BREAKFAST

tel: 01749 679612 **Coxley BA5 1QZ**
email: amberhouse.wells@gmail.com
dir: *On A39 in village, 0.25m S past Pound Inn on right*

Located less than two miles south of the centre of Wells, and ideally placed for touring the area's historic sites and countryside, this friendly family home offers a relaxed atmosphere. Bedrooms are well equipped; some look out over open countryside and farmland to the rear. A traditional English breakfast is served at separate tables in the cosy dining room, which guests are welcome to use at other times.

Rooms 3 en suite **Facilities** FTV DVD tea/coffee WiFi ⛁ **Parking** 3 **Notes** ⊗ ⊛

19 St Cuthbert Street

★★ BED AND BREAKFAST

tel: 01749 673166 **BA5 2AW**
dir: *At bottom of High St opposite St Cuthbert's Church*

Guests are assured of a friendly welcome at this charming terrace house, which is within walking distance of the cathedral and the bus station. The accommodation is fresh, light and comfortable and the atmosphere homely. Bedrooms are well appointed and there is a relaxing lounge. Breakfast, featuring home-made marmalade, is served in the dining room around a family table.

Rooms 2 rms S £38-£42; D £60-£65* **Facilities** FTV TVL tea/coffee **Notes** ⊗ No Children 5yrs ⊛

Crapnell Farm

Ⓤ

tel: 01749 342683 **Dinder BA5 3HG**
email: pamkeen@yahoo.com **web:** www.crapnellfarm.co.uk
dir: *M5 junct 23 signed Glastonbury/Wells. Onto A371 signed Shepton Mallet. Follow signs for Dinder*

Currently the rating for this establishment is not confirmed. This may be due to a change of ownership or because it has only recently joined the AA rating scheme.

Rooms 3 en suite (2 fmly) S £55; D £75-£85* **Facilities** FTV TVL tea/coffee WiFi ⚞ ⌕ 18 Riding ⛁ **Parking** 8 **Notes** LB ⊗ Closed 20 Dec-5 Jan ⊛

Crossways Inn

★★★★ INN

tel: 01278 783756 **fax:** 01278 501117 **Withy Rd TA9 3RA**
email: info@crosswaysinn.com **web:** www.crosswaysinn.com
dir: *On main A38 between M5 junct 22 & 23*

Crossways is a family-run traditional 17th-century coaching inn serving good food and offering a very high standard of accommodation accompanied by warm friendly service. Bedrooms are very comfortable, and offer a host of extras such as iPod docks and WiFi.

Rooms 7 en suite (2 GF) **Facilities** FTV iPod docking station tea/coffee Dinner available Lift WiFi Pool table ⛁ Skittle alley **Parking** 72

Premier Collection

Church House

★★★★★ ≋ BED AND BREAKFAST

tel: 01934 633185 **27 Kewstoke Rd, Kewstoke BS22 9YD**
email: churchhouse@kewstoke.net **web:** www.churchhousekewstoke.co.uk
dir: *From M5 junct 21 follow signs for Kewstoke 2.5m, next to Kewstoke Church*

In a peaceful location at the foot of Monk's Hill, Church House is a delightful property that enjoys wonderful views of the Bristol Channel and as far as Wales on clear days. The bedrooms are stylish and spacious, with lots of thoughtful extras and well-appointed en suites. Public areas include a pleasant conservatory and an elegant dining room where impressive breakfasts are served. AA Friendliest B&B of the Year Finalist 2014-2015.

Rooms 5 en suite S fr £70; D fr £85* **Facilities** tea/coffee WiFi **Parking** 10 **Notes** LB

Oakover Guest House

★★★★ GUEST HOUSE

tel: 01934 620125 **fax:** 01934 620173 **25 Clevedon Rd BS23 1DA**
email: info@oakover.co.uk **web:** www.oakover.co.uk
dir: *Exit A370 (Beach Rd) near Sea Life Aquarium into Clevedon Rd*

Oakover is a substantial Victorian property situated a short level walk from the town centre and seafront. Bedrooms and bathrooms offer very good levels of quality and comfort, and a varied breakfast menu is offered in the bright dining room. The friendly resident proprietor maintains an easy-going and welcoming establishment.

Rooms 6 en suite (2 GF) S £45-£75; D £60-£100 **Facilities** FTV DVD tea/coffee WiFi **Parking** 7 **Notes** ⊗ No Children 12yrs

Camellia Lodge

★★★★ BED AND BREAKFAST

tel: 01934 613534 **fax:** 01934 613534 **76 Walliscote Rd BS23 1ED**
email: dachefs@aol.com **web:** www.camellialodge.net
dir: *200yds from seafront*

Guests return regularly for the warm welcome at Camellia Lodge, an immaculate Victorian family home, which is just off the seafront and within walking distance of the town centre. Bedrooms have a range of thoughtful touches, and carefully prepared breakfasts are served in the relaxing dining room.

Rooms 5 en suite (2 fmly) S £35-£45; D £70-£75 **Facilities** FTV DVD tea/coffee WiFi

Jamesfield Guest House

★★★★ GUEST HOUSE

tel: 01934 642898 **1A Ellenborough Park North BS23 1XH**
email: jamesfield1@aol.com **web:** www.jamesfieldguesthouse.co.uk

A well-maintained property in an ideal location, Jamesfield Guest House is a short walk from the seafront and only a few minutes' stroll from town. The bedrooms are comfortably furnished and well decorated, and include rooms on the ground floor. Guests are welcome to use the relaxing lounge, and the property also benefits from its own car park.

Rooms 7 rms (6 en suite) (1 pri facs) (1 fmly) (2 GF) S £35; D £60* **Facilities** FTV TVL tea/coffee WiFi **Parking** 9 **Notes** ⊗

Linden Lodge Guest House

★★★★ GUEST ACCOMMODATION

tel: 01934 645797 **27 Clevedon Rd BS23 1DA**
email: info@lindenlodge.com **web:** www.lindenlodge.com
dir: *Follow signs to seafront. 0.5m S of grand pier turn into Clevedon Rd*

Just a short walk from the town centre and the seafront, Linden Lodge offers welcoming hospitality and guest care in a traditional style. Bedrooms come in a range of shapes and sizes, and all are well decorated and equipped. A good selection is offered at breakfast which is served in the pleasant conservatory.

Rooms 5 en suite (1 fmly) **Facilities** tea/coffee **Parking** 3 **Notes** ⊗

Goodrington Guest House

★★★ GUEST HOUSE

tel: 01934 623229 **23 Charlton Rd BS23 4HB**
email: vera.bishop@talk21.com **web:** www.goodrington.info
dir: *A370 Beach Rd S onto Uphill Rd, left into Charlton Rd*

The owners of Goodrington Guest House make every effort to ensure guests enjoy their stay at this charming Victorian house, tucked away in a quiet residential area. The bedrooms are comfortably furnished, and there is an attractive lounge. Families are especially welcome and this makes a good holiday base.

Rooms 3 rms (2 en suite) (1 pri facs) (1 fmly) (1 GF) S £35-£50; D £56-£60* **Facilities** FTV DVD TVL tea/coffee Dinner available WiFi **Notes** LB ⊗ Closed Oct-Etr ⊗

Parasol Guest House

★★★ GUEST HOUSE

tel: 01934 636409 & 07592 357619 **49 Walliscote Rd BS23 1EE**
email: parasol49@hotmail.com **web:** www.parasolguesthouse.co.uk

Located in a residential area with the seafront and town centre just a short stroll away, Parasol Guest House offers a range of well-decorated bedrooms in various sizes. Breakfast is served at individual tables in the comfortable dining room. WiFi is among the welcome extras available in the bedrooms.

Rooms 8 en suite (2 fmly) (1 GF) S £25-£35; D £45-£70* **Facilities** FTV DVD iPod docking station tea/coffee WiFi ⚭ Pass available to fitness club **Parking** 2 **Notes** LB ⊗

Corbiere Guest House

★★★ GUEST HOUSE

tel: 01934 629607 **24 Upper Church Rd BS23 2DX**
email: corbierehotel@btinternet.com
dir: *M5 junct 21, take 2nd exit to seafront*

Located on a residential street just a few minutes walk from the seafront, this relaxed and welcoming accommodation offers a range of shapes and sizes in terms of bedrooms and bathrooms. All are well furnished and have comfortable beds and bedding. Breakfast is served in the lower ground floor dining room and offers a good selection of hot and cold dishes.

Rooms 10 en suite (4 fmly) (2 GF) S £25-£35; D £50-£60 **Facilities** FTV DVD Lounge TVL tea/coffee Dinner available **Notes** LB ⊗

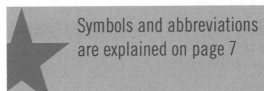

Symbols and abbreviations
are explained on page 7

WHEDDON CROSS

Map 3 SS93

The Rest and Be Thankful Inn

★★★★ INN

tel: 01643 841222 **fax:** 01643 841813 **TA24 7DR**
email: stay@restandbethankful.co.uk **web:** www.restandbethankful.co.uk
dir: M5 junct 25, A358 to Minehead, left onto B3224 at Wheddon Cross sign

The Rest and Be Thankful Inn is situated in the highest village on Exmoor, overlooking Dunkery Beacon. The comfortable bedrooms are extremely well equipped with extras such as mini-bars and trouser presses. The convivial bar, complete with crackling log fires, is a popular meeting point for locals and visitors alike. A range of wholesome dishes is offered in the bar, the restaurant or outside on the patio, from where lovely countryside views can be enjoyed.

Rooms 8 en suite (1 fmly) **Facilities** FTV tea/coffee Dinner available Direct Dial WiFi Pool table Skittle alley Table Tennis **Extras** Mini-bar - chargeable **Conf** Max 50 Class 50 Board 50 **Parking** 10 **Notes** Closed 25 Dec

WILLITON

Map 3 ST04

Arden Cottage B&B

★★★★ BED AND BREAKFAST

tel: 01984 634090 & 07794 656484 **33 Long St TA4 4QU**
email: enquiries@ardencottagewilliton.co.uk
web: www.ardencottagebedandbreakfast.co.uk
dir: M5 junct 23 to Bridgwater, then A39 signed Minehead. In Williton, over railway line, 0.5m on right

Located in the pleasant village of Williton, Arden Cottage is full of character and history. A friendly welcome is assured, and if the timing is right may include tea and home-made cakes served in the large rear garden or the conservatory. Bedrooms offer a range of shapes and sizes, all with very comfortable beds.

Breakfast utilises a good range of quality local ingredients, and a number of pubs are within easy walking distance for evening meals.

Rooms 3 en suite (1 fmly) S £37.50-£45; D £72-£80* **Facilities** iPod docking station TVL tea/coffee WiFi ⚓ Holistic massage Shibashi Tai Chi **Extras** Home-made biscuits, speciality toiletries **Parking** 3 **Notes** ⊜

The White House

★★★★ GUEST ACCOMMODATION

tel: 01984 632306 **11 Long St TA4 4QW**
email: whitehouselive@btconnect.com **web:** www.whitehousewilliton.co.uk
dir: A39 Bridgwater to Minehead, in Williton on right prior to Watchet turning

This Grade II listed Georgian house is in the perfect location for guests wishing to explore the beautiful Somerset countryside and coast. Many original features have been retained and add to the character of the house. Rooms are well equipped, and guests have a choice of rooms in the main house or in the courtyard. Additional facilities include a bar and lounge.

Rooms 8 rms (7 en suite) (1 pri facs) 6 annexe en suite (2 fmly) (6 GF) **Facilities** FTV TVL TV13B Licensed WiFi ⚓ **Parking** 12

WINSFORD

Map 3 SS93

Royal Oak Inn

★★★★ ⇒ INN

tel: 01643 851455 **Halse Ln TA24 7JE**
email: enquiries@royaloakexmoor.co.uk **web:** www.royaloakexmoor.co.uk
dir: M5 junct 27 onto A361 Tiverton bypass. At 1st rdbt turn right onto A396, 0.5m after Bridgetown turn left signed Winsford

Dating back to the 12th century, this former farmhouse and dairy is located in the heart of Exmoor and is a perfect base for exploring this stunning area. For many years, this picturesque thatched inn has been providing a warm welcome for weary travellers looking for rest and relaxation. Bedrooms, all of which offer great comfort and quality, include a number with four-posters, and all have modern bathrooms. The menu makes use of great local produce and can be enjoyed either in the bar or restaurant. A well-appointed guest lounge is also available.

Rooms 8 en suite 2 annexe en suite (2 GF) S £55-£75; D £100-£140 **Facilities** iPod docking station Lounge TVL Dinner available Direct Dial WiFi ⌣ Fishing Riding ⚓ **Parking** 14

WITHYPOOL

Map 3 SS83

Premier Collection

Kings Farm

★★★★★ 🏠 BED AND BREAKFAST

tel: 01643 831381 **TA24 7RE**
email: info@kingsfarmexmoor.co.uk **web:** www.kingsfarmexmoor.co.uk
dir: Off B3223 to Withypool, over bridge & sharp left to farm

This delightful farmhouse is set in over two acres of landscaped gardens in an idyllic valley beside the River Barle. It combines the character and charm of its 19th-century origins with modern comforts. From the carefully planned bedrooms to the sumptuously furnished sitting room, delicious home-cooked breakfasts and the warmest of welcomes, top quality is most definitely the hallmark of Kings Farm. Both stabling and fishing are available.

Rooms 2 rms (1 en suite) (1 pri facs) S £65; D £85-£105* **Facilities** STV FTV Lounge tea/coffee WiFi Fishing ⚓ **Extras** Speciality toiletries, fruit, chocolates - free **Parking** 3 **Notes** No Children 14yrs

The Royal Oak Inn

★★★★ 🛏 INN

tel: 01643 831506 **TA24 7QP**
email: enquiries@royaloakwithpool.co.uk web: www.royaloakwithpool.co.uk

Set in the heart of Exmoor, this long established and popular inn continues to provide rest and sustenance for weary travellers. The atmosphere is warm and engaging with the bar always frequented by cheery locals, happy to offer helpful suggestions for making the most of a stay in this beautiful area. Bedrooms and bathrooms are stylish and well appointed with all the required necessities to ensure a comfortable stay. Menus feature excellent local produce and can be enjoyed either in the bars or the elegant restaurant.

Rooms 8 en suite S £55-£60; D £80-£100* **Facilities** FTV Dinner available Direct Dial WiFi ⌇ 18 🔒 **Conf** Max 20 Thtr 20 Class 20 Board 20 **Parking** 10 **Notes** No coaches

YEOVIL
See also Crewkerne

Map 4 ST51

Premier Collection

Little Barwick House

★★★★★ ◉◉◉ 🍽 RESTAURANT WITH ROOMS

tel: 01935 423902 **fax:** 01935 420908 **Barwick Village BA22 9TD**
email: littlebarwick@hotmail.com web: www.littlebarwickhouse.co.uk
dir: From Yeovil A37 towards Dorchester, left at 1st rdbt, 1st left, 0.25m on left

Situated in a quiet hamlet in three and half acres of gardens and grounds, this listed Georgian dower house is an ideal retreat for those seeking peaceful surroundings and good food. Just one of the highlights of a stay here is a meal in the restaurant, where good use is made of local ingredients. Each of the bedrooms has its own character, and a range of thoughtful extras such as fresh flowers, bottled water and magazines is provided.

Rooms 6 en suite **Facilities** FTV iPod docking station tea/coffee Dinner available Direct Dial **Parking** 30 **Notes** No Children 5yrs RS Sun eve & Mon closed No coaches

The Masons Arms

★★★★ 🍽 🛏 INN

tel: 01935 862591 **fax:** 01935 862591 **41 Lower Odcombe BA22 8TX**
email: paula@masonsarmsodcombe.co.uk web: www.masonsarmsodcombe.co.uk
dir: From A303 take A3088 to Yeovil, follow signs to Montacute after village, 3rd turning on right

Dating back to the 16th century, The Masons Arms claims to be the oldest building in this small country village on the outskirts of Yeovil. The spacious bedrooms are contemporary in style, with clean lines, a high level of comfort and a wide range of considerate extras. The friendly hosts run their own micro brewery, and their ales are available at the bar along with other brews. Public areas include a bar-restaurant, which offers a full menu of freshly prepared dishes, along with a choice of lighter snacks.

Rooms 6 en suite (1 fmly) (6 GF) **Facilities** FTV tea/coffee Dinner available Direct Dial WiFi 🔒 **Extras** Mineral water/beer in room fridge **Conf** Max 15 Class 15 Board 15 **Parking** 35 **Notes** No coaches

The Manor

★★★★ INN

tel: 01935 423116 **fax:** 01935 706607 **Hendford BA20 1TG**
email: manor.yeovil@oldenglishinns.co.uk web: www.oldenglish.co.uk
dir: A303 onto A3088 to Yeovil. Over River Yeo, 2nd exit at rdbt immediately left into Hendford

The Manor, dating from 1735, stands in the centre of Yeovil and has the benefit of its own spacious car park. There is a bar and an open-plan lounge area where afternoon tea may be enjoyed. Breakfast and dinner are served in the light and airy conservatory dining area.

Rooms 21 rms (20 en suite) (1 pri facs) 21 annexe en suite (10 GF) **Facilities** tea/coffee Dinner available Direct Dial WiFi **Conf** Max 150 Thtr 120 Class 80 Board 60 **Parking** 60 **Notes** ⊗ Civ Wed 60

The Halfway House Inn Country Lodge

★★★ INN

tel: 01935 840350 & 849005 **fax:** 01935 849006 **Ilchester Rd BA22 8RE**
email: paul@halfwayhouseinn.com web: www.halfwayhouseinn.com
dir: A303 onto A37 (Yeovil road) at Ilchester, inn 2m on left

This roadside inn offers comfortable accommodation, which consists of bedrooms in the main house, in addition to contemporary annexe rooms, each with its own front door; all bedrooms are bright and well equipped. Meals are available in the cosy restaurant and bar where friendly staff ensure a warm welcome.

Rooms 11 en suite 9 annexe en suite (7 fmly) (9 GF) S £51.95-£61.95; D £69.95-£75.95* **Facilities** STV Lounge tea/coffee Dinner available WiFi Fishing Pool table **Conf** Max 90 Thtr 90 Class 60 Board 60 **Parking** 49 **Notes** LB

At Your Service B&B

★★★ BED AND BREAKFAST

tel: 01935 706932 & 07590 960339 **102 West Coker Rd BA20 2JG**
email: randall9ee@btinternet.com web: http://atyourserviceuk.wordpress.com

Conveniently located on the main through-road, this relaxed bed and breakfast makes an ideal base from which to explore the various nearby attractions. Bedrooms come in a range of shapes and sizes including some on the ground floor. There is a car park to the rear of the property.

Rooms 4 en suite (4 GF) S £40-£45; D £55-£70* **Facilities** FTV tea/coffee **Parking** 4 **Notes** LB Closed 24-26 Dec

The Half Moon Inn

★★★ INN

tel: 01935 850289 **fax:** 01935 850842 **Main St, Mudford BA21 5TF**
email: enquiries@thehalfmooninn.co.uk web: www.thehalfmooninn.co.uk
dir: A303 at Sparkford onto A359 to Yeovil, 3.5m on left

Situated north of Yeovil, this delightful village inn dates from the 17th century. It has a wealth of character including exposed beams and flagstone floors. The inn proves very popular for its extensive range of wholesome food, and there is a choice of bar and dining areas. Most of the spacious, well-equipped bedrooms are on the ground floor and are situated in an adjacent building.

Rooms 14 en suite (4 fmly) (9 GF) S £49.95-£59.95; D £49.95-£64.95 (room only)* **Facilities** STV FTV tea/coffee Dinner available WiFi 🔒 **Parking** 36 **Notes** ⊗ Closed 25-26 Dec

STAFFORDSHIRE

Marsh Farm *(SK069261)*

★★★★ FARMHOUSE

tel: 01283 840323 **WS15 3EJ**
email: marshfarm@meads1967.co.uk **web:** www.marshfarmstaffs.co.uk
dir: *1m N of Abbots Bromley on B5013*

Guests are welcome to walk around the fields at this working farm and watch the activities. The farmhouse has been modernised, and bedrooms are carefully furnished and equipped; three rooms are located in a sympathetic barn conversion. Comprehensive breakfasts are served in the spacious cottage-style dining room, which operates as a popular tea room during the summer.

Rooms 2 rms (1 en suite) (1 pri facs) 3 annexe en suite (1 fmly) (1 GF) S £30-£45; D £60-£65 **Facilities** FTV TVL tea/coffee WiFi 🛁 **Extras** Fresh milk **Parking** 6 **Notes** Closed 25-27 Dec ⊛ 20 acres mixed

Offley Grove Farm *(SJ761270)*

★★★ FARMHOUSE

tel: 01785 280205 & 07792 641984 **Eccleshall ST20 0QB**
email: enquiries@offleygrovefarm.co.uk **web:** www.offleygrovefarm.co.uk
dir: *3m from A519 between Shebdon & Adbaston*

This attractive farm dates back to the 1800s, and is quietly located between Eccleshall and Newport making it convenient for visiting attractions such as Alton Towers, Ironbridge and the Potteries. Bedrooms are traditional, comfortable and well equipped. The lounge and gardens also provide additional space for guests to relax in. A small conference room is available along with outdoor activities.

Rooms 2 en suite (1 fmly) S £38; D £60 **Facilities** FTV DVD TVL tea/coffee WiFi Fishing 🛁 4x4 Land Rover courses Air rifle shooting **Conf** Max 20 Thtr 20 Class 12 Board 12 **Parking** 20 **Notes** ⊛ Civ Wed 40 45 acres beef

Amber House

★★★ 🛏 BED AND BREAKFAST

tel: 01283 792154 & 07812 202415 **18 Burton Rd DE13 7BB**
email: gill@lichfieldhotels.net **web:** www.lichfieldhotels.net
dir: *A38 onto A513, follow signs to Alrewas. Amber House situated on A38 slip road after Royal British Legion & garage. Signed*

A stone's throw from the National Memorial Arboretum, Amber House is within easy reach of the A38, M6 Toll, Birmingham International Airport and the NEC. It is a real home from home, offering well-equipped, comfortable bedrooms and a spacious lounge. Breakfast is a highlight, featuring local produce with home-made breads and preserves and eggs laid by the resident hens. Evening meals are available by prior arrangement.

Rooms 3 rms (2 en suite) (1 pri facs) (1 GF) S £40-£55; D £60-£85 **Facilities** FTV DVD TVL tea/coffee Dinner available WiFi 🛁 **Extras** Speciality toiletries **Conf** Max 20 Board 20 **Parking** 4 **Notes** LB

The Three Horseshoes

★★★★ 🍺 INN

tel: 01283 716268 **2 Station Rd DE13 8DR**
email: enquiries@3horseshoesbarton.co.uk **web:** www.3horseshoesbarton.co.uk

This popular inn has been lovingly transformed with a contemporary twist. Bedrooms are a new addition to the inn and are individually styled. Bit 'n' Cherry restaurant, located in a converted cobbler's workshop, offers a wide selection of imaginative meals.

Rooms 3 en suite S £60; D £70* **Facilities** FTV tea/coffee Dinner available WiFi **Parking** 14

The Riverside

★★★ INN

tel: 01283 511234 **fax:** 01283 511441 **Riverside Dr, Branston DE14 3EP**
email: 6498@greeneking.co.uk **web:** www.oldenglish.co.uk
dir: *From A38 onto A5121 to Burton upon Trent, property on right entering Branston*

With its quiet residential location and well-kept terraced garden stretching down to the River Trent, this inn has all the ingredients for a relaxing stay. Many of the tables in the Garden Room restaurant have views over the garden. Bedrooms are tastefully furnished and provide a good range of extras.

Rooms 23 en suite (15 GF) **Facilities** TVL tea/coffee Dinner available Direct Dial WiFi ⚓ 18 Fishing **Conf** Max 150 Thtr 150 Class 30 Board 40 **Parking** 60 **Notes** Civ Wed 170

CHEADLE
Map 10 SK04

Park View Guest House
★★★★ GUEST ACCOMMODATION

tel: 01538 755412 fax: 01538 755412 **15 Mill Rd ST10 1NG**
email: enquiries@parkviewguesthouse.co web: www.parkviewguesthouse.co

Located in a residential area overlooking the municipal park, this Victorian property, with a purpose-built, self-contained accommodation block, offers thoughtfully equipped and comfortable bedrooms. Guests have their own entrance to the rear of the house. All rooms overlook the garden which includes a summer house and a small games room. Off-road parking and WiFi are available.

Rooms 7 rms (6 en suite) (1 pri facs) (5 fmly) (4 GF) S £35-£55; D £55-£75*
Facilities FTV TVL tea/coffee WiFi Pool table 🔒 **Parking** 7

CHEDDLETON
Map 16 SJ95

Prospect House
★★★★ GUEST HOUSE

tel: 01782 550639 **334 Cheadle Rd ST13 7BW**
email: prospect@talk21.com web: www.prospecthouse.tv
dir: *4m S of Leek on A520*

Prospect House was built from local stone in 1838, and is situated between Cheddleton and Wetley Rocks. Bedrooms are in a converted coach house behind the house, and facilities include an attractive dining room together with a cosy lounge, and a pleasant garden with a conservatory.

Rooms 4 en suite (1 GF) S £30; D £70* **Facilities** FTV TVL tea/coffee WiFi 🔒
Parking 4 **Notes** LB ⊗

ECCLESHALL
Map 15 SJ82

Slindon House Farm (SJ826324)
★★★★ 🏠 FARMHOUSE

tel: 01782 791237 **Slindon ST21 6LX**
email: bonsall@btconnect.com web: www.slindonhousefarm.co.uk
dir: *2m N of Eccleshall on A519*

This large, charming, Victorian farmhouse is fronted by a lovely garden and situated on a dairy, arable and livestock farm in the village of Slindon, some two miles from Eccleshall. It has one twin and one double-bedded room, both of which are thoughtfully equipped. Breakfast is served at individual tables in the traditionally furnished combined breakfast room and lounge.

Rooms 2 rms (1 en suite) (1 pri facs) S £45-£50; D £70* **Facilities** FTV DVD TVL tea/coffee WiFi **Parking** 4 **Notes** ⊗ Closed 23 Dec-3 Jan 🖐 175 acres arable/dairy/sheep/beef

HALMER END
Map 15 SJ74

The Lodge B&B
★★★★ GUEST ACCOMMODATION

tel: 01782 729047 & 07973 776797 **Red Hall Ln ST7 8AX**
email: freelancedobies@aol.com web: www.thelodge-halmerend.co.uk
dir: *M6 junct 16 onto A500, exit signed Audley, turn right into Alsager Rd. 2nd exit at rdbt, then left into Limbrick Rd (B5367). Turn right into Red Hall Ln*

Set in a peaceful location, this newly converted barn offers warm traditional hospitality. The lodge is adjacent to Bateswood Nature reserve. The accommodation is well equipped and very comfortable. Breakfast is served in the dining room on the ground floor. WiFi is available.

Rooms 2 en suite (1 fmly) S fr £34; D fr £68* **Facilities** FTV TVL tea/coffee WiFi Fishing **Parking** 2

The Church Farm Bed & Breakfast

The Church Farm is conveniently situated less than a mile from The Churnet Valley Steam Railway and six miles from Alton Towers. On the edge of the Peak District and the Staffordshire Moorlands, there is some outstanding scenery to walk, drive, ride or boat through, wooded valleys to rugged peaks and gentle farmland. The beautiful market towns of Leek, Bakewell, Ashbourne and Buxton are all nearby.

Our three rooms are individually decorated and have beverage making facilities, freeview/combi TVs and toiletries with many extras for your enjoyment. Pretty gardens and ample off road parking. Two en-suite doubles and a Bunk bedroom sleeping a maximum of 6 persons.

Tariff
Adults £30.00 to £35.00 • Children 12 years and under £20.00 • Single £40

Holt Lane, Kingsley, Stoke-on-Trent, Staffordshire ST10 2BA • Tel: 01538 754759
Email: thechurchfarm@yahoo.co.uk • Website: www.bandbatthechurchfarm.co.uk

KINGLEY
Map 10 SK04

The Church Farm (SK013466)

★★★★ FARMHOUSE

tel: 01538 754759 **Holt Ln ST10 2BA**
email: thechurchfarm@yahoo.co.uk **web:** www.bandbatthechurchfarm.co.uk
dir: From A52 in Kingsley into Holt Ln, 150mtrs on right opposite school drive

A warm welcome is assured at this charming farmhouse situated in the village of Kingsley. Thoughtfully equipped bedrooms with stylish furnishings are available in the main house. A hearty breakfast is served on individual tables overlooking the cottage gardens.

Rooms 3 en suite D £65-£75 **Facilities** FTV DVD TVL TV2B tea/coffee WiFi garden
Extras Speciality toiletries - complimentary **Parking** 6 **Notes** LB ⊗ Closed 23 Dec-2 Jan ⏚ 100 acres beef/mixed

See advert on page 323

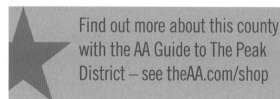

Find out more about this county with the AA Guide to The Peak District – see theAA.com/shop

LICHFIELD
Map 10 SK10

Premier Collection

Pipe Hill House

★★★★★ BED AND BREAKFAST

tel: 01543 255751 & 07779 291219 **fax:** 0871 978 9286
Walsall Rd, Pipehill WS13 8JU
email: nick@pipehillhouse.co.uk **web:** www.pipehillhouse.co.uk
dir: From A5 rdbt at junct with A461 towards Lichfield. 1m on right

Located two miles from the centre of the cathedral city of Lichfield, this beautiful 300-year-old Georgian house is personally run by owners Nick and Annmarie. Individually designed bedrooms offer high levels of comfort and warm hospitality ensures an enjoyable stay. The comprehensive breakfast features free-range eggs and locally sourced produce, while gluten free, dairy free, low sodium and diabetic diets are catered for. Full business services are available in an adjoining barn conversion.

Rooms 3 en suite D £90-£130 **Facilities** FTV iPod docking station Lounge tea/coffee Licensed WiFi **Extras** Speciality toiletries - free; robes, slippers **Parking** 4 **Notes** ⊗ No Children 16yrs

Premier Collection

Netherstowe House

★★★★★ ⊛ GUEST HOUSE

tel: 01543 254270 **fax:** 01543 419998 **Netherstowe Ln WS13 6AY**
email: reception@netherstowehouse.com **web:** www.netherstowehouse.com
dir: A38 onto A5192, 0.3m on right into Netherstowe Ln. 1st left, 1st right down private drive

Netherstowe House is located in a residential area a few minutes' drive from the city centre, and provides a range of bedrooms, some of which are quite spacious. Comprehensive breakfasts are taken in a cosy dining room and a comfortable guest lounge is also available, along with a well-equipped gym.

Rooms 9 en suite 8 annexe en suite (8 fmly) (4 GF) **Facilities** STV FTV DVD Lounge tea/coffee Dinner available Licensed WiFi ⅃ 18 Gym ⏚ **Extras** Robes, fruit, flowers - chargeable **Conf** Max 14 Thtr 14 Class 14 Board 14 **Parking** 35 **Notes** ⊗ No Children 12yrs

Innkeeper's Lodge Lichfield

★★★ INN

tel: 0845 112 6071 **Stafford Rd WS13 8JB**
email: info@innkeeperslodge.com **web:** www.innkeeperslodge.com

Conveniently located close to the M6 Toll, M42 and Birmingham, and ideal for both the business and leisure traveller. This 18th-century property has been beautifully restored. Bedrooms are all attractively presented; well-equipped and free WiFi is available. There is a very popular restaurant, with large gardens suitable for alfresco dining.

Rooms 9 en suite (2 fmly) **Facilities** FTV tea/coffee Dinner available Direct Dial WiFi **Parking**

The Hawthorns

★★★ BED AND BREAKFAST

tel: 01543 250151 & 07794 709240 **30 Norwich Close WS13 7SJ**
email: bambrushton@hotmail.com **web:** www.thehawthorns-bedandbreakfast.co.uk
dir: *1m N of city centre. Exit A5192 (Eastern Av) near Bristol Street Motors left into Norwich Close*

Located in a residential area on the outskirts of the city, this modern house provides two homely bedrooms with separate side entrance. Breakfast is taken in an attractive kitchen-dining room overlooking a pretty rear garden.

Rooms 2 en suite (2 GF) S £38; D £50 **Facilities** FTV tea/coffee WiFi 🔒 **Parking** 2 **Notes** LB ⊗ No Children 16yrs ⊛

| **OAKAMOOR** | **Map 10 SK04** |

Crowtrees Farm (SK049459)

★★★★ FARMHOUSE

tel: 01538 702260 **Eaves Ln ST10 3DY**
email: dianne@crowtreesfarm.co.uk **web:** www.crowtreesfarm.co.uk
dir: *Exit B5417 in village N into Eaves Ln, farm 1m on left*

This impeccably maintained 200-year-old farmhouse is convenient for the Potteries, the Peak District and Alton Towers. Bedrooms are comfortable and well equipped. It is still a working farm and has splendid views. The friendly owners, along with their collection of pets, create a relaxing atmosphere.

Rooms 2 en suite 5 annexe en suite (3 fmly) (4 GF) **Facilities** FTV tea/coffee WiFi **Parking** 8 **Notes** ⊗ Closed 25-26 Dec 70 acres sheep

| **RUGELEY** | **Map 10 SK01** |

Premier Collection

Colton House

★★★★★ 🏠 🍴 GUEST HOUSE

tel: 01889 578580 **fax:** 01889 578580 **Colton WS15 3LL**
email: mail@coltonhouse.com **web:** www.coltonhouse.com
dir: *1.5m N of Rugeley. Exit B5013 into Colton, 0.25m on right*

Set in the pretty village of Colton, this elegant early 18th-century house has bags of original character and provides high standards of comfort and facilities. Bedrooms have a wealth of thoughtful extras. Public areas include a cosy bar, a comfortable lounge and a large garden. Dinner is by arrangement and hearty breakfasts are served in the elegant dining room.

Rooms 11 en suite S £74-£116; D £94-£204 **Facilities** FTV TVL tea/coffee Dinner available Licensed WiFi 🔒 **Conf** Max 25 Thtr 25 Class 25 Board 25 **Parking** 15 **Notes** ⊗ No Children 13yrs

The Shoulder of Mutton

★★★ 🍴 INN

tel: 01889 504488 & 07967 805111 **Yoxall Rd WS15 3RZ**
email: shoulderhamstall@aol.com **web:** www.theshoulderofmuttoninn.co.uk

This village inn dates back to 1834, when it was known as the Rose and Crown. Today, The Shoulder of Mutton is the hub of the village. There is a friendly locals' bar with hand-pulled ales; and a cosy lounge bar with dining room that offers good home-cooked food. Bedrooms are comfortable. A large car park is available.

Rooms 4 en suite (2 fmly) **Facilities** FTV TVL tea/coffee Dinner available WiFi ⅃ 18 Fishing **Extras** Slippers, robes **Conf** Max 30 **Parking** 25 **Notes** ⊗ No coaches

| **STAFFORD** | **Map 10 SJ92** |

Rooks Nest (SJ960268)

★★★★ FARMHOUSE

tel: 01889 270624 & 07966 732953 **Rooks Nest Farm, Weston ST18 0BA**
email: info@rooksnest.co.uk **web:** www.rooksnest.co.uk
dir: *From Stafford on A518 towards Weston. Left to Rooks Nest Farm, 1st property*

Rooks Nest is in a peaceful location with panoramic views over the Trent Valley and countryside. This modern farmhouse has comfortable bedrooms with homely extras. The establishment is handy for visiting the County Showground and Stafford University, with easy access to all Staffordshire's attractions.

Rooms 2 en suite (1 fmly) S £37.50; D £60* **Facilities** FTV DVD tea/coffee WiFi **Parking** 4 **Notes** ⊗ ⊛ 220 acres arable/beef

Leonards Croft

★★★ GUEST HOUSE

tel: 01785 223676 **fax:** 01785 223676 **80 Lichfield Rd ST17 4LP**
email: leonardscroft@hotmail.com **web:** www.leonardscroft.co.uk
dir: *A34 from town centre signed Cannock, 0.5m on left*

Located south of the town centre, this well-proportioned late Victorian house is conveniently positioned to appeal to both business and leisure guests. Bedrooms are practically furnished, with two situated on the ground floor. A spacious lounge and complimentary WiFi are also provided. The gardens are extensive.

Rooms 9 en suite (3 fmly) (2 GF) S £40-£50; D £60-£75* **Facilities** FTV TVL tea/coffee Dinner available Licensed WiFi **Parking** 12

STAFFORD *continued*

The Old School

★★★ BED AND BREAKFAST

tel: 01785 780358 **fax:** 01785 780358 **Newport Rd, Haughton ST18 9JH**
email: info@theoldsc.co.uk **web:** www.theoldsc.co.uk
dir: *A518 W from Stafford, 3m to Haughton, Old School next to church*

In the heart of Haughton, this Grade II listed former Victorian school has a range of bedrooms; a single, a double and a twin. All are appropriately equipped and complimentary WiFi is also provided. Breakfast is served at a family table in the homely dining room.

Rooms 3 rms (3 GF) **Facilities** FTV tea/coffee WiFi **Parking** 3 **Notes** No Children 14yrs
⊜

STONE   Map 10 SJ93

Field House

★★★ BED AND BREAKFAST

tel: 01785 605712 **fax:** 01785 605712 **59 Stafford Rd ST15 0HE**
email: fieldhouse@ntlworld.com
dir: *From A34, NW into town centre, right into Stafford Rd, opposite Walton Grange*

This family home stands in secluded, pretty gardens close to the town centre. The Georgian house has traditionally furnished bedrooms, some with family pieces. Guests breakfast together in the lounge-dining room, and hospitality is very welcoming.

Rooms 2 rms (1 en suite) (1 pri facs) **Facilities** STV FTV TVL tea/coffee Art tuition on request **Parking** 4 **Notes** ⊗ ⊜

TAMWORTH   Map 10 SK20

Premier Collection

Oak Tree Farm

★★★★★ GUEST ACCOMMODATION

tel: 01827 56807 **fax:** 01827 67271 **Hints Rd, Hopwas B78 3AA**
email: oaktreefarm1@aol.com **web:** www.oaktreefarmhotel.co.uk
dir: *2m NW of Tamworth. Off A51 in Hopwas*

A warm welcome is assured at this well-loved farmhouse, located in peaceful rural surroundings yet only a short drive from the NEC. Spacious bedrooms are filled with homely extras. The elegant dining room, adorned with Oriental artefacts, is the setting for memorable breakfasts. A small conference room is available.

Rooms 4 en suite 10 annexe en suite (4 fmly) (7 GF) S £35-£69; D £65-£85* **Facilities** FTV TVL tea/coffee WiFi ⊗ Fishing **Conf** Max 15 Thtr 15 Class 9 Board 15 **Parking** 20

Globe Inn

★★★ INN

tel: 01827 60455 **fax:** 01827 63575 **Lower Gungate B79 7AW**
email: info@theglobetamworth.com **web:** www.theglobetamworth.com

Located in the centre of Tamworth, this popular inn provides well-equipped and pleasantly decorated accommodation. The public areas include a spacious lounge bar and a relaxed dining area where a varied selection of dishes is available. There is also a function room and adjacent parking.

Rooms 18 en suite (2 fmly) (18 smoking) **Facilities** STV FTV tea/coffee Dinner available WiFi ♪ **Conf** Thtr 90 Class 90 Board 90 **Parking** 30 **Notes** ⊗ Closed 25 Dec, 1 Jan

The Gungate

★★★ ⌂ GUEST ACCOMMODATION

tel: 01827 63120 & 07802 987283 **62 Upper Gungate B79 8AA**

The Gungate sits within a moment's walk of the town centre with the benefit of on-site parking. Bedrooms and bathrooms have benefited from recent investment, showcasing the Victorian splendour of the main house, whilst the coach house annexe rooms are more contemporary in their appeal. Families, leisure and business guests are well catered for. A number of popular visitor attractions are located nearby.

Rooms 10 en suite (2 fmly) (1 GF) S £35-£50; D £50-£60* **Facilities** FTV DVD TVL tea/coffee Direct Dial Licensed WiFi ⊜ **Conf** Max 30 Thtr 30 Class 20 Board 20 **Parking** 10 **Notes** LB

UTTOXETER   Map 10 SK03

High View Cottage

★★★★ GUEST ACCOMMODATION

tel: 01889 568183 & 07980 041670 **Toothill Rd ST14 8JU**
email: info@highviewcottage.co.uk **web:** www.highviewcottage.com
dir: *1m S of town centre. Exit B5017 (Highwood Rd) into Toothill Rd*

Situated on the edge of Uttoxeter and close to the racecourse, High View Cottage offers comfortable, well-equipped accommodation and a friendly atmosphere. Bedrooms are equipped with lots of thoughtful extras, and hearty breakfasts are served in the attractive Garden Room which overlooks the courtyard.

Rooms 5 en suite (2 fmly) (5 GF) **Facilities** FTV DVD tea/coffee WiFi **Conf** Max 8 Board 8 **Parking** 10 **Notes** ⊗

SUFFOLK

ALDEBURGH Map 13 TM45

The Toll House

★★★★ GUEST HOUSE

tel: 01728 453239 **50 Victoria Rd IP15 5EJ**
email: mail@tollhousealdeburgh.com **web:** www.tollhousealdeburgh.com
dir: B1094 into town until rdbt, on right

Expect a warm welcome at this delightful red-brick property situated just a short walk from the seafront and town centre. Bedrooms are tastefully furnished, have co-ordinated fabrics and many thoughtful touches. Breakfast is served at individual tables in the smart dining room, which overlooks the garden.

Rooms 7 en suite (3 GF) S £65-£70; D £80-£85* **Facilities** FTV DVD tea/coffee WiFi **Parking** 6 **Notes** ⊗

BURY ST EDMUNDS Map 13 TL86

Premier Collection

Clarice House

★★★★★ ⊚ GUEST ACCOMMODATION

tel: 01284 705550 **fax:** 01284 716120 **Horringer Court, Horringer Rd IP29 5PH**
email: bury@claricehouse.co.uk **web:** www.claricehouse.co.uk
dir: 1m SW from town centre on A143 towards Horringer

Clarice House is a large country property set amid pretty landscaped grounds a short drive from the historic town centre. The spacious, well-equipped bedrooms have co-ordinated fabrics and many thoughtful touches. Public rooms have a wealth of charm and include a smart lounge bar, an intimate restaurant, a further lounge and a conservatory. The property also has superb leisure facilities.

Rooms 13 en suite S £80; D £100-£140 **Facilities** FTV Lounge tea/coffee Dinner available Direct Dial Lift Licensed WiFi ⊛ Sauna Gym Spa & Beauty facilities **Conf** Max 50 Thtr 50 Class 50 Board 50 **Parking** 85 **Notes** LB ⊗ No Children 5yrs Closed 24-26 Dec & 31 Dec-1 Jan Civ Wed 70

The Chantry

★★★★ GUEST ACCOMMODATION

tel: 01284 767427 **fax:** 01284 760946 **8 Sparhawk St IP33 1RY**
email: chantryhotel1@aol.com **web:** www.chantryhotel.com
dir: From cathedral S into Crown St, left into Honey Hill then right into Sparhawk St

The Chantry is an attractive Georgian property, just a short walk from the town centre. The individually decorated bedrooms are furnished with well-chosen pieces and have many extra thoughtful touches. Breakfast is served in the smart restaurant, and there is a cosy lounge-bar.

Rooms 11 en suite 3 annexe en suite (1 fmly) (1 GF) S £75-£99; D £95-£135* **Facilities** FTV Lounge tea/coffee Direct Dial Licensed WiFi ♨ **Parking** 14 **Notes** LB

Grange Farm (TL974614)

★★★★ FARMHOUSE

tel: 01359 241143 & 07740 780460 **Woolpit Green, Woolpit IP30 9RG**
email: grangefarm@btinternet.com **web:** www.grangefarm-woolpit.co.uk
dir: A14 junct 47 from slip road turn left. 1st right signed Woolpit, after 0.25m 1st left signed Woolpit Green. 0.75m on left

This charming Grade II listed farmhouse enjoys a peaceful rural location in the heart of Suffolk, convenient for the pretty village of Woolpit and the busy town of Bury St Edmunds. Bedrooms are all generously sized and attractively presented, along with a host of thoughtful guest accessories. This arable farm has been worked by the family since the 1830s. There is also a self-catering cottage adjacent to the house.

Rooms 3 rms (2 en suite) (1 pri facs) S £45-£47.50; D £75-£77.50* **Facilities** FTV TVL tea/coffee WiFi Fishing ♨ **Parking** 12 **Notes** Closed 23 Dec-2 Jan 124 acres arable

The Old Pear Tree Bed & Breakfast

★★★★ ☖ BED AND BREAKFAST

tel: 01284 850470 **The Old Pear Tree, Whepstead IP29 4UD**
email: jenny@theoldpeartree.co.uk **web:** www.theoldpeartree.co.uk

Surrounded by rolling countryside and just five miles from historic Bury St Edmunds, The Old Pear Tree Bed & Breakfast enjoys a peaceful rural location yet is close to the main road network. Bedrooms are all beautifully presented, most comfortable and very well equipped. This charming house is an ideal base for walkers and is close to Ickworth House (National Trust) and Newmarket racecourse.

Rooms 3 rms (2 en suite) (1 pri facs) (1 fmly) **Facilities** FTV TVL tea/coffee WiFi ♨ **Parking** 4 **Notes** ⊗

The Abbey

★★★★ GUEST ACCOMMODATION

tel: 01284 762020 **fax:** 01284 330279 **35 Southgate St IP33 2AZ**
email: reception@abbeyhotel.co.uk **web:** www.abbeyhotel.co.uk
dir: A14 junct 44, A1302 to town centre, into Southgate St, premises 400yds

The Abbey is well placed for visiting the historic town centre. The property is split between several old buildings, the main core dating from the 15th century. The public rooms in the Tudor inn section feature a comfortable lounge and an informal dining area. Bedrooms vary in size and style, but all are comfortably furnished and well equipped.

Rooms 12 en suite (1 fmly) (2 GF) S £88-£118; D £98-£138* **Facilities** FTV Lounge tea/coffee WiFi **Parking** 12 **Notes** LB ⊗

83 Whiting Street

★★★★ BED AND BREAKFAST

tel: 01284 704153 & 07703 601072 **83 Whiting St IP33 1NX**
email: gordon.wagstaff@btinternet.com **web:** www.83whitingstreetbandb.co.uk
dir: In town centre

An attractive, three-storey terrace property convenient for exploring this popular town. The spacious, individually decorated bedrooms are furnished with pine and equipped with modern facilities. Breakfast is served in the beamed dining room, where there is an open fireplace and a wall painting dating from 1530.

Rooms 4 en suite (1 fmly) S £45; D £70* **Facilities** FTV tea/coffee WiFi ♨ **Notes** ⊗ ✉

BURY ST EDMUNDS *continued*

St Andrews Lodge

★★★★ BED AND BREAKFAST

tel: 01284 756733 **30 Saint Andrews Street North IP33 1SZ**
email: standrewslodge@hotmail.com **web:** www.thestandrewslodge.co.uk
dir: *A14 junct 43, A134 towards town centre, left into Saint Andrews St North. Lodge on right*

This delightful property is situated close to the A14 and the town centre. The well-equipped modern bedrooms are on the ground floor of a separate, purpose-built area to the rear of the house. Breakfast is served at individual tables in the smart dining room, which overlooks the neat courtyard.

Rooms 3 annexe en suite (3 GF) S £50; D £68* **Facilities** FTV DVD tea/coffee WiFi **Parking** 3

The Six Bells at Bardwell

★★★★ ⊜ INN

tel: 01359 250820 **fax:** 01359 250820 **The Green, Bardwell IP31 1AW**
email: sixbellsbardwell@aol.com **web:** www.sixbellsbardwell.co.uk
dir: *8m NE, off A143 on edge of village. Follow brown signs from A143*

This 16th-century inn lies in the peaceful village of Bardwell. The bedrooms, in a converted stable block next to the main building, are furnished in a country style and thoughtfully equipped. Public rooms have original character and provide a choice of areas in which to relax.

Rooms 10 annexe en suite (1 fmly) (10 GF) S £50-£80; D £62.50-£130*
Facilities FTV Lounge tea/coffee Dinner available WiFi ⚓ **Parking** 50 **Notes** LB
Closed 25 Dec-3 Jan

Dog & Partridge, The Old Brewers House

★★★ ⊜ INN

tel: 01284 764792 **29 Crown St IP33 1QU**
email: 1065@greeneking.co.uk **web:** www.oldenglish.co.uk
dir: *In town centre. Exit A134 (Parkway) into Westgate St & left into Crown St*

This charming inn is situated just a short walk from the town centre. Public rooms include a smart conservatory, a lounge bar and a a small dining area. The smartly decked terrace to the rear of the property is useful for alfresco dining. Bedrooms are pleasantly decorated, have co-ordinated fabrics, natural wood furniture and many thoughtful touches.

Rooms 9 en suite (2 fmly) (3 GF) **Facilities** STV tea/coffee Dinner available Direct Dial **Parking** 11 **Notes** ⊗

Hamilton House

★★★ BED AND BREAKFAST

tel: 01284 703022 & 07787 146553 **4 Nelson Rd IP33 3AG**
email: hamiltonhouse@hotmail.co.uk
dir: *A14 junct 42, follow A1302 across rdbt, then 1st right*

A warm welcome awaits at Hamilton House, a relaxing Edwardian villa, situated in a quiet side road just a short walk from the town centre. The bedrooms are brightly decorated with co-ordinated fabrics and have a good range of facilities. Breakfast is served at a large communal table in the dining room.

Rooms 4 rms (2 en suite) (1 fmly) S £27-£35; D £55-£60* **Facilities** FTV DVD tea/coffee WiFi ⚓ **Notes** ⊗ ⊜

The Old Cannon Brewery

★★★ INN

tel: 01284 768769 **86 Cannon St IP33 1JR**
email: stay@oldcannonbrewery.co.uk **web:** www.oldcannonbrewery.co.uk
dir: *A14 junct 43, A134 towards town centre. At rdbt after Tesco left then sharp right into Cadney Ln, left into Cannon St, on left*

Originally a beer house and brewery, this delightful Victorian property is sure to please. The brewery's finished products can be sampled in the bar. The open-plan bar and dining area features the polished stainless steel mash tun and kettle. The well-equipped bedrooms are located in an adjacent building, and visitors will find a bottle of beer each waiting for them after they check in.

Rooms 7 annexe en suite (3 GF) S fr £90; D fr £120* **Facilities** STV tea/coffee Dinner available WiFi ⚓ **Parking** 7 **Notes** ⊗ No coaches

Abbotts Guest House

★★★ GUEST ACCOMMODATION

tel: 01284 755484 **2 Newmarket Rd IP33 3SN**
email: info@abbottsguesthouse.co.uk **web:** www.abbottsguesthouse.co.uk

Abbotts Guest House is conveniently located and is a short walk to the centre of Bury St Edmunds. Ample secure parking is available along with free WiFi for guests. Breakfast is served in the conservatory breakfast room and includes many tasty choices. Bedrooms are all smartly presented and comfortable.

Rooms 11 en suite (1 fmly) (4 GF) S £45; D £65* **Facilities** FTV tea/coffee WiFi ⚓ **Extras** Sweets **Parking** 11 **Notes** LB

The Black Boy

★★★ INN

tel: 01284 752723 **69 Guildhall St IP33 1QD**
web: www.theblackboypublichouse.co.uk
dir: *Exit A14 to town centre*

The Black Boy is a popular inn situated in the centre of this historic town. The spacious bedrooms have co-ordinated fabrics, pine furniture and many thoughtful touches. Public areas feature a large open-plan bar with a good selection of ales, and a range of bar snacks are available.

Rooms 5 en suite S £35-£40; D £60-£70* **Facilities** FTV tea/coffee Dinner available WiFi Pool table **Parking** 6 **Notes** ⊗ No coaches

6 Orchard Street

★★★ BED AND BREAKFAST

tel: 07946 590265 **IP33 1EH**
email: mariellascarlett@me.com **web:** www.number6orchardstreet.co.uk
dir: *In town centre near St John's Church on one-way system; Northgate St turn right into Looms Ln, 2nd right into Well St, straight on into Orchard St*

Expect a warm welcome from the caring hosts at this terrace property, situated just a short walk from the town centre. The pleasant bedrooms are comfortably appointed and have a good range of useful extras. Breakfast is served at a large communal table in the cosy dining room.

Rooms 3 rms (2 en suite) (1 pri facs) S £40-£45; D £48-£65* **Facilities** FTV tea/coffee WiFi ⚓ **Notes** No Children 6yrs ⊜

CAVENDISH
Map 13 TL84

The George

★★★★ ◎◎ 🛏 RESTAURANT WITH ROOMS

tel: 01787 280248 **The Green CO10 8BA**
email: thegeorgecavendish@gmail.com **web:** www.thecavendishgeorge.co.uk
dir: A1092 into Cavendish, The George next to village green

The George is situated in the heart of the pretty village of Cavendish and has five very stylish bedrooms. The front-facing rooms overlook the village; the comfortable, spacious bedrooms retain many of their original features. The award-winning restaurant is very well appointed and dinner should not be missed. Guests are guaranteed to receive a warm welcome, attentive friendly service and great food.

Rooms 5 en suite (1 fmly) S £50; D £75-£90 **Facilities** FTV DVD tea/coffee Dinner available WiFi ♨ **Extras** Speciality toiletries, mineral water, sweets **Notes** Closed 25 Dec & 1 Jan

CLARE
Map 13 TL74

Ship Stores

★★★★ GUEST ACCOMMODATION

tel: 01787 277834 **fax:** 01787 277183 **22 Callis St CO10 8PX**
email: shipclare@aol.com **web:** www.ship-stores.co.uk
dir: A1092 to Clare, onto B1063, pass church, 100yds on right

Ship Stores is a charming property situated in the heart of an historic market town. Bedrooms are split between the main house and a converted stable block; each room is furnished in a country style with bright, co-ordinated soft furnishings and many thoughtful touches. Public areas include a contemporary breakfast room with a stripped-pine floor.

Rooms 4 en suite 2 annexe en suite (1 fmly) (3 GF) S £50-£65; D £70-£75* **Facilities** tea/coffee WiFi **Parking** 3 **Notes** LB ❌

ELMSWELL
Map 13 TL96

Kiln Farm Guest House

★★★★ GUEST HOUSE

tel: 01359 240442 **Kiln Ln IP30 9QR**
email: davejankilnfarm@btinternet.com
dir: A14 junct 47 onto A1088. Entrance to Kiln Ln off E'bound slip road

Kiln Farm Guest House is a delightful Victorian farmhouse situated in a peaceful rural location amid three acres of landscaped grounds. The bedrooms are housed in converted farm buildings, and each one is smartly decorated and furnished in country style. Breakfast is served in the smart conservatory and there is also a cosy lounge and bar area.

Rooms 2 en suite 6 annexe en suite (2 fmly) (6 GF) S £35-£40; D £70-£80* **Facilities** FTV DVD Lounge TVL tea/coffee Dinner available Licensed WiFi ♨ **Extras** Fruit, snacks, chocolates **Parking** 20

ELVEDEN
Map 13 TL88

Premier Collection

The Elveden Inn

★★★★★ 🛏 INN

tel: 01842 890876 **fax:** 01842 221822 **Brandon Rd IP24 3TP**
email: enquiries@elvedeninn.com **web:** www.elvedeninn.com
dir: Off A11 (dual carriageway) onto B1106 (Brandon Road) towards Bury St Edmunds

This charming country inn has been totally refurbished and offers a range of beautifully presented bedrooms and sleek modern bathrooms. Enjoying a peaceful location in the heart of East Anglia, the inn is part of the Guinness family-owned Elveden Estate. The bar is full of character and the terrace is a popular dining venue on warmer days. The Elveden courtyard shops are nearby and the café is very popular.

Rooms 4 en suite (2 fmly) D £105 **Facilities** FTV tea/coffee Dinner available Direct Dial WiFi **Extras** Speciality toiletries, fruit, bottled water - free **Parking** 100 **Notes** LB

EYE
Map 13 TM17

The White Horse Inn

★★★★ INN

tel: 01379 678222 **fax:** 01379 678800 **Stoke Ash IP23 7ET**
email: mail@whitehorse-suffolk.co.uk **web:** www.whitehorse-suffolk.co.uk
dir: On A140 halfway between Ipswich & Norwich

The White Horse Inn is on the main A140 midway between Norwich and Ipswich. It has been run by the same family for over a decade, offering home-made, good quality food in a friendly and comfortable environment. This is complemented by well-kept local ales and cider. Accommodation is set in the quiet grounds by the 17th-century coaching inn. The modern, purpose-built motel-style rooms are comfortable and offer beds of double size or larger along with large, professionally laundered towels and superior toiletries. Many rooms also have air conditioning. Complimentary WiFi is available in the public areas and bedrooms.

Rooms 11 annexe en suite (1 fmly) (9 GF) **Facilities** FTV tea/coffee Dinner available Direct Dial WiFi **Conf** Max 50 Thtr 50 Class 50 Board 20 **Parking** 60 **Notes** LB ❌

Find out more about this county with the AA Guide to Suffolk & Norfolk – see theAA.com/shop

Boundary Farm

★★★★ BED AND BREAKFAST

tel: 01728 723401 **Saxmundham Rd IP13 9NU**
email: info@boundaryfarm.biz **web:** www.boundaryfarm.biz
dir: *From Framlingham on B1119 towards Saxmundham. After 1.5m left at 1st x-rds signed Cransford & Badingham*

Expect peace and tranquillity at this traditional 17th-century Suffolk farmhouse. All rooms are individually decorated and reflect the style of the building; in addition, all rooms offer a range of amenities to enhance comfort. Original paintings by a resident artist adorn the house. Guests can relax in the guest lounge, or by the pond during the warm months of the year.

Rooms 4 rms (3 en suite) (1 pri facs) D £80-£95 **Facilities** FTV DVD TVL TV3B tea/coffee WiFi 🔒 **Extras** Snacks, chocolates **Parking** 6 **Notes** ⊗ 🐾

Church Farm *(TM605267)*

★★★★ FARMHOUSE

tel: 01728 723532 **Church Rd, Kettleburgh IP13 7LF**
email: jbater@suffolkonline.net **web:** www.churchfarmkettleburgh.co.uk
dir: *Off A12 to Wickham Market, signs to Easton Farm Park & Kettleburgh 1.25m, house behind church*

This is a charming 300-year-old farmhouse situated close to the village church surrounded by superb grounds that include a duck pond, mature shrubs and sweeping lawns. The property retains exposed beams and open fireplaces. Bedrooms are pleasantly decorated and equipped with useful extras, and ground-floor rooms are available.

Rooms 2 rms (1 en suite) (1 pri facs) 2 annexe rms 1 annexe en suite (1 pri facs) (3 GF) S £35-£40; D £70-£80* **Facilities** TVL tea/coffee Dinner available WiFi Fishing 🔒 **Extras** Home-made biscuits - complimentary **Parking** 10 **Notes** 🐾 70 acres mixed

Colston Hall *(TM316672)*

★★★★ 🏠 FARMHOUSE

tel: 01728 638375 **Badingham IP13 8LB**
email: liz@colstonhall.com **web:** www.colstonhall.com
dir: *On A1120 between Badingham & Peasenhall*

Set in a peaceful rural location, Colston Hall offers a range of individually designed spacious bedrooms. This authentic Elizabethan farmhouse has many original

features including brick floors and oak beams. Bedrooms have lovely countryside views, overlooking the lakes and the pretty kitchen garden. The hearty breakfasts are not to be missed and the home-made marmalade is rather special.

Rooms 3 en suite 3 annexe rms 2 annexe en suite (1 pri facs) (3 GF) S £50-£65; D £90-£110 **Facilities** FTV DVD Lounge TVL tea/coffee WiFi Fishing Snooker Pool table 🔒 **Conf** Max 50 Thtr 50 Class 50 Board 50 **Parking** 22 **Notes** LB ⊗ 27 acres sheep

Premier Collection

Valley Farm

★★★★★ 🏠 BED AND BREAKFAST

tel: 01986 874521 & 07971 669270 **Bungay Rd IP19 8LY**
email: mail@valleyfarmholton.co.uk **web:** www.valleyfarmholton.co.uk
dir: *A144 onto B1123 to Holton, left at fork in village, left at school, 500yds on left*

Expect a warm welcome from the caring hosts at this charming red-brick farmhouse situated in a peaceful rural location just a short drive from Halesworth. The individually decorated bedrooms are tastefully appointed with co-ordinated soft furnishings and many thoughtful touches. Breakfast, which features locally sourced and home-grown produce, is served at a large communal table in the smartly appointed dining room. The property has lovely landscaped grounds, a summer house, and an indoor heated swimming pool.

Rooms 2 en suite (1 fmly) **Facilities** FTV DVD Lounge tea/coffee WiFi 🕭 🛶 🔒 Boules piste **Extras** Speciality toiletries, sweets **Parking** 15 **Notes** ⊗

INGHAM — Map 13 TL87

The Cadogan Arms

★★★★ ⓘ INN

tel: 01284 728443 **The Street IP31 1NG**
email: info@thecadogan.co.uk web: www.thecadogan.co.uk
dir: *4m from Bury St Edmunds, follow A134 towards Thetford*

The Cadogan Arms is a popular inn situated four miles from the centre of Bury St Edmunds. The smartly appointed bedrooms have been thoughtfully designed and have many useful extras. The open-plan public rooms are contemporary in style and they include a range of seating areas with plush leather sofas and a smart restaurant.

Rooms 7 en suite S £35.50-£80; D £71-£100 (room only)* **Facilities** FTV tea/coffee Dinner available WiFi **Extras** Bottled water **Parking** 30 **Notes** LB

IXWORTH — Map 13 TL97

Premier Collection

Ixworth House

★★★★★ 🍽 BED AND BREAKFAST

tel: 01359 230639 & 07887 903047 **St Edmund Close IP31 2HP**
email: sharyn@ixworthhouse.co.uk web: www.ixworthhouse.co.uk
dir: *A143 to Ixworth, opposite Fordhams Garage turn into St Edmund Close*

Built in 1908, this fine Edwardian house has been sympathetically restored and has retained many of its original features. Ixworth House enjoys a prominent position on a quiet cul de sac and is a short walk from the pretty village of Ixworth. The three spacious bedrooms are beautifully presented and there is a real sense of luxury. Hospitality is first class and freshly cooked breakfasts served in the very well appointed dining room are not to be missed.

Rooms 3 en suite (1 fmly) S £65-£80; D £90-£100* **Facilities** FTV TVL tea/coffee WiFi 🚲 **Parking** 3 **Notes** ⊗

LAVENHAM — Map 13 TL94

Premier Collection

Lavenham Great House 'Restaurant With Rooms'

★★★★★ ⓘ ⓘ 🍽 RESTAURANT WITH ROOMS

tel: 01787 247431 fax: 01787 248007 **Market Place CO10 9QZ**
email: info@greathouse.co.uk web: www.greathouse.co.uk
dir: *Exit A1141 into Market Ln, behind cross on Market Place*

The 18th-century frontage on Market Place conceals a 15th-century timber-framed building that is now a restaurant with rooms. Lavenham Great House is a little slice of France, offering high-quality rural cuisine served by French staff. The spacious bedrooms are individually decorated and thoughtfully equipped with many useful extras; some rooms have a separate lounge area.

Rooms 5 en suite (1 fmly) S £95-£195; D £95-£225 (room only)* **Facilities** FTV DVD tea/coffee Dinner available Direct Dial WiFi 🚲 Free bicycle use for guests **Extras** Mini-bar, fruit, sherry - complimentary **Notes** LB ⊗ Closed Jan RS Sun eve & Mon Restaurant closed No coaches

LEISTON — Map 13 TM46

Field End

★★★★ GUEST HOUSE

tel: 01728 833527 & 07946 287451 **1 Kings Rd IP16 4DA**
email: herbert@herbertwood.wanadoo.co.uk web: www.fieldendguesthouse.co.uk
dir: *In town centre off B1122*

This Edwardian house has been appointed to a high standard and is impeccably maintained by the present owners. Bedrooms have co-ordinated soft furnishings and many thoughtful touches. Breakfast is served in an attractive dining room, which has a large sofa and a range of puzzles and games.

Rooms 5 rms (2 en suite) (1 pri facs) (1 fmly) (1 GF) **Facilities** FTV DVD TVL tea/coffee WiFi **Extras** Fridges **Parking** 5 **Notes** ⊗ No Children 6mths 📧

LOWESTOFT — Map 13 TM59

Wavecrest Guest House

★★★★ GUEST HOUSE

tel: 01502 561268 **31 Marine Pde NR33 0QN**
email: wavecrestguesthouse@gmail.com web: www.thewavecrest.com
dir: *On seafront just S of Lowestoft Bridge*

This Victorian terrace house is situated on the seafront, overlooking the award-winning beach and within easy walking distance of the town centre. The bedrooms are smartly decorated with co-ordinated soft furnishings, and all are equipped with modern facilities. Public areas include an elegant dining room where breakfast is served at individual tables.

Rooms 5 rms (4 en suite) (1 pri facs) (1 fmly) S £34-£45; D £54-£65* **Facilities** FTV DVD tea/coffee WiFi 🚲 **Notes** ⊗ Closed 24-31 Dec

Somerton Guest House

★★★ GUEST ACCOMMODATION

tel: 01502 565665 **7 Kirkley Cliff NR33 0BY**
email: somerton7@hotmail.co.uk web: www.somertonguesthouse.co.uk
dir: *On old A12, 200mtrs from Claremont Pier*

This fine Grade II listed Georgian terraced house has panoramic sea views and is part of the Lowestoft conservation area. Individually styled bedrooms are all well appointed and the friendly new owners are gradually refurbishing bedrooms. The menu at breakfast offers an extensive choice and free WiFi is available. The town centre is a short walk away and the house overlooks the popular promenade. Well-behaved pets are welcome although conditions do apply.

Rooms 7 rms (5 en suite) (2 pri facs) (1 fmly) (1 GF) S £38; D £62-£75* **Facilities** FTV tea/coffee WiFi 🚲 **Extras** Fridge, bottled water

Coventry Guest House

★★★ GUEST ACCOMMODATION

tel: 01502 573865 **8 Kirkley Cliff NR33 0BY**
email: john.e54@uwclub.net

The Coventry Guest House is a beautiful Victorian building which has retained many original features along with plenty of charm. Front-facing rooms overlook the award-winning gardens and beyond. Rooms with private facilities are ideal for the cost conscious travellers. The freshly cooked breakfast is served in a homely setting.

Rooms 6 rms (4 en suite) (2 pri facs) (3 fmly) **Facilities** STV FTV DVD iPod docking station WiFi 🚲 **Notes** LB

MILDENHALL   Map 12 TL77

AA FUNKIEST B&B OF THE YEAR
2014–2015

Premier Collection

The Bull Inn

★★★★★ @ INN

tel: 01638 711001 fax: 01638 712003 **The Street, Barton Mills IP28 6AA**
email: bookings@bullinn-bartonmills.com web: www.bullinn-bartonmills.com
dir: *A11 between Newmarket & Mildenhall, signed Barton Mills. Inn by Five Ways rdbt*

This delightful 16th-century coaching inn is lovingly cared for by the owners. Public rooms offer a choice of bars, a brasserie-style restaurant and a further lounge area. The contemporary bedrooms are tastefully appointed with co-ordinated soft furnishings and many thoughtful touches. All are individually designed with designer wallpaper, bespoke glass walls and many other unique elements.

Rooms 13 en suite 2 annexe en suite (1 fmly) (2 GF) S £80-£115; D £95-£175*
Facilities FTV Lounge tea/coffee Dinner available Direct Dial WiFi 🐾
Extras Speciality toiletries **Conf** Max 30 Thtr 30 Class 20 Board 20 **Parking** 50
Notes ⊗ Closed 25 Dec

See advert on opposite page

NEWMARKET   Map 12 TL66

Premier Collection

The Packhorse Inn

★★★★★ @@@ INN

tel: 01638 751818 **Bridge St, Moulton CB8 8SP**
email: info@thepackhorseinn.com web: www.thepackhorseinn.com
dir: *A14 junct 39 onto B1506. After 1.5m turn left at x-rds onto B1085 (Moulton Rd). In Moulton, left into Bridge St*

The Packhorse Inn has been totally refurbished, and reopened in late 2013. The property is situated just a short drive from Newmarket in the heart of a village close to the River Kennet. The property has four individually designed bedrooms (four more are on the way). All are tastefully appointed, with many thoughtful touches and views of the surrounding hills, after which the rooms are named. The open-plan public rooms include a choice of seating and dining areas with an eclectic collection of furniture.

Rooms 4 en suite (1 fmly) S £85-£100; D £100-£175* **Facilities** FTV tea/coffee Dinner available WiFi 🐾 18 🐾 **Extras** Speciality toiletries - free; mineral water **Conf** Max 30 Thtr 30 Class 20 Board 30 **Parking** 30

Pavilion House Bed and Breakfast

★★★★ BED AND BREAKFAST

tel: 01638 508005 & 07776 197709 **133 Station Rd, Dullingham CB8 9UT**
email: info@pavilionhousebandb.co.uk web: www.pavilionhousebandb.co.uk
dir: *500yds N of Dullingham Rail Station*

Surrounded by a one acre garden, Pavilion House enjoys a peaceful rural setting, a short drive from both Newmarket and Cambridge and just a three-minute walk to the railway station. Individually styled bedrooms are all attractively presented and very well equipped with a host of thoughtful little extras. Free WiFi is available for guests along with secure parking. Breakfast is not to be missed and the delicious free-range eggs come from their own "Bluebelle" chickens. Dinner is also available by prior arrangement.

Rooms 3 rms (1 en suite) (2 pri facs) (1 fmly) (3 GF) S £55-£60; D £85-£90*
Facilities FTV Lounge tea/coffee Dinner available WiFi 🐾🐾 🐾 **Parking** 4

SIBTON   Map 13 TM36

Sibton White Horse Inn

★★★★ @ INN

tel: 01728 660337 **Halesworth Rd IP17 2JJ**
email: info@sibtonwhitehorseinn.co.uk web: www.sibtonwhitehorseinn.co.uk
dir: *From A12 in Yoxford take A1120 signed Sibton & Peasenhall. 3m, in Peasenhall right opposite butcher's shop. White Horse 600mtrs*

The Sibton White Horse Inn is a delightful Grade II listed 16th-century Tudor property set in open countryside, a few miles from the Suffolk coast. Public rooms include a traditional beamed bar with exposed brick fireplaces and a choice of dining areas. The attractive bedrooms are situated in a converted building adjacent to the inn.

Rooms 6 annexe en suite (3 GF) S £60-£80; D £70-£90* **Facilities** FTV DVD tea/coffee Dinner available WiFi 🐾 **Extras** Bottled water **Parking** 50 **Notes** LB No Children 12yrs Closed 26-27 Dec No coaches

SOUTHWOLD
Map 13 TM57

Sutherland House
★★★★★ ◎◎ RESTAURANT WITH ROOMS

tel: 01502 724544 **56 High St IP18 6DN**
email: enquiries@sutherlandhouse.co.uk **web:** www.sutherlandhouse.co.uk
dir: A1095 into Southwold, on High St on left after Victoria St

Situated in the heart of the bustling town centre, this delightful 16th-century house has a wealth of character - oak beams, exposed brickwork, open fireplaces and two superb ornate plasterwork ceilings. The stylish bedrooms are tastefully decorated using co-ordinated fabrics and include many thoughtful touches. Public rooms feature a large open-plan contemporary restaurant with plush furniture. There's a modern British menu created with care, and the food miles are listed alongside each dish.

Rooms 4 en suite (1 fmly) S £85-£120; D £140-£195 **Facilities** FTV DVD tea/coffee Dinner available Direct Dial WiFi **Conf** Max 80 Thtr 80 Class 30 Board 30 **Parking** 1 **Notes** ⊗ RS Mon Restaurant closed in winter Oct-Mar No coaches

STOKE-BY-NAYLAND
Map 13 TL93

The Angel Inn
★★★★ INN

tel: 01206 263245 & 07748 484619 **Polstead St CO6 4SA**
email: info@angelinnsuffolk.co.uk **web:** www.angelinnsuffolk.co.uk
dir: From A134 onto Bear St (B1087), 2m on right in Stoke-by-Nayland

This charming inn has welcomed guests since the 16th century. Today it is still popular with the locals and is well known for its food and ambiance. Public areas have a wealth of character and offer a choice of dining rooms that include a smart restaurant with an original well. Bedrooms are pleasantly decorated and thoughtfully equipped.

Rooms 6 en suite S £75-£130; D £85-£150* **Facilities** FTV Lounge tea/coffee Dinner available WiFi ⓑ **Conf** Max 25 Thtr 15 Class 18 Board 18 **Parking** 12 **Notes** LB

SUDBURY
Map 13 TL84

The Case Restaurant with Rooms
★★★★ ◎ RESTAURANT WITH ROOMS

tel: 01787 210483 **fax:** 01787 211725 **Further St, Assington CO10 5LD**
email: restaurant@thecaserestaurantwithrooms.co.uk **web:** www.thecaserestaurantwithrooms.co.uk
dir: Exit A12 at Colchester onto A134 to Sudbury. 7m, establishment on left

The Case Restaurant with Rooms offers dining in comfortable surroundings, along with luxurious accommodation in bedrooms that all enjoy independent access. Some bathrooms come complete with corner jacuzzi, while internet access comes as standard. In the restaurant, local produce is used in all dishes, and bread and delicious desserts are made fresh every day.

Rooms 7 en suite (2 fmly) (7 GF) S fr £69; D £145* **Facilities** FTV Lounge tea/coffee Dinner available WiFi **Extras** Speciality toiletries - free; snacks - charged **Parking** 25 **Notes** LB ⊗

THORNHAM MAGNA
Map 13 TM17

Thornham Hall
★★★★★ GUEST ACCOMMODATION

tel: 01379 783314 **fax:** 01379 788347 **IP23 8HA**
email: info@thornhamhall.com **web:** www.thornhamhall.com
dir: Turn off A140 at Stoke Ash White Horse pub. After 350mtrs right before Four Horseshoes pub. Through village, pass church & into drive signed Thornham Hall

Set in a formal park, Thornham Hall enjoys a picturesque setting and the comfortable, individually styled bedrooms overlook the extensive gardens. There is a choice of reception rooms in which to relax and the Thornham estate offers guests over ten miles of walks through ancient woodland and farmland. The walled garden has recently been restored and contains many rare apple trees. The charming town of Eye is nearby and Framlingham is a short drive away.

Rooms 3 en suite D £100-£130* **Facilities** Lounge TVL tea/coffee Licensed WiFi ⊰ ⊱ Fishing ⓑ **Parking** 10 **Notes** ⊗

WINGFIELD
Map 13 TM27

Holly Tree House

★★★★ ≋ BED AND BREAKFAST

tel: 01379 384854 **Bleach Green IP21 5RG**
email: sharon@hollytreehousebandb.co.uk **web:** www.hollytreehousebandb.co.uk

This beautiful 16th-century timber-framed house enjoys a peaceful rural location on the Suffolk/Norfolk border. Guests are served refreshment on arrival in the garden or in the cosy lounge, depending on the weather. Bedrooms are beautifully presented and are very well equipped. The house has been sympathetically restored in recent years, and boasts many eye-catching original features as well as lovely gardens. AA Friendliest B&B of the Year Finalist 2014-2015.

Rooms 2 en suite S fr £60; D £85-£95* **Facilities** FTV DVD iPod docking station Lounge tea/coffee WiFi ⬥ **Extras** Speciality toiletries, snacks **Parking** 4 **Notes** No Children ⊗

WOODBRIDGE
Map 13 TM24

Cherry Tree Inn

★★★★ ⬭ INN

tel: 01394 384627 & 385213 **73 Cumberland St IP12 4AG**
email: info@thecherrytreepub.co.uk **web:** www.thecherrytreepub.co.uk

Cherry Tree Inn is a charming 17th-century inn located close to the town of Woodbridge. This authentic inn has many original features including oak beams, low ceilings and log fires. There is a great atmosphere in the bar and evening meals feature an extensive choice of freshly prepared traditional dishes. There is a good choice of cask ales available and the bedrooms are all spacious and very comfortable.

Rooms 3 annexe en suite (1 fmly) (2 GF) S £90-£100; D £100-£120* **Facilities** STV FTV DVD tea/coffee Dinner available Direct Dial WiFi ⬥ **Extras** Home-made biscuits, still/sparkling water **Parking** 30

Grove House

★★★★ ⬭ GUEST ACCOMMODATION

tel: 01394 382202 & 386236 **39 Grove Rd IP12 4LG**
email: reception@grovehousehotel.ltd.uk **web:** www.grovehousehotel.ltd.uk
dir: W of town centre on A12

Grove House is conveniently located on the outskirts of the pretty village of Woodbridge and is the perfect base from which to explore the beautiful Suffolk coastline. There is an extensive choice of rooms including a family room, as well as five that are on the ground floor with easy access. The refurbished bedrooms are all attractively presented and individually styled. There is a comprehensive choice on the dinner menu, and the comfortable lounge is ideal for pre-dinner drinks.

Rooms 11 en suite (1 fmly) (5 GF) D £65-£95* **Facilities** FTV DVD TVL tea/coffee Dinner available Licensed WiFi ⬥ **Parking** 12 **Notes** LB ⊗

YAXLEY
Map 13 TM17

Premier Collection

The Auberge

★★★★★ ◉◉ ≋ RESTAURANT WITH ROOMS

tel: 01379 783604 **fax:** 01379 788486 **Ipswich Rd IP23 8BZ**
email: aubmail@the-auberge.co.uk **web:** www.the-auberge.co.uk
dir: On A140 between Norwich & Ipswich at x-rds with B1117

A warm welcome awaits at The Auberge, a charming 15th-century property, which was once a rural pub but is now a smart restaurant with rooms. The restaurant has gained two AA Rosettes for the good use of fresh, quality produce in well-crafted dishes. The public areas have a wealth of character, such as exposed brickwork and beams, and the grounds are particularly well kept and attractive. The spacious bedrooms are tastefully appointed and have many thoughtful touches; one bedroom has a four-poster.

Rooms 11 annexe en suite (2 fmly) (6 GF) **Facilities** FTV tea/coffee Dinner available Direct Dial WiFi ⬥ **Conf** Max 46 Thtr 30 Class 30 Board 20 **Parking** 40 **Notes** LB ⊗ No coaches

SURREY

ALBURY
Map 6 TQ04

The Drummond at Albury

★★★ ⬭ INN

tel: 01483 202039 **fax:** 01483 205361 **High St GU5 9AG**
web: www.thedrummondarms.co.uk

The Drummond is centrally located in this picturesque village, with attractive gardens running down to a small river at the rear of the property. The bedrooms are individually appointed and offer all the modern comforts. Breakfast is served in the light and airy conservatory while the restaurant offers mouth-watering dishes.

Rooms 9 en suite **Facilities** Dinner available **Conf** Max 40 Thtr 40 Class 40

CAMBERLEY
Map 6 SU86

Hatsue Guest House

★★★★ ⬭ GUEST ACCOMMODATION

tel: 01276 22160 & 07791 267620 **fax:** 01276 671415 **17 Southwell Park Rd GU15 3PU**
email: welcome@hatsueguesthouse.com **web:** www.hatsueguesthouse.com
dir: M3 junct 4, A331 N, A30 E, at Arena sports centre turn right. At T-junct, turn right, 2nd house on left before church

Hatsue Guest House offers comfortable, well-appointed accommodation in a period house, which has been sympathetically updated to meet the needs of the modern guest. Flat-screen TV and free WiFi are examples of the amenities provided. The breakfast room overlooks the quiet rear garden. Ample parking is available.

Rooms 5 en suite S £60; D £70 **Facilities** FTV tea/coffee Direct Dial WiFi **Parking** 5 **Notes** ⊗

CHARLWOOD

For accommodation details see under Gatwick Airport (London), (Sussex, West)

CHERTSEY

Map 6 TQ06

Hamilton's

★★★★ RESTAURANT WITH ROOMS

tel: 01932 560745 **23 Windsor St KT16 8AY**
email: bookings@hamiltons23.com **web:** www.hamiltons23.com
dir: *M25 junct 11 St Peters Way (A317). At rdbt 1st exit, Chertsey Rd (A317), next rdbt 2nd exit into Free Prae Rd, then Pound Rd. Left into London St, opposite church*

Hamilton's is an intimate and attractive building close to the cricket ground. The en suite rooms are beautifully appointed and equipped with all modern amenities. The restaurant offers a fine dining menu from Wednesday to Saturday, while a freshly cooked breakfast ensures a good start to the day. Free parking is available.

Rooms 5 en suite S £68-£80; D £80-£95* **Facilities** STV FTV DVD tea/coffee Dinner available WiFi **Parking** 3 **Notes** ⊗ No Children 18yrs RS Sun-Tue Restaurant closed No coaches

CHIDDINGFOLD

Map 6 SU93

Premier Collection

The Crown Inn

★★★★★ INN

tel: 01428 682255 **fax:** 01428 683313 **The Green, Petworth Rd GU8 4TX**
email: enquiries@thecrownchiddingfold.com **web:** www.thecrownchiddingfold.com

Set in a tranquil location in a picturesque village, the inn dates back to the early 13th century. This charming property offers stylish, modern accommodation that has been tastefully finished without losing any period features. Breakfast and dinner can be enjoyed in the oak-panelled dining room, and there is a spacious bar, outside seating and small courtyard.

Rooms 8 en suite (4 fmly) **Facilities** FTV DVD iPod docking station Lounge tea/coffee Dinner available Direct Dial WiFi **Conf** Max 40 Thtr 40 Class 25 Board 28 **Parking** 15 **Notes** ⊗

The Swan Inn

★★★★★ ⊛ INN

tel: 01428 684688 **fax:** 01428 685991 **Petworth Rd GU8 4TY**
email: info@theswaninnchiddingfold.com **web:** www.theswaninnchiddingfold.com
dir: *M25 junct 10, A3 to Milford junct. At rdbt 1st exit onto A283, left at lights. At next rdbt 2nd exit, 5m to Swan Inn*

The Swan Inn offers well-sourced, seasonal food in an elegant environment. The well-appointed bedrooms are air conditioned and equipped to meet the needs of both the leisure and business traveller. The rear garden is a peaceful option during the warm months.

Rooms 10 en suite (1 fmly) D fr £100* **Facilities** STV DVD tea/coffee Dinner available Direct Dial WiFi **Extras** Speciality toiletries - complimentary **Conf** Max 20 Thtr 20 Class 20 Board 20 **Parking** 30 **Notes** No coaches

CRANLEIGH

Map 6 TQ03

The Cranley

★★★ INN

tel: 01483 272827 **fax:** 01483 548576 **The Common GU6 8SQ**
email: thecranleyhotel@gmail.com **web:** www.thecranleyhotel.co.uk
dir: *From Guildford on A281 left to Cranleigh*

This traditional pub, located in the picturesque village of Cranleigh, offers freshly prepared food, at both lunch and dinner, using local produce. Regular entertainment is provided, and the rear garden is popular with families. The comfortable bedrooms have TVs and tea- and coffee-making facilities.

Rooms 7 en suite **Facilities** TVL tea/coffee Dinner available WiFi Pool table **Parking** 50 **Notes** ⊗

DORKING

Map 6 TQ14

Denbies Farmhouse B&B (TQ168510)

★★★★ FARMHOUSE

tel: 01306 876777 **fax:** 01306 888930 **London Rd RH5 6AA**
email: bandb@denbiesvineyard.co.uk **web:** www.denbies.co.uk
dir: *Off A24*

Denbies Farmhouse enjoys a wonderful location in the heart of England's largest vineyard and is a short walk to the historic market town of Dorking. Very popular with ramblers, there are many beautiful walks nearby. Bedrooms have been refurbished and delicious breakfasts are served in the conservatory with its wonderful views of the vineyard.

Rooms 7 en suite (2 fmly) (2 GF) S £95; D £105 **Facilities** STV FTV tea/coffee Licensed WiFi ⚓ **Extras** Speciality toiletries - complimentary **Parking** 14 **Notes** LB ⊗ 650 acres wine

EFFINGHAM

Map 6 TQ15

Sir Douglas Haig

★★★ INN

tel: 01372 456886 **fax:** 01372 450987 **The Street KT24 5LU**
email: sirdouglashaig@hotmail.com **web:** www.sirdouglashaig.co.uk
dir: *M25 junct 9, A243 then A24, at rdbt take 2nd exit onto A246. Through Bookham, at lights with golf club on left, turn right. Pub on right*

A traditional public house located in the village centre, the Sir Douglas Haig has retained a country atmosphere and offers comfortable accommodation for the modern traveller. The bar is well stocked and provides regular entertainment whilst the restaurant serves a choice of traditional dishes. Ample parking is available.

Rooms 7 en suite (1 fmly) S £65-£75; D £70-£80 (room only)* **Facilities** FTV DVD tea/coffee Dinner available WiFi ⚓ **Parking** 15 **Notes** LB

FARNHAM
Map 5 SU84

Sandiway

★★★ BED AND BREAKFAST

tel: 01252 710721 **24 Shortheath Rd GU9 8SR**
email: john@shortheath.freeserve.co.uk **web:** www.sandiwayfarnham.co.uk
dir: *Onto A287 Hindhead, at lights at top of hill right into Ridgway Rd, past green on left, Sandiway 300yds on right*

Guests are warmly welcomed at this delightful house, set in attractive gardens in a quiet residential area. Smart bedrooms have a thoughtful range of facilities and share a spacious, well-appointed bathroom. Guests have use of a comfortable lounge during the day and evening, which doubles as the dining room at breakfast.

Rooms 3 rms S £30-£40; D £50 **Facilities** FTV TVL tea/coffee WiFi 🔒 **Extras** Bottled water **Parking** 3 **Notes** ⊗ No Children 10yrs Closed 21-31 Dec ⊜

GODALMING
Map 6 SU94

Innkeeper's Lodge Godalming

★★★★ ⊜ INN

tel: 0845 112 6102 & 155 1551 **Ockford Rd GU7 1RH**
email: info@innkeeperslodge.com **web:** www. innkeeperslodge.com

At Innkeeper's Lodge you'll find accommodation with comfort and character in equal measure, and everything needed for a relaxing stay, from easy check-in and free parking to complimentary breakfast and a cosy pub serving great value food and drink on the doorstep. Each Lodge has quality rooms, and there are Lodges in a variety of locations from towns and cities to countryside settings across the UK.

Rooms 14 en suite (4 fmly) **Facilities** FTV tea/coffee Dinner available Direct Dial WiFi **Conf** Max 28 Class 24 Board 20 **Parking Notes** ⊗

The Squirrel Inn

★★★ INN

tel: 01483 860223 **Hurtmore Rd GU7 2RN**
email: info@thesquirrel-hurtmore.co.uk **web:** www.thesquirrel-hurtmore.co.uk
dir: *A3 Hurtmore junct, on slip road*

Situated in the village of Hurtmore, near Godalming and Guildford, with easy access just off the A3. Accommodation is in refurbished 16th-century cottages, offering five double and three single rooms. All rooms have flat-screen TVs, DVD players, tea and coffee making facilities and are ideal for those on business, leisure weekends or just visiting family or friends. Food is available with daily changing specials.

Rooms 8 rms (7 en suite) (1 pri facs) (3 GF) S £50; D £70-£75* **Facilities** STV FTV DVD iPod docking station Lounge tea/coffee Dinner available WiFi ⌁ 18 **Conf** Max 25 Class 25 Board 25 **Parking** 90

GUILDFORD
Map 6 SU94

Asperion Hillside

★★★★ ⊜ GUEST ACCOMMODATION

tel: 01483 232051 **fax:** 01483 233716 **Perry Hill, Worplesdon GU3 3RF**
email: info@thehillsidehotel.com **web:** www.asperionhillside.com

Located just a short drive from central Guildford, this accommodation is popular with both business and leisure travellers. Bedrooms are comfortable and well

equipped with good facilities. Public areas include a spacious lounge bar where dinner is served, and a bright well-styled breakfast room. Gardens are well maintained and are enhanced by a guest terrace. Small meetings and events can also be catered for here.

Rooms 15 en suite (6 GF) S £70; D £85-£135* **Facilities** FTV Lounge tea/coffee Dinner available Licensed WiFi **Conf** Max 20 Thtr 20 Class 10 Board 12 **Parking** 12 **Notes** ⊗ Closed 21 Dec-2 Jan

The Angel

★★★★ GUEST ACCOMMODATION

tel: 01483 564555 **fax:** 01483 533770 **81 High St GU1 3DP**
email: reservations@angelpostinghouse.com **web:** www.angelpostinghouse.com
dir: *From A281 (Horsham Rd), turn left into High St. 200yds on left*

On the high street, in the heart of Guildford and within the popular Angel Gate area with its shops and restaurants, this historic property features a range of rooms including spacious suites and traditional doubles. All have flat-screen TVs, free WiFi, and high-quality bathrooms with power showers, some with separate baths. Rates are room-only; breakfast is available in the adjacent 'Bills' restaurant, which is also open for lunch and dinner.

Rooms 22 en suite S £99-£199; D £99-£199 (room only)* **Facilities** STV FTV Lounge tea/coffee Dinner available Direct Dial Lift Licensed WiFi ⌁ 18 🔒 **Conf** Max 60 Thtr 60 Class 30 Board 30 **Notes** ⊗ Civ Wed 50

Asperion

★★★★ ⊜ GUEST ACCOMMODATION

tel: 01483 579299 **fax:** 01483 457977 **73 Farnham Rd GU2 7PF**
email: enquiries@asperion.co.uk **web:** www.asperion.co.uk
dir: *Exit A3 at Surrey University only, 2nd exit from rdbt into Chase Rd. Right into Agraria Rd to Farnham Rd junct. Turn right into Farnham Rd (A31), 3rd on right*

The stylish Asperion provides comfortable, modern and contemporary styled bedrooms in a convenient location close to the city centre. The owners are committed to a 'more than for profit' business ethos, part of which involves a healthy organic breakfast.

Rooms 15 rms (14 en suite) (1 pri facs) (1 fmly) (9 GF) **Facilities** FTV TVL tea/coffee Dinner available Direct Dial Licensed WiFi **Extras** Bottled water - complimentary **Parking** 11 **Notes** ⊗ No Children 12yrs Closed 21 Dec-2 Jan

HASLEMERE
Map 6 SU93

The Wheatsheaf Inn

★★★ ⊜ INN

tel: 01428 644440 **fax:** 01428 641285 **Grayswood Rd, Grayswood GU27 2DE**
email: ken@thewheatsheafgrayswood.co.uk **web:** www.thewheatsheafgrayswood.co.uk
dir: *1m N of Haslemere on A286 in Grayswood*

Situated in a small village just outside Haslemere, this well-presented inn has a friendly atmosphere. The smart conservatory restaurant, complements the attractive dining area and popular bar. Bedrooms are furnished to a good standard; all but one on the ground floor.

Rooms 7 en suite (6 GF) S fr £59; D fr £79* **Facilities** FTV tea/coffee Dinner available Direct Dial WiFi **Parking** 21 **Notes** No coaches

HORLEY

For accommodation details see under Gatwick Airport (London), (Sussex, West)

SUNBURY

See London Plan 2 A1

The Flower Pot

★★★★ 🛏 INN

tel: 01932 780741 **fax:** 01932 325464 **Thames St TW16 6AA**
email: info@theflowerpotsunbury.co.uk **web:** www.theflowerpotsunbury.co.uk
dir: M3 junct 1, at Sunbury Cross rdbt take 6th exit (Green St). Bear left into Church Rd, right at mini rdbt into Thames St

This upmarket coaching inn has benefited from complete refurbishment throughout, and now provides high-quality boutique en suite accommodation; each room is equipped with a wide-screen TV, an espresso machine and free WiFi. A range of tasty dishes is available in the dining area.

Rooms 8 en suite (1 fmly) D £89-£109* **Facilities** FTV Lounge TVL tea/coffee Dinner available WiFi ⅃ 18 🅿 **Extras** Speciality toiletries, coffee machines **Parking** 4 **Notes** LB

WEYBRIDGE   Map 6 TQ06

Innkeeper's Lodge Weybridge

★★★ INN

tel: 0845 112 6111 **25 Oatlands Chase KT13 9RW**
email: info@innkeeperslodge.com **web:** www.innkeeperslodge.com

At Innkeeper's Lodge you'll find accommodation with comfort and character in equal measure, and everything needed for a relaxing stay, from easy check-in and free parking to complimentary breakfast and a cosy pub serving great value food and drink on the doorstep. Each Lodge has quality rooms, and there are Lodges in a variety of locations from towns and cities to countryside settings across the UK.

Rooms 19 en suite (5 fmly) (2 GF) **Facilities** FTV tea/coffee Dinner available Direct Dial WiFi **Parking**

WOKING   Map 6 TQ05

Innkeeper's Lodge Woking

★★★ INN

tel: 0845 112 6112 **Chobham Rd, Horsell GU21 4AL**
email: info@innkeeperslodge.com **web:** www.innkeeperslodge.com

Just a short walk from Woking station, a 25-minute commute from central London, this establishment is ideal for both the business or leisure traveller. It offers comfortable en suite bedrooms and attractive public areas with cosy open fires and friendly, welcoming staff. Food is served daily in The Wheatsheaf. The free on-site parking is a plus.

Rooms 33 en suite (3 fmly) (13 GF) **Facilities** FTV tea/coffee Dinner available WiFi **Parking** 28

Made In Sud

[U]

tel: 01483 723080 **14 The Broadway GU21 5AP**
email: dminardi@btinternet.com

Currently the rating for this establishment is not confirmed. This may be due to a change of ownership or because it has only recently joined the AA rating scheme.

Rooms 8 en suite S £50-£70*

EAST SUSSEX

BECKLEY   Map 7 TQ82

Chestnut Lodge B&B

★★★★ BED AND BREAKFAST

tel: 01797 260877 & 07966 181825 **Main St TN31 6RS**
email: info@chestnutlodgebeckley.com **web:** www.chestnutlodgebeckley.com
dir: On B2088 Main St

Chestnut Lodge is located in the quiet village of Beckley, just a short drive from Rye, Hastings and Tunbridge Wells. This Grade II listed Georgian house has been refurbished to offer modern and stylish accommodation including en suite bathrooms and modern amenities such as digital TVs, and free WiFi throughout. The orangery is a spacious addition to this house, where guests can enjoy breakfast each day.

Rooms 2 en suite S £90-£110; D £95-£110* **Facilities** FTV tea/coffee WiFi **Extras** Fridge, milk, bottled water, fruit - free **Parking** 3 **Notes** ⊗ No Children 12yrs 🅦

Woodgate Farm

★★★★ BED AND BREAKFAST

tel: 01797 260763 **Church Ln TN31 6UH**
email: info@woodgate-farm.co.uk **web:** www.woodgate-farm.co.uk
dir: Off B2088 into Church Ln or off A268 into Stoddards Ln

Set in 22 acres of tranquil countryside, yet convenient for both Rye and Hastings, this B&B offers two comfortably appointed bedrooms with modern decor and furnishings. The owners also offer a friendly welcome and home-made refreshments. Guests are free to explore the property's garden and meadows. A hearty cooked breakfast or continental option is served each morning in the open-plan kitchen.

Rooms 2 rms (1 en suite) (1 pri facs) (2 GF) S £75-£85; D £90-£95* **Facilities** STV Lounge tea/coffee WiFi 🅦 Jacuzzi Table tennis **Extras** Speciality toiletries, filtered water **Parking** 4 **Notes** LB ⊗ No Children Closed Xmas wk 🅦

BOREHAM STREET   Map 6 TQ61

Premier Collection

Boreham House

★★★★★ 🏠 BED AND BREAKFAST

tel: 01323 833719 **Boreham Hill BN27 4SF**
email: enquiries@borehamhouse.com **web:** www.borehamhouse.com
dir: *On A271 between Herstmonceux & Battle, 100mtrs from Bull's Head pub*

This recently restored Georgian manor is in a quiet location just a short drive from Bodiam Castle, Hastings and Pevensey Bay. Both sides of the property enjoy excellent views of the High Wield or across the Pevensey Marshes to the sea. Bedrooms and bathrooms are contemporary in style, yet retain many original features. There is a guest lounge, and an excellent pub just 100 metres away. Guests can enjoy a hearty cooked or continental breakfast served in the dining room, all items locally sourced.

Rooms 3 en suite (1 fmly) S £70-£130; D £90-£150* **Facilities** FTV Lounge tea/coffee WiFi 🅿 **Parking** 3 **Notes** ⊗ ⊛

BRIGHTON & HOVE   Map 6 TQ30

Blanch House

★★★★ 🏠 GUEST ACCOMMODATION

tel: 01273 603504 **17 Atlingworth St BN2 1PL**
email: info@blanchhouse.co.uk **web:** www.blanchhouse.co.uk
dir: *Left at pier onto A259. Left into Lower Rock Gardens, right into Saint James St & right into Atlingworth St*

Blanch House is located in the heart of Kemp Town with the seafront and town centre just a couple of minutes walk away. Bedrooms are individual in their design and style yet all are of a very high quality and comfort. There's a spacious function suite ideal for private meetings, dinners or weddings. There is a bar (open daily) where guests can enjoy cocktails or champagne, and the award-wining breakfast offers a range of both cooked and continental dishes.

Rooms 12 en suite S £79-£209; D £89-£219* **Facilities** FTV Lounge tea/coffee Licensed WiFi In-house massage therapies available **Extras** Speciality toiletries, home-made biscuits, robes **Conf** Max 40 Thtr 40 Class 16 Board 20 **Notes** ⊗ No Children 15yrs Civ Wed 40

Five

★★★★ GUEST ACCOMMODATION

tel: 01273 686547 **fax:** 0871 522 7472 **5 New Steine BN2 1PB**
email: info@fivehotel.com **web:** www.fivehotel.com
dir: *On A259 towards E, 8th turn on left into square*

Five is an attractive town house in a traditional Georgian square just a stone's throw from the famous Brighton beaches, cafés and shops. Comfortable bedrooms and bathrooms are well equipped. A copious organic breakfast is served each day by cheerful hosts in the spacious, contemporary dining room.

Rooms 10 en suite **Facilities** FTV TVL tea/coffee WiFi **Conf** Max 20 Board 20 **Notes** ⊗ No Children 5yrs

New Steine

★★★★ 🏠 ⊜ GUEST ACCOMMODATION

tel: 01273 695415 & 681546   **fax:** 01273 622663 **10-11 New Steine BN2 1PB**
email: reservation@newsteinehotel.com **web:** www.newsteinehotel.com
dir: *A23 to Brighton Pier, left into Marine Parade, New Steine on left after Wentworth St*

Close to the seafront, off the Esplanade, the New Steine provides spacious and well-appointed accommodation. The Bistro offers simple yet appealing dishes with a French and British influence; produce from farms in Sussex is used for the breakfasts. There are two meeting rooms suitable for a variety of occasions. Street parking can be arranged.

Rooms 20 rms (16 en suite) (4 pri facs) (4 fmly) (2 GF) S £39-£69.50; D £55-£135 **Facilities** FTV Lounge tea/coffee Dinner available Direct Dial Licensed WiFi 🅿 **Extras** Speciality toiletries **Conf** Max 50 Thtr 50 Class 20 Board 26 **Notes** LB No Children 4yrs

The Twenty One

★★★★ GUEST ACCOMMODATION

tel: 01273 686450 **21 Charlotte St, Marine Pde BN2 1AG**
email: enquiries@thetwentyone.co.uk **web:** www.thetwentyone.co.uk
dir: *From Brighton Pier turn left into Marine Parade, 16th left turn*

This stylishly-appointed town house property is situated in Kemp Town, within easy reach of clubs, bars and restaurants, and just a short walk from the beach. Bedrooms are elegantly furnished and comfortable, with an abundance of thoughtful extras provided. The smart dining room is the setting for a delicious, freshly-cooked breakfast.

Rooms 7 en suite S £65-£75; D £99-£155 **Facilities** FTV DVD iPod docking station Lounge tea/coffee WiFi 🅿 **Extras** iPads **Notes** LB ⊗ No Children 10yrs

BRIGHTON & HOVE *continued*

The White House

★★★★ 🏠 GUEST ACCOMMODATION

tel: 01273 626266 **6 Bedford St BN2 1AN**
email: info@whitehousebrighton.com **web:** www.whitehousebrighton.com
dir: *A23 to Brighton, follow signs to town centre. At rdbt opposite pier 1st exit, through 2 sets of lights, left into Bedford St*

The White House is a small Regency residence only 100 metres from the seafront, and a short walk from Brighton's centre. There are sea views from the south-facing rooms and a courtyard garden where guests may sit and relax. All rooms are smartly and stylishly decorated and there is a relaxed atmosphere. Breakfast is served in the dining room, or alfresco. The extensive breakfast menu uses only the best quality ingredients.

Rooms 10 rms (8 en suite) (2 GF) **Facilities** FTV DVD iPod docking station tea/coffee WiFi **Notes** ⊗

Brighton House

★★★★ 🏠 GUEST ACCOMMODATION

tel: 01273 323282 **52 Regency Square BN1 2FF**
email: info@brighton-house.co.uk **web:** www.brighton-house.co.uk
dir: *Opposite West Pier*

Situated close to the seafront is the elegant and environmentally-friendly Brighton House. Comfortably appointed bedrooms and bathrooms come in a variety of sizes and are located on four floors. An impressively abundant, organic continental breakfast is served in the spacious and elegant dining room. Parking is in the nearby underground car park.

Rooms 16 en suite (2 fmly) S £40-£69; D £80-£110 **Facilities** FTV tea/coffee Licensed WiFi **Notes** ⊗ No Children 12yrs

Four Seasons Guest House

★★★★ GUEST ACCOMMODATION

tel: 01273 673574 **3 Upper Rock Gardens BN2 1QE**
email: info@4seasonsbrighton.co.uk **web:** www.4seasonsbrighton.co.uk
dir: *A23 signed town centre & seafront to Brighton Pier. At rdbt 1st exit, left into Marine Parade. At next lights left into Lower Rock Gardens*

Caring hosts William and Thommy provide smart accommodation with a variety of stylish contemporary bedrooms, each with ample facilities including WiFi and hairdryers. A healthy breakfast is served in the sunny dining room. Beaches, restaurants and shops are all within easy walking distance.

Rooms 7 rms (6 pri facs) (1 GF) **Facilities** FTV tea/coffee WiFi **Notes** LB ⊗ No Children 10yrs

Gullivers

★★★★ GUEST ACCOMMODATION

tel: 01273 681546 & 695415 **fax:** 01273 622663 **12a New Steine BN2 1PB**
email: reservation@gullivershotel.com **web:** www.gullivershotel.com
dir: *A23 to Brighton Pier, left into Marine Parade, premises 300yds on left*

Situated in an impressive Regency square close to the town and seafront, Gullivers has much to offer. Compact rooms use clever design and contemporary colours to ensure comfort, and some have quality shower rooms en suite. The lounge and brasserie, decorated with fine art, are super areas in which to relax and dine.

Rooms 12 rms (9 en suite) (3 pri facs) (2 GF) (4 smoking) S £39-£65; D £55-£129 **Facilities** FTV Lounge tea/coffee Dinner available Direct Dial Licensed WiFi 🛁

Extras Speciality toiletries - complimentary **Conf** Max 30 Thtr 30 Class 10 Board 20 **Notes** LB ⊗ No Children 4yrs

Marine View

★★★★ GUEST ACCOMMODATION

tel: 01273 603870 **fax:** 01273 357257 **24 New Steine BN2 1PD**
email: info@mvbrighton.co.uk **web:** www.mvbrighton.co.uk
dir: *From A23, left into Marine Pde, left into New Steine, 300mtrs*

Overlooking the elegant Steine Square with the sea just a glance away, this 18th-century property offers comfortable, well-designed accommodation. Plenty of accessories are provided, including free WiFi. A hearty breakfast is available in the bright lounge-dining room.

Rooms 11 rms (8 en suite) (1 pri facs) (2 fmly) (2 GF) S £35-£65; D £59-£120* **Facilities** Lounge tea/coffee WiFi **Notes** LB ⊗

Snooze

★★★★ GUEST ACCOMMODATION

tel: 01273 605797 **25 St George's Ter BN2 1JJ**
email: info@snoozebrighton.com **web:** www.snoozebrighton.com
dir: *Follow A23 to seafront/pier. Turn left at mini rdbt opposite pier, then left into Bedford St, 2nd right into St George's Terrace*

This splendid Victorian terraced property is close to the beach and the popular Kemp Town bars and restaurants. Bedrooms have a distinctly 'retro' feel and all are comfortably presented. A choice of hearty breakfasts is served in the spacious dining room that is enhanced by large bay windows.

Rooms 8 en suite (2 GF) **Facilities** FTV DVD iPod docking station tea/coffee WiFi **Extras** Speciality toiletries **Notes** ⊗

Motel Schmotel

★★★ 🏠 GUEST ACCOMMODATION

tel: 01273 326129 **37 Russell Square BN1 2EF**
email: info@motelschmotel.co.uk **web:** www.motelschmotel.co.uk

The quirkily named Motel Schmotel is a charming, family-run establishment situated in a quiet square just minutes away from the beach and the shops. The bright en suite bedrooms include thoughtful amenities such as free WiFi and Freeview TV. The substantial breakfast menu uses fresh, local produce and is served in the comfort of the guest's own room or in the breakfast room.

Rooms 8 en suite (1 fmly) (2 GF) **Facilities** FTV tea/coffee WiFi **Parking** 2 **Notes** ⊗

Regency Landsdowne Guest House

★★★ GUEST ACCOMMODATION

tel: 01273 321830 **fax:** 01273 777067 **45 Landsdowne Place BN3 1HF**
email: rlgh@btconnect.com **web:** www.regencylansdowne.co.uk
dir: *A23 to Brighton Pier, right onto A259, 1m right into Lansdowne Place, house on left before Western Rd*

A warm welcome is guaranteed at this Regency house, located only minutes from the seafront. Comfortable bedrooms are functionally equipped with a good range of facilities, and an extensive continental breakfast is served each day at a communal table overlooking attractive gardens. On-road parking is a short walk away.

Rooms 7 rms (5 en suite) (2 pri facs) S £32-£58; D £48-£99* **Facilities** FTV tea/coffee Lift WiFi **Notes** ⊗ Closed 20-27 Dec

Avalon

★★★ GUEST ACCOMMODATION

tel: 01273 692344 **7 Upper Rock Gardens BN2 1QE**
email: info@avalonbrighton.co.uk **web:** www.avalonbrighton.com
dir: *A23 to Brighton Pier, left into Marine Parade, 300yds at lights left into Lower Rock Gdns, over lights, Avalon on left*

The Avalon is situated a short walk from the seafront and The Lanes. The en suite bedrooms vary in size and style but all are attractively presented with plenty of useful accessories. Parking vouchers are available for purchase from the proprietor.

Rooms 7 en suite (3 fmly) (1 GF) **Facilities** FTV DVD tea/coffee WiFi

Innkeeper's Lodge Brighton, Patcham

★★★ INN

tel: 0845 112 6097 **Black Lion Harvester, London Rd, Patcham BN1 8YQ**
email: info@innkeeperslodge.com **web:** www.innkeeperslodge.com

At Innkeeper's Lodge you'll find accommodation with comfort and character in equal measure, and everything needed for a relaxing stay, from easy check-in and free parking to complimentary breakfast and a cosy pub serving great value food and drink on the doorstep. Each Lodge has quality rooms, and there are Lodges in a variety of locations from towns and cities to countryside settings across the UK.

Rooms 17 en suite (6 fmly) (1 GF) **Facilities** FTV tea/coffee Dinner available Direct Dial WiFi **Parking**

The Iron Duke

 ★★★ INN

tel: 01273 734806 **3 Waterloo St BN3 1AQ**
email: info@irondukebrighton.co.uk **web:** www.irondukebrighton.co.uk

Located right off of the seafront in Hove yet within just a short walking distance of Brighton's town centre, this inn offers nine spacious bedrooms, ideal for both business and leisure guests. The pub is traditional in style yet offers a vibrant Thai menu served daily. Breakfast is served in the main bar area.

Rooms 9 rms (6 en suite) (2 fmly) **Facilities** FTV TVL tea/coffee Dinner available WiFi
🔒 **Notes** No coaches

Westbourne Guest House

★★★ GUEST ACCOMMODATION

tel: 01273 686920 **fax:** 01273 686920 **46 Upper Rock Gardens BN2 1QF**
email: welcome@westbournehotel.net **web:** www.westbournehotel.co.uk
dir: *A23 to Brighton Pier, left into Marine Parade, 100yds left at lights, premises on right*

Just a short walk from the seafront, this Victorian house is run by friendly owners. The attractive bedrooms are bright and well furnished, and some have flat-screen TVs. A spacious dining area is complemented by a large bay window.

Rooms 11 rms (7 en suite) (1 fmly) (2 GF) S £35-£65; D £45-£120* **Facilities** FTV tea/coffee Licensed WiFi **Parking** 1 **Notes** ✶ Closed 23-30 Dec

The Bear Inn & Burwash Motel

★★★ INN

tel: 01435 882540 **fax:** 01435 882260 **High St TN19 7ET**
email: enquiries@bear-inn-hotel-burwash.co.uk **web:** www.bear-inn-hotel-burwash.co.uk

Located in the village of Burwash, this country inn offers en suite bedrooms with external access. The inn is traditional in style and benefits from uninterrupted views of the Sussex countryside. Traditional bar meals are available daily and guests can enjoy a cooked or continental breakfast in the restaurant.

Rooms 8 en suite (8 GF) S £55; D £80* **Facilities** FTV DVD TVL tea/coffee Dinner available WiFi ➋ ⚓ 36 Fishing Pool table 🔒 **Conf** Max 50 Thtr 50 Class 35 Board 35 **Parking** 8

The Gallivant

★★★★★ INN

tel: 01797 225057 **New Llyd Rd TN31 7RB**
email: beachbistro@thegallivanthotel.com **web:** www.thegallivanthotel.com

The Gallivant is located right on the edge of Camber Sands and just a short drive from the historic town of Rye. Following a complete refurbishment the inn offers guests modern, coastal-styled accommodation with light airy decor and reconditioned driftwood furniture. Rooms are well equipped and ideal for both business and leisure guests. There's a bar and the award-winning Beach Bistro serves food daily. The large function suite is open year round and is perfect for parties or weddings. The sand dunes and beach are just across the road in front of the inn.

Rooms 16 en suite 4 annexe en suite (4 fmly) (20 GF) S £110-£150; D £115-£175
Facilities FTV DVD Lounge tea/coffee Dinner available Direct Dial WiFi ⚓ 18 🔒
Extras Speciality toiletries **Conf** Max 120 Thtr 120 Class 60 Board 40 **Parking** 25
Notes Civ Wed 150

Premier Collection

Tovey Lodge

★★★★★ GUEST ACCOMMODATION

tel: 01273 256156 & 07515 753802 **fax:** 01273 256156 **Underhill Ln BN6 8XE**
email: info@toveylodge.co.uk **web:** www.toveylodge.co.uk
dir: *From Ditchling N on Beacon Rd. 0.5m, left into Underhill Ln, 100yds, 1st drive on left*

Tovey Lodge is set within three acres of gardens and has great views of the South Downs. There is an indoor swimming pool, sauna and hot tub. Bedrooms and bathrooms are spacious and stylishly decorated. Bedrooms also include WiFi and DVD plasma TVs. There is a guest lounge which backs on to a patio a lovely place to spend time on a summer's day. The lounge is spacious and features a 50-inch plasma TV. A cooked or continental breakfast can be enjoyed in the dining room.

Rooms 5 en suite (4 fmly) (2 GF) **Facilities** FTV DVD iPod docking station TVL tea/coffee Dinner available Licensed WiFi 🔊 ⚓ 18 Riding Sauna Gym 🔒 Hot tub spa **Extras** Speciality toiletries, sweets - complimentary **Conf** Max 12 Thtr 12 Board 12 **Parking** 28

DITCHLING *continued*

The Bull

★★★★ INN

tel: 01273 843147 **fax:** 01273 843147 **2 High St BN6 8TA**
email: info@thebullditchling.com **web:** www.thebullditchling.com
dir: *Exit A23 signed Pyecombe, left onto A273 signed Hassocks. Up hill, pass Pyecombe Golf Club on right, 2nd right into New Rd (B2112) to Ditchling. Right at mini rdbt, next left into car park*

Dating back to 1563, The Bull is one of the oldest buildings in this famously pretty Sussex village. First used as an overnight resting place for travelling monks, the inn has also served as a courthouse and staging post for the London-Brighton coach. Home-cooked meals and local ales are available in the restaurant. There is a landscaped garden with seating that enjoys stunning views over the South Downs. Bedrooms have been refurbished and are very comfortable, offering many stylish features and a range of amenities. An extensive cooked and continental breakfast is served daily in the restaurant.

Rooms 4 en suite D £100-£140* **Facilities** FTV DVD iPod docking station Dinner available WiFi ♨ 18 🔒 **Extras** Speciality toiletries, mineral water, chocolates **Parking** 30 **Notes** LB No coaches

See advert on page 339

See advert on page 339

EASTBOURNE   Map 6 TV69

Premier Collection

Ocklynge Manor

★★★★★ BED AND BREAKFAST

tel: 01323 734121 & 07979 627172 **Mill Rd BN21 2PG**
email: ocklyngemanor@hotmail.com **web:** www.ocklyngemanor.co.uk
dir: *From Eastbourne Hospital follow town centre/seafront sign, 1st right into Kings Av, Ocklynge Manor at top of road*

This charming home has seen a variety of uses since serving as a commanderie for the Knights of St John in the 12th century. An air of peace and relaxation is evident in the delightful public rooms, well-tended gardens and the spacious, comfortable bedrooms that come filled with thoughtful extras, including free WiFi. The hospitality is noteworthy, and home-baked bread is just one of the delights at breakfast.

Rooms 3 rms (2 en suite) (1 pri facs) S £60-£120; D £100-£120* **Facilities** FTV DVD Lounge tea/coffee WiFi 🔒 **Extras** Snacks - complimentary **Parking** 3 **Notes** ⊗ No Children 18yrs ⊕ Civ Wed

The Berkeley

★★★★ GUEST ACCOMMODATION

tel: 01323 645055 **3 Lascelles Ter BN21 4BJ**
email: info@theberkeley.net **web:** www.theberkeley.net
dir: *Follow seafront from pier, take 7th turn on right*

The Berkeley is an attractive Victorian property located close to The Devonshire Park Theatre along with being only a few minutes walk from the seafront. The beautifully decorated bedrooms are comfortable with a wide range of accessories on offer. Breakfast is served in the dining room with black pudding and haggis sourced from Scotland.

Rooms 13 en suite (3 fmly) (1 GF) **Facilities** STV DVD Lounge tea/coffee WiFi 🔒

The Camelot Lodge

★★★★ GUEST ACCOMMODATION

tel: 01323 725207 **35 Lewes Rd BN21 2BU**
email: info@camelotlodgehotel.com **web:** www.camelotlodgehotel.com
dir: *A22 onto A2021, premises 0.5m after hospital on left*

The Camelot Lodge occupies a delightful Edwardian property, within walking distance of the seafront and local amenities. The beautifully styled bedrooms feature a range of facilities including free WiFi access, and there is a spacious lounge-bar area. Meals are served in the conservatory dining room, and dinner is available by arrangement.

Rooms 8 en suite (3 fmly) (1 GF) S £29.95-£50; D £59.95-£80 **Facilities** FTV Lounge TVL tea/coffee Dinner available Licensed WiFi **Extras** Fridge **Parking** 8 **Notes** LB ⊗

Gyves House Guesthouse

★★★★ GUEST ACCOMMODATION

tel: 01323 721709 **20 St Aubyns Rd BN22 7AS**
email: book@gyveshouse.com **web:** www.gyvesguesthouse.co.uk
dir: *On seafront between Redoubt Fortress & pier, into St Aubyns Rd, 1st house*

This property is located just 30 metres from the seafront and within a short walking distance of the both the town centre and pier. Bedrooms are comfortably appointed throughout and are modern in style with high quality soft furnishings. Complimentary WiFi and digital TVs are provided in addition to well stocked beverage trays. A range of cooked and continental dishes are served daily in the main dining room.

Rooms 6 en suite **Facilities** FTV tea/coffee WiFi ⚓ 18 🔒 **Extras** Bottled water **Notes** ⊗

The Mowbray

★★★★ GUEST ACCOMMODATION

tel: 01323 720012 **fax:** 01323 733579 **2 Lascelles Ter BN21 4BJ**
email: info@themowbray.com **web:** www.themowbray.com
dir: *Opposite Devonshire Park Theatre*

The Mowbray is an elegant town house located opposite The Devonshire Park Theatre and a few minutes' walk from the seafront. Bedrooms are accessible by a lift to all floors, and vary in size, but all are attractively furnished and comfortable. Public areas include a spacious well presented lounge, small modern bar and a stylish dining room. Breakfast is home-cooked, as are evening meals, available by prior arrangement.

Rooms 13 en suite (1 fmly) (1 GF) **Facilities** FTV DVD TVL tea/coffee Dinner available Lift Licensed WiFi 🔒 **Extras** Superior rooms - fruit, bottled water, slippers **Conf** Max 20 Thtr 20 Class 10 Board 10

Arden House

★★★★ GUEST ACCOMMODATION

tel: 01323 639639 **fax:** 0872 113 0639 **17 Burlington Place BN21 4AR**
email: info@theardenhotel.co.uk **web:** www.theardenhotel.co.uk
dir: *On seafront, towards W, 5th turn after pier*

This attractive Regency property sits just minutes away from the seafront and town centre. Bedrooms are comfortable and bright, most with en suite bathrooms. Guests can enjoy a hearty breakfast at the beginning of the day then relax in the cosy lounge in the evening.

Rooms 11 rms (10 en suite) (1 pri facs) (1 fmly) S £37-£43; D £58-£69* **Facilities** STV FTV DVD TVL tea/coffee WiFi 🔒 **Parking** 3 **Notes** LB

The Bay Lodge

★★★★ GUEST ACCOMMODATION

tel: 01323 732515 **61-62 Royal Pde BN22 7AQ**
email: baylodge@hotmail.co.uk **web:** www.baylodge.org.uk
dir: *From A22 follow signs to seafront. Bay Lodge on right opposite Pavilion Tea Gardens*

A family-run guest accommodation, The Bay Lodge offers a warm welcome in comfortable surroundings opposite the Redoubt and Pavilion Gardens. Bedrooms are bright and spacious, some with balconies. There is a sun lounge, and a cosy bar that enjoy superb sea views.

Rooms 10 en suite (2 fmly) (2 GF) S £35-£40; D £60-£80* **Facilities** FTV Lounge tea/coffee Licensed WiFi 🔒 **Parking** 6 **Notes** LB ⊗ No Children 5yrs Closed 23 Dec-3 Jan

Bella Vista

★★★★ GUEST ACCOMMODATION

tel: 01323 724222 **30 Redoubt Rd BN22 7DH**
email: stay@thebellavista.com **web:** www.thebellavista.com
dir: *500yds NE of town centre. Off A259 (Seaside Rd)*

Situated on the east side of town, just off the seafront, this is an attractive flint house with the bonus of a car park. Bedrooms are generally spacious, comfortable and neatly appointed with modern facilities including free WiFi. There is a large lounge and a dining room where dinner and breakfast is served.

Rooms 9 en suite (3 GF) D £64-£80* **Facilities** FTV TVL tea/coffee Dinner available WiFi **Parking** 10 **Notes** LB ⊗

Ivydene

★★★★ GUEST ACCOMMODATION

tel: 01323 720547 **fax:** 01323 411247 **5-6 Hampden Ter, Latimer Rd BN22 7BL**
email: ivydenehotel@hotmail.co.uk **web:** www.ivydenehotel-eastbourne.co.uk
dir: *From town centre/pier NE along seafront, towards Redoubt Fortress, into St Aubyns Rd, 1st right into Hampden Terrace*

Ivydene is a friendly, family-run property situated a short walk from the pier and seafront. Bedrooms are bright and cheerful with comfortable, stylish furnishings. Public areas include a spacious lounge-bar, sunny conservatory and attractive dining room.

Rooms 14 en suite (2 fmly) (1 GF) S £35-£40; D £65-£80* **Facilities** FTV TVL tea/coffee Licensed WiFi **Notes** LB ⊗

EASTBOURNE *continued*

The Royal

★★★★ GUEST ACCOMMODATION

tel: 01323 649222 **fax:** 0560 1500 065 **8-9 Marine Pde BN21 3DX**
email: info@royaleastbourne.org.uk **web:** www.royaleastbourne.org.uk
dir: *On seafront 100mtrs E of pier*

The Royal enjoys a central seafront location close to the pier and within easy walking distance of the town centre. Spectacular uninterrupted sea views are guaranteed. This eco-friendly property has comfortable modern bedrooms with flat-screen TVs and free WiFi. One of the ten rooms has private facilities, while the others are en suite. A substantial continental breakfast is served. The Royal offers a full pet-sitting service and dogs stay free of charge.

Rooms 10 rms (9 en suite) (1 pri facs) (1 fmly) (1 GF) S £40-£59; D £75-£98*
Facilities STV FTV DVD tea/coffee WiFi ♿ 18 Free Wi-fi **Extras** Speciality toiletries -
complimentary **Notes** LB No Children 12yrs

The Sheldon

★★★★ GUEST ACCOMMODATION

tel: 01323 724120 **fax:** 01323 644327 **9-11 Burlington Place BN21 4AS**
email: info@thesheldonhotel.co.uk **web:** www.thesheldonhotel.co.uk
dir: *Just off The Grand Parade near bandstand*

The Sheldon has comfortable accommodation where the rooms have flat-screen TVs with 110 satellite channels, and the public areas have been finished to a very high standard. These factors, together with an excellent location, make for a very enjoyable stay. Ample, secure parking is available.

Rooms 20 en suite (4 fmly) (2 GF) S £25-£68; D £65-£145* **Facilities** STV FTV
Lounge tea/coffee Lift WiFi ♿ 18 **Extras** Speciality toiletries **Conf** Max 20 Thtr 20
Class 10 Board 10 **Parking** 21 **Notes** ⊗

The Sherwood

★★★★ GUEST HOUSE

tel: 01323 724002 & 07851 716706 **fax:** 01323 400133 **7 Lascelles Ter BN21 4BJ**
email: info@thesherwood.net **web:** www.thesherwood.net
dir: *Follow signs to seafront. At pier turn into Grand Parade (towards Beachy Head). Right into Lascelles Terrace*

The Sherwood is an attractive Victorian property just a minute's walk from the seafront, offering well-appointed bedrooms with comfortable, co-ordinated furnishings. The cosy lounge is great to relax in, and the attractive dining room serves a robust breakfast.

Rooms 11 en suite (2 fmly) (1 GF) S £30-£54; D £53-£110* **Facilities** FTV DVD TVL
tea/coffee Licensed WiFi 🐾 **Extras** Bottled water **Notes** ⊗

Beachy Rise Guest House

★★★ GUEST HOUSE

tel: 01323 639171 **fax:** 01323 645006 **5 Beachy Head Rd BN20 7QN**
email: susanne234@hotmail.com **web:** www.beachyrise.com
dir: *1m SW of town centre. Off B2103 Upper Dukes Rd*

This friendly, family-run guest house has a quiet residential location close to Meads. Bedrooms are individually styled with co-ordinated soft furnishings and feature some useful extras. Breakfast is served in the light and airy dining room overlooking the garden, where guests are free to wander.

Rooms 4 en suite (2 fmly) S £40-£50; D £60-£70* **Facilities** FTV tea/coffee WiFi
Notes ⊗

EWHURST GREEN   Map 7 TQ82

AA GUEST ACCOMMODATION OF THE YEAR FOR ENGLAND 2014–2015

Premier Collection

Prawles Court B&B

★★★★★ 🏠 BED AND BREAKFAST

tel: 01580 830136 & 07799 576187 **Shoreham Ln TN32 5RG**
email: info@prawlescourt.com **web:** www.prawlescourt.com
dir: *A21 after Hurst Green, turn left signed Bodiam. Through x-rds, over level crossing, 2nd left into Shoreham Ln. 200yds on right*

Prawles Court is a country house set within 27 acres of gardens and located in the quiet village of Ewhurst Green, just a short walk from Bodiam Castle. The guest lounge features wood panelling, traditional decor and a large open fire place. Guests can relax and enjoy home-made refreshments on arrival. Bedrooms are stylish and offer a mix of the building's original features in addition to luxury furnishings. Breakfast offers an excellent range of both cooked and continental dishes.

Rooms 4 en suite D £140-£170 **Facilities** FTV DVD Lounge tea/coffee Licensed
WiFi 🐾 **Extras** Speciality toiletries, home-made biscuits, fruit **Parking** 10
Notes ⊗ No Children 12yrs Closed Xmas-New Year

FOREST ROW
Map 6 TQ43

The Roebuck
★★★ INN

tel: 01342 823811 fax: 01342 824790 **Wych Cross RH18 5JL**
email: 6499@greeneking.co.uk web: www.oldenglish.co.uk

A 17th-century country house, The Roebuck is located just minutes from Forest Row just off the A22. Public areas have many original features and log fires are lit during the winter months. Free WiFi is available throughout. Bedrooms are well equipped and offer comfortable facilities. Dinner and breakfast are served in Antlers Restaurant.

Rooms 28 en suite (8 GF) **Facilities** TVL tea/coffee Dinner available Direct Dial WiFi Pool table **Conf** Max 100 Thtr 10 Class 20 **Parking** 100 **Notes** Civ Wed 100

HALLAND
Map 6 TQ41

Beechwood B&B
★★★★★ Ⓐ GUEST ACCOMMODATION

tel: 01825 840936 fax: 01825 840936 **Eastbourne Rd BN8 6PS**
email: chyland1956@aol.com web: www.beechwoodbandb.co.uk
dir: *On A22 directly before speed camera in Halland*

Set in an acre of mature gardens with a large lawn, Beechwood B&B is an attractive property offering stylish bedrooms, each with its own colour theme. Although evening meals are not served, the owners are very happy to recommend local pubs and restaurants. A comprehensive breakfast is served family-style in the kitchen, and uses local or home-made produce wherever possible.

Rooms 3 rms (2 en suite) (1 pri facs) (1 fmly) **Facilities** TVL tea/coffee WiFi ⤵ Hot tub **Parking** 5

The Black Lion Inn
★★★ INN

tel: 01825 840304 **Lewes Rd BN8 6PN**
email: nigel.fright@btconnect.com web: www.theblacklioninn-halland.co.uk

This traditional inn is located on the A22 between Eastbourne and Uckfield. There is a cosy restaurant and bar area with many original features and an open fireplace; traditional pub food is served daily. Bedrooms are modern and very comfortable with digital TV and free WiFi throughout. A cooked and continental breakfast is served in the bar area.

Rooms 7 rms **Facilities** Dinner available

The Forge
★★★ INN

tel: 01825 840456 fax: 01825 840773 **BN8 6PW**
dir: *Off A22, 4m S of Uckfield*

Reputedly built on the site of the village forge, this convenient roadside inn offers a spacious lounge bar and popular carvery restaurant. Bedrooms are on two floors in a separate motel-style annexe and have a practical layout and close parking.

Rooms 17 annexe en suite (2 fmly) (8 GF) S £65; D £75* **Facilities** FTV TVL tea/coffee Dinner available Direct Dial WiFi 🔒 **Conf** Max 60 Thtr 60 Board 40 **Parking** 70 **Notes** ⊗

HASTINGS & ST LEONARDS
Map 7 TQ80

Stream House
★★★★★ BED AND BREAKFAST

tel: 01424 814916 & 0794 191 1378 **Pett Level Rd, Fairlight TN35 4ED**
email: info@stream-house.co.uk web: www.stream-house.co.uk
dir: *4m NE of Hastings. Exit A259 onto unclassified road between Fairlight & Cliff End*

Lovingly converted from three cottages, the Stream House stands in three acres of tranquil grounds, just one mile from Winchelsea beach. If you arrive before 6pm, you will be greeted with a complimentary cup of tea and slice of Sandra's home-made cake. The well-appointed bedrooms are beautifully decorated, and among the delightful extras provided are sherry and chocolates, along with speciality toiletries in the bathrooms. Delicious breakfasts are served in the lounge-dining room which has an original inglenook fireplace, and during warmer months you can enjoy the extensive garden with its rippling stream and Koi pond.

Rooms 3 en suite S £50-£60; D £80-£100 **Facilities** STV Lounge tea/coffee WiFi 🔒 **Extras** Speciality toiletries, snacks **Parking** 4 **Notes** LB ⊗ No Children 5yrs Closed Dec-Feb 🚭

HASTINGS & ST LEONARDS *continued*

The Cloudesley

★★★★★ GUEST ACCOMMODATION

tel: 01424 722759 & 07507 000148 **7 Cloudesley Rd TN37 6JN**
email: info@thecloudesley.co.uk **web:** www.thecloudesley.co.uk
dir: *A21 (London Rd) onto A2102, left into Tower Rd. Right into Cloudesley Rd, house on left*

The Cloudesley is located just minutes from Hastings in the quiet residential area of St Leonards, and offers high standards of quality and comfort. The bedrooms have been environmentally designed - the walls have been eco-limewashed, the hand-made beds have Siberian goosedown pillows, and the shampoos are free of parabens and sodiam lauryl sulphate. There is a treatment room for holistic therapies. The two guest lounges are stylish and decorated with photographs taken by the proprietor. An extensive selection of cooked and continental dishes is available for breakfast, which includes locally sourced, organic ingredients.

Rooms 5 en suite **Facilities** iPod docking station Lounge tea/coffee Dinner available Licensed WiFi Holistic therapies & massage **Extras** Speciality toiletries, mini-fridge **Notes** ⊗ No Children 6yrs ⊜

Seaspray Bed & Breakfast

★★★★ 🅰 GUEST HOUSE

tel: 01424 436583 **54 Eversfield Place TN37 6DB**
email: jo@seaspraybb.co.uk **web:** www.seaspraybb.co.uk
dir: *A21 to town centre & seafront, Seaspray 100yds W of pier*

This attractive house occupies a prime location overlooking the seafront and many rooms enjoy lovely views. Bedrooms are well equipped, smartly appointed and brightly decorated. The breakfast room has separate tables.

Rooms 10 rms (8 en suite) (2 pri facs) (1 fmly) (1 GF) S £30-£45; D £65-£80
Facilities FTV DVD tea/coffee WiFi 🔔 **Notes** LB ⊗ Closed 10 Jan-10 Feb ⊜

Eagle House

★★★ GUEST ACCOMMODATION

tel: 01424 430535 & 437771   **fax:** 01424 400035 **Pevensey Rd TN38 0JZ**
email: info@eaglehousehotel.co.uk **web:** www.eaglehousehotel.co.uk
dir: *Exit seafront into London Rd, 5th turn on left into Pevensey Rd. 150mtrs on right*

Eagle House is a Victorian property situated in a peaceful residential area within easy walking distance of the shops, college and seafront. Public areas are sumptuously decorated in a traditional style and the spacious 'retro' bedrooms are simply furnished. A hearty breakfast can be enjoyed in the dining room, which overlooks the gardens.

Rooms 19 en suite (3 fmly) (3 GF) S £45-£55; D £70-£90* **Facilities** FTV Lounge TVL tea/coffee Licensed WiFi **Parking** 9 **Notes** ⊗

HEATHFIELD	Map 6 TQ52

Holly Grove

★★★★ BED AND BREAKFAST

tel: 01435 863375 & 07814 398854   **Little London TN21 0NU**
email: andy.christie@btconnect.com **web:** www.hollygrovebedandbreakfast.co.uk
dir: *A267 to Horam, turn right at Little London garage into Spinney Ln, proceed to bottom of lane*

Holly Grove is set in a quiet rural location with heated outdoor swimming pool, satellite TV, WiFi and parking facilities. Bedrooms are appointed to a very high standard. There is a separate lounge available for guests, and breakfast is served in the dining room or on the terrace, weather permitting.

Rooms 4 rms (3 en suite) (1 pri facs) (1 fmly) (2 GF) S £65-£110; D £75-£120*
Facilities STV TVL tea/coffee Dinner available WiFi ⚓ 🔔 **Parking** 7

HERSTMONCEUX	Map 6 TQ61

Wartling Place

★★★★★ GUEST ACCOMMODATION

tel: 01323 832590 **fax:** 01323 831558 **Wartling Place, Wartling BN27 1RY**
email: accom@wartlingplace.prestel.co.uk **web:** www.wartlingplace.co.uk
dir: *2.5m SE of Herstmonceux. Exit A271 to Wartling. Wartling Place opposite village church*

Located in a sleepy village, this beautiful Grade II listed country home is set in two acres of well-tended gardens. The individually decorated bedrooms, two featuring four-poster beds, are luxurious and have a host of thoughtful extras. Delicious breakfasts are served in the elegant dining room. Guests can also enjoy free broadband access.

Rooms 4 en suite (1 fmly) **Facilities** tea/coffee Dinner available **Conf** Max 12 **Parking** 10 **Notes** ⊗

HOVE

See Brighton & Hove

LEWES

Map 6 TQ41

The Blacksmiths Arms

★★★★ 🍴 INN

tel: 01273 472971 **London Rd, Offham BN7 3QD**
email: blacksmithsarms@shineadsl.co.uk **web:** www.theblacksmithsarms-offham.co.uk
dir: *1m N of Lewes. On A275 in Offham*

Situated just outside Lewes, this is a great location for touring the south coast, offering high-quality accommodation in comfortable bedrooms. Enjoyable meals are available in the cosy bar downstairs, and this is where the hearty cooked breakfast is also served.

Rooms 4 en suite **Facilities** FTV tea/coffee Dinner available WiFi **Extras** Bottled water, fruit, toiletries, sweets **Parking** 22 **Notes** ⊗ No coaches

NORTHIAM

Map 7 TQ82

Premier Collection

Knelle Dower B&B

★★★★★ 🏠 GUEST ACCOMMODATION

tel: 01797 253163 **Rye Rd TN31 6NJ**
email: knelledower@btconnect.com **web:** www.knelledower.co.uk
dir: *A21 to Flimwell onto A268, then A28. In Northiam onto B2088 opposite primary school, on left between Talisman & Boundary House*

Located in a rural location close to both Rye and the village of Northiam, this converted barn hosts a prime location with uninterrupted countryside views. The accommodation is spacious with high-quality decor and furnishings, and there is a private terrace leading off the main living area for guests to enjoy during summer months. Breakfast can be served here or in the main house.

Rooms 1 annexe en suite (1 GF) S £110-£120; D £120-£130* **Facilities** FTV DVD iPod docking station tea/coffee WiFi 🍵 🎣 18 🎯 **Parking** 2 **Notes** ⊗ No Children 3yrs Closed 21-28 Dec

ROTTINGDEAN

Map 6 TQ30

White Horse

★★★ INN

tel: 01273 300301 **fax:** 01273 308716 **Marine Dr BN2 7HR**
email: 5308@greeneking.co.uk **web:** www.oldenglish.co.uk
dir: *A27 Lewes towards Rottingdean on B1223*

The White Horse is conveniently located just a couple of miles from Brighton, and is right on the seafront enjoying uninterrupted sea views. Bedrooms are comfortable with modern fixtures and fittings, and there is free WiFi throughout. Dinner is served daily and a cooked or continental breakfast can be enjoyed in the restaurant. There is plenty of outside seating available.

Rooms 19 en suite (2 fmly) S £25-£85; D £45-£120* **Facilities** FTV tea/coffee Dinner available Direct Dial WiFi **Conf** Max 120 Thtr 100 Class 80 Board 40 **Parking** 40 **Notes** LB

Find out more about the AA Friendliest B&B of the Year on page 17

RYE
Map 7 TQ92

See also Hastings & St Leonards

Premier Collection

Jeake's House
★★★★★ 🛏 GUEST ACCOMMODATION

tel: 01797 222828 **Mermaid St TN31 7ET**
email: stay@jeakeshouse.com **web:** www.jeakeshouse.com
dir: *Approach from High St or The Strand*

Previously a 16th-century wool store and then a 19th-century Baptist school, this delightful house stands on a cobbled street in one of the most beautiful parts of this small, bustling town. The individually decorated bedrooms combine elegance and comfort with modern facilities. Breakfast is served at separate tables in the galleried dining room, and there is an oak-beamed lounge as well as a stylish, book-lined bar complete with old pews.

Rooms 11 rms (10 en suite) (1 pri facs) (2 fmly) S £75-£100; D £90-£140*
Facilities FTV iPod docking station Lounge tea/coffee Licensed WiFi 🛎
Parking 20 **Notes** LB No Children 5yrs

See advert on opposite page

Premier Collection

Manor Farm Oast
★★★★★ 🛏 BED AND BREAKFAST

tel: 01424 813787 & 07866 818952   **fax:** 01424 813787 **Windmill Ln TN36 4WL**
email: manor.farm.oast@lineone.net **web:** www.manorfarmoast.co.uk
dir: *4m SW of Rye. A259 W past Icklesham church, left at x-rds into Windmill Ln, after sharp left bend, left (follow sign) into farmland*

Manor Farm Oast is a charming 19th-century, environmentally-friendly oast house peacefully located amid orchards in open countryside. Spacious bedrooms are individually styled and include numerous thoughtful extras including free WiFi. A choice of lounges is available, one heated by a roaring log fire during the winter.

Rooms 3 rms (2 en suite) (1 pri facs) (1 fmly) S £90-£105; D £105* **Facilities** FTV Lounge tea/coffee Licensed WiFi 🛎 **Extras** Speciality toiletries, fruit, chocolates **Conf** Max 20 Thtr 20 Board 12 **Parking** 8 **Notes** LB ⊗ No Children 11yrs Closed 31 Dec

Premier Collection

White Vine House
★★★★★ 🍴 RESTAURANT WITH ROOMS

tel: 01797 224748 **24 High St TN31 7JF**
email: info@whitevinehouse.co.uk **web:** www.whitevinehouse.co.uk
dir: *In town centre*

Situated in the heart of the ancient Cinque Port town of Rye, this property's origins go back to the 13th century. The cellar is the oldest part, but the current building dates from 1560 and boasts an impressive Georgian frontage. The original timber framework is visible in many areas and certainly adds to the house's sense of history. The bedrooms have period furniture along with luxury bath or shower rooms; one bedroom has an antique four-poster.

Rooms 7 en suite (1 fmly) **Facilities** tea/coffee Dinner available WiFi **Conf** Max 30 Thtr 30 Class 30 Board 30 **Notes** ⊗ No coaches Civ Wed 30

Premier Collection

Willow Tree House

★★★★★ GUEST ACCOMMODATION

tel: 01797 227820 & 07715 991325 **Winchelsea Rd TN31 7EL**
email: info@willow-tree-house.com **web:** www.willow-tree-house.com
dir: On A259, 500mtrs from town centre

Willow Tree House is an early 17th-century farmhouse which has been sympathetically refurbished to retain many of its charming original features. There are six individually furnished bedrooms, all appointed to a high standard - four doubles, one four-poster bedroom and a king size/twin; each has an en suite shower room. There is also ample free parking in the secure on-site car park. Willow Tree House is only ten minutes' walk away from Rye town centre with its antique shops restaurants, pubs, and cobbled streets.

Rooms 6 en suite (2 fmly) S £85–£100; D £90–£130* **Facilities** FTV iPod docking station Lounge tea/coffee Licensed WiFi ⅃ 18 **Extras** Speciality toiletries **Parking** 6 **Notes** LB ⊗ No Children 11yrs

Strand House

★★★★ 🛏 🍴 GUEST ACCOMMODATION

tel: 01797 226276 **fax:** 01797 224806 **Tanyards Ln, Winchelsea TN36 4JT**
email: info@thestrandhouse.co.uk **web:** www.thestrandhouse.co.uk
dir: M20 junct 10, A2070 to Lydd. A259 through Rye to Winchelsea, house in 2m

This charming 15th-century house is just a few miles from Rye. Traditional character is maintained in comfortably appointed rooms and the public areas, while the annexe rooms offer a more contemporary style. Local produce is a feature of the home-cooked evening meals and breakfasts.

Rooms 10 rms (9 en suite) (1 pri facs) 3 annexe en suite (4 fmly) (3 GF) S £55–£125; D £70–£180* **Facilities** FTV DVD iPod docking station Lounge tea/coffee Dinner available Licensed WiFi 🔒 **Extras** Mini-fridge in annexe rooms **Parking** 15 **Notes** LB No Children 5yrs RS wknds (high season) 2 night bookings only Civ Wed 30

See advert on page 350

The Kings Head Inn

★★★★ 🍴 INN

tel: 01797 225962 & 07762 404958 **Rye Hill TN31 7HN**
email: info@kingsheadrye.co.uk **web:** www.kingsheadrye.co.uk

This recently refurbished inn is located just a couple of miles from the centre of Rye. Bedrooms are stylish and contemporary in style and very comfortable and are split between the main pub and converted annexe rooms with private parking. The pub and restaurant is an ideal place to relax and enjoy a traditional pub lunch or dinner. Breakfast is served in this area daily.

Rooms 5 en suite 4 annexe en suite (3 fmly) (4 GF) S £75–£140; D £85–£140 **Facilities** FTV tea/coffee Dinner available WiFi **Parking** 40 **Notes** No coaches

RYE *continued*

Little Saltcote

★★★★ GUEST ACCOMMODATION

tel: 01797 223210 & 07940 742646 **fax:** 01797 224474 **22 Military Rd TN31 7NY**
email: info@littlesaltcote.co.uk **web:** www.littlesaltcote.co.uk
dir: *0.5m N of town centre. Exit A268 into Military Rd signed Appledore, house 300yds on left*

This delightful family-run establishment stands in quiet surroundings within walking distance of Rye town centre. The bright and airy en suite bedrooms are equipped with modern facilities including WiFi, and guests can enjoy afternoon tea in the garden conservatory. A hearty breakfast is served at individual tables in the dining room.

Rooms 4 en suite (2 fmly) (1 GF) S £40-£75; D £70-£85 **Facilities** FTV DVD tea/coffee WiFi 🔒 **Parking** 5 **Notes** LB Closed 25-26 Dec

The Windmill Guest House

★★★★ GUEST ACCOMMODATION

tel: 01797 224027 **Ferry Rd TN31 7DW**
email: info@ryewindmill.co.uk **web:** www.ryewindmill.co.uk

This white smock windmill has been a Rye landmark since 1820 and was more recently a bakery. Bedrooms located in the purpose-built extension have good beds and en suite facilities and are generously proportioned. Breakfast, taken in the old granary, is a freshly-cooked affair using well-sourced local ingredients including butchers' sausages and some good fruit juices.

Rooms 10 en suite (4 GF) **Facilities** FTV Lounge TVL tea/coffee Licensed WiFi 🔒 **Extras** Mineral water - complimentary **Conf** Max 30 Thtr 25 Class 30 Board 12 **Parking** 12 **Notes** No Children 12yrs Closed 24-26 Dec

Cliff Farm (TQ933237)

★★★ FARMHOUSE

tel: 01797 280331 **fax:** 01797 280331 **Military Rd, Iden Lock TN31 7QD**
email: info@cliff-farm.com **web:** www.cliff-farm.com
dir: *2m along Military Rd to Appledore, turn left at hanging milk churn*

Beautiful views and wonderful hospitality are what you'll find at this farmhouse, situated in a peaceful rural location just a short drive from Rye and Hastings. Bedrooms are pleasantly decorated and comfortably furnished. Breakfast is served at individual tables in the dining room, and there is also a cosy sitting room with a wood-burning stove and TV.

Rooms 3 rms (1 en suite) (2 pri facs) (1 fmly) S fr £40; D £60-£70* **Facilities** TVL tea/coffee WiFi **Parking** 6 **Notes** LB Closed Nov-Feb 🌐 6 acres small holding

Tower House

★★★ BED AND BREAKFAST

tel: 01797 226865 & 07940 817438 **fax:** 01797 226865 **Hilders Cliff TN31 7LD**
web: www.towerhouse-rye.co.uk
dir: *Follow one-way system, signs to town centre. Through medieval archway, 30mtrs on right*

This expansive Georgian property is conveniently located in the heart of historic Rye. Benefiting from off-road parking, the house is set back off the road within its own well-tended and gated gardens. Bedrooms are traditionally decorated, and there is a TV lounge, as well as a spacious dining room where guests can enjoy a cooked or continental breakfast.

Rooms 3 rms (2 en suite) (1 pri facs) (1 GF) S £60-£65; D £85-£95* **Facilities** TVL tea/coffee Licensed 🔒 **Parking** 3 **Notes** ⊗ No Children 12yrs Closed Dec-Wed before Etr 🌐

ST LEONARDS

See Hastings & St Leonards

SEAFORD
Map 6 TV49

Ab Fab Rooms

★★★★ 🛏 BED AND BREAKFAST

tel: 01323 895001 & 07713 197915 fax: 0705 360 3204 **11 Station Rd, Bishopstone BN25 2RB**
email: stay@abfabrooms.co.uk web: www.abfabrooms.co.uk

Just a short walk from Bishopstone station and sandy beaches, this is a perfect base for visiting local sights and attractions. Contemporary-styled bedrooms offer superior comfort and amenities. Breakfast, served in the garden conservatory, includes home-made jams and local Sussex produce.

Rooms 3 en suite S £55-£65; D £70-£80* **Facilities** STV DVD iPod docking station tea/coffee WiFi **Parking** 2 **Notes** ⊗ ⊗

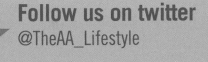

Follow us on twitter
@TheAA_Lifestyle

The Avondale

★★★ GUEST ACCOMMODATION

tel: 01323 890008 **fax:** 01323 490598 **Avondale Rd BN25 1RJ**
email: info@theavondale.co.uk **web:** www.theavondale.co.uk
dir: *In town centre, off A259 behind war memorial*

A warm welcome is offered by the caring owners at this friendly, family-run guest accommodation which is ideally placed for the Newhaven to Dieppe ferry service. The bedrooms are pleasantly furnished and thoughtfully equipped. Breakfast is served in the attractive dining room and guests also have the use of a cosy lounge.

Rooms 14 rms (8 en suite) (4 fmly) S £35-£50; D £40-£90 **Facilities** FTV DVD TVL tea/coffee Lift Licensed WiFi **Conf** Max 15 Class 15 Board 15 **Notes** LB ⊗

SEDLESCOMBE
Map 7 TQ71

Kester House B&B

★★★★ 🛏 BED AND BREAKFAST

tel: 01424 870035 & 07875 996107 **The Street TN33 0QB**
email: derek@kesterhouse.co.uk **web:** www.kesterhouse.co.uk
dir: *A21 onto B2244 signed Sedlescombe, after 0.75m enter village, Kester House on right opposite Bridge Antiques*

This 16th-century, Grade II listed house is located in the tranquil village of Sedlescombe, close to Hastings, Battle and Rye. The bedrooms have been tastefully appointed to offer stylish, comfortable accommodation while still retaining many of the building's original features. There is a guest lounge next to the dining room area where guests can enjoy home-made refreshments on arrival, and a hearty cooked or continental breakfast which features top quality, locally sourced produce. AA Friendliest B&B of the Year Finalist 2014-2015.

Rooms 3 rms (1 en suite) (2 pri facs) (1 fmly) S £50-£75; D £75-£105 **Facilities** FTV DVD iPod docking station Lounge tea/coffee WiFi 🚲 Arrangement with local riding stables **Extras** Robes **Notes** ⊗ No Children 7yrs Closed 20 Dec-5 Jan

UCKFIELD
Map 6 TQ42

Old Copwood B&B

[U]

tel: 07889 272560 **Rocks Rd TN22 3PT**
email: dialproperties@yahoo.co.uk

Currently the rating for this establishment is not confirmed. This may be due to a change of ownership or because it has only recently joined the AA rating scheme.

Rooms 3 rms (1 en suite) (2 pri facs) S £50; D £80* **Notes** ☺

WADHURST
Map 6 TQ63

Little Tidebrook Farm (TQ621304)

★★★★ FARMHOUSE

tel: 01892 782688 & 07970 159988 **Riseden TN5 6NY**
email: info@littletidebrook.co.uk **web:** www.littletidebrook.co.uk
dir: A267 from Tunbridge Wells to Mark Cross, left onto B2100, 2m, right at Best Beech Inn, left after 1m into Riseden Rd, farm on left

This traditional farmhouse has cosy log fires in winter and wonderful garden dining in warm months. The imaginative decor sits well with modern amenities, such as WiFi, to provide both leisure and business guests with excellent accommodation. It is close to Bewl Water and Royal Tunbridge Wells.

Rooms 3 rms (2 en suite) (1 pri facs) D £50-£90* **Facilities** FTV TVL tea/coffee WiFi ⚓ **Parking** 8 **Notes** No Children 12yrs ☺ 50 acres horses

The Greyhound Inn

★★★ INN

tel: 01892 783224 **High St TN5 6AP**
email: info@thegreyhoundwadhurst.co.uk **web:** www.thegreyhoundwadhurst.co.uk
dir: In village centre

This 16th-century inn is located in the centre of Wadhurst. The pub and restaurant area are traditional in style and feature a large open fireplace. Breakfast, lunch and dinner are served daily. Bedrooms are all annexed and have been converted from the original stable blocks. They are spacious and comfortable and combine traditional features such as exposed oak beams with modern decor and furnishings.

Rooms 5 en suite (1 fmly) (3 GF) S £65; D £79* **Facilities** FTV DVD tea/coffee Dinner available WiFi **Parking** 5 **Notes** RS Sun-Mon Restaurant closed☺

WILMINGTON
Map 6 TQ50

Crossways

★★★★ ◉◉ RESTAURANT WITH ROOMS

tel: 01323 482455 **fax:** 01323 487811 **Lewes Rd BN26 5SG**
email: stay@crosswayshotel.co.uk **web:** www.crosswayshotel.co.uk
dir: On A27 between Lewes & Polegate, 2m E of Alfriston rdbt

Proprietors Davis Stott and Clive James have been welcoming guests to this elegant restaurant with rooms for over 25 years. Crossways sits amid stunning gardens and attractively tended grounds. The well-presented bedrooms are tastefully decorated and provide an abundance of thoughtful amenities including free WiFi. Guest comfort is paramount and the naturally warm hospitality ensures guests often return.

Rooms 7 en suite S £85-£90; D £145-£180 **Facilities** FTV tea/coffee Dinner available Direct Dial WiFi ⚓ **Extras** Speciality toiletries, mini-bar, fresh milk **Parking** 30 **Notes** LB ⊗ No Children 12yrs Closed 24 Dec-23 Jan No coaches

WEST SUSSEX

AMBERLEY
Map 6 TQ01

Woody Banks Cottage

★★★★ BED AND BREAKFAST

tel: 01798 831295 & 07719 916703 **Crossgates BN18 9NR**
email: enquiries@woodybanks.co.uk **web:** www.woodybanks.co.uk
dir: Off B2139 into village, right at Black Horse pub, Woody Banks 0.5m on left past Sportsman pub

Located close to Arundel on an elevated position with stunning views over the Wildbrooks, this immaculately maintained house and gardens is very popular with walkers. It provides two comfortable, homely bedrooms filled with thoughtful extras. Imaginative breakfasts are served in the spacious lounge-dining room.

Rooms 2 rms (1 pri facs) (1 fmly) S £40-£50; D £70-£80* **Facilities** FTV DVD TVL tea/coffee ⚓ **Parking** 2 **Notes** LB ⊗ No Children 6yrs Closed 24-27 Dec ☺

ANGMERING
Map 6 TQ00

Angmering Manor

★★★★ ⌂ GUEST ACCOMMODATION

tel: 01903 859849 **fax:** 01903 783268 **High St BN16 4AG**
email: angmeringmanor@thechapmansgroup.co.uk **web:** www.relaxinnz.co.uk
dir: Follow A27 towards Portsmouth, exit A280, follow signs for Angmering

This former manor house in the heart of the village has been stylishly appointed. It offers good food, a bar, an indoor pool, and good parking. Staff are friendly and helpful and rooms are very comfortable.

Rooms 17 en suite (3 fmly) (4 GF) **Facilities** FTV TVL tea/coffee Dinner available Direct Dial Licensed WiFi ☖ Sauna Gym Beauty salon **Parking** 25 **Notes** ⊗ Civ Wed 50

ARUNDEL
Map 6 TQ00

See also Amberley

Hanger Down House B&B

☆☆☆☆☆ BED AND BREAKFAST

tel: 01903 882904 & 07753 595191 **Priory Ln, Tortington BN18 0BG**
email: aayling@btinternet.com **web:** www.hangerdownhouse.co.uk
dir: *A27 to Arundel, take road signed Ford/Climping at Arundel rdbt. Priory Ln 0.5m on right*

Set in picturesque Sussex countryside, Hanger Down House is conveniently and quietly located one mile from the historic town of Arundel. All three bedrooms are stylishly decorated and provide comfortable accommodation for guests. Bedrooms include king-size beds, a leather sofa, fridge, digital LCD TVs and free WiFi. There are great views of the local countryside and a walled garden which guests are free to use. A cooked or continental breakfast can be enjoyed in the dining room.

Rooms 3 en suite (2 fmly) (1 GF) S £60-£90; D £90-£120* **Facilities** FTV Lounge tea/coffee WiFi ⛄ Pool table 🛁 Trampoline Football pitch Outdoor table tennis **Extras** Speciality toiletries - complimentary; fridges **Parking** 5 **Notes** LB ⊗ ⊜

The Town House

☆☆☆☆☆ ⊛⊛ RESTAURANT WITH ROOMS

tel: 01903 883847 **65 High St BN18 9AJ**
email: enquiries@thetownhouse.co.uk **web:** www.thetownhouse.co.uk
dir: *A27 to Arundel, into High Street, establishment on left at top of hill*

This is an elegant, Grade II listed Regency building overlooking Arundel Castle, just a short walk from the shops and centre of the town. Bedrooms and public areas retain the building's unspoilt character. The ceiling in the dining room is particularly spectacular and originated in Florence in the 16th century.

Rooms 4 en suite S £75-£95; D £95-£130* **Facilities** FTV iPod docking station tea/coffee Dinner available WiFi 🛁 **Extras** Speciality toiletries **Notes** ⊗ Closed 2wks Etr & 2wks Oct RS Sun-Mon Restaurant closed No coaches

White Swan

★★★★ INN

tel: 01903 882677 **fax:** 01903 684154 **16 Chichester Rd BN18 0AD**
email: thewhiteswan.arundel@pebblehotels.com **web:** www.pebblehotels.com

The White Swan offers very comfortable and stylish accommodation. There is a character bar, a lounge and a restaurant, and an informal service is provided by the friendly team. Substantial snacks and meals can be ordered throughout the day and evening. Complimentary WiFi is available in the public areas.

Rooms 20 en suite (6 GF) **Facilities** FTV TVL tea/coffee Dinner available Direct Dial WiFi **Conf** Max 100 Thtr 100 **Parking** 100 **Notes** Civ Wed 70

April Cottage B&B

★★★★ 🄰 BED AND BREAKFAST

tel: 01903 885401 & 07885 488213 **Crossbush Ln BN18 9PQ**
email: april.cott@btinternet.com **web:** www.april-cottage.co.uk
dir: *E from Arundel station on A27, at top of hill turn left into Crossbush Ln. 500mtrs on right*

April Cottage is based around three cottages, thought to be from the 17th century, and is run by a family team headed by Richard and Tanya. Set in the South Downs National Park, there are plenty of opportunities for cycling and walking, as well as visits to nearby attractions like Bognor Regis, Goodwood, Chichester and Worthing. Guests have their own private entrance, super king-size beds, plenty of off-road parking, a cycle storage area, a patio garden, cooler fridges and the use of a safe.

Rooms 2 en suite S £50-£90; D £70-£120* **Facilities** FTV Lounge tea/coffee WiFi 🛁 **Extras** Fridge with fresh milk, safe **Parking** 3 **Notes** ⊗ ⊜

BOGNOR REGIS
Map 6 SZ99

Hayleys Corner

★★★★ GUEST ACCOMMODATION

tel: 01243 826139 **14 Limmer Ln, Felpham PO22 7EJ**
email: hayleyscornerbandb@yahoo.co.uk **web:** www.hayleyscorner.co.uk
dir: *Off A259 into Felpham village. Left into Limmer Ln, opposite St Mary's Church*

Hayleys Corner is located in a quiet and tranquil area of Felpham, close to Bognor Regis, Portsmouth and Chichester. Bedrooms are modern in style yet retain some traditional features. All offer digital TV and free WiFi. Guests can enjoy a cooked or continental breakfast in the dining room and for dinner there are several pubs, restaurants and cafés within a short walking distance.

Rooms 5 rms (3 en suite) (2 pri facs) S £45-£60; D £80-£120* **Facilities** FTV Lounge tea/coffee WiFi 🛁 **Parking** 3 **Notes** LB ⊗

Find out more about the AA's guest accommodation rating scheme on page 8

BOGNOR REGIS *continued*

The Old Priory

★★★★ GUEST HOUSE

tel: 01243 863580 **fax:** 01243 826597 **80 North Bersted St PO22 9AQ**
email: old.priory@btinternet.com **web:** www.old-priory.com
dir: *1.6m NW of Bognor. Off A259 (Chichester road) to North Bersted. Old Priory sign on left*

Located in the mainly residential area of North Bersted, this 400-year-old property retains many original features. Bedrooms, which are all individual in style, are homely and one has a four-poster waterbed and a double air bath. There is an outdoor pool and attractive grounds, perfect for the summer.

Rooms 3 rms (2 en suite) (1 pri facs) 3 annexe en suite (3 GF) S £50; D £80-£110* **Facilities** STV tea/coffee WiFi ⚡ 🔒 Hot tub **Parking** 6

Jubilee Guest House

★★★ GUEST ACCOMMODATION

tel: 01243 863016 **5 Gloucester Rd PO21 1NU**
email: info@jubileeguesthouse.com
dir: *A259 to seafront, house opposite Day Entrance to Butlins*

This property is conveniently located opposite Butlins and close to the seafront and town centre. Comfortably appointed bedrooms come well equipped with free WiFi, flat-screen digital TVs and heating/cooling systems. A cooked breakfast can be enjoyed in the attractive dining room.

Rooms 6 rms (2 en suite) (4 pri facs) (3 fmly) S £25-£55; D £50-£80* **Facilities** FTV tea/coffee WiFi **Parking** 4 **Notes** LB ⊗

BOLNEY
Map 6 TQ22

8 Bells Bed & Breakfast

★★★★ ➡ INN

tel: 01444 881396 **The Long House, The Street RH17 5QP**
email: stay@8bellsbandb.com web: www.8bellsbandb.com
dir: *A23/A272 junct. Village situated between Ansty & Cowfold on A272*

This Tudor property is situated in a peaceful village and close to both Heathfield and Crawley. Many original features, including exposed beams, remain, along with high-quality, modern and comfortable accommodation. Guests check in at the pub located directly opposite and it is here that breakfast, lunch and dinner can be enjoyed.

Rooms 3 en suite (1 fmly) (1 GF) **Facilities** FTV DVD Lounge tea/coffee Dinner available WiFi Pool table **Extras** Bottled water - complimentary **Parking** 15 **Notes** LB ⊗

BOSHAM
Map 5 SU80

White Barn Guest House

★★★★ ➡ BED AND BREAKFAST

tel: 01243 573113 **fax:** 01243 573113 **Crede Ln PO18 8NX**
email: chrissie@whitebarn.biz web: www.whitebarn.biz
dir: *A259 Bosham rdbt, turn S signed Bosham Quay, 0.5m to T-junct, left signed White Barn, 0.25m turn left signed White Barn, 50yds turn right*

This delightful, single-storey property is close to Bosham Harbour, Goodwood Race Circuit, Chichester and Portsmouth, and has cosy bedrooms with colour co-ordinated soft furnishings and many thoughtful extras. The open-plan dining room overlooks an attractive garden, where breakfast is served if the weather permits.

Rooms 2 en suite 1 annexe en suite (3 GF) **Facilities** FTV DVD tea/coffee WiFi **Parking** 3 **Notes** LB ⊗ No Children 12yrs Closed Xmas & New Year

CHARLTON
Map 6 SU81

The Fox Goes Free

★★★★ INN

tel: 01243 811461 **fax:** 01243 811946 **PO18 0HU**
email: enquiries@thefoxgoesfree.com web: www.thefoxgoesfree.com
dir: *In village centre*

This former hunting lodge has retained much original character and is located in lovely countryside at the foot of the South Downs National Park. The bedrooms are well appointed and the pub boasts low ceilings, brick floors and three inglenook fireplaces. The inn serves its own ale and has an inviting, daily-changing menu. During the summer months, guests can take advantage of the rear garden.

Rooms 5 en suite (2 GF) S £65-£175; D £90-£175* **Facilities** FTV tea/coffee Dinner available WiFi ✆ **Parking** 50

CHICHESTER
Map 5 SU80

See also Bosham & West Marden

Premier Collection

Rooks Hill

★★★★★ ➡ BED AND BREAKFAST

tel: 01243 528400 **Lavant Rd, Lavant PO18 0BQ**
email: enquiries@rookshill.co.uk web: www.rookshill.co.uk

Rooks Hill is in a convenient and picturesque location near Goodwood and the city of Chichester. The warm and friendly proprietors create a wonderful home-from-home atmosphere. Rooms have power showers and additional thoughtful extras. A delicious breakfast, served in the stylish dining room or on the patio overlooking the pretty gardens in warmer weather provides a substantial start to the day.

Rooms 3 en suite (1 GF) **Facilities** FTV Lounge tea/coffee WiFi ✆ 19 **Extras** Speciality toiletries **Parking** 6 **Notes** ⊗ No Children 12yrs

CHICHESTER *continued*

The Royal Oak Inn

★★★★★ ⚜ ≜ INN

tel: 01243 527434 **Pook Ln, East Lavant PO18 0AX**
email: info@royaloakeastlavant.co.uk **web:** www.royaloakeastlavant.co.uk
dir: *2m N of Chichester. Exit A286 to East Lavant centre*

Located close to the Goodwood estate and Rolls Royce HQ this delightful inn is full of character with beamed ceilings, timber floors and open fires in the public areas. Bedrooms are finished to a very high standard with comfortable beds and state-of-the-art electronic equipment. AA Rosette award-winning meals are served in the popular restaurant.

Rooms 3 en suite 5 annexe en suite (1 fmly) (2 GF) S £90-£145; D £125-£220*
Facilities FTV DVD iPod docking station tea/coffee Dinner available Direct Dial WiFi ⅃ 27 Riding **Extras** Speciality toiletries, chocolate, fresh milk - free of charge **Parking** 25 **Notes** ⊗ No coaches

Old Chapel Forge

★★★★ ≜ BED AND BREAKFAST

tel: 01243 264380 **Lower Bognor Rd, Lagness PO20 1LR**
email: info@oldchapelforge.co.uk **web:** www.oldchapelforge.co.uk
dir: *4m SE of Chichester. Exit A27 (Chichester bypass) at Bognor rdbt signed Pagham & Runcton, onto B2166 (Pagham Rd & Lower Bognor Rd). Old Chapel Forge on right*

Great local produce features in the hearty breakfasts at this comfortable, eco-friendly property, an idyllic 17th-century house and chapel set in mature gardens with panoramic views of the South Downs. Old Chapel Forge is a short drive from Chichester, Goodwood, Pagham Harbour Nature Reserve and the beach. Bedrooms, including suites in the chapel, are luxurious, and all have internet access.

Rooms 3 annexe en suite (1 fmly) (3 GF) S £45-£112.50; D £65-£125* **Facilities** FTV DVD tea/coffee Dinner available WiFi ⅃ 18 **Parking** 6 **Notes** LB

Richmond House Boutique B&B

★★★★ ≜ BED AND BREAKFAST

tel: 01243 771464 & 07909 971736 **230 Oving Rd PO19 7EJ**
email: richmondhousechichester@hotmail.co.uk
web: www.richmondhousechichester.co.uk
dir: *From A27 bypass enter Chichester from lights E of city on Oving Rd. 1m on left*

Richmond House is conveniently located within a short walking distance of the town centre. Bedrooms and bathrooms are stylishly decorated and offer guests high quality comfort. All bedrooms come equipped with digital TVs, free WiFi and beverage making facilities. An extensive cooked or continental breakfast can be enjoyed in the private dining area.

Rooms 3 en suite S £85-£165; D £95-£170* **Facilities** FTV iPod docking station tea/coffee WiFi ⚓ **Extras** Speciality toiletries, home-made snacks - free **Parking** 1 **Notes** LB ⊗

The Bulls Head

★★★★ INN

tel: 01243 839895 **99 Fishbourne Road West PO19 3JP**
email: enquiries@bullsheadfishbourne.net **web:** www.bullsheadfishbourne.net
dir: *A27 onto A259, 0.5m on left*

Located in Fishbourne, yet just a short drive from the centre of Chichester, and within easy access of Portsmouth, The Bulls Head offers comfortably appointed bedrooms in a former coach house. The bedrooms are light and airy with modern decor and furnishings. The pub is traditional in style and offers a wide selection of home-cooked pub classics as well as a good range of cask ales. Breakfast is served in the restaurant daily.

Rooms 4 annexe en suite (1 fmly) (4 GF) **Facilities** FTV DVD tea/coffee Dinner available WiFi 🔒 **Parking** 35

See advert below

82 Fishbourne

★★★★ 🏠 BED AND BREAKFAST

tel: 07854 051013 **82 Fishbourne Road West PO19 3JL**
email: nik@nikwestacott.plus.com **web:** www.82fishbourne.co.uk
dir: *A27 at Chichester rdbt, towards Fishbourne & Bosham on A259. 0.5m on right diagonally opposite Woolpack pub*

Warm and friendly hospitality abounds at 82 Fishbourne, which is just a short drive from historic Chichester. Accommodation is spacious and well equipped. Breakfast provides a substantial start to the day and includes delicious fresh eggs from the free-range hens that live in the back garden. Scheduled activities include 'mushroom hunts', and wine tastings are held throughout the year.

Rooms 3 en suite (1 fmly) (1 GF) D £77–£170* **Facilities** FTV tea/coffee Dinner available Licensed WiFi 🔒 Cookery lessons, fly fishing trips **Parking** 3 **Notes** LB

CHICHESTER *continued*

Horse and Groom
★★★★ INN

tel: 01243 575339 **East Ashling PO18 9AX**
email: info@thehorseandgroomchichester.co.uk
web: www.thehorseandgroomchichester.co.uk
dir: *3m N of Chichester, on B2178 towards Rowland's Castle*

The Horse and Groom is a 17th-century country pub and restaurant offering spacious and comfortable accommodation and warm, friendly hospitality. The substantial, freshly prepared breakfasts, lunches and dinners make good use of fresh fish and locally sourced ingredients.

Rooms 11 en suite (11 GF) S £50-£60; D £80-£90* **Facilities** FTV tea/coffee Dinner available WiFi 🔒 **Parking** 40 **Notes** RS Sun eve Bar & Restaurant close 6pm

Musgrove House
★★★★ 🏠 BED AND BREAKFAST

tel: 01243 790179 & 07885 586344 **63 Oving Rd PO19 7EN**
email: enquiries@musgrovehouse.co.uk **web:** www.musgrovehouse.co.uk
dir: *From A27 onto B2144 towards city centre, at corner of Oving Rd & St James Rd*

Located just outside Chichester city centre, this establishment offers three stylish bedrooms with light, airy decor and modern fixtures and fittings, including free WiFi and digital TVs. Expect a friendly welcome on arrival and a choice of both cooked and continental dishes at breakfast, which makes good use of high-quality and locally sourced produce.

Rooms 3 en suite S £65-£90; D £70-£100* **Facilities** FTV DVD iPod docking station tea/coffee WiFi 🔒 **Extras** Speciality toiletries **Parking** 3 **Notes** ⊗ No Children 12yrs

The George & Dragon
★★★ INN

tel: 01243 785660 **51 North St PO19 1NQ**
email: info@georgeanddragoninn.co.uk **web:** www.georgeanddragoninn.co.uk
dir: *On North St, off A286, near Chichester Festival Theatre*

This recently refurbished inn, located at one end of Chichester's high street boasts attractively styled rooms and a friendly atmosphere. Rooms are comfortable with all the amenities needed for a pleasant night's stay. There is a light and airy dining room set apart from the popular central bar area where dinner and breakfast is served. Regional ales are available.

Rooms 10 annexe en suite (5 GF) **Facilities** FTV tea/coffee Dinner available WiFi **Notes** No coaches

The Vestry
★★★ INN

tel: 01243 773358 **fax:** 08720 220801 **23 Southgate PO19 1ES**
email: info@the-vestry.com **web:** www.the-vestry.co.uk

The Vestry is conveniently located in the town centre. Bedrooms are spacious and well equipped including beverage making facilities and WiFi. The bar and restaurant are spacious with comfortable seating areas; during the winter months guests can keep cosy in front of the log fires. Lunch and dinner are served daily; both continental and a range of wholesome cooked breakfasts are available.

Rooms 11 en suite (2 fmly) **Facilities** FTV tea/coffee Dinner available WiFi **Notes** Closed 24-26 Dec & 31 Dec-1 Jan

CRAWLEY

For accommodation details see Gatwick Airport (London)

GATWICK AIRPORT (LONDON)   Map 6 TQ24

Acorn Lodge Gatwick
★★★★ GUEST ACCOMMODATION

tel: 01293 774550 **fax:** 01293 782865 **79 Massetts Rd RH6 7EB**
email: info@acornlodgegatwick.co.uk **web:** www.acornlodgegatwick.co.uk
dir: *M23 junct 9, A23 into Horley, off A23 Brighton Rd*

This property provides a 24-hour transfer service to the airport and has on-site parking. Bedrooms are comfortably furnished, come with a practical desk area and useful touches. The breakfasts served in the comfortable dining room make a good start to the day; dinner is also available.

Rooms 15 en suite (4 fmly) (7 GF) **Facilities** FTV TVL tea/coffee Dinner available Licensed WiFi **Parking** 20 **Notes** ⊗

The Lawn Guest House
★★★★ GUEST HOUSE

tel: 01293 775751 **fax:** 01293 821803 **30 Massetts Rd RH6 7DF**
email: info@lawnguesthouse.co.uk **web:** www.lawnguesthouse.com
dir: *M25 junct 7, M23 S towards Brighton/Gatwick Airport. Exit at junct 9. At either South or North Terminal rdbts take A23 towards Redhill. At 3rd rdbt (Esso garage on left) take 3rd exit. (Texaco garage on right). In 200yds right at lights into Massetts Rd. Guest house 400yds on left*

Once a Victorian school, this friendly guest house is well-positioned on a quiet leafy street close to Gatwick. Bedrooms are spacious with thoughtful amenities such as free WiFi, and fans for use in warm weather. Airport parking is available.

Rooms 12 en suite (4 fmly) S £40-£55; D £49-£69 **Facilities** STV tea/coffee Direct Dial WiFi 🔒 **Parking** 4

Vulcan Lodge Guest House

★★★★ BED AND BREAKFAST

tel: 01293 771522 & 07980 576012   **fax:** 01737 720153 **27 Massetts Rd RH6 7DQ**
email: reservations@vulcan-lodge.com **web:** www.vulcan-lodge.com
dir: M23 junct 9, A23 into Horley, off A23 Brighton Rd

A particularly warm and friendly welcome is offered by the hosts of Vulcan Lodge,
a charming period house, which sits back from the main road and is convenient for
Gatwick Airport. Bedrooms are well equipped and feature many thoughtful extras.
A choice of breakfast is offered, including vegetarian, and is served in a delightful
dining room.

Rooms 4 rms (3 en suite) (1 pri facs) (1 fmly) S £47-£54; D £64-£68* **Facilities** FTV
TVL tea/coffee WiFi **Parking** 13 **Notes** Closed 23-27 Dec & 31 Dec-2 Jan

Gainsborough Lodge

★★★ GUEST ACCOMMODATION

tel: 01293 783982 **fax:** 01293 785365 **39 Massetts Rd RH6 7DT**
email: enquiries@gainsborough-lodge.co.uk **web:** www.gainsborough-lodge.co.uk
dir: 2m NE of airport off A23 Brighton Rd

Close to Gatwick, this fine Edwardian house offers a courtesy service to and from
the airport. The bright bedrooms are comfortably appointed, and a varied breakfast,
including a vegetarian option is served in the cheerful conservatory-dining room.
There is also an attractive lounge.

Rooms 15 rms (14 en suite) (1 pri facs) 7 annexe en suite (5 fmly) (12 GF)
Facilities FTV TVL tea/coffee WiFi **Parking** 20 **Notes** ⊗

Linchens Bed & Breakfast London Gatwick

★★★ BED AND BREAKFAST

tel: 01342 713085 & 07749 821057   **Herons Close RH10 3HF**
email: aas.linchens@btinternet.com **web:** www.linchens.co.uk

This family run B&B is located in a quiet residential area yet just a 10-minute drive
from Gatwick Airport. Bedrooms are traditional in style and comfortably appointed;
all rooms have digital TV and free WiFi. A cooked and continental breakfast is
served daily in the dining room. Plenty of secure parking is available.

Rooms 3 en suite (1 fmly) (1 GF) S £40-£50; D £65-£75 **Facilities** STV FTV DVD TVL
tea/coffee WiFi ↜ ⅃ 18 Riding ⌂ **Conf** Max 6 Board 6 **Parking** 16 **Notes** LB ⊗
Closed Xmas

Gatwick White House

★★ GUEST ACCOMMODATION

tel: 01293 402777 & 0800 612 3605   **fax:** 01293 424135 **50-52 Church Rd RH6 7EX**
email: hotel@gwhh.com **web:** www.gwhh.com
dir: In Horley centre off A23 (Brighton Rd)

Convenient for the airport and major routes, this establishment offers efficient and
functional accommodation. There is a bar and a restaurant that serves good curries
as well as traditional dishes. The house has ample parking, and a 24-hour transfer
service to Gatwick is available on request.

Rooms 27 en suite (2 fmly) (10 GF) S £39-£49; D £45-£55 **Facilities** FTV TVL tea/
coffee Dinner available Direct Dial Licensed WiFi **Parking** 30 **Notes** ⊗

HORSHAM   Map 6 TQ13

Springfields

★★★★ GUEST ACCOMMODATION

tel: 01403 246770 **Springfield Park Rd RH12 2PW**
email: enquiries@springfieldhotel.co.uk

This purpose-built guest accommodation is located in the very heart of Horsham,
bedrooms are modern in style, spacious and come well equipped with stylish
furnishings, free WiFi, digital TV and well stocked beverage trays. Breakfast is
served in the main dining room on the ground floor and ample parking is available
on site. There are a number of restaurants within walking distance including a good
selection of traditional meals at the neighbouring pub.

Rooms 11 rms

LINDFIELD   Map 6 TQ32

The Pilstyes

★★★★ BED AND BREAKFAST

tel: 01444 484101 **106-108 High St RH16 2HS**
email: carol@sussex-bedandbreakfast.co.uk **web:** www.sussex-bedandbreakfast.co.uk
dir: On High Street (B2028), S of church

The Pilstyes is a Grade II listed village house that was built around 1575. The
spacious bedrooms are beautifully furnished and provide all the comforts of home.
A healthy breakfast is served in the charming country kitchen or, on sunny days, in
the flower-filled cottage courtyard.

Rooms 2 en suite **Facilities** FTV TVL tea/coffee WiFi **Parking** 6 **Notes** ⊗
No Children 8yrs

LITTLEHAMPTON	Map 6 TQ00

Berry House

★★★★★ ⌂ GUEST ACCOMMODATION

tel: 01903 726260 & 07799 425136 **fax:** 0872 110 8713 **Berry Ln BN17 5HD**
email: info@berryhouse.biz **web:** www.berryhouse.biz

Berry House is located in the heart of Littlehampton and has spacious, modern and comfortably appointed accommodation. The house was built in 2012, so all rooms have modern facilities including complimentary WiFi and digital TV. Breakfast is served in the main dining room and there is a wide selection of both cooked and continental dishes. Secure off-road parking is provided, and there are gardens for guests to enjoy during the summer months.

Rooms 4 en suite (1 fmly) (2 GF) S £70-£135; D £80-£145* **Facilities** STV FTV tea/coffee WiFi ⌁ 18 🔒 **Extras** Bottled water - complimentary; fruit, chocolates **Parking** 7 **Notes** ⊗ No Children 16yrs

East Beach Guest House

★★★★ GUEST HOUSE

tel: 01903 714270 **fax:** 01903 714270 **71 South Ter BN17 5LQ**
email: admin@eastbeachguesthouse.co.uk **web:** www.eastbeachguesthouse.co.uk
dir: On South Terrace, opposite beach, 200mtrs from junct with Pier Rd

This guest house offers individually styled and comfortable accommodation; all rooms are equipped with a good range of amenities including flat-screen TVs and WiFi; some bedrooms have sea views. A freshly cooked breakfast, using local produce, is served in the first-floor breakfast room that overlooks the sea.

Rooms 9 en suite (2 fmly) (2 GF) S £50-£76; D £70-£102 **Facilities** FTV DVD TVL tea/coffee WiFi 🔒 **Extras** Speciality toiletries - complimentary **Notes** LB ⊗ No Children 3yrs

Leeside

★★★★ GUEST ACCOMMODATION

tel: 01903 723666 & 07791 797131 **Rope Walk BN17 5DE**
email: leeside1@tiscali.co.uk **web:** www.leesidebandb.com
dir: From A259 into Ferry Rd signed Rope Walk & West Beach. 1m, turn right into Rope Walk, Leeside on right

Leeside is a bright bungalow, close to local sailing clubs, the River Arun and the beach. Visitors will enjoy a warm welcome, and comfortable modern bedrooms have flat-screen TVs and free WiFi. The hearty breakfasts make a good start to the day.

Rooms 4 en suite (3 GF) **Facilities** FTV TVL tea/coffee WiFi 🔒 **Parking** 4 **Notes** ⊗ No Children 14yrs

Marina Gardens Bed & Breakfast

[U]

tel: 01903 730180 & 07909 513036 **2 Irvine Rd BN17 5JJ**
email: marinagardens@hotmail.co.uk **web:** www.marinagardensbandb.co.uk
dir: A284 left into Franciscan Way. 2nd exit at rdbt into Beach Rd, at next rdbt 3rd exit continue on Beach Rd. 1st right after church into Irvine Rd, last house on left

Currently the rating for this establishment is not confirmed. This may be due to a change of ownership or because it has only recently joined the AA rating scheme.

Rooms 2 en suite S £35-£55; D £65-£85* **Facilities** FTV DVD TVL tea/coffee WiFi **Parking** 2 **Notes** ⊗

LODSWORTH	Map 6 SU92

The Halfway Bridge Inn

★★★★★ ◉ ⌂ INN

tel: 01798 861281 & 07971 872655 **fax:** 01798 861576
Halfway Bridge GU28 9BP
email: enquiries@halfwaybridge.co.uk **web:** www.halfwaybridge.co.uk
dir: From Petworth on A272 towards Midhurst, 3m on right

This refurbished inn, located between Petworth and Midhurst, has attractively styled rooms in a converted barn setting; the spacious rooms, each with their own contemporary country-style decor, are spacious and have many thoughtful extras. The popular inn offers warming fires, and intimate dining areas where guests can enjoy award-winning cuisine. The central bar is popular and guest ales feature strongly. The friendly team are key to the business here, making for a memorable stay.

Rooms 7 en suite (1 fmly) (7 GF) S fr £85; D £140-£230* **Facilities** FTV DVD iPod docking station tea/coffee Dinner available WiFi **Extras** Speciality toiletries, fresh milk - complimentary **Parking** 30 **Notes** No coaches

MIDHURST	Map 6 SU82

See also Rogate

Loves Farm (SU912235)

★★★★ FARMHOUSE

tel: 01730 813212 & 07789 228400 **Easebourne St GU29 0BG**
email: lovesl@btinternet.com **web:** www.lovesfarm.com
dir: 2m NE of town centre. Exit A272 at Easebourne church into Easebourne St, follow signs for Loves Farm

This 17th-century farmhouse is set on a 300-acre farm with wonderful views of the South Downs from the windows. The comfortable rooms have their own entrance and benefit from king size beds and en suite or private facilities. This is a great location for access to Midhurst, Cowdray Park and Goodwood.

Rooms 3 rms (2 en suite) (1 pri facs) (2 fmly) (1 GF) S £55-£65; D £80-£100* **Facilities** FTV tea/coffee WiFi **Parking** 3 **Notes** ⊗ ☯ 300 acres arable/horses

PETWORTH	Map 6 SU92

Willow Barns

★★★★ BED AND BREAKFAST

tel: 01798 867493 & 07747 634011 **Graffham GU28 0NU**
email: infowillowbarns@aol.com **web:** www.willowbarns.co.uk

This bed and breakfast comprises five en suite bedrooms set in modern converted barns overlooking an RHS Silver Gilt awarded, professionally designed courtyard. This makes a fabulous choice for those walking the South Downs Way. Cyclists and horse riders are also welcomed, with stabling and turn-out facilities available by prior arrangement. Breakfasts are served around a family-style table.

Rooms 5 en suite (2 fmly) (5 GF) D £90-£120* **Facilities** FTV DVD Lounge tea/coffee Dinner available Licensed WiFi **Parking** 5 **Notes** ⊗ No Children 12yrs Closed 2wks Xmas

The Old Railway Station

★★★★ GUEST ACCOMMODATION

tel: 01798 342346 **fax:** 01798 343066 **Station Rd GU28 0JF**
email: info@old-station.co.uk **web:** www.old-station.co.uk
dir: *1.6m S of Petworth on A285*

This building, once the railway station for Petworth, retains much of its railway history and atmosphere. Guest rooms are available in both the Station House and the fully restored Edwardian Pullman railway carriages. The original ticket windows can still be seen in the reception area. Breakfast is served in the 'waiting room' which has a six-metre high vaulted ceiling; weather permitting, breakfast can be taken outside on the platform. Both WiFi and parking are available.

Rooms 2 en suite 8 annexe en suite (1 GF) S £58-£150; D £78-£230* **Facilities** FTV Lounge tea/coffee Licensed WiFi 🐾 **Extras** Speciality toiletries **Parking** 11 **Notes** LB ⊗ No Children 10yrs Closed 24-26 Dec

ROGATE	Map 5 SU82

Premier Collection

Mizzards Farm

★★★★★ BED AND BREAKFAST

tel: 01730 821656 **fax:** 01730 821655 **GU31 5HS**
email: francis@mizzards.co.uk
dir: *0.6m S from Rogate x-rds, over river & signed 300yds on right*

This charming 16th-century house stands near the River Rother in two acres of beautifully landscaped gardens that feature a lake and the proprietor's own sculptures. Guests can relax in either the conservatory or the split-level drawing room, and the airy, well-appointed bedrooms look over the grounds. There is an impressive entrance hall, and the swimming pool is available to guests in summer.

Rooms 3 en suite S £50-£60; D £85-£95* **Facilities** FTV Lounge tea/coffee WiFi ⚡ 🌿 🐾 **Parking** 12 **Notes** ⊗ No Children 9yrs Closed Xmas 🚭

RUSTINGTON	Map 6 TQ00

Kenmore Guest House

★★★★ GUEST ACCOMMODATION

tel: 01903 784634 **Claigmar Rd BN16 2NL**
email: enquiries@kenmoreguesthouse.co.uk **web:** www.kenmoreguesthouse.co.uk
dir: *A259 follow signs for Rustington, turn for Claigmar Rd by war memorial. Kenmore on right as Claigmar Rd bends*

A warm welcome is assured at this Edwardian house, located close to the sea and convenient for touring West Sussex. Spacious bedrooms, all individually decorated, are provided with many useful extras. There is a comfortable lounge in which to relax and a bright dining room where a good choice of breakfast is served.

Rooms 8 rms (7 en suite) (1 pri facs) (1 fmly) (2 GF) **Facilities** FTV Lounge tea/coffee WiFi 🐾 **Parking** 7 **Notes** ⊗ No Children 6yrs

Rustington Manor

★★★★ 🍴 GUEST ACCOMMODATION

tel: 01903 788782 **12 Broadmark Ln BN16 2HH**
email: enquiries@rustingtonmanor.com **web:** www.rustingtonmanor.co.uk

A warm welcome is assured at family-run Rustington Manor where guests are made to feel at home. Attentive service and excellent food make for a wonderful dining

experience. Six comfortable, en suite rooms offer all the amenities that the modern guest requires. The property is just a short walk from the beach.

Rooms 6 en suite S £55-£65; D £75-£90* **Facilities** FTV DVD TVL tea/coffee Dinner available Direct Dial Licensed WiFi ♿ **Conf** Max 40 Thtr 40 Class 40 Board 40 **Parking** 14 **Notes** ⊗

SIDLESHAM	Map 5 SZ89

Premier Collection

The Crab & Lobster

★★★★★ 🏵️🏵️ RESTAURANT WITH ROOMS

tel: 01243 641233 **Mill Ln PO20 7NB**
email: enquiries@crab-lobster.co.uk **web:** www.crab-lobster.co.uk
dir: *A27 onto B2145 signed Selsey. 1st left after garage at Sidlesham into Rookery Ln to Crab & Lobster*

Hidden away on the south coast near Pagham Harbour and only a short drive from Chichester is the stylish Crab & Lobster. Bedrooms are superbly appointed, and bathrooms are a feature with luxury toiletries and powerful 'raindrop' showers. Guests can enjoy lunch or dinner in the smart restaurant where the menu offers a range of locally caught fresh fish together with other regionally-sourced, seasonal produce.

Rooms 4 en suite S £90; D £155-£195 **Facilities** FTV DVD iPod docking station tea/coffee Dinner available WiFi **Extras** Speciality toiletries, fresh milk **Parking** 12 **Notes** ⊗ No coaches

The Jolly Fisherman B&B

★★★★ BED AND BREAKFAST

tel: 01243 641544 **Selsey Rd PO20 7LS**
email: pamela.brett@btinternet.com **web:** www.thejollyfisherman.info
dir: *From Chichester take B2145 (Selsey Rd)*

The Jolly Fisherman B&B benefits from its location halfway between the historic city of Chichester and Selsey. It is perfect for exploring the south coast harbours and ideal for Goodwood. Accommodation is comfortable and a traditional substantial breakfast is available in the dining room or on the rear patio overlooking fields, weather permitting.

Rooms 3 en suite **Facilities** FTV WiFi ⚡ **Parking** 3 **Notes** ⊗ 🚭

TILLINGTON	Map 6 SU92

The Horse Guards Inn

★★★★ 🏵️ INN

tel: 01798 342332 **fax:** 01798 345126 **GU28 9AF**
email: info@thehorseguardsinn.co.uk **web:** www.thehorseguardsinn.co.uk
dir: *Off A272 to Tillington, up hill opposite All Hallows church*

This inn is conveniently located close to Petworth and Midhurst in a quiet village setting opposite the quaint church, and is perfect for exploring the beautiful surrounding countryside. The comfortable bedrooms are simply decorated, and delicious breakfasts are prepared to order using the finest local ingredients. The same principles apply to the substantial and flavoursome meals served in the cosy restaurant-bar dining areas.

Rooms 2 en suite 1 annexe en suite (1 fmly) S £85-£115; D £95-£120* **Facilities** FTV DVD tea/coffee Dinner available WiFi

WEST CHILTINGTON   Map 6 TQ01

The Roundabout

★★★★ GUEST ACCOMMODATION

tel: 01798 817336 **Monkmead Ln RH20 2PF**
email: roundabout@relax.co.uk

The refurbished Roundabout was originally designed by Reginald Wells in 1925, and many of the original features have been retained and sympathetically blended with contemporary touches to create accommodation that is suitable for the modern traveller. There is a choice of room types, comfortable public areas, a restaurant, and meeting rooms. The rear garden offers peace and tranquillity.

Rooms 26 en suite

WEST DEAN   Map 5 SU81

The Dean Ale & Cider House

★★★★ INN

tel: 01243 811465 **Main Rd PO18 0QX**
email: thebar@thedeaninn.co.uk **web:** www.thedeaninn.co.uk
dir: On A286, opposite West Dean primary school

The Dean Ale & Cider House, formerly The Selsey Arms, is located in the heart of West Dean village and has been the local village watering hole for the past 200 years. Set in the valley of the River Lavant in the South Downs, The Dean is five miles north of Chichester and five miles south of Midhurst. Newly refurbished, the inn boasts a new restaurant extension and large courtyard with decked garden. The barns at the rear of the pub have been sympathetically renovated and now house comfortable bed and breakfast accommodation. A robust breakfast is part of the offering with plenty of on site parking available.

Rooms 6 annexe en suite (3 GF) **Facilities** FTV tea/coffee Dinner available WiFi **Parking** 30 **Notes** No coaches

WEST MARDEN   Map 5 SU71

Grandwood House

★★★★ GUEST ACCOMMODATION

tel: 07971 845153 & 023 9263 1436 **Watergate PO18 9EG**
email: info@grandwoodhouse.co.uk **web:** www.grandwoodhouse.co.uk

Set in the South Downs and built in 1907, Grandwood House was originally a lodge belonging to Watergate House, which was accidentally burnt down by troops during WWII. All rooms are en suite and enjoy views of the garden, open farmland or both. Large security gates leading onto the driveway ensure secure parking at all times. Only a short walk away, in nearby Walderton, is the local pub which serves lunches and evening meals.

Rooms 4 annexe en suite (4 GF) S £60-£100; D £75-£100* **Facilities** FTV DVD tea/coffee WiFi Riding 🐴 **Parking** 8 **Notes** LB

WORTHING   Map 6 TQ10

The Beacons

★★★★ GUEST ACCOMMODATION

tel: 01903 230948 **18 Shelley Rd BN11 1TU**
email: thebeacons@btconnect.com **web:** www.beaconsworthing.com
dir: 0.5m W of town centre. Exit A259 Richmond Rd into Crescent Rd, 3rd left

This splendid Edwardian property is ideally situated close to the shopping centre, marine garden and pier. Bedrooms are bright, spacious and attractively furnished with many thoughtful amenities, including free WiFi. Guests can enjoy the comfortable lounge with honesty bar, and breakfast is served in the sunny dining room.

Rooms 8 en suite (1 fmly) (3 GF) S £48-£60; D £75-£85* **Facilities** FTV Lounge tea/coffee Licensed WiFi **Parking** 8 **Notes** ⊗

The Burlington

★★★★ GUEST ACCOMMODATION

tel: 01903 211222 **fax:** 01903 209561 **Marine Pde BN11 3QL**
email: info@theburlingtonworthing.co.uk **web:** www.theburlingtonworthing.co.uk
dir: On seafront 0.5m W of Worthing Pier, Wordsworth Rd junct opposite Heene Terrace

This imposing seafront building has a modern contemporary look that appeals to a mainly youthful clientele. The light bar and terrace extends to a night club open at the weekends. Bedrooms are spacious and thoughtfully furnished, with some modern touches. The staff are friendly.

Rooms 26 en suite (6 fmly) S £70-£85; D £85-£105* **Facilities** FTV Lounge tea/coffee Dinner available Direct Dial Licensed WiFi **Conf** Max 100 Thtr 50 Class 35 Board 40 **Notes** ⊗

The Conifers

★★★★ 🏠 GUEST ACCOMMODATION

tel: 01903 265066 & 07947 321096 **43 Parkfield Rd BN13 1EP**
email: conifers@hews.org.uk **web:** www.theconifers.org.uk
dir: A24 or A27 onto A2031 at Offington rdbt, over lights, Parkfield Rd 5th right

The Conifers is located in a quiet residential area of west Worthing close to the town centre and seafront. Bedrooms are traditionally decorated and offer guests comfortable accommodation. There are a number of thoughtful extras which make this a true home-from-home experience. Guests can enjoy a selection of both cooked and continental dishes for breakfast which has achieved an AA Breakfast Award. There is a well-kept garden for guests to enjoy during the summer months.

Rooms 2 rms (1 pri facs) (2 fmly) S £50-£60; D £80-£100* **Facilities** FTV tea/coffee WiFi **Extras** Chocolates, water, magazines - free; robes **Notes** LB ⊗ No Children 12yrs Closed Xmas & New Year

Merton House

★★★★ GUEST ACCOMMODATION

tel: 01903 238222 & 07767 163059 **96 Broadwater Rd BN14 8AW**
email: stay@mertonhouse.co.uk **web:** www.mertonhouse.co.uk
dir: A24 into Worthing, on left past Manor Green

This family run establishment is located on the A24 leading into Worthing, just a couple of minutes from the town centre and seafront. There are seven en suite bedrooms, all of a very traditional style yet providing up-to-date facilities including free WiFi and digital TV. A cooked and continental breakfast is served daily in the dining room. Parking available on site.

Rooms 7 en suite (2 GF) S £47-£60; D £75-£85* **Facilities** FTV Lounge tea/coffee Dinner available WiFi 🐴 **Parking** 5 **Notes** ⊗ No Children 12yrs

Moorings

★★★★ GUEST ACCOMMODATION

tel: 01903 208882 **4 Selden Rd BN11 2LL**
email: themooringsworthing@hotmail.co.uk **web:** www.mooringsworthing.co.uk
dir: 0.5m E of pier off A259 towards Brighton

Moorings is a well-presented Victorian house, located in a quiet residential street just a short walk from the seafront and town centre. Bedrooms are attractively co-ordinated with plenty of extras such as WiFi and Freeview TV. Breakfast is served in a smart dining room and there is a small lounge with books and games.

Rooms 7 en suite (1 fmly) (1 GF) **Facilities** FTV DVD Lounge tea/coffee Direct Dial WiFi 🔒 **Notes** ⊗ No Children 3yrs

High Beach Guest House

★★★ GUEST ACCOMMODATION

tel: 01903 236389 **201 Brighton Rd BN11 2EX**
email: info@highbeachworthing.com **web:** www.highbeachworthing.com
dir: On A259, 200yds past Aquarena swimming pool

High Beach Guest House is situated within a short walk of Worthing town centre, and its seafront location offers uninterrupted sea views from front-facing rooms and the breakfast room. Bedrooms are traditionally decorated and come well equipped. A conservatory with comfortable seating leads onto the front garden where guests can sit during summer months.

Rooms 7 rms (3 en suite) (1 GF) S £28-£40; D £60-£75 **Facilities** FTV Lounge TVL tea/coffee WiFi 🔒 **Parking** 3 **Notes** ⊗

Marina Guest House

★★★ GUEST ACCOMMODATION

tel: 01903 207844 **191 Brighton Rd BN11 2EX**
email: marinaworthing@ntlworld.com
dir: M27 onto A259 to Worthing; or M23 onto A24 to Worthing

This Victorian establishment is in a great location with uninterrupted sea views, and is a short distance from the town centre. The property is well maintained with comfortable accommodation. A cooked breakfast can be enjoyed in the family-style breakfast room that looks out over the sea.

Rooms 5 rms (2 en suite) (2 fmly) **Facilities** tea/coffee Direct Dial WiFi **Notes** ⊗

Park House

[U]

tel: 01903 207939 **4 St Georges Rd BN11 2DS**
email: theparkhouse@aol.com

Currently the rating for this establishment is not confirmed. This may be due to a change of ownership or because it has only recently joined the AA rating scheme.

Rooms 5 rms S £25-£50; D £40-£80*

BIRTLEY Map 19 NZ25

Bowes Incline

★★★★ 🔒 INN

tel: 0191 410 2233 **fax:** 0191 410 4756 **Northside DH3 1RF**
email: info@thebowesinclinehotel.co.uk **web:** www.thebowesinclinehotel.co.uk
dir: From rdbt on A1231 NE of Washington follow Wreckenton sign. Pass lakes on left, approx 0.5m 1st left (signed). Approx 0.5m

Located just one mile from the A1 but surrounded by open countryside, close to the protective arms of the Angel of the North. The family run inn takes its name from the Bowes Incline Railway & Museum located close by. Bedrooms are of a good size and very well appointed with modern en suites. The large bar and restaurant offers award winning food chosen from the large blackboards. The hands on team are friendly and welcoming making this inn a perfect base to tour the North East.

Rooms 18 en suite (2 fmly) (18 GF) S £55-£65; D £65-£75* **Facilities** FTV tea/coffee Dinner available Direct Dial WiFi **Parking** 40 **Notes** ⊗ Closed 24 Dec-2 Jan No coaches

GATESHEAD Map 21 NZ26

Premier Collection

Hedley Hall Bed & Breakfast & Country Cottages

★★★★★ GUEST ACCOMMODATION

tel: 01207 231835 **Hedley Ln NE16 5EH**
email: hedleyhall@aol.com **web:** www.hedleyhall.com

(For full entry see Sunniside)

NEWCASTLE UPON TYNE Map 21 NZ26

Kenilworth

★★★★ GUEST ACCOMMODATION

tel: 0191 281 8111 **fax:** 0191 281 9476 **44 Osborne Rd, Jesmond NE2 2AL**
email: info@kenilworthhotel.co.uk **web:** www.kenilworthhotel.co.uk
dir: A1058 signed Tynemouth for 1m. Left at lights into Osborne Rd, 0.5m on right

This property is located in the heart of Jesmond; an area that has a cosmopolitan feel due to its many hotels and bars. On-going refurbishment of bedrooms and en suites is creating comfortable modern accommodation. Public areas are limited but the bar and restaurant are informal and staff are friendly.

Rooms 11 en suite (5 fmly) (1 GF) S £40-£65; D £50-£90* **Facilities** FTV DVD TVL tea/coffee Dinner available Licensed WiFi 🔒 Access to leisure centre nearby **Parking** 11

SOUTH SHIELDS
Map 21 NZ36

Forest Guest House

★★★★ GUEST HOUSE

tel: 0191 454 8160 & 07834 690989   **fax:** 0191 454 8160 **117 Ocean Rd NE33 2JL**
email: enquiries@forestguesthouse.com **web:** www.forestguesthouse.com

Forest Guest House is centrally located, close to both beach and town centre. It offers comfortable and modern bedrooms and many thoughtful extras provided as standard. The hospitable owners are always on hand to offer help and recommendations. A well-cooked breakfast is served on individual tables giving a great start to the day.

Rooms 6 rms (5 en suite) (1 pri facs) (2 fmly) S £33-£38; D £60-£75* **Facilities** STV FTV DVD tea/coffee WiFi ☕ **Notes** ⊗

Cross Arms

★★★ INN

tel: 0191 454 2139 & 07968 949856   **fax:** 0191 406 7537 **Barrington St NE33 1AN**
email: info@crossarmshotel.com **web:** www.crossarmshotel.com
dir: In town centre, adjacent to market square

Centrally located in the heart of South Shields overlooking the market square, this property is currently undergoing a full refurbishment. Work in the pub has been completed and now the accommodation is to benefit from investment. Continental breakfast is on a self-service basis whilst this kitchen area is available for the guest to use in the evenings and throughout the day.

Rooms 9 rms (2 en suite) (3 pri facs) (1 fmly) S £25-£30; D £45-£50* **Facilities** FTV DVD TVL tea/coffee WiFi Pool table **Parking** 7 **Notes** RS 25 Dec Closed for check-in

The Sir William Fox

★★★ GUEST ACCOMMODATION

tel: 0191 456 4554 **fax:** 0191 247 5781 **5 Westoe Village NE33 3DZ**
email: enquiries@sirwilliamfoxhotel.com **web:** www.sirwilliamfoxhotel.com
dir: A194 into John Reid Rd, then King George Rd into Sunderland Rd. Over rdbt, turn right & right again

Located in the picturesque village of Westoe in the heart of South Shields, The Sir William Fox offers value-for-money accommodation. It benefits from some off-road parking and is within easy walking distance of the Metro, and South Tyneside College. Dinner is available and the property is fully licensed.

Rooms 15 en suite (4 fmly) (2 GF) S £34.50-£40; D £55-£65 **Facilities** FTV DVD TVL tea/coffee Dinner available Direct Dial Licensed WiFi ☕ **Parking** 10

SUNNISIDE
Map 19 NZ25

Premier Collection

Hedley Hall Bed & Breakfast & Country Cottages

★★★★★ GUEST ACCOMMODATION

tel: 01207 231835 **Hedley Ln NE16 5EH**
email: hedleyhall@aol.com **web:** www.hedleyhall.com
dir: From A1 follow signs for Lamsely, at mini rdbt turn right 2m, left at Birkheads Garden/Nursery sign. Straight over x-rds, turn left to Hedley Hall Bed & Breakfast & Country Cottages

Located within easy reach of Beamish, Hedley Hall was once a working farm that was part of the late Queen Mother's estate. A warm welcome and quality accommodation is guaranteed. The stylish modern bedrooms, one with a super-king size bed, are very thoughtfully equipped. Delightful day rooms include a spacious lounge with deep sofas. Breakfast is served in the conservatory or the elegant dining room.

Rooms 4 en suite (1 fmly) **Facilities** DVD Lounge TVL tea/coffee WiFi ☕ **Extras** Fruit, snacks **Parking** 6 **Notes** LB ⊗ Closed 22 Dec-2 Jan

WHITLEY BAY
Map 21 NZ37

Park Lodge

★★★★ GUEST HOUSE

tel: 0191 253 0288 **158-160 Park Av NE26 1AU**
email: parklodgehotel@hotmail.com **web:** www.parklodgewhitleybay.com
dir: From S A19 through Tyne Tunnel, right onto A1058 to seafront. Left, after 2m left at lights onto A191. On left

Set on a leafy avenue, overlooking the park and just minutes from the town centre and coastline, you can expect a friendly atmosphere at this Victorian house. Bedrooms are very comfortable, stylishly furnished and feature homely extras. A hearty breakfast is served and free WiFi is available.

Rooms 5 en suite (1 fmly) (2 GF) S £65-£95; D £95-£100* **Facilities** FTV DVD iPod docking station TVL tea/coffee WiFi ☕ **Parking** 2

Sandsides Guest House

★★★ GUEST ACCOMMODATION

tel: 0191 253 0399 & 07947 447695 **122 Park Av NE26 1AY**
email: sandsides@btinternet.com
dir: A19 Tyne Tunnel exit A1058. At rdbt follow A192 Whitley Bay, next rdbt turn left. Located in one-way system

Situated opposite the park and close to the beach and town centre, Sandsides Guest House offers a variety of room sizes, two with en suite shower rooms and the others with shared facilities. Freshly-cooked breakfasts are served in the dining room.

Rooms 5 rms (2 en suite) (2 fmly) D £50-£60* **Facilities** FTV DVD tea/coffee WiFi ☕ **Parking** 1 **Notes** LB ⊗ ☺

WARWICKSHIRE

ALDERMINSTER
Map 10 SP24

The Bell at Alderminster

★★★★ INN

tel: 01789 450414 **Shipston Rd CV37 8NY**
email: info@thebellald.co.uk **web:** www.thebellald.co.uk

This former 18th-century coaching inn is situated in Alderminster just a few miles away from Stratford-upon-Avon. It's a warm and friendly place where guests can enjoy a range of home-cooked dishes and a range of ales and fine wines. The accommodation is smart, stylish and contemporary in design and bedrooms offer a high level of comfort with many thoughtful extras. The Bell is a Runner Up in the AA Funkiest B&B of the Year 2014-2015.

Rooms 4 en suite 5 annexe en suite (2 fmly) (3 GF) **Facilities** FTV iPod docking station tea/coffee Dinner available Direct Dial WiFi **Extras** Speciality toiletries, home-made biscuits, milk **Conf** Max 12 Thtr 12 Class 12 Board 12 **Parking** 50

ARMSCOTE
Map 10 SP24

The Fuzzy Duck

★★★★ INN

tel: 01608 682635 **Ilmington Rd CV37 8DD**
email: info@fuzzyduckarmscote.com **web:** www.fuzzyduckarmscote.com

The Fuzzy Duck has recently been renovated by the family behind Bayliss & Harding, who are renowned for their quality toiletries. This English country pub now offers boutique bed and breakfast. The bedrooms are sumptuous providing guests with lovely accessories such as luxury robes, and fluffy socks and slippers. Dinner can be enjoyed in the sophisticated restaurant where the chef uses only the finest quality and fresh ingredients.

Rooms 4 en suite (2 fmly) S £110-£160; D £110-£160* **Facilities** FTV iPod docking station Lounge Dinner available WiFi **Extras** Sherry, robes, fruit, snacks, slippers **Conf** Max 20 **Parking** 15

BAGINTON
Map 11 SP37

The Oak

★★★ INN

tel: 024 7651 8855 **fax:** 024 7651 8866 **Coventry Rd CV8 3AU**
email: thebagintonoak@aol.com **web:** www.thebagintonoak.co.uk

Located close to major road links and Coventry Airport, this popular inn serves a wide range of food throughout the themed, open-plan public areas. Families are especially welcome. Modern, well-equipped bedrooms are situated in a separate accommodation building.

Rooms 13 annexe en suite (1 fmly) (6 GF) S £45-£60; D £45-£60* **Facilities** FTV tea/coffee Dinner available WiFi **Conf** Max 40 Thtr 40 Class 40 Board 25 **Parking** 110

BIDFORD-ON-AVON
Map 10 SP15

Buckle House Bed and Breakfast

★★★★ 🏠 BED AND BREAKFAST

tel: 01789 778183 & 07834 810804 **Honeybourne Rd, Bickmarsh B50 4PD**
email: enquiries@bucklehouse.com **web:** www.bucklehouse.com
dir: *From Stratford or M40/M42 to Bidford-on-Avon. At traffic island follow signs for Honeybourne. Buckle House in 1.5m*

Set back from the road and surrounded by attractive gardens, Buckle House is peacefully located, within easy reach of Stratford-upon-Avon and the Cotswolds. The house offers very comfortable bedrooms, all with modern bathrooms, and a large wood burning stove which adds to the homely atmosphere in the sitting room. Breakfast is served overlooking the gardens, and uses fresh local produce including eggs from the neighbouring farm, home grown seasonal vegetables and home-made jams. Hospitality provided by owners Mark and Donna is excellent. AA Friendliest B&B of the Year Finalist 2014-2015.

Rooms 4 rms (3 en suite) (1 pri facs) (2 fmly) S £55-£60; D £70-£90* **Facilities** STV FTV Lounge tea/coffee WiFi 🛎 **Extras** Fridge, milk **Conf** Board 10 **Parking** 10 **Notes** LB ⊗

COLESHILL
Map 10 SP28

Coleshill

★★★ INN

tel: 01675 465527 **fax:** 01675 464013 **152 High St B46 3BG**
email: 9130@greeneking.co.uk **web:** www.oldenglish.co.uk
dir: *M6 junct 4, A446 signed Coleshill & Lichfield. Turn right (across dual carriageway) into Coventry Rd to Coleshill. Straight on at mini rdbt, establishment on left*

The Coleshill is in a convenient location for both the NEC and Birmingham International Airport. Bedrooms, some of which are in a separate house opposite, provide comfortable and well-equipped facilities. The bar and bistro are attractively appointed, and there are additional features including a car park and self-contained function suite.

Rooms 15 en suite 8 annexe en suite (3 fmly) (3 GF) **Facilities** tea/coffee Direct Dial **Parking** 30

Innkeeper's Lodge Birmingham (NEC) Coleshill

★★★ INN

tel: 0845 112 6061 **High St B46 3BL**
email: info@innkeeperslodge.com **web:** www.innkeeperslodge.com

At Innkeeper's Lodge you'll find accommodation with comfort and character in equal measure, and everything needed for a relaxing stay, from easy check-in and free parking to complimentary breakfast and a cosy pub serving great value food and drink on the doorstep. Each Lodge has quality rooms, and there are Lodges in a variety of locations from towns and cities to countryside settings across the UK.

Rooms 33 en suite (7 fmly) (1 GF) **Facilities** FTV tea/coffee Dinner available Direct Dial WiFi **Parking** 44

DORSINGTON
Map 10 SP14

Church Farm *(SP132497)*

★★★ FARMHOUSE

tel: 01789 720471 **CV37 8AX**
email: marianwalters2012@btinternet.com **web:** www.churchfarmstratford.co.uk
dir: *From Stratford on B439 (Evesham Road) for 4m. Turn left signed Welford, then after 1m turn right by shop, signed Dorsington. After 0.75m, left signed Dorsington, on right in 1.25m*

Located in the picturesque Warwickshire village of Dorsington, this friendly working farm is just a short drive from the edge of the Cotswolds and Stratford-upon-Avon. Rooms are all en suite, well equipped with small fridge and microwave; free WiFi and a comfortable guest lounge are also available. A warm welcome is assured.

Rooms 1 en suite 3 annexe en suite (2 fmly) (3 GF) S £36-£42; D £58-£70
Facilities FTV Lounge TVL tea/coffee WiFi ⚓ **Parking** 4 **Notes** LB 130 acres calves/sheep/horses

FILLONGLEY
Map 10 SP28

Heart of England Conference & Events Centre

★★★★ GUEST ACCOMMODATION

tel: 01676 540333 **fax:** 01676 540365 **Meriden Rd CV7 8DX**
email: pa@heartofengland.co.uk **web:** www.heartofengland.co.uk

The Heart of England Conference & Events Centre is a charming stone-built house that offers attractively presented, well-equipped bedrooms and sleek modern bathrooms. This fine old house has bags of character and the spacious, comfortable lounge has a wood-burning stove, which proves a real bonus on cooler evenings. Delicious hot breakfasts are served at individual tables in the well-appointed breakfast room. The nearby Quicken Tree restaurant serves an extensive choice of imaginative dishes and makes a good choice for evening meals. As the name implies, first-rate conference and business facilities are available on site.

Rooms 7 en suite (1 GF) **Facilities** FTV TVL tea/coffee Dinner available Direct Dial Licensed WiFi Fishing **Conf** Max 450 Thtr 450 Class 200 Board 50 **Parking** 36 **Notes** LB ⊗ Civ Wed 200

KENILWORTH
Map 10 SP27

Ferndale House

★★★★ GUEST HOUSE

tel: 01926 853214 **fax:** 01926 858394 **45 Priory Rd CV8 1LL**
email: info@kenilworth-guesthouse-accommodation.com **web:** www.kenilworth-guesthouse-accommodation.com
dir: *From M40 junct 15 onto A46 towards Coventry, then onto A452, Priory Rd on right*

Ferndale House is situated five-minutes' walk away from Kenilworth, and is on the local bus route close to the university. Each of the bedrooms is attractively designed with a modern style, and the beds provide a very good night's sleep. Both parking and WiFi are free.

Rooms 7 en suite (1 fmly) S £38-£39; D £60-£65* **Facilities** FTV TVL tea/coffee WiFi **Parking** 4

Milsoms Kenilworth

★★★★ ⊜ INN

tel: 01926 515450 **fax:** 01926 515451 **Clarendon House Hotel, High St CV8 1LZ**
email: kenilworth@milsomshotel.co.uk **web:** www.milsomshotel.co.uk
dir: *A452 signs to town centre, at small rdbt with clock tower, 2nd exit Abbey Hill. At lights, Milsoms immediately on left*

Milsoms enjoys a prominent position in the heart of Kenilworth and benefits from secure parking for guests. The bedrooms are beautifully appointed and very well equipped; complimentary WiFi is available. Dinner in the Loch Fyne Restaurant should be not be missed as guests are assured of great food along with attentive and friendly service. There is also a charming bar and a comfortable lounge. The NEC and Birmingham Airport are a short drive away.

Rooms 28 en suite 3 annexe en suite (1 fmly) (5 GF) **Facilities** FTV Lounge tea/coffee Dinner available WiFi ⚓ **Extras** Bottled water - complimentary **Conf** Max 25 Thtr 16 Class 18 **Parking** 19 **Notes** ⊗ No coaches

Stoneleigh Park Lodge

★★★★ GUEST HOUSE

tel: 024 7669 0123 **fax:** 024 7669 0789 **Stoneleigh Park CV8 2LZ**
email: info@stoneleighparklodge.com **web:** www.stoneleighparklodge.com
dir: *2m E of Kenilworth in Stoneleigh Park*

This house lies within the grounds of the National Agricultural Centre and provides modern, well-equipped accommodation. Meals, using local produce, are served in the Park View Restaurant overlooking the showground. Various conference and meeting facilities are available.

Rooms 58 en suite (4 fmly) (26 GF) S £55-£120; D £65-£130* **Facilities** FTV TVL tea/coffee Dinner available Direct Dial Licensed WiFi Fishing **Conf** Max 10 **Parking** 60 **Notes** Closed Xmas

LEAMINGTON SPA (ROYAL)
Map 10 SP36

The Adams

★★★★ GUEST ACCOMMODATION

tel: 01926 450742 **fax:** 01926 313110 **22 Avenue Rd CV31 3PQ**
email: bookings@adams-hotel.co.uk **web:** www.adams-hotel.co.uk
dir: *500yds W of town centre. Exit A452 (Adelaide Rd) into Avenue Rd*

Just a short walk from the town centre, this elegant 1827 Regency house offers a relaxing setting and quality accommodation. Public areas include a lounge bar with leather armchairs, and a pretty garden. The attractive bedrooms are very well appointed, and have modem points and bathrobes.

Rooms 10 en suite (2 GF) **Facilities** FTV Lounge tea/coffee Direct Dial Licensed WiFi ⚓ **Parking** 14 **Notes** ⊗ No Children 16yrs Closed 23 Dec-2 Jan

---

■ LONG COMPTON Map 10 SP23

The Red Lion
★★★★ INN

tel: 01608 684221 **fax:** 01608 684968 **Main St CV36 5JS**
email: info@redlion-longcompton.co.uk **web:** www.redlion-longcompton.co.uk
dir: *5m S of Shipston on Stour on A3400*

Located in the pretty rural village of Long Compton, this mid 18th-century posting house retains many original features which are complemented by rustic furniture in the public areas. A good range of ales is offered, and interesting menus capitalise on quality local produce. The bedrooms are well appointed, and have a good range of facilities.

Rooms 5 en suite (1 fmly) S £60; D £90-£140* **Facilities** tea/coffee Dinner available WiFi children's play area **Extras** Speciality toiletries **Parking** 60 **Notes** No coaches

Tallet Barn B&B
★★★★ BED AND BREAKFAST

tel: 01608 684248 **fax:** 01608 684248 **Yerdley Farm CV36 5LH**
email: talletbarn@googlemail.com **web:** www.countryaccom.co.uk/yerdley-farm
dir: *From A3400 in village into Vicarage Ln opposite village store, 3rd entrance on right at sharp bend*

This converted barn and grain store, in the heart of an unspoiled Cotswold village, provides comfortable bedrooms with thoughtful extras. Comprehensive breakfasts are served in the elegant, beamed dining room in the main house.

Rooms 2 annexe en suite (1 GF) S £50; D £75-£80 **Facilities** tea/coffee **Parking** 2 **Notes** ⊛ No Children 6yrs ⊛

■ RUGBY Map 11 SP57

Innkeeper's Lodge Rugby, Dunchurch
★★★ INN

tel: 0845 112 6073 **The Green, Dunchurch CV22 6NJ**
email: info@innkeeperslodge.com **web:** www.innkeeperslodge.com

At Innkeeper's Lodge you'll find accommodation with comfort and character in equal measure, and everything needed for a relaxing stay, from easy check-in and free parking to complimentary breakfast and a cosy pub serving great value food and drink on the doorstep. Each Lodge has quality rooms, and there are Lodges in a variety of locations from towns and cities to countryside settings across the UK.

Rooms 16 en suite (2 fmly) (6 GF) **Facilities** FTV tea/coffee Dinner available Direct Dial WiFi **Parking**

Diamond House
AA Advertised

tel: 01788 572701 **28-30 Hillmorton Rd CV22 5AA**
email: diamondhouse2830@aol.com

Diamond House is a privately-run guest house, just three minutes' walk from Rugby town centre and Rugby School. There are single, double, and a choice of family room sizes. There's plenty of private parking, and a 24-hour laundry service is available.

Rooms 19 rms S £38-£50; D £56-£60*

■ SHIPSTON ON STOUR Map 10 SP24

Holly End Bed & Breakfast
★★★★ BED AND BREAKFAST

tel: 01608 664064 **London Rd CV36 4EP**
email: hollyend.hunt@btinternet.com **web:** www.holly-end.co.uk
dir: *0.5m S of Shipston on Stour on A3400, just beyond Methodist church*

Located between Oxford and Stratford-upon-Avon and a short walk from the town centre, this immaculate detached house offers bedrooms with lots of thoughtful extras. Accommodation is all you would expect from a four-star establishment yet still manages to maintain a home-from-home atmosphere. Comprehensive breakfasts use the best of local produce and comprise an award-winning range of options, one of which is full English.

Rooms 2 rms (1 en suite) (1 pri facs) **Facilities** FTV iPod docking station tea/coffee WiFi **Extras** Speciality toiletries, bottled water - free **Parking** 6 **Notes** LB ⊛ No Children 9yrs ⊜

■ STRATFORD-UPON-AVON Map 10 SP25

Premier Collection

Cherry Trees
★★★★★ GUEST HOUSE

tel: 01789 292989 **Swans Nest Ln CV37 7LS**
email: cherrytreesstratforduponavon@gmail.com
web: www.cherrytrees-stratford.co.uk
dir: *M40 junct 15 to A439, one-way system (A3400) over bridge, pass Cherry Trees, continue on to rdbt & double back. Then take 1st left into Swan's Nest Ln*

Near to the theatre and the centre of Stratford, Cherry Trees offers three spacious, luxurious and well-equipped suites. The Garden Suite and the Terrace Suite each have a conservatory while the Tiffany Suite has its own private TV room. All the rooms have king size beds with many extra touches, such as Roberts radios and fridges.

Rooms 3 en suite (3 GF) S £85-£110; D £110-£135 **Facilities** FTV tea/coffee WiFi 🛁 **Extras** Home-made biscuits - complimentary **Parking** 4 **Notes** LB ⊛ No Children 12yrs Closed Jan

Adelphi Guest House
★★★★ GUEST ACCOMMODATION

tel: 01789 204469 **39 Grove Rd CV37 6PB**
email: info@adelphi-guesthouse.com **web:** www.adelphi-guesthouse.com
dir: *M40 junct 15 onto A46 towards Stratford, then A3400. Straight over at 2 rdbts, at lights right into Arden St (A4390). This becomes Grove Rd, on left opposite park*

Based in the centre of Stratford-upon-Avon, the Adelphi is ideally located for those visiting the Royal Shakespeare, Swan or Courtyard Theatres. The bedrooms offer comfort throughout and are all tastefully decorated in period design with many thoughtful extras. All guests will receive a warm and friendly welcome, and breakfast is not to be missed with a wide selection of high-quality dishes offered. Free parking and WiFi are also available.

Rooms 6 rms (5 en suite) (1 pri facs) (1 fmly) (1 GF) S £40-£45; D £75-£95* **Facilities** FTV DVD iPod docking station tea/coffee WiFi 🛁 **Parking** 5 **Notes** LB ⊛ No Children 10yrs

STRATFORD-UPON-AVON *continued*

Ambleside Guest House

★★★★ GUEST HOUSE

tel: 01789 297239 **41 Grove Rd CV37 6PB**
email: peter@amblesideguesthouse.com **web:** www.amblesideguesthouse.com
dir: *250mtrs from town centre on A4390 opposite Firs Gdns*

Ambleside is a very comfortable house in the heart of Stratford. Breakfast is served in the bright and airy dining room, which overlooks the park at the front. Free on-site parking and WiFi are provided.

Rooms 7 rms (5 en suite) (2 pri facs) (2 fmly) (2 GF) S £38-£45; D £70-£88 **Facilities** FTV tea/coffee WiFi 🔒 **Parking** 9 **Notes** ⊗ No Children 10yrs

Hunters Moon Guest House

★★★★ GUEST ACCOMMODATION

tel: 01789 292888 & 07799 833373 **fax:** 01789 292888 **150 Alcester Rd CV37 9DR**
email: thehuntersmoon@ntlworld.com **web:** www.huntersmoonguesthouse.com
dir: *M40 junct 15 onto A46 to Stratford. 1st rdbt take 2nd exit (Stratford Rd), next rdbt 1st exit onto A46. Next rdbt 1st exit onto A422, on left*

This recently renovated guest house is situated midway between the town centre and Anne Hathaway's Cottage, and only a ten-minute walk from the train station. A friendly welcome will be offered by Gary and Sally at this attractive property. Bedrooms are modern in design and lots of thoughtful accessories are provided, including free WiFi. An enjoyable breakfast will round off a pleasant stay. Parking is available.

Rooms 4 en suite **Facilities** FTV DVD tea/coffee WiFi 🔒 **Extras** Mini fridge, bottled water - complimentary **Parking** 4 **Notes** ⊗ No Children 12yrs

Symbols and abbreviations are explained on page 7

Arden Way Guest House

★★★★ GUEST HOUSE

tel: 01789 205646 **fax:** 01789 205646 **22 Shipston Rd CV37 7LP**
email: info@ardenwayguesthouse.co.uk **web:** www.ardenwayguesthouse.co.uk
dir: *On A3400, S of River Avon, 100mtrs on left*

A warm welcome is assured at this non-smoking house, located within easy walking distance of the Butterfly Farm and cricket ground. The homely bedrooms are filled with lots of thoughtful extras and an attractive dining room, overlooking the pretty rear garden, is the setting for comprehensive breakfasts.

Rooms 6 en suite (1 fmly) (2 GF) S £40-£56; D £60-£76* **Facilities** FTV DVD tea/coffee WiFi 🔒 **Parking** 6 **Notes** LB ⊗

Monk's Barn Farm *(SP206516)*

★★★★ FARMHOUSE

tel: 01789 293714 & 205886 **Shipston Rd CV37 8NA**
email: ritameadows@btconnect.com **web:** www.monksbarnfarm.co.uk
dir: *2m S of Stratford on A3400, on right after bungalows on left*

With stunning views of the surrounding countryside, a warm welcome awaits at this impressive house. Bedrooms, some of which are located in former outbuildings, are filled with a wealth of thoughtful extras. Memorable breakfasts are served in the spacious and cosy lounge-dining room.

Rooms 2 en suite 3 annexe en suite (1 fmly) (3 GF) S £31-£35; D £62-£67 **Facilities** FTV DVD Lounge TVL tea/coffee WiFi 🔒 **Extras** Snacks **Parking** 7 **Notes** LB ⊗ Closed 25-27 Dec 75 acres mixed

Moonraker House

★★★★ GUEST ACCOMMODATION

tel: 01789 268774 **fax:** 01789 268774 **40 Alcester Rd CV37 9DB**
email: info@moonrakerhouse.com **web:** www.moonrakerhouse.com
dir: *200yds from rail station on A422 (Alcester Rd)*

Just a short walk from the railway station and the central attractions, this establishment provides a range of stylish bedrooms. The sitting area during the day is the setting for the freshly cooked breakfasts. The attractive exterior is enhanced by a magnificent floral display during the warmer months.

Rooms 7 en suite (1 fmly) (2 GF) **Facilities** FTV tea/coffee WiFi **Parking** 7 **Notes** ⊗ No Children 6yrs

Twelfth Night

★★★★ GUEST ACCOMMODATION

tel: 01789 414595 **13 Evesham Place CV37 6HT**
email: twelfthnight@fsmail.net **web:** www.twelfthnight.co.uk
dir: *In town centre off A4390 Grove Rd*

This delightful Victorian villa is within easy walking distance of the town centre. Quality decor and furnishings enhance the charming original features, and the elegant dining room is the setting for imaginative English breakfasts.

Rooms 7 rms (6 en suite) (1 pri facs) **Facilities** tea/coffee **Parking** 6 **Notes** ⊗ Closed 11-25 Feb

Barbette Guest House

★★★ BED AND BREAKFAST

tel: 01789 297822 **165 Evesham Rd CV37 9BP**
email: barbette@sitgetan.demon.co.uk
dir: B439 S, 0.5m from town centre

Expect a friendly welcome at this B&B, a compact but comfortable establishment close to the main road, with parking and a landscaped rear garden. Bedrooms are comfortable and well equipped, and guests have use of a TV lounge.

Rooms 4 rms (2 en suite) **Facilities** FTV TVL tea/coffee WiFi **Parking** 5 **Notes** ⊗ ⊜

Stretton House

★★★ GUEST ACCOMMODATION

tel: 01789 268647 **38 Grove Rd CV37 6PB**
email: shortpbshort@aol.com **web:** www.strettonhouse.co.uk
dir: On A439 in town centre road behind police station

This attractive, Edwardian terrace house is within easy walking distance of the railway station and Shakespeare's birthplace. Bedrooms are carefully decorated, well equipped, and many have modern shower rooms en suite. The pretty front garden is a welcoming feature.

Rooms 6 rms (5 en suite) (1 pri facs) (3 fmly) (1 GF) S £35-£40; D £65-£75*
Facilities FTV tea/coffee WiFi 🛁 **Parking** 6 **Notes** ⊗

Salamander Guest House

★★★ 🅰 GUEST HOUSE

tel: 01789 205728 **fax:** 01789 205728 **40 Grove Rd CV37 6PB**
email: p.delin@btinternet.com **web:** www.salamanderguesthouse.co.uk
dir: 250yds W of town centre on A439 ring road, opposite Firs Garden

Ideally located within easy walking distance of central attractions, this well-maintained Edwardian house provides a range of thoughtfully furnished bedrooms with the benefit of modern and efficient en suite shower rooms. Breakfast is served in an attractive dining room overlooking a pretty park, and private parking is also available.

Rooms 7 rms (6 en suite) (1 pri facs) (5 fmly) (1 GF) **Facilities** FTV tea/coffee Dinner available WiFi **Parking** 12 **Notes** ⊗

TEMPLE GRAFTON — Map 10 SP15

The Blue Boar

★★★ INN

tel: 01789 750010 **fax:** 01789 750635 **B49 6NR**
email: info@theblueboar.co.uk **web:** www.theblueboar.co.uk
dir: From A46 (Stratford-upon-Avon - Alcester), turn left, Blue Boar at 1st x-rds

A warm welcome is guaranteed at this country inn. The bedrooms are comfortable and homely, and the dining room and bar menus offer extensive choice, plus additional specials. There is also a beer garden to sit in when the weather allows.

Rooms 14 en suite (5 fmly) (1 GF) **Facilities** FTV Dinner available WiFi **Conf** Max 30 Thtr 30 Class 40 Board 30 **Parking** 35

WELLESBOURNE — Map 10 SP25

Innkeeper's Lodge Stratford-upon-Avon

★★★ INN

tel: 0845 112 6075 **Warwick Rd CV35 9LX**
email: info@innkeeperslodge.com **web:** www.innkeeperslodge.com

At Innkeeper's Lodge you'll find accommodation with comfort and character in equal measure, and everything needed for a relaxing stay, from easy check-in and free parking to complimentary breakfast and a cosy pub serving great value food and drink on the doorstep. Each Lodge has quality rooms, and there are Lodges in a variety of locations from towns and cities to countryside settings across the UK.

Rooms 9 en suite (2 fmly) **Facilities** FTV tea/coffee Dinner available Direct Dial WiFi **Parking** 35

WEST MIDLANDS

BIRMINGHAM
Map 10 SP08

Black Firs

★★★★ GUEST HOUSE

tel: 0121 779 2727 **fax:** 0121 778 1149 **113 Coleshill Rd, Marston Green B37 7HT**
email: julie@b-firs.co.uk **web:** www.b-firs.co.uk
dir: *M42 junct 6, A45 W, onto B4438, follow signs for Marston Green*

This elegant house is set in immaculate gardens in a mainly residential area close to the NEC. Thoughtfully equipped bedrooms with WiFi access are complemented by smart shower rooms. Memorable breakfasts are served in an attractive dining room, and a lounge is also available.

Rooms 6 en suite **Facilities** TVL tea/coffee WiFi **Conf** Max 14 **Parking** 6 **Notes** ⊗ ➡

Westbourne Lodge

★★★★ GUEST ACCOMMODATION

tel: 0121 429 1003 **fax:** 0121 429 7436 **25-31 Fountain Rd, Edgbaston B17 8NJ**
email: info@westbournelodge.co.uk **web:** www.westbournelodge.co.uk
dir: *100yds from A456*

Located on a quiet residential avenue close to Hagley Road, this well-maintained property provides a range of non-smoking, thoughtfully furnished bedrooms, one of which is on the ground floor. Breakfasts are served in the attractive dining room overlooking a pretty patio garden. A comfortable sitting room and lounge bar are also available.

Rooms 12 en suite (4 fmly) (1 GF) S £49.50-£69.50; D £69.50-£89.50* **Facilities** FTV TVL tea/coffee Licensed WiFi 🛝 **Parking** 12 **Notes** Closed 24 Dec-1 Jan

Tri-Star

★★★ GUEST ACCOMMODATION

tel: 0121 782 1010 & 782 6131 **fax:** 0121 782 6131 **Coventry Rd, Elmdon B26 3QR**
email: info@tristarhotel.co.uk **web:** www.tristarhotel.co.uk
dir: *On A45*

Just a short drive from the airport, Birmingham International station and the NEC, this owner-managed property provides a range of thoughtfully furnished bedrooms with modern bathrooms. The open-plan ground-floor area includes a bright, attractive dining room and a comfortable lounge and bar. A separate room is available for conferences or functions.

Rooms 15 en suite (3 fmly) (6 GF) **Facilities** FTV TVL tea/coffee Dinner available Licensed WiFi Pool table Games room **Conf** Max 20 Thtr 20 Class 10 Board 20 **Parking** 25 **Notes** ⊗

Innkeeper's Lodge Birmingham West (Quinton)

★★★ INN

tel: 0845 112 6066 **563 Hagley Road West, Quinton B32 1HP**
email: info@innkeeperslodge.com **web:** www.innkeeperslodge.com

At Innkeeper's Lodge you'll find accommodation with comfort and character in equal measure, and everything needed for a relaxing stay, from easy check-in and free parking to complimentary breakfast and a cosy pub serving great value food and drink on the doorstep. Each Lodge has quality rooms, and there are Lodges in a variety of locations from towns and cities to countryside settings across the UK.

Rooms 24 en suite (8 fmly) (8 GF) **Facilities** FTV tea/coffee Dinner available Direct Dial WiFi **Parking**

BIRMINGHAM (NATIONAL EXHIBITION CENTRE)

See Solihull

COVENTRY
Map 10 SP37

Innkeeper's Lodge Birmingham (NEC) Meriden

★★★★ ➡ INN

tel: 0845 112 6072 **Main Rd, Meriden CV7 7NN**
email: info@innkeeperslodge.com **web:** www.innkeeperslodge.com

At Innkeeper's Lodge you'll find accommodation with comfort and character in equal measure, and everything needed for a relaxing stay, from easy check-in and free parking to complimentary breakfast and a cosy pub serving great value food and drink on the doorstep. Each Lodge has quality rooms, and there are Lodges in a variety of locations from towns and cities to countryside settings across the UK.

Rooms 13 en suite (3 fmly) (4 GF) **Facilities** FTV tea/coffee Dinner available Direct Dial WiFi **Parking**

MERIDEN
Map 10 SP28

Grove House Bed & Breakfast

★★★★ BED AND BREAKFAST

tel: 01676 523295 **8 Whichcote Av CV7 7LR**
email: enquiries@grovehousebandb.co.uk **web:** www.grovehousebandb.co.uk
dir: *M42 junct 6, A45, A452, at rdbt onto B4102 signed Meriden. At next rdbt 3rd exit. Pass Bulls Head on left, 3rd left into Leys Ln, Whichcote Av on left*

In the quiet village of Meriden, just ten minutes from Birmingham International Airport and the NEC, a warm welcome is guaranteed at Grove House. Bedrooms are spacious and well equipped providing impressive quality and comfort. Ground-floor areas include a comfortable lounge in addition to the cosy breakfast room that overlooks the garden.

Rooms 2 rms (1 en suite) (1 pri facs) **Facilities** FTV TVL tea/coffee Dinner available WiFi **Parking** 6 **Notes** LB ⊗ ➡

SOLIHULL
Map 10 SP17

Premier Collection

Hampton Manor

★★★★★ ⑨⑨ 🍴 RESTAURANT WITH ROOMS

tel: 01675 446080 **fax:** 01675 443838
Swadowbrook Ln, Hampton-in-Arden B92 0EN
email: info@hamptonmanor.eu **web:** www.hamptonmanor.eu
dir: *M42 junct 6 follow signs for A45 (Birmingham). At 1st rdbt, 1st exit onto B4438 (Catherine de Barnes Ln). Left into Shadowbrook Ln*

Hampton Manor is set within 45 acres of mature woodland, only minutes from Birmingham's major air, rail and road links and the NEC. The manor has received major renovation and now offers luxurious accommodation with a contemporary and sophisticated style whilst maintaining many of its original features and heritage. The bedrooms are all beautifully and uniquely designed and boast sumptuous beds. Fine dining can be enjoyed at Peel's restaurant, which is a fabulous venue for innovative cooking, and will prove the highlight of any stay.

Rooms 15 en suite (3 fmly) (1 GF) S £150-£340; D £150-£340 (room only)* **Facilities** FTV DVD iPod docking station Lounge tea/coffee Dinner available Direct Dial WiFi 🛝 18 **Extras** Bottled water, home-made cookies **Conf** Max 120 Thtr 120 Board 35 **Parking** 30 **Notes** LB ⊗ Civ Wed 120

The Gate House

★★★ BED AND BREAKFAST

tel: 01675 443274 **Barston Ln, Barston B92 0JN**
email: enquiries@gatehousesolihull.co.uk web: www.gatehousesolihull.co.uk
dir: *4m E of Solihull. Off B4101 or B4102 to Barston, on W side of village*

This elegant Victorian building stands in landscaped grounds, has secure parking and is within easy driving distance of the NEC and Birmingham. A warm welcome and a comfortable night's rest are guaranteed. Enjoy breakfast in the elegant dining room, overlooking the gardens, which are stunning in spring and summer.

Rooms 4 rms (2 en suite) **Facilities** tea/coffee WiFi **Parking** 20 **Notes** ⊛ No Children 5yrs ⊛

Innkeeper's Lodge Solihull, Knowle

★★★ INN

tel: 0845 112 6070 **Warwick Rd, Knowle B93 0EE**
email: info@innkeeperslodge.com web: www.innkeeperslodge.com

At Innkeeper's Lodge you'll find accommodation with comfort and character in equal measure, and everything needed for a relaxing stay, from easy check-in and free parking to complimentary breakfast and a cosy pub serving great value food and drink on the doorstep. Each Lodge has quality rooms, and there are Lodges in a variety of locations from towns and cities to countryside settings across the UK.

Rooms 11 en suite (1 fmly) **Facilities** FTV tea/coffee Dinner available Direct Dial WiFi **Parking**

WILTSHIRE

ALDBOURNE	Map 5 SU27

The Crown Aldbourne

★★★ INN

tel: 01672 540214 & 07773 219579 **2 The Square SN8 2DU**
email: bookings@thecrownaldbourne.co.uk web: www.thecrownaldbourne.co.uk
dir: *M4 junct 15 S on A346. After 1m turn left at garage onto Ridgeway. Turn right after 1.5m onto B4192*

The Crown is located in a beautiful village popular with visitors and locals alike. The accommodation consists of well-equipped en suite rooms, all located in the main house. The restaurant has a friendly atmosphere and offers a wide range of freshly prepared dishes. There is a large drinks selection, including beers and wines, which is available all day.

Rooms 4 en suite S £55-£65; D £65-£80* **Facilities** FTV DVD Lounge TVL tea/coffee Dinner available WiFi ⌣ 18 Riding ⚓ **Conf** Max 24

AMESBURY	Map 5 SU14

Mandalay

★★★★ GUEST ACCOMMODATION

tel: 01980 623733 **15 Stonehenge Rd SP4 7BA**
email: nick.ramplin@btinternet.com web: www.mandalayguesthouse.com
dir: *500yds W of town centre, exit High St into Church St & Stonehenge Rd*

Quietly located on the edge of the town, yet within easy reach of Stonehenge and Salisbury Cathedral, this delightful property provides individually decorated rooms. Freshly cooked breakfasts are served in the pleasant breakfast room, which overlooks the landscaped gardens. Please note that a 48-hour cancellation policy is in operation.

Rooms 5 en suite (1 fmly) (1 GF) S £50-£60; D £65-£80 **Facilities** FTV iPod docking station Lounge tea/coffee WiFi ⚓ **Parking** 5 **Notes** ⊛

Park House Motel

★★★★ GUEST ACCOMMODATION

tel: 01980 629256 **fax:** 01980 629256 **SP4 0EG**
email: info@parkhousemotel.com web: www.parkhousemotel.co.uk
dir: *5m E of Amesbury. Junct A303 & A338*

This family-run establishment offers a warm welcome and is extremely convenient for the A303. Bedrooms are practically equipped with modern facilities and come in a variety of sizes. There is a large dining room where dinner is served during the week, and a cosy bar in which to relax.

Rooms 30 rms (27 en suite) (1 pri facs) (9 fmly) (25 GF) **Facilities** STV FTV TVL tea/coffee Dinner available Licensed WiFi **Parking** 40

BOWERCHALKE	Map 5 SU02

Greenbank Bed & Breakfast

★★★★ BED AND BREAKFAST

tel: 01722 780350 & 07812 486045 **Church St SP5 5BE**
email: enquiries@greenbank101.com web: www.greenbank101.com
dir: *A354 from Salisbury to Coombe Bissett. Right at 1st junct, follow signs for Broad Chalke. Left by public house & follow signs for Bowerchalke*

Located in the scenic Chalke Valley, a short drive out from Salisbury, Greenbank offers contemporary style en suite accommodation. There is ample off-road parking and a warm welcome from your hosts Sue and Paul who will ensure that your stay is a relaxing and pleasurable experience. Accommodation consists of two non-smoking, en suite double rooms. Guests also have use of a fridge and their own conservatory-lounge where there is access to all indoor and outdoor areas, games, magazines and items of local interest.

Rooms 2 en suite (2 GF) S £45-£55; D £75-£85* **Facilities** FTV Lounge tea/coffee WiFi **Extras** Fruit, snacks - complimentary **Parking** 4 **Notes** ⊛ No Children 12yrs

BOX	Map 4 ST86

Premier Collection

The Northey Arms

★★★★★ ⊜ INN

tel: 01225 891166 **Bath Rd SN13 8AE**
web: www.ohhcompany.co.uk

This stylish inn combines modern facilities and quality with relaxed and welcoming hospitality. The bedrooms and bathrooms are especially comfortable and well equipped, with large walk-in showers, luxurious towels and toiletries. Food is served throughout the day and utilises high quality produce on a menu which has something for everyone.

Rooms 3 en suite **Facilities** Dinner available

BRADFORD-ON-AVON   Map 4 ST86

The Muddy Duck

★★★★ ◎ INN

tel: 01225 858705 **Monkton Farleigh BA15 2QH**
email: dishitup@themuddyduckbath.co.uk web: www.themuddyduckbath.co.uk
dir: *A363 from Bath towards Bradford-on-Avon. Left towards Monkton Farleigh, then left into village*

The Muddy Duck is full of character and is quietly located in a pleasant village almost mid-way between Bath and Bradford-on-Avon. Bedrooms and bathrooms vary in terms of space but all are very well furnished and equipped. One bedroom in particular is very large. A menu offering carefully prepared dishes to suit all tastes is available at both lunch and dinner. Breakfast offers a range of high quality produce and a generous choice of hot dishes. Outdoor seating is available to both the front and rear of the inn.

Rooms 3 en suite 2 annexe en suite (2 GF) S £115-£225; D £115-£225*
Facilities FTV DVD iPod docking station TVL tea/coffee Dinner available Direct Dial WiFi ♨ **Parking** 20 **Notes** ⊗ No coaches

The Beeches Farmhouse

★★★★ BED AND BREAKFAST

tel: 01225 865170 fax: 01225 865170 **Molt Rd BA15 1TS**
email: stay@beeches-farmhouse.co.uk web: www.beeches-farmhouse.co.uk
dir: *1m E of Bradford-on-Avon on B3107, on left just past garden centre*

Peacefully located and surrounded by delightful countryside, this relaxed and welcoming accommodation offers guest bedrooms in well furnished, converted barns and stables adjacent to the main building. There are various leisure facilities in the grounds including a games room. Breakfast is served in the conservatory of the main farmhouse.

Rooms 1 en suite 4 annexe en suite (1 fmly) (4 GF) S £65-£115; D £85-£115*
Facilities FTV DVD Lounge tea/coffee WiFi ch fac ♨ 18 Pool table ♨ **Extras** Mineral water, fruit, local biscuits & fudge **Conf** Max 8 Board 8 **Parking** 11 **Notes** LB RS Xmas & New Year room only (no breakfast)

Serendipity

★★★★ BED AND BREAKFAST

tel: 01225 722380 & 07941 778397 **19f Bradford Rd, Winsley BA15 2HW**
email: vanda.shepherd@tesco.net
dir: *A36 onto B3108, 1.5m right into Winsley, establishment on right on main road*

Set in a quiet residential area, Serendipity is convenient for visiting nearby Bath. The proprietors are friendly and welcoming, and bedrooms are brightly decorated and equipped with a range of extras. Two bedrooms are on the ground floor. Guests can watch badgers and other wildlife in the gardens during the evening. Breakfast is served in the conservatory overlooking the garden.

Rooms 3 en suite (1 fmly) (2 GF) S £59-£78; D £69-£79* **Facilities** FTV DVD tea/coffee WiFi ☜♨ 72 ♨ **Parking** 5 **Notes** LB ⊗ ⊗ ⊜

The Tollgate Inn

★★★★ ⊜ INN

tel: 01225 782326 **Ham Green, Holt BA14 6PX**
email: laura@tollgateinn.co.uk web: www.tollgateholt.co.uk
dir: *A363 Bradford-on-Avon turn left onto B3105, left onto B3107, 100yds on right at W end of Holt*

The Tollgate Inn combines the comforts of a traditional hostelry with excellent food, all served in delightful surroundings. It stands near the village green in Holt, only a short drive from Bath. The bedrooms, varying in size, are comfortable and thoughtfully equipped with welcome extras. An on-site café, deli and farm shop provide lunches and interesting picnic items.

Rooms 4 en suite S £70-£110; D £70-£110* **Facilities** FTV DVD tea/coffee Dinner available Direct Dial WiFi Farm shop & animals **Extras** Fresh fruit, still & sparkling mineral water **Parking** 30 **Notes** ⊗

BROMHAM   Map 4 ST96

Wayside

★★★ BED AND BREAKFAST

tel: 01380 850695 & 07770 774460 fax: 01380 850696 **Chittoe Heath SN15 2EH**
email: mail@waysideofwiltshire.co.uk web: www.waysideofwiltshire.co.uk
dir: *From A342 take road signed Spye Park & Chittoe, Wayside 1st on right*

Peacefully located yet only just off the main road, Wayside offers relaxed and comfortable accommodation and bedrooms in a range of shapes and sizes. Guests are welcome to use the lounge and there is even a wood to the rear of the property where guests can enjoy a quiet walk. Good quality ingredients are offered at breakfast, and there is a wide choice of local inns and restaurants for dinner.

Rooms 3 rms (2 en suite) (1 pri facs) (1 fmly) (2 GF) (3 smoking) S £40-£45; D £70-£75 **Facilities** STV FTV DVD TVL tea/coffee WiFi ♨ 18 Riding ♨ 12 acres of private woodland **Parking** 3 **Notes** LB ⊜

BURCOMBE   Map 5 SU03

Burcombe Manor B&B

★★★★ BED AND BREAKFAST

tel: 01722 744288 & 07967 594449 **Burcombe Ln SP2 0EJ**
email: enquiries@burcombemanor.co.uk web: www.burcombemanor.co.uk
dir: *A30 from Wilton, after 0.75m turn left over bridge. At T-junct turn right, 100mtrs on left*

Located in the village of Burcombe, only five miles west of Salisbury, this family home is set at the edge of a 1300-acre farm with views out over the water meadows. Bedrooms, including two en suite rooms, offer comfortable accommodation. Breakfast is served in one of the drawing rooms and there is a spacious lounge for guests to relax in.

Rooms 3 rms (2 en suite) (1 pri facs) **Facilities** Lounge tea/coffee WiFi **Parking** 6

BURTON   Map 4 ST87

Premier Collection

The Old House at Home

★★★★★ ⊜ INN

tel: 01454 218227 **SN14 7LT**
email: office@ohhcompany.co.uk web: www.ohhcompany.co.uk
dir: *M4 junct 18, A46, B4040 to Acton Turvill, right onto B4039. 1.5m to Burton*

In a pleasant setting, just a couple of miles from the delightful village of Castle Combe, this well-established country inn is run personally by the resident proprietors and their family. Six purpose-built, high-quality bedrooms and bathrooms provide plenty of welcome extras, and are located in a stylish block adjacent to the main building. Dinner here should not be missed, with a varied selection of carefully prepared ingredients used in the dishes, including the daily specials.

Rooms 6 annexe en suite (6 GF) **Facilities** FTV tea/coffee Dinner available Direct Dial WiFi **Parking** 20 **Notes** LB ⊗ Closed 25 Dec

CALNE
Map 4 ST97

The White Horse
★★★★ @ ≗ INN

tel: 01249 813118 **Compton Bassett SN11 8RG**
email: info@whitehorse-comptonbassett.co.uk
web: www.whitehorse-comptonbassett.co.uk
dir: M4 junct 16 onto A3102, after Hilmarton village turn left to Compton Bassett

Nestled in the Wiltshire countryside, this free house offers a warm welcome and remains part of the local community. Inside the pub there is a modern, comfortable restaurant where high-quality food is served at breakfast, lunch and dinner. Bedrooms are located externally to the rear and offer individually styled accommodation.

Rooms 8 annexe en suite (3 fmly) (6 GF) **Facilities** FTV DVD tea/coffee Dinner available WiFi Boules **Extras** Home-made cookies, crisps, bottled water - free **Parking** 40

The Lansdowne
★★★ INN

tel: 01249 812488 **fax:** 01249 815323 **The Strand SN11 0EH**
email: lansdowne@arkells.com **web:** www.lansdownestrand.co.uk

Situated in a picturesque market town, The Lansdowne was built in the 16th century as a coaching inn, and it still retains much of the charm and character of that era. Bedrooms are spacious and furnished in a traditional style. Guests can enjoy dinner in the pleasant bistro, in either of the bar areas, or choose from a varied room-service menu. An outdoor courtyard seating area is also available.

Rooms 21 en suite 4 annexe en suite (2 fmly) S £40-£55; D £65-£85* **Facilities** FTV tea/coffee Dinner available WiFi 🔒 **Conf** Max 50 Thtr 45 Class 45 Board 50

CASTLE COMBE
Map 4 ST87

Fosse Farmhouse Chambre d'Hote
★★★★ BED AND BREAKFAST

tel: 01249 782286 **fax:** 01249 783066 **Nettleton Shrub SN14 7NJ**
email: caroncooper@fossefarmhouse.com **web:** www.fossefarmhouse.com
dir: 1.5m N from Castle Combe on B4039, left at Gib, 1m on right

Set in quiet countryside not far from Castle Combe, this bed and breakfast has well-equipped bedrooms decorated in keeping with its 18th-century origins. Excellent dinners are served in the farmhouse, and cream teas can be enjoyed in the old stables or the delightful garden.

Rooms 2 en suite (1 fmly) S £85-£95; D £95-£135* **Facilities** FTV DVD Lounge tea/coffee Dinner available Licensed WiFi 🔒 Badminton & ping pong in garden **Extras** Speciality toiletries, bottled water, flowers **Conf** Max 15 Thtr 10 Class 10 Board 10 **Parking** 12 **Notes** LB

CHIPPENHAM
Map 4 ST97

The Old Rectory
★★★★ BED AND BREAKFAST

tel: 01249 730335 & 07824 377321 **fax:** 01249 730166 **Cantax Hill, Lacock SN15 2JZ**
email: sexton@oldrectorylacock.co.uk **web:** www.oldrectorylacock.co.uk
dir: M4 junct 17 onto A350, around Chippenham. After 6m, turn left at double set of lights. Old Rectory 1st on right

Located in the historic village of Lacock and ideal for visiting Lacock Abbey and other National Trust properties in rural Wiltshire. Family run, offering comfortable accommodation in a peaceful setting, The Old Rectory itself is a fine example of Gothic architecture dating back to 1866. Breakfast is served in the large dining room overlooking the orchard. A warm welcome is assured

Rooms 6 rms (4 en suite) (2 pri facs) (2 fmly) (1 GF) S £50-£60; D £80-£95* **Facilities** FTV TVL tea/coffee WiFi ⬇ 🔒 18 🔒 **Extras** Speciality toiletries, water - complimentary **Conf** Max 20 Board 20 **Parking** 7 **Notes** LB ⊗ No Children 5yrs Closed 24-29 Dec

Diana Lodge Bed & Breakfast
★★★ BED AND BREAKFAST

tel: 01249 650306 **Grathie Cottage, 72 Marshfield Rd SN15 1JR**
email: diana.lodge@talktalk.net **web:** www.dianalodgebedandbreakfast.co.uk
dir: 500yds NW of town centre on A420, into West End Club car park

A cheerful welcome awaits at Diana Lodge Bed & Breakfast, a late 19th-century cottage that is within walking distance of the town centre and the railway station. The comfortable bedrooms are well appointed, and adjacent parking is available.

Rooms 5 rms (3 en suite) (2 pri facs) (1 fmly) (2 GF) **Facilities** FTV tea/coffee WiFi **Parking** 1 **Notes** ⊗

COLLINGBOURNE KINGSTON
Map 5 SU25

Manor Farm B&B (SU238556)
★★★★ FARMHOUSE

tel: 01264 850859 **SN8 3SD**
email: stay@manorfm.com **web:** www.manorfm.com
dir: Opposite church in centre of village

An attractive, Grade II listed farmhouse with comfortable and spacious rooms on a working family farm. Manor Farm is the ideal base from which to explore the surrounding countryside by walking or cycling directly from the farm. All rooms have been individually appointed and offer a range of practical amenities. Sumptuous traditional, vegetarian and special diet breakfasts are served at the communal table in the dining room.

Rooms 3 rms (2 en suite) (1 pri facs) (2 fmly) S £45-£60; D £70-£85 **Facilities** FTV tea/coffee WiFi 🔒 **Extras** Speciality toiletries, bottled water - free **Parking** 6 **Notes** LB ⊗ No Children 8yrs 550 acres arable

CORSHAM
Map 4 ST87

The Methuen Arms
★★★★★ ◉ ◉ INN

tel: 01249 717060 **2 High St SN13 0HB**
email: info@themethuenarms.com web: www.themethuenarms.com
dir: *M4 junct 17, A350 towards Chippenham, at rdbt take A4 towards Bath. 1m after lights, at next rdbt sharp left into Pickwick Rd, establishment 0.5m on left*

This well-established inn, in the centre of the thriving town of Corsham, provides very high levels of quality and comfort. The bedrooms are modern and stylish with large comfortable beds and spacious, well-equipped bathrooms. Guests can enjoy a drink in the relaxing bar, a light snack in the day or evening, and should not miss the carefully prepared, award-winning dishes at dinner.

Rooms 14 en suite (3 fmly) S £85-£125; D £100-£175* **Facilities** FTV tea/coffee Dinner available WiFi ⚓ 18 **Extras** Speciality toiletries, digital radios **Conf** Max 60 Thtr 50 Board 14 **Parking** 50

Pickwick Lodge Farm B&B *(ST857708)*
★★★★ ⌂ FARMHOUSE

tel: 01249 712207 **Guyers Ln SN13 0PS**
email: bandb@pickwickfarm.co.uk web: www.pickwickfarm.co.uk
dir: *Exit A4, Bath side of Corsham, into Guyers Ln, farmhouse at end on right*

This Grade II listed, 17th-century farmhouse is peacefully located on a 300-acre beef and arable farm, within easy reach of Bath. The spacious bedrooms are well equipped with modern facilities and many thoughtful extras. A hearty breakfast, using the best local produce, is served at a communal table in the dining room.

Rooms 3 rms (2 en suite) (1 pri facs) **Facilities** FTV TVL tea/coffee WiFi Fishing ⚓ **Extras** Speciality toiletries, fruit, home-made cake **Parking** 6 **Notes** LB ⊗ No Children 12yrs 300 acres arable/beef

CRICKLADE
Map 5 SU09

The Red Lion Inn
★★★★ ◉ ⌂ INN

tel: 01793 750776 **74 High St SN6 6DD**
email: info@theredlioncricklade.co.uk web: www.theredlioncricklade.co.uk
dir: *Off A419*

This historic pub is proud to feature real ales from its very own microbrewery on site along with ciders and other guest ales. A range of menu options are available from pub classics to modern British dishes. There are five spacious en suite bedrooms, all designed individually and providing a high level of quality and comfort. Dogs are welcome in some of the accommodation.

Rooms 5 annexe en suite (2 GF) S £80-£90; D £80-£90* **Facilities** FTV DVD iPod docking station tea/coffee Dinner available WiFi ⚓ **Notes** No coaches

DEVIZES
Map 4 SU06

Blounts Court Farm
★★★★★ ⌂ BED AND BREAKFAST

tel: 01380 727180 **Coxhill Ln, Potterne SN10 5PH**
email: carys@blountscourtfarm.co.uk web: www.blountscourtfarm.co.uk
dir: *A360 to Potterne, into Coxhill Ln opposite George & Dragon, at fork turn left, follow drive uphill to farmhouse*

A warm welcome is assured at this peacefully located, delightful arable farm, overlooking the village cricket field. The character barn has been converted to provide three attractive bedrooms on the ground floor - one has a four-poster bed. The elegant decor is in keeping with the character of the house. Breakfast, which features home-made and local produce, is served in the farmhouse dining room.

Rooms 3 en suite (3 GF) S £50-£55; D £75-£86* **Facilities** FTV DVD iPod docking station TVL tea/coffee WiFi ⚓ **Extras** Speciality toiletries **Parking** 5 **Notes** ⊗ No Children 8yrs

Avalon Lodge
★★★★ ⌂ BED AND BREAKFAST

tel: 01380 728189 fax: 08723 520921 **Devizes Rd, Rowde SN10 2LU**
email: stay@avalonlodge.co.uk web: www.avalonlodge.co.uk
dir: *1m from Devizes on A342. On left*

Avalon Lodge, located on the outskirts of Devizes, offers a great base for visiting a host of local historical sites. Expect a very warm welcome from owners Nick and Jenny. Rooms are individually decorated, offering very good levels of comfort, with lots of thoughtful extras provided.

Rooms 3 en suite S £50-£65; D £70-£85* **Facilities** FTV DVD iPod docking station Lounge tea/coffee Dinner available Licensed WiFi ⚓ **Extras** Fresh milk - complimentary; snacks - chargeable **Parking** 6 **Notes** LB ⊗ No Children 12yrs

Glebe House
★★★★ ⌂ BED AND BREAKFAST

tel: 01380 850864 & 07767 608841 **Chittoe SN15 2EL**
email: ginnyscrope@gmail.com web: www.glebehouse-chittoe.co.uk
dir: *Off A342 to Chittoe & Spye Park Ln, over x-rds, 2nd on left*

Located in the quiet and rural location of Chittoe, and close to attractions such as Avebury, Bath and Stonehenge, Glebe House offers comfortable accommodation in quiet surroundings. Both breakfast and dinner are available, and ingredients are all locally sourced where possible. A warm welcome will certainly be received by Ginny and her friendly dogs.

Rooms 3 rms (2 en suite) (1 pri facs) (1 GF) S £50-£60; D £85-£95 **Facilities** TVL tea/coffee Dinner available WiFi ⚓ **Parking** 4 **Notes** LB

Rosemundy Cottage Bed and Breakfast

★★★★ 🏠 BED AND BREAKFAST

tel: 01380 727122 **fax:** 01380 720495 **London Rd SN10 2DS**
email: info@rosemundycottage.co.uk **web:** www.rosemundycottage.co.uk
dir: *A361, pass old Barracks, at rdbt continue over. 300yds, after pedestrian crossing turn left into lane between two brick walls, Rosemundy Cottage faces canal*

Rosemundy Cottage is the ideal base for exploring Devizes and the surrounding area. All rooms are en suite and offer comfort and practical amenities. The lounge is the perfect venue in which to relax, and the award-winning breakfast is served at individual tables in the dining room. Parking is available.

Rooms 4 en suite (1 fmly) (1 GF) S £42.50–£45; D £72–£75* **Facilities** FTV DVD TVL tea/coffee WiFi ⬥ 🔒 **Extras** Trouser press, safe, speciality toiletries **Parking** 4 **Notes** ⊗

Vine Cottage Bed & Breakfast

★★★★ 🏠 BED AND BREAKFAST

tel: 01380 728360 & 07501 504948 **26 Bunnies Ln, Rowde SN10 2QB**
email: vinecottagebb@btinternet.com **web:** www.vinecottagebb.co.uk
dir: *2m from town centre on A342, signed Chippenham. At George & Dragon pub take 2nd left into Bunnies Ln*

Vine Cottage is located in the quiet village of Rowde and is a good base for exploring the Wiltshire countryside. All rooms offer comfortable accommodation and are well equipped. The award-winning breakfast is served at the communal table in the cosy breakfast room. Parking available.

Rooms 3 en suite (1 fmly) (1 GF) S £50–£65; D £70–£95* **Facilities** FTV DVD Lounge tea/coffee WiFi Sauna 🔒 **Extras** Speciality toiletries, robes, bottled water, fruit **Parking** 4 **Notes** ⊗

EDINGTON   Map 4 ST95

Premier Collection

The Three Daggers

★★★★★ 🍴 INN

tel: 01380 830940 **Westbury Rd BA13 4PG**
email: hello@threedaggers.co.uk **web:** www.threedaggers.co.uk
dir: *A36 towards Warminster, A350 to Westbury, B3098 to Edington*

Stylishly refurbished to offer luxurious standards of quality and comfort throughout, The Three Daggers combines traditional hospitality with contemporary furnishings and decor. Bedrooms and bathrooms are in a range of shapes and sizes but all are appointed with high quality Egyptian cotton bedding, large shower heads and a generous range of welcome extras. The bar and dining area menus offer high quality, carefully prepared ingredients at both dinner and breakfast. A large lounge with a real fire and comfortable seating is also available to guests. The recently opened adjoining farm shop and brewery are further enhancements to any visit.

Rooms 3 rms (2 en suite) (1 pri facs) (1 fmly) S £85–£105; D £100–£165* **Facilities** FTV DVD iPod docking station TVL Dinner available WiFi Riding **Extras** Fruit, speciality toiletries, fresh flowers **Conf** Max 14 **Parking** 45 **Notes** LB

FONTHILL BISHOP   Map 4 ST93

The Riverbarn

★★★ 🍴 GUEST HOUSE

tel: 01747 820232 **SP3 5SF**
web: www.theriverbarn.org.uk
dir: *From Wincanton towards Amesbury on A303 take B3089, through Hindon to Fonthill Bishop. Property on right. Or from Amesbury on A303 left onto unclassified road after Wylye signed Fonthill Bishop. Property on left*

Surrounded by lawns stretching down to the river, The Riverbarn is the central hub of the village of Fonthill Bishop. Parts of the barn are 600 years old and it has operated as a business for the last 100 years. The annexe bedrooms are spacious and well appointed. The café-bar offers sumptuous cakes and cream teas, light lunches and evening meals.

Rooms 3 annexe en suite (3 GF) **Facilities** FTV DVD tea/coffee Dinner available Licensed WiFi 🔒 **Parking** 20 **Notes** ⊗ No Children 14yrs

FOXHAM   Map 4 ST97

The Foxham Inn

★★★★ 🍴 INN

tel: 01249 740665 **fax:** 0872 111 3867 **SN15 4NQ**
email: info@thefoxhaminn.co.uk **web:** www.thefoxhaminn.co.uk
dir: *Off B4069 between Sutton Benger & Lyneham*

The Foxham Inn is an unpretentious family-run country inn, which serves award-winning food, real ale and fine wines. The two rooms are well configured and have been completed to a very good standard, and both offer a range of amenities including free WiFi. The main restaurant is a versatile venue suitable for a range of different occasions.

Rooms 2 en suite S £65–£75; D £80–£95 **Facilities** FTV Lounge tea/coffee Dinner available WiFi Fishing Riding 🔒 **Conf** Max 40 Thtr 40 Class 40 Board 20 **Parking** 20 **Notes** Closed 2-14 Jan RS Mon No coaches

HEYTESBURY   Map 4 ST94

The Resting Post

★★★★ BED AND BREAKFAST

tel: 01985 840204 **fax:** 01985 840204 **67 High St BA12 0ED**
email: enquiries@therestingpost.co.uk **web:** www.therestingpost.co.uk
dir: *From A36 Warminster bypass rdbt into Heytesbury. Pass Red Lion & church on right, 200yds past church on right*

This Grade II listed building is located in the main High Street and was formerly the village Post Office. Bedrooms and bathrooms are all comfortably furnished and include some welcome extras. Parking is available on the main road outside although one private parking space is also available to the rear of the property. Two pubs are within a short stroll. Breakfast is served in the cosy dining room.

Rooms 3 en suite (1 fmly) S £50–£60; D £70–£80 **Facilities** FTV tea/coffee WiFi 🔒 **Notes** ⊗

HINDON
Map 4 ST93

The Lamb at Hindon
★★★★ ⊛ INN

tel: 01747 820573 **fax:** 01747 820605 **SP3 6DP**
email: info@thelambathindon.co.uk **web:** www.lambathindon.co.uk
dir: Off B3089 in village centre

This 17th-century coaching inn is in a pretty village within easy reach of Salisbury and Bath. It has been appointed in an eclectic style, and some of the well-equipped bedrooms have four-poster beds. Enjoyable, freshly prepared dishes are available at lunch and dinner in the restaurant or bar, where log fires provide a welcoming atmosphere on colder days.

Rooms 13 en suite 6 annexe en suite (1 fmly) (3 GF) D £95-£125* **Facilities** FTV tea/coffee Dinner available Direct Dial WiFi Boules court **Extras** Speciality toiletries **Conf** Max 40 Thtr 40 Class 16 Board 24 **Parking** 16 **Notes** LB

HORNINGSHAM
Map 4 ST84

The Bath Arms at Longleat
★★★★★ ⊛⊛ INN

tel: 01985 844308 **fax:** 01985 845187 **Longleat Estate BA12 7LY**
email: enquiries@batharms.co.uk **web:** www.batharms.co.uk
dir: In village, on Longleat Estate

Peacefully located at the edges of the Longleat Estate, the style of this delightful inn is perhaps best described as 'quirky luxury'. Bedrooms come in a variety of shapes and sizes; each individually decorated in a range of styles and designs. High-quality produce is used to prepare delicious, award-winning dinners which are served in the relaxed main restaurant.

Rooms 9 en suite 7 annexe en suite (9 fmly) (7 GF) **Facilities** FTV DVD Lounge tea/coffee Dinner available Direct Dial WiFi ⅃ 18 **Extras** Flavoured vodka - complimentary **Parking** 6

LOWER CHICKSGROVE
Map 4 ST92

Compasses Inn
★★★★ ⊛ INN

tel: 01722 714318 **fax:** 01722 714318 **SP3 6NB**
email: thecompasses@aol.com **web:** www.thecompassesinn.com
dir: Exit A30 signed Lower Chicksgrove, 1st left into Lagpond Ln, single-track lane to village

This charming 17th-century inn, within easy reach of Bath, Salisbury, Glastonbury and the Dorset coast, offers comfortable accommodation in a peaceful setting.

Carefully prepared dinners are enjoyed in the warm atmosphere of the bar-restaurant, while breakfast is served in a separate dining room.

Rooms 5 en suite (2 fmly) S £50-£65; D £65-£85 **Facilities** FTV iPod docking station tea/coffee Dinner available WiFi ⛫ **Conf** Max 16 Thtr 16 Class 16 Board 14 **Parking** 40 **Notes** LB Closed 25-26 Dec

MALMESBURY
Map 4 ST98

Kings Arms
★★★ INN

tel: 01666 823383 **29 High St SN16 9AA**

Located on Malmesbury high street, a stones throw from the Abbey. A traditional coaching inn split between either side of the original delivery passage. One side features a cosy bar, the ideal place to enjoy a pint of Arkell's ale, whilst the more contemporary restaurant and bar is perfect for dining and breakfast and is located opposite. Bedrooms are en suite and located above the main pub building or in the former coach house and stables at the rear. Owned by the Arkell's family brewers, a great range of traditionally brewed beers are available.

Rooms 12 en suite

MARLBOROUGH
Map 5 SU16

Premier Collection

Poulton Grange (SU194698)
★★★★★ ≘ FARMHOUSE

tel: 01672 516888 & 07786 958712 **Poulton Grange Farm Estate SN8 2LN**
email: sheppard@poultongrange.com **web:** www.poultongrange.com

The Marlborough Downs are the backdrop of Poulton Grange, a farmhouse that offers high-quality accommodation with all the modern amenities. The award-winning Aga-cooked breakfast is served either at the communal table in the family kitchen or in the formal dining room. Ample parking is available, as well as a Finnish-style, self-catering cottage.

Rooms 2 en suite S £75; D £120* **Facilities** FTV iPod docking station TVL tea/coffee WiFi ⛫ **Extras** Speciality toiletries, robes, fruit **Parking** 5 **Notes** LB ⊗ No Children 10yrs 450 acres arable/sheep

The Lamb Inn
★★★ ≘ INN

tel: 01672 512668 & 07885 275568 **fax:** 01672 512668 **The Parade SN8 1NE**
email: thelambinnmarlboro@fsmail.net **web:** www.thelambinnmarlborough.com
dir: From High St, right into The Parade, establishment 50yds on left

Located in a quiet area of Marlborough, yet just a couple of minutes from the bustle of the main street, this traditional inn provides a friendly welcome and relaxed ambience. Bedrooms vary in size and are located above the main inn, and in modernised stables adjacent to the pleasant rear garden. Dinner here is a highlight with a good selection of very well-cooked and presented dishes using fresh ingredients.

Rooms 3 en suite 3 annexe en suite (1 fmly) **Facilities** tea/coffee Dinner available WiFi ⅃ 18 ⛫ **Conf** Max 24 **Notes** No coaches

MELKSHAM
Map 4 ST96

The Conigre Rooms and Restaurant

★★★★ ⌂ GUEST ACCOMMODATION

tel: 01225 702229 **Semington Rd SN12 6BZ**
email: enquiries@theconigrehotel.co.uk

This family-run Grade II listed former farmhouse is only a short walk from Melksham, and within easy reach of Longleat, Lacock and the historic city of Bath. All rooms are en suite, individually decorated and comfortably furnished. Dinner is served Tuesday to Saturday and is not to be missed. Service is relaxed and friendly - a warm welcome is assured.

Rooms 8 en suite S £60-£65; D £79-£95* **Facilities** Dinner available

MERE
Map 4 ST83

Chetcombe House

★★★★ GUEST ACCOMMODATION

tel: 01747 860219 & 07983 389854   **fax:** 0872 113 8613 **Chetcombe Rd BA12 6AZ**
email: info@chetcombehouse.co.uk **web:** www.chetcombehouse.co.uk
dir: *From E on A303, exit at Mere, off slip road on left. From W, exit A303 at Stourhead & follow signs to Mere. Pass fire station on left, right into Chatcombe Rd. 6th house on right*

Chetcombe House is a delightful detached property on the outskirts of Mere, convenient for local pubs and restaurants and just a short drive from both Stourhead Gardens and Longleat. Bedrooms and bathrooms are comfortably furnished and include some welcome extras. There are pleasant surrounding gardens and plenty of off-street car parking. Breakfast utilises local quality produce and includes a fine range of options.

Rooms 5 en suite (1 fmly) S £50-£60; D £75-£85* **Facilities** Lounge tea/coffee WiFi ♨ **Extras** Speciality toiletries, home-made cakes/biscuits - free of charge **Parking** 8 **Notes** ⊗ Closed 20 Dec-3 Jan

PEWSEY
Map 5 SU15

Premier Collection

Red Lion Freehouse

★★★★★ ⊚⊚⊚ INN

tel: 01980 671124 **East Chisenbury SN9 6AQ**
email: enquiries@redlionfreehouse.com **web:** www.redlionfreehouse.com
dir: *A345 to Upavon, left at T-junct, right signed East Chisenbury*

The Red Lion Freehouse at East Chisenbury offers an interesting blend of sumptuous accommodation and food, yet it retains the informality and laidback atmosphere of a traditional pub. Each of the five rooms have been individually appointed and offer plenty of in-room amenities coupled with beautiful views of the surrounding countryside.

Rooms 5 en suite (1 fmly) (5 GF) S £130-£230; D £130-£230* **Facilities** FTV tea/coffee Dinner available WiFi ♨ 18 Fishing **Extras** Speciality toiletries, snacks, juice, robes **Parking** 5 **Notes** LB No coaches

RAMSBURY
Map 5 SU27

The Bell at Ramsbury

★★★★★ ⊚ INN

tel: 01672 520230 **The Square SN8 2PE**
email: thebell@thebellramsbury.com **web:** www.thebellramsbury.com
dir: *From Hungerford on B4192 towards Swindon. After 3.5m, left into Newton Rd. 1m on right*

Owned by the local Ramsbury Brewery, this inn offers excellent en suite accommodation. Various dining options are available; traditional pub classics served in the bar or garden for a relaxed experience, formal dining options in the restaurant, and also Café Bella (open daily) offering delicious cakes and much more.

Rooms 6 en suite 3 annexe en suite **Facilities** FTV tea/coffee Dinner available WiFi ♨ 18 ♨ **Conf** Max 8 Board 8 **Parking** 20 **Notes** Closed 25 Dec

REDLYNCH
Map 5 SU22

Rookseat B&B

★★★★ BED AND BREAKFAST

tel: 01725 512522 & 07748 550481 **Grove Ln SP5 2NR**
email: deanransome@btinternet.com **web:** www.rookseat.co.uk

Expect a friendly welcome at this family-run bed and breakfast situated in the quiet New Forest village of Redlynch, perfect for visiting Salisbury and Bournemouth. Comfortable bedrooms all have en suite shower rooms. A delicious breakfast with plenty of choice is served in the dining room.

Rooms 3 en suite **Facilities** FTV tea/coffee WiFi ♨ **Parking** 3 **Notes** ⊗ No Children 12yrs ⊜

ROWDE
Map 4 ST96

The George & Dragon

★★★★ ⊚⊚ RESTAURANT WITH ROOMS

tel: 01380 723053 **High St SN10 2PN**
email: thegandd@tiscali.co.uk **web:** www.thegeorgeanddragonrowde.co.uk
dir: *1.5m from Devizes on A350 towards Chippenham*

The George & Dragon dates back to the 14th century when it was a meeting house. Exposed beams, wooden floors, antique rugs and open fires create a warm atmosphere in the bar and restaurant. Bedrooms and bathrooms are very well decorated and equipped with some welcome extras. Dining in the bar or restaurant should not be missed, as local produce and fresh fish deliveries from Cornwall are offered on the daily-changing blackboard menu.

Rooms 3 rms (2 en suite) (1 pri facs) (1 fmly) D £75-£115* **Facilities** FTV DVD iPod docking station Lounge TVL tea/coffee Dinner available WiFi ♨ **Extras** Mini-bar, snacks - free of charge **Parking** 15 **Notes** No coaches

SALISBURY

Map 5 SU12

See also Amesbury

Websters

★★★★ GUEST HOUSE

tel: 01722 339779 **11 Hartington Rd SP2 7LG**
email: enquiries@websters-bed-breakfast.com **web:** www.websters-bed-breakfast.com
dir: *From city centre onto A360 (Devizes Rd), 1st turn on left*

A warm welcome is assured at this delightful property, located in a quiet cul-de-sac close to the city centre. The charming, well-presented bedrooms are equipped with numerous extras including broadband. There is one ground-floor room with easier access.

Rooms 5 en suite (1 GF) **Facilities** FTV TVL tea/coffee WiFi **Parking** 5 **Notes** ⊗ No Children 12yrs Closed 31 Dec & 1 Jan RS Xmas & New Year continental breakfast only at Xmas

Cricket Field House

★★★★ GUEST ACCOMMODATION

tel: 01722 322595 **fax:** 01722 444970 **Skew Bridge, Wilton Rd SP2 9NS**
email: cricketfieldcottage@btinternet.com **web:** www.cricketfieldhouse.co.uk
dir: *A36, 1m W of Salisbury, towards Wilton & Warminster*

A 19th-century gamekeeper's cottage in award-winning gardens overlooking the South Wiltshire Cricket Ground. Within walking distance of the city centre and railway station, Cricket Field House provides a high level of accommodation, hospitality and customer care.

Rooms 7 en suite 10 annexe en suite (10 GF) S £50-£75; D £95-£150* **Facilities** FTV tea/coffee Licensed WiFi 🔒 **Conf** Thtr 20 Class 14 Board 16 **Parking** 25 **Notes** ⊗ No Children 14yrs RS 24-26 Dec room only

Newton Farmhouse *(SU230223)*

★★★★ FARMHOUSE

tel: 01794 884416 **Southampton Rd SP5 2QL**
email: lizzie@newtonfarmhouse.com **web:** www.newtonfarmhouse.com

(For full entry see Whiteparish)

2 Park Lane

★★★★ GUEST ACCOMMODATION

tel: 01722 321001 **2 Park Ln SP1 3NP**
web: www.2parklane.co.uk

2 Park Lane is a stylish, family-run period property usefully located within walking distance of the city centre and its attractions. This Victorian house has been sympathetically modernised, with a contemporary feel enhancing the Victorian features. Light, airy rooms, comfortable beds and good off-road parking are available.

Rooms 6 en suite S £50-£65; D £60-£85 **Facilities** FTV tea/coffee WiFi **Parking** 6 **Notes** ⊗ No Children 6yrs

The Devizes Inn

★★★ INN

tel: 01722 327842 **53-55 Devizes Rd SP2 7LQ**
email: pennyburden1969@btinternet.com

The Devizes Inn is a community pub located on the edge of Salisbury and is popular with visitors and locals alike. The accommodation consists of soundly equipped rooms all located in the main house. The pub has a friendly atmosphere and offers a large drinks selection including beers and wines. Limited parking is also available.

Rooms 4 rms S £50-£100; D £65-£120* **Facilities** Dinner available

Old Mill

★★★ ⌂ INN

tel: 01722 327517 **fax:** 01722 333367 **Town Path SP2 8EU**
email: theoldmill@simonandsteve.com **web:** www.simonandsteve.com
dir: *A338 onto A3094, turn 3rd right*

Full of character, the Old Mill has an interesting history going back well over five hundred years. Located in tranquil water meadows, the medieval city of Salisbury is just a ten-minute walk along the footpath. Bedrooms come in a range of shapes and sizes and include two above the lively bar. Dinner here is a highlight; the carefully prepared dishes, utilising local produce, should suit all tastes.

Rooms 11 en suite **Facilities** FTV DVD tea/coffee Dinner available Direct Dial WiFi Fishing 🔒 **Extras** Bottled water - complimentary **Conf** Max 43 Class 43 Board 28 **Parking** 17

STOURTON

Map 4 ST73

Spread Eagle Inn

★★★★ ⌂ INN

tel: 01747 840587 **Church Lawn BA12 6QE**
email: enquiries@spreadeagleinn.com **web:** www.spreadeagleinn.com
dir: *0.5m W off B3092 at entrance to Stourhead Gardens*

Set in the beautiful grounds of Stourhead House with its Palladian temples, lakes and inspiring vistas, the Spread Eagle Inn is an impressive red-brick building with a good reputation for simple, honest and locally-sourced food. In the bedrooms, National Trust antiques sit side by side with modern comforts. The large Georgian windows, low ceilings and uneven floors add to the authentic atmosphere of this delightful place.

Rooms 5 en suite **Facilities** tea/coffee Dinner available Direct Dial WiFi **Conf** Max 30 Thtr 30 Board 20 **Notes** ⊗

Stourhead B&B

Ⓤ

tel: 01747 840002 & 07955 311577 **87/88 Church Lawn, Stourhead Gardens BA12 6QE**
email: bb@stourhead.org **web:** www.stourhead.org
dir: *From A303 exit signed B3092 (Mere), follow brown signs to Stourhead House & Gardens*

Currently the rating for this establishment is not confirmed. This may be due to a change of ownership or because it has only recently joined the AA rating scheme.

Rooms 2 rms (1 en suite) (1 pri facs) (2 fmly) S £70; D £95 **Facilities** STV FTV WiFi ⌕ 18 Fishing Riding **Parking** 2 **Notes** LB ⊗ ⌂

SWINDON Map 5 SU18

Sun Inn
★★★★ INN

tel: 01793 523292 **Coate SN3 6AA**

Located on the outskirts of Swindon adjacent to the popular Coate Water Country Park; featuring a large garden and children's play area with a thatched summer house. Accommodation has been recently completed suitable for both business and leisure guests, offering free WiFi throughout. A regularly-changing blackboard menu offers great dishes, well prepared and available throughout the day and evening. The popular Sunday lunch should not be missed. Owned by the Arkell's family brewers, a great range of traditionally brewed beers are available.

Rooms 10 en suite

The Angel
★★★★ INN

tel: 01793 851161 **47 High St, Royal Wootton Bassett SN4 7AQ**

Located on directly on the high street of the historic Royal Wootton Bassett, The Angel is the perfect place to stop; everything from morning coffee in the lounge, a drink at the bar or a bite in the popular restaurant. Public areas are intimate and comfortably furnished. Accommodation is located at the rear of the property in a purpose built wing overlooking the courtyard. Its location makes it ideal for both corporate guests and those exploring the local area. The property also includes a boardroom and larger function room.

Rooms 17 en suite

Ardecca
★★★★ GUEST ACCOMMODATION

tel: 01793 721238 & 07791 120826 **Fieldrise Farm, Kingsdown Ln, Blunsdon SN25 5DL**
email: chris-graham.ardecca@fsmail.net **web:** www.ardecca-bedandbreakfast.co.uk
dir: A419 onto B4019 to Blunsdon/Highworth, then into Turnpike Rd at Cold Harbour pub, left into Kingsdown Ln

Ardecca is quietly located in 16 acres of pastureland with easy access to Swindon and the Cotswolds. All bedrooms are on the ground floor and are well furnished and equipped. An especially friendly welcome is provided and arts and crafts workshops are available on site.

Rooms 4 rms (4 pri facs) (1 fmly) (4 GF) **Facilities** FTV tea/coffee WiFi Art & Crafts workshops **Conf** Class 16 **Parking** 5 **Notes** ⊗ No Children 6yrs ⊛

The Old Post Office Guest House
★★★★ GUEST HOUSE

tel: 01793 823114 **fax:** 01793 823441 **Thornhill Rd, South Marston SN3 4RY**
email: theoldpostofficeguesthouse@yahoo.co.uk
web: www.theoldpostofficeguesthouse.co.uk
dir: M4 junct 15, A419 signed Cirencester/Swindon (East), approx 3m, left onto A420 towards Oxford, at next rdbt 2nd exit into Merlin Way, 0.3m, at White Hart rdbt 3rd exit onto A420. At Gablecross rdbt follow South Marston signs

This attractive property is about two miles from Swindon. Guests are welcomed by the enthusiastic owner, a professional opera singer with a wonderful sense of humour. The comfortable bedrooms vary in size, and all are equipped with numerous facilities. An extensive choice is offered at breakfast, which is freshly cooked and uses the best local produce.

Rooms 5 en suite (1 fmly) **Facilities** STV tea/coffee WiFi **Parking** 6 **Notes** ⊗

Tawny Owl
★★★★ INN

tel: 01793 706770 **fax:** 01793 706785 **Queen Elizabeth Dr, Taw Hill SN25 1WR**
email: tawnyowl@arkells.com **web:** www.arkells.com
dir: 2.5m NW of town centre, signed from A419

Expect a genuinely friendly welcome from the staff at this modern inn on the north-west outskirts of Swindon. It has comfortable, well-equipped bedrooms and bathrooms. A varied selection of enjoyable home-cooked meals is on offer at both lunch and dinner together with a range of Arkell's ales and wines. A private function room is available.

Rooms 5 en suite (1 fmly) **Facilities** TVL tea/coffee Dinner available Direct Dial Stairlift **Conf** Max 55 Thtr 55 Class 55 Board 55 **Parking** 75 **Notes** ⊗ RS Xmas/New Year Civ Wed 50

Fairview Guest House
★★★ GUEST HOUSE

tel: 01793 852283 **52 Swindon Rd, Royal Wootton Bassett SN4 8EU**
email: fairviewguesthouse@hotmail.com **web:** www.fairviewguesthouse.com
dir: On A3102 to Royal Wootton Bassett. 1.25m from M4 junct 16. 5m from Swindon centre

A welcoming, family-run property with easy access to the M4 and Swindon. Bedrooms are split between the main house and the bungalow annexe, and breakfast is served in an open-plan dining-sitting room where an open fire blazes on cooler mornings.

Rooms 8 rms (3 en suite) 4 annexe rms 3 annexe en suite (1 pri facs) (2 fmly) (4 GF) S £32-£39.50; D £55-£65* **Facilities** FTV DVD Lounge TVL tea/coffee WiFi ⌨ **Parking** 14 **Notes** LB ⊗

Heart in Hand
★★★ INN

tel: 01793 721314 **fax:** 01793 727026 **43 High St, Blunsdon SN26 7AG**
email: leppardsteve@aol.com
dir: Exit A419 into High St, 200yds on right

Right in the village centre, this family-run inn offers a friendly welcome together with a wide selection of home-cooked food. Bedrooms are spacious, well equipped and offer a number of useful extras. A pleasant patio and rear garden with seating is also available.

Rooms 4 en suite (1 fmly) **Facilities** tea/coffee Dinner available **Parking** 17 **Notes** ⊗

Internos B&B
★★★ BED AND BREAKFAST

tel: 01793 721496 **fax:** 01793 721496 **3 Turnpike Rd, Blunsdon SN26 7EA**
web: www.internos-bedandbreakfast.co.uk
dir: 4m N of Swindon. Alongside A419 access from Cold Harbour End

Situated just off the A419, Internos B&B offers comfortable accommodation in a relaxed and informal atmosphere. The gardens open onto a field, which is a haven for wildlife. Guests can enjoy the freshly-cooked breakfasts, served in the dining room, and a cosy lounge is also available.

Rooms 3 rms (1 fmly) S £28-£35; D fr £48* **Facilities** FTV TVL tea/coffee WiFi **Parking** 6 **Notes** ⊗ ⊛

SWINDON *continued*

Saracens Head

★★ INN

tel: 01793 762284 **fax:** 01793 767869 **High St, Highworth SN6 7AG**
email: saracenshead@arkells.com **web:** www.arkells.com
dir: *5m NE of Swindon*

The Saracens Head stands on the main street of a pleasant market town, close to Swindon. It offers plenty of character, including a popular bar dating from 1828. A fine selection of real ales and home-cooked food are highlights. Bedrooms, which vary in size, are generally compact. A rear car park and a patio area are available.

Rooms 12 en suite (1 fmly) **Facilities** tea/coffee Dinner available WiFi **Conf** Max 10 Thtr 10 Class 10 Board 10 **Parking** 30

UPTON LOVELL	Map 4 ST94

Prince Leopold

U

tel: 01985 850460 **54 Upton Lovell BA12 0JP**
email: info@princeleopold.co.uk

Currently the rating for this establishment is not confirmed. This may be due to a change of ownership or because it has only recently joined the AA rating scheme.

Rooms 6 rms S £65-£75; D £75-£95*

WANBOROUGH	Map 5 SU28

The Harrow Inn

★★★ INN

tel: 01793 791792 **SN4 0AE**
email: info@theharrowwanborough.co.uk **web:** www.theharrowwanborough.co.uk

Steeped in history and with many original features retained this cosy inn provides a warm welcome. The three en suite bedrooms are set in the 'old forge' opposite the main pub and all have their own external entrance. Hearty meals using much locally sourced produce are available daily.

Rooms 3 annexe en suite (3 GF) **Facilities** FTV DVD tea/coffee Dinner available WiFi 🔒 **Parking** 50

WARMINSTER	Map 4 ST84

The Dove Inn

★★★★ 🏵 INN

tel: 01985 850109 **fax:** 01985 851041 **Corton BA12 0SZ**
email: info@thedove.co.uk **web:** www.thedove.co.uk
dir: *5m SE of Warminster. Exit A36 to Corton*

Quietly located in the village of Corton, this traditional inn has undergone many changes and provides a friendly welcome, and plenty of quality and comfort. In addition to lighter options, a range of well-sourced, quality produce is used to create the enjoyable dinners served in the main restaurant. There is a choice of standard bedrooms adjacent to the inn, and two more luxurious rooms in a cottage appointed to high standards.

Rooms 1 en suite 12 annexe en suite (1 fmly) (6 GF) S £80-£100; D £90-£140*
Facilities STV FTV tea/coffee Dinner available WiFi 🔒 **Extras** Speciality toiletries, mineral water **Parking** 24 **Notes** LB

Home Farm B&B (ST893442)

★★★★ FARMHOUSE

tel: 01985 213266 & 07831 311846 **221 Boreham Rd, Boreham BA12 9HF**
email: theleggs221@aol.com **web:** www.homefarmboreham.com
dir: *A36 from Salisbury, at Cotley Hill rdbt onto B3414 towards Warminster. 1.5m on right, pass 30mph limit sign*

This charming farmhouse was built in the 1830s, and is situated on the edge of Warminster and the Wylye valley, making it an ideal base for a visit to Longleat. All rooms are on the first floor of the main house and are comfortably furnished and equipped. The dining room is also available as a guest lounge where freshly cooked breakfasts utilising local produce are served.

Rooms 3 en suite (1 fmly) (1 GF) **Facilities** FTV Lounge tea/coffee WiFi 🔒 **Parking** 20 **Notes** LB ⊗ No Children 2yrs 100 acres mixed

WEST GRAFTON	Map 5 SU26

Mayfield Bed & Breakfast

★★★★ 🛏 BED AND BREAKFAST

tel: 01672 810339 & 07771 996811 **fax:** 01672 811158 **SN8 3BY**
email: countess.an@virgin.net **web:** www.mayfieldbandb.com
dir: *M4 junct 14 onto A338, through Hungerford. Turn left to West Grafton, 300mtrs on right*

This 15th-century, cosy bed and breakfast is located in a quiet hamlet just seven miles from the famous market town of Marlborough. Bedrooms are comfortable with many thoughtful extras. Hearty breakfasts consisting of much home-made produce is served around a family-style table.

Rooms 4 rms (2 en suite) (2 fmly) S £55-£70; D £80-£100* **Facilities** STV FTV TVL tea/coffee Dinner available WiFi ⛷ 🏂 🔒 **Extras** Fruit, snacks - complimentary **Parking** 8 **Notes** ⊗ Closed Xmas

WHITEPARISH	Map 5 SU22

Newton Farmhouse (SU230223)

★★★★ FARMHOUSE

tel: 01794 884416 **Southampton Rd SP5 2QL**
email: lizzie@newtonfarmhouse.com **web:** www.newtonfarmhouse.com
dir: *7m SE of Salisbury on A36, 1m S of A27 junct*

Dating back to the 16th century, this delightful farmhouse was gifted to Lord Nelson's family as part of the Trafalgar estate. The house has comfortable bedrooms, most with four-poster beds, and all adorned with personal touches. Delicious breakfasts are available in the relaxing conservatory. The pleasant gardens include an outdoor swimming pool.

Rooms 6 en suite 2 annexe en suite (3 fmly) (4 GF) **Facilities** FTV DVD TVL tea/coffee WiFi ⛷ 🏂 🔒 **Extras** Speciality toiletries, sweets **Parking** 8 **Notes** LB ⊗ 2.5 acres non-working

WOODFALLS	Map 5 SU12

The Woodfalls Inn

★★★ INN

tel: 01725 513222 **The Ridge SP5 2LN**
email: enquiries@woodfallsinn.co.uk

The Woodfalls Inn has been offering rest and relaxation to travellers for many a decade, a tradition that is just as strong today. Situated close to the New Forest, it is an ideal base from which to explore this beautiful area. Bedrooms have everything necessary to ensure a comfortable stay, while public areas have charm and character. The menu offers a range of interesting and flavoursome dishes served in the light and airy conservatory restaurant.

Rooms 9 rms

ZEALS   Map 4 ST73

Cornerways Cottage

★★★★ BED AND BREAKFAST

tel: 01747 840477 **Longcross BA12 6LL**
email: cornerways.cottage@btinternet.com **web:** www.cornerwayscottage.co.uk
dir: *A303 onto B3092 signed Stourhead. At bottom of slip road, right under bridge, follow signs for Zeals. On left by 40mph sign*

A warm friendly welcome, comfortable rooms and hearty breakfasts await in Cornerways Cottage, a charming 250-year-old stone building. Situated right on the borders of Somerset, Dorset and Wiltshire it is ideal for visiting Longleat, Stourhead House and Gardens. Horseriding, fishing, the Wiltshire Cycleway and plenty of great walks are all on the doorstep.

Rooms 3 rms (2 en suite) (1 pri facs) S £50-£60; D £65-£70 **Facilities** FTV Lounge TVL tea/coffee WiFi ⌘ 9 ⚓ **Extras** Speciality toiletries, bottled water **Parking** 10 **Notes** ⊗ No Children Closed Xmas & New Year

WORCESTERSHIRE

ALVECHURCH   Map 10 SP07

Alcott Farm (SP056739)

★★★ Ⓐ FARMHOUSE

tel: 01564 824051 **fax:** 01564 829799 **Icknield St, Weatheroak B48 7EH**
email: alcottfarm@btinternet.com **web:** www.alcottfarm.co.uk
dir: *2m NE of Alvechurch. M42 junct 3, A435 for Birmingham, left signed Weatheroak, left at x-rds down steep hill, left opposite pub, farm 0.5m on right up long driveway*

Located in a peaceful rural setting, this house dates from the 18th century and works have resulted in homely bedrooms complemented by efficient modern bathrooms. Breakfast is taken at one family table in the attractive open-plan kitchen, overlooking a terrace with a pond which is teeming with koi carp.

Rooms 4 en suite (1 GF) **Facilities** FTV TVL tea/coffee WiFi Fishing **Parking** 20 **Notes** No Children 10yrs 66 acres horses

ASTWOOD BANK   Map 10 SP06

Corner Cottage

★★★ BED AND BREAKFAST

tel: 01527 459122 & 07917 582884 **fax:** 01527 459122 **1194 Evesham Rd B96 6AA**
email: marilyn_alan1194@hotmail.co.uk **web:** www.corner-cottagebb.co.uk
dir: *A441 through Astwood Bank, Corner Cottage at lights*

A warm welcome awaits you at Corner Cottage, a beautiful Victorian cottage set in a delightful village location within walking distance of pubs, shops and restaurants. Convenient for Stratford-upon-Avon, Evesham, Warwick, Birmingham and Worcester.

Rooms 3 rms (2 en suite) (1 pri facs) S £40; D £55-£60* **Facilities** FTV TVL tea/coffee WiFi ⚓ **Notes** LB ⊗ ⊗ 🍽

BECKFORD   Map 10 SO93

The Beckford Inn

★★★★ INN

tel: 01386 881532 **Cheltenham Rd GL20 7AN**
email: enquiries@thebeckford.com **web:** www.thebeckford.com
dir: *M5 junct 9, A46 towards Evesham, inn on left*

Looking more like a country mansion than a typical inn, this is a superb Cotswold stone building with 18th-century origins. Comfortable accommodation is provided and there's a good range of choices at dinner and breakfast; a snug is available with a widescreen TV. The Beckford is a good venue for parties, weddings or conferences. There is ample parking and disabled access.

Rooms 8 en suite 2 annexe en suite (2 fmly) S fr £75; D fr £90 **Facilities** FTV DVD iPod docking station tea/coffee Dinner available WiFi **Conf** Max 100 Thtr 100 Class 60 Board 100 **Parking** 70 **Notes** LB Civ Wed 60

BEWDLEY   Map 10 SO77

Premier Collection

Kateshill House

★★★★★ 🏠 GUEST ACCOMMODATION

tel: 01299 401563 **Red Hill DY12 2DR**
email: info@kateshillhouse.co.uk **web:** www.kateshillhouse.co.uk
dir: *A456 onto B4195 signed Bewdley. Bear left over bridge, 1st left into Severnside South. Right into Lax Ln, at T-junct turn left, up hill on right*

A very warm welcome awaits at Kateshill House, a Georgian manor house overlooking Bewdley. Two acres of landscaped gardens provide a dramatic backdrop to the house, as well as fruit for breakfasts and home-made jams. The elegant bedrooms are individually styled, sumptuously decorated with rich fabrics and period furniture, and equipped with a wealth of amenities for guests' use. Small private functions are also catered for.

Rooms 7 en suite S £65-£70; D £85-£100* **Facilities** FTV Lounge TVL tea/coffee WiFi ⚓ **Parking** 10 **Notes** LB ⊗

Premier Collection

Number Thirty

★★★★★ BED AND BREAKFAST

tel: 01299 402404 **30 Gardners Meadow DY12 2DG**
email: info@numberthirty.net **web:** www.numberthirty.net
dir: *From A456 take B4195 (Stourport Rd) signed Bewdley. Bear left, over Bewdley Bridge (Load St). 1st left into Severnside South, 2nd right into Gardners Meadow*

Number Thirty is a smart, modern house, just a short stroll from the River Severn and the Georgian town centre. Bedrooms are luxuriously furnished and have lots of thoughtful extras. Comprehensive breakfasts are taken in an attractive dining room that overlooks the immaculate gardens and cricket ground; guests can enjoy watching a game from a raised sun deck. A sumptuous guest lounge is also available.

Rooms 3 en suite S fr £60; D fr £80* **Facilities** STV DVD iPod docking station Lounge TVL tea/coffee WiFi ⌘ 18 ⚓ **Extras** Sherry, sweets - complimentary; robes **Parking** 6 **Notes** ⊗ No Children 10yrs 🍽

BEWDLEY *continued*

The Mug House Inn

★★★★ INN

tel: 01299 402543 **12 Severnside North DY12 2EE**
email: drew@mughousebewdley.co.uk **web:** www.mughousebewdley.co.uk
dir: *In town centre on riverfront*

Located on the opposite side of the River Severn to Bewdley Rowing Club, this 18th-century inn combines high standards of comfort and facilities with many original features. Bedrooms are thoughtfully furnished, there is a separate breakfast room, and imaginative dinners are served in the restaurant.

Rooms 4 en suite 3 annexe en suite (1 GF) S £67-£87; D £77-£97* **Facilities** FTV tea/coffee Dinner available WiFi **Notes** No Children 10yrs No coaches

Royal Forester Country Inn

★★★★ INN

tel: 01299 266286 **Callow Hill DY14 9XW**
email: royalforesterinn@btinternet.com **web:** www.royalforesterinn.co.uk

Located opposite the Wyre Forest on the town's outskirts, this inn dates back to 1411 and has been sympathetically restored to provide high standards of comfort. Stylish modern bedrooms are complemented by smart bathrooms, and equipped with many thoughtful extras. Decor styles throughout the public areas highlight the many period features, and the restaurant serves imaginative food featuring locally sourced produce.

Rooms 7 en suite (2 fmly) **Facilities** STV FTV tea/coffee Dinner available WiFi **Parking** 40 **Notes** LB No coaches

Welchgate Guest House

★★★★ GUEST HOUSE

tel: 01299 402655 **1 Welch Gate DY12 2AT**
email: info@welchgate-guesthouse.co.uk **web:** www.welchgate-guesthouse.co.uk

Welchgate Guest House is a 400-year-old former inn providing modern comfort and good facilities. Bedrooms are equipped with fine furnishings and thoughtful extras, and have smart, modern en suite shower rooms. Hearty breakfasts are taken in a rustic-look café, which is also open to the public during the day.

Rooms 4 en suite **Facilities** tea/coffee Licensed WiFi ✆ **Notes** LB ⊗ No Children

Bank House

★★★ BED AND BREAKFAST

tel: 01299 402652 **14 Lower Park DY12 2DP**
email: fleur.nightingale@virgin.net **web:** www.bewdley-accommodation.co.uk
dir: *In town centre. From junct High St & Lax Ln, Bank House after junct on left*

Once a private bank, this Victorian house retains many original features and offers comfortable accommodation. The cosy dining room is the setting for tasty English breakfasts served at one family table. Owner Mrs Nightingale has a comprehensive knowledge of the town and its history. AA Friendliest B&B of the Year Finalist 2014-2015.

Rooms 4 rms (1 fmly) S £36-£39; D £60-£64* **Facilities** FTV tea/coffee WiFi ✆ **Parking** 2 **Notes** ⊗ Closed 24-26 Dec 🐾

Woodcolliers Arms

★★★ INN

tel: 01299 400589 **fax:** 01299 488490 **76 Welch Gate DY12 2AU**
email: roger@woodcolliers.co.uk **web:** www.woodcolliers.co.uk
dir: *Exit A456, follow road behind church, left into Welch Gate (B4190)*

Dating from before 1780, the Woodcolliers Arms is a family-run establishment located in the renowned Georgian town of Bewdley. This is a traditional inn offering an interesting menu with both British pub food favourites and a speciality Russian menu. Accommodation is comfortable and rooms are well equipped.

Rooms 5 rms (4 en suite) (1 pri facs) S £30-£48; D £50-£66 (room only)* **Facilities** FTV DVD tea/coffee Dinner available WiFi ✆ **Parking** 2 **Notes** LB ⊗ No Children 12yrs

---

BROADWAY   Map 10 SP03

Premier Collection

Abbots Grange

★★★★★ 🏠 GUEST HOUSE

tel: 020 8133 8698 **Church St WR12 7AE**
email: rooms@abbotsgrange.com **web:** www.abbotsgrange.com
dir: *M5 junct 9 follow signs to Evesham & Broadway*

A warm welcome awaits at Abbots Grange, a 14th-century monastic manor house believed to be the oldest dwelling in Broadway. A Grade II listed building, it stands proudly in eight acres of grounds. The bedrooms are luxurious and comprise twin and four-poster suites. Among the thoughtful extras in the rooms are fruit bowls and a selection of alcoholic drinks. The stunning medieval Great Hall is the guests' lounge and makes a romantic setting with its log fire and candles. Tea and cake is offered on arrival, and quality breakfasts are served at the large communal table in the wood-panelled dining room. Abbots Grange has a tennis court and croquet lawn along with a helicopter landing pad.

Rooms 4 rms (3 en suite) (1 pri facs) S £150-£175; D £150-£175* **Facilities** STV FTV DVD iPod docking station Lounge tea/coffee WiFi 🍵 🍽 🔒 **Extras** Port, whisky, sherry, soft drinks, mineral water **Conf** Board 10 **Parking** 8 **Notes** ⊗ No Children 6yrs

East House

⭐⭐⭐⭐⭐ 🏠 GUEST ACCOMMODATION

tel: 01386 853789 & 07738 290855 **162 High St WR12 7AJ**
email: enquiries@easthouseuk.com **web:** www.easthouseuk.com
dir: *M40 junct 8 then A44 to Broadway, left at mini rdbt to Upper High Street. 600mtrs on left*

East House is a fine house, located in a quiet residential area of Broadway. Day rooms include an elegant reception room with open fire, a drawing room with grand piano and a cosy breakfast room where memorable breakfasts are served. Individually furnished bedrooms, equipped with many thoughtful extras, are decorated and furnished in keeping with the rest of the house. Off-road parking is a bonus.

Rooms 4 en suite D £165-£195 **Facilities** FTV DVD iPod docking station Lounge tea/coffee WiFi 🔒 Table tennis Treadmill **Extras** Speciality toiletries **Parking** 7 **Notes** ⊗ No Children 18yrs

Mill Hay House

⭐⭐⭐⭐⭐ 🏠 GUEST ACCOMMODATION

tel: 01386 852498 **Snowshill Rd WR12 7JS**
email: info@millhay.co.uk **web:** www.millhay.co.uk
dir: *0.7m S of Broadway towards Snowshill, house on right*

Set in three acres of immaculate grounds beside a medieval watermill, this impressive early 18th-century stone house has many original features complemented by quality decor, period furniture and works of art. The spacious bedrooms are filled with thoughtful extras and one has a balcony. Imaginative breakfasts are served in the elegant dining room, and there is a spacious drawing room.

Rooms 3 en suite S £135-£210; D £155-£230* **Facilities** FTV TVL tea/coffee Direct Dial WiFi 🔒 **Extras** Mineral water - complimentary **Parking** 15 **Notes** LB ⊗ No Children 12yrs

Russell's

⭐⭐⭐⭐⭐ ⓦ 🍴 RESTAURANT WITH ROOMS

tel: 01386 853555 **fax:** 01386 853964 **20 High St WR12 7DT**
email: info@russellsofbroadway.co.uk **web:** www.russellsofbroadway.co.uk
dir: *Opposite village green*

Situated in the centre of picturesque Broadway, this restaurant with rooms makes a great base for exploring local attractions. The superbly appointed bedrooms, each with its own character, have air conditioning and a wide range of extras. The cuisine is a real draw here with skilful use made of freshly-prepared, local produce.

Rooms 4 en suite 3 annexe en suite (4 fmly) (2 GF) S £98-£275; D £115-£300* **Facilities** FTV DVD iPod docking station tea/coffee Dinner available Direct Dial WiFi **Conf** Max 12 Board 12 **Parking** 16 **Notes** No coaches

Bowers Hill Farm (SP086420)

⭐⭐⭐⭐ FARMHOUSE

tel: 01386 834585 & 07966 171861 **Bowers Hill, Willersey WR11 7HG**
email: sarah@bowershillfarm.com **web:** www.bowershillfarm.com
dir: *3m NW of Broadway. A44 onto B4632 to Willersey, at mini rdbt signs to Badsey & Willersey Industrial Estate, farm 2m on right by post box*

An impressive Victorian house set in immaculate gardens on a diverse farm, where point-to-point horses are bred. The house provides very comfortable bedrooms with modern bathrooms. Breakfast is served in the elegant dining room or the magnificent conservatory, and a lounge, with an open fire, is available to guests.

Rooms 3 en suite (1 fmly) S £55-£65; D £70-£85* **Facilities** FTV DVD Lounge TVL tea/coffee WiFi 🔒 **Conf** Max 8 Class 8 Board 8 **Parking** 6 **Notes** LB ⊗ 98 acres horse breeding/grassland

Cowley House

★★★★ GUEST ACCOMMODATION

tel: 01386 858148 **Church St WR12 7AE**
email: joan.peter@cowleyhouse-broadway.co.uk **web:** www.cowleyhouse-broadway.co.uk
dir: *Follow signs for Broadway. Church St adjacent to village green, 3rd on left*

A warm welcome is assured at this 18th-century Cotswold-stone house, just a stroll from the village green. Fine period furniture enhances the interior, and the elegant hall has a polished flagstone floor. Tastefully equipped bedrooms include thoughtful extras and smart modern shower rooms. Comprehensive breakfasts feature local produce.

Rooms 8 rms (7 en suite) (1 pri facs) (2 fmly) (2 GF) S £69-£96; D £79-£106* **Facilities** FTV TVL TV7B tea/coffee WiFi 🔒 **Parking** 8 **Notes** LB

BROADWAY *continued*

Horse & Hound

★★★★ INN

tel: 01386 852287 fax: 01386 853784 **54 High St WR12 7DT**
email: djttruesdale@msn.com web: www.horse-and-hound.co.uk
dir: *Off A46 to Evesham*

The Horse & Hound is at the heart of the beautiful Cotswold village of Broadway, and there are many areas of interest to visit within easy distance of this well-established inn. A warm welcome is guaranteed from hosts David and Diane whether dining in the inviting pub or staying overnight in one of the attractive and well-appointed bedrooms. Breakfast and dinner provide quality ingredients which are freshly prepared.

Rooms 4 en suite **Facilities** FTV tea/coffee Dinner available WiFi 🔒 **Parking** 15 **Notes** RS Winter

BROMSGROVE   Map 10 SO97

The Vernon

★★★★ ⊛ INN

tel: 01527 821236 fax: 01527 821137 **Droitwich Rd, Hanbury B60 4DB**
email: info@thevernonhanbury.com web: www.thevernonhanbury.com
dir: *M5 junct 5, A38 to Droitwich. Turn left into Bromsgrove Rd (B4065). Left into Hanbury Rd (B4090), opposite junction*

Situated in the rural parish of Hanbury close to Bromsgrove and Droitwich, The Vernon has undergone major renovation. This 18th-century property is sometimes known as the 'Birthplace of the Archers', because Godfrey Baseley, the original creator of the famous soap, was a regular. The inn boasts modern and comfortable accommodation, and fine dining can be enjoyed in the attractive restaurant.

Rooms 5 en suite S £65; D £85-£105* **Facilities** STV FTV Lounge TVL tea/coffee Dinner available Direct Dial WiFi **Parking** 74 **Notes** ⊗

Manor Hill House

★★★★ ⚑ BED AND BREAKFAST

tel: 01527 861200 **Manor Hill, Swan Ln, Upton Warren B61 9HE**
email: info@manorhillhouse.co.uk web: www.manorhillhouse.co.uk

A sweeping gravel drive leads up to the front door of Manor Hill House, the family home of Michael and Emma Moffett. The light and spacious rooms come complete with Egyptian cotton bed linen, complimentary hospitality trays and free WiFi, as well as some lovely views of the West Midlands countryside. The full English breakfast is served family style, and is prepared from mainly locally sourced produce. Manor Hill House is very popular as a wedding venue.

Rooms 5 en suite

EVESHAM   Map 10 SP04

South House Alpacas Bed & Breakfast

★★★★ BED AND BREAKFAST

tel: 01386 830848 & 07956 254990 **South House, Main St WR11 8TJ**
email: enquiry@southhousealpacas.com web: www.southhousealpacas.com
dir: *From Evesham take B4035 signed Badsey. In Badsey left onto B4085 signed Bidford. In South Littleton, house on right*

South House is a stunning Grade II listed property, located in a quiet Worcestershire village within easy reach of the Cotswolds and historic Stratford. Both spacious en

suite rooms are located in the eves of the former coach house. Guests are welcome to relax in the elegant drawing room in the main house. Aga-cooked breakfasts are washed down with home-pressed apple juice. A warm welcome is assured from the owners and friendly alpacas. Alpaca trekking is available by prior arrangement.

Rooms 2 annexe en suite D £110-£120* **Facilities** FTV TVL tea/coffee Dinner available WiFi ⚲ ☺ Gym ⚑ Alpaca trekking/feeding **Extras** Speciality toiletries, home-made biscuits **Conf** Max 14 Board 14 **Parking** 6 **Notes** ⊗ No Children 14yrs

FLYFORD FLAVELL   Map 10 SO95

The Boot Inn

★★★★ ⚌ INN

tel: 01386 462658 fax: 01386 462547 **Radford Rd WR7 4BS**
email: enquiries@thebootinn.com web: www.thebootinn.com
dir: *In village centre, signed from A422*

An inn has occupied this site since the 13th century, though The Boot itself dates from the Georgian period. Much historic charm remains in the pub, while the bedrooms, furnished in antique pine, are equipped with practical extras and have modern bathrooms. A range of ales, wines and imaginative food is offered in the cosy public areas, which include an attractive conservatory and patio.

Rooms 5 annexe en suite (2 GF) S £50-£60; D £65-£90* **Facilities** FTV DVD iPod docking station Lounge tea/coffee Dinner available WiFi ⚲ 27 Pool table **Parking** 30 **Notes** LB

HIMBLETON
Map 10 SO95

Phepson Farm

★★★★ ☰ GUEST ACCOMMODATION

tel: 01905 391205 **WR9 7JZ**
email: info@phepsonfarm.co.uk **web:** www.phepsonfarm.co.uk
dir: M5 junct 5 onto A38 (Droitwich). Left at 1st lights, left at next lights onto B4090. After 2m right to Himbleton. Phepson Farm 2m on right

Set in 50 acres of peaceful Worcestershire countryside, Phepson Farm has a one and a half acre coarse fishing lake. The farm is run in an eco-friendly manner and guests are welcome to walk the wildlife route. There are six individually styled bedrooms; two large rooms are in the main farmhouse, two rooms are in The Granary, and two are in the converted stables that have their own entrances. Award-winning breakfasts include asparagus in season, damsons and plums from the farm, and locally sourced sausages and bacon. There is a guest lounge.

Rooms 2 en suite 4 annexe en suite (4 GF) S £50; D £75* **Facilities** FTV TVL tea/coffee WiFi Fishing **Parking** 6 **Notes** LB Closed Xmas & New Year

KEMPSEY
Map 10 SO84

Walter de Cantelupe Inn

★★★ INN

tel: 01905 820572 **Main Rd WR5 3NA**
email: info@walterdecantelupe.co.uk **web:** www.walterdecantelupe.co.uk
dir: On A38 in village centre

This inn provides cosy bedrooms with smart bathrooms, and is convenient for the M5 and Worcester. The intimate, open-plan public areas are the setting for a range of real ales, and imaginative food featuring local produce and a fine selection of British cheeses.

Rooms 3 rms (2 en suite) (1 pri facs) (1 fmly) **Facilities** DVD iPod docking station Lounge tea/coffee Dinner available WiFi **Parking** 24 **Notes** No coaches

MALVERN
Map 10 SO74

Ashbury Bed & Breakfast

★★★★ BED AND BREAKFAST

tel: 01684 574225 **Ashbury, Old Hollow WR14 4NP**
email: ashburybandb@btinternet.com **web:** www.ashburybedandbreakfast.co.uk
dir: A449 onto B4053, 2nd left into Hornyold Rd. Right at T-junct into Cowleigh Rd, 250yds on left

A warm and friendly welcome awaits you from Karen and Graham at Ashbury Bed & Breakfast. This beautiful and grand Victorian property offers modern, comfortable and stylish bedrooms; the many period features that have been retained add to the overall charm of the house. An enjoyable breakfast made with all fresh ingredients can be enjoyed with some views across the Malvern countryside. This is a good location for those wishing to go walking in the Malvern area. Free WiFi is available.

Rooms 3 en suite (2 GF) S £50-£75; D £70-£110* **Facilities** FTV TVL tea/coffee WiFi ⓐ **Extras** Home-made biscuits - complimentary **Parking** 4 **Notes** LB ⊗ No Children 12yrs

The Old Rectory

★★★★ ☰ ⊜ GUEST ACCOMMODATION

tel: 01886 880109 **Cradley WR13 5LQ**
email: oldrectorycradley@btinternet.com **web:** www.oldrectorycradley.com
dir: M5 junct 7 onto A4103. Turn left to Cradley opposite Millbank Garage. 0.75m through village, on left by church

This stunning Georgian building situated in the quiet village of Cradley, close to the Malvern Hills, offers a quiet retreat in beautiful surroundings. Public areas have a certain charm, and walls are adorned with owner Claire's fabulous artwork. Each bedroom is spacious and thoughtfully decorated. The house can be let separately for private dinners, celebrations, or shoot parties, which can be accommodated in the formal dining room, where wonderful home-cooked cuisine is served.

Rooms 3 en suite **Facilities** Lounge TVL tea/coffee Dinner available WiFi ⇔ ⅃ 18 ⓐ **Extras** Speciality toiletries, snacks, sweets - free **Conf** Max 30 Thtr 30 Board 20 **Parking** 8

Appleby

★★★★ BED AND BREAKFAST

tel: 01684 562106 **213 Worcester Rd WR14 1SP**
email: davidwatkins_07@hotmail.co.uk
dir: On A449, opposite United Reform church

Appleby is a Victorian building on the main road leading into Great Malvern, and where a warm and friendly welcome can be expected from the friendly host, David Watkins. The bedrooms are spacious, comfortable and offer modern facilities including WiFi. Breakfast, in the dining room, is freshly prepared and served with impeccable style. There is a small lounge for guests, and some parking is available at the rear of the property.

Rooms 2 rms (1 en suite) (1 pri facs) S fr £40; D fr £70* **Facilities** DVD TVL tea/coffee WiFi **Extras** Bottled water - complimentary **Parking** 6 **Notes** ⊗ No Children 7yrs Closed Xmas & New Year ⊜

Puddle Lane Bed & Breakfast

★★★★ BED AND BREAKFAST

tel: 01684 572720 **54 Barnards Green Rd WR14 3LW**
email: puddlelanemalvern@hotmail.co.uk **web:** www.puddlelanemalvern.co.uk
dir: From Barnards Green up hill (Barnards Green Rd), 200mtrs opposite Wilton Rd junct

Friendly hospitality can be expected at this B&B, located just a 15-minute walk away from the centre of Malvern, close to the theatre and all local amenities. Bedrooms are homely and lots of useful accessories provided. An enjoyable breakfast with fresh ingredients and home-made produce is served daily.

Rooms 3 en suite (1 fmly) (3 GF) S £45-£60; D £70-£85* **Facilities** FTV DVD iPod docking station Lounge tea/coffee WiFi ⓐ **Extras** Fruit, mineral water **Parking** 3 **Notes** LB ⊜

MALVERN *continued*

Wyche Inn

★★★★ INN

tel: 01684 575396 **fax:** 01384 577227 **74 Wyche Rd WR14 4EQ**
email: thewycheinn@googlemail.com **web:** www.thewycheinn.co.uk
dir: *1.5m S of Malvern. On B4218 towards Malvern & Colwall. Off A449 (Worcester to Ross/Ledbury road)*

Located in an elevated position on the outskirts of Malvern, this inn is popular with locals and visiting walkers. The thoughtfully furnished bedrooms provide good levels of comfort with suitable guest extras; all bathrooms have a bath and shower. Each bedroom benefits from stunning countryside views. The menus feature home-cooked dishes, including good-value options, and a comprehensive range of real ales is available from the bar.

Rooms 4 en suite 2 annexe rms (2 pri facs) (1 GF) **Facilities** FTV DVD tea/coffee Dinner available WiFi Pool table **Extras** Speciality toiletries, bottled mineral water **Parking** 6 **Notes** LB No coaches

The Pembridge

★★★ GUEST ACCOMMODATION

tel: 01684 574813 **fax:** 01684 566885 **114 Graham Rd WR14 2HX**
email: info@thepembridge.co.uk **web:** www.thepembridge.co.uk
dir: *From A449 into Church St, 1st left*

Located on a leafy residential road close to the town centre, this large Victorian house retains many original features, including a superb staircase. Bedrooms, which include a ground-floor room, are well equipped. Other areas include a comfortable sitting room and an elegant dining room.

Rooms 8 en suite (1 fmly) (1 GF) S £48-£53; D £64-£69* **Facilities** FTV TVL tea/coffee Direct Dial WiFi ✆ **Parking** 10 **Notes** LB ⊗ No Children 7yrs RS 25-26 Dec No cooked English breakfast

Portocks End House

★★★ BED AND BREAKFAST

tel: 01684 310276 **Little Clevelode WR13 6PE**
email: email@portocksendbandb.co.uk **web:** www.portocksendbandb.co.uk
dir: *On B4424, 4m N of Upton upon Severn, opposite Riverside Caravan Park*

Peacefully located, yet convenient for the showground and major road links, this period house retains many original features; the traditional furnishings and decor highlight its intrinsic charm. The bedrooms are equipped with lots of thoughtful extras, and breakfasts are taken in a cosy dining room overlooking the pretty garden.

Rooms 2 rms (1 en suite) (1 pri facs) (1 fmly) S £35; D £56-£60* **Facilities** Lounge tea/coffee WiFi ✆ **Extras** Speciality toiletries - complimentary **Parking** 4 **Notes** Closed Dec-Feb ✉

Sidney House

★★★ GUEST ACCOMMODATION

tel: 01684 574994 **40 Worcester Rd WR14 4AA**
email: info@sidneyhouse.co.uk **web:** www.sidneyhouse.co.uk
dir: *On A449, 200yds N from town centre*

This impressive Grade II listed Georgian house is close to Malvern's central attractions and has stunning views. Bedrooms are filled with thoughtful extras, and some have small, en suite shower rooms. The spacious dining room overlooks the Cotswold escarpment and a comfortable lounge is also available.

Rooms 8 rms (6 en suite) (2 pri facs) (1 fmly) **Facilities** FTV TVL tea/coffee Licensed WiFi ✆ **Parking** 9 **Notes** Closed 24 Dec-3 Jan

Four Hedges

★★ GUEST ACCOMMODATION

tel: 01684 310405 **The Rhydd, Hanley Castle WR8 0AD**
email: fredgies@aol.com
dir: *4m E of Malvern at junct of B4211 & B4424*

Situated in a rural location, this detached house stands in mature grounds with wild birds in abundance. The bedrooms are equipped with thoughtful extras. Tasty English breakfasts, using free-range eggs, are served in a cosy dining room at a table made from a 300-year-old elm tree.

Rooms 4 rms (2 en suite) S fr £25; D fr £50* **Facilities** FTV iPod docking station Lounge TVL TV2B tea/coffee ⚓ Fishing ✆ **Extras** Snacks, fruit, flowers **Parking** 5 **Notes** No Children 1yr Closed Xmas ✉

| PERSHORE | Map 10 SO94 |

Evesham Lodge Bed & Breakfast

★★★★ BED AND BREAKFAST

tel: 01386 710285 & 07816 203960 **Evesham Lodge, Bricklehampton WR10 3HQ**
email: kerry@eveshamlodge.co.uk **web:** www.eveshamlodge.co.uk
dir: *B4084 Pershore to Evesham road, exit signed Bricklehampton. At T-junct turn right, through village, road bears right, 2nd on right*

Evesham Lodge is a 19th-century gate lodge, sympathetically renovated and offering two well-appointed en suite rooms, one of which has a balcony overlooking the countryside. It is set in a quiet location and perfect for exploring the Cotswolds and the Malvern Hills. A freshly cooked breakfast using free-range local produce is served in the dining room.

Rooms 2 en suite **Facilities** FTV DVD Lounge tea/coffee WiFi ✆ **Extras** Speciality toiletries, water, home-made biscuits **Parking** 2 **Notes** ⊗ ✉

| UPTON UPON SEVERN | Map 10 SO84 |

The Swan

★★★★ INN

tel: 01684 594948 & 07501 223754 **Waterside WR8 0JD**
email: info@theswanhotelupton.co.uk **web:** www.theswanhotelupton.co.uk

Based in the historic riverside town of Upton upon Severn this 400-year-old inn offers plenty of charm and quirkiness. The bedrooms provide good comfort and practicality and are modern in design, with some having views of the river. Enjoy good quality bar meals and cask conditioned ales in the waterside bar. A separate restaurant is also available for functions.

Rooms 6 en suite S £55-£95; D £75-£115 **Facilities** FTV tea/coffee Dinner available Direct Dial ✆ **Extras** Slippers **Notes** No coaches

WICHENFORD
Map 10 SO76

Laughern Hill Estate
★★★★★ GUEST ACCOMMODATION

tel: 01886 888065 **Laughern Hill WR6 6YB**
email: enquiries@laughernhill.co.uk **web:** www.laughernhill.co.uk
dir: From A443 onto B4204 (Martley Rd). Located at Willow Rd junct, with white gates

This charming and attractive Grade II listed manor house, nestled in the Worcestershire countryside, offers a quiet and relaxing stay. A wonderful location for civil ceremonies and private parties. The bedrooms have been elegantly furnished with some thoughtful extras, and breakfast can be enjoyed in the grand dining room. Stables and livery are also available for guests.

Rooms 4 rms (3 en suite) (1 pri facs) (4 fmly) **Facilities** STV FTV DVD Lounge tea/coffee WiFi ☕ Riding 🐾 **Extras** Robes **Parking** 8 **Notes** LB Closed 24-26 Dec ⊛ Civ Wed 100

WORCESTER
Map 10 SO85

Church House Bed & Breakfast *(SO849587)*
★★★★ FARMHOUSE

tel: 01905 452366 & 07909 968938   **fax:** 01905 452366
Church House, Claines WR3 7RL
email: wr37rl@btinternet.com **web:** www.churchhousebandb.co.uk
dir: M5 junct 6 onto A449, after 3m at rdbt take 1st exit. 1st drive on right before Claines church

Church House Bed & Breakfast is situated on a working farm in a peaceful area of Worcestershire, within easy reach of the motorway network. This Grade II listed Georgian building offers relaxing and comfortable accommodation. Each bedroom is en suite, with WiFi and large screen TVs. The comfortable beds offer a good night's sleep, and the enjoyable breakfast, with home-made produce from the farm, will provide a good start for the day.

Rooms 3 en suite S £50-£65; D £70-£85* **Facilities** FTV tea/coffee WiFi ☕ Fishing 🐾 **Extras** Home-made biscuits - complimentary **Parking** 10 **Notes** No Children 12yrs ⊛ 600 acres mixed

Oaklands B&B
★★★★ GUEST ACCOMMODATION

tel: 01905 458871 **Claines WR3 7RS**
email: oaklandsbb@btinternet.com **web:** www.oaklandsbandb.com
dir: M5 junct 6, A449. At rdbt take 1st exit signed Claines. 1st left into School Bank. Oaklands 1st house on right

A warm welcome is guaranteed at this converted stable, which is in a peaceful setting, just a short drive from major routes. The property stands in abundant mature gardens, and the well-appointed bedrooms are mostly spacious. There is also a snooker room. Parking is available.

Rooms 4 en suite (2 fmly) S £45; D £75 **Facilities** FTV DVD Lounge tea/coffee WiFi Snooker 🐾 **Parking** 7 **Notes** LB Closed Xmas & New Year ⊛

Wyatt Guest House
★★★★ GUEST HOUSE

tel: 01905 26311 **40 Barbourne Rd WR1 1HU**
email: wyatt.guest@virgin.net **web:** www.wyattguest.co.uk
dir: On A38 0.5m N from city centre

Located within easy walking distance of shops, restaurants and central attractions, this lovely Victorian house provides a range of thoughtfully furnished bedrooms. Breakfast is served in an attractive dining room, a warm welcome is assured, and the attractive frontage is a regular winner in Worcester's 'Britain in Bloom' competition.

Rooms 8 rms (7 en suite) (1 fmly) (1 GF) S £40-£50; D £65 **Facilities** FTV DVD Lounge tea/coffee WiFi

Ye Olde Talbot
★★★★ INN

tel: 01905 23573 **fax:** 01905 612760 **Friar St WR1 2NA**
email: 9250@greeneking.co.uk **web:** www.oldenglish.co.uk

In the heart of the city, Ye Olde Talbot has attractive and cosy public areas where guests can relax and enjoy a wide range of imaginative food, wine and real ales. Bedrooms are thoughtfully furnished. Parking is available at the adjacent NCP.

Rooms 29 en suite (6 fmly) (6 GF) **Facilities** FTV tea/coffee Direct Dial WiFi **Notes** ⊗

BEVERLEY
Map 17 TA03

Newbegin House
★★★★★ 🏠 BED AND BREAKFAST

tel: 01482 888880 **10 Newbegin HU17 8EG**
email: wsweeney@wsweeney.karoo.co.uk **web:** www.newbeginhousebbbeverley.co.uk

Newbegin House is a delightful Georgian manor house located on a quiet one way street in the centre of this historic market town. It is an impressive family home, very spacious and with many original period features and a homely, inviting feel. Excellent breakfasts are served in the grand dining room. The walled garden is also available for guests to enjoy and private parking is provided.

Rooms 3 en suite (1 fmly) **Facilities** FTV DVD iPod docking station TVL tea/coffee WiFi ch fac 🐾 **Conf** Max 30 Thtr 30 Class 20 Board 12 **Parking** 3 **Notes** ⊗ RS Closed owners annual holiday ⊛

BEVERLEY *continued*

Trinity Guest House

★★★★ GUEST HOUSE

tel: 01482 869537 **Trinity Ln, Station Square HU17 0AR**
email: trinity_house@hotmail.com **web:** www.trinityguesthouse.com
dir: *Opposite railway station*

This well presented Victorian town house is located next to the train station in the historic town centre. Guests simply need to cross the quiet street if they arrive by train. There is a convenient public car park opposite the house or permits are available for on-street parking. The house combines traditional and modern decor with a comfortable lounge also provided. WiFi access is also available. A secluded, walled garden provides additional space for guests to relax in warmer weather.

Rooms 6 en suite (2 fmly) S £40-£48; D £60-£70* **Facilities** FTV DVD TVL tea/coffee WiFi 🔒 **Notes** ⊗

| BRIDLINGTON | Map 17 TA16 |

Premier Collection

Marton Grange

★★★★★ GUEST ACCOMMODATION

tel: 01262 602034 & 07891 682687 **fax:** 01262 602034
Flamborough Rd, Marton cum Sewerby YO15 1DU
email: info@marton-grange.co.uk **web:** www.martongrange.co.uk
dir: *2m NE of Bridlington. On B1255, 600yds W of Links golf club*

This Grade II listed former farmhouse is set in well-maintained gardens and offers high levels of comfort, service and hospitality. Bedrooms are well appointed with quality fixtures and fittings and public areas offer wonderful views of the gardens. Thoughtful extras, provided as standard, help create a delightful guest experience.

Rooms 11 en suite (3 GF) **Facilities** FTV DVD iPod docking station Lounge TVL tea/coffee Lift Licensed WiFi ⅃ 18 🔒 **Extras** Home-made shortbread, speciality toiletries **Parking** 11 **Notes** LB RS Nov-Jan restricted opening for refurbishments

Bestworth House

★★★★ BED AND BREAKFAST

tel: 01262 262728 **fax:** 01262 262264 **51-53 High St YO16 4PR**
email: david@bestworthhouse.co.uk **web:** www.bestworthhouse.co.uk
dir: *Follow signs for Historic Old Town. At double rdbt into Market Place. Left at junct, on right*

On one side of this impressive Grade II* listed, 17th-century house is the High Street with shops, tearooms and galleries, whilst the other side offers a peaceful retreat in the beautiful walled garden. There are three bedrooms; two in the main house and the other with private access from the garden. All feature king-size beds, large televisions and luxurious bathrooms.

Rooms 2 rms (1 en suite) (1 pri facs) 1 annexe en suite (1 GF) S £50-£75; D £70-£95* **Facilities** FTV tea/coffee WiFi 🔒 **Extras** Fridge, milk, Nespresso machine, bottled water **Parking** 3 **Notes** ⊗

The Brockton

★★★★ GUEST ACCOMMODATION

tel: 01262 673967 & 401771 **fax:** 01262 401771 **4 Shaftesbury Rd YO15 3NP**
email: brocktonhotel@yahoo.co.uk **web:** www.brocktonhotelbridlington.co.uk
dir: *Off A167 coast road, right at golf course, through lights, 2nd on left*

Located close to the seafront, this family-run property offers comfortable bedrooms, some with sea views, and all with en suite shower rooms. A lounge and bar area is available, and dinner and breakfast are served in the dining room.

Rooms 10 en suite (1 fmly) (2 GF) S £35-£38; D £64-£70* **Facilities** FTV DVD Lounge TVL tea/coffee Dinner available Licensed WiFi ⅃ 18 🔒 **Conf** Max 20 **Parking** 10 **Notes** LB ⊗

Burlington Quays

★★★★ GUEST ACCOMMODATION

tel: 01262 676052 **20 Meadowfield Rd YO15 3LD**
email: burlingtonquays@axis-connect.com **web:** www.burlington-quays.co.uk
dir: *A165 into Bridlington, 1st right past golf course into Kingston Rd. Bear left to seafront, take 3rd left*

In a peaceful street close to the seafront, this spacious house features modern, well-appointed bedrooms, all with en suite bath or shower rooms. Guests also have use of a comfortable lounge and a cosy, fully licensed bar. Tasty breakfasts are served in the pleasant dining room at individual tables.

Rooms 5 en suite (4 fmly) S £40-£50; D £66-£75 **Facilities** FTV DVD TVL tea/coffee Licensed WiFi 🔒 **Parking** 2 **Notes** LB ⊗

Rosebery House

★★★★ GUEST HOUSE

tel: 01262 670334 **1 Belle Vue YO15 2ET**
email: info@rosebery-house.com **web:** www.rosebery-house.com
dir: *From B1254 (Promenade) into Tennyson Ave, Belle Vue on left*

This beautiful, quietly positioned Grade II listed Georgian house is only 100 metres from the seafront and promenade. The harbour is only a few minutes' walk and within five to ten minutes guests can walk to a wide choice of shops, restaurants and cafés or explore the historic Old Town. Private parking, parking permits and secure cycle storage are all provided as well as free WiFi access. Bedrooms are comfortable and the front rooms have views of the garden, public gardens and the sea beyond.

Rooms 7 en suite (3 fmly) **Facilities** FTV TVL tea/coffee WiFi 🔒 **Parking** 6 **Notes** ⊗ Closed Nov-Feb

The Royal Bridlington

★★★★ GUEST ACCOMMODATION

tel: 01262 672433 **fax:** 01262 672118 **1 Shaftesbury Rd YO15 3NP**
email: info@royalhotelbrid.co.uk **web:** www.royalhotelbrid.co.uk
dir: *A615 N to Bridlington (Kingsgate), right into Shaftesbury Rd*

Just off the promenade, this immaculate property has a range of thoughtfully furnished bedrooms with smart modern bathrooms. The spacious public areas include a large dining room, conservatory-sitting room, and a cosy TV lounge. Freshly-cooked dinners are a feature and a warm welcome is assured.

Rooms 14 rms (13 en suite) (1 pri facs) 4 annexe en suite (7 fmly) (4 GF) S £40-£50; D £70-£80* **Facilities** FTV DVD Lounge TVL tea/coffee Dinner available Licensed WiFi ⅃ 18 🔒 **Conf** Max 85 Thtr 85 Class 20 Board 40 **Parking** 7 **Notes** LB ⊗ No Children 12yrs

The Marina

★★★★ GUEST HOUSE

tel: 01262 677138 & 0800 970 0591 **8 Summerfield Rd YO15 3LF**
email: themarina8@hotmail.com **web:** www.themarina-bridlington.com
dir: *From A165 take 1st right after Broadacres pub on left. Onto promenade, take 5th left*

A few yards from the seafront in a quiet part of Bridlington, The Marina is ideal for short or long breaks, and offers seven rooms, including a ground-floor twin for the less mobile. Guests can relax in the cosy bar and enjoy a freshly prepared breakfast. All rooms come with expected amenities. Cyclists may make use of a lockable shed, and there is an outdoor mains plug available for wheelchair or mobility scooter charging.

Rooms 7 en suite (1 fmly) (1 GF) S £25-£32; D £45-£60 (room only)* **Facilities** FTV DVD tea/coffee Dinner available Licensed WiFi 🔒 **Notes** LB ⊗ No Children 7yrs

DRIFFIELD
Map 17 TA05

The Red Lion

★★★ INN

tel: 01377 255907 **57 Middle Street North YO25 6SS**
email: redliondriffield@live.co.uk **web:** www.redliondriffield.co.uk

The Red Lion is within walking distance of the town centre and offers a wide range of food and drink and comfortable en suite bedrooms. There is a good menu choice using quality fresh ingredients. Speciality evenings, quiz nights and live entertainment at the weekend makes the Red Lion a popular venue with the locals. Complimentary WiFi and ample car parking are provided.

Rooms 4 en suite (1 fmly) S £25-£35; D £50-£60* **Facilities** FTV DVD tea/coffee Dinner available WiFi Pool table 🔒 **Parking** 15 **Notes** ⊗ No coaches

HUGGATE
Map 19 SE85

The Wolds Inn

★★★ INN

tel: 01377 288217 **Driffield Rd YO42 1YH**
email: woldsinn@gmail.com **web:** www.woldsinn.co.uk
dir: *Huggate signed off A166 & brown signs to Wolds Inn*

At the end of the highest village in the Yorkshire Wolds, midway between York and the coast, this ancient inn is a rural haven beside the Wolds Way walk. Substantial meals are served in the dining room and a good range of well-kept beers is available in the bar. Bedrooms, varying in size, are well equipped and comfortable.

Rooms 3 en suite S £53; D £83 **Facilities** FTV tea/coffee Dinner available WiFi 🔒
Extras Bottled water - complimentary **Parking** 30 **Notes** ⊗

KILHAM
Map 17 TA06

St Quintin Arms

★★★ INN

tel: 01262 490329 **Main St, Harpham YO25 4QY**
email: burdaz3@o2.co.uk

This friendly local inn specialises in food, the owners have their own farm, producing prize winning lamb, they also use lots of other local produce in the restaurant. Bedrooms are pleasantly appointed and spacious. A cosy bar and pleasant restaurant form the public areas, and there is generous parking available.

Rooms 4 rms **Parking Notes** Closed 2-10 Jan

MARKET WEIGHTON
Map 17 SE84

Robeanne House

★★★ GUEST ACCOMMODATION

tel: 01430 873312 & 07720 468811 **fax:** 01430 879142
Towthorpe Ln, Shiptonthorpe YO43 3PW
email: enquiries@robeannehouse.co.uk **web:** www.robeannehouse.co.uk
dir: *1.5m NW on A614*

Set back off the A614 in a quiet location, this delightful, modern family home was built as a farmhouse. York, the coast, and the Yorkshire Moors and Dales are within easy driving distance. All bedrooms have country views and include a large family room. A charming wooden chalet is available in the garden.

Rooms 2 en suite 6 annexe en suite (3 fmly) (3 GF) S £45-£50; D £65-£75
Facilities FTV TVL tea/coffee Dinner available WiFi 🔒 **Extras** Guest kitchen, robes - complimentary **Conf** Max 8 Board 8 **Parking** 10 **Notes** LB

WILLERBY
Map 17 TA03

Innkeeper's Lodge Hull, Willerby

★★★ INN

tel: 0845 112 6036 **Beverley Rd HU10 6NT**
email: info@innkeeperslodge.com **web:** www.innkeeperslodge.com

Conveniently located for the city centre which is just five minutes away and also close to the M62 and the Humber Bridge. Bedrooms are modern and offer good space and comfort. There is a Toby Carvery pub on site where guests can enjoy a wide range of drinks and food, including fresh roast dinners. Complimentary WiFi is provided and there is on-site parking also.

Rooms 32 en suite (12 fmly) (8 GF) **Facilities** FTV tea/coffee Dinner available Direct Dial WiFi **Parking** 70

NORTH YORKSHIRE

AMPLEFORTH
Map 19 SE57

Premier Collection

Shallowdale House

★★★★★ 🏠 ☕ GUEST ACCOMMODATION

tel: 01439 788325 **fax:** 01439 788885 **West End YO62 4DY**
email: stay@shallowdalehouse.co.uk **web:** www.shallowdalehouse.co.uk
dir: Off A170 at W end of village, on turn to Hambleton

An outstanding example of an architect-designed 1960s house, Shallowdale lies in two acres of hillside gardens. There are stunning views from every room, and the elegant public rooms include a choice of lounges. Spacious bedrooms blend traditional and 1960s style with many home comforts. Expect excellent service and genuine hospitality from Anton and Phillip. The very imaginative, freshly cooked dinners are not to be missed.

Rooms 3 rms (2 en suite) (1 pri facs) S £90-£105; D £110-£135* **Facilities** FTV Lounge tea/coffee Dinner available Licensed WiFi 🛁 **Extras** Speciality toiletries - complimentary **Parking** 3 **Notes** ⊗ No Children 12yrs Closed Xmas & New Year

ARKENGARTHDALE
Map 18 NY90

Charles Bathurst Inn

★★★★ ◉ 🏠 INN

tel: 01748 884567 **fax:** 01748 884599 **DL11 6EN**
email: info@cbinn.co.uk **web:** www.cbinn.co.uk
dir: B6270 to Reeth, at Buck Hotel turn N to Langthwaite, pass church on right, inn 0.5m on right

The CB Inn, as it is known to locals, is surrounded by magnificent scenery high in the Dales. Food is the focus of the pub, where a choice of rustic eating areas makes for atmospheric dining. The well-equipped bedrooms blend contemporary and traditional styles, and cosy lounge areas are available. A function suite is also available.

Rooms 19 en suite (3 fmly) (5 GF) S £81-£91; D £99-£110* **Facilities** FTV Lounge tea/coffee Dinner available Direct Dial WiFi Fishing Riding Pool table 🛁 **Extras** Speciality toiletries, home-made shortbread **Conf** Max 70 Thtr 70 Class 30 Board 30 **Parking** 35 **Notes** LB Closed 25 Dec Civ Wed 70

ASENBY
Map 19 SE37

Premier Collection

Crab Manor

★★★★★ ◉◉ 🍴 RESTAURANT WITH ROOMS

tel: 01845 577286 **fax:** 01845 577496 **YO7 3QL**
web: www.crabandlobster.co.uk
dir: A1(M) junct 49, on outskirts of village

This stunning, 18th-century Grade II listed Georgian manor is located in the heart of the North Yorkshire Dales. Each bedroom is themed around the world's most famous hotels and has high-quality furnishings, beautiful wallpaper, and thoughtful extras. Scandinavian log cabins are also available in the grounds, which have their own terrace with hot tubs. There is a comfortable lounge bar where guests can relax in the Manor before enjoying dinner next door in the Crab & Lobster Restaurant, which specialises in fresh local seafood. The attractive gardens offer a lovely backdrop.

Rooms 8 en suite 6 annexe en suite (3 fmly) **Facilities** FTV tea/coffee Dinner available WiFi Sauna **Conf** Max 16 Board 16 **Parking** 90 **Notes** ⊗ No coaches Civ Wed 105

ASKRIGG
Map 18 SD99

The White Rose Inn

★★★★ INN

tel: 01969 650515 **fax:** 01969 650176 **Main St DL8 3HG**
email: stay@thewhiterosehotelaskrigg.co.uk **web:** www.thewhiterosehotelaskrigg.co.uk
dir: M6 or A1 onto A685, follow signs to Askrigg, White Rose Inn in village centre

This family-run inn, set in the small village of Askrigg, provides a perfect place to stay and dine in the North Yorkshire Dales. The accommodation offers standard as well as king-sized rooms, some with original fireplaces. The large bar-lounge is welcoming with its open fire and real ales, and there is a spacious dining room. Private off-road parking is also available.

Rooms 12 en suite D £75-£85* **Facilities** FTV tea/coffee Dinner available WiFi **Parking** 20 **Notes** LB Closed 24-25 Dec

---

| **AUSTWICK** | **Map 18 SD76** |

The Traddock

✯✯✯✯✯ ◉◉ 🍴 RESTAURANT WITH ROOMS

tel: 015242 51224 **fax:** 015242 51796 **LA2 8BY**
email: info@thetraddock.co.uk **web:** www.thetraddock.co.uk
dir: *From Skipton take A65 towards Kendal, 3m after Settle turn right signed Austwick, cross hump back bridge, 100yds on left*

Situated within the Yorkshire Dales National Park and a peaceful village environment, this fine Georgian country house with well-tended gardens offers a haven of calm and good hospitality. There are two comfortable lounges with real fires and fine furnishings, as well as a cosy bar and an elegant dining room serving fine cuisine. Bedrooms are individually styled with many homely touches.

Rooms 12 en suite (2 fmly) (1 GF) S £85-£95; D £95-£200* **Facilities** FTV DVD Lounge tea/coffee Dinner available Direct Dial WiFi ⬤⬤ 18 ⬤ **Extras** Speciality toiletries, fruit, bottled water - free **Conf** Max 24 Thtr 24 Class 16 Board 16 **Parking** 20 **Notes** LB No coaches

---

| **AYSGARTH** | **Map 19 SE08** |

The Aysgarth Falls

✯✯✯✯ 🍴 INN

tel: 01969 663775 **DL8 3SR**
email: info@aysgarthfallshotel.com **web:** www.aysgarthfallshotel.com
dir: *On A684 between Leyburn & Hawes*

A friendly, high-quality inn, perfect for exploring the Yorkshire Dales, and the grounds lead down to Aysgarth Falls. Excellent meals are served throughout the bar and dining areas, and also on the outdoor terraces in warmer weather. Bedrooms are contemporary, featuring comfortable beds, flat-screen TVs and luxurious en suites. Residents also have use of drying rooms for waterproofs and boots.

Rooms 11 en suite (2 fmly) **Facilities** FTV DVD tea/coffee Dinner available WiFi ⬤ **Parking** 30 **Notes** No coaches

---

| **BAINBRIDGE** | **Map 18 SD99** |

Premier Collection

Yorebridge House

✯✯✯✯✯ ◉◉◉ 🍴 RESTAURANT WITH ROOMS

tel: 01969 652060 **fax:** 01969 650258 **DL8 3EE**
email: enquiries@yorebridgehouse.co.uk **web:** www.yorebridgehouse.co.uk
dir: *A648 to Bainbridge. Yorebridge House N of centre on right before river*

Yorebridge House is situated by the river on the edge of Bainbridge, in the heart of the North Yorkshire Dales. In the Victorian era this was a schoolmaster's house and school, the building now offers luxury boutique-style accommodation. Each bedroom is individually designed with high-quality furnishings and thoughtful extras. All rooms have stunning views of the Dales and some have their own terrace with hot tub. There is a comfortable lounge bar where guests can relax before enjoying dinner in the attractive and elegant dining room.

Rooms 7 en suite 4 annexe en suite (11 fmly) (5 GF) **Facilities** STV FTV DVD iPod docking station Lounge tea/coffee Dinner available Direct Dial WiFi ⬤ Fishing **Extras** Speciality toiletries **Conf** Max 70 Thtr 70 Class 60 Board 30 **Parking** 30 **Notes** No coaches Civ Wed 100

| **BEDALE** | **Map 19 SE28** |

Three Coopers

✯✯✯ INN

tel: 01677 422153 & 07568 336472 **2 Emgate DL8 1AL**
dir: *In town centre (Market Pl) turn into Emgate at monument, Three Coopers on right*

This traditional pub, located in the small town of Bedale is a delight to visit, with its wooden floor, real ales, beer garden and high speed WiFi throughout. The bedrooms are modern and comfortable with bathrooms to match. The food is home-cooked and includes traditional Yorkshire offerings. The welcome is always warm and friendly. There is no on-site parking but there is free parking near by.

Rooms 5 en suite S £40; D £70-£90* **Facilities** FTV tea/coffee Dinner available WiFi

---

| **BISHOP MONKTON** | **Map 19 SE36** |

Lamb & Flag Inn

✯✯✯✯ INN

tel: 01765 677322 **Boroughbridge Rd HG3 3QN**
email: carol@lambandflagbarn.co.uk **web:** www.lambandflagbarn.co.uk
dir: *From A61 turn E into Moor Rd (cross Knaresbrough Rd)*

The Lamb & Flag Inn is a delightful country hostelry near to Harrogate, York and Leeds. The inn provides a warm welcome and freshly-prepared local food. The three comfortably furnished and equipped bedrooms are a conversion from a barn and are annexed next to the pub. A continental-style breakfast is provided in your bedroom.

Rooms 3 annexe en suite (1 fmly) (3 GF) D £60-£70* **Facilities** FTV tea/coffee Dinner available WiFi Pool table **Parking** 20 **Notes** ⊗ No coaches

BOLTON ABBEY   Map 19 SE05

Howgill Lodge

★★★★ GUEST ACCOMMODATION

tel: 01756 720655 **Barden BD23 6DJ**
email: info@howgill-lodge.co.uk **web:** www.howgill-lodge.co.uk
dir: B6160 from Bolton Abbey signed Burnsall, 3m right at Barden Tower signed
Appletreewick, Howgill Lodge 1.25m on right at phone box

In an idyllic position high above the valley, this converted stone granary provides a
quality get-away. The stylish bedrooms provide a host of thoughtful touches and are
designed to feature original stonewalls, flagstone floors and timber beams. All of
the rooms boast spectacular, memorable views. Breakfasts make excellent use of
fresh local ingredients.

Rooms 4 en suite (1 fmly) (4 GF) S £50-£80; D £80* **Facilities** FTV tea/coffee
Extras Fridge **Parking** 6 **Notes** LB ⊗ Closed 24-26 Dec

BOROUGHBRIDGE   Map 19 SE36

Premier Collection

The Crown Inn

★★★★★ ◉ ⌂ RESTAURANT WITH ROOMS

tel: 01423 322300 **fax:** 01423 322033 **Roecliffe YO51 9LY**
email: info@crowninnroecliffe.com **web:** www.crowninnroecliffe.com
dir: A1(M) junct 48, follow signs for Boroughbridge. At rdbt exit towards Roecliffe &
brown tourist signs

The Crown is a 16th-century coaching inn providing an excellent combination of
traditional charm and modern comforts. Service is friendly and professional and
food is a highlight of any stay. The kitchen team use the finest of Yorkshire
produce from the best local suppliers to create a weekly-changing seasonal
menu. Bedrooms are attractively furnished with stylish en suite bathrooms.

Rooms 4 en suite (1 fmly) S £80-£90; D £90-£120 **Facilities** FTV DVD tea/coffee
Dinner available WiFi ⌕ **Extras** Sherry, Espresso coffee machine, chocolate
Conf Max 100 Thtr 100 Class 60 Board 30 **Parking** 40 **Notes** No coaches Civ Wed
120

Grantham Arms

★★★★ ◉ RESTAURANT WITH ROOMS

tel: 01423 323980 **Milby YO51 9BW**
email: info@granthamarms.co.uk **web:** www.granthamarms.co.uk

The Grantham Arms is a real gem of a place, from the neat and tidy garden area at
the front, to the flamboyant and extravagant design of the interior. The public areas
are a real feature with mood lighting, contemporary furniture and wooden floorings.
Bedrooms are very well appointed with quality throughout. Food is a highlight of
any visit with fresh seasonal and local produce being a feature on all menus.
Dinner, lunch and afternoon tea are available. Staff are wonderfully friendly and
make this quite an exceptional place to visit.

Rooms 7 en suite 1 annexe en suite (1 fmly) (1 GF) S £75-£100; D £85-£100*
Facilities FTV iPod docking station Lounge tea/coffee Dinner available Direct Dial
WiFi ⌕ **Extras** Speciality toiletries **Parking** 10 **Notes** LB ⊗

BURNSALL   Map 19 SE06

The Devonshire Fell

★★★★★ ◉◉ RESTAURANT WITH ROOMS

tel: 01756 729000 & 718111 **fax:** 01756 729009 **BD23 6BT**
email: manager@devonshirefell.co.uk **web:** www.devonshirefell.co.uk
dir: On B6160, 6m from Bolton Abbey rdbt, A59 junct

Located on the edge of the attractive village of Burnsall, this establishment offers
comfortable, well-equipped accommodation in a relaxing atmosphere. There is an
extensive menu featuring local produce, and meals can be taken either in the bar
area or the more formal restaurant. A function room with views over the valley is
also available.

Rooms 12 en suite (2 fmly) S £105-£200; D £110-£240* **Facilities** STV FTV DVD tea/
coffee Dinner available Direct Dial WiFi Fishing Free use of spa facilities at sister
hotel **Conf** Max 50 Thtr 50 Class 30 Board 24 **Parking** 40 **Notes** LB Civ Wed 120

CLAPHAM   Map 18 SD76

Brookhouse Guest House

★★★★ ⌂ GUEST HOUSE

tel: 015242 51580 **Station Rd LA2 8ER**
email: admin@brookhouseclapham.co.uk **web:** www.brookhouse-clapham.co.uk
dir: Off A65 into village

Beside the river, in the pretty conservation village of Clapham, this personally run
guest house provides comfortable accommodation and warm hospitality.
Brookhouse also provides an evening bistro, popular with locals, which offers an
interesting selection of home-made meals. Secure storage for cycles is also
available.

Rooms 3 rms (2 en suite) (1 pri facs) (1 fmly) **Facilities** FTV tea/coffee Dinner
available Licensed WiFi ⌕⌕ 18 **Notes** ⊗ ⌂

CLOUGHTON   Map 19 TA09

Blacksmiths Arms

★★★★ INN

tel: 01723 870244 **High St YO13 0AE**
email: enquiries@blacksmithsarmsinn.co.uk **web:** www.blacksmithsarmsinn.co.uk
dir: On A171 in village centre. 6m N of Scarborough

Situated six miles north of Scarborough, this inn features smartly furnished
bedrooms. Four are in converted stone buildings that have private entrances. A

good range of dishes is served in the bar and dining room, which have the ambience of a country inn, including open fires and traditional furniture.

Rooms 6 en suite 4 annexe en suite (1 fmly) (4 GF) **Facilities** FTV tea/coffee Dinner available WiFi **Parking** 35 **Notes** LB ⊗ RS 25-27 Dec No breakfast or room service No coaches

CONEYSTHORPE
Map 19 SE77

Lime Kiln House
★★★★★ Ⓐ BED AND BREAKFAST

tel: 01653 648213 **YO60 7DD**
email: gillianharris_slt@yahoo.co.uk **web:** www.limekiln-coneysthorpe.com
dir: *From York on A64, turn left at sign for Castle Howard. After 0.5m turn right then 1st left*

With tasteful and spacious rooms, Lime Kiln House is a sympathetically modernised traditional Yorkshire stone property. Breakfast produce is locally sourced and served in the guest sitting room, which boasts features such as an open fireplace, an antique leather rocking chair and views across the village green to Castle Howard. Coneysthorpe is convenient for A64, the charming market town of Malton, York and the Yorkshire coast. This is an ideal area for foodies and nature lovers.

Rooms 1 en suite (1 fmly) D £80-£95 **Facilities** FTV DVD TVL tea/coffee WiFi 🌢 **Extras** Speciality toiletries, home-made biscuits - free **Parking** 4 **Notes** LB

CONONLEY
Map 18 SD94

Throstle Nest Farm (SD985481)
★★★★ FARMHOUSE

tel: 07894 283004 **Woodside Ln BD20 8PE**
email: throstlenestfarmbandb@gmail.com **web:** www.throstlenestfarmbandb.co.uk
dir: *From Skipton on A6131 towards Keighley, take 1st right past Tesco garage. After 1m bear left signed Lothersdale, 1m on left*

Located on the edge of the Aire Valley, yet only two minutes from the market town of Skipton, this beautifully presented house is perfect for exploring the Yorkshire Dales. The house is set in five acres of land and the family also have rare breed sheep. The attractive bedrooms (each with high-quality en suite shower room) have views over the rolling countryside. There is a spacious lounge and dining room with an inglenook fireplace.

Rooms 5 en suite (1 fmly) **Facilities** FTV DVD Lounge tea/coffee WiFi 🌢 **Parking** 6 **Notes** ⊗ 5 acres sheep

CRAYKE
Map 19 SE57

The Durham Ox
★★★★ Ⓐ RESTAURANT WITH ROOMS

tel: 01347 821506 **fax:** 01347 823326 **Westway YO61 4TE**
email: enquiries@thedurhamox.com **web:** www.thedurhamox.com
dir: *A19 to Easingwold. Through market place to Crayke, 1st left up hill*

The Durham Ox is some 300 years old. The owners pride themselves on offering a friendly and efficient service, plus traditional pub food using only the best local ingredients. The pub has breathtaking views over the Vale of York on three sides, and a charming view up the hill to the medieval church on the other. Accommodation is mainly in four converted farm cottages. Crayke is in the heart of 'Herriot Country' and less than 20 minutes from York city centre.

Rooms 1 en suite 5 annexe en suite (1 fmly) (3 GF) **Facilities** DVD tea/coffee Dinner available WiFi Shooting, fishing, riding by arrangement **Extras** Speciality toiletries **Parking** 35 **Notes** LB No coaches

ELLERBY
Map 19 NZ71

Ellerby Residential Country Inn
★★★★ INN

tel: 01947 840342 **fax:** 01947 841221 **12-14 Ryeland Ln TS13 5LP**
email: relax@ellerbyhotel.co.uk **web:** www.ellerbyhotel.co.uk

This friendly, family-run inn is in a quiet country setting just eight miles from Whitby and a short drive from the North York Moors National Park. There is a traditional bar with open fire and real ales as well as a spacious restaurant. There is also a beautiful secluded garden and a residents' conservatory lounge. A range of bedrooms is available including ground-floor rooms, family rooms and a disabled accessible room. Complimentary WiFi is also provided and there is secure bicycle storage.

Rooms 10 en suite (5 fmly) (4 GF) S £60-£90; D £90-£120* **Facilities** FTV Lounge tea/coffee Dinner available Direct Dial WiFi 🌢 **Extras** Fresh milk - complimentary **Parking** 30 **Notes** LB

FILEY
Map 17 TA18

Premier Collection

All Seasons Guesthouse
★★★★★ 🏠 GUEST HOUSE

tel: 01723 515321 & 07870 267945 **11 Rutland St YO14 9JA**
email: lesley@allseasonsfiley.co.uk **web:** www.allseasonsfiley.co.uk

This immaculately presented, contemporary guest house is a short stroll from the seafront and is also close to the Crescent Gardens and town centre. There is a friendly, welcoming atmosphere and a lovely lounge for guests to relax in. Bedrooms and bathrooms are stylish and very comfortable. They include a luxury suite, a king-size room, family and twin rooms. Breakfast is a highlight of any stay with all produce either locally sourced or home-made. Complimentary WiFi is also provided. AA Friendliest B&B of the Year Finalist 2014-2015.

Rooms 6 en suite (2 fmly) S £60-£97; D £80-£117* **Facilities** FTV DVD TVL tea/coffee WiFi ⌣ ⅃ 19 🌢 **Extras** Dressing gowns, slippers - complimentary **Notes** LB ⊗ No Children 10yrs

FLIXTON
Map 17 TA07

Orchard Lodge

★★★★ GUEST ACCOMMODATION

tel: 01723 890202 **fax:** 01723 890202 **North St YO11 3UA**
email: c.pummell@btinternet.com **web:** www.orchard-lodge.com
dir: Off A1039 in village centre

Located six miles south of Scarborough, just off the main road, this establishment offers spacious and comfortable bedrooms. It is a good base for touring the coast, the North York Moors or the Wolds. Hearty breakfasts feature home-made preserves.

Rooms 6 en suite D fr £70* **Facilities** FTV tea/coffee **Parking** 8 **Notes** LB ⊗ No Children 3yrs Closed Jan-Feb

FYLINGTHORPE
Map 19 NZ90

Flask Inn

★★★★ INN

tel: 01947 880305 & 880592 **YO22 4QH**
email: info@flaskinn.com **web:** www.theflaskinn.co.uk
dir: On A171 from Whitby, on left

This traditional inn has been recently refurbished and now offers spacious bar and dining areas along with smart, contemporary bedrooms. The rooms are very well equipped and feature modern en suites. There is a friendly atmosphere and food is a highlight of any stay with a high standard of cooking and a wide choice on the appealing menus. The inn has a very convenient location, close to the main road offering a scenic drive between Whitby and Scarborough and set in the beautiful North Yorkshire countryside.

Rooms 9 en suite (2 fmly) (3 GF) S £45-£60; D £60-£80* **Facilities** FTV tea/coffee Dinner available WiFi Pool table ⚓ **Extras** Bottled water **Parking** 25 **Notes** LB No coaches

GIGGLESWICK
Map 18 SD86

Harts Head Inn

★★★★ ⚑ INN

tel: 01729 822086 & 07703 559325 **Belle Hill BD24 0BA**
email: info@hartsheadinn.co.uk **web:** www.hartsheadinn.co.uk
dir: On B6480, 1m from A65

This traditional and welcoming inn provides well-equipped accommodation that includes a spacious family room complete with bunks, and a smart barn conversion in the grounds. Local beers, an extensive menu, roaring fires and a genuine community spirit ensure a convivial atmosphere prevails.

Rooms 7 en suite 2 annexe en suite (1 fmly) **Facilities** STV FTV tea/coffee Dinner available WiFi ⚓ 9 Snooker Pool table ⚓ **Conf** Max 30 Class 30 Board 20 **Parking** 25 **Notes** LB

GOLDSBOROUGH
Map 19 SE35

Premier Collection

Goldsborough Hall

★★★★★ ⌑ GUEST ACCOMMODATION

tel: 01423 867321 **fax:** 08723 310728 **Church St HG5 8NR**
email: info@goldsboroughhall.com **web:** www.goldsboroughhall.com
dir: A1(M) junct 47, A59 to Knaresborough. 2nd left into Station Rd, at T-junct left into Church St

It's not every day that you get the chance to stay in the former residence of a Royal Princess, in this case HRH Princess Mary (1897-1965), who was one of the Queen's aunts. Hospitality at Goldsborough Hall is second to none. The luxury bedrooms are appointed to the highest standards, and the bathrooms have a real 'wow' factor. Bedrooms feature hand-made mahogany four-poster beds, chesterfields and 50 inch TVs. Royal Afternoon Tea is served in the Jacobean Library or the Drawing Room and reservations for dinner from non-residents are welcomed.

Rooms 6 en suite (4 fmly) S £95-£195; D £115-£495 (room only)* **Facilities** FTV DVD iPod docking station Lounge tea/coffee Dinner available Direct Dial Lift Licensed WiFi ⚓♨ 18 ⚓ Outdoor Hot tub **Extras** Speciality toiletries; mini-bar - chargeable **Conf** Max 150 Thtr 150 Class 50 Board 30 **Parking** 50 **Notes** LB Closed 24-26 Dec & 31 Dec-1 Jan Civ Wed 150

GRASSINGTON
Map 19 SE06

Premier Collection

Grassington House

★★★★★ ⊛⊛ ⌑ RESTAURANT WITH ROOMS

tel: 01756 752040 **fax:** 01756 752050 **5 The Square BD23 5AQ**
email: bookings@grassingtonhousehotel.co.uk
web: www.grassingtonhousehotel.co.uk
dir: A59 into Grassington, in town square opposite post office

Located in the square of the popular village of Grassington, this beautifully converted Georgian house is personally run by owners John and Sue. Delicious food, individually designed bedrooms and warm hospitality ensure an enjoyable stay. There is a stylish lounge bar looking out to the square and the restaurant is split between two rooms; here guests will find the emphasis is on fresh, local ingredients and attentive, yet friendly service.

Rooms 9 en suite (2 fmly) S £95-£132.50; D £110-£220* (incl.dinner) **Facilities** STV FTV tea/coffee Dinner available Direct Dial WiFi **Conf** Thtr 26 Class 20 Board 20 **Parking** 25 **Notes** LB ⊗ Civ Wed 44

Premier Collection

Ashfield House

★★★★★ 🏛 ☕ GUEST ACCOMMODATION

tel: 01756 752584 **fax:** 07092 376562 **Summers Fold BD23 5AE**
email: sales@ashfieldhouse.co.uk **web:** www.ashfieldhouse.co.uk
dir: *B6265 to village centre, from main street left into Summers Fold*

Guests are greeted like old friends at this beautifully maintained 17th-century house, peacefully tucked away a few yards from the village square. The smart lounges offer a high level of comfort and an honesty bar. The freshly prepared three-course dinner (by arrangement) is a highlight of any stay. The attractive bedrooms are well furnished and thoughtfully equipped.

Rooms 7 rms (6 en suite) (1 pri facs) 1 annexe en suite S £65–£90; D £80–£200*
Facilities FTV Lounge tea/coffee Dinner available Licensed WiFi **Extras** Home-baked cookies, speciality toiletries **Conf** Max 8 Board 8 **Parking** 8 **Notes** LB ⊗ No Children 5yrs RS Nov–Mar No dinner on Sun & Wed eve

---

GREAT AYTON   Map 19 NZ51

Royal Oak

★★★ INN

tel: 01642 722361 & 723270 **fax:** 01642 724047 **123 High St TS9 6BW**
email: info@royaloak-hotel.co.uk **web:** www.royaloak-hotel.co.uk
dir: *Off the A173, on High Street*

This 18th-century former coaching inn is very popular with locals and visitors alike. Bedrooms are all comfortably equipped. The restaurant and public bar retain many original features and offer a good selection of fine ales; an extensive range of food is available all day and is served in the bar or the dining room.

Rooms 5 rms (4 en suite) **Facilities** tea/coffee Dinner available Direct Dial WiFi
Conf Max 30 Thtr 30 Class 30 Board 30 **Notes** Closed 25 Dec

---

HACKNESS   Map 19 SE99

Troutsdale Lodge

★★★★ GUEST ACCOMMODATION

tel: 01723 882209 **Troutsdale YO13 0BS**
email: captroutsdale@yahoo.co.uk **web:** www.troutsdalelodge.co.uk
dir: *Off A170 at Snainton signed Troutsdale*

Commanding magnificent views across a peaceful valley and the forest beyond, this Edwardian house showcases many original features combined with modern art. Bedrooms offer good all-round comfort and guests receive fine hospitality from the resident owners.

Rooms 4 en suite (1 fmly) (4 GF) **Facilities** TVL tea/coffee Dinner available Licensed
🐾 **Parking** 8 **Notes** ⊛

HARROGATE   Map 19 SE35

Premier Collection

The Grafton Boutique B&B

★★★★★ 🏛 GUEST ACCOMMODATION

tel: 01423 508491 **fax:** 01423 523168 **1-3 Franklin Mount HG1 5EJ**
email: enquiries@graftonhotel.co.uk **web:** www.graftonhotel.co.uk
dir: *Follow signs to International Centre, into Kings Rd (with Centre on left), Franklin Mount 450yds on right*

The Grafton is a stylish townhouse, in a quiet location, just a short walk from the conference centre and town. It is a period property but with a contemporary interior design throughout and a luxurious feel. There is a beautifully appointed lounge looking out to the garden, and breakfast is served in a spacious and striking dining room. Complimentary WiFi is provided.

Rooms 13 en suite (1 GF) D £85–£115 **Facilities** FTV Lounge tea/coffee Direct Dial Licensed WiFi ♨ 18 ☕ **Parking** 1 **Notes** LB ⊗ Closed 15 Dec–6 Jan

HARROGATE *continued*

Shelbourne House

★★★★ 🛏 GUEST ACCOMMODATION

tel: 01423 504390 **78 Kings Rd HG1 5JX**
email: sue@shelbournehouse.co.uk **web:** www.shelbournehouse.co.uk
dir: *Follow signs to International Centre, over lights by Holiday Inn, premises on right*

Situated opposite the conference centre and close to the town centre, this elegant Victorian house features attractive well-equipped bedrooms. There is a beautifully presented guest lounge and smart dining room. The friendly owners provide attentive service and offer a wide choice at breakfast, with emphasis on local ingredients. Complimentary WiFi access is provided.

Rooms 8 en suite (2 fmly) **Facilities** FTV DVD iPod docking station TVL tea/coffee WiFi **Conf** Board 16 **Parking** 1 **Notes** LB ⊗

Wynnstay House

★★★★ 🛏 GUEST ACCOMMODATION

tel: 01423 560476 **60 Franklin Rd HG1 5EE**
email: wynnstayhouse@tiscali.co.uk **web:** www.wynnstayhouse.com
dir: *Exit A61 in town centre into Kings Rd, right into Strawberry Dale, left at top of road into Franklin Rd*

This double fronted Victorian villa is beautifully maintained. It is located in a residential area a short distance from the conference centre, shops and attractions and is ideal for both business and leisure guests. There is a friendly, welcoming atmosphere. The bedrooms are individually decorated and thoughtfully equipped. Delicious breakfasts are a highlight and are served in the elegant dining room.

Rooms 5 en suite S £50-£80; D £80-£90* **Facilities** FTV iPod docking station Lounge tea/coffee WiFi 🛁 **Notes** LB ⊗ No Children 14yrs

The Cavendish

★★★★ GUEST HOUSE

tel: 01423 509637 **fax:** 01423 504434 **3/5 Valley Dr HG2 0JJ**
email: cavendishhotel@gmail.com **web:** www.cavendishhotelharrogate.co.uk
dir: *Follow signs to town centre, then signs for Valley Gardens & Pump Museum. Turn left before zebra crossing*

This spacious Victorian property is located at the top of the valley gardens and is just a short walk from the town centre. The interior has been fully refurbished in a contemporary style. There is a well-stocked bar and guest lounge and a wide choice is offered for breakfast in the attractive dining room. A range of bedrooms are offered including a family room and a four-poster room. Off-site parking is available.

Rooms 14 en suite (1 fmly) (1 GF) S £50; D £85 **Facilities** TVL tea/coffee Direct Dial Licensed WiFi **Notes** ⊗

Harrogate Brasserie with Rooms

★★★★ 🍴 GUEST ACCOMMODATION

tel: 01423 505041 **fax:** 01423 722300 **28-30 Cheltenham Pde HG1 1DB**
email: info@harrogatebrasserie.co.uk **web:** www.harrogatebrasserie.co.uk
dir: *On A61 town centre behind theatre*

This town centre establishment is distinctly continental in style. The brasserie covers three cosy dining areas, richly decorated and adorned with artefacts. Live jazz is featured on Wednesday, Friday and Sunday nights. The individual bedrooms feature period collectibles; many rooms have DVD players and all have lots of reading material.

Rooms 13 en suite 3 annexe en suite (3 fmly) S £85; D £110* **Facilities** FTV tea/coffee Dinner available Direct Dial Licensed WiFi 🛁 **Parking** 12 **Notes** LB

Innkeeper's Lodge Harrogate (West)

★★★★ INN

tel: 0845 112 6034 **Beckwith Knowle, Otley Rd HG3 1UE**
email: info@innkeeperslodge.com **web:** www.innkeeperslodge.com

Located close to town in Beckwith Knowle, this period property is ideal for exploring historic and vibrant Harrogate and the Yorkshire Dales National Park. The building has been restored and refurbished to a high standard and the spacious public areas are stylish and full of character. Seasonally-changing menus feature traditional favourites as well as Mediterranean influences and the chef's daily specials. Bedrooms are modern, spacious and well furnished. Complimentary WiFi is provided.

Rooms 12 en suite (4 fmly) **Facilities** FTV tea/coffee Dinner available Direct Dial WiFi **Parking** 60

Ruskin

★★★ GUEST ACCOMMODATION

tel: 01423 502045 **fax:** 01423 506131 **1 Swan Rd HG1 2SS**
email: ruskin.hotel@virgin.net **web:** www.ruskinhotel.co.uk
dir: *Off A61(Ripon road), left opposite The Majestic Hotel*

Ruskin, a mid 19th-century house, stands in secluded tree-studded gardens, only a five minute walk from the town centre. It retains many original features and has a relaxing lounge. Breakfasts are served in the elegant dining room, and the thoughtfully equipped bedrooms range from compact to spacious, all furnished in stylish Victorian pine.

Rooms 7 en suite (2 fmly) (1 GF) **Facilities** tea/coffee Direct Dial Licensed **Parking** 7

HAWES	Map 18 SD88

Ebor House

★★★★ GUEST HOUSE

tel: 01969 667337 **Burtersett Rd DL8 3NT**
email: eborhousehawes@yahoo.co.uk **web:** www.eborhouse.co.uk

This beautifully restored three-storey house is just a short walk from the centre of Hawes and is perfectly located for visiting all the attractions that the Yorkshire Dales National Park has to offer. The house has been fully refurbished to provide attractively presented bedrooms with modern bathrooms, whilst retaining many period features. The owners are friendly with all guests made to feel very welcome. There is space at the rear of the property for four cars to make use of the private parking and for the secure storage of bicycles. Complimentary WiFi access is also available. AA Friendliest B&B of the Year Finalist 2014-2015.

Rooms 6 rms (5 en suite) (1 pri facs) S £60-£85; D £80-£90* **Facilities** FTV DVD tea/coffee WiFi 🛁 **Parking** 4 **Notes** ⊗ No Children 18yrs Closed Dec-Jan 🐾

HAWNBY	Map 19 SE58

The Inn at Hawnby

★★★★ 🍴 INN

tel: 01439 798202 **fax:** 01439 798344 **YO62 5QS**
email: info@innathawnby.co.uk **web:** www.innathawnby.co.uk
dir: *Exit B1257 between Stokesley & Helmsley*

This charming 19th-century inn is located in a peaceful village. Service is attentive and friendly, with guests able to relax and browse menus in the cosy bar where there is a good wine list and range of ales. Delicious, home-cooked meals are served in the restaurant, overlooking the gardens and surrounding countryside. Bedrooms are well equipped, with some in the converted stables.

Rooms 6 en suite 3 annexe en suite (1 fmly) (3 GF) S £75-£79; D £85-£99* **Facilities** FTV DVD tea/coffee Dinner available Direct Dial WiFi Fishing Riding **Extras** Speciality toiletries, sherry - complimentary **Conf** Max 20 Thtr 12 Class 20 **Parking** 9 **Notes** LB Closed 25 Dec RS Feb & Mar Restricted lunch service Mon & Tue

Laskill Grange

★★★★ GUEST ACCOMMODATION

tel: 01439 798268 & 798265 **YO62 5NB**
email: laskillgrange@tiscali.co.uk **web:** www.laskillgrange.co.uk
dir: From York A19 to Thirsk, A170 to Helmsley then B1257 N, after 6m sign on left to Laskill Grange

Lovers of the countryside will enjoy this charming 19th-century farmhouse. Guests can take a walk in the surrounds, fish the River Seph which runs through the grounds or visit nearby Rievaulx Abbey. The comfortable, well-furnished bedrooms are in the main house and are supplied with many thoughtful extras.

Rooms 3 rms (2 en suite) (1 pri facs) (3 GF) S £45; D £90* **Facilities** FTV Lounge TVL tea/coffee Dinner available Licensed WiFi ch fac Fishing Riding Outdoor activity area Hot tubs **Extras** Speciality toiletries - complimentary **Conf** Max 20 **Parking** 20 **Notes** LB Civ Wed 620

HELMSLEY	Map 19 SE68

See also Hawnby

Premier Collection

Shallowdale House

★★★★★ GUEST ACCOMMODATION

tel: 01439 788325 **fax:** 01439 788885 **West End YO62 4DY**
email: stay@shallowdalehouse.co.uk **web:** www.shallowdalehouse.co.uk

(For full entry see Ampleforth)

The Feathers

★★★★ INN

tel: 01439 770275 **fax:** 01439 771101 **Market Place YO62 5BH**
email: reservations@feathershotelhelmsley.co.uk **web:** www.feathershotelhelmsley.co.uk
dir: A1(M) junct 49 onto A168 signed Thirsk. Bear left, then take 2nd exit at rdbt onto A170. In Market Place

This fine old property enjoys a prominent position overlooking the busy town square in pretty Helmsley. The bar and lounge areas are full of character and real fires glow on the cooler evenings. There is an extensive dinner menu along with a nightly specials board, which uses the best in local, seasonal produce. Bedrooms have been refurbished to a high standard and are most comfortable. Ample secure parking is available for guests at the rear of the inn. The Feathers is an ideal base from which to explore the North York Moors National Park, and Helmsley is situated on the Cleveland Way walk.

Rooms 21 en suite 2 annexe en suite (2 fmly) S £70; D £80-£99* **Facilities** FTV tea/coffee Dinner available WiFi 18 **Parking** 15 **Notes** LB Closed 24-25 Dec

Plumpton Court

★★★★ GUEST ACCOMMODATION

tel: 01439 771223 **High St, Nawton YO62 7TT**
email: mail@plumptoncourt.com **web:** www.plumptoncourt.com
dir: 2.5m E of Helmsley. Exit A170 in Nawton, signed

Situated in the small village of Nawton between Helmsley and Kirkbymoorside, Plumpton Court has six modern and individually decorated bedrooms. Guests can relax in front of a real fire in the homely lounge with a bottle of wine from the well-stocked bar and enjoy a leisurely breakfast with locally sourced ingredients. Chris is a convivial host and takes delight in helping guests make the most of their visit to North Yorkshire. To the rear of the house is a private, secure car park and a secluded garden.

Rooms 6 en suite (1 GF) S £55-£65; D £72-£78* **Facilities** FTV DVD Lounge tea/coffee Licensed WiFi 18 **Parking** 8 **Notes** No Children 12yrs Closed 22-29 Dec

HETTON	Map 18 SD95

Premier Collection

The Angel Inn

★★★★★ RESTAURANT WITH ROOMS

tel: 01756 730263 **fax:** 01756 730363 **BD23 6LT**
email: info@angelhetton.co.uk **web:** www.angelhetton.co.uk
dir: B6265 from Skipton towards Grassington. At Rylstone turn left by pond, follow signs to Hetton

This roadside inn is steeped in history; parts of the building go back more than 500 years. The restaurant and bar are in the main building, which has ivy and green canopies at the front. Food is a highlight of any stay, offering excellent ingredients, skilfully prepared and carefully presented. The large and stylish bedrooms are across the road in a converted barn which has great views of the Dales, its own wine cave and private parking.

Rooms 9 en suite (3 GF) S £135-£185; D £150-£200* **Facilities** FTV tea/coffee Dinner available Direct Dial WiFi Wine tasting cave **Conf** Max 16 Board 14 **Parking** 40 **Notes** LB Closed 25 Dec & 1wk Jan No coaches Civ Wed 40

HUNTON	Map 19 SE19

The Countryman's Inn

★★★ INN

tel: 01677 450554 & 07734 556845 **South View DL8 1PY**
email: tony@countrymansinn.co.uk **web:** www.countrymansinn.co.uk
dir: Exit A1(M) at Leeming Bar onto A684 towards Bedale/Leyburn. Through Patrick Brompton, right at x-rds. After 1.25m turn left signed Hunton

This traditional country pub offers a friendly atmosphere, cask ales and great food. The bar features a real fire and beamed ceiling and there is a beer garden for warmer weather. A wide choice of freshly prepared meals are served and there is a smartly presented dining room. Bedrooms and bathrooms are more contemporary with a fresh, bright style with good provision made for families and a designated 'pet friendly' room. Other facilities include complimentary WiFi and private parking. Discounted rounds of golf can be arranged at Catterick Golf Club.

Rooms 4 en suite (2 fmly) **Facilities** FTV tea/coffee Dinner available WiFi **Parking**

INGLETON
Map 18 SD67

Gale Green Cottage
★★★★ BED AND BREAKFAST

tel: 015242 41245 & 077867 82088 **Westhouse LA6 3NJ**
email: jill@galegreen.com **web:** www.galegreen.com
dir: *2m NW of Ingleton. S of A65 at Masongill x-rds*

Peacefully located in a rural hamlet, this 300-year-old house has modern facilities without compromising original charm and character. Thoughtfully furnished bedrooms feature smart, modern en suite shower rooms, and a guest lounge is also available.

Rooms 3 en suite (1 fmly) S £42-£45; D £64-£70* **Facilities** FTV TVL tea/coffee WiFi **Extras** Free toiletries **Parking** 6 **Notes** Closed Xmas & New Year

KETTLEWELL
Map 18 SD97

Belk's Bed & Breakfast
[U]

tel: 01756 761188 & 07979 149019 **Middle Ln BD23 5QX**
email: davidbelk23@gmail.com
dir: *Into Kettlewell on B6160, turn opposite Racehorses Hotel, 200mtrs on right*

Currently the rating for this establishment is not confirmed. This may be due to a change of ownership or because it has only recently joined the AA rating scheme.

Rooms 3 en suite S £39; D £85* **Facilities** FTV DVD tea/coffee Licensed WiFi **Parking** 2 **Notes** LB No Children Closed Jan-Feb

KEXBY
Map 17 SE65

Premier Collection

Kexby House
★★★★★ GUEST ACCOMMODATION

tel: 01759 380254 **Kexby YO41 5LE**
email: info@bradfordowen.com **web:** www.kexbyhouse.co.uk
dir: *On A1079, E of York*

This beautifully presented 18th-century Georgian farmhouse is just a few miles outside of York, yet enjoys an idyllic setting in 13 acres of grounds, with 400 yards of private fishing. The marble floored hall leads to an impressive and elegant dining room and the three bedrooms in the main house are individually furnished with bathrooms featuring cast iron roll top baths. The Cottage Room is located within the grounds and gives guests the added benefits of a kitchenette, living room and private patio. Delicious breakfasts feature free range eggs from the owners' own hens.

Rooms 3 en suite 1 annexe en suite (1 fmly) (1 GF) S £90-£115; D £90-£115* **Facilities** DVD tea/coffee WiFi Fishing **Parking** 8 **Notes** No Children 11yrs Closed 30 Nov-15 Jan

KIRKBY FLEETHAM
Map 19 SE29

Premier Collection

The Black Horse
★★★★★ ◎◎ RESTAURANT WITH ROOMS

tel: 01609 749010 & 749011 **fax:** 01423 507836 **Lumley Ln DL7 0SH**
email: gm@blackhorsekirkbyfleetham.com **web:** www.blackhorsekirkbyfleetham.com
dir: *A1 onto A648 towards Northallerton. Left into Ham Hall Ln, through Scruton. At T-junct left into Fleetham Ln. Through Great Fencote to Kirkby Fleetham, into Lumley Ln, inn on left past post office*

Set in a small village, The Black Horse provides everything needed for a getaway break including award-winning food. The spacious bedrooms, named after famous racehorses, are beautifully designed in New England-French style with pastel colours, co-ordinating fabrics and excellent beds; many of the superb bathrooms feature slipper or roll-top baths. There is a large dining room and bar that attracts locals as well as visitors from further afield.

Rooms 7 en suite (1 fmly) (2 GF) S £100-£140; D £120-£180* **Facilities** FTV tea/coffee Dinner available WiFi 18 Fishing Quoits pitch **Conf** Max 40 Thtr 40 Class 30 Board 24 **Parking** 90 **Notes** LB

KIRKBYMOORSIDE
Map 19 SE68

The George and Dragon
AA Advertised

tel: 01751 433334 **Market Place YO62 6AA**
email: reception@georgeanddragon.net **web:** www.georgeanddragon.net
dir: *From A1 onto A168 to Thirsk. Continue on A150 towards Scarborough, exit signed Kirkbymoorside*

Set in the market town of Kirkbymoorside, The George and Dragon is privately owned and run by Alison and David Nicholas and their daughter Laura Moore. The feel is relaxed and personal. The restaurant, bar and bistro all serve excellent, locally sourced food, local real ales, and a great selection of wines. Bedrooms have modern amenities blended with traditional charm.

Rooms 20 annexe en suite (2 fmly) (5 GF) S £60-£75; D £90-£140* **Facilities** tea/coffee Dinner available Licensed WiFi 18 **Conf** Max 30 Thtr 30 Class 20 Board 20 **Parking** 14 **Notes** LB

KNARESBOROUGH
Map 19 SE35

Premier Collection

General Tarleton Inn
★★★★★ ◎◎ RESTAURANT WITH ROOMS

tel: 01423 340284 **fax:** 01423 340288 **Boroughbridge Rd, Ferrensby HG5 0PZ**
email: gti@generaltarleton.co.uk **web:** www.generaltarleton.co.uk
dir: *A1(M) junct 48 at Boroughbridge, take A6055 to Knaresborough. 4m on right*

This 18th-century coaching inn is both beautiful and stylish. Though the physical aspects are impressive, the emphasis here is on food with high-quality, skilfully prepared dishes served in the smart bar-brasserie and in the Orangery. There is also a richly furnished cocktail lounge with a galleried private dining room above it. Bedrooms are very comfortable and business guests are also well catered for.

Rooms 13 en suite (7 GF) S £75-£107; D £129-£150* **Facilities** FTV Lounge tea/coffee Dinner available Direct Dial WiFi **Extras** Speciality toiletries, home-made biscuits **Conf** Max 40 Thtr 40 Class 35 Board 20 **Parking** 40 **Notes** LB Closed 24-26 Dec, 1 Jan No coaches

Newton House

★★★★ 🏠 GUEST ACCOMMODATION

tel: 01423 863539 **5-7 York Place HG5 0AD**
email: info@newtonhousehotel.com **web:** www.newtonhouseyorkshire.com
dir: A1(M) junct 47 onto A59 towards Knaresborough. Right at 1st rdbt, continue to town centre, on right before lights

This elegant Georgian guest accommodation is only a short walk from the river, castle and market square; the property is entered by an archway into the courtyard. Attractive, very well-equipped bedrooms include some four-poster beds and also king-sized double rooms. There is a comfortable lounge with honesty bar and memorable breakfasts are served in the attractive dining rooms.

Rooms 9 rms (8 en suite) (1 pri facs) 3 annexe en suite (2 fmly) (4 GF) **Facilities** FTV TVL tea/coffee Direct Dial Licensed WiFi ⚓ 18 **Parking** 9

Innkeeper's Lodge Harrogate (East)

★★★ INN

tel: 0845 112 6033 **Wetherby Rd, Plompton HG5 8LY**
email: info@innkeeperslodge.com **web:** www.innkeeperslodge.com

This country pub and lodge is convenient for Harrogate, with its tourist attractions, shops and tearooms as well as the Conference Centre. It is also well located for visiting picturesque Knaresborough, Ripon and the Yorkshire Dales. Hearty, seasonal food and cask ales are noteworthy, along with real fires and a range of areas in which to relax. There is a lovely beer garden when the weather's warmer. Bedrooms are comfortable. Complimentary WiFi and on-site parking are also provided.

Rooms 10 en suite (2 fmly) **Facilities** FTV tea/coffee Dinner available Direct Dial WiFi **Parking**

LEEMING BAR · Map 19 SE57

Little Holtby

★★★★ 🅰 BED AND BREAKFAST

tel: 01609 748762 **DL7 9LH**
email: littleholtby@yahoo.co.uk **web:** www.littleholtby.co.uk
dir: 0.5m N of A684 (junct with A1)

All the guest rooms at Little Holtby have wonderful views over rolling countryside, as well as many useful facilities. On cooler evenings log fires are lit in the sitting and dining rooms, ideal for relaxation.

Rooms 3 en suite S £50; D £85-£90* **Facilities** FTV DVD TVL tea/coffee WiFi ⚓ 18 **Extras** Speciality toiletries, fruit, snacks - free **Parking** 6 **Notes** LB ⊗ No Children 12yrs 🐾

Visit theAA.com/shop
for the latest Hotel, Pub and Restaurant Guides

LEVISHAM · Map 19 SE89

Moorlands Country House

★★★★★ 🏠 🍽 GUEST HOUSE

tel: 01751 460229 & 07733 980392 **YO18 7NL**
email: info@moorlandslevisham.co.uk **web:** www.moorlandslevisham.co.uk
dir: A169 from Pickering or Whitby, take turn signed Lockton/Levisham. Through Lockton to Levisham

An elegant and luxuriously appointed house located in the peaceful village of Levisham in the heart of the North York Moors National Park. The gardens are beautiful and the view over the valleys beyond is stunning. The lounge, dining room and bedrooms are richly furnished and there is a wealth of personal touches and thoughtful accessories. Food is also a highlight, with delicious evening meals and impressive breakfasts offered.

Rooms 4 en suite **Facilities** FTV DVD iPod docking station Lounge tea/coffee Dinner available Licensed WiFi ⚓ 18 Riding 🐎 **Extras** Snacks **Parking** 9 **Notes** ⊗ No Children Closed Nov-May

The Horseshoe Inn

★★★★ 🍽 INN

tel: 01751 460240 **fax:** 01751 460052 **Main St YO18 7NL**
email: info@horseshoelevisham.co.uk **web:** www.horseshoelevisham.co.uk
dir: From Pickering on A169, after 4m past Fox & Rabbit Inn on right. 0.5m left to Lockton, then steep winding road to village

The Horseshoe Inn is a charming 19th-century inn with a peaceful location in Levisham village. The spacious bar and dining area are traditionally furnished and food is a highlight with a wide choice and generous portions. The attractive bedrooms include two garden rooms, and most rooms in the main house have lovely views of the village.

Rooms 9 en suite (3 fmly) (3 GF) S £40; D £90* **Facilities** FTV tea/coffee Dinner available WiFi **Parking** 30 **Notes** LB No coaches

LEYBURN · Map 19 SE19

Capple Bank Farm

★★★★★ BED AND BREAKFAST

tel: 01969 625825 & 07836 645238 **West Witton DL8 4ND**
email: julian.smithers@btinternet.com **web:** www.capplebankfarm.co.uk
dir: A1 to Bedale, onto A684 to Leyburn, turn left to Hawes, through Wensley, 1st left in West Witton. Up hill, left bend, gates straight ahead

Ideal for walking and touring in the Yorkshire Dales National Park, Capple Bank Farm is a spacious house. Guests have use of a lovely lounge with a real fire lit on cooler days, and breakfast is served at a beautiful table in the open-plan kitchen and dining room. All bedrooms are en suite with bath and a shower.

Rooms 2 en suite 1 annexe en suite S £60; D £90* **Facilities** STV FTV Lounge tea/coffee WiFi 🐎 **Extras** Toiletries, hairdryers **Parking** 6 **Notes** ⊗ No Children 10yrs Closed Xmas

LEYBURN *continued*

Premier Collection

Low Mill Guest House

★★★★★ 🛏 🍴 GUEST HOUSE

tel: 01969 650553 & 07802 888725 **fax:** 01969 650553 **Bainbridge DL8 3EF**
email: lowmillguesthouse@gmail.com **web:** www.lowmillguesthouse.co.uk
dir: *A1 junct 51 onto A684 towards Hawes. In Bainbridge turn right by junct on village green*

A truly unique, luxurious retreat tucked away in the beautiful Dales village of Bainbridge. Grade II listed, Low Mill Guest House has been refurbished to an impressive standard with the original mill works and waterwheel restored. Bedrooms are spacious with original features blended with stylish design. There is a stunning lounge with working range, and an attractive dining room where breakfast and candlelit evening meals are served. Low Mill Guest House was the AA Guest Accommodation of the Year for England 2013-14.

Rooms 3 en suite S £75-£125; D £100-£170 **Facilities** FTV DVD iPod docking station TVL tea/coffee Dinner available Direct Dial Licensed WiFi Fishing 🛇 **Extras** Speciality toiletries, home-made biscuits - free **Parking** 3 **Notes** LB No Children 10yrs

Premier Collection

Braithwaite Hall

★★★★★ 🛏 BED AND BREAKFAST

tel: 01969 640287 **East Witton DL8 4SY**
email: info@braithwaitehall.co.uk **web:** www.braithwaitehall.co.uk
dir: *1.5m from East Witton on single track road*

This impressive 17th-century building is set in open farmland in Coverdale with views over the Pennines bordering Wensleydale. Inside are many period features including antique furnishings and a stunning oak staircase. The drawing room comes complete with oak panelling from the 1660s. Bedrooms are spacious and very comfortable. Delicious breakfasts are served in the elegant dining room and there is a friendly, welcoming atmosphere.

Rooms 3 rms (2 en suite) (1 pri facs) S £65-£75; D £95-£120 **Facilities** FTV DVD tea/coffee WiFi 🎣 Fishing **Extras** Speciality toiletries, fruit, port **Parking** 8 **Notes** ⊗ No Children 12yrs Closed Dec-Feb 🖼

The Queens Head

★★★★ 🍴 INN

tel: 01677 450259 **Westmoor Ln, Finghall DL8 5ND**
email: enquiries@queensfinghall.co.uk **web:** www.queensfinghall.co.uk
dir: *From Bedale follow A684 W towards Leyburn, just after pub & caravan park turn left signed to Finghall. Follow road, on left*

Located in the quiet village of Finghall, this country inn dates back to the 18th century and has original oak beams. A wide choice of freshly prepared meals are served in either the bar or more contemporary restaurant, which has lovely views of the surrounding countryside. Bedrooms are spacious and located in an adjacent annexe.

Rooms 3 annexe en suite (1 fmly) (3 GF) **Facilities** FTV DVD tea/coffee Dinner available 🛇 **Parking** 40

LITTON
Map 18 SD97

The Queens Arms

★★★ INN

tel: 01756 770096 **BD23 5QJ**
email: info@queensarmslitton.co.uk **web:** www.queensarmslitton.co.uk
dir: *A59 N of Skipton onto B6265 Grassington Rd. Through Kilnsey & Arncliffe to Litton*

The Queens Arms is a traditional, family-run village inn set in the Yorkshire countryside, and is a cosy pub with a very homely atmosphere. It has welcoming fires in the bar and a log burner in the dining room. Bedrooms are traditionally decorated, with crisp linen and extremely comfortable beds. Evening meals are served in the bar or in the dining room, and breakfast is sure to set you up for the day.

Rooms 6 rms (4 en suite) (2 pri facs) (1 fmly) S £65.50-£73.50; D £88.50-£95* **Facilities** Lounge tea/coffee Dinner available WiFi Fishing 🛇 **Extras** Speciality toiletries **Notes** LB RS Mon in winter No coaches

---

LONG PRESTON
Map 18 SD85

The Boars Head

★★★ 🍴 INN

tel: 01729 840217 **fax:** 01729 840217 **9 Main St BD23 4ND**
email: boardsheadhotel@hotmail.co.uk **web:** www.boarsheadlongpreston.co.uk

Situated in the pleasant village of Long Preston, the inn was built in the 18th century and features beamed ceilings and open fires. It's a lively inn with entertainment including live bands, discos, bingo and quizzes. A wide range of food and ales are available in the pub restaurant. Bedrooms are en suite and comfortable. The property has ample parking.

Rooms 5 en suite **Facilities** FTV DVD tea/coffee Dinner available WiFi Pool table 🛇 **Parking** 26

LOW ROW
Map 18 SD99

The Punch Bowl Inn

★★★★ 🛏 🍴 INN

tel: 01748 886233 **fax:** 01748 886945 **DL11 6PF**
email: info@pbinn.co.uk **web:** www.pbinn.co.uk
dir: *From Scotch Corner take A6108 to Richmond then B6270 to Low Row*

This friendly inn is appointed in a contemporary style. Real ales and freshly-cooked meals are served in either the spacious bar or dining room. The modern bedrooms are stylish yet simply furnished, with well-equipped bathrooms. Guests also have use of a lounge which has stunning views of the Dales.

Rooms 9 en suite 2 annexe en suite (1 fmly) (1 GF) **Facilities** FTV Lounge tea/coffee Dinner available Direct Dial WiFi Fishing **Extras** Speciality toiletries, home-made shortbread **Parking** 20 **Notes** Closed 25 Dec

---

MALHAM
Map 18 SD96

The Lister Arms

★★★★ INN

tel: 01729 830330 **BD23 4DB**
email: relax@listerarms.co.uk **web:** www.listerarms.co.uk
dir: *From A59 into Malham, right in centre of village*

Located in Malham in the Yorkshire Dales National Park, The Lister Arms is a traditional country inn with wood beams and open fires. It is close to the village green and a babbling stream. The accommodation is comfortable and well equipped, and a wide selection of imaginative dishes, together with real ales and fine wines, are served in the busy bar and restaurant, where the atmosphere is relaxed and comfortable.

Rooms 15 en suite (3 fmly) **Facilities** FTV tea/coffee Dinner available WiFi **Parking** 20 **Notes** LB No coaches

River House

★★★★ 🛏 🍽 GUEST HOUSE

tel: 01729 830315 **fax:** 01729 292315 **BD23 4DA**
email: info@riverhousehotel.co.uk **web:** www.riverhousemalham.co.uk
dir: Off A65, N to Malham

Expect a warm welcome at River House, which dates from 1664. The house is nestled right in the centre of this scenic Malhamdale village and is perfect for walking and cycling routes. Bedrooms are bright and comfortable, with one on the ground floor. Public areas include an inviting lounge and a large, well-appointed dining room. The establishment is also licensed and offers excellent evening meals for groups of six or more. Breakfast is another highlight with delicious Dales cooked breakfasts featuring eggs from the owners' own hens. Other facilities also include free WiFi and secure storage for bikes.

Rooms 8 en suite (1 GF) S £55-£80; D £70-£90* **Facilities** FTV Lounge tea/coffee Dinner available Licensed WiFi Fishing 🚲 Drying room **Extras** Wine, flowers, fruit - chargeable **Parking** 5 **Notes** LB No Children 12yrs Closed 21-26 Dec

The Buck Inn at Malham

★★★ INN

tel: 01729 830317 **fax:** 01729 830605 **Cove Rd BD23 4DA**
email: buck-inn@btconnect.com **web:** www.thebuckinnmalham.co.uk
dir: From Skipton on A65 towards Kendal, after 2.5m turn right to Malham. Follow road to village

The friendly owners and staff ensure guests are well looked after when they arrive at this traditional 19th-century coaching inn in the centre of Malham. Cask beers and a wide choice of hearty meals are served at lunchtimes and throughout evenings, with a log fire adding to the cosy atmosphere in the lounge bar. The Hikers Bar features a Yorkshire flagstone floor, and dogs, families and muddy boots are all welcome. Free WiFi is available and there is also a heated patio.

Rooms 12 en suite (1 fmly) S £45-£90; D £50-£90* **Facilities** tea/coffee Dinner available WiFi 🚲 **Conf** Max 40 Thtr 40 Class 20 Board 20 **Parking** 20

Lindon Guest House

★★★ GUEST HOUSE

tel: 01729 830418 **Airton, Malham Dale BD23 4BE**
email: lindonguesthouse@googlemail.com **web:** www.lindonguesthouse.co.uk
dir: From A65 onto Malham road, on left in village of Airton

This attractive stone building was originally a barn and has been carefully converted into a friendly, family-run guest house. The location is idyllic, in the heart of the Yorkshire Dales National Park and with panoramic views across Malhamdale. The house is ideal for walkers and cyclists with the Pennine Way passing just outside. Bedrooms are compact but furnished well and with lots of character including original beams. There is also an inviting, spacious lounge and dining room.

Rooms 5 en suite S £40-£55; D £55-£70* **Facilities** TVL tea/coffee Dinner available Licensed WiFi 🚲 **Parking** 8 **Notes** LB Closed 24-26 Dec

Beck Hall

★★★ GUEST HOUSE

tel: 01729 830332 **Cove Rd BD23 4DJ**
email: alice@beckhallmalham.com **web:** www.beckhallmalham.com
dir: A65 to Gargrave, turn right to Malham. Beck Hall 100yds on right after mini rdbt

A small stone bridge over Malham Beck leads to this delightful property. Dating from 1710, the house has true character, and bedrooms come complete with four-poster beds. Delicious afternoon teas are available in the colourful garden in warmer months, while roaring log fires welcome guests in the winter.

Rooms 11 en suite 7 annexe en suite (4 fmly) (4 GF) **Facilities** STV Lounge tea/coffee Licensed WiFi 🚲 **Parking** 40

| OLDSTEAD | Map 19 SE57 |

Premier Collection

The Black Swan at Oldstead

★★★★★ ⊛⊛⊛ 🍽 RESTAURANT WITH ROOMS

tel: 01347 868387 **YO61 4BL**
email: enquiries@blackswanoldstead.co.uk **web:** www.blackswanoldstead.co.uk
dir: Exit A19, 3m S Thirsk for Coxwold, left in Coxwold, left at Byland Abbey for Oldstead

The Black Swan is set amidst the stunning scenery of the North York Moors National Park, and parts of the building date back to the 16th century. Well appointed, very comfortable bedrooms and bathrooms provide the perfect get-away. Open fires, a traditional bar and a restaurant, serving award-winning food, is the icing on the cake for this little gem of a property.

Rooms 4 en suite (4 GF) D £195-£390* (incl.dinner) **Facilities** FTV DVD tea/coffee Dinner available WiFi **Extras** Home-made biscuits/brownies, speciality toiletries **Parking** 24 **Notes** ⊛ No Children 16yrs Closed 2wks Jan No coaches

| OSMOTHERLEY | Map 19 SE49 |

Premier Collection

Cleveland Tontine

★★★★★ ⊛ 🍽 RESTAURANT WITH ROOMS

tel: 01609 882671 **fax:** 01609 882660 **Staddlebridge DL6 3JB**
email: bookings@theclevelandtontine.co.uk **web:** www.theclevelandtontine.co.uk
dir: Just off A172 junct on A19 Nbound

This iconic destination restaurant with rooms is a stunning place. Contemporary public areas sit alongside a traditional restaurant with open fires, tiled flooring and great food. Afternoon tea can be taken in the conservatory overlooking the gardens. Bedrooms are individually designed, with modern furniture and feature bathrooms. The service is friendly and relaxed, there is ample parking and major road links are close by.

Rooms 7 en suite (4 fmly) S £130-£190; D £130-£190* **Facilities** STV FTV Lounge tea/coffee Dinner available Direct Dial WiFi ✤ Riding 🚲 **Extras** Speciality toiletries **Conf** Max 70 Thtr 56 Class 28 Board 38 **Parking** 60 **Notes** ⊛

PATELEY BRIDGE
Map 19 SE16

Roslyn House

★★★★ ≜ GUEST ACCOMMODATION

tel: 01423 711374 **fax:** 01423 715995 **9 King St HG3 5AT**
email: enquiries@roslynhouse.co.uk **web:** www.roslynhouse.co.uk
dir: B6165 into Pateley Bridge, right at end of High St at newsagents into King St, house 200yds on left

You are assured of a warm welcome at well-maintained Roslyn House in the centre of the village. Bedrooms are attractively furnished, with homely touches and contemporary en suites. A comfortable lounge is provided and hearty breakfasts will ensure you are set up for the day. Complimentary WiFi is also available. Cyclists and walkers on the famous Nidderdale Way are well catered for.

Rooms 7 en suite S £55-£59; D £78-£79* **Facilities** FTV TVL tea/coffee WiFi **Extras** Chocolates, water, sweets - complimentary **Conf** Max 8 Board 8 **Parking** 6 **Notes** LB ⊗ No Children 3yrs

PICKERING
Map 19 SE78

Premier Collection

17 Burgate

★★★★★ ≜ GUEST ACCOMMODATION

tel: 01751 473463 **17 Burgate YO18 7AU**
email: info@17burgate.co.uk **web:** www.17burgate.co.uk
dir: From A170 follow sign to Castle. 17 Burgate on right

An elegant house close to the centre of Pickering and the castle, 17 Burgate offers comfortable, individually designed bedrooms with all modern facilities, including free broadband, iPod docks, DVD/CD player and comfy sofas. Public areas include a restful lounge bar, and breakfast includes a wide choice of local, healthy foods. The proprietors here make every effort to maintain green and sustainable credentials.

Rooms 5 en suite S £70-£95; D £75-£105* **Facilities** FTV DVD iPod docking station Lounge tea/coffee Licensed WiFi **Extras** Chocolate, snacks - chargeable **Conf** Max 12 Thtr 12 Class 12 Board 12 **Parking** 7 **Notes** LB No Children 10yrs Closed Xmas RS 15-29 Dec

Fox & Hounds Country Inn

★★★★ ⚘ INN

tel: 01751 431577 **fax:** 01751 432791 **Main St, Sinnington YO62 6SQ**
email: fox.houndsinn@btconnect.com **web:** www.thefoxandhoundsinn.co.uk
dir: 3m W of Pickering. Off A170 between Pickering & Helmsley

An attractive village inn offering smart, well-equipped bedrooms. The public areas include a bar, a cosy lounge and a restaurant which offers an impressive range of well presented and well cooked dishes. Food here has been awarded an AA Rosette.

Rooms 10 en suite (4 GF) S £59-£94; D £60-£170* **Facilities** FTV Lounge tea/coffee Dinner available Direct Dial WiFi **Parking** 40 **Notes** LB Closed 25-27 Dec Civ Wed

Grindale House

★★★★ 🅰 GUEST ACCOMMODATION

tel: 01751 476636 **123 Eastgate YO18 7DW**
email: info@grindalehouse.com **web:** www.grindalehouse.com

Close to the North York Moors National Park and North Riding Forest Park, Grindale House is a charming stone building with self-catering cottages to the side and behind. The guest accommodation is comfortable and attractive and breakfasts are memorable. Much of the produce that goes into it has come from local farms and suppliers. There is also on-site parking, WiFi, and secure bike lock-up.

Rooms 6 rms (5 en suite) (1 pri facs) 3 annexe en suite (3 fmly) (3 GF) S fr £55; D £85-£100* **Facilities** FTV TVL tea/coffee WiFi **Parking** 8 **Notes** LB ⊗ Closed mid Dec-Mar

PICKHILL
Map 19 SE38

Nags Head Country Inn

★★★★ ⚘⚘ INN

tel: 01845 567391 **fax:** 01845 567212 **YO7 4JG**
email: reservations@nagsheadpickhill.co.uk **web:** www.nagsheadpickhill.co.uk
dir: Leave A1 junct 50 (travelling N) onto A6055; junct 51 (travelling S) onto A684, then A6055

This country inn, situated in the centre of the attractive village, is only a mile from the A1, and nine miles northwest of Thirsk. It is renowned for the excellence of its food and traditional real ales, complemented by the atmosphere and character of its cosy bars. Some bedrooms are in a cottage next door, and they all have en suite bathrooms and are very well equipped. The smartly appointed restaurant and cocktail bar is open for dinner to both residents and non-residents.

Rooms 7 en suite 6 annexe en suite (1 fmly) (3 GF) **Facilities** FTV TVL tea/coffee Dinner available Direct Dial WiFi 👍 ♿ 18 **Extras** Fruit **Conf** Thtr 30 Class 18 Board 16 **Parking** 40 **Notes** ⊗ Closed 25 Dec

REDCAR
Map 19 NZ62

Springdale House

★★★★ BED AND BREAKFAST

tel: 01642 297169 & 07834 615147 **3 Nelson Ter TS10 1RX**
email: reservations@springdalehouse.co.uk **web:** www.springdalehouse.co.uk

Springdale House is a Victorian town house situated on a quiet terraced row and has delightful and friendly accommodation with a focus on quality furnishings and comfort. Each room is individually decorated and has flat-screen TV with Freeview. It is situated only five minutes' walk from the town's bars and restaurants, and near to the promenade.

Rooms 5 rms (4 en suite) (1 pri facs) S £42-£59; D £75-£80* **Facilities** FTV TV4B tea/coffee WiFi **Notes** ⊗ No Children 16yrs

RICCALL
Map 16 SE63

White Rose Villa

★★★★ 🅰 BED AND BREAKFAST

tel: 01757 248115 **33 York Rd YO19 6QG**
email: whiterosevilla@btinternet.com **web:** www.whiterosevilla.info
dir: S of York, from A19, signed Riccall, 50mtrs on right

Expect a warm and friendly welcome from Viv and Steve when visiting White Rose Villa. Conveniently located in the heart of the Yorkshire countryside, the popular village of Riccall is close to both York and Selby. All bedrooms are en suite and well equipped. There is a guest TV lounge to relax in, complete with a selection of DVDs, CDs, books and board games. Breakfast is served in the sunny dining room, and special diets are catered to by prior arrangement.

Rooms 3 en suite (2 fmly) S £35-£40; D £65-£70* **Facilities** FTV DVD TVL tea/coffee WiFi **Extras** Speciality toiletries **Parking** 4 **Notes** LB ⊗ Closed 24-26 & 31 Dec

Per Bacco at The Park View

★★★ RESTAURANT WITH ROOMS

tel: 01757 249146 **20 Main St YO19 6PX**
email: gianlucasechi@hotmail.co.uk web: www.per-bacco.co.uk
dir: *A19 from Selby, left for Riccall by water tower, house 100yds on right*

This spacious detached property is located in a quiet residential area and is convenient for York. The ground floor has been converted into an authentic Italian restaurant and there is a wide choice of fresh, home-made dishes and a friendly atmosphere. The restaurant is the main part of the business but there is also a range of comfortable en suite bedrooms. Ample parking is available.

Rooms 4 en suite (2 fmly) **Facilities** STV FTV iPod docking station Lounge tea/coffee Dinner available WiFi ♨ 🔒 **Parking** 30 **Notes** No coaches

| RICHMOND | Map 19 NZ10 |

Rosedale Guest House

★★★★ 🏠 GUEST HOUSE

tel: 01748 823926 & 07854 698027 **2 Pottergate DL10 4AB**
email: gary53uk@hotmail.com web: www.richmondbedandbreakfast.co.uk
dir: *A1(M), A6108 to Richmond. Pottergate 0.5m before town centre*

A short stroll away from the centre of the small town of Richmond, Rosedale Guest House is an attractive Grade II listed building which has been tastefully decorated throughout. Warm hospitality abounds alongside stylishly furnished and comfortably equipped bedrooms. The public rooms include a dining area and a private lounge offering free WiFi.

Rooms 4 en suite (1 fmly) S £55-£70; D £70-£88* **Facilities** FTV Lounge tea/coffee WiFi 🔒 **Notes** LB ⊗ No Children 5yrs

Whashton Springs Farm (NZ149046)

★★★★ FARMHOUSE

tel: 01748 822884 fax: 01748 826285 **DL11 7JS**
email: whashtonsprings@btconnect.com web: www.whashtonsprings.co.uk
dir: *In Richmond N at lights towards Ravensworth, 3m down steep hill, farm at bottom on left*

A friendly welcome awaits at Whashton Springs Farm, situated in the heart of the countryside yet convenient for major routes. Bedrooms are split between the courtyard rooms and the main farmhouse. Hearty breakfasts are served in the spacious dining room overlooking the gardens.

Rooms 3 en suite 5 annexe en suite (2 fmly) (5 GF) **Facilities** FTV tea/coffee WiFi **Conf** Max 16 Board 16 **Parking** 10 **Notes** ⊗ No Children 3yrs Closed late Dec-Jan ⊗ 600 acres arable/beef/mixed/sheep

The Frenchgate Guest House

★★★★ GUEST HOUSE

tel: 01748 823421 & 07889 768696   fax: 01748 823421 **66 Frenchgate DL10 7AG**
email: info@66frenchgate.co.uk web: www.66frenchgate.co.uk
dir: *From Scotch Corner, enter Richmond, straight over rdbt & lights. Left at 2nd rdbt, turn left after 100mtrs, drive to top of Frenchgate*

Tucked away on a charming cobbled street in an historic market town, this attractively presented Victorian town house has an elevated position with stunning views. Bedrooms are comfortable and well equipped with complimentary WiFi access provided. The spacious conservatory-lounge and breakfast room has panoramic south-facing views of the Swale Valley and Easby Abbey.

Rooms 8 rms (7 en suite) (1 pri facs) (3 fmly) (2 GF) D £62-£98 **Facilities** FTV Lounge tea/coffee WiFi ♨ 18 🔒 **Extras** Fridges, bottled water, fruit **Conf** Max 20 Thtr 15 Class 15 Board 15 **Notes** LB ⊗ No Children 5yrs

| RIPON | Map 19 SE37 |

Premier Collection

Mallard Grange (SE270704)

★★★★★ 🏠 FARMHOUSE

tel: 01765 620242 & 07720 295918   fax: 01765 620242 **Aldfield HG4 3BE**
email: maggie@mallardgrange.co.uk web: www.mallardgrange.co.uk
dir: *B6265 W fom Ripon, Mallard Grange 2.5m on right*

Located near Fountains Abbey, a genuine welcome is always guaranteed at Mallard Grange. The original features of this early 16th-century, Grade II listed farmhouse are highlighted by quality furnishings and decor. Bedrooms, two of which are in a converted smithy, are filled with a wealth of thoughtful extras, and comprehensive breakfasts feature home-reared and local produce.

Rooms 2 en suite 2 annexe en suite (2 GF) D £80-£100* **Facilities** FTV iPod docking station Lounge tea/coffee WiFi **Extras** Speciality toiletries, home-made biscuits **Parking** 6 **Notes** LB ⊗ No Children 12yrs Closed Xmas & New Year 500 acres mixed/beef/sheep/arable

RIPON *continued*

The Old Coach House

★★★★★ 🅰 GUEST ACCOMMODATION

tel: 01765 634900 & 07912 632296 **fax:** 01765 635352
2 Stable Cottages, North Stainley HG4 3HT
email: enquiries@oldcoachhouse.info **web:** www.oldcoachhouse.info
dir: *From Ripon take A6108 to Masham. Once in North Stainley, on left opposite Staveley Arms*

The Old Coach House has been part of the local community for over twenty years, so if you need information on the local area, don't hesitate to ask. This 18th-century building stands in the grounds of North Stainley Hall. All bedrooms are designed to a high specification and are individually decorated. Each room is named after a famous Yorkshire landmark or place and each offers a range of facilities. All rooms are en suite and some have wet rooms.

Rooms 8 en suite (4 GF) D £70-£110* **Facilities** FTV iPod docking station tea/coffee Direct Dial WiFi ⬇ 18 🔒 **Extras** Speciality toiletries - complimentary **Parking** 8 **Notes** ⊗ No Children 14yrs

Bay Tree Farm (SE263685)

★★★★ 🏠 FARMHOUSE

tel: 01765 620394 **fax:** 01765 620394 **Aldfield HG4 3BE**
email: val@baytreefarm.co.uk **web:** www.baytreefarm.co.uk
dir: *4m W of Ripon. S off B6265 in village of Aldfield*

A warm welcome awaits at Bay Tree Farm, a well presented farmhouse set in the countryside close to Fountains Abbey and Studley Park. Bedrooms are comfortable, with flat-screen TVs, WiFi and luxury toiletries. There is a cosy lounge with a log-burning stove in winter and plenty of outside space for the summer months. Food is a highlight of any stay with delicious breakfasts served at the large farmhouse table. Memorable home cooked dinners are also available by prior arrangement.

Rooms 4 en suite 2 annexe en suite (1 fmly) (3 GF) S £60-£80; D £90-£95 **Facilities** FTV Lounge tea/coffee Dinner available WiFi **Parking** 10 **Notes** LB 400 acres beef/arable

St George's Court (SE237697)

★★★★ 🏠 FARMHOUSE

tel: 01765 620618 **Old Home Farm, Grantley HG4 3PJ**
email: info@stgeorgescourt.co.uk **web:** www.stgeorges-court.co.uk
dir: *B6265 W from Ripon, up hill 1m past Risplith sign & next right, 1m on right*

This renovated farmhouse is in a great location, in the delightful countryside close to Fountains Abbey. The attractive, well-equipped, ground-floor bedrooms are located around a central courtyard. Imaginative breakfasts are served in the breakfast room, and a guest lounge is available, both with views of the surrounding countryside.

Rooms 4 en suite (1 fmly) (4 GF) **Facilities** Lounge tea/coffee WiFi Fishing 🔒 **Conf** Max 12 **Parking** 12 **Notes** 20 acres beef/sheep/pigs

The Black A Moor Inn

★★★★ 🍺 INN

tel: 01765 603511 & 07880 745756 **Boroughbridge Rd, Bridge Hewick HG4 5AA**
email: info@blackamoorinn.co.uk **web:** www.blackamoorinn.co.uk

This friendly family run inn offers good food, a welcoming atmosphere and individually styled bedrooms. The location is ideal for Ripon Racecourse, Newby Hall and Fountains Abbey. The inn has been refurbished and provides a relaxing, airy

feel but with the traditional style and character retained. There is a lounge with comfortable seating, traditional bar and a spacious restaurant. Guests can expect log fires, real ales and a wide choice on the seasonal menus that change regularly. There is on-site parking and complimentary WiFi access is available.

Rooms 5 en suite (2 fmly) (1 GF) S fr £55; D fr £75* **Facilities** FTV DVD Lounge tea/coffee Dinner available WiFi 🔒 **Conf** Max 30 Class 30 **Parking** 30 **Notes** ⊗

The George at Wath

★★★★ 🏅 INN

tel: 01765 641324 **Main St, Wath HG4 5EN**
email: reception@thegeorgeatwath.co.uk **web:** www.thegeorgeatwath.co.uk
dir: *From A1 (dual carriageway) N'bound, left signed Melmerby & Wath. From A1 S'bound, exit at slip road signed A61. Right at T-junct signed Ripon. Approx 0.5m, right for Melmerby & Wath*

Located in the centre of the beautiful North Yorkshire village of Wath, this popular village inn provides well-equipped and pleasantly decorated accommodation. The public areas include a spacious lounge bar complete with log burning stove, and a relaxed dining area where a varied selection of dishes is available. WiFi is available throughout.

Rooms 5 en suite (1 fmly) **Facilities** FTV iPod docking station tea/coffee Dinner available WiFi Pool table 🔒 **Extras** Home-made cookies **Conf** Max 45 Thtr 45 Class 32 Board 20 **Parking** 25 **Notes** Civ Wed 60

The Royal Oak

★★★★ 🏅 INN

tel: 01765 602284 **36 Kirkgate HG4 1PB**
email: info@royaloakripon.co.uk **web:** www.royaloakripon.co.uk
dir: *In town centre*

Ideally located in the heart of the city centre close to the cathedral and museum, The Royal Oak offers modern, stylish, and comfortable en suite rooms with a genuine, warm welcome on arrival. The inn has a restaurant and separate bar area which organises food and wine tasting events on a regular basis. The menu boasts a varied range of traditional dishes with a European influence in the attractively designed restaurant. A good selection of Timothy Taylor ales can be found along with a varied selection of wines.

Rooms 6 en suite (1 fmly) S £55-£65; D £65-£100* **Facilities** FTV DVD tea/coffee Dinner available WiFi 🔒 **Parking** 4

| **RUNSWICK** | Map 19 NZ81 |

The Firs

★★★★ 🏅 🍴 GUEST HOUSE

tel: 01947 840433 **fax:** 01947 841616 **26 Hinderwell Ln TS13 5HR**
email: mandy.shackleton@talk21.com **web:** www.the-firs.co.uk
dir: *From Whitby on A174, turn right signed Runswick. At T-junct turn left, 150yds on right*

The Firs is a spacious, family-run property located in the picturesque village of Runswick on the stunning North Yorkshire coast. The house is just eight miles north of Whitby and is on the edge of the North York Moors National Park. Free private parking, complimentary WiFi and comfortable bedrooms are offered along with a friendly welcome. The ground floor rooms are wheelchair accessible and have en suite wet rooms. Dinner reservations can be made by residents and non-residents; menus change daily and feature traditional, freshly prepared dishes and generous portions.

Rooms 9 en suite (3 fmly) (6 GF) S fr £65; D fr £85* **Facilities** FTV DVD iPod docking station Lounge tea/coffee Dinner available Direct Dial WiFi 🔒 **Extras** Sweets, mineral water, home-made cake **Parking** 12 **Notes** LB No Children 2yrs Closed Nov-Mar 🍴

▮ SCARBOROUGH
Map 17 TA08

Amrock Guest House

★★★★ GUEST HOUSE

tel: 01723 374423 & 07712 515564 **11 Victoria Park Av YO12 7TR**
email: info@amrockguesthouse.co.uk **web:** www.amrockguesthouse.co.uk
dir: A64 follow brown signs for North Bay. With Peasholm Park on right, turn right from Northstead Manor Dr, straight over rdbt. 500yds on left

This well maintained Edwardian house is located in the North Bay area close to Peasholm Park. Accommodation is over three floors and is clean and comfortable. All bedrooms are en suite and have flat-screen TVs, DVD players and complimentary WiFi access. Parking permits can be provided for the on-street parking.

Rooms 6 en suite (1 fmly) S £25-£30; D £50-£60* **Facilities** FTV DVD tea/coffee WiFi **Notes** LB ⊗

Downe Arms Country Inn

★★★★ INN

tel: 01723 862471 **fax:** 01723 865096 **Main Rd, Wykeham YO13 9QB**
email: info@downearmshotel.co.uk **web:** www.downearmshotel.co.uk
dir: On A170 Pickering to Scarborough road in Wykeham

Downe Arms Country Inn is a family-orientated inn on the doorstep of the North York Moors National Park and close to the coast and tourist areas in and around York. Part of the Dawnay estate, this 17th-century former farmhouse has been tastefully modernised. Expect comfortable public areas supported by good cooking, utilising local produce. Bedrooms are well appointed and equipped with a contemporary feel. The property also caters well for functions and is a popular wedding venue. Ample car parking is available.

Rooms 10 en suite (2 fmly) **Facilities** FTV Lounge tea/coffee Dinner available WiFi **Conf** Max 150 Thtr 150 Class 90 Board 50 **Parking** 85 **Notes** Civ Wed 120

Foulsyke Farm House B&B (TA008912)

★★★★ FARMHOUSE

tel: 01723 507423 **Barmoor Ln, Scalby YO13 0PG**
email: foulsykebandb@btinternet.com **web:** www.foulsykefarmhouse.co.uk
dir: A171 from Scarborough follow signs to Whitby. Pass through Newby & Scalby. Left into Barmoor Ln, 50yds past pond

Foulsyke Farm is situated in the quiet village of Scalby, some three miles north of Scarborough. The B&B is on a working farm which is part of the Duchy of Lancaster estate. Bedrooms all provide a good level of comfort, and the loft room offers luxury accommodation with wine, chocolates and flowers, ideal for a special occasion. Gardens offer space to sit and enjoy the surrounding peaceful countryside.

Rooms 4 en suite S £50-£65; D £65-£90* **Facilities** FTV tea/coffee WiFi ⬚ **Extras** Speciality toiletries, snacks in some rooms **Parking** 8 **Notes** LB ⊗ No Children arable/beef/dairy/sheep

The Grainary (SE965959)

★★★★ ⬚ FARMHOUSE

tel: 01723 870026 **Keesbeck Hill Farm, Harwood Dale YO13 0DT**
email: info@grainary.co.uk **web:** www.grainary.co.uk
dir: From N - exit A171 signed Harwood Dale. From S - exit A171 in Burniston, into Stone Quarry Rd

The Grainary is a delightful property set in acres of its own land with animal enclosures and duck ponds for the children and families. The tea room has stunning views over the countryside and is a real delight, with home-baked produce being a feature. Evening meals are also served and the Grainary is also licensed. The accommodation is comfortable and very well presented. Public areas are a real feature. True Yorkshire hospitality guarantees a warm welcome and attentive service.

Rooms 14 en suite (3 fmly) (4 GF) S £37-£43; D £69-£80* **Facilities** FTV DVD Lounge TVL tea/coffee Dinner available Licensed WiFi Fishing Pool table ⬚ **Parking** 20 **Notes** LB Closed Dec-Jan 200 acres mixed

Olivers

★★★★ GUEST ACCOMMODATION

tel: 01723 368717 **34 West St YO11 2QP**
email: info@olivershotelscarborough.co.uk **web:** www.olivershotel.scarborough.co.uk
dir: Take A64 to B1427 (Margarets Rd). Right onto A165 (Filey Rd). 2nd left into Granville Rd

Well-equipped, spacious bedrooms are a feature of this old Victorian gentleman's residence; one bedroom was originally the nursery. Close to the cliff lift which takes you down to the spa, beaches and gardens, and centrally located on the South Cliff.

Rooms 6 en suite (2 fmly) (1 GF) S £28-£36; D £56-£64* **Facilities** FTV DVD tea/coffee WiFi **Notes** LB ⊗ Closed 20-28 Dec

Paragon

★★★★ GUEST ACCOMMODATION

tel: 01723 372676 **fax:** 01723 372676 **123 Queens Pde YO12 7HU**
web: www.paragonhotel.com
dir: On A64, follow signs for North Bay. Establishment on clifftop

This welcoming Victorian terrace house has been carefully renovated to provide stylish, thoughtfully equipped, non-smoking accommodation. Hearty English breakfasts are served in the attractive dining room and there is also a lounge bar with a fabulous sea view.

Rooms 14 en suite (1 fmly) S £35-£38; D £62-£74 **Facilities** Lounge tea/coffee Direct Dial Licensed WiFi **Parking** 6 **Notes** LB Closed 20 Nov-24 Jan

The Whiteley

★★★★ GUEST ACCOMMODATION

tel: 01723 373514 **fax:** 01723 373007 **99-101 Queens Pde YO12 7HY**
email: whiteleyhotel@bigfoot.com **web:** www.yorkshirecoast.co.uk/whiteley
dir: A64, A165 to North Bay & Peasholm Park, right into Peasholm Rd, 1st left

The Whiteley is an immaculately run, sea-facing home-from-home. Bedrooms, though compact, are carefully decorated and have many thoughtful extras. There's a small garden at the rear, a choice of lounges and a bar. The establishment has superb views, and the owners provide personal attention and a substantial breakfast.

Rooms 10 en suite (3 fmly) (1 GF) S £33.50-£37; D £59-£70 **Facilities** TVL tea/coffee Licensed WiFi **Parking** 8 **Notes** LB ⊗ No Children 3yrs Closed 30 Nov-Jan

SCARBOROUGH *continued*

Howdale

★★★★ 🄰 GUEST HOUSE

tel: 01723 372696 **121 Queens Pde YO12 7HU**
email: mail@howdale.co.uk **web:** www.howdale.co.uk
dir: *Left at lights opposite railway station, stay in left lane. Straight over at next lights into Northway then Columbus Ravine. Right into Victoria Park, continue into Queens Parade*

Within easy walking distance of Scarborough's beach and many other attractions, Howdale offers a comfortable lounge with TV, games console and lots of board games. All bedrooms have digital LCD TVs, along with many other useful facilities. Some rooms with sea views are available. Full English breakfast is offered.

Rooms 15 rms (13 en suite) (1 fmly) S £26-£29; D £52-£72* **Facilities** FTV TVL tea/coffee WiFi **Parking** 9 **Notes** LB Closed Nov-Feb

The Wharncliffe

★★★★ 🄰 GUEST ACCOMMODATION

tel: 01723 374635 **26 Blenheim Ter YO12 7HD**
email: info@thewharncliffescarborough.co.uk
web: www.thewharncliffehotelscarborough.co.uk
dir: *Follow signs to Castle, left into Blenheim St, left into Blenheim Ter*

This delightfully furnished and friendly establishment stands near the castle with fine views over the bay. There is a cosy bar, lounge and dining room, and the bedrooms are thoughtfully equipped.

Rooms 10 en suite D £65-£75* **Facilities** FTV DVD TVL tea/coffee Licensed WiFi **Notes** LB ⊗ No Children 18yrs

The Barrington Guest House

★★★ GUEST HOUSE

tel: 01723 379494 **3 Palace Hill, Eastborough YO11 1NL**
email: valeriehotchin@talktalk.net **web:** www.barringtonguesthouse.co.uk
dir: *From A64 follow signs for South Bay, left into Eastborough, on right*

This charming house is in an elevated position just a short walk from the sandy beaches of South Bay and all the amenities of the town. Bedrooms are ranged over three floors and all are tastefully decorated in a contemporary style; they include family rooms and en suite rooms.

Rooms 6 en suite (2 fmly) S £25-£35; D £55-£60* **Facilities** FTV tea/coffee WiFi **Notes** LB Closed 24 Dec-2 Jan

North End Farm Country Guesthouse

★★★ GUEST ACCOMMODATION

tel: 01723 862965 **88 Main St, Seamer YO12 4RF**
email: northendfarm@tiscali.co.uk **web:** www.northendfarmseamer.co.uk
dir: *A64 N onto B1261 through Seamer, next to rdbt*

Located in Seamer, a village inland from Scarborough, this 18th-century guest accommodation contains comfortable, well-equipped en suite bedrooms. Breakfast is served at individual tables in the smart dining room, and the cosy lounge has a large-screen TV.

Rooms 3 en suite (1 fmly) S £40-£45; D £70-£75* **Facilities** FTV TVL tea/coffee WiFi 🅿 **Parking** 6 **Notes** ⊗

Peasholm Park

★★★ GUEST ACCOMMODATION

tel: 01723 500954 **21-23 Victoria Park YO12 7TS**
email: peasholmparkhotel@btconnect.com **web:** www.peasholmpark.co.uk
dir: *Opposite entrance to Peasholm Park, off Columbus Ravine*

A warm welcome awaits you at Peasholm Park a family-run guest accommodation, which is within easy walking distance of the beach or the town centre. Bedrooms are comfortable, and feature homely extras. Breakfast is served at individual tables in the dining room, which looks over Peasholm Park. Free WiFi is also available.

Rooms 12 en suite (3 fmly) S £33-£38; D £64-£74* **Facilities** FTV TVL tea/coffee Licensed WiFi **Parking** 2 **Notes** LB ⊗ No Children 6yrs Closed Dec-Mar

The Phoenix Guest House

★★★ GUEST HOUSE

tel: 01723 368319 & 07847 102337 **157 Columbus Ravine YO12 7QZ**
email: jnnlms@aol.co.uk **web:** www.thephoenixguesthouse.co.uk
dir: *From railway station at junct of A64 & A165, take A165 signed North Bay. On right, 100mtrs from Peasholm Park*

Located close to Peasholm Park and just a few minutes' walk from the North Bay, this friendly guest house offers clean, comfortable bedrooms. There is a cosy lounge where guests can relax, exchange books or play games at the card table. Complimentary WiFi is provided and packed lunches can also be purchased.

Rooms 6 en suite (2 fmly) D £52-£56* **Facilities** FTV DVD TVL tea/coffee WiFi **Notes** LB ⊗ 🍽

The Dolphin Guesthouse

★★★ A GUEST HOUSE

tel: 01723 341914 **fax:** 08715 284118 **151 Columbus Ravine YO12 7QZ**
email: dolphinguesthouse@btinternet.com **web:** www.thedolphin.info
dir: *At train station left into Northway, into Columbus Ravine, guest house on right*

The Dolphin Guesthouse is a privately run establishment that offers six spacious bedrooms. A friendly welcome is guaranteed and service is very good. The Dolphin is close to all Scarborough's amenities, and is ideal for those exploring Yorkshire's moors and dales. Rooms include the full range of guest necessities. Free parking permits for guests.

Rooms 6 rms (5 en suite) (1 pri facs) (4 fmly) S £30; D £54-£56* **Facilities** FTV TVL tea/coffee WiFi 🔒 **Notes** LB ⊗ Closed 22-26 Dec

Lyness Guest House

★★★ A GUEST HOUSE

tel: 01723 375952 **fax:** 01723 372550 **145 Columbus Ravine YO12 7QZ**
email: info@thelyness.co.uk **web:** www.thelyness.co.uk
dir: *Follow signs for North Bay, leading onto Northway. Continue onto Columbus Ravine, over 2 rdbts, 200mtrs on right*

Set on the valley road of Columbus Ravine, Lyness is a family-run guest house that welcomes young families. Close to all local amenities and the town centre, it is also only a short walk from the cliffs. Traditional English breakfast is served along with a range of alternatives including porridge or pancakes. There is a range of rooms and a travel cot and high chair are available when required.

Rooms 6 rms (5 en suite) (1 pri facs) (2 fmly) S £27-£29; D £58-£62 **Facilities** FTV tea/coffee WiFi **Notes** LB ⊗ Closed 20 Dec-3 Jan

The Sheridan

★★★ A GUEST ACCOMMODATION

tel: 01723 372094 **108 Columbus Ravine YO12 7QZ**
email: kim@thesheridan.co.uk **web:** www.thesheridan.co.uk
dir: *From railway station left into Northway, over 2 mini rdbts, establishment 300yds on left*

Set on an attractive, tree-lined road close to all North Bay attractions, and only five minutes' walk away from the beach, The Sheridan is a welcoming place to stay. At breakfast, try a full English - special diets are catered for. Traditional Yorkshire cuisine is available in the evening.

Rooms 8 en suite (2 fmly) (1 GF) **Facilities** FTV tea/coffee Dinner available WiFi **Parking** 5 **Notes** LB ⊗ No Children 5yrs Closed Xmas & New Year

The Albert

U

tel: 01723 447260 & 07792 902745 **58 North Marine Rd YO12 7PE**
email: alberthotel@btinternet.com

Currently the rating for this establishment is not confirmed. This may be due to a change of ownership or because it has only recently joined the AA rating scheme.

Rooms 3 en suite (2 fmly) S £60; D £60-£100* **Facilities** FTV tea/coffee Dinner available Licensed WiFi Pool table 🔒 **Parking** 6 **Notes** LB

SCOTCH CORNER   Map 19 NZ20

The Vintage

★★★ A INN

tel: 01748 824424 & 822961 **fax:** 01748 826272 **DL10 6NP**
email: thevintagescotchcorner@btinternet.com **web:** www.thevintagehotel.co.uk
dir: *Exit A1 at Scotch Corner onto A66 towards Penrith, premises 200yds on left*

A warm welcome and attentive service awaits you at The Vintage, a family-run establishment. Bedrooms come in a variety of styles and sizes and all are well equipped. You can choose either a continental or a cooked breakfast, and a tempting selection of evening meals is available either in the bar or restaurant.

Rooms 8 rms (5 en suite) S £25-£40; D £40-£60 (room only)* **Facilities** FTV TVL tea/coffee Dinner available WiFi **Extras** Snacks - complimentary **Conf** Max 40 Thtr 40 Class 24 Board 20 **Parking** 40 **Notes** LB Closed Xmas & New Year

---

SETTLE   Map 18 SD86

See also Clapham

The Lion at Settle

★★★★ INN

tel: 01729 822203 **Duke St BD24 9DU**
email: relax@thelionsettle.co.uk **web:** www.thelionsettle.co.uk
dir: *In town centre opposite Barclays Bank*

Located in the heart of the market town of Settle, this is a traditional coaching inn with an inglenook fireplace. The accommodation is comfortable and well equipped. A wide selection of imaginative dishes, together with real ales and fine wines, is served in the busy bar, and also the restaurant where the atmosphere is relaxed and comfortable; alfresco dining is possible in the courtyard.

Rooms 14 en suite (3 fmly) S £55-£107; D £61-£113* **Facilities** FTV tea/coffee Dinner available WiFi 🔒 **Notes** LB

Whitefriars Country Guesthouse

★★★★ GUEST ACCOMMODATION

tel: 01729 823753 **Church St BD24 9JD**
email: info@whitefriars-settle.co.uk **web:** www.whitefriars-settle.co.uk
dir: *Off A65 through Settle market place, premises signed 50yds on left*

This friendly, family-run house stands in peaceful gardens just a stroll from the town centre and railway station. Bedrooms, some quite spacious, are attractively furnished in a traditional style and thoughtfully equipped. A hearty breakfast is served in the beamed dining room, and a cosy lounge is available.

Rooms 8 rms (6 en suite) (1 pri facs) (1 fmly) S fr £41; D fr £72* **Facilities** FTV Lounge TVL tea/coffee WiFi **Parking** 10 **Notes** ⊗ Closed 25 Dec 📧

SKIPTON   Map 18 SD95

Clay Hall

★★★★ GUEST ACCOMMODATION

tel: 01756 794391 **Broughton Rd BD23 3AA**
dir: *On A6069, 1m from Skipton towards Broughton*

A warm welcome is assured here at Clay Hall on the outskirts of the town and next to the Leeds and Liverpool canal. The house offers carefully furnished bedrooms with smart modern shower rooms en suite, and a wealth of thoughtful extras. Comprehensive breakfasts are served in an attractive dining room.

Rooms 2 en suite **Facilities** tea/coffee **Parking** 4 **Notes** ⊗ No Children 12yrs 📧

SKIPTON *continued*

Westfield House

★★★★ 🛏 GUEST HOUSE

tel: 01756 790849 **50 Keighley Rd BD23 2NB**
dir: *500yds S of town centre on A6131, S of canal bridge*

Just a stroll from the town centre, this friendly, non-smoking guest house provides smart accommodation. Bedrooms are well presented and most have large beds and many accessories including bath robes. A hearty breakfast is served in the cosy dining room. Hospitality here is warm and nothing is too much trouble for the owners.

Rooms 4 en suite D £65–£70* **Facilities** tea/coffee **Notes** ⊗ No Children 🚭

The Woolly Sheep

★★★★ 🍺 INN

tel: 01756 700966 **38 Sheep St BD23 1HY**
email: woolly.sheep@btconnect.com **web:** www.woollysheepinn.co.uk
dir: *At bottom of High St*

Situated right in the centre of Skipton's vibrant market town, close to the medieval castle and railway station, this popular inn offers good quality and comfortable accommodation. All bedrooms are en suite and well equipped with traditional pine furniture, colour TV and tea/coffee making facilities. Good home-cooked food is served alongside a range of Timothy Taylor real ales. There is an attractive courtyard seating area and free secure parking to the rear.

Rooms 9 en suite (3 fmly) **Facilities** FTV tea/coffee Dinner available WiFi **Parking** 14 **Notes** ⊗ No coaches

Low Skibeden House *(SD013526)*

★★★ FARMHOUSE

tel: 01756 793849 **Harrogate Rd BD23 6AB**
web: www.lowskibeden.co.uk
dir: *1m E of Skipton on right before A59/A65 rdbt, set back from road*

Low Skibeden House is a lovely stone-built 16th-century farmhouse just a mile from Skipton and surrounded by open countryside. Bedrooms are traditionally furnished

and there is a spacious, comfortable lounge where guests are offered tea or coffee and cake on arrival, and supper time drinks from hosts, Bill and Heather.

Rooms 3 rms (2 en suite) (1 pri facs) (2 fmly) S £40–£56; D £68–£76 **Facilities** TVL tea/coffee 🛁 **Parking** 4 **Notes** LB ⊗ No Children 14yrs 40 acres sheep/non-working

Rockwood House

★★★ GUEST ACCOMMODATION

tel: 01756 799755 & 07976 314980 **fax:** 01756 799755 **14 Main St, Embsay BD23 6RE**
email: rockwood@steadonline.com **web:** www.stayinyorkshire.co.uk
dir: *2m NE of Skipton. Off A59 into Embsay village centre*

This Victorian terrace house has a peaceful location in the village of Embsay. Bedrooms are thoughtfully furnished, individually styled and reassuringly comfortable. The traditionally styled dining room sets the venue for hearty breakfasts. Hospitality is a feature here with a genuine and friendly welcome.

Rooms 3 en suite (1 fmly) (1 GF) S £40–£60; D £72–£85 **Facilities** DVD TVL tea/coffee WiFi ♿ 18 🛁 **Parking** 3 **Notes** LB ⊗ No Children 3yrs

The Wilson Arms

★★★ 🍺 INN

tel: 01947 602552 **Beacon Way YO22 5HS**
email: dawn1990@hotmail.co.uk

The Wilson Arms is set in the picturesque village of Sneaton on the way to Whitby. It is a traditional inn with open fires, real ale and really friendly service. Home-cooked food from the proprietors is also a real feature along with a great Sunday lunch. Accommodation is all en suite and the room are well appointed and comfortable. Families and pets are welcome at the inn. Ample off-road parking.

Rooms 7 en suite **Facilities** Dinner available

Harmony House

★★★★ 🅰 GUEST HOUSE

tel: 01904 720933 & 07889 808749 **fax:** 01904 720933 **The Green YO19 6SH**
email: hilary@harmonyhouseyork.com **web:** www.harmonyhouseyork.com
dir: *From York on A19 towards Selby, through Escrick (on dual carriageway). Right onto B1222 signed Stillingfleet. 2m to village. Right signed Naburn. 1st left into The Green, house on right*

Just six miles from York, Harmony House is in a peaceful country setting. The house has an interesting history, having been a reading room, a Sunday school, agricultural cottages and the village post office. Some parts date back to the 17th century, but renovation and modernisation have made it into a smart, characterful place to stay.

There are log fires in winter, a guest lounge that overlooks the Green, and the offer of tea and cakes on arrival. Afternoon tea or midweek evening meals are available (by prior arrangement) and friends or family are welcome to come along. Hilary is a trained chef and runs a small cookery school. Harmony House is not child friendly, however the self-catering family annexe can accommodate a family of four.

Rooms 3 en suite S £45-£65; D £75-£80* **Facilities** FTV DVD iPod docking station TVL tea/coffee Dinner available WiFi **Extras** Mini fridge **Parking** 3 **Notes** LB ⊗ No Children 17yrs Closed 23 Dec-2 Jan

■ **SUTTON-ON-THE-FOREST**   Map 19 SE56

The Blackwell Ox Inn

★★★★ ❀ INN

tel: 01347 810328 **fax:** 01347 812738 **Huby Rd YO61 1DT**
email: enquiries@blackwelloxinn.co.uk **web:** www.blackwelloxinn.co.uk
dir: A1237 onto B1363 to Sutton-on-the-Forest. Left at T-junct, 50yds on right

Standing in this lovely village, the inn and restaurant offers very good bedrooms and pleasing public rooms. Built in 1823, the Blackwell Ox was named after a locally-bred animal that weighed 2278lbs when it was slaughtered in 1779. The kitchen sources local produce from North Yorkshire, to create simple, honest cooking that has achieved an AA Rosette.

Rooms 7 en suite **Facilities** FTV tea/coffee Dinner available Direct Dial Lift WiFi **Parking** 18 **Notes** LB ⊗ Closed 25 Dec & 1 Jan No coaches

■ **TADCASTER**   Map 16 SE44

The Old Presbytery Guest House

★★★ BED AND BREAKFAST

tel: 01937 557708 **London Rd, Saxton LS24 9PU**
email: guest@presbytery.plus.com **web:** www.presbyteryguesthouse.co.uk
dir: 4m S of Tadcaster on A162. 100yds N of Barkston Ash on E side of road

Dating from the 18th century, this former dower house has been modernised to provide comfortable accommodation, while retaining many original features. The hall lounge features a wood-burning stove, and delicious breakfasts are served at an old oak dining table in a cosy breakfast room. The beautiful gardens are a feature in their own right, with an attractive wooden bower providing sheltered outdoor seating space. Secure parking and complimentary WiFi are provided.

Rooms 4 rms (3 en suite) (1 pri facs) (1 fmly) S £46.50-£56.50; D £88* **Facilities** FTV TVL tea/coffee WiFi ⅃ 18 🔒 **Parking** 6 **Notes** ⊗ Closed 21 Dec-6 Jan

■ **THIRSK**   Map 19 SE48

Premier Collection

Spital Hill

★★★★★ 🛏 ☺ GUEST ACCOMMODATION

tel: 01845 522273 **fax:** 01845 524970 **York Rd YO7 3AE**
email: spitalhill@spitalhill.entadsl.com **web:** www.spitalhill.co.uk
dir: 1.5m SE of town, set back 200yds from A19, driveway marked by 2 white posts

Set in pleasant gardens, this substantial Victorian country house is delightfully furnished. The spacious bedrooms are thoughtfully equipped with many extras, one even has a piano, but no TVs or kettles; the proprietor prefers to offer tea as a service. Delicious meals feature local and home-grown produce and are served house-party style around one table in the interesting dining room.

Rooms 3 rms (2 en suite) (1 pri facs) 2 annexe en suite (1 GF) **Facilities** TVL Dinner available Direct Dial Licensed WiFi 🐾 ⅃ **Extras** Fruit **Parking** 6 **Notes** ⊗ No Children 12yrs ☺

Meadowcroft Bed & Breakfast

★★★★ BED AND BREAKFAST

tel: 01845 527497 & 07798 768129 **86 Topcliffe Rd YO7 1RY**
email: sue@meadowcroft-thirsk.co.uk **web:** www.meadowcroft-thirsk.co.uk
dir: A1(M) junct 49 onto A168. After 5m onto B1448, B&B on left just past school in 1.5m

This attractive detached family home was built in 1937 and has many original art deco features. The house is very spacious and is set in attractive, mature gardens in a peaceful location just a short stroll from the town centre. Guests can expect warm hospitality, and breakfasts feature local and home-made produce including eggs from the friendly owner's own hens. The three bedrooms are very well equipped with thoughtful accessories, comfortable beds and flat-screen TV's.

Rooms 3 rms (2 en suite) (1 pri facs) S £40-£65; D £70-£90* **Facilities** FTV DVD tea/coffee WiFi 🔒 **Extras** Mineral water - complimentary **Parking** 4 **Notes** LB ⊗ No Children 11yrs

Newsham Grange Farm Bed and Breakfast

★★★★ BED AND BREAKFAST

tel: 01845 588047 & 07808 903044 **fax:** 01845 587798
Newsham Grange Farm YO7 4DF
email: sue@newshamgrange farm.co.uk **web:** www.newshamgrangefarm.co.uk
dir: A1(M) junct with A61, follow signs to Thirsk for 4m. Left at rdbt onto A167, 3m on left

This impressive Georgian farmhouse is set in extensive grounds on the outskirts of Thirsk. It's family run and the friendly owners have refurbished the property to a high standard. The two spacious bedrooms feature luxurious touches, such as under-floor heating, and can also be reconfigured to provide a family room. Complimentary WiFi is also available. The grounds are stunning with a decked terrace, outdoor swimming pool and hot tub adding to the idyllic setting overlooking the orchard. Secure parking with CCTV and lockable storage for bicycles add to the range of facilities.

Rooms 2 en suite (1 fmly) (2 GF) S £70-£80; D £80-£90* **Facilities** FTV tea/coffee WiFi ⅃ 18 🔒 Hot tub **Parking** 4 **Notes** LB ⊗ No Children 7yrs

■ **WESTOW**   Map 19 SE76

Woodhouse Farm (SE749637)

★★★★ FARMHOUSE

tel: 01653 618378 & 07904 293422 **fax:** 01653 618378 **YO60 7LL**
email: stay@wood-house-farm.co.uk **web:** www.wood-house-farm.co.uk
dir: Exit A64 to Kirkham Priory & Westow. Right at T-junct, farm drive 0.5m out of village on right

The owners of this house are a young farming family who offer caring hospitality in their rural home. Bedrooms are spacious and there is a comfortable lounge also available for guests. Complimentary WiFi is provided. Home-made bread, preserves and farm produce turn breakfast into a feast, and the views from the house across open fields are splendid.

Rooms 2 en suite (1 fmly) S £40-£50; D £65-£80* **Facilities** FTV DVD iPod docking station TVL tea/coffee WiFi ch fac Fishing 🔒 **Extras** Robes **Parking** 12 **Notes** LB ⊗ Closed Xmas, New Year & mid Mar-mid Apr ☺ 500 acres arable/sheep/beef

WEST WITTON
Map 19 SE08

Premier Collection

The Wensleydale Heifer
★★★★★ ⊛ ⌂ RESTAURANT WITH ROOMS

tel: 01969 622322 **Main St DL8 4LS**
email: info@wensleydaleheifer.co.uk **web:** www.wensleydaleheifer.co.uk
dir: A1 to Leeming Bar junct, A684 towards Bedale for approx 10m to Leyburn, then towards Hawes 3.5m to West Witton

Describing itself as 'boutique style', this 17th-century former coaching inn is very much of the 21st century. The bedrooms, with Egyptian cotton linen and Molton Brown toiletries as standard, are each designed with an interesting theme - for example, Black Sheep, Night at the Movies, True Romantics and Shooters, and for chocolate lovers there's a bedroom where they can eat as much chocolate as they like! The food is very much the focus here in both the informal fish bar and the contemporary style restaurant. The kitchen prides itself on sourcing the freshest fish and locally reared meats.

Rooms 9 en suite 4 annexe en suite (2 fmly) (2 GF) S £100-£160; D £140-£200*
Facilities FTV DVD Lounge tea/coffee Dinner available Direct Dial WiFi
Extras Speciality toiletries, fruit, snacks **Parking** 30 **Notes** LB

WHITBY
Map 19 NZ81

Abbotsleigh of Whitby
★★★★ ⌂ GUEST HOUSE

tel: 01947 606615 & 07866 880707 **5 Argyle Rd YO21 3HS**
email: enquiries@abbotsleighofwhitby.co.uk **web:** www.abbotsleighofwhitby.co.uk
dir: From train station onto Bagdale. At mini rdbt turn right onto Chubb Hill. At next rdbt take 2nd exit & right at next rdbt. Right into Argyle Rd

Guests can be sure of friendly service at this immaculately presented Victorian house where tea and home-made cake are offered on arrival. The attractively furnished bedrooms, and stylish en suite wet rooms have a luxurious feel. Thoughtful accessories such as coffee machines, iPod docking stations and DVD players are provided. Complimentary WiFi is also available.

Rooms 5 en suite (1 GF) D £90-£100* **Facilities** STV DVD iPod docking station tea/coffee WiFi **Extras** Speciality toiletries, home-made biscuits, milk **Parking** 3 **Notes** LB ⊗ No Children 12yrs ⊗

Estbek House
★★★★ ⊛⊛ ⌂ RESTAURANT WITH ROOMS

tel: 01947 893424 **fax:** 01947 893625 **East Row, Sandsend YO21 3SU**
email: info@estbekhouse.co.uk **web:** www.estbekhouse.co.uk
dir: From Whitby take A174. In Sandsend, left into East Row

The speciality seafood restaurant on the first floor is the focus of this listed building in a small coastal village north west of Whitby. The seasonal menu is based on local fresh local ingredients, and is overseen by Tim the chef, who has guided his team to 2 AA Rosette standard. There is also a small bar and breakfast room, and four individually appointed bedrooms offering high levels of comfort.

Rooms 4 rms (3 en suite) (1 pri facs) **Facilities** tea/coffee Dinner available WiFi **Conf** Board 20 **Parking** 6 **Notes** ⊗ No Children 14yrs No coaches

Netherby House
★★★★ ⌂ ⌘ GUEST ACCOMMODATION

tel: 01947 810211 **fax:** 01947 810211 **90 Coach Rd, Sleights YO22 5EQ**
email: info@netherby-house.co.uk **web:** www.netherby-house.co.uk
dir: In village of Sleights, off A169 (Whitby-Pickering road)

This fine Victorian house offers thoughtfully furnished, individually styled bedrooms together with delightful day rooms. There is a fine conservatory and the grounds are extensive, with exceptional views from the summer house at the bottom of the garden. Imaginative dinners feature produce from the extensive kitchen garden.

Rooms 6 en suite 5 annexe en suite (1 fmly) (5 GF) S £41.50-£51; D £83-£102*
Facilities FTV Lounge TVL tea/coffee Dinner available Licensed WiFi ⌘ ⌘
Parking 17 **Notes** LB ⊗ No Children 2yrs Closed 25-26 Dec

Overdale Guest House
★★★★ GUEST HOUSE

tel: 01947 605612 **39 Prospect Hill YO21 1QE**
email: jayneoates@hotmail.co.uk **web:** www.overdaleguesthouse.co.uk
dir: A171 to Whitby, onto A174 signed Town Centre. Guest house on right

This fine Victorian terraced house has been sympathetically refurbished in recent years and offers guests four charming, very well appointed bedrooms. Built originally for a local sea captain, the house is a short walk from the town centre and Whitby's lovely beaches. Free WiFi is available throughout the house and parking is available for guests. A warm welcome is guaranteed and breakfast is served at individual tables in the light-filled breakfast room.

Rooms 4 en suite (2 fmly) D £85-£110* **Facilities** FTV Lounge tea/coffee WiFi ⌘ **Parking** 6 **Notes** ⊗

Sandpiper Guest House

★★★★ GUEST HOUSE

tel: 01947 600246 **4 Belle Vue Ter YO21 3EY**
email: enquiries@sandpiperhouse.wanadoo.co.uk **web:** www.sandpiperhouse.co.uk
dir: *From A169 2nd left at rdbt signed Whitby, follow signs to West Cliff on N Prom, 4th right, take Esplanade straight into Belle Vue Terrace. Guest house on left*

This well presented Victorian house is just a few minutes' walk from Whitby's golden sands and the quaint streets of its historic harbour area. The contemporary bedrooms vary in size with a choice of singles, twins, a four-poster room and family room available. Hearty breakfasts are served in the cheerful lower ground-floor dining room.

Rooms 7 en suite (1 fmly) (1 GF) **Facilities** tea/coffee WiFi **Parking** 3 **Notes** ⊗ No Children 4yrs ⊜

Argyle House

★★★★ GUEST ACCOMMODATION

tel: 01947 602733 & 821877 **18 Hudson St YO21 3EP**
email: argyle-house@fsmail.net **web:** www.argyle-house.co.uk
dir: *Follow signs for West Cliff & Whitby Pavillion, with the sea on left, turn into Royal Crescent & exit through the rear of crescent. Hudson St is also known as Abbey Terrace*

Built originally in the 1850s and enjoying a prominent position in a conservation area, Argyle House is a short walk from Whitby's town centre, harbour and beaches. Recently restored, there are a range of comfortable, well-appointed bedrooms. Guests are guaranteed a warm welcome from the friendly owners and delicious breakfast are served at individual tables in the light-filled breakfast room. Free WiFi is available throughout.

Rooms 7 en suite (1 fmly) D £58-£86* **Facilities** STV FTV DVD iPod docking station tea/coffee WiFi **Extras** Fruit **Notes** LB ⊗ No Children 5yrs

Boulmer Guest House

★★★★ GUEST HOUSE

tel: 01947 604284 **23 Crescent Av YO21 3ED**
email: info@boulmerguesthouse.co.uk **web:** www.boulmerguesthouse.co.uk
dir: *Follow signs for West Cliff, from Royal Crescent into Crescent Av, pass church on right. Road bears to right, 3rd house on left before sorting office*

This friendly guest house is just a short walk from the beautiful beach and Whitby Pavilion on the picturesque West Cliff, and is also convenient for shops, cafés and restaurants. The range of attractively presented bedrooms include family rooms, a twin, a single, and with prior arrangement, dog-friendly bedrooms. Modern facilities are provided including complimentary WiFi. Free on-street parking is available.

Rooms 7 rms (5 en suite) (2 fmly) (1 GF) **Facilities** FTV DVD TVL tea/coffee WiFi 🔒 **Notes** ⊜

Chiltern Guest House

★★★★ GUEST HOUSE

tel: 01947 604981 **13 Normanby Ter, West Cliff YO21 3ES**
email: Jjchiltern@aol.com **web:** www.chilternwhitby.co.uk
dir: *Whalebones next to Harbour, sea on right. Royal Hotel on left, 200yds. Royal Gardens turn left, 2nd road on left, 6th house on right*

In a Victorian terrace, the Chiltern Guest House offers a warm welcome and comfortable accommodation within walking distance of the town centre and seafront. Public areas are smartly decorated and include a bright, attractive dining room. Bedrooms are thoughtfully equipped and many have modern en suites.

Rooms 9 en suite (2 fmly) S fr £35; D £60-£65* **Facilities** FTV tea/coffee WiFi ⌁ 18 🔒 **Notes** LB ⊗

Corra Lynn

★★★★ GUEST ACCOMMODATION

tel: 01947 602214 **fax:** 01947 602214 **28 Crescent Av YO21 3EW**
dir: *On corner of A174 & Crescent Av*

Occupying a prominent corner position, Corra Lynn mixes traditional values with a trendy and artistic style. Bedrooms are thoughtfully equipped, individually furnished and have bright colour schemes. However, it is the delightful dining room with corner bar, and a wall adorned with clocks that catch the eye.

Rooms 5 en suite (1 fmly) D fr £74* **Facilities** STV FTV tea/coffee Direct Dial Licensed **Parking** 5 **Notes** ⊗ Closed 21 Dec-14 Feb ⊜

Kimberley House

★★★★ GUEST ACCOMMODATION

tel: 01947 604125 **fax:** 01947 604125 **7 Havelock Place YO21 3ER**
email: enquiries@kimberleyhouse.com **web:** www.kimberleyhouse.com
dir: *Follow signs for West Cliff, close to Whalebone Arch and Captain Cook Monument, behind Royal Crescent at corner of Hudson St*

Warm and genuine hospitality is offered at this attractive house in the centre of Whitby, just a short stroll away from the local attractions. Bedrooms are pleasantly co-ordinated and comfortably furnished, with an attic family suite available. Freshly prepared breakfasts are served in the attractive ground floor dining room which has a cosy sitting area, where guests can enjoy complimentary teas and coffees.

Rooms 9 rms (8 en suite) (1 pri facs) (1 fmly) (1 GF) S £35-£40; D £60-£72* **Facilities** FTV DVD TVL tea/coffee WiFi 🔒 **Extras** Speciality toiletries **Notes** LB ⊗

Rosslyn Guest House

★★★★ GUEST HOUSE

tel: 01947 604086 **11 Abbey Ter YO21 3HQ**
email: rosslynhouse@googlemail.com **web:** www.rosslynhousewhitby.co.uk

Guests are sure of a friendly atmosphere, high standards of cleanliness and comfortable bedrooms at this lovely house, close to the seafront. Breakfast is served in a beautifully appointed dining room. Additional facilities include a small guest kitchen, complimentary WiFi, Sky TV and secure outside storage for bikes.

Rooms 6 en suite (2 fmly) (1 GF) S £35-£60; D £55-£75* **Facilities** STV tea/coffee WiFi 🔒 **Parking** 1 **Notes** LB ⊗

Whitehaven Guest House

★★★★ GUEST ACCOMMODATION

tel: 01947 601569 **29 Crescent Av YO21 3EW**
email: simon@whitehavenguesthouse.co.uk **web:** www.whitehavenguesthouse.co.uk
dir: *Follow signs to West Cliff, A174 into Crescent Av*

Occupying a corner position close to the sports complex and indoor swimming pool, this house provides colourful bedrooms in contrasting styles. All rooms have mini-fridges and most have DVD players. Vegetarian options are available at breakfast, which is served in the attractive dining room. Complimentary WiFi access is also available.

Rooms 4 rms (3 en suite) (1 pri facs) (1 fmly) D £75-£80 **Facilities** FTV DVD tea/coffee WiFi 🔒 **Notes** LB ⊗ Closed 23-26 Dec ⊜

WOMBLETON
Map 19 SE68

New Buckland

★★★★ BED AND BREAKFAST

tel: 01751 433369 & 07738 430519 **Flatts Ln YO62 7RU**
email: junedrake138@btinternet.com web: www.new-buckland-apartment.co.uk
dir: *From A170 turn right 3m from Helmsley, left at Plough Inn follow round, last property on right*

New Buckland offers two attractive bedrooms and excellent bathrooms in a well-presented countryside property. Whether one or both rooms are booked, guests have exclusive use of the spacious, contemporary lounge and a very well-equipped small kitchen. Complimentary WiFi access is available. Guests also have use of an area of the attractive garden with summer house and garden furniture.

Rooms 2 rms (2 pri facs) **Facilities** FTV TVL WiFi **Parking** 2 **Notes** ⊗ No Children

YORK
Map 16 SE65

See also Sutton-on-the-Forest

Ascot House

★★★★ GUEST ACCOMMODATION

tel: 01904 426826 fax: 01904 431077 **80 East Pde YO31 7YH**
email: admin@ascothouseyork.com web: www.ascothouseyork.com
dir: *0.5m NE of city centre. Exit A1036 (Heworth Green) into Mill Ln, 2nd left*

Ascot House is a 15-minute walk from York Minster. All bedrooms are en suite and many have been refurbished. The first-floor rooms all have four-poster or antique canopy beds and attractive period furniture, while those on the second floor have a more contemporary style. All rooms are well equipped with TV and free WiFi. The dining room offers a range of breakfast options including traditional English, vegetarian and continental. The comfortable residents' lounge is the ideal place to enjoy tea or coffee, or something stronger from the Butler's Pantry.

Rooms 12 en suite (3 fmly) (2 GF) S £70-£85; D £85-£110* **Facilities** FTV TVL tea/coffee Licensed WiFi ♨ **Extras** Bottled water - complimentary **Parking** 13 **Notes** LB Closed 21-28 Dec

Guy Fawkes Inn

★★★★ ◉ INN

tel: 01904 623716 **25 High Petergate YO1 7HP**
email: enquiry@gfyork.com web: www.gfyork.com
dir: *A64 onto A1036 signed York & inner ring road. Over bridge into Duncombe Place, right into High Petergate*

This inn is only feet away from the Minster and was the birthplace of the notorious plotter, Guy Fawkes. Steeped in history, it is full of character and has many original features including the timber staircase, gas lighting and open fires. The bar is a real gathering place for locals and visitors to the city. The bedrooms are wonderfully appointed with antique furniture, Italian fabrics and luxury beds; some of the modern bathrooms have roll-top baths. An outside courtyard at the back of the inn provides ample space for dining and enjoying a drink.

Rooms 13 en suite (1 fmly) (2 GF) **Facilities** FTV tea/coffee Dinner available Direct Dial WiFi

The Lamb & Lion

★★★★ ◉ INN

tel: 01904 612078 & 654112 **2-4 High Petergate YO1 7EH**
email: enquiry@lambandlionyork.com web: www.lambandlionyork.com
dir: *A64 onto A1036. 3.5m, at rdbt 3rd exit, continue on A1036. 2m, right into High Petergate*

This inn, steeped in history and full of character, stands in the shadows of the medieval city gate on Bootham Bar. The stylish bedrooms are well appointed and have wonderfully comfortable beds; some benefit from views of the city wall and the Minster itself. The public areas have winding passages leading to a parlour-type dining room complete with church pews and open fire; cosy little rooms off the corridor afford much privacy.

Rooms 12 en suite **Facilities** FTV tea/coffee Dinner available WiFi **Conf** Max 20 Thtr 20 Class 20 Board 20

Ashley Guest House

★★★★ ⌂ GUEST HOUSE

tel: 01904 647520 & 07955 250271 **76 Scott St YO23 1NS**
email: stay@ashleyguesthouse.co.uk web: www.ashleyguesthouse.co.uk
dir: *From A64 take York West exit onto A1036 (Tadcaster Rd) follow city centre signs. After racecourse (on right) at 2nd lights right into Scarcroft Rd. Scott St 2nd last street before lights*

Ashley Guest House is a Victorian end-terrace that has been given modern treatment resulting in stylish interiors and a distinctive character. Attractively furnished bedrooms and caring hospitality are hallmarks of this well-located city centre establishment.

Rooms 6 rms (5 en suite) (1 pri facs) (1 fmly) S £40-£55; D £50-£86* **Facilities** FTV Lounge tea/coffee WiFi ♨ **Notes** ⊗ No Children 5yrs

City Guest House

★★★★ GUEST ACCOMMODATION

tel: 01904 622483 **68 Monkgate YO31 7PF**
email: info@cityguesthouse.co.uk **web:** www.cityguesthouse.co.uk
dir: *NE of city centre on B1036*

Just a five-minute walk from York Minster and close to the city wall and other sights, this charming Victorian town house is well located for business, shopping and sightseeing. Carefully furnished bedrooms are attractively presented and offer a range of thoughtful touches. The traditional and beautifully presented dining room provides a pleasant venue for the hearty breakfast.

Rooms 7 rms (6 en suite) (1 pri facs) (1 fmly) (1 GF) S £44-£48; D £68-£78*
Facilities FTV iPod docking station Lounge tea/coffee WiFi ⅃ 9 🔒 **Parking** 6 **Notes** ⊗ No Children 8yrs Closed Xmas & 1st 2wks Jan

Fifth Milestone Cottage

★★★★ GUEST HOUSE

tel: 01904 489361 & 07885 502420 **fax:** 01904 489308 **Hull Rd YO19 5LR**
email: mismartyn@hotmail.com **web:** www.milestonecottage.co.uk
dir: *From A64 onto A1079 towards Hull. On left after Philip Welch Garage*

As the name suggests, this spacious cottage is just five miles from York centre. The property is set in large, well-kept grounds with private parking. Guests can relax in the pretty garden where there is also a large decked area. There is a wide range of bedrooms available from doubles, including a four-poster room, to twins and family rooms. Some also have their own terrace and several offer very good disabled facilities and good access for wheelchair users.

Rooms 4 en suite 3 annexe en suite (2 fmly) (5 GF) **Facilities** FTV DVD iPod docking station tea/coffee WiFi 🔒 Animal farm **Parking** 12 **Notes** ⊗ RS 25-26 Dec room only

The Heathers Guest House

★★★★ GUEST ACCOMMODATION

tel: 01904 640989 **fax:** 01904 640989 **54 Shipton Rd, Clifton-Without YO30 5RQ**
email: aabbg@heathers-guest-house.co.uk **web:** www.heathers-guest-house.co.uk
dir: *N of York on A19, halfway between A1237 ring road & York city centre*

This spacious detached house offers off-street parking and a peaceful setting, only a short drive or walk from the city centre. Each room is individually designed, using quality fabrics. The light, airy breakfast room looks out onto the beautiful large rear garden, which is visited daily by local wildlife. Complimentary WiFi access is provided.

Rooms 6 rms (5 en suite) (1 pri facs) S £64-£98; D £68-£102 **Facilities** FTV Lounge tea/coffee WiFi 🔒 **Parking** 9 **Notes** ⊗ No Children 12yrs Closed Xmas

Holly Lodge

★★★★ GUEST ACCOMMODATION

tel: 01904 646005 **204-206 Fulford Rd YO10 4DD**
email: geoff@thehollylodge.co.uk **web:** www.thehollylodge.co.uk
dir: *On A19 south side, 1.5m on left from A64/A19 junct, or follow A19 Selby signs from city centre to Fulford Rd*

Located just a short walk from the historic centre, this pleasant Georgian property has colour co-ordinated, well-equipped bedrooms. The spacious lounge houses a grand piano, and hearty breakfasts are served in the cosy dining room. You may also enjoy the delightful walled garden. Complimentary WiFi is also available.

Rooms 5 en suite (1 fmly) (1 GF) S £68-£88; D £78-£88* **Facilities** FTV Lounge tea/coffee WiFi **Parking** 6 **Notes** ⊗ No Children 7yrs Closed 24-27 Dec

Holmwood House

★★★★ GUEST ACCOMMODATION

tel: 01904 626183 **fax:** 01904 670899 **112/114 Holgate Rd YO24 4BB**
email: info@holmwoodhousehotel.co.uk **web:** www.holmwoodhousehotel.co.uk

A 15-minute walk from Holmwood House takes you into the centre of York. The individually styled bedrooms are richly decorated and smartly furnished with many antiques. There is a comfortable lounge and a substantial breakfast is served in the pleasant basement dining room. Private parking and complimentary WiFi are also available.

Rooms 14 en suite (1 fmly) (3 GF) S £50-£100; D £69-£150* **Facilities** FTV Lounge tea/coffee Licensed WiFi 🔒 **Parking** 8 **Notes** LB ⊗ Closed 24-27 Dec

Midway House

★★★★ 🅐 GUEST ACCOMMODATION

tel: 01904 659272 **fax:** 01904 638496 **145 Fulford Rd YO10 4HG**
email: info@midwayhouseyork.co.uk **web:** www.midwayhouseyork.co.uk
dir: *A64 to York, 3rd exit A19 to York city centre, over 2nd lights, house 50yds on right*

This well-presented, large Victorian corner house offers comfortable accommodation in well-equipped bedrooms, one on the ground floor. Breakfast is served in the attractive dining room.

Rooms 12 rms (10 en suite) (3 fmly) (1 GF) S £60-£84; D £72-£96* **Facilities** FTV TVL tea/coffee WiFi **Parking** 14 **Notes** LB ⊗ No Children 6yrs Closed 18 Dec-20 Jan

YORK *continued*

The Crescent Guest House

★★★ GUEST HOUSE

tel: 01904 623216 **77 Bootham YO30 7DQ**
email: enquiries@crescentguesthouseyork.co.uk

Located just a short walk from York's city walls and the main shopping and business district, The Crescent Guest House offers a range of well-appointed and comfortable bedrooms. York Minster is just a five-minute walk away, and the racecourse is a short drive. This guest house makes an ideal base from which to explore the historic city and the beautiful county of North Yorkshire. Delicious breakfasts are served at individual tables in the light-filled breakfast room, and free WiFi is available for guests.

Rooms 10 rms

Adam's House

★★★ GUEST HOUSE

tel: 01904 655413 **fax:** 01904 643203 **5 Main St, Fulford YO10 4HJ**
email: adams.house2@yahoo.co.uk **web:** www.adamshouseyork.co.uk
dir: *A64 onto A19, 200yds on right after lights*

Adam's House offers comfortable accommodation, in the suburb of Fulford and not far from York centre, close to the university. It has many fine period features, pleasant, well-proportioned bedrooms, and an attractive dining room. The resident owners are friendly and attentive.

Rooms 8 rms (7 en suite) (4 fmly) (2 GF) **Facilities** FTV tea/coffee WiFi **Parking** 8 **Notes** ⊗

Greenside

★★★ GUEST HOUSE

tel: 01904 623631 **fax:** 01904 623631 **124 Clifton YO30 6BQ**
email: greenside@onebillnet.co.uk **web:** www.greensideguesthouse.co.uk
dir: *A19 N towards city centre, over lights for Greenside, on left opposite Clifton Green*

Overlooking Clifton Green, this charming detached conservation house is within walking distance of the city centre. Accommodation consists of comfortably furnished bedrooms and the traditional full English breakfast is served in the dining room. Secure parking and WiFi are additional bonuses.

Rooms 6 rms (3 en suite) (2 fmly) (3 GF) S £32-£35; D £60-£70 **Facilities** FTV tea/coffee WiFi **Parking** 6 **Notes** LB Closed Xmas & New Year ⊗

Monkgate Guest House

AA Advertised

tel: 01904 655947 **65 Monkgate YO31 7PA**
email: 65monkgate@btconnet.com **web:** www.monkgateguesthouse.com

Monkgate Guest House provides family-friendly accommodation in York city centre, as well as B&B for business travellers. Tastefully renovated in keeping with its age, it has a cosy atmosphere, and was originally three 18th-century cottages. Families with small children are particularly welcome, and the family suite is on the ground floor. A folder is provided with lots of info on nearby family-friendly attractions, restaurants and shops.

Rooms 8 rms (6 en suite) (2 pri facs) (1 fmly) (2 GF) **Facilities** DVD tea/coffee WiFi ⚓ **Parking** 5 **Notes** ⊗ Closed Xmas

---

SOUTH YORKSHIRE

■ DONCASTER Map 16 SE50

Innkeeper's Lodge Doncaster, Bessacarr

★★★ INN

tel: 0845 112 6032 **Bawtry Rd, Bessacarr DN4 7BS**
email: info@innkeeperslodge.com **web:** www.innkeeperslodge.com

Comfortable, modern accommodation ideal for Doncaster racecourse and also convenient for Doncaster airport. There is a Toby Carvery offering a friendly pub atmosphere and roast dinners every day. There is also a pub menu, free WiFi throughout and Sky Sports is shown in the bar. Ample on-site parking is also available.

Rooms 25 en suite (3 fmly) (6 GF) **Facilities** FTV tea/coffee Dinner available Direct Dial WiFi **Parking**

■ ROTHERHAM Map 16 SK49

The Stonecroft

★★★★ BED AND BREAKFAST

tel: 01709 540922 **fax:** 01709 540922 **138 Main St, Bramley S66 2SF**
email: stonecrofthotel@btconnect.com **web:** www.stonecrofthotel.com
dir: *3m E of Rotherham. Off A631 into Bramley village centre*

These converted stone cottages in the centre of Bramley provide a good base for visiting Rotherham or Sheffield. Some bedrooms are around a landscaped courtyard with private parking, and there is a lounge with a bar. Imaginative home-cooked meals are available.

Rooms 3 en suite 1 annexe en suite (1 fmly) (1 GF) S £49-£57; D £65-£72* **Facilities** FTV TVL tea/coffee Dinner available Licensed WiFi ⚡ 18 **Parking** 7 **Notes** LB ⊗ Closed 24 Dec-2 Jan

■ SHEFFIELD Map 16 SK38

Cross Scythes

★★★★ ☕ INN

tel: 0114 236 0204 **Baslow Rd, Totley S17 4AE**
email: enquiries@cross-scythes.com **web:** www.cross-scythes.com

Located approximately five miles south of Sheffield city centre and just ten minutes' drive from Chatsworth House, this 18th-century building has been sympathetically renovated. There are four tastefully decorated double rooms and all are en suite. Food is served all day throughout the spacious public areas.

Rooms 4 en suite D fr £59 (room only)* **Facilities** FTV tea/coffee Dinner available WiFi ⚡ 18 **Parking** 51 **Notes** ⊗

Follow us on twitter
@TheAA_Lifestyle

Dog & Partridge

★★★★ INN

tel: 01226 763173 **fax:** 01226 379731 **Bord Hill, Flouch S36 4HH**
email: info@dogandpartridgeinn.co.uk **web:** www.dogandpartridgeinn.co.uk
dir: M1 junct 37 onto A628. At Flouch rdbt, straight over follow signs for Manchester. 1m
on left

This comfortable family-run inn is located within the Peak District National
Park. Bedrooms are situated in the 18th-century barn adjoining the inn, all rooms
are comfortably furnished and some superior rooms are available. The beer garden
has stunning views of the surrounding moorland and a selection of real ales and
imaginative food is served in the public areas.

Rooms 10 en suite (2 fmly) (7 GF) S £60-£85; D £70-£100* **Facilities** FTV tea/coffee
Dinner available Direct Dial WiFi 🛁 **Conf** Max 50 Thtr 50 Class 36 Board 20
Parking 70 **Notes** ✖ Closed 25-27 Dec Civ Wed 80

Innkeeper's Lodge Hathersage, Peak District

★★★ INN

tel: 0845 112 6041 **Hathersage Rd, Longshaw S11 7TY**
email: info@innkeeperslodge.com **web:** www.innkeeperslodge.com

At Innkeeper's Lodge you'll find accommodation with comfort and character in equal
measure, and everything needed for a relaxing stay, from easy check-in and free
parking to complimentary breakfast and a cosy pub serving great value food and
drink on the doorstep. Each Lodge has quality rooms, and there are Lodges in a
variety of locations from towns and cities to countryside settings across the UK.

Rooms 9 en suite (6 fmly) (4 GF) **Facilities** FTV tea/coffee Dinner available Direct
Dial WiFi **Parking**

Alara Bed & Breakfast

AA Advertised

tel: 0114 234 0108 **fax:** 0114 234 0108 **981-987 Penistone Rd S6 2DH**
email: alara1@btconnect.com **web:** www.alara-bb.co.uk

Opened around a decade ago, Alara is a family-run bed and breakfast on the A61
North between Hillsborough Stadium and Hillsborough Park. Rooms come in a
variety of sizes, and include TV, tea and coffee-making facilities and WiFi.

Rooms 18 en suite (4 fmly) (4 GF) S £25-£40; D £45-£70* **Facilities** STV FTV DVD
TVL tea/coffee Dinner available WiFi 🛁 **Parking** 10 **Notes** ✖

| THROAPHAM | Map 16 SK58 |

Throapham House

★★★★★ 🄰 GUEST ACCOMMODATION

tel: 01909 562208 **fax:** 01909 212005 **Oldcotes Rd S25 2QS**
email: enquiries@throapham-house.co.uk **web:** www.throapham-house.co.uk
dir: M1 junct 31, A57 E towards Worksop. 1m, left at rdbt, at rdbt 2nd exit into Common
Rd. In Throapham, 200yds on left after sign

Throapham House is an 18th-century, Grade II listed property that has been home to
Ann and Robert Holland since 1993. It provides guest accommodation in three
spacious, en suite double rooms. Drinks are served on arrival in the stylish guest
lounge. Breakfast includes vegetarian and gluten-free options, and uses local and
home-grown produce where possible. Free WiFi is available.

Rooms 3 en suite S £65-£85; D £80-£95* **Facilities** FTV TVL tea/coffee WiFi 🛁
Extras Fruit, snacks **Parking** 3 **Notes** LB ✖

| TODWICK | Map 16 SK48 |

The Red Lion

★★★ INN

tel: 01909 771654 **fax:** 01909 773704 **Worksop Rd S26 1DJ**
email: 7933@greeneking.co.uk **web:** www.oldenglish.co.uk
dir: On A57, 1m from M1 junct 31 towards Worksop

Originally a roadside public house, The Red Lion is now a popular bar and
restaurant offering a wide range of food and drink. Bedrooms are well equipped,
modern and comfortable, and there are ample parking facilities.

Rooms 27 en suite (1 fmly) (14 GF) **Facilities** tea/coffee Direct Dial **Parking** 80

WEST YORKSHIRE

| ADDINGHAM | Map 16 SE04 |

Craven Heifer

★★★★★ ◉◉ RESTAURANT WITH ROOMS

tel: 01943 830106 **Main St LS29 0PL**
email: info@wellfedpubs.co.uk **web:** www.thecravenheifer.com

The Craven Heifer is located close to the town of Skipton and boasts themed rooms
based on Yorkshire celebrities. The bar is a traditional 'Dalesway' inn with stone
and oak floors, open fires, leather seating, real ale and outstanding food. The two
AA Rosette cuisine is beautifully complemented by a carefully chosen wine list. A
warm and very friendly welcome from the well-informed staff is guaranteed.

Rooms 7 en suite S £60-£135; D £75-£150 (room only)* **Facilities** FTV TVL tea/
coffee Dinner available WiFi **Conf** Max 20 **Parking** 10 **Notes** LB

| CASTLEFORD | Map 16 SE42 |

The Wheldale & Boot Room Sports Bar

Ⓤ

tel: 01977 553403 **fax:** 01977 232077 **Wheldon Rd WF10 2SD**

Currently the rating for this establishment is not confirmed. This may be due to a
change of ownership or because it has only recently joined the AA rating scheme.

Rooms 7 en suite

| HALIFAX | Map 19 SE02 |

Shibden Mill Inn

★★★★★ ◉◉ INN

tel: 01422 365840 **fax:** 01422 362971 **Shibden Mill Fold, Shibden HX3 7UL**
email: enquiries@shibdenmillinn.com **web:** www.shibdenmillinn.com
dir: 3m NE of Halifax off A58

Nestling in a fold of Shibden Dale, this 17th-century inn features exposed beams
and open fires. Guests can dine well in the two lounge-style bars, the restaurant, or
outside in summer. The stylish bedrooms come in a variety of sizes, and all are
thoughtfully equipped and have access to a free video library. Service is friendly
and obliging.

Rooms 11 en suite (1 GF) **Facilities** FTV DVD tea/coffee Dinner available Direct Dial
WiFi 🛁 18 Free use of local fitness centre **Conf** Max 50 Thtr 50 Class 21 Board 24
Parking 100 **Notes** Closed 25-26 Dec & 1 Jan

| HAWORTH | Map 19 SE03 |

Ashmount Country House

★★★★★ ⊛ 🏠 GUEST HOUSE

tel: 01535 645726 & 643822   **fax:** 01535 642550 **Mytholmes Ln BD22 8EZ**
email: info@ashmounthaworth.co.uk **web:** www.ashmounthaworth.co.uk
dir: *M65 junct 13A Laneshaw Bridge, turn right over moors to Haworth. Turn left after car park on right, 100yds on right*

Ashmount Country House is a stunning property in the heart of Brontë Country, just a short stroll from the centre of Haworth. It is an ideal location for those seeking a relaxing retreat with luxury touches. Each bedroom is designed with high-quality furnishings, attractive decor and many thoughtful extras; some have their own terrace with hot tub or sauna. There is also a comfortable lounge bar and an elegant dining room. The restaurant closes on Monday and Tuesday but a substantial snack menu is offered to residents. The landscaped gardens provide a lovely backdrop and a pleasant location to relax or enjoy afternoon tea on the lawn.

Rooms 8 en suite 4 annexe en suite (5 GF) S £55-£150; D £95-£245*
Facilities FTV iPod docking station Lounge tea/coffee Dinner available Licensed WiFi ✤ 🔒 **Extras** Fruit, home-made biscuits, sherry - complimentary **Conf** Max 25 Class 25 Board 15 **Parking** 12 **Notes** ⊗ No Children 10yrs Civ Wed 40

Wilsons

★★★★ GUEST ACCOMMODATION

tel: 01535 643209 **fax:** 01535 642509 **15 West Ln BD22 8DU**
email: enquire@wilsonsofhaworth.co.uk **web:** www.wilsonsofhaworth.co.uk

This charming property, named after the friendly owners, is located on the historic cobbled main street in the centre of picturesque Haworth. It is next to the Brontë Parsonage Museum with a couple of the bedrooms even looking onto it. There are lots of period features combined with modern facilities in the individually styled bedrooms and a boutique feel throughout. A cosy lounge area provides additional space for guests to relax and delicious breakfasts featuring only locally sourced produce are served in the light, airy dining room. Complimentary WiFi is also provided.

Rooms 5 en suite (1 GF) S £55; D £89-£110* **Facilities** FTV DVD iPod docking station Lounge tea/coffee Licensed WiFi **Notes** LB ⊗ No Children 16yrs Closed mid Dec-Feb

| HOLMFIRTH | Map 16 SE10 |

Rooms at the Nook

★★★★ GUEST ACCOMMODATION

tel: 01484 682373 & 07841 646308 **Victoria Square HD9 2DN**
email: office@thenookbrewhouse.co.uk **web:** www.roomsatthenook.co.uk
dir: *From A6024 in Holmfirth. On A635 (Victoria St), at bottom of Victoria St*

A warm welcome is assured at this centrally-located former 18th-century inn, where recent major investment has created eight stylish bedrooms from the former owners' accommodation. The Nook pub retains many original features and benefits from an on-site microbrewery serving award-winning ales and a good wine selection. An adjacent bar and restaurant, known as The Tap House, specialises in tapas with a Yorkshire twist.

Rooms 8 en suite (3 fmly) **Facilities** FTV DVD TVL tea/coffee Dinner available Licensed WiFi 👣 18 Pool table 🔒 **Notes** ⊗

| HUDDERSFIELD | Map 16 SE11 |

315 Bar and Restaurant

★★★★★ ⊛ RESTAURANT WITH ROOMS

tel: 01484 602613 **315 Wakefield Rd, Lepton HD8 0LX**
email: info@315barandrestaurant.co.uk **web:** www.315barandrestaurant.co.uk
dir: *M1 junct 38, A637 towards Huddersfield. At rdbt take A642 towards Huddersfield. Establishment on right in Lepton*

In a wonderful setting, 315 Bar and Restaurant is very well presented and benefits from countryside views from the well-appointed dining room and conservatory areas. The interior is modern with open fires that add character and ambiance, while the chef's table gives a real insight into the working of the kitchen. Bedrooms are well appointed and modern, and most have feature bathrooms. Staff are friendly and attentive, and there are excellent parking facilities.

Rooms 10 en suite (3 fmly) S fr £80; D £90-£110* **Facilities** FTV DVD TV8B tea/coffee Dinner available Lift WiFi **Conf** Max 150 Thtr 100 Class 75 Board 60 **Parking** 97 **Notes** ⊗ Civ Wed 120

Woodman Inn

★★★★ 🍽 INN

tel: 01484 605778 **Thunder Bridge Ln HD8 0PX**
email: info@woodman-inn.com **web:** www.woodman-inn.com

(For full entry see Kirkburton)

Innkeeper's Lodge Huddersfield, Kirkburton

★★★ INN

tel: 0845 112 6035 **36a Penistone Rd, Kirkburton HD8 0PQ**
email: info@innkeeperslodge.com **web:** www.innkeeperslodge.com

Situated on the Penistone Road, with easy reach of the National Coal Mining Museum and Huddersfield town centre. The lodge provides modern bedrooms and is attached to the Foxglove Vintage Inn; an attractive 19th-century building with real fires and spacious dining areas. A continental buffet breakfast is complimentary for all guests - a cooked option available at a supplement. Free WiFi is available throughout plus ample parking space.

Rooms 23 en suite (3 fmly) (13 GF) **Facilities** FTV tea/coffee Dinner available Direct Dial WiFi **Parking**

| ILKLEY | Map 19 SE14 |

Innkeeper's Lodge Ilkley

★★★ INN

tel: 0845 112 6037 **Hangingstone Rd LS29 8BT**
email: info@innkeeperslodge.com **web:** www.innkeeperslodge.com

This Innkeeper's Lodge is a 19th-century Victorian property idyllically located in the Yorkshire Dales, with stunning views over Wharfedale. Perfect for walkers, browsing the spa town of Ilkley, close to Ben Rhydding golf course and only a short drive from Leeds and Bradford. There is lots of period charm in the inviting public areas, where hearty food and cask ales are served. The bedrooms are modern and comfortable. Complimentary WiFi is provided.

Rooms 13 en suite (2 fmly) **Facilities** FTV tea/coffee Dinner available Direct Dial WiFi **Parking**

KIRKBURTON
Map 16 SE11

Woodman Inn

★★★★ ⊜ INN

tel: 01484 605778 **Thunder Bridge Ln HD8 0PX**
email: info@woodman-inn.com **web:** www.woodman-inn.com
dir: *1m SW of Kirkburton. Off A629 in Thunder Bridge*

The Woodman Inn is extremely popular with locals. The popular bar offers a wide selection of real ales, lagers and draught ciders. Bedrooms have been recently refurbished and are comfortable and comprehensively furnished, making this an ideal base for walking, visiting the National Mining Museum, or simply escaping to the country.

Rooms 10 en suite (3 fmly) (3 GF) S £50-£70; D £60-£80* **Facilities** FTV tea/coffee Dinner available Direct Dial WiFi ⅃ 18 **Conf** Max 60 Thtr 50 Class 60 Board 30 **Parking** 60 **Notes** Civ Wed 80

LEEDS
Map 19 SE23

Hinsley Hall

★★★ GUEST ACCOMMODATION

tel: 0113 261 8000 **fax:** 0113 224 2406 **62 Headingley Ln LS6 2BX**
email: info@hinsley-hall.co.uk **web:** www.hinsley-hall.co.uk
dir: *On A660 Leeds to Skipton road, past university & Hyde Park lights. Turn right into Oakfield*

Set in extensive landscaped gardens, Hinsley Hall enjoys a peaceful setting just a short drive from Leeds city centre and the nearby university. Bedrooms are all comfortable, well equipped and well appointed. A lounge is available for guests along with a small bar area. There are large conferencing facilities on site along with a number of meeting rooms. Headingley Stadium is a 10 minute walk away.

Rooms 50 rms (47 en suite) (3 pri facs) (1 fmly) (4 GF) S £39.50-£49.95; D £49.50-£67.50 **Facilities** FTV Lounge TVL TV9B tea/coffee Dinner available Licensed WiFi ⬛ **Conf** Max 90 Thtr 90 Class 50 Board 36 **Parking** 100 **Notes** ⊗ Closed 24 Dec-2 Jan

Innkeeper's Lodge Leeds Calverley

★★★ INN

tel: 0845 112 6043 **Calverley Ln, Pudsey LS28 5QQ**
email: info@innkeeperslodge.com **web:** www.innkeeperslodge.com

A striking 19th-century Victorian lodge peacefully located in the picturesque village of Calverley, yet very convenient for Bradford and Leeds and only six miles from Leeds Bradford International Airport. The spacious bar and dining areas are comfortable, with cask ales and a wide choice of food offered. Bedrooms are spacious and suitably equipped, and there is a large garden with outside seating. Complimentary WiFi is also provided.

Rooms 14 en suite (5 fmly) **Facilities** FTV tea/coffee Dinner available Direct Dial WiFi **Parking**

Find out more about beds in B&Bs - see page 24

MIRFIELD
Map 16 SE21

The Mirfield Monastery B&B

★★ GUEST ACCOMMODATION

tel: 01924 483346 & 494318 **Stocks Bank Rd WF14 0BN**
email: enquiries@mirfield.org.uk **web:** www.monastery-stay.co.uk
dir: *M62 junct 25 towards Mirfield. At rdbt, fork left onto A62 (Leeds). 1st right at lights, 0.5m*

This is a quiet haven; set within the walls of Mirfield Monastery, in beautiful gardens tended by the resident monks. Rooms are modestly appointed and decorated in calming neutral tones. WiFi is available. A continental breakfast is provided on a self service basis. The emphasis is on peace and quiet, with guests welcome to attend services if they wish.

Rooms 8 en suite S £40-£43; D £50-£53* **Facilities** FTV Lounge tea/coffee Licensed WiFi **Conf** Max 70 Thtr 70 Class 40 Board 25 **Parking** 10 **Notes** ⊗ No Children 5yrs

NORMANTON
Map 16 SE32

The Grange

★★★★ BED AND BREAKFAST

tel: 01924 892203 & 07970 505157 **2 Snydale Rd WF6 1NT**
email: enquiries@thegrangenormanton.co.uk **web:** www.thegrangenormanton.co.uk

The house has been in Sarah's family for over 100 years, and is a well maintained property with gardens that were designed by 2002 Chelsea Flower Show winner, Peter Garnett-Orme. The individually styled bedrooms are well appointed and have many thoughtful extras. Guests have use of the lounge with large screen TV. Full English breakfast is served in the dining room.

Rooms 3 rms (2 en suite) (1 pri facs) (1 fmly) S £45; D £70-£90* **Facilities** FTV TVL tea/coffee Dinner available WiFi ⬛ **Extras** Fruit juice, bottled water **Parking** 4 **Notes** LB ⊗ No Children 18mths Closed 24-29 Dec

OSSETT
Map 16 SE22

Heath House

★★★★ GUEST ACCOMMODATION

tel: 01924 260654 & 07890 385622 **fax:** 01924 263131 **Chancery Rd WF5 9RZ**
email: bookings@heath-house.co.uk **web:** www.heath-house.co.uk
dir: *M1 junct 40, A638 towards Dewsbury, at end dual carriageway exit rdbt 2nd left, house 20yds on right*

Heath House is a spacious Victorian family home standing in four acres of tranquil gardens a short distance from the M1. It has elegant en suite bedrooms, and the courteous and friendly owners provide healthy, freshly-cooked breakfasts.

Rooms 2 en suite 2 annexe en suite (1 fmly) (1 GF) **Facilities** FTV DVD tea/coffee WiFi ⬛ **Parking** 16

TODMORDEN
Map 18 SD92

Stoodley Hunting Lodge

[U]

tel: 01706 810275 **Stoodley Ln OL14 6HA**
email: info@stoodleyhuntinglodge.co.uk **web:** www.stoodleyhuntinglodge.co.uk

Currently the rating for this establishment is not confirmed. This may be due to a change of ownership or because it has only recently joined the AA rating scheme.

Rooms 3 en suite (1 fmly) S £79.95-£99.95; D £99.95-£119.95* **Facilities** STV FTV DVD iPod docking station Lounge tea/coffee Dinner available Direct Dial WiFi ch fac ⅃ 9 Fishing Riding Snooker Pool table ⬛ Beauty salon **Extras** Speciality toiletries, sweets, fridge available **Conf** Class 8 Board 8 **Parking** 6 **Notes** LB

CHANNEL ISLANDS
JERSEY

ST AUBIN   Map 24

Premier Collection

The Panorama

★★★★★ 🏠 GUEST ACCOMMODATION

tel: 01534 742429 & 07797 742429   **fax:** 01534 745940
La Rue du Crocquet JE3 8BZ
email: info@panoramajersey.com **web:** www.panoramajersey.com
dir: *In village centre*

Having spectacular views across St Aubin's Bay, The Panorama is a long-established favourite with visitors. The welcome is genuine and many of the well-equipped bedrooms have wonderful views; the bathrooms are finished to a high standard. Public areas also look seaward and have attractive antique fireplaces. Breakfast is excellent and served in two dining areas.

Rooms 14 en suite (3 GF) S £50-£82; D £104-£168* **Facilities** STV Lounge tea/coffee WiFi 🛜 **Extras** Robes, slippers **Notes** ⊗ No Children 18yrs Closed mid Oct-mid Apr

Harbour View

★★★★ GUEST HOUSE

tel: 01534 741585 **fax:** 01534 499460 **Le Boulevard JE3 8AB**
email: harbourview@localdial.com **web:** www.harbourviewjersey.com

Harbour View is situated in a beautiful location overlooking St Aubin Harbour. The guest house has been lovingly restored over recent years and it retains many

original features. Bedrooms are all smartly presented and come with a host of facilities. Food can be taken at 'Danny's at the Harbour View' and parking is an added bonus. A substantial continental breakfast, along with cooked options, is available in the well-appointed breakfast room.

Rooms 16 en suite (4 fmly) (2 GF) **Facilities** STV TVL tea/coffee Licensed WiFi 🛜 18 **Parking** 8 **Notes** Closed Dec-Feb

Peterborough House

★★★ GUEST ACCOMMODATION

tel: 01534 741568 **fax:** 01534 746787 **La Rue du Crocquet JE3 8BZ**
email: fernando@localdial.com **web:** www.jerseyisland.com/peterborough-house.html
dir: *A13 to St Aubin, left at La Haule Slip, 1st left. Left fork, half way down on left*

Situated on the old St Aubin high street, this well-presented house dates back to 1690. The bedrooms are comfortably appointed and the sea-facing rooms are always in high demand. One of the two lounge areas has a bar, or guests can enjoy the view with a drink on the outdoor terrace. Breakfast has a choice of traditional and continental options.

Rooms 14 rms (12 en suite) (1 fmly) (2 GF) S £33.10-£44.75; D £56.20-£79.50* **Facilities** Lounge TVL tea/coffee Licensed WiFi **Notes** LB ⊗ No Children 12yrs Closed Nov-Feb

ST HELIER   Map 24

Bay View Guest House

★★★★ GUEST ACCOMMODATION

tel: 01534 720950 & 07700 720100   **fax:** 01534 720950 **12 Havre des Pas JE2 4UQ**
email: bayview.guesthouse@jerseymail.co.uk **web:** www.bayviewjersey.com
dir: *Through tunnel, right at rdbt, down Green St & left, 100yds on left*

The Bay View is just across the road from the Havre des Pas Lido and beach, and a ten-minute walk from the centre of St Helier. The bedrooms are well equipped, and extra facilities include a bar and a TV lounge both with Sky TV channels. Free WiFi is available throughout the property. There is a small patio garden to the front of the establishment, and at the rear, another secluded terrace and a hot tub.

Rooms 12 rms (12 pri facs) (3 fmly) S £38-£54; D £76-£128* **Facilities** FTV DVD iPod docking station TVL tea/coffee Licensed WiFi 🛜 Hot tub **Extras** Speciality toiletries, robes, fridge **Notes** LB ⊗

ISLE OF MAN

PORT ST MARY   Map 24 SC26

Premier Collection

Aaron House

★★★★★ 🏠 GUEST HOUSE

tel: 01624 835702 **fax:** 01624 837731 **The Promenade IM9 5DE**
web: www.aaronhouse.co.uk
dir: *Follow signs for South & Port St Mary, left at Post Office. House in centre of Promenade*

Aaron House is truly individual. From the parlour down to the cast-iron baths, the house, overlooking the harbour, has maintained its Victorian origins. The family work hard to offer the best quality, whether its providing luxury and comfort in the bedrooms, or offering home-made cakes on arrival.

Rooms 4 rms (3 en suite) (1 pri facs) **Facilities** TVL TV1B tea/coffee **Notes** ⊗ No Children 12yrs Closed 21 Dec-3 Jan 🚭

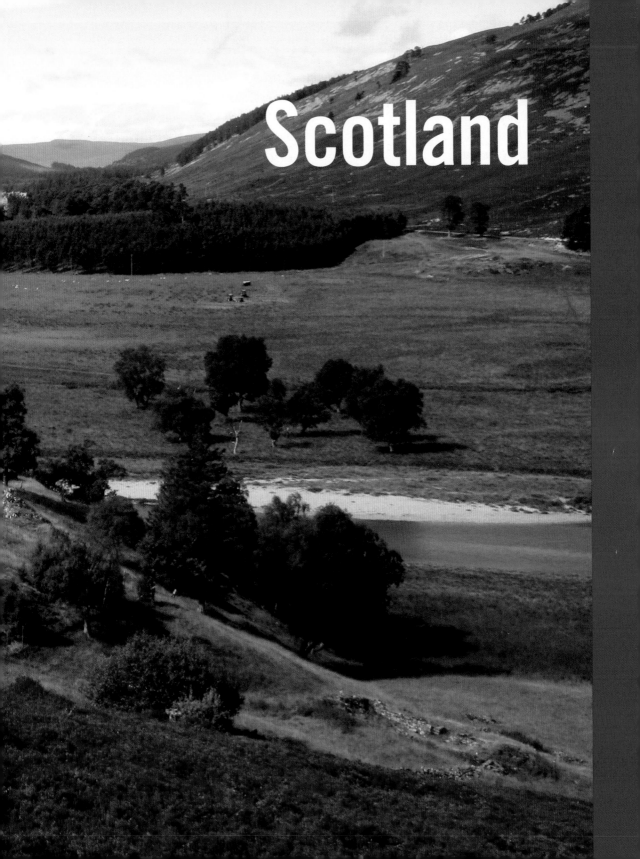

Scotland

CITY OF ABERDEEN

ABERDEEN
Map 23 NJ90

The Jays Guest House

★★★★ GUEST HOUSE

tel: 01224 638295 **422 King St AB24 3BR**
email: alice@jaysguesthouse.co.uk **web:** www.jaysguesthouse.co.uk
dir: *From S on A90, cross river, at next rdbt right into Holburn St (A9013). At lights right into Union St. Becomes King St. Guest house on right*

Guests are warmly welcomed to this attractive granite house on the north side of the city. Maintained in first-class order throughout, it offers attractive bedrooms, smartly furnished to appeal to business guests and tourists. Freshly prepared breakfasts are enjoyed in the carefully appointed dining room. A private car park is a definite plus.

Rooms 10 rms (8 en suite) (2 pri facs) (1 GF) S fr £60; D fr £100 (room only)*
Facilities STV FTV tea/coffee WiFi **Parking** 9 **Notes** ✱ No Children 12yrs Closed mid Dec-mid Jan

Arkaig Guest House

★★★ GUEST HOUSE

tel: 01224 638872 **fax:** 01224 622189 **43 Powis Ter AB25 3PP**
email: info@arkaig.co.uk **web:** www.arkaig.co.uk
dir: *On A96 at junct with Bedford Rd*

Arkaig Guest House offers a friendly welcome and relaxed atmosphere, situated on the north side of the city close to the university and city centre. Bedrooms vary in size, are attractively decorated, and are all thoughtfully equipped to appeal to business and leisure guests. There is a comfortable lounge and an attractive breakfast room where delicious, freshly cooked breakfasts are served. Parking is also available.

Rooms 9 rms (7 en suite) (1 fmly) (5 GF) **Facilities** FTV TVL tea/coffee Direct Dial **Parking** 10

ABERDEENSHIRE

ABOYNE
Map 23 NO59

The Lodge on the Loch of Aboyne

★★★★ 🍴 GUEST ACCOMMODATION

tel: 013398 86444 **Aboyne Loch Golf Centre AB34 5BR**
email: info@thelodgeontheloch.com **web:** www.thelodgeontheloch.com
dir: *1m E of Aboyne on A93*

The beautiful location of this lochside property ensures stunning views and a peaceful stay. The wide range of facilities include a nine-hole golf centre with driving range, osprey viewing deck, fitness centre and a wide range of treatments offered in the Reflect Spa. Dining options include the restaurant and the bistro bar, with very good function and wedding facilities also available.

Rooms 14 en suite (2 fmly) (7 GF) D £100-£150* **Facilities** FTV TVL tea/coffee Dinner available Direct Dial Licensed WiFi ⬇ ⬆ 9 Sauna Gym 🔑 Hot tub Holistic spa treatments **Conf** Max 80 Thtr 80 Class 40 Board 25 **Parking** 30 **Notes** LB Civ Wed 120

BALLATER
Map 23 NO39

The Auld Kirk

★★★★ GUEST HOUSE

tel: 01339 755762 & 07918 698000 **Braemar Rd AB35 5RQ**
email: info@theauldkirk.com **web:** www.theauldkirk.com
dir: *From Aboyne on A93 into Ballater, through village, past The Old Railway Station, 250yds on right*

This Victorian Scottish Free Church building has been carefully converted to make an unusual bed and breakfast. Many original features of the kirk have been restored and incorporated in the design, and all seven rooms are purpose-built and situated on the first floor, accessed by a wide staircase from the large entrance hallway. Breakfasts using the finest local produce are served in the Spirit restaurant, where private dining is available by appointment. Packed lunches can also be provided.

Rooms 7 en suite (1 fmly) S £60-£90; D £100-£125* **Facilities** FTV Lounge tea/coffee Direct Dial Licensed WiFi ⬆ 18 🔑 **Extras** Mineral water **Parking** 4 **Notes** Closed 24-25 Dec & Jan

BRAEMAR
Map 23 NO19

Callater Lodge Guest House

★★★★ GUEST HOUSE

tel: 01339 741275 **9 Glenshee Rd AB35 5YQ**
email: info@hotel-braemar.co.uk **web:** www.callaterlodge.co.uk
dir: *Next to A93, 300yds S of Braemar centre*

Located in the picturesque village of Braemar, this grand Victorian villa is very well presented with stunning views and lots of period features. Bedrooms are attractively decorated with many thoughtful extras, and the spacious lounge is inviting and homely. Breakfast is served at individual tables and uses quality local ingredients. The gardens are a very pleasant feature. AA Friendliest B&B of the Year Finalist 2014-2015.

Rooms 6 en suite (1 fmly) S £36-£80; D £72-£160* **Facilities** FTV Lounge tea/coffee Licensed WiFi ⬆ 18 🔑 **Parking** 6 **Notes** ✱ Closed Xmas

ELLON
Map 23 NJ93

AA GUEST ACCOMMODATION OF THE YEAR FOR SCOTLAND 2014–2015

Premier Collection

Aikenshill House *(NJ968218)*

★★★★★ FARMHOUSE

tel: 01358 742990 **Aikenshill, Foveran AB41 6AT**
email: enquiries@aikenshill.co.uk **web:** www.aikenshill.co.uk
dir: *From Aberdeen N on A90, pass Cock & Bull restaurant & Trump International Golf Links. Turn left signed Aikenshill, 500mtrs at end of road*

This farmhouse enjoys spectacular views from its elevated position overlooking Donald Trump's golf course and the Aberdeenshire coastline beyond. Located close to Aberdeen, the house is well situated for either a peaceful getaway or a city break. Decorated and furnished to an impressive standard, the modern feel of the property is complemented by friendly hospitality from the whole family. Memorable breakfasts include the best ingredients, and dinners by request are also available.

Rooms 4 en suite S £140-£280; D £160-£320* **Facilities** FTV TVL Dinner available WiFi ⬇ 🔑 **Parking Notes** 300 acres arable

KILDRUMMY
Map 23 NJ41

Kildrummy Inn
★★★★ ◎◎ INN

tel: 01975 571227 **fax:** 01975 571227 **AB33 8QS**
email: enquiries@kildrummyinn.co.uk **web:** www.kildrummyinn.co.uk
dir: On A97, 2m from junct with A944 at Mossat in direction of Strathdon & Cairngorms National Park

Located in the heart of rural Aberdeenshire, this popular inn is the perfect base for touring the Grampian Mountains and beyond. Personally run and with a unique history, Kildrummy Inn provides four comfortable bedrooms, all en suite and featuring TV, DVD player and free WiFi. The lounge bar with roaring fire and a good selection of beers and whiskies is a great place in which to while away the time. No visit would be complete without sampling the food on offer with skilfully created dishes highlighting the best in local produce.

Rooms 4 en suite D £79.50-£89.50* **Facilities** FTV DVD Lounge tea/coffee Dinner available Licensed WiFi Fishing ▲ **Conf** Max 12 Board 12 **Parking** 20 **Notes** ⊗ Closed Jan

STONEHAVEN
Map 23 NO88

The Ship Inn
★★★ INN

tel: 01569 762617 **fax:** 01569 767074 **5 Shorehead AB39 2JY**
email: enquiries@shipinnstonehaven.com **web:** www.shipinnstonehaven.com
dir: From A90 follow signs to Stonehaven, then signs to harbour

This popular inn overlooks the harbour in Stonehaven, and has been a fixture since 1771. Recently refurbished bedrooms and bathrooms offer good levels of comfort; many with views of the harbour. The Lounge Bar serves a host of whiskys and real ales, while the Captain's Table restaurant specialises in fresh local fish and some spectacular meats. Close to Aberdeen and the A90, the property is in an excellent location for those looking for some peace and tranquillity.

Rooms 11 en suite (2 fmly) S £75-£100; D £105-£135* **Facilities** FTV tea/coffee Dinner available WiFi **Notes** ⊗ No coaches

TARLAND
Map 23 NJ40

The Commercial
Ⓤ

tel: 01339 881922 **fax:** 01339 881922 **The Square, Aboyne AB34 4TX**
email: info@thecommercial-hotel.co.uk **web:** www.thecommerical-hotel.co.uk
dir: From Aboyne on A93 follow signs for Tarland. In village turn left into The Square, on right by monument

This property benefits from a stunning location in the heart of Royal Deeside in the 'Howe O' Cromar'. Near to Aberdeen, the Grampian Mountains and the Cairngorm National Park, The Commercial is ideally located, is family-run and has been recently refurbished. On offer is comfortable accommodation and a range of dining options including the cosy lounge bar or the more formal Cromar restaurant.

Rooms 9 en suite S £54-£65; D £89-£99* **Facilities** FTV DVD iPod docking station tea/coffee Dinner available Licensed WiFi Pool table ▲ **Extras** Bottled water - complimentary **Parking** 12

ANGUS

ARBROATH
Map 21 NO64

Hayswell Guest House
★★★ BED AND BREAKFAST

tel: 01241 430385 **29 Hayswell Rd DD11 1TU**
email: info@hayswellguesthouse.co.uk **web:** www.hayswellguesthouse.co.uk

This small Victorian property is situated close to the centre of Arbroath and the historic Abbey where the 'Declaration of Arbroath', recognising Scotland's right to a sovereign state, was signed in 1320. The two bedrooms are presented to a good standard with fridges and flat-screen TVs as standard. Warm hospitality is provided throughout any stay here, whether relaxing in the attractive lounge or enjoying one of the signature breakfasts in the dining room. Parking is easy to find next to the house. AA Friendliest B&B of the Year Finalist 2014-2015.

Rooms 2 rms (1 en suite) (1 pri facs) (1 GF) S £40-£45; D £65-£70* **Facilities** FTV Lounge tea/coffee WiFi ⅃ 18 ▲ **Notes** ⊗ ⊜

INVERKEILOR
Map 23 NO64

Premier Collection

Gordon's
★★★★★ ◎◎◎ 🍽 RESTAURANT WITH ROOMS

tel: 01241 830364 **Main St DD11 5RN**
email: gordonsrest@aol.com **web:** www.gordonsrestaurant.co.uk
dir: Exit A92 between Arbroath & Montrose into Inverkeilor

It's worth a detour off the main road to this family-run restaurant with rooms set in the centre of the village. The award-winning evening meals and the excellent breakfasts are equally memorable. A huge fire dominates the restaurant on cooler evenings. The attractive bedrooms are tastefully decorated and thoughtfully equipped; the larger two are furnished in pine.

Rooms 4 en suite 1 annexe en suite (1 GF) S fr £110; D £110-£150*
Facilities FTV tea/coffee Dinner available WiFi ▲ **Parking** 6 **Notes** ⊗ No Children 12yrs Closed 3wks Jan No coaches

MONTROSE
Map 23 NO75

Oaklands Guest House
★★★ GUEST HOUSE

tel: 01674 672018 **fax:** 01674 672018 **10 Rossie Island Rd DD10 9NN**
email: oaklands1@btopenworld.com **web:** www.oaklands.sm4.biz
dir: On A92 at S end of town

A genuine welcome and attentive service are assured at Oaklands Guest House, a smart, detached house situated on the south side of the town. Bedrooms come in a variety of sizes and are neatly presented. There is a lounge on the ground floor next to the attractive dining room, where hearty breakfasts are served. Motorcycle guided tours can be arranged for those travelling with their own motorbikes.

Rooms 7 en suite (1 fmly) (1 GF) S £35-£45; D £60-£70 **Facilities** FTV TVL tea/coffee WiFi ▲ **Extras** Mints - complimentary **Parking** 8 **Notes** ⊗

ARGYLL & BUTE

APPIN
Map 20 NM94

Pineapple House
★★★★ GUEST HOUSE

tel: 01631 740350 **Duror PA38 4BP**
email: info@pineapplehouse.co.uk **web:** www.pineapplehouse.co.uk
dir: In Duror, off A828. 5m S of A82

Situated in the pretty village of Duror on the Argyll Coastal Route, Pineapple House is within easy reach of both Fort William and Oban. The property is in an excellent location for tourists, walkers and cyclists who wish to explore the Highlands. Appointed to a very high standard, the guest house is family run and all bedrooms have en suite facilities. Bike storage and drying facilities are also available. The hearty breakfasts and warm hospitality make for a memorable stay.

Rooms 6 en suite (1 fmly) S £48; D £80-£95* **Facilities** FTV TVL tea/coffee WiFi 🅟 **Extras** Sweets, bottled water, speciality toiletries **Parking** 8 **Notes** ⊗ No Children 7yrs Closed mid Nov-mid Feb

BARCALDINE
Map 20 NM94

Premier Collection

Ardtorna
★★★★★ 🏡 BED AND BREAKFAST

tel: 01631 720125 & 07867 785524 **Mill Farm PA37 1SE**
email: info@ardtorna.co.uk **web:** www.ardtorna.co.uk
dir: N from Connel on A828, 0.5m from Scottish Sea Life Sanctuary

Purpose-built as a luxury bed and breakfast, Ardtorna enjoys a commanding position overlooking the Firth of Lorn near Oban. Warm hospitality can always be found here. Floor-to-ceiling windows in the bedrooms let you watch the glorious sunsets in comfort, and the excellent king-size beds will provide a great night's sleep. Bathrooms have luxury toiletries and huge towels. Breakfast will leave you spoilt for choice. 'Butler' and 'romantic' packages are also available for those wishing to be pampered further. Ardtorna was Guest Accommodation of the Year for Scotland 2013-14.

Rooms 4 en suite (4 GF) **Facilities** FTV DVD iPod docking station tea/coffee WiFi 🛁♨ 9 🅟 Leisure facilities available at nearby hotel **Extras** Fresh fruit, flowers, malt whisky, Baileys **Parking** 10 **Notes** LB ⊗ No Children 12yrs

CAIRNDOW
Map 20 NN11

Cairndow Stagecoach Inn
★★★ INN

tel: 01499 600286 & 600252 **fax:** 01499 600220 **PA26 8BN**
email: enq@cairndowinn.com **web:** www.cairndowinn.com
dir: From N, take either A82 to Tarbet, A83 to Cairndow, or A85 to Palmally, A819 to Inveraray & A83 to Cairndow

A relaxed, friendly atmosphere prevails at the 18th-century Cairndow Stagecoach Inn, overlooking the beautiful Loch Fyne. Bedrooms offer individual decor and thoughtful extras. Traditional public areas include a comfortable beamed lounge, a well-stocked bar where food is served throughout the day, and a spacious restaurant with conservatory extension. Deluxe bedrooms offer more space and luxury.

Rooms 13 en suite 5 annexe en suite (2 fmly) (5 GF) **Facilities** STV FTV Lounge tea/coffee Dinner available Direct Dial WiFi ♨ 9 Sauna 🅟 **Conf** Max 30 Thtr 30 Class 30 Board 30 **Parking** 30

CONNEL
Map 20 NM93

Premier Collection

Ards House
★★★★★ 🏡 GUEST HOUSE

tel: 01631 710255 & 07703 438341 **fax:** 01631 710857 **PA37 1PT**
email: info@ardshouse.com **web:** www.ardshouse.com
dir: On A85, 4m N of Oban

This delightful Victorian villa on the approaches to Loch Etive has stunning views over the Firth of Lorne and the Morven Hills beyond. The stylish bedrooms come with added touches such as mineral water and home-made shortbread. There is an inviting drawing room complete with piano, games and books, plus a fire on cooler evenings. The attractive dining room is the setting for delicious breakfasts.

Rooms 4 en suite **Facilities** FTV Lounge TVL tea/coffee WiFi **Parking** 12 **Notes** ⊗ No Children 10yrs Closed mid Dec-mid Jan

LUSS
Map 20 NS39

The Inn on Loch Lomond
★★★★ 🍴 INN

tel: 01436 860678 **fax:** 01436 860203 **Inverbeg G83 8PD**
email: inverbeg.reception@loch-lomond.co.uk **web:** www.innonlochlomond.co.uk
dir: A82 N of Balloch

Dating back to the 18th century this inn offers very stylish, comfortable bedrooms, bathrooms, and equally attractive public areas that boast open fires and cow-hide sofas. Food is as much of a feature as the property itself; a number of quirky dishes including deep-fried Mars bars and Irn Bru sorbet are offered. The Beach House accommodation, just a short walk from the inn, is a real treat for those looking for a little more privacy.

Rooms 25 en suite 8 annexe en suite (1 fmly) (5 GF) S £59-£200; D £69-£260* **Facilities** TVL tea/coffee Dinner available WiFi 🅟 **Parking** 60 **Notes** LB Civ Wed 60

OBAN
Map 20 NM82

Premier Collection

Blarcreen House
★★★★★ GUEST HOUSE

tel: 01631 750272 & 07557 977225 **Ardchattan, Connel PA37 1RG**
email: info@blarcreenhouse.com **web:** www.blarcreenhouse.com
dir: N over Connel Bridge, turn right signed Bonawe, 6.7m to Blarcreen

This elegant Victorian mansion house on the side of Loch Etive is the ideal base for exploring the Highlands. Warm hospitality and log fires await guests arriving at this property, where they can relax and enjoy comfortable bedrooms and fantastic views. Evening meals are also available by prior arrangement.

Rooms 3 en suite S £80-£100; D £100-£120* **Facilities** FTV DVD iPod docking station TVL tea/coffee Dinner available Licensed WiFi 🅟 **Extras** Speciality toiletries, chocolates - complimentary **Parking** 5 **Notes** No Children 16yrs

Glenburnie House

★★★★ 🛏 GUEST HOUSE

tel: 01631 562089 **fax:** 01631 562089 **The Esplanade PA34 5AQ**
email: graeme.strachan@btinternet.com **web:** www.glenburnie.co.uk
dir: On Oban seafront. Follow signs for Ganavan

This impressive Victorian seafront house has been lovingly appointed to a high standard. The bedrooms (including a four-poster room and a mini-suite) are beautifully decorated and very well equipped. There is a cosy ground-floor lounge and an elegant dining room, where hearty traditional breakfasts are served at individual tables.

Rooms 12 en suite (2 GF) D £85-£120 **Facilities** FTV DVD Lounge tea/coffee WiFi Massage **Parking** 12 **Notes** LB ⊗ No Children 12yrs Closed Dec-Feb

MacKay's Guest House

★★★★ 🛏 GUEST HOUSE

tel: 01631 563121 & 566356 **Corran Esplanade PA34 5AQ**
email: info@mackaysguesthouse.co.uk **web:** www.mackaysguesthouse.co.uk
dir: A85 into town, at rdbt 2nd exit to seafront (Corran Esplanade). Pass Cathedral, 300yds on right

Boasting fantastic views across Oban Bay, this newly renovated property offers comfort and quality as well as warm traditional hospitality. All front facing bedrooms are spacious and very well appointed. Award winning breakfast is served in the bright conservatory and breakfast room. Dedicated off-road parking and outdoor seating overlooking the bay add to this wonderful guest experience.

Rooms 8 en suite (2 GF) **Facilities** FTV DVD iPod docking station TVL tea/coffee WiFi **Extras** Robes, snacks, water, sherry - complimentary **Parking** 10 **Notes** ⊗ No Children 15yrs Closed 13 Nov-21 Mar

The Barriemore Guest House

★★★★ GUEST HOUSE

tel: 01631 566356 **Corran Esplanade PA34 5AQ**
email: reception@barriemore-hotel.co.uk **web:** www.barriemore-hotel.co.uk
dir: A85 into Oban, 1st rdbt exit towards sea. Right at 2nd rdbt, continue with sea on left, last guest house on right

This splendid three-storey Victorian town house enjoys a fantastic location on Oban's seafront and enjoys great views over Oban Bay. Spacious rooms with modern decor and friendly service can be found at this family-run property. A hearty Scottish breakfast will keep guests going for the day ahead.

Rooms 15 en suite (4 fmly) (2 GF) D £45-£70* **Facilities** FTV DVD iPod docking station Lounge tea/coffee WiFi **Extras** Fruit, bottled water, sherry, robes - free **Parking** 14 **Notes** ⊗ Closed Nov-Apr

The Glenrigh Guest House

★★★★ GUEST HOUSE

tel: 01631 562991 **Corran Esplanade PA34 5AQ**
email: reception@barriemore-hotel.co.uk **web:** www.barriemore-hotel.co.uk
dir: Down hill into Oban, turn right (with sea on left), along esplanade

This former Victorian mansion has fantastic views of Oban Bay and the far away islands, and has the added bonus of on-site parking. Close to the heart of Oban town centre, it is also within walking distance of local amenities. Glenrigh offers comfortable bedrooms, impressive bathrooms and a hearty breakfast. A friendly team are waiting to make your stay memorable.

Rooms 15 en suite (3 fmly) (3 GF) **Facilities** FTV DVD iPod docking station TVL tea/coffee WiFi 🔓 **Extras** Snacks, drinks **Parking** 20 **Notes** ⊗ Closed Nov-Mar

Lancaster

★★ GUEST ACCOMMODATION

tel: 01631 562587 **fax:** 01631 562587 **Corran Esplanade PA34 5AD**
email: lancasteroban@btconnect.com **web:** www.lancasteroban.co.uk
dir: On seafront next to Columba's Cathedral

Lancaster is a family-run establishment on the esplanade that offers budget accommodation; many bedrooms boast lovely views out over the bay towards the Isle of Mull. Public areas include a choice of lounges and bars that also benefit from the panoramic views. A swimming pool, sauna and spa bath are added benefits.

Rooms 27 rms (24 en suite) (3 fmly) (10 smoking) **Facilities** FTV Lounge TVL tea/coffee Dinner available Licensed WiFi ⟳ Sauna Pool table 🔓 Spa Steam room **Conf** Max 30 Thtr 30 Class 20 Board 12 **Parking** 20 **Notes** LB

LARGS	Map 20 NS25

South Whittlieburn Farm

★★★★ BED AND BREAKFAST

tel: 01475 675881 & 675080 **fax:** 01475 675080 **Brisbane Glen KA30 8SN**
email: largsbandb@southwhittlieburnfarm.freeserve.co.uk
web: www.smoothhound.co.uk/hotels/whittlie.html
dir: 2m NE of Largs off A78 signed Brisbane Glen, after Vikingar centre

This comfortable and welcoming farmhouse is on a working farm surrounded by gently rolling countryside. The attractive bedrooms are well equipped, with all having Sky TV and DVD players. There is a spacious ground-floor lounge and a bright airy dining room where delicious breakfasts are served.

Rooms 3 en suite (1 fmly) S £39.50-£45; D £65-£70 **Facilities** STV FTV DVD TVL tea/coffee WiFi ⬇ 18 🔓 **Parking** 10 **Notes** LB ⊗ RS Xmas ⊛

AYR	Map 20 NS32

26 The Crescent

★★★★★ GUEST HOUSE

tel: 01292 287329 **fax:** 01292 201003 **26 Bellevue Crescent KA7 2DR**
email: enquiries@26crescent.co.uk **web:** www.26crescent.co.uk
dir: Exit A79 at rdbt, 3rd exit into King St. Left into Bellevue Crescent

Located in a quiet residential area of Ayr, close to the seafront, town centre and race course, this guest house offers a traditional warm welcome with well-appointed and comfortable bedrooms. Bathrooms are of a high standard, as is the hearty breakfast served at individual tables in the charming dining room.

Rooms 5 en suite **Facilities** FTV DVD iPod docking station Lounge tea/coffee WiFi **Extras** Speciality toiletries - complimentary **Notes** LB ⊗ No Children 2yrs

AYR *continued*

Daviot House

★★★★ 🏠 GUEST HOUSE

tel: 01292 269678 **12 Queens Ter KA7 1DU**
email: daviothouse@hotmail.com **web:** www.daviothouse.com
dir: *Exit A719 into Wellington Sq & Bath Place, turn right*

This well-maintained Victorian house stands in a peaceful location close to the beach and town centre. Bedrooms are modern in style and well equipped. Hearty breakfasts are served in the dining room. Daviot House is a member of Golf South Ayrshire - a golf booking service for local municipal courses, so let your hosts know if you'd like a round to be organised.

Rooms 6 rms (5 en suite) (1 pri facs) (1 fmly) (1 GF) **Facilities** FTV tea/coffee WiFi
Notes ⊗

DUMFRIES & GALLOWAY

| CASTLE DOUGLAS | Map 21 NX76 |

Craigadam

★★★★ 🏠 🍴 GUEST HOUSE

tel: 01556 650233 & 650100 **fax:** 01556 650233 **Craigadam DG7 3HU**
email: inquiry@craigadam.com **web:** www.craigadam.com
dir: *From Castle Douglas E on A75 to Crocketford. In Crocketford turn left on A712 for 2m. House on hill*

Set on a farm, this elegant country house offers gracious living in a relaxed environment. The large bedrooms, most set around a courtyard, are strikingly individual in style. Public areas include a billiard room with comprehensive honesty bar, and the panelled dining room which features a magnificent 15-seater table, the setting for Celia Pickup's delightful meals.

Rooms 10 en suite (2 fmly) (7 GF) S £47-£67; D £94-£110* **Facilities** FTV Lounge TVL tea/coffee Dinner available Licensed WiFi ch fac 🦢 Fishing Snooker Private fishing & shooting **Conf** Max 22 **Parking** 12 **Notes** LB Closed Xmas & New Year Civ Wed 150

| DUMFRIES | Map 21 NX97 |

Wallamhill House

★★★★ BED AND BREAKFAST

tel: 01387 248249 **Kirkton DG1 1SL**
email: wallamhill@aol.com **web:** www.wallamhill.co.uk
dir: *3m N of Dumfries. Off A701 signed Kirkton, 1.5m on right*

Wallamhill House is set in well-tended gardens, in a delightful rural area three miles from Dumfries. Bedrooms are spacious and extremely well equipped. There is a peaceful drawing room, and a mini health club with sauna, steam shower and gym equipment.

Rooms 3 en suite (1 fmly) (3 GF) S fr £40; D fr £65 **Facilities** FTV TVL tea/coffee WiFi 🦢 Sauna Gym 🛁 Steam room Hot tub **Extras** Fridge **Parking** 6 **Notes** LB ⊗

Rivendell

★★★★ GUEST HOUSE

tel: 01387 252251 **fax:** 0872 111 7592 **105 Edinburgh Rd DG1 1JX**
email: info@rivendellbnb.co.uk **web:** www.rivendellbnb.co.uk
dir: *On A701 Edinburgh Rd, 400yds S of A75 junct*

Situated just north of the town and close to the bypass, this lovely 1920s house, standing in extensive landscaped gardens, has been restored to reflect the period style of the property. Bedrooms are thoughtfully equipped, many are spacious and all offer modern facilities. Traditional breakfasts are served in the elegant dining room.

Rooms 7 rms (6 en suite) (1 pri facs) 3 annexe en suite (2 fmly) (5 GF) **Facilities** FTV iPod docking station tea/coffee WiFi **Parking** 12 **Notes** LB ⊗

Southpark House

★★★★ GUEST ACCOMMODATION

tel: 01387 711188 & 0800 970 1588 **fax:** 01387 711155
Quarry Rd, Locharbriggs DG1 1QR
email: info@southparkhouse.co.uk **web:** www.southparkhouse.co.uk
dir: *3.5m NE of Dumfries. Exit A701 in Locharbriggs into Quarry Rd, last house on left*

With a peaceful location commanding stunning views, this well-maintained property offers comfortable, attractive and well-equipped bedrooms. The peaceful lounge has a log fire on colder evenings, and fax and email facilities are available. Friendly proprietor Ewan Maxwell personally oversees the hearty Scottish breakfasts served in the conservatory breakfast room.

Rooms 4 en suite (1 fmly) **Facilities** STV FTV Lounge TVL tea/coffee WiFi 2 acres of garden **Parking** 13 **Notes** ⊗

| GRETNA (WITH GRETNA GREEN) | Map 21 NY36 |

Barrasgate House

★★★★ GUEST ACCOMMODATION

tel: 01461 337577 & 07711 661938 **fax:** 01461 337577 **Mill Hill DG16 5HU**
email: info@barrasgate.co.uk **web:** www.barrasgate.co.uk
dir: *From N: A74 (M) junct 22 signed Gretna Green/Longtown. At 2nd rdbt right, signed Longtown. Approx 1.5m, establishment on right. From S: M6 junct 45 take A6071 signed Longtown. Approx 1m turn 2nd left, signed Gretna Green/Springfield. 1st left*

This detached house lies in attractive gardens in a rural setting near Gretna, the Blacksmith Centre and motorway links. Bedrooms are well presented and equipped. Hearty breakfasts, featuring local produce, are taken in an attractive dining room, overlooking the gardens.

Rooms 4 en suite (1 fmly) (1 GF) S £35-£45; D £65-£75* **Facilities** FTV tea/coffee WiFi 🛁 **Parking** 10 **Notes** LB Closed Jan-Feb

Surrone House

★★★ GUEST ACCOMMODATION

tel: 01461 338341 **Annan Rd DG16 5DL**
email: enquiries@surronehouse.co.uk **web:** www.surronehouse.co.uk
dir: In town centre on B721

Guests are assured of a warm welcome at this well-maintained property in attractive gardens set back from the road. Bedrooms are sensibly furnished and include a delightful honeymoon suite. Dinner, drinks and light refreshments are available.

Rooms 6 en suite (3 fmly) (1 GF) S fr £40; D fr £70* **Facilities** FTV TVL tea/coffee Dinner available Licensed WiFi 🔒 **Parking** 10 **Notes** ⊗

LANGHOLM — Map 21 NY38

Glengarth Guest Rooms

★★★★ GUEST ACCOMMODATION

tel: 01387 380777 & 07802 771137 **Maxwell Rd DG13 0DX**
email: info@glengarthguestrooms.co.uk **web:** www.glengarthguestrooms.co.uk
dir: M6 junct 44, A7. In Langholm 500yds past Co-op

Glengarth Guest Rooms is located in a quiet residential area in the Borders town of Langholm. Strong hospitality and customer care is provided. Bedrooms and en suites are well appointed, comfortable, and cater well for the needs of the guest. Quality breakfast is served in the lounge/dining room using locally sourced produce.

Rooms 2 en suite (2 GF) S £60; D £70 **Facilities** STV FTV DVD Lounge TVL tea/coffee WiFi ⟊ 9 Fishing **Parking** 2 **Notes** LB ⊗ No Children

MOFFAT — Map 21 NT00

Bridge House

★★★★ GUEST HOUSE

tel: 01683 220558 **fax:** 01683 220558 **Well Rd DG10 9JT**
email: info@bridgehousemoffat.co.uk **web:** www.bridgehousemoffat.co.uk
dir: Exit A708 (The Holm) into Burnside, bear right into Well Rd, house 0.5m on left

A fine Victorian property, Bridge House stands in attractive gardens in a quiet residential area on the outskirts of the town. The atmosphere is very friendly and relaxed. The chef-proprietor provides interesting dinners (by prior arrangement) featuring local produce. There is a cosy guest lounge, and free WiFi is available.

Rooms 7 en suite (1 fmly) S £55; D £70-£100* **Facilities** FTV Lounge tea/coffee Dinner available WiFi 🔒 **Parking** 7 **Notes** LB ⊗ No Children 2yrs Closed Xmas & New Year

Hartfell House & The Limetree Restaurant

★★★★ ⊛ GUEST HOUSE

tel: 01683 220153 **Hartfell Crescent DG10 9AL**
email: enquiries@hartfellhouse.co.uk **web:** www.hartfellhouse.co.uk
dir: From High St at war memorial into Well St & Old Well Rd. Hartfell Crescent on right

Built in 1850, this impressive Victorian house is in a peaceful terrace high above the town and has lovely countryside views. Beautifully maintained, the bedrooms offer high quality and comfort. The attractive dining room is transformed in the evening into The Limetree Restaurant, offering chef Matt Seddon's culinary delights.

Rooms 7 en suite (2 fmly) (1 GF) S £40-£45; D £60-£75 **Facilities** FTV Lounge tea/coffee Dinner available Licensed WiFi ⟊ 18 **Parking** 6 **Notes** LB ⊗ Closed Xmas

Limetree House

★★★★ GUEST ACCOMMODATION

tel: 01683 220001 **Eastgate DG10 9AE**
email: limetreehousemoffat@yahoo.co.uk **web:** www.limetreehouse.co.uk
dir: From High St into Well St, left into Eastgate, house 100yds on left

A warm welcome is assured at this well-maintained property, quietly situated behind the main high street. Recognisable by its many colourful flower baskets in season, it provides an inviting lounge and a bright, cheerful breakfast room. Bedrooms are smartly furnished and include a large family room.

Rooms 6 en suite (1 fmly) (1 GF) S £50-£55; D £70-£90* **Facilities** FTV TVL tea/coffee WiFi ⟊ 18 🔒 **Parking** 3 **Notes** LB No Children 5yrs RS Xmas & New Year

MOFFAT *continued*

No 29 Well Street

★★★★ BED AND BREAKFAST

tel: 01683 221905 **29 Well St DG10 9DP**
email: mcleancamm1956@btinternet.com **web:** www.moffatbandb.co.uk
dir: *M74 junct 15 follow signs to High St, Well St on right*

Located in the heart of Moffat, just a few minutes' drive from the rolling countryside of the Scottish Borders, this is a very comfortable and well-presented property offering high standards of hospitality and service. The bedrooms are well appointed with many useful extras provided as standard. Breakfasts are hearty with local produce used to good effect.

Rooms 3 en suite (2 GF) S £38–£45; D £58–£68* **Facilities** FTV DVD tea/coffee WiFi 🔒 **Extras** Speciality toiletries - complimentary **Parking** 1 **Notes** No Children 10yrs Closed 24-26 & 31 Dec, 1 Jan

Barnhill Springs Country Guest House

★★ GUEST ACCOMMODATION

tel: 01683 220580 **DG10 9QS**
email: barnhillsprings@yahoo.co.uk
dir: *A74(M) junct 15, A701 towards Moffat. Barnhill Rd 50yds on right*

This former farmhouse is in a quiet, rural location south of the town and within easy reach of the M74. Bedrooms are well proportioned and have private bathrooms. There is a comfortable lounge and separate dining room. Barnhill Springs continues to welcome pets.

Rooms 3 rms (3 pri facs) (1 GF) S £39; D £78* **Facilities** TVL tea/coffee 🔒 **Parking** 10 **Notes** LB 🐾

WEST DUNBARTONSHIRE

BALLOCH Map 20 NS38

The Waterhouse Inn

★★★★ INN

tel: 01389 752120 **fax:** 01389 752125 **34 Balloch Rd G83 8LE**
email: info@waterhouseinn.co.uk **web:** www.waterhouseinn.co.uk
dir: *M8 junct 30 onto M898. Over Erskine bridge, take exit for Crianlarich onto A82 head towards Loch Lomond. Right at rdbt onto A811*

The Waterhouse Inn is located on the high street of Balloch, close to the park and the mouth of Loch Lomond. Bedrooms are well equipped and spacious, with modern bright bathrooms. The inn is welcoming and friendly, with a café that serves home-cooked food throughout the day, and is a perfect base for touring Loch Lomond and the Trossachs National Park.

Rooms 7 en suite (2 fmly) S £59–£69; D £69–£89* **Facilities** STV FTV Lounge TVL tea/coffee Dinner available WiFi 🔒 **Notes** ⊗

Innkeeper's Lodge Loch Lomond

★★★ INN

tel: 0845 112 6006 **Balloch Rd G83 8LQ**
email: info@innkeeperslodge.com **web:** www.innkeeperslodge.com

This property enjoys an excellent location, a stone's throw from Loch Lomond and the nearby Balloch Castle Country Park. The historical lodge has been refurbished

to provide modern, spacious accommodation. The cosy and welcoming lounge bar is a popular place to dine below the exposed wooden beams. Enjoy a cask ale by the open fire or a dish from their wide and varying menu. Parking available on site.

Rooms 11 en suite (4 fmly) **Facilities** FTV tea/coffee Dinner available Direct Dial WiFi **Parking** 52

CITY OF EDINBURGH

EDINBURGH Map 21 NT27

See also Livingston (West Lothian)

Premier Collection

Kew House

★★★★★ GUEST ACCOMMODATION

tel: 0131 313 0700 **fax:** 0131 313 0747 **1 Kew Ter, Murrayfield EH12 5JE**
email: info@kewhouse.com **web:** www.kewhouse.com
dir: *W of city centre on A8*

Forming part of a listed Victorian terrace, Kew House lies within walking distance of the city centre, and is convenient for Murrayfield Stadium and tourist attractions. Meticulously maintained throughout in contemporary style, it offers attractive bedrooms in a variety of sizes, all thoughtfully equipped to suit business and leisure guests. There is a comfortable lounge. Both parking and WiFi are complimentary.

Rooms 6 en suite (1 fmly) (2 GF) S £81–£99; D £99–£179* **Facilities** FTV Lounge tea/coffee Direct Dial WiFi 🔒 **Extras** Speciality toiletries, sherry, chocolates, fridge **Parking** 6 **Notes** LB ⊗ Closed approx 5-23 Jan

Six Brunton Place

★★★★★ 🏠 GUEST HOUSE

tel: 0131 622 0042 & 07748 858892 **6 Brunton Place EH7 5EG**
email: contact@sixbruntonplace.com **web:** www.sixbruntonplace.com
dir: *On London Road (B1350), opposite London Road Gardens*

This award-winning Georgian town house is located within easy walking distance of the centre of Edinburgh. The building and its lovingly restored features cannot help but impress, and the warmth and hospitality make this a 'little gem'. Bedrooms are extremely well equipped with quality and comfort a given. Guests can also relax in either the walled garden or attractive lounge area.

Rooms 4 en suite (1 fmly) (1 GF) S £89-£139; D £109-£199 **Facilities** STV FTV DVD iPod docking station Lounge tea/coffee WiFi ⚓ 18 🔔 **Extras** Speciality toiletries, home-baked goods - free **Notes** ⊗ No Children 10yrs

23 Mayfield

★★★★★ 🏠 GUEST ACCOMMODATION

tel: 0131 667 5806 **fax:** 0131 667 6833 **23 Mayfield Gardens EH9 2BX**
email: info@23mayfield.co.uk **web:** www.23mayfield.co.uk
dir: *A720 bypass S, follow city centre signs. Left at Craigmillar Park, 0.5m on right*

23 Mayfield continues to go from strength to strength, with many new additions to the property, and the garden that now has a hot tub. It is well located for access to Edinburgh and has the added benefit of secure off-road parking. The spacious accommodation has retained many of original period features. Breakfast is a real delight, with the very best local produce used to give guests a great start to their day.

Rooms 8 en suite (2 fmly) (1 GF) **Facilities** FTV DVD iPod docking station Lounge tea/coffee WiFi 🔔 Bike hire Hot tub **Parking** 8 **Notes** LB ⊗

21212

★★★★★ ⚜⚜⚜⚜ RESTAURANT WITH ROOMS

tel: 0131 523 1030 & 0845 222 1212 **3 Royal Ter EH7 5AB**
email: reservations@21212restaurant.co.uk **web:** www.21212restaurant.co.uk
dir: *Calton Hill, city centre*

A real jewel in Edinburgh's crown, this establishment takes its name from the number of choices at each course on the five-course dinner menu. Located on the prestigious Royal Terrace this is a light and airy, renovated Georgian town house stretching over four floors. The four individually designed bedrooms epitomise luxury living and the bathrooms certainly have the wow factor. At the heart of this restaurant with rooms is the creative, award-winning cooking of Paul Kitching. Service throughout is friendly and very attentive.

Rooms 4 en suite D £95-£325 **Facilities** STV FTV iPod docking station Lounge Dinner available WiFi **Extras** Speciality toiletries, mineral water, sloe gin **Notes** ⊗ No Children 5yrs Closed 1wk Jan & 1wk Autumn RS Sun & Mon restaurant closed No coaches

The Witchery by the Castle

★★★★★ ⚜ 🏠 RESTAURANT WITH ROOMS

tel: 0131 225 5613 **fax:** 0131 220 4392 **Castlehill, The Royal Mile EH1 2NF**
email: mail@thewitchery.com **web:** www.thewitchery.com
dir: *Top of Royal Mile at gates of Edinburgh Castle*

Originally built in 1595, The Witchery by the Castle is situated in a historic building at the gates of Edinburgh Castle. The two luxurious and theatrically decorated suites, known as the Inner Sanctum and the Old Rectory are located above the restaurant and are reached via a winding stone staircase. Filled with antiques, opulently draped beds, large roll-top baths and a plethora of memorabilia, this ancient and exciting establishment is often described as one of the country's most romantic destinations.

Rooms 4 en suite 5 annexe en suite (1 GF) D £325-£370* **Facilities** STV FTV DVD tea/coffee Dinner available Direct Dial WiFi **Extras** Bottled water - complimentary **Notes** ⊗ No Children 12yrs Closed 25-26 Dec No coaches

Bonnington Guest House

★★★★ 🏠 GUEST HOUSE

tel: 0131 554 7610 **202 Ferry Rd EH6 4NW**
email: booking@thebonningtonguesthouse.com **web:** www.thebonningtonguesthouse.com
dir: *On A902, near corner of Ferry Rd & Newhaven Rd*

This delightful Georgian house offers individually furnished bedrooms on two floors that retain many of their original features. Family rooms are also available. A substantial freshly prepared breakfast is served in the dining room. Off-street parking is an added bonus.

Rooms 7 rms (5 en suite) (2 pri facs) (2 fmly) (1 GF) S £65-£115; D £75-£136* **Facilities** FTV tea/coffee WiFi **Extras** Speciality toiletries, sherry - free; robes **Parking** 9 **Notes** ⊗ Closed Nov-Mar RS 27 Dec-2 Jan Open for New Year

EDINBURGH *continued*

Fraoch House

★★★★ ≣ GUEST ACCOMMODATION

tel: 0131 554 1353 **66 Pilrig St EH6 5AS**
email: info@fraochhouse.com **web:** www.fraochhouse.com
dir: *1m from Princes St*

Situated within walking distance of the city centre and convenient for many attractions, Fraoch House, which dates from the 1900s, has been appointed to offer well-equipped and thoughtfully furnished bedrooms. Delicious, freshly cooked breakfasts are served in the charming dining room on the ground floor.

Rooms 9 rms (7 en suite) (2 pri facs) (1 fmly) (1 GF) **Facilities** FTV tea/coffee WiFi Free use of DVDs and CDs & internet access **Notes** ⊗

Kingsway Guest House

★★★★ ≣ GUEST HOUSE

tel: 0131 667 5029 **5 East Mayfield EH9 1SD**
email: room@edinburgh-guesthouse.com **web:** www.edinburgh-guesthouse.com
dir: *A701 to city centre, after 4m road name changes to Mayfield Gdns. Right at lights into East Mayfield*

Well situated for the city centre and with off-road parking, this well-presented Victorian building maintains a number of original features, and genuine and warm hospitality is assured. All the bedrooms are comfortable, and the quality Scottish breakfasts make an excellent start to the day.

Rooms 7 rms (6 en suite) (1 pri facs) (2 fmly) S £45-£75; D £65-£110*
Facilities FTV DVD iPod docking station Lounge tea/coffee WiFi ⌕ 18 🅿 **Parking** 4
Notes ⊗

Southside Guest House

★★★★ ≣ GUEST HOUSE

tel: 0131 668 4422 **fax:** 0131 667 7771 **8 Newington Rd EH9 1QS**
email: info@southsideguesthouse.co.uk **web:** www.southsideguesthouse.co.uk
dir: *E end of Princes St into North Bridge to Royal Mile, continue S, 0.5m, house on right*

Situated within easy reach of the city centre and convenient for the major attractions, Southside Guest House is an elegant sandstone building. Bedrooms are individually styled, comfortable and thoughtfully equipped. Traditional, freshly cooked Scottish breakfasts are served at individual tables in the smart, ground-floor dining room.

Rooms 8 en suite (2 fmly) (1 GF) S £65-£90; D £90-£190 **Facilities** FTV DVD tea/coffee Direct Dial Licensed WiFi **Extras** Speciality toiletries **Notes** LB ⊗ No Children 10yrs

Ashlyn Guest House

★★★★ GUEST HOUSE

tel: 0131 552 2954 **42 Inverleith Row EH3 5PY**
email: info@ashlynguesthouse.com **web:** www.ashlynguesthouse.com
dir: *Adjacent to Edinburgh Botanic Gardens. Follow signs for North Edinburgh & Botanics*

The Ashlyn Guest House is a warm and friendly Georgian home, ideally located to take advantage of Edinburgh's attractions. The city centre is within walking distance and the Royal Botanical Gardens are minutes away. Bedrooms are all individually decorated and furnished to a high standard. A generous and hearty breakfast gives a great start to the day.

Rooms 6 rms (3 en suite) (3 pri facs) (1 fmly) S £40; D £75-£95* **Facilities** FTV Lounge tea/coffee WiFi 🅿 **Extras** Mineral water **Notes** ⊗ No Children 7yrs Closed 23-28 Dec

Buckstone Bed and Breakfast

★★★★ BED AND BREAKFAST

tel: 0131 445 1430 & 07761 013286 **58 Buckstone Ter EH10 6RQ**
email: harrison453@btinternet.com
dir: *From City by-pass (A720) exit at Fairmilehead onto A702 signed city centre. Straight on at lights, pass Tusitala restaurant on right. B&B approx 50yds on left*

Family-run property with commanding views over Edinburgh and across to Fife. Just minutes from the by-pass and on a main route into the city centre. The versatile bedroom has its own lounge that can be used as a further bedroom for a larger family. Comfortable and well appointed with freedom of space. The breakfast offers a good start to the day with homemade preserves adding to the quality.

Rooms 1 en suite S £40-£60; D £70-£100* **Facilities** DVD TVL tea/coffee WiFi ch fac
🛁 **Parking** 1 **Notes** ⊗ ☺

Heriott Park Guest House

★★★★ GUEST HOUSE

tel: 0131 552 3456 **256 Ferry Rd, Goldenacre EH5 3AN**
email: reservations@heriottpark.co.uk **web:** www.heriottpark.co.uk
dir: *1.5m N of city centre on A902*

A conversion of two adjoining properties, which retain many original features, Heriott Park Guest House is on the north side of the city and has lovely panoramic views of the Edinburgh skyline, including the castle and Arthur's Seat. The attractive bedrooms are well equipped and have excellent en suite bathrooms.

Rooms 15 en suite (7 fmly) (1 GF) S £45-£120; D £70-£130* **Facilities** FTV tea/coffee WiFi **Notes** ⊗

The International Guest House

★★★★ GUEST HOUSE

tel: 0131 667 2511 & 0845 241 7551   **fax:** 0131 667 1112 **37 Mayfield Gardens EH9 2BX**
email: intergh1@yahoo.co.uk **web:** www.accommodation-edinburgh.com
dir: *On A701 1.5m S of Princes St*

Guests are assured of a warm and friendly welcome at this attractive Victorian terraced house, situated to the south of the city centre. The smartly presented bedrooms are thoughtfully decorated, comfortably furnished and well equipped. Hearty Scottish breakfasts are served at individual tables in the traditionally styled dining room, which boasts a beautiful ornate ceiling.

Rooms 9 en suite (3 fmly) (1 GF) S £35-£85; D £50-£150 **Facilities** FTV tea/coffee Direct Dial WiFi **Parking** 3 **Notes** LB ⊗

Sherwood Guest House

★★★★ GUEST HOUSE

tel: 0131 667 1200 **fax:** 0131 667 2344 **42 Minto St EH9 2BR**
email: enquiries@sherwood-edinburgh.com **web:** www.sherwood-edinburgh.com
dir: *On A701, S of city centre*

Lying on the south side of the city, this guest house is immaculately maintained and attractively presented throughout. Bedrooms vary in size, the smaller ones being thoughtfully appointed to make the best use of space. All include iron and ironing board, and several come with a fridge and microwave. Continental breakfast is served in the elegant dining room.

Rooms 6 rms (5 en suite) (1 pri facs) (2 fmly) (1 GF) S £50-£70; D £60-£100* **Facilities** FTV tea/coffee WiFi **Extras** Bottled water & toiletries - complimentary **Parking** 3 **Notes** LB ⊗ Closed 20-29 Dec & 5 Jan-2 Mar

EDINBURGH *continued*

Ravensdown Guest House

★★★★ Ⓐ GUEST HOUSE

tel: 0131 552 5438 **248 Ferry Rd EH5 3AN**
email: david@ravensdownhouse.com **web:** www.ravensdownhouse.com
dir: *N of city centre, close to Royal Botanic Gardens, A902 Goldenacre*

This substantial end-of-terrace house enjoys wonderful views of the city skyline. It offers comfortable, individually styled bedrooms with smart bathrooms. Guests are made to feel welcome with good hospitality and customer care. Freshly prepared breakfasts are served at individual tables in the dining room.

Rooms 7 en suite (5 fmly) (1 GF) **Facilities** FTV iPod docking station tea/coffee WiFi
🔒 **Parking** 2 **Notes** ⊗

Arden Guest House

★★★ GUEST HOUSE

tel: 0131 664 3985 **fax:** 0131 621 0866 **126 Old Dalkeith Rd EH16 4SD**
email: ardenguesthouse@btinternet.com **web:** www.ardenedinburgh.co.uk
dir: *2m SE of city centre near Craigmillar Castle. On A7, 200yds W of hospital*

Arden Guest House is well situated on the south-east side of the city, close to the hospital, and benefits from off-road parking. Many thoughtful extras are provided as standard, including WiFi. Attentive and friendly service enhances the guest experience.

Rooms 8 en suite (2 fmly) (3 GF) **Facilities** STV FTV DVD tea/coffee WiFi **Parking** 8
Notes Closed 22-27 Dec

Elder York Guest House

★★★ GUEST HOUSE

tel: 0131 556 1926 **fax:** 0131 624 7140 **38 Elder St EH1 3DX**
email: reception@elderyork.co.uk **web:** www.elderyork.co.uk
dir: *Close to Princes St, next to bus station*

Elder York Guest House is centrally located just minutes from the bus station, Harvey Nichols and the St James Shopping Centre. Accommodation is situated up flights of stairs and all bedrooms are well appointed with many thoughtful extras including WiFi. Quality breakfast is served on individual tables overlooking Queen Street.

Rooms 12 rms (11 en suite) (1 pri facs) (1 fmly) **Facilities** FTV tea/coffee WiFi
Notes ⊗

Averon Guest House

★★★ GUEST HOUSE

tel: 0131 229 9932 **44 Gilmore Place EH3 9NQ**
email: info@averon.co.uk **web:** www.averon.co.uk
dir: *From W end of Princes St onto A702, right at Kings Theatre*

Situated within walking distance of the west end of the city and close to the Kings Theatre, Averon Guest House offers comfortable, good-value accommodation, with a secure car park to the rear.

Rooms 10 rms (6 en suite) (1 pri facs) (3 fmly) (5 GF) **Facilities** tea/coffee
Parking 19 **Notes** ⊗

See advert on opposite page

Innkeeper's Lodge Edinburgh, Corstorphine

★★★ INN

tel: 0845 112 6002 **St Johns Rd, Corstorphine EH12 8AX**
email: info@innkeeperslodge.com **web:** www.innkeeperslodge.com

At Innkeeper's Lodge you'll find accommodation with comfort and character in equal measure, and everything needed for a relaxing stay, from easy check-in and free parking to complimentary breakfast and a cosy pub serving great value food and drink on the doorstep. Each Lodge has quality rooms, and there are Lodges in a variety of locations from towns and cities to countryside settings across the UK.

Rooms 28 en suite (4 fmly) (6 GF) **Facilities** FTV tea/coffee Dinner available Direct Dial WiFi **Parking** 46 **Notes** ⊗ No coaches

Mingalar

★★★ GUEST HOUSE

tel: 0131 556 7000 & 558 7868 **2 East Claremont St EH7 4JP**
email: mingalar@mingalar.info **web:** www.mingalar.info
dir: *A1 onto A900 (Elm Row), left into Annandale St. At end, turn left into East Claremont St*

Located on the edge of Edinburgh's New Town, Mingalar is a period building boasting many original features including the shutters at the front-facing bedroom windows. Many thoughtful extras are provided in the bedrooms and a small kitchenette is available for guests' use. Family-style breakfasts are served in the charming basement garden room with the old stove used to good effect. Limited off-road parking is available on a first-come-first served basis.

Rooms 7 en suite (3 fmly) (3 GF) **Facilities** FTV tea/coffee WiFi 🔒 **Extras** Fridge **Parking** 2 **Notes** LB ⊗

See advert on page 434

Sonas Guest House

★★★ Ⓐ GUEST HOUSE

tel: 0131 667 2781 & 07866 843659 **3 East Mayfield EH9 1SD**
email: info@sonasguesthouse.com **web:** www.sonasguesthouse.com
dir: *A720 Straiton junct follow city signs. At 6th set of lights turn right into East Mayfield*

Bright and cheerful in both atmosphere and appearance, Sonas Guest House offers bedrooms with many thoughtful touches. A full Scottish breakfast can be enjoyed in the attractive dining room.

Rooms 7 en suite (2 fmly) (1 GF) S £40-£95; D £55-£120* **Facilities** FTV DVD iPod docking station WiFi ⅃ 18 **Parking** 5 **Notes** LB ⊗

Halcyon House

★★ GUEST HOUSE

tel: 0131 556 1033 & 556 1032   **fax:** 0131 556 1383 **8 Royal Ter EH7 5AB**
email: patricia@halcyon-hotel.com **web:** www.halcyon-hotel.com

Halcyon House benefits from a fantastic location, and has retained many of its original Georgian features. It is within easy walking distance of the theatre and the centre of Edinburgh. Rooms are split over three floors, come in a variety of sizes, and are decorated in a basic but comfortable fashion. Front or back rooms offer wonderful views of the gardens or views across to the Forth.

Rooms 14 rms (11 en suite) (1 pri facs) (7 fmly) (2 GF) S £55-£97; D £77-£182 **Facilities** TVL tea/coffee WiFi **Notes** LB ⊗

| RATHO | Map 21 NT17 |

The Bridge Inn at Ratho

★★★★ 🛏 ☕ INN

tel: 0131 333 1320 **fax:** 0131 333 3480 **27 Baird Rd EH28 8RA**
email: info@bridgeinn.com **web:** www.bridgeinn.com

Located beside the Union Canal and in use as a hostelry since the 19th century, this inn offers modern, spacious and well-furnished bedrooms with views of the canal. The busy bistro's kitchen uses home-grown produce to create award-winning food. Outdoor seating is an added bonus as are the two restaurant barges that serve lunch, afternoon tea and dinner. The Bridge Inn is the AA Pub of the Year for Scotland 2014-2015.

Rooms 4 en suite S £65-£95; D £80-£95* **Facilities** FTV tea/coffee Dinner available WiFi 🏊 **Extras** Speciality toiletries - complimentary **Parking** 40 **Notes** Closed 25 Dec Civ Wed 80

| SOUTH QUEENSFERRY | Map 21 NT17 |

Innkeeper's Lodge Edinburgh South Queensferry

★★★ INN

tel: 0845 112 6001 **7 Newhalls Rd EH30 9TA**
email: info@innkeeperslodge.com **web:** www.innkeeperslodge.com

At Innkeeper's Lodge you'll find accommodation with comfort and character in equal measure, and everything needed for a relaxing stay, from easy check-in and free parking to complimentary breakfast and a cosy pub serving great value food and drink on the doorstep. Each Lodge has quality rooms, and there are Lodges in a variety of locations from towns and cities to countryside settings across the UK.

Rooms 14 en suite (5 fmly) (3 GF) **Facilities** FTV tea/coffee Dinner available Direct Dial WiFi **Parking** 40

FALKIRK

| FALKIRK | Map 21 NS88 |

Ashbank Guest House

★★★★ BED AND BREAKFAST

tel: 01324 716649 & 07963 885931 **105 Main St FK2 9UQ**
email: ashbankguesthouse@gmail.com **web:** www.bandbfalkirk.com
dir: M9 junct 5 onto A9. After 200yds turn left, through x-rds then 2nd right. Ashbank on right

Ashbank Guest House is set in attractive gardens and has stunning views over the Ochil Hills. The property is a good base for touring the central belt and some of Scotland's major attractions while also making a good business base. Bedrooms and bathrooms are spaciously appointed. There is also private parking and free WiFi for all guests.

Rooms 4 en suite (1 fmly) **Facilities** FTV tea/coffee WiFi 🏊 **Parking** 4 **Notes** ⊗ Closed 15 Dec-15 Jan

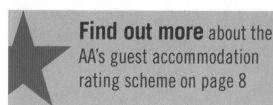

FIFE

ANSTRUTHER
Map 21 NO50

The Spindrift

★★★★ ☗ ⇔ GUEST HOUSE

tel: 01333 310573 & 07713 597996   **fax:** 01333 310573 **Pittenweem Rd KY10 3DT**
email: info@thespindrift.co.uk **web:** www.thespindrift.co.uk
dir: *Enter town from W on A917, 1st building on left*

This immaculate Victorian villa stands on the western edge of the village. The attractive bedrooms offer a wide range of extra touches; the Captain's Room, a replica of a wood-panelled cabin, is a particular feature. The inviting lounge has an honesty bar, while imaginative breakfasts, and enjoyable home-cooked meals by arrangement, are served in the cheerful dining room. Free WiFi is available. AA Friendliest B&B of the Year Finalist 2014-2015.

Rooms 8 rms (7 en suite) (1 pri facs) (2 fmly) S £40-£100; D £60-£100
Facilities FTV DVD iPod docking station TVL tea/coffee Dinner available Direct Dial Licensed WiFi ⅃ 18 ☖ **Extras** Speciality toiletries - complimentary **Parking** 12
Notes LB No Children 10yrs Closed Xmas-late Jan

The Bank

★★★★ INN

tel: 01333 310189 **23-25 High Street East KY10 3DQ**
email: enquiries@thebank_anstruther.co.uk **web:** www.thebank-anstruther.co.uk
dir: *From St Andrews, in Anstruther turn right towards Pittenweem. 50mtrs on left*

Located in the heart of Anstruther where the Dreel Burn meets the Forth, this friendly inn serves real ales and great pub food; there is a separate building next door for the accommodation. Modern, high quality, en suite bedrooms cater well for guests' needs and some offer great views. The beer garden is a real suntrap and has a children's play area.

Rooms 8 en suite (1 fmly) (1 GF) **Facilities** STV tea/coffee Dinner available Direct Dial WiFi ⅃ 18 Pool table **Extras** Bottled water - complimentary; fridge, safe **Parking** 3 **Notes** ⊗

INVERKEITHING
Map 21 NT18

The Roods

★★★★ BED AND BREAKFAST

tel: 01383 415049 **fax:** 01383 415049 **16 Bannerman Av KY11 1NG**
email: isobelmarley@hotmail.com **web:** www.the-roods.co.uk
dir: *N of town centre off B981(Church St/Chapel Place)*

This charming house stands in secluded, well-tended gardens close to the train station. Bedrooms are individually styled and have state-of-the-art bathrooms. There is an inviting lounge, and breakfast is served at a large shared table in an attractive conservatory.

Rooms 3 en suite (2 GF) S £35-£40; D £70-£85 **Facilities** FTV DVD iPod docking station TVL tea/coffee Direct Dial WiFi ☖ **Parking** 4 **Notes** LB ⊗

PEAT INN
Map 21 NO40

Premier Collection

The Peat Inn

★★★★★ ◎◎◎ RESTAURANT WITH ROOMS

tel: 01334 840206 **KY15 5LH**
email: stay@thepeatinn.co.uk **web:** www.thepeatinn.co.uk
dir: At junct of B940 & B941, 5m SW of St Andrews

This 300-year-old former coaching inn enjoys a rural location, and is close to St Andrews. The Peat Inn is spacious, very well appointed, and offers rooms that all have lounge areas. The inn is steeped in history and for years has proved a real haven for food lovers. The three dining areas create a romantic setting, and chef/owner Geoffrey Smeddle produces excellent, award-winning dishes. Expect welcoming open fires and a relaxed ambiance. An extensive continental breakfast selection is served to guests in their bedrooms each morning.

Rooms 8 annexe en suite (3 fmly) (8 GF) S £175-£205; D £195-£225*
Facilities FTV Lounge tea/coffee Dinner available Direct Dial WiFi ♨
Extras Speciality toiletries, fruit, sherry - free **Parking** 24 **Notes** LB ⊗
Closed 25-26 Dec, 2wks Jan, 1wk Nov RS Sun-Mon closed No coaches

ST ANDREWS
Map 21 NO51

Premier Collection

The Paddock

★★★★★ ⌂GUEST ACCOMMODATION

tel: 01334 850888 **fax:** 01334 850870 **Sunnyside, Strathkinness KY16 9XP**
email: thepaddock@btinternet.com **web:** www.thepadd.co.uk
dir: 3m W from St Andrews off B939. The Paddock signed from village centre

Situated in a peaceful village overlooking rolling countryside, this friendly, family-run guest accommodation offers stylish and very well-equipped bedrooms. Superb fish tanks, one freshwater, the other salt, line the entrance hall and contain beautiful and unusual fish. The conservatory is a lovely setting for the delicious breakfasts. Beauty treatments are also available on site.

Rooms 4 en suite (1 fmly) (2 GF) **Facilities** FTV tea/coffee WiFi **Parking** 8 **Notes** ⊗
No Children 12yrs Closed Nov-Mar

Nethan House

★★★★ ⌂GUEST HOUSE

tel: 01334 472104 **fax:** 01334 850870 **17 Murray Park KY16 9AW**
email: enquiries@nethan-standrews.com **web:** www.nethan-standrews.com
dir: A91 towards St Andrews, over 2nd rdbt into North St, Murray Park on left before cinema

This large Victorian terrace house is set in the heart of St Andrews; a short walk from the main tourist attractions and the famous golf course. The bright bedrooms are stylish and well appointed. The freshly cooked breakfast is a highlight and is served in the attractive dining room.

Rooms 7 en suite (1 fmly) (1 GF) **Facilities** FTV TVL tea/coffee WiFi **Notes** ⊗
Closed 24-26 Dec

The Inn at Lathones

★★★★ ◎◎ INN

tel: 01334 840494 **fax:** 01334 840694 **Largoward KY9 1JE**
email: lathones@theinn.co.uk **web:** www.theinn.co.uk
dir: 5m S of St Andrews on A915, 0.5m before village of Largoward on left just after hidden dip

This lovely country inn, parts of which are 400 years old, is full of character and individuality. The friendly staff help to create a relaxed atmosphere. Smart contemporary bedrooms are in two separate wings. The colourful, cosy restaurant is the main focus, where the menu offers modern interpretations of Scottish and European dishes.

Rooms 21 annexe en suite (1 fmly) (18 GF) **Facilities** STV TVL tea/coffee Dinner available Direct Dial WiFi **Conf** Max 40 Thtr 40 Class 10 Board 20 **Parking** 35 **Notes** Closed 26 Dec & 3-16 Jan RS 24 Dec Civ Wed 45

Lorimer House

★★★★ ⚠ GUEST HOUSE

tel: 01334 476599 **fax:** 01334 476599 **19 Murray Park KY16 9AW**
email: info@lorimerhouse.com **web:** www.lorimerhouse.com
dir: A91 to St Andrews, left into Golf Place, right into The Scores, right into Murray Park

A warm and friendly welcome is assured at Lorimer House, set in a delightful Victorian terrace, situated within easy reach of the famous Old Course, the seafront and town centre. Bedrooms are attractive, comfortably furnished and well equipped. Freshly prepared Scottish breakfasts are served in the stylish dining room, which also has a lounge area and offers free broadband internet access.

Rooms 5 en suite (1 GF) S £40-£80; D £80-£130* **Facilities** STV FTV TVL tea/coffee WiFi ♨ **Extras** Chilled water, use of fridge **Notes** ⊗ No Children 12yrs

CITY OF GLASGOW

GLASGOW
Map 20 NS56

The Arthouse Glasgow

★★★★ GUEST ACCOMMODATION

tel: 0141 221 6789 **fax:** 0141 221 6777 **129 Bath St G2 2SZ**
email: reservationsglasgow@abodehotels.co.uk **web:** www.abodehotels.co.uk

Located a moment's walk from Glasgow's shopping centres and central transport links, The Arthouse provides comfortable accommodation with a boutique feel. Bedrooms are tastefully appointed and offer a range of facilities and accessories for today's traveller. Snacks are served in the intimate lounge, whilst 24 hour room service is also provided for those that wish to dine in the comfort of their room. A hearty traditional Scottish breakfast sets you up for the day ahead.

Rooms 59 en suite

Clifton Guest House

★★★ GUEST HOUSE

tel: 0141 334 8080 **fax:** 0141 337 3468
26-27 Buckingham Ter, Great Western Rd G12 8ED
email: enquiries@cliftonhotelglasgow.co.uk **web:** www.cliftonhotelglasgow.co.uk
dir: 1.25m NW of city centre off A82 (Inverquhomery Rd)

Located north-west of the city centre, the Clifton Guest House forms part of an elegant terrace and is ideal for business and leisure. The attractive bedrooms are spacious, and there is an elegant lounge. Hearty breakfasts are served at individual tables in the dining room.

Rooms 23 rms (17 en suite) (6 fmly) (3 GF) **Facilities** STV FTV TVL tea/coffee Direct Dial WiFi **Parking** 8 **Notes** ✖

Georgian House

★★ GUEST HOUSE

tel: 0141 339 0008 & 07973 971563 **29 Buckingham Ter, Great Western Rd G12 8ED**
email: thegeorgianhouse@yahoo.com **web:** www.thegeorgianhousehotel.com
dir: *M8 junct 17 towards Dumbarton, through 4 sets of lights & right into Queen Margaret Dr, then right into Buckingham Ter*

Georgian House offers good-value accommodation and is situated at the west end of the city in a peaceful tree-lined Victorian terrace near the Botanic Gardens. Bedrooms vary in size and are furnished in a modern style. A continental style breakfast is served in the first-floor lounge-dining room.

Rooms 11 rms (10 en suite) (1 pri facs) (4 fmly) (3 GF) **Facilities** FTV tea/coffee WiFi **Parking** 6

HIGHLAND

ARDELVE — Map 22 NG82

Caberfeidh House

★★★ GUEST HOUSE

tel: 01599 555293 **IV40 8DY**
email: info@caberfeidh.plus.com **web:** www.caberfeidh.plus.com
dir: *A87 over Dornie Bridge 1st left into Ardelve, 100yds on right*

Set in a peaceful location overlooking Lochs Alsh and Duich, Caberfeidh House offers good value, comfortable accommodation in relaxed and friendly surroundings. A stone's throw from Eilean Donan Castle, the property enjoys great views of this historic building. Bedrooms are traditionally furnished and thoughtfully equipped, and there is a cosy lounge with a wide selection of books, games and magazines. Hearty breakfasts are served at individual tables in the dining room. Discount available for stays of two or more nights.

Rooms 5 rms (4 en suite) (1 pri facs) (3 fmly) S £30-£32; D £60-£64 **Facilities** FTV Lounge tea/coffee WiFi **Parking** 4 **Notes** ✖ Closed 25-26 Dec

AVIEMORE — Map 23 NH81

Eriskay Bed & Breakfast

★★★ BED AND BREAKFAST

tel: 01479 810717 & 07702 009614 **fax:** 0872 110 3520 **Craig Na Gower Av PH22 1RW**
email: enquiries@eriskay-aviemore.co.uk **web:** www.eriskay-aviemore.co.uk
dir: *From S turn left into Craig Na Gower Av, follow signs to Aviemore dental practice. At end of lane next to dentist*

This family-run B&B enjoys a quiet location close to the centre of Aviemore and is a great base for exploring the Cairngorms National Park and further afield. All bedrooms have en suite facilities and provide comfortable accommodation. A spacious guest lounge is also provided. Warm hospitality and a memorable breakfast are major aspects of any stay here. Newly built, self-contained ecopods in the grounds of the property are an alternative to the main accommodation.

Rooms 3 en suite (1 fmly) (3 GF) S £40-£60; D £60-£80* **Facilities** FTV TVL tea/coffee WiFi **Parking** 3 **Notes** LB ♨

BOAT OF GARTEN — Map 23 NH91

Moorfield House

★★★★ Ⓐ GUEST HOUSE

tel: 01479 831646 **Deshar Rd PH24 3BN**
email: enquiries@moorfieldhouse.com **web:** www.moorfieldhouse.com
dir: *Off A9 at Carrbridge junct. Follow signs for Boat of Garten, in centre next to church*

Moorfield House is a charming family-run Victorian guest house, close to the Cairngorms. Bedrooms, named after tartans, are en suite and have flat-screen satellite TV and a variety of useful amenities. Breakfast offers a wide choice and evening meals are available on request. The owners are happy to advise on local walks and attractions. The premises is licensed.

Rooms 6 en suite (1 GF) **Facilities** STV Lounge tea/coffee Dinner available Licensed WiFi ⅃ 18 ♣ **Extras** Sweets, bottled water - complimentary **Parking** 6 **Notes** ✖ No Children 12yrs Closed 31 Oct-26 Dec

BRACHLA — Map 23 NH53

Premier Collection

Loch Ness Lodge

★★★★★ GUEST ACCOMMODATION

tel: 01456 459469 **fax:** 01456 459439 **Loch Ness-Side IV3 8LA**
email: escape@loch-ness-lodge.com **web:** www.loch-ness-lodge.com
dir: *A9 from Inverness onto A82 signed Fort William, 9m, at 30mph sign. Lodge on right immediately after Clansman Hotel*

This house enjoys a prominent position overlooking Loch Ness, and each of the individually designed bedrooms enjoys views of the loch. The bedrooms are of the highest standard, and are beautifully presented with a mix of traditional luxury and up-to-date technology, including WiFi. There is a spa with a hot tub, sauna and a therapy room offering a variety of treatments. Guests have a choice of attractive lounges which feature real fires in the colder months and where decadent afternoon teas are served.

Rooms 7 en suite (1 GF) **Facilities** Direct Dial Licensed WiFi ⅃ 18 Fishing Sauna Hot tub Therapy room **Conf** Max 14 Thtr 14 Class 10 Board 14 **Parking** 10 **Notes** ✖ No Children 16yrs Closed 2-31 Jan Civ Wed 24

CARRBRIDGE

Map 23 NH92

Dalrachney Lodge

★★★ GUEST ACCOMMODATION

tel: 01479 841252 & 841245 **Grantown Rd PH23 3AT**
email: dalrachney@aol.com web: www.dalrachney.co.uk
dir: *A9 onto A95, then B9153. Join A938, signed on right*

This former Victorian hunting lodge has played host to King George V, and sits on the banks of the River Dulnain in the picturesque village of Carrbridge. Bedrooms feature Egyptian cotton bedsheets and a host of modern amenities. A range of spacious public areas include a comfortable lounge and popular bar and bistro, and this is an ideal base for tourists and for hunting, fishing and shooting parties.

Rooms 12 rms (9 en suite) (3 pri facs) (3 fmly) (1 GF) **Facilities** STV FTV Lounge tea/coffee Dinner available Licensed WiFi Fishing 🚗 **Parking** 20 **Notes** No Children 7yrs

Cairn

★★★ INN

tel: 01479 841212 **Main Rd PH23 3AS**
email: info@cairnhotel.co.uk

Conveniently located in the centre of the Cairngorms National Park, this property is the hub of the local community. The traditional bar and restaurant are complemented by a range of cosy bedrooms featuring modern touches. Guests can relax in front of the log fire with a cask ale or local malt whisky. The inn is an ideal base from which to participate in a number of outdoor activities with activity breaks and packages available to book.

Rooms 7 rms S £30-£45; D £60-£80*

The Pines Country House

★★★ BED AND BREAKFAST

tel: 01479 841220 fax: 01479 841520 **Duthil PH23 3ND**
email: lynn@thepines-duthil.co.uk web: www.thepines-duthil.co.uk
dir: *2m E of Carrbridge in Duthil on A938*

A warm welcome is assured at this comfortable home in the Cairngorms National Park. The bright bedrooms are traditionally furnished and offer good amenities. Enjoyable home-cooked fare is served around a communal table. Guests can relax in the conservatory-lounge and watch squirrels feed in the nearby wood.

Rooms 3 en suite (1 fmly) S £45-£46; D £63.50-£65* **Facilities** STV FTV DVD Lounge tea/coffee Dinner available WiFi ch fac 🚗 **Parking** 4 **Notes** LB

DORNOCH

Map 23 NH78

2 Quail

★★★★★ 🏠 GUEST ACCOMMODATION

tel: 01862 811811 **Castle St IV25 3SN**
email: theaa@2quail.com web: www.2quail.com
dir: *On main street, 200yds from cathedral*

The saying 'small is beautiful' applies to this property set in the main street. The cosy public rooms are ideal for conversation, but there are masses of books for those just wishing to relax. The stylish, individual bedrooms match the character of the house and are thoughtfully equipped to include DVD players.

Rooms 3 en suite S £70-£90; D £85-£120 **Facilities** FTV DVD Lounge tea/coffee Direct Dial Licensed WiFi ⚡ **Extras** Speciality toiletries **Notes** ⊗ No Children 8yrs Closed Xmas & 2wks Feb/Mar RS Nov-Mar winter hours - check when booking

FORT WILLIAM

Map 22 NN17

See also Spean Bridge

Mansfield Guest House

★★★★ GUEST HOUSE

tel: 01397 772262 & 0845 6449432 **Corpach PH33 7LT**
email: mansefield@btinternet.com web: www.fortwilliamaccommodation.com
dir: *2m N of Fort William. A82 onto A830, house 2m on A830 in Corpach*

Peacefully set in its own well-tended garden this friendly, family-run guest house provides comfortable, attractively decorated and well-equipped accommodation. There is a cosy lounge, where a roaring coal fire burns on cold evenings, and an attractive dining room where delicious, home-cooked evening meals and breakfasts are served at individual tables.

Rooms 6 en suite (1 GF) S £35-£40; D £65-£68* **Facilities** FTV DVD TVL tea/coffee Dinner available WiFi ⚡ 18 🚗 **Parking** 7 **Notes** LB ⊗ No Children 12yrs

FOYERS

Map 23 NH42

The Craigdarroch Inn

★★★★ INN

tel: 01456 486400 fax: 01456 286111 **IV2 6XU**
email: info@hotel-loch-ness.co.uk web: www.hotel-loch-ness.co.uk
dir: *Take B862 from either end of loch, then B852 signed Foyers*

Craigdarroch Inn is located in an elevated position, high above Loch Ness on the south side. Bedrooms vary in style and size but all are comfortable and well equipped; those that are front-facing have wonderful views. This friendly inn offers relaxed dining, many tables have loch views, and the staff are friendly and welcoming.

Rooms 8 en suite (1 fmly) S £70-£120; D £70-£140 **Facilities** FTV Lounge TVL tea/coffee Dinner available WiFi 🚗 **Conf** Max 30 Thtr 30 Class 30 Board 30 **Parking** 24 **Notes** No coaches Civ Wed 30

Foyers Bay Country House

★★★ GUEST HOUSE

tel: 01456 486624 **Lochness IV2 6YB**
email: info@foyersbay.co.uk **web:** www.foyersbay.co.uk
dir: *Off B852 into Lower Foyers*

Situated in sloping grounds with pines and abundant colourful rhododendrons, this delightful Victorian villa has stunning views of Loch Ness. The attractive bedrooms vary in size and are well equipped. There is a comfortable lounge next to the plant-filled conservatory-café, where delicious evening meals and traditional breakfasts are served.

Rooms 7 en suite (1 GF) D £80-£110* **Facilities** FTV TVL tea/coffee Dinner available Licensed WiFi 🔒 **Conf** Max 20 Thtr 20 Class 20 Board 20 **Parking** 7 **Notes** LB ⊗ No Children 16yrs

| GRANTOWN-ON-SPEY | Map 23 NJ02 |

PREMIER COLLECTION

The Dulaig

★★★★★ ≜ BED AND BREAKFAST

tel: 01479 872065 **Seafield Av PH26 3JF**
email: enquiries@thedulaig.com **web:** www.thedulaig.com
dir: *A9 onto A95 to B9102. Into High St, left into Seafield Av for 200mtrs, past Rhuarden Court, The Dulaig on left*

Presented to an exceptional standard, this guest house benefits from a tranquill setting in 1.5 acres of stunning gardens. Featuring a summer house, duck pond and an array of wildlife, the grounds provide a relaxing backdrop to the house. Located only a short walk from the centre of the town, features include luxurious, spacious bedrooms with Arts and Crafts antique furniture and immaculately presented bathrooms featuring luxury toiletries. A welcoming drawing room is available for guest use. Memorable breakfasts served around a large shared table feature the best in local produce and include eggs from their collection of hens. Carol and Gordon provide memorable hospitality which is appreciated by their many regular guests.

Rooms 3 en suite S £115-£130; D £155-£170* **Facilities** STV DVD Lounge tea/coffee WiFi 🔒 **Extras** Speciality toiletries, fruit, chocolates - free **Parking** 6 **Notes** LB ⊗ No Children 12yrs Closed 15 Dec-8 Jan

| INVERNESS | Map 23 NH64 |

Premier Collection

Daviot Lodge

★★★★★ ≜ GUEST ACCOMMODATION

tel: 01463 772215 **Daviot Mains IV2 5ER**
email: margaret.hutcheson@btopenworld.com **web:** www.daviotlodge.co.uk
dir: *Exit A9 5m S of Inverness onto B851 signed Croy. 1m on left*

Standing in 80 acres of peaceful pasture land, this impressive establishment offers attractive, well-appointed and well-equipped bedrooms. The master bedroom is furnished with a four-poster bed. There is a tranquil lounge with deep sofas and a real fire, and a peaceful dining room where hearty breakfasts featuring the best of local produce are served. Full disabled access for wheelchairs is provided.

Rooms 4 en suite (1 GF) **Facilities** FTV DVD Lounge TVL tea/coffee Licensed WiFi **Extras** Speciality toiletries, snacks **Parking** 10 **Notes** No Children 5yrs Closed 23 Dec-2 Jan

Premier Collection

Trafford Bank

★★★★★ ≜ GUEST HOUSE

tel: 01463 241414 **96 Fairfield Rd IV3 5LL**
email: info@traffordbankguesthouse.co.uk **web:** www.traffordbank.co.uk
dir: *Exit A82 at Kenneth St, 2nd left into Fairfield Rd, 600yds on right*

This impressive Victorian house lies in a residential area close to the canal. Lorraine Pun has utilised her interior design skills to blend the best in contemporary styles with the house's period character and the results are simply stunning. Delightful public areas offer a choice of lounges, while breakfast is taken in a beautiful conservatory featuring eye-catching wrought-iron chairs. Each bedroom is unique in design and has TV, DVD and CDs, sherry, silent mini-fridges and much more.

Rooms 5 en suite (2 fmly) **Facilities** STV FTV TVL tea/coffee WiFi **Parking** 10 **Notes** ⊗

See advert on page 441

INVERNESS *continued*

Avalon Guest House

★★★★ GUEST HOUSE

tel: 01463 239075 & 07936 226241 **fax:** 01463 709827 **79 Glenurquhart Rd IV3 5PB**
email: avalon@inverness-loch-ness.co.uk **web:** www.inverness-loch-ness.co.uk

Avalon Guest House is just a short walk from the city centre, and five minutes' drive from Loch Ness. Breakfast can be taken in the well-appointed dining room where fresh local produce is the highlight of the menu. Bedrooms are spacious with a host of thoughtful extras including WiFi, fridges, fluffy towels and complimentary toiletries. A guest lounge is also provided.

Rooms 6 rms (5 en suite) (1 pri facs) (4 GF) D £60-£95* **Facilities** FTV DVD iPod docking station TVL tea/coffee WiFi **Extras** Fridge, chocolates, flowers **Parking** 10 **Notes** No Children 10yrs

Ballifeary Guest House

★★★★ GUEST HOUSE

tel: 01463 235572 **fax:** 01463 717583 **10 Ballifeary Rd IV3 5PJ**
email: info@ballifearyguesthouse.co.uk **web:** www.ballifearyguesthouse.co.uk
dir: *Exit A82, 0.5m from town centre, left into Bishops Rd, sharp right into Ballifeary Rd*

This charming detached house has a peaceful residential location within easy walking distance of the town centre and Eden Court Theatre. The attractive bedrooms are carefully appointed and well equipped. There is an elegant ground-floor drawing room and a comfortable dining room, where delicious breakfasts, featuring the best of local produce, are served at individual tables.

Rooms 7 en suite (1 GF) S £45-£50; D £72-£85 **Facilities** FTV DVD Lounge tea/coffee WiFi ♨ **Extras** Mineral water - complimentary **Parking** 6 **Notes** LB ⊗ No Children 15yrs Closed 24-28 Dec

The Ghillies Lodge

★★★★ BED AND BREAKFAST

tel: 01463 232137 & 07817 956533 **16 Island Bank Rd IV2 4QS**
email: info@ghillieslodge.com **web:** www.ghillieslodge.com
dir: *1m SW from town centre on B862, pink house facing river*

Situated on the banks of the River Ness, not far from the city centre, The Ghillies Lodge offers comfortable accommodation in a relaxed, peaceful environment. The attractive bedrooms, one of which is on the ground floor, are all en suite, and are individually styled and well equipped. There is a comfortable lounge-dining room, and a conservatory that overlooks the river

Rooms 3 en suite (1 GF) S £45-£65; D £69-£78* **Facilities** STV FTV tea/coffee WiFi ♨ **Parking** 4 **Notes** ⊗

Moyness House

★★★★ GUEST ACCOMMODATION

tel: 01463 233836 **fax:** 01463 233836 **6 Bruce Gardens IV3 5EN**
email: stay@moyness.co.uk **web:** www.moyness.co.uk
dir: *Off A82 (Fort William road), almost opposite Highland Regional Council headquarters*

Situated in a quiet residential area just a short distance from the city centre, this elegant Victorian villa dates from 1880 and offers beautifully decorated, comfortable bedrooms and well-appointed bathrooms. There is an attractive sitting room and an inviting dining room, where traditional Scottish breakfasts are served. Guests are welcome to use the secluded and well-maintained back garden.

Rooms 6 en suite (1 fmly) (2 GF) S £60-£90; D £69-£110* **Facilities** FTV Lounge tea/coffee WiFi **Extras** Speciality toiletries, robes **Parking** 10 **Notes** LB ⊗ No Children 6yrs

Trafford Bank
Guest House

Built in 1873 Trafford Bank Guest House, this former Bishop's home, has been refurbished from top to bottom and mixes antique and contemporary furniture, some of which has been designed by Lorraine Pun herself – an accomplished interior designer.

The home boasts a wealth of character and original features. You will be amazed by the dining room chairs, unusual lighting and original art presented throughout the house.

This guesthouse is within a few minutes walk of Inverness city centre, and the Caledonian Canal.

Luxury B&B accommodation and warm Highland hospitality go hand in hand at Trafford Bank.

The establishment is non-smoking throughout. The house is surrounded by mature gardens that the guests can enjoy and has ample parking.

Trafford Bank is ideally situated to suit both business and holiday visitors and offers guests free wireless internet connection if they have a laptop.

AA
Breakfast
Award

AA ★★★★★

Trafford Bank Guest House
96 Fairfield Road, Inverness, Highland IV3 5LL
Tel: 01463 241414
E-Mail: info@traffordbankhotel.co.uk

www.traffordbankhotel.co.uk

INVERNESS *continued*

Heathcote B&B

★★★★ BED AND BREAKFAST

tel: 01463 236596 & 07833 730849 **fax:** 0871 528 3915 **59 Glenurquhart Rd IV3 5PB**
email: info@heathcotebandb.co.uk **web:** www.heathcotebandb.co.uk

Only a few minutes' walk from the Eden Court Theatre and the centre of Inverness, this Victorian town house is ideally situated for touring Inverness and beyond, whether you are searching for the Loch Ness Monster or just castle-hunting. Modern bedrooms and bathrooms offer spacious and comfortable accommodation. Friendly hospitality and memorable breakfasts are also features here. Ample off street-private parking is provided.

Rooms 3 en suite (1 fmly) S £40-£80; D £50-£90* **Facilities** FTV tea/coffee WiFi ⚓ **Extras** Bottled water **Parking** 6 **Notes** ⊗

Lyndon Guest House

★★★★ GUEST HOUSE

tel: 01463 232551 **fax:** 01463 225827 **50 Telford St IV3 5LE**
email: lyndon@invernessbedandbreakfast.com **web:** www.invernessbedandbreakfast.com
dir: *A9 onto A82, over Friars Bridge, right at rdbt into Telford St. House on right*

A warm Highland welcome awaits at Lyndon Guest House, family-run accommodation close to the centre of Inverness. All bedrooms are en suite and are equipped with plenty of useful facilities including full internet access. Gaelic is spoken here.

Rooms 6 en suite (4 fmly) (2 GF) S £30-£50; D £60-£80* **Facilities** FTV TVL tea/coffee WiFi ⚓ **Parking** 7 **Notes** ⊗ Closed 20 Dec-5 Jan

Strathness House

★★★★ GUEST HOUSE

tel: 01463 232765 **fax:** 01463 232970 **4 Ardross Ter IV3 5NQ**
email: info@strathnesshouse.com **web:** www.strathnesshouse.co.uk
dir: *From A9, A96 to city centre, pass Eastgate shopping centre. At bottom of Academy St turn left, follow river (on left), cross bridge & turn immediate left, Ardross Terrace on corner*

Strathness House offers comfortable accommodation and heartwarming hospitality in the centre of Inverness. Eight of the well-equipped bedrooms have either river or castle views. Scottish breakfasts are served in a room overlooking the river.

Rooms 12 en suite (3 fmly) **Facilities** FTV Lounge tea/coffee Direct Dial WiFi **Extras** Soft drinks - chargeable **Notes** ⊗ No Children 6yrs Closed 3wks Xmas-New Year

Westbourne Guest House

★★★★ 🛎 GUEST ACCOMMODATION

tel: 01463 220700 **50 Huntly St IV3 5HS**
email: richard@westbourne.org.uk **web:** www.westbourne.org.uk
dir: *A9 onto A82 at football stadium over 3 rdbts, at 4th rdbt 1st left into Wells St & Huntly St*

The immaculately maintained Westbourne Guest House looks across the River Ness to the city centre. This friendly, family-run house has bright modern bedrooms of varying size, all are attractively furnished in pine and very well equipped. A relaxing lounge with internet access, books, games and puzzles is available.

Rooms 9 en suite (2 fmly) S £50-£60; D £80-£90* **Facilities** FTV DVD Lounge tea/coffee WiFi ⚓ **Parking** 6 **Notes** LB Closed Xmas & New Year

Sunnyholm

★★★ GUEST ACCOMMODATION

tel: 01463 231336 **12 Mayfield Rd IV2 4AE**
email: sunnyholm@aol.com **web:** www.invernessguesthouse.com
dir: *500yds SE of town centre. Exit B861 (Culduthel Rd) into Mayfield Rd*

Situated in a peaceful residential area within easy walking distance of the city centre, Sunnyholm offers comfortably proportioned and well-equipped bedrooms. A spacious conservatory-lounge overlooks the rear garden, and there is a another lounge next to the bright, airy dining room.

Rooms 4 en suite (4 GF) S £40-£45; D £65-£70 **Facilities** FTV DVD Lounge tea/coffee WiFi ⚓ **Extras** Snacks - complimentary **Parking** 6 **Notes** ⊗ No Children 3yrs 🚭

Acorn House

★★★ GUEST HOUSE

tel: 01463 717021 & 240000   fax: 01463 714236 **2A Bruce Gardens IV3 5EN**
email: enquiries@acorn-house.freeserve.co.uk **web:** www.acorn-house.freeserve.co.uk
dir: *From town centre onto A82, on W side of river, right into Bruce Gardens*

This attractive detached house is just a five-minute walk from the town centre and occupies a quiet location set back from the road. Bedrooms are smartly presented and well equipped. Breakfast is served at individual tables in the spacious dining room.

Rooms 6 en suite (2 fmly) **Facilities** STV TVL tea/coffee WiFi Sauna Hot tub **Parking** 7 **Notes** Closed 25-26 Dec

Fraser House

★★★ GUEST ACCOMMODATION

tel: 01463 716488 & 07900 676799   fax: 01463 716488 **49 Huntly St IV3 5HS**
email: fraserlea@btopenworld.com **web:** www.fraserhouse.co.uk
dir: *A82 W over bridge, left into Wells St leading into Huntly St, house in 100yds*

Situated on the west bank of the River Ness, Fraser House has a commanding position overlooking the city, and is within easy walking distance of the central amenities. Bedrooms, all en suite, vary in size and are comfortably furnished and well equipped. The ground-floor dining room is the setting for freshly cooked Scottish breakfasts.

Rooms 5 en suite (2 fmly) S £40-£45; D £65-£70* **Facilities** FTV DVD iPod docking station tea/coffee WiFi **Notes** Closed Feb-Mar

Dunhallin Guest House

★★★★ GUEST HOUSE

tel: 01463 220824 **fax:** 01463 229814 **164 Culduthel Rd IV2 4BH**
email: relax@dunhallin.co.uk **web:** www.dunhallin.co.uk
dir: *From city centre follow Castle St then Culduthel Rd for 1m. At mini rdbt take 1st exit, right at lights. 100mtrs on right*

Located in the Highland capital, this comfortable guest house offers a relaxing home-from-home. Margaret and Sandy love what they do and this shows in the friendly hospitality and helpful service they provide to all guests. Breakfasts are a feature of any stay here with a wide range of dishes offering something for everybody. Bedrooms are spaciously appointed with a great range of modern accessories including flat screen TVs, DVD players and iPod docks. Complimentary parking on site.

Rooms 5 en suite S £45-£98; D £55-£108 **Facilities** FTV DVD iPod docking station Lounge tea/coffee WiFi **Parking** 5 **Notes** LB No Children 12yrs

Premier Collection

The Cross

★★★★★ @@ 🏠 RESTAURANT WITH ROOMS

tel: 01540 661166 **Tweed Mill Brae, Ardbroilach Rd PH21 1LB**
email: relax@thecross.co.uk **web:** www.thecross.co.uk
dir: *From lights in Kingussie centre take Ardbroilach Rd, 300yds left into Tweed Mill Brae*

Built as a water-powered tweed mill in the late 19th century, The Cross is situated in the picturesque Cairngorms National Park and surrounded by four acres of riverside grounds that teem with an abundance of wildlife. Comfortable lounges and a selection of well-appointed bedrooms are offered, and dinners are served by an open fire in the stone-walled and wood-beamed restaurant.

Rooms 8 en suite (1 fmly) S £80-£170; D £100-£170* **Facilities** FTV DVD Lounge tea/coffee Dinner available Direct Dial WiFi Riding **Extras** Bottled water **Conf** Max 20 Thtr 20 Class 20 Board 20 **Parking** 20 **Notes** Closed Jan No coaches

Allt Gynack Guest House

★★★ A GUEST HOUSE

tel: 01540 661081 **fax:** 0872 115 3205 **Gynack Villa, 1 High St PH21 1HS**
email: alltgynack@tiscali.co.uk **web:** www.alltgynack.com
dir: *A9 onto A86 through Newtonmore, 2m to Kingussie, on left after bridge*

Allt Gynack Guest House is family-owned and situated at the west end of the high street beside the River Gynack. Set in its own grounds, it has a private car park at the rear plus secure parking for motorbikes and bicycles. Evening meals are not available, but the owners are happy to make recommendations for the many excellent restaurants in the area. Pets are welcome in designated bedrooms only.

Rooms 5 rms (3 en suite) (2 pri facs) S £32-£35; D £64-£70 **Facilities** FTV tea/coffee WiFi 18 **Parking** 4 **Notes** No Children 15yrs

Premier Collection

Pool House

★★★★★ 🏠 ⌂ GUEST HOUSE

tel: 01445 781272 **fax:** 01445 781403 **IV22 2LD**
email: stay@pool-house.co.uk **web:** www.pool-house.co.uk
dir: *6m N of Gairloch on A832 in the centre of village by bridge*

Set on the shores of Loch Ewe where the river meets the bay, the understated roadside façade gives little hint of its splendid interior, nor of the views facing the bay. Memorable features include delightful public rooms and stunningly romantic suites, each individually designed and with feature bathrooms. Pool House is run very much as a country house - the hospitality and guest care by the Harrison family are second to none.

Rooms 4 en suite (1 fmly) S £175-£195; D £225-£250 **Facilities** FTV DVD iPod docking station Lounge tea/coffee Dinner available Direct Dial Licensed WiFi Snooker **Extras** Sherry, speciality toiletries - complimentary **Parking** 10 **Notes** LB No Children 12yrs Closed Nov-mid Mar

ROY BRIDGE
Map 22 NN28

Homagen

★★★ BED AND BREAKFAST

tel: 01397 712411 **PH31 4AN**
email: stay@homagen.co.uk web: www.homagen.co.uk
dir: *On A86, opposite Roy Bridge Hotel*

Homagen is a family-run property in a great location for touring the Highlands, with links to Fort William, Aviemore and beyond. Bedrooms feature modern decor and comfortable beds. Hearty breakfasts are served in the dining room at a communal table. Free WiFi is provided. Packed lunches are available for those making day trips.

Rooms 4 rms (3 en suite) (1 pri facs) S £30-£35; D £60-£70* **Facilities** FTV Lounge tea/coffee WiFi Fishing ♨ **Parking** 6 **Notes** LB Closed 23 Dec-3 Jan

SHIEL BRIDGE
Map 22 NG91

Grants at Craigellachie

★★★★ ◉ RESTAURANT WITH ROOMS

tel: 01599 511331 **Craigellachie, Ratagan IV40 8HP**
email: info@housebytheloch.co.uk web: www.housebytheloch.co.uk
dir: *From A87 exit for Glenelg, 1st right to Ratagan, opposite Youth Hostel sign*

Sitting on the tranquil shores of Loch Duich and overlooked by the Five Sisters mountains, Grants really does occupy a stunning location. The restaurant has a well deserved reputation for its cuisine, and the bedrooms are stylish and come with all the creature comforts. Guests are guaranteed a warm welcome at this charming house.

Rooms 2 en suite 2 annexe en suite (3 GF) S £70-£122.50; D £100-£185* **Facilities** STV DVD tea/coffee Dinner available WiFi Riding **Extras** Speciality toiletries, bottled water - free; robes **Parking** 8 **Notes** LB No Children 12yrs Closed Dec-mid Feb RS mid Feb-Nov reservation only No coaches

SOUTH BALLACHULISH
Map 22 NN05

Craiglinnhe House

★★★★ GUEST HOUSE

tel: 01855 811270 **Lettermore PH49 4JD**
email: info@craiglinnhe.co.uk web: www.craiglinnhe.co.uk
dir: *From village A82 onto A828, Craiglinnhe 1.5m on left*

Built during the reign of Queen Victoria, Craiglinnhe House enjoys an elevated position with stunning views across Loch Linnhe to the village of Onich, and up to the Ballachulish Bridge and the Pap of Glencoe. The attractive bedrooms vary in size, are stylishly furnished, and are well equipped. There is a ground-floor lounge and a charming dining room where delicious breakfasts, and evening meals (by prior arrangement) are served at individual tables.

Rooms 5 en suite D £66-£85* **Facilities** FTV iPod docking station Lounge tea/coffee Dinner available Licensed WiFi **Parking** 5 **Notes** LB ⊗ No Children 13yrs Closed 24-26 Dec

SPEAN BRIDGE
Map 22 NN28

Smiddy House

★★★★ ◎◎ 🍴 RESTAURANT WITH ROOMS

tel: 01397 712335 fax: 01397 712043 **Roy Bridge Rd PH34 4EU**
email: enquiry@smiddyhouse.com web: www.smiddyhouse.com
dir: *In village centre, A82 onto A86*

Set in the Great Glen which stretches from Fort William to Inverness, this was once the village smithy, and is now a very friendly establishment. The attractive bedrooms, named after places in Scotland, are comfortably furnished and well equipped. A relaxing garden room is available for guest use. Delicious evening meals are served in Russell's restaurant.

Rooms 4 en suite (1 fmly) **Facilities** FTV Lounge tea/coffee Dinner available WiFi **Extras** Speciality toiletries, mineral water - free **Parking** 15 **Notes** No coaches

Distant Hills Guest House

★★★★ 🍴 GUEST HOUSE

tel: 01397 712452 **Roy Bridge Rd PH34 4EU**
email: enquiry@distanthills.com web: www.distanthillsspeanbridge.co.uk
dir: *From A82 onto A86 signed Newtonmore. 0.5m on right*

Distant Hills Guest House in the heart of the Highlands offers stylish bedrooms, award-winning breakfasts and friendly hospitality. Set amongst wonderful scenery, the house enjoys a quiet setting in its own impressive grounds. An ideal base for touring Fort William, Oban, Inverness and the Highlands whether walking, climbing or driving. Off road parking and free WiFi are some of the many features of the house. AA Friendliest B&B of the Year Finalist 2014-2015.

Rooms 7 en suite (7 GF) S £62-£80; D £80-£93* **Facilities** FTV DVD TVL tea/coffee WiFi ♨ 9 ♨ **Extras** Speciality toiletries **Parking** 10 **Notes** ⊗ No Children 12yrs Closed 15 Nov-1 Mar

Achnabobane Farmhouse *(NN195811)*

★★★ FARMHOUSE

tel: 01397 712919 **PH34 4EX**
email: enquiries@achnabobane.co.uk **web:** www.achnabobane.co.uk
dir: *2m S of Spean Bridge on A82*

With breathtaking views of Ben Nevis, Aonach Mhor and the Grey Corries, this farmhouse offers comfortable, good-value accommodation in a friendly, family environment. Bedrooms are traditional in style and well equipped. Breakfast is served in the conservatory-dining room. Pets are welcome.

Rooms 4 rms (1 en suite) (1 fmly) (1 GF) **Facilities** FTV DVD TVL tea/coffee WiFi **Parking** 5 **Notes** No Children 7yrs Closed Xmas red deer/woodland

---

STRATHPEFFER	Map 23 NH45

Inver Lodge

★★★ GUEST HOUSE

tel: 01997 421392 **IV14 9DL**
email: derbyshire@inverlg.fsnet.co.uk **web:** www.inverlodgestrathpeffer.com
dir: *A834 through Strathpeffer centre, turn beside Spa Pavilion signed Bowling Green, Inver Lodge on right*

You are assured of a warm welcome at this Victorian lodge, secluded in its own tree-studded gardens yet within easy walking distance of the town centre. Bedrooms are comfortable and well equipped, and the cosy lounge is ideal for relaxation. Breakfasts, and evening meals (by arrangement), are served at a communal table.

Rooms 2 rms (1 fmly) S £32-£35; D £50-£55* **Facilities** FTV tea/coffee Dinner available WiFi ⅃ 18 🔒 **Parking** 2 **Notes** LB ⊗ Closed Xmas & New Year ⊛

TOMATIN	Map 23 NH82

Glenan Lodge Guest House

★★★★ GUEST HOUSE

tel: 01808 511217 **fax:** 08082 801125 **IV13 7YT**
email: enquiries@glenanlodge.co.uk **web:** www.glenanlodge.co.uk
dir: *Off A9 to Tomatin, turn left to distillery, then right into distillery drive. Proceed to top of hill, take right fork & follow road to Glenan Lodge*

Peacefully located on the edge of the village, this relaxed and homely guest house offers a warm welcome. The comfortable bedrooms are traditionally furnished and suitably equipped. An inviting lounge is available, and delicious home-cooked evening meals and breakfasts are served in the dining room. A two mile stretch of the River Findhorn is available for fly-fishing, and golfers, walkers and bird watchers are also well provided for locally.

Rooms 7 en suite (1 fmly) **Facilities** FTV DVD TVL tea/coffee Dinner available Licensed WiFi Fishing **Parking** 7 **Notes** ⊗ No Children 5yrs

---

TORRIDON	Map 22 NG95

The Torridon Inn

★★★★ ⊜ INN

tel: 01445 791242 **fax:** 01445 712253 **IV22 2EY**
email: inn@thetorridon.com **web:** www.thetorridon.com/inn

The Torridon Inn enjoys an idyllic location and is set in 58 acres of parkland, overlooking Loch Torridon and surrounded by steep mountains on all sides.

Bedrooms are lodge style with adjacent parking and are smartly appointed with comfy beds and modern facilities. Freshly prepared food is served in the adjacent inn, where over 80 whiskies, and several real ales including a local Torridon Ale, are firm favourites.

Rooms 12 en suite (3 fmly) (5 GF) **Facilities** STV tea/coffee Dinner available WiFi ⅃ Fishing Pool table 🔒 Outdoor adventure activities available **Parking** 12 **Notes** LB Closed Jan Civ Wed 55

ULLAPOOL	Map 22 NH19

The Arch Inn

★★★ INN

tel: 01854 612454 **10-11 West Shore St IV26 2UR**
email: info@thearchinn.co.uk **web:** www.thearchinn.co.uk

The Arch Inn is situated on Ullapool waterfront on the shores of Loch Broom, only a two-minute walk from the Outer Hebrides ferry terminal. The accommodation provided is comfortable, and most rooms have stunning views over the loch to the mountains in the distance. The relaxed bar and grill offers a selection of fresh local produce including seafood.

Rooms 10 en suite (1 fmly) (2 GF) **Facilities** FTV tea/coffee Dinner available WiFi Pool table **Conf** Max 60 Thtr 40 Class 30 Board 35 **Parking** 5 **Notes** ⊗

WICK	Map 23 ND35

The Clachan

★★★★ BED AND BREAKFAST

tel: 01955 605384 **13 Randolph Place, South Rd KW1 5NJ**
email: enquiry@theclachan.co.uk **web:** www.theclachan.co.uk
dir: *Off A99 0.5m S of town centre*

A warm welcome is assured at this immaculate detached home, by the main road on the south edge of the town. The bright, airy bedrooms (all on the ground floor) though compact, are attractively furnished to make good use of available space. Breakfast offers an extensive choice and is served at individual tables in the cosy dining room. AA Friendliest B&B of the Year Finalist 2014-2015.

Rooms 3 en suite (3 GF) S £60-£65; D £76-£86 **Facilities** FTV tea/coffee WiFi 🔒 **Parking** 3 **Notes** ⊗ No Children 12yrs Closed Xmas & New Year ⊛

NORTH LANARKSHIRE

MOTHERWELL	Map 20 NS75

Innkeeper's Lodge Glasgow

★★★ INN

tel: 0845 112 6004 **fax:** 0870 191 0932 **1 Hamilton Rd ML1 3RB**
email: info@innkeeperslodge.com **web:** www.innkeeperslodge.com

This property enjoys an excellent location for those travelling to and from Scotland, or as a base for visiting anywhere in the central belt. The inn is located just off the M74 with links to nearby Glasgow and Edinburgh. Modern, spacious bedrooms occupy an attractive building, where friendly service, wide-ranging breakfasts, free WiFi and complimentary parking are also available. Next door is the ever-popular Toby Carvery where food and real ales are available all day.

Rooms 28 en suite (10 fmly) (14 GF) S £42-£56* **Facilities** FTV tea/coffee Dinner available WiFi ⅃ 18 **Conf** Max 35 Thtr 35 Class 35 Board 35 **Parking** 150 **Notes** LB ⊗

SOUTH LANARKSHIRE

STRATHAVEN   Map 20 NS74

Rissons at Springvale

★★★ ◉ RESTAURANT WITH ROOMS

tel: 01357 521131 & 520234   **fax:** 01357 521131 **18 Lethame Rd ML10 6AD**
email: info@rissons.co.uk **web:** www.rissonsrestaurant.co.uk
dir: *A71 into Strathaven, W of town centre off Townhead St*

Guests are assured of a warm welcome at this charming establishment close to the town centre. The bedrooms and bathrooms are stylish and well equipped. The main attraction here is the food - a range of interesting, well-prepared dishes served in Rissons Restaurant.

Rooms 9 en suite (1 fmly) (1 GF) S £47.50; D £85 **Facilities** FTV Lounge TVL tea/coffee Dinner available WiFi ⚓ 18 🅿 **Parking** 10 **Notes** ⊗ Closed 1st wk Jan No coaches

EAST LOTHIAN

ABERLADY   Map 21 NT47

Ducks at Kilspindie

★★★★ ◉◉ RESTAURANT WITH ROOMS

tel: 01875 870682 **fax:** 01875 870504 **Main St EH32 0RE**
email: kilspindie@ducks.co.uk **web:** www.ducks.co.uk
dir: *A1 (Bankton junct) take 1st exit to North Berwick. At next rdbt 3rd exit onto A198 signed Longniddry, left towards Aberlady. At T-junct, facing river, right to Aberlady*

The name of this restaurant with rooms is referenced around the building - Ducks Restaurant for award-winning cuisine; Donald's Bistro and the Ducklings informal coffee shop. The warm and welcoming public areas include a great bar offering real ales and various objets d'art. The bedrooms are comfortable and well-appointed with stylish en suites. The team are informal and friendly, taking the time to chat to their guests.

Rooms 23 en suite (1 fmly) (6 GF) S £60-£105; D £80-£120* **Facilities** STV FTV Lounge TVL tea/coffee Dinner available Direct Dial WiFi ⚓ 18 🅿 **Conf** Max 100 Thtr 100 Class 60 Board 30 **Parking** 15

EAST LINTON   Map 21 NT57

The Linton

★★★★ ◉ ☖ RESTAURANT WITH ROOMS

tel: 01620 860202 **3 Bridgend EH40 3AF**
email: infolinton@aol.com **web:** www.thelintonhotel.co.uk
dir: *From A1, follow signs for East Linton, 3m*

The Linton is located in a quiet conservation village within easy distance of Edinburgh, the East Lothian coast and numerous golf courses. Award-winning food promotes local suppliers with a menu that has something for everybody. The pub serves real ales and is warm and welcoming. Bedrooms are individually appointed with many useful extras provided as standard. The rear garden is a real suntrap with just the chimes of the church clock to disturb the peace.

Rooms 7 en suite (2 fmly) **Facilities** FTV DVD iPod docking station tea/coffee Dinner available WiFi 🅿

HADDINGTON   Map 21 NT57

Redshill Bed & Breakfast *(NT521651)*

★★★★ ☖ FARMHOUSE

tel: 01620 810406 & 07971 115848 **Redshill Farm, Gifford EH41 4JN**
email: redshill@btinternet.com **web:** www.redshill.co.uk
dir: *A1 to Haddington, take S exit & follow signs to Gifford on B6369. Exit village, with golf course on right, signed old farmhouse*

Dating back to the early 19th century and fully refurbished to provide modern comfortable luxuries in the well-appointed bedrooms, Redshill is located on a working arable farm. It is ideally located for the whole of East Lothian and Edinburgh whilst still offering a peaceful rural setting. A welcoming lounge is where refreshments are served on arrival, and breakfast uses the very best local suppliers from around the region.

Rooms 3 en suite (2 GF) S £55-£70; D £70-£85* **Facilities** FTV DVD TVL WiFi 🅿 Drying room **Extras** Mineral water, robes **Parking** 3 **Notes** ⊗ 300 acres arable

WEST LOTHIAN

BLACKBURN   Map 21 NS96

Cruachan B&B

★★★★ GUEST ACCOMMODATION

tel: 01506 655221 **fax:** 01506 652395 **78 East Main St EH47 7QS**
email: enquiries@cruachan.co.uk **web:** www.cruachan.co.uk
dir: *On A705 in Blackburn, 1m from M8 junct 4*

This B&B is ideally located for both leisure and business travellers, with Edinburgh just 30 minutes away by train and Glasgow only 35 minutes by car. Cruachan is the comfortable, friendly home of the Harkins family. Bedrooms are bright, attractive and very well equipped. Breakfast, featuring the best of local produce is served at individual tables in the ground-floor dining room.

Rooms 4 rms (3 en suite) (1 pri facs) (1 fmly) S £45-£50; D £65-£70* **Facilities** FTV DVD tea/coffee WiFi 🅿 **Parking** 5 **Notes** ⊗

EAST CALDER
Map 21 NT06

Ashcroft Farmhouse

★★★★ GUEST HOUSE

tel: 01506 881810 & 07788 926239 fax: 01506 884327 **EH53 0ET**
email: ashcroftinfo@aol.com **web:** www.ashcroftfarmhouse.com

(For full entry see Livingston)

Whitecroft Bed & Breakfast

★★★★ BED AND BREAKFAST

tel: 01506 882494 **fax:** 01506 882598 **7 Raw Holdings EH53 0ET**
email: lornascot@aol.com **web:** www.whitecroftbandb.co.uk

(For full entry see Livingston)

KIRKNEWTON
Map 21 NT16

Highfield House

★★★ BED AND BREAKFAST

tel: 01506 881489 **EH27 8BJ**
email: jill@hunter-gordon.co.uk

Dating back to 1735, this was originally the manse for the church across the road. Set in its own gardens with great transportation links into Edinburgh and the Lothians, Highfield House is an ideal location for both leisure and corporate guests. Many original features of the house remain and bedrooms are comfortable and well appointed. Breakfast uses plenty of local produce, and is served in a wonderful dining room around a large oval table.

Rooms 3 rms

LINLITHGOW
Map 21 NS97

Premier Collection

Arden Country House

★★★★★ GUEST ACCOMMODATION

tel: 01506 670172 fax: 01506 670172 **Belsyde EH49 6QE**
email: info@ardencountryhouse.com **web:** www.ardencountryhouse.com
dir: *1.3m SW of Linlithgow. A706 over Union Canal, entrance 200yds on left at Lodge Cottage*

Situated in the picturesque grounds of the Belsyde country estate and close to the Royal Burgh of Linlithgow, Arden Country House offers immaculate, stylishly furnished and spacious bedrooms. There is a cosy ground-floor lounge and a charming dining room where delicious breakfasts feature the best of local produce.

Rooms 3 en suite (1 GF) **Facilities** FTV DVD iPod docking station Lounge tea/coffee WiFi **Extras** Savoury snacks, chocolates **Parking** 4 **Notes** LB ⊗ No Children 12yrs Closed 25-26 Dec

Belsyde House

★★★★ GUEST ACCOMMODATION

tel: 01506 842098 **fax:** 01506 234134 **Lanark Rd EH49 6QE**
email: info@belsydehouse.com **web:** www.belsyde.com
dir: *1.5m SW on A706, 1st left over Union Canal*

Reached by a tree-lined driveway, this welcoming farmhouse is peacefully situated in attractive grounds close to the Union Canal. There are well-proportioned bedrooms including a family room; all are nicely furnished and well equipped. Breakfast, including a vegetarian menu, is served at good-sized tables in the dining room, next to the lounge.

Rooms 3 en suite (1 fmly) **Facilities** FTV TVL tea/coffee WiFi **Extras** Speciality toiletries, robes - complimentary **Parking** 10 **Notes** ⊗ No Children 12yrs Closed Xmas

LINLITHGOW *continued*

Bomains Farm Guest House

★★★★ GUEST HOUSE

tel: 01506 822188 & 822861   **fax:** 01506 824433 **Bo'ness EH49 7RQ**
email: bunty.kirk@onetel.net **web:** www.bomains.co.uk
dir: *A706, 1.5m N towards Bo'ness, left at golf course x-rds, 1st farm on right*

From its elevated location this friendly farmhouse has stunning views of the Firth of Forth. The bedrooms, which vary in size, are beautifully decorated and well-equipped with many thoughtful extra touches. Delicious home-cooked fare, featuring the best local produce, is served in a stylish lounge-dining room.

Rooms 6 rms (4 en suite) (1 pri facs) (1 fmly) (2 GF) **Facilities** STV FTV DVD Lounge TVL tea/coffee WiFi ⅃ 18 Fishing ♨ **Parking** 12

Kirkland House

★★★★ BED AND BREAKFAST

tel: 01506 822188 & 07974 736480 **Bomains Farm EH49 7RQ**
email: bunty.kirk@onetel.net **web:** www.bomains.co.uk
dir: *A706, 1.5m N towards Bo'ness, left at golf course x-rds, 1st farm on right*

Kirkland House is a new purpose-built property adjacent to the family-run Bomains Farm Guest House, where a number of guest services are provided. Large bedrooms come with high quality fixtures and fittings, and patio doors that lead onto the garden which has a children's play area and views onto the River Forth. All in all, a peaceful location within striking distance of Linlithgow, Edinburgh and the Central Belt.

Rooms 3 en suite (1 fmly) (3 GF) **Facilities** FTV TVL tea/coffee WiFi ⅃ 18 Fishing **Parking** 6 **Notes** ⊗ ⊜

■ **LIVINGSTON**   **Map 21 NT06**

Ashcroft Farmhouse

★★★★ ≘ GUEST HOUSE

tel: 01506 881810 & 07788 926239   **fax:** 01506 884327 **East Calder EH53 0ET**
email: ashcroftinfo@aol.com **web:** www.ashcroftfarmhouse.com
dir: *On B7015, off A71, 0.5m E of East Calder, near Almondell Country Park*

With over 40 years' experience in caring for guests, Derek and Elizabeth Scott ensure a stay at Ashcroft will be memorable. Their modern home sits in lovely, award-winning landscaped gardens and provides attractive and well-equipped ground-floor bedrooms. The comfortable lounge includes a video and DVD library. Breakfast, featuring home-made sausages and the best of local produce, is served at individual tables in the stylish dining room. Free WiFi is available, and a Park and Ride facility is nearby.

Rooms 6 en suite (2 fmly) (6 GF) S £50-£60; D £80-£90 **Facilities** FTV TVL tea/coffee WiFi ♨ **Parking** 8 **Notes** ⊗

Whitecroft Bed & Breakfast

★★★★ BED AND BREAKFAST

tel: 01506 882494 **fax:** 01506 882598 **7 Raw Holdings, East Calder EH53 0ET**
email: lornascot@aol.com **web:** www.whitecroftbandb.co.uk
dir: *A71 onto B7015, establishment on right*

A relaxed and friendly atmosphere prevails at Whitecroft, a charming, modern bed and breakfast. The bedrooms, all of which are on the ground floor, are attractively colour co-ordinated, well-equipped and contain many thoughtful extra touches. Breakfast is served at individual tables in the smart dining room.

Rooms 3 en suite (3 GF) S £40-£60; D £70-£80* **Facilities** FTV DVD tea/coffee WiFi **Parking** 5 **Notes** No Children 12yrs

MIDLOTHIAN

DALKEITH
Map 21 NT36

The Sun Inn

★★★★★ ⊛ ≘ INN

tel: 0131 663 2456 **Lothian Bridge EH22 4TR**
email: thesuninn@live.co.uk **web:** www.thesuninnedinburgh.co.uk
dir: *On A7 towards Galashiels, opposite Newbattle Viaduct*

The Sun Inn dates back to 1697 and is situated within easy striking distance of Edinburgh. It has boutique-style bedrooms (one featuring a copper bath) and modern bathrooms. High quality, award-winning food is served in stylish surroundings; drinks can be enjoyed in the terraced garden area.

Rooms 5 en suite S £75-£100; D £95-£150* **Facilities** STV FTV tea/coffee Dinner available WiFi ⌁ 18 Fishing **Parking** 50 **Notes** LB ⊛

ROSLIN
Map 21 NT26

The Original Rosslyn Inn

★★★★ INN

tel: 0131 440 2384 **fax:** 0131 440 2514 **4 Main St EH25 9LE**
email: enquiries@theoriginalhotel.co.uk **web:** www.theoriginalhotel.co.uk
dir: *From A701 at rdbt take B7003 signed Roslin & Rosewell, into Roslin. At T-junct, inn opposite. Or from mini rdbt on A701 at Bilston take B7006 to Roslin. Inn on left*

Whether on *The Da Vinci Code* trail or in the area on business, this property is ideally placed for a well-worth visit to the famous Rosslyn Chapel, which is just a short walk away. It is a delightful village inn that offers well-equipped bedrooms with en suites; four of the bedrooms have four-poster beds. The Grail Restaurant, the lounge and conservatory offer a comprehensive selection of dining options.

Rooms 7 en suite (2 fmly) **Facilities** FTV DVD Lounge tea/coffee Dinner available WiFi ⌁ **Conf** Max 130 Thtr 130 Class 80 Board 60 **Parking** 8 **Notes** Civ Wed 180

MORAY

FORRES
Map 23 NJ05

Cluny Bank

★★★★ ⊛ RESTAURANT WITH ROOMS

tel: 01309 674304 **fax:** 01309 638206 **69 St Leonards Rd IV36 1DW**
email: info@clunybankhotel.co.uk **web:** www.clunybankhotel.co.uk

Historic, listed Cluny Bank occupies a quiet location within walking distance of the centre of Forres, and is an ideal base for exploring the North East of Scotland. Family-run, the building retains many original architectural features. Public areas include the 'Altyre Bar' with a wide range of whiskies, and 'Franklin's Restaurant' where a real taste of Moray can be experienced. Room service, complimentary WiFi and memorable breakfasts are also provided for guests.

Rooms 6 en suite 1 annexe en suite (2 GF) S £75-£82.50; D £125-£155*
Facilities FTV iPod docking station Lounge tea/coffee Dinner available Direct Dial WiFi **Parking** 7 **Notes** LB ⊛ No coaches

PERTH & KINROSS

ALYTH
Map 23 NO24

Premier Collection

Tigh Na Leigh Guesthouse

★★★★★ 🏠 🍴 GUEST ACCOMMODATION

tel: 01828 632372 **fax:** 01828 632279 **22-24 Airlie St PH11 8AJ**
email: bandcblack@yahoo.co.uk **web:** www.tighnaleigh.co.uk
dir: *In town centre on B952*

Situated in the heart of this charming country town, Tigh Na Leigh (Gaelic for 'The House of the Doctor') is an equally charming property. It has an imposing, yet welcoming appearance, and inside has been completely restored to blend its Victorian architecture with contemporary interior design. Bedrooms, including a superb suite, have state-of-the-art bathrooms and spa baths. There are three lounges, and delicious meals are served in the conservatory/dining room overlooking a spectacular landscaped garden. Free WiFi is provided.

Rooms 5 en suite (1 GF) S £55; D £89-£130* **Facilities** FTV DVD iPod docking station Lounge TVL tea/coffee Dinner available Licensed WiFi ♨ 18 🏌
Extras Fruit, mineral water **Parking** 5 **Notes** No Children 12yrs Closed Dec-Feb

BLAIR ATHOLL
Map 23 NN86

The Firs

★★★★ GUEST HOUSE

tel: 01796 481256 **PH18 5TA**
email: kirstie@firs-blairatholl.co.uk **web:** www.firs-blairatholl.co.uk
dir: *A9 follow signs to Blair Atholl, 1st left after Blair Atholl garage*

The Firs is located in the peaceful village of Blair Atholl, home of Europe's only legal private army, the Atholl Highlanders. This is a well-presented property with lovely gardens. Bedrooms are comfortable and have quality decor. Public areas are warm and welcoming, and are enhanced by a log fire, while breakfast is served in the conservatory at individual tables.

Rooms 6 en suite (3 fmly) (2 GF) S £45-£65; D £70-£90 **Facilities** FTV DVD Lounge tea/coffee WiFi 🏌 **Parking** 7 **Notes** LB Closed Nov-Feb

CALVINE
Map 23 NN86

The Struan Inn

★★★★ GUEST ACCOMMODATION

tel: 01796 483714 **PH18 5UB**
email: thestruan.calvine@btinternet.com **web:** www.thestruan-inn.co.uk
dir: *From N - A9 turn right onto B847, turn right for Kinloch Rannoch. Under bridge, 1st right. From S - A9 turn left onto B847, turn right for Kinloch Rannoch, then as for From N*

Located on the edge of the Cairngorms National Park, this location is very peaceful, although it is just two minutes from the A9. Inside there is a residents' bar with a log fire, comfortable lounge, and dinner served by prior arrangement. Bedrooms are well appointed with modern features. Hospitality is warm and traditional.

Rooms 3 en suite (1 fmly) (1 GF) S £40-£70; D £65-£100* **Facilities** STV DVD iPod docking station TVL tea/coffee Dinner available Licensed WiFi 🏌 **Parking** 6 **Notes** ⊗

CRIEFF
Map 21 NN82

Merlindale

★★★★ BED AND BREAKFAST

tel: 01764 655205 **fax:** 01764 655205 **Perth Rd PH7 3EQ**
email: jandjclifford@gmail.com **web:** www.merlindale.co.uk
dir: *On A85, 350yds from E end of High St*

Situated in a quiet residential area within walking distance of the town centre, this delightful detached house stands in well-tended grounds and offers a warm welcome. The pretty bedrooms are comfortably furnished and well equipped. There is a spacious lounge, an impressive library, and an elegant dining room where traditional breakfasts are served.

Rooms 3 en suite (1 fmly) **Facilities** STV FTV Lounge TVL tea/coffee WiFi **Parking** 3 **Notes** LB ⊗ Closed 9 Dec-10 Feb

MEIKLEOUR
Map 21 NO13

Meikleour Arms

★★★★ INN

tel: 01250 883206 & 883406 **fax:** 01250 883309 **PH2 6EB**
email: contact@meikleourarms.co.uk **web:** www.meikleourarms.co.uk
dir: *N of Perth on A93*

This family-run country inn has been a popular venue for almost 200 years. It was first established as a coach and posting house. Today it welcomes both locals and visitors who come to the area for fishing and shooting. Bedrooms are spacious and comfortable with impressive bathrooms. An attractive restaurant serves high quality local produce, and the lounge bar is a cosy area where beer connoisseurs can sample the property's own real ale.

Rooms 5 en suite 4 annexe en suite (2 fmly) (7 GF) S £65–£100; D £75–£110* **Facilities** FTV Lounge tea/coffee Dinner available WiFi ⅃ 45 Fishing Snooker 🦪 **Extras** Speciality toiletries, bottled water, sherry - free of charge **Parking** 25

■ MUTHILL   Map 21 NN81

Barley Bree Restaurant with Rooms

★★★★ ◉◉ RESTAURANT WITH ROOMS

tel: 01764 681451 **fax:** 01764 910055 **6 Willoughby St PH5 2AB**
email: info@barleybree.com **web:** www.barleybree.com
dir: A9 onto A822 in centre of Muthill

Situated in the heart of the small village of Muthill, and just a short drive from Crieff, genuine hospitality and quality food are obvious attractions at this charming restaurant with rooms. The stylish bedrooms are appointed to a very high standard. The restaurant has a rustic feel with exposed stonework, wooden floors and a log-burning fire in the centre. Choices range from set, carte and tasting menus. Children are welcome too.

Rooms 6 en suite (1 fmly) S £70–£85; D £110–£150 **Facilities** FTV DVD Lounge tea/coffee Dinner available WiFi ⅃ 9 🦪 **Parking** 10 **Notes** LB ⊗ Closed see website for closures RS Mon & Tue restaurant closed to public No coaches

■ PERTH   Map 21 NO12

Cherrybank Guesthouse

★★★★ ≘ GUEST ACCOMMODATION

tel: 01738 451982 **fax:** 01738 561336 **217-219 Glasgow Rd PH2 0NB**
email: m.r.cherrybank@blueyonder.co.uk
dir: 1m SW of town centre on A93

Convenient for the town and major roads, Cherrybank Guesthouse offers well equipped and beautifully presented bedrooms, one of which is on the ground floor. The delightful lounge is ideal for relaxation, while delicious breakfasts are served at individual tables in the bright airy dining room.

Rooms 5 rms (4 en suite) (1 pri facs) (2 fmly) (1 GF) **Facilities** tea/coffee WiFi **Parking** 4 **Notes** ⊗

Ballabeg Guest House

★★★ BED AND BREAKFAST

tel: 01738 620434 **14 Keir St PH2 7HJ**
email: ballabeg@btopenworld.com **web:** www.ballabegguesthouse.co.uk
dir: NE of city centre, Keir St accessed from A93 (E of river) or from A94 (Strathmore St)

Well situated for the town centre and benefiting from off-road parking, this property offers modern, comfortable bedrooms of a good overall size with a number of extras provided as standard. Well-cooked breakfasts together with warm and genuine hospitality ensure a pleasant stay. All major credit cards are accepted.

Rooms 4 rms (3 en suite) (1 pri facs) D £39–£63* **Facilities** FTV DVD tea/coffee WiFi 🦪 **Parking** 4 **Notes** ⊗ No Children 16yrs Closed Dec-Jan

■ PITLOCHRY   Map 23 NN95

Craigroyston House

★★★★ GUEST HOUSE

tel: 01796 472053 **fax:** 01796 472053 **2 Lower Oakfield PH16 5HQ**
email: reservations@craigroyston.co.uk **web:** www.craigroyston.co.uk
dir: In town centre near information centre car park

The Maxwell family delight in welcoming guests to their home, an impressive detached Victorian villa set in a colourful garden. The bedrooms have pretty colour schemes and are comfortably furnished in period style. There is an inviting sitting room, complete with deep sofas for those wishing to relax and enjoy the peaceful atmosphere. Scottish breakfasts are served at individual tables in the attractive dining room.

Rooms 8 en suite (1 fmly) (1 GF) D £80–£98 **Facilities** FTV Lounge tea/coffee WiFi **Parking** 9 **Notes** LB ⊗ ⊜

Wellwood House

★★★★ GUEST HOUSE

tel: 01796 474288 **fax:** 01796 474299 **13 West Moulin Rd PH16 5EA**
email: wellwoodhouse@aol.com **web:** www.wellwoodhouse.com
dir: In town centre opposite town hall

Set in lovely grounds on an elevated position overlooking the town, Wellwood House has stunning views of the Vale of Atholl and the surrounding countryside. The comfortably proportioned bedrooms are attractively decorated and well equipped. The elegant lounge has an honesty bar and a fire on cooler evenings, and the spacious dining room is the setting for hearty breakfasts served at individual tables.

Rooms 10 rms (8 en suite) (2 pri facs) (1 fmly) (1 GF) S £50–£70; D £75–£89 **Facilities** FTV Lounge TVL tea/coffee Licensed WiFi ⅃ 18 🦪 **Extras** Honesty bar **Parking** 20 **Notes** ⊗ Closed 10 Nov-14 Feb Civ Wed 24

SCOTTISH BORDERS

■ BROUGHTON   Map 21 NT13

The Glenholm Centre

★★★ ≘ GUEST ACCOMMODATION

tel: 01899 830408 **ML12 6JF**
email: info@glenholm.co.uk **web:** www.glenholm.co.uk
dir: 1m S of Broughton. Off A701 to Glenholm

Surrounded by peaceful farmland, this former schoolhouse has a distinct African theme. The home-cooked meals and baking have received much praise and are served in the spacious lounge-dining room. The bright airy bedrooms are thoughtfully equipped, and the service is friendly and attentive. Computer courses are available.

Rooms 3 en suite 1 annexe en suite (1 fmly) (2 GF) S £38–£45; D £66* **Facilities** FTV DVD TVL tea/coffee Dinner available Licensed WiFi 🦪 **Parking** 10 **Notes** LB Closed 20 Dec-1 Feb

DENHOLM
Map 21 NT51

Auld Cross Keys Inn

★★★ ⬢ INN

tel: 01450 870305 **fax:** 01450 420007 **Main St TD9 8NU**
email: bookings@crosskeysdenholm.co.uk **web:** www.crosskeysdenholm.co.uk

Located in the village of Denholm in the heart of the Borders, and built in the 1800s, originally as a bakehouse but converted to a coaching inn, the Auld Cross Keys offers bedrooms of various sizes and styles. All are well presented and appointed with comfortable beds. Public and lounge bars boast a good selection of malts with real ale on tap and a separate restaurant for dining. The gardens to the rear are a welcome addition, allowing guests to make the best of the summer weather.

Rooms 7 rms (6 en suite) (1 pri facs) 5 annexe en suite (1 fmly) (3 GF) S fr £45; D fr £70* **Facilities** FTV tea/coffee Dinner available WiFi ⬡ 18 Pool table ⬢ **Parking** 10 **Notes** LB

EDDLESTON
Map 21 NT24

The Horseshoe Restaurant with Rooms

★★★★★ ⬤⬤ ⬢ RESTAURANT WITH ROOMS

tel: 01721 730225 **fax:** 01721 730268 **EH45 8QP**
email: reservations@horseshoeinn.co.uk **web:** www.horseshoeinn.co.uk
dir: A703, 5m N of Peebles

The Horseshoe is five miles north of Peebles and only 18 miles south of Edinburgh. Originally a blacksmith's shop, it has a very good reputation for its delightful atmosphere and excellent cuisine. There are eight luxuriously appointed and individually designed bedrooms. Please note: children are welcome, but dinner is not served to under fives except in the private dining room.

Rooms 8 en suite (1 fmly) (6 GF) S £90-£110; D £120-£140* **Facilities** FTV Lounge tea/coffee Dinner available Direct Dial WiFi **Extras** Speciality toiletries, fruit, mineral water - free of charge **Parking** 20 **Notes** LB Closed 25 Dec, 1st 2wks Jan & 1st 2wks Sep RS Mon & Tue closed

INNERLEITHEN
Map 21 NT33

Caddon View

★★★★ ⬢ ⬢ GUEST ACCOMMODATION

tel: 01896 830208 **14 Pirn Rd EH44 6HH**
email: stay@caddonview.co.uk **web:** www.caddonview.co.uk
dir: Signed from A72 in Innerleithen

Set in its own well maintained gardens this well-presented Victorian house was originally built in the 1850s. Caddon View offers high standards of accommodation along with wonderful hospitality and customer care awareness. Located in the beautiful Tweed Valley, it's ideally located for all the border areas as well as Edinburgh. The property is licensed and serves quality evening meals (by prior arrangement), in a bright, welcoming and well-appointed dining room.

Rooms 8 rms (7 en suite) (1 pri facs) (2 fmly) (2 GF) S £50-£55; D £70-£110* **Facilities** FTV DVD Lounge tea/coffee Dinner available Licensed WiFi ⬢ **Parking** 7 **Notes** Closed 25-26 Dec RS Sun & Mon no dinner available

JEDBURGH
Map 21 NT62

Ferniehirst Mill Lodge

★★ GUEST HOUSE

tel: 01835 863279 **TD8 6PQ**
email: ferniehirstmill@aol.com **web:** www.ferniehirstmill.co.uk
dir: 2.5m S of Jedburgh on A68, onto private track to end

Reached by a narrow farm track and a rustic wooden bridge, this chalet-style house has a secluded setting by the River Jed. Bedrooms are small and functional, and there is a comfortable lounge in which to relax. Home-cooked and hearty breakfasts are served in the cosy dining room.

Rooms 7 en suite (1 GF) **Facilities** TVL tea/coffee Fishing Riding ⬢ **Parking** 10

MELROSE
Map 21 NT53

Fauhope Country House

★★★★★ ⬢ GUEST HOUSE

tel: 01896 823184 & 07816 346768 **fax:** 01896 823184 **Gattonside TD6 9LU**
email: info@fauhopehouse.com **web:** www.fauhopehouse.com
dir: 0.7m N of Melrose over River Tweed. N off B6360 at Gattonside 30mph sign (E) up long driveway

It's hard to imagine a more complete experience than a stay at Fauhope Country House, set high on a hillside on the north-east edge of the village. Hospitality is first class, breakfasts are excellent, and the delightful country house has a splendid interior. Bedrooms are luxurious, each individual and superbly equipped. Public areas are elegantly decorated and furnished, and enhanced by beautiful floral arrangements; the dining room is particularly stunning.

Rooms 3 en suite S £70-£85; D £95-£140* **Facilities** FTV DVD Lounge tea/coffee Dinner available WiFi ⊌ Riding Treatment room **Extras** Speciality toiletries, fruit, sherry - free **Parking** 10 **Notes** LB

NEWCASTLETON   Map 21 NY48

Liddesdale

★★★★ INN

tel: 01387 375255 **fax:** 01387 752577 **Douglas Sq TD9 0QD**
email: reception@theliddesdalehotel.co.uk **web:** www.theliddesdalehotel.co.uk

Liddesdale is located in the peaceful 17th-century village of Newcastleton, overlooking the village square. There are well-appointed bedrooms and bathrooms, and the public areas offer various locations in which to dine. The welcoming public bar is well used by locals and residents alike, and there is also a beer garden. Relaxed and informal menus use the best local produce available.

Rooms 6 en suite (2 fmly) **Facilities** STV FTV Lounge TVL tea/coffee Dinner available Direct Dial WiFi ⊌ ⌁ 9 Fishing ⚿ **Conf** Max 60 Thtr 40 Class 40 Board 40

STIRLING

CALLANDER   Map 20 NN60

Lubnaig House

★★★★ 🅐 GUEST HOUSE

tel: 01877 330376 **fax:** 01877 330376 **Leny Feus FK17 8AS**
email: info@lubnaighouse.co.uk **web:** www.lubnaighouse.co.uk
dir: From town centre take A84 W, 1st street on right after Poppies Hotel

Lubnaig House is set in a delightful tree-lined secluded garden, just a five-minute walk from the town centre. The house, built in 1864, has comfortable, well-appointed bedrooms. There are two cosy lounges, and an impressive dining room where hearty traditional breakfasts are served at individual tables.

Rooms 6 en suite 2 annexe en suite (4 GF) S £45-£60; D £70-£80* **Facilities** FTV iPod docking station Lounge tea/coffee WiFi ⚿ **Parking** 10 **Notes** LB ⊗ No Children 7yrs Closed Nov-1 Apr

LOCHEARNHEAD   Map 20 NN52

Tigh Na Crich

★★★★ BED AND BREAKFAST

tel: 01567 830235 **FK19 8PR**
email: johntippett2@aol.com **web:** www.tighnacrich.co.uk
dir: At junct of A84 & A85, next to village shop

Tich Na Crich is located in the heart of the small village of Lochearnhead, surrounded by mountains on three sides and Loch Earn on the fourth. Inside is very well presented accommodation with many thoughtful extras provided. The generous breakfast is served in the comfortable dining room on individual tables looking out to the front of the property.

Rooms 3 en suite (1 fmly) S £45-£50; D £70-£85* **Facilities** FTV DVD Lounge tea/coffee WiFi ⚿ **Parking** 3 **Notes** Closed Xmas-New Year ⊜

STIRLING   Map 21 NS79

Linden Guest House

★★★★ GUEST HOUSE

tel: 01786 448850 & 07974 116573   **fax:** 01786 448850 **22 Linden Av FK7 7PQ**
email: fay@lindenguesthouse.co.uk **web:** www.lindenguesthouse.co.uk
dir: 0.5m SE of city centre off A9

Situated within walking distance of the town centre, this friendly guest house offers attractive and very well-equipped bedrooms, including a large family room that sleeps five comfortably. There is a bright dining room where delicious breakfasts are served at individual tables with quality Wedgwood crockery.

Rooms 4 en suite (2 fmly) (1 GF) **Facilities** STV FTV DVD iPod docking station tea/coffee WiFi **Parking** 2 **Notes** LB

STRATHYRE
Map 20 NN51

Premier Collection

Creagan House

★★★★★ ◉◉ 🍽 RESTAURANT WITH ROOMS

tel: 01877 384638 **fax:** 01877 384319 **FK18 8ND**
email: eatandstay@creaganhouse.co.uk **web:** www.creaganhouse.co.uk
dir: 0.25m N of Strathyre on A84

Originally a farmhouse dating from the 17th century, Creagan House has operated as a restaurant with rooms for many years. The baronial-style dining room provides a wonderful setting for the cuisine which is classic French with some Scottish influences. The warm hospitality and attentive service are noteworthy.

Rooms 5 en suite (1 fmly) (1 GF) S £90-£100; D £130-£150 **Facilities** FTV Lounge tea/coffee Dinner available WiFi 🔒 **Extras** Speciality toiletries **Conf** Max 35 Thtr 35 Class 12 Board 35 **Parking** 16 **Notes** LB Closed 29 Oct-26 Mar RS Wed & Thu closed

SCOTTISH ISLANDS

ISLE OF ARRAN

BRODICK
Map 20 NS03

Allandale Guest House

★★★★ GUEST HOUSE

tel: 01770 302278 **KA27 8BJ**
email: info@allandalehouse.co.uk **web:** www.allandalehouse.co.uk
dir: 500yds S of Brodick Pier, off A841 towards Lamlash, up hill 2nd left at Corriegills sign

This comfortable guest house, run by enthusiastic owners, is set in delightful gardens in beautiful countryside. Guests can relax in the lounge with its attractive garden views. Bedrooms vary in size and have pleasing colour schemes and mixed modern furnishings, along with thoughtful amenities. In a peaceful location, Allandale Guest House is convenient for the CalMac ferry and Brodick centre.

Rooms 4 rms (3 en suite) (1 pri facs) 2 annexe en suite (3 fmly) (2 GF) **Facilities** FTV Lounge tea/coffee WiFi **Parking** 6 **Notes** ⊗ Closed Nov-Feb

Dunvegan House

★★★★ GUEST HOUSE

tel: 01770 302811 **fax:** 01770 302811 **Dunvegan Shore Rd KA27 8AJ**
email: dunveganhouse1@hotmail.com **web:** www.dunveganhouse-arran.co.uk
dir: Turn right from ferry terminal, 500yds along Shore Rd

Situated close to the shore and enjoying spectacular views of the bay, this establishment is a popular choice for visitors to the island. The property benefits from having a hands-on approach from the friendly owner whilst public areas and bedrooms have great views.

Rooms 9 en suite (3 GF) S £55; D £95* **Facilities** FTV Lounge tea/coffee Dinner available Licensed WiFi 🔒 **Parking** 8 **Notes** ⊗ Closed 23 Dec-3 Jan ⊛

ISLE OF HARRIS

SCARISTA (SGARASTA BHEAG)
Map 22 NG09

Scarista House

★★★★ ◉◉ 🍽 RESTAURANT WITH ROOMS

tel: 01859 550238 **HS3 3HX**
email: timandpatricia@scaristahouse.com **web:** www.scaristahouse.com
dir: On A859, 15m S of Tarbert

A former manse, Scarista House is a haven for food lovers and those who seek to explore this magnificent island. The house enjoys breathtaking views of the Atlantic and is just a short stroll from miles of golden sandy beaches. The house is run in a relaxed country-house manner by the friendly hosts. Expect wellies in the hall and masses of books and CDs in one of the lounges. Bedrooms are cosy, and delicious set dinners and memorable breakfasts are provided.

Rooms 3 en suite 3 annexe en suite (1 fmly) (2 GF) D £210-£235* **Facilities** Lounge tea/coffee Dinner available WiFi 🔒 **Extras** Speciality toiletries, fruit **Parking** 12 **Notes** LB Closed Xmas, Jan & Feb No coaches Civ Wed 40

ISLE OF ISLAY

BOWMORE
Map 20 NR36

The Harbour Inn and Restaurant

★★★★ ◉◉ 🍽 RESTAURANT WITH ROOMS

tel: 01496 810330 **fax:** 01496 810990 **The Square PA43 7JR**
email: info@harbour-inn.com **web:** www.harbour-inn.com
dir: Next to harbour

The humble whitewashed exterior of the Harbour Inn conceals a sophisticated environment that draws discerning travellers from all over the world. Spacious bedrooms are appointed to a high standard and the conservatory-lounge has stunning views over Loch Indaal to the peaks of Jura. The cosy bar is popular with locals, and the smart dining room showcases some excellent seafood. Welcoming peat fires burn in cooler months.

Rooms 7 en suite (1 fmly) (1 GF) **Facilities** Lounge tea/coffee Dinner available Direct Dial WiFi ⚓ 18 Fishing Riding Gym **Extras** Speciality toiletries - complimentary **Notes** ⊗ No Children 10yrs No coaches

LISMORE

BACHUIL
Map 20 NM84

Bachuil Country House
★★★★ GUEST ACCOMMODATION

tel: 01631 760256 **PA34 5UL**
email: anita@clanlivingstone.com **web:** www.bachuilcountryhouse.co.uk
dir: *On Isle of Lismore - 45 minute car ferry from Oban or 10 minute passenger ferry from Port Appin. There is no fuel available on Lismore*

Situated on the Isle of Lismore, the most easterly of the southern Hebrides, Bachuil Country House provides a great place to enjoy the tranquillity of this historic and picturesque island. Hearty breakfasts and enjoyable dinners are provided daily. Guests can relax in the drawing room and enjoy open log fires.

Rooms 3 en suite D £100-£120* **Facilities** iPod docking station TVL tea/coffee Dinner available WiFi 🐟 Fishing 🔒 **Extras** Fruit, snacks - complimentary **Parking** 4 **Notes** No Children 8yrs Closed Nov-Mar

ISLE OF MULL

TOBERMORY
Map 22 NM55

Harbour View Bed and Breakfast
★★★★ BED AND BREAKFAST

tel: 01688 301111 **1 Argyll Ter PA75 6PB**
email: swanandalan@gmail.com **web:** www.tobermorybandb.com
dir: *A848 to Tobermory. At mini rdbt 1st left signed Dervaig, over bridge, immediately 1st right signed Tobermory & Breadelbane St. Approx 300yds right into Breadelbane St. 3rd right into Victoria St, down hill. B&B 50yds on right, on corner, opposite church*

As the name suggests, you are guaranteed to get a stunning view of the Tobermory harbour from some of the rooms in this former Victorian fisherman's cottage, which sits in an elevated position. Recently refurbished to a high standard, rooms contain many original features including exposed brick walls and fireplaces. The dining room also has great views; the best place to enjoy a freshly cooked breakfast while gazing down at the Sound of Mull.

Rooms 3 en suite 1 annexe en suite (1 fmly) (1 GF) S £40-£65; D £50-£90* **Facilities** STV FTV DVD Dinner available WiFi ⚓ 9 🔒 **Notes** LB ⊗ 📧

Find out more about beds in B&Bs - see page 24

SHETLAND

LERWICK
Map 24 HU44

Glen Orchy House
★★★★ GUEST HOUSE

tel: 01595 692031 **fax:** 01595 692031 **20 Knab Rd ZE1 0AX**
email: glenorchy.house@virgin.net **web:** www.guesthouselerwick.com
dir: *Next to coastguard station*

This welcoming and well-presented house lies above the town with views over the Knab, and is within easy walking distance of the town centre. Bedrooms are modern in design and there is a choice of lounges with books and board games, one with an honesty bar. Substantial breakfasts are served, and the restaurant offers a delicious Thai menu.

Rooms 24 en suite (4 fmly) (4 GF) S £80; D £105* **Facilities** STV FTV Lounge TVL tea/coffee Dinner available Licensed WiFi **Parking** 10

ISLE OF SKYE

EDINBANE
Map 22 NG35

Shorefield House
★★★★ GUEST HOUSE

tel: 01470 582444 **Edinbane IV51 9PW**
email: stay@shorefield-house.com **web:** www.shorefieldhouse.com
dir: *12m from Portree & 8m from Dunvegan, off A850 into Edinbane, 1st on right*

Shorefield House stands in the village of Edinbane and looks out to Loch Greshornish. Bedrooms range from single to family options, and one of the ground-floor rooms has easy access. All rooms are thoughtfully equipped and have WiFi, fridges, safes, DVD and CD players. The choices at breakfast are impressive, and the house has a child-friendly garden.

Rooms 3 en suite (2 fmly) (2 GF) S £50-£60; D £89-£115* **Facilities** STV FTV DVD TVL tea/coffee WiFi 🔒 **Parking** 10 **Notes** LB ⊗ Closed Oct-Apr

| GLENDALE | Map 22 NG15 |

Six Willows B&B

★★ GUEST ACCOMMODATION

tel: 01470 511351 fax: 0872 115 3513 6-7 Feriniquarrie IV55 8WN
email: oceanandscotty@btinternet.com web: www.sixwillows-skye.co.uk
dir: A863, left at Dunvegan to Glendale. After 8m right at Ferinquarrie, left at T-junct, 1st house on left

Situated in sweeping countryside, Six Willows is in an ideal location for walkers and divers. There is a meditation room, and the proprietor offers a range of treatments and therapies. The menu is eclectic, and offers a notable range of dietary options, essentially vegetarian, but able to cater for most dietary preferences, including Halal.

Rooms 2 rms (1 en suite) (1 pri facs) (1 fmly) (2 GF) S £39-£51; D £54-£66* Facilities DVD iPod docking station Lounge tea/coffee Dinner available WiFi Therapies available Parking 3 Notes LB Closed 22 Dec-Feb

| STAFFIN | Map 22 NG46 |

The Glenview

★★★ ◉◉ RESTAURANT WITH ROOMS

tel: 01470 562248 Culnacnoc IV51 9JH
email: enquiries@glenviewskye.co.uk web: www.glenviewskye.co.uk
dir: 12m N of Portree on A855

The Glenview is located in one of the most beautiful parts of Skye with stunning sea views; close to the famous rock formation The Old Man of Storr. The individually styled bedrooms are very comfortable and front-facing rooms enjoy the dramatic views. Evening meals should not to be missed as the restaurant has a well deserved reputation for its treatment of locally sourced produce.

Rooms 5 en suite (1 GF) D £90-£120* Facilities tea/coffee Dinner available WiFi Parking 12 Notes ⊗ RS Sun & Mon closed No coaches

| STRUAN | Map 22 NG33 |

Premier Collection

Ullinish Country Lodge

★★★★★ ⌂ RESTAURANT WITH ROOMS

tel: 01470 572214 fax: 01470 572341 IV56 8FD
email: ullinish@theisleofskye.co.uk web: www.theisleofskye.co.uk
dir: Take A863 N. Lodge signed on left

Set in some of Scotland's most dramatic landscape, with views of the Black Cuillin and MacLeod's Tables, this lodge has lochs on three sides. Samuel Johnson and James Boswell stayed here in 1773 and were impressed with the hospitality even then. Hosts Brian and Pam hope to extend the same welcome to their guests today. As you would expect, all bedrooms have amazing views, and come with half-tester beds. The AA Rosette award for the Ullinish Country Lodge is currently suspended due to a change in chef. AA Rosettes may be awarded after the inspectors have assessed the food created by the new kitchen regime.

Rooms 6 en suite S £80-£110; D £110-£160* Facilities FTV Lounge tea/coffee Dinner available WiFi Parking 8 Notes LB ⊗ No Children 16yrs Closed 24 Dec-Jan No coaches

| UIG | Map 22 NG36 |

Woodbine House

★★★ GUEST ACCOMMODATION

tel: 01470 542243 & 07904 267561 IV51 9XP
email: contact@skyeactivities.co.uk web: www.skyeactivities.co.uk
dir: From Portree into Uig Bay, pass Ferry Inn, right onto A855 (Staffin road), house 300yds on right

Built in the late 19th century, Woodbine House occupies an elevated position overlooking Uig Bay and the surrounding countryside, and is well suited for walking and bird-watching enthusiasts. The ground-floor dining room has lovely sea views, as do the front-facing bedrooms.

Rooms 5 en suite (1 fmly) (1 GF) S £45-£58; D £66-£75* Facilities FTV TVL tea/coffee WiFi ♨ Archery Mountain Bike/Sea kayak hire Boat trips Parking 5 Notes LB ⊗ RS Nov-Feb long stays or group bookings only

Wales

ISLE OF ANGLESEY

BEAUMARIS   Map 14 SH67

Premier Collection

Ye Olde Bulls Head Inn

★★★★★ ◎◎◎ INN

tel: 01248 810329 **fax:** 01248 811294 **Castle St LL58 8AP**
email: info@bullsheadinn.co.uk **web:** www.bullsheadinn.co.uk
dir: *Located on Main St in town centre*

Both Charles Dickens and Samuel Johnson visited this inn, and the interior still features exposed beams and antique weaponry. Bedrooms are richly decorated and traditional, while The Townhouse, just across a side street, offers additional boutique bedrooms, each with vibrant decor. The food continues to attract praise in both the Loft Restaurant and the less formal Brasserie, and cask-conditioned ales are served in the traditional bar. Meeting and functions can be catered for.

Rooms 25 en suite 1 annexe en suite (2 fmly) (5 GF) S £82.50-£90; D £105-£175* **Facilities** FTV Lounge tea/coffee Dinner available Direct Dial Lift WiFi ⚓ 18 **Extras** Speciality toiletries **Parking** 10 **Notes** LB Closed 25 & 26 Dec No coaches

HOLYHEAD   Map 14 SH28

Blackthorn Farm

★★★★ Ⓐ GUEST ACCOMMODATION

tel: 01407 765262 **fax:** 01407 765336 **Penrhosfeilw, Trearddur Bay LL65 2LT**
email: enquiries@blackthornfarm.co.uk **web:** www.blackthornleisure.co.uk
dir: *A55 to Holyhead, take 1st exit at rdbt, turn immediately right between two pubs. At end of road, turn right, 0.5m on left*

Blackthorn Farm is a family-run establishment that is also a camping and touring site. Set in 18 peaceful acres on Holy Island, the farm enjoys outstanding panoramic views of the Irish Sea, Snowdonia, and coastal views of Anglesey. Within easy reach are a beach and coastal trails. A full Welsh breakfast is served. Please note pets are welcome.

Rooms 8 rms (6 en suite) (3 fmly) (1 GF) S £62-£78; D £75-£105* **Facilities** FTV DVD tea/coffee Licensed WiFi ⚓ **Conf** Thtr 25 Class 25 Board 20 **Parking** 10 **Notes** LB Closed 22-31 Dec

MENAI BRIDGE   Map 14 SH57

Bulkeley Arms

Ⓤ

tel: 01248 712715 **fax:** 01248 712718 **Uxbridge Square LL59 5DF**
email: tafarnwr@gmail.com **web:** www.bulkeleyarms.co.uk

Currently the rating for this establishment is not confirmed. This may be due to a change of ownership or because it has only recently joined the AA rating scheme.

Rooms 3 en suite (1 fmly) S £45-£55; D fr £65* **Facilities** FTV tea/coffee Dinner available Licensed WiFi Pool table ⚓ **Parking** 6 **Notes** LB

RHOSNEIGR   Map 14 SH37

Cefn Dref

★★★★ ⌂ BED AND BREAKFAST

tel: 01407 810714 **LL64 5JH**
email: bookings@cefndref.co.uk
dir: *A55 junct 5 (signed Rhosneigr), onto A4080 to Llanfaelog. Turn right signed Rhosneigr, 1st house on right after 30mph sign*

Enjoying stunning coastal views, this welcoming Edwardian shooting lodge has been transformed into a quality bed and breakfast. Bedrooms, complemented by smart, stylish bathrooms, are very well equipped, and contain extras including Freeview television and free WiFi. Breakfast is a memorable experience, with home-made or locally sourced produce on an extensive and imaginative menu. The town centre, with many dining options, is a ten-minute walk away, as is the sea.

Rooms 3 en suite (1 fmly) S £60-£70; D £80-£120* **Facilities** FTV DVD tea/coffee WiFi ⚓ 18 ⚓ **Extras** Speciality toiletries, fridges in rooms **Parking** 10 **Notes** ⊗ Closed Nov-Feb

CARDIFF

CARDIFF   Map 9 ST17

Innkeeper's Lodge Cardiff

★★★★ INN

tel: 029 2034 3443 & 0845 112 6178
The Beverley Hotel, 75-77 Cathedral Rd CF11 9PG
email: central.reservations@mbplc.com **web:** www.innkeeperslodge.com/cardiff
dir: *M4 junct 29 (from E) onto A48. Left onto A4119, 0.5m left again (Cathedral Rd). Lodge on right*

Located in the Pontcanna district of Cardiff, this former Victorian villa has been tastefully restored as an inn. The refurbished modern bedrooms are equipped to a good standard offering a range of extras for both the business and leisure traveller. The popular bar and restaurant offers home-cooked classics, with a number of real ales on tap. Just a short walk away are the Swalec Stadium, Cardiff University and the Millennium Centre.

Rooms 17 en suite (9 fmly) **Facilities** FTV tea/coffee WiFi **Notes** ⊗ No coaches

CARMARTHENSHIRE

CARMARTHEN   Map 8 SN42

Sarnau Mansion

★★★★ GUEST ACCOMMODATION

tel: 01267 211404 **fax:** 01267 211404 **Llysonnen Rd SA33 5DZ**
email: d.fernihough@btinternet.com **web:** www.sarnaumansion.co.uk
dir: *5m W of Carmarthen. Exit A40 onto B4298, becomes Bancyfelin road (signed Bancyfelin), Sarnau Mansion on right*

Located west of Carmarthen in 16 acres of grounds and gardens, including a tennis court, this large Grade II listed, late Georgian house retains much original character and is stylishly decorated. There is a lounge with a log fire, an elegant dining room, and spacious bedrooms with stunning rural views.

Rooms 4 rms (3 en suite) (1 pri facs) S £39-£50; D £80-£90 **Facilities** DVD TVL tea/coffee Dinner available WiFi ⚓ 18 ⚓ **Parking** 10 **Notes** ⊗ No Children 5yrs

FELINGWM UCHAF   Map 8 SN52

Allt Y Golau Farmhouse (SN510261)

★★★★ 🏠 FARMHOUSE

tel: 01267 290455 **Allt Y Golau Uchaf SA32 7BB**
email: alltygolau@btinternet.com **web:** www.alltygolau.com
dir: A40 onto B4310, N for 2m. 1st on left after Felingwm Uchaf

This delightful Georgian farmhouse has been furnished and decorated to a high standard by the present owners, and enjoys panoramic views over the Tywi Valley to the Black Mountains beyond. Guests are welcome to take a relaxing walk through two acres of mature garden. Many thoughtful extras are provided in the comfortable bedrooms, and there is a separate lounge. Breakfast is provided in the cosy dining room and served around a communal table.

Rooms 3 rms (2 en suite) (1 pri facs) (2 GF) S £45; D £70 **Facilities** TVL tea/coffee WiFi �— **Extras** Speciality toiletries, snacks **Parking** 3 **Notes** ⊗ Closed 20 Dec–2 Jan 🐾 2 acres small holding

LAUGHARNE   Map 8 SN31

Broadway Country House

★★★★ 🏠 GUEST ACCOMMODATION

tel: 01994 427969 **Broadway SA33 4NU**

This family-run business offers a relaxed and peaceful retreat. Set in seven acres of grounds and gardens it has delightful views over Carmarthen Bay and the Gower Peninsula. Bedrooms and bathrooms are well decorated and furnished and include some welcome extras. Both dinner and breakfast offer a range of carefully prepared quality ingredients and are a highlight of any visit.

Rooms 8 en suite **Facilities** Dinner available

LLANARTHNE   Map 8 SN51

Premier Collection

Llwyn Helyg Country House

★★★★★ 🏠 BED AND BREAKFAST

tel: 01558 668778 & 07794 064834 **SA32 8HJ**
email: enquiries@llwynhelygcountryhouse.co.uk
web: www.llwynhelygcountryhouse.co.uk
dir: A48 onto B4310, at rdbt at entrance of National Botanic Gardens of Wales take 1st exit (B4310). After 0.3m turn right at farm along lane then sharp left, 1m on left

The owners of Llwyn Helyg, a newly-built 'country house', have used the finest quality materials to create this luxury bed and breakfast accommodation. Situated in three acres of landscaped gardens and surrounded by countryside, it's on the outskirts of Llanarthne, midway between Carmarthen and Llandeilo. All the individually designed, en suite bedrooms have 6-foot wide beds and luxurious Vi-Spring mattresses. Private parking is available. Llwyn Helyg was the AA Guest Accommodation of the Year for Wales 2013-14.

Rooms 3 en suite D £125-£149* **Facilities** FTV DVD iPod docking station Lounge TVL tea/coffee WiFi �— 🌊 Therapy/Holistic treatment room **Extras** Speciality toiletries, fruit, snacks - free **Conf** Max 6 Board 6 **Parking** 10 **Notes** LB ⊗ No Children 16yrs Closed Xmas & New Year

LLANDOVERY   Map 9 SN73

Llanerchindda Farm

★★★ 🏠 GUEST HOUSE

tel: 01550 750274 **fax:** 01550 750300 **Cynghordy SA20 0NB**
email: info@cambrianway.com **web:** www.cambrianway.com
dir: A483 Llandovery to Builth Wells road, after 40mph sign turn left at brown tourist sign (Llanerchindda), 2.75m to farm

Set in 50 acres of Welsh countryside with spectacular views over the Black Mountains and the Brecon Beacons, this farmhouse-style accommodation is the ideal base for various activities including walking, fishing, quad bike riding and bird watching. Bedrooms and bathrooms are comfortable and guests also have use of the lounge. In addition to a substantial breakfast, dinner is also available by prior arrangement and features delicious home cooking.

Rooms 9 en suite (1 fmly) (2 GF) S £38-£42.50; D £76-£85* **Facilities** FTV Lounge TVL tea/coffee Dinner available Licensed WiFi 🎣 18 Fishing 🌊 Clay pigeon shooting Quad bike trekking **Parking** 31 **Notes** LB Closed 2-16 Jan

LLANWRDA   Map 9 SN73

Premier Collection

Tyllwyd Hir Bed & Breakfast

★★★★★ 🏠 BED AND BREAKFAST

tel: 01550 777362 & 07850 330218 **Tyllwyd Hir SA19 8AS**
email: info@bandbwestwales.co.uk **web:** www.bandbwestwales.co.uk
dir: From Llanwrda on A482 Lampeter Rd for 1.5m, entrance on right with green name sign. 0.5m along lane through neighbouring farmland

A warm welcome from hosts Philip and Jennifer is promised at this luxury bed and breakfast, which has a superb setting with stunning views out across the Brecon Beacons. Recently renovated, the old building has been brought back to life, yet has retained many of its original features. Set near the village of Llanwrda, it is within easy reach of Lampeter and Landovery. Bedrooms are very comfortable and modern with a host of extras provided. All three bedrooms have en suite facilities of high quality. Breakfast is a highlight of any stay, with well-prepared fresh ingredients, including eggs from Tyllwyd Hir's own hens.

Rooms 3 en suite **Facilities** FTV DVD TVL tea/coffee WiFi 🌊 **Extras** Fruit, chocolates - free; robes, slippers **Parking** 10 **Notes** LB ⊗ No Children RS wknds & BHs 2 nights stay min

ST CLEARS
Map 8 SN21

Premier Collection

Coedllys Country House

★★★★★ BED AND BREAKFAST

tel: 01994 231455 **fax:** 01994 231441 **Coedllys Uchaf, Llangynin SA33 4JY**
email: coedllys@btinternet.com **web:** www.coedllyscountryhouse.co.uk
dir: A40 St Clears rdbt, take 3rd exit, at lights turn left. After 100yds turn right, 3m to Llangynin, pass village sign. 30mph sign on left, turn immediately down track (private drive)

Set in a peaceful valley, Coedllys is the home of the Harbers, who make visitors feel like honoured guests. Bedrooms are lavishly furnished, and the thoughtful and useful extras make a stay most memorable. There is a cosy, well-furnished lounge, and an extensive breakfast choice is served in the pleasant dining room. A further cottage-style annexe, suitable as a self-catering let, is also available. For the energetic there is a fitness suite, but guests can also relax in the sauna or small indoor pool.

Rooms 3 en suite 1 annexe en suite (1 GF) D £90-£110 **Facilities** FTV DVD iPod docking station Lounge tea/coffee WiFi ✪ Sauna Gym ✚ **Extras** Speciality toiletries, home-made biscuits - free **Parking** 6 **Notes** LB No Children 12yrs Closed 22-28 Dec

Lolfa Cynin

★★★★ GUEST ACCOMMODATION

tel: 01994 232773 & 231516 **fax:** 01994 232773
Llety Cynin Leisure Club, Llangynin Rd SA33 4JR
email: info@lolfacynin.co.uk **web:** www.lolfa-cynin.co.uk
dir: A40 to St Clears, pass slip road to rdbt. Take 3rd exit to St Clears. Left at lights, turn towards Llangynin. 1.4m on right

Peacefully located on a working dairy farm, this converted coach house has well equipped bedrooms and very comfortable beds. The Wales Coast Path and the home town of Dylan Thomas are just a short drive away. Guests can enjoy the use of the attached leisure club with pool and sauna, and a coffee lounge with snacks is also open during the day. Breakfast is served in the comfortable dining room with an excellent selection of well-prepared dishes.

Rooms 8 en suite (5 fmly) (1 GF) S £55.50-£70; D £74-£89* **Facilities** FTV DVD Lounge TVL tea/coffee Licensed WiFi ✪ Sauna Gym Spa treatments availabe **Conf** Max 60 Thtr 60 Class 40 Board 30 **Parking** 40 **Notes** LB ✷ Closed 17-28 Dec

CEREDIGION

ABERAERON
Map 8 SN46

Premier Collection

Ty Mawr Mansion

★★★★★ ◉◉ 🍴 RESTAURANT WITH ROOMS

tel: 01570 470033 **Cilcennin SA48 8DB**
email: info@tymawrmansion.co.uk **web:** www.tymawrmansion.co.uk
dir: On A482 (Lampeter to Aberaeron road), 4m from Aberaeron

Surrounded by rolling countryside in its own naturally beautiful gardens, this fine country mansion house is a haven of peace and tranquillity. Careful renovation has restored it to its former glory and, combined with lush fabrics, top quality beds and sumptuous furnishings, the accommodation is spacious, superbly equipped and very comfortable. Award-winning chefs create mouth-watering dishes from local and seasonal produce. There is even a 27-seat cinema. Martin and Cath McAlpine offer the sort of welcome which makes every visit to Ty Mawr a memorable one.

Rooms 8 en suite 1 annexe en suite (1 fmly) (2 GF) **Facilities** FTV DVD Lounge tea/coffee Dinner available Direct Dial WiFi Fishing ✚ Cinema **Extras** Speciality toiletries, home-made biscuits, robes **Conf** Max 25 Thtr 25 Class 25 Board 16 **Parking** 20 **Notes** ✷ No Children 12yrs Closed 28 Dec-10 Jan No coaches Civ Wed 30

Premier Collection

Feathers Royal

★★★★★ 🍴 INN

tel: 01545 571750 **fax:** 01545 571760 **Alban Square SA46 0AQ**
email: enquiries@feathersroyal.co.uk **web:** www.feathersroyal.co.uk
dir: A482, Lampeter Road, Feathers Royal opposite recreation grounds

This is a family-run inn, ideally located in the picturesque Georgian town of Aberaeron. It is a charming Grade II listed property, built in 1815 as a traditional coaching house, and later transformed to coincide with the town's bicentenary celebrations. Accommodation is very comfortable with modern fittings and accessories provided, and the public areas are well appointed. There is a large suite available for private or business functions. A friendly welcome can be expected.

Rooms 13 en suite (2 fmly) S £79; D £120* **Facilities** FTV Lounge tea/coffee Dinner available Direct Dial WiFi ✚ **Conf** Max 200 Thtr 200 Class 100 Board 50 **Parking** 20 **Notes** LB ✷ Civ Wed 200

The Castle

★★★★ 🍴 INN

tel: 01545 570205 **fax:** 01545 571442 **Market St SA46 0AU**
email: castle_hotel@btconnect.com **web:** www.the-castlehotel.co.uk
dir: On A487, in centre of town

The Castle is a Grade II listed building in the coastal town of Aberaeron, situated close to many walks including the Llanerchaeron Trail. The ground-floor café bar serves food daily, and the restaurant menu can also be offered downstairs in the evening for less-mobile customers. The modern bedrooms have flat-screen TVs, WiFi, Egyptian linen and duck down duvets.

Rooms 6 en suite (1 fmly) **Facilities** FTV tea/coffee Dinner available WiFi ✚ **Conf** Max 45 Thtr 30 Class 40 Board 20 **Notes** LB

Aromatherapy Reflexology Centre

★★★ BED AND BREAKFAST

tel: 01974 202581 **The Barn House, Pennant Rd SY23 5LZ**
email: aromareflex@googlemail.com **web:** www.aromatherapy-breaks-wales.co.uk
dir: S of Aberystwyth to Llanon, leave village, turn left at 40mph sign. 2nd left to Barn House

Expect a warm welcome from this family-run bed and breakfast where Welsh is spoken. Set in its own grounds in a tranquil position with lovely views of Cardigan Bay. Bedrooms are comfortable and smartly presented, and there is a choice of traditional, vegetarian or vegan breakfasts. Aromatherapy and reflexology are available at the centre.

Rooms 3 rms (2 en suite) (1 pri facs) S £39-£45; D £69-£75 **Facilities** FTV DVD tea/coffee WiFi 🛁 Massage/Reflexology by appointment **Parking** 7 **Notes** LB 🖂

ABERYSTWYTH	Map 8 SN58

Premier Collection

Awel-Deg

★★★★★ BED AND BREAKFAST

tel: 01970 880681 **Capel Bangor SY23 3LR**
email: awel-deg@tiscali.co.uk **web:** www.awel-deg.co.uk
dir: 5m E of Aberystwyth. On A44 in Capel Bangor

Located five miles from the historic university town of Aberystwyth, this attractive bungalow, set in pretty gardens, provides high standards of hospitality, comfort and facilities. Immaculately maintained throughout, spacious bedrooms are equipped with a wealth of thoughtful extras and smart, modern en suite shower rooms. Comprehensive breakfasts are served at one table in the elegant dining room and a choice of lounges is available.

Rooms 2 en suite (2 GF) D £59* **Facilities** FTV TVL tea/coffee WiFi **Parking** 8 **Notes** LB 🛇 No Children 11yrs Closed 20-30 Dec 🖂

Premier Collection

Nanteos Mansion

★★★★★ 🏛 🍽 RESTAURANT WITH ROOMS

tel: 01970 600522 **Rhydyfelin SY23 4LU**
email: info@nanteos.com **web:** www.nanteos.com
dir: A487 onto A4120 signed Devil's Bridge then immediately right onto B4340 towards Trawscoed. Take 1st left fork, along narrow road, Nanteos Mansion signed

This historic mansion sits in delightfully peaceful countryside. Staff are keen to please, and proud of the cuisine served here. The restaurant offers good menu choices and a very pleasant wine list, and retains many of the grand features of the original house. The well-appointed bedrooms are splendid, and many are very spacious. Public areas are also roomy, and breakfast is taken in the Buttery, which was once the original kitchen.

Rooms 10 en suite 4 annexe en suite (4 fmly) (3 GF) **Facilities** FTV iPod docking station Lounge tea/coffee Dinner available Direct Dial WiFi 🍴 🎣 18 Fishing **Extras** Speciality toiletries, fridge, robes, welcome gift **Conf** Max 80 Thtr 80 Class 40 Board 40 **Parking** 60 **Notes** LB Civ Wed 100

Bodalwyn Guest House

★★★★ GUEST HOUSE

tel: 01970 612578 **fax:** 01970 639261 **Queen's Av SY23 2EG**
email: enquiries@bodalwyn.co.uk **web:** www.bodalwyn.co.uk
dir: 500yds N of town centre. Exit A487 (Northgate St) into North Rd to end

Located a short walk from the promenade, this imposing Edwardian house, built for a college professor, has been appointed to provide high standards of comfort and good facilities. Smart modern bathrooms complement the spacious bedrooms, which are equipped with a wealth of thoughtful extras; family rooms are available. Comprehensive Welsh breakfasts are served in the elegant conservatory-dining room.

Rooms 7 en suite (2 fmly) S £45-£55; D £70-£76* **Facilities** FTV DVD tea/coffee WiFi **Notes** 🛇 Closed 22 Dec-2 Jan 🖂

Glyn-Garth

★★★★ GUEST HOUSE

tel: 01970 615050 **South Rd SY23 1JS**
email: glyngarth@aol.com **web:** www.glyngarth.cjb.net
dir: In town centre. Off A487 into South Rd, off South Promenade

Privately owned and personally run by the same family for over 50 years, this immaculately maintained guest house provides a range of thoughtfully furnished bedrooms with smart modern bathrooms. Breakfast is served in the attractive dining room and a lounge is also available.

Rooms 10 rms (6 en suite) (2 fmly) (1 GF) S £33-£60; D £66-£82* **Facilities** STV FTV TVL tea/coffee WiFi 🎣 18 🛁 **Parking** 2 **Notes** 🛇 🖂

Yr Hafod

★★★★ GUEST HOUSE

tel: 01970 617579 **1 South Marine Ter SY23 1JX**
email: johnyrhafod@aol.com **web:** www.yrhafod.co.uk
dir: On south promenade between harbour & castle

Yr Hafod is an immaculately maintained end of terrace Victorian house with a commanding location overlooking South Bay. The spacious bedrooms are comfortable, some with delightful sea views and many have particularly well-appointed bathrooms. Breakfast is served in the attractive front-facing dining room.

Rooms 6 rms (3 en suite) S £33-£35; D £66-£88* **Facilities** STV FTV TVL tea/coffee WiFi 🛁 **Extras** Chocolates, mineral water - complimentary **Parking** 1 **Notes** 🛇 Closed Xmas & New Year 🖂

ABERYSTWYTH *continued*

Y Gelli

★★★ GUEST HOUSE

tel: 01970 617834 **Dolau, Lovesgrove SY23 3HP**
email: pat@plasdolau.co.uk **web:** www.plasdolau.co.uk
dir: *Off A44 2.75m E of town centre*

Set in spacious grounds on the town's outskirts, this modern detached house contains a range of practical furnished bedrooms, with three further rooms available in an adjacent Victorian property. Comprehensive breakfasts are served in the attractive dining room with evening meals available on request. A comfortable lounge is also available for guests' use.

Rooms 6 rms (3 en suite) 3 annexe rms 1 annexe en suite (3 fmly) (1 GF)
Facilities TVL TV8B tea/coffee Dinner available Snooker Pool table Table tennis
Stabling can be provided **Conf** Thtr 30 Class 30 Board 20 **Parking** 20 **Notes** ⊗

NEW QUAY   Map 8 SN35

Cambrian Inn & Restaurant

★★★ INN

tel: 01545 560295 **New Rd SA45 9SE**
email: cambrianhotel@gmail.com **web:** www.cambrianhotel-newquay.co.uk
dir: *From A487 at Llanarth onto B4342 for 2m*

Situated in a quiet location on the outskirts of popular New Quay, this family-run inn offers a good selection of dishes at both lunch and dinner. Bedrooms include a range of sizes and are all located on the first floor. Breakfast is served in the conservatory restaurant, and a garden with outdoor seating is also available.

Rooms 4 en suite S £40-£45; D £60-£70* **Facilities** FTV TVL tea/coffee Dinner available WiFi ⚓ **Extras** Trouser press **Parking** 9 **Notes** LB RS Jan-15 Mar bar & restaurant closed

PONTERWYD   Map 9 SN78

Ffynnon Cadno Guest House

★★★★ 🅰 BED AND BREAKFAST

tel: 01970 890224 **SY23 3AD**
email: ffynnoncadno@btinternet.com **web:** www.ffynnoncadno.co.uk
dir: *Adjacent to A44 (Aberystwyth to Llangurig road), on Aberystwyth side of village*

In the foothills of the Cambrian mountains, Ffynnon Cadno has large gardens and is just outside the small village of Ponterwyd, a short drive from Aberystwyth. Ffynnon Cadno is ideal for walkers, cyclists or anyone who enjoys beautiful countryside. The three rooms include all expected amenities, including TV with Freeview channels, DVD player, WiFi, and king-size beds.

Rooms 3 rms (2 en suite) (1 pri facs) (1 fmly) S £20-£35; D £40-£70* **Facilities** STV FTV DVD TVL tea/coffee WiFi Pool table ⚓ **Parking** 6 **Notes** ⊗ No Children 3yrs

TREGARON   Map 8 SN65

Y Talbot

★★★★ ⚍ INN

tel: 01974 298208 **The Square SY25 6JL**
email: info@ytalbot.com **web:** www.ytalbot.com
dir: *From Lampeter or Aberystwyth on A485, in Tregaron turn opposite NatWest, 100yds in Square*

Located in the heart of this quiet town, Y Talbot has been appointed to provide a range of very high-quality bedrooms and bathrooms with luxury showers. Some smaller standard rooms are also available. There is a traditional bar serving real ales and a contemporary-style main restaurant and lounge. Dinner offers a very good selection of dishes using quality produce.

Rooms 11 en suite 2 annexe en suite (3 fmly) (1 GF) S £60-£90; D £80-£130*
Facilities FTV iPod docking station Lounge tea/coffee Dinner available WiFi ⌁ 9 ⚓
Drying room **Extras** Mineral water, home-made shortcake **Conf** Max 120 Thtr 80
Class 120 Board 40 **Parking** 7 **Notes** LB Civ Wed 140

CONWY

ABERGELE   Map 14 SH97

Premier Collection

The Kinmel Arms

★★★★★ ⚍ ◉◉ RESTAURANT WITH ROOMS

tel: 01745 832207 **fax:** 01745 822044 **The Village, St George LL22 9BP**
email: info@thekinmelarms.co.uk **web:** www.thekinmelarms.co.uk
dir: *From A55 junct 24a to St George. E on A55, junct 24. 1st left to Rhuddlan, 1st right into St George. 2nd right*

This converted 17th-century coaching inn stands close to the church in the village of St George, in the beautiful Elwy Valley. The popular restaurant specialises in produce from Wales and north-west England, and friendly and helpful staff ensure you will have an enjoyable stay. The four attractive suites are luxuriously furnished and feature stunning bathrooms. Substantial continental breakfasts are served in the rooms.

Rooms 4 en suite (2 GF) D £115-£175 **Facilities** STV DVD Lounge tea/coffee Dinner available ⌁ 18 ⚓ **Extras** Speciality toiletries, fruit, snacks - free **Parking** 50 **Notes** LB No Children 16yrs Closed 25 Dec & 1 Jan RS Sun & Mon closed (ex BHs) No coaches

The Black Lion

★★★★ ⌂ INN

tel: 01745 720205 **Swan Square, Llanfair Talhaiarn LL22 8RY**
web: www.theblacklionnorthwales.co.uk

A warm Welsh welcome awaits you at this country inn. Well-cooked, hearty meals are served in the restaurant or in the more casual bar by the fire. Local real ales feature on the bar, alongside much local produce on the menus. Bedrooms are very comfortable with thoughtful extras.

Rooms 5 en suite (2 fmly) S £70; D £75-£85* **Facilities** FTV tea/coffee Dinner available WiFi Pool table **Parking** 15 **Notes** ⊗

BETWS-Y-COED	Map 14 SH75

Premier Collection

Penmachno Hall

★★★★★ ⌂ GUEST ACCOMMODATION

tel: 01690 760410 **fax:** 01690 760410 **Penmachno LL24 0PU**
email: stay@penmachnohall.co.uk **web:** www.penmachnohall.co.uk
dir: 4m S of Betws-y-Coed. A5 onto B4406 to Penmachno, over bridge, right at Eagles pub signed Ty Mawr. 500yds at stone bridge

Set in more than two acres of mature grounds including a mountain stream and woodland, this impressive Victorian rectory provides high standards of comfort and good facilities. Stylish decor and quality furnishings highlight the many original features throughout the ground-floor areas, and the bedrooms have a wealth of thoughtful extras. Alongside the main building is a superb two-bedroom, self-catering unit in a former coach house. Pre-booked set menu, party-style evening meals are served on Saturday nights, while buffet-style meals are served Tuesday through Friday.

Rooms 3 en suite D £90-£100 **Facilities** STV DVD Lounge tea/coffee Dinner available Licensed WiFi ⚓ **Extras** Fruit - complimentary; robes **Parking** 5 **Notes** LB ⊗ Closed Xmas & New Year RS Sun-Mon no evening meals

Afon View Guest House

★★★★ GUEST HOUSE

tel: 01690 710726 **fax:** 01690 710726 **Holyhead Rd LL24 0AN**
email: welcome@afon-view.co.uk **web:** www.afon-view.co.uk
dir: On A5, 150yds E of HSBC bank

A warm welcome is assured at this elegant Victorian house, located between Waterloo Bridge and the village centre. Bedrooms are equipped with lots of thoughtful extras, and day rooms include an attractive dining room and comfortable guest lounge.

Rooms 7 en suite (1 fmly) **Facilities** FTV Lounge tea/coffee WiFi ⚓ **Parking** 7 **Notes** LB ⊗ No Children 5yrs Closed 23-26 Dec

Bryn Bella Guest House

★★★★ GUEST HOUSE

tel: 01690 710627 **Lon Muriau, Llanrwst Rd LL24 0HD**
email: welcome@bryn-bella.co.uk **web:** www.bryn-bella.co.uk
dir: A5 onto A470, 0.5m right onto driveway signed Bryn Bella

Located in an elevated position on the town's outskirts, with stunning views of the surrounding countryside, this elegant Victorian house provides a range of thoughtfully equipped bedrooms and smart, modern bathrooms. A fine collection of memorabilia adorns the public areas, which include an attractive dining room and a comfortable lounge. A warm welcome is assured and guest services include a daily weather forecast.

Rooms 5 en suite (1 GF) D £70-£85 **Facilities** FTV DVD TVL tea/coffee WiFi ⚓ **Parking** 6 **Notes** LB ⊗ No Children 16yrs

Cwmanog Isaf Farm (SH799546)

★★★★ FARMHOUSE

tel: 01690 710225 & 07808 421634 **Fairy Glen LL24 0SL**
email: h.hughes165@btinternet.com **web:** www.cwmanogisaffarmholidays.co.uk
dir: 1m S of Betws-y-Coed off A470 before stone bridge, 500yds on farm lane

Peacefully located in 30 acres of undulating land, where the Fairy Glen (a well known beauty spot on the River Conwy) can be found, this 200-year-old house on a working livestock farm has been restored to provide comfortable, thoughtfully furnished bedrooms. Breakfasts use home-reared or organic produce. The property's elevated position provides stunning views of the surrounding countryside.

Rooms 3 rms (2 en suite) (1 pri facs) (1 GF) S £50-£65; D £65-£75* **Facilities** STV Lounge tea/coffee ⚓ **Parking** 4 **Notes** ⊗ No Children 15yrs Closed Nov-15 Mar 🐾 30 acres sheep

Park Hill

★★★★ GUEST HOUSE

tel: 01690 710540 **fax:** 0872 111 6197 **Llanrwst Rd LL24 0HD**
email: welcome@park-hill.co.uk **web:** www.park-hill.co.uk
dir: 0.5m N of Betws-y-Coed on A470 (Llanrwst road)

A warm welcome is assured at this guest house, which benefits from a peaceful location overlooking the village and valley beyond. Well-equipped bedrooms, including one with a four-poster, offer comfortable beds and thoughtful extras. There are a choice of lounges, a heated swimming pool, sauna and whirlpool bath for guests' use.

Rooms 8 en suite S £60-£90; D £66-£99.50* **Facilities** FTV DVD Lounge tea/coffee WiFi 🏊 ♨ 9 Sauna ⚓ **Parking** 11 **Notes** LB ⊗ No Children 8yrs

Ty Gwyn Inn

★★★ ⌂ INN

tel: 01690 710383 **fax:** 01690 710383 **LL24 0SG**
email: mratcl1050@aol.com **web:** www.tygwynhotel.co.uk
dir: Junct of A5 & A470, by Waterloo Bridge

Situated on the edge of the village, close to the Waterloo Bridge, this historic coaching inn retains many original features. Quality furnishings and memorabilia enhance its intrinsic charm. Bedrooms, some with antique beds, are equipped with thoughtful extras. Imaginative food is provided in the cosy bars and the restaurant.

Rooms 13 rms (10 en suite) (3 fmly) (1 GF) **Facilities** TVL tea/coffee Dinner available WiFi **Parking** 14 **Notes** Closed Mon-Wed in Jan

CAPEL CURIG
Map 14 SH75

Bryn Tyrch Inn
★★★★ ⊛ INN

tel: 01690 720223 & 07855 762791 **LL24 0EL**
email: info@bryntyrchinn.co.uk **web:** www.bryntyrchinn.co.uk
dir: *On A5 at top end of village*

Dating from the early Victorian period, this former posting house has been sympathetically refurbished to provide public areas of real character and stylish modern bedrooms with smart en suite bath or shower rooms. Hog and lamb roasts are a feature on certain days throughout the year and the enthusiastic proprietors, assisted by a friendly team, are constantly making improvements to ensure a visit to Bryn Tyrch is a memorable one.

Rooms 11 en suite S £65-£90; D £79-£120* **Facilities** FTV Lounge tea/coffee Dinner available WiFi ♨ 9 Drying facilities **Extras** Home-made biscuits **Parking** 30 **Notes** LB Closed 15-27 Dec & 3-20 Jan RS Feb-Mar open wknds only & school hols No coaches Civ Wed 75

COLWYN BAY
Map 14 SH87

Bryn Woodlands House
★★★★ GUEST HOUSE

tel: 01492 532320 **fax:** 01492 532320 **14 Woodland Rd LL29 7DT**
email: enquiries@brynwoodlandshouse.co.uk **web:** www.brynwoodlandshouse.co.uk

Opposite the parish church, on a tree-lined road within a few minutes' walk of the town centre, this elegant late Victorian house has been sympathetically renovated to provide good levels of comfort and facilities. Bedrooms are well equipped and include en suite shower rooms, and a fine collection of artwork and ornaments is on display throughout the interior. In addition to comprehensive breakfasts, dinner is available by arrangement and a warm welcome is assured.

Rooms 8 en suite (1 fmly) (1 GF) S £55-£70; D £65-£85* **Facilities** STV FTV DVD TVL tea/coffee Dinner available Licensed WiFi ♨ **Parking** 7 **Notes** ⊗

The Northwood
★★★★ GUEST HOUSE

tel: 01492 549931 **47 Rhos Rd, Rhos-on-Sea LL28 4RS**
email: welcome@thenorthwood.co.uk **web:** www.thenorthwood.co.uk
dir: *Exit at A55 junct 22 (Old Colwyn). At T-junct right, to next T-junct (facing sea). Left, pass pier, opposite harbour left into Rhos Rd. On left adjacent to church*

A short walk from the seafront and shops, The Northwood is a constantly improving guest house with a warm and friendly atmosphere and many regular guests. The bedrooms are furnished in a modern style, and the freshly prepared meals utilising fresh produce (some home-grown), can be enjoyed in the spacious dining room that overlooks the pretty patio.

Rooms 11 rms (10 en suite) (1 pri facs) (3 fmly) (2 GF) **Facilities** TVL tea/coffee Dinner available Licensed WiFi **Conf** Max 20 Class 20 Board 20 **Parking** 12

Whitehall Guest House
★★★★ GUEST HOUSE

tel: 01492 547296 **51 Cayley Promenade, Rhos-on-Sea LL28 4EP**
email: mossd.cymru@virgin.net **web:** www.whitehall-hotel.co.uk
dir: *A55 onto B5115 (Brompton Av), right at rdbt into Whitehall Rd to seafront*

Overlooking the Rhos-on-Sea promenade, this popular, family-run establishment is convenient for the shops and local amenities. Attractively appointed bedrooms include family rooms and a room on the ground floor; all benefit from an excellent

range of facilities such as video and CD players as well as air-conditioning. Facilities include a bar and a foyer lounge. Home-cooked dinners are available.

Rooms 12 en suite (4 fmly) (1 GF) S £32; D £64-£80* **Facilities** FTV DVD TVL tea/coffee Dinner available Direct Dial Licensed WiFi ♨ **Parking** 5 **Notes** LB

CONWY
Map 14 SH77

Premier Collection

The Groes Inn
★★★★★ ⊛ INN

tel: 01492 650545 **fax:** 01492 650855 **Tyn-y-Groes LL32 8TN**
email: enquiries@thegroes.com **web:** www.groesinn.com
dir: *A55, over Old Conwy Bridge, 1st left through Castle Walls on B5106 (Trefriw Road), 2m on right*

Located in the picturesque Conwy Valley, this historic inn dates from 1573 and was the first licensed house in Wales. The exterior and gardens have an abundance of shrubs and seasonal flowers that create an impressive welcome, which is matched by the friendly and professional staff. Public areas are decorated and furnished with flair to highlight the many period features. The spacious bedrooms, in renovated outbuildings, are equipped with a wealth of thoughtful extras; many have balconies overlooking the countryside.

Rooms 14 en suite (1 fmly) (6 GF) S £100-£175; D £125-£200* **Facilities** FTV tea/coffee Dinner available Direct Dial WiFi ♨ 18 Petanque **Conf** Max 20 Thtr 20 Class 20 Board 20 **Parking** 100 **Notes** LB Civ Wed 100

DWYGYFYLCHI
Map 14 SH77

The Gladstone
★★★★ INN

tel: 01492 623231 **Ygborwen Rd LL34 6PS**
email: thegladstonepub@hotmail.co.uk **web:** www.thegladstone.co.uk
dir: *A55 junct 16 turn left, then left again towards Dwygyfylchi, 0.25m on right*

The Gladstone offers modern seaside accommodation; the comfortable, stylish bedrooms are individually designed, equipped with plenty of thoughtful extras and luxurious bathrooms. The bar and front bedrooms have views of Puffin Island and Anglesey; there is seating outside for alfresco dining and for enjoying the sunsets. Off-road parking is available.

Rooms 6 en suite S £60-£80; D £70-£120 **Facilities** FTV Lounge TVL tea/coffee Dinner available WiFi ♨ **Conf** Max 20 Board 20 **Parking** 25 **Notes** LB ⊗ Civ Wed 40

LLANDUDNO
Map 14 SH78

Premier Collection

Bryn Derwen
★★★★★ BED AND BREAKFAST

tel: 01492 876804 **fax:** 01492 876804 **34 Abbey Rd LL30 2EE**
email: brynderwen34@btinternet.com **web:** www.bryn-derwen.co.uk
dir: *A470 into Llandudno, left at The Parade promenade to cenotaph, left, over rdbt, 4th right into York Rd, Bryn Derwen at top*

A warm welcome is assured at this impressive Victorian house, which retains original tiled floors and some fine stained-glass windows. Quality decor and furnishings highlight the historic charm of the property, which is apparent in the sumptuous lounges and attractive dining room, the setting for imaginative breakfasts. Bedrooms are equipped with a wealth of thoughtful extras.

Rooms 9 en suite (1 fmly) S £50-£56; D £78-£100* **Facilities** FTV DVD iPod docking station Lounge TVL tea/coffee Licensed WiFi ⚓ 18 🔒 **Extras** Speciality toiletries, water, chocolates - free **Parking** 9 **Notes** LB ⊗ No Children 12yrs Closed Dec-Jan

Abbey Lodge

★★★★ GUEST HOUSE

tel: 01492 878042 **14 Abbey Rd LL30 2EA**
email: enquiries@abbeylodgeuk.com **web:** www.abbeylodgeuk.com
dir: A546 to N end of town, into Clement Av, right into Abbey Rd

This impressive Victorian villa is on a leafy avenue within easy walking distance of the promenade. Abbey Lodge has been lovingly restored, and the stylish decor and furniture add to its charm. Bedrooms come with a wealth of thoughtful extras, and there is a sumptuous lounge. Breakfasts are served around the elegant dining table.

Rooms 4 en suite S £45-£50; D £75-£80* **Facilities** FTV Lounge tea/coffee WiFi 🔒 **Extras** Speciality toiletries, chocolates **Parking** 4 **Notes** ⊗ Closed Dec-1 Mar 🐾

Brigstock House

★★★★ GUEST HOUSE

tel: 01492 876416 **fax:** 01492 879292 **1 St David's Place LL30 2UG**
email: brigstockguesthouse@gmail.com **web:** www.brigstockhouse.co.uk
dir: A470 into Llandudno, left into The Parade promenade, left into Lloyd St, left into St David's Rd & left into St David's Place

This impressive Edwardian property is in a quiet residential cul-de-sac within easy walking distance of the seafront and central shopping area. The attractive bedrooms are well equipped, and a comfortable lounge is available. Substantial breakfasts and dinners, by arrangement, are served in the elegant dining room.

Rooms 8 en suite S £38-£55; D £70-£90* **Facilities** FTV DVD TVL tea/coffee Dinner available Licensed WiFi 🔒 **Parking** 6 **Notes** LB ⊗ No Children 12yrs Closed Dec-Jan

The Cliffbury

★★★★ GUEST ACCOMMODATION

tel: 01492 877224 **34 St David's Rd LL30 2UH**
email: info@thecliffbury.co.uk **web:** www.thecliffbury.co.uk

Located on a leafy avenue within easy walking distance of the town centre, this elegant Edwardian house provides high standards of comfort. Bedrooms, furnished in minimalist style, provide a range of practical and thoughtful extras and smart modern bath/shower rooms are an additional benefit. Breakfast is taken in an attractive dining room and a warm welcome is assured.

Rooms 6 en suite D £68-£80* **Facilities** FTV DVD tea/coffee WiFi **Parking** 6 **Notes** LB ⊗ No Children 11yrs

St Hilary Guest House

★★★★ GUEST ACCOMMODATION

tel: 01492 875551 **fax:** 01492 877538 **16 Craig-y-Don Pde, The Promenade LL30 1BG**
email: info@sthilaryguesthouse.co.uk **web:** www.sthilaryguesthouse.co.uk
dir: 0.5m E of town centre. On B5115 seafront road near Venue Cymru

A warm welcome is assured at this constantly improving guest accommodation, located at the Craig-y-Don end of The Promenade, and many of the thoughtfully furnished bedrooms have superb sea views. Day rooms include a spacious and attractive front-facing dining room. A cosy guest lounge is also available.

Rooms 9 en suite (1 GF) S £43-£46; D £66-£86* **Facilities** FTV iPod docking station Lounge tea/coffee WiFi **Notes** LB ⊗ No Children 8yrs Closed mid Dec-mid Jan

Stratford House

★★★★ GUEST ACCOMMODATION

tel: 01492 877962 **8 Craig-y-Don Pde, The Promenade LL30 1BG**
email: stratfordhtl@aol.com **web:** www.thestratfordbandb.com
dir: A470 at rdbt take 4th exit, on Queens Rd to promenade, on right

This immaculately presented spacious house is located on the seafront with spectacular views. Bedrooms are attractively decorated, some with four-poster beds, and all have an excellent range of accessories, such as flat-screen TVs. The traditionally decorated dining room is also beautifully presented. The friendly owners are very welcoming.

Rooms 9 en suite (1 fmly) (1 GF) S £50-£70; D £60-£75* **Facilities** FTV tea/coffee WiFi **Extras** Chocolates - complimentary **Notes** LB ⊗ No Children 8yrs Closed Jan RS Dec & Feb

Britannia Guest House

★★★★ GUEST HOUSE

tel: 01492 877185 & 07890 765071 **fax:** 01492 233300
15 Craig-y-Don Pde, The Promenade LL30 1BG
email: info@thebritanniaguesthouse.co.uk **web:** www.thebritanniaguesthouse.co.uk
dir: A55 onto A470 to Llandudno, at rdbt take 4th exit signed Craig-y-Don, right at promenade

This family-run Victorian guest house offers a warm welcome and friendly service. The bedrooms are very comfortable and well equipped, and many have fantastic views of Llandudno's bay. Ground-floor rooms are available, and hearty breakfasts are served in the dining room that has sea views.

Rooms 10 en suite (2 GF) D £68-£86* **Facilities** FTV DVD tea/coffee WiFi **Notes** LB ⊗ No Children 10yrs Closed 28 Nov-13 Feb

LLANDUDNO *continued*

Can-Y-Bae

★★★★ GUEST ACCOMMODATION

tel: 01492 874188 **fax:** 01492 868376
10 Mostyn Crescent, Central Promenade LL30 1AR
email: canybae@btconnect.com **web:** www.can-y-baehotel.com
dir: *A55 junct 19, A470, signed Llandudno/Promenade. Can-Y-Bae on seafront promenade between Venue Cymru Theatre & band stand*

A warm welcome is assured at this tastefully renovated house, centrally located on the Promenade. Bedrooms are equipped with both practical and homely extras and upper floors are serviced by a modern lift. Day rooms include a panoramic lounge, cosy bar and attractive basement dining room.

Rooms 16 en suite (2 GF) S £40-£90; D £80-£90 **Facilities** FTV Lounge tea/coffee Dinner available Direct Dial Lift Licensed WiFi **Extras** Speciality toiletries, mineral water - free **Notes** LB No Children 12yrs

Epperstone

★★★★ GUEST ACCOMMODATION

tel: 01492 878746 **fax:** 01492 871223 **15 Abbey Rd LL30 2EE**
email: epperstonehotel@btconnect.com **web:** www.theepperstone.co.uk
dir: *A550, A470 to Mostyn St. Left at rdbt, 4th right into York Rd. Epperstone at junct of York Rd & Abbey Rd*

This delightful property is located in wonderful gardens in a residential part of town, within easy walking distance of the seafront and shopping area. Bedrooms are attractively decorated and thoughtfully equipped. Two lounges and a Victorian-style conservatory are available.

Rooms 8 en suite (5 fmly) (1 GF) **Facilities** FTV Lounge tea/coffee Dinner available Direct Dial Licensed WiFi **Parking** 8

Glenavon Guest House

★★★★ GUEST HOUSE

tel: 01492 877687 **fax:** 0870 706 2247 **27 St Mary's Rd LL30 2UB**
email: postmaster@glenavon.plus.com **web:** www.glenavon-llandudno.co.uk
dir: *From A470 signed Llandudno, left at lights into Trinity Av. 3rd right into St Mary's Rd. Glenavon on right*

Supporters of Liverpool Football Club are especially welcome here and they can admire the extensive range of memorabilia throughout the comfortable day rooms. Bedrooms are equipped with thoughtful extras and Welsh breakfasts provide a good start to the day.

Rooms 7 en suite (1 fmly) S £45-£50; D £70-£75* **Facilities** FTV TVL tea/coffee WiFi **Parking** 4 **Notes** LB ⊗

The Lilly Restaurant with Rooms

★★★★ ◉ ⌂ RESTAURANT WITH ROOMS

tel: 01492 876513 **fax:** 01492 550100 **West Pde, West Shore LL30 2BD**
email: thelilly@live.co.uk **web:** www.thelilly.co.uk
dir: *Phone for detailed directions*

Located on the seafront on the West Shore with views over the Great Orme, this establishment has bedrooms that offer high standards of comfort, and good facilities. Children are very welcome here, and a relaxed atmosphere is found in Madhatter's Brasserie, which takes its name from Lewis Carroll's *Alice in Wonderland*, some of which may have been written while the author was staying on the West Shore. A fine dining restaurant is also available.

Rooms 5 en suite **Facilities** FTV iPod docking station Lounge tea/coffee Dinner available Direct Dial WiFi **Extras** Speciality toiletries **Conf** Max 35 Thtr 25 Board 20 **Notes** ⊗ No coaches

See advert on opposite page

The Lilly
Restaurant With Rooms

Here at The Lilly we have a true passion for great food, and our aim is to make sure that each and every one of our guests experience the ultimate dining experience, along with the highest possible standard of customer service.

We have a beautiful a-la-carte restaurant, which has stunning views right across the entire sea front, where you will taste some amazing dishes from our 5-course menu.

Or for a more relaxed atmosphere, we also have our Madhatters Brasserie, where you can relax and have a bite to eat or drink all day every day!

Our accommodation includes 5 modern sea view rooms, two of which are Superior Sea-View doubles, which all offer extreme comfort and King Size beds.

And to finish off your stay, wake up to our AA award-winning Full Welsh Breakfast served in our Brasserie.

AA
Breakfast
Award

AA ✿

AA ★★★★

The Lilly Restaurant With Rooms
West Parade, Llandudno. LL30 2BD
Tel. 01492 876513   E-Mail. enquiries@thelilly.co.uk

www.thelilly.co.uk

LLANDUDNO *continued*

Minion

★★★ GUEST ACCOMMODATION

tel: 01492 877740 **21-23 Carmen Sylva Rd, Craig-y-Don LL30 1EQ**
dir: A55 junct 19, A470 to Llandudno. At 4th rdbt take Craig-y-Don exit. 2nd right after park

Situated in a quiet residential area just a few minutes' walk from the eastern promenade, the Minion has been owned by the same family for over 60 years and continues to extend a warm welcome. The bedrooms are smart and comfortable, and two are on the ground floor. There is a cosy bar and a colourful garden.

Rooms 10 en suite (1 fmly) (2 GF) **Facilities** FTV TVL tea/coffee Dinner available Licensed **Parking** 8 **Notes** No Children 2yrs Closed Nov-Mar ⊕

The Trevone

★★★ GUEST ACCOMMODATION

tel: 01492 876314 **fax:** 01492 877597 **10 St Georges Crescent LL30 2LF**
email: info@trevone.net **web:** www.trevone.net
dir: A55 follow signs for Llandudno & central promenade

The Trevone is in a splendid location right on the seafront. Bedrooms and bathrooms come in a range of shapes and sizes; some have excellent sea views. Guests are welcome to use the lounge and the bar, and dinner is usually available by prior arrangement. Entertainment is provided for group bookings during the week.

Rooms 24 en suite (5 fmly) (1 GF) S £36-£38; D £72-£96* **Facilities** FTV Lounge tea/coffee Dinner available Lift Licensed WiFi **Notes** LB ⊗ Closed Jan-Feb

LLANRWST   Map 14 SH86

The Eagles

Ⓤ

tel: 01492 640454 **Ancaster Square LL26 0LG**
email: info@theeagleshotel.com **web:** www.theeagleshotel.com
dir: A5 onto A470 to Llanrwst. Pass bridge on left, 50yds on left

Currently the rating for this establishment is not confirmed. This may be due to a change of ownership or because it has only recently joined the AA rating scheme.

Rooms 7 en suite S £55; D £85-£130* **Facilities** FTV tea/coffee Dinner available Direct Dial Licensed WiFi Fishing Pool table 🍴 **Conf** Max 150 Thtr 150 Class 150 Board 20 **Parking** 35 **Notes** Civ Wed 150

RHOS-ON-SEA   Map 14 SH88
See also Colwyn Bay

Premier Collection

Plas Rhos

★★★★★ ≜ GUEST ACCOMMODATION

tel: 01492 543698 **fax:** 0872 115 4361 **Cayley Promenade LL28 4EP**
email: info@plasrhos.co.uk **web:** www.plasrhos.co.uk
dir: A55 junct 20 onto B5115 for Rhos-on-Sea, right at rdbt into Whitehall Rd to promenade

Stunning sea views are a feature of this lovely Victorian house, which provides high standards of comfort and hospitality. Cosy bedrooms are filled with a wealth of thoughtful extras, and public areas include a choice of sumptuous lounges featuring smart decor, quality soft furnishings and memorabilia. Breakfast is served in the attractive dining room, overlooking the pretty patio garden.

Rooms 5 en suite S £60-£65; D £80-£105* **Facilities** FTV Lounge TVL tea/coffee Licensed WiFi 🍴 **Parking** 4 **Notes** LB ⊗ No Children 12yrs Closed Nov-Feb

TREFRIW
Map 14 SH76

Premier Collection

Yr Hafod Country House and Grill

★★★★★ 🍴 🍽 RESTAURANT WITH ROOMS

tel: 01492 642444 **LL27 0RQ**
email: enquiries@hafod-house.co.uk **web:** www.hafod-house.co.uk
dir: *From N - A470 onto B5279, after 1m left onto B5106. 5.5m to Trefriw, over bridge 200mtrs on left. From S - A470 into Llanrwst, left over bridge onto B5106. 1.5m on right*

Situated in tranquil countryside and ideally located for the Conwy valley and Snowdonia National Park, this cosy restaurant with rooms offers very well appointed bedrooms, which are tastefully designed and comfortable, each with separate access and its own balcony. Dinner and breakfast are not to be missed, and dishes are freshly prepared using as much home-grown and local produce as possible. The small friendly team are particularly welcoming.

Rooms 3 en suite S £79; D £89* **Facilities** FTV DVD Lounge tea/coffee Dinner available 🚫 **Extras** Speciality toiletries, sweets, bottled water **Parking** 3 **Notes** ⊗ Closed Dec-13 Feb No coaches

Ty Newydd B&B

★★★ GUEST ACCOMMODATION

tel: 01492 641210 **Conwy Rd LL27 0JH**
email: tynewyddtrefriw@aol.com **web:** www.tynewyddtrefriw.co.uk
dir: *In village centre, near post office*

Nestled in a small village in the unspoilt Conwy Valley, Ty Newydd is just a short drive from Llandudno. The hosts of this large Victorian house offer a genuine warm Welsh welcome on arrival. Comfortable rooms are well equipped, and the property is within easy walking distance of a number of pubs and restaurants.

Rooms 4 rms (2 en suite) (2 pri facs) (1 fmly) S £30; D £60* **Facilities** STV FTV TVL tea/coffee WiFi 🚫 **Notes** Closed 24-25 Dec

DENBIGHSHIRE

CORWEN
Map 15 SJ04

Bron-y-Graig

★★★★ 🍴 GUEST HOUSE

tel: 01490 413007 **LL21 0DR**
email: info@north-wales-hotel.co.uk **web:** www.north-wales-hotel.co.uk
dir: *On A5 on E edge of Corwen*

A short walk from the town centre, Bron-y-Graig is an impressive Victorian house that has retained many original features including fireplaces, stained glass, and a tiled floor in the entrance hall. Bedrooms, complemented by luxurious bathrooms, are thoughtfully furnished; two are to be found in a coach house. Ground-floor areas include a traditionally furnished dining room and a comfortable lounge. A warm welcome, attentive service and imaginative food is assured.

Rooms 7 en suite 2 annexe en suite (4 fmly) S £39-£55; D £59-£68 **Facilities** STV FTV DVD Lounge tea/coffee Dinner available Direct Dial Licensed WiFi 🚫 **Conf** Max 20 Class 20 Board 15 **Parking** 15 **Notes** LB

Plas Derwen Country House

★★★★ GUEST ACCOMMODATION

tel: 01490 412742 & 07773 965874 **London Rd LL21 0DR**
email: bandb@plasderwen.supanet.com **web:** www.plasderwen.co.uk
dir: *On A5 0.5m E of Corwen*

Set in four acres of mature gardens and fields, in an elevated position with superb views of the River Dee, this elegant late 18th-century house has been restored to provide top-notch levels of comfort and facilities. Quality furnishings and stylish decor highlight the many original features, and a warm welcome is assured.

Rooms 2 en suite (2 fmly) **Facilities** FTV TVL tea/coffee WiFi 🚫 **Parking** 6 **Notes** ⊗ Closed Dec-Jan

LLANDYRNOG
Map 15 SJ16

Premier Collection

Pentre Mawr Country House

★★★★★ 🍽 GUEST ACCOMMODATION

tel: 01824 790732 **fax:** 01824 790441 **LL16 4LA**
email: info@pentremawrcountryhouse.co.uk **web:** www.pentremawrcountryhouse.co.uk
dir: *From Denbigh follow Bodfari/Llandyrnog signs. Left at rdbt to Bodfari, 50yds, left into country lane, Pentre Mawr on left*

Expect a warm welcome from Graham and Bre at this superb family country house, set in nearly 200 acres of meadows, park and woodland. The property has been in Graham's family for over 400 years. Bedrooms are individually decorated, very spacious, and each is thoughtfully equipped. Breakfast and dinner are served in the conservatory-restaurant overlooking the salt water swimming pool on the terrace. A formal dining room is available for larger parties. There are also six luxury Safari lodges and two suites, all with private hot tubs.

Rooms 3 en suite 8 annexe en suite (7 GF) **Facilities** FTV DVD iPod docking station Lounge tea/coffee Dinner available Licensed WiFi ⚡ 🍴 Fishing 🚫 **Extras** Robes **Conf** Max 20 Class 20 Board 20 **Parking** 14 **Notes** No Children 13yrs

LLANGOLLEN
Map 15 SJ24

See also Corwen

Geufron Hall Boo-tique Bed and Breakfast

★★★★ 🛏 BED AND BREAKFAST

tel: 01978 860676 & 07726 943770 **fax:** 01978 211100 **Geufron LL20 8DY**
email: enquiries@geufronhall.co.uk **web:** www.geufronhall.co.uk
dir: *From A5 in Llangollen into Castle St (signed Ruthin), over river. At T-junct right, 1st left after hotel & taxidermy studio. Up hill, over canal. At next T-junct left into Dinbren Rd, 0.75m, sharp right (just before double yellow lines end), single track road, follow to end*

Set in a rural location, only moments from the centre of Llangollen, Geufron Hall Boo-tique Bed and Breakfast offers an elegant home-from-home. Guests are encouraged to spend time in the house - the property is licensed and offers stunning views to enjoy, especially in fine weather, with a cold drink, and cosy fires to curl up by on chilly days. Children are genuinely welcomed. Breakfasts are served in a room overlooking the Vale of Llangollen, and feature home-made produce, including some home-reared meats.

Rooms 4 en suite (3 fmly) S £50-£60; D £80-£150 **Facilities** FTV DVD Lounge tea/coffee Licensed WiFi 🚫 **Extras** Home-made biscuits & cakes - complimentary **Parking** 6 **Notes** LB ⊗

LLANGOLLEN *continued*

Tyn Celyn Farmhouse

★★★★ BED AND BREAKFAST

tel: 01978 861117 **Tyndwr LL20 8AR**
email: j.m.bather-tyncelyn@talk21.com web: www.tyncelyn-bnb-llangollen.co.uk
dir: *A5 to Llangollen, pass golf club on right, next left signed Tyndwr outdoor centre, 0.5m sharp left into Tyndwr Rd, past outdoor centre on left. Tyn Celyn 0.5m on left*

This 300-year-old timber-framed farmhouse has stunning views over the Vale of Llangollen. Bedrooms, one of which is located on the ground floor, provide a range of thoughtful extras in addition to fine period furniture. Breakfast is served at a magnificent carved table in a spacious sitting-dining room.

Rooms 3 en suite (1 fmly) (1 GF) D £62-£66* **Facilities** DVD TVL tea/coffee WiFi 🛇 **Parking** 5 **Notes** LB ⊗ ⊜

RUTHIN	Map 15 SJ15

Premier Collection

Firgrove Country House B&B

★★★★★ 🏠 ⊜ BED AND BREAKFAST

tel: 01824 702677 **fax:** 01824 702677 **Firgrove, Llanfwrog LL15 2LL**
email: meadway@firgrovecountryhouse.co.uk web: www.firgrovecountryhouse.co.uk
dir: *0.5m SW of Ruthin. A494 onto B5105, 0.25m past Llanfwrog church on right*

Standing in immaculate mature gardens in a peaceful rural location, this well-proportioned house retains many original features, highlighted by the quality decor and furnishings throughout the interior. Bedrooms, complemented by smart modern bathrooms, are equipped with a wealth of thoughtful extras. Memorable breakfasts, using home-made or local produce, are served in an elegant dining room. Imaginative dinners are also available by prior arrangement and a warm welcome is assured.

Rooms 2 en suite 1 annexe en suite (1 GF) D £90-£120 **Facilities** FTV Lounge tea/coffee Dinner available WiFi 🛇 **Extras** Mineral water, fresh milk - complimentary; fridge **Parking** 4 **Notes** ⊗ No Children Closed Dec-Feb

Tyddyn Chambers *(SJ102543)*

★★★★ FARMHOUSE

tel: 01824 750683 & 07745 589946 **Pwllglas LL15 2LS**
email: ella.williams@btconnect.com web: www.tyddynchambers.co.uk
dir: *3m S of Ruthin. W from A494 after Fox & Hounds pub in Pwllglas, signed*

This charming little farmhouse offers carefully appointed, modern accommodation, which includes one family room. The pleasant, traditionally furnished breakfast room has separate tables and a lounge is also available. The house stands in an elevated position with panoramic views.

Rooms 3 en suite (1 fmly) S £38-£42; D £60-£70 **Facilities** TVL tea/coffee **Parking** 3 **Notes** ⊗ No Children 4yrs Closed Xmas & New Year ⊜ 180 acres beef/sheep

ST ASAPH — Map 15 SJ07

Premier Collection

Tan-Yr-Onnen Guest House

★★★★★ 🏠 GUEST HOUSE

tel: 01745 583821 **fax:** 01745 583821 **Waen LL17 0DU**
email: tanyronnenvisit@aol.com **web:** www.northwalesbreaks.co.uk
dir: *W on A55 junct 28, turn left in 300yds*

A warm welcome is assured at Tan-Yr-Onnen Guest House, which is quietly located in six acres of gardens, conveniently close to the A55. The very well-equipped accommodation includes four ground-floor rooms with French windows that open onto the terrace. Upstairs, there are two luxury suites with lounge areas. Hearty breakfasts are served in the dining room overlooking the gardens, and a conservatory-lounge and WiFi access are also available.

Rooms 6 en suite (1 fmly) (4 GF) **Facilities** FTV tea/coffee Dinner available Licensed WiFi **Parking** 8

Bach-Y-Graig *(SJ075713)*

★★★★ FARMHOUSE

tel: 01745 730627 **fax:** 01745 730627 **Tremeirchion LL17 0UH**
email: anwen@bachygraig.co.uk **web:** www.bachygraig.co.uk
dir: *3m SE of St Asaph. Exit A525 at Trefnant onto A541 to x-rds with white railings, left, down hill, over bridge, right*

Dating from the 16th century, this Grade II listed building is said to be the earliest brick-built house in Wales and retains many original features, including a wealth of exposed beams and inglenook fireplaces. Bedrooms are furnished with fine period pieces and quality soft fabrics. Ground-floor areas include a quiet lounge and a combined sitting and dining room, featuring a superb Jacobean oak table.

Rooms 3 rms (2 en suite) (1 pri facs) (1 fmly) S £45-£55; D £80* **Facilities** FTV DVD TVL tea/coffee WiFi Fishing Woodland trail **Parking** 3 **Notes** LB ⊗ Closed Xmas & New Year 200 acres dairy/mixed

FLINTSHIRE

NANNERCH — Map 15 SJ16

The Old Mill Guest Accommodation

★★★★ GUEST ACCOMMODATION

tel: 01352 741542 **Melin-Y-Wern, Denbigh Rd CH7 5RH**
email: mail@old-mill.co.uk **web:** www.old-mill.co.uk
dir: *A541, NW from Mold, 7m into Melin-Y-Wern, Old Mill on right*

This converted stone stable block was once part of a Victorian watermill complex. Immediately adjacent is The Cherry Pie Inn where evening meals can be taken. The non-smoking accommodation offers modern, well-equipped bedrooms with en suite bathrooms.

Rooms 6 en suite (1 fmly) (2 GF) **Facilities** FTV Lounge tea/coffee Direct Dial WiFi 🐾 **Parking** 12 **Notes** ⊗ Closed Feb

GWYNEDD

BALA — Map 14 SH93

Erw Feurig Guest House *(SH965394)*

★★★★ FARMHOUSE

tel: 01678 530262 & 07786 168399 **fax:** 01678 530262 **Cefnddwysarn LL23 7LL**
email: erwfeurig@yahoo.com **web:** www.erwfeurig.com
dir: *3m NE of Bala off A494. 2nd left after x-rds at Cefnddwysarn, turn at B&B sign*

A warm welcome is assured at this delightful and peaceful farm cottage situated on a hillside with panoramic views of the Berwyn Mountains. The comfortable, individually styled bedrooms have a range of additional extras. A cosy lounge and a cheerful ground-floor breakfast room are available.

Rooms 4 rms (2 en suite) (2 pri facs) (1 GF) S £40-£45; D £65-£70* **Facilities** FTV Lounge tea/coffee WiFi Fishing 🐾 **Parking** 6 **Notes** LB ⊗ No Children Closed Jan-Feb ⊛ 45 acres grazing

BANGOR — Map 14 SH57

Gors-Yr-Eira Guest House B&B

★★★★ BED AND BREAKFAST

tel: 01248 601353 & 07887 394611 **Mynyddllandega LL57 4DZ**
email: einir@gorsyreira.co.uk
dir: *A55 onto A5, follow Betws-y-Coed road to Bethesda. Right onto B4409, after 1m turn left, up steep hill, B&B on brow of hill*

A warm welcome is assured at this detached extended property with lovely country views, located between Bangor and Bethesda and also convenient for Llanberis and Mount Snowdon. Bedrooms and bathrooms vary in size and all are equipped with good furnishings, homely and practical extras including free WiFi. Hearty breakfasts are taken in a conservatory dining room overlooking the rear garden which is home to chickens, ducks and goats.

Rooms 3 en suite **Facilities** FTV DVD TVL tea/coffee WiFi 🐾 **Parking** 3

BANGOR *continued*

Tregarth Homestay B&B

★★★ BED AND BREAKFAST

tel: 01248 600532 & 07711 710364 **Llain-Y-Grug, Dob, Tregarth LL57 4PW**
email: tregarth.homestay@btinternet.com **web:** www.tregarth-homestay.com
dir: *From A55 junct 11 onto A5 (Betwys), then 1st right onto A4244. Left onto B4409 signed Tregarth. Take 3rd right after chapel*

Ideally located for both Bangor and Llanberis, this modern split-level house has cosy bedrooms at the lower level, with fine views over the pretty rear garden, surrounding coast and mountains. Hearty breakfasts utilise quality local produce and there is a choice of good eating pubs a ten minute drive away.

Rooms 3 rms (1 en suite) (2 pri facs) **Facilities** FTV TVL tea/coffee WiFi 🔒 **Parking** 3 **Notes** ⊗

| BARMOUTH | Map 14 SH61 |

See also Dyffryn Ardudwy

Morwendon House

★★★★ 🛏 🍴 GUEST ACCOMMODATION

tel: 01341 280566 **fax:** 07092 197785 **Llanaber LL42 1RR**
email: info@morwendon-house.co.uk **web:** www.morwendon-house.co.uk
dir: *A496 at Llanaber N of Barmouth. On seaward side 250yds past Llanaber Church*

With its impressive location overlooking Cardigan Bay, Morwendon House is an ideal base for exploring the surrounding area and its many attractions. The bedrooms are well equipped, and many rooms have sea views. Dinner is available by arrangement, and meals are taken in the attractive dining room overlooking the bay. There is also a comfortable lounge, again, with views over the bay.

Rooms 5 en suite 1 annexe en suite (1 GF) **Facilities** FTV DVD Lounge tea/coffee Dinner available Licensed WiFi ⚓ 18 🔒 **Parking** 6 **Notes** ⊗ No Children 12yrs Closed 24-27 Dec

Richmond House

★★★★ GUEST HOUSE

tel: 01341 281366 & 07800 583815 **High St LL42 1DW**
email: info@barmouthbedandbreakfast.co.uk **web:** www.barmouthbedandbreakfast.co.uk
dir: *In town centre. Car park at rear on Jubilee Rd*

A warm welcome awaits at Richmond House, a lovely Victorian building, which has been appointed to provide good quality and thoughtfully equipped accommodation. Two of the bedrooms have sea views, as do the lounge and dining room, where there are separate tables. There is also a pleasant garden.

Rooms 4 en suite (1 fmly) S £65-£70; D £80-£90* **Facilities** FTV DVD Lounge tea/coffee WiFi 🔒 **Parking** 5 **Notes** LB ⊗

Llwyndu Farmhouse

★★★★ 🍴 GUEST ACCOMMODATION

tel: 01341 280144 **Llanaber LL42 1RR**
email: intouch@llwyndu-farmhouse.co.uk **web:** www.llwyndu-farmhouse.co.uk
dir: *A496 towards Harlech where street lights end, on outskirts of Barmouth, take next right*

This converted 16th-century farmhouse offers warm hospitality and traditional guest accommodation. Many original features are retained, including inglenook fireplaces, exposed beams and timbers. There is a cosy lounge and meals can be enjoyed in the licensed restaurant. Bedrooms are comfortable and well equipped, and some have four-poster beds. Four bedrooms are in the old dairy building.

Rooms 3 en suite 4 annexe en suite (2 fmly) S fr £60; D £90-£120* **Facilities** FTV TVL tea/coffee Dinner available Licensed WiFi 🔒 **Extras** Speciality toiletries, fruit, snacks - free **Conf** Max 10 **Parking** 10 **Notes** LB Closed 25-26 Dec RS Sun no dinner

| BEDDGELERT | Map 14 SH54 |

Tanronnen Inn

★★★★ INN

tel: 01766 890347 **fax:** 01766 890606 **LL55 4YB**
email: tanbedd@12freeukisp.co.uk **web:** www.tanronnen.co.uk
dir: *In village centre opposite river bridge*

This delightful inn offers comfortable, well-equipped and attractively appointed accommodation, including rooms suitable for families. There is also a selection of pleasant and relaxing public areas. The wide range of bar food is popular with tourists, and more formal meals are served in the restaurant.

Rooms 7 en suite (3 fmly) S £55-£65; D £100-£120* **Facilities** FTV tea/coffee Dinner available Direct Dial 🔒 **Parking** 9 **Notes** LB ⊗ No coaches

| BETWS GARMON | Map 14 SH55 |

Betws Inn

★★★★ 🍴 BED AND BREAKFAST

tel: 01286 650324 **LL54 7YY**
email: stay@betws-inn.co.uk **web:** www.betws-inn.co.uk
dir: *On A4085 (Caernarfon to Beddgelert), opposite Bryn Gloch Caravan Park*

Set in the western foothills of Snowdonia, this 17th-century former inn is an establishment of immense charm. A warm welcome and caring service are assured. Bedrooms have a wealth of homely extras, and imaginative dinners feature local produce. Breakfast includes home-made bread and preserves.

Rooms 3 en suite **Facilities** FTV iPod docking station TVL tea/coffee Dinner available WiFi **Parking** 3 **Notes** ⊗

CAERNARFON　　　　　　　　　　　Map 14 SH46

Premier Collection

Plas Dinas Country House

★★★★★ 🛏 🍽 GUEST ACCOMMODATION

tel: 01286 830214 **fax:** 0872 111 4641 **Bontnewydd LL54 7YF**
email: info@plasdinas.co.uk **web:** www.plasdinas.co.uk
dir: *3m S of Caernarfon, off A487, 0.5m down private drive*

Situated in 15 acres of beautiful grounds in Snowdonia, this delightful Grade II listed building dates back to the mid-17th century, but has many Victorian additions. It was once the home of the Armstrong-Jones family, so there are many family portraits, memorabilia and original pieces of furniture on view. The bedrooms are individually decorated and include four-poster beds along with modern facilities. There is a stylish drawing room where a fire burns in the winter, and fresh local produce features on the dinner menu.

Rooms 10 en suite (2 fmly) (1 GF) S £89-£249; D £89-£249 **Facilities** FTV Lounge tea/coffee Dinner available Licensed WiFi **Extras** Speciality toiletries, mini-bar **Conf** Max 14 Board 14 **Parking** 16 **Notes** No Children 12yrs Civ Wed 32

Black Boy Inn

★★★★ INN

tel: 01286 673604 **fax:** 01286 674955 **LL55 1RW**
email: office@black-boy-inn.com **web:** www.black-boy-inn.com
dir: *A55 junct 9, A487, follow signs for Caernarfon. Inn within town walls between castle & Victoria Dock*

Located within Caernarfon's historic town walls, this fine 16th-century inn has low ceilings, narrow staircases and thick wooden beams originally from old ships. It is one of the oldest inns in north Wales, and has a wealth of charm and character. The bedrooms provide modern accommodation, and hearty meals are available in both the restaurant and bar area. On-site parking is available.

Rooms 16 en suite 10 annexe en suite (5 fmly) (3 GF) **Facilities** FTV tea/coffee Dinner available Direct Dial WiFi ♨ 18 🐕 **Conf** Max 40 Thtr 40 Class 20 Board 30 **Parking** 26 **Notes** LB ⊗

CRICCIETH　　　　　　　　　　　Map 14 SH43

Bron Rhiw

★★★★ 🛏 GUEST ACCOMMODATION

tel: 01766 522257 **Caernarfon Rd LL52 0AP**
email: clairecriccieth@yahoo.co.uk **web:** www.bronrhiwhotel.co.uk
dir: *From High St onto B4411*

A warm welcome, and high standards of comfort and facilities are assured at Bron Rhiw, a constantly improving Victorian property, just a short walk from the seafront. Bedrooms are equipped with lots of thoughtful extras and ground-floor areas include a sumptuous lounge, a cosy bar, and an elegant dining room, the setting for imaginative breakfasts.

Rooms 9 en suite (2 fmly) S £47-£48; D £72-£78* **Facilities** FTV Lounge tea/coffee Licensed WiFi 🐕 **Parking** 3 **Notes** LB ⊗ No Children 10yrs Closed Nov-Feb

Min Y Gaer

★★★★ GUEST HOUSE

tel: 01766 522151 **Porthmadog Rd LL52 0HP**
email: info@minygaer.co.uk **web:** www.minygaer.co.uk
dir: *On A497 200yds E of junct with B4411*

The friendly, family-run Min Y Gaer has superb views from many of the rooms. Min Y Gaer is Welsh for 'near the fort', and so some of the fine views are of Criccieth Castle. The smart, modern bedrooms are furnished in pine, and the welcoming proprietors also provide a bar and a traditionally furnished lounge.

Rooms 10 en suite (1 fmly) S £43-£45; D £72-£82* **Facilities** FTV DVD Lounge tea/coffee Licensed WiFi 🐕 **Parking** 12 **Notes** Closed 11 Nov-mid Mar

DOLGELLAU
Map 14 SH71

AA GUEST ACCOMMODATION OF THE YEAR FOR WALES 2014–2015

Premier Collection

Tyddynmawr Farmhouse (SH704159)

★★★★★ FARMHOUSE

tel: 01341 422331 **Cader Rd, Islawrdref LL40 1TL**
email: olwynevans@btconnect.com **web:** www.wales-guesthouse.co.uk
dir: *From town centre left at top of square, left at garage into Cader Rd for 3m. 1st farm on left after Gwernan Lake*

A warm welcome is assured at this 18th-century farmhouse which lies at the foot of Cader Idris amid breathtaking scenery. The bedrooms are spacious and have Welsh oak furniture; the upper room has a balcony and the ground-floor room has a patio area. The bathrooms are large and luxurious. Breakfast offers an excellent choice of home-made items including bread, preserves, muesli or smoked fish. Self-catering cottages are also available.

Rooms 2 en suite (1 GF) S £65; D £82-£85 **Facilities** Lounge TVL tea/coffee WiFi
🔒 **Parking** 8 **Notes** ⊗ No Children Closed Dec-Jan 🐾 800 acres beef/sheep

Plas Gwyn B&B and Holiday Cottage

★★★★ BED AND BREAKFAST

tel: 01341 388176 & 07411 228477   **fax:** 08713 140334 **Cader Rd LL40 1RH**
email: plasgwyn@hotmail.co.uk **web:** www.plasgwynbandb.co.uk
dir: *From A470 Arran Rd (signed Dolgellau), cross bridge after 1m. At High St bear left at Ty Siamas building, 500mtrs on left*

Located in the centre with easy walking to all shops, cafés and inns this welcoming B&B provides plenty of character and quality. Rooms are named after previous residents and offer a range of shapes and sizes, with plenty of welcome extras to add to guest comfort. A car park and garden are available to the rear. Breakfast utilises local, quality produce and is served around one large table in the comfortably furnished dining room.

Rooms 3 en suite S £45-£55; D £55-£75* **Facilities** STV FTV iPod docking station tea/coffee Dinner available WiFi 🔒 **Extras** Mini-bar, snacks **Parking** 13 **Notes** LB ⊗ No Children 10yrs

Dolgun Uchaf Guesthouse

★★★★ GUEST HOUSE

tel: 01341 422269 **Dolgun Uchaf LL40 2AB**
email: dolgunuchaf@aol.com **web:** www.guesthousessnowdonia.com
dir: *Exit A470 at Little Chef just S of Dolgellau. Dolgun Uchaf 1st property on right*

Located in a peaceful area with stunning views of the surrounding countryside, this 500-year-old, late medieval hall house retains many original features including exposed beams and open fireplaces. The bedrooms are equipped with thoughtful extras, and a lounge for guests is available.

Rooms 3 en suite 1 annexe en suite (1 GF) **Facilities** TVL tea/coffee Dinner available WiFi 🔒 **Parking** 6 **Notes** No Children 5yrs

DYFFRYN ARDUDWY
Map 14 SH52

Cadwgan Inn
★★★★ INN

tel: 01341 247240 **LL44 2HA**
email: cadwgan.hotel@virgin.net **web:** www.cadwganhotel.co.uk
dir: *In Dyffryn Ardudwy into Station Rd, over railway crossing*

Privately-owned Cadwgan Inn stands in grounds close to Dyffryn Ardudwy station, between Barmouth and Harlech, with the beach just a short walk away. The good-quality, well-equipped modern accommodation includes family rooms and a room with a four-poster bed. Public areas include an attractive dining room, popular bar and a beer garden.

Rooms 6 en suite (3 fmly) **Facilities** TVL tea/coffee Dinner available Sauna Gym Pool table **Notes** ⊗ No coaches Civ Wed 60

LLANBEDR
Map 14 SH52

Bryn Artro Country House
★★★★ GUEST ACCOMMODATION

tel: 01341 241619 **LL45 2LE**
email: enquiries@llanbedr-brynartro.com

This former Victorian gentleman's residence is set in the Snowdonia National Park. Built from traditional Welsh slate and stone, this delightful property has attractive gardens, and the richly furnished dining room leads onto a landscaped terrace area. The dining room is open to non-residents and offers an extensive menu, including more exotic dishes such as crocodile and zebra. Bedrooms are individually designed and well equipped, some rooms have four-poster beds and spa baths.

Rooms 7 rms

Victoria Inn
★★★★ INN

tel: 01341 241213 **fax:** 01341 241644 **LL45 2LD**
email: junevicinn@aol.com **web:** www.vic-inn.co.uk
dir: *In village centre*

A former coaching inn, the Victoria Inn lies beside the River Artro in a very pretty village. Many original features remain, including the Settle bar with its flagstone floor, black polished fireplace and unusual circular wooden settle. The menu is extensive and is supplemented by blackboard specials. Bedrooms are spacious and thoughtfully furnished.

Rooms 5 en suite (1 fmly) S £55; D £85-£105* **Facilities** FTV tea/coffee Dinner available 🔒 **Conf** Max 40 **Parking** 75 **Notes** LB

MALLWYD
Map 14 SH81

Tafarn y Brigand's Inn
[U]

tel: 01650 511999 **fax:** 01650 531208 **SY20 9HJ**
email: bookings@brigandsinn.com **web:** www.brigandsinn.com
dir: *In village at junct A458 & A470*

Currently the rating for this establishment is not confirmed. This may be due to a change of ownership or because it has only recently joined the AA rating scheme.

Rooms 9 en suite (1 fmly) S £85; D £115* **Facilities** STV FTV Lounge tea/coffee Dinner available Direct Dial Licensed WiFi **Extras** Home-made biscuits, fresh milk **Parking** 50 **Notes** LB

PORTHMADOG
Map 14 SH53

Tudor Lodge
★★★★ GUEST ACCOMMODATION

tel: 01766 515530 **Tan-Yr-Onnen, Penamser Rd LL49 9NY**
email: res@tudorlodge.co.uk **web:** www.tudor-lodge.co.uk
dir: *From main Porthmadog rdbt into Criccieth Rd, house 40mtrs on left*

Tudor Lodge is a large property conveniently situated within a short walk of the town centre. It has good quality, modern accommodation, including family rooms. Separate tables are provided in the breakfast room, where a substantial self-service continental breakfast buffet is provided. There is also a pleasant garden for guests to use.

Rooms 13 en suite (3 fmly) (6 GF) S £49; D £75-£85* **Facilities** STV tea/coffee WiFi ⌁ 18 🔒 **Parking** 25 **Notes** LB ⊗

PWLLHELI
Map 14 SH33

The Old Rectory
★★★★★ BED AND BREAKFAST

tel: 01758 721519 **Boduan LL53 6DT**
email: theashcrofts@theoldrectory.net **web:** www.theoldrectory.net
dir: *From Pwllheli take A497 signed Nefyn. Continue 3m, after villlage sign for Boduan turn left. 1st house on right*

The Old Rectory is a lovely Georgian property set in delightful grounds. Ideally located for the marina in Abersoch, it is centrally placed for walkers on the Welsh Coast Path. The proprietors take great pride in their home and provide very well appointed bedrooms, spacious public areas and super gardens. Breakfast is also a delight, featuring local produce and taken at a large communal table in the dining room.

Rooms 4 en suite (1 fmly) S £75-£90; D £75-£110* **Facilities** FTV TVL tea/coffee WiFi ⌁ 18 🔒 **Extras** Chocolates, sherry **Parking** 6 **Notes** LB ⊗ Closed 24-27 Dec

MERTHYR TYDFIL

MERTHYR TYDFIL
Map 9 SO00

The Mount Pleasant Inn
★★★★ INN

tel: 01443 693555 & 07918 763640 **Mount Pleasant CF48 4TD**
email: jwacmorgan@aol.com **web:** www.themountpleasantinn.co.uk
dir: *A470 at Abercynnon rdbt onto A4054 towards Aberfan. 2.5m to Mount Pleasant*

With pleasant views across the valley, this friendly and welcoming inn provides guests with a relaxed and homely ambience. Bedrooms offer a range of shapes and sizes and are well equipped. Dinner is available every night except Sunday, when a popular roast lunch is served during the day. Guests may enjoy a drink on the terrace to the rear of the inn.

Rooms 5 en suite (1 fmly) **Facilities** STV FTV DVD Lounge TVL tea/coffee Dinner available WiFi 🔒 **Extras** Speciality toiletries - complimentary **Notes** ⊗ Closed 23 Dec-2 Jan No coaches

PONTSTICILL
Map 9 SO01

Penrhadw Farm
★★★★ GUEST HOUSE

tel: 01685 723481 & 722461 **fax:** 01685 722461 **CF48 2TU**
email: treghotel@aol.com **web:** www.penrhadwfarm.co.uk
dir: *5m N of Merthyr Tydfil*

Expect a warm welcome at this 19th-century former farmhouse in the glorious Brecon Beacons National Park. The house is appointed to provide quality modern accommodation. The well-equipped, spacious bedrooms include two large suites in cottages adjacent to the main building. There is also a comfortable lounge. Separate tables are provided in the cosy breakfast room.

Rooms 5 en suite 5 annexe en suite (5 fmly) (1 GF) **Facilities** FTV TVL tea/coffee Dinner available WiFi ⌕ 18 ⚓ **Conf** Max 10 Thtr 10 Class 10 **Parking** 22 **Notes** ⊗

MONMOUTHSHIRE

ABERGAVENNY
Map 9 SO21

Kings Arms
★★★★ ⌣ INN

tel: 01873 855074 **29 Nevill St NP7 5AA**
email: enquiries@kingsarmsabergavenny.co.uk **web:** www.kingsarmsabergavenny.co.uk

This characterful inn has plenty of history and is located in the centre of the town, just one minute's walk from the high street. The Kings Arms is a traditional inn where access to some of the bedrooms is via steep stairs. All rooms are well decorated and equipped and come in a range of shapes and sizes. A good range of beers is available and both lunch and dinner offer a selection of well-cooked and presented quality ingredients.

Rooms 11 en suite (2 fmly) S fr £65; D £85-£110* **Facilities** FTV DVD tea/coffee Dinner available WiFi ⌕ 18 ⚓ **Extras** Speciality toiletries **Conf** Max 50 Thtr 50 Class 40 Board 30 **Notes** LB

Brynhonddu Country House B&B
★★★ BED AND BREAKFAST

tel: 01873 890535 **fax:** 01873 890792 **Bwrch Trewyn Estate, Pandy NP7 7PD**
email: kdwhite@brynhonddu.co.uk **web:** www.brynhonddu.co.uk
dir: *From Abergavenny N on A465 towards Hereford. After 6m turn left at Old Pandy Inn into Longtown Rd. Turn left after 300mtrs, then right into long tree-lined drive, after 700mtrs*

Peacefully located and surrounded by walks from its doorstep, this delightful building has parts dating back to the 17th century. Bedrooms and bathrooms offer a range of shapes and sizes and are traditionally furnished. Breakfast is served around one large table in the comfortable dining room. Please call ahead for directions here as Sat Nav will often not be successful.

Rooms 4 en suite S £35-£40; D £70-£80 **Facilities** STV FTV Lounge tea/coffee WiFi ⚓ **Parking** 6 **Notes** Closed Xmas ⊛

LLANDOGO
Map 4 SO50

The Sloop Inn
★★★★ INN

tel: 01594 530291 **NP25 4TW**
email: thesloopinn@btconnect.com **web:** www.thesloopinn.co.uk
dir: *On A466 in village centre*

This welcoming inn is centrally located in the village of Llandogo, close to the River Wye in an outstandingly beautiful valley. The Sloop Inn offers a selection of traditional food, as well as friendly hospitality. The dining room has delightful views over the valley, and the spacious bedrooms and bathrooms are equipped for both business and leisure guests.

Rooms 4 en suite (1 fmly) **Facilities** tea/coffee Dinner available Pool table **Parking** 50 **Notes** RS Mon-Fri closed between 3-6

LLANTRISANT
Map 9 ST39

Greyhound Inn
★★★★ A INN

tel: 01291 673447 & 672505 **NP15 1LE**
email: enquiry@greyhound-inn.com **web:** www.greyhound-inn.com
dir: *M4 junct 24, A449, 1st exit for Usk, 2.5m from town square, follow Llantrisant signs*

The Greyhound Inn has been run by the same family for more than thirty years. Built as a farmhouse in the 17th century, and first established as an inn in 1845, its traditional features and character have been carefully maintained. Choose from four dining areas, relax in the garden, browse the Antique Pine Shop, or just curl up in front of a winter-warming log fire. There's also a small cocktail lounge, and a stable bar popular with locals. Bedrooms are situated in a converted stable block, and are all en suite.

Rooms 10 en suite (2 fmly) (5 GF) S £66; D £88* **Facilities** tea/coffee Dinner available Direct Dial WiFi **Parking** 75 **Notes** LB Closed 25-26 Dec RS Sun eve no food No coaches

MONMOUTH
Map 10 SO51

Bistro Prego
★★★★ ⊛⊛ RESTAURANT WITH ROOMS

tel: 01600 712600 **fax:** 01600 716016 **7 Church St NP25 3BX**
email: enquiries@pregomonmouth.co.uk **web:** www.pregomonmouth.co.uk
dir: *Travelling N A40 at lights left turn, T-junct left turn, 2nd right, Bistro Prego at rear of car park*

Located in the middle of Monmouth, this Italian-style restaurant with rooms is open all day for a selection of teas, coffees, lunches and light snacks. At dinner, a delicious choice of dishes using local produce is available in the popular bistro-style dining area. Rooms are located above the dining room and come in a range of shapes and sizes.

Rooms 8 en suite (2 fmly) S £35-£40; D £55-£60* **Facilities** FTV DVD tea/coffee Dinner available WiFi ⚓ **Notes** Closed 24-26 & 31 Dec

The Inn at Penallt

★★★★ @ INN

tel: 01600 772765 **Penallt NP25 4SE**
email: enquiries@theinnatpenallt.co.uk **web:** www.theinnatpenallt.co.uk
dir: *From Monmouth on B4293 towards Trellech. After 2m turn left signed Penallt, at village x-rds turn left, 0.3m on right*

This 17th-century farmhouse and inn underwent a renovation when Andrew and Jackie Murphy took over. Food is very much to the fore here, and fresh, local produce is sourced by head chef Peter Hulsmann. There are two bedrooms in the Barn, separate to the inn, and two bedrooms within the main building; all are smartly presented and comfortable. The bar, with beams and a wood-burner, offers a good selection of beers and spirits and a sound wine list. There is a conservatory lounge to relax in, as well as a garden.

Rooms 2 en suite 2 annexe en suite (2 GF) S £50–£57.50; D £80* **Facilities** STV FTV DVD iPod docking station Lounge tea/coffee Dinner available WiFi **Extras** Bottled water, home-made Welsh cakes **Parking** 26 **Notes** LB Closed 5-22 Jan No coaches

Penylan Farm

★★★★ 🄰 BED AND BREAKFAST

tel: 01600 716435 **fax:** 01600 719391 **The Hendre NP25 5NL**
email: penylanfarm@gmail.com **web:** www.penylanfarm.co.uk
dir: *5m NW of Monmouth. B4233 through Rockfield towards Hendre. 0.5m before Hendre turn right towards Newcastle. After 1.5m turn left, farm 0.5m on right*

This converted barn was originally part of the Hendre Estate, once owned by the Rolls family. The bedrooms, housed in a former granary, have private entrances and are equipped with many thoughtful extras. Breakfast, focusing on local produce, home-made preserves and eggs from the farm's own hens, is served by the welcoming, friendly owners. Extensive walking trails can be accessed from the farm. A self-catering cottage is also available.

Rooms 3 en suite 3 annexe en suite (1 fmly) (2 GF) S £40–£55; D £68–£95* **Facilities** tea/coffee Dinner available WiFi 🌢 🔒 **Parking** 10 **Notes** LB ⊗ Closed Xmas & New Year

Church Farm Guest House

★★★ GUEST HOUSE

tel: 01600 712176 **Mitchel Troy NP25 4HZ**
email: info@churchfarmguesthouse.eclipse.co.uk **web:** www.churchfarmmitcheltroy.co.uk
dir: *From A40 S, left onto B4293 for Trelleck before tunnel, 150yds turn left and follow signs to Mitchel Troy. Guest House on main road on left, 200yds beyond campsite*

Located in the village of Mitchel Troy, this 16th-century former farmhouse retains many original features including exposed beams and open fireplaces. There is a range of bedrooms and a spacious lounge, and breakfast is served in the traditionally furnished dining room. Dinner is available by prior arrangement.

Rooms 8 rms (6 en suite) (2 pri facs) (3 fmly) S £35–£37; D £70–£74 **Facilities** FTV TVL tea/coffee Dinner available WiFi ch fac 🔒 **Parking** 12 **Notes** LB Closed Xmas

ROCKFIELD	Map 9 SO41

The Stonemill & Steppes Farm Cottages

★★★★ @@ RESTAURANT WITH ROOMS

tel: 01600 775424 **NP25 5SW**
email: bookings@thestonemill.co.uk **web:** www.steppesfarmcottages.co.uk
dir: *A48 to Monmouth, take B4233 to Rockfield. 2.6m*

Located in a small hamlet just west of Monmouth, close to the Forest of Dean and the Wye Valley, this establishment offers accommodation comprising six very well-appointed cottages. The comfortable rooms (for self-catering or on a B&B basis) have been lovingly restored to retain many original features. In a separate, converted 16th-century barn is the Stonemill Restaurant, with oak beams, vaulted ceilings and an old cider press. Breakfast is served in the cottages on request. The location is handy for golfers, with a choice of many courses in the area.

Rooms 6 en suite (6 fmly) (6 GF) **Facilities** FTV DVD TVL tea/coffee Dinner available WiFi ⅃ 18 🔒 Free golf **Conf** Max 60 Thtr 60 Class 56 Board 40 **Parking** 53 **Notes** LB ⊗ RS Sun eve & Mon closed No coaches Civ Wed 120

SKENFRITH	Map 9 SO42

The Bell at Skenfrith

★★★★★ @@ 🍴 RESTAURANT WITH ROOMS

tel: 01600 750235 **fax:** 01600 750525 **NP7 8UH**
email: enquiries@skenfrith.co.uk **web:** www.skenfrith.co.uk
dir: *On B4521 in Skenfrith, opposite castle*

The Bell is a beautifully restored, 17th-century former coaching inn which still retains much original charm and character. It is peacefully situated on the banks of the Monnow, a tributary of the River Wye, and is ideally placed for exploring the numerous delights of the area. Natural materials have been used to create a relaxing atmosphere, while the bedrooms, which include full suites and rooms with four-poster beds, are stylish, luxurious and equipped with DVD players. Fresh produce from the garden is used by the kitchen brigade who produce award-winning food for relaxed dining in the welcoming restaurant.

Rooms 11 en suite (2 fmly) **Facilities** STV FTV Lounge tea/coffee Dinner available Direct Dial WiFi 🔒 **Extras** Speciality toiletries, home-made shortbread **Conf** Max 20 Thtr 20 Board 20 **Parking** 36 **Notes** No Children 8yrs RS Nov-Mar closed Tue

TINTERN PARVA	Map 4 SO50

Parva Farmhouse Riverside Guest House & Restaurant

★★★★ ⟲ GUEST HOUSE

tel: 01291 689411 **Monmouth Rd NP16 6SQ**
email: parvahoteltintern@hotmail.co.uk **web:** www.parvafarmhouse.co.uk
dir: *On A466 at N edge of Tintern. Next to St Michael's Church on the riverside*

Parva Farmhouse is a relaxed and friendly family-run guest house, situated on a sweep of the River Wye with far-reaching views of the valley. Dating from the 17th century, this establishment has many excellent features, providing character and comfort in an informal atmosphere. The cosy Inglenook Restaurant is the place for quality ingredients at breakfast and dinner. The individually designed bedrooms are tastefully decorated and enjoy pleasant views; one has a four-poster.

Rooms 8 en suite (2 fmly) S £58–£72; D £75–£85* **Facilities** FTV Lounge tea/coffee Dinner available Licensed WiFi ⓑ **Parking** 8 **Notes** No Children 12yrs

USK	Map 9 SO30

Newbridge on Usk

★★★★★ ⊛ ⌂ RESTAURANT WITH ROOMS

tel: 01633 451000 & 410262 **Tredunnock NP15 1LY**
email: newbridgeonusk@celtic-manor.com **web:** www.celtic-manor.com
dir: *M4 junct 24, signed Newport, onto B4236. At Ship Inn turn right, over mini rdbt onto Llangybi/Usk road. Turn right opposite Cwrt Bleddyn Hotel, signed Tredunnock, through village & down hill*

This cosy gastro-pub is tucked away in a beautiful village setting with the River Usk nearby. The well-equipped bedrooms, in a separate building, provide comfort and a good range of extras. Guests can eat at rustic tables around the bar or in the upstairs dining room where award-winning, seasonal food is served; there is also a small private dining room. Breakfast is one of the highlights of a stay with quality local ingredients offered in abundance.

Rooms 6 en suite (2 fmly) (4 GF) S £73–£241; D £85–£260 **Facilities** FTV DVD tea/coffee Dinner available Direct Dial WiFi ⓢ ⓢ ⓛ 18 Fishing Sauna Gym Facilities available at Celtic Manor Resort **Extras** Speciality toiletries - complimentary **Conf** Max 14 Thtr 14 Class 14 Board 14 **Parking** 60 **Notes** LB Civ Wed 80

WHITEBROOK	Map 4 SO50

Premier Collection

The Crown at Whitebrook

★★★★★ ⊛⊛⊛ ⌂ RESTAURANT WITH ROOMS

tel: 01600 860254 **NP25 4TX**
email: info@crownatwhitebrook.co.uk **web:** www.crownatwhitebrook.co.uk
dir: *4m from Monmouth on B4293, left at sign to Whitebrook, 2m on unclassified road, on right*

Peacefully located and surrounded by woods and rivers, this delightful restaurant with rooms offers a peaceful escape. All the bedrooms are located above the main restaurant and come in a range of shapes and sizes. All are very comfortably decorated and furnished. Dinner utilises the finest of local produce and the relaxing surroundings and friendly service provide a memorable dining experience. The team lead by chef-owner Chris Harrod, who trained under Raymond Blanc, has recently earned 3 AA Rosettes for The Crown.

Rooms 8 en suite S £80–£105; D £115–£140* **Facilities** FTV Lounge tea/coffee Dinner available Direct Dial WiFi **Parking** 20 **Notes** ⊗ No Children 12yrs Closed 2-15 Jan No coaches

NEATH PORT TALBOT

NEATH	Map 9 SS79

Cwmbach Cottages Guest House

★★★★ GUEST HOUSE

tel: 01639 639825 **Cwmbach Rd, Cadoxton SA10 8AH**
email: l.morgan5@btinternet.com **web:** www.cwmbachguesthouse.co.uk
dir: *1.5m NE of Neath. A465 onto A474 & A4230 towards Aberdulais, left opposite Cadoxton church, guest house signed*

Cwmbach Cottages is a terrace of former miners' cottages that has been restored to provide a range of thoughtfully furnished bedrooms, with one on the ground floor for easier access. Spacious public areas include a comfortable lounge and a pleasant breakfast room with separate tables. A superb decked patio overlooks a wooded hillside rich with wildlife.

Rooms 5 en suite (2 fmly) (1 GF) S £40–£55; D £60–£80* **Facilities** FTV DVD iPod docking station Lounge TVL tea/coffee WiFi ⓛ 18 ⓑ **Parking** 9 **Notes** LB ⊗

NEWPORT

NEWPORT	Map 9 ST38

Labuan Guest House

★★★★ GUEST HOUSE

tel: 01633 664533 **fax:** 01633 664533 **464 Chepstow Rd NP19 8JF**
email: patricia.bees@ntlworld.com **web:** www.labuanhouse.co.uk
dir: *M4 junct 24, 1.5m on B4237*

Expect a warm welcome from owners Pat and John at this delightful guest house, set on the main road into Newport. Accommodation is comfortable and includes a ground-floor twin room; all bedrooms are of a good size and bathrooms feature a wide range of extras. The hearty breakfasts, with a good choice on the menu, are taken in the welcoming dining room at separate tables. Off-street parking is available.

Rooms 5 rms (3 en suite) (2 pri facs) (1 GF) S £40–£50; D £70–£75* **Facilities** FTV DVD TVL tea/coffee Dinner available WiFi ⓑ **Extras** Chocolate, sweets - complimentary **Parking** 6 **Notes** LB

Kepe Lodge Guest House

★★★ GUEST HOUSE

tel: 01633 262351 **fax:** 01633 262351 **46A Caerau Rd NP20 4HH**
email: kepelodge@hotmail.com
dir: *500yds W of town centre. M4 junct 27, town centre signs, 2nd lights left, premises on right*

This attractive guest house in a quiet residential area is set back from the road in pleasant gardens. Guests can expect attentive service and comfortable homely bedrooms. Breakfast is served at individual tables in the well-appointed dining room, and a comfortable lounge is also available.

Rooms 8 rms (3 en suite) S £30–£40; D £60* **Facilities** FTV tea/coffee **Parking** 12 **Notes** ⊗ No Children 10yrs ⓐ

REDWICK — Map 9 ST48

Brickhouse Country Guest House

★★★★ GUEST HOUSE

tel: 01633 880230 **fax:** 01633 882441 **North Row NP26 3DX**
email: brickhouse@compuserve.com **web:** www.brickhouseguesthouse.co.uk
dir: M4 junct 23A, follow steelworks road for 1.5m. Left after sign for Redwick, Brickhouse 1.5m on left

This impressive country house is in a peaceful location with attractive, well-tended gardens. The friendly hosts are most attentive and provide a relaxing atmosphere. Bedrooms are spacious and traditionally furnished, while the public areas include a choice of lounges. Dinners featuring home-grown produce are available by prior arrangement.

Rooms 7 rms (5 en suite) (2 pri facs) (1 fmly) S £40-£50; D £65* **Facilities** FTV Lounge TVL tea/coffee Dinner available Licensed WiFi Parking 7

PEMBROKESHIRE

FISHGUARD — Map 8 SM93

Premier Collection

Erw-Lon Farm (SN028325)

★★★★★ FARMHOUSE

tel: 01348 881297 **Pontfaen SA65 9TS**
email: lilwenmcallister@btinternet.com **web:** www.erwlonfarm.co.uk
dir: 5.5m SE of Fishguard on B4313

Located in the Pembrokeshire Coast National Park, with stunning views of the Gwaun Valley, this attractive farmhouse has been converted to provide modern well-equipped bedrooms with a wealth of homely extras. The McAllisters give the warmest of welcomes, and their memorable dinners feature the finest local produce.

Rooms 3 en suite S £50-£60; D £70-£80* **Facilities** FTV TVL tea/coffee Dinner available WiFi **Parking** 5 **Notes** LB ⊗ No Children 10yrs Closed Dec-Mar 128 acres beef/sheep

HAVERFORDWEST — Map 8 SM91

See also Narberth

Premier Collection

The Paddock (SM990217)

★★★★★ FARMHOUSE

tel: 01437 731531 & 07973 636510 **Lower Haythog, Bethlehem SA62 5QL**
email: joss@thepaddockwales.co.uk **web:** www.thepaddockwales.co.uk
dir: From Haverfordwest on A40 towards Fishguard. At next rdbt, 3rd exit onto B4329, 4.5m to Bethlehem, on right

Peacefully located and surrounded by pleasant countryside, this modern, detached accommodation stands alongside the traditional farmhouse building and has been recently refurbished to provide high levels of quality and comfort. Spacious bedrooms and bathrooms are all on the ground floor and include some welcome extras. Both breakfast and dinner (available by prior arrangement) utilise a range of high quality produce.

Rooms 3 en suite (3 GF) S £60-£75; D £80-£95* **Facilities** FTV DVD Lounge tea/coffee Dinner available WiFi **Extras** Speciality toiletries, fridge, water **Parking** 4 **Notes** ⊗ No Children 12yrs 250 acres dairy

College Guest House

★★★★ GUEST HOUSE

tel: 01437 763710 **93 Hill St, St Thomas Green SA61 1QL**
email: colinlarby@aol.com **web:** www.collegeguesthouse.com
dir: In town centre, along High St, pass church, keep in left lane. 1st exit by Stonemason Arms pub, follow signs for St Thomas Green/Leisure Centre/Police Station. 300mtrs on left by No Entry sign

Situated in a mainly residential area within easy walking distance of Haverdfordwest's attractions, this impressive Georgian house offers good levels of comfort and facilities. There is a range of practically equipped bedrooms, along with public areas that include a spacious lounge (with internet access) and an attractive pine-furnished dining room - the setting for comprehensive breakfasts.

Rooms 8 en suite (4 fmly) **Facilities** FTV DVD TVL tea/coffee WiFi **Extras** Bottled water

MANORBIER   Map 8 SS09

Castlemead

★★★★ RESTAURANT WITH ROOMS

tel: 01834 871358 **fax:** 01834 871358 **SA70 7TA**
email: castlemeadhotel@aol.com **web:** www.castlemeadhotel.com
dir: *A4139 towards Pembroke, B4585 into village, follow signs to beach & castle, establishment on left*

Benefiting from a superb location with spectacular views of the bay, the Norman church and Manorbier Castle, this family-run business is friendly and welcoming. Bedrooms, which include some in a converted former coach house at ground floor level, are generally quite spacious and have modern facilities. Public areas include a sea-view residents' lounge and a restaurant accessed by stairs, which is open to non-residents, along with a cosy bar. There are extensive gardens to the rear of the property.

Rooms 5 en suite 3 annexe en suite (2 fmly) (3 GF) **Facilities** FTV Lounge tea/coffee Dinner available Direct Dial WiFi 🔒 **Parking** 20 **Notes** Closed Jan-Feb RS Nov maybe B&B only No coaches

NARBERTH   Map 8 SN11

Premier Collection

The Grove

★★★★★ ◉◉◉ 🍴 RESTAURANT WITH ROOMS

tel: 01834 860915 **Molleston SA67 8BX**
email: info@thegrove-narberth.co.uk **web:** www.thegrove-narberth.co.uk
dir: *A48 to Carmarthen, A40 to Haverfordwest. At A478 rdbt 1st exit to Narberth, through town towards Tenby. At bottom of hill right, 1m, The Grove on right*

The Grove is an elegant 18th-century country house set on a hillside in 24 acres of rolling countryside. The owners have lovingly restored the building with care, combining period features with excellent modern decor. There are bedrooms in the main house, and additional rooms in separate buildings; all are appointed with quality and comfort. Some bedrooms are on the ground floor, and most have fantastic views out over the Preseli Hills. There are two sumptuous lounge areas, one with an open fire and a small bar, and two separate dining rooms that offer award-winning cuisine. Self-catering cottages are available.

Rooms 14 en suite 6 annexe en suite (3 fmly) (3 GF) S £170-£310; D £180-£320* **Facilities** FTV DVD Lounge tea/coffee Dinner available Direct Dial WiFi **Extras** Speciality toiletries, Welsh cakes **Conf** Max 40 Thtr 40 Class 40 Board 40 **Parking** 45 **Notes** LB Civ Wed 100

Canaston Oaks

★★★★★ 🅐 BED AND BREAKFAST

tel: 01437 541254 **fax:** 01437 541595 **Canaston Bridge SA67 8DE**
email: enquiries@canastonoaks.co.uk **web:** www.canastonoaks.co.uk
dir: *Turn left off A40 at Canaston Bridge onto A4075. 600yds on left*

Canaston Oaks is a skilful blend of converted traditional farm stables with modern additions, all designed and built by Pembrokeshire craftsmen. The decor blends classic and contemporary elements to produce high levels of comfort in a peaceful setting.

Rooms 2 en suite 5 annexe en suite (2 fmly) (7 GF) S £85-£115; D £95-£180* **Facilities** FTV DVD iPod docking station tea/coffee WiFi 🔒 **Extras** Bottled water, chocolates - complimentary **Parking** 10 **Notes** LB ⊗

NEVERN   Map 8 SN04

Trewern Arms

★★★★ INN

tel: 01239 820395 **fax:** 01239 820173 **SA42 0NB**
email: info@trewern-arms.co.uk **web:** www.trewern-arms.co.uk
dir: *Off A48. Midway between Cardigan & Fishguard*

Set in a peaceful and picturesque village, this charming 16th-century inn is well positioned to offer a relaxing stay. There are many original features to be seen in the two character bars and attractive restaurant, and the spacious bedrooms are appointed to a high standard and include some family rooms.

Rooms 10 en suite (4 fmly) **Facilities** FTV Lounge tea/coffee Dinner available WiFi Fishing Riding Pool table 🔒 **Conf** Thtr 80 Class 40 Board 30 **Parking** 100 **Notes** ⊗

NEWPORT   Map 8 SN03

Premier Collection

Y Garth Boutique B&B

★★★★★ 🍴 BED AND BREAKFAST

tel: 01348 811777 & 07814 917920 **Dinas Cross SA42 0XR**
email: enquiries@y-garth.co.uk **web:** www.bedandbreakfast-pembrokeshire.co.uk
dir: *A487 from Fishguard, in Dinas Cross turn left after tennis courts. 200yds on right*

A warm welcome can be expected from proprietor Joyce Evans at this boutique-style B&B. The sea is close by and the house is set in a quiet location some three miles from Newport; St Davids and the Pembrokeshire Coast National Park are also within easy driving distance. The bedrooms offer quality soft furnishings with sumptuous beds and many guest extras; two are en suite and one has a luxury private bathroom. There is a smart and cosy lounge plus a conservatory for guests. An award-winning breakfast is provided.

Rooms 3 rms (2 en suite) (1 pri facs) D £85-£105* **Facilities** FTV DVD iPod docking station TVL tea/coffee WiFi ⌇ 18 🔒 **Extras** Chocolates, flowers - free; robes **Parking** 3 **Notes** LB ⊗ No Children 14yrs

Llys Meddyg

★★★★ ◎◎ RESTAURANT WITH ROOMS

tel: 01239 820008 **East St SA42 0SY**
email: contact@llysmeddyg.com **web:** www.llysmeddyg.com
dir: On A487 in centre of town

Llys Meddyg is a Georgian town house offering a blend of old and new, with elegant furnishings, deep sofas and a welcoming fire. The owners of this property employed local craftsmen to create a lovely interior that has an eclectic style. The focus of the quality restaurant menu is the use of fresh, seasonal, locally sourced ingredients. The spacious bedrooms are comfortable and contemporary in design; bathrooms vary in style.

Rooms 5 en suite 3 annexe en suite (3 fmly) (1 GF) S £70-£150; D £100-£160*
Facilities FTV DVD iPod docking station Lounge tea/coffee Dinner available WiFi
⛵ 18 Riding 🛎 **Extras** Speciality toiletries, mini-bar **Conf** Max 20 Class 20 Board 20
Parking 8 **Notes** LB No coaches Civ Wed 90

Salutation Inn

★★★ 🅰 INN

tel: 01239 820564 & 07793 488262 **fax:** 01239 820355 **Filindre Farchog SA41 3UY**
email: johndenley@aol.com **web:** www.salutationcountryhotel.co.uk
dir: On A487 between Cardigan & Fishguard. 3m N of Newport

John and Gwawr Denley offer a warm welcome at this 16th-century coaching inn near Newport, in the heart of the Pembrokeshire Coast National Park. The old part of the inn blends well with the modern and well equipped bedrooms. Guests can enjoy a relaxing drink or a meal in one of the two bars; both offer oak beams and old country atmosphere. The inn overlooks lawned gardens that lead down to the river. All bedrooms are ground floor, en suite, and equipped with flat-screen TV.

Rooms 8 en suite (2 fmly) (8 GF) **Facilities** FTV tea/coffee Dinner available Direct Dial WiFi ⛵ 18 Pool table **Conf** Max 25 Thtr 25 Class 12 Board 12 **Parking** 60
Notes LB

ST DAVIDS Map 8 SM72
See also Solva

Premier Collection

Ramsey House

★★★★★ 🏠 ⬤ GUEST HOUSE

tel: 01437 720321 & 07795 575005 **fax:** 01437 701321 **Lower Moor SA62 6RP**
email: info@ramseyhouse.co.uk **web:** www.ramseyhouse.co.uk
dir: From Cross Sq in St Davids towards Porthclais, house 0.25m on left

This pleasant guest house, under the ownership of Suzanne and Shaun Ellison, offers the ideal combination of professional management and the warmth of a family-run guest house. The property is quietly located on the outskirts of St Davids and is surrounded by unspoilt countryside. It provides modern, well-equipped bedrooms, most with en suite bathrooms, along with a good range of welcome extras. Carefully prepared dinners by chef Shaun feature quality, local Welsh produce and breakfast provides a choice of home-made items, including breads and preserves.

Rooms 6 rms (5 en suite) (1 pri facs) (3 GF) S £60-£115; D £90-£115*
Facilities FTV Lounge tea/coffee Dinner available Licensed WiFi 🛎
Extras Speciality toiletries - complimentary **Parking** 10 **Notes** LB ⊗ No Children 16yrs Closed Nov-13 Feb

ST DAVIDS *continued*

Lochmeyler Farm Guest House (SM855275)

★★★★★ FARMHOUSE

tel: 01348 837724 **fax:** 01348 837622 **Llandeloy, Pen-y-Cwm SA62 6LL**
email: stay@lochmeyler.co.uk **web:** www.lochmeyler.co.uk

(For full entry see SOLVA)

The Waterings

★★★★ BED AND BREAKFAST

tel: 01437 720876 **fax:** 01437 720876 **Anchor Dr, High St SA62 6QH**
email: enquiries@waterings.co.uk **web:** www.waterings.co.uk
dir: *On A487 on E edge of St Davids*

Situated a short walk from the centre of St Davids, The Waterings offers spacious bedrooms that are accessed from a courtyard garden; most bedrooms have their own separate seating area. Breakfast, made from a good selection of local produce, is served in a smart dining room in the main house.

Rooms 2 en suite 5 annexe en suite (4 fmly) (5 GF) **Facilities** FTV tea/coffee Licensed WiFi ⌣ ♿ 9 **Conf** Max 15 Board 15 **Parking** 20 **Notes** No Children 5yrs

The City Inn

★★★ INN

tel: 0845 347 3102 & 01437 720829 **New St SA62 6SU**
email: info@cityinnstdavids.co.uk **web:** www.cityinnstdavids.co.uk

Located just a ten minute walk from St Davids Cathedral and even closer to the main town, this well-furnished accommodation provides a relaxed and informal atmosphere. Guests can choose from a range of bar and restaurant menus at both dinner and lunch. Meals are served in the main dining room. A car park is a welcome feature.

Rooms 9 en suite (5 fmly) S £50-£52.50; D £70-£75* **Facilities** FTV Dinner available WiFi ♿ 9 Pool table ♿ **Parking** 12 **Notes** Closed 23-26 Dec

SOLVA	Map 8 SM82

Crug-Glas Country House

★★★★★ ☕ 🍴 RESTAURANT WITH ROOMS

tel: 01348 831302 **Abereiddy SA62 6XX**
email: janet@crugglas.plus.com **web:** www.crug-glas.co.uk
dir: *From Solva to St Davids on A487. From St Davids take A487 towards Fishguard. 1st left after Carnhedryn, house signed*

This house, on a dairy, beef and cereal farm of approximately 600 acres, is situated about a mile from the coast on the St Davids peninsula. Comfort, relaxation and flawless attention to detail are provided by the charming host, Janet Evans. Each spacious bedroom has the hallmark of assured design plus a luxury bathroom with both bath and shower; one suite on the top floor has great views. In addition there are two suites in separate buildings.

Rooms 7 en suite (1 fmly) (2 GF) **Facilities** FTV tea/coffee Dinner available WiFi **Conf** Max 200 Thtr 200 Class 200 Board 200 **Parking** 10 **Notes** ⊗ No Children 12yrs Closed 24-27 Dec Civ Wed 220

Lochmeyler Farm Guest House (SM855275)

★★★★★ FARMHOUSE

tel: 01348 837724 **fax:** 01348 837622 **Llandeloy, Pen-y-Cwm SA62 6LL**
email: stay@lochmeyler.co.uk **web:** www.lochmeyler.co.uk
dir: *From Haverfordwest A487 (St Davids road) to Pen-y-Cwm, right to Llandeloy*

On a 220-acre dairy farm in a beautiful area, with easy access to the Pembrokeshire coastline, Lochmeyler provides high levels of comfort and excellent facilities. The spacious bedrooms, of which four are cottage-style converted outbuildings, are equipped with a wealth of thoughtful extras and have private sitting rooms. One bedroom is in the main house, and has its own separate entrance. Comprehensive breakfasts are served in the spacious dining room; a bar and pleasant lounge are also available.

Rooms 1 en suite 4 annexe en suite (4 fmly) (4 GF) S £47.50-£52.50; D £75-£85 **Facilities** FTV DVD Lounge tea/coffee Direct Dial Licensed WiFi & Pet area **Extras** Speciality toiletries, home-made Welsh cakes **Parking** 5 **Notes** LB 220 acres dairy

See advert below

TENBY
Map 8 SN10

Esplanade

★★★★ GUEST ACCOMMODATION

tel: 01834 842760 & 843333   **fax:** 01834 845633 1 The Esplanade SA70 7DU
email: esplanadetenby@googlemail.com **web:** www.esplanadetenby.co.uk
dir: Follow signs to South Beach, exit South Parade into St Florence Parade. Premises on seafront adjacent to town walls

Located beside the historic town walls of Tenby, with stunning views over the sea to Caldey Island, the Esplanade provides a range of standard and luxury bedrooms, some ideal for families. Breakfast is offered in the elegant front-facing dining room, which contains a comfortable lounge-bar area.

Rooms 14 en suite (4 fmly) (1 GF) S £50-£95; D £80-£130* **Facilities** FTV DVD Lounge tea/coffee Direct Dial Licensed WiFi & **Extras** Mineral water - complimentary **Notes** LB Closed 15-27 Dec

---

POWYS

BRECON
Map 9 SO02

See also Sennybridge

Premier Collection

Peterstone Court

★★★★★ ⚜ RESTAURANT WITH ROOMS

tel: 01874 665387 **Llanhamlach LD3 7YB**
email: info@peterstone-court.com **web:** www.peterstone-court.com
dir: 3m from Brecon on A40 towards Abergavenny

Situated on the edge of the Brecon Beacons, this establishment affords stunning views overlooking the River Usk. The atmosphere is friendly and informal, without any unnecessary fuss. No two bedrooms are alike, but all share comparable levels of comfort, quality and elegance. Public areas reflect similar standards, eclectically styled with a blend of the contemporary and the traditional. Quality produce is cooked with care in a range of enjoyable dishes.

Rooms 8 en suite 4 annexe en suite (2 fmly) **Facilities** FTV DVD iPod docking station Lounge tea/coffee Dinner available Direct Dial WiFi ⚓ Fishing Riding Sauna Gym & Pool open mid Apr-1 Oct Spa facilities **Conf** Max 100 Thtr 100 Class 100 Board 60 **Parking** 60 **Notes** LB Civ Wed

Llanddetty Hall Farm (SO124205)

★★★ FARMHOUSE

tel: 01874 676415 **fax:** 01874 676415 **Talybont-on-Usk LD3 7YR**
dir: SE of Brecon. Off B4558

This impressive Grade II listed, 17th-century farmhouse in the beautiful Usk Valley is full of character, and the friendly proprietors ensure a comfortable stay. Bedrooms are very pleasant and feature traditional furnishings, exposed timbers and polished floorboards. Welcoming log fires are lit during cold weather in the comfortable lounge, and guests dine around one table in the dining room.

Rooms 3 rms (2 en suite) (1 pri facs) 1 annexe en suite (1 GF) **Facilities** TVL TV1B tea/coffee **Parking** 6 **Notes** ⊗ No Children 12yrs Closed 15 Dec-15 Jan RS Feb-Apr restricted service at lambing season 🐑 48 acres sheep

---

BRECON *continued*

The Beacons Guest House

★★★ GUEST HOUSE

tel: 01874 623339 **fax:** 01874 623339 **16 Bridge St LD3 8AH**
email: guesthouse@thebreconbeacons.co.uk **web:** www.thebreconbeacons.co.uk
dir: *On B4601 opposite Christ College*

Located west of the historic town centre over the bridge, this 17th-century former farmhouse by the river has a range of homely bedrooms, some in converted barns and outbuildings. There is a guests' lounge and a cosy bar. This is a non-smoking establishment.

Rooms 11 rms (9 en suite) (2 pri facs) 3 annexe en suite (4 fmly) (3 GF) S £40-£85; D £60-£85* **Facilities** FTV Lounge TVL tea/coffee Licensed WiFi 🔔 **Conf** Max 30 Thtr 30 Class 25 Board 20 **Parking** 20 **Notes** LB ⊗

Borderers Guesthouse

★★★ GUEST ACCOMMODATION

tel: 01874 623559 **47 The Watton LD3 7EG**
email: info@borderers.com **web:** www.borderers.com
dir: *200yds SE of town centre on B4601, opposite church*

A warm welcome awaits at Borderers Guesthouse, originally a 17th-century drovers' inn. On offer are comfortable, attractively decorated bedrooms, some in the main building; annexe bedrooms are centred around a courtyard that provides secure car and bike parking. A private chalet is also available. Hearty breakfasts are served in the original part of the inn.

Rooms 4 rms (3 en suite) (1 pri facs) 5 annexe en suite (2 fmly) (4 GF) **Facilities** FTV tea/coffee WiFi **Parking** 6

The Lansdowne

★★★ GUEST ACCOMMODATION

tel: 01874 623321 **fax:** 01874 610438 **The Watton LD3 7EG**
email: reception@lansdownehotel.co.uk **web:** www.lansdownehotel.co.uk
dir: *A40, A470 onto B4601*

Privately-owned and personally-run, this Georgian house is conveniently located close to the town centre. The accommodation is well equipped and includes family rooms and a bedroom on ground-floor level. There is a comfortable lounge, a small bar and an attractive split-level dining room where dinner is available to residents.

Rooms 9 en suite (2 fmly) (1 GF) S £45; D £65* **Facilities** FTV Lounge tea/coffee Dinner available Direct Dial Licensed **Notes** LB No Children 5yrs

BUILTH WELLS Map 9 SO05

Rhedyn Guest House

★★★★ 🍴 GUEST HOUSE

tel: 01982 551944 & 07703 209721 **Rhedyn, Cilmery LD2 3LH**
email: info@rhedynguesthouse.co.uk **web:** www.rhedynguesthouse.co.uk
dir: *From Builth Wells on A483 towards Garth. Rhedyn Guest House on right*

This detached property stands just off the main road outside Cilmery, which is a short drive from Builth Wells. Three comfortable bedrooms provide all the modern facilities including WiFi and a range of guest extras. Two bedrooms are on the ground floor with their own entrances. Dinner, bookable at the time of reservation, offers imaginative menus. A hearty breakfast, including a selection of home-made preserves, is served in the delightful dining room around a communal table. Access to the guest house is via two gates through a field.

Rooms 1 en suite 2 annexe en suite (2 GF) S £80; D £90* **Facilities** STV FTV DVD Lounge tea/coffee Dinner available WiFi Riding 🔔 **Extras** Sherry/Welsh cakes - complimentary **Parking** 3 **Notes** ⊛

CEMMAES Map 14 SH80

The Penrhos Arms

★★★★ INN

tel: 01650 511243 & 07808 589349 **fax:** 01650 511643 **SY20 9PR**
email: dawndavies8@hotmail.com **web:** www. penrhosarms.com

The Penrhos Arms provides a warm welcome to new and returning guests alike, an historic inn with a charming and comfortable interior. Bedrooms are smartly appointed and have very comfortable beds. A hearty range of menu choices are offered, much of which uses local produce.

Rooms 5 en suite 2 annexe en suite (1 fmly) **Facilities** FTV DVD TVL tea/coffee Dinner available WiFi ⚓ Pool table 🔔 **Conf** Max 40 **Notes** LB Civ Wed 50

CRICKHOWELL Map 9 SO21

The Bear

★★★★ ⍟ INN

tel: 01873 810408 **NP8 1BW**
email: info@bearhotel.co.uk **web:** www.bearhotel.co.uk
dir: *Town centre, off A40 (Brecon road). 6m from Abergavenny*

The Bear is a favourite with locals as well as visitors; the character and friendliness of this 15th-century coaching inn are renowned. The bedrooms come in a variety of sizes and include some with four-posters. The bar and restaurant are furnished in keeping with the style of the building, and provide comfortable areas in which to enjoy some of the very popular dishes that use the finest locally-sourced ingredients, served from a menu to suit all tastes.

Rooms 34 en suite (4 fmly) (6 GF) **Facilities** FTV Lounge tea/coffee Dinner available Direct Dial WiFi Fishing 🔔 **Parking** 40

CRIGGION
Map 15 SJ21

Brimford House (SJ310150)

★★★★ FARMHOUSE

tel: 01938 570235 **SY5 9AU**
email: info@brimford.co.uk **web:** www.brimford.co.uk
dir: Exit B4393 after Crew Green left for Criggion, Brimford 1st on left after pub

This elegant Georgian house stands in lovely open countryside and is a good base for touring central Wales and the Marches. The bedrooms are spacious, and thoughtful extras enhance guest comfort. A cheery log fire burns in the lounge during colder weather; the hospitality is equally warm and creates a relaxing atmosphere throughout.

Rooms 3 en suite S fr £50; D fr £80 **Facilities** FTV TVL tea/coffee WiFi Fishing **Parking** 4 **Notes** LB 250 acres arable/beef/sheep

ERWOOD
Map 9 SO04

Hafod-y-Garreg

★★★★ ⌂ BED AND BREAKFAST

tel: 01982 560400 **LD2 3TQ**
email: john-annie@hafod-y.wanadoo.co.uk **web:** www.hafodygarreg.co.uk
dir: 1m S of Erwood. Off A470 at Trericket Mill, sharp right, up track past cream farmhouse towards pine forest, through gate

This remote Grade II listed farmhouse dates in part from 1401 and has been confirmed, by dendrochronology, as the 'oldest dwelling in Wales'. As you would expect, the house has tremendous character, and is decorated and furnished to befit its age; even so, the bedrooms have all the modern facilities. There is an impressive dining room and a lounge with an open fireplace. Warm hospitality from John and Annie is a major strength here.

Rooms 2 en suite D £89 **Facilities** STV iPod docking station tea/coffee Dinner available WiFi ⌂ **Extras** Speciality toiletries, sherry, mags/books - free **Parking** 6 **Notes** No Children Closed Xmas ⊛

HAY-ON-WYE
Map 9 SO24

See also Erwood

Old Black Lion Inn

★★★★ ⊛ INN

tel: 01497 820841 **fax:** 01497 822960 **26 Lion St HR3 5AD**
email: info@oldblacklion.co.uk **web:** www.oldblacklion.co.uk
dir: From B4348 in Hay-on-Wye into Lion St. Inn on right

This fine old coaching inn, with a history stretching back several centuries, has a wealth of charm and character. It was occupied by Oliver Cromwell during the siege

of Hay Castle. Privately-owned and personally-run, it provides cosy and well-equipped bedrooms, some located in an adjacent building. A wide range of well-prepared food is provided, and the service is relaxed and friendly.

Rooms 6 rms (5 en suite) (1 pri facs) 4 annexe en suite (2 GF) S £45-£55; D £79-£99* **Facilities** FTV tea/coffee Dinner available Direct Dial WiFi ⌂ **Parking** 12 **Notes** ⊛ Closed 24-26 Dec

KNIGHTON
Map 9 SO27

Pilleth Oaks

★★★★★ GUEST ACCOMMODATION

tel: 01547 560272 **Whitton LD7 1NP**
email: hoods@pillethoaks.co.uk **web:** www.pillethoaks.co.uk
dir: A488 W from Knighton, left onto B4356 signed Presteigne. 1m on right

Peacefully located with delightful views over the surrounding countryside in all directions, this large, detached house provides guests with plenty of quality and comfort. In addition to well-furnished bedrooms of various shapes and sizes, guests are welcome to use the very comfortable lounge. Breakfast utilises good quality local produce and is served around one large table.

Rooms 3 en suite **Facilities** FTV DVD Lounge tea/coffee WiFi Fishing ⌂ **Parking** 4 **Notes** ⊛ No Children 10yrs Closed 23-25 Dec ⊛

LLANDRINDOD WELLS
Map 9 SO06

Holly Farm (SO045593)

★★★★ FARMHOUSE

tel: 01597 822402 **fax:** 01597 822402 **Holly Ln, Howey LD1 5PP**
web: www.hollyfarmbandb.co.uk
dir: 2m S on A483 of Llandrindod Wells near Howey

This working farm dates from Tudor times. The bedrooms are homely and full of character, and the comfortable lounge has a warming log fire in cooler months. The traditional home cooking, using local produce, can be enjoyed in the dining room.

Rooms 3 en suite (1 fmly) S £38-£42; D £66-£72* **Facilities** FTV DVD TVL tea/coffee Dinner available WiFi **Parking** 4 **Notes** LB 70 acres beef/sheep

LLANGAMMARCH WELLS
Map 9 SN94

The Cammarch
★★★★ GUEST ACCOMMODATION

tel: 01591 620545 **LD4 4BY**
email: mail@cammarch.com **web:** www.cammarch.com
dir: Exit A483 at Garth, signed Llangammarch Wells, opposite T-junct

This property dates from the 1850s and was built as a hotel by the railway company. Owner Kathryn Dangerfield offers a warm welcome to all guests and the establishment provides modern, well-equipped bedrooms that are tastefully decorated. There is a comfortable spacious bar and lounge, with a log-burning fire, ideal for colder evenings. The conservatory dining room, overlooking the attractive gardens and pond, offers fresh local produce on the dinner menu and the hearty Welsh breakfast makes a good start to the day. Parking is provided at the side of the property.

Rooms 12 en suite (2 fmly) S £69; D £89 **Facilities** FTV DVD Lounge TV11B tea/coffee Dinner available Licensed WiFi ⇘ Fishing 🛎 **Extras** Speciality toiletries **Conf** Max 20 Thtr 20 Class 15 Board 15 **Parking** 16 **Notes** LB RS Xmas-New Year

LLANGEDWYN
Map 15 SJ12

Plas Uchaf Country House
★★★★ ➡ GUEST HOUSE

tel: 01691 780588 & 07817 419747 **SY10 9LD**
email: info@plasuchaf.com **web:** www.plasuchaf.com
dir: Mile End services Oswestry A483/Welshpool. After 2m right at White Lion public house, 4.5m Llangedwyn. 150yds after school on right

Located in an elevated position in extensive mature parkland, this elegant Queen Anne house provides high standards of comfort and facilities. The interior flooring was created from recycled ship timbers taken from the Armada fleet of 1588, and furnishing styles highlight the many period features. Imaginative dinners are available, and a warm welcome is assured.

Rooms 6 en suite (1 fmly) (1 GF) S £61.50; D £87-£102* **Facilities** FTV DVD iPod docking station Lounge tea/coffee Dinner available Licensed WiFi ⛲⇘ 🛎 **Conf** Max 15 Thtr 15 Class 15 Board 15 **Parking** 30 **Notes** LB Civ Wed 50

Symbols and abbreviations are explained on page 7

LLANGURIG
Map 9 SN97

The Old Vicarage
★★★★ GUEST HOUSE

tel: 01686 440280 **fax:** 01686 440280 **SY18 6RN**
email: info@theoldvicaragellangurig.co.uk **web:** www.theoldvicaragellangurig.co.uk
dir: A470 onto A44, signed

Located in pretty, mature grounds, which feature a magnificent holly tree, this elegant Victorian house provides a range of thoughtfully furnished bedrooms, some with fine period objects. Breakfast is served in a spacious dining room, and a comfortable guest lounge is also available.

Rooms 4 en suite (1 fmly) S £42; D £68* **Facilities** DVD TVL tea/coffee Licensed WiFi 🛎 **Parking** 6 **Notes** LB ➡

LLANIDLOES
Map 9 SN98

Mount Inn
★★★ INN

tel: 01686 412247 **China St SY18 6AB**
email: mountllani@aol.com
dir: In town centre

Mount Inn is believed to occupy part of the site of an old motte and bailey castle, and started life as a coaching inn. The traditional bars are full of character, with exposed beams and timbers as well as cobbled flooring and log fires. Bedrooms, which include some in a separate building, are carefully furnished and equipped with practical and thoughtful extras.

Rooms 3 en suite 6 annexe en suite (3 fmly) (3 GF) S £47; D £70* **Facilities** FTV Lounge TVL tea/coffee Dinner available WiFi ⛲ 9 Pool table 🛎 **Conf** Max 20 Thtr 12 Class 20 Board 12 **Parking** 12

LLANWRTYD WELLS
Map 9 SN84

Carlton Riverside
★★★★ ◉◉ RESTAURANT WITH ROOMS

tel: 01591 610248 **Irfon Crescent LD5 4SP**
email: carltonriverside@hotmail.co.uk **web:** www.carltonriverside.com
dir: *In town centre beside bridge*

Guests are made to feel part of the family at this character property, set beside the river in the smallest town in Wales. Carlton Riverside offers award-winning cuisine which Mary Ann Gilchrist produces using the very best of local ingredients. The set menu is complemented by a well-chosen wine list and dinner is served in the stylish restaurant which offers a memorable blend of traditional comfort, modern design and river views. Four comfortable bedrooms have tasteful combinations of antique and contemporary furniture, along with welcome personal touches.

Rooms 4 en suite S £50; D £65-£100* **Facilities** FTV Lounge tea/coffee Dinner available WiFi 🔒 **Notes** LB Closed 20-30 Dec No coaches

Lasswade Country House
★★★★ ◉◉ RESTAURANT WITH ROOMS

tel: 01591 610515 **fax:** 01591 610611 **Station Rd LD5 4RW**
email: info@lasswadehotel.co.uk **web:** www.lasswadehotel.co.uk
dir: *Exit A483 into Irfon Terrace, right into Station Rd, 350yds on right*

This friendly establishment on the edge of the town has impressive views over the countryside. Bedrooms are comfortably furnished and well equipped, while the public areas consist of a tastefully decorated lounge, an elegant restaurant with a bar, and an airy conservatory which looks towards the neighbouring hills. The kitchen utilises fresh, local produce to provide an enjoyable dining experience.

Rooms 8 en suite (1 fmly) S £70-£90; D £80-£120* **Facilities** FTV Lounge TVL tea/coffee Dinner available WiFi ⚓ Riding 🔒 **Conf** Max 20 Thtr 20 Class 20 Board 20 **Parking** 6 **Notes** LB No coaches

SENNYBRIDGE
Map 9 SN92

Maeswalter
★★★★ GUEST ACCOMMODATION

tel: 01874 636629 **Heol Senni LD3 8SU**
email: bb@maeswalter.co.uk **web:** www.maeswalter.co.uk
dir: *A470 onto A4215, 2.5m left for Heol Senni, 1.5m on right over cattle grid*

Set in a peaceful country location with splendid views of the Senni Valley, this 17th-century farmhouse offers a friendly and relaxing place to stay. The accommodation is well maintained and includes a suite on the ground floor of an adjacent building. A lounge-dining room is provided, and freshly cooked farmhouse breakfasts are a pleasure.

Rooms 4 en suite (1 fmly) (2 GF) **Facilities** STV FTV TVL tea/coffee Dinner available **Parking** 12 **Notes** ⊗ No Children 5yrs

WELSHPOOL
Map 15 SJ20

See also Criggion

Heath Cottage *(SJ239023)*
★★★ 🏚 FARMHOUSE

tel: 01938 580453 **fax:** 01938 580453 **Kingswood, Forden SY21 8LX**
email: heathcottagewales@tiscali.co.uk
dir: *4m S of Welshpool. Off A490 behind Forden Old Post Office, opposite Parrys Garage*

The furnishings and decor at Heath Cottage highlight the original features of this early 18th-century farmhouse. Bedrooms have stunning country views, and a choice of lounges, one with a log fire. Memorable breakfasts feature free-range eggs and home-made preserves.

Rooms 3 en suite (1 fmly) S fr £35; D fr £70* **Facilities** TVL tea/coffee WiFi 🔒 **Parking** 4 **Notes** ⊗ Closed Oct-Etr 🐾 6 acres poultry/sheep

SWANSEA

LLANGENNITH
Map 8 SS49

Kings Head
★★★★ INN

tel: 01792 386212 **fax:** 01792 386477 **Town House SA3 1HX**
email: info@kingsheadgower.co.uk **web:** www.kingsheadgower.co.uk
dir: *M4 junct 47 follow signs for Gower A483. At next rdbt, 2nd left follow signs to Gowerton. At lights right onto B495, through old walls, keep left at fork. Kings Head on right*

The Kings Head is made up of three 17th-century buildings set behind a splendid rough stone wall; it stands opposite the church in this coastal village. The well-equipped bedrooms, including some on the ground floor, are in two of the buildings. This is an ideal base for exploring the Gower Peninsula, whether for walking, cycling or surfing. Evening meals and breakfasts can be taken in the inn.

Rooms 27 en suite (3 fmly) (14 GF) S £99-£150; D £125-£150* **Facilities** FTV tea/coffee Dinner available Direct Dial Pool table 🔒 **Parking** 35 **Notes** LB Closed 25 Dec RS 24 Dec closed for check-in

MUMBLES
Map 8 SS68

Premier Collection

Little Langland
★★★★★ GUEST ACCOMMODATION

tel: 01792 369696 **2 Rotherslade Rd, Langland SA3 4QN**
email: enquiries@littlelangland.co.uk **web:** www.littlelangland.co.uk
dir: *Exit A4067 in Mumbles into Newton Rd, 4th left at lights into Langland Rd, 2nd left into Rotherslade Rd*

Little Langland is only five miles from Swansea's city centre and within easy access of the stunning Gower Peninsula with its many coves and bays. The bedrooms are stylish, comfortable, and include free broadband. There is a café bar, ideal for a relaxing drink, and also a bar menu of freshly prepared snacks. Breakfast is served in the comfortable dining area.

Rooms 6 en suite S £70; D £90 **Facilities** FTV tea/coffee Dinner available Direct Dial Licensed WiFi **Parking** 5 **Notes** ⊗ No Children 8yrs

PARKMILL (NEAR SWANSEA)   Map 8 SS58

Parc-le-Breos House *(SS529896)*

★★★★ FARMHOUSE

tel: 01792 371636 **fax:** 01792 371287 **SA3 2HA**
email: info@parclebreos.co.uk **web:** www.parc-le-breos.co.uk
dir: *On A4118, right 300yds after Shepherds shop, next left, signed*

This imposing, early 19th-century house is at the end of a forest drive and set in over 60 acres of delightful grounds. Many charming original features have been retained in the public rooms, which include a lounge and a games room. The bedrooms have comfortable furnishings, and many are suitable for families.

Rooms 10 en suite (7 fmly) (1 GF) **Facilities** FTV Lounge TVL tea/coffee Dinner available Licensed WiFi Fishing Riding Pool table **Conf** Max 30 Thtr 30 **Parking** 12 **Notes** LB ⊗ Closed 25-26 Dec 65 acres arable/horses/pigs/chickens

REYNOLDSTON   Map 8 SS48

Premier Collection

Fairyhill

★★★★★ ◉◉ ≜ RESTAURANT WITH ROOMS

tel: 01792 390139 **fax:** 01792 391358 **SA3 1BS**
email: postbox@fairyhill.net **web:** www.fairyhill.net
dir: *M4 junct 47, A483, at next rdbt right onto A484. At Gowerton take B4295 for 10m*

Peace and tranquillity are never far away at this charming Georgian mansion set in the heart of the beautiful Gower Peninsula. Bedrooms are furnished with care and are filled with many thoughtful extras. There is also a range of comfortable seating areas, with crackling log fires, to choose from. The smart restaurant offers menus based on local produce that are complemented by an excellent wine list.

Rooms 8 en suite S £170-£270; D £190-£290* **Facilities** FTV DVD iPod docking station Lounge TVL tea/coffee Dinner available Direct Dial WiFi ⚓ Holistic treatments **Extras** Speciality toiletries **Conf** Max 32 Thtr 32 Board 16 **Parking** 50 **Notes** LB No Children 8yrs Closed 26 Dec & 5-30 Jan No coaches Civ Wed 40

SWANSEA   Map 9 SS69

The Alexander

★★★★ GUEST ACCOMMODATION

tel: 01792 470045 **fax:** 01792 476012 **3 Sketty Rd, Uplands SA2 0EU**
email: reception@alexander-hotel.co.uk **web:** www.alexander-hotel.co.uk

Located in fashionable Uplands between The Gower and the city centre, this Victorian house has been modernised to provide good levels of comfort and facilities. Bedrooms include family rooms, doubles and twins, and all are filled with a very good range of practical extras. Other areas include a cosy dining room where a hearty breakfast is served, and a comfortably furnished lounge with a guest bar.

Rooms 9 rms (8 en suite) (1 pri facs) (4 fmly) **Facilities** FTV Lounge tea/coffee Direct Dial Licensed WiFi **Notes** ⊗

The White House

★★★★ GUEST ACCOMMODATION

tel: 01792 473856 & 07729 414273   fax: 01792 455300 **4 Nyanza Ter SA1 4QQ**
email: reception@thewhitehousehotel.co.uk **web:** www.thewhitehousehotel.co.uk
dir: *On A4118, 1m W of city centre at junct with Eaton Crescent*

Part of a short early-Victorian terrace in fashionable Uplands, this house retains many of its original features. It has been restored to provide thoughtfully furnished, comfortable accommodation, with all bedrooms having en suite facilities. Breakfast offers a very good selection of hot and cold dishes including a cooked Welsh breakfast. On-road parking is available and there is easy access to local restaurants and shops.

Rooms 9 en suite (2 fmly) **Facilities** FTV Lounge tea/coffee WiFi

Hurst Dene Guest House

★★★ GUEST HOUSE

tel: 01792 280920 **fax:** 01792 280920 **10 Sketty Rd, Uplands SA2 0LJ**
email: hurstdenehotel@yahoo.co.uk **web:** www.hurstdene.co.uk
dir: *1m W of city centre. A4118 through Uplands shopping area into Sketty Rd, Hurst Dene on right*

This friendly guest house has a private car park and provides soundly maintained bedrooms with modern furnishings and equipment. Facilities include an attractive breakfast room with separate tables and a small comfortable lounge.

Rooms 10 rms (8 en suite) (3 fmly) (1 GF) S £38-£50; D £65* **Facilities** FTV TVL tea/coffee WiFi **Parking** 7 **Notes** ⊗ Closed 22 Dec-1 Jan

See advert on opposite page

VALE OF GLAMORGAN

BONVILSTON   Map 9 ST07

Plas Hen Country Guest House

★★★★ BED AND BREAKFAST

tel: 01446 781345 & 07967 756627   **Heol-y-March CF5 6TS**
email: helen@plashen.co.uk **web:** www.plashen.co.uk
dir: *M4 junct 33 onto A4232 to Culverhouse Cross interchange. A48 to Cowbridge, take right turn to Welsh St Donats*

Plas Hen is welcoming accommodation surrounded by pleasant countryside, with easy access to nearby Cardiff or the popular town of Cowbridge. Bedrooms are well decorated and are all located on the first floor. A comfortable guest lounge is available, in addition to car parking and a large garden. Breakfast is cooked to order on the Aga, and is served in the kitchen/dining room around one large table.

Rooms 4 en suite (1 fmly) S £50-£65; D £79-£89* **Facilities** FTV DVD Lounge TVL tea/coffee WiFi ⌧ 18 Riding Sauna Gym **Extras** Fresh milk, Welsh cakes **Parking** 5 **Notes** LB ⊗

HENSOL   Map 9 ST07

Premier Collection

Llanerch Vineyard

★★★★★ ◉ 🛏 GUEST ACCOMMODATION

tel: 01443 222716 **CF72 8GG**
email: info@llanerch-vineyard.co.uk **web:** www.llanerch-vineyard.co.uk
dir: *M4 junct 34, follow brown signs*

Llanerch Vineyard is delightfully set on a working Welsh vineyard with views over the vines to the countryside beyond. Bedrooms and bathrooms come in a range of shapes and sizes including sumptuously appointed suites in the main building. The Cariad Restaurant & Bistro is open during the day for lunch, afternoon tea and dinner, with outdoor seating on the terrace in the warmer months. The vineyard's own wines are available to purchase in the small shop area, and are also on the wine list at dinner.

Rooms 3 en suite 7 annexe en suite (3 fmly) (7 GF) S £70-£200; D £80-£220* **Facilities** FTV DVD TVL tea/coffee Dinner available Direct Dial Licensed WiFi ⌧ 18 **Parking** 100 **Notes** LB

LLANCARFAN   Map 9 ST07

Fox and Hounds

★★★★ 🍽 INN

tel: 01446 781287 **CF62 3AD**
email: foxandhoundsllancarfan@gmail.com **web:** www.foxandhoundsllancarfan.co.uk
dir: *M4 junct 33, at rdbt 4th exit onto A48. Left onto A4226, turn right signed Fox and Hounds*

Located in a peaceful village, this country-style inn offers a relaxed ambience combined with an excellent choice of dishes with good quality ingredients utilised at both dinner and breakfast. Bedrooms and bathrooms are all located on this first floor of the inn and come in a range of shapes and sizes. Outdoor seating is also available.

Rooms 8 en suite (1 fmly) S £65; D £90-£100 **Facilities** FTV tea/coffee Dinner available Direct Dial WiFi ⌧ 18 **Parking** 18 **Notes** ⊗ Closed 25-27 Dec No coaches

WREXHAM

LLANARMON DYFFRYN CEIRIOG   Map 15 SJ13

The Hand at Llanarmon

★★★★ ◉ INN

tel: 01691 600666 **fax:** 01691 600262 **LL20 7LD**
email: reception@thehandhotel.co.uk **web:** www.thehandhotel.co.uk
dir: *Exit A5 at Chirk onto B4500 signed Ceiriog Valley, 11m to village*

Appointed to a high standard, this inn provides a range of thoughtfully furnished bedrooms, with smart modern bathrooms. Public areas retain many original features including exposed beams and open fires. Imaginative food utilises the finest of local produce. A warm welcome and attentive service ensure a memorable guest experience.

Rooms 13 en suite (4 GF) S £50-£65; D £90-£127.50 **Facilities** Lounge tea/coffee Dinner available Direct Dial WiFi Pool table **Conf** Max 15 Thtr 10 Class 10 Board 15 **Parking** 19 **Notes** LB

WREXHAM   Map 15 SJ35

Buck House

★★★ INN

tel: 01978 780336 & 07515 709883   **fax:** 01978 781101 **High St LL13 0BU**
email: buckhousehotel@aol.com **web:** www.buckhousehotel.co.uk

Standing in the centre of the historic village, Buck House is a traditional inn located just a short drive from the racecourse. Bedrooms are comfortable and well equipped and there is a choice of bars with a good selection of real ales on tap. Whether choosing to dine in one of the bars or in the restaurant there is a good range of home-made classics on offer.

Rooms 4 en suite (1 fmly) S fr £35; D fr £60* **Facilities** FTV DVD Lounge TVL tea/coffee Dinner available Direct Dial WiFi Fishing Pool table ◈ **Conf** Max 60 Thtr 60 Class 50 Board 30 **Parking** 20

Ireland

NORTHERN IRELAND

COUNTY ANTRIM

BUSHMILLS Map 1 C6

Premier Collection

Causeway Lodge

★★★★★ ⌂ GUEST HOUSE

tel: 028 2073 0333 **fax:** 0800 756 5433
52 Moycraig Rd, Dunseverick BT57 8TB
email: stay@causewaylodge.com **web:** www.causewaylodge.com

Causeway Lodge offers high-quality, contemporary accommodation in an idyllic setting on the north Antrim coast. Each of the individually designed bedrooms is thoughtfully presented and the Causeway Suite is very stylish. The house is close to the Giant's Causeway, Carrick-A-Rede rope bridge and the famous Bushmills Distillery. WiFi is available and a warm welcome is assured from the friendly owners. Causeway Lodge was the AA Guest Accommodation of the Year for Northern Ireland 2013-14.

Rooms 4 en suite 1 annexe en suite (2 fmly) (1 GF) S £80-£100; D £90-£140* **Facilities** STV FTV iPod docking station TVL tea/coffee WiFi 🏃 **Extras** Speciality toiletries, fridge, bottled water, milk **Parking** 6 **Notes** ⊗

AA GUEST ACCOMMODATION OF THE YEAR FOR NORTHERN IRELAND 2014–2015

Premier Collection

Whitepark House

★★★★★ GUEST ACCOMMODATION

tel: 028 2073 1482 **150 Whitepark Rd, Ballintoy BT54 6NH**
email: bob@whiteparkhouse.com **web:** www.whiteparkhouse.com
dir: On A2 at Whitepark Bay, 6m E of Bushmills

Whitepark House nestles above a sandy beach and has super views of the ocean and Scotland's Western Isles. The house features bijouterie gathered from Far Eastern travels, while the traditional bedrooms are homely. Breakfasts are served around a central table in the open-plan hallway, and hospitality is warm and memorable.

Rooms 3 en suite S £80; D £120 **Facilities** Lounge tea/coffee WiFi **Extras** Bottled water, robes **Parking** 6 **Notes** ⊗ No Children 10yrs

BELFAST

BELFAST Map 1 D5

Tara Lodge

★★★★ GUEST ACCOMMODATION

tel: 028 9059 0900 **fax:** 028 9059 0901 **36 Cromwell Rd BT7 1JW**
email: info@taralodge.com **web:** www.taralodge.com
dir: M1 onto A55, left onto A1, right into Fitzwilliam St, left into University Rd, proceed to Botanic Av

Friendly staff and comfortable bedrooms make Tara Lodge popular for those on holiday or on business. The stylish dining room is the scene for memorable breakfasts, while secure off-road parking is a bonus so close to the city centre.

Rooms 19 en suite 15 annexe en suite (3 GF) S £69-£89; D £79-£119* **Facilities** STV FTV DVD TVL tea/coffee Direct Dial Lift WiFi **Parking** 19 **Notes** LB ⊗ Closed 24-28 Dec

Springfield B&B

★★★ BED AND BREAKFAST

tel: 07711 971188 **16 Springfield Rd BT12 7AG**
email: k.obrien@live.co.uk

Located just 10-15 minutes' walk from the city centre, Springfield B&B offers budget accommodation and genuine hospitality. Bedrooms and en suites are generally compact but cater well for the guest. Complimentary WiFi and good sized TVs feature throughout. Breakfast offers a great start to the day with the traditional Ulster Fry - not for the faint hearted, but not to be missed.

Rooms 5 en suite

COUNTY DOWN

DONAGHADEE Map 1 D5

Pier 36

★★★★ 🅰 GUEST HOUSE

tel: 028 9188 4466 **fax:** 028 9188 4636 **36 The Parade BT21 0HE**
email: info@pier36.co.uk **web:** www.pier36.co.uk
dir: A2 left onto flyover before Bangor, follow signs for Donaghadee (right across bridge). In 3m take 3rd exit at rdbt towards harbour. Pier 36 on right

Pier 36 is right on the quayside of Donaghadee Harbour. The en suite bedrooms are well furnished, and both superior and standard rooms are available, all with fabulous views over the harbour and Copeland Islands. The breakfast menu is extensive, and there's is also a restaurant where guests can enjoy anything from sirloin and fillet steaks to a wide range of seafood, or a home-made scone beside the fire. Entertainment is offered most weekends.

Rooms 6 en suite (2 fmly) **Facilities** STV FTV TVL tea/coffee Dinner available Licensed WiFi ⅃ 18 🏃 **Conf** Max 14 Thtr 14 Class 14 Board 14

COUNTY FERMANAGH

ENNISKILLEN   Map 1 C5

Belmore Court & Motel

★★★★ GUEST ACCOMMODATION

tel: 028 6632 6633 **fax:** 028 6632 6362 **Tempo Rd BT74 6HX**
email: info@motel.co.uk **web:** www.motel.co.uk
dir: On A4, opposite Tesco on corner of Tempo Rd (B80)

Situated in the centre of Enniskillen, the Belmore Court offers an ideal location for visiting the north west and Fermagh lakes. The accommodation offered has a range of styles from rooms with small kitchen areas to executive suites. All are stylish and have the modern attractions of flat-screen TVs and free WiFi. Some also come with espresso coffee makers. The public areas are also modern, and the breakfast room catches all the morning sun. Free parking.

Rooms 30 en suite 30 annexe en suite (17 fmly) (12 GF) **Facilities** FTV DVD iPod docking station TVL tea/coffee Direct Dial Lift WiFi ⚓ 18 **Conf** Max 45 Thtr 45 Class 25 Board 16 **Parking** 60 **Notes** ⊗ Closed 24-27 Dec

COUNTY LONDONDERRY

COLERAINE   Map 1 C6

Premier Collection

Greenhill House (C849210)

★★★★★ ⌂ FARMHOUSE

tel: 028 7086 8241 & 07719 884103 **fax:** 028 7086 8365
24 Greenhill Rd, Aghadowey BT51 4EU
email: greenhill.house@btinternet.com **web:** www.greenhill-house.co.uk
dir: A29 from Coleraine, S for 7m, left onto B66 (Greenhill Rd) for 300yds. House on right (AA sign at front gate)

Set in the tranquil Bann Valley, overlooking the Antrim Hills, this delightful Georgian house nestles in well-tended gardens with views to open rolling countryside. Public rooms are traditionally styled and include a comfortable lounge and an elegant dining room. The pleasant bedrooms vary in size and style and have a host of thoughtful extras.

Rooms 4 en suite (1 fmly) S £45; D £70 **Facilities** FTV TVL tea/coffee Direct Dial WiFi ⚓ **Extras** Snacks, bottled water, fruit **Parking** 10 **Notes** ⊗ Closed Nov-Feb RS Mar-Oct 150 acres beef

REPUBLIC OF IRELAND

COUNTY CARLOW

CARLOW   Map 1 C3

Avlon House Bed & Breakfast

★★★★ BED AND BREAKFAST

tel: 059 9174222 **fax:** 059 9173829 **Green Ln, Dublin Rd**
email: avlonhouse@eircom.net **web:** www.carlowbedandbreakfast.com
dir: N of town centre

Avlon House is a property built with visiting guests in mind. Located on the main approach from Dublin, there is secure parking and an attractively landscaped garden terrace. All of the bedrooms are well appointed, and guests have the choice of two comfortable lounge areas. While it is a non-smoking house, there is a dedicated smoking lodge in the garden.

Rooms 5 en suite (1 fmly) **Facilities** STV FTV TVL tea/coffee Dinner available Direct Dial WiFi **Parking** 7 **Notes** ⊗

Barrowville Town House

★★★★ GUEST HOUSE

tel: 059 9143324 & 086 2520013 **Kilkenny Rd**
email: barrowvilletownhouse@eircom.net **web:** www.barrowville.com
dir: Carlow Town, N9 Kilkenny Rd near Institute of Technology

The Smyths are the friendly owners of this carefully maintained 18th-century town house. Many of the very comfortable bedrooms are spacious, and the public rooms are elegant and relaxing. The conservatory, with its fruiting vine, is where Barrowville's breakfasts are served, overlooking well tended gardens. Ample parking is available.

Rooms 7 en suite (3 fmly) S €40-€55; D €70-€100* **Facilities** STV TVL tea/coffee Direct Dial WiFi **Parking** 11 **Notes** LB ⊗ Closed 24-26 Dec

COUNTY CLARE

BALLYVAUGHAN   Map 1 B3

Ballyvaughan Lodge

★★★ ⌂ GUEST HOUSE

tel: 065 7077292 & 086 2511512
email: ballyvaughanlodge@yahoo.ie **web:** www.ballyvaughanlodge.com
dir: From Galway take N6. Exit at junct 19 onto N18 (Oranmore). In Kilcolgan right onto N69 signed Ennistimon. Lodge on right on entering Ballyvaughan

The warm and welcoming home of the O'Sullivans is the ideal base for touring the wonderful Burren region and Galway Bay. The village has a number of craft shops and atmospheric pubs, most of which serve evening meals. Bedrooms are comfortably appointed and the relaxing lounges include a sun room, with reading material, guides and some interesting pieces of original art. Breakfast is a delight; an array of fresh and poached fruits and local farmhouse cheeses followed by a selection of options cooked to order by Pauline.

Rooms 11 en suite (1 fmly) (5 GF) S €45-€60; D €70-€90* **Facilities** FTV Lounge TVL tea/coffee Direct Dial WiFi ⚓ **Extras** Bottled water, snacks, chocolates **Parking** 11 **Notes** Closed 23-28 Dec

Follow us on twitter
@TheAA_Lifestyle

CRATLOE
Map 1 B3

Premier Collection

Highbury House

★★★★★ ☰ BED AND BREAKFAST

tel: 061 357212 & 086 3304648 **Ballymoris**
email: cormston@iol.ie **web:** www.highbury.homestead.com
dir: On N18, 2m S of Bunratty Castle

Rosemary and Jack Ormston's wonderful family home is set in secluded landscaped gardens on the main road from Shannon to Limerick. Each of the four comfortably appointed rooms is individually decorated, with lots of reading material and personal touches to ensure guests have a relaxing time. A recent addition is a light-filled lounge overlooking the gardens. The atmospheric breakfast room is the location for Rosemary's range of breakfast delights, featuring home-made preserves and baking, together with chatty anecdotes from Jack. There is plenty of parking, and a children's play area is available if required.

Rooms 4 en suite (4 fmly) (4 GF) S €45; D €76-€80 **Facilities** FTV Lounge TVL tea/coffee WiFi 🍴 **Extras** Snacks, sweets, magazines **Parking** 6 **Notes** LB ⊗ Closed 15 Dec-10 Jan

DOOLIN
Map 1 B3

Cullinan's Seafood Restaurant & Guest House

★★★ ◉◉ ☰ GUEST HOUSE

tel: 065 7074183
email: info@cullinansdoolin.com **web:** www.cullinansdoolin.com
dir: In town centre at x-rds between McGanns Pub & O'Connors Pub

A charming guest house and restaurant, where dinner is served in the conservatory dining room (in season; closed Wed and Sun) overlooking the River Aille. Chef-patron James Cullinan features locally caught fresh fish on the dinner menu, which also includes steaks, lamb and vegetarian dishes, and there is a popular Early Bird menu. Bedrooms are attractively decorated in a traditional style. There is a cosy guest lounge and ample off-street parking.

Rooms 8 en suite 2 annexe en suite (3 fmly) (3 GF) S €40-€75; D €60-€110 **Facilities** STV FTV Lounge TVL tea/coffee Dinner available Direct Dial WiFi **Parking** 15 **Notes** ⊗ Closed mid Dec-mid Feb

Visit theAA.com/shop
for the latest Hotel, Pub and Restaurant Guides

LAHINCH
Map 1 B3

Premier Collection

Moy House

★★★★★ ◉◉ ☰ GUEST HOUSE

tel: 065 7082800 **fax:** 065 7082500
email: moyhouse@eircom.net **web:** www.moyhouse.com
dir: 1km from Lahinch on Miltown Malbay Rd, signed from Lahinch N67

Moy House, an 18th-century former hunting lodge, overlooks Lahinch Bay, the world-famous surfing beach and championship golf links. Individually designed bedrooms and suites are decorated with luxurious fabrics and fine antique furniture. The elegant drawing room has an open turf fire and guests can enjoy breathtaking views of the ocean while enjoying a pre-dinner drink from the honesty bar. The Conservatory Restaurant adjoins the elegant dining room and features award-winning cookery. The menu is based on local seafood and seasonal produce from small independent farmers. A gourmet tasting menu is served on selected nights. Dinner must be pre-booked. Breakfast is also a treat, with a number of healthy options on offer together with the traditional Irish selection.

Rooms 9 en suite (2 fmly) (4 GF) S €140-€280; D €185-€360* **Facilities** STV FTV DVD TVL Dinner available Direct Dial Licensed WiFi 🍴 Private access to beach **Extras** Speciality toiletries **Conf** Max 16 Board 16 **Parking** 30 **Notes** LB ⊗ Closed Nov-Feb Civ Wed 35

LISCANNOR
Map 1 B3

Moher Lodge (R043917)

★★★★ FARMHOUSE

tel: 065 7081269 **fax:** 065 7081589 **Cliffs of Moher**
email: moherlodge@gmail.com **web:** www.cliffsofmoher-ireland.com
dir: 1m from Cliffs of Moher on R478

This very comfortable farmhouse is within walking distance of the world famous Cliffs of Moher. Three of the well appointed bedrooms are on the ground floor. There is a cosy sitting room with a turf fire and guests are greeted with tea and Mary's Guinness cake on arrival; there is a selection of dishes and freshly baked scones for breakfast. The locality offers restaurants, pubs with Irish music, ferries to the Aran Islands and the links golf course at Lahinch.

Rooms 4 en suite (1 fmly) (3 GF) **Facilities** FTV TVL tea/coffee WiFi **Parking** 4 **Notes** ⊗ Closed Nov-Mar 🐄 300 acres dairy/beef

LISDOONVARNA
Map 1 B3

Ballinsheen House

★★★★ BED AND BREAKFAST

tel: 065 7074806 & 087 1241872 **Galway Rd**
email: ballinsheenhouse@hotmail.com **web:** www.ballinsheen.com
dir: On N67

Ballinsheen House is situated on an elevated site overlooking the spa town of Lisdoonvarna. Guests can enjoy the scenery from the lovely garden or relax in the cosy guest sitting room by the turf fire. A delicious breakfast is served in the conservatory dining room and includes Mary Gardiner's home baking and locally smoked salmon. The bedrooms offer good space and are attractively decorated, some are suitable for families. This is an ideal base for exploring the Burren region on walking or bicycle trips. Secure off-street parking is available.

Rooms 4 en suite (2 fmly) **Facilities** STV Lounge TVL tea/coffee WiFi 📶 18 🍴 **Parking** 9 **Notes** ⊗ Closed Nov-Feb

Wild Honey Inn

★★★★ ◎◎ RESTAURANT WITH ROOMS

tel: 065 7074300 **fax:** 065 7074490 **Kincora**
email: info@wildhoneyinn.com **web:** www.wildhoneyinn.com
dir: *N18 from Ennis to Ennistymon. Continue through Ennistymon towards Lisdoonvarna, located on the right at edge of town*

Set in a former hotel dating from the 1860s, when the town prospered as a Spa, the Wild Honey Inn has created a solid reputation for its cuisine. 'Modern bistro style' is Aidan McGrath's description of the food on offer, served in the comfortable atmospheric bar at both lunch and dinner. Great attention is paid to the provenance of the ingredients, most of which are organic and sourced as close to County Clare as possible. Reservations are not taken. Bedrooms come in a number of styles, and the garden rooms have private patios. Residents have the use of a relaxing lounge, filled with reading material, not surprisingly featuring food and cookery. Breakfast is also a highlight of any visit, with a range of interesting options.

Rooms 14 en suite (3 GF) **Facilities** STV Lounge Dinner available Direct Dial WiFi ⌚
Notes LB ⊗ No Children 4yrs Closed early Jan-mid Feb RS Nov-Dec & Jan-Apr
Open Thu-Sun No coaches

TUAMGRANEY
Map 1 B3

Clareville House

★★★★ ⌂ BED AND BREAKFAST

tel: 061 922925 & 087 6867548 **fax:** 061 922925
email: info@clarevillehouse.net **web:** www.clarevillehouse.net
dir: *On R352 in village adjacent to Scarriff*

Clareville House is situated in the pretty lakeside village of Tuamgraney. Bedrooms are attractively decorated and furnished to a high standard, and there is a cosy guest sitting room. Teresa's breakfast is a special treat. Walking tours are organised by Derek, who knows all about fishing and golf in the area, and also offers a taxi service and airport collection.

Rooms 4 en suite (4 fmly) S €45-€50; D fr €75 **Facilities** FTV TVL tea/coffee WiFi ⌚ 18 Riding ⌚ **Extras** Bottled water, magazines **Parking** 8 **Notes** LB ⊗

COUNTY CORK

BALTIMORE
Map 1 B1

Rolfs Country House

★★★ ◎ RESTAURANT WITH ROOMS

tel: 028 20289 **Baltimore Hill**
email: info@rolfscountryhouse.com **web:** www.rolfscountryhouse.com
dir: *Before village turn sharp left up hill. House signed*

Situated on a hill above the fishing village of Baltimore, these 400-year-old stone buildings have been successfully converted by the Haffner family. There are ten traditionally furnished en suite bedrooms in an annexe, a cosy bar with an open fire, and a rustic restaurant on two levels. Dinner is served nightly during the high season and at weekends in the winter; the menu features quality meats, artisan cheeses and fish landed at the busy pier. This is a lovely place to stay and the hosts are very friendly.

Rooms 10 annexe en suite S €50-€60; D €80-€100* **Facilities** FTV tea/coffee Dinner available WiFi **Parking** 60 **Notes** LB Closed 20-26 Dec No coaches

BANDON
Map 1 B2

Glebe Country House

★★★★ ⌂ BED AND BREAKFAST

tel: 021 4778294 & 086 3680202 **fax:** 021 4778456 **Ballinadee**
email: info@glebecountryhouse.ie **web:** www.glebecountryhouse.com
dir: *Exit N71 at Innishannon Bridge signed Ballinadee, 8km (along river bank), left after village sign*

Situated in the charming village of Ballinadee, Glebe Country House stands in well-kept gardens, and is run with great attention to detail. Antique furnishings predominate throughout this comfortable home-from-home, which has an elegant lounge and dining room. Bedrooms are spacious and well appointed. There is an interesting breakfast menu featuring local and garden produce, and a country-house style dinner is available by arrangement.

Rooms 4 en suite (2 fmly) **Facilities** TVL tea/coffee Dinner available Direct Dial WiFi ch fac ⌚ **Parking** 10 **Notes** Closed 21 Dec-3 Jan

CLONAKILTY
Map 1 B2

Duvane House (W349405)

★★★★ ⌂ FARMHOUSE

tel: 023 8833129 **Ballyduvane**
email: duvanefarm@eircom.net **web:** www.duvanehouse.com
dir: *1km SW from Clonakilty on N71*

This Georgian farmhouse is on the N71 Skibbereen road. Bedrooms are comfortable and include four-poster and brass beds. There is a lovely sitting room and dining room, and a wide choice is available at breakfast (dinner is available by arrangement). Local amenities include Blue Flag beaches, riding and golf.

Rooms 4 en suite (1 fmly) **Facilities** TVL tea/coffee Dinner available WiFi ⌚ 9 Fishing Pool table ⌚ **Parking** 20 **Notes** ⊗ Closed Nov-Mar ⌚ 100 acres beef/dairy/mixed/sheep/horses

Springfield House (W330342)

★★★★ FARMHOUSE

tel: 023 8840622 **fax:** 023 8840622 **Kilkern, Rathbarry, Castlefreke**
email: jandmcallanan@eircom.net **web:** www.springfieldhousebandb.com
dir: *N71 from Clonakilty for Skibbereen, 0.5km left after Pike Bar & signed for 5km*

Springfield House is a Georgian-style farmhouse in a picturesque rural setting. Maureen and John Callanan are genuine and welcoming hosts, and their comfortable home has well-appointed bedrooms and lovely gardens. You are welcome to watch the cows being milked. Home cooking is a speciality.

Rooms 4 rms (3 en suite) (2 fmly) **Facilities** TVL TV3B **Parking** 8 **Notes** ⊗ Closed 20-27 Dec ⌚ 130 acres dairy/beef

CLONAKILTY *continued*

An Sugan Guesthouse

★★★ GUEST HOUSE

tel: 023 8833719 & 023 8833498 **fax:** 023 8833825 **Long Quay**
email: info@ansugan.com **web:** www.ansugan.com
dir: *N71 Cork to Clonakilty, in Clonakilty straight over rdbt, take 1st left*

This historic house was built in the late 1800s and has a good standard of accommodation. Bedrooms are attractively decorated, and the dining room and guest sitting room are comfortably furnished. Breakfast is a real treat with Mrs O'Crowley's home baking and quality local produce. Guests check in at An Sugan Restaurant and Bar next door, where seafood and steaks are available throughout the day and evening.

Rooms 7 en suite (1 fmly) (1 GF) D €70-€100* **Facilities** FTV iPod docking station Lounge tea/coffee Direct Dial WiFi **Parking** 3 **Notes** ⊗ Closed 23-26 Dec RS Nov-Jan group bookings only

| CORK | Map 1 B2 |

Garnish House

★★★★ GUEST HOUSE

tel: 021 4275111 **fax:** 021 4273872 **1 Aldergrove, Western Rd**
email: garnish@iol.ie **web:** www.garnish.ie
dir: *Opposite Cork University College*

Garnish House is a very welcoming house, with tea and scones offered on arrival. Bedrooms vary in size and are furnished with comfort in mind, some have jacuzzi baths, fridges and safes. There is a cosy sitting room and a spacious, bright dining room where breakfast is served. Expect a wide choice of dishes including home-baked breads and preserves. Situated close to UCC and the city centre and convenient for the ferry and airport. Off-street parking is available.

Rooms 21 en suite (4 fmly) (1 GF) (10 smoking) **Facilities** STV FTV TVL tea/coffee Direct Dial WiFi **Parking** 20 **Notes** ⊗

| DURRUS | Map 1 B2 |

Blairscove House & Restaurant

★★★★★ ◎◎ RESTAURANT WITH ROOMS

tel: 027 61127 **fax:** 027 61487
email: mail@blairscove.ie **web:** www.blairscove.ie
dir: *From Durrus on R591 towards Crookhaven, 2.4km, house (blue gate) on right*

Blairscove comprises four elegant suites located in the courtyard of a Georgian country house outside the pretty village of Durrus near Bantry; each room is individually decorated in a contemporary style and has stunning views over Dunmanus Bay and the mountains. The restaurant is renowned for its wide range of hors d'oeuvres and its open wood-fire grill. The piano playing and candle light add to a unique dining experience.

Rooms 4 annexe en suite (1 fmly) (4 smoking) **Facilities** STV DVD tea/coffee Dinner available Direct Dial 🔒 **Extras** Sherry - complimentary; wine - chargeable **Parking** 30 **Notes** ⊗ Closed Nov-Feb No coaches Civ Wed 30

| GOLEEN | Map 1 A1 |

The Heron's Cove

★★★★ ◎ ☖ BED AND BREAKFAST

tel: 028 35225 & 0868 073072 **fax:** 028 35422 **The Harbour**
email: suehill@eircom.net **web:** www.heronscove.com
dir: *By harbour in Goleen*

There are charming views of the harbour, fast-flowing stream and inland hills from The Heron's Cove, at Ireland's most south-westerly point, near Mizen Head. Bedrooms are comfortably furnished, some with balconies. The restaurant and wine bar is run by chef-patron Sue Hill, where the freshest fish and local produce feature and guests can choose their own wines from the cocktail bar shelves. Breakfast is a special treat and the best of West Cork ingredients can be enjoyed while watching the herons on the cove.

Rooms 5 en suite (2 fmly) S €45-€60; D €70-€90 **Facilities** STV DVD iPod docking station tea/coffee Dinner available Direct Dial Licensed WiFi 🔒 **Extras** Bottled water **Parking** 10 **Notes** LB ⊗ Closed Xmas & New Year RS Oct-Mar bookings essential

| KINSALE | Map 1 B2 |

Premier Collection

Friar's Lodge

★★★★★ GUEST HOUSE

tel: 086 2895075 & 021 4777384 **fax:** 021 4774363 **5 Friars St**
email: mtierney@indigo.ie **web:** www.friars-lodge.com
dir: *In town centre next to parish church*

This family-run and owned lodge was purpose-built and is near the Friary, on a quiet street just a short walk from Kinsale, renowned for its restaurants and bars. Bedrooms and suites are particularly spacious and furnished with comfort in mind. Being close to The Old Head Golf Club, and many others, there is storage for clubs and a drying room available, with secure parking to the rear. There is a cosy lounge where a wine and snack menu is available. The elegant dining room is the setting for imaginative Irish breakfasts.

Rooms 18 en suite (2 fmly) (4 GF) **Facilities** STV tea/coffee Direct Dial Lift WiFi **Parking** 20 **Notes** Closed Xmas ◎

Premier Collection

The Old Bank House

★★★★★ GUEST HOUSE

tel: 021 4774075 **fax:** 021 4774296 **11 Pearse St**
email: info@oldbankhousekinsale.com **web:** www.oldbankhousekinsale.com
dir: *On main road into Kinsale from Cork Airport (R600). House on right at start of Kinsale, next to Post Office*

The Fitzgerald family maintains this delightful Georgian house with pride. The en suite bedrooms, with period furniture and attractive decor, combine charm with modern comforts. Sailing, deep-sea fishing and horse riding can be arranged. Dinner is available at the sister Blue Haven Hotel.

Rooms 17 en suite (3 fmly) S €59-€85; D €70-€220* **Facilities** FTV TVL tea/coffee Direct Dial Lift WiFi 🔒 **Conf** Max 15 Thtr 15 Class 10 Board 12 **Notes** LB ⊗ Closed 23-28 Dec

The White House

★★★★ @ RESTAURANT WITH ROOMS

tel: 021 4772125 **fax:** 021 4772045 **Pearse St, The Glen**
email: info@whitehouse-kinsale.ie **web:** www.whitehouse-kinsale.ie
dir: *In town centre*

Centrally located among the narrow, twisting streets of the charming maritime town of Kinsale, this restaurant with rooms dates from 1850. It is a welcoming hostelry with smart, comfortably appointed contemporary bedrooms. The atmospheric bar and bistro are open for lunch and dinner, with Restaurant d'Antibes also open during the evenings. The varied menu features local fish and beef. The courtyard at the rear makes a perfect setting in summer and there is regular entertainment in the bar.

Rooms 10 en suite (2 fmly) **Facilities** STV tea/coffee Dinner available Direct Dial WiFi **Notes** ⊗ Closed 24-25 Dec

Woodlands House B&B

★★★★ BED AND BREAKFAST

tel: 021 4772633 **Cappagh**
email: info@woodlandskinsale.com **web:** www.woodlandskinsale.com
dir: *R605 NW from Kinsale, pass St Multose's Church, 0.5km on left*

Situated in an elevated position overlooking the town, about a 10-minute walk away on the Bandon road, this house offers great comfort and the personal attention of Brian and Valerie Hosford. Rooms are individually decorated, some with views towards the harbour. Breakfast is a particular pleasure, featuring home-made breads and preserves. Free WiFi is also available.

Rooms 6 en suite (1 fmly) (2 GF) **Facilities** FTV TVL tea/coffee Direct Dial WiFi ⛳ 18 **Parking** 8 **Notes** ⊗ Closed 16 Nov-Feb

MALLOW
Map 1 B2

Greenfield House B&B

★★★★ BED AND BREAKFAST

tel: 022 50231 & 08723 63535 **Navigation Rd**
email: greenfieldhouse@hotmail.com **web:** www.greenfieldhousemallow.com
dir: *Exit N20 at Mallow rdbt onto N72 (Killarney road), last house, 300mtrs on left*

This purpose-built bed and breakfast is situated within walking distance of the town centre of Mallow, the railway station and Cork Racecourse. The bedrooms offer good space and are well appointed. There is a cosy guest sitting room and the breakfast menu includes gluten-free and vegetarian dishes as well as the full Irish breakfast. There is ample off-street parking available.

Rooms 6 en suite (1 GF) S €45; D €70* **Facilities** STV Lounge TVL tea/coffee WiFi 🍴 **Parking** 10

SHANAGARRY
Map 1 C2

Premier Collection

Ballymaloe House

★★★★★ @@ 🏠 GUEST HOUSE

tel: 021 4652531 **fax:** 021 4652021
email: res@ballymaloe.ie **web:** www.ballymaloe.ie
dir: *N25 onto R630 at Midleton rdbt. After 0.5m, left onto R631 to Cloyne. 2m after Cloyne on Ballycotton road*

This charming country house is on a 400-acre farm, part of the Geraldine estate in east Cork. Bedrooms upstairs in the main house retain many original features, and the ground floor and courtyard rooms have garden patios. The relaxing drawing room and dining rooms have enchanting old-world charm. Ballymaloe House is renowned for excellent meals, many of which are created using ingredients produced on the farm. There are a craft shop, café, tennis and small golf course on the estate.

Rooms 21 en suite 9 annexe en suite (2 fmly) (3 GF) **Facilities** TVL Dinner available Direct Dial Licensed WiFi 🎣 ♨ 🏊 ⛳ 9 Fishing Children's sand pit/slide **Conf** Max 200 Thtr 200 Class 50 Board 50 **Parking** 50 **Notes** Closed 23-26 Dec, 8-28 Jan Civ Wed 170

COUNTY DONEGAL

CARRIGANS
Map 1 C5

Mount Royd Country Home

★★★★ 🏠 BED AND BREAKFAST

tel: 074 914 0163 **fax:** 074 914 0400
email: jmartin@mountroyd.com **web:** www.mountroyd.com
dir: *From Letterkenny on N14. At Dry Arch rdbt 2nd exit onto N13. At next rdbt 2nd exit onto N14 towards Lifford. Left at R236 to Carrigans. Or from Derry take A40 to Carrigans*

Mount Royd is a creeper-clad house with lovely gardens in the pretty village of Carrigans, a short distance from Derry. The friendly Martins have brought hospitality to new heights - nothing is too much trouble for them. Breakfast is a feast of choices including home baking and eggs from their own hens. Bedrooms are very comfortable, with lots of personal touches.

Rooms 4 en suite (1 fmly) (1 GF) S €40; D €70* **Facilities** FTV TVL tea/coffee WiFi **Parking** 7 **Notes** LB ⊗ No Children 12yrs RS Nov-Feb 🐾

Who are the AA's award-winning B&Bs? For details see pages 12-16

Follow us on Facebook
www.facebook.com/TheAAUK

DONEGAL
Map 1 B5

The Red Door Country House

★★★★ ⊕ RESTAURANT WITH ROOMS

tel: 074 9360289 **Fahan, Inishowen**
email: info@thereddoor.ie **web:** www.thereddoor.ie
dir: In Fahan village, church on right, The Red Door signed on left

Nestled among mature trees and landscaped gardens, this warm and welcoming restaurant with rooms stands proudly on the shore of Lough Swilly, in the historic village of Fahan, just south of Buncrana. Dating from 1789, the original features of the house are cleverly combined with contemporary styling. Bedrooms are cosy and comfortable, each individually decorated and all en suite. The house has a fine reputation in the region for the quality of its restaurant for evening dining, and alfresco lunches. Breakfast is also a highlight and is designed to be lingered over.

Rooms 4 en suite **Facilities** FTV Lounge tea/coffee Dinner available WiFi ⚓ 18 **Conf** Max 100 Thtr 100 Board 100 **Parking** 40 **Notes** RS Mon & Tue closed Civ Wed 160

DUBLIN

DUBLIN
Map 1 D4

Premier Collection

Glenogra Town House

★★★★★ GUEST HOUSE

tel: 01 6683661 **fax:** 01 6683698 **64 Merrion Rd, Ballsbridge**
email: info@glenogra.com **web:** www.glenogra.com
dir: Opposite Royal Dublin Showgrounds & Four Seasons Hotel

This fine 19th-century red brick house is situated across from the RDS and close to the Aviva Stadium. The bedrooms are comfortably appointed and include many thoughtful extras; three bedrooms are on the ground floor. There is an elegant drawing room and dining room, and the interesting breakfast menu offers a range of dishes. Secure parking is available, and The Aircoach and city-centre buses stop in Merrion Road; the DART rail is around the corner.

Rooms 13 en suite (1 fmly) (3 GF) S €59-€149; D €89-€199* **Facilities** STV TVL tea/coffee Direct Dial WiFi ⚓ **Parking** 10 **Notes** LB ⊗ Closed 23-28 Dec

Premier Collection

Harrington Hall

★★★★★ GUEST HOUSE

tel: 01 4753497 **fax:** 01 4754544 **69-70 Harcourt St**
email: harringtonhall@eircom.net **web:** www.harringtonhall.com
dir: St Stephen's Green via O'Connell St, in Earlsfort Ter pass National Concert Hall & right into Hatch St, right into Harcourt St

Harrington Hall is a Georgian house on a one-way street, just off St Stephen's Green in the centre of the city. The spacious bedrooms are well appointed and include comfortable suites. A lovely plasterwork ceiling adorns the relaxing drawing room, and an extensive breakfast menu is served in the basement dining room. A lift, porter service and limited off-street parking are available.

Rooms 28 en suite (3 fmly) (3 GF) **Facilities** STV tea/coffee Direct Dial Lift **Conf** Max 20 Thtr 20 Class 6 Board 12 **Parking** 8 **Notes** ⊗

Charleville Lodge Guest House

★★★★ GUEST HOUSE

tel: 01 8386633 **fax:** 01 8385854 **268/272 North Circular Rd, Phibsborough**
email: info@charlevillelodge.ie **web:** www.charlevillelodge.ie
dir: N from O'Connell St to Phibsborough, left fork at St Peter's Church, house 250mtrs on left

Situated close to the city centre near Phoenix Park, this elegant terrace of Victorian houses provides accommodation of a high standard. The two interconnecting lounges are welcoming, and the smart dining room offers a choice of breakfasts. Bedrooms are very comfortable with pleasant decor, and there is a secure car park.

Rooms 30 en suite (2 fmly) (4 GF) S €50-€150; D €70-€300 **Facilities** STV FTV Lounge TVL Direct Dial Licensed WiFi ⚓ 18 **Conf** Max 10 Thtr 10 Class 10 Board 10 **Parking** 18 **Notes** LB ⊗

Glenshandan Lodge

★★★★ GUEST ACCOMMODATION

tel: 01 8408838 & 08765 92114 **fax:** 01 8408838 **Dublin Rd, Swords**
email: glenshandan@eircom.net **web:** www.glenshandan.ie
dir: Beside Topaz on airport side of Swords Main St

Glenshandan Lodge is a warm and friendly, family-run guest accommodation with hospitable proprietors and good facilities. Bedrooms come in a number of sizes, and are particularly suited to large family groups. They are comfortable and well appointed, with a relaxing seating area on the mezzanine, together with a limited kitchen area. Located on the south side of Swords, Dublin Airport is easily accessible. There is ample parking available, and buses to the airport and the city pass the front door. Facilities for dogs can be arranged.

Rooms 9 en suite (5 fmly) (5 GF) **Facilities** FTV TVL tea/coffee WiFi ⚓ 36 **Conf** Max 20 **Parking** 10 **Notes** Closed Xmas & New Year

Ardagh House

★★★ GUEST HOUSE

tel: 01 4977068 **fax:** 01 4973991 **1 Highfield Rd, Rathgar**
email: enquiries@ardahouse.com **web:** www.ardahouse.com
dir: S of city centre through Rathmines

Ardagh House is an early 19th-century house with modern additions, and stands in a premier residential area on the outskirts of the city, close to local restaurants and pubs. It retains many original features and has a relaxing lounge that overlooks a delightful garden. There is an attractive dining room where hearty breakfasts are served at individual tables. The comfortable bedrooms vary in size. Ample off-street parking is available.

Rooms 19 en suite (4 fmly) (1 GF) S €60-€95; D €70-€150 **Facilities** FTV TVL tea/coffee Direct Dial WiFi **Parking** 20 **Notes** ⊗ Closed 22 Dec-3 Jan

Leeson Bridge Guest House

★★★ GUEST HOUSE

tel: 01 6681000 & 6682255 **fax:** 01 6681444 **1 Upper Leeson St**
email: info@leesonbridgehouse.ie **web:** www.leesonbridgehouse.ie
dir: At junct of N11 & N7, Leeson St

This guest house is located right by Leeson Street Bridge, close to the city centre and is easily accessible from the ferry ports. Centred around a Georgian house, many of its original architectural features are retained. It offers a range of en suite bedroom styles, some with spa baths, sauna or galley kitchenette. Residents have access to ample parking at the rear. A take-away breakfast is offered to guests departing early in the morning.

Rooms 20 en suite (1 fmly) (2 GF) (10 smoking) **Facilities** STV FTV TVL tea/coffee Direct Dial Lift WiFi Fishing **Parking** 18 **Notes** LB ⊗

COUNTY DUBLIN

RUSH
Map 1 D4

Sandyhills Bed & Breakfast

★★★★ 🏠 BED AND BREAKFAST

tel: 01 8437148 & 086 242 3660   **fax:** 01 8437148 **Sandyhills**
email: mary@sandyhills.ie **web:** www.sandyhills.ie
dir: *M1 exit 4, right to Lusk on R127. 3rd exit at rdbt in Lusk to Rush R128. Right towards church car park, right to Corrs Ln, then 2nd right, 3rd house on right*

Set just a stroll from the sea and the village of Rush, within easy reach of Dublin Airport, Sandyhills has spacious bedrooms, all well equipped with thoughtful extra facilities. Breakfast is a special treat featuring local produce along with Mary Buckley's preserves, freshly-baked cakes and breads. There is a cosy sitting room and a lovely garden with secure parking.

Rooms 5 en suite (2 fmly) **Facilities** FTV tea/coffee Direct Dial WiFi ♨ 18 **Parking** 20 **Notes** LB ⊗ No Children 12yrs

COUNTY GALWAY

CLIFDEN
Map 1 A4

Ardmore House *(L589523)*

★★★★ FARMHOUSE

tel: 095 21221 & 076 6030227 **Sky Rd**
email: info@ardmore-house.com **web:** www.ardmore-house.com
dir: *N59 from Galway to Clifden. Just N of Clifden centre follow signs on left for 'Sky Road', 5km, house on left*

Ardmore House is set among the wild scenery of Connemara, between hills and the sea on the Sky Road. Bedrooms are attractively decorated and the house is very comfortable throughout. A pathway leads from the house to the coast. A good hearty breakfast is provided featuring home baking.

Rooms 6 en suite (3 fmly) (6 GF) S €45-€55; D €70-€80* **Facilities** STV FTV TVL tea/coffee WiFi **Parking** 8 **Notes** LB ⊗ Closed Oct-Mar ⊜ 25 acres non-working

Faul House *(L650475)*

★★★★ FARMHOUSE

tel: 095 21239 **fax:** 095 21998 **Ballyconneely Rd**
email: info@ireland.com **web:** www.faulhouse.com
dir: *1.5km from town right at rugby pitch signed Rockglen Hotel*

Faul House, a fine modern farmhouse, stands on a quiet and secluded road overlooking Clifden Bay. It is smart and comfortable with large bedrooms, all well furnished and with good views. Kathleen offers a hearty breakfast with home baking. There are Connemara ponies available for trekking.

Rooms 6 en suite (3 fmly) (3 GF) **Facilities** FTV TVL tea/coffee WiFi **Parking** 10 **Notes** Closed Nov-26 Mar ⊜ 35 acres sheep/ponies/hens/ducks

Mallmore House

★★★★ BED AND BREAKFAST

tel: 095 21460 **Ballyconneely Rd**
email: info@mallmore.ie **web:** www.mallmorecountryhouse.com
dir: *1.5km from Clifden towards Ballyconneely take 1st right*

Mallmore House is a charming Georgian-style house built in the 17th century and lovingly maintained. It is situated close to the town and has a beautiful garden and mature woodland, and overlooks Clifden Bay. Bedrooms are spacious and very well appointed with antique furniture. The drawing room is delightfully relaxing with a turf fire. There is a wide choice available at breakfast including home baking and locally smoked fish. Mallmore is a lovely place to stay and enjoy the peace and quiet of Connemara.

Rooms 6 en suite (2 fmly) (6 GF) S €60-€70; D €80-€90 **Facilities** FTV DVD Lounge tea/coffee WiFi **Parking** 15 **Notes** ⊗ Closed Oct-1 Apr ⊜

Ben View House

★★★ GUEST HOUSE

tel: 095 21256 **fax:** 095 21226 **Bridge St**
email: benviewhouse@ireland.com **web:** www.benviewhouse.com
dir: *Enter town on N59, opposite Esso fuel station*

This house is well located in the centre of the town with ample on-street parking. Dating from 1824, it offers good quality accommodation at a moderate cost. The breakfast room and lounge feature an old world atmosphere, with antique furniture and sparkling silverware in everyday use.

Rooms 10 rms (9 en suite) (3 fmly) **Facilities** TVL TV9B tea/coffee **Notes** ⊗

GALWAY
Map 1 B3

Marian Lodge Guest House

★★★★ GUEST HOUSE

tel: 091 521678 **fax:** 091 528103 **Knocknacarra Rd, Salthill Upper**
email: celine@iol.ie **web:** www.marian-lodge.com
dir: *From Galway to Salthill on R336, through Salthill, 1st right after Spinnaker Hotel into Knocknacarra Rd*

This large modern house is only 50 metres from the seafront. The fully equipped bedrooms have orthopaedic beds and en suite facilities. There is also a lounge and separate breakfast room available.

Rooms 6 en suite (4 fmly) **Facilities** STV TVL tea/coffee Direct Dial **Parking** 10 **Notes** ⊗ No Children 3yrs Closed 23-28 Dec

Find out more about beds in B&Bs - see page 24

COUNTY KERRY

DINGLE (AN DAINGEAN)	Map 1 A2

Premier Collection

Gormans Clifftop House & Restaurant
★★★★★ ◎ GUEST HOUSE

tel: 066 9155162 & 083 0033133   **fax:** 066 9155003 **Glaise Bheag, Ballydavid**
email: info@gormans-clifftophouse.com **web:** www.gormans-clifftophouse.com
dir: R559 to An Mhuirioch, turn right at T-junct, N for 3km

Sile and Vincent Gorman's guest house and restaurant is perched over the cliffs on the western tip of the Slea Head Peninsula near Ballydavid village. The beauty of the rugged coastline, rhythm of the sea and the sun going down on Smerwick Harbour can be enjoyed over a delicious dinner in the smart dining room. The menu includes produce from the garden, local seafood and lamb. Bedrooms are comfortably proportioned and thoughtfully equipped and have breathtaking views of the ocean or mountains, the ground-floor rooms are adapted for the less mobile. Bracing cliff walks can be accessed across from the house.

Rooms 8 en suite (2 fmly) (4 GF) **Facilities** tea/coffee Dinner available Direct Dial Licensed WiFi Bicycles for hire **Parking** 15 **Notes** ⊗ Closed 24-26 Dec RS Oct-Mar reservation only Civ Wed 25

An Bothar Pub
★★★ GUEST HOUSE

tel: 066 9155342 **Cuas, Ballydavid**
email: botharpub@eircom.net **web:** www.botharpub.com

This traditional guest house and pub is located close to the town of Dingle on the Slea Head Drive at the foot of Mount Brandon. The Walsh family has been welcoming guests for three generations and the pub is famous for music and dancing. Fresh fish, their own farm produce and home baking are included on the daily menu. Walking, cycling, horse riding, golf, swimming and windsurfing are all locally available activities. The comfortable bedrooms are attractively decorated and furnished, some suitable for families.

Rooms 7 en suite (2 fmly) S €45; D €80* **Facilities** STV FTV TVL Dinner available Direct Dial Licensed Pool table ⚓ **Parking** 30 **Notes** ⊗ Closed 24-25 Dec RS Oct-Mar No evening meals available

Barr na Sraide Inn
★★★ GUEST HOUSE

tel: 066 9151331 & 9151446   **fax:** 066 9151446 **Upper Main St**
email: barrnasraide@eircom.net **web:** www.barrnasraide.com

Barr na Sraide Inn is a family-run guest house which has its very own traditional pub on site and free parking at the rear. It is situated in the heart of Dingle town and just a stroll from many restaurants, traditional music venues and shops. The en suite bedrooms are attractively decorated and comfortably furnished. There is a cosy guest sitting room and a hearty breakfast can be chosen from the breakfast menu which includes Patricia's home-baked breads.

Rooms 26 en suite (7 fmly) (4 GF) **Facilities** STV FTV TVL tea/coffee Direct Dial Licensed WiFi ch fac ⚓ 18 Riding ⚓ **Parking** 18 **Notes** ⊗ Closed 19-25 Dec

Hurleys Farm (Q392080)
★★★ FARMHOUSE

tel: 066 9155112 & 0862 142580   **An Dooneen, Kilcooley**
email: andooneen@eircom.net **web:** www.hurleysbandb.com
dir: 11km W of Dingle town on Ballydavid-Muirioch road

Hurleys Farm is tucked away behind the church in Kilcooley, 1.5 kilometres from the beach and sheltered by Mount Brandon, a popular place for hill walkers. Accommodation includes a cosy TV room, dining room and comfortable en suite bedrooms, graced by some special pieces of high quality furniture. The whole area is rich in early historic and prehistoric relics: ogham stones, ring forts and the famous dry-stone masonry 'beehive' huts.

Rooms 5 en suite (2 GF) **Facilities** TVL WiFi **Parking** 6 **Notes** ⊗ Closed Nov-Mar ⊛ 38 acres non-working

KENMARE	Map 1 B2

Davitts
★★★★ GUEST HOUSE

tel: 064 6642741 **fax:** 064 6642757 **Henry St**
email: info@davitts-kenmare.com **web:** www.davitts-kenmare.com
dir: On N22 (Cork-Killarney rd) at Kenmare junct (R569). In town centre

This family-run guest house is situated in the centre of the heritage town of Kenmare. With the popular Davitts Bar Bistro at street level serving excellent food, it is the perfect location for an enjoyable holiday all under the one roof. The spacious, well-appointed bedrooms are decorated in a contemporary style, and there is a cosy sitting room available on the first floor, with secure parking to the rear.

Rooms 11 en suite (1 fmly) **Facilities** STV FTV TVL Dinner available Direct Dial Licensed WiFi **Parking** 4 **Notes** ⊗ Closed 1-14 Nov & 24-26 Dec

Kenmare House B&B
★★★★ BED AND BREAKFAST

tel: 064 6641283 **fax:** 064 6642765 **Sneem Rd**
email: info@kenmarehousebandb.com **web:** www.kenmarehousebandb.com
dir: From Kenmare left onto N70 towards Sneem & Ring of Kerry. House 500mtrs on right

Kenmare House is owned and run by the O'Sullivan family; it is situated on the Ring of Kerry road (N70) only minutes from Kenmare town. Bedrooms are spacious and comfortably furnished to accommodate families and there are two ground floor rooms. The relaxing guest sitting room has books, maps and information on the area. The extensive breakfast menu includes Fionnuala's home baking, and Danny will advise on tours and activities available.

Rooms 6 en suite (3 fmly) (2 GF) **Facilities** FTV TVL tea/coffee WiFi **Parking** 11 **Notes** ⊗ Closed 26 Oct-Apr ⊛

Follow us on twitter
@TheAA_Lifestyle

Muxnaw Lodge

★★★★ BED AND BREAKFAST

tel: 064 6641252 & 087 2922895 **Casletownbere Rd**
email: muxnaw@eircom.net **web:** www.muxnawlodge.ie

Located on the Castletownbere Road, within easy walking distance of Kenmare town, this warm and friendly house is a former hunting lodge dating from the early 19th century. It is set on an elevated site in mature gardens. Bedrooms and en suites are individually decorated, with some enjoying views of the Kenmare River. The lounge retains much of its original character, in addition to the bright and airy sun room. Ample parking is available to the rear.

Rooms 5 en suite (1 fmly) D €70-€90 **Facilities** STV DVD TVL tea/coffee WiFi 🏝
Parking 5 **Notes** ⊗ Closed 24-25 Dec 🛍

Sea Shore Farm Guest House

★★★★ GUEST HOUSE

tel: 064 6641270 & 6641675 **fax:** 064 6641270 **Tubrid**
email: seashore@eircom.net **web:** www.seashorekenmare.com
dir: 1.6km from Kenmare off N70 Ring of Kerry road. Signed at junct N70 & N71

Overlooking Kenmare Bay on the Ring of Kerry road, this modern farm guest house is close to town and has spacious bedrooms. Ground-floor rooms open onto the patio and have easier access. Guests are welcome to enjoy the farm walks through the fields to the shore, and nearby salmon and trout fishing on the Roughty River. There is a comfortable sitting room and dining room and a delightful garden.

Rooms 6 en suite (2 fmly) (2 GF) S €65-€75; D €90-€110* **Facilities** FTV Lounge tea/coffee Direct Dial WiFi ♨ 18 🛡 **Extras** Speciality toiletries, snacks - complimentary **Parking** 10 **Notes** ⊗ Closed Nov-19 Mar

| KILLARNEY | Map 1 B2 |

Fairview Guest House

★★★★★ 🛏 GUEST HOUSE

tel: 064 6634164 & 087 2351900 **fax:** 064 6671777 **College St**
email: info@fairviewkillarney.com **web:** www.killarneyfairview.com
dir: In town centre off College St

Great attention to detail is demonstrated in the design of this smart guest house, handily located in the town centre close to the bus/railway station. Bedrooms include some with air conditioning and jacuzzi baths, and all are comfortable, with quality furnishings and fittings. There is a lift to all floors, and the impressive penthouse suite enjoys views over the town towards the Kerry mountains. There is a relaxing sitting area and the breakfast menu offers a selection of dishes cooked to order. Local activities and excursions include lake cruises, championship golf courses and the Killarney National Park.

Rooms 29 en suite (2 fmly) (1 GF) (2 smoking) S €50-€150* **Facilities** STV DVD TVL tea/coffee Dinner available Direct Dial Lift Licensed WiFi ♨ 18 Jacuzzi suites available **Parking** 11 **Notes** LB

Find out more about the AA Friendliest B&B of the Year on page 17

Foleys Town House

★★★★★ 😋 GUEST HOUSE

tel: 064 6631217 **fax:** 064 6634683 **22/23 High St**
email: info@foleystownhouse.com **web:** www.foleystownhouse.com
dir: In town centre

Charming, individually-designed bedrooms are a feature of this well-established town house right in the centre of the town. Bedrooms are all well appointed and decorated with elegance. A warm welcome is assured at this property, which is family-owned and run by Carol Hartnett who is also the chef in the adjoining popular bar and restaurant that specialises in seafood. There is a relaxing first-floor lounge reserved for guests, together with secure off-street parking to the rear.

Rooms 28 en suite S €55-€80; D €90-€130 **Facilities** STV Lounge TVL tea/coffee Dinner available Direct Dial Lift Licensed WiFi 🛡 **Parking** 60 **Notes** LB ⊗ Closed 6 Nov-16 Mar

Old Weir Lodge

★★★★★ GUEST HOUSE

tel: 064 6635593 **fax:** 064 6635583 **Muckross Rd**
email: oldweirlodge@eircom.net **web:** www.oldweirlodge.com
dir: On N71 (Muckross Rd), 500mtrs from Killarney

This purpose-built Tudor-style guest house is situated within walking distance of the town on the road to the National Park and the INEC Centre. There are two relaxing lounges, and the dining room is a lovely bright area with a conservatory that overlooks the rear garden. The spacious and comfortable bedrooms are equipped to a high standard; those upstairs can be accessed by lift. A varied range of tasty options is available at breakfast including Maureen's freshly baked breads, and special dietary requirements can be facilitated with notice. Dermot will help with boat trips on the Killarney Lakes, golf, fishing and walking tours. There is also a drying room and ample off-road parking.

Rooms 30 en suite (2 fmly) (6 GF) **Facilities** STV TVL tea/coffee Dinner available Direct Dial Lift Licensed WiFi ♨ 18 **Parking** 30 **Notes** ⊗ Closed 23-26 Dec

Ashville House

★★★★ GUEST HOUSE

tel: 064 6636405 **fax:** 064 6636778 **Rock Rd**
email: info@ashvillekillarney.com **web:** www.ashvillekillarney.com
dir: In town centre. Exit at N end of High St into Rock Rd

This inviting house is just a stroll from the town centre and near the N22 (Tralee road). Bedrooms are comfortably furnished, and there is a pleasant sitting room and dining room. There is a private car park, and tours can be arranged.

Rooms 12 en suite (4 fmly) (4 GF) **Facilities** STV FTV TVL tea/coffee Direct Dial WiFi 🛡 **Parking** 13 **Notes** ⊗ Closed Nov-1 Mar

KILLARNEY *continued*

Kingfisher Lodge

★★★★ GUEST HOUSE

tel: 064 6637131 & 087 2580351 **fax:** 064 6639871 **Lewis Rd**
email: info@kingfisherlodgekillarney.com **web:** www.kingfisherkillarney.com
dir: *Dublin link straight through 1st rdbt. Right at next rdbt towards town centre, Lodge on left*

This welcoming, modern guest house is home to the Carroll family. It is situated within walking distance of the town centre, and has comfortable and well-appointed bedrooms, all of which are en suite. A delicious breakfast is served in the attractively decorated dining room and there is also a relaxing lounge and conservatory with WiFi. A drying room is available for fishing and wet gear. Golf, walking and fishing trips can be arranged. There is ample parking, and complimentary pick-up from the bus and train station are offered.

Rooms 10 en suite (1 fmly) (2 GF) S €35-€70; D €64-€110 **Facilities** STV FTV Lounge TVL tea/coffee Direct Dial WiFi ⚓ 18 🔒 Walking Fishing Horseriding Golf can be booked **Parking** 12 **Notes** LB Closed 15 Dec-13 Feb

| KILLORGLIN | Map 1 A2 |

Premier Collection

Carrig House Country House & Restaurant

★★★★★ 🏅 🍽 GUEST HOUSE

tel: 066 9769100 **fax:** 066 9769166 **Caragh Lake**
email: info@carrighouse.com **web:** www.carrighouse.com
dir: *N70 to Killorglin*

Located on the shores of Lake Caragh a short drive from Killorglin, amid natural green woodlands, this family-run house is the perfect retreat for a relaxing break. There is a range of room styles on offer, with some having lake views. Each is decorated to a high standard, with guest comfort in mind. Public rooms include elegant drawing rooms and cosy nooks. There is a true passion for food in evidence at dinner, where local seafood and seasonal produce is cooked and presented with care in the Lakeshore Restaurant. With over fifteen golf courses and a range of other outdoor pursuits available, there is something to suit all tastes.

Rooms 16 en suite **Facilities** Lounge TVL Dinner available Direct Dial Licensed WiFi ⚓ 18 Fishing **Extras** Bottled water **Parking** 20 **Notes** ⊗ No Children 8yrs Closed Oct-Feb Civ Wed 63

O'Regan's Country Home & Gardens

★★★★ BED AND BREAKFAST

tel: 066 9761200 & 087 8651333 **fax:** 066 9761200 **Bansha**
email: jeromeoregan@eircom.net **web:** www.oreganscountryhomeandgardens.com
dir: *1.6km from Killorglin on N70, turn right at sign for An Bainseach*

The O'Regan family have been welcoming guests to their family home for many years, with some returning regularly. Set in beautifully kept gardens overlooking the Kerry Mountains, the house is particularly comfortable and welcoming. The lounge and breakfast room overlook the gardens. The bedrooms are well appointed, and breakfast features a wide selection, including Christina's delicious home baking.

Rooms 4 en suite (1 fmly) (4 GF) **Facilities** TVL tea/coffee WiFi ⚓ 18 **Parking** 8 **Notes** ⊗ Closed Nov-Feb

COUNTY KILDARE

| ATHY | Map 1 C3 |

Premier Collection

Coursetown Country House

★★★★★ 🛏 BED AND BREAKFAST

tel: 059 8631101 **fax:** 059 8632740 **Stradbally Rd**
web: www.coursetown.com
dir: *M7 exit to M9, then exit at Ballitore onto N78 to Athy, take R428*

This charming Victorian country house stands on a 100-hectare tillage farm and bird sanctuary. All bedrooms are furnished to the highest standards, with a comfortable lounge and bright, airy breakfast room. Convalescent or disabled guests are especially welcome, and Iris and Jim Fox are happy to share their knowledge of the Irish countryside and its wildlife. Breakfast is a highlight of a visit to this welcoming house.

Rooms 5 en suite (1 GF) **Facilities** TVL tea/coffee Direct Dial **Parking** 22 **Notes** No Children 12yrs Closed 15 Nov-15 Mar

COUNTY KILKENNY

| KILKENNY | Map 1 C3 |

Butler House

★★★★ GUEST HOUSE

tel: 056 7765707 & 7722828 **fax:** 056 7765626 **Patrick St**
email: res@butler.ie **web:** www.butler.ie
dir: *In centre near Kilkenny Castle*

Once the dower house of Kilkenny Castle, this fine Georgian building fronts onto the main street, with secluded gardens at the rear, through which you stroll to have a full Irish breakfast in the Kilkenny Design Centre. A continental breakfast is served in the bedrooms, which all feature contemporary decor. There is a comfortable foyer lounge and conference/banqueting suites.

Rooms 13 en suite (4 fmly) S €60-€120; D €99-€250 **Facilities** STV FTV Lounge tea/coffee Direct Dial WiFi 🔒 **Extras** Bottled water - complimentary; safe in all rooms **Conf** Max 120 Thtr 120 Class 40 Board 40 **Parking** 24 **Notes** LB ⊗ Closed 24-29 Dec Civ Wed 80

COUNTY LAOIS

| PORTLAOISE | Map 1 C3 |

Mahers B&B

★★★★ BED AND BREAKFAST

tel: 087 212 9236 **Rathleague**
email: mahersbandb@rathleague.com **web:** www.mahers-bnb.com

This Georgian home has been creatively renovated with attention to every detail, keeping original features where possible together with every modern facility. Built in the late 1700s, it has been in the Maher family for over 100 years. Outbuildings include storage for bikes, fishing tackle and hiking gear, and there is even an ornamental plant nursery on the site. Above all, it is the natural warm welcome from the family that endears visitors to this fine family home.

Rooms 4 rms (2 en suite) (2 pri facs) (3 fmly) S €34.50-€45; D €69-€80 **Facilities** STV FTV TVL tea/coffee WiFi ch fac ⚓ 18 **Conf** Max 20 Thtr 20 Class 16 Board 20 **Parking** 10

COUNTY LIMERICK

ADARE
Map 1 B3

Berkeley Lodge
★★★★ BED AND BREAKFAST

tel: 061 396857 fax: 061 396857 **Station Rd**
email: berlodge@iol.ie **web:** www.adare.org
dir: *N21, at rdbt turn to village centre*

Situated in the pretty village of Adare, this homely bed and breakfast has very comfortably furnished and attractively decorated bedrooms. The lounge leads on to a pleasant conservatory-style breakfast room, which offers Bridie's home baking and a choice of hot dishes. Adare Manor and many other golf courses and horse-riding stables are close by.

Rooms 6 en suite (2 fmly) (1 GF) **Facilities** iPod docking station TVL tea/coffee WiFi 🔒 **Parking** 6 **Notes** ⊗

COUNTY LOUTH

CARLINGFORD
Map 1 D4

Ghan House
★★★★ ⊛⊛ 🍴 GUEST ACCOMMODATION

tel: 042 9373682 & 086 6000399   fax: 042 9373772
email: info@ghanhouse.com **web:** www.ghanhouse.com
dir: *M1 junct 18 signed Carlingford, 5mtrs on left after 50kph speed sign*

Dating from 1727, Ghan House oozes charm and comfort. Set in two acres of walled gardens, the house is within 50 metres of the centre of the medieval village of Carlingford, making it an ideal base for walking and touring the Cooley peninsula. Bedrooms are warm and well appointed, either in the house itself or in a converted barn in the grounds. The public rooms are comfortable, featuring log fires and relaxing armchairs; perfect for getting lost in a good book. Food is an important element of the business, with a successful cookery school operating here for many years. Dinner is a highlight of a visit, with an emphasis on artisan produce and, given its location, renowned Cooley Lamb. Breakfast is a real treat with a great choice of fruit compôtes and preserves.

Rooms 4 en suite 8 annexe en suite (3 fmly) (4 GF) S €70-€95; D €145-€250 **Facilities** iPod docking station Lounge tea/coffee Dinner available Licensed WiFi 🏌 18 Riding 🔒 **Extras** Home-made biscuits **Conf** Max 50 Thtr 50 Class 26 Board 32 **Parking** 35 **Notes** LB ⊗ Civ Wed 45

COUNTY MAYO

BALLINA
Map 1 B4

Red River Lodge B&B
★★★★ BED AND BREAKFAST

tel: 096 22841 **Iceford, The Quay Rd**
email: redriverlodge@eircom.net **web:** www.redriverlodgebnb.com
dir: *3km from quay*

Located on the N59 five miles from Ballina, Red River Lodge is a very comfortable family home set in half an acre of beautifully landscaped gardens. Bedrooms are very well appointed in a contemporary style, with many of them having spectacular views of the estuary of the River Moy. Dolores and Mark are perfect hosts. Breakfast is served in the bright and airy conservatory. This is an ideal location for visitors touring the counties of Mayo and Sligo.

Rooms 4 en suite (2 fmly) (1 GF) S €40-€45; D €65-€70* **Facilities** STV FTV TVL WiFi 🏌 18 🔒 **Parking** 6 **Notes** ⊗ Closed 30 Sep-1 May

CASTLEBAR
Map 1 B4

Lough Lannagh Lodge
★★★ GUEST ACCOMMODATION

tel: 094 9027111 **fax:** 094 9027295 **Old Westport Rd**
email: info@loughlannagh.ie **web:** www.loughlannagh.ie
dir: *N5 around Castlebar. 3rd rdbt, 2nd exit. Next left, past playground, 1st building on right*

Lough Lannagh Lodge is in a delightful wooded area within walking distance of Castlebar. There is a conference centre, fitness centre, tennis, table tennis, laundry and drying facilities, a private kitchen, and many activities for children. Bedrooms are well appointed and breakfast is served in the café. Dinner is available by appointment for groups.

Rooms 24 en suite (24 fmly) (12 GF) S €59; D €79 **Facilities** FTV Lounge TVL Dinner available Direct Dial WiFi ch fac ⊛ 🏌 18 🔒 **Conf** Max 100 Thtr 100 Class 54 Board 34 **Parking** 24 **Notes** LB ⊗ Closed mid Dec-mid Jan RS Sun no arrivals

WESTPORT
Map 1 B4

Bertra House (L903823)
★★★ FARMHOUSE

tel: 098 64833 & 086 0667233   **fax:** 098 64833 **Thornhill, Murrisk**
email: bertrahse@eircom.net **web:** www.bertrahouse.com
dir: *W of Westport off R335, near Croagh Patrick on L1833*

This attractive bungalow overlooks the Blue Flag Bertra beach. Four bedrooms are en suite and the fifth has its own bathroom. Breakfast is generous and Mrs Gill offers tea and home-baked cakes in the cosy lounge on arrival.

Rooms 5 rms (4 en suite) (1 pri facs) (1 fmly) (5 GF) S €40-€45; D €60-€70 **Facilities** FTV Lounge TVL tea/coffee WiFi **Parking** 7 **Notes** LB ⊗ No Children 6yrs Closed 15 Nov-15 Mar ⊜ 40 acres beef

COUNTY MEATH

SLANE
Map 1 D4

Premier Collection

Tankardstown
★★★★★ ⊛⊛ 🍴 GUEST ACCOMMODATION

tel: 041 9824621 **fax:** 041 9884911
email: info@tankardstown.ie **web:** www.tankardstown.ie
dir: *N51 (Navan-Slane road), take turn directly opposite main entrance to Slane Castle, signed Kells. Continue for 5km*

Tankardstown is a magical place. Set in 80 acres of parkland, it has many strings to its bow. The main house is host to elegant rooms, with others in cottages in the converted stableyard. Each is individually decorated to a very high standard. The cottages have the benefit of spacious kitchens and living areas, ideal for longer stays. The property is also host to Brabazon, a fine dining restaurant, and there's a bistro for more casual fare. Excellent breakfasts are served in the main house, with the option of having it delivered to the cottages. This fine property is ideal for family gatherings and intimate wedding celebrations. There is a small gym in the grounds, together with a hot tub and all-weather tennis court. Tankardstown was the AA Guest Accommodation of the Year for the Republic of Ireland 2013-14.

Rooms 7 en suite 15 annexe en suite (6 fmly) **Facilities** STV FTV DVD Lounge TVL tea/coffee Dinner available Direct Dial Licensed WiFi 🏌 36 Fishing 🔒 Hot tub **Extras** Still water - free; mini-bar - chargeable **Conf** Max 150 Thtr 150 Class 80 Board 50 **Parking** 200 **Notes** Closed 5-30 Jan Civ Wed 200

COUNTY MONAGHAN

GLASLOUGH
Map 1 C5

Premier Collection

The Castle at Castle Leslie Estate

★★★★★ GUEST HOUSE

tel: 047 88100 fax: 047 88256
email: info@castleleslie.com web: www.castleleslie.com
dir: M1 junct 14, N2 to Monaghan then N12 onto N185 for Glaslough

Set in 1000 acres of rolling countryside, The Castle is the centre of the Leslie Estate which has been in the family since the 1660s. Bedrooms are all decorated in keeping with the age and style of the period, and are ideal for relaxing breaks where guests enjoy the peace and tranquillity of the property without any interference from televisions or other distractions. With a successful equestrian centre and a private fishing lake, this is an ideal location for those who enjoy country pursuits.

Rooms 20 rms (19 en suite) (1 pri facs) S €170-€250; D €190-€270*
Facilities Lounge TVL Direct Dial Lift Licensed WiFi ⌂ ⚓ 18 Fishing Riding Snooker Spa treatment rooms Private cinema Falconry Extras Speciality toiletries Conf Max 280 Thtr 260 Class 150 Board 65 Parking 100 Notes LB ⊗ Closed 22-27 Dec Civ Wed 80

COUNTY SLIGO

BALLYSADARE
Map 1 B5

Seashore House

★★★ BED AND BREAKFAST

tel: 071 9167827 fax: 071 9167827 Lisduff
email: seashore@oceanfree.net web: www.seashoreguests.com
dir: N4 onto N59 W at Ballisadore, in 4km Seashore signed on right. Turn down road, 600mtrs on right

Seashore House is an attractive dormer bungalow in a quiet seashore location. A comfortable lounge with open turf fire and sunny conservatory-dining room look out over attractive landscaped gardens and further sea and mountain views. Bedrooms are attractively appointed and comfortable, and there is also a tennis court and bicycle storage. Credit cards only accepted during high season.

Rooms 5 rms (4 en suite) (2 fmly) (3 GF) Facilities STV FTV TVL WiFi ⌂ Fishing ⚓ Parking 6 Notes ⊗ No Children

GRANGE
Map 1 B5

Rowanville Lodge

★★★★ BED AND BREAKFAST

tel: 071 9163958 & 087 6138019 fax: 071 9139200 Moneygold
email: rowanville@hotmail.com web: www.rowanville.com
dir: On N15, 1km N of Grange village

Located in an elevated position near Grange, on the main route from Sligo to Donegal, this warm and welcoming B&B offers really high standards of accommodation in a bright, contemporary style, with complimentary WiFi provided. Taking breakfast in the bright and airy sunroom is a real treat, with breath-taking views of Benbulben Mountain. The breakfast choice is wide, featuring home-baked goods and preserves. Patricia and Mattie are natural hosts, happy to offer suggestions for the many activities in the region.

Rooms 4 en suite (4 fmly) (2 GF) Facilities STV FTV TVL tea/coffee WiFi ⚓ 18 Parking 9 Notes LB Closed Nov-1 Mar

STRANDHILL
Map 1 B5

Strandhill Lodge and Suites

★★★★ GUEST HOUSE

tel: 071 9122122 fax: 071 9122795 Top Rd
email: info@strandhilllodgeandsuites.com web: http://strandhilllodgeandsuites.com
dir: From Sligo onto R292 for Strandhill

Located in the centre of Strandhill village, just five kilometres from Sligo, this property offers particularly spacious accommodation, finished to a very high standard. Many of the rooms have stunning views of the bay. Public areas are open plan in design, with a bright and airy breakfast room where continental breakfast is served. This is an ideal property for those playing golf or participating in the many other pursuits available in the region. There is a meeting room on the first floor, and ample parking to the rear. A number of cosy pubs and quality restaurants are located in the village.

Rooms 21 en suite 1 annexe en suite (7 fmly) (8 GF) Facilities STV FTV DVD iPod docking station Lounge TVL tea/coffee Direct Dial Lift WiFi ⌂ ⚓ 18 Fishing Riding ⚓ Extras Bottled water Conf Max 20 Thtr 20 Class 10 Board 8 Parking 22 Notes ⊗ Closed Jan-5 Feb

COUNTY TIPPERARY

CASHEL
Map 1 C3

Ard Ri House

★★★★ BED AND BREAKFAST

tel: 062 63143 fax: 062 63037 Dualla Rd
email: ardrihouse@gmail.com web: www.ardrihouse.com
dir: From town centre, 1st right after Information Office onto R688, left after church onto R691, 1km on right

A warm welcome awaits you at this non-smoking house, on the Kilkenny Road, only a short distance from the town. All of the bedrooms are comfortably furnished with thoughtful extras, and are on the ground floor. Breakfast features locally sourced ingredients from a varied menu. Facilities are available for children.

Rooms 4 en suite (1 fmly) (4 GF) Facilities TVL tea/coffee WiFi Parking 8 Notes ⊗ Closed Nov-Feb

Symbols and abbreviations are explained on page 7

Ashmore House

★★★ BED AND BREAKFAST

tel: 062 61286 & 0861 037010   **fax:** 062 62789 **John St**
email: info@ashmorehouse.ie **web:** www.ashmorehouse.ie
dir: Exit N8 in town centre, into John St, house 100mtrs on right

Ashmore House is a Georgian building set in a colourfully planted walled garden, right in the centre of the town, within walking distance of the Rock of Cashel. There is secure parking at the rear. Guests have use of a large sitting and dining room, and bedrooms come in a variety of sizes from big family rooms to a more compact double. Children are welcome and guests have WiFi access.

Rooms 5 en suite (2 fmly) **Facilities** STV FTV TVL tea/coffee Dinner available WiFi **Parking** 10 **Notes** ⊗

| THURLES | Map 1 C3 |

Premier Collection

The Castle

★★★★★ BED AND BREAKFAST

tel: 0504 44324 **fax:** 0504 44352 **Twomileborris**
email: bandb@thecastletmb.com **web:** www.thecastletmb.com
dir: 7km E of Thurles. On N75 200mtrs W of Twomileborris at Castle

Pierce and Joan are very welcoming hosts. Their fascinating house, sheltered by a 16th-century tower house, has been in the Duggan family for 200 years. Bedrooms are comfortable and spacious, there is a relaxing lounge, and the dining room overlooks the delightful garden. Golf, fishing, hill walking, and traditional pubs and restaurants are all nearby. Dinner is available by arrangement.

Rooms 4 en suite (3 fmly) **Facilities** STV FTV TVL tea/coffee Dinner available WiFi ♨ ♨ ⚓ 18 Fishing Pool table 🏺 **Conf** Max 40 Board 20 **Parking** 30 **Notes** ⊗

Premier Collection

Inch House Country House & Restaurant

★★★★★ ⚜ 🍴 GUEST HOUSE

tel: 0504 51348 & 51261
email: mairin@inchhouse.ie **web:** www.inchhouse.ie
dir: 6.5km NE of Thurles on R498

This lovely Georgian house, at the heart of a working farm, was built in 1720 and is lovingly maintained by the Egan family. The elegant drawing room ceiling is particularly outstanding among the grand public rooms, and the five spacious bedrooms are delightfully appointed. Reservations are essential in the fine restaurant, where an imaginative choice of freshly prepared dishes is on offer, with an emphasis on local produce. Some of the produce from the kitchen is available in a number of specialist outlets throughout the country.

Rooms 5 en suite (1 fmly) S €45-€55; D €80-€110 **Facilities** TVL tea/coffee Dinner available Direct Dial Licensed WiFi **Parking** 40 **Notes** LB ⊗ Closed 2wks Xmas RS Sun & Mon Restaurant closed during day Civ Wed 50

| TIPPERARY | Map 1 C3 |

Ach-na-Sheen House

★★★ GUEST HOUSE

tel: 062 51298 & 0879 746589   **fax:** 062 80467 **Clonmel Rd**
email: info@achnasheen.ie **web:** www.achnasheen.ie
dir: In town centre

This large, modern bungalow, set in a lovely garden, is only five minutes' walk from the main street of Tipperary, on the N24 to Clonmel. This is a family-run house where guests are made to feel very much at home. The public areas include a spacious sitting room and bright and airy breakfast room. The bedrooms are comfortably appointed and there is good off-street parking available.

Rooms 8 en suite (5 fmly) (6 GF) S €35-€50; D €60-€80 **Facilities** STV Lounge tea/coffee WiFi 🏺 **Parking** 13 **Notes** ⊗ Closed 11 Dec-8 Jan

---

Aisling

★★★ BED AND BREAKFAST

tel: 062 33307 & 087 2278230 **Glen of Aherlow**
email: ladygreg@oceanfree.net **web:** www.aislingbedandbreakfast.com
dir: From town centre R664 for 2.4km, past golf club

Aisling is close to Tipperary on the R664, Glen of Aherlow road. The bedrooms are well furnished and attractively decorated. There is a comfortable guest sitting room and a delightful garden with patio seating. Marian and Bob are helpful hosts, happy to arrange day trips, and provide maps and information on the locality.

Rooms 5 rms (4 en suite) (1 pri facs) (2 fmly) (5 GF) (2 smoking) **Facilities** FTV Lounge TVL WiFi ♨ 🏺 **Extras** Wine, chocolate, bottled water - complimentary **Conf** Max 6 Class 6 **Parking** 5 **Notes** LB

| COUNTY WATERFORD | |
| BALLYMACARBRY | Map 1 C2 |

Premier Collection

Hanoras Cottage

★★★★★ ⚜ GUEST HOUSE

tel: 052 6136134 & 6136442 **Nire Valley**
email: hanorascottage@eircom.net **web:** www.hanorascottage.com
dir: From Clonmel or Dungarvan R672 to Ballymacarbry, at Melodys Bar turn into Nire Valley, establishment by bridge beside church

Nestling in the beautiful Nire Valley, Hanoras Cottage is very popular with hill and forest walkers, bird watchers and nature lovers. Run by two generations of the Wall family, it offers spacious, comfortably-appointed bedrooms that are beautifully decorated. There are cosy lounge areas and the award-winning restaurant serves dinner from an interesting menu that features local produce. Those with special dietary needs are well catered for. Breakfast is a particular treat, with home baking and a range of hearty and healthy options.

Rooms 10 en suite S €99; D €120-€125* **Facilities** STV FTV Lounge TVL tea/coffee Dinner available Direct Dial Licensed WiFi ♨ 18 Fishing 🏺 Jacuzzi in all rooms **Conf** Class 40 **Parking** 15 **Notes** LB ⊗ No Children 12yrs Closed Xmas wk RS Sun Restaurant closed Civ Wed 40

TRAMORE | Map 1 C2

Cloneen

★★★★ BED AND BREAKFAST

tel: 051 381264 **fax:** 051 381264 **Love Ln**
email: cloneen@iol.ie **web:** www.cloneen.net
dir: *N25 onto R675 to Tramore, Majestic Hotel on right, continue up hill until road bears left, take 1st left*

This pleasant family home is situated on a quiet residential area off the coast road and within walking distance of the seaside town of Tramore. Bedrooms are stylishly furnished with guest comfort in mind; some of the ground-floor rooms have their own patio overlooking the lovely garden. Guests can relax in the conservatory-style sitting room and enjoy a hearty breakfast in the bright dining room.

Rooms 6 en suite (2 fmly) (4 GF) **Facilities** TVL tea/coffee WiFi ⌕ 18 **Extras** Bottled water - complimentary **Parking** 8 **Notes** ⊗

Seacourt

★★★★ BED AND BREAKFAST

tel: 051 386244 **fax:** 051 386244 **Tivoli Rd**
email: seacourthouse@gmail.com **web:** www.seacourt.ie
dir: *Leave Waterford City on R675 to Tramore. Over 2 rdbts, at 3rd rdbt (boat in middle) straight over, 1st B&B on left*

Seacourt is a very comfortable house situated in the seaside town close to Splashworld, the beach and Tramore Race Course, with many other tourist attractions available locally. Bedrooms are comfortably furnished with a spacious family room on the ground floor. There is a cosy guest sitting room, a wide choice of cooked breakfast served in the dining room, and ample off-street parking is available.

Rooms 5 rms (5 pri facs) (1 fmly) (1 GF) **Facilities** STV TVL tea/coffee WiFi ⌕ 18 ⊛ **Parking** 10 **Notes** No Children 6yrs Closed Oct-2 Apr

WATERFORD | Map 1 C2

Belmont House

★★★ BED AND BREAKFAST

tel: 051 832174 **Belmont Rd, Rosslare Rd, Ferrybank**
email: belmonthouse@eircom.net
dir: *Exit N25 at Luffany rdbt onto N29. At Slieverue rdbt follow R711 (Waterford N). Belmont House 4km from junct, 2nd B&B on left after service station*

This comfortable bed and breakfast is within walking distance of the city centre. A hospitality tray is available in the relaxing guest sitting room and a hearty breakfast is served in the dining room at separate tables. Bedrooms are well appointed and offer good quality and space.

Rooms 6 rms (4 en suite) (3 fmly) S €45-€50; D €60-€76 **Facilities** TVL WiFi **Parking** 6 **Notes** ⊗ No Children 7yrs Closed Nov-Apr ⊜

COUNTY WESTMEATH

HORSELEAP | Map 1 C4

Woodlands Farm House (N286426)

★★★★ FARMHOUSE

tel: 044 9226414 **Streamstown**
email: maxwells.woodlandsfarm@gmail.com
dir: *From N6 N onto R391 at Horseleap, farm signed 4km*

This very comfortable and charming house has a delightful setting on a farm. The spacious sitting and dining rooms are very relaxing, and there is a hospitality kitchen where tea and coffee are available at all times.

Rooms 5 rms (4 en suite) (1 pri facs) (2 fmly) (2 GF) **Facilities** TVL **Parking** **Notes** Closed Nov-Feb ⊛ 120 acres mixed

COUNTY WEXFORD

CAMPILE | Map 1 C2

Premier Collection

Kilmokea Country Manor & Gardens

★★★★★ ⌂ GUEST ACCOMMODATION

tel: 051 388109 & 086 6641946 **fax:** 051 388776 **Great Island**
email: stay@kilmokea.com **web:** www.kilmokea.com
dir: *R733 from New Ross to Campile, right before village for Great Island & Kilmokea Gardens*

This fine property is an 18th-century former rectory, lovingly restored and maintained by the hospitable Emma Hewlett and her husband Mark. The house is located in wooded and beautifully landscaped gardens that are in themselves a popular visitor attraction. In the grounds there is a spa with an indoor heated swimming pool, and aromatherapy treatments are available. The bedrooms are richly furnished in a mix of styles, but all have particularly comfortable beds. The drawing and reading rooms reflect 18th-century style and proportions, and there is an honesty bar. Dinner is available by prior arrangement, in what was the original dining room of the house, or in the conservatory in summer.

Rooms 4 en suite 2 annexe en suite (1 fmly) (2 GF) S fr €75; D €150-€220* **Facilities** STV Lounge TVL TV2B tea/coffee Dinner available Direct Dial Licensed WiFi ch fac ⌂ ⌕⌁⌕ 18 Fishing Riding Sauna Gym Pool table ⊛ Aromatherapy treatments Meditation room Jacuzzi **Conf** Max 75 Thtr 40 Class 30 Board 25 **Parking** 23 **Notes** LB RS Nov-end Jan Civ Wed 60

WEXFORD | Map 1 D3

Killiane Castle (T058168)

★★★★ ⌂ FARMHOUSE

tel: 053 9158885 **fax:** 053 9158885 **Drinagh**
email: killianecastle@yahoo.com **web:** www.killianecastle.com
dir: *Off N25 between Wexford and Rosslare*

This 17th-century house is run by the Mernagh family on a dairy farm close to Wexford town. The house is part of a 13th-century Norman castle. The comfortable reception rooms and bedrooms are beautifully furnished. Breakfast is a real treat and includes farm produce and Kathleen's baking and preserves. There is a hard tennis court, croquet lawn, a golf driving range and walks through the farm.

Rooms 8 en suite (2 fmly) S €65-€85; D €90-€130* **Facilities** Lounge TVL Dinner available Licensed WiFi ⌁⌕⌕ Driving range 18 hole pitch & putt **Parking** 8 **Notes** ⊗ Closed Dec-Feb 230 acres dairy

Maple Lodge

★★★★ BED AND BREAKFAST

tel: 053 9159195 **fax:** 053 9159195 **Castlebridge**
email: sreenan@eircom.net **web:** www.maplelodgewexford.com
dir: *5km N of Wexford. On R741, N on outskirts of Castlebridge, pink house on left*

This imposing house, set in extensive mature gardens, is in a peaceful location close to Curracloe Beach. Eamonn and Margaret Sreenan offer warm hospitality in their comfortable home. There is a varied breakfast menu offered and secure parking in the grounds.

Rooms 4 en suite (2 fmly) **Facilities** STV TVL WiFi **Parking** 5 **Notes** ⊗ No Children 10yrs Closed mid Nov-mid Mar

COUNTY WICKLOW

DUNLAVIN Map 1 C3

Tynte House *(N870015)*

★★★★ FARMHOUSE

tel: 045 401561 **fax:** 045 401586
email: info@tyntehouse.com **web:** www.tyntehouse.com
dir: *N81 at Hollywood Cross, right at Dunlavin, follow finger signs for Tynte House, past market house in town centre*

This 19th-century farmhouse stands in the square of the quiet country village of Dunlavin, in the west of County Wicklow. The friendly hosts have carried out a lot of restoration resulting in cosy bedrooms and a relaxing guest sitting room. Breakfast, featuring Caroline's home baking, is a highlight of a visit to this house. An all-weather tennis court is located in the grounds, together with an indoor games room. This house is an ideal base for touring the Wicklow and Kildare areas with their many sporting attractions.

Rooms 7 en suite (2 fmly) **Facilities** Lounge TVL tea/coffee Direct Dial WiFi ch fac ⌣ ⌿ 18 Playground Games room **Parking** 16 **Notes** Closed 16 Dec-9 Jan 200 acres beef/tillage

COUNTY MAPS

England

1 Bedfordshire
2 Berkshire
3 Bristol
4 Buckinghamshire
5 Cambridgeshire
6 Greater Manchester
7 Herefordshire
8 Hertfordshire
9 Leicestershire
10 Northamptonshire
11 Nottinghamshire
12 Rutland
13 Staffordshire
14 Warwickshire
15 West Midlands
16 Worcestershire

Scotland

17 City of Glasgow
18 Clackmannanshire
19 East Ayrshire
20 East Dunbartonshire
21 East Renfrewshire
22 Perth & Kinross
23 Renfrewshire
24 South Lanarkshire
25 West Dunbartonshire

Wales

26 Blaenau Gwent
27 Bridgend
28 Caerphilly
29 Denbighshire
30 Flintshire
31 Merthyr Tydfil
32 Monmouthshire
33 Neath Port Talbot
34 Newport
35 Rhondda Cynon Taff
36 Torfaen
37 Vale of Glamorgan
38 Wrexham

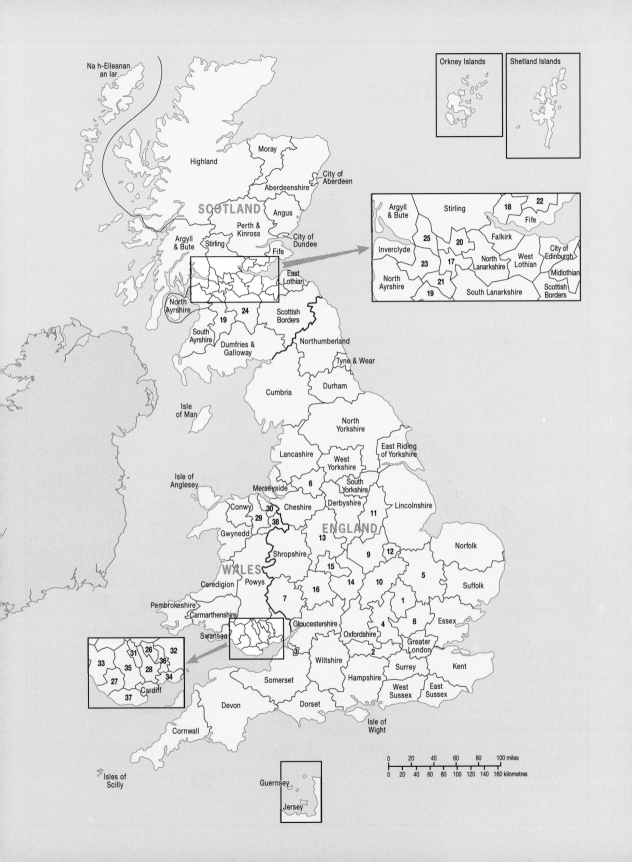

Na h-Eileanan
an Iar

Highland

Moray

Aberdeenshire

City of
Aberdeen

SCOTLAND

Angus

Perth &
Kinross

City of
Dundee

Argyll
& Bute

Stirling

Fife

East
Lothian

North
Ayrshire

19   24

Scottish
Borders

South
Ayrshire

Dumfries &
Galloway

Northumberland

Orkney Islands

Shetland Islands

Argyll
& Bute

Stirling

18   22

Fife

25

20

Falkirk

Inverclyde

23   17

North
Lanarkshire

West
Lothian

City of
Edinburgh

North
Ayrshire

21

19

South Lanarkshire

Midlothian

Scottish
Borders

Cumbria

Tyne & Wear

Durham

Isle
of Man

North
Yorkshire

East Riding
of Yorkshire

Lancashire

West
Yorkshire

Isle of
Anglesey

Merseyside

6

South
Yorkshire

Lincolnshire

Conwy

30

Cheshire

Derbyshire

29   38

11

ENGLAND

Gwynedd

13

Norfolk

Shropshire

9   12

WALES

15

Ceredigion

Powys

16   14   10

5

Suffolk

Pembrokeshire

7

1

Carmarthenshire

Gloucestershire

8

Essex

Swansea

4

3

Oxfordshire

Greater
London

33 31 26 32

36

2

Kent

35 28 34

Wiltshire

Surrey

27

Cardiff

Hampshire

37

West
Sussex

East
Sussex

Somerset

Devon

Dorset

Isle of
Wight

Cornwall

Isles of
Scilly

Guernsey

Jersey

| 0 | 20 | 40 | 60 | 80 | 100 miles |

| 0 | 20 | 40 | 60 | 80 | 100 | 120 | 140 | 160 kilometres |

KEY TO ATLAS

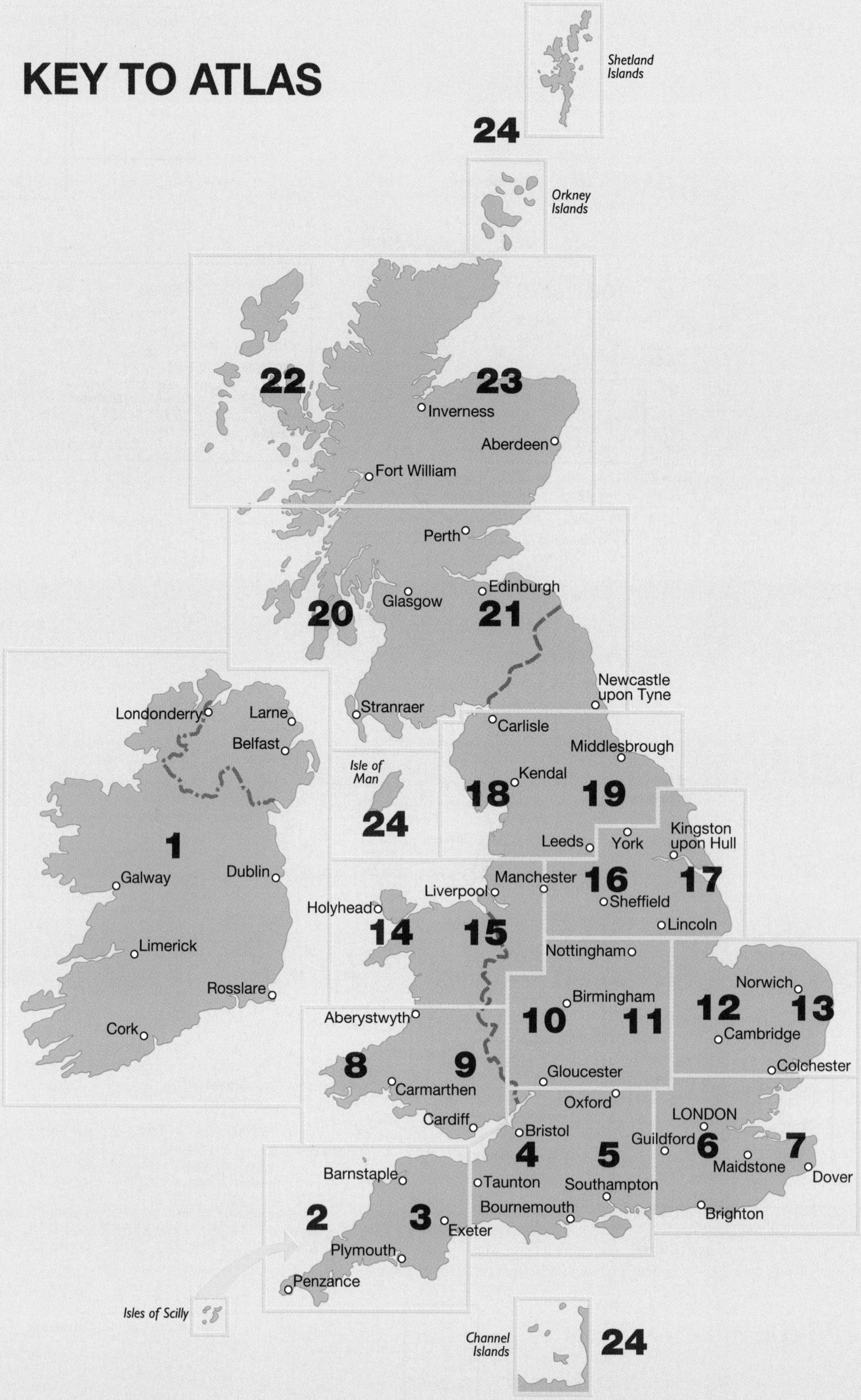

24 Shetland Islands

Orkney Islands

22 **23**
Inverness
Aberdeen
Fort William

Perth

20 Glasgow Edinburgh **21**

Newcastle upon Tyne

Londonderry Larne
Belfast
Stranraer
Carlisle
Middlesbrough
Isle of Man
Kendal
18 **19**
24
Leeds York Kingston upon Hull

1
Galway Dublin
Manchester **16** **17**
Liverpool
Sheffield
Holyhead
Lincoln
Limerick
Nottingham
14 **15**
Rosslare
Norwich
Birmingham
Aberystwyth
12 **13**
Cork
10 **11**
Cambridge
Gloucester
Colchester
8 **9**
Oxford
Carmarthen
LONDON
Cardiff
Guildford **6**
Bristol
4 **5**
Maidstone
Barnstaple
Southampton **7**
Taunton
Brighton Dover
2 **3**
Bournemouth
Plymouth Exeter

Penzance

Isles of Scilly

Channel Islands **24**

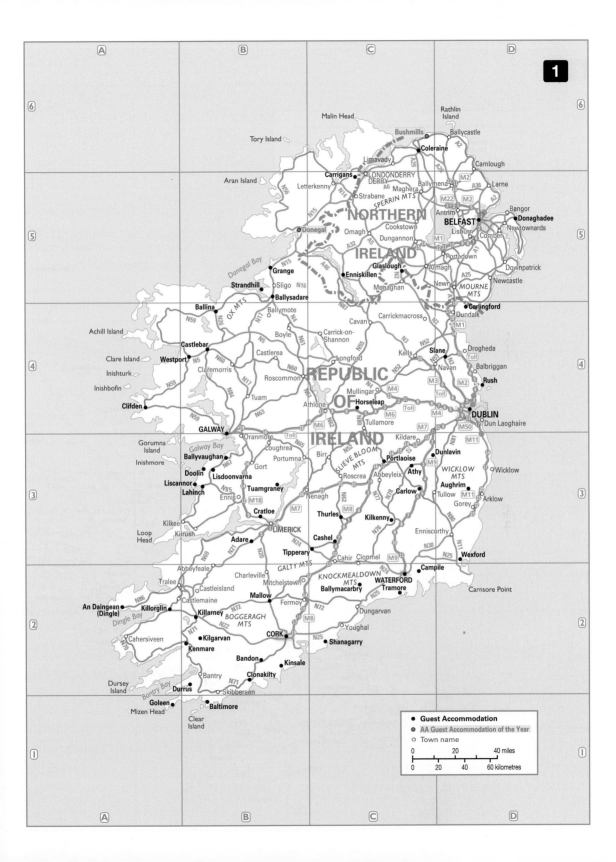

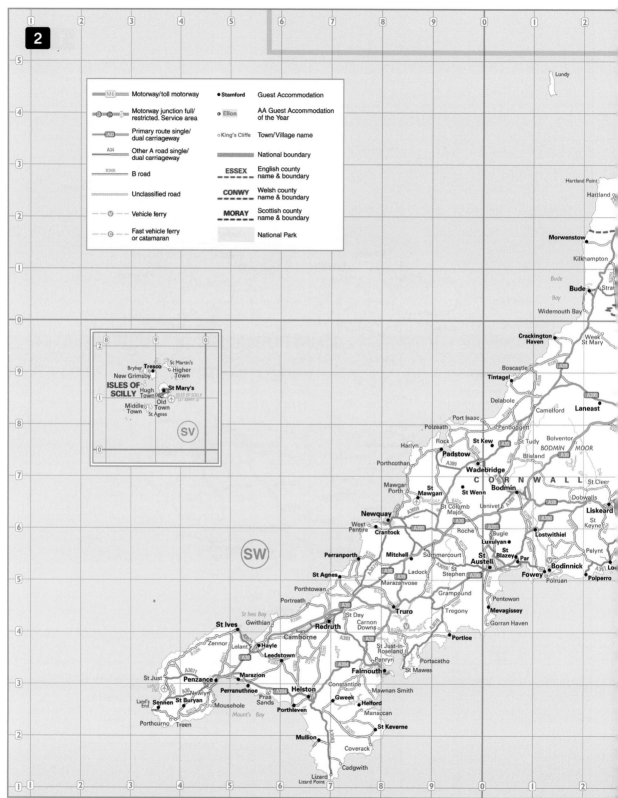

Legend

M6	Motorway/toll motorway
	Motorway junction full/restricted. Service area
A31	Primary route single/dual carriageway
A34	Other A road single/dual carriageway
B3400	B road
	Unclassified road
V	Vehicle ferry
C	Fast vehicle ferry or catamaran
● Stamford	Guest Accommodation
● Ellon	AA Guest Accommodation of the Year
○ King's Cliffe	Town/Village name
	National boundary
ESSEX	English county name & boundary
CONWY	Welsh county name & boundary
MORAY	Scottish county name & boundary
	National Park

Lundy

Hartland Point
Hartland

Morwenstow

Kilkhampton

Bude
Bude Bay
Bude Strat

Widemouth Bay

Crackington Haven
Week St Mary

Boscastle
Tintagel

Delabole

Camelford
Laneast

Port Isaac

Polzeath
Pendoggett
Bolventor
BODMIN MOOR

Harlyn
Rock
St Kew
St Tudy

Padstow
Blisland

Porthcothan
A389
Wadebridge
Bodmin

C O R N W A L L
St Cleer

Dobwalls

Mawgan Porth
St Mawgan
St Wenn

St Columb Major
Lanivet
Liskeard
St Keyne

Newquay
Roche
Bugle

West Pentire
Crantock
Luxulyan
St Blazey
Lostwithiel

Perranporth
Mitchell
Summercourt
St Austell
Par
Pelynt

St Agnes
Ladock
St Stephen
Fowey
Bodinnick
Lo

Marazanvose
Polruan
Polperro

Porthtowan
Grampound
Pentewan

Portreath
St Day
Tregony
Mevagissey

Truro
Gorran Haven

St Ives
Gwithian
Redruth
Carnon Downs
Portloe

Zennor
Camborne

Lelant
Hayle
A393
St Just-in-Roseland

Leedstown
Penryn
Portscatho

St Just
Marazion
Falmouth
St Mawes

Penzance
Helston
Constantine
Mawnan Smith

Newlyn
Perranuthnoe
Gweek
Helford

Land's End
St Buryan
Praa Sands
Porthleven
Manaccan

Sennen
Mousehole
St Keverne

Porthcurno
Treen
Mount's Bay

Mullion

Coverack

Cadgwith

Lizard
Lizard Point

ISLES OF SCILLY

Tresco
St Martin's
Higher Town

Bryher
New Grimsby

Hugh Town
St Mary's
ISLES OF SCILLY ST MARY'S

Middle Town
Old Town
St Agnes

SV

SW

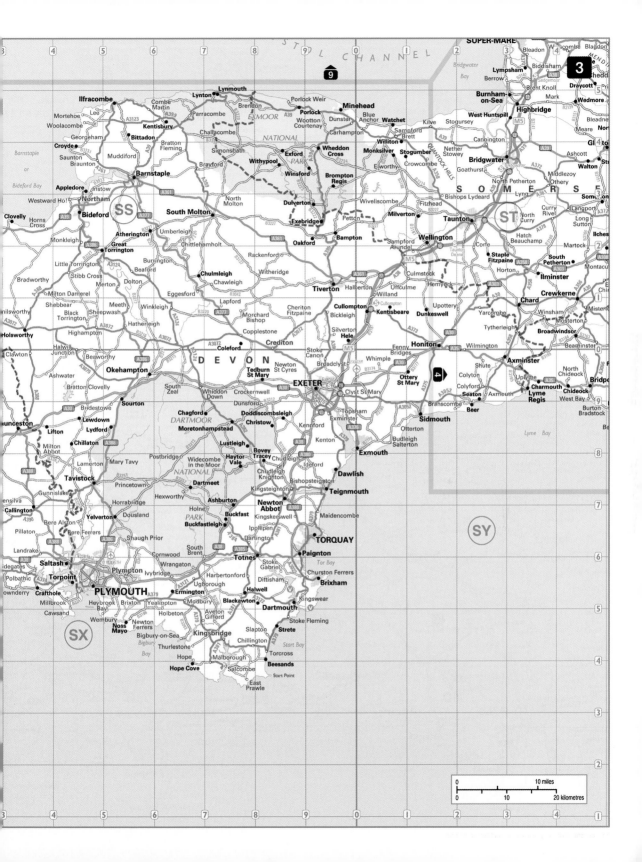

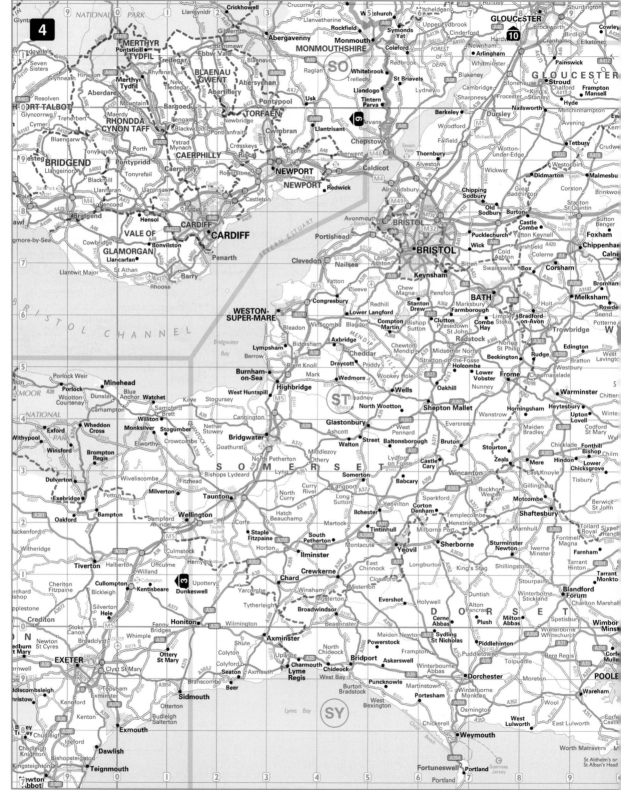

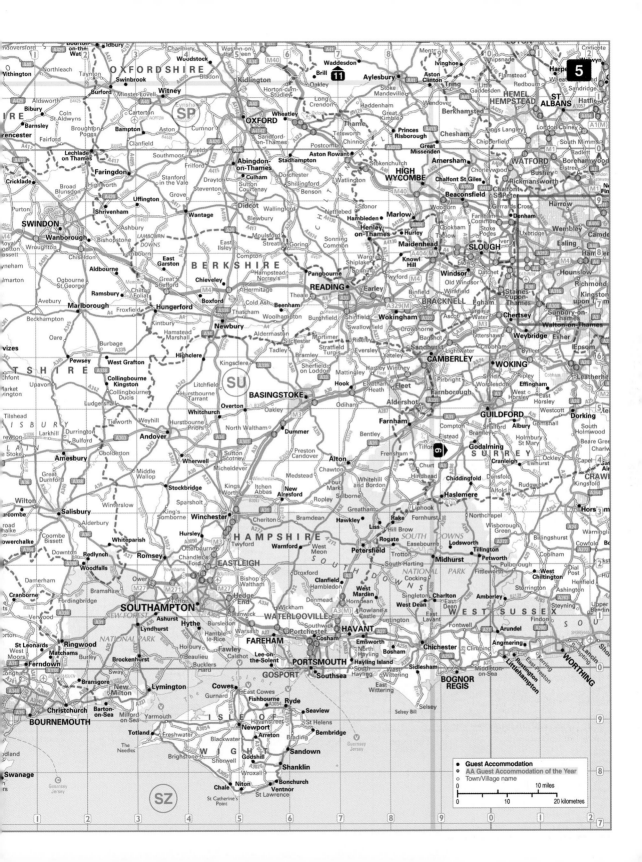

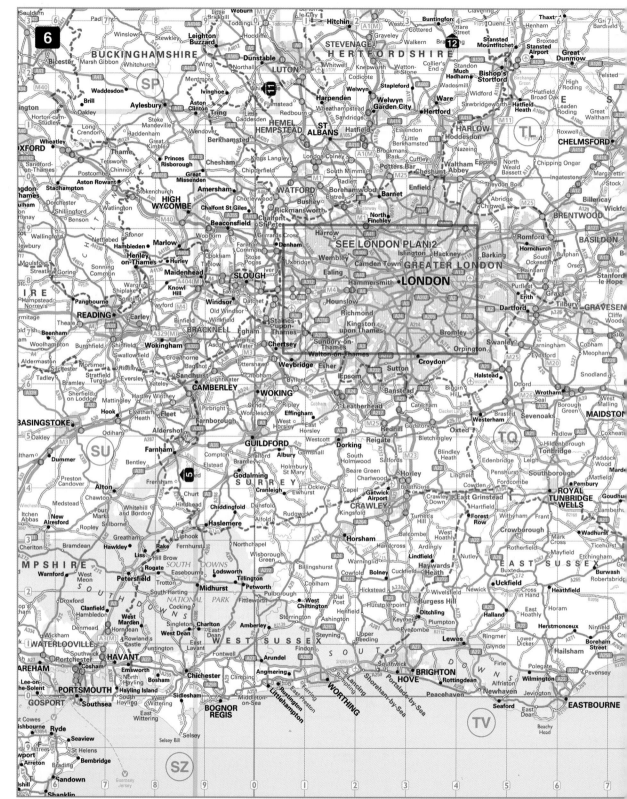

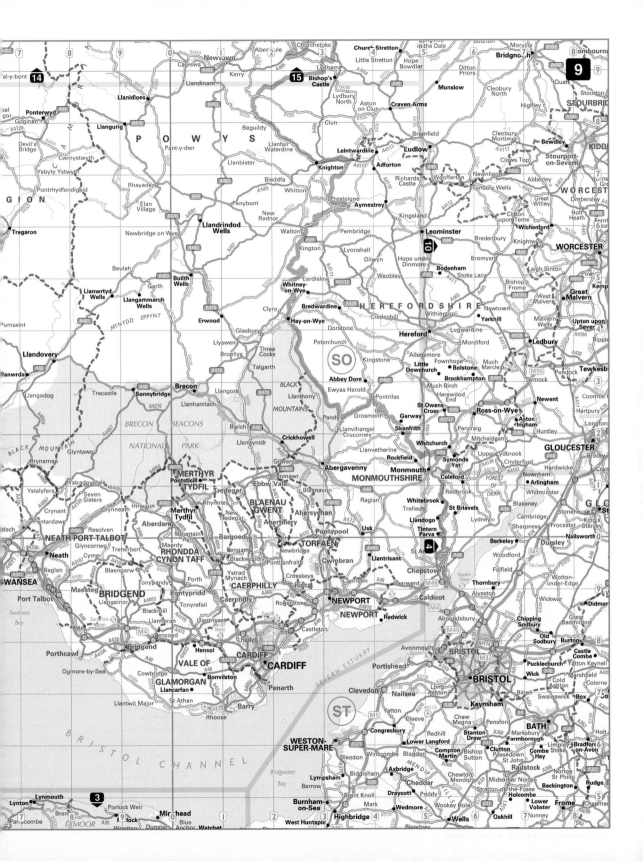

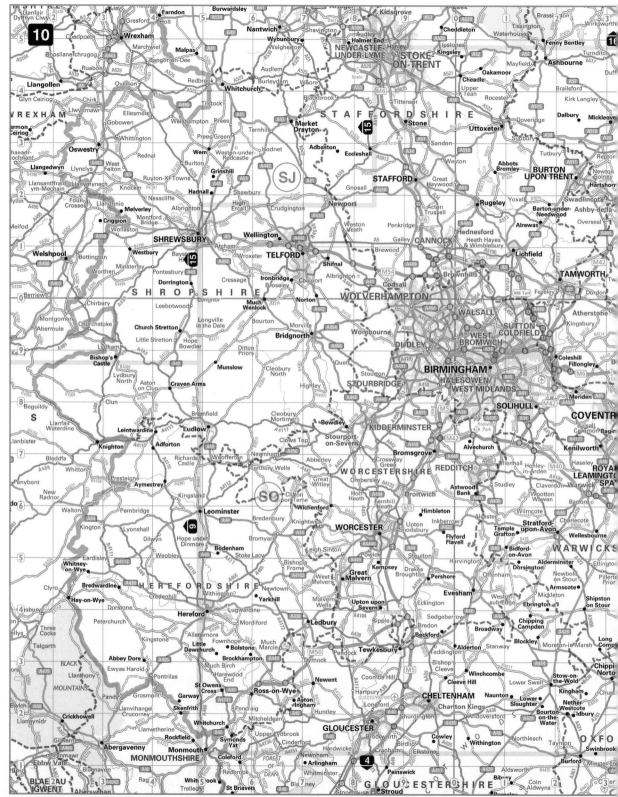

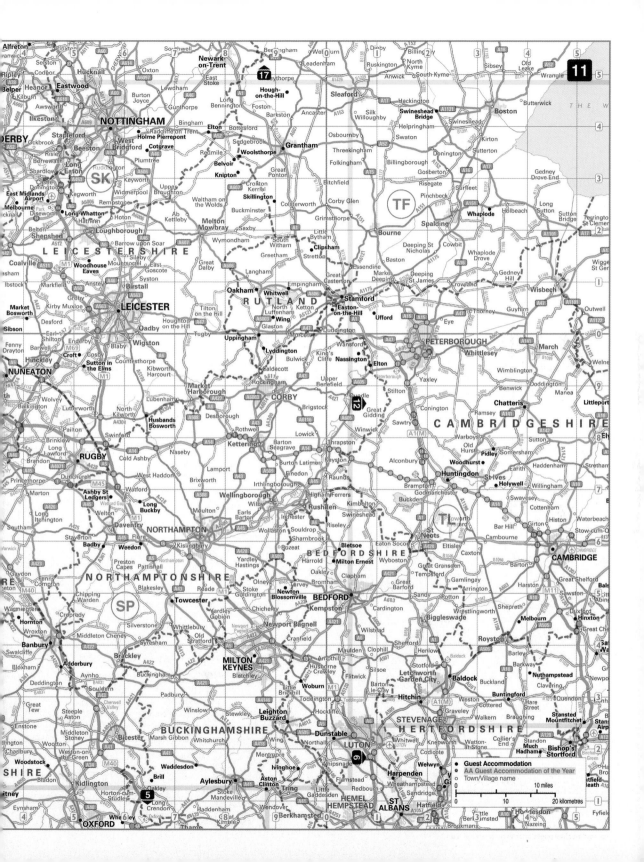

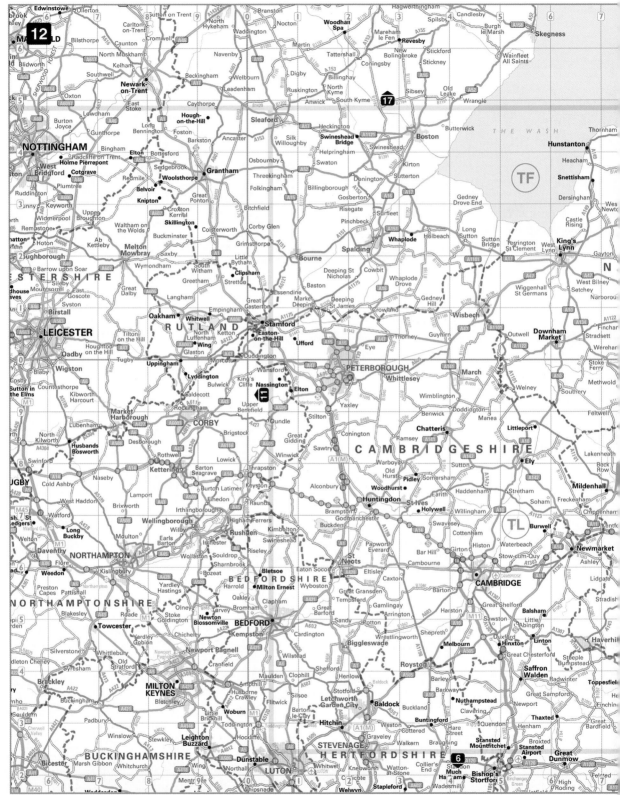

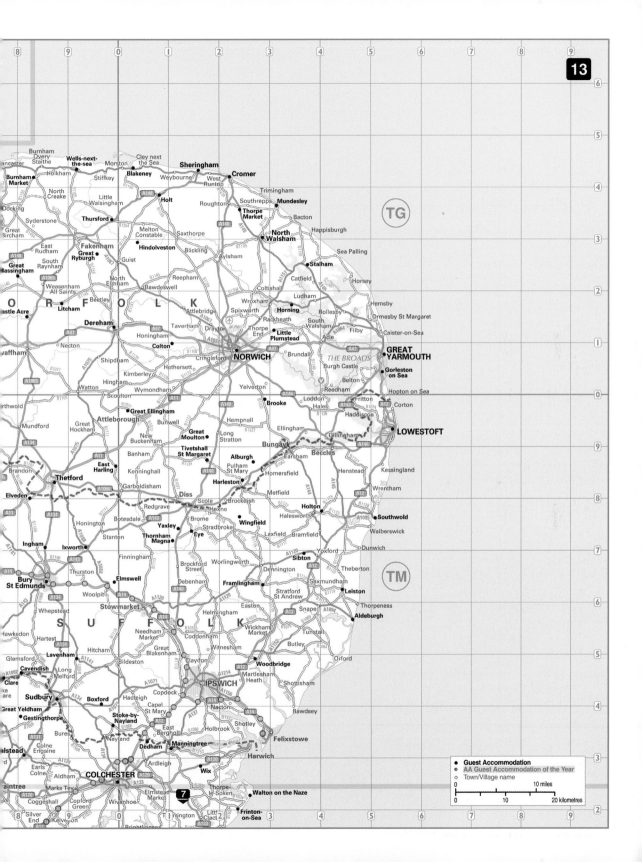

ISLE OF ANGLESEY

Cemaes

Amlwch

Holyhead

Llanfachraeth

Llanerchymedh

Benllech

Red Wharf Bay

Llangoed

Llandudno

Rhôs-on-Sea

Colwyn Bay

Aberg

Trearddur Bay

Holy Island

Deganwy

Llanddulas

Dwygyfylchi

Conwy

Llansanffraid Glan Conwy

Penmaenmawr

Rhosneigr

Llangefni

Beaumaris

Menai Bridge

Bangor

Llanfairfechan

Betws-yn-Rhos

Llanfair P·G

Aberffraw

Y Felinheli

Llanllechid

Bethesda

Tal-y-Cafn

Tal-y-Bont

Llangernyw

Llanfair Talhaiarn

Llansanna

Newborough

Caernarfon

Llanrug

Trefriw

Llanrwst

Bylchau

Bontnewydd

Llanwnda

Llanberis

Capel Curig

CONWY

Caernarfon Bay

Llandwrog

Betws Garmon

Betws-y-Coed

Dolwyddelan

Penygroes

Rhyd-Ddu

Penmachno

Pentrefoelas

Cerrigydrudion

Clynnog-fawr

SH

Beddgelert

Blaenau Ffestiniog

Y Ma

Llanaelhaearn

Prenteg

Tremadog

Maentwrog

Ffestiniog

Morfa Nefyn

Nefyn

PENINSULA

Llanystumdwy

Porthmadog

Penrhyndeudraeth

SNOWDONIA

Llande

Bodfuan

LLEYN

Criccieth

Borth-y-Gest

Talsarnau

Trawsfynydd

NATIONAL

Bala

Sarn

Pwllheli

Harlech

GWYNEDD

Llanuwchllyn

PARK

Llanbedrog

Llanbedr

Ganllwyd

Aberdaron

Y Rhiw

Abersoch

Dyffryn Ardudwy

Llanw

Bardsey Island

Tal-y-bont

Barmouth

Dolgellau

Dinas-Mawddwy

Fairbourne

Mallwyd

Llangad

Llwyngwril

Corris

Cemmaes Road

Cemmaes

Llanbrynmair

Bryncrug

Tywyn

Pennal

Machynlleth

Carno

SN

Aberdyfi

Borth

Tal-y-bont

Llandre

9

Llanidloes

Aberystwyth

Capel Bangor

Ponterwyd

Goginan

Guest Accommodation
AA Guest Accommodation of the Year
Town/Village name

0   10 miles

0   10   20 kilometres

For continuation pages refer to numbered arrows

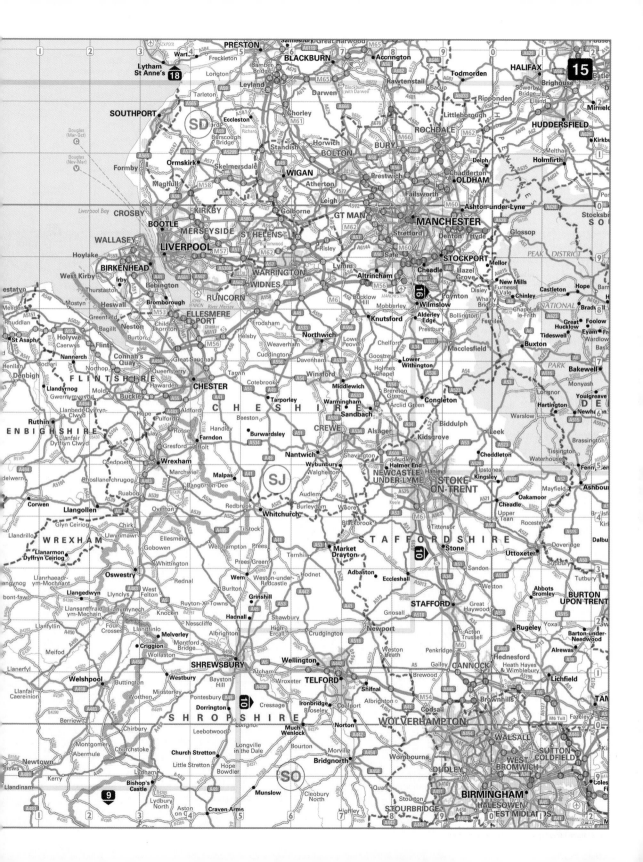

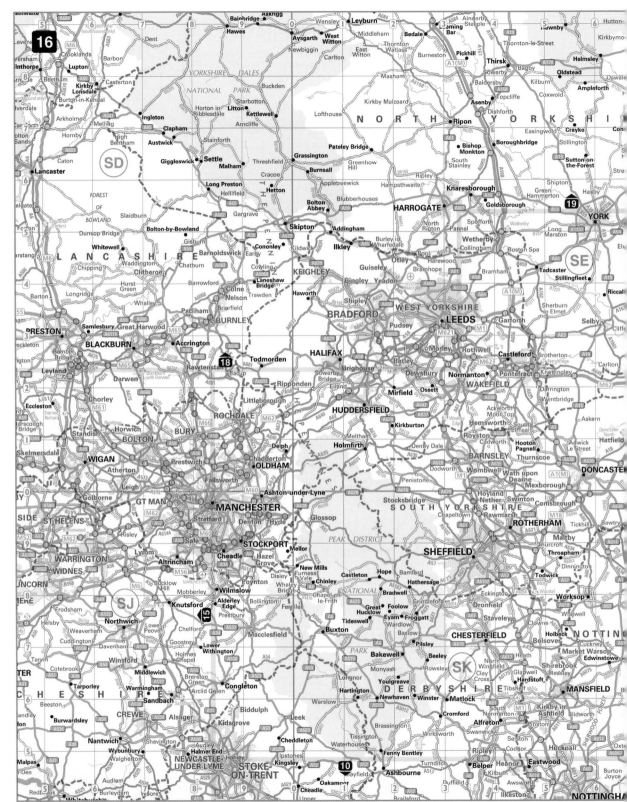

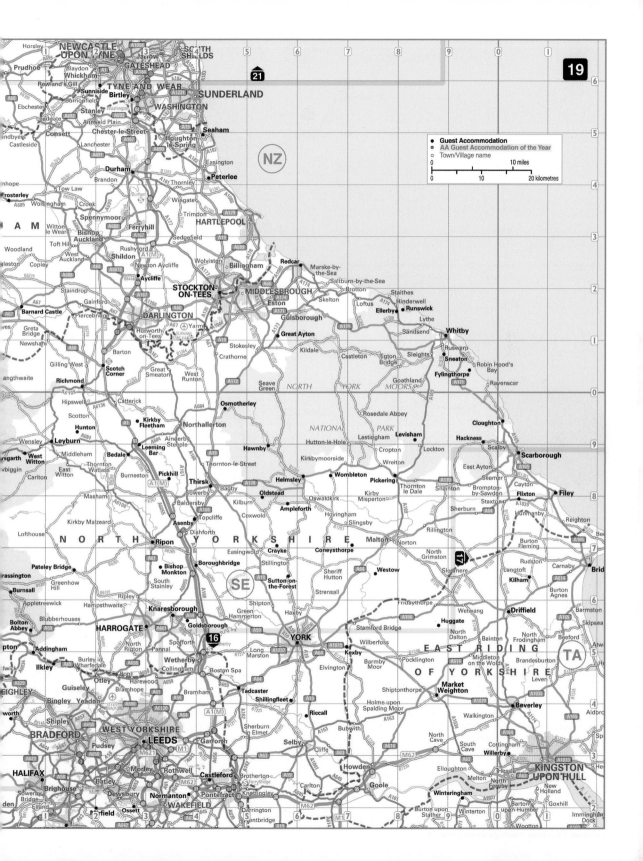

22

PERTH
KINROSS

Fort William
Kinlochleven

Acharacle

Point of
Ardnamurchan

Coll
Arinagour

Tobermory

South
Ballachulish   Ballachulish

ISLE

OF

Tiree
Scarinish

Lochaline

Appin
Bachuil
Lismore   Barcaldine
Connel

NM

MULL

NN

Killin

Ulva

Kerrera   Oban

Tyndrum

Iona
Fionnphort

Dalmally   Crianlarich

Lochearnhead

Strathyre

Firth of Lorne

LOCH LOMOND

Luing

ARGYLL   AND

BUTE

STIRLING

Callander

Scarba

Inveraray

Cairndow

AND THE TROSSACHS

Colonsay
Scalasaig

Oronsay

NATIONAL PARK

Luss

Lochgilphead

J U R A

Helensburgh   Balloch
W
DUNS   Kilsyth
GREENOCK   Dumbarton   E DUNS

Sound of Jura

Dunoon
Colintraive

INVER

Port Askaig

Tarbert

Bute
Rothesay

C GLAS
GLASGOW

Bowmore
I S L A Y

Kennacraig

RENS   PAISLEY

Portnahaven

Claonaig

Great
Cumbrae
Island

Largs

E RENS   EAST
KILBRIDE

Port
Ellen

Gigha

Kilbirnie   Beith

Sound
of Bute

Stewarton   Strathaven

NR

K I N T Y R E

ARRAN

Ardrossan

NORTH AYRSHIRE
Kilwinning

KILMARNOCK   LA

Brodick
Lamlash

Irvine

Galston

NS

Campbeltown

Troon
Prestwick
Ayr

Cumnock

EAST
AYRSHIRE

Mull of Kintyre

(May-Sept)

Maybole

Ailsa Craig

Girvan

SOUTH
AYRSHIRE

DUMF
GA

Ballantrae

North   Channel

Cairnryan

NX

Newton Stewart

New
Gallo

Stranraer

Wigtown

Gatehouse
of Fleet

NW

Portpatrick

Kirkcudbright

Luce Bay

Wigtown
Bay

Whithorn

Drummore

Burrow Head

Mull of
Galloway

C EDIN	City of Edinburgh
C GLAS	City of Glasgow
CLACKS	Clackmannanshire
C DUND	City of Dundee
E DUNS	East Dunbartonshire
E RENS	East Renfrewshire
INVER	Inverclyde
MDLOTH	Midlothian
N LANS	North Lanarkshire
RENS	Renfrewshire
W DUNS	West Dunbartonshire
W LOTH	West Lothian

For continuation pages refer to numbered arrows

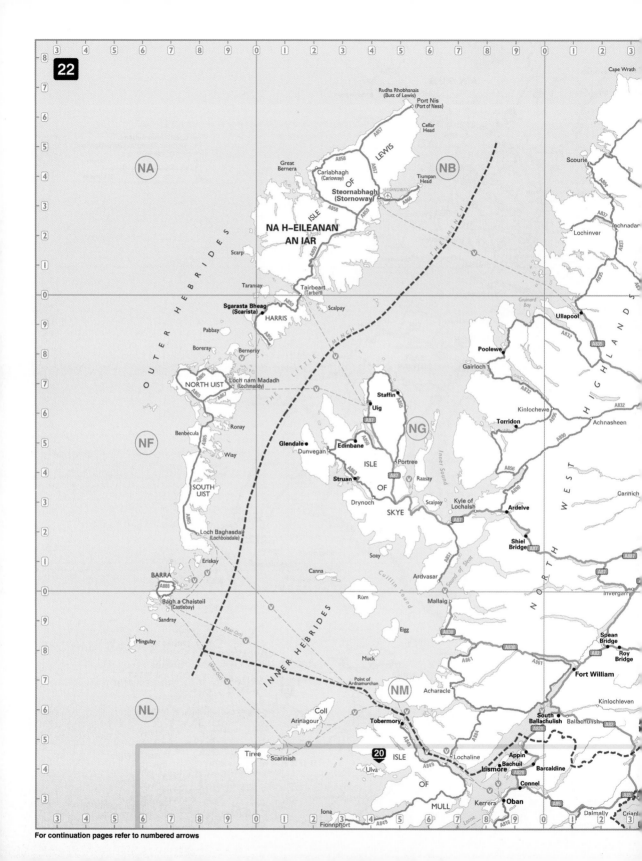

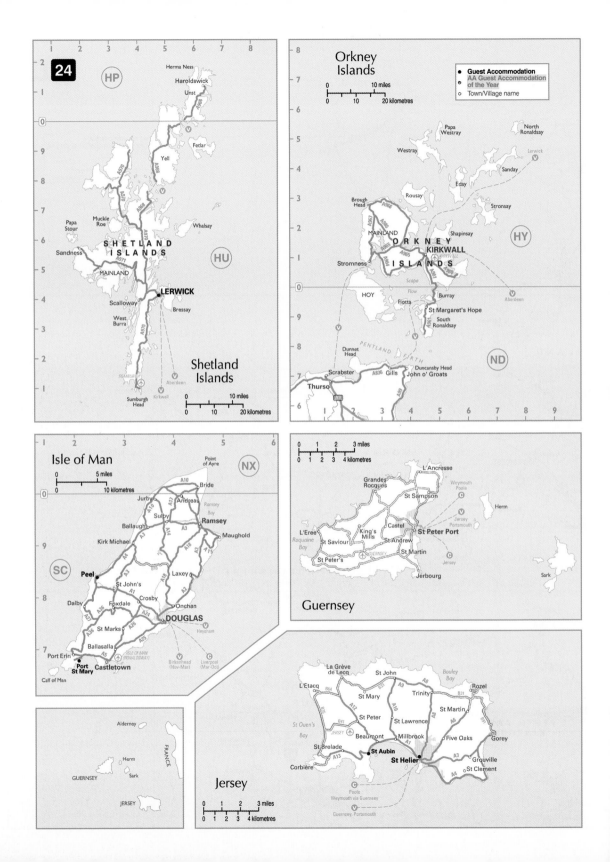

24

HP

Herma Ness
Haroldswick
Unst
A968

0

Fetlar
Yell
A970
A968

Papa
Stour
Muckle
Roe
Whalsay
S H E T L A N D
I S L A N D S
HU
Sandness
A971
A970
MAINLAND
LERWICK
Scalloway
Bressay
West
Burra
A970
Sumburgh
SUMBURGH
Aberdeen
Kirkwall
Sumburgh
Head

Shetland Islands

0   10 miles
0   10   20 kilometres

Orkney Islands

Guest Accommodation
AA Guest Accommodation
of the Year
Town/Village name

0   10 miles
0   10   20 kilometres

Papa
Westray
North
Ronaldsay
Westray
Lerwick
Sanday
Rousay
Eday
Brough
Head
A966
Stronsay
A960
A986
MAINLAND
O R K N E Y
Shapinsay
KIRKWALL
A965
Stromness
A964
A961
I S L A N D S
Aberdeen
Scapa
Flow
Burray
HOY
Flotta
St Margaret's Hope
South
Ronaldsay
Loch
PENTLAND   FIRTH
Dunnet
Head
Duncansby Head
John o' Groats
Scrabster
A836
Gills
A99
Thurso
A9

HY

ND

Isle of Man

Point
of Ayre
NX
0   5 miles
0   10 kilometres
A10
Bride
Jurby
A10
Andreas
A17
Ramsey
Bay
Sulby
Ballaugh
A3
Ramsey
Kirk Michael
A3
A18
Maughold
A14
A4
A2
A18
A15
SC
B10
Peel
Laxey
A1
St John's
A18
A2
Crosby
Dalby
Foxdale
A24
Onchan
A27
A36
DOUGLAS
St Marks
A26
Heysham
A5
Ballasalla
A25
Port Erin
ISLE OF MAN
(RONALDSWAY)
Birkenhead
(Nov-Mar)
Liverpool
(Mar-Oct)
Port
St Mary
Castletown
Calf of Man

0   1   2   3 miles
0   1   2   3   4 kilometres

L'Ancresse
Grandes
Rocques
Weymouth
Poole
St Sampson
Herm
L'Eree
King's
Mills
Castel
St Peter Port
Jersey
Portsmouth
Roquaine
Bay
St Saviour
St Andrew
St Peter's
GUERNSEY
St Martin
Jersey
Sark
Jerbourg

Guernsey

Alderney
Herm
FRANCE
GUERNSEY
Sark
JERSEY

Jersey

0   1   2   3 miles
0   1   2   3   4 kilometres

La Grève
de Lecq
St John
Bouley
Bay
L'Etacq
B64
St Mary
A9
A8
Rozel
Trinity
B31
A12
St Peter
A10
St Martin
St Lawrence
A6
St Ouen's
Bay
B41
JERSEY
Beaumont
Millbrook
Five Oaks
Gorey
St Brelade
A1
St Aubin
St Helier
A3
Grouville
Corbière
A13
St Clement
A4
Poole
Weymouth via Guernsey
Guernsey, Portsmouth

Central London

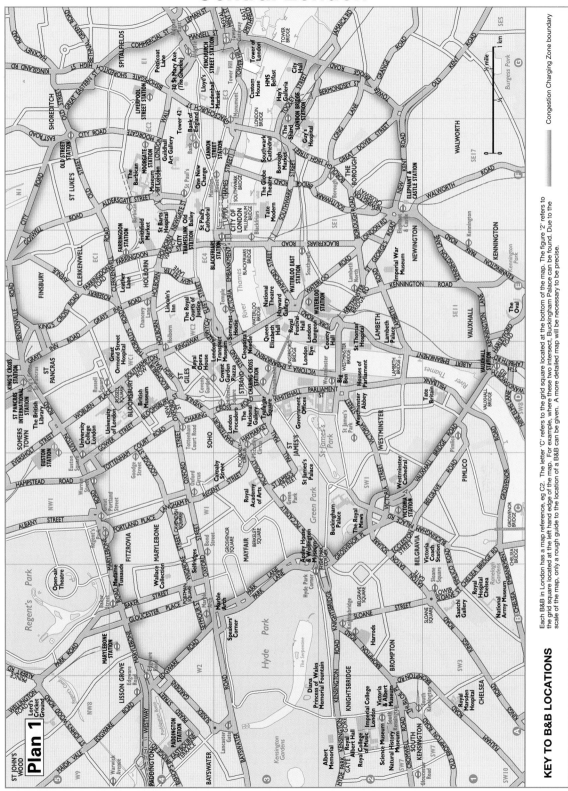

Plan 1

KEY TO B&B LOCATIONS

Each B&B in London has a map reference, eg C2. The letter 'C' refers to the grid square located at the left hand edge of the map. The figure '2' refers to the grid square located at the bottom of the map. For example, where these two intersect, Buckingham Palace can be found. Due to the scale of the map, only a rough guide to the location of a B&B can be given. A more detailed map will be necessary to be precise.

Congestion Charging Zone boundary

Index of Bed & Breakfasts

D

Acknowledgements

The Automobile Association wishes to thank the following photographers and organisations for their assistance in the preparation of this book.

Abbreviations for the picture credits are as follows – (t) top; (b) bottom; (l) left; (r) right; (c) centre; (AA) AA World Travel Library

Front Cover: © Superstock / Alamy

England Opener AA/Adam Burton;
Scotland Opener AA/Jonathan Smith;
Wales Opener AA/Mark Bauer;
Ireland Opener AA/Caroline Jones

003 Strand House, East Sussex; 004 © Scottish Viewpoint/Alamy; 009 © Arcaid Images/Alamy; 010 Dorain House, Somerset; 012–013 AA/Royalty Free disc; 012 River Garth Guest House, Penrith; 013l The Bull Inn, Suffolk; 013r Sydney House Chelsea, London; 014–015 AA/Royalty Free disc; 014l Prawles Court, East Sussex; 014r Aikenshill House, Aberdeenshire; 015l Tyddyn Mawr Farmhouse, Gwynedd; 015r WhitePark House, County Antrim; 016–017 Cumbria Life/Danny Fowler; 020–021 © Adam Burton/Alamy; 023 © TIM GRAHAM /Alamy; 024 The Marble Arch by Montcalm, London; 076 AA/Adam Burton; 182 AA/Rebecca Duke; 419 © Photoshot Holdings Ltd/Alamy; 431 AA/Karl Blackwell; 448 AA/Karl Blackwell; 457 © Mark ferguson/Alamy; 492–493 AA/AJ Hopkins; 513 AA/Steve Day.

Every effort has been made to trace the copyright holders, and we apologise in advance for any unintentional omissions or errors. We would be pleased to apply any corrections in a following edition of this publication.